P9-CBQ-436

IBM 370 Assembly Language With ASSIST, Structured Concepts, and Advanced Topics

Charles J. Kacmar
Texas A & M University

PRENTICE HALL, *Englewood Cliffs, New Jersey 07632*

Library of Congress Cataloging-in-Publication Data

KACMAR, CHARLES J.

IBM 370 assembly language with ASSIST, structured concepts, and advanced topics.

Bibliography: p.

Includes index.

1. IBM 370 (Computer)—Programming. 2. Assembler language (Computer program language) 3. ASSIST (Computer program) I. Title.

QA76.8.I123K33 1987 005.2'25 87-11362

ISBN 0-13-455742-5

Editorial/production supervision and
interior design: **Ellen B. Greenberg**
Cover design: **Photo Plus Art**
Manufacturing buyer: **Barbara Kelly Kittle**

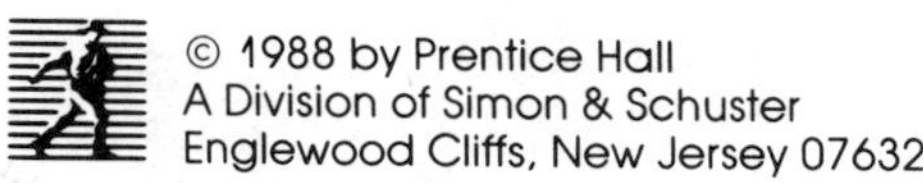

© 1988 by Prentice Hall
A Division of Simon & Schuster
Englewood Cliffs, New Jersey 07632

All rights reserved. No part of this book may be reproduced, in any form or by any means, without permission in writing from the publisher.

Printed in the United States of America

10 9 8 7 6 5 4 3 2

ISBN 0-13-455742-5 025

Prentice-Hall International (UK) Limited, *London*
Prentice-Hall of Australia Pty. Limited, *Sydney*
Prentice-Hall Canada Inc., *Toronto*
Prentice-Hall Hispanoamericana, S.A., *Mexico*
Prentice-Hall of India Private Limited, *New Delhi*
Prentice-Hall of Japan, Inc., *Tokyo*
Simon & Schuster Asia Pte. Ltd., *Singapore*
Editora Prentice-Hall do Brasil, Ltda., *Rio de Janeiro*

to Micki

Contents

Preface xi

Acknowledgments xiii

1 The Programming Environment 1

Understanding the Problem and Developing a Solution 2
Components of the Computer System 4
Program Transformations and Transformation Agents 8
Data Formats and Data Processing 13
Programming and Languages 15
Study Questions 16

2 Data Representation and Number Systems 17

Memory Denominations 17
Registers and Data Addressing 19
Decimal, Hexadecimal, and Binary Number Systems 23
Binary and Hexadecimal Operations 27
Negative Numbers and Operations 30
Data Types and Their Most Common Representation 32
Zoned and Packed Decimal Representation 36
Study Questions 41

3 The Assembly Language Program 43

Assembly Language Statement Format 43
Beginning the Assembly Language Program 45
Body of the Assembly Language Program 54
Data Elements and their Definitions 54
Logical Data Structures 60
Boundary and Alignment 63
Exiting an Assembly Language Program 65
Ending the Assembly Language Program 68

Constructing A Complete Program 69
Reading An Output Listing 71
Helping Program Readability 85
The EQU Instruction 91
Study Questions 95

4 Processing Character Data and Performing I/O Operations 97

Types of Machine Instructions 97
How Programs Are Executed 103
Processing Character Data 109
Sequential File Input/Output in Assembly Language 113
The I/O Macro Instructions 118
Readying and Terminating File Processing—OPEN and CLOSE 121
Processing Data Records—GET and PUT 122
JCL To Run an Assembly Language Program 123
Sequential File Processing Using ASSIST 126
ASSIST Input and Output Instructions—XREAD and XPRNT 126
JCL and ASSIST Control Statements 128
Label Print Program 128
Controlling Line Spacing—Carriage Controls 132
Character Data Literals 133
Assembly Time and Date Values 136
Study Questions 143
Programming Problems 146

5 Processing Binary Data, Input and Output of Binary Fields, the Full IBM Linkage Conventions 147

Register-to-Register Instructions 147
Register-to-Storage Instructions 152
The IBM Linkage Conventions 155
Input and Output of Binary Information 163
Halfword Processing Instructions 168
Fullword and Halfword Literals 171
Report Formatting and Carriage Controls 172
ASSIST Arithmetic Conversion Instructions—XDECI and XDECO 177
Study Questions 184
Programming Problems 186

6 Controlling Program Flow: Looping, Comparisons, and Branching 187

Overview of Program Control 187
Testing the Condition Code Value 190

Comparing Fields and Testing Values (IF-THEN Constructs) 196
Extended Mnemonic Instructions 200
Defining Your Own Mnemonics (OPSYN) 202
Loop Constructs: A General Overview 204
Counter Loops 205
WHILE and UNTIL Loop Constructs 210
End-of-File and Trailer Record Processing 211
Compound Conditions 216
Mailing Label Print Program Example 218
Study Questions 230
Programming Problems 231

7 Processing with Packed-Decimal Data 233

Review of Packed-Decimal Format 233
Defining and Initializing Packed-Decimal Fields 234
Input and Output of Packed-Decimal Fields 237
  Editing or Formatting Numeric Output 239
  Negative Signs and Floating Characters 245
Packed-Decimal Instructions 251
Adding and Subtracting Packed-Decimal Fields 254
Handling Decimal Overflow Conditions 254
Multiplying, Dividing and Zapping Packed-Decimal Data 256
Digits to the Left and Right of the Decimal 261
Decimal Data Programming Example 263
Study Questions 271
Programming Problems 272

8 Program Debugging 274

Syntax Errors 275
Execution Errors 280
Diagnosing Errors: Abend Codes 281
Defensive Programming: Debugging Tools 285
The Debugging Process Using Dumps 296
Program Debugging Examples 316
Study Questions 335

9 Internal and External Subroutines 338

What is a Module or a Function? 338
Packaging Logical Functions into Modules 340
Internal Subroutines 343
Internal Subroutine Packaging and Data Access 347
Defining Multiple-Base Registers 348

Passing Data to Subroutines by Following the Linkage Conventions 349
External Subroutines 355
Internal and External Subroutines in the Same Program 359
Execute JCL Statement Parameters 361
I/O Operations Across Module Boundaries 363
Testing DCB's When Used as Parameters 365
Assembly Language and COBOL Communications 368
Study Questions 382
Programming Problems 384

10 Macros and Conditional Assembly 386

Overview of Macro Processing 386
Basic Structure and Coding of a Macro 390
Using Macros in Your Program 391
The Macro Prototype Statement 395
The Macro Body and a Complete Macro Example 399
The Length Attribute 401
The Macro Language 402
Character Variables, Concatenation, and String Processing 411
Sublists Within Macro Parameters 413
The Type and Count Data Attributes 415
Conditional Assembly 419
Study Questions 421
Programming Problems 423

11 Extended Instructions and Advanced Techniques 425

Using R13 as a Base Register 425
Byte-Processing RS Instructions—ICM STCM, and CLM 426
The Execute Instruction 429
Translating Data Areas 433
Searching for Characters within Fields 436
Single-Dimensional Array Processing 440
Multidimensional Arrays 442
Table Processing 448
The Move and Compare Long Instructions 451
AND, OR, and EXCLUSIVE OR Processing 454
Alternate Move Instructions—MVO, MVN, and MVZ 459
The Logical Instructions 462
The Shift Instructions 464
Study Questions 468
Programming Problems 469

12 Floating-Point Processing 472

Internal Representation and Conversions 472
Defining Floating-Point Storage Areas 479
Load and Store Instructions 480
Normalization and the Guard Digit 482
Arithmetic Floating-Point Operations 483
Additional Floating-Point Load Instructions 485
Rounding Floating-Point Values 485
Comparison Between Floating-Point Values 486
Conversion of Floating-Point Data For I/O 486
Floating-Point Programming Example 488
Study Questions 504
Programming Problems 505

13 More Advanced Topics 507

Dummy Control Sections (DSECT's) 507
Copy Libraries 511
Locate Mode Processing 513
Tape Processing 518
Variable-Length Record Processing 520
System Support Macros and Services 525
  Abnormal Program Termination 525
  Invoking External Subroutines 527
  Obtaining the Current Date and Time 529
  Sending Messages to the Operator 530
  Reentrant Programming 532
Study Questions 539
Programming Problems 539

14 Random File Processing 541

General Overview 541
Relative File Processing 542
  Defining A Relative Record Dataset 543
  Dumping the Contents of a Relative Dataset 545
  Updating A Relative Dataset 547
  Sequentially Processing Records in a Relative File 552
Indexed File Processing Using ISAM 552
  Structure of An ISAM Dataset 553
  Creating An ISAM Dataset 554
  Processing An ISAM Dataset Sequentially 555
  Obtaining a Dump of An ISAM Dataset 557
  Randomly Processing An ISAM File 558
Event Completion Using The WAIT Macro Instruction 563
Study Questions 564
Programming Problems 565

15 VSAM File Processing 567

Overview of VSAM File Structures 567
Overview of IDCAMS 570
Creating an ESDS 572
Creating an RRDS 574
Creating a KSDS 574
Defining an Alternate Index 575
Using IDCAMS to Print a VSAM Dataset 577
Deleting a VSAM Cluster 579
VSAM Dataset Verification 579
Obtaining Dataset Statistics 580
Copying Application Data 580
Overview of the VSAM I/O Instructions 582
Processing a VSAM ESDS Sequentially for Output 585
Processing a VSAM RRDS Sequentially for Output 587
Processing a VSAM KSDS Sequentially for Output 588
Testing the Success of an I/O Operation 589
End-of-File Processing 596
Sequential Input Processing on VSAM Clusters 597
Randomly Processing a VSAM Dataset 598
Generating the ACB and RPL at Execution Time 600
Variable-Length Record Processing 611
Overview of VSAM Alternate Indexes 612
Processing an Alternate Index Sequentially 614
Updating Base Cluster Records Through The Alternate Index 615
Reentrant VSAM Coding 617
Study Questions 620
Programming Problems 620

Appendix A: Bibliography 623

Appendix B: Instruction Summary 624

Appendix C: Instruction Reference 629

Appendix D: ANSI Carriage Control Characters 653

Appendix E: Common Program Abends (Exceptions) 654

Answers to the Chapter Study Questions 655

Index 674

Preface

As a student, teacher, consultant, programmer, and computer user, I have been fortunate to be exposed to many processing environments, languages, and techniques. Throughout my brief career, I have learned through my contacts and experiences and have hoped that someone along the way could benefit by what I had to say and offer. Although, at times, my students may have felt that my purpose was to inflict pain upon them, I hope that they have realized that my goal was to develop a skill in them which they might not have known they had; namely, the ability to think and solve problems using a computer.

This textbook is yet another effort to provide guidance in the art of software development. In particular, this textbook approaches assembly language programming from a real world viewpoint using current programming methodologies. Structured programming techniques are discussed early and used throughout the text. Comparisons are made pro and con as to some of the various programming styles that one might find in assembly language systems. It is hoped that justification for certain strategies can influence your decisions when choosing implementation techniques.

When I began this project, I wanted to serve three audiences. First, I wanted to develop a textbook that was easy to read and one that offered the first term or beginning assembly language programmer an effective tool for learning. Secondly, I wanted to develop a textbook that offered an advanced student some techniques or strategies that could not be found in manuals and that might be used when developing more sophisticated applications. Lastly, I wanted this textbook to serve as a reference for all levels of students as well as the professional programmer. As a programmer, I sometimes find it difficult to extract information from manuals that can be used to solve problems. Hopefully, this textbook can assist in this task.

Another goal of this project was to provide a textbook that could be used in a multiterm assembly language programming sequence. With respect to entry level assembly language texts, the market is quite abundant with successful publications. However, as we move away from in-stream files and sequential processing to more advanced techniques, the availability of materials for the advanced student or the professional programmer is not as abundant. As a result, it's common to find upper division classes and programmers being forced into using manuals before they have the background to fully understand how a manual can be used. In fact, manuals may have been the only viable resource that the instructor felt was available for the class being taught. This textbook bridges the gap between entry level and advanced courses, and can serve as an acceptable resource for any assembly language class or business setting.

The text spans the typical realm of assembly language programming found in most entry-level classes. The text also includes a detailed discussion of floating-point processing, system macro instructions, standard assembly language I/O procedures, and random file processing, including VSAM. End of chapter questions and programming problems that further challenge and extend the concepts discussed in the text are also included.

SUPPLEMENTARY MATERIALS

A complete instructor's guide is provided, which includes solutions to many end of chapter programming problems, an exam question pool, and exercise sheets that highlight the major concepts of each chapter. Through these facilities, it is hoped that a complete package has been provided; one that can be of benefit to both the experienced and beginning assembly language instructor.

The instructor's manual comes with a complete 370 emulation system. This package, developed by Donald Higgins, allows the student to develop and execute mainframe 370 programs on IBM-compatible personal computers. Hence, it's not necessary for students to have access to an IBM mainframe to study and learn the concepts in this text. Through the power of the micro computer and the genius of Donald Higgins, this power and capability has been brought to the individual user level.

The PC/370 package is provided on a 360K floppy diskette. It is completely installed and comes with editor, debugger, assembler, linker, and support files. It supports almost all of the 370 instructions including the ASSIST facilities. For a nominal membership fee, enrollment in the PC/370 Society can provide additional materials and updates with respect to the 370 package.

As distributed, the package may be copied and distributed to students in classes. Documentation is provided in the instructor's manual and on the distribution diskette. A selection of sample programs are also available on the diskette which exhibit just some of the extended capabilities of this system. Our only request in using the system is that you acknowledge the efforts of the system's author, Donald Higgins, by registering as a PC/370 user and by sending a small honorarium to his attention when you begin your adoption usage. The honorarium should be directed to Donald Higgins, 6365–32nd Avenue North, St. Petersburg, Florida, 33710.

Acknowledgments

The process of developing a textbook involves the cooperation and dedication of many individuals. Ideas, concerns, comments, and even criticisms are shared among all involved. It is for this reason that I wish to thank the many people that have helped in the development of this text.

Clearly, this text is intended for students and it is to them that I direct my first acknowledgment. In particular, I wish to thank the many students who have worked through the end of chapter questions and programming problems and who have assisted in building the solutions manual. There are too many individuals to acknowledge separately at this time, but I thank them all for their attention and patience.

Next, I wish to acknowledge the exceptional dedication and efforts on the part of Marcia Horton, Computer Science Editor, and Ellen Greenberg, Editorial Production Editor, at Prentice Hall. These are the people who really produce a textbook and they deserve the credit for an outstanding performance. It is through their encouragement, guidance, and unwaivering patience that this text has been formed. Yet, even though they are responsible for the end product, I still am responsible for any and all errors that this text may contain.

The production of a textbook requires several reviews by practicing professionals in the field. Theresa M. Phinney, Texas A&M University, James F. Peters III, St. John's University, and Charles J. Dowling, Catonsville Community College, all served as reviewers for the manuscript. Their efforts have brought many valuable ideas to the text during the various stages of production. I am extremely grateful to them all.

The ultimate test of any text is hands-on use in the classroom. It is for this reason that I express my gratitude to Tim Stone at Illinois State University. Tim put the text through its initial workout in his assembly language programming class. Working with spiral bound notebooks, students and teacher provided many valuable comments and suggestions. For their efforts, I am forever indebted.

In a similar manner, I wish to express my sincere thanks to Robert Lee Moulic at Illinois State University. He, too, provided many comments concerning textual material, programming matters, and issues of presentation. His experience and suggestions have brought a great deal to the later chapters of this text. For this we are all grateful.

As I said earlier, the production of a text requires the cooperation of many individuals and a tremendous amout of resources. With no exception, this text required many computer hours in order to validate the examples in the text, implement the end of chapter problems for the instructor's manual, and in some cases, produce camera copy to be incorporated directly into the manuscript. It is with great appreciation that I offer my thanks to the Computer Science Department at Texas A&M University and the Applied Computer Science Department of Illinois State University. These institutions graciously offered their resources to assist in my endeavor. Clearly, it would not be fitting to produce such a document without acknowledging their assistance in this project.

Finally, I wish to express my sincere appreciation to my wife. This has been a long project and yet, she has never waivered in her support. She has worn the hat of sounding board, reviewer, reader, and a host of other roles. It is for this reason that this text is dedicated to her.

Charles J. (Chuck) Kacmar

1

The Programming Environment

Programming languages come in many sizes, shapes, and forms. The popular languages, such as COBOL, PL/I, BASIC, PASCAL, and FORTRAN, have established themselves as the primary languages of computer software. Available now or on the horizon are fourth- and fifth-generation languages that allow the easier definition and implementation of a computerized solution to a problem in a shorter time. These new tools also allow software developers to generate the appropriate lower-level code for the computer solution. Hence, by allowing the software developers to remove themselves from the minute details of the computer system and to focus more of their attention on the problem, the languages allow quicker and more accurate software development.

Although a great deal of emphasis will continue to be placed on **application development tools,** we must remember that the basis for all languages is machine code. All languages, no matter what generation, must be converted into machine language since computers typically execute only machine language instructions. Thus conversion is typically done by an **assembler** for second-generation languages, a **compiler** for third-generation languages, and a **preprocessor/compiler** or **preprocessor/assembler** for fourth- and fifth-generation languages. These **language translators** convert higher level statements into machine language for execution by the computer.

The power of the higher level language is dependent on the ability to convert the statements into machine language. Where the capabilities of a machine are not usable because certain functions cannot be described and converted by the translator, such limitations can be resolved by implementing applications in an assembly language.

An **assembly language** is the most powerful of all languages since it is closest to the machine level. Any operation or function supported on the machine is available in an assembly language. On the other hand, assembly languages have some disadvantages. Assembly languages are generally difficult to read since they are typically oriented around cryptic instructions and machine-level operations. Assembly languages do not easily lend themselves to structured programming constructs (which will be discussed in detail later). Assembly languages are machine dependent, that is, an application developed using IBM 370 assembly language cannot usually be used on another computer system without rewriting the application. On the other hand, an application developed in COBOL may be used completely on another computer system with few, if any, changes. Finally, assembly languages are difficult to understand (for those just learning about the assembly language) since they require a detailed understanding of the computer system being used. Considering all these factors, application software developed using assembly language generally takes more time to develop and is generally more difficult to maintain or keep up to date when compared to software developed using a higher level language.

Why then should we study or learn to develop computer applications in assembly language? Looking at the reverse side of the coin, assembly languages have distinct advantages over the higher level languages. The most important is the speed at which applications are processed. Assembly languages generally allow the development of the application efficiently to obtain the best performance possible from the computer. Although good performance development is possible with higher level languages, it is generally not as high as with assembly language. Further, the machine-level code generated by the higher level language translator may not be as efficient as that in assembly language since the translator's design may not produce the most efficient machine level code. Since assembly language code is most comparable to machine code, the performance of an assembly language program is directly related to the level of understanding that the developer has of the computer and language itself.

Functionality is the second most important advantage. As stated earlier, since assembly language programming is closest to machine level programming, it can use all available functions of the computer hardware. These advantages are the primary reasons to implement applications in assembly language rather than in a higher level language. With the market moving more toward packaged software, users require control and speed, which are easily obtained through assembly languages.

Another type of language translator is an **interpreter.** An interpreter does not convert higher level language statements into machine code, but processes each program statement by *simulating* the execution of the instructions within the program. For example, if an instruction requests that elements A and B are to be added, the interpreter performs the addition by obtaining the values for A and B, checking to see that they are within the specified ranges, and then performing the addition. The extra step of checking the validity of the data is one of the most powerful features of the interpreter since such functions are not typically performed by assemblers, compilers, or preprocessors. In other words, the interpreter monitors the execution of a program and provides better and more complete diagnostic information should a problem arise during execution. On the negative side, the simulation is slower since one source machine instruction may require execution of several hundred instructions within the interpreter. However, programmers generally sacrifice performance for the diagnostics and added verification provided by an interpreter, especially during program testing.

Throughout the text, we will give examples that use the **ASSIST** assembly language interpreter as an alternative to the more common method of processing and executing assembly language programs. ASSIST is a software package that simulates program execution and provides an easier method for program debugging and monitoring. Without further discussion, let's begin our study of assembly language programming.

UNDERSTANDING THE PROBLEM AND DEVELOPING A SOLUTION

The first step to implement any application is to understand what the computer is to do. Although we might be able to immediately begin typing the computer program to solve a problem, most of us gradually develop our solution by thinking about the problem before beginning the coding process. As stated earlier, developing programs in assembly language is generally more difficult than in higher level languages. Therefore, we'll first review the basics within the problem solving process, forming guidelines for program development.

When beginning the development of an application program, we typically want to know what data is to be processed, what processing is required, and what outputs are desired. To determine these, we sit down with the user and discuss what he has and what he needs from the program. Using this information, we develop a strategy for implementing their application on the computer. This information gathering process is called **analysis.** Typical outputs from this phase of the development process are written documents that outline and define the user's requirements as well as establish a plan for arriving at the desired goals. In a classroom environment, most of the analysis has already been done by the professor who generally gives a set of specifications for a project to be implemented on the computer. The problem has been defined and the professor knows the expected results. However, *we* must also know what is to be derived from the solution to the problem and so we must perform some analysis by reading the project specifications and asking questions to clarify anything not understood.

Once we have a firm grasp of the problem and understand what is desired from the computer, we can now begin the **design** phase. Here we form our solution by considering the programming language to be used, by finding the existence and location of available and needed data, by establishing testing procedures for the ultimate solution, and by considering many other important factors too numerous and detailed to discuss here. In short, we will arrive at a solution to the problem. Of course, we'll hope that the solution is correct and will solve the problem, but designs generally have to be reconsidered over and over since a few details are usually forgotten during this part of the development process. The end product of design is generally a set of detailed algorithms for each component of our solution. For each component, we identify all of the inputs and describe the outputs from the element. We also describe how the input data is transformed into the output data. This transformation is described using flowcharts or pseudocode or some other algorithmic form. The main point is that we have a solution—maybe not the only solution to the problem—but a solution nonetheless. If we've arrived at several possible solutions, we must determine which solution to follow in the development.

The next phase can be described as the **coding** phase where we implement our algorithms in a programming language. As was said earlier, the implementation could use machine language, assembly language, a higher-level language such as COBOL or PL/I, or a fourth- or fifth-generation language. Regardless of the choice, the ultimate product of the coding and implementation is an executable program. This is the component that will process data and produce results.

To many the next phase, **testing,** is the longest in the development life cycle. **Testing** an application and verifying its results is a time consuming and frustrating experience. With each test of our solution, we must fix any bugs and rerun or retest the implementation. Often, testing involves redesign since we discover a situation not allowed for in an earlier part of the development process. When this occurs, we can generalize and say that we didn't understand the problem to begin with or that we didn't have adequate information to develop a complete and accurate solution. In either case, the algorithm and ultimate solution are reworked to meet the new specifications. In fact, this process of test–review–redesign continues iteratively (over and over) until a correct solution is reached. When we obtain the correct results, the project is completed—but is it? We forgot the documentation.

Documentation is probably the worst word that a student has ever heard. Perhaps too often, it's something that is added to a program *after* the program has been completed. Quite frankly, documentation will be appreciated with more exposure to specifications, designs, algorithms, and programs developed by others. Documentation is really an ongoing process that starts with the first thoughts about a system until the system is implemented and has been turned over to another group for maintenance and operation. Inadequate documentation is expensive because it takes more time to understand a component or phase of a system than if proper and complete documentation were available. We've encountered similar situations—we developed a program and didn't comment it; later, when going back to add the comments, we couldn't understand the code and had to spend some time relearning what we had already developed. If we had commented properly the first time, this time would have been saved.

Proper documentation must be stressed when applications are implemented in assembly language. Since assembly language is inherently difficult to read, it becomes increasingly important that programs be properly commented. As we progress through the text, we'll see several different techniques for commenting assembly language programs. With the professor, we will decide which method of documentation is appropriate.

Is the system done yet? Can we start on something else at this point? Well, not quite. To complete the development life cycle, we should **review** what we've done. Let's return to the analysis and design documentation to see that we've implemented all aspects of the problem. Verify the results and double check to make sure that the program(s) is producing what the user wanted. Finally, review the programs and see that they are properly commented, contain the proper and approved structuring constructs, and that no part of the solution is "tricky" or contains a technique that will not meet with approval.

These are the basic phases in the development of a system. Again, these phases are not language dependent, that is, this development process applies to machine language, assembly language, or higher level implementation. By stressing this process for application development, it is hoped that fewer problems will occur. Also, we should be able to achieve our results faster and with more accuracy than before.

COMPONENTS OF THE COMPUTER SYSTEM

The basic components of a computer system are hardware and software. Hardware components are the physical devices within the computer system, while software is the program that is executed or run by the computer. Typical hardware consists of a central processing unit (CPU), memory, channels (input/output processors), line printers, card readers, disk drives, and terminals. Software for the computer system consists of the operating system, utility or support programs, assemblers, compilers, preprocessors, and application programs. Let's look at each of these components so that we may further understand what we'll be working with.

Data is stored within a computer system in many formats and on many hardware devices. Figure 1.1 illustrates a **punched card** (called a **Hollerith card**), which allows 80 characters of data to be entered into the computer system.

As we can see from Fig. 1.1, each column on the punched card allows one character to be represented as holes in the card. Holes are punched in the card with a card punch machine. After data or a program is punched in the cards, the cards are fed into a **card reader,** which "reads" or interprets the hole punches and transmits the characters represented by the holes into the computer system. Punched cards are one of the oldest forms of data representation. They are quickly being replaced with terminals, mark-sensing machines, and machines that can read printed material directly from typed pages.

Probably the most abundant modern input device is the **terminal.** The terminal is much more reliable, quieter, and allows for easier correction of mistakes. For example, if a mistake is made on a punched card, the entire card must be repunched, but an error made on a terminal can be corrected by backspacing to the error and retyping the data

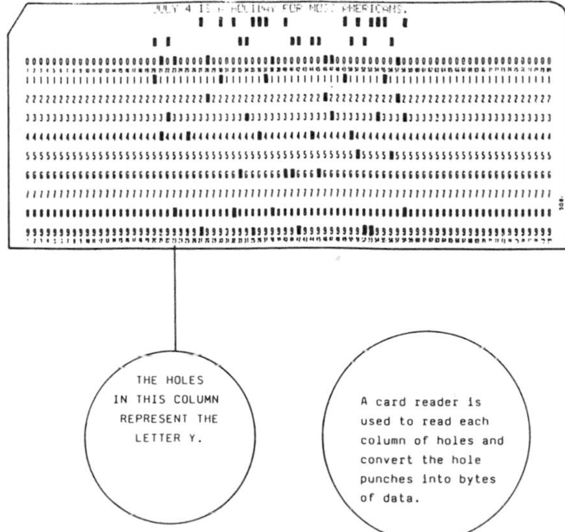

Figure 1.1 The punched card.

correctly. See Fig. 1.2. Terminals are also aesthetically more pleasing since they occupy much less space than a keypunch, come in a variety of forms and colors (coordinated to your office environment), and allow developers to spend countless hours trying to decide which color is to be used for each field on a terminal display screen. Clearly, they are the industry standard, regardless of the fact that they are also the brunt of many cartoons and jokes directed at the computer industry.

Data may also be supplied to the computer through magnetic recording devices, such as **disk drives** and **tape drives** (see Fig. 1.3). Here, data is recorded magnetically by

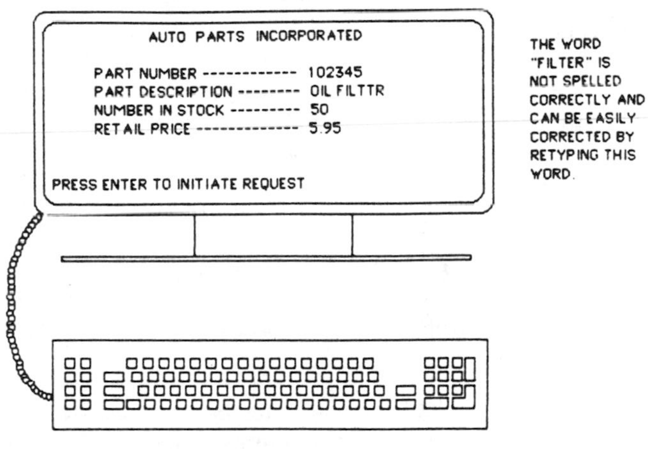

Figure 1.2 An on-line terminal.

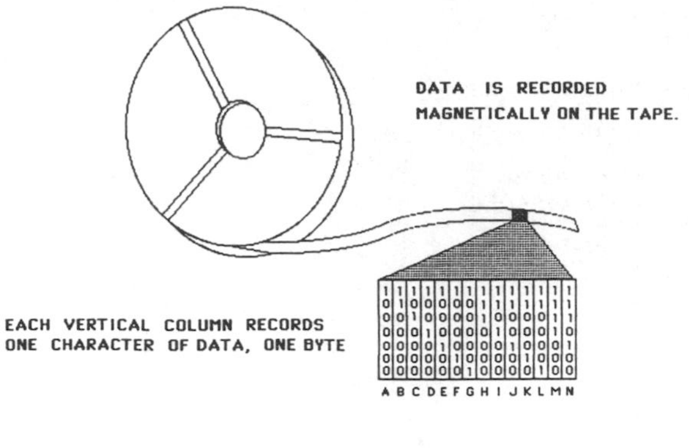

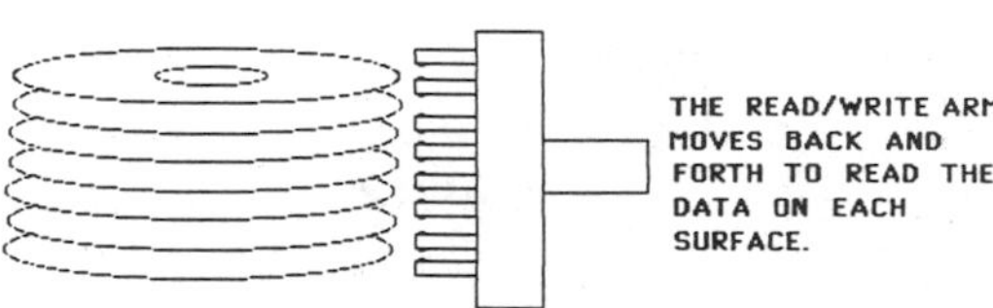

Figure 1.3 Tape and disk storage.

the device and can be reread by the computer after it is stored. Additionally, tapes and disks can be used over and over; a punched card can only be used to represent one set of data.

The primary advantage of these devices is the long-term storage of information. Excluding failure of the devices themselves, information may be stored almost indefinitely on tapes or disks. Further, data may be retrieved quite rapidly and made available to an application program when needed. In contrast to computer memory, external storage is a slower form of data access, but it offers the advantages of larger capacity and longer term storage than the more volatile computer memory.

Information can be directed from the computer to a line printer, graphics plotting device, or to typical devices such as a tape drive, disk drive, card punch, or terminal. Through these devices, data and programs can be brought into the computer, processed, and results sent out of the computer for use by humans or other computers. In fact, the terminology used most often to describe the general format of processing is input, processing, and output. See Fig. 1.4. The umbrella components within the realm of data processing are **input,** consisting of programs and data; **processing,** consisting of the program instructions used to process the data; and **output,** consisting of printed lines or terminal displays. Successful processing is based on valid input and correct processing. If either the input is garbage or the processing is incorrect, the output will be garbage (gigo: garbage in, garbage out).

The hardware devices discussed previously are generally referred to as **peripherals** or peripheral devices. They *support* the execution of the computer and service the programs operating within the computer system. Considering the computer system, its three main components are memory, channels, and the CPU (central processing unit).

The **memory** of the computer holds programs and data to be processed. The **channels** allow data to come in and go out of the computer. The **CPU** performs calculations and makes decisions based on the instructions and data being processed. Further, the

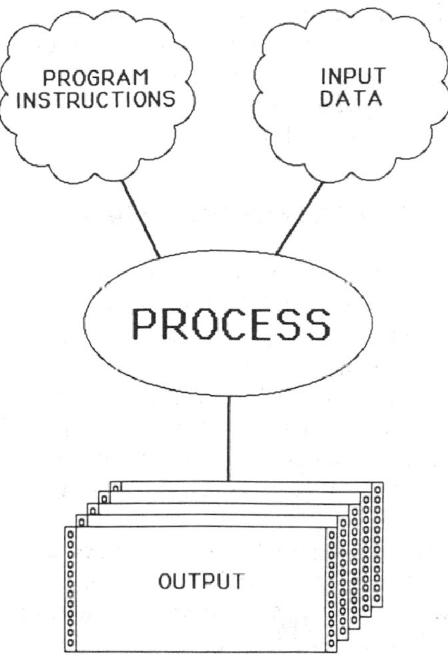

Figure 1.4 Logical processing overview.

CPU controls the flow of execution within a program by performing the instructions within the program.

The hardware alone doesn't make a computer system. One of the most important components is its software. Although software consists of the operating system, utilities or support programs, assemblers, compilers, preprocessors, and the application programs, the computer could not function without the operating system. Hence, the most important component to *manage* the operation of the computer environment is the operating system.

The **operating system** is simply a set of programs, usually supplied by the computer manufacturer, to manage and control the processing within the computer. Generally, the operating system is written in assembly language (what a coincidence!) or some *souped up* higher level language. The components of the operating system interact to control the flow of data in and out of the computer (by interacting with the channels), control the processing and scheduling of activity within the computer, and handle problems if they occur during processing. For example, suppose that a component of the computer begins to fail during processing. The operating system could detect the failure and inform the computer operator that there is a problem and that a service representative should be called.

The **utility** or **support programs** help the programmers or the operating system to manage the data within the computer system, prepare programs and data to be processed by the computer, and assist the programmer by performing repetitive functions. Utility programs are supplied by the computer manufacturer as part of the operating system or are purchased or developed by the programming staff within the computer center. Utility programs are an important component in the day-to-day processing within the computer although they are not themselves an integral part of the operating system.

Since we already discussed the role of an assembler or compiler, the last software component found within a computer system is the **application software** developed to support the company or business. This software, too, is supplied by the computer manufacturer, purchased from a third party, or developed by the in-house programming staff. Application software supports the end user by processing input data and producing output. This is the component on which we are going to concentrate in this text, specifically, application software developed in assembly language.

PROGRAM TRANSFORMATIONS AND TRANSFORMATION AGENTS

Solutions or programs can undergo many transformations before they can be executed by a computer system. If a solution is implemented in machine language, then little or no transformation is necessary. If a solution is implemented in a higher level language, then a compiler or assembler must convert the program into machine language before it can be executed by the computer. Fourth- and fifth-generation languages require a preprocessor to convert the statements into a subordinate form (higher level language, second- or third-generation form) and then a compiler or assembler converts the subordinate form into machine language. Figure 1.5 illustrates the various phases of software conversion.

As stated earlier, the compiler or assembler converts programs from one form into another. Which device is used depends upon the language used to implement the computer solution. Two other elements must also be understood within this transformation process. These elements are the **linkage editor** and the **loader.**

Both the linkage editor and loader are programs. They are generally supplied by IBM (or other computer manufacturers) as part of the computer system. Although they assist in program processing, they are generally not considered as an integral part of the computer's operating system. Instead, they are considered agents or elements that assist

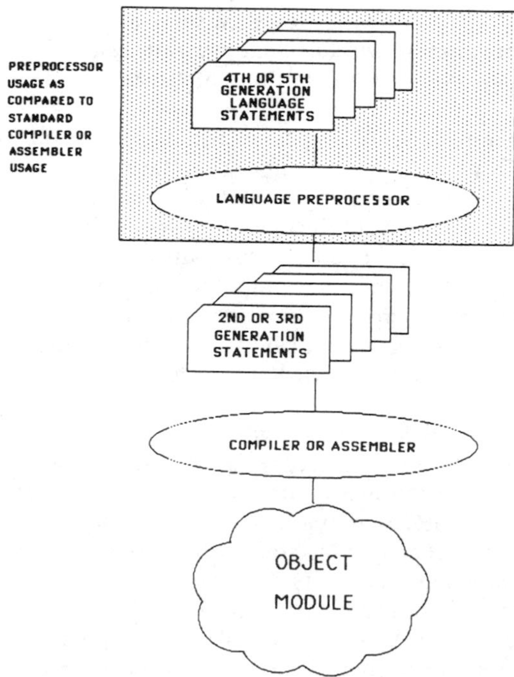

Figure 1.5 Program transformations.

in the preparation of programs so that they can be executed by the computer. These programs are also called **support programs** since they support or assist in the processing of other programs. To understand their operation and where they are used in a programming environment, we must first understand each of the general forms of a program during its development.

A program solution can be found in one of several states: executable or machine format, source format, object format, and load module format. The characteristics of each state are described in Fig. 1.6.

As seen in Fig. 1.6, two of the forms (machine and load module format) produce something that is executable by the computer and the other forms (source and object) do not generally produce executable elements.

Machine code, an executable format, is the lowest level format of a program solution. Programs implemented in this fashion are very difficult, if not impossible, to read and maintain. Programs are not usually developed directly in this format due to its complexity, although this format may be derived through some other process. Some higher level of sophistication for entering programs is used even if it may be an assembly language source code format. In later chapters, we'll discuss machine code format and present examples of its difficulty in use and understanding.

Source code is the format of a program that contains human readable statements and is the most common form of a program. Typical source programs consist of COBOL, PL/I, or assembly language instructions. This form can be more easily read and maintained and serves as the primary method of program development. This is the format that we will use when we develop and implement our programs in assembly language.

An **object module** or **object program** is created by a compiler or assembler after translating or converting the higher level language or assembly language statements. Although the object module is made up of machine code, it is still *not* executable. The object program must be processed once more before it is in a format that can be executed by a computer. The object module consists of machine instructions and data *work areas* (not necessarily the data itself) that will be used by the program during execution. Transforming object modules into executable formats is done through the linkage editor or the loader.

State	Characteristics
Machine format	Can be executed by the computer. Format of the solution in the most basic format and the format most closely related to the characteristics of the machine.
Source format	Cannot be directly executed by the computer unless through interpretation. Format of the solution as entered by the programmer in human readable form.
Object format	Cannot be executed by the computer. Format of the solution after processing by either a compiler or an assembler.
Load module format	Can be executed by the computer. Format of the solution after the object form of the solution is processed by a special program called a linkage editor.

Figure 1.6 Program formats.

The **linkage editor** converts an object module into a load module format while the **loader** converts an object module into an executable machine format. Although both process programs after the programs are compiled, there are definite differences between the functions of these service programs or utilities. For our purposes, we'll give their primary difference.

The linkage editor converts an object program into a load module program and stores the load module program on a direct-access storage device (disk drive). The load module can then be called or fetched into memory (by the operating system) and then executed by the computer. In fact, the load module can be called upon over and over to perform its function.

The loader does not create a load module. The loader creates an executable program, places that program directly into the computer's memory, and then begins the execution of that program. In other words, an object module processed by the loader is immediately executed by the computer while an object module processed by the linkage editor is not executed until the programmer instructs the operating system to fetch and execute the program. Since the loader does not produce a load module, the converted object program is usable for only *one* execution. If that program must be executed again, the object program must be reloaded and executed (using the loader).

Again, the primary difference is the executable end product. Using the loader creates no *permanent* executable program. On the other hand, the linkage editor creates a program that when **fetched** by the operating system is executed. Programs created by the linkage editor can be stored in this format for long periods of time. Hence, one-time or single-use programs are generally processed by the loader and multiple-use or long-term usage programs are generally processed by the linkage editor. Figure 1.7 clarifies the use of these utilities.

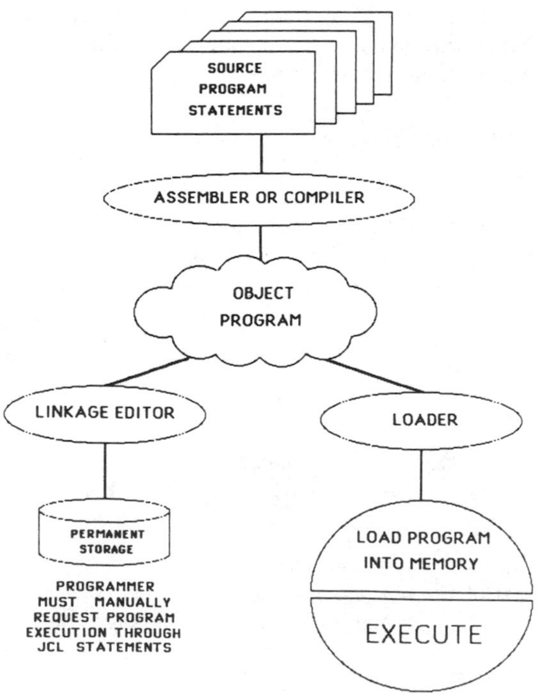

Figure 1.7 Functions of the linkage editor and the loader.

When discussing the linkage editor and loader, we must also consider the assembler or compiler. As stated earlier, the compiler and assembler do not produce executable elements. Whenever a compiler converts source code statements into object code, either the linkage editor or loader converts the object code into an executable format. In data processing, terminology is used to identify each of the phases that programs go through before they are in an executable format. When the source code is converted by a compiler into object code, that code has been **compiled.** When an assembler converts assembly language source code statements into an object program, that program has been **assembled.** Converting an object program into a load module is called **link editing,** and converting and executing an object program using the loader is called **load and go.**

Combining all the terminology, we get: higher level language programs are processed using a **compile and go** procedure (compilation followed by loading and execution), or they may be processed using a **compile, link, and go** procedure (compilation followed by link editing and then a specific request for execution initiated by a programmer). Assembly language programs are processed using an **assemble and go** procedure (assembly followed by loading and execution), or they may be processed using an **assemble, link, and go** procedure similar to higher level language processing. The terminology is quite descriptive since it identifies each component in the processing of a source program. Figures 1.8, 1.9, and 1.10 illustrate these processes.

It is important to remember that with the linkage editor programs are not executed until the *programmer* informs the operating system. This decision must be made specifically by the programmer since it is not an automatic process as is the case with the loader. In a later section, we'll discuss how a programmer requests services from the operating system.

Earlier, we discussed the function of an interpreter as compared to the assembler or the compiler. In discussing the linkage editor and the loader, we must return to the inter-

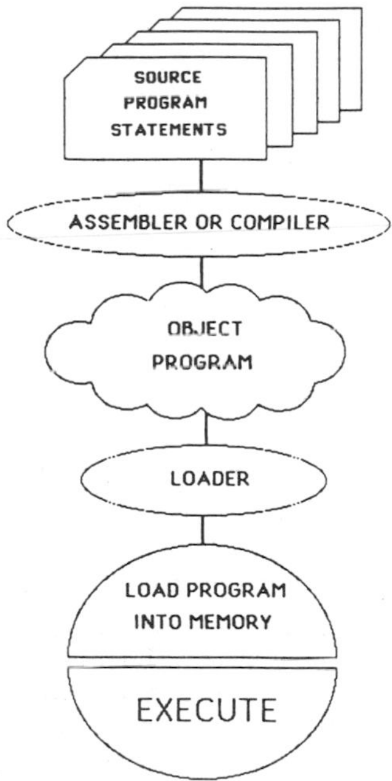

Figure 1.8 Assemble/compile and execute procedure.

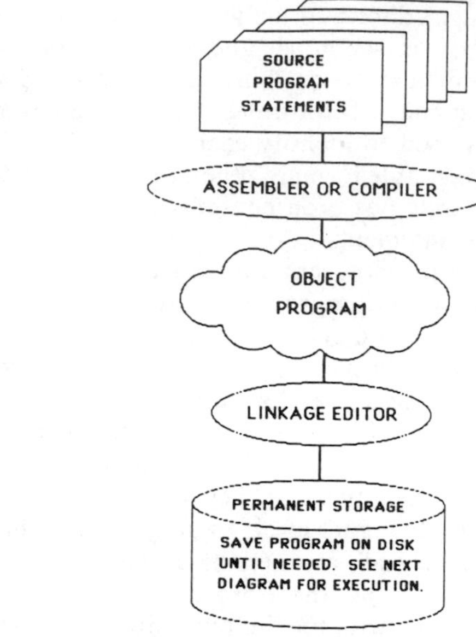

Figure 1.9 Assemble/compile and link edit procedure.

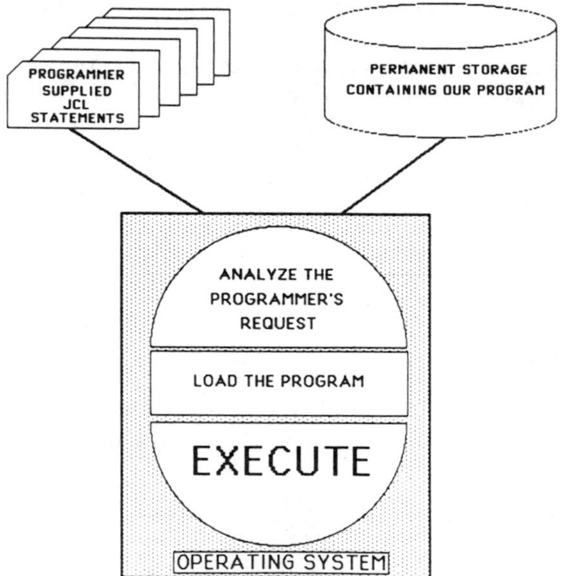

Figure 1.10 Program execution after link editing.

preter. If you recall, an interpreter simulates the execution of instructions. Since source programs are *not* converted into machine code, no object module is produced. Therefore, the linkage editor and the loader are not used if source programs are processed by an interpreter. The interpreter processes the source programs and simulates their execution all in one step, using the necessary input data and allowing the program to print or produce the appropriate output. Although the more common methods of compile-link-go, compile–load/go, and so on are the eventual methods for implementing applications, interpreters are quite important in program testing and in student programming environments where more complete and immediate feedback concerning the execution of a program are needed. We will be using the ASSIST assembly language interpreter throughout the text.

DATA FORMATS AND DATA PROCESSING

Source programs, object programs, and load modules are data to the computer system. How that data is processed by programs and the computer determines its usefulness and importance. A source program is input data to a compiler or to an assembler and an object program is the output of a compilation or assembly. Although these elements are in fact data, we generally regard data as something else, that is, information that is collected, processed, and produced to support a business, research, or academic environment.

Information can be produced in many different formats, such as written, spoken, or recorded. In order for that information to be meaningful to a computer program, however, it must be supplied to the computer in a specific format. Earlier, we discussed punched cards and terminals and stated that these were the primary devices to input data to a computer. In fact, there are many other input devices that present data to a computer in a variety of ways. The many devices and how they interact with the computer are not within the scope of this text, rather, we want to understand how data is stored and processed by the application programs.

Each character of data that passes through a computer is represented as a string of on and off magnetic or electronic pulses. An **on** pulse is generally represented by the digit **1** (one) and an **off** pulse is represented by the **0** (zero) digit. Since only two possible values may be represented with a 0 or 1, it is not feasible for only these two digits to represent all possible alphabet characters. Instead, these digits must be combined to form a string of digits. Thus, the longer the string, the more combinations of on and off pulses. This allows representation of more characters.

Each 0 or 1 value is called a **bit.** A bit has two values—off/on, zero/one, 0/1, no/yes, and so on. When IBM developed their computer systems, they built their computers to process individual bits, but more commonly the computers operate on a group of eight bits at a time called a **byte**. With eight bits, all possible characters of the alphabet and all digits could be represented. In fact, since each bit has two possible values, the number of different combinations of zeros and ones in an eight-bit string is $2*2*2*2*2*2*2*2 = 2^8$, or 256. Hence, IBM allows 256 different characters to be represented within the computer. But there are only 26 characters in the alphabet. Why are 256 combinations needed?

Although there are only 26 characters in the alphabet, there are also 10 digits, special characters such as !, @, #, $, %, &, *, (,), and each character must be represented in upper case as well as lower case. This set of characters and digits alone requires 71 different representations. The number of representations is quickly used or assigned as the number of possible character combinations are developed. Some of these combinations of the eight bits, however, represent unfamiliar characters. Many combinations are used internally within the computer or by the hardware to represent data in one form or another. For example, some of the eight-bit combinations specify how data is to be displayed at a terminal. Depending on the type of terminal being used, these bit patterns may require that data be displayed in a highlighted or bright format, a dark or hidden format, or in a color such as red, green, or blue. Although we don't actually see these special characters on the terminal screen, we do see their impact when looking at the data.

The collection of all combinations that can be represented by eight bits is called a **set** or **character set.** The eight-bits-per-byte character set is called the **EBCDIC** (**Ex**tended **B**inary **C**oded **D**ecimal **I**nterchange **C**ode) character set. There are many other character sets used in the computer industry, but the two most common are the EBCDIC character set and the **ASCII** (**A**merican National **S**tandard **C**ode for **I**nformation **I**nterchange) character set. The basic difference between the two character sets is the number of bits that are grouped together to form characters. EBCDIC uses eight bits per byte to represent its data and ASCII uses seven bits per byte to represent its characters. If you are thinking that 2 to the 7th power (2^7) allows 128 characters to be represented, you are correct. How then can a computer system that allows only 128 different characters succeed when another computer system requires 256 different character possibilities? Simply, both character sets do the job on their respective computer systems. It's almost like comparing tires or engines on an automobile; not all cars have the same tires nor do they all have the same engine, yet they accomplish the task of going from point A to point B. In fact, we generally don't even consider the details of the character sets until we want an ASCII computer system to share data or communicate with an EBCDIC computer system. Since the two characters sets are not identical, some translation must be done to convert ASCII to EBCDIC (or EBCDIC or ASCII), process the data, and convert the results back into the ASCII (or EBCDIC) form so that they are understandable on the original computer. Since this text is concerned with IBM assembly language, we will be studying the EBCDIC character set throughout the remainder of the text.

Although it is possible to process individual bits within a byte, we generally do not perform arithmetic operations on bit data. Bits are generally used as *flags* to signal certain conditions within a program or within a record. For example, an employee record may contain bits set 0 or 1 to indicate that the employee belongs or doesn't belong to the retirement program, participates or doesn't participate in the insurance program, and so on. In general, the smallest unit of data processed by a program running on the IBM computer is a byte.

Each character of source code is converted into a byte within the computer. As the source program is converted into an object program and so on, new bytes of data are formed. Bytes are stored internally within the computer (in the computer's memory area) or on data storage devices such as tape or disk mechanisms. Each character printed by the printer or displayed on a terminal is a byte of data and each column of holes punched on a Hollerith card represents a byte of data. Clearly, the computer must be capable of handling thousands or millions of bytes at a time. The number of bytes that can be stored within the computer at any one instant is dependent on a number of factors, the primary factor being the size of the computer's memory.

When a computer is purchased, computer memory is obtained. Computer memory size is measured in bytes. The more bytes of memory available to the computer, the more data that can be held within the computer. This reduces the need to obtain data from an external source. Further, large memory size increases the overall performance of a program since the program doesn't have to wait for data to be brought into the computer. More memory allows the programmer to write larger programs, programs to do more and process larger amounts of data than was available on smaller computer systems.

Since computer memories run into the hundreds, thousands, or millions of bytes, it is difficult to discuss computer memory in terms of bytes. A similar situation occurs with money. For example, if we spoke only in terms of cents, then a new car may cost 1,000,000 cents rather than 10,000 dollars. Similarly, terminology has been developed to reduce the large numbers of computer memory. One **kilobyte** (commonly referred to as one **K**) represents 1024 bytes of data. When we talk of computers with 256K of memory, that represents 262,144 (256 times 1024) bytes of data. Larger computers contain thousands of kilobytes, requiring the term **megabyte** (commonly called a **meg**) to represent 1024 kilobytes. A computer system having 10M of memory actually contains 10,240 kilobytes of memory, or 10,485,760 bytes. Believe it or not, there are some storage devices that hold thousands of megabytes of data. In this instance, **gigabyte** refers to thousands of megabytes of memory. One gigabyte is equal to 1024M, 1,048,576K, or quite simply, a lot of bytes. Whether the data is in program form, punched-card form, magnetic form or whatever, all characters are represented by eight bits (one byte) in the EBCDIC character set. The next chapter will discuss further denominations (less than one kilobyte) that are common terms to assembly language programmers. For now, these terms should suffice since they are generic and not specific to assembly language programmers. They allow us to discuss, in a general manner, the operation and overview of the computer system.

PROGRAMMING AND LANGUAGES

Now that we understand some of the major hardware and software components of a computer system, let's put them into perspective with respect to programmers and programming.

Programs are developed and communicate with the operating system through programming languages. As discussed earlier, programming languages range from the bare-boned machine language to application development tools such as fourth- and fifth-generation languages. Although we addressed these application languages before, we have yet to address a very important and necessary language for data processing, the **control language.**

The control language for the computer system is a special language that communicates with the operating system. Through the control languages, the programmer instructs the operating system to perform the required processing for their program(s). This may include identifying the input data to be processed, specifying the programs to be executed to process the data, and directing the output of processing to the printer or to some other storage device.

IBM's control language is more commonly known as **JCL** (**J**ob **C**ontrol **L**anguage). Within the title, the word **job** is significant in that the control language is specifically related to the control and processing of units of work within the computer. All units of work or processing steps performed by your program make up your job to the operating system. Students just learning JCL often find it difficult, but if you remember that it is a programming language and is a necessary and powerful tool in the development of an application, it makes the learning process a little easier.

At this point in the text, we'll simply use JCL and discuss its capabilities briefly as they are needed to support the execution of our applications. What we want to remember is that it is through JCL that we instruct the operating system to assemble (or compile) our source code, invoke the loader or linkage editor to convert our object program into an executable program or into a load module, and, finally, to direct the input and output of data to our program. Again, as we feel the need to perform these functions, we will call upon JCL to identify the processing steps required by our jobs.

The concepts that we discussed in this chapter will be carried throughout the remainder of the text. We do not want to forget our development life cycle nor do we want to lose track of the interaction between hardware and software. The next chapter will expand our knowledge base by looking more closely at the memory organization of the computer as it relates to the assembly language programmer. We will also discuss how data is referenced, processed, and stored by an assembly language program. As we build our knowledge base, we will begin to develop increasingly sophisticated programs, hoping to reach the level of a relatively competent computer professional by the end of the text.

STUDY QUESTIONS

1. A program that converts source programs into object programs is called a ____________ or a ____________.
2. A more common name for second-generation programming languages is ____________.
3. Two higher level languages are ____________ and ____________.
4. Although most components in a development cycle are ongoing processes, the step most common to all phases of a development cycle is ____________.
5. Proper and thorough ____________ generally reduces time and frustration during the ____________ phase of a development cycle.
6. The three primary components of a computer system are ____________, ____________, and ____________.
7. The two most common character sets are ____________ and ____________.
8. Devices that support the central computer, such as card readers, printers, and terminals, are more commonly referred to as ____________.
9. Computer memory is organized (from smallest to largest) denominations as follows: ____________, ____________, ____________, ____________, and ____________.
10. A ____________ converts and executes an object program, but a ____________ only converts the object program and stores it on a direct-access storage device (disk) for later execution.
11. ____________ characters of data may be punched on one Hollerith card.
12. The component of the computer system that controls program processing, scheduling, and access to data is called the ____________.
13. There are ____________ bytes in 5K of memory.
14. A general-purpose program, usually supplied by the computer manufacturer and used for day-to-day processing of general-purpose requests, is called a ____________.
15. A program in executable format and stored on a direct-access storage device is commonly called a ____________.
16. Converting a higher level language program from source format into executable format and executing the program is referred to as a ____________ and ____________.
17. The number of bits per byte in the EBCDIC character set is ____________.
18. A ____________ provides input and output capabilities to the computer.
19. The first step in the development cycle involves understanding the problem and gathering information in order to solve the problem. This phase in the life cycle is called ____________.
20. The computer language closest to that of the hardware level is called ____________.

2

Data Representation and Number Systems

Bits, bytes, kilobytes, megabytes, and gigabytes were some of the concepts discussed in Chapter 1. We will now expand our understanding of memory organization within the IBM 370 series of computers by looking at memory from a programmer's point of view. This viewpoint will uncover many new terms and many new concepts, all very important to the assembly language programmer. Further, the concepts and terms that you'll learn in this chapter are applicable to other languages. Some reference to higher level languages such as COBOL or PL/I will be made where appropriate, but such references will be kept to a minimum since our purpose is not to compare and contrast languages but to learn assembly language programming techniques.

MEMORY DENOMINATIONS

The terms bit and byte were the two smallest denominations of memory that we have encountered so far. If you recall, a **bit** is a single binary digit that has a value of 0 or 1 at any given instant. Groups of eight bits form **bytes,** which represent the letters of the alphabet in upper and lower case, digits, and special symbols such as the dollar sign, ampersand, left parenthesis, and so on. Once again, eight bits per byte is characteristic of the EBCDIC character set.

The bit is the smallest element of data that may be processed by any program running in an IBM computer system. As we remarked earlier, bits are generally used as flags to indicate true/false, on/off, or yes/no situations. An assembly language program may process individual bits within a byte, but a COBOL program cannot, that is, the COBOL compiler cannot produce the necessary instructions to allow a COBOL program to turn on or off individual bits within the computer system. As stated earlier, assembly language programming is the closest level of programming to the machine and allows the most functions. This illustrates that some capabilities of the machine can be used at the assembly language level that cannot be used in a higher level language. In contrast to COBOL, PL/I *does* allow access to data at the bit level.

Bits are grouped into bytes. Bits are not found by themselves within the computer, but are always associated within a byte of storage. If a programmer needs to use just one bit for a certain function, the remaining seven bits within that byte will be wasted or not used. Remember, the smallest denomination of memory is the byte and although certain programs (such as assembly language and PL/I) may access individual bits within the computer, those bits must still be contained within a byte of storage.

Between the terms byte and kilobyte there are several more denominations of memory. The next highest level is called the **halfword,** which consists of two consecutive bytes, or 16 bits. Although halfwords may hold many different types of data, they most often hold binary integer data. Of the 16 bits within a halfword, only the rightmost 15 bits hold a numeric value. The leftmost bit indicates the sign of the number, that is, a value of 0 in the leftmost bit indicates a positive number and a 1 in the leftmost bit indicates a negative number. Halfwords are very important to programmers in any language because they are commonly associated with fast numeric processing. Halfwords are used as subscripts or counters since these data elements typically hold binary integer data (no digits to the right of the decimal) whose value is less than $2^{15} - 1$, or 32,767. Further, there are special instructions on the IBM computer systems to process halfword data storage areas. These instructions are called **halfword instructions** and their primary purpose is to process integer data.

The next highest memory denomination is the **fullword,** which is four consecutive bytes of storage, or 32 bits. Fullwords are the most common denomination of memory in the IBM computer since they are used for arithmetic operations, referencing data, and controlling the flow of execution within a program. Since they are the most used of the memory denominations and since they are the basic unit for controlling program processing, they are commonly referred to simply as **words.**

Fullwords are used extensively for integer operations as well as memory addressing. Fullwords, as was the case with halfwords, are used primarily for binary integer processing. The rightmost 31 bits of the fullword hold the value of the number and the leftmost bit again holds the sign. The largest value that can be stored in a fullword is 2,147,483,647.

The next and last memory denomination is the **doubleword,** which contains eight consecutive bytes, that is, two fullwords, four halfwords, or 64 bits. Doublewords are *not*

Term	Use
Bit	Used as a flag or indicator for situations that have only two options such as yes/no, true/false, and so on. Not used for arithmetic processing.
Byte	Holds 1 character of data. Used to hold integer data as large as +255, but not generally used in this way.
Halfword	Used for numeric integer data processing. Allows values up to 32,767 to be processed.
Fullword	Used primarily for processing numeric integer data and for values less than 2,147,483,647.
Doubleword	Used for floating point or scientific applications. Also used for converting data between external and internal representation.

Figure 2.1 Memory denominations.

generally used for integer computation, but instead are used in floating-point or scientific computation. You may have seen a number such as 1.23×10^2 to represent the number 123. This representation, also written as 1.23E + 02, is associated with scientific representation and floating-point numbers. Although doublewords are primarily used for this purpose, they are also used heavily to convert data from one form to another. Data coming into the computer is generally represented in character format and cannot be processed numerically by the computer's instructions. For numeric data to be processed, it must be converted into binary integer form, decimal form, or floating-point form. The doubleword is used, with appropriate instructions, to aid in this conversion process. Figure 2.1 summarizes the discussion on memory denominations and their use.

In the previous chapter, we discussed the terms kilobyte, megabyte, and gigabyte. Although you should be familiar with these terms, they are not as important as the terms that we have just discussed. The terms halfword, fullword, and doubleword are everyday terms in the life of assembly language programmers and ones that must be carefully understood to fully understand assembly language.

REGISTERS AND DATA ADDRESSING

Now that we understand the basic memory divisions, we can see how data is referenced in the computer.

Referencing a byte of storage is called **addressing.** A program references a byte or group of bytes by telling the computer system the location of the bytes from the beginning of memory. To give the address of data, we can use the term **offset** as well as **address** (we think of them as being synonymous) to describe how far data is from the beginning of memory. The first byte of memory is at offset 0 and the second byte of memory is at offset 1. Another way to think of an address or an offset is to think of the number of bytes *before* the data that you want to reference. If you want to reference the tenth byte of memory, you immediately know that there are nine bytes of memory before it. Hence, the offset or address of the data that begins at the tenth byte of memory is 9. Again, the first byte of memory is at offset 0, the second byte is at offset 1, the third byte is at offset 2, and so on, thus placing the two hundreth byte of memory at offset 199.

The number of bytes of storage available in a computer depends on a number of factors, primarily, the cost of the memory and the manner in which memory can be addressed. If cost is no object, then, in general, the amount of memory that can be accessed by a program depends on *how* the memory is addressed. Most IBM computer systems use 24-bit binary numbers to reference areas in the computer. These **addresses** allow memory locations 0 through $2^{24} - 1$ bits of data to be addressed or 16,777,216 bytes (16 megabytes) of storage. Although fullwords are the most common memory denomination used to hold addresses, only the rightmost 24 bits of the fullword are actually used to hold a memory address. The leftmost eight bits are not used in addressing.

Newer IBM computers use even larger addresses that allow 31 bits of addressing. To distinguish between these computer models and the older computers, a special term has been given to this new type of addressing: **extended addressing** or **extended architecture,** more commonly known by its acronym, XA. The bounds of the computer memory have been extended by using seven more bits in addressing data. As a result, $2^{31} - 1$ bits of data can be referenced for a total of 2,147,483,648 bytes.

The computer program can reference data by using a distinctive set of fullwords called **registers.** A register is a special memory area in the computer that is 32 bits long (one fullword). A register addresses data and can be used for other functions, such as performing integer operations, moving data from one place in the computer to another, and controlling the flow of instruction execution within an application program.

Registers are not part of the normal memory or storage available on a computer system. Registers are located in a special part of the computer, but are available to all application programs. As each program within the computer executes, the registers are set to values needed by that program. When it becomes another program's turn to execute, the registers are loaded with values and addresses appropriate for the new program.

A register is four bytes long. Each byte within the register has a name, with the leftmost byte being called **byte 0,** the next byte being called **byte 1,** and so on, as shown in Fig. 2.2. The leftmost byte is also referred to as the **high-order byte** and the rightmost byte is called the **low-order byte.** See Fig. 2.3. The leftmost bit in the register is called **bit 0** and the rightmost bit is called **bit 31.** Figure 2.4 illustrates this nomenclature.

The leftmost bit in a register also assumes the role of the sign bit described earlier. The **sign bit** denotes whether the remaining bits in the register define a positive or a negative number. A value of 0 in the leftmost bit indicates that the number in the register is positive and a 1 bit indicates that the number is negative. Note that when discussing the concept of addressing, we do not speak of it in terms of positive and negative numbers. The lowest byte is at address 0, that is, there are no negative addresses. The largest address depends on which form of addressing our computer supports—24-bit or 31-bit addressing.

For our purposes, the computer contains 16 fullword registers, more commonly called **general-purpose registers,** and 4 doubleword registers, which are called **floating-point registers.** Although there are other registers that control the actual processing and execution within the computer, they are not available to the applications programmer. Hence, we will discuss only the registers available to us and only those that can be used by our programs to process or reference data elements.

The general-purpose registers are referred to using numbers such as 0, 1, 2, 3, . . . , 14, 15, and the floating-point registers are referred to as 0, 2, 4, and 6. For now,

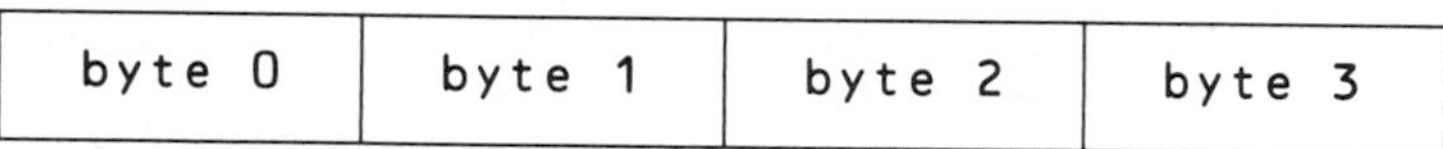

Figure 2.2 Format of a register.

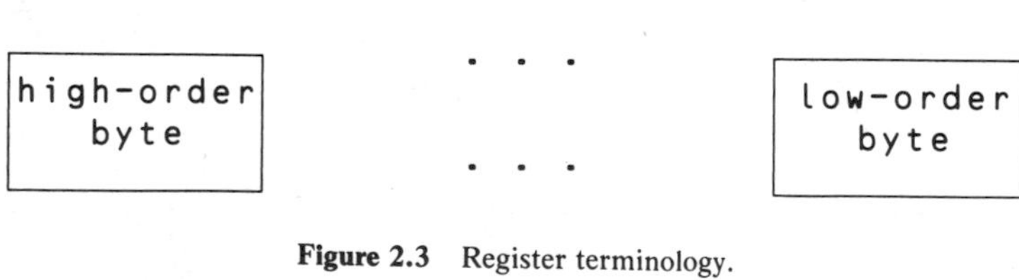

Figure 2.3 Register terminology.

bit: 0 1 2 3 . . . 31

Figure 2.4 Register bit position terminology.

we are concerned only with the general-purpose registers and how they are used in referencing data and program processing. Floating-point registers will be discussed in a later chapter.

An address in an IBM computer is represented in two primary forms, **absolute** and **logical**. The form of addressing that we use will be based on the instructions selected to perform our processing, however, most instructions require logical addressing.

Absolute addressing can be used when our data is located between the first byte and the 4096th byte in the computer. If our data is located beyond or after the 4096th byte, then we must use logical addressing. Further, the first 100,000 (or so) bytes of computer memory are used by the operating system to control the execution of our program and all other programs in the computer. Therefore, we will be *required* to use logical addressing for all but our most advanced processing requirements, since our data and program statements will always be located after the 4096th byte in the computer. As you can clearly see, it is extremely important that you fully understand logical addressing since it is the form of addressing that we will use most often.

The general format in which an address is written is **D(B),** which is a special format called **base-displacement** addressing. The location of the data that we want to process is located at the address that is contained in register **B** (meaning **base**) with an additional offset of **D** bytes. For example, if register 4 contains a value of 200,000, then the address 0(4) informs the computer that our data is at location 0 + 200000 or 200,000. Had we written the address as 6(4), then the computer would have referred to the data at location 6 + 200000 or 200,006.

In these two examples, the digit before the left parenthesis is called the **displacement** and the (4) is called the **base** reference; hence, we coin the term **base-displacement addressing.** Register 4 acts as a reference point in the memory of the computer. Since register 4's value is 200,000, then the reference point is at this location. From this reference point, we want to reference a data item that is 6 bytes beyond this location. Hence, 6(4) allows us to reference the memory location 200,006 in the computer. The value 6 is the distance away from the reference point that our data is to be referenced. In other words, the value 6 is the **displacement** value.

There are really two different forms of base-displacement addressing. One form is written as **D(B)** and the other is written as **D(X,B).** At execution time, both forms will determine an **effective address,** that is, they identify the location of data to be processed. When we develop our programs and write them in source code form, we must be familiar with both forms because each instruction uses one or the other form of addressing.

As you can see in Fig. 2.5, one form uses a comma and an index register within the address and the other form does not. When we coded 0(4) we did not use a comma, but had we coded 0(,4) then we'd immediately know which addressing form was used [D(X,B)]. In fact, the D(X,B) form may be written several ways. Each of the following are valid representations of a D(X,B) address: D(X,B), D(,B), D(X,), and D(X). The last form, D(X), looks similar to that of the base-no index-displacement [D(B)] form of addressing. Although the format is the same, the instruction selected to process the data in memory will determine which of the two addressing formats has actually been selected.

A register's value may change during processing, which can impact the location of

```
D(X,B)     displacement (index register, base register)
D(B)       displacement (base register)
```

Figure 2.5 Addressing formats.

memory being referenced. Suppose, for example, that a D(X,B) address of 4(5,6) references a memory location. The displacement value in this example is 4, the index register is 5, and the base register is 6. If register 5's value changes each time the memory is referenced, using this address form will obviously reference a different memory location. Even if the base register's value (register 6) does not change, any change in register 5 will cause a different location to be referenced.

This is a powerful feature of the addressing mechanism. As an example, consider a list of consecutive fullwords of memory that are to be processed. If a base register contains the address of the first element in this list, then an index register can be used to move from element to element. An initial value of 0 in the index register allows us to process the first fullword and subsequent values of 4, 8, 12, and so on allow us to move through the list to process the remaining fullword areas.

Let's do another example concerning base-displacement addressing. Suppose that register 4 contains the base-10 number 200,000 and register 5 contains the base-10 number 50. What memory location is referenced by the address 8(5,4)?

The answer is found by adding the contents of registers 4 and 5 to the value of 8. In other words, 200,000 + 50 + 8 will yield a memory location of 200,058. This is the location referenced with this address.

In Fig. 2.5, each of the forms use registers inside parentheses to assist in addressing. An **effective address** is calculated by the computer by adding the displacement to the contents of the index register (if there is one) and the contents of the base register. Address computation is further illustrated in Fig. 2.6.

Suppose that register 9 contains the value 6. 11(9) allows us to reference offset 17 in the computer (the data starting at the eighteenth byte). This example is particularly important in that I want to emphasize the difference between an address and the displacement. A **displacement** is coded *before* the parenthesis and must be a positive number greater than or equal to zero and less than or equal to 4095. A displacement *must always be coded* whenever you are using base-displacement addressing.

Displacements are always assumed to be specified as base-10 numbers. In other words, the displacement 35 is much different than a displacement coded as X'35' (we'll discuss this format later; it means hexadecimal value 35). If we assume that register 7 contains the value 10,000, Fig. 2.7 gives the memory locations that will be referenced with several different addressing forms.

```
  D(B) address = D + contents of register B
D(X,B) address = D + contents of register X
                   + contents of register B
```

Figure 2.6 Effective address computation.

Address	Memory Location Referenced
35(7)	10,035
X'35'(7)	10,053
B'0011'(7)	10,003

Figure 2.7 Examples of address computations.

Although most displacements are typically coded in base-10 notation, it is sometimes desirable to code them in binary or hexadecimal form. The examples above are coded properly if hexadecimal and binary forms of displacement coding are to be used.

For now, the terms **index register** and **base register** are just that, terms. We will discuss the full meaning of each of these terms in later chapters, but for now these terms will mean any of the 16 general-purpose registers. Don't be misled into thinking that there are special index registers and base registers that are different from the general-purpose registers—they are one and the same. Figure 2.8 illustrates proper coding of address representations.

The last example in Fig. 2.8 may be confusing, but, in fact, it's quite simple. The *contents* of register 0 are *not* used in computing an address. If a value of 0 is coded where a register number is expected, a *value* of 0 and not the *contents* of register zero are used in computing the address. Make sure that you distinguish between *value* and *contents* when understanding addressing and address computation. This situation only occurs when register 0 is used.

DECIMAL, HEXADECIMAL, AND BINARY NUMBER SYSTEMS

At this point you should be in the habit of counting from 0 rather than from 1. This is something that assembly language programmers must become familiar with when they develop applications. In order to fully understand assembly language instructions, program processing, and data types, we must learn a new number system. You're familiar with the number system we use most often that counts from 0 as follows: 0, 1, 2, 3, 4, 5, 6, 7, 8, 9, 10, . . . , 20, 21, and so on. But what does the value 21 mean? The number 21 means that there are two groups of 10, or 10 + 10, along with 1, giving a total of 21. The basis or base of our number system is the number 10. We must now learn a number system whose base is 16.

Assume that R3 contains the value 10,
R4 contains the value 15,
R5 contains the value 20.

Address	Result
3(3,4)	Reference data at location 28.
3	Reference data at location 3 (this is an absolute address).
(3)	Invalid, displacement not coded.
0(4)	Reference data at location 15.
100(5,)	Reference data at location 120.
100(,5)	Reference data at location 120.
100(5)	Reference data at location 120.
5(3,4,5)	Invalid, too many operands.
54321(3)	Invalid, displacement too large.
−35(3,5)	Invalid, displacements cannot be less than 0.
20(0,0)	Reference data at location 20.

Figure 2.8 Proper and improper address coding.

The base-16 number system is called the **hexadecimal** number system. In this number system, we count as follows: 0, 1, 2, 3, 4, 5, 6, 7, 8, 9, A, B, C, D, E, F, 10, 11, 12, 13, 14, and so on. In other words, some of the numbers are represented by letters of the alphabet. In particular, letters A through F, respectively, represent the numbers we generally call 10 through 15. Hexadecimal 13 is really sixteen plus three, or nineteen. Hexadecimal 3A is really three groups of 16, or 16 + 16 + 16, plus 10, or 58. A value in any number system can be understood if you remember the following concepts:

1. Each position in the number system represents a number of groups of the base number.
2. The value of the number is the sum of all groups represented.

The number 1234 in base 10 is

1 group of 1000 +
2 groups of 100 +
3 groups of 10 +
4 groups of 1

The number 1AF3 in hexadecimal is equivalent to a base-10 or decimal value of 6,899.

1 group of 16*16*16 or 1 * 4096 +
10 groups of 16*16 or 10 * 256 +
15 groups of 16 or 15 * 16 +
3 groups of 1 or 3 * 1

Each digit position within the number is related to a power of the base number. The number 2048 in base 10 has four digit positions. They are related to the powers of 10 in the following way:

____	____	____	____
10^3	10^2	10^1	10^0

If we convert from power representation to decimal representation, each of the digit positions have values of

____	____	____	____
1000	100	10	1

Base-16 or hexadecimal representation occurs in a similar manner.

. . . ____	____	____	____
16^3	16^2	16^1	16^0

. . . ____	____	____	____
4096	256	16	1

As you can see, it's easy to convert from base 16 to base 10; you simply need to remember the power representation of each digit position.

Now, let's convert from base 10 to base 16. The table given in Fig. 2.9 helps significantly in this conversion. Each column of the table represents a hexadecimal digit position. The largest hexadecimal number in the table is six digits long and has the hexadecimal value of FFFFFF.

Using the table in Fig. 2.9, let's convert the base-10 number 5555 to base-16 repre-

HEXADECIMAL AND DECIMAL CONVERSION *

From hex: locate each hex digit in its corresponding column position and note the decimal equivalents. Add these to obtain the decimal value.

From decimal: (1) locate the largest decimal value in the table that will fit into the decimal number to be converted, and (2) note its hex equivalent and hex column position. (3) Find the decimal remainder. Repeat the process on this and subsequent remainders.

Note: Decimal, hexadecimal, (and binary) equivalents of all numbers from 0 to 255 are listed on panels 9 – 12.

HEXADECIMAL COLUMNS											
6		5		4		3		2		1	
HEX	DEC	HEX	DEC	HEX	DEC	HEX	DEC	HEX	DEC	HEX	DEC
0	0	0	0	0	0	0	0	0	0	0	0
1	1,048,576	1	65,536	1	4,096	1	256	1	16	1	1
2	2,097,152	2	131,072	2	8,192	2	512	2	32	2	2
3	3,145,728	3	196,608	3	12,288	3	768	3	48	3	3
4	4,194,304	4	262,144	4	16,384	4	1,024	4	64	4	4
5	5,242,880	5	327,680	5	20,480	5	1,280	5	80	5	5
6	6,291,456	6	393,216	6	24,576	6	1,536	6	96	6	6
7	7,340,032	7	458,752	7	28,672	7	1,792	7	112	7	7
8	8,388,608	8	524,288	8	32,768	8	2,048	8	128	8	8
9	9,437,184	9	589,824	9	36,864	9	2,304	9	144	9	9
A	10,485,760	A	655,360	A	40,960	A	2,560	A	160	A	10
B	11,534,336	B	720,896	B	45,056	B	2,816	B	176	B	11
C	12,582,912	C	786,432	C	49,152	C	3,072	C	192	C	12
D	13,631,488	D	851,968	D	53,248	D	3,328	D	208	D	13
E	14,680,064	E	917,504	E	57,344	E	3,584	E	224	E	14
F	15,728,640	F	983,040	F	61,440	F	3,840	F	240	F	15
0 1 2 3		4 5 6 7		0 1 2 3		4 5 6 7		0 1 2 3		4 5 6 7	
BYTE				BYTE				BYTE			

Figure 2.9 Hexadecimal and decimal conversion table. Reprinted by permission from *IBM System/370 Reference Summary* (GX20-1850). Copyright 1981 by International Business Machines Corporation.

sentation. We begin by looking in the table to find the largest decimal number that is less than or equal to 5555. The value is 4096. The number 4096 is under the fourth column from the right and is associated with the hexadecimal value 1. We therefore will have a four-digit hexadecimal number whose leftmost digit is 1.

1 ____ ____ ____

Now find the difference between 5555 and 4096. 5555 minus 4096 leaves 1459. Find the largest number in the table that is less than or equal to 1459. According to the table, 1280 is the number closest to 1459 and is associated with the hexadecimal value 5. Hence, the third digit position has a value 5.

1 5 ____ ____

The difference between 1459 and 1280 is 179. The largest number in the table less than or equal to 179 is 176 and is associated with the hexadecimal digit B (decimal 11). Hence, the second digit of our number is B (remember, we want to end up with a hexadecimal number).

1 5 B ____

The difference between 179 and 176 is 3. The rightmost digit of our number is 3. Therefore, the base-10 or decimal number 5555 is equal to the hexadecimal or base-16 number 15B3.

1 5 B 3

In other words,

1 times 4096	=	4096
5 times 256	=	1280
B times 16	=	176
3 times 1	=	3
		5555

There's another method for converting from base 10 to hexadecimal, and it involves the process of division. Let's now discuss this technique.

Dividing 5555 by 16, we get 347 with a remainder of 3. The remainder gives us our *rightmost* digit. Dividing 347 by 16, we arrive at a value of 21 with a remainder of 11. Eleven or B gives us our next number (working from right to left). Twenty-one divided by 16 gives us 1 with a remainder of 5. Five is our third digit. One divided by 16 gives us 0 with a remainder of 1 and so our last digit is a 1.

Although we arrived at the same value, we went about it in a different way. One method worked from left to right and the other worked from right to left. The disadvantage with the table lookup method is that it only allows us to convert numbers with less than or equal to six hexadecimal digits whereas the division/remainder method works with a decimal number of any size.

Each hexadecimal digit can be represented by four bits. Hexadecimal representation is commonly used with addressing and address computation. Since addresses are 24 bits long, the largest number of hexadecimal digits needed to represent a 24-bit address is 6 (24 divided by 4 gives 6). Since most hexadecimal operations involve addresses, IBM felt that a table of six-digit hexadecimal numbers was sufficient. However, if you need to convert numbers larger than 24 bits, then they must be converted using the division/remainder method. (Incidentally, you can buy a calculator that converts from hexadecimal to decimal and vice versa at the touch of a button.)

Binary data is represented by a series of 0's and 1's. Binary data can also represent numbers, and, in fact, all data in the computer is actually processed and represented in binary form. The disadvantage of binary representation is that it is cumbersome and requires a lot of paper for all of the bits that you have to write down.

The basis of the binary number system is the number 2. We count in the binary number system as follows: 0, 1, 10, 11, 100, 101, 110, 111, 1000, 1001, 1010, 1011, 1100, and so on. I'm sure that you agree that it's quite awkward and very difficult to read. Let's take a binary number and apply the techniques that we've been using to convert the binary number to base 10.

The number 101101 is a six-digit binary number. Each digit position, represented by a power of 2, is expressed in the following way:

1	0	1	1	0	1
2^5	2^4	2^3	2^2	2^1	2^0
32	16	8	4	2	1

In this example, we have one group of 32 plus one group of 8 plus one group of 4 plus one group of 1, or a base-10 number of 45. Just look at the difference in representation: we write a two-digit number (45) in base 10 whereas a six-digit number must be written when base 2 is used. You can easily see that large numbers are difficult to represent and understand.

Rather than writing binary numbers using 0's and 1's, it is more common to represent binary data using hexadecimal numbers. There is a direct relationship between hexadecimal digits and binary digits since each hexadecimal digit can be represented by four binary digits (four bits). Figure 2.10 illustrates the relationship between decimal, binary, and hexadecimal digits.

If we return to the binary number of 101101 and convert this base-2 number into a base-16 number, we arrive at a number that is shorter in length and hopefully easier to understand. Before starting the conversion process, we must first expand the number so that its length is a multiple of four. The original number 101101 is six bits long, which is not an even multiple of four. We must, therefore, add two bits to the *left* of the number. These bits will have a value of 0. We do this because numeric data is right justified and *padded* (filled in) on the *left* with *zeros*. Now, starting from the right side of the number, we can cut the number into groups of four binary digits. Doing so, we arrive at the binary number **00**10-1101. Using the table in Fig. 2.10, we can now convert this binary number into hexadecimal, arriving at the hexadecimal number 2D. Hexadecimal 2D is equal to 32 plus 13, or 45 base 10.

From this point on, we want to represent binary numbers in hexadecimal format. We will be converting from one form to another frequently throughout the text and so it is wise to practice your conversions by completing the study questions at the end of the chapter.

BINARY AND HEXADECIMAL OPERATIONS

The assembly language programmer may be required to perform addition and subtraction of hexadecimal numbers, decimal numbers, and to convert between hex and decimal quite often. Occasionally, operations between binary numbers must also be performed, but, as we studied earlier, binary numbers can be easily converted into hexadecimal numbers, thus allowing us to perform operations on hex numbers instead of binary.

Addition and subtraction of hexadecimal numbers is handled in a manner similar to decimal operations, except that you're working in base 16 rather than base 10. For example, hexadecimal 30 plus hexadecimal 20 gives hexadecimal 50 (0 plus 0 gives 0, and 3 plus 2 gives 5). Hexadecimal 40 plus hexadecimal 60 gives hexadecimal A0 (0 plus 0

Decimal	Hexadecimal	Binary
0	0	0000
1	1	0001
2	2	0010
3	3	0011
4	4	0100
5	5	0101
6	6	0110
7	7	0111
8	8	1000
9	9	1001
10	A	1010
11	B	1011
12	C	1100
13	D	1101
14	E	1110
15	F	1111

Figure 2.10 Decimal-hexadecimal-binary digit relationship.

gives 0, and 4 plus 6 gives 10, which is represented by the letter A in hexadecimal notation).

Let's add the hexadecimal numbers 3E7B and 2F7. Working from right to left,

> B + 7 is the same as adding decimal 11 and 7. The result, 18, is written as hex 12. Hence, the result of adding B plus 7 is 2 carry a 1.
>
> One (carried) plus 7 plus F is 8 plus F, or 8 plus 15, which is 23. Twenty-three in hexadecimal is 17, or 7 carry at 1.
>
> One (carried) plus E plus 2 is F plus 2, or 15 plus 2 (in decimal), which is 17. Seventeen in hexadecimal is 11, or 1 carry a 1.
>
> One (carried) plus 3 is 4. The result is 4172.

```
  3E7B
+  2F7
------
  4172
```

Subtracting the two numbers, we proceed as follows:

> B minus 7 is the same as 11 minus 7, or 4. Therefore, the rightmost digit is 4.
>
> Seven minus F will not work without borrowing from the position to the left. When we borrow, we are actually borrowing a group of **16** (since we're in base 16) and not a group of 10. After the borrow, we have 7 + 16 minus 15, or 23 minus 15, which is 8.
>
> D (since we borrowed one from the original E) minus 2 is the same as 13 minus 2, or 11 (hex B).
>
> Three minus 0 is 3.

```
  3E7B
-  2F7
------
  3B84
```

Let's focus our attention on binary operations for a minute. Suppose that we want to add the numbers 1011001 and 110111. Again, working from right to left:

```
                 1
                +1
                --
                 0 carry a 1

                1 (carried)
                0
               +1
               --
                0 carry a 1

               1 (carried)
               0
              +1
              --
               0 carry a 1

              1 (carried)
              1
             +0
             --
              0 carry a 1

             1 (carried)
             1
            +1
            --
             1 carry a 1 (1 + 1 + 1 is 3, which is 11 in binary)

            1 (carried)
            0
           +1
           --
            0 carry a 1

           1 (carried)
          +1
          --
           0 carry a 1

          1 (carried)
          -
          1

             1 0 1 1 0 0 1
          +    1 1 0 1 1 1
          -----------------
           1 0 0 1 0 0 0 0
```

As you can see, there is a lot of carrying during binary operations. Had we converted these binary numbers to hexadecimal, it may have been easier:

Number 1	B'1011001' = B'01011001'	(add pad digits)
	B'01011001' = X'59'	(convert)
Number 2	B'110111' = B'00110111'	(add pad digits)
	B'00110111' = X'37'	(convert)

What we now have is hexadecimal 59 plus hexadecimal 37, which we can add as follows:

```
  9
 +7
 --
  0 carry a 1

  1 (carried)
  5
+ 3
---
  9
```

Therefore, the result of X'59' + X'37' is X'90', or if we write the result in binary:

1 0 0 1 0 0 0 0

Incidentally, some of you may wish to convert the numbers into decimal, perform the operation, and then convert back into the required base. Although this technique works, it takes substantially more time than learning hex and binary operations. Consider examination time when you may have to do several operations of this type in a limited time span. You don't want to spend most of your time converting from one base to another as the test time ticks away. Practicing these operations is the best way to become familiar with them. Again, the study questions at the end of the chapter may help you during your practice sessions.

NEGATIVE NUMBERS AND OPERATIONS

Up to this point, we've avoided negative numbers and, in practice, assembly language programmers do not have to convert or manually work with negative numbers too often. Most manual calculations performed by assembly language programmers involve addresses, and, as we know, addresses are always positive numbers (since the lowest address value is 0). Even if we have to subtract one address from another, we'll always have a positive result because there are no negative addresses. We'll always take away the smaller address from the larger address to yield a positive number.

Although most of our manual calculations involve positive numbers and addresses, it is no excuse to avoid the subject of negative numbers because we will be working with them as we process our data. We must know how negative numbers are represented and how to perform operations on them so that we can recognize and understand them when needed.

Negative binary numbers (note that we're talking only about binary numbers) are represented in a format called the **two's complement** notation. This form will seem rather peculiar since the resulting negative number is not easily recognized. In order to know the value of a negative number in this form, you must convert the number into its **complementary form** and append a negative sign to the front of it.

Two's complement form will be used for binary integer numbers that occupy halfwords or fullwords of storage. Rarely do you see the two's complement form used in any other place within assembly language. In particular, two's complement will be most often used with registers—representing numbers in registers and performing operations on numbers stored in registers.

We have already discussed the format of a register, a halfword, and a fullword, and, as you know, the leftmost bit in a register represents the sign of the number: 0

meaning positive and 1 meaning negative. The base-10 number 43 represented in binary (base 2) would appear as follows:

43 (base 10) = 16 + 16 + 11 = X'2B' = B'00101011'

But, as we've shown the number so far, it is not in a complete fullword or halfword representation. Converting the number to its fullword or halfword format (32 or 16 bits, respectively), we arrive at

0000000000101011	halfword representation
00000000000000000000000000101011	fullword representation

The leftmost bit, bit 0, is 0 and so the number is positive. The negative representation of 43, −43 in other words, would be as follows:

1111111111010101	halfword representation
11111111111111111111111111010101	fullword representation

Before we discuss how we arrived at the negative value of 43, let's add negative 43 and positive 43 to see if we get zero.

```
   0000000000101011
 + 1111111111010101
 ------------------
  10000000000000000
```

As you can see, we have a *leftover* value of 1 that carries beyond the normal 16 bits of the halfword values. Such a condition is called an **overflow** since the last *carry* causes a bit to be dropped from the number. However, the resulting 16 bits (the rightmost 16 bits, that is) will all be zero, thus illustrating that −43 plus +43 gives 0.

At this time, we're not concerned about overflow. An assembly language programmer may be concerned at times about overflow, but we are not at this point. When appropriate, we will discuss overflow in detail and how it may be handled.

The negative representation of a number can be arrived at by performing the following steps:

1. Encode the number in its positive binary form.
2. Change all 0's to 1's and all 1's to 0's within the number. Here we are finding the **one's complement** of the number.
3. Add 1.

Applying this process to the number 43, we have:

1. 0000000000101011
2. 1111111111010100
3. 1111111111010101

Step 3 gives us the two's complement form of negative 43. Hence, −43 (base 10) is equal to 1111111111010101 (base 2).

Using a smaller number and only four bits, let's represent the value −7.

1. represent in binary	0111
2. switch bit values	1000
3. add 1	1001

Now let's suppose that we have −7 (in binary) and we want to convert it to a positive number. Performing the same set of steps, we should get +7.

1. negative 7 1001
2. switch bits 0110
3. add 1 0111

We've been working with binary values up to this point, so now let's practice with hexadecimal numbers. Using fullword representation, let's represent −43.

1. represent in hex 0000002B
2. switch bits FFFFFFD4
3. add 1 FFFFFFD5

This may have been a little confusing, so let's look at this example again in binary.

1. in binary 00000000000000000000000000101011
2. switch bits 11111111111111111111111111010100
3. add 1 11111111111111111111111111010101
4. in hex F F F F F F D 5

If you look at the leftmost bit in the result, you see it has a value of 1 and so the result is a negative number.

It is important to remember that our discussion so far has centered around binary integer numbers. We have not discussed decimal numbers (numbers with digits to the right of the decimal) nor have we discussed floating-point (scientific representation) numbers. These will be discussed in later chapters.

As a review, the two's complement or negative representation of a number may be found by first finding the one's complement of the number and then adding 1. If the number is a negative number, then the two's complement gives the positive representation of the number. The process for converting from the negative representation to the positive representation is the same: find the one's complement and then add 1.

DATA TYPES AND THEIR MOST COMMON REPRESENTATION

We've worked with binary numbers and have spent some time on bit, byte, halfword, and fullword representations of binary numbers. We have also discussed character data and that each character of the alphabet requires eight bits in the computer. An assembly language programmer chooses instructions when implementing his program based on the type of data that is being processed. Each type of data has its own set of instructions that *must* be used in order to process the data correctly.

When choosing the instructions in which to implement the program, the programmer must understand the different forms of data available in the IBM computer systems. The programmer may also consider the speed at which the instructions operate in order to build a program that performs faster. Bit data instructions generally process faster than binary instructions, binary instructions are generally faster than character data instructions, character data faster than decimal, and decimal instructions are generally faster than floating-point instructions. The programmer may choose to represent data in one form over another and may even choose a form not typical for the data being stored to gain better performance from the program. The data types and their purposes are listed in Fig. 2.11.

Data Type	Use or Explanation
Character	Represents data that people can easily understand, such as letters of the alphabet. Each character to be represented requires eight bits or one byte of memory.
Binary	Primarily used to represent integer data in positive or negative form and as 16-bit (halfword) or 32-bit (fullword) numbers.
Bit	One of eight bits in a byte of storage that can indicate a condition for the program, such as yes/no, true/false, and so on, as set by the programmer's instructions within that or another program.
Packed decimal	Represents decimal numbers, that is, numbers with digits to the left and/or right of the decimal point.
Zoned decimal	Used in conjunction with packed decimal form to represent decimal numbers during input and output operations to the computer.
Floating point	Represents scientific numbers or numbers that require extreme precision to the right of the decimal. Provides automatic handling of the decimal point.
Address	Used heavily by assembly programmers to reference data and other instructions within an assembly program.

Figure 2.11 Data types and their usage.

Since we've already discussed bit, binary, and address, and since we are going to discuss floating point later, let's concentrate our efforts by looking at character and decimal representation.

As we have said, each character requires eight bits to represent it. Figure 2.12 gives the most common characters and their corresponding representations.

First Column-character
Second Column-hexadecimal representation
Third Column-binary representation

space	40	01000000

.	4B	01001011	<	4C	01001100
(	4D	01001101	+	4E	01001110
&	50	01010000	!	5A	01011010
$	5B	01011011	*	5C	01011100
)	5D	01011101	;	5E	01011110
-	60	01100000	/	61	01100001
¦	6A	01101010	,	6B	01101011
%	6C	01101100	_	6D	01101101
>	6E	01101110	?	6F	01101111
:	7A	01111010	#	7B	01111011
@	7C	01111100	'	7D	01111101
=	7E	01111110	"	7F	01111111
a	81	10000001	b	82	10000010
c	83	10000011	d	84	10000100
e	85	10000101	f	86	10000110

Figure 2.12 Character representation table.

g	87	10000111	h	88	10001000
i	89	10001001	j	91	10010001
k	92	10010010	l	93	10010011
m	94	10010100	n	95	10010101
o	96	10010110	p	97	10010111
q	98	10011000	r	99	10011001
s	A2	10100010	t	A3	10100011
u	A4	10100100	v	A5	10100101
w	A6	10100110	x	A7	10100111
y	A8	10101000	z	A9	10101001
A	C1	11000001	B	C2	11000010
C	C3	11000011	D	C4	11000100
E	C5	11000101	F	C6	11000110
G	C7	11000111	H	C8	11001000
I	C9	11001001	J	D1	11010001
K	D2	11010010	L	D3	11010011
M	D4	11010100	N	D5	11010101
O	D6	11010110	P	D7	11010111
Q	D8	11011000	R	D9	11011001
S	E2	11100010	T	E3	11100011
U	E4	11100100	V	E5	11100101
W	E6	11100110	X	E7	11100111
Y	E8	11101000	Z	E9	11101001

Figure 2.12 (continued)

¢	4A	01001010
|	4F	01001111
¬	5F	01011111
[	8B	10001011
]	9B	10011011
[	AD	10101101
]	BD	10111101
≠	BE	10111110
\	E0	11100000
|	FA	11111010

Figure 2.12 (continued)

What do the following hexadecimal characters mean in readable form?

D385819995899587408 1A2A285948293859940

93819587A48187854089A24086A4955A5A5A5A

Using the Table in Fig. 2.12, we can convert each of the two-digit hexadecimal representations (two hexadecimal digits make one byte of storage, or one character) into the phrase "Learning assembler language is fun!!!!"

Each byte of data requires two hexadecimal digits to form the full character consisting of eight bits. Remember, each hexadecimal digit occupies four bits, and so eight bits will require two hexadecimal digits.

ZONED AND PACKED-DECIMAL REPRESENTATION

The character table in Fig. 2.12 did not contain representations for the digits 0, 1, 2, . . ., 9. Although digits are characters, we want to address them at this time since they are more often used in calculations and arithmetic operations rather than simply to represent characters. It is also an appropriate opportunity to discuss the relationship between data external to the computer, data internal to the computer, and the relationship of data to instructions.

Information that we understand is in what is called **human readable form,** that is, it is information that we can look at and easily determine what it means. As you read the words on this page, you understand what they mean. If this textbook was printed in hexadecimal or binary, I doubt if you would be able to understand it. This is what is meant by human readable form. In fact, information that is to be entered into the computer and information that is printed or output from the computer must usually be converted from human readable to machine readable format. Within the computer, that same information must be in a format that the computer's instructions can process as needed by the programs written by the programmer. As we stated earlier, a specific set of instructions are available on IBM systems to process character data, binary data, float-

0	F0	11110000
1	F1	11110001
2	F2	11110010
3	F3	11110011
4	F4	11110100
5	F5	11110101
6	F6	11110110
7	F7	11110111
8	F8	11111000
9	F9	11111001

Figure 2.13 Character representation of digits.

ing-point data, and addresses. Very few of these instructions may be used on another set of data unless, of course, you want errors to occur.

Two other data forms, **packed decimal** and **zoned decimal,** use digits in their representations. However, these forms are peculiar to processing numeric data; although they are used to represent numeric information, the representations may not appear exactly as shown in Fig. 2.13. Their primary goal is to allow numbers to be used in computation and we must distinguish between their representations and those of character digit representations.

Character-digit data (also called **character-decimal data**) is the numeric information you see on punched cards, on a terminal screen, or on printed output. The table in Fig. 2.13 gives you the representations for each of these digits as well as their binary equivalents. On the other hand, **zoned-decimal** information is used to convert human readable (character) data into packed-decimal format. **Packed-decimal** format is an internal representation of numeric decimal data in the computer that allows us to perform calculations. You might say that zoned-decimal data is *sandwiched* between character and packed-decimal representation. Zoned decimal is used to convert character-decimal format into packed-decimal format and packed-decimal format into character-decimal format. As an assembly language programmer, it is very important that you understand that operations such as addition and subtraction *cannot* be performed on either zoned or character-decimal format (without errors occurring).

Data represented in character-decimal form usually contains a plus sign (+) or a minus sign (−) to indicate whether the data is positive or negative. Zoned-decimal data uses hexadecimal digits to denote whether the data is positive or negative. Hexadecimal digits A, C, E, and F may all be used by the computer to indicate a positive number and the digits B and D are used to indicate a negative number. Consider the number +432, which may be represented in character-decimal format as 4EF4F3F2. In zoned-decimal format, the plus sign is removed from the number and its rightmost byte is converted so that it now contains the sign. The number +432 in zoned format is represented as F4F3C2.

Each byte of a zoned-decimal number contains two portions: the left half of the byte (four bits long and the first hex digit in the byte) is called the **zone** portion of the number and the right half (the second hex digit in the byte) is called the **digit** portion. Most zone values are the hexadecimal letter F, except for the rightmost byte. The rightmost byte, which in the example above for the value +432 is C2, contains the digit 2 as well as the sign of the number, C (positive). In other words, zoned-decimal format represents digits according to the format described in Fig. 2.14.

All digits *to the left of the rightmost byte* are represented in the standard character-decimal format with each byte divided in half and called the zone portion and digit portion, respectively, of the byte.

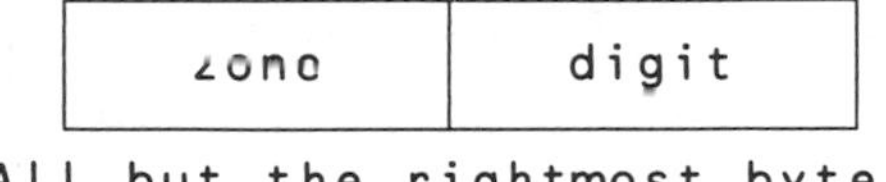

All but the rightmost byte.

The *rightmost byte* consists of two parts, the left half being the sign and the right half being the digit of the number.

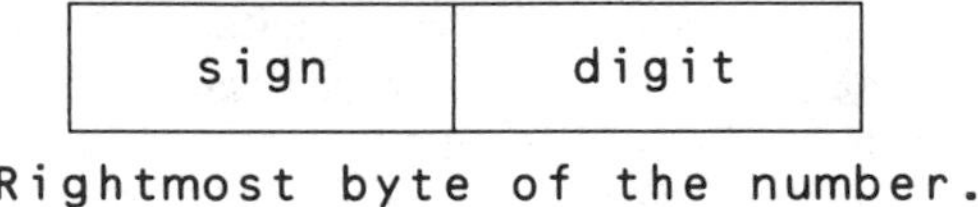

Rightmost byte of the number.

Figure 2.14 Zoned-decimal representation.

The rightmost byte of the number is divided in half, four bits dedicated to holding the sign of the number and four bits dedicated to representing the last digit of the number. The left half is called the **sign portion** of the byte and the right half is called the **digit portion.** Generally, the sign portion contains the hexadecimal digit F or C to indicate a positive number and a sign value D to indicate a negative number. The letters A and E are rarely used to represent positive numbers (although they may) and the letter B is rarely used to represent negative numbers.

Figure 2.15 illustrates a few more examples of data in both character and zoned formats.

Human Readable	Character Format	Zoned Format
0	F0	C0
3	F3	C3
−3	60F3	D3
256	F2F5F6	F2F5C6
−21678	60F2F1F6F7F8	F2F1F6F7D8
+487	4EF4F8F7	F4F8C7

Figure 2.15 Examples of zoned and character formats.

If our ultimate goal is to perform operations on data, then the data must be in binary format, floating-point format, or packed-decimal format. These are the only formats for which there are instructions on the IBM computers to add, subtract, multiply, or divide numbers. If the data has been entered on the terminal or punched on data cards, then this data will be entered in character format. In order to perform arithmetic operations on the data, we must convert it into zoned format *and then into* binary format, floating-point format, or packed-decimal format. Since we've already discussed binary format and we'll discuss floating-point format in a later chapter, let's concentrate our efforts at this time on packed-decimal format.

Packed-decimal data format is derived from zoned-decimal format. The primary use of packed-decimal data is to perform arithmetic operations. Although binary data may also be used to perform arithmetic operations, packed-decimal data allows us to process data having digits to the left and right of the decimal point. Although binary data can be used to process data with digits to the left and right of the decimal, it's more difficult to do so in binary than it is in packed decimal. As we stated earlier, binary data is most often used with integer arithmetic.

Further, binary data was limited to numbers no larger than 2,147,483,647 whereas packed-decimal data is limited to numbers that are up to 31 digits long. This is quite a substantial difference between the two forms of numeric processing. Typically, packed-decimal processing is *the* most commonly used form of numeric processing in business environments. Further, packed-decimal processing is one of the most common forms used by higher level languages such as COBOL and PL/I.

Figure 2.16 describes the internal format of a packed-decimal number. Again, the rightmost byte of a packed-decimal value is divided in half, but it is divided in a slightly different way as described in the figure.

All digits *to the left of the rightmost byte* are stored *without* zones. In other words, packed-decimal data can be considered as a *compressed* data format. Further, packed-decimal data is not readable when printed on a printer or on the screen of an on-line terminal since each byte of a packed decimal field may or may not convert into a human understandable character.

digit	digit

Data to the left of the rightmost byte.

The *rightmost byte* is again split into two parts, but this time the position of the sign and digit portions within this byte are reversed. The left half contains the digit value and the right half contains the sign. Comparing this to zoned decimal, you'll see that the position of the sign and digit have been switched.

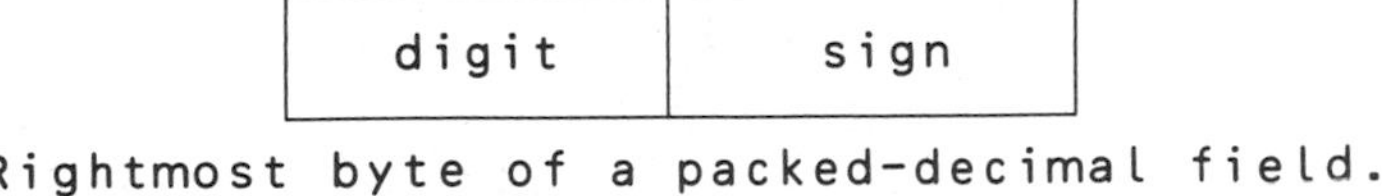

Rightmost byte of a packed-decimal field.

Figure 2.16 Packed-decimal representation.

Combining the above descriptions, we have the full format for packed-decimal numbers as shown below.

The sign of the number is located in the rightmost half byte of the number and all digits within the number are encoded in four-bit fields to the left of the sign.

Figure 2.16 (continued)

The table in Fig. 2.17 gives examples of each data format and how several numerical values would appear in the computer if stored in the various formats.

Let's look carefully at two examples in Fig. 2.17, specifically, the representations for 256 and −13. The number 256 is stored in packed-decimal format in what appears to be human readable format, but remember that no zones are associated with any of the digits. Look carefully at each byte in the packed-decimal number; you'll see that the bytes have values X'25' and X'6C'. Referring to the character and digit tables illustrated in Figs. 2.12 and 2.13, respectively, you'll see that hexadecimal 25 isn't in the tables. Hence, it does not represent a character that we are familiar with although the computer will know its value when appropriate packed-decimal instructions are used to process this data.

The second byte's value is X'6C', which again, according to the table in Fig. 2.12, represents the percent sign (%). Considering the bytes as characters, they do not form a normal representation of the number 256 as far as we're concerned, but as a packed decimal field, the computer will recognize both bytes *together* as positive 256 when the appropriate instructions are used to process that data.

The number −13 reveals another interesting feature that you've seen before, namely, padding. *Only full bytes may be represented in the computer* and so the value of any packed decimal field that does not completely fill a byte requires padding on the left side with zeros. As you can see, −13 in packed-decimal format is represented by X'013D'. The leading zero was added automatically by instructions that converted our data from zoned-decimal format into packed-decimal format so that only full bytes would be represented.

Human Readable	Zoned Decimal	Packed Decimal
0	C0	0C
3	C3	3C
−3	D3	3D
256	F2F5C6	256C
−21678	F2F1F6F7D8	21678D
+487	F4F8C7	487C
−13	F1D3	013D

Figure 2.17 Human readable format compared with zoned- and packed-decimal examples.

The packed-decimal format is one of the most important formats used in business environments and business programming and is one that should be very familiar to an assembly language programmer. Although we've covered a great many concepts in this chapter, it is impossible to rank them in order of importance since they are all equally important to the assembly programmer. In fact, all of the concepts that we've discussed will be found in most higher level languages as well. Figure 2.18 shows the relationship between the elements that we've discussed to that of PL/I and COBOL programs.

Concept	PL/I Equivalent	COBOL Equivalent
binary	FIXED BINARY	COMPUTATIONAL
character	CHARACTER	X (alphanumeric)
packed	FIXED DECIMAL	COMPUTATIONAL-3
zoned	PIC '99 . . . 9'	display 9's
address	BASED	linkage section
floating pt.	FLOAT	COMPUTATIONAL-1 COMPUTATIONAL-2

Figure 2.18 Data format representation in the PL/I and COBOL languages.

It's surprising to see the similarity between the various languages, especially the most common business languages. In fact, this similarity is not a coincidence. Data created by an assembler program may be processed by a COBOL, PL/I, or FORTRAN program as long as the standard forms of storage are used to represent the data.

To enhance your understanding of data conversion and data representation, you are strongly encouraged to complete the study questions at the end of this chapter.

STUDY QUESTIONS

1. The number system represented by a base of 16 is called the _____ number system.
2. The size of a register is _____ bits, _____ halfwords, or _____ bytes.
3. Registers are used to _____ memory and to perform _____ operations on _____ data.
4. Each character requires _____ bits to represent that character in the computer.
5. Perform the following conversions:
   (a) 10111011101 (base 2) into base 10
   (b) 2FEDA (base 16) into base 2
   (c) 2FEDA (base 16) into base 10
   (d) 15075 (base 10) into base 16
   (e) 491 (base 10) into base 2
6. Perform the following conversions:
   (a) −587 (base 10) into binary halfword
   (b) −3BA2 (base 16) into packed decimal
   (c) −25 (base 10) into binary fullword
   (d) −3274 (base 10) into packed decimal
7. Perform the following *hexadecimal* operations:

```
(a)   1EF5      (b)   951      (c)    EF
    +  7AB           -CD             +A9
    ------           ---             ---
```

8. Perform the following binary operations:

(a) 10111011 + 010101 (b) 1100001 − 11111 (c) 101 + 11

```
(a)   10111011      (b)   1100001      (c)   101
    +   010101          −   11111          +  11
```

9. Assume the following and give the resulting effective addresses using the D(B) or D(X,B) formats given below:

R1 = X'00004CA0'
R2 = X'00001234'
R3 = X'0007ACDE'

(a) 240(R1,R2) = X'________________'
(b) 0(R2) = X'________________'
(c) 4(R3,) = X'________________'
(d) −3(,R1) = X'________________'
(e) 5048 = X'________________'

10. The base-10 number 12,582,912 needs to be represented in memory. How many bytes will be required to hold the number if it is to be stored in the formats below? (Assume the number is positive.) Write the representation of the number in each of the formats.

Format	Number of Bytes	Representation of the Number
(a) binary	______	__________
(b) zoned	______	__________
(c) character	______	__________
(d) packed	______	__________

11. If a computer has 2,500 words of memory, how many bytes of memory are available on the machine?

12. Each of the following addresses are either in the D(B) or the D(X,B) format. Identify which format is used in each instance.

(a) 3(4,5)
(b) 100
(c) 3(,5)
(d) 250(1)
(e) 12(13)

13. What data types are used to represent and process numeric data on an IBM computer system?

14. How are negative numbers represented within the various data types?

15. Most addresses are 24 bits long, but in some cases, 31 bit addresses may be used. In what case(s) can 31 bit addresses be used in a program?

3

The Assembly Language Program

Developing an assembly language program is similar to developing a program in any other programming language in that certain statements start and end the program. Other statements define data elements and process the data elements. In this chapter, we will learn the basic format of an assembly language program as well as learn more terminology related to assembly language programming. By the end of the chapter, we should be able to implement a very simple program.

ASSEMBLY LANGUAGE STATEMENT FORMAT

Although there are very few rules that must be followed when programming in assembly language, some standards have been developed for coding assembly language programs. The assembly language statement consists of six basic components:

label area: starts in column 1
mnemonic area: starts in column 10
operands area: starts in column 16
comment area: starts in column 40
continuation indicator: contained in column 72
sequence number: columns 73–80

There are not many hard-and-fast rules to statement coding except for the label area (also called the symbol area), which must begin in column 1. The mnemonic area can start before or after column 10 as long as there is at least one blank column that separates the mnemonic area from the label area. The operands area may start in, before, or after column 16 as long as one blank separates the mnemonic from the operands. The only other rule is the position of the continuation indicator, which must be coded in column 72.

The **label area** (symbol area) of a statement identifies a data element or a location in a program. Assembly language statement labels are usually one to eight characters in length, but the latest IBM assemblers allow 63-character labels. I suggest that you stay with the old standard of one- to eight-character labels since most industries use this format. The statement label may begin with any letter of the alphabet or the special characters @, #, or $, and may be followed by any of these characters or the digits 0 to 9. The new assemblers also allow the use of the underscore character (_) within the label as long as it is not the first character of the label. Figure 3.1 gives some examples of valid and invalid statement labels.

A label is an identifier similar to your name. Labels allow referencing statements or data elements by name rather than by the D(B) or D(X,B) address forms. Referencing data areas using labels is called **implicit addressing** whereas referencing data areas using specific D(B) or D(X,B) address formats is called **explicit addressing.** As a general rule, we want to use implicit (labeled) addressing whenever possible. Placing a label on a statement or on a data element helps you to refer to it later. However, there is a slight difference between human names and those in assembly language programs. Not only do labels have a different format, but they must also be unique. No label may appear more than once in the same assembly language program, but many people may have the same name (just look in the phone book under Brown, Jones, or Smith).

This is a good point to distinguish between **machine language** and **assembly (assembler) language.** In many settings, these terms are used synonymously. However, we should be aware that writing programs in machine language can be very difficult. Machine language does not allow labels, thus causing programs to be almost impossible to read. All storage areas must be addressed using explicit addressing forms. Through the power of the assembler and hence assembly languages, programmers can write programs that are easier to develop and maintain. Therefore, we will study only *assembly* language programming in this text. In fact, it's very rare to find someone who develops programs in true *machine* language.

The **mnemonic** area in a statement contains the actual instruction code or instruction identifier. Although we haven't seen any mnemonics yet, we'll soon see the actual instructions used by assembly language programmers. The mnemonic is the *heart* of the assembly language instruction since it determines the processing to be performed by the computer.

The **operands** in an instruction identify the data to be processed *as related to the mnemonic.* Each instruction requires specific operands that must be coded in a specific format and order, and that reference appropriate data elements.

If you make an error in coding the assembly language statement, the assembler will not fully convert your program into an object module so that it may be executed. Instead, the assembler will *flag* your statement (indicate that there's an error) with a **syntax error message.** Misspelling a label, not coding the label in a proper format, coding a nonexistent mnemonic, or coding a D(X,B) address instead of a D(B) address when required are examples of syntax errors. If the assembler does not find any syntax error, then the program is converted into object code and sent on for further processing.

Errors that occur during execution are called **execution-time errors** or **run-time errors** and are generally caused by logical problems within the program solution. Execu-

```
LOOP          valid
@LOOP         valid
LOOP1         valid
1LOOP         invalid, doesn't begin properly
@123          valid
$SUBTOTAL     too long in old assemblers
SUB-TOT       invalid, can't use a dash
MAIN PGM      invalid, can't use space
```

Figure 3.1 Valid and invalid statement labels.

tion-time errors are generally more difficult and take more time to fix than syntax errors since they tend to be related to several statements rather than to one statement, as is usually the case with syntax errors.

The **comment** area in an assembly language statement allows a short comment for each instruction. The comment area is also called a **line comment** since the comment is contained on the line to which it refers. We've indicated that the line comment should begin in column 40, but, in fact, it may start anywhere after the operands area as long as the two areas are separated by at least one space. Although the line comment area is quite small, you'd be surprised how terse you can be when it comes to describing the instruction being processed. In fact, there's a tendency to be too terse, giving comments that do not help the readability of the program. For example, consider the LR (load register) instruction. This instruction has two operands, both of which are registers. Further, LR copies the register contents from *right to left*. Suppose that we want to copy the contents of register 4 into register 3. The examples in Fig. 3.2 copy the contents of register 4 into register 3 and illustrate several examples of line commenting.

Which of these comments would you rather see on the instruction? It's obvious that some comments are much more descriptive than others. The last example in Fig. 3.2 is the type of line comment to use so that other programmers (or even ourselves) will understand the processing being done. (In contrast, the person who wrote the comment "3=4" must be in another number system.)

An assembly language instruction may be continued over more than one line by typing a character in column 72. *DO NOT* type in column 72 unless you are continuing an instruction. Column 72, the **continuation column,** indicates to the assembler that the instruction will continue on the next line. Rarely will you have to use this option since most assembly language instructions, and their operands, easily fit on one line. There will be cases, however, where we will need to provide continuation and those will be pointed out as we come to them.

The last field is called the **sequence number** field and is used to number the statements in the program. When using punched cards for program development, it is important to use this field and number each statement in your program. The numbering scheme is not important as long as you know the order of the statements in your program. Should you drop the punched cards, you can easily put them back in order using the numbers in columns 73 to 80. To provide some security, you can place your initials in this area to prevent others from easily duplicating your program. Those programs would contain your initials in the rightmost columns, easily detectable by anyone.

BEGINNING THE ASSEMBLY LANGUAGE PROGRAM

There are many ways to begin an assembly language program. They often begin with comments describing the elements and the processing within the program. Aside from comments, an assembly language program typically begins with either the **CSECT** or the

```
LR     3,4     LOAD REGISTER 4 INTO 3
LR     3,4     3=4
LR     3,4     R3=R4
LR     3,4     TOTAL=INITIAL
LR     3,4     SET TOTAL TO AN INITIAL VALUE
```

Figure 3.2 Line comments.

START statement. Although there are some important differences in their use, we will use their most basic format, thus allowing us to use them interchangeably for now.

An assembly language program is called a **control section** from which the mnemonic CSECT is derived. On the other hand, since our program is being "started," the START statement may also be used to begin an assembly language program. The general format for coding the CSECT and START statements is described in Fig. 3.3.

By following these steps, we have named our program and indicated where it begins. Incidentally, we'll discuss the meaning of the zero (in the operands area) in the START statement later in this chapter.

The next decision we must make is to select one of the 16 general-purpose registers to be our **base register** or **reference register.** Before we do, however, we must know how the general-purpose registers will be used by our program during processing. We cannot select a register as a base register that will be used to perform an addition, subtraction, or any other operation within the program. The register can only be used as the base register and should not be used for any other purpose.

A base register simply contains an address, which is very important since it serves as a reference point for our program. When we discussed the organization of memory in an earlier chapter, we indicated that the first 100,000 bytes or so of memory are used by the operating system. Let's suppose that our program is 500 bytes long and begins at location 200,000 in the computer. As you know, data is referenced using absolute or logical addressing. Since absolute addressing can only be used to reference data within the first 4096 bytes of the computer, we generally do not use absolute addressing in our program. Logical addressing uses a reference point to access data or other instructions within the program.

If we associate logical addressing (sometimes referred to as **relative addressing**) to the real world, you may be able to understand the concept more clearly. Suppose that a town called Middletown is 150 miles from Chicago, Illinois, and 200 miles from St. Louis, Missouri, as illustrated in Fig. 3.4.

1. Assign a name for your routine (one to eight characters) and code this name in the label area on the statement (columns 1 to 8).
2. Code either the word CSECT or the word START in the mnemonic area of the statement (column 10)
3. If you coded the START statement, then code the number zero (0) in column 16.

For example,

```
MAINPGM    CSECT
MAINPGM    START    0
```

Figure 3.3 Coding the CSECT or START instructions.

Figure 3.4 Logical reference points.

If Chicago is our reference point, then we can say that Middletown is 150 miles from Chicago and St. Louis is 350 miles from Chicago. The distance between Middletown and St. Louis is therefore 350 minus 150 or 200 miles. In other words, all distances are measured from Chicago.

Applying this idea to that of addressing, let's assume that address 200,000 is our reference point. A data element in our program that is located at address 200,050 is 50 bytes from the beginning of our program, or 200,050 minus 200,000. We can now say that the data element is at offset or displacement 50 with respect to the beginning of our program. If register 12 contains the value 200,000, then we can represent the location of the data element through D(B) or D(X,B) addressing format as 50(12) or 50(,12) or 50(12,). Although any of these formats will work, remember to use the proper format related to the instruction that we are coding to reference or process the data element.

Register 12 is serving as a reference point—register 12 is our base register. All data elements or instructions are measured in terms of their distances from the address in this register. The location of all data areas in a program is thus relative to the base register's value. If the base register contains the address 100,000, then all data areas are relative to address 100,000. If the program is executed again and begins at location 200,000 instead of 100,000, data areas are now relative to location 200,000. The base register determines the logical reference point, also referred to as the relative reference point. Hence the terms "logical addressing" and "relative addressing" are used to describe this addressing technique.

When selecting a base register, remember that some registers are "special" and should be used very carefully *if at all.* In particular, registers 0, 1, 13, 14, and 15 are special registers whose important uses we'll see later. For now, let's restrict ourselves to registers 2 to 12 for our base register *and* for our processing. On the other hand, ASSIST allows use of most of the special registers without any problem. ASSIST compensates for any "misuse" of the registers. However, remember that this is not good practice since you *must* abide by the rules when you're coding programs and running them outside of the ASSIST programming environment.

A base register may be used to address a *maximum* of 4096 bytes of storage. In other words, the **range** of a base register is 4096 bytes. Programs equal to or shorter than 4096 bytes will need only one base register and programs longer than 4096 bytes will require one base register *for each* 4096 bytes. Clearly, lengthy programs may require many base registers. Building programs in terms of modules relieves the strain on register use and allows more registers for standard processing. The more registers assigned for base register tasks, the fewer available for standard processing operations. Most of our programs will be less than 4096 bytes or we will modularize our programs to obtain components whose sizes are less than 4096 bytes. Therefore, we can select one register to be our base register. Let's select register 12.

To define the base register to the assembler, you must code the **USING** statement. The USING statement informs the assembler about the base register and indicates the reference point for our program. Assuming that the program is named MAINPGM, it would be coded as shown in Fig. 3.5. It is important to note that the example in Fig. 3.5 is not complete: it will not work as coded. It is only a partial example of beginning a program.

```
MAINPGM   CSECT
          USING    MAINPGM,12
```

Figure 3.5 Beginning an assembly language program.

What's in register 12? Your guess is as good as mine at this point. If you recall, registers are inherited from the operating system. Whatever was in register 12 from the operating system is what's in register 12 when our program gets control.

What should register 12 contain? Since we want register 12 to be our base register, then it should contain the address of the beginning of our program. For register 12 to contain our address so that it can be used as our base register, we must place a value into register 12 that is equal to the address of the beginning of our program.

Remember the special registers 0, 1, 13, 14, and 15? When our program gets control from the operating system, register 15 contains the **entry point address** or starting point of our program. If we copy the value of register 15 into register 12, then we'll have set register 12 equal to the beginning address of our program. Do you remember how to copy the contents of one register into another? We can do this with the **load register** instruction.

As discussed earlier, the load register instruction copies the contents of one register into another. We can use this instruction to copy the contents of register 15 into register 12 (they will then be equal) to establish our base register. Figure 3.6 continues our program development.

At this point in our discussion, we need to make a distinction. The CSECT and USING statements are **assembly language instructions** and the LR instruction is a **machine instruction.** Machine instructions are converted by the assembler into executable machine code and are executed by the computer. Assembly language instructions are simply information to the assembler so that it can convert the program into an executable format as you desire. You do not have to use assembly language instructions, but you must use machine instructions to execute your program. However, we don't think about writing programs without assembly instructions since it makes a program impossible to write and maintain as discussed earlier.

You're probably wondering why we did not use register 15 as our base register, especially since it already contained the proper entry point address for our program. This is a good question, and again it relates to the use of the special registers by the operating system. As we pointed out, you *can* use register 15 as a base register. However, if you want to learn to program using industry techniques, then you must learn to use a register, other than 15, for the base register. On the other hand, using register 15 for a base register is a common practice in ASSIST, especially for beginning students and for the first few programming projects. We'll discuss this technique in a later section in this chapter. However, this is not an industry standard. Therefore, instead of learning a technique which we'll have to discard later, let's learn how to begin an assembly language program in the proper manner.

Later we will discuss how to bring data into the computer and send data out of the computer. Input and output of information requires the use of register 15; in fact, registers 0, 1, 14, and 15 are *all* required for input/output processing. If we were using any of these registers for our base register or for our normal processing, we'd be in trouble because the values in these registers are changed by the operating system during input or output processing. Clearly, if we had selected register 15 as our base register and if it were

```
MAINPGM  CSECT
         LR     12,15
         USING  MAINPGM,12
```

Figure 3.6 Establishing a base register.

destroyed, we would lose our reference point and not be able to properly reference our data areas or statement labels after the I/O operation.

This problem brings up an interesting philosophy that we are going to adopt, namely, we want to preserve the environment of our program and the other programs using the computer. In general, excluding ASSIST for now, an I/O operation causes most of registers 0, 1, 14, and 15 to be altered. Clearly, any values in these special registers are destroyed. The operating system file access routines are not very friendly to our programs when we perform I/O. Regardless of the operating system's actions, we want to preserve the operating environment for our program and other programs. It is easily done and requires just one instruction, the **STM (store multiple)** instruction.

When the program begins execution, a special data area is set aside by the operating system for our use. The address of this data area is contained in register 13 (another special register). This data area is large enough to hold 15 of the 16 general-purpose registers (register 13's contents are handled in a special manner). As we discussed in the last chapter, all programs use the same set of general-purpose registers. To protect one program from another, each program is responsible for setting aside the contents of the registers *before* using them. The STM instruction will do this job for us and will use the special **register save area** addressed by register 13.

As Fig. 3.7 shows, these four instructions are the key to properly beginning an assembly language program. However, this is not the only way to begin a program nor are these instructions the only instructions that we must code. These instructions identify the name of our program to the assembler and tell the assembler which register is our base register (CSECT and USING). At execution time, we preserve the registers by using the special area addressed by register 13 (using the STM instruction). Then, we copy the entry point address (address of the first executable instruction) of our program contained in register 15 into register 12 to set up our base register (using the LR instruction).

Although these are the primary instructions for entering a program, a few more are needed. The example in Fig. 3.7 would work properly if our program did not call for any other programs or performed any input or output operations. However, since most programs perform input and output, we must code a few more instructions before we've fully completed the code to enter our program properly.

When our program was invoked, register 13 pointed to a special register save area in the computer, which was established by the operating system for our use. If we want to perform I/O (which requires a call to an operating system subroutine) or use a subroutine that we've written, then *we* must set up a similar register save area for the routine that we will be using. To do this, we define a register save area in the data area portion of our program using a DS or DC instruction. We then use the proper instructions to assign the memory location of the save area into register 13, just as the operating system had provided for our program when *we* began execution. These instructions are **LA (load address), ST (store register),** and **LR (load register).** Let's look at the required code. In a later chapter, we'll go into detail about why we're using this code and how it works. Figure 3.8 gives the complete code to enter a program.

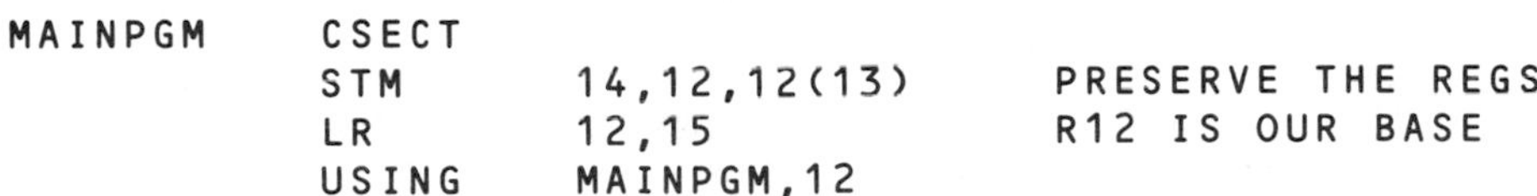

```
MAINPGM  CSECT
         STM    14,12,12(13)     PRESERVE THE REGS
         LR     12,15            R12 IS OUR BASE
         USING  MAINPGM,12
```

Figure 3.7 Preserving register contents.

```
MAINPGM    CSECT
           STM      14,12,12(13)      PRESERVE THE REGS
           LR       12,15             R12 IS OUR BASE
           USING    MAINPGM,12
           LA       11,SAVEAREA       ADDRESS OUR SAVE AREA
           ST       13,4(11)          SAVE CURRENT R13 VALUE
           ST       11,8(13)          INFORM THE O.S.
           LR       13,11             ESTABLISH NEW SAVE AREA
```

Figure 3.8 Entering a program and establishing a save area.

The data element called SAVEAREA will be defined within our program. You'll see how to define this field soon.

Now let's see the code using the START statement. Figure 3.9 illustrates how this may be done.

```
MAINPGM    START    0
           STM      14,12,12(13)      PRESERVE THE REGS
           LR       12,15             R12 IS OUR BASE
           USING    MAINPGM,12
           LA       11,SAVEAREA       POINT TO SAVE AREA
           ST       13,4(11)          SAVE CURRENT R13 VALUE
           ST       11,8(13)          INFORM THE O.S.
           LR       13,11             ESTABLISH NEW SAVE AREA
```

Figure 3.9 Starting a program and establishing a save area.

Before we go further, we need to clean up a few loose ends. Have you noticed that the USING statement contains the name of the program that is also coded on the CSECT or START statement? This is *not* a coincidence. When a program begins execution, register 15 contains the entry point address, the address or memory location of the first executable instruction in our program. In the program sections shown in Figs. 3.8 and 3.9, the first machine instruction is the STM instruction. The CSECT statement is not a machine instruction and will therefore not occupy any memory during execution. If our program begins at memory location 200,000, then the first instruction that the computer will find at that location is the STM instruction.

Although the USING statement tells the assembler about our base register, it is very important that the base register value and the USING statement reference point refer to the same location in our program.

The USING operands—MAINPGM and 12—indicate that register 12 is the base register and that the reference point for the program, from the assembler's point of view, is at the location whose label is MAINPGM. Since MAINPGM is the beginning of the program and since the contents of base register R12 also point to the beginning of the program, we say that the reference point established by the USING and the base register contents agree. If they don't agree, the program will not execute correctly. Figure 3.10 gives an example of a program that does not work because the USING and base register contents do not agree.

```
            THIS CODE WILL NOT WORK PROPERLY
MAINPGM     CSECT
            STM       14,12,12(13)
            USING     MAINPGM,12
            LA        11,SAVEAREA          POINT TO SAVE AREA
            ST        13,4(11)             SAVE CURRENT R13 VALUE
            ST        11,8(13)             INFORM THE O.S.
            LR        13,11                ESTABLISH NEW SAVE AREA
```

Figure 3.10 Incorrectly establishing an entry point.

What did we forget? We didn't load register 12 with the entry point address contained in register 15. Hence, we don't know what register 12 will contain, but the assembler will *assume* that register 12 is all right and use MAINPGM as the reference point.

```
            THIS CODE WILL NOT WORK PROPERLY
MAINPGM     CSECT
            STM       14,12,12(13)
            LR        10,15
            USING     MAINPGM,12
            LA        11,SAVEAREA          POINT TO SAVE AREA
            ST        13,4(11)             SAVE CURRENT R13 VALUE
            ST        11,8(13)             INFORM THE O.S.
            LR        13,11                ESTABLISH NEW SAVE AREA
```

Figure 3.11 Incorrectly specifying a base register.

Figure 3.11 illustrates an even more blatant error. We've told the assembler via the USING that register 12 would be our base register, but we've loaded register *10* with the entry point address from register 15. Our program will fail during execution, and, if we don't see this error immediately, we could spend hours trying to fix the program. Incidentally, did you notice that this type of error was an execution error and not a syntax error? We did not make a coding mistake, rather we made a logical mistake by misusing the registers.

Why must the USING and base register contents agree? The answer is not simple since it involves base registers, addressing, and instruction formats. However, we should understand the answer before we continue our discussion of assembly language programming.

Recall our discussion on D(B) and D(X,B) addresses. Each of these formats has the letter **B** for **base register** and the letter **D** for **displacement**. All data elements in our program are located in memory, a certain number of bytes from the base reference point. When we use a label to define a data element and later reference that data element using a machine instruction, the assembler converts the label reference of the data element into a D(B) or D(,B) address format.

Here's an example. Suppose that a fullword binary data element called AMOUNT is to be added to the contents of register 5. The add instruction shown in Fig. 3.12 adds the value in AMOUNT to the contents of register 5.

```
            A      5,AMOUNT
```

Figure 3.12 Adding fullword contents to a register.

The result of the addition is held in register 5. When this instruction is converted into machine code by the assembler, the label AMOUNT is converted into a D(X,B) address since the second operand of the A (add) instruction requires the D(X,B) format. If the data element AMOUNT is 50 bytes from the beginning of our program, then the resulting D(X,B) address will be **C032** after conversion. The first number indicates the base register being used in the program, in this case, C or 12. The next three digits, 032, represent the displacement or number of bytes that AMOUNT is from the reference point. The hexadecimal value 032 is equal to 50 in base 10 (48 plus 2). Hence, the location referenced by this base-displacement address is 50 bytes from the beginning of our program (which R12 addresses).

Labels do not require an index register and so for instructions utilizing D(X,B) addressing, the typical label will convert into a D(,B) address format. This is still a D(X,B) format except that the index register is assigned a value of 0—it is unused.

All labels must be converted into D(B) or D(,B) address formats by the assembler. Further, labels will convert into a two-byte field; the first *half byte* is the base register, whose range must encompass the data element, and the remaining *one and one-half bytes* give the displacement of the data element from the base reference point (identified by the USING statement). The largest value for the displacement is hexadecimal FFF, or decimal 4095. Hence, this is the reason why a base register can only support reference of 4096 bytes of data.

If the USING statement tells the assembler a reference point that does not agree with the base register's value, the program will not access the data correctly during execution, and in fact the program may fail.

In the example shown in Fig. 3.13, the base register points to the first instruction in the program since register 12's value is taken directly from the contents of register 15. On the other hand, the USING statement tells the assembler that the reference point is at location POINTA. The two do not agree. The difference between the MAINPGM location and the POINTA location is the STM instruction that is between the two. The STM instruction is a machine instruction that occupies four bytes of memory after it is converted by the assembler into machine format. Therefore, all references to our data areas will be off by four bytes. Think carefully about this. If we attempt to reference a fullword of storage, we won't be able to do it properly. The base register and USING statement reference points are off by four bytes, and, since the fullword is four bytes long, when we attempt to reference the fullword area, we'll just miss it.

The base register and USING statements must agree. Figure 3.14 generalizes our discussion and shows a typical method for establishing a base register. In this example, Rx is any register R2 through R10. In this example, Rx is any register R2 through R10, or R12. R11 can't be selected because it's used in the instructions that follow the USING. If

```
THIS CODE WILL NOT WORK PROPERLY
MAINPGM    CSECT
           STM      14,12,12(13)
POINTA     LR       12,15
           USING    POINTA,12
           LA       11,SAVEAREA
           ST       13,4(11)
           ST       11,8(13)
           LR       13,11
```

Figure 3.13 Mismatching the USING and base register values.

```
MAINPGM    CSECT
           STM      14,12,12(13)
           LR       Rx,15
           USING    MAINPGM,Rx
           LA       11,SAVEAREA
           ST       13,4(11)
           ST       11,8(13)
           LR       13,11
```

Figure 3.14 General format for entering a program.

some other register is used in place of R11 then R11 could be established as the program's base register.

Let's look closely at the STM instruction. It tells the computer to store registers 14 *through* register 12 into the location whose address is 12 bytes from register 13. In other words, place the contents of the registers 14, 15, 0, 1, 2, . . ., 11, 12 into the memory area whose address is 12(13). In the last operand, 12(13), the number 12 is simply the displacement from the location whose address is in register 13. If register 13 contains the address 300,000, then the registers will be stored into the area starting at location 300,012. Let's not worry why the displacement is 12, since we'll discuss this in a later chapter, rather, let's simply use the instruction for now as we continue to build our knowledge base about assembly language programming.

As I pointed out earlier, much of our discussion may be ignored when programming in ASSIST. Since the ASSIST package compensates for nonstandard register usage, we can enter ASSIST programs with less code than was required for standard assembly language processing. Figure 3.15 illustrates a typical method for entering an ASSIST program and establishing register 12 as a base register.

```
PROGRAM    CSECT
           LR       12,15
           USING    PROGRAM,12
```

Figure 3.15 Entering a program developed in ASSIST.

As illustrated, you do not have to establish a register save area. In fact, register 15 could have been used as the base register simply by coding the CSECT and USING statements as shown in Fig. 3.16.

```
PROGRAM    CSECT
           USING    PROGRAM,15
```

Figure 3.16 Using R15 as a base register in an ASSIST Program.

Clearly, this is easier to remember as to what to do to enter a program. However, it is not how things are done in the real world and it's the real world that counts! Although ASSIST allows these shortcuts, they will not become our standard throughout the remainder of the text. All programs will be implemented in the full fashion so that errors are minimized, if not eliminated, and so that you'll have an easier transition from classroom to office when you finish this text.

BODY OF THE ASSEMBLY LANGUAGE PROGRAM

The main component of the assembly language program is the **body**. Here data areas are defined so that they may be used in processing and to produce results. We will also code the necessary assembly language and machine instructions to operate on that data.

Machine language instructions are coded depending on the function to be performed and the data to be processed. To process binary data, for example, you would use binary data instructions whereas packed-decimal instructions are used to process packed-decimal data. As we discuss the instructions to process each data type in later chapters, you will become more familiar with the various machine instructions that you may code within the body of your program.

Machine instruction choice impacts performance as we discussed in an earlier chapter. Bit data instructions generally process faster than binary, binary than character, character than packed decimal, and packed decimal than floating point. Floating-point instructions are among the slowest instructions in the computer system, but they are among the most powerful.

Performance and processing speed is not only related to the type of data being processed, but is also related to where the data is processed. Data processed in registers is processed much faster than data processed in memory. Whenever possible, you should use registers to process data to improve performance. However, there are two flaws in this thinking. First, there are very few registers, and, second, not all data may be processed by registers. When we consider that only registers 2 to 12 are available for use and that at least one of these must be designated as the base register, that leaves only 10 registers to work with. That's not very many.

The body of the assembly language program is coded based on the design of the program, the data being processed, and any performance considerations incorporated into the program. Although the design of the program is more crucial, some consideration to data types and processing speed should be given by the assembly language programmer.

DATA ELEMENTS AND THEIR DEFINITIONS

Another component within the body of the assembly language program is the data area definitions. Here we define the **variables** or **data elements** that process the input data and give the desired results. Variables hold data that can be processed by instructions.

It is very simple to define data elements since they have only two basic formats. One format simply sets aside the required storage for the data element and does not **initialize** or give a default value to the area, and the other format defines *and* initializes the data area.

To define and initialize a data area, we use the **define constant (DC)** assembly language instruction. Note that an *assembly language* instruction is used instead of a machine instruction. The instruction sets aside the appropriate amount of storage and assigns the value that you specified to that storage area. You may give a name to the area by placing a label in column 1 just as you've seen before. Again, labels are one to eight characters long and must begin with A to Z, @, #, or $. Figure 3.17 illustrates the method for defining an unnamed fullword binary data area and initializing the area to the value zero.

```
         DC    F'0'
```

Figure 3.17 Defining and initializing a fullword of storage.

If we also want to give the storage area a name, such as TOTAL, we may do so as shown in Fig. 3.18.

```
TOTAL   DC    F'0'
```

Figure 3.18 Naming a defined constant storage area.

As you can see, we simply code the instruction **DC,** place a label on the statement (if appropriate), and use the data type identifier (in this case, the letter F, meaning *fullword*) to set aside storage. The area is initialized by placing the default value for the area inside a set of single quotes (apostrophes) immediately after the data type identifier. You may place a comment on the statement as long as one blank column separates the end of the data element definition from the first character of your line comment.

There are many data types in assembly language, and the table in Fig. 3.19 lists the most common data types that are used to define storage areas.

Identifier	Result
B	Defines bits (within a byte) of storage.
X	Defines a hexadecimal byte of storage.
H	Defines a halfword of storage.
F	Defines a fullword of storage.
D	Defines a doubleword of storage.
C	Defines a character storage area.
P	Defines a packed-decimal area.
A	Defines a fullword that will hold an address

Figure 3.19 Most common data types.

The data type identifier may be preceded by a number that allows the request of several identical storage areas. This number is called the **repetition factor** or **duplication factor** and is useful in defining many similar data areas that are adjacent to each other. For example, the instruction **DC 10F'0'** defines 10 fullwords of storage, all initialized to the binary value zero.

```
FIELDS  DC    10F'0'
```

Figure 3.20 Using the repetition factor.

The instruction in Fig. 3.20 defines 10 fullword fields, all initialized to the value zero. The first field *and only the first field* will be named. This raises a major drawback to the use of the repetition factor, namely, when using the repetition factor, the name of the field only applies to the first field in the definition. Subsequent fields must be referenced through displacement addressing.

At this time, we can now define the field called SAVEAREA that is so important to entering our assembly language program. If you recall, SAVEAREA was a field that was established as the new register save area in the event that our program performed I/O or called a subroutine.

```
SAVEAREA  DC    18F'0'
```

Figure 3.21 Defining a register save area.

Wait, there are only *16* general-purpose registers, but, as shown in Fig. 3.21, SAVEAREA defines 18 fullwords of storage. Yes, there are only 16 registers, but, we must abide by the rules for assembly language programming on an IBM 370 system. One of the rules states that the register save area must be *18* fullwords in length. Again, if we simply use this code for now, we'll eventually get to the point where we can discuss why we must enter our programs in this way and why we must define an 18-fullword save area.

In addition to the special repetition qualifier, another qualifier may be coded with the identifiers A, C, P, and X. This qualifier, called the **length (L) qualifier,** modifies or qualifies the length of the field that you are defining. Suppose that we want to define a character field that is 20 bytes long. We can do it in two ways as illustrated in Fig. 3.22.

```
DC    20C' '
DC    CL20' '
```

Figure 3.22 Defining and initializing 20 bytes of storage.

In Fig. 3.22, both definitions result in the same amount of storage, and both storage areas are initialized to the character blank (space). However, if we now try to put some other value in this field, two different results will be obtained.

```
DC    20C'AUTO PARTS'
DC    CL20'AUTO PARTS'
```

Figure 3.23 Defining and initializing a storage area with a default value longer than a byte.

The first example in Fig. 3.23 will define 20 consecutive strings, all having the value 'AUTO PARTS'. This will yield the value 'AUTO PARTSAUTO PARTSAUTO PARTS. . .' and so on for this field definition. Since this is probably not what we wanted, let's now look at the second data definition in this example.

The second line in Fig. 3.23 requested *one* 20-byte area of storage. Since this area is greater than or equal to the length of our string, the string will fit into the area. The string 'AUTO PARTS' is less than 20 characters long, but the area defined is 20 characters long. When the string is placed into the storage area as part of the initialization process, 10 characters of storage will be unaccounted for. In situations like this, the assembler will place the string into the area from *left to right,* filling in the remaining or leftover positions with blanks (since we are defining character data). This action is called **padding.**

In an earlier chapter, we discussed padding numeric fields. We noted that leading zeros were added to the left side of a number and the number was placed from *right to left* into a field. Numeric fields are **right justified** and padded on the left with zeros. Character fields are **left justified** and padded on the right with blanks. Therefore, using the lower case letter b with a line through it to indicate a blank, our character field looks as shown in Fig. 3.24 *inside the computer* (*not* on the printout of our program).

```
DC      CL20'AUTO PARTSƀƀƀƀƀƀƀƀƀƀ'
```

Figure 3.24 Internal value of an initialized string.

To avoid padding, we can also define character, X, or P fields in yet another way. In this method, we do not use either the repetition factor or the length qualifier. We also do not allow the assembler to pad the data areas and so we save storage. Using our AUTO PARTS character string as an example, we can define it as illustrated in Fig. 3.25.

```
DC      C'AUTO PARTS'
```

Figure 3.25 String definition without repetition or length qualification.

In Fig. 3.25, the data is defined and occupies only 10 bytes in the computer. In other words, this method uses only the storage necessary to hold the data. This method is very efficient, but how long is the area? In order to determine its length, *we* have to manually count the number of characters of data within the quotes. When we used the length qualifier, we knew immediately the length of the field since part of the field's definition was its length. For short fields, the method above is acceptable although it may be easier to determine the length of a field if the length qualifier were used.

We may define hexadecimal fields by using the X operand. If we convert each character of our string into hexadecimal, we can define it as a 20-character field using the X identifier as shown in Fig. 3.26.

```
DC      XL20'C1E4E3D640D7C1D9E3E240404040404040404040'
```

or

```
DC      X'C1E4E3D640D7C1D9E3E2'
```

Figure 3.26 Defining fields using hexadecimal notation.

In Fig. 3.26, the hexadecimal representation of a blank is 40. Again, we used the L qualifier (in the first example) to indicate that we were defining a single area of 20 characters and not 20 individual characters. The second example in Fig. 3.26 defines the same string of characters, but does not waste 10 additional bytes of memory.

If I would have defined our area in yet another way, we would have obtained a totally different definition. What is the result of Fig. 3.27's definition?

```
DC      XL20'C1E4E3D640D7C1D9E3E2'
```

Figure 3.27 Padding within hexadecimal fields.

I've defined the same field, but entered only the necessary characters of my character string. As you know, padding will occur. What you don't know is that padding is different when defining hexadecimal fields than when defining character fields.

Padding of hexadecimal fields is performed by the assembler by filling in positions with the hexadecimal value 00, but it occurs on the left since a hexadecimal field is really a *numeric* field! When we defined our field using the C data type, padding was done using blanks and on the right. Not so here. Clearly, we must be very careful when defining fields so that we don't incur unwanted characters. Yes, we may be able to define the same field in a number of different ways, but we must be careful when doing so since the actual value of the field in memory may be different, depending on the pad character and where the data is padded (left or right side). The actual value of our field, with the X'00' pad characters is given in Fig. 3.28.

```
DC      XL20'0000000000000000000000C1E4E3D640D7C1D9E3E2'
```

Figure 3.28 Internal value of a partially filled hexadecimal field.

The table in Fig. 3.29 gives examples of defining storage areas using the DC instruction.

Operation	Implementation
Define one fullword and initialize to a value of 5.	DC F'5'
Define 10 fullwords, all initialized to 5.	DC 10F'5'
Define 50 characters each initialized to the letter Z.	DC 50C'Z'
Define one 50-character area initialized to 'ABC'.	DC CL50'ABC'
Define a packed area to hold five digits and initialized to the value +456.	DC PL3'+456'
Define one byte initialized to '1'	DC C'1'
and a halfword initialized to 1.	DC H'1'
Define a one-fullword area to hold the address of the area called X.	DC A(X)
Define a three-byte area to hold the 24-bit address of X.	DC AL3(X)
Define one fullword and two halfwords, initialized respectively to the values 1, 2, and 3.	DC F'1',H'2',H'3'

Figure 3.29 Examples of defining constant fields.

We may define a storage area, give it a name (if desired), and *not* initialize it by using the **define storage** assembly language instruction. The mnemonic for this instruction is **DS** and it is used in a manner similar to the DC instruction, except that you cannot initialize fields. Figure 3.30 illustrates its use.

Let's look at a few examples in Fig. 3.30. The packed-decimal field, defined as PL3, is three bytes long and allows storage of five digits. From the previous chapter, you'll recall that the packed-decimal format is a compressed format and stores two digits per byte, except for the rightmost byte, which holds only one digit. A three-byte packed area can therefore hold (6 − 1) digits, or five digits of data.

Since storage addresses are only 24 bits long (on computers without the extended architecture (XA) feature), the A operand may be qualified to set aside only enough storage to hold 24 bits of data. The typical A operand sets aside one fullword of storage. Since

Operation	Implementation
Define one fullword.	DS F
Define 10 fullwords.	DS 10F
Define 50 characters.	DS 50C
Define one 50-character area.	DS CL50
Define a packed area to hold five digits.	DS PL3
Define one byte.	DS C
Define a one-fullword area to hold an address.	DS A
Define a three-byte area to hold a 24-bit address.	DS XL3
	DS 3X
	DS AL3
Define one fullword, two halfwords, and a character string able to hold 50 characters.	DS F,2H,CL50

Figure 3.30 Defining fields without initialization.

we know that addresses are generally only 24 bits long, we do not need to waste a byte of storage to store the address.

The last example in Fig. 3.30 is particularly interesting since it illustrates the power of the assembler to accept many data definitions on a single line. As shown in Fig. 3.29, you can do the same with the DC instruction and give each field an initial value.

As we said earlier, the assembly language program is made up of assembly language instructions and machine instructions. Further, you do not have to use assembly instructions, but it's to your advantage to do so. Figure 3.31 is an example of a program that *will* execute but tends to be a little more difficult to read than other programs.

```
DC      X'90ECD00C18CF41300005414000061A345030C01807FE000000000000'
```

Figure 3.31 Executable program in machine code format.

The program in Fig. 3.31 will add the numbers 5 and 6 and store them into a data area within the program. I used the hexadecimal data definition instruction DC to define each of the bytes within the area. In fact, this area contains both instructions and an area to hold the results of the addition. Clearly, this is not how we want to write our assembly language programs. Through the use of meaningful labels (symbols), machine instructions, assembly language instructions, and comments, our programs can be much more readable and maintainable than the code above. Just imagine a program that is 10 times longer than this. How would you like to code it or maintain it? Incidentally, before assemblers and higher level languages were available, this is basically how you had to program.

To further illustrate the importance and function of the assembler, consider what would happen if all of your programs had to be written in the form above. Since every reference to a storage area would have to be made in an explicit manner, no labels could be used to define storage areas. Whenever the slightest change was made to the program, you'd have to reenter most of the instructions and recompute the displacements to each of the data areas since most of the displacements to the storage areas would have probably changed. The assembler eliminates this work since it converts all labels into proper address forms for us.

The program above can be written in a more standard format as shown in Fig. 3.32.

```
MAINPGM  CSECT
         STM   14,12,12(13)      SAVE THE REGS
         LR    12,15             R12 IS OUR BASE REG
         USING MAINPGM,12        TELL THE ASSEMBLER OF OUR BASE REG
         LA    3,5               PUT 5 IN R3
         LA    4,6               PUT 6 IN R4
         AR    3,4               ADD THE NUMBERS
         ST    3,SUM             SAVE RESULT IN STORAGE
         BCR   B'1111',14        RETURN TO OS
SUM      DS    F                 RESULT AREA
         END   MAINPGM
```

Figure 3.32 Standard coding of the assembly language program of Fig. 3.31.

This program is more readable, but not much since we're not yet familiar with the assembly language instructions and machine instructions to understand what is happening. Let's put it aside for now and continue with our discussion of data definition.

LOGICAL DATA STRUCTURES

Single data elements are easy to define and are the most common types of data definitions within your first assembly language programs. As you become more experienced, however, you will define more sophisticated data definitions.

Single data elements are more commonly referred to as **scalar variables.** Such variables may not be closely related to any other variables within the program unless by coincidence. Although programs could not survive without such variables, it is even more important to understand relationships between several data elements. Consider information about you—your name, address, city, state, zip code, age, height, weight, and so on. All the individual pieces of data are called scalar elements, but together they constitute a **logical data structure.** Relating this concept to the real world, let's think of a highrise building. Each of the components, such as the concrete, iron, glass, plastic, and so on, make up the actual materials within the building. The building itself is generally called a **structure.** Hence, the structure is made up of its component parts. In data processing, similar relationships may be used to describe application data. Each of the pieces of information about you is a component and the whole information constitutes your data structure. If we now collect your data and store it on the computer, we switch terminology slightly and refer to each component as a **field.** The sum of all fields makes up a **record.** The collection of records for the people we are gathering forms a **file.** Figure 3.33 further illustrates the terminology that we've been developing.

If we want to define your record in assembly language, we do so by constructing a hierarchical relationship using the DS instruction. Although we could define your record using the DC instruction, it doesn't make sense to do so since we would need a separate definition for each person in the file. If our file contained several hundred records, we'd have a very large data area within our program. By using the DS instruction, we will define a **generic** set of data elements that we'll use over and over for each person's data in the file as shown in Fig. 3.34.

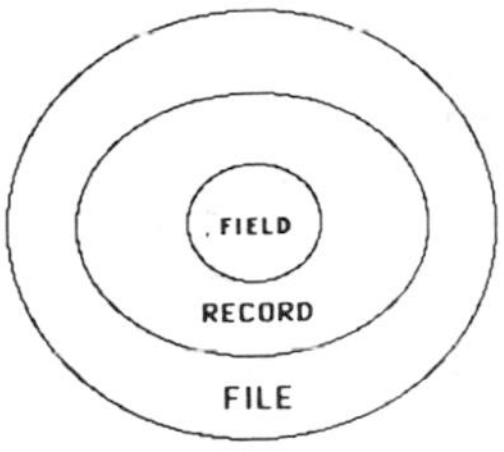

FIELDS ARE SUBORDINATE TO RECORDS.
RECORDS ARE SUBORDINATE TO FILES.

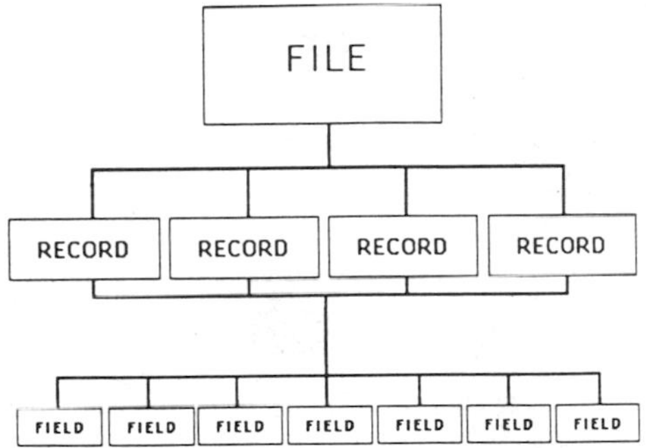

Figure 3.33 Field, record, file relationship.

```
PERSON   DS   0CL86
NAME     DS   CL30
STREET   DS   CL25
CITY     DS   CL20
STATE    DS   CL2
ZIP      DS   CL5
AGE      DS   PL2
HEIGHT   DS   H
```

Figure 3.34 Generic data structure for a person's data.

This data structure in Fig. 3.34 is called PERSON, and within a person's record are the fields NAME, STREET, CITY, STATE, ZIP, AGE, and HEIGHT. PERSON is the name of the record and NAME, STREET, and so on are the names of the fields that make up the record.

In the structure shown in Fig. 3.35, we really have several data structures. The relationship between the various structures is further illustrated in Fig. 3.36.

EMPLOYEE is the highest level in the structure and is called the **major structure name** or simply the **record name.** Within EMPLOYEE, there are two other structures, STARTED and HOURS. These elements are called **minor structures.** You can easily identify the data elements and the major and minor structures by looking at the data definitions. For the definitions EMPLOYEE, STARTED, and HOURS, you see that the data type identifier is preceded by a repetition factor value of zero (0). This means that no

```
EMPLOYEE  DS   0CL103
NAME      DS   CL30
STREET    DS   CL25
CITY      DS   CL20
STATE     DS   CL2
ZIP       DS   CL5
SALARY    DS   PL5
STARTED   DS   0CL6
MM        DS   CL2
DD        DS   CL2
YY        DS   CL2
HOURS     DS   0XL10
REGULAR   DS   PL5
OVERTIME  DS   PL5
```

Figure 3.35 An employee record data structure.

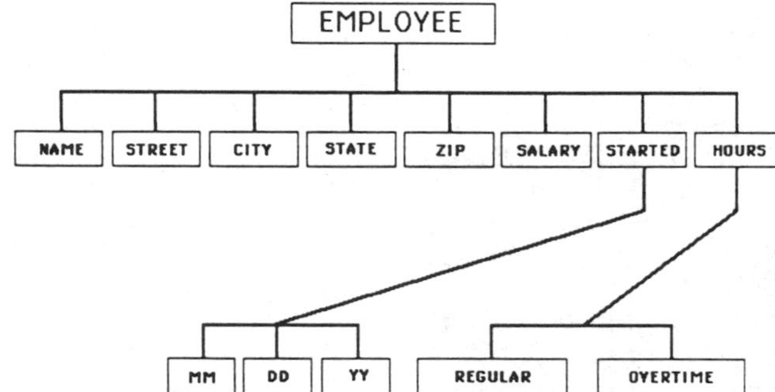

Figure 3.36 Hierarchy diagram for an employee record structure.

storage is to be set aside for this variable—it is simply being used to name the next set of fields below it and to give an overall length to the structural description. EMPLOYEE refers to the next 103 bytes of data that follow its definition; STARTED refers to the next six bytes of data that follow its definition; HOURS refers to the next 10 bytes of data that follow its definition. Organizing data in this manner helps the assembly language programmer since it identifies the boundary or range of a structure definition. In this example, the major structure EMPLOYEE defines a record that is 103 bytes long.

It would be helpful if we could use indentation to help define structures in our assembly language programs. The example in Fig. 3.37 clearly illustrates which fields are subordinate to the others and clearly separates the major and minor structures from the field elements.

As you know, all labels (symbols) *must* begin in column 1. Although this representation clearly distinguishes major structures, minor structures, and fields, it does not work. The assembler requires that *all* labels begin in column 1, and so we cannot indent as we've done.

We will be using data structures quite often in later sections of this text. Scalar variables will also be used for program processing, but as we progress, we'll utilize record descriptions more frequently.

```
THIS EXAMPLE WILL NOT WORK CORRECTLY

EMPLOYEE     DS   0CL103
  NAME       DS   CL30
  STREET     DS   CL25
  CITY       DS   CL20
  STATE      DS   CL2
  ZIP        DS   CL5
  SALARY     DS   PL5
  STARTED    DS   0CL6
    MM       DS   CL2
    DD       DS   CL2
    YY       DS   CL2
  HOURS      DS   0XL10
    REGULAR  DS   PL5
    OVERTIME DS   PL5

12345678901234567890123456   columns
```

Figure 3.37 Incorrect coding of a data structure using indentation.

BOUNDARY AND ALIGNMENT

As data elements are defined, the assembly language programmer must be aware of the terms **boundary** and **alignment.** These terms are related to the way that data is defined as well as to the instructions that will process the data.

As you know, memory is a long string of bytes that begins with location 0 and usually ends 16 megabytes later. Although memory is just that—a string of bytes—certain instructions require that the data elements they process be located at certain positions within memory. Instructions that process halfword data fields require that the data field begin at a memory location whose rightmost address digit is either 0, 2, 4, 6, 8, A, C, or E (in other words, an address evenly divisible by 2). Fullword instructions require that data be at locations ending in 0, 4, 8, or C (divisible by 4). Doubleword instructions require addresses that end with 0 or 8 (divisible by 8). These requirements are called **alignment** or **boundary alignment** and are completely dependent on the instructions used to define and process the data.

How much concern should you give to alignment? Well, it depends on your computer. Older computer systems require data alignment. If you try to process data that is not aligned, your program will abnormally terminate (**abend**) or will not assemble. Newer systems do not require alignment and will compensate for misaligned data without abending your program. Even though such compensation is made, you still may want to give attention to alignment since aligned data generally processes faster than nonaligned data.

Figure 3.38 gives examples of addresses and their alignment characteristics.

Meanings: H, halfword
F, fullword
D, doubleword

Address	Type of alignment
000000	H, F, D
0A143C	H, F
012345	None
01C010	H, F, D

Figure 3.38 Examples of storage area alignment.

Alignment is most often a concern when processing halfword, fullword, or doubleword binary data. Again, it is the instruction that requires us to align our data. In general, instructions that process binary numeric data require alignment. Alignment is also needed when we convert from character format into packed-decimal format to process numeric data in packed-decimal or floating-point format.

Let's look at address 012345. Since this address is not evenly divisible by 2, 4, or 8, we say that the memory location at this address is not aligned on an address evenly divisible by 2, 4, or 8. Therefore, alignment is specifically related to where the data is located in memory. For those fields that are not aligned on an address that is evenly divisible by 2, 4, or 8, we say that those fields are **byte aligned** or are aligned at the *next available byte.* If the address is evenly divisible by 2, then we say that the data area is aligned on a **halfword boundary.** If the address is evenly divisible by 4, then it is aligned on a **fullword boundary.** Data whose address is evenly divisible by 8 is said to be aligned on a **doubleword boundary.**

The assembler will automatically align data on its proper boundary when you code your DC or DS instructions. The data type identifier (X, C, H, F, D, . . .) not only tells the assembler the type of data you are defining, the length of the field, and the repetition factor (number of times you want this data defined), but it also indicates alignment. Whenever you use the data identifiers H, F, A, and D, *without qualifying them with the length qualifier,* the assembler will automatically align those fields on halfword, fullword, fullword, and doubleword boundaries, respectively. When you use the L qualifier, the assembler does not align data defined using these identifiers. In fact, anytime that the length qualifier is used, the data will not be aligned. See Fig. 3.39.

```
DS   F          fullword alignment
DC   F'0'       fullword alignment
DC   F'3'       fullword alignment
DS   CL10       byte alignment
DS   10C        byte alignment
DS   X          byte alignment
DS   AL3        byte alignment
DC   H'256'     halfword alignment
```

Figure 3.39 Impact of storage definitions on alignment.

Alignment can be a negative factor as well for the assembly language programmer. Since a base register has a range of only 4096 bytes, the assembly language programmer may have to be concerned with the length or size of a program. Alignment effects program size in that it causes the assembler to waste bytes of your program. In the example shown in Fig. 3.40, several *consecutive* fields are defined. The address of each field is given for reference.

```
Location          Definition          Alignment
________       _______________        _________
00A000       A  DS   CL5              none
00A005       B  DC   CL2'HI'          none
00A008       C  DS   H                halfword
00A00C       D  DC   F'200'           fullword
```

Figure 3.40 Alignment and its impact on storage definition.

Field A is five bytes long and starts at location X'00A000'. Field A will therefore occupy locations X'00A000', X'00A001', X'00A002', X'00A003', and X'00A004'. The next available location is X'00A005' and this is where field B starts since it does not require alignment. Field B is two bytes long, which allows the next field to start at location X'00A005' plus X'000002', or X'00A007'. However, field C is a halfword field requiring alignment, and so field C must *begin* on an address that is evenly divisible by 2. The next address greater than or equal to X'00A007' that is evenly divisible by 2 is X'00A008', and so this is where field C starts.

But, what is stored at location X'00A007'? If field B starts at location X'00A005' and is two characters long, then field B occupies memory locations X'00A005' and X'00A006'. Field C doesn't start until X'00A008', which leaves location X'00A007' vacant or undefined. This is what we mean when we say that bytes may be wasted by the assembler when data is aligned. It's not the assembler's fault, however, it's simply a result of defining data elements in a manner so that they can be processed by the instructions on the computer system.

Continuing, field C starts at location X'00A008' and is a halfword long, two bytes. Field C occupies locations X'00A008' and X'00A009'. Field D does not begin until location X'00A00C' since it requires fullword alignment (an address evenly divisible by 4). Clearly, memory locations X'00A00A' and X'00A00B' are wasted.

What you want to be aware of is that the *order* of the fields impacts alignment. Figure 3.41 defines the same fields, but in a different order. Look at the difference that ordering can make.

Location	Definition			Alignment
00A000	D	DC	F'200'	fullword
00A004	C	DS	H	halfword
00A006	A	DS	CL5	none
00A00B	B	DC	CL2'HI'	none

Figure 3.41 Ordering fields to reduce storage waste caused by alignment.

The same set of fields can be defined but no bytes need to be wasted. Instead of occupying 16 bytes of storage, these same fields will now only require 13 bytes of memory. If possible, order your fields in such a way as to save memory within your program.

Many of the techniques that we've discussed can cause an assembly language programmer to worry too much about the field ordering and definition of data within their program. Although there may be times to worry at this level, we are going to take the stand that our programs will be small enough so that we won't have to worry about wasted bytes. Further, our techniques for programming will be of a structured nature and emphasize the use of modules or program components to perform tasks. Modular programming generally reduces the size of your programs and hence, does not require you to spend a great deal of time worrying about lost storage bytes. This is a much more productive use of your time than continually worrying about each possible byte within your program or within the computer.

EXITING AN ASSEMBLY LANGUAGE PROGRAM

A program is generally called by the operating system or the loader. After the program performs its processing, the program has the responsibility to give control back to the operating system so that other programs may be executed. In an earlier section, we learned how to enter an assembly language program by establishing a control section (CSECT), how to save the register contents, and how to load our entry point address into our base register. We also learned how to inform the assembler what our base register would be to convert all statement and data element labels into D(B) or D(,B) addresses, how to establish a register save area, and how to set register 13 to address that new save area. We must now learn how to give control back to the system so that other programs may be run. Incidentally, most programs are allowed only a certain number of seconds in the computer. If our program does not give control back in this time, the operating system will take control back.

Giving control back to the operating system is easy since it requires just a few instructions. Logically, the instructions perform the following:

1. Restore R13 to its original value so that it addresses the register save area established by the operating system.
2. Restore the registers to their state when our program first obtained control.
3. Place a value into register 15 that indicates whether our program executed successfully or if there was a problem during execution.
4. Return control to the operating system.

When we entered our program, we saved the registers and set up a new register save area. We then forced R13 to address the new save area that we established. In order to return properly to the operating system, we return R13 to its original value before continuing the exiting process. This is done with the instruction shown in Fig. 3.42.

```
         L     13,4(13)        RESTORE OLD R13 VALUE
```

Figure 3.42 Restoring the contents of register 13.

The second instruction that must be performed does the opposite function of the STM (store multiple) instruction. This function is performed using the **LM (load multiple)** instruction. While store multiple saves a copy of the registers specified, load multiple restores values for the registers specified. When our program received control, we saved registers 14, 15, 0, 1, . . . , 10, 11, and 12, and so we must reload those registers from the same location where they were stored. By doing so, we return the registers to their original values, thus preserving the environment as if our program hadn't even executed.

If you recall, the STM instruction saved the register contents into an area that was offset 12 bytes from the address in register 13. We'll reload the registers from the same location as shown in Fig. 3.43.

```
LM     14,12,12(13)       RESTORE THE REGISTER CONTENTS
```

Figure 3.43 The LM instruction restores the original register contents.

We must now clear register 15 so that its value is zero. A value of zero means that our program completed normally. If we don't clear register 15, the operating system may interpret the value of register 15 as indicating that we did not perform our processing successfully. Register 15 may be cleared by subtracting its contents from itself. The value of anything minus itself is zero and so the contents of register 15 minus the contents of register 15 is zero. We'll use the **SR (subtract register)** instruction to perform this function as shown in Fig. 3.44.

```
SR      15,15          SET REGISTER 15 TO 0
```

Figure 3.44 Setting register 15 to a value of 0.

Finally, to return control to the operating system, we issue the instruction in Fig. 3.45.

```
BCR     B'1111',14          RETURN TO THE O.S.
```

Figure 3.45 Return control to the operating system.

The **BCR (branch on condition register)** instruction causes our program to give control back to the operating system, in other words, to end processing. When our program ends, another program may be started. Therefore, the complete set of instructions to return control from our program are contained in Fig. 3.46.

```
L       13,4(13)            RESTORE R13 TO O.S. SAVEAREA
LM      14,12,12(13)        RESTORE THE REGISTERS
SR      15,15               INDICATE THAT ALL WENT OK
BCR     B'1111',14          END OUR PROGRAM
```

Figure 3.46 Exiting a program.

Let's review this code. Again, registers 13, 14, and 15 are used. These registers are part of the special registers that we discussed earlier. Register 13 addresses a storage area in which we can save the contents of the registers when our program begins execution and where we can reclaim the values of those registers when we've finished processing.

Register 15 tells the system whether we completed normally or if our program encountered a problem during processing. In almost all cases, we'll want to set register 15 to zero.

Register 14 is one of the most important special registers. It contains an address within the operating system. The BCR instruction causes the computer to process instructions starting at the address given in register 14. When processing starts at this point, our program is finished.

If you recall, our program began execution because the operating system told the computer to begin executing instructions at the location that was contained in register 15. Register 15 contained the entry point address or first instruction of our program. When the computer started executing instructions at this address, our program started executing. When we are finished processing, we direct the computer to execute instructions within the operating system; the operating system regains control and proceeds to process other programs or to print our program.

If we want to tell the operating system that something unusual happened during processing, we must place a value, other than zero, into register 15. This value is usually less than 4096. For example, the typical error codes are given in Fig. 3.47.

Error Code Value	Meaning
0	Everything went OK.
4	Warning: we processed all records but there may have been a minor problem
8	Minor error: a problem has occurred; check all results and possibly run the program again.
12	Error: a severe error has occurred and the program has not processed all the data. The program must be rerun.
16 or greater	Abandon ship!

Figure 3.47 Common return code values and their meanings.

These error codes are very misleading. First, the error codes are made up between you, your fellow programmers, and possibly your user. In fact, the operating system won't do anything with the error code other than print out its value on your listing. Whatever values you decide for the error codes, that's what they will be. Generally, any error code greater than or equal to 16 means that something is seriously wrong and that the program or the data processed by the program needs to be fixed. Error codes less than or equal to 8 generally mean that you processed all of the data but there may have been a few [minor] errors.

For example, if one or more employee records indicate that the employees worked more than 80 hours in one week, your payroll program may set a value of 4 or 8 in register 15. Your payroll program may set an error code of 16 to indicate that all employees in the company worked no hours for the week. Clearly, this is a severe problem for a payroll program and something has to be fixed to pay the employees on payday.

ENDING THE ASSEMBLY LANGUAGE PROGRAM

An assembly language program must be ended. In the previous section, we talked about ending the *execution* of an assembly language program by issuing certain machine instructions. What is meant here is that we want to tell the assembler that there are no more instructions for the assembler to convert from source code format into object code format. We must indicate the end of our program to the assembler or we will receive a syntax error during assembly.

An assembly language program is ended by using the **END** statement. There's not much to the END statement, so let's see how it's coded in Fig. 3.48.

```
               END     <label>

Column  123456789012345678901234567890. . . .
```

Figure 3.48 Coding the physical end of the assembly language program.

In column 16 of the statement, you see that a label is coded. This label is the name of your program coded on your CSECT or START statement. If the name of your main program was MAINPGM, then this would be the value of the label that we'd code in column 16 on the END statement.

Although the <label> is optional, I suggest that you code it. In later sections of the text, the END statement serves a very important function, especially when our programs consist of several modules. For now, let's simply get into the habit of coding the END statement with the name of our program on it.

CONSTRUCTING A COMPLETE PROGRAM

Now that we have discussed each of the elements within an assembly language program, we can draw them together to form a complete unit. Since we've discussed assembly language and ASSIST programming as two separate elements, we will continue to treat their development in different manners. Again, ASSIST provides many services that standard programming does not. Hence, many shortcuts may be taken, especially to the linkage conventions, thus making the construction of programs within the two processors significantly different.

The general layout of a program using either processor is shown in Figure 3.49.

Using the structure above and integrating our previous discussion into this format, we arrive at an ASSIST program layout in Figures 3.50 and 3.51. Figure 3.50 gives the complete format for a typical ASSIST program which uses register 15 as the base register for the program. Figure 3.51 gives the program format when using another register, in this case register 12, as the base register for the program. Note that in both examples, the programs do not adhere to the true linkage conventions (although the programs could be rewritten to do so).

```
´label`     CSECT or START

            [entry code]

            [body of the program]

            [exit code]

            [data definitions]

            END      ´label`
```

Figure 3.49 General format of an assembly language program.

```
ASISTPGM  CSECT
          USING  ASISTPGM,15       USE R15 AS A BASE REGISTER

          [ body of the program ]

          BCR    B´1111´,14        RETURN CONTROL TO THE SYSTEM

          [ data definitions ]

          END    ASISTPGM
```

Figure 3.50 ASSIST program format using R15 as a base register.

```
ASISTPGM  CSECT
          LR     12,15              COPY THE E.P.A. INTO R12
          USING  ASISTPGM,12        USE R12 AS A BASE REGISTER

          [ body of the program ]

          BCR    B'1111',14         RETURN CONTROL TO THE SYSTEM

          [ data definitions ]

          END    ASISTPGM
```

Figure 3.51 ASSIST program format using R12 as a base register.

Figure 3.52 illustrates the construction of a complete assembly language program. Immediately, you notice the additional instructions needed to perform the entry and exit linkage standards. You should remember however that these standards are arbitrary and it's up to you whether or not to adhere to them. In fact, you could construct your programs like the ASSIST formats presented in Figures 3.50 and 3.51. However, in order to avoid problems, you should follow the format presented in Figure 3.52. In Figure 3.52, register 12 has been selected as the base register for the program. Again, any of the registers 2 through 12 could have been selected for this task.

```
ASMPGM    CSECT
          STM    14,12,12(13)     SAVE THE CALLER'S REGISTERS
          LR     12,15            COPY THE E.P.A. INTO R12
          USING  ASMPGM,12        ESTABLISH R12 AS THE BASE REGISTER
          LA     11,SAVEAREA      ADDRESS OUR REGISTER SAVE AREA
          ST     13,SAVEAREA+4    SAVE THE CALLER'S SAVE AREA ADDRESS
          ST     11,8(13)         INFORM THE CALLER OF OUR SAVE AREA
          LR     13,11            OUR SAVE AREA IS NOW THE CURRENT ONE

          [ body of the program ]

          L      13,4(13)         RESTORE THE SAVE AREA ADDRESS
          LM     14,12,12(13)     RESTORE THE CALLER'S REGISTERS
          SR     15,15            SET THE RETURN CODE TO ZERO
          BCR    B'1111',14       RETURN CONTROL TO THE SYSTEM

SAVEAREA  DS     18F              REGISTER SAVE AREA FOR OUR PROGRAM

          [ other data definitions ]

          END    ASMPGM
```

Figure 3.52 Assembly language program format.

READING AN OUTPUT LISTING

In this section, we're going to look at actual assembly language program listings. The programs that were processed by the assembler are very simple and perform the enter and exit instructions that we developed throughout this chapter. We're actually going to look at several listings, each illustrating another feature of assembly language programming. Finally, we're going to look at the same program executed by the interpreter called ASSIST and point out some of the similarities and differences between ASSIST and standard 370 assembly language listings.

The standard assembly language program listing will consist of many components. The first line is called the title line and allows space for a string of characters to identify the program. The title line also contains the page number that is useful in larger programs.

The body of the assembly listing consists of (from left to right): the location counter, object code, operand addresses, statement number, and the source statement. Let's describe each of these components in detail.

The **location counter** is an address or, more accurately, it is a displacement. For each instruction or data area in your program, the assembler gives you the displacement of that instruction or data area with respect to the beginning of the program. For example, the CSECT and USING statements do not occupy any storage at execution time, but the STM and LR instructions occupy four and two bytes of storage, respectively. Each source statement machine instruction converts into object code that occupies a certain number of bytes of storage in memory. The location counter tells you the address of that instruction with respect to the first statement in the program.

```
Location Counter           Program Instruction
________________           ___________________
   000000            MAINPGM  CSECT
   000000                     STM      14,12,12(13)
   000004                     LR       12,15
                              USING    MAINPGM,12
   000006                     LA       11,SAVEAREA
   00000A                     ST       13,4(11)
   00000E                     ST       11,8(13)
   000012                     LR       13,11
```

Figure 3.53 Location counter values as related to instructions.

As shown in Fig. 3.53, the values of the location counter increase as each *machine instruction* is processed. The USING statement does not have a location counter value since the USING statement is not an executable instruction (it is an assembly language instruction). The CSECT statement does have a location counter, but this is simply a reference to indicate that the first instruction in the program is at offset 0.

Since the LR instruction begins at offset four and is two bytes long (when converted into machine code), the next machine instruction, "LA 11,SAVEAREA", begins at offset 6.

The next component on the listing is the **object code** section. Here you see the actual machine code that results from converting your source statements into executable format. In the next chapter, we'll discuss the format of machine code, but, for now, Fig. 3.54 illustrates what you might see based on this same set of instructions.

```
Object Code        Source Program Instruction
                   MAINPGM  CSECT
90EC D00C                   STM     14,12,12(13)
18CF                        LR      12,15
                            USING   MAINPGM,12
```

Figure 3.54 Object code generation from assembly.

The CSECT statement and the USING statement are not machine instructions and so they do not generate any object code. You only see object code for machine instructions or those instructions that will require storage during execution time.

The next set of fields on the listing are **ADDR1** and **ADDR2**. These fields are important when labels are used to help the programmer verify that the data elements being referenced are properly converted into D(B) or D(X,B) formats. Let's skip these two fields for now.

The **source statement number** field helps you identify the number of source code statements that are in your program. This field is also helpful if your program contains

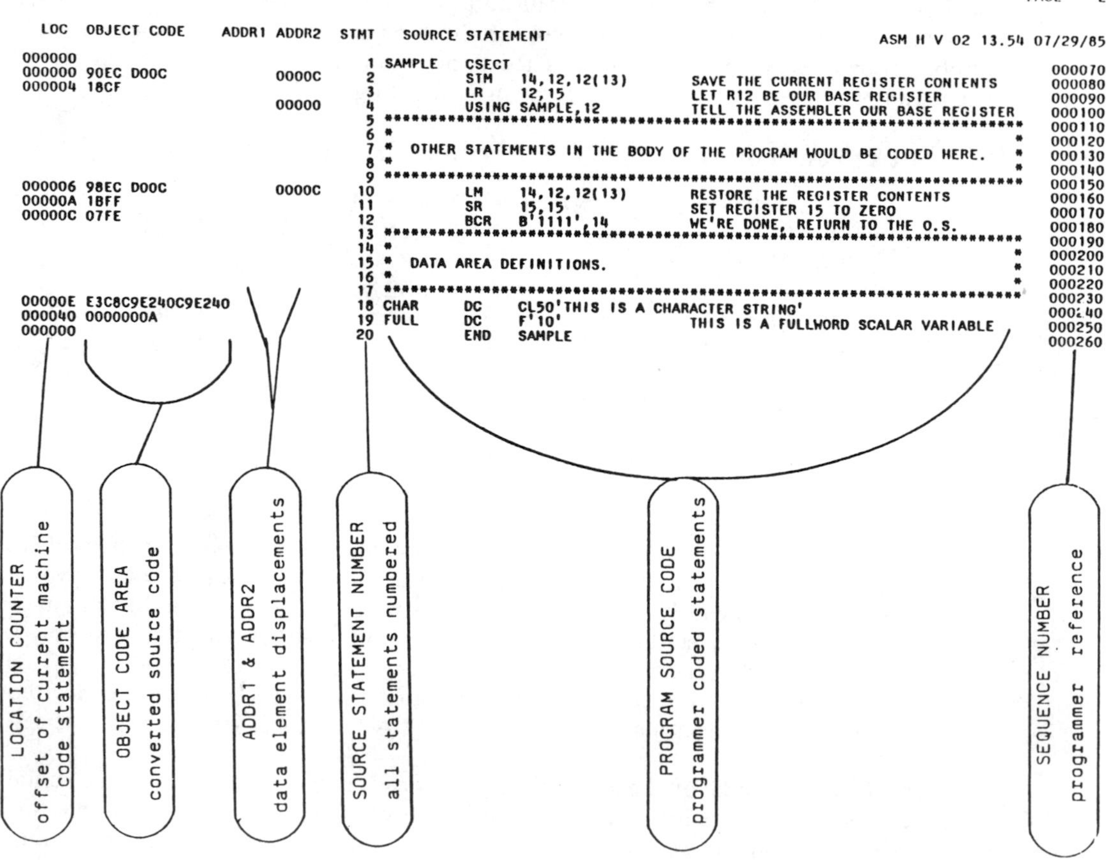

Figure 3.55 Components of an assembly language listing.

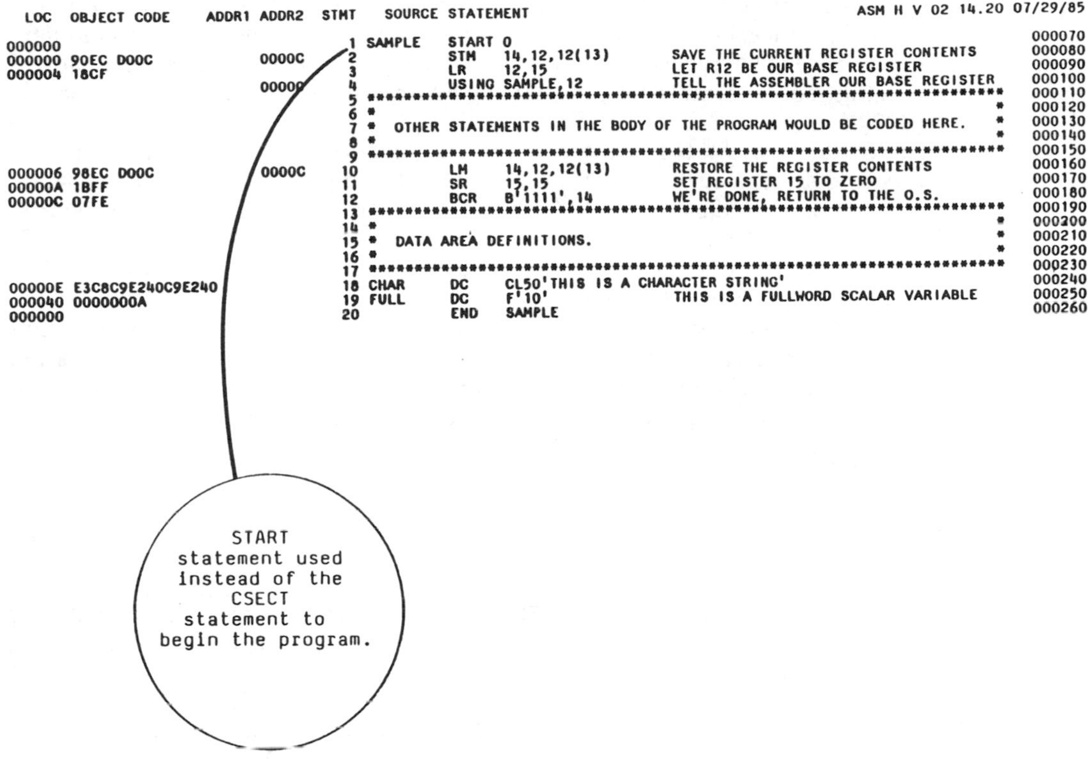

```
                                                                                     PAGE    2
  LOC  OBJECT CODE    ADDR1 ADDR2  STMT   SOURCE STATEMENT                                  ASM H V 02 14.20 07/29/85
000000                                1 SAMPLE   START 0                                                        000070
000000 90EC D00C            0000C     2          STM   14,12,12(13)       SAVE THE CURRENT REGISTER CONTENTS    000080
000004 18CF                           3          LR    12,15              LET R12 BE OUR BASE REGISTER          000090
                            00000     4          USING SAMPLE,12          TELL THE ASSEMBLER OUR BASE REGISTER  000100
                                      5 *********************************************************************** 000110
                                      6 *                                                                     * 000120
                                      7 *   OTHER STATEMENTS IN THE BODY OF THE PROGRAM WOULD BE CODED HERE.  * 000130
                                      8 *                                                                     * 000140
                                      9 *********************************************************************** 000150
000006 98EC D00C            0000C    10          LM    14,12,12(13)       RESTORE THE REGISTER CONTENTS         000160
00000A 1BFF                          11          SR    15,15              SET REGISTER 15 TO ZERO               000170
00000C 07FE                          12          BCR   B'1111',14         WE'RE DONE, RETURN TO THE O.S.        000180
                                     13 *********************************************************************** 000190
                                     14 *                                                                     * 000200
                                     15 *   DATA AREA DEFINITIONS.                                            * 000210
                                     16 *                                                                     * 000220
                                     17 *********************************************************************** 000230
00000E E3C8C9E240C9E240              18 CHAR     DC    CL50'THIS IS A CHARACTER STRING'                         000240
000040 0000000A                      19 FULL     DC    F'10'              THIS IS A FULLWORD SCALAR VARIABLE    000250
000000                               20          END   SAMPLE                                                   000260
```


Figure 3.56 Example of coding the START instruction.

any syntax errors. If a statement contains a syntax error, a message is printed describing the error and the number of the statement in error is also given. You can read the error message and refer directly to the statement to find and fix your programming problem.

The last field within the body of your source listing is the **source statement area.** This field shows you a copy of each of your source statements so that you may read your program as you view your listing. Figure 3.55 gives a complete example of an assembly listing and each of its components.

We can use the START statement instead of the CSECT statement to begin our program and obtain a listing that looks identical to the program listing that began with CSECT. Figure 3.56 illustrates this coding technique.

We can also use a very powerful feature of the START statement that the CSECT statement does not have. In column 16 of the START statement, we typically code the value zero. This value is used to set the location counter so that statement offsets in the listing begin with offset X'000000'. On some computer systems, it may be possible to know where in memory your program will be placed and executed. For example, if we knew that our program would *always* be placed into memory at decimal (base 10) location 300, then we could code a START statement like the one shown in Fig. 3.57.

```
OURPGM   START   300
```

Figure 3.57 Forcing a nonzero location counter value through the use of the START instruction.

Using this feature, the assembler adjusts the location counter so that the first statement appears at offset 300 in the program listing rather than at offset 0. Actually, the program begins at location 304 since a program must begin on a doubleword boundary and 300 is not evenly divisible by 8. However, 304 is the next highest and closest address that meets this requirement. Hence, the starting address of the program is at location 304 or X'000130'.

This feature is useful to fix program problems that occur during execution since all references to data at execution time must be done through addresses. If our location counter began at zero, then we would have to convert from an offset of 0 into the true location in memory where our program executed. The START statement eliminates this conversion on the part of the programmer; thus, the process of fixing programs (called debugging) becomes faster and easier. The listing in Fig. 3.58 illustrates the use of the START statement to set the location counter to an initial value other than zero. Note that the value 300 is converted into hexadecimal (by the assembler) before the location counter is displayed. If we had wanted the location counter to reflect the hexadecimal value 300, then we could have coded our START statement as specified in Figure 3.59.

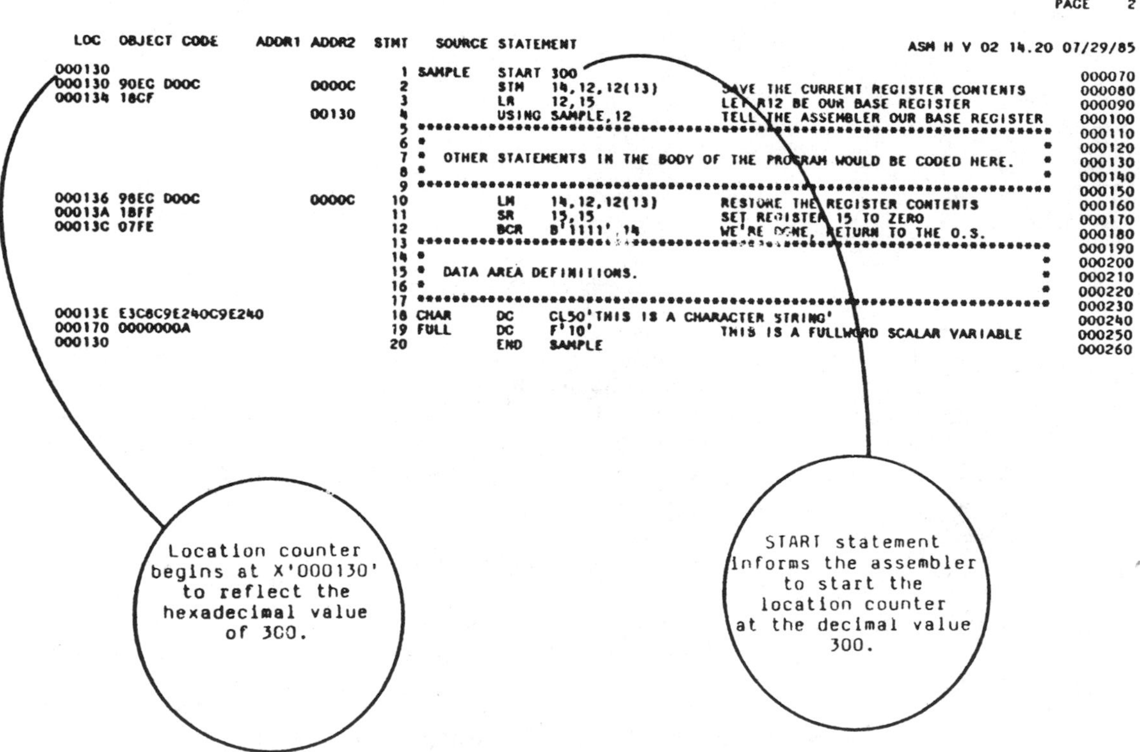

```
                                                                                                   PAGE    2
  LOC  OBJECT CODE    ADDR1 ADDR2  STMT   SOURCE STATEMENT                                ASM H V 02 14.20 07/29/85
000130                                1 SAMPLE   START 300                                                 000070
000130 90EC D00C            0000C     2          STM   14,12,12(13)     SAVE THE CURRENT REGISTER CONTENTS 000080
000134 18CF                           3          LR    12,15            LET R12 BE OUR BASE REGISTER       000090
                            00130     4          USING SAMPLE,12        TELL THE ASSEMBLER OUR BASE REGISTER 000100
                                      5 ********************************************************************* 000110
                                      6 *                                                                   * 000120
                                      7 *  OTHER STATEMENTS IN THE BODY OF THE PROGRAM WOULD BE CODED HERE.  * 000130
                                      8 *                                                                   * 000140
                                      9 ********************************************************************* 000150
000136 98EC D00C            0000C    10          LM    14,12,12(13)     RESTORE THE REGISTER CONTENTS      000160
00013A 1BFF                          11          SR    15,15            SET REGISTER 15 TO ZERO            000170
00013C 07FE                          12          BCR   B'1111',14       WE'RE DONE, RETURN TO THE O.S.     000180
                                     13 ********************************************************************* 000190
                                     14 *                                                                   * 000200
                                     15 *  DATA AREA DEFINITIONS.                                           * 000210
                                     16 *                                                                   * 000220
                                     17 ********************************************************************* 000230
00013E E3C8C9E240C9E240              18 CHAR     DC    CL50'THIS IS A CHARACTER STRING'                    000240
000170 0000000A                      19 FULL     DC    F'10'            THIS IS A FULLWORD SCALAR VARIABLE 000250
000130                               20          END   SAMPLE                                              000260
```


Figure 3.58 The START statement can impact the starting value of the location counter.

```
SAMPLE   START   X'300'
```

Figure 3.59 Setting the location counter value using hexadecimal notation.

Now let's turn our attention to other components in a standard assembly language printout. Although these pages actually come *before* the program pages that we just discussed, we generally think of them as secondary to the program listing itself. Hence, we'll discuss them at this time.

The first page of the listing is called the **job log** page, which indicates the time that your program started execution and the time that it finished as shown on Fig. 3.60. Other information, varying from installation to installation, might tell you the total number of statements in your complete job, the number of lines printed on your listing, and so on.

The main use of the job log page occurs during debugging. As illustrated in Fig. 3.61, some error messages appear in the top part of the job log page. Look for such error messages when you run your program.

The next page of a listing is called the **job control** or **JCL** page. The operating system lists all of the control language statements that were used in processing your program. In Fig. 3.62, you can see the two phases of processing within an assemble-and-go procedure. Each phase begins with a statement containing the word **EXEC** or **EXECUTE** and the characters // in the first two columns of the statement.

The **allocation and messages** page follows the JCL page. This page contains important information about the success or failure of each processing phase in your job. Of immediate importance are the fields called **COND CODE** (condition codes) that are shown in Figs. 3.63 through 3.66, indicating the success or failure of each of your pro-

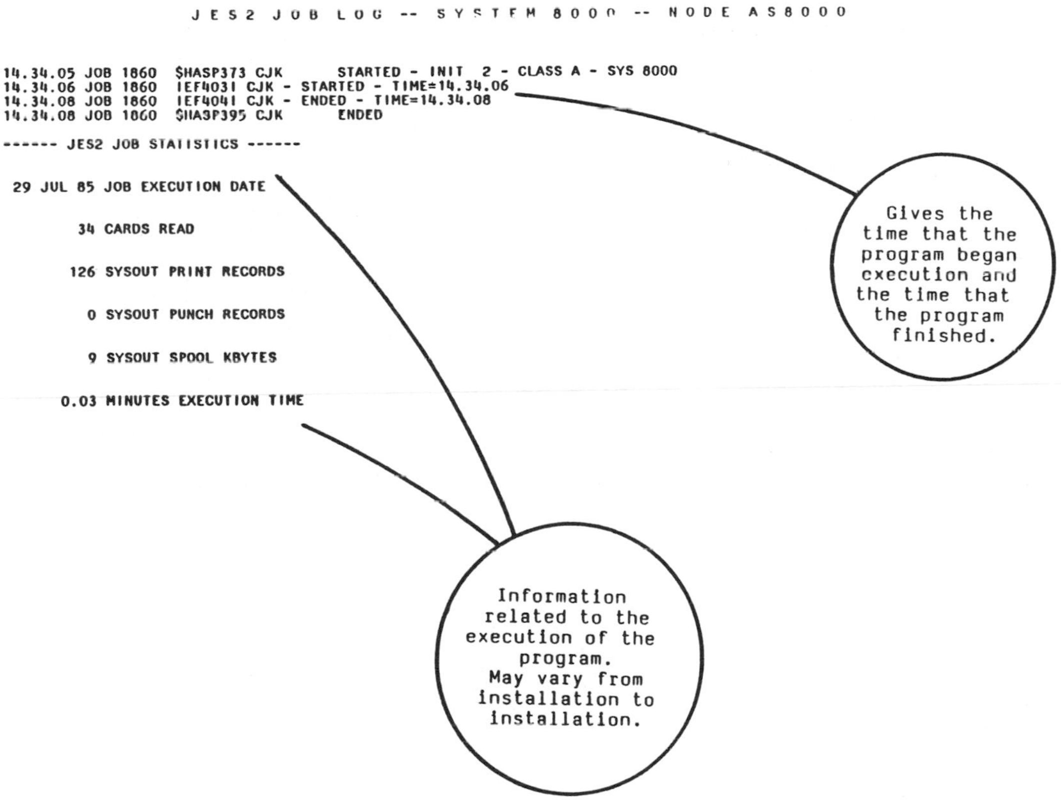

```
                    J E S 2   J O B   L O G  --  S Y S T E M  8 0 0 0  --  N O D E   A S 8 0 0 0

14.34.05 JOB 1860  $HASP373 CJK       STARTED - INIT  2 - CLASS A - SYS 8000
14.34.06 JOB 1860  IEF403I CJK - STARTED - TIME=14.34.06
14.34.08 JOB 1860  IEF404I CJK - ENDED - TIME=14.34.08
14.34.08 JOB 1860  $HASP395 CJK       ENDED

------ JES2 JOB STATISTICS ------

 29 JUL 85 JOB EXECUTION DATE

        34 CARDS READ

       126 SYSOUT PRINT RECORDS

         0 SYSOUT PUNCH RECORDS

         9 SYSOUT SPOOL KBYTES

      0.03 MINUTES EXECUTION TIME
```


Figure 3.60 The JES job log page.

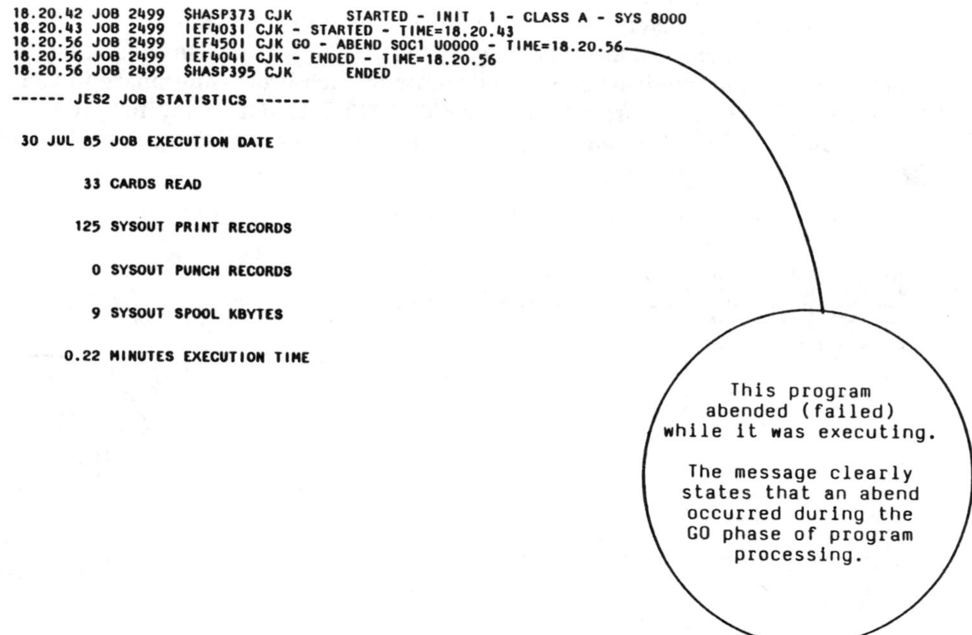

```
                    J E S 2  J O B  L O G  --  S Y S T E M  8 0 0 0  --  N O D E  A S 8 0 0 0

18.20.42 JOB 2499  $HASP373 CJK      STARTED - INIT  1 - CLASS A - SYS 8000
18.20.43 JOB 2499  IEF403I CJK - STARTED - TIME=18.20.43
18.20.56 JOB 2499  IEF450I CJK GO - ABEND SOC1 U0000 - TIME=18.20.56
18.20.56 JOB 2499  IEF404I CJK - ENDED - TIME=18.20.56
18.20.56 JOB 2499  $HASP395 CJK      ENDED
------ JES2 JOB STATISTICS ------

 30 JUL 85 JOB EXECUTION DATE

        33 CARDS READ

       125 SYSOUT PRINT RECORDS

         0 SYSOUT PUNCH RECORDS

         9 SYSOUT SPOOL KBYTES

      0.22 MINUTES EXECUTION TIME
```


Figure 3.61 Abend messages appear within the job log page.

```
1     //CJK    JOB (ISU,                                                   JOB 1860
      //                XXXXXXXXXXXXXXX),CJK,                                  0010
      //       CLASS=A,PRTY=8,MSGCLASS=A                                     000030
      ***ROUTE PRINT 16670                                                    00004
2     //  EXEC  ASMSCG                                                       000050
3     XXASMSCG    PROC R=1024,MAC1='SYS1.MACLIB',MAC2='SYS1.MACLIB',       00000010
      XX               MAC3='SYS1.ASISTMAC',LIST=,OUT=$                    00000020
4     XXASM       EXEC PGM=IEV90,PARM='DECK,OBJ,&LIST',REGION=&R.K         00000030
5     XXSYSLIB    DD    DSN=&MAC1,DISP=SHR,DCB=BLKSIZE=23440               00000040
6     XX          DD    DSN=&MAC2,DISP=SHR,DCB=BLKSIZE=23440               00000050
7     XX          DD    DSN=&MAC3,DISP=SHR,DCB=BLKSIZE=23440               00000060
8     XXSYSPRINT DD     SYSOUT=&OUT                                        00000070
9     XXSYSPUNCH DD     DUMMY                                              00000080
10    XXSYSUT1    DD    UNIT=VIO,SPACE=(CYL,10)                            00000090
11    XXSYSUT2    DD    UNIT=VIO,SPACE=(CYL,10)                            00000100
12    XXSYSUT3    DD    UNIT=VIO,SPACE=(CYL,10)                            00000110
13    XXSYSLIN    DD    UNIT=VIO,DSN=&&LOADSET,SPACE=(TRK,(2,1)),          00000120
      XX               DISP=(NEW,PASS),DCB=(RECFM=FB,LRECL=80,BLKSIZE=800) 00000130
14    //ASM.SYSIN  DD  *                                                     000060
15    XXGO        EXEC PGM=ISULOADR,COND=(4,LT,ASM)                        00000140
16    XXSYSLIN    DD    DSN=&&LOADSET,DISP=(OLD,DELETE)                    00000150
17    XXSYSLOUT   DD    SYSOUT=&OUT                                        00000160
      //                                                                   000290
```


Figure 3.62 The JCL listing.

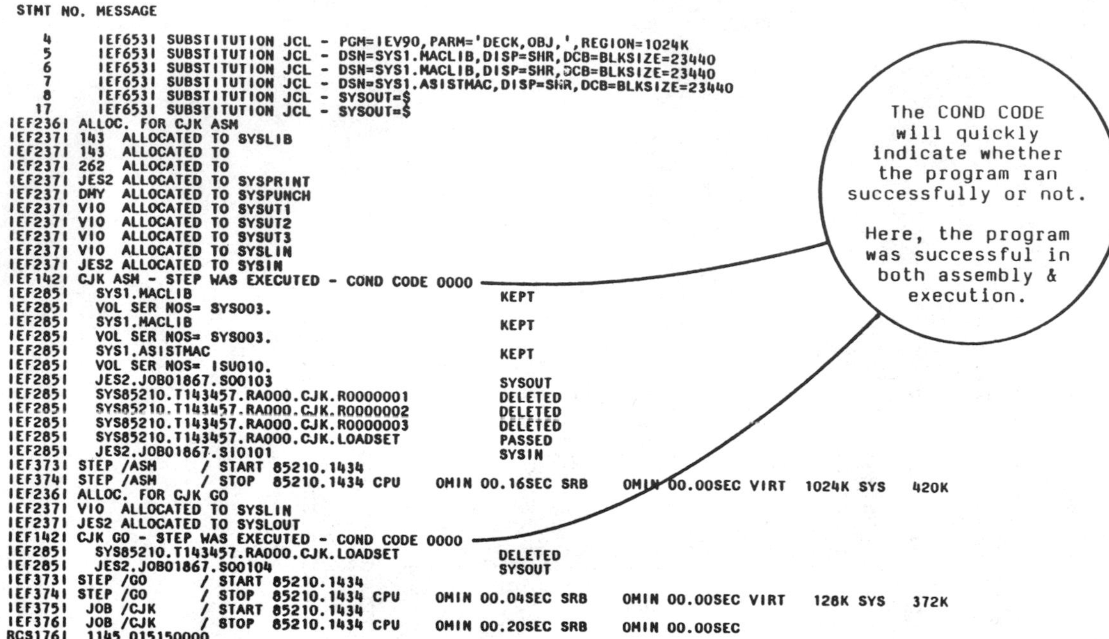

```
STMT NO. MESSAGE

    4      IEF653I SUBSTITUTION JCL - PGM=IEV90,PARM='DECK,OBJ,',REGION=1024K
    5      IEF653I SUBSTITUTION JCL - DSN=SYS1.MACLIB,DISP=SHR,DCB=BLKSIZE=23440
    6      IEF653I SUBSTITUTION JCL - DSN=SYS1.MACLIB,DISP=SHR,DCB=BLKSIZE=23440
    7      IEF653I SUBSTITUTION JCL - DSN=SYS1.ASISTMAC,DISP=SHR,DCB=BLKSIZE=23440
    8      IEF653I SUBSTITUTION JCL - SYSOUT=$
   17      IEF653I SUBSTITUTION JCL - SYSOUT=$
IEF236I ALLOC. FOR CJK ASM
IEF237I 143  ALLOCATED TO SYSLIB
IEF237I 143  ALLOCATED TO
IEF237I 262  ALLOCATED TO
IEF237I JES2 ALLOCATED TO SYSPRINT
IEF237I DMY  ALLOCATED TO SYSPUNCH
IEF237I VIO  ALLOCATED TO SYSUT1
IEF237I VIO  ALLOCATED TO SYSUT2
IEF237I VIO  ALLOCATED TO SYSUT3
IEF237I VIO  ALLOCATED TO SYSLIN
IEF237I JES2 ALLOCATED TO SYSIN
IEF142I CJK ASM - STEP WAS EXECUTED - COND CODE 0000
IEF285I   SYS1.MACLIB                                  KEPT
IEF285I   VOL SER NOS= SYS003.
IEF285I   SYS1.MACLIB                                  KEPT
IEF285I   VOL SER NOS= SYS003.
IEF285I   SYS1.ASISTMAC                                KEPT
IEF285I   VOL SER NOS= ISU010.
IEF285I   JES2.JOB01867.S00103                         SYSOUT
IEF285I   SYS85210.T143457.RA000.CJK.R0000001          DELETED
IEF285I   SYS85210.T143457.RA000.CJK.R0000002          DELETED
IEF285I   SYS85210.T143457.RA000.CJK.R0000003          DELETED
IEF285I   SYS85210.T143457.RA000.CJK.LOADSET           PASSED
IEF285I   JES2.JOB01867.SI0101                         SYSIN
IEF373I STEP /ASM     / START 85210.1434
IEF374I STEP /ASM     / STOP  85210.1434 CPU    0MIN 00.16SEC SRB    0MIN 00.00SEC VIRT   1024K SYS   420K
IEF236I ALLOC. FOR CJK GO
IEF237I VIO  ALLOCATED TO SYSLIN
IEF237I JES2 ALLOCATED TO SYSLOUT
IEF142I CJK GO - STEP WAS EXECUTED - COND CODE 0000
IEF285I   SYS85210.T143457.RA000.CJK.LOADSET           DELETED
IEF285I   JES2.JOB01867.S00104                         SYSOUT
IEF373I STEP /GO      / START 85210.1434
IEF374I STEP /GO      / STOP  85210.1434 CPU    0MIN 00.04SEC SRB    0MIN 00.00SEC VIRT    128K SYS   372K
IEF375I  JOB /CJK     / START 85210.1434
IEF376I  JOB /CJK     / STOP  85210.1434 CPU    0MIN 00.20SEC SRB    0MIN 00.00SEC
RCS176I  1145 015150000
```


Figure 3.63 Using CONDition CODEs to determine execution success or failure.

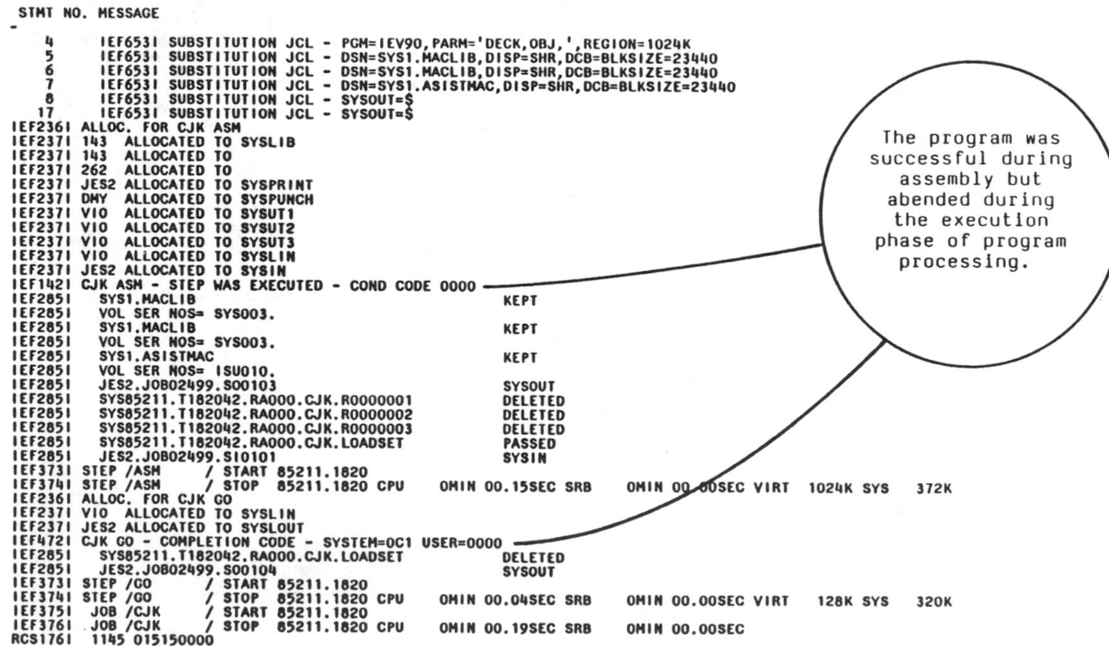

```
STMT NO. MESSAGE

    4      IEF653I SUBSTITUTION JCL - PGM=IEV90,PARM='DECK,OBJ,',REGION=1024K
    5      IEF653I SUBSTITUTION JCL - DSN=SYS1.MACLIB,DISP=SHR,DCB=BLKSIZE=23440
    6      IEF653I SUBSTITUTION JCL - DSN=SYS1.MACLIB,DISP=SHR,DCB=BLKSIZE=23440
    7      IEF653I SUBSTITUTION JCL - DSN=SYS1.ASISTMAC,DISP=SHR,DCB=BLKSIZE=23440
    8      IEF653I SUBSTITUTION JCL - SYSOUT=$
   17      IEF653I SUBSTITUTION JCL - SYSOUT=$
IEF236I ALLOC. FOR CJK ASM
IEF237I 143  ALLOCATED TO SYSLIB
IEF237I 143  ALLOCATED TO
IEF237I 262  ALLOCATED TO
IEF237I JES2 ALLOCATED TO SYSPRINT
IEF237I DMY  ALLOCATED TO SYSPUNCH
IEF237I VIO  ALLOCATED TO SYSUT1
IEF237I VIO  ALLOCATED TO SYSUT2
IEF237I VIO  ALLOCATED TO SYSUT3
IEF237I VIO  ALLOCATED TO SYSLIN
IEF237I JES2 ALLOCATED TO SYSIN
IEF142I CJK ASM - STEP WAS EXECUTED - COND CODE 0000
IEF285I   SYS1.MACLIB                                  KEPT
IEF285I   VOL SER NOS= SYS003.
IEF285I   SYS1.MACLIB                                  KEPT
IEF285I   VOL SER NOS= SYS003.
IEF285I   SYS1.ASISTMAC                                KEPT
IEF285I   VOL SER NOS= ISU010.
IEF285I   JES2.JOB02499.S00103                         SYSOUT
IEF285I   SYS85211.T182042.RA000.CJK.R0000001          DELETED
IEF285I   SYS85211.T182042.RA000.CJK.R0000002          DELETED
IEF285I   SYS85211.T182042.RA000.CJK.R0000003          DELETED
IEF285I   SYS85211.T182042.RA000.CJK.LOADSET           PASSED
IEF285I   JES2.JOB02499.SI0101                         SYSIN
IEF373I STEP /ASM     / START 85211.1820
IEF374I STEP /ASM     / STOP  85211.1820 CPU    0MIN 00.15SEC SRB    0MIN 00.00SEC VIRT   1024K SYS   372K
IEF236I ALLOC. FOR CJK GO
IEF237I VIO  ALLOCATED TO SYSLIN
IEF237I JES2 ALLOCATED TO SYSLOUT
IEF472I CJK GO - COMPLETION CODE - SYSTEM=0C1 USER=0000
IEF285I   SYS85211.T182042.RA000.CJK.LOADSET           DELETED
IEF285I   JES2.JOB02499.S00104                         SYSOUT
IEF373I STEP /GO      / START 85211.1820
IEF374I STEP /GO      / STOP  85211.1820 CPU    0MIN 00.04SEC SRB    0MIN 00.00SEC VIRT    128K SYS   320K
IEF375I  JOB /CJK     / START 85211.1820
IEF376I  JOB /CJK     / STOP  85211.1820 CPU    0MIN 00.19SEC SRB    0MIN 00.00SEC
RCS176I  1145 015150000
```


Figure 3.64 Completion codes (abend codes) also appear within the messages page.

```
STMT NO. MESSAGE

    4       IEF653I SUBSTITUTION JCL - PGM=IEV90,PARM='DECK,OBJ,',REGION=1024K
    5       IEF653I SUBSTITUTION JCL - DSN=SYS1.MACLIB,DISP=SHR,DCB=BLKSIZE=23440
    6       IEF653I SUBSTITUTION JCL - DSN=SYS1.MACLIB,DISP=SHR,DCB=BLKSIZE=23440
    7       IEF653I SUBSTITUTION JCL - DSN=SYS1.ASISTMAC,DISP=SHR,DCB=BLKSIZE=23440
    8       IEF653I SUBSTITUTION JCL - SYSOUT=$
   17       IEF653I SUBSTITUTION JCL - SYSOUT=$
IEF236I ALLOC. FOR CJK ASM
IEF237I 143  ALLOCATED TO SYSLIB
IEF237I 143  ALLOCATED TO
IEF237I 262  ALLOCATED TO
IEF237I JES2 ALLOCATED TO SYSPRINT
IEF237I DMY  ALLOCATED TO SYSPUNCH
IEF237I VIO  ALLOCATED TO SYSUT1
IEF237I VIO  ALLOCATED TO SYSUT2
IEF237I VIO  ALLOCATED TO SYSUT3
IEF237I VIO  ALLOCATED TO SYSLIN
IEF237I JES2 ALLOCATED TO SYSIN
IEF142I CJK ASM - STEP WAS EXECUTED - COND CODE 0008
IEF285I   SYS1.MACLIB                                  KEPT
IEF285I   VOL SER NOS= SYS003.
IEF285I   SYS1.MACLIB                                  KEPT
IEF285I   VOL SER NOS= SYS003.
IEF285I   SYS1.ASISTMAC                                KEPT
IEF285I   VOL SER NOS= ISU010.
IEF285I   JES2.JOB02502.S00103                         SYSOUT
IEF285I   SYS85211.T182201.RA000.CJK.R0000001          DELETED
IEF285I   SYS85211.T182201.RA000.CJK.R0000002          DELETED
IEF285I   SYS85211.T182201.RA000.CJK.R0000003          DELETED
IEF285I   SYS85211.T182201.RA000.CJK.LOADSET           PASSED
IEF285I   JES2.JOB02502.SI0101                         SYSIN
IEF373I STEP /ASM     / START 85211.1822
IEF374I STEP /ASM     / STOP  85211.1822 CPU    0MIN 00.15SEC SRB    0MIN 00.00SEC VIRT  1024K SYS   412K
IEF202I CJK GO - STEP WAS NOT RUN BECAUSE OF CONDITION CODES
IEF272I CJK GO - STEP WAS NOT EXECUTED.
IEF373I STEP /GO      / START 85211.1822
IEF374I STEP /GO      / STOP  85211.1822 CPU    0MIN 00.00SEC SRB    0MIN 00.00SEC VIRT     0K SYS     0K
IEF285I   SYS85211.T182201.RA000.CJK.LOADSET           DELETED
IEF375I  JOB /CJK     / START 85211.1822
IEF376I  JOB /CJK     / STOP  85211.1822 CPU    0MIN 00.15SEC SRB    0MIN 00.00SEC
RCS176I  1145 015150000
```

The program did not assemble correctly.

A syntax error was discovered by the assembler.

Since the program did not assemble properly, the system did not try to execute the program.

Figure 3.65 Condition codes indicate program failure in this example.

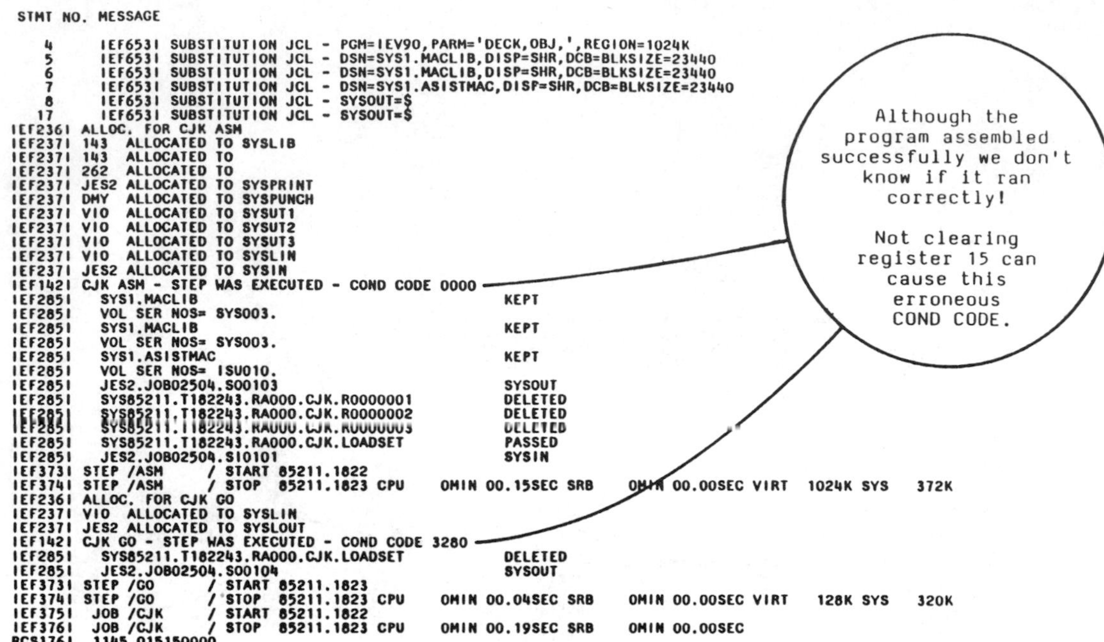

```
STMT NO. MESSAGE

    4      IEF653I SUBSTITUTION JCL - PGM=IEV90,PARM='DECK,OBJ,',REGION=1024K
    5      IEF653I SUBSTITUTION JCL - DSN=SYS1.MACLIB,DISP=SHR,DCB=BLKSIZE=23440
    6      IEF653I SUBSTITUTION JCL - DSN=SYS1.MACLIB,DISP=SHR,DCB=BLKSIZE=23440
    7      IEF653I SUBSTITUTION JCL - DSN=SYS1.ASISTMAC,DISP=SHR,DCB=BLKSIZE=23440
    8      IEF653I SUBSTITUTION JCL - SYSOUT=$
   17      IEF653I SUBSTITUTION JCL - SYSOUT=$
IEF236I ALLOC. FOR CJK ASM
IEF237I 143  ALLOCATED TO SYSLIB
IEF237I 143  ALLOCATED TO
IEF237I 262  ALLOCATED TO
IEF237I JES2 ALLOCATED TO SYSPRINT
IEF237I DMY  ALLOCATED TO SYSPUNCH
IEF237I VIO  ALLOCATED TO SYSUT1
IEF237I VIO  ALLOCATED TO SYSUT2
IEF237I VIO  ALLOCATED TO SYSUT3
IEF237I VIO  ALLOCATED TO SYSLIN
IEF237I JES2 ALLOCATED TO SYSIN
IEF142I CJK ASM - STEP WAS EXECUTED - COND CODE 0000
IEF285I   SYS1.MACLIB                                  KEPT
IEF285I   VOL SER NOS= SYS003.
IEF285I   SYS1.MACLIB                                  KEPT
IEF285I   VOL SER NOS= SYS003.
IEF285I   SYS1.ASISTMAC                                KEPT
IEF285I   VOL SER NOS= ISU010.
IEF285I   JES2.JOB02504.S00103                         SYSOUT
IEF285I   SYS85211.T182243.RA000.CJK.R0000001          DELETED
IEF285I   SYS85211.T182243.RA000.CJK.R0000002          DELETED
IEF285I   SYS85211.T182243.RA000.CJK.R0000003          DELETED
IEF285I   SYS85211.T182243.RA000.CJK.LOADSET           PASSED
IEF285I   JES2.JOB02504.S10101                         SYSIN
IEF373I STEP /ASM     / START 85211.1822
IEF374I STEP /ASM     / STOP  85211.1823 CPU    0MIN 00.15SEC SRB    0MIN 00.00SEC VIRT  1024K SYS   372K
IEF236I ALLOC. FOR CJK GO
IEF237I VIO  ALLOCATED TO SYSLIN
IEF237I JES2 ALLOCATED TO SYSLOUT
IEF142I CJK GO - STEP WAS EXECUTED - COND CODE 3280
IEF285I   SYS85211.T182243.RA000.CJK.LOADSET           DELETED
IEF285I   JES2.JOB02504.S00104                         SYSOUT
IEF373I STEP /GO      / START 85211.1823
IEF374I STEP /GO      / STOP  85211.1823 CPU    0MIN 00.04SEC SRB    0MIN 00.00SEC VIRT   128K SYS   320K
IEF375I  JOB /CJK     / START 85211.1822
IEF376I  JOB /CJK     / STOP  85211.1823 CPU    0MIN 00.19SEC SRB    0MIN 00.00SEC
RCS176I  1145 015150000
```


Figure 3.66 The program may not have cleared register 15 before returning control to the operating system.

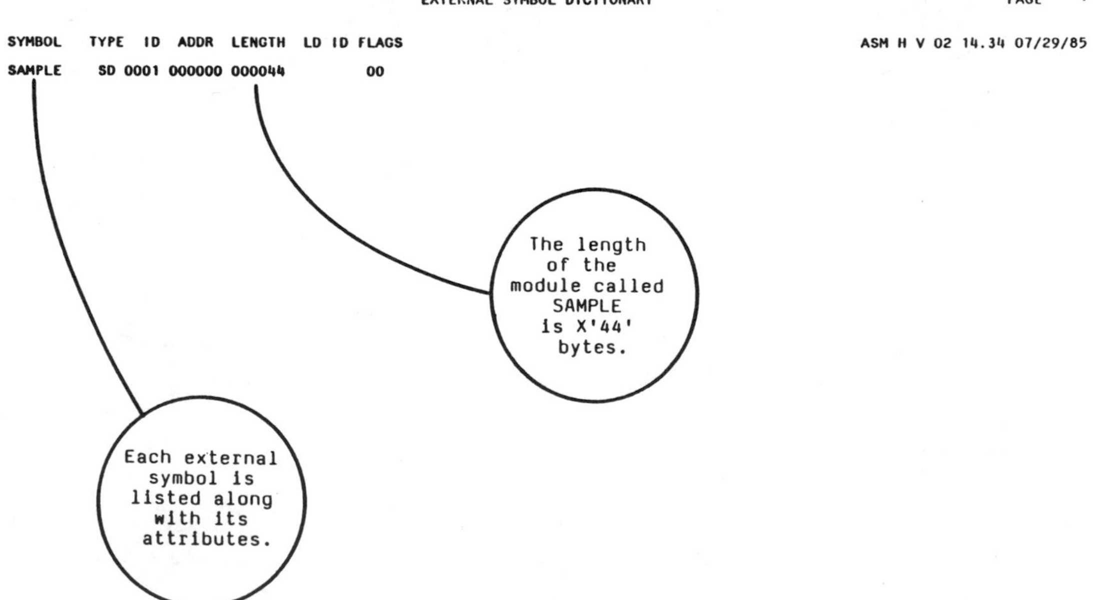

```
                                   EXTERNAL SYMBOL DICTIONARY                                   PAGE    1

SYMBOL   TYPE  ID  ADDR  LENGTH  LD ID FLAGS                                    ASM H V 02 14.34 07/29/85

SAMPLE    SD 0001 000000 000044          00
```


Figure 3.67 The external symbol dictionary.

cessing steps. For example, if the assembler detects a syntax error while converting your program into machine language, the COND CODE value will not be zero. Without flipping through many pages of a listing, you can quickly look here to see if your program worked or if it failed.

When your program executes or does not, we pointed out that register 15 indicates the success or failure during execution. The value placed in register 15 by your program will appear in the COND CODE area, again allowing you to quickly determine if your program was successful or not.

The **external symbol dictionary** usually follows the allocation and messages page, but in some installations this page may not appear. Each module within your program or any modules needed by your program (but were not coded within your program) are listed. Since we have only been using single-module programs, we only have one entry on this page.

As you can see in Fig. 3.67, our program called SAMPLE is hexadecimal 44 bytes long (68 bytes in decimal).

After the body of our program is listed, we come to the pages that end the program listing. The first is called the **cross-reference** page as shown in Fig. 3.68. Again, the importance that you place on this page will depend on how you use it and how often you use it.

This page lists each label in your program, the length of the area it defines, the statement number in which it was defined, and *each* statement in which it was used or

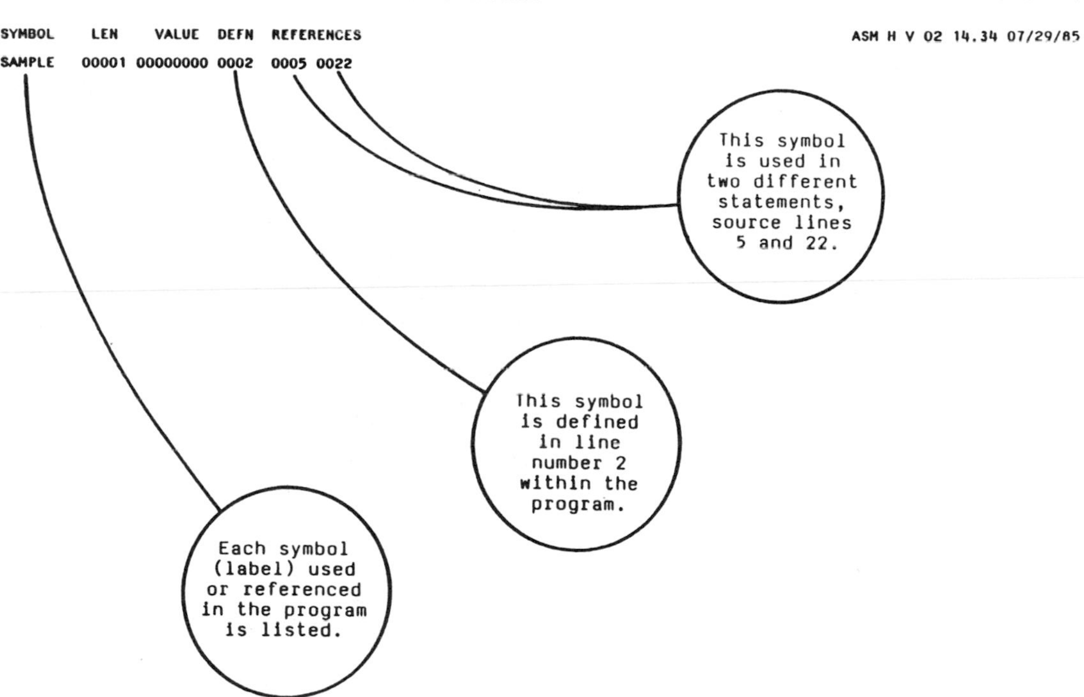

Figure 3.68 The cross-reference page.

referenced. This is quite valuable to an assembly language programmer since it allows review for unused elements. If a data element that has not been referenced is found, it can be removed from the program or the program may be looked over carefully to see if the element should have been used within the program. The page also allows the programmer to quickly find all statements that reference a particular field. Hence, if a programmer needs to change the definition or use of a field, the impact of that change on each reference of the field can be first reviewed to see if any other errors may occur as a result of the proposed change.

The **diagnostic summary** page (as shown in Fig. 3.69) has to be one of the most important pages to a programmer because it lists all of the syntax errors that were found in the program. Again, each syntax error is listed with a reference to the line where the error occurred as shown in Figs. 3.70 and 3.71.

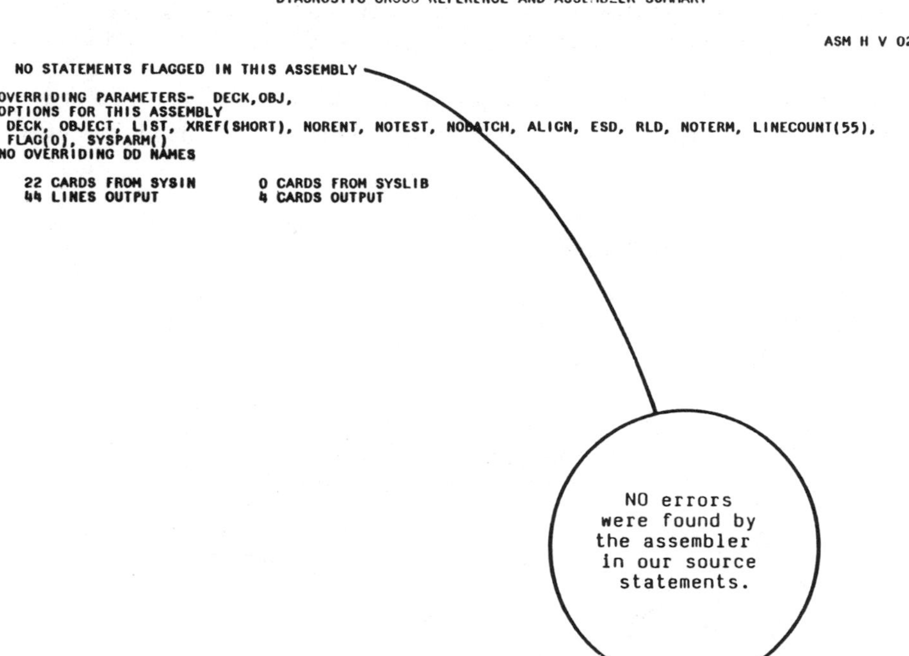

```
                         DIAGNOSTIC CROSS REFERENCE AND ASSEMBLER SUMMARY                    PAGE    5

                                                                             ASM H V 02 14.34 07/29/85
  NO STATEMENTS FLAGGED IN THIS ASSEMBLY

OVERRIDING PARAMETERS-  DECK,OBJ,
OPTIONS FOR THIS ASSEMBLY
 DECK, OBJECT, LIST, XREF(SHORT), NORENT, NOTEST, NOBATCH, ALIGN, ESD, RLD, NOTERM, LINECOUNT(55),
 FLAG(0), SYSPARM()
NO OVERRIDING DD NAMES

   22 CARDS FROM SYSIN         0 CARDS FROM SYSLIB
   44 LINES OUTPUT             4 CARDS OUTPUT
```


Figure 3.69 No syntax errors were found in this program by the assembler.

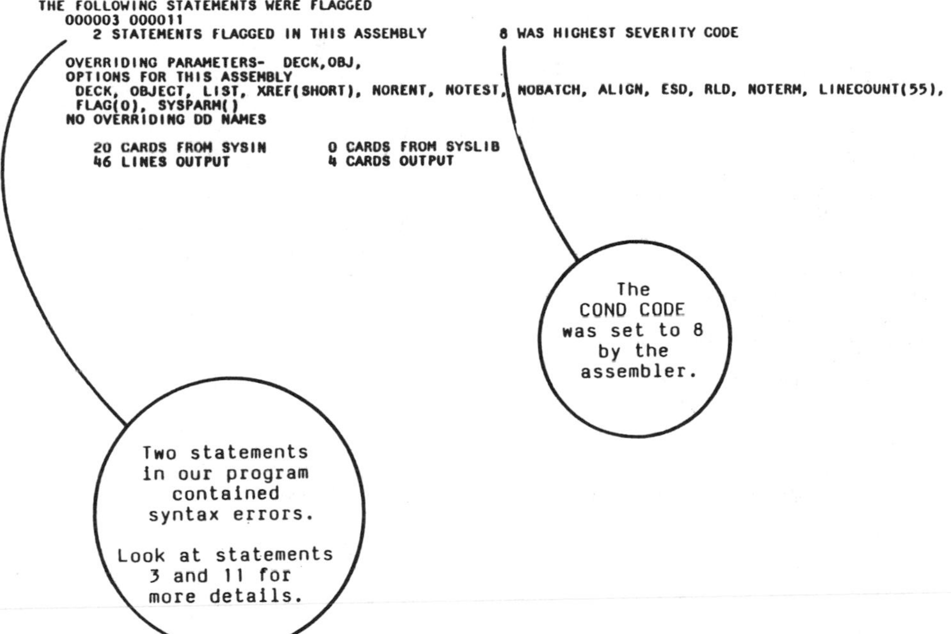

Figure 3.70 Two syntax errors have been found in the program.

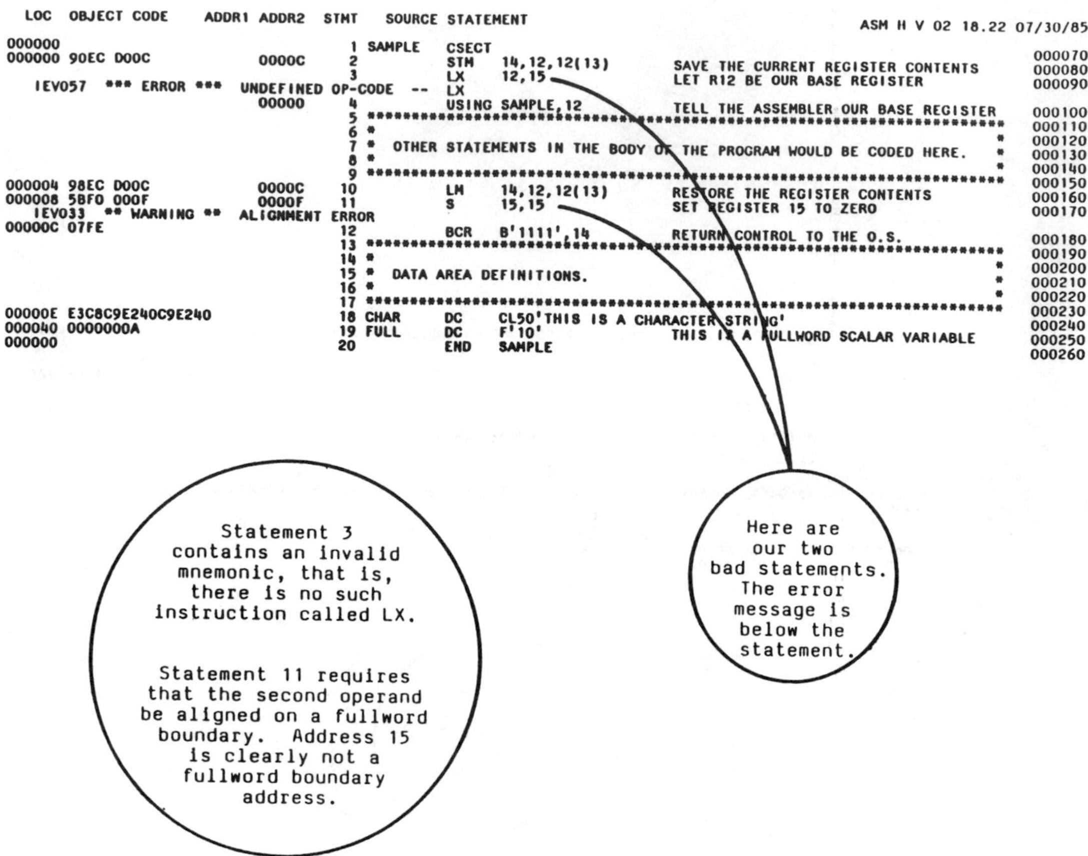

```
                                                                                                   PAGE    2
  LOC  OBJECT CODE    ADDR1 ADDR2  STMT   SOURCE STATEMENT                                ASM H V 02 18.22 07/30/85
000000                                1 SAMPLE   CSECT
000000 90EC D00C            0000C     2          STM   14,12,12(13)       SAVE THE CURRENT REGISTER CONTENTS     000070
                                      3          LX    12,15              LET R12 BE OUR BASE REGISTER           000080
   IEV057  *** ERROR ***  UNDEFINED OP-CODE --   LX                                                          000090
                            00000     4          USING SAMPLE,12          TELL THE ASSEMBLER OUR BASE REGISTER   000100
                                      5 ****************************************************************     000110
                                      6 *                                                              *     000120
                                      7 *  OTHER STATEMENTS IN THE BODY OF THE PROGRAM WOULD BE CODED HERE. * 000130
                                      8 *                                                              *     000140
                                      9 ****************************************************************     000150
000004 98EC D00C            0000C    10          LM    14,12,12(13)       RESTORE THE REGISTER CONTENTS          000160
000008 5BF0 000F            0000F    11          S     15,15              SET REGISTER 15 TO ZERO                000170
   IEV033  ** WARNING **  ALIGNMENT ERROR
00000C 07FE                          12          BCR   B'1111',14         RETURN CONTROL TO THE O.S.             000180
                                     13 ****************************************************************     000190
                                     14 *                                                              *     000200
                                     15 *  DATA AREA DEFINITIONS.                                      *     000210
                                     16 *                                                              *     000220
                                     17 ****************************************************************     000230
00000E E3C8C9E240C9E240              18 CHAR     DC    CL50'THIS IS A CHARACTER STRING'                      000240
000040 0000000A                      19 FULL     DC    F'10'              THIS IS A FULLWORD SCALAR VARIABLE     000250
000000                               20          END   SAMPLE                                                000260
```


Figure 3.71 Locating the errors within your source program.

The last page in the listing, before any output produced by your program, is the **loader messages** or **linkage editor messages** page. If we're doing an assemble-load/go procedure, then we'll have loader produced messages; an assemble-and-link procedure will generate a linkage editor messages page.

Figure 3.72 illustrates a loader produced messages page. This page gives the total length of the executable module and the memory location where the program was placed into the computer to be executed (called the entry point address). Here is where we would find the entry point address to place on the START statement if our program was consistently loaded at the same memory location in the computer from execution to execution. Be careful when you use the START statement in this way, however, because if your program is ever not loaded into the computer at this address, you'll have an even more difficult time converting into the actual memory location than if you defaulted the location counter value to zero. We'd use the START statement to set our location counter to X'11C010' as illustrated in Figure 3.73.

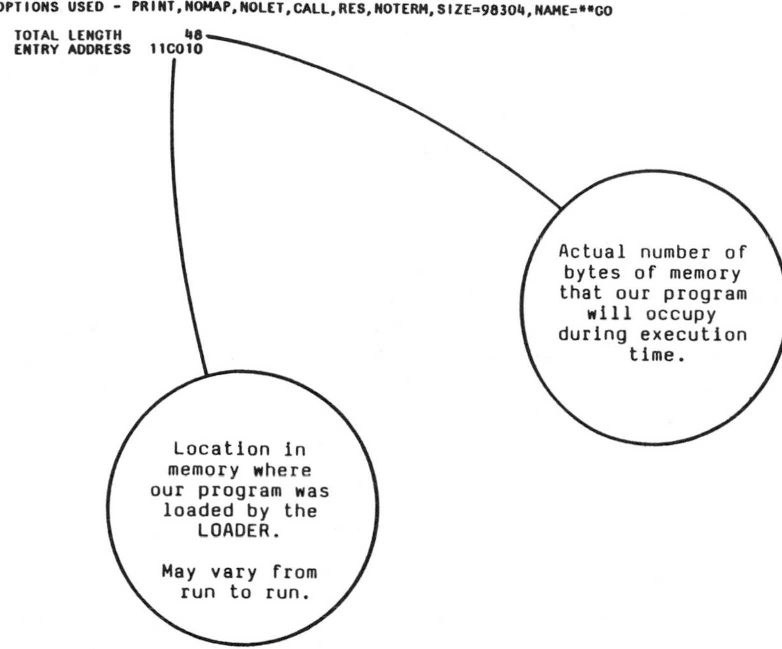

Figure 3.72 The entry point address and the length of your program are printed on the Loader messages page.

```
SAMPLE   START   X'11C010'
```

Figure 3.73 Specifying a known entry point address using the START instruction.

HELPING PROGRAM READABILITY

The first line on every page in the body of an assembly listing is the **title line**. This line allows you to place up to 100 characters of information on the top of each page to identify each part of the assembly language program. To place information into the title area, you must use the **TITLE instruction**. The TITLE instruction may be coded anywhere and as often as you desire within your program. It is an assembly language instruction and it is not executable. See Fig. 3.74.

Since the TITLE instruction allows up to 100 characters of information, you may need to continue the instruction from one source line to the next. Again, an assembly language instruction may be continued by typing the instruction up to and into column 71, placing any character in column 72, and then continuing on the next line *starting in column 16*. You *must* start in column 16 and not before. Figure 3.74 illustrates the proper format for continuing an instruction and in using the TITLE statement.

```
                  1         1         .    .    .    .    .         7
Columns  1234567890123456789012345678901234567890123
                  TITLE 'THIS IS A LOT OF INFORMATX
                        ION AND WILL NOT FIT ALL OX
                        N ONE LINE'
```

Figure 3.74 Continuing an instruction.

The TITLE statement mnemonic is coded in column 10 and the information for the title area begins in column 16 with a single quote. Type the information that you want in the title area and end the information with another single quote.

Wherever the TITLE instruction is coded, a page eject will immediately occur and the *next page* of your source listing will contain the information that you have coded in the TITLE statement. We'll see a complete example shortly (Fig. 3.77). Figure 3.75 illustrates the proper coding of the TITLE statement.

```
TITLE   'ENTER AND EXIT SAMPLE PROGRAM'
```

Figure 3.75 Coding the TITLE instruction.

If the information that you want to type into the title area contains a single quote (apostrophe), then you must **double quote** your data for it to appear properly as shown in Fig. 3.76.

```
TITLE     'JOHN' 'S AUTO PARTS'
```

Figure 3.76 Coding a quote within the TITLE value.

We now turn our attention to ASSIST program listings instead of standard assembly language program listings. If you recall, ASSIST simulates the execution of machine instructions. It generally is used in academic environments since it provides easy-to-understand messages when errors occur. ASSIST is an interpreter and does not convert source code to executed object code. Hence, the loader and the linkage editor are not used with the ASSIST package.

As shown in Fig. 3.78, an ASSIST printout is much smaller and uses less pages than the standard assembler printout. Although ASSIST listings contain the same elements, students generally find them easier to follow and understand until they get used to the standard assembler listings.

To further enhance the readability of your program, you can use the **EJECT** and **SPACE** assembly language instructions. Each time that the EJECT instruction is coded, the statements that *follow* the instruction will be placed at the top of the next page.

The SPACE instruction may be used within the program listing to place blank lines between current lines of code. One, two, or three blank lines may be inserted by coding the appropriate instruction as shown in Fig. 3.79.

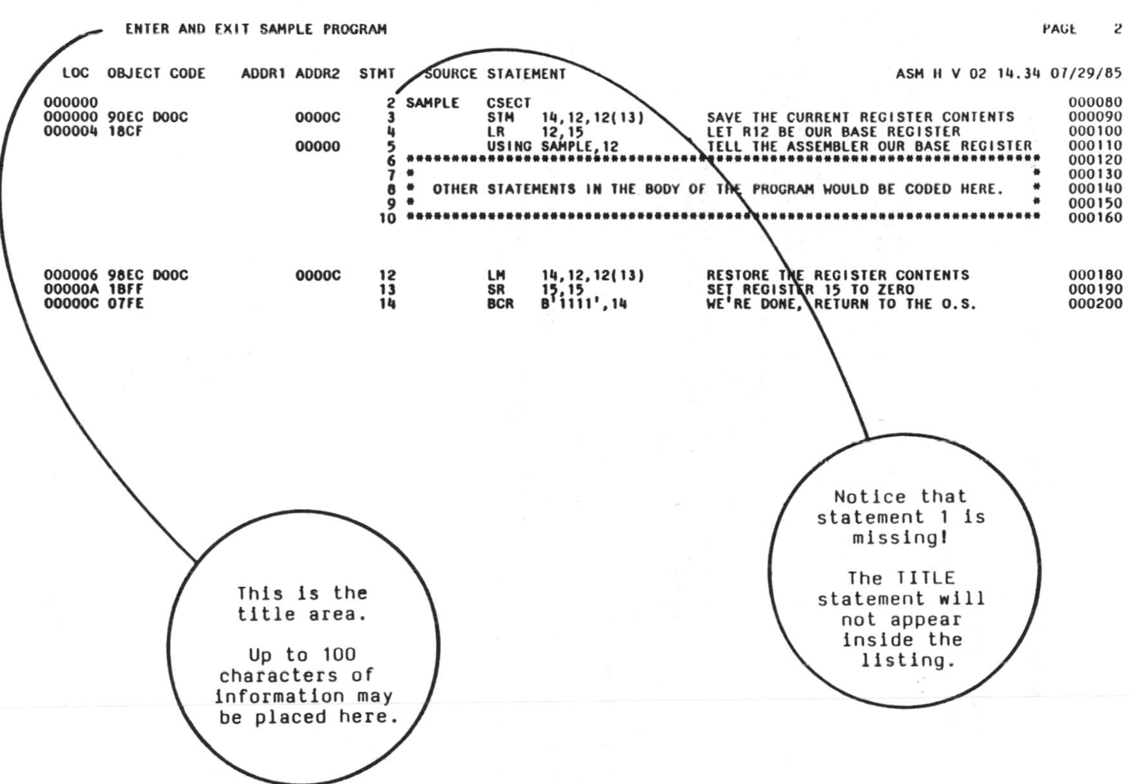

Figure 3.77 Using the TITLE instruction to label sections of code.

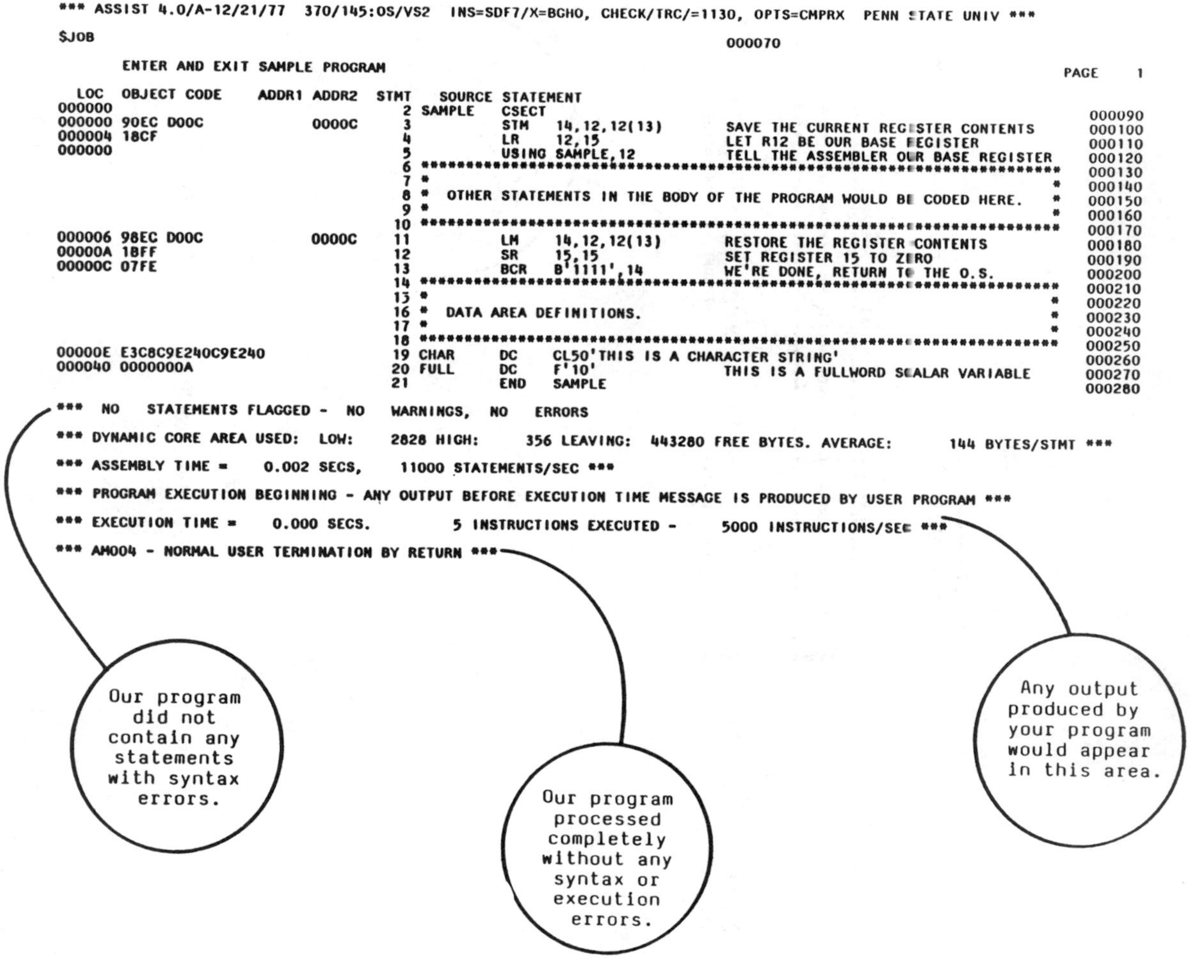

```
*** ASSIST 4.0/A-12/21/77  370/145:OS/VS2  INS=SDF7/X=BGHO, CHECK/TRC/=1130, OPTS=CMPRX  PENN STATE UNIV ***
$JOB                                                                     000070
       ENTER AND EXIT SAMPLE PROGRAM                                                              PAGE    1
  LOC  OBJECT CODE    ADDR1 ADDR2  STMT   SOURCE STATEMENT
000000                               2 SAMPLE   CSECT                                                      000090
000000 90EC D00C            0000C    3          STM   14,12,12(13)      SAVE THE CURRENT REGISTER CONTENTS    000100
000004 18CF                          4          LR    12,15             LET R12 BE OUR BASE REGISTER          000110
000000                               5          USING SAMPLE,12         TELL THE ASSEMBLER OUR BASE REGISTER  000120
                                     6 ********************************************************************** 000130
                                     7 *                                                                  *   000140
                                     8 *  OTHER STATEMENTS IN THE BODY OF THE PROGRAM WOULD BE CODED HERE.  *  000150
                                     9 *                                                                  *   000160
                                    10 ********************************************************************** 000170
000006 98EC D00C            0000C   11          LM    14,12,12(13)      RESTORE THE REGISTER CONTENTS         000180
00000A 1BFF                         12          SR    15,15             SET REGISTER 15 TO ZERO               000190
00000C 07FE                         13          BCR   B'1111',14        WE'RE DONE, RETURN TO THE O.S.        000200
                                    14 ********************************************************************** 000210
                                    15 *                                                                  *   000220
                                    16 *  DATA AREA DEFINITIONS.                                          *   000230
                                    17 *                                                                  *   000240
                                    18 ********************************************************************** 000250
00000E E3C8C9E240C9E240             19 CHAR     DC    CL50'THIS IS A CHARACTER STRING'                        000260
000040 0000000A                     20 FULL     DC    F'10'             THIS IS A FULLWORD SCALAR VARIABLE    000270
                                    21          END   SAMPLE                                                  000280
*** NO  STATEMENTS FLAGGED - NO  WARNINGS, NO  ERRORS
*** DYNAMIC CORE AREA USED:  LOW:    2828 HIGH:     356 LEAVING:  443280 FREE BYTES. AVERAGE:      144 BYTES/STMT ***
*** ASSEMBLY TIME =    0.002 SECS,    11000 STATEMENTS/SEC ***
*** PROGRAM EXECUTION BEGINNING - ANY OUTPUT BEFORE EXECUTION TIME MESSAGE IS PRODUCED BY USER PROGRAM ***
*** EXECUTION TIME =    0.000 SECS.         5 INSTRUCTIONS EXECUTED -     5000 INSTRUCTIONS/SEC ***
*** AM004 - NORMAL USER TERMINATION BY RETURN ***
```


Figure 3.78 Components of an ASSIST printout.

```
SPACE 1
SPACE 2
SPACE 3
```

Figure 3.79 Forcing blank lines into the program listing to aid readability.

The sample program listings in Figs. 3.80 and 3.81 illustrate the use of the EJECT and SPACE instructions.

Finally, throughout all of our examples, we have been using comments to help identify various parts within the assembly language program. A **comment** line is simply a line of information to yourself or to other programmers. Comments are not machine instructions and so they are not executable, and they do not generate object code. Comments may be coded on lines by themselves by placing an asterisk in column 1 and typing any information between columns 2 and 71. Be careful about typing into column 72.

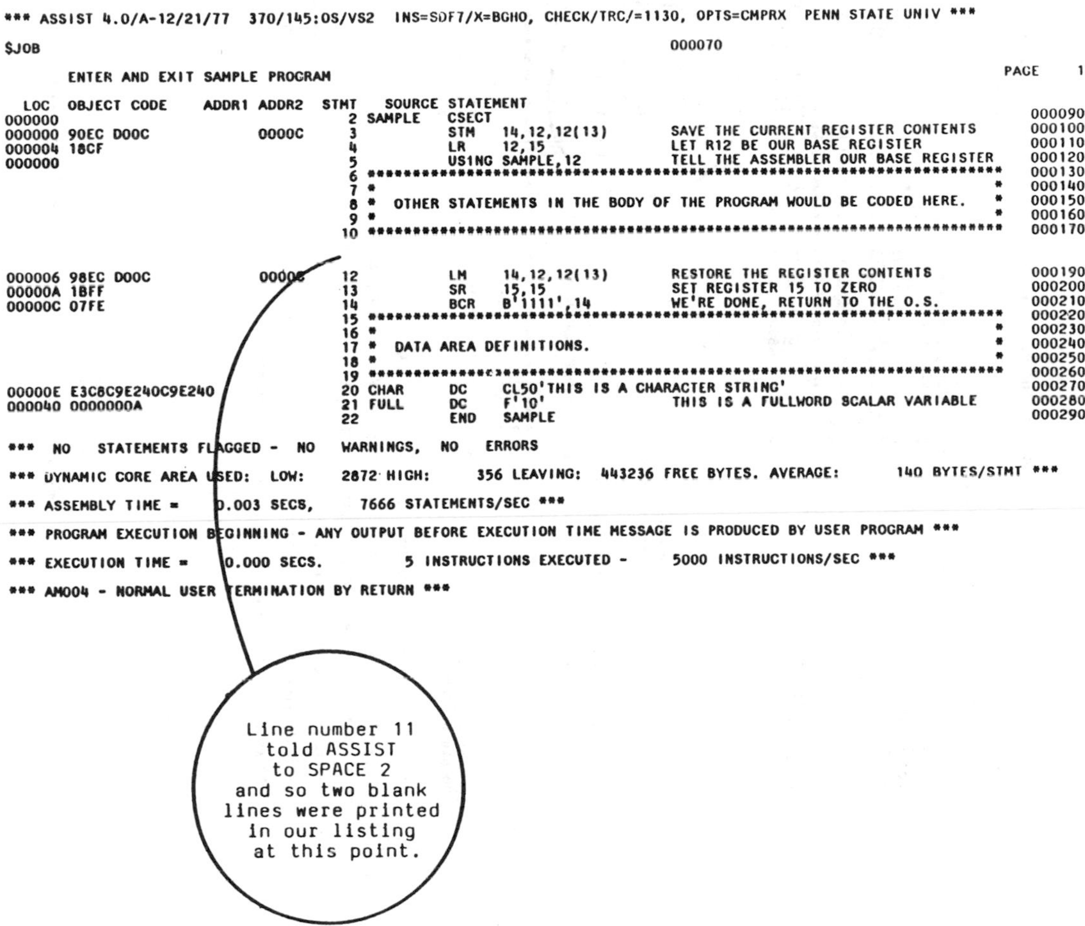

```
*** ASSIST 4.0/A-12/21/77  370/145:OS/VS2  INS=SDF7/X=BGHO, CHECK/TRC/=1130, OPTS=CMPRX  PENN STATE UNIV ***

$JOB                                                                      000070

      ENTER AND EXIT SAMPLE PROGRAM                                                                  PAGE    1

  LOC  OBJECT CODE    ADDR1 ADDR2  STMT   SOURCE STATEMENT
000000                                2 SAMPLE   CSECT                                                      000090
000000 90EC D00C            0000C     3          STM   14,12,12(13)        SAVE THE CURRENT REGISTER CONTENTS    000100
000004 18CF                           4          LR    12,15               LET R12 BE OUR BASE REGISTER          000110
000000                                5          USING SAMPLE,12           TELL THE ASSEMBLER OUR BASE REGISTER  000120
                                      6 *********************************************************************** 000130
                                      7 *                                                                     * 000140
                                      8 *  OTHER STATEMENTS IN THE BODY OF THE PROGRAM WOULD BE CODED HERE.   * 000150
                                      9 *                                                                     * 000160
                                     10 *********************************************************************** 000170


000006 98EC D00C            0000C    12          LM    14,12,12(13)        RESTORE THE REGISTER CONTENTS         000190
00000A 1BFF                          13          SR    15,15               SET REGISTER 15 TO ZERO               000200
00000C 07FE                          14          BCR   B'1111',14          WE'RE DONE, RETURN TO THE O.S.        000210
                                     15 *********************************************************************** 000220
                                     16 *                                                                     * 000230
                                     17 *  DATA AREA DEFINITIONS.                                             * 000240
                                     18 *                                                                     * 000250
                                     19 *********************************************************************** 000260
00000E E3C8C9E240C9E240              20 CHAR     DC    CL50'THIS IS A CHARACTER STRING'                         000270
000040 0000000A                      21 FULL     DC    F'10'               THIS IS A FULLWORD SCALAR VARIABLE    000280
                                     22          END   SAMPLE                                                   000290

***  NO   STATEMENTS FLAGGED -  NO   WARNINGS,  NO   ERRORS

*** DYNAMIC CORE AREA USED:  LOW:    2872 HIGH:     356 LEAVING:  443236 FREE BYTES. AVERAGE:      140 BYTES/STMT ***

*** ASSEMBLY TIME =    0.003 SECS,     7666 STATEMENTS/SEC ***

*** PROGRAM EXECUTION BEGINNING - ANY OUTPUT BEFORE EXECUTION TIME MESSAGE IS PRODUCED BY USER PROGRAM ***

*** EXECUTION TIME =    0.000 SECS.        5 INSTRUCTIONS EXECUTED -    5000 INSTRUCTIONS/SEC ***

*** AM004 - NORMAL USER TERMINATION BY RETURN ***
```


Figure 3.80 Using the SPACE instruction to enhance readability.

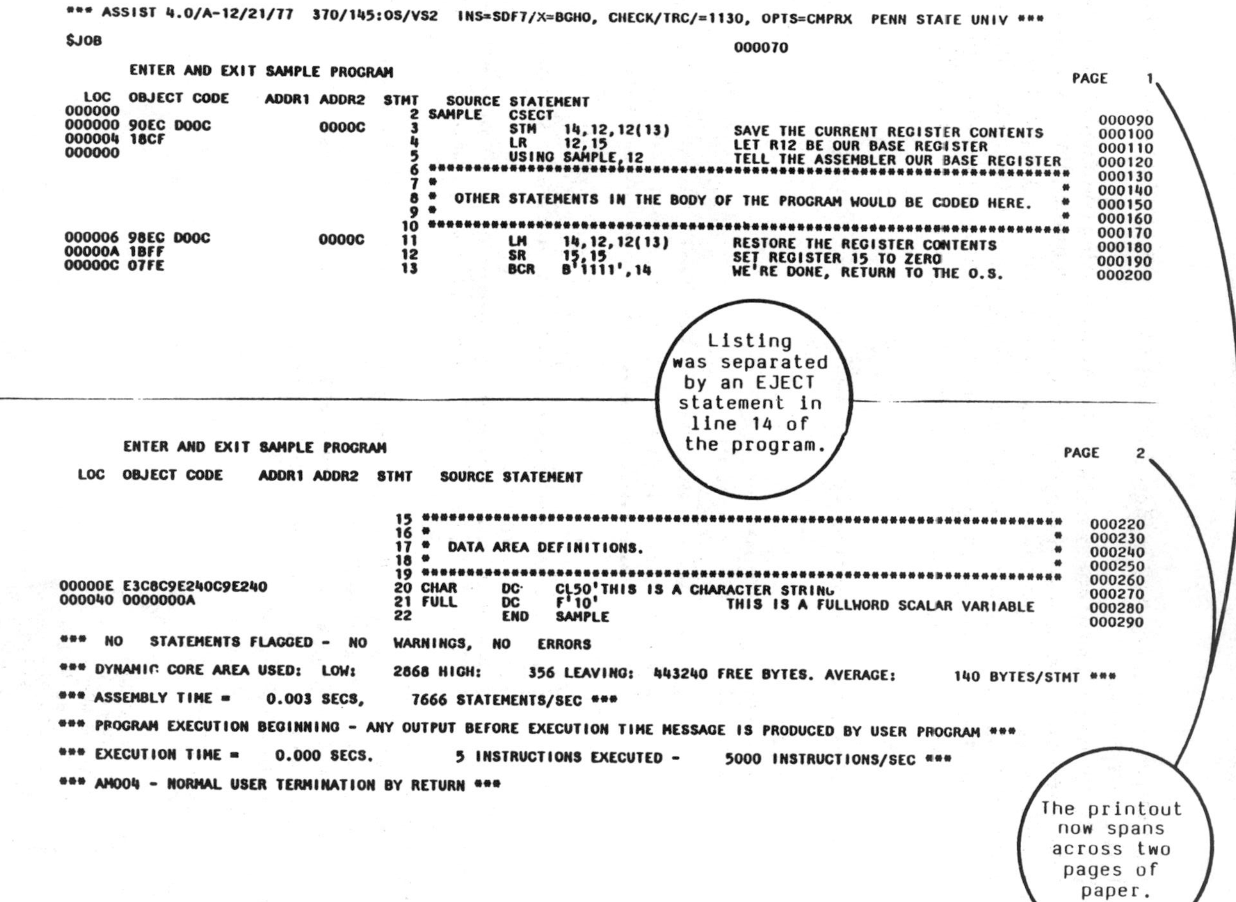

```
*** ASSIST 4.0/A-12/21/77  370/145:OS/VS2  INS=SDF7/X=BGHO, CHECK/TRC/=1130, OPTS=CMPRX  PENN STATE UNIV ***
$JOB                                                                          000070
        ENTER AND EXIT SAMPLE PROGRAM                                                          PAGE    1
  LOC  OBJECT CODE    ADDR1 ADDR2  STMT   SOURCE STATEMENT
000000                                2 SAMPLE   CSECT                                                  000090
000000 90EC D00C            0000C     3          STM   14,12,12(13)      SAVE THE CURRENT REGISTER CONTENTS   000100
000004 18CF                           4          LR    12,15             LET R12 BE OUR BASE REGISTER        000110
000000                                5          USING SAMPLE,12         TELL THE ASSEMBLER OUR BASE REGISTER 000120
                                      6 ********************************************************************* 000130
                                      7 *                                                                   * 000140
                                      8 *  OTHER STATEMENTS IN THE BODY OF THE PROGRAM WOULD BE CODED HERE. * 000150
                                      9 *                                                                   * 000160
                                     10 ********************************************************************* 000170
000006 98EC D00C            0000C    11          LM    14,12,12(13)      RESTORE THE REGISTER CONTENTS        000180
00000A 1BFF                          12          SR    15,15             SET REGISTER 15 TO ZERO              000190
00000C 07FE                          13          BCR   B'1111',14        WE'RE DONE, RETURN TO THE O.S.       000200

        ENTER AND EXIT SAMPLE PROGRAM                                                          PAGE    2
  LOC  OBJECT CODE    ADDR1 ADDR2  STMT   SOURCE STATEMENT

                                     15 ********************************************************************* 000220
                                     16 *                                                                   * 000230
                                     17 *  DATA AREA DEFINITIONS.                                           * 000240
                                     18 *                                                                   * 000250
                                     19 ********************************************************************* 000260
00000E E3C8C9E240C9E240              20 CHAR     DC    CL50'THIS IS A CHARACTER STRING                        000270
000040 0000000A                      21 FULL     DC    F'10'             THIS IS A FULLWORD SCALAR VARIABLE   000280
                                     22          END   SAMPLE                                                 000290
***  NO   STATEMENTS FLAGGED -  NO   WARNINGS,  NO   ERRORS
*** DYNAMIC CORE AREA USED:  LOW:     2868 HIGH:     356 LEAVING:  443240 FREE BYTES. AVERAGE:     140 BYTES/STMT ***
*** ASSEMBLY TIME =    0.003 SECS,     7666 STATEMENTS/SEC ***
*** PROGRAM EXECUTION BEGINNING - ANY OUTPUT BEFORE EXECUTION TIME MESSAGE IS PRODUCED BY USER PROGRAM ***
*** EXECUTION TIME =    0.000 SECS.       5 INSTRUCTIONS EXECUTED -     5000 INSTRUCTIONS/SEC ***
*** AM004 - NORMAL USER TERMINATION BY RETURN ***
```


Figure 3.81 EJECT forces lines of code to the next page.

When discussing the format of a machine instruction, we pointed out that machine instructions may also contain comments. These comments usually started in columns 35 or 40 and contained a terse description of the instruction. As we noted then and as we note now, the line comment may not be sufficient to describe all that is happening. Hence, full line comments may be needed.

Placing borders around comment lines aids in readability and helps construct what is commonly called a **comment block**. For our final sample page (see Fig. 3.82), we return to the standard assembler printout to view the small line comment, the full line comment, and the comment block.

THE EQU INSTRUCTION

The last instruction that we want to discuss in this chapter is the **EQU** instruction. It too will help enhance the readability of your program.

The EQU instruction is an assembly language instruction that allows you to define a new symbol to be **equ**ivalent to another symbol. Typically, the EQU instruction is used with register numbers to provide a more meaningful way of representing registers in the program.

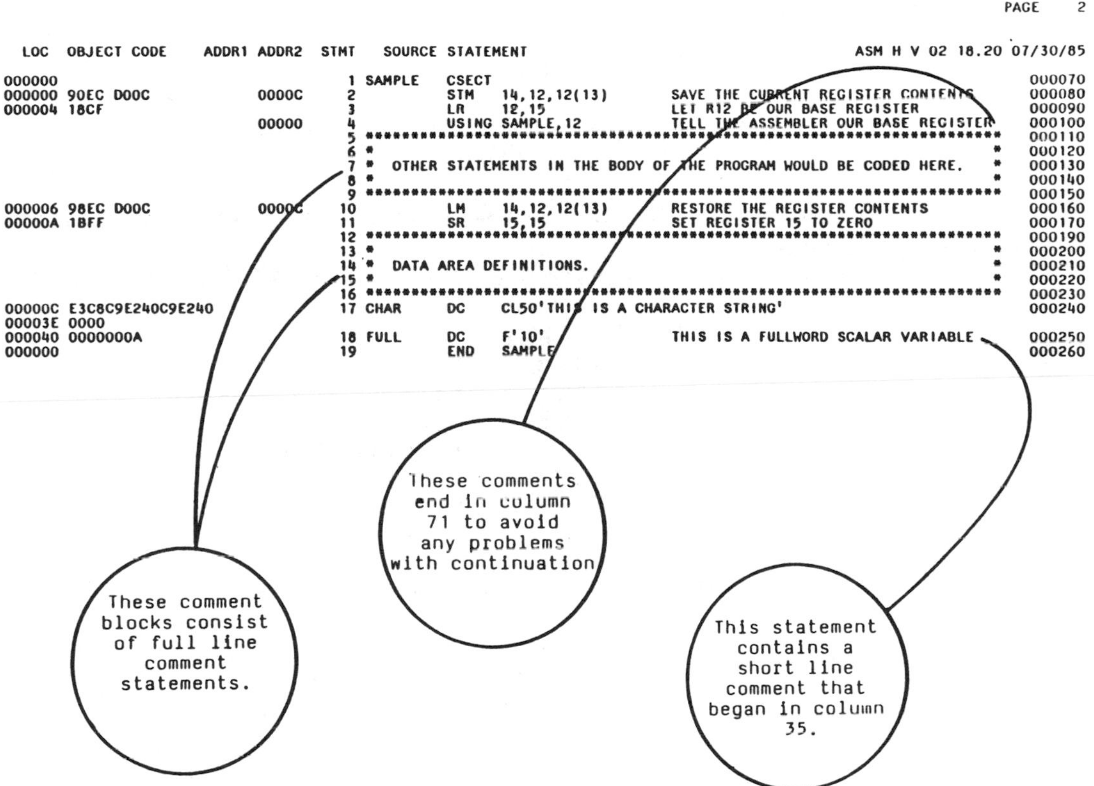

```
                                                                                     PAGE    2

  LOC  OBJECT CODE    ADDR1 ADDR2  STMT   SOURCE STATEMENT                  ASM H V 02 18.20 07/30/85

000000                                1 SAMPLE   CSECT                                           000070
000000 90EC D00C            0000C     2          STM   14,12,12(13)       SAVE THE CURRENT REGISTER CONTENTS  000080
000004 18CF                           3          LR    12,15              LET R12 BE OUR BASE REGISTER        000090
                            00000     4          USING SAMPLE,12          TELL THE ASSEMBLER OUR BASE REGISTER 000100
                                      5 *********************************************************************** 000110
                                      6 *                                                                     * 000120
                                      7 *  OTHER STATEMENTS IN THE BODY OF THE PROGRAM WOULD BE CODED HERE.   * 000130
                                      8 *                                                                     * 000140
                                      9 *********************************************************************** 000150
000006 98EC D00C            0000C    10          LM    14,12,12(13)       RESTORE THE REGISTER CONTENTS       000160
00000A 1BFF                          11          SR    15,15              SET REGISTER 15 TO ZERO             000170
                                     12 *********************************************************************** 000190
                                     13 *                                                                     * 000200
                                     14 *  DATA AREA DEFINITIONS.                                             * 000210
                                     15 *                                                                     * 000220
                                     16 *********************************************************************** 000230
00000C E3C8C9E240C9E240              17 CHAR     DC    CL50'THIS IS A CHARACTER STRING'                      000240
00003E 0000
000040 0000000A                      18 FULL     DC    F'10'              THIS IS A FULLWORD SCALAR VARIABLE  000250
000000                               19          END   SAMPLE                                            000260
```


Figure 3.82 Line and block commenting.

As you know, registers are numbered 0 through 15. As appropriate, the register number is coded on the instruction in its proper place as illustrated in Fig. 3.83.

```
LR      3,4
```

Figure 3.83 Standard coding of register numbers on machine instructions.

Here, the contents of register 4 are copied into register 3. Since this instruction uses only registers, it is relatively clear that each of the operands is a register. The example in Fig. 3.84 may not easily distinguish registers from other operands.

```
A       6,8(2,5)
```

Figure 3.84 A potentially confusing instruction.

The fullword data, at a location eight bytes from the sum of the addresses contained in registers 2 and 5, is to be added to the contents of register 6. The result is placed into register 6. The second operand is where the "readability problem" is, namely, it may be difficult to distinguish between register numbers and displacements when addressing data in this format. The EQU instruction can help by allowing us to code the instruction as illustrated in Fig. 3.85.

```
A       R6,8(R2,R5)
```

Figure 3.85 Enhancing readability by using the Rx Notation.

The displacement clearly stands out here as we've used the letter **R** as a prefix to each register number.

Compare the two sections of code shown in Figs. 3.86 and 3.87 for readability.

```
MAINPGM  CSECT
         STM    14,12,12(13)
         LR     12,15
         USING  MAINPGM,12
         LA     11,SAVEAREA
         ST     13,4(11)
         ST     11,8(13)
         LR     13,11
```

Figure 3.86 Coding example without the Rx notation.

```
MAINPGM  CSECT
         STM   R14,R12,12(R13)
         LR    R12,R15
         USING MAINPGM,R12
         LA    R11,SAVEAREA
         ST    R13,4(R11)
         ST    R11,8(R13)
         LR    R13,R11
```

Figure 3.87 Coding example with the Rx Notation.

I hope that you agree that the second example, Fig. 3.87, is at least a little more readable than the first. The use of the prefix R does help distinguish between registers and nonregisters in an instruction.

To use the R symbol in this way, we must tell the assembler that the **symbols** 2 and R2 are the same, that is, when we write R2, we really mean the symbol 2. Using a real world point of view, we can relate this to full names and nicknames. Both names identify the same person—they are labels for the same person—but they are spelled differently.

The assembler may be instructed to equate these symbols by using the EQU instruction as follows:

1. In column 1, place a symbol that you want to be equivalent to the old symbol.
2. In column 10, place the mnemonic EQU.
3. In column 16, code the old symbol.

Hence, to equate symbol R2 with symbol 2, we'd code the statement given in Fig. 3.88.

```
R2           EQU   2
<new symbol> EQU   <old symbol>
```

Figure 3.88 Using the EQU instruction.

Typically, you'd find a complete set of equates at the beginning of a program to equate the symbols R*x* to the symbol *x*. Although the **register equates** may be placed anywhere in the program, they generally appear as part of the entry conventions for the program. They are coded in their full format as shown in Fig. 3.89.

As you can see, some of the register numbers have been equated to two different symbols, one symbol for decimal representation and the other for hexadecimal representation of the register number. It is not suggested that you interchange the usage of the register symbols, however. Identify one set and use it consistently throughout your program. Multiple equates to the same register number are shown here simply for illustration.

The equate symbol may also help program readability in other ways. For example, if a register is being used as a counter or as a running total, then it may be more helpful to refer to the register by a more meaningful name. The example in Fig. 3.90 defines a symbol called TOTAL, which is to be logically associated with symbol 5. A value [symbol] of 12 is to be assigned to the symbol called BASE.

```
R0    EQU  0
R1    EQU  1
R2    EQU  2
R3    EQU  3
R4    EQU  4
R5    EQU  5
R6    EQU  6
R7    EQU  7
R8    EQU  8
R9    EQU  9
R10   EQU  10
RA    EQU  10
R11   EQU  11
RB    EQU  11
R12   EQU  12
RC    EQU  12
R13   EQU  13
RD    EQU  13
R14   EQU  14
RE    EQU  14
R15   EQU  15
RF    EQU  15
```

Figure 3.89 The register equates.

```
TOTAL    EQU    5
BASE     EQU    12
```

Figure 3.90 Equating symbols for other uses.

These equates might be used for the instructions shown in Fig. 3.91.

```
MAINPGM  CSECT
         LR       BASE, R15           OBTAIN ENTRY POINT ADDRESS
         USING    MAINPGM,BASE        ESTABLISH OUR BASE REGISTER
            .
            .
            .
         A        TOTAL,TAXES         ADD TAXES TO TOTAL
            .
            .
            .
```

Figure 3.91 Using equated symbols on program instructions.

There are many other situations in which the EQU instruction can enhance the readability of our program and increase the maintainability of the code that we write. In the cases above, for example, equating registers causes each register reference to be listed on the cross reference page since the *Rx* symbols are now regarded as *labels*. Clearly, this aids in debugging and maintenance. As other situations arise in which the EQU instruction can provide these enhancements, we'll discuss them further.

STUDY QUESTIONS

1. Register ____________ contains an address within the operating system that returns control to the operating system when our program is finished processing.
2. The rules governing the use of the registers are referred to as the ____________ ____________.
3. The reference point for accessing data elements is set by coding the ____________ assembly language statement.
4. Any register from ____________ through ____________ may be selected as the base register of the program.
5. The range of addressibility for a register is limited to ____________ bytes.
6. All labels convert into a two-byte field. The first half byte is the ____________ ____________ and the next one and one-half bytes give the ____________ of the field from the base reference point.
7. From the lowest to the highest level, the logical structure for data elements is ____________, ____________, and ____________ .
8. Within a ____________, data elements may be grouped together to form ____________ ____________ and ____________ ____________.
9. Data may be defined and initialized using the ____________ instruction.
10. A packed-decimal field capable of holding numbers between +99999 and −99999 would be defined as ____________.
11. Data elements are forced on certain memory boundaries by a principal called ____________.
12. The instruction that returns control to the operating system is ____________.
13. Program readability may be enhanced by using ____________, ____________, ____________, or the ____________ instructions.
14. Two types of errors may occur in an assembly language program; they are called ____________ and ____________ errors.
15. Column ____________ is the continuation column.
16. The address of the first instruction, which is contained in register 15 when your program gets control, is more appropriately referred to as the ____________ ____________ ____________.
17. ____________ ____________ instructions are not executable and do not generate object code and ____________ instructions are executed by the computer and occupy memory within the computer.
18. To define many identical fields, the programmer may code a ____________ ____________ on the data type identifier when the field(s) is(are) defined.

19. Character data is ____________ justified and padded on the ____________ with ____________ and numeric data is ____________ justified and padded on the ____________ with ____________.

20. The address X'01C010' would be aligned on a ____________ boundary.

21. How many bytes of storage are defined in each of the following instructions?

```
(a) DC    3F'25'
(b) DS    H,A
(c) DS    25C
(d) DS    4D
```

22. Which of the following labels are legal?

```
(a) MAINLOOP
(b) GO_SUB
(c) BYEBYE
(d) RATE3.5
(e) TEAFOR2
(f) X25@20
```

23. Write an instruction to perform each of the following:

(a) specify register 3 as the program's base register
(b) copy the contents of register 4 into register 8
(c) begin a program called PROJECT1
(d) indicate to the assembler the end of program PROJECT1
(e) define a 20 byte storage area called LASTNAME
(f) copy the entry point address into register 7

24. Which of the following instructions contain errors? If any do contain errors, identify the error and indicate how it can be corrected.

```
(a)           AR     R5,TOTAL        ADD TOTAL TO R5
(b) MAINPGM   CSECT  X'100'
(c) FIVE      DS     F'5'            CONSTANT VALUE 5
(d)           USING  PROJECT1,R25    ESTABLISH A BASE REGISTER
(e)           BC     B'1111',14      RETURN TO THE OPERATING SYSTEM
(f) R25       EQU    2+5             EQUATE THE SYMBOL R25 WITH 7
```

25. Write a complete program which does nothing, that is, it obtains control from the operating system and immediately exits. Write this program in standard assembly language.

26. Redo problem 25 but write the program in ASSIST. Use the shortest method possible and don't necessarily adhere to the linkage conventions.

Processing Character Data and Performing I/O Operations

4

Our first exposure to machine instructions and assembly language programming involves character data. As we discussed earlier, there are many different data formats and data types processed within an IBM computer system. Character data is one type, and, with the instructions available, we can process single characters or strings of data in assembly language.

Before we begin, we need to understand how programs are executed. Although we know that our program is loaded into the computer by the operating system or loader and that specific instructions process related data types, we haven't discussed how this takes place. Therefore, the first few sections will cover processing all data types under all situations. This knowledge will be used throughout the text and surface many times, especially when we discuss the *art* of program debugging.

TYPES OF MACHINE INSTRUCTIONS

Within the IBM computer system, information is processed using specific instructions. As you have seen, the instructions that we code in our programs are *not* the instructions that are actually processed by the computer. Our instructions are converted into machine language by either a compiler or an assembler before they are in a format that can be used by a computer. There are six basic types of machine instructions available on an IBM computer system. Each relates directly to the type of data that may be processed by that instruction type. Additionally, each instruction type is simply a format for the instructions within that type; there are over 100 instructions on an IBM computer within these six instruction types. Clearly, several instructions are of the same type and, as a result, make up a set of instructions that process certain types of data. Figure 4.1 identifies the six instruction types and the type of data that they commonly process.

From Fig. 4.1, you can see that each instruction is 2, 4, or 6 bytes long. If your program consists of 100 SS instructions, then it occupies 600 bytes of memory. Of course, programs do not consist of just one instruction type. We use a combination of several instructions and instruction types to develop programs that solve our problems.

I did not list the data type processed by S instructions since we will not be using them in our programs. They are generally used only within the operating system and not

Instruction Type	Length	Data Processed
RR	2 bytes	binary
RX	4 bytes	binary
RS	4 bytes	binary
SI	4 bytes	any form
S	4 bytes	
SS	6 bytes	packed decimal or character

Figure 4.1 Instruction types.

by application programmers. As a result, we've already reduced our study to the five listed in Fig. 4.2.

Instruction Type	Meaning
RR	register-to-register
RX	register-to-storage (with index)
RS	register-to-storage (no index)
SI	storage-to-immediate
SS	storage-to-storage

Figure 4.2 Instruction types and associated meanings.

The various instruction types affect the performance of our program. For example, RR instructions generally process faster than SS instructions. The instruction types listed in Fig. 4.2 are ordered from fastest to slowest, giving you a rough idea as to their comparative performance rates.

Each instruction type is directly related to how it is stored in memory. When the compiler or assembler converts our source programs into object programs, the resulting object program contains instructions in specific byte formats. For example, **RR instructions** occupy two bytes of memory. An RR instruction in source code format has the general form shown in Fig. 4.3.

```
mnemonic  op1,op2
```

Figure 4.3 Format of an RR source instruction.

The mnemonic of the instruction is coded in column 10 and the two operands are coded beginning in column 16. The instruction may contain a label in column 1 or line comments somewhere after the second operand. When the RR instruction is converted into executable format, it appears within the computer system as illustrated in Fig. 4.4:

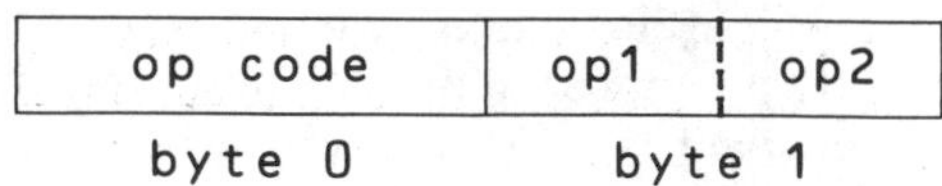

Figure 4.4 Machine format of an RR instruction.

As you can see, the second byte of the instruction is split in half, with the first half holding the first operand and the second half holding the second operand. The **operation code** or **op code** defines the instruction to the computer system, telling the computer what it is to do. The op code is a one-byte hexadecimal number unique to each instruction. For example, in the last chapter, you were introduced to the LR (load register) instruction, which copied the contents of one register into another. That is an RR instruction. If we code the instruction given in Fig. 4.5, the assembler converts that source instruction into the object code also given in the figure.

Source Instruction		Resulting Object Code
LR	12,15	18CF

Figure 4.5 Example of source to object conversion.

The op code is X'18', which to the computer means *load register.* The first operand, register 12, is denoted by hexadecimal C and the second operand, register 15, is denoted by the hexadecimal letter F. When the computer comes to this two-byte instruction, it copies the contents of register 15 into register 12.

The source instruction given in Fig. 4.6 adds the contents of register 5 to that of register 4, placing the result in register 4. The conversion of this source code into object code is also shown in the figure.

Source Instruction		Resulting Object Code
AR	4,5	1A45

Figure 4.6 Source to object conversion for the add register instruction.

All RR instructions are two bytes long with the first byte containing an op code and the next byte containing the two operands. Since RR instructions only allow operations between registers and since each register can be expressed within a four-bit field, only one byte or eight bits of storage are needed to store the two operand register numbers.

RR instructions are one of the easiest and one of the most used instruction types. We will use them to add, subtract, multiply, divide, copy, and compare values between registers. We've already used them to establish our program environment by copying and setting up the base register for our program. Chapter 5 is primarily devoted to a discussion of RR instructions and processing binary data.

RX instructions process binary fullword data between register(s) and memory. With these instructions, you can copy data from memory into a register, copy data from a register into memory, add a fullword from memory to a register, subtract a fullword value in memory from a value stored in a register, and multiply or divide a value in a register with a value in memory.

The general format of an RX *source* instruction is shown in Fig. 4.7.

```
mnemonic  R,D(X,B)
```

Figure 4.7 Format of an RX instruction.

Did you notice the D(X,B) address in the second operand? We discussed addressing earlier in the text and so this should be familiar. The first operand in the RX instruction is a register and the second defines a location in memory. If you recall, a memory location can be described using a label or through explicit coding of the displacement, index, and base register. Since either can reference a memory location, it is up to you as to how to reference your data. In most cases, you'll probably use labels, but if you don't, Fig. 4.8 shows the conversion of an RX instruction into machine code when either of the memory addressing forms is used.

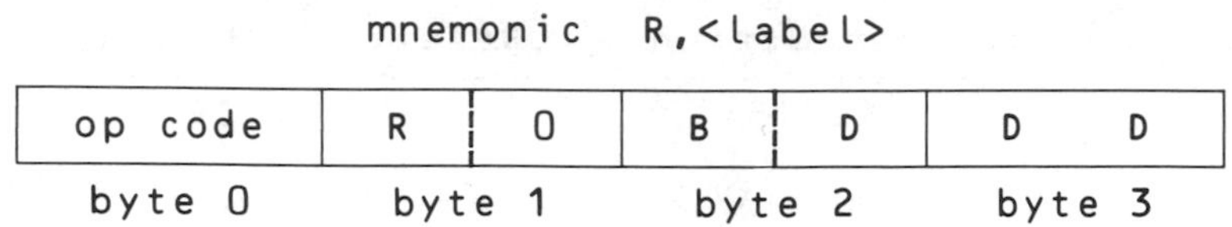

Figure 4.8 RX machine code format.

Again, the op code occupies the first byte of the machine instruction. The first operand, a register, occupies the next half byte. Since all *labels* convert into a D(0,B) format (no index register and hence a value of zero), the second half of byte 1 contains the value 0 to indicate that there is no index register specified.

Bytes 2 and 3 make up the label address by containing the base register number and the displacement or offset of the data element with respect to the base reference point. Again, a displacement can only occupy one and one-half bytes, which limits the value of the displacement to 4095 (X'FFF').

By coding the second operand specifically (without using a label), the programmer can use the index register position. With the A (add) instruction as an example (since the add instruction is an RX instruction), the source code to add the contents from the memory location "40 bytes off registers 5 and 7" *to* the contents of register 1 is coded and converted as shown in Fig. 4.9.

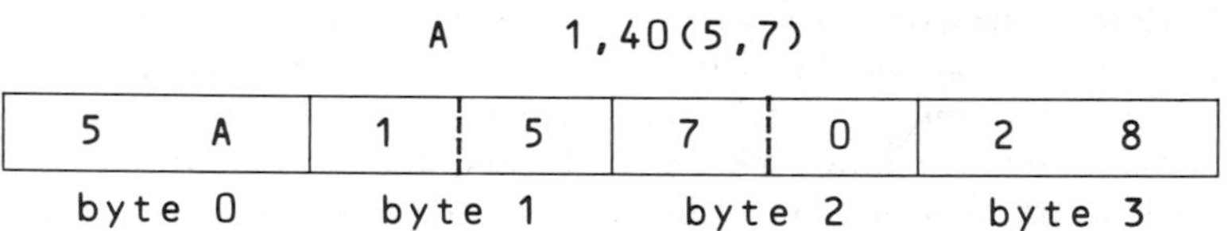

Figure 4.9 Conversion of the RX add instruction to machine code.

In order to understand this example, remember that hexadecimal 28 equals 40 base 10. Also, the add instruction mnemonic is converted into op code 5A. Hence, op code 5A specifies the RX add. The first operand, register 1, is contained in the first half of the second byte of the instruction. The index register, specified in the second operand address, is contained in the second half of the second byte. Finally, the base and displacement values for the explicit address comprise the last two bytes of the instruction.

If you're wondering how I arrived at the op codes, it's not difficult at all. When IBM built the 370 computer systems, they defined a set of machine instructions that can be processed by the computers. You are seeing those instructions now. For each instruction type, IBM defined a specific format in which the instruction must be coded to be

Edwin N. Strickland

understood by the computer. (Each type of instruction and its format may be found in *IBM SYSTEM/370 REFERENCE SUMMARY* (IBM publication GX20-1850) or *IBM SYSTEM/370 PRINCIPLES OF OPERATION* (GA22-7000).)

RS instructions allow programmers to process binary data one to four bytes long. Due to the diversity of the RS instructions, we can't say that RS instructions are used for this or that specific purpose. You've already seen RS instructions when we discussed entering and leaving our program. The instructions LM (load multiple) and STM (store multiple) are RS instructions. Let's use them to illustrate the general format of an RS instruction as shown in Fig. 4.10.

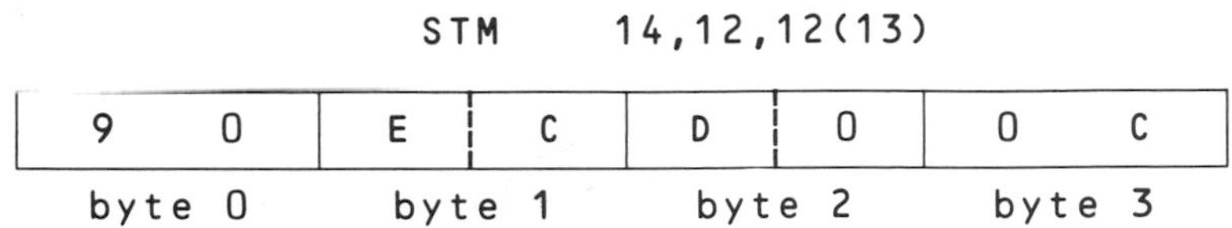

Figure 4.10 Conversion of the RS store multiple instruction.

The last operand is a D(B) address, occupying bytes 2 and 3 within the instruction. Since this operand is a D(B) address and not a D(X,B) address, we immediately know that a label (an **implicit** form of addressing) could replace the **explicit** format of the memory address that we've coded and that an index register may not be coded. In the example shown in Fig. 4.10, the letter D stands for register 13 and the value 00C stands for the displacement of 12 bytes. The op code for the store multiple instruction is X'90'.

The load multiple instruction has an op code of 98 and appears as shown in Fig. 4.11 when converted to machine code format.

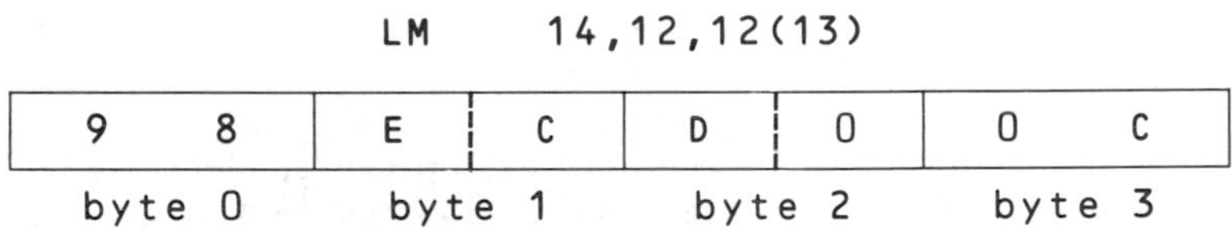

Figure 4.11 Conversion of the RS load multiple instruction.

SI instructions generally move or compare single bytes of data within memory. They may also turn on and off individual bits in memory and test the value of individual bits within storage. Assembler language is one of the few programming languages that allows processing individual bits within a byte. It is through the use of the SI instructions that this feature is possible.

SI instructions are four bytes long and are simple in form. Let's use one of the instructions that we'll discuss later in this chapter as an example.

The MVI (move immediate) instruction moves one byte of data into storage. For example, if I want to store the byte value X'00' into the memory location 50 bytes off register 10, I would code the instruction as shown in Fig. 4.12.

```
MVI     50(10),X'00'
```

Figure 4.12 Example of an SI instruction (MVI).

When the assembler encounters this instruction, it converts our source code into the machine code as shown in Fig. 4.13.

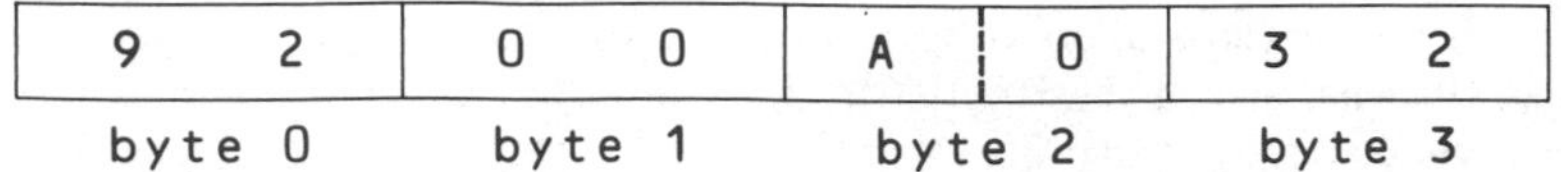

Figure 4.13 Machine code for the MVI instruction.

Byte 0 contains the op code for the move immediate instruction, byte 1 contains the **immediate value** to be moved, and bytes 2 and 3 contain the location of the target memory area. Considering bytes 2 and 3 in more detail, we see that these bytes contain a displacement of one and one-half bytes that is related to a base reference register number. In the instruction given in Figs. 4.12 and 4.13, the displacement value is X'032' and this displacement is related to register A (10). The displacement value, when added to the address in register 10, identifies a computer storage area into which our single character may be moved.

The last instruction type is the storage-to-storage instructions or **SS instructions.** SS instructions are among the slowest instructions on an IBM computer system, but they are also among the most powerful.

SS instructions are the longest instructions since they occupy six bytes of memory for each instruction. They are also some of the most complex instructions since there are three different forms and they utilize operands and features that we have not seen. Let's describe their format in a slightly different manner as shown in Fig. 4.14.

```
mnemonic    D1(L,B1),D2(B2)
```

Figure 4.14 First format of an SS instruction.

The first SS instruction format has two operands, which are both memory locations, as you can clearly determine from the D(B) address formats. The first operand looks rather peculiar in that it has an additional element L. This element is called the **length** operand, which qualifies processing between the two operands. Without going into more detail about this type of SS instruction, let's look at its machine code format as shown in Fig. 4.15.

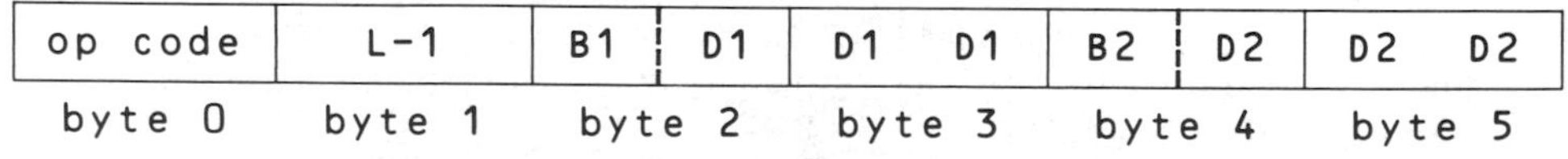

Figure 4.15 Machine code format of an SS instruction.

The op code is again contained in the first byte of the machine instruction. The length operand value, minus one, occupies the entire second byte or byte 1. The first memory location D1(B1) is defined in bytes 2 and 3 and the second operand's memory location is defined in bytes 4 and 5. Displacements D1 and D2 each occupy three half bytes to allow a maximum displacement of 4095 (X'FFF').

The second form of an SS instruction allows two length operands, one for each memory address. This format is illustrated in Fig. 4.16.

```
mnemonic   D1(L1,B1),D2(L2,B2)
```

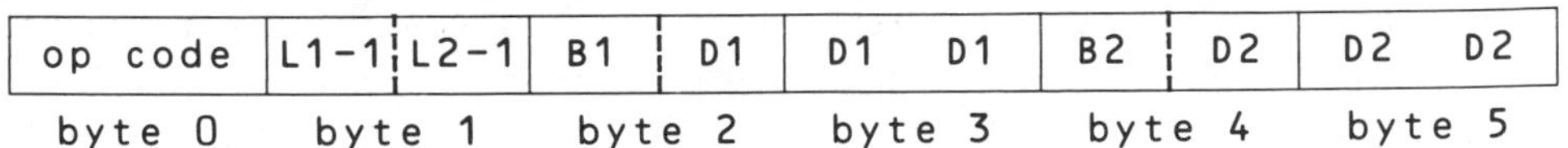

Figure 4.16 Second form of an SS instruction.

This SS instruction format is similar to the previous format except that L1 − 1 must now share byte 1 with L2 − 1. Since they must share a byte, they are limited to a value no greater than four bits or a maximum value of 15 (X'F'). When L − 1 occupied byte 1 by itself, it could attain a value as high as 255 (X'FF'). This situation may not seem important now, but when we discuss packed-decimal processing in Chapter 7, you'll see where the length operands come into play and how they are used to impact program processing.

The final SS format is quite different since it has three operands as shown in Fig. 4.17.

```
mnemonic   D1(L1,B1),D2(B2),M3
```

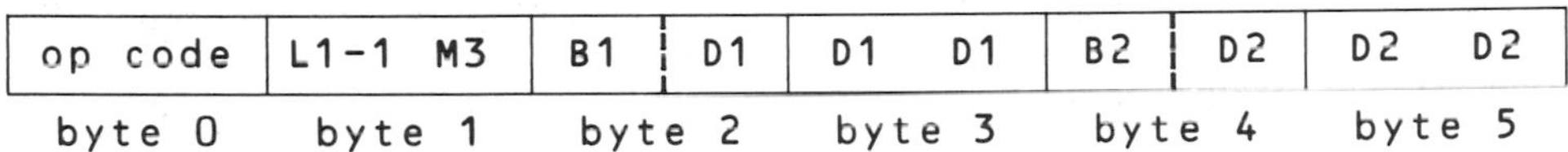

Figure 4.17 Third form of an SS instruction.

Again, L1—1 shares byte 1 with M3. Incidentally, I wrote M3 rather than M1 to indicate that this is the third operand in the instruction. M3 can have a maximum value of 15 (X'F') since it is restricted to only four bits of storage. The memory locations D1(B1) and D2(B2) occupy their usual two bytes of storage with the displacements of each memory address occupying 75 percent of that space.

It's important to realize that the length operand values are stored in the instructions as one less than the values coded on the source statement. This is a peculiarity of SS instructions that will become increasingly important as we progress through the text.

The six instruction types form the basis for the many instructions that we will learn throughout the text. The six instruction types may not seem important to you now, and, in fact, you may not understand their importance. However, their importance becomes more apparent as we implement increasingly difficult computer solutions.

HOW PROGRAMS ARE EXECUTED

Programs are converted from one format to another as they are processed. Source programs are converted into object programs, object programs can be converted into load modules and stored on disk, object programs can be converted into executable format and then executed, or load modules can be executed. The compiler or assembler converts source programs to object form and the linkage editor and loader convert object programs to load module and/or executable format. Once our programs are in executable format, they may be processed by the computer. Let's now discuss how programs are executed when we want them to be processed.

The operating system controls all processing within the computer. When it is our turn to execute, our program is loaded into memory (either by the loader or by the operating system). The process of loading into memory is called a **program fetch.** When our program is loaded into memory, it begins at a certain memory location. Since either the operating system or loader has placed our program at this location, execution can start by transferring control to our program. In other words, the program is treated as a subroutine to be called by the operating system or loader.

The instructions within our program, or for any program, are processed by the computer system (not the operating system). As each instruction is processed, our program moves closer and closer to completion and, hopefully, will arrive at the correct results. Our program continues to execute until one of the following situations occurs:

1. The program ends normally and gives control back to the operating system as we discussed in a previous chapter.
2. The program abnormally terminates, that is, an error occurs within the program; the operating system detects it and stops the processing.
3. The program runs out of time. In general, all programs run on an IBM computer system have only a limited number of seconds to do their processing. JCL tells the operating system how much time is required by the program to do its job. If the programmer underestimates the time required or if the program contains a logical error that causes it to go into an infinite loop, the program could exceed its time limit. When a program runs out of time, the operating system abnormally ends (abends) the program.

All programs, except for operating system programs, are executed in this manner. Operating system programs usually do not have to abide by the time limit restrictions although they may abnormally terminate for some other reason; they may contain errors. In fact, most computer manufacturers continually update their operating systems when bugs are found and corrected. They distribute a new release of the system or send users **PTF** (program temporary fix) information so that fixes or patches to the system may be made. Application programs are also fixed in a similar manner. Users that find software problems can call hotlines or write to report the problems that they've found so that their problem can be fixed and that a PTF will soon arrive.

This general overview of program execution is not sufficient for our needs, however. We need to look more deeply at program execution, in particular, we need to fully understand how both operating system programs and application programs are executed.

The instructions within any program, whether contained within the operating system or within an application, are processed by the computer hardware and another set of software called **micro code.** Micro code is a special computer language that *controls the hardware* and *interprets the machine instructions* in our programs. Micro code is not generally used in the development of operating systems or application programs, although there is some movement to write components of the operating system at the micro code level. Although we will not study micro code programming or its instructions, we will try to learn how the micro code operates on our machine instructions to allow our programs to execute.

As the instructions in the operating system or in our applications are encountered by the micro code, it instructs the hardware to process our instructions. A special eight-byte area in the computer tells the micro code the address of the *next* instruction to be processed. This special area, the **program status word** or **PSW,** is located in memory at location 0.

When instructions are executed sequentially, the PSW is updated by a value of 2, 4, or 6, depending on the length of the current instruction. As long as the PSW is up to date, the micro code will know the location of the next instruction to be processed.

When an instruction is processed by the micro code, the next instruction is retrieved from memory at the location given in the PSW. The micro code then updates the PSW based on the length of the instruction just retrieved. This process continues until the computer has nothing to process or is turned off. This execution process is described in Fig. 4.18 using structured English, or pseudo code.

```
1. Using the address in the PSW, retrieve eight bytes
   of memory from the computer and place this
   data into a special instruction processing
   area accessible only by the micro code.
2. Repeat the next steps until idle or until the
   computer is turned off.
   2.a if the instruction type is RR then
        add 2 to the instruction location in the PSW
       otherwise
       if the instruction type is RX, RS, or SI
        add 4 to the instruction location in the PSW
       otherwise
        add 6 to the instruction location in the PSW
   2.b interpret the instruction within the program,
       in other words, execute the instruction
   2.c fetch the next instruction from memory as
       specified by the address in the PSW
```

Figure 4.18 Instruction execution.

In instruction processing by the micro code, eight bytes of memory are fetched to ensure that the longest instruction is obtained in one fetch operation. Further, eight bytes are fetched to decrease the number of fetching operations required. For example, if two four-byte instructions are fetched, then only one fetching operation is needed for the two instructions. If four 2-byte instructions are fetched, then 3 fetching operations are saved since each instruction is not fetched individually. However, if two 6-byte instructions are coded one after the other, then in one fetch operation the system will obtain one complete instruction and only one-third of another instruction. Clearly, no savings result in this case since another instruction fetch must be done to retrieve the second 6-byte instruction in its entirety.

The entire process of executing programs begins with the micro code. Using a simplistic viewpoint, we say that the computer is *started* by the computer operator by pressing the **IPL button** (**I**nitial **P**rogram **L**oad) on the computer's control panel. When the computer is IPL'd, the micro code is loaded into the computer. In fact, the micro code is loaded into its own memory area and uses its own set of registers for processing. After the micro code is loaded, it **boots** or loads parts of the operating system. The micro code then loads the PSW with the address of the first component of the operating system and begins to process instructions within the operating system. As the operating system starts processing, it continues to load more and more parts of itself until the entire operating system is loaded. Once loaded, the operating system allows application programs to be submitted into the computer and application processing begins.

Once the micro code has completed its initial booting and begins to process instructions as specified in the PSW, it turns the control of processing over to the operating system. It is the operating system that now determines which application programs will run and in what order. However, the micro code is still underlying all processing by interpreting and controlling the hardware based on the instructions within the operating system or within the application programs.

The PSW contains more information than just the address of the next instruction to be executed. Within the eight bytes of the PSW, there are approximately nine separate fields. The **next instruction address** field is just one of these nine fields. Further, many fields within the PSW are referenced at the bit level, that is, each bit within some fields has a specific meaning. The fields and bit meanings within the PSW are given in Fig. 4.19.

The last field in the PSW is the next instruction address field that we've been discussing. As you can see, there are many more fields in the PSW, so let's see how they are used to control program processing.

The first field within the PSW is the **channel mask** field. If you recall from Chapter 1, channels were devices that allowed data to come in and out of the computer system. The channel mask field consists of many individual bits that indicate to the system whether or not input or output may be directed to or accepted from a particular channel. An IBM computer may have many channels attached to it. Each channel is uniquely identified to the computer and has an associated bit within the channel mask area in the PSW. For example, the fourth channel attached to our computer would be controlled by the fourth bit within the channel mask area (bit number 3 since bit numbering begins at zero). During an I/O operation, this channel may supply or obtain data from the CPU. If the channel mask bit for this channel is set to 1, then the channel *can* **interrupt** the CPU. This simply means that the operating system must stop what it's doing, respond to the channel, and then go back to what it was doing (before it was interrupted).

Channel interrupts, however, can be suppressed by the CPU. For example, suppose that the operating system is doing something so important that it is not to be interrupted by a channel. Setting all channel mask bits to 0 prevents any channel from interrupting the CPU. Only when a channel mask is set to 1 may it interrupt the operating system (CPU) to allow input or output to occur.

The **external mask** bit works in the same manner as the channel mask bits. A computer operator usually monitors the processing within the computer. Although the operating system actually controls processing, the operator can override the operating system and instruct it to process one job before another. Again, if the operating system is doing something very important and cannot respond to the operator immediately, it can *mask* the external interrupt bit by setting it to zero. Only when the external interrupt bit is set back to 1 may the operator again communicate with the operating system.

The operating system protects a program from another program by using the **protection key** field within the PSW. In fact, every application program is assigned a different protection key value while it is executing. Further, the protection key value covers the entire area of memory owned by the program when it began execution. When a program tries to reference or store data into any memory location, the system compares the protect key of the program with the protect key of the memory area into which the program wants

Field Name	Bit Positions	Meaning or Use
channel mask	0-6	Allows or suppresses I/O to the system through the various channels.
external mask	7-7	Allows the system to be interrupted by the computer operator.
protection key	8-11	Protects one program from another.
CMWP	12-15	C-application mode or operating system mode of processing. M-hardware error ignore indicator. W-system is waiting for work. P-determines which instructions may be processed by the micro code.
interrupt code	16-31	Contains abend code when the program fails.
instruction length code	32-33	Gives the length of the instruction currently being processed (in halfwords).
condition code	34-35	Helps control program branching during execution.
program mask	36-39	Allows or suppresses certain types of error conditions.
instruction address	40-63	Address of the next instruction to be processed by the micro code.

Figure 4.19 Components of the program status word (PSW).

to reference. If both protect keys match, the system lets the application program perform the operation since the program is accessing its own memory area. If the protect keys do not match, then the program is abnormally terminated since it has attempted to access data from an area not owned by that program. This situation is called a **protection excep-**

tion and happens often to applications that are being developed by programmers. If a program was allowed to reference another program's memory area, you can imagine what might occur—programs or data areas could be destroyed, information could be stolen, and so on. System protection is an automatic feature that cannot be suppressed as can channel and external masking. All programs are protected at all times while they are executing.

The **CMWP** field is another set of masks that indicate whether the operating system or an application program is executing. When the operating system is executing, the **problem state** bit, or P bit (bit 15), is set to 0, and when the application program is executing, the P bit is set to 1. When the computer is idle, the W(**wait bit**) is set to 1, and when the computer is processing, the wait bit is set to 0. The M (**machine check mask**) bit is usually set to 1. Should damage occur to the computer while it is processing, this bit allows the operating system or micro code to respond to that problem. If this bit were 0, then any damage to the system would not cause an interrupt and could seriously impact the integrity of data or programs within the computer. The last bit in this field is the C (**extended control mode**) bit which is set to 0 when our application is running and 1 when the operating system is executing (and performing special tasks). There are two forms of the PSW—**basic control mode PSW form** and **extended control mode PSW form.** The extended control mode is used only by the operating system and so we'll not discuss it.

The **interrupt code** field within the PSW will be helpful when we discuss program debugging. When a program fails, and depending on how the program has failed, this field contains a value that helps us determine *why* our program abended. When we cover program debugging in a later chapter, we'll discuss this field.

The **ILC** or **instruction length code** field occupies bit positions 32 and 33 in the PSW. This field is set by the micro code depending on the length of the *current* instruction being processed. In fact, this field updates the PSW so that the next instruction address field addresses the upcoming instruction to be executed. Although the instruction length code field occupies only two bits, it properly represents the length of each instruction type. RR instructions are two bytes long and are represented by the bit code 01. RX, RS, and SI instructions are four bytes long and are represented by the bit code 10. SS instructions are represented by the bit code 11. The ILC bit codes 01, 10, and 11 represent the values 1, 2, and 3, respectively (in binary or base-2 representation).

Each bit pair of the ILC indicates the number of *halfwords* that the current instruction occupies. An RR instruction two bytes long occupies one halfword. Hence, the bit code for an RR or 2-byte instruction is 01, indicating that it occupies one halfword of storage. A bit code of 10 (a value of 2) indicates that two halfwords or four bytes of storage are required for the instruction, and a bit code of 11 indicates that three halfwords or six bytes of storage are required. The ILC is also very valuable during debugging because the length of the current instruction (given by the ILC) can be subtracted from the next instruction address in the last field in the PSW. The result gives the address of the *current* instruction being executed by the computer as shown in Fig. 4.20.

The **condition code** is one of the most important fields in the PSW to a programmer. It is a two-bit field that can contain a value of 00, 01, 10, or 11, and controls the

```
 next instruction address
-length of current instruction
------------------------------
 address of current instruction
```

Figure 4.20 Determining the address of the current instruction being executed.

execution of an application program. In particular, the condition code is used after comparisons to help the program determine the relationship between data elements. It is also used by the program to control branching and looping. In Chapter 6, we'll discuss the condition code field in detail when we talk about looping and the instructions used to set and test the value of the condition code.

Program masks are bits within the PSW that may be set by an application program. They suppress or allow certain operations to occur without abending the application program. When the value of these mask bits is 1, program processing may be interrupted, and a bit value of 0 suppresses the occurrence of such interrupts. In particular, the program mask bits control overflow, underflow, and significance when arithmetic operations are performed. For example, two very large numbers that are multiplied may result in an answer that is too long to fit into the field specified. The computer abnormally terminates your program when this occurs if the overflow bit(s) are set to 1. If the overflow bits are set to 0, the overflow situation is ignored by the computer and the operation continues as if nothing had happened. This could be disasterous since you may lose some data (since the field was too small to hold the full result). In general, it is not good practice to turn these bits off to suppress the overflow and underflow interrupt conditions. We'll discuss this further in a later chapter.

The last field in the PSW is the **instruction address** field, which contains the address of the *next* instruction to be executed by the computer. It is important that you remember that the *next* instruction's address is stored in the PSW and not the *current* instruction's address. Since the PSW and especially this field are used heavily during debugging, it is important that you know which instruction is being addressed by this field.

The PSW is a very important element in program processing. The instructions in the operating system and those in our programs are monitored and controlled through the program status word. Program execution and the flow of processing within a program are directly related to the address in the last field in the PSW. Finally, the instructions that we process and the order in which they are processed are of no concern to either the micro code or the operating system. As long as we abide by the rules for using the computer and do not attempt to violate any resources that we want to use, it is up to us and our program coding whether our programs will correctly or incorrectly process our data.

PROCESSING CHARACTER DATA

Any byte within the computer is a character of data. If that byte contains information that is valid or human readable, then it has meaning to us; if not, it doesn't. We can take this seemingly oversimplified approach to character data processing because the instructions have few if any limitations. They do not require alignment, they don't care what the data is that you are processing, and they don't care whether or not the information that you're processing is human readable or valid. In fact, they can be considered dangerous instructions since they rely totally on the programmer for verification.

There are just two character data processing instructions that we want to cover at this time. Both move data from one location in memory to another. One instruction moves only one byte of data and the other instruction moves 1 to 256 bytes of data. You might wonder why we need two instructions that move one byte of data. Although both instructions can move one byte, only one can move more than one byte. When only one byte of data needs to be moved, it is more efficient to use the single-byte moving instruction than the multiple-byte moving instruction. However, the single-byte moving instruction is limited as to where the data to be moved may come from. With this instruction, the byte to be moved is contained *within the instruction* whereas the multibyte moving instruction may move one byte of data from any allowable area in the computer to any other allowable area in the computer.

The two instructions are **MVI (move immediate)** and **MVC (move character)**. We saw the MVI instruction earlier and recognize that it moves just one byte of data. It is the MVC instruction that allows us to move as much as 256 bytes of data from one location in memory to another.

The formats of the MVI and MVC instructions are quite different since the MVI instruction is an SI instruction and the MVC instruction is an SS instruction. Figure 4.21 gives the source and instruction formats for these two instructions.

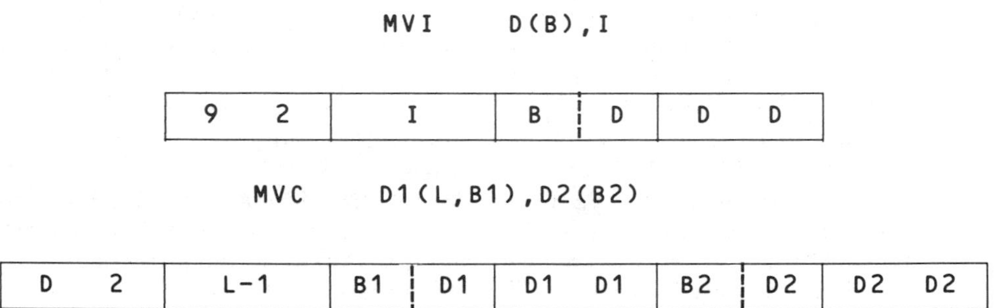

Figure 4.21 Source and machine formats for the MVI and MVC instructions.

Both instructions contain D(B) address formats. The MVI instruction requires the programmer to specify one D(B) address either explicitly (by coding the displacement and base register number) or implicitly (by coding a label). The MVC instruction requires two such addresses.

The second operand of the MVI instruction is the **immediate data operand,** which defines one byte of storage that is stored *within the instruction.* This is the data element value that is to be moved to some other location in memory. The operands for the MVC instruction refer to data areas in memory, usually not contained within the instruction, that are accessible by the program. If the program contains an error and either the MVI or MVC instructions result in a reference to an address outside of the bounds of the program, a protection exception abend occurs.

The MVI instruction does not allow moving one byte of data from any allowable area in memory to any other allowable area. Further, this instruction requires the programmer to define a specific *static* or *nonchanging* byte of data that is to be moved. On the other hand, the MVC instruction allows the programmer to move data from some location (which can be changed as often as desired within the program) to another location in memory. For example, to move character A to a location labeled STUFF, the MVI instruction is coded as in Fig. 4.22.

```
         MVI      STUFF,C'A'
```

Figure 4.22 Moving an immediate byte into a field using MVI.

Since character A may be expressed in hexadecimal as X'C1', we could have coded the instruction as illustrated in Fig. 4.23.

```
MVI     STUFF,X'C1'
```

Figure 4.23 Alternate form of coding an immediate character.

The bits B'11000001' also represent character A, thus allowing us to move the letter A to STUFF by coding the instruction as shown in Fig. 4.24.

```
MVI     STUFF,B'11000001'
```

Figure 4.24 Bit form of expressing an immediate byte value.

Of course, the first method shown in Fig. 4.22 is the most meaningful since it is the most readable. Since we want readable programs, we will continue to use the format for data representation that describes the data in the most human readable form. Figure 4.22 illustrates this coding technique.

STUFF is a label on some storage area within our program, that is, it is accessible by our program. STUFF can be defined as a field of one byte or larger. The MVI instruction moves our data to the *first byte* of STUFF *without changing the remaining bytes of this field.* The MVI and MVC instructions do not pad fields; they simply move the data into the area (from left to right) and leave alone any remaining data.

Two data fields defined in Fig. 4.25 illustrate the MVC instruction. These fields are initialized so that you can see what happens between each MVC instruction.

```
A       DC      CL5'ABC'
B       DC      CL7'1234567'
```

Figure 4.25 Field definitions used in Fig. 4.26–4.31 examples.

Fields A and B are five and seven bytes long, respectively. Field A contains the data C'ABCbb' since it is defined as a five-byte field but only initialized with three characters (padding *does* apply when *defining* fields). Since field B is defined as a seven-byte field and is initialized with seven characters, no padding occurs. Therefore, B's value is C'1234567'.

```
MVC     A(5),B
```

Figure 4.26 Using the MVC instruction.

In the MVC instruction coded in Fig. 4.26, the length operand tells the computer to move five bytes *from B to A.* This may seem backward since we read left to right, however, the MVC instruction, as with most IBM instructions, operates from *right to left.* Hence, B is moved to A. The length operand further qualifies the movement by specifying that only five bytes of data are to be moved. Since B's value does not change, A's new value is C'12345'.

With A and B at their original values, let's go through another example as shown in Fig. 4.27.

```
MVC     A(2),B
```

Figure 4.27 Qualifying the number of bytes moved.

Two bytes from B are moved into A. The two leftmost characters in B are the character digits 1 and 2. They are moved into A starting *from the left.* Figure 4.28 illustrates the outcome of this move instruction. The three right characters of A are not altered since no data was moved into them.

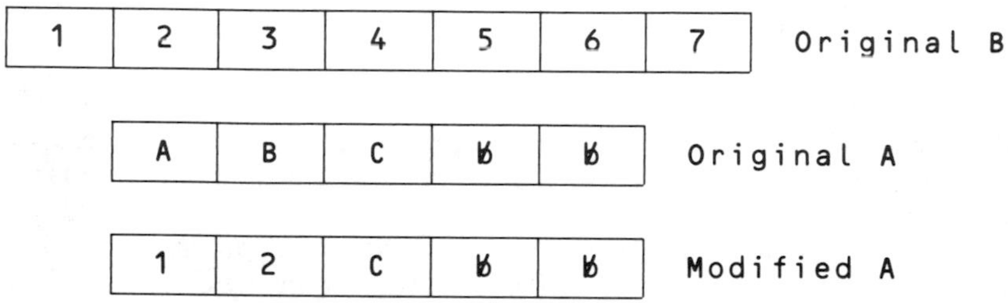

Figure 4.28 Outcome of the MVC given in Fig. 4.27.

With A and B again at their original values, consider the MVC instruction given in Fig. 4.29. What do you expect to be moved here?

```
MVC     A,B
```

Figure 4.29 Using implicit lengths on an MVC instruction.

We forgot the length operand. When the length operand is not coded, the assembler will supply a length for you. To do this, the assembler looks at how the first operand, field A, is defined. Since A was defined with the CL5 qualifier, the assembler will supply a length of **5** to our instruction. Therefore, our instruction becomes that coded in Fig. 4.30.

```
MVC     A(5),B
```

Figure 4.30 Result of an unqualified length MVC.

If A was defined as C'ABC' instead of CL5'ABC', we'd have a much different result. Explicitly coding the length qualifier value of 5 informs the assembler that we are defining a field that is five bytes long. Without the length qualifier, our field becomes three bytes long and does not contain the two extra padded blank bytes as shown earlier. Defining field A in this way causes the assembler to give a value of 3 to our implicit length operand in the MVC instruction. We must be very careful when we do not explicitly code the length operand. If you do not code an explicit length, the assembler will determine the length for you. It is your responsibility to define the data element so that the assembler can determine its *correct* length.

Often, the length determined by the assembler is not the length wanted. In general, whenever an instruction calls for a length operand, code it explicitly within the instruction or use the "length attribute" definition (which we'll discuss in a later chapter). This feature also supplies lengths of fields to the instructions of our program if the attribute is coded properly and the fields are defined properly. Since the length attribute requires consideration when it is used and since we're still in the early stages of learning assembly language programming, let's study the instructions with explicitly coded length operands. If you're interested in using the length attribute in your coding, refer to the discussion in Chapter 10 at this time.

```
MVC     A(7),B
```

Figure 4.31 Length qualifier larger than the target field.

Let's suppose that I coded my MVC instruction as given in Fig. 4.31. Here, seven bytes of data are to be moved from field B to field A. But field A is only five bytes long. The computer will move seven bytes of data. However, since field A only holds five of the seven bytes, the remaining two bytes either destroy some other data element in our program or cause our program to abend with a protection exception. As I pointed out earlier, with the MVC and MVI instructions, you *must* know how much data you want to move and to where.

SEQUENTIAL FILE INPUT/OUTPUT IN ASSEMBLY LANGUAGE

Almost every program requires input or output processing. Therefore, we need to learn how I/O is done before we go any further.

An IBM system allows a program to create and process many different file types. Sequential, relative, direct, and indexed files make up most of the files used by a programmer; see Fig. 4.32. The most common and easiest file type to process is the sequential file and this is the file that we need to do our most common input and output processing.

Sequential files are used to print information to the printer or some other device, or to read records, one after the other and in the order that they were stored, into our program. A sequential file may contain many records, but each record may only be accessed by processing all records that come before it. For example, to process the tenth record in the file, our program would have to read and process records 1 through 9 first. The order in which the information is stored is the order in which it can be accessed later.

To process sequential files in assembly language, the programmer must learn several assembly language instructions, not machine instructions. Specifically, the instructions generally used to perform I/O in assembly language are called **macros**.

A **macro** is a set of source code statements that generate machine instructions. When the assembler finds a macro instruction in our program, it replaces the macro instruction by many machine instructions. In other words, the macro instruction defines an entire sequence of machine instructions. Rather than coding the entire set of machine instructions, we simply code a one- or two-line macro instruction, which is expanded into

File Type	Processing Description
sequential	Records are processed in the order placed into the file. No record may be processed until those before it in the file have been processed.
relative	Records may be processed randomly, that is, record 5 may be processed before records 1, 2, 3, or 4. The program can process any record at any time simply by telling the system that record *n* is to be processed at this time.
direct	Records may be processed randomly by the program. Records are processed based on where they are stored on a disk device and not on the position of the record within the file. This type of processing is rarely used.
indexed	Records may be processed randomly based on character identifiers. A person's name, their address, a zip code, or any other field may be used to access records as long as the programmer has informed the system that these fields are to be used. This type of access is one of the most powerful since it allows the programmer to reference the data in the most meaningful manner.

Figure 4.32 Common file structures and their usage.

its full form, and our program can now be processed by the system to allow input and output to our program. Figures 4.33 and 4.34 illustrate this concept.

The instructions generated by the macro expansion request services from various program operating system components to help us in the I/O processing. Our program doesn't perform the processing, but it is done by the operating system, giving us the data we want. We rely on the operating system to make our job of programming easier. By using macros, we have fewer instructions to code, and by using the operating system components, we can be assured that our requests will be handled quickly and accurately.

Although you may wonder how macros impact program performance, this should not be a concern. Macros do require processing time by the assembler, but the machine instructions generated by the macro are no more or less efficient than those entered by code. Macro processing increases the assembly time of our program, but it does not have a significant impact on its execution. Since their benefits far outweigh the small performance disadvantage, we'll not consider performance as a factor in using or selecting macros to support processing.

The operating system component that performs I/O is a program called the **access method**. There are several access methods on an IBM system and the access method used is related to a file structure. For example, the **QSAM (queued sequential access method)** processes sequential files and the **ISAM (indexed sequential access method)** processes indexed files. Figure 4.35 lists the common access methods and the most common file types that they process.

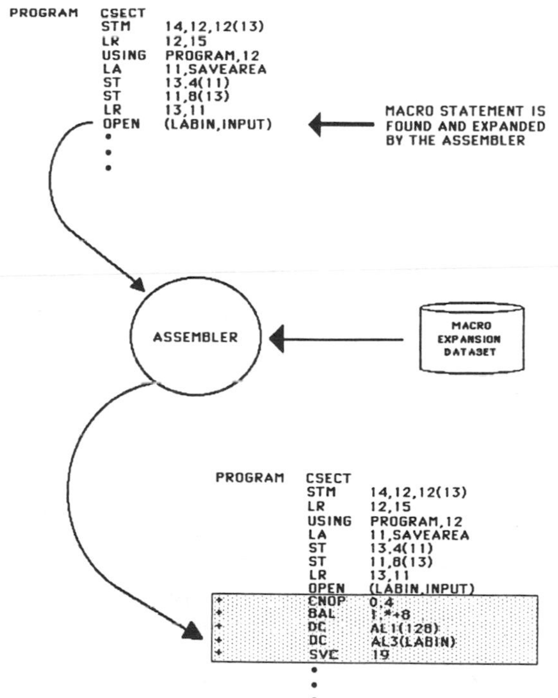

Figure 4.33 Result of macro expansion.

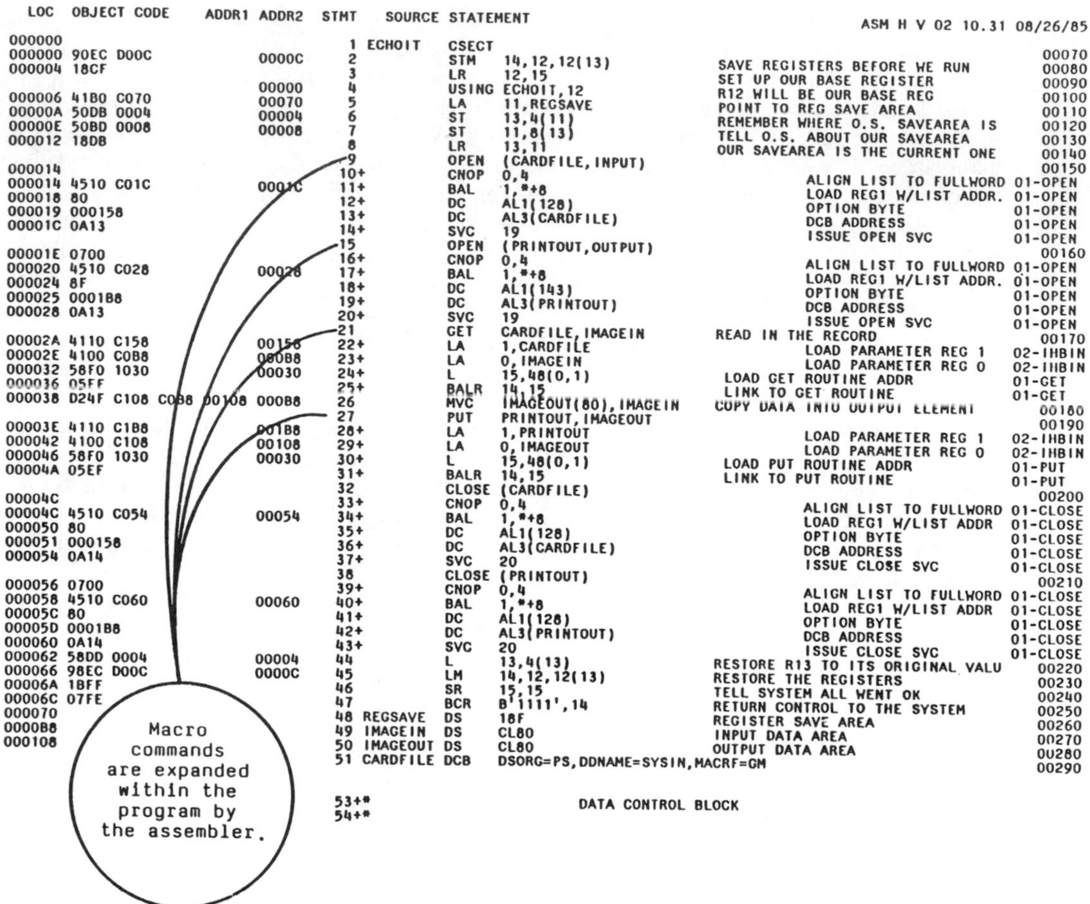

```
                                                                                            PAGE    2
  LOC  OBJECT CODE     ADDR1 ADDR2  STMT   SOURCE STATEMENT                           ASM H V 02 10.31 08/26/85
000000                                 1 ECHOIT   CSECT                                                     00070
000000 90EC D00C             0000C     2          STM   14,12,12(13)       SAVE REGISTERS BEFORE WE RUN     00080
000004 18CF                            3          LR    12,15              SET UP OUR BASE REGISTER         00090
                             00000     4          USING ECHOIT,12          R12 WILL BE OUR BASE REG         00100
000006 41B0 C070             00070     5          LA    11,REGSAVE         POINT TO REG SAVE AREA           00110
00000A 50DB 0004             00004     6          ST    13,4(11)           REMEMBER WHERE O.S. SAVEAREA IS  00120
00000E 50BD 0008             00008     7          ST    11,8(13)           TELL O.S. ABOUT OUR SAVEAREA     00130
000012 18DB                            8          LR    13,11              OUR SAVEAREA IS THE CURRENT ONE  00140
                                       9          OPEN  (CARDFILE,INPUT)                                    00150
000014                                10+         CNOP  0,4                        ALIGN LIST TO FULLWORD 01-OPEN
000014 4510 C01C             0001C    11+         BAL   1,*+8                      LOAD REG1 W/LIST ADDR. 01-OPEN
000018 80                             12+         DC    AL1(128)                   OPTION BYTE            01-OPEN
000019 000158                         13+         DC    AL3(CARDFILE)              DCB ADDRESS            01-OPEN
00001C 0A13                           14+         SVC   19                         ISSUE OPEN SVC         01-OPEN
                                      15          OPEN  (PRINTOUT,OUTPUT)                                   00160
00001E 0700                           16+         CNOP  0,4                        ALIGN LIST TO FULLWORD 01-OPEN
000020 4510 C028             00028    17+         BAL   1,*+8                      LOAD REG1 W/LIST ADDR. 01-OPEN
000024 8F                             18+         DC    AL1(143)                   OPTION BYTE            01-OPEN
000025 0001B8                         19+         DC    AL3(PRINTOUT)              DCB ADDRESS            01-OPEN
000028 0A13                           20+         SVC   19                         ISSUE OPEN SVC         01-OPEN
                                      21          GET   CARDFILE,IMAGEIN   READ IN THE RECORD               00170
00002A 4110 C158             00158    22+         LA    1,CARDFILE                 LOAD PARAMETER REG 1   02-IHBIN
00002E 4100 C0B8             000B8    23+         LA    0,IMAGEIN                  LOAD PARAMETER REG 0   02-IHBIN
000032 58F0 1030             00030    24+         L     15,48(0,1)          LOAD GET ROUTINE ADDR         01-GET
000036 05FF                           25+         BALR  14,15               LINK TO GET ROUTINE           01-GET
000038 D24F C108 C0B8 00108 000B8     26          MVC   IMAGEOUT(80),IMAGEIN COPY DATA INTO OUTPUT ELEMENT  00180
                                      27          PUT   PRINTOUT,IMAGEOUT                                   00190
00003E 4110 C1B8             001B8    28+         LA    1,PRINTOUT                 LOAD PARAMETER REG 1   02-IHBIN
000042 4100 C108             00108    29+         LA    0,IMAGEOUT                 LOAD PARAMETER REG 0   02-IHBIN
000046 58F0 1030             00030    30+         L     15,48(0,1)          LOAD PUT ROUTINE ADDR         01-PUT
00004A 05EF                           31+         BALR  14,15               LINK TO PUT ROUTINE           01-PUT
                                      32          CLOSE (CARDFILE)                                          00200
00004C                                33+         CNOP  0,4                        ALIGN LIST TO FULLWORD 01-CLOSE
00004C 4510 C054             00054    34+         BAL   1,*+8                      LOAD REG1 W/LIST ADDR  01-CLOSE
000050 80                             35+         DC    AL1(128)                   OPTION BYTE            01-CLOSE
000051 000158                         36+         DC    AL3(CARDFILE)              DCB ADDRESS            01-CLOSE
000054 0A14                           37+         SVC   20                         ISSUE CLOSE SVC        01-CLOSE
                                      38          CLOSE (PRINTOUT)                                          00210
000056 0700                           39+         CNOP  0,4                        ALIGN LIST TO FULLWORD 01-CLOSE
000058 4510 C060             00060    40+         BAL   1,*+8                      LOAD REG1 W/LIST ADDR  01-CLOSE
00005C 80                             41+         DC    AL1(128)                   OPTION BYTE            01-CLOSE
00005D 0001B8                         42+         DC    AL3(PRINTOUT)              DCB ADDRESS            01-CLOSE
000060 0A14                           43+         SVC   20                         ISSUE CLOSE SVC        01-CLOSE
000062 58DD 0004             00004    44          L     13,4(13)           RESTORE R13 TO ITS ORIGINAL VALU 00220
000066 98EC D00C             0000C    45          LM    14,12,12(13)       RESTORE THE REGISTERS            00230
00006A 1BFF                           46          SR    15,15              TELL SYSTEM ALL WENT OK          00240
00006C 07FE                           47          BCR   B'1111',14         RETURN CONTROL TO THE SYSTEM     00250
000070                                48 REGSAVE  DS    18F                REGISTER SAVE AREA               00260
0000B8                                49 IMAGEIN  DS    CL80               INPUT DATA AREA                  00270
000108                                50 IMAGEOUT DS    CL80               OUTPUT DATA AREA                 00280
                                      51 CARDFILE DCB   DSORG=PS,DDNAME=SYSIN,MACRF=GM                      00290

                                      53+*                     DATA CONTROL BLOCK
                                      54+*
```


Figure 4.34 Macro expansion within the program listing.

Our programs will call upon the access method to perform the I/O operation we want. For example, to input a file, we tell the access method of our choice. Each time we want a record, we call upon the access method to get it for us. If we want to print records, we'll present the line of output to the access method and it will take care of the printing operation.

When we want to process a file, we inform the operating system through the JCL. We tell the access method how the file is to be processed (input or output), the file's record length, position of the key if any, and so on by using a macro instruction called the **DCB (data control block)** instruction. The DCB and the JCL are connected through an element called the DDNAME (data definition name). Therefore, to perform an I/O operation, the DCB tells the access method how to process the file, the DCB connects the program to the file through JCL, and the operating system takes care of the request. Figure 4.36 logically describes these connections.

Access Method Acronym	Full Name	Logical Type of Files Processed
QSAM	queued sequential access method	sequential
BDAM	basic direct access method	relative, direct
ISAM	indexed sequential access method	indexed, sequential
BPAM	basic partitioned access method	partitioned, sequential
VSAM	virtual storage access method	indexed, relative, sequential

Figure 4.35 Access methods and associated file types.

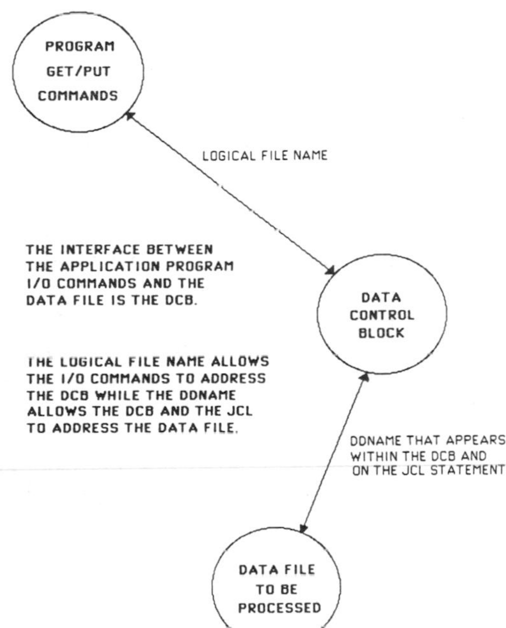

Figure 4.36 Relationship between I/O instructions, the DCB, and the external file as identified in the JCL.

The access method must know how the file is to be processed—input or output. The DCB gives this information to the access method, but the programmer also uses special macro instructions for input processing and other instructions for output processing. The input processing instruction for processing sequential files is **GET,** and the output instruction is **PUT**. Again, a connection between the DCB and the GET/PUT instructions informs the access method of the processing requirements. This connection occurs through an element called the DCB name, or more commonly, the **logical file name.**

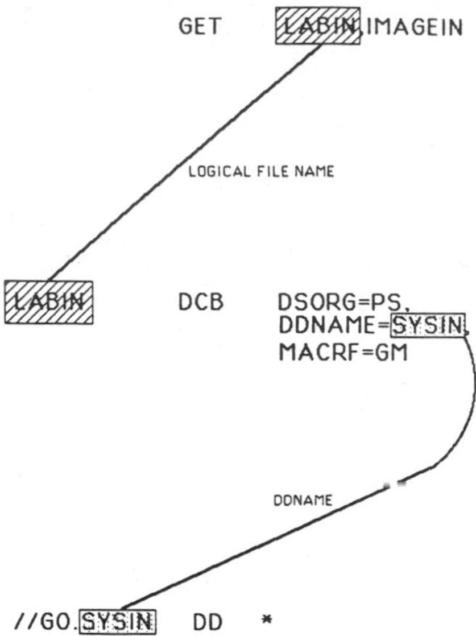

Figure 4.37 The relationship between the GET instruction, DCB instruction, and JCL statement.

When a DCB is defined, it is given a name, which is used throughout the program to reference the DCB. When a DCB is referenced through the proper input or output instructions, I/O occurs. Figure 4.37 illustrates the coding and relationship between the GET instruction, the DCB instruction, and the JCL.

The last set of instructions to process files are **OPEN** and **CLOSE**. The OPEN macro instruction informs the access method that we are about to process the file and to get it ready for processing. The **OPEN** instruction actually connects our program to the file, through the DCB and JCL. When the file processing is completed, we **CLOSE** the file. The CLOSE instruction disconnects our program from the file and informs the access method that we will not issue any more GET/PUT instructions for this file. As a programmer, you must be very careful when performing I/O. You *must* make sure that you OPEN the file *before* you issue any GET or PUT instructions, and you must make sure that you CLOSE the file before you end your program and return control to the operating system. If you don't adhere to these rules, your program will abend.

Logically speaking, our program would look something like the coding example 4.1 (if we omit the JCL for now).

As you can see, the file(s) are opened *before* any GET or PUT instructions are issued, and the files are closed before we return control to the operating system. In the coding example 4.1, the files are closed just before control is returned to the operating system. Actually, the files may be closed at any time as long as they're closed before we return control to the operating system. Files may be opened at any time as long as they're opened before we attempt to process them.

The I/O Macro Instructions

Since the DCB is the focal point of I/O processing, let's see how it's coded and the operands it contains.

The DCB macro instruction is coded with a label in column 1, with mnemonic DCB in column 10, and with the operands in column 16. Since the operands for the DCB

```
PROGRAM    CSECT
           STM     14,12,12(13)
           LR      12,15
           USING   PROGRAM,12
           LA      11,REGSAVE
           ST      13,4(11)
           ST      11,8(13)
           LR      13,11
           OPEN    .......

(body of our program containing GET and PUT instructions)

           CLOSE   .......
           L       13,4(13)
           LM      14,12,12(13)
           SR      15,15
           BCR     B'1111',14

      (data areas used by the program)

REGSAVE    DS      18F
           DCB     .......
           END     PROGRAM
```

Example 4.1 General program format with I/O.

generally do not fit on one line, it is often necessary to continue onto more than one line. This is done by ending the current line with a comma or by typing up and into column 71, placing some character in column 72, and then continuing the DCB operands on the next line starting in column 16. For example, a file that we'll call CARDFILE might require a DCB instruction as shown in Fig. 4.38. Or it may be coded as shown in Fig. 4.39.

```
CARDFILE  DCB    DSORG=PS,DDNAME=SYSIN,MACRF=GM
```

Figure 4.38 Example of a DCB instruction.

```
CARDFILE  DCB    DSORG=PS,                                X
                 DDNAME=SYSIN,                            X
                 MACRF=GM
```

Figure 4.39 Example of continuing a DCB instruction.

The DCB instructions in Figures 4.38 and 4.39 identify a **logical file** called CARDFILE; in fact, CARDFILE is called a **logical file name**. This name is how *our program* identifies the file; it is *not* how the operating system or access method identifies the file. The operating system/access method identifies the file through the DDNAME parameter and through the JCL as stated earlier.

The order in which the operands on the statement are coded does not matter. The first operand on the statement indicates that the **d**ata**s**et **org**anization of the file is **p**hysical **s**equential (DSORG=PS), that is, we are processing a sequential file. We'll code this parameter on most of our DCB statements.

The second operand, DDNAME, connects the DCB statement with our JCL statement. The JCL statement for an in-stream card file (a set of data cards that immediately follows the program and is submitted to the system at the same time that the program is submitted) is very simple and is coded as given in Figure 4.40.

```
//GO.SYSIN   DD   *
```

Figure 4.40 JCL statement for an in-stream card file.

Between the words SYSIN and DD, DD and the star (asterisk) are one or more blank columns. The // in the first two columns indicate that this statement is a JCL statement. **GO.** indicates that this JCL statement is to be used during the GO or execution phase of our program and not the assembly phase. **DD, D**ata **D**efinition, indicates that a file is being defined to the operating system. The star (asterisk) means that the data to be processed immediately follows this statement.

The last DCB operand informs the access method that the **G**et instruction is to be used and that **M**ove mode processing is also to be used. We'll not go into a discussion of move mode processing at this time.

```
PRINTOUT  DCB    DSORG=PS,DDNAME=PRINT,MACRF=PM,     X
                 RECFM=F,LRECL=80,BLKSIZE=80
```

Figure 4.41 DCB for a print file.

A DCB that may be used to send 80-byte line images to the printer might be coded as shown in Fig. 4.41. In this example, the name of our file is PRINTOUT. Again, we are processing sequentially (DSORG=PS), but this DCB is connected to the JCL statement called PRINT instead of SYSIN. The MACRF (macro facility) parameter indicates that the **PUT** instruction and **m**ove mode processing will be used. Each record in our file has the same length or has what is referred to as fixed length (RECFM=F, that is, record format = fixed), each record is 80 characters long (LRECL=80, that is, logical record length = 80), and each logical record makes up one physical record rather than multiple logical records being contained within one physical record (BLKSIZE=80, that is, block size = 80). Logical and physical records are quite important to a programmer.

A program processes logical records and the channel processes physical records. Physical records may be stored permanently on disk or tape or some other device, but logical records exist only within the mind of the programmer. The programmer tells the access method the size of the records to be stored on disk, tape, or whatever. If the logical and physical record sizes are the same, that is, the LRECL and BLKSIZE values are equal, we say that the logical to physical relationship is one to one. Storing records in a one-to-one relationship is not very efficient, and so to utilize our storage devices more efficiently, we **block** our logical records, which means that more than one logical record may be stored within a single physical record. This is done simply by assigning a value to the BLKSIZE operand equal to an integer multiple of the LRECL. With an LRECL of 80, we could assign a value of 80, 160, 240, 320, and so on to the BLKSIZE parameter. In general, but not in all cases, the larger the BLKSIZE value, the better the I/O performance. However, the BLKSIZE value must not exceed 32,760 and must be an integer multiple of the LRECL.

If the LRECL and BLKSIZE are not the same value, we must change the RECFM value to indicate that the records are to be blocked. RECFM=FB,LRECL=80,BLKSIZE=4000 is an example of this. Figure 4.42 illustrates the approximate efficiency for processing and storing blocked and nonblocked records whose lengths are 80 bytes on an IBM 3350 disk storage device. As you can see, the efficiency of storing the data increases with the BLKSIZE value.

Block Size	Records per Device	Efficiency
80	1,198,800	30%
800	3,163,500	81%
8000	3,330,000	98%

Figure 4.42 Efficiency of storing 80-byte records on an IBM 3350-type disk storage device.

Readying and Terminating File Processing—OPEN and CLOSE

Before we can process a file, it must be opened. The OPEN instruction is very simple and is coded as shown in Fig. 4.43.

```
OPEN  (filename,direction)
```

Figure 4.43 General form of the OPEN macro instruction.

According to our DCB's, our filenames are CARDFILE and PRINTOUT, which are to be processed as INPUT and OUTPUT files, respectively. The OPEN macro statements for these files would be coded as shown in Fig. 4.44.

```
OPEN  (CARDFILE,INPUT)
OPEN  (PRINTOUT,OUTPUT)
```

Figure 4.44 Example of opening files.

We can combine these two requests into one OPEN statement by coding the single OPEN instruction given in Figure 4.45.

```
OPEN  (CARDFILE,INPUT,PRINTOUT,OUTPUT)
```

Figure 4.45 Opening two files with one OPEN instruction.

Our files may be closed by coding the statements shown in Fig. 4.46.

```
CLOSE  (CARDFILE)
CLOSE  (PRINTOUT)
```

Figure 4.46 Closing files after processing.

On the other hand, our files may also be closed using another form of the CLOSE instruction as shown in Fig. 4.47.

```
CLOSE  CARDFILE
CLOSE  PRINTOUT
```

Figure 4.47 Alternate form of the CLOSE instruction (note that parentheses are not coded).

Again, the two CLOSE instructions may be combined into one as shown in Fig. 4.48.

```
CLOSE   (CARDFILE,,PRINTOUT)
```

Figure 4.48 Closing two files in a single CLOSE instruction.

In the example given in Figure 4.48, parentheses are required, and, yes, I *did* mean to code two commas together. There is an additional operand that can be coded after the filename that we will not use. Since that operand was not coded, its omission is indicated by coding two consecutive commas.

It doesn't matter whether you code two OPEN or CLOSE statements or just one. Although one OPEN/CLOSE statement is slightly more efficient than two, the difference in performance is very small. Use the technique that is most comfortable, unless you've been told otherwise.

Processing Data Records—GET and PUT

Finally, the GET and PUT instructions may be coded to perform the input or output operations. Both instructions have two operands with the same format, which is illustrated in Fig. 4.49.

```
mnemonic   filename,location
```

Figure 4.49 General format for the GET and PUT instructions.

The mnemonics are, of course, GET or PUT. The filename coded in the first operand identifies the DCB for our file. In the case of our examples, if you're doing input processing using the GET instruction, then code the filename CARDFILE. If you're doing output printing using the PUT instruction, then code the filename PRINTOUT. Be careful not to mix up the filenames or the GET/PUT commands. If you do, your program will abend, and this is not an easy problem to find.

The second operand identifies an area into which the input data is to be placed (if you're using the GET instruction) or an area to be printed (if you're using the PUT instruction). Since 80-byte line images are being read by our program, then the input area must be at least 80 bytes. According to our PRINTOUT DCB (see Fig. 4.41), the output area must also be at least 80 bytes. If your input area is smaller than the input record size, parts of your program will be destroyed, or a protection exception will occur (just as in the example about the MVC instruction). If your output area is smaller than the length of the records to be written to the printer, then you'll print some garbage on your printout. Again, it's very important that all lengths match properly. Areas should be exactly equal to the lengths that you are processing to avoid processing problems.

A simple program that will read in one 80-byte record and print it out is done using the program coding example 4.2. The program reads one record into the area called IMAGEIN, uses an MVC instruction to move a copy of the data from this area to the area called IMAGEOUT, and then writes a copy of that area to the printer. We didn't need two separate data areas as we could have read the data into IMAGEIN and written directly from this same area. However, to illustrate use of the MVC instruction, this method was selected instead. Incidentally, although the areas IMAGEIN, IMAGEOUT,

```
ECHOIT     CSECT
           STM    14,12,12(13)
           LR     12,15
           USING  ECHOIT,12
           LA     11,REGSAVE
           ST     13,4(11)
           ST     11,8(13)
           LR     13,11
*
           OPEN   (CARDFILE,INPUT)
           OPEN   (PRINTOUT,OUTPUT)
           GET    CARDFILE,IMAGEIN
           MVC    IMAGEOUT(80),IMAGEIN
           PUT    PRINTOUT,IMAGEOUT
           CLOSE  (CARDFILE)
           CLOSE  (PRINTOUT)
*
           L      13,4(13)
           LM     14,12,12(13)
           SR     15,15
           BCR    B'1111',14
*
IMAGEIN    DS     CL80
IMAGEOUT   DS     CL80
REGSAVE    DS     18F
CARDFILE   DCB    DSORG=PS,DDNAME=SYSIN,MACRF=GM
PRINTOUT   DCB    DSORG=PS,DDNAME=PRINT,MACRF=PM,      X
                  RECFM=F,LRECL=80,BLKSIZE=80
           END    ECHOIT
```

Example 4.2 Program to read and print a single record.

CARDFILE, and PRINTOUT can be located anywhere in the data areas section of your program, you must remember that they are data areas and are *not* executable instructions.

Now, let's wrap JCL around this program to inform the operating system that we want our program assembled and executed (using the loader). The coding example 4.3 illustrates the necessary JCL and our complete program a second time.

After assembly, we will obtain a listing of our program and the results of our processing. Don't be surprised when you obtain this listing since it will be much longer than the few lines of code given in the coding example 4.3. In other words, the assembler and the operating system print many more messages related to the processing of our program. Clearly, these additional messages and the output produce a much larger set of output lines than what we originally coded. In fact, input and output macros cause significant amounts of code to be added to our programs. Remember, a macro is expanded into the machine code necessary to carry out its function. Figure 4.50 shows the expansion of our PRINTOUT DCB macro as we'd see it in our program listing.

JCL To Run an Assembly Language Program

The first JCL statement in our **job** is called the **job card**. A job card defines the processing requirements to the operating system by identifying who we are, how much time is needed to execute, how much memory the program requires, and several other elements about the program. Since the job card statement varies substantially in each installation, you'll have to determine the format to use on your computer system.

The second JCL statement "// EXEC ASMFCG" tells the operating system that version F of the assembler is to be executed (**ASM**FCG). It also tells the system that you want to assemble (ASMF**C**G) and then execute (ASMFC**G**) or make the program go. The

```
//job card
//        EXEC   ASMFCG
//ASM.SYSIN      DD       *
ECHOIT           CSECT
                 STM      14,12,12(13)
                 LR       12,15
                 USING    ECHOIT,12
                 LA       11,REGSAVE
                 ST       13,4(11)
                 ST       11,8(13)
                 LR       13,11
*
                 OPEN     (CARDFILE,INPUT)
                 OPEN     (PRINTOUT,OUTPUT)
                 GET      CARDFILE,IMAGEIN
                 MVC      IMAGEOUT(80),IMAGEIN
                 PUT      PRINTOUT,IMAGEOUT
                 CLOSE    (CARDFILE)
                 CLOSE    (PRINTOUT)
*
                 L        13,4(13)
                 LM       14,12,12(13)
                 SR       15,15
                 BCR      B'1111',14
*
IMAGEIN          DS       CL80
IMAGEOUT         DS       CL80
REGSAVE          DS       18F
CARDFILE         DCB      DSORG=PS,DDNAME=SYSIN,MACRF=GM
PRINTOUT         DCB      DSORG=PS,DDNAME=PRINT,MACRF=PM,    X
                          RECFM=F,LRECL=80,BLKSIZE=80
                 END      ECHOIT
//GO.SYSUDUMP DD          SYSOUT=$
//GO.PRINT       DD       SYSOUT=$,OUTLIM=1000
//GO.SYSIN       DD       *
 HERE IS OUR INPUT DATA CARD TO BE PRINTED TO THE PRINTER
//
```

Example 4.3 Complete program with JCL to read and print a single record.

operating system supplies additional JCL to complete the processing. Incidentally, some systems do not use the ASMFCG **procedure name**. Instead, ASMCG, ASMXCG, or some other directive may perform an assemble-and-go procedure.

The next JCL statement "//ASM.SYSIN DD *" tells the system that the assembly language program follows this statement and that the program is to be input to the assembler and converted into object code.

To support the execution *of our program,* we supply JCL statements qualified with the **GO.** parameter. Referring to the coding example 4.3, you'll notice that these statements *follow* the body of our assembly language program. The statement "//GO.SYSUDUMP DD SYSOUT=$" is a standard that we always want to code when writing assembly language programs as it is used in program debugging. We'll discuss debugging later, but, for now, let's always code this statement in our program.

The next two JCL statements (referring back to example 4.3) are used by the system to connect our program to the printer and input card data, respectively. Statement "//GO.PRINT DD SYSOUT=$,OUTLIM=1000" informs the system that we want to output to the printer (SYSOUT=$). The OUTLIM parameter is a debugging aid that we'll always code to help prevent infinite loops. Here, we're telling the system that we will print no more than 1000 lines of output. If our program attempts to print more than 1000 lines, the operating system will abend our program. Incidentally, the dollar sign ($) after

```
  LOC  OBJECT CODE     ADDR1 ADDR2  STMT   SOURCE STATEMENT                                  ASM H V 02 10.31 08/26/85

                                    108+*
0001B8                              109+PRINTOUT DC    0F'0'                 ORIGIN ON WORD BOUNDARY          01-DCB
                                    111+*                        DIRECT ACCESS DEVICE INTERFACE

0001B8 0000000000000000             113+         DC    BL16'0'               FDAD,DVTBL                       01-DCB
0001C8 00000000                     114+         DC    A(0)                  KEYLE,DEVT,TRBAL                 01-DCB
                                    116+*                        COMMON ACCESS METHOD INTERFACE

0001CC 00                           118+         DC    AL1(0)                BUFNO                            01-DCB
0001CD 000001                       119+         DC    AL3(1)                BUFCB                            01-DCB
0001D0 0000                         120+         DC    AL2(0)           BUFL                                  01-DCB
0001D2 4000                         121+         DC    BL2'0100000000000000'        DSORG                     01-DCB
0001D4 00000001                     122+         DC    A(1)                  ICQE/IOBAD                       01-DCB
                                    124+*                        FOUNDATION EXTENSION

0001D8 00                           126+         DC    BL1'00000000'             BFTEK,BFLN,HIARCHY           01-DCB
0001D9 000001                       127+         DC    AL3(1)                EODAD                            01-DCB
0001DC 80                           128+         DC    BL1'10000000'         RECFM                            01-DCB
0001DD 000000                       129+         DC    AL3(0)                EXLST                            01-DCB
                                    131+*                        FOUNDATION BLOCK

0001E0 D7D9C9D5E3404040             133+         DC    CL8'PRINT'            DDNAME                           01-DCB
0001E8 02                           134+         DC    BL1'00000010'         OFLGS                            01-DCB
0001E9 00                           135+         DC    BL1'00000000'                   IFLG                   01-DCB
0001EA 0050                         136+         DC    BL2'0000000001010000' MACR                             01-DCB
                                    138+*                        BSAM-BPAM-QSAM INTERFACE

0001EC 00                           140+         DC    BL1'00000000'                                     RER1 01-DCB
0001ED 000001                       141+         DC    AL3(1)                CHECK, GERR, PERR                01-DCB
0001F0 00000001                     142+         DC    A(1)                  SYNAD                            01-DCB
0001F4 0000                         143+         DC    H'0'                  CIND1, CIND2                     01-DCB
0001F6 0050                         144+         DC    AL2(80)               BLKSIZE                          01-DCB
0001F8 00000000                     145+         DC    F'0'                  WCPO, WCPL, OFFSR, OFFSW         01-DCB
0001FC 00000001                     146+         DC    A(1)                  IOBA                             01-DCB
000200 00                           147+         DC    AL1(0)                NCP                              01-DCB
000201 000001                       148+         DC    AL3(1)                EOBR, EOBAD                      01-DCB
                                    150+*                        QSAM INTERFACE

000204 00000001                     152+         DC    A(1)                  RECAD                            01-DCB
000208 0000                         153+         DC    H'0'                  QSWS                             01-DCB
00020A 0050                         154+         DC    AL2(80)         LRECL                                  01-DCB
00020C 00                           155+         DC    BL1'00000000'         EROPT                            01-DCB
00020D 000001                       156+         DC    AL3(1)                CNTRL                            01-DCB
000210 00000000                     157+         DC    F'0'                  PRECL                            01-DCB
000214 00000001                     158+         DC    A(1)                  EOB                              01-DCB
000000                              159          END   ECHOIT                                                  00320
```

This entire page is just part of the macro expansion for the file called PRINTOUT.

Figure 4.50 DCB macro expansion.

the operand **SYSOUT=** may not be accepted by your system. Instead, an asterisk (*), the letter A, the letter D, or some other symbol, may be needed to properly direct your output to the printer.

The "//GO.SYSIN DD *" statement is immediately followed by the data card that we want to read and print. This JCL statement identifies our input data card and gives a name to our data to be processed (SYSIN).

Our program is ended with "//", called the **null JCL statement,** which informs the operating system that there are no more statements to be processed.

Although this was a very simple program, it is the basis for all our subsequent processing. In every program, we'll use the same instructions to do I/O—OPEN, GET, PUT, CLOSE, and DCB. JCL will wrap around our program so that we can properly communicate our processing requirements to the operating system.

SEQUENTIAL FILE PROCESSING USING ASSIST

As we discussed in an earlier chapter, ASSIST is a student assembler that provides better diagnostics than standard assembly language programming. ASSIST also allows us to process files sequentially. Therefore, let's implement the same program (read and print a single card image) in ASSIST.

ASSIST Input and Output Instructions—XREAD and XPRNT

To perform input and output processing in ASSIST, you only need to know two instructions, XREAD and XPRNT. XREAD brings data into your program and XPRNT sends data from your program to the printer. These instructions replace the GET and PUT instructions used in the earlier program. Further, ASSIST does *not* require use of OPEN, CLOSE, or to code the DCB statement. Quite simply, ASSIST makes our job easier so we can concentrate on problem solving rather than on the statements required to support program execution. We must keep in mind, however, the overall usefullness of ASSIST. ASSIST is not used in industry since it is an interpreter and generally processes slower than a program already in executable format. Further, ASSIST is not as powerful as standard assembly language programming and so some techniques that we'll want to do later cannot be done under ASSIST. Although ASSIST does have some limitations, it nonetheless is a useful package in which to learn assembly language programming.

Input operations in ASSIST are controlled through the **XREAD** instruction. The XREAD instruction calls for ASSIST to do the I/O for you. ASSIST in turn calls the access method just as our program did in the last section. ASSIST acts as an interface between our program and the real I/O access routines. ASSIST makes a lot of assumptions for our program, thus allowing one instruction instead of the many required for I/O.

The XREAD instruction has two operands. The first operand identifies the area into which the data is to be read. In fact, the first operand is the same as the second operand on the GET instruction.

The second operand on the XREAD instruction indicates the amount of data that you want to read. ASSIST allows you to read 1, 2, 3, . . . , as many as 80 bytes of data from a data card. In the real I/O processing mode, you didn't have a choice, you had to read all 80 characters of data. To be consistent with the standard method for performing I/O and to use ASSIST to process as close to the real world as possible, let's always read 80 characters of data from data cards. Figure 4.51 illustrates the proper coding of an XREAD instruction.

```
XREAD   IMAGEIN,80
```

Figure 4.51 Reading an input record in ASSIST.

To output a line of data to the printer, we use the XPRNT statement. Don't spell this statement incorrectly by adding the letter I. Although we are printing, the mnemonic for the instruction is X-P-R-N-T. Figure 4.52 illustrates the proper coding for the XPRNT instruction.

```
XPRNT IMAGEOUT,80
```

Figure 4.52 Proper coding of the XPRNT instruction.

Again, XREAD and XPRNT are ASSIST instructions not available in standard assembly language programming. Since these instructions are all that are needed for an ASSIST program, we can now write the program to read and print our single record as we did earlier. The coding example 4.4 contains the complete program.

To execute an ASSIST program, we must again wrap some JCL around our source program. However, ASSIST requires a few other control statements to process our program. The complete program with JCL, ASSIST control statements, our program, and our data card is contained in the coding example 4.5.

```
ECHOIT     CSECT
           STM     14,12,12(13)
           LR      12,15
           USING   ECHOIT,12
           LA      11,REGSAVE
           ST      13,4(11)
           ST      11,8(13)
           LR      13,11
*
           XREAD   IMAGEIN,80
           MVC     IMAGEOUT(80),IMAGEIN
           XPRNT   IMAGEOUT,80
*
           L       13,4(13)
           LM      14,12,12(13)
           SR      15,15
           BCR     B'1111',14
*
IMAGEIN    DS      CL80
IMAGEOUT   DS      CL80
REGSAVE    DS      18F
           END     ECHOIT
```

Example 4.4 Reading and printing a single record in ASSIST.

```
//job card
//    EXEC     ASSIST
//SYSIN        DD      *
$JOB
ECHOIT         CSECT
               STM     14,12,12(13)
               LR      12,15
               USING   ECHOIT,12
               LA      11,REGSAVE
               ST      13,4(11)
               ST      11,8(13)
               LR      13,11
*
               XREAD   IMAGEIN,80
               MVC     IMAGEOUT(80),IMAGEIN
               XPRNT   IMAGEOUT,80
*
               L       13,4(13)
               LM      14,12,12(13)
               SR      15,15
               BCR     B'1111',14
*
IMAGEIN        DS      CL80
IMAGEOUT       DS      CL80
REGSAVE        DS      18F
               END     ECHOIT
$ENTRY
 HERE IS OUR INPUT DATA CARD TO BE PRINTED TO THE PRINTER
//
```

Example 4.5 Complete ASSIST program with all control statements.

JCL and ASSIST Control Statements

In the coding example 4.5, the $JOB statement tells ASSIST where our source program begins and the $ENTRY statement separates our source program from the data to be processed. In other words, the $JOB statement acts as the "//ASM.SYSIN DD *" statement and the $ENTRY statement as the "//GO.SYSIN DD *" statement. Note that the SYSUDUMP and other GO. JCL statements are not required when using the ASSIST package since ASSIST provides its own debugging features and has a built-in facility for sending output to the printer.

Your installation may require slightly different JCL statements than those shown in example 4.5. The word ASSIST indicates to the operating system that I am running the ASSIST interpreter system. Other systems may use the directive ASCG instead of ASSIST or some other **procedure name**. Most of the other statements are the same except perhaps for $JOB and $ENTRY. Your installation may use *JOB or *ENTRY, replacing the dollar sign with a star. You'll have to know this before running ASSIST programs on your system.

LABEL PRINT PROGRAM

One of the most common programs used is for the printing of mailing labels. Have you ever given thought to how the mailing labels are produced? Let's write a program that reads in one person's record consisting of their name, street address, city, state, and zip code, and then construct and print a mailing label. Further, let's use structures to define the record to be processed and use the MVC instruction to build the lines of our mailing label. Finally, let's implement our program in standard assembly language as well as in ASSIST.

Suppose that our input record has a format as described in Fig. 4.53. The last field is not named since it does not contain any meaningful data. The *important* information is contained within the first 72 bytes of our data card, but in order to account for all 80 bytes, we have to add a field of eight bytes at the end of our data structure to fullfill our standard processing requirements.

```
PERSON   DS    0CL80
NAME     DS    CL25
STREET   DS    CL25
CITY     DS    CL15
STATE    DS    CL2
ZIP      DS    CL5
         DS    CL8
```

Figure 4.53 Input record format example.

A line of a mailing label holds approximately 30 characters of information. Some labels allow up to 40 characters, but for our purposes, let's assume a 30-character label line. To form our label here's what our program will do:

1. Read in the data card.
2. Move the name to the label line.
3. Print the label line.

4. Clear the label line.
5. Move the street to the label line.
6. Print the label line.
7. Clear the label line.
8. Move the city to the label line.
9. Print the label line.
10. Clear the label line.
11. Move the state and zip to the label line.
12. Print the label line.
13. Quit.

If you notice, steps 4, 7, and 10 clear the label line. In other words, we're going to define one label line and use it over and over. As long as we use it and clear it before using it again, we won't have any garbage printed on any of the label lines.

Incidentally, we could have defined separate label lines for each component of the person's information, requiring more storage and adding several more fields to our program. Both methods work. However, let's continue as we started.

The coding example 4.6 contains the complete program in standard assembly language.

```
//job card
//      EXEC      ASMFCG
//ASM.SYSIN    DD      *
LABEL     CSECT
          STM      14,12,12(13)         SAVE THE REGISTERS
          LR       12,15                MAKE R12 THE BASE
          USING    LABEL,12             FINISH THE JOB
          LA       11,REGSAVE           POINT TO OUR SAVE AREA
          ST       13,4(11)             SAVE CURRENT R13
          ST       11,8(13)             INFORM THE O.S.
          LR       13,11                ESTABLISH NEW R13
*
          OPEN     (LABIN,INPUT)        OPEN INPUT FILE
          OPEN     (LABOUT,OUTPUT)      OPEN OUTPUT FILE
          GET      LABIN,PERSON         READ IN THE RECORD
          MVC      LABLINE(25),NAME     MOVE NAME TO LABEL LINE
          PUT      LABOUT,LABLINE       PRINT THE NAME
          MVC      LABLINE(30),BLANKS   CLEAR LABEL LINE
          MVC      LABLINE(25),STREET   MOVE STREET INTO LABEL
          PUT      LABOUT,LABLINE       PRINT THE STREET LINF
          MVC      LABLINE(30),BLANKS   CLEAR LABEL LINE
          MVC      LABLINE(15),CITY     MOVE CITY INTO LABEL
          PUT      LABOUT,LABLINE       PRINT THE CITY LINE
          MVC      LABLINE(30),BLANKS   CLEAR LABEL LINE AGAIN
          MVC      LABLINE(2),STATE     MOVE STATE INTO LINE
          MVI      LABLINE+2,C','       MOVE COMMA AFTER STATE
          MVC      LABLINE+4(5),ZIP     MOVE ZIP AFTER STATE
          PUT      LABOUT,LABLINE       PRINT STATE/ZIP LINE
          CLOSE    (LABIN)
          CLOSE    (LABOUT)
*
          L        13,4(13)             RESTORE R13 TO ORIGINAL
          LM       14,12,12(13)         RESTORE THE REGS
          SR       15,15                EVERYTHING WENT OK
          BCR      B'1111',14           RETURN TO THE SYSTEM
```

Example 4.6 Program to print a mailing label.

```
*
PERSON    DS    0CL80                  DEFINE PERSON STRUCTURE
NAME      DS    CL25
STREET    DS    CL25
CITY      DS    CL15
STATE     DS    CL2
ZIP       DS    CL5
          DS    CL8
*
LABLINE   DC    CL30' '                DEFINE AND INITIALIZE
*
BLANKS    DC    CL30'                  USED TO CLEAR LABLINE
*
REGSAVE   DS    18F
LABIN     DCB   DSORG=PS,DDNAME=LABIN,MACRF=GM
LABOUT    DCB   DSORG=PS,DDNAME=LABOUT,MACRF=PM,                       X
                RECFM=F,LRECL=30,BLKSIZE=30
          END   LABEL
//GO.SYSUDUMP   DD   SYSOUT=$
//GO.LABOUT     DD   SYSOUT=$,OUTLIM=1000
//GO.LABIN      DD   *
CHUCK KACMAR     100 OAK STREET    AUSTIN     TX    78731
//
```

Example 4.6 (cont.)

Since our program is only printing thirty-byte output lines, I've changed the output DCB to reflect this length accordingly. The DCB has changed in yet another way. In example 4.6, the label on the DCB and the DDNAME parameters are the same, which helps relate the logical name of our files within the program directly with the JCL file names on our **GO.** statements. Many assembly language programmers do this, but it's your option whether or not to choose this method for coding your DCB and JCL statements.

```
MVC    LABLINE(2),STATE       MOVE STATE INTO LINE
MVI    LABLINE+2,C','         MOVE COMMA AFTER STATE
MVC    LABLINE+4(5),ZIP       MOVE ZIP AFTER STATE
```

Figure 4.54 Extracted lines from the program for purposes of illustration.

Let's look at the lines that place the state and zip code into the label line. Figure 4.54 contains the lines as extracted from the coding example. The first MVC moves the state code into the first two bytes of the label line. The second instruction, MVI, places a comma into the label line at offset 2; in other words, **LABLINE+2** tells the system to move the character C',' two bytes past the beginning of LABLINE. Therefore, the comma is placed into the *third* byte of the area LABLINE, thus placing it immediately after the two-character state code. The last instruction places the zip code into LABLINE starting at offset 4, or, actually, in byte **5** of the area. Since nothing was moved into byte 4, then it remains as it was, set to a blank value as a result of the MVC just above this code. When this label is printed, it will appear as shown in Fig. 4.55.

```
CHUCK KACMAR
100 OAK STREET
AUSTIN
TX, 78731

123456789012345678901234567890
```

Figure 4.55 Sample output label produced by our program.

Implementing the same program in ASSIST gives us the results contained in the coding example 4.7.

```
                         BE CAREFUL ABOUT THIS PROGRAM

                      it looks like it works but it's got a bug

//job card
//     EXEC     ASSIST
//SYSIN   DD      *
$JOB
LABEL     CSECT
          STM      14,12,12(13)         SAVE THE REGISTERS
          LR       12,15                MAKE R12 THE BASE
          USING    LABEL,12             FINISH THE JOB
          LA       11,REGSAVE           POINT TO OUR SAVE AREA
          ST       13,4(11)             SAVE CURRENT R13
          ST       11,8(13)             INFORM THE O.S.
          LR       13,11                POINT TO NEW SAVE AREA
          XREAD    PERSON,80            READ IN THE RECORD
          MVC      LABLINE(25),NAME     MOVE NAME TO LABEL LINE
          XPRNT    LABOUT,30            PRINT THE NAME
          MVC      LABLINE(30),BLANKS   CLEAR LABEL LINE
          MVC      LABLINE(25),STREET   MOVE STREET INTO LABEL
          XPRNT    LABOUT,30            PRINT THE STREET LINE
          MVC      LABLINE(30),BLANKS   CLEAR LABEL LINE
          MVC      LABLINE(15),CITY     MOVE CITY INTO LABEL
          XPRNT    LABOUT,30            PRINT THE CITY LINE
          MVC      LABLINE(30),BLANKS   CLEAR LABEL LINE AGAIN
          MVC      LABLINE(2),STATE     MOVE STATE INTO LINE
          MVI      LABLINE+2,C','       MOVE COMMA AFTER STATE
          MVC      LABLINE+4(5),ZIP     MOVE ZIP AFTER STATE
          XPRNT    LABOUT,30            PRINT STATE/ZIP LINE
          L        13,4(13)             RESTORE R13 TO ORIGINAL
          LM       14,12,12(13)         RESTORE THE REGS
          SR       15,15                EVERYTHING WENT OK
          BCR      B'1111',14           RETURN TO THE SYSTEM
*
PERSON    DS       0CL80                DEFINE PERSON STRUCTURE
NAME      DS       CL25
STREET    DS       CL25
CITY      DS       CL15
STATE     DS       CL2
ZIP       DS       CL5
          DS       CL8
*
LABLINE   DC       CL30' '              DEFINE AND INITIALIZE
*
BLANKS    DC       CL30' '              USED TO CLEAR LABLINE
REGSAVE   DS       18F
          END      LABEL
$ENTRY
CHUCK KACMAR         100 OAK STREET    AUSTIN     TX    78731
//
```

Example 4.7 Mailing label program in ASSIST with a bug.

I'm sure that you'd agree that the ASSIST program is much easier to read and is much smaller than the assembly language version. Also, it is much easier to see that 80 bytes of data are being read by the program and only 30 bytes are printed per label line. To recognize this in the assembly language version, you must look at the DCBs to obtain this information or at the record descriptions used to hold the input and output data records.

CONTROLLING LINE SPACING—CARRIAGE CONTROLS

The ASSIST version of our program doesn't work. There's something subtly wrong with it. The problem is in the print instructions; they're syntactically correct, but they will not work as desired at execution time. The reason is something that we haven't discussed about ASSIST.

In general, *but not always,* when information is sent to the printer, the first character of each line controls line spacing. The printer works as a big typewriter in that it performs carriage return operations depending on the first character of every line. When sitting at a typewriter, you can put in a new page of paper and begin typing; when you reach the end of the line, you return the carriage and start typing on the next line. If you return the carriage twice before typing, you end up with one blank line and you type on the second. The more times that you return before typing, the more blank lines you have between lines of type. The printer works in much the same manner, but its spacing is controlled by the first character of every line.

This is an IBM industry standard and you *must* be familiar with it. ASSIST *always* requires us to account for line spacing controls, but we can ignore such controls in standard assembly language. That is why the assembly language version worked, but the ASSIST version didn't. Let's look more carefully into this situation.

```
LABOUT   DCB   DSORG=PS,DDNAME=LABOUT,MACRF=PM,         X
               RECFM=F,LRECL=30,BLKSIZE=30
```

Figure 4.56 DCB for the mailing label print file.

In assembly language, the DCB describes our input and output records. If we look carefully at the DCB called LABOUT, as shown in Fig. 4.56, we see that it defines our output records as 30 characters in length. The RECFM parameter indicates that the records are of fixed length. Nowhere in this DCB does it indicate that the printer is to use the first character of each record as a line control or a carriage control. If we want to use carriage controls, we have to alter our DCB slightly. We have to code our RECFM parameter as RECFM=F*A* to indicate that the records are of fixed length *and* that **ANSI** (American National Standards Institute) carriage control characters are being used by our program for this output file.

ASSIST does not allow this choice; we must always allow for carriage controls. It is not an option.

To allow for carriage controls in this application, we must remember that only 30 characters of information may be printed on a label. The carriage control character is not printed but simply absorbed by the printer and used to control line spacing. Hence, instead of a 30-character line, we define our label line as 31 characters, the first character holding our carriage control and the remaining 30 characters holding our actual label data. Figure 4.57 illustrates this structure in a logical manner.

Figure 4.57 Logical line structure with carriage control.

The characters that may be used to control line spacing according to the ANSI guidelines are listed in the table of Fig. 4.58. These carriage controls are used in almost all languages in one form or another. COBOL, PL/I, FORTRAN, and **ASSIST** all use these carriage controls to impact line spacing on IBM systems. In our label print program, however, we don't want carriage controls since we're not skipping to the top of a page and we're not double spacing, triple spacing, or overprinting any lines. Hence, we'll just use a blank carriage control value for all lines to be printed.

Carriage Control Character	Action Taken by the Printer
1	Begin printing at the top of the next page.
blank	Return and print on the next line (single space).
0	Return twice and print on the second line (double space to leave one line blank between each line printed).
-	Return three times and print on the third line (triple space, two blank lines between each line printed).
+	Do not return (print over top of the current line).

Figure 4.58 ANSI carriage control characters and their usage.

To allow for carriage control, we'll define a one-byte field, initialized to a blank, just before the label line. By modifying only our output statements, we can easily get our program to execute and to account for the required carriage controls. The coding example 4.8 contains a modified assembly language program that utilizes carriage control and the coding example 4.9 contains the corrected ASSIST program to print our mailing label.

This application is not a full example of carriage control use since only one carriage control character was utilized. We will see many more examples of using carriage controls, and, in fact, this is one of the few applications that we'll develop in the text that does not require full use of carriage controls.

CHARACTER DATA LITERALS

The assembler or ASSIST allows yet another format for defining and using data elements within an assembly language program. It is called **literal** processing and is quite useful

```
//job card
//      EXEC     ASMFCG
//ASM.SYSIN    DD       *
LABEL     CSECT
          STM      14,12,12(13)        SAVE THE REGISTERS
          LR       12,15               MAKE R12 THE BASE
          USING    LABEL,12            FINISH THE JOB
          LA       11,REGSAVE          POINT TO OUR SAVE AREA
          ST       13,4(11)            SAVE CURRENT R13
          ST       11,8(13)            INFORM THE O.S.
          LR       13,11               ESTABLISH NEW SAVE AREA
          OPEN     (LABIN,INPUT)       OPEN INPUT FILE
          OPEN     (LABOUT,OUTPUT)     OPEN OUTPUT FILE
          GET      LABIN,PERSON        READ IN THE RECORD
          MVC      LABLINE(25),NAME    MOVE NAME TO LABEL LINE
          PUT      LABOUT,LABCC        PRINT THE NAME
          MVC      LABLINE(30),BLANKS  CLEAR LABEL LINE
          MVC      LABLINE(25),STREET  MOVE STREET INTO LABEL
          PUT      LABOUT,LABCC        PRINT THE STREET LINE
          MVC      LABLINE(30),BLANKS  CLEAR LABEL LINE
          MVC      LABLINE(15),CITY    MOVE CITY INTO LABEL
          PUT      LABOUT,LABCC        PRINT THE CITY LINE
          MVC      LABLINE(30),BLANKS  CLEAR LABEL LINE AGAIN
          MVC      LABLINE(2),STATE    MOVE STATE INTO LINE
          MVI      LABLINE+2,C','      MOVE COMMA AFTER STATE
          MVC      LABLINE+4(5),ZIP    MOVE ZIP AFTER STATE
          PUT      LABOUT,LABCC        PRINT STATE/ZIP LINE
          CLOSE    (LABIN)
          CLOSE    (LABOUT)
          L        13,4(13)            RESTORE ORIGINAL R13
          LM       14,12,12(13)        RESTORE THE REGS
          SR       15,15               EVERYTHING WENT OK
          BCR      B'1111',14          RETURN TO THE SYSTEM
*
PERSON    DS       0CL80               DEFINE PERSON STRUCTURE
NAME      DS       CL25
STREET    DS       CL25
CITY      DS       CL15
STATE     DS       CL2
ZIP       DS       CL5
          DS       CL8
*
LABCC     DC       C' '                SINGLE SPACING
LABLINE   DC       CL30' '             DEFINE AND INITIALIZE
*
BLANKS    DC       CL30' '             USED TO CLEAR LABLINE
REGSAVE   DS       18F
LABIN     DCB      DSORG=PS,DDNAME=LABIN,MACRF=GM
LABOUT    DCB      DSORG=PS,DDNAME=LABOUT,MACRF=PM,                       X
                   RECFM=FA,LRECL=31,BLKSIZE=31
          END      LABEL
//GO.SYSUDUMP      DD   SYSOUT=$
//GO.LABOUT        DD   SYSOUT=$,OUTLIM=1000
//GO.LABIN         DD   *
CHUCK KACMAR        100 OAK STREET    AUSTIN     TX    78731
//
```

Example 4.8 Assembly language program with carriage controls.

for all types of data. However, data defined in this format *does not have a name* and is not usually referenced through typical implicit or explicit addressing.

A **literal** is a piece of data that has a value that doesn't change. A program usually does not change the value of a literal unless accidentally through a bad instruction or an invalid address. A literal is a constant term that may be used on an instruction in place of defining a separate data element through a DC instruction. For example, in the program

```
//job card
//    EXEC     ASSIST
//SYSIN   DD        *
$JOB
LABEL     CSECT
          STM      14,12,12(13)         SAVE THE REGISTERS
          LR       12,15                MAKE R12 THE BASE
          USING    LABEL,12             FINISH THE JOB
          LA       11,REGSAVE           POINT TO OUR SAVE AREA
          ST       13,4(11)             SAVE CURRENT R13
          ST       11,8(13)             INFORM THE O.S.
          LR       13,11                ESTABLISH NEW SAVE AREA
          XREAD    PERSON,80            READ IN THE RECORD
          MVC      LABLINE(25),NAME     MOVE NAME TO LABEL LINE
          XPRNT    LABCC,31             PRINT THE NAME
          MVC      LABLINE(30),BLANKS   CLEAR LABEL LINE
          MVC      LABLINE(25),STREET   MOVE STREET INTO LABEL
          XPRNT    LABCC,31             PRINT THE STREET LINE
          MVC      LABLINE(30),BLANKS   CLEAR LABEL LINE
          MVC      LABLINE(15),CITY     MOVE CITY INTO LABEL
          XPRNT    LABCC,31             PRINT THE CITY LINE
          MVC      LABLINE(30),BLANKS   CLEAR LABEL LINE AGAIN
          MVC      LABLINE(2),STATE     MOVE STATE INTO LINE
          MVI      LABLINE+2,C','       MOVE COMMA AFTER STATE
          MVC      LABLINE+4(5),ZIP     MOVE ZIP AFTER STATE
          XPRNT    LABCC,31             PRINT STATE/ZIP LINE
          L        13,4(13)             RESTORE ORIGINAL R13
          LM       14,12,12(13)         RESTORE THE REGS
          SR       15,15                EVERYTHING WENT OK
          BCR      B'1111',14           RETURN TO THE SYSTEM
*
PERSON    DS       0CL80                DEFINE PERSON STRUCTURE
NAME      DS       CL25
STREET    DS       CL25
CITY      DS       CL15
STATE     DS       CL2
ZIP       DS       CL5
          DS       CL8
*
LABCC     DC       C' '                 SINGLE SPACING
LABLINE   DC       CL30' '              DEFINE AND INITIALIZE
*
BLANKS    DC       CL30' '              USED TO CLEAR LABLINE
REGSAVE   DS       18F
          END      LABEL
$ENTRY
CHUCK KACMAR         100 OAK STREET   AUSTIN     TX    78731
//
```

Example 4.9 Corrected ASSIST mailing label program.

listing shown in coding example 4.8, the field BLANKS clears the value of the label line as each line of the label was constructed and printed. Since BLANKS does not change during the execution of the program, we could have used a literal in its place. Hence, for BLANKS, we could have used a literal that defined a data area of 30 blank characters.

To code a literal, simply code an equals sign and then code the *operands area* of a DC instruction. Since literals must be given a value, you cannot use them as if defining a DS storage area. Most importantly, literals *are not* coded within the data area in your program. A literal is coded directly on the instruction in which you want to use it. For example, we cleared the area called LABLINE by using the field BLANKS as shown in Fig. 4.59. To clear that same area using a literal, code the instruction shown in Fig. 4.60.

The second operand defines a character area of length 30 that is initialized to all blanks. The leftmost character of the area is set to a blank and the remaining 29 characters are padded with blanks to give us a complete 30-byte blank field. If you look care-

```
MVC     LABLINE(30),BLANKS
```

Figure 4.59 Moving BLANKS to the label line.

```
MVC     LABLINE(30),=CL30' '
```

Figure 4.60 Using a literal in place of DC defined fields.

fully, there's not much difference between this definition and that of the field called BLANKS. Other than the fact that there's no name for this field, the two fields have the same value.

Let's do another example not related to the label program. To set the five-byte field called STUFF to the value ABCDE, we can code either of the instructions given in Fig. 4.61. Since the second operand in these examples yields the same value, it doesn't make any difference which form we use.

When a literal is encountered by the assembler, the assembler defines the literal much as if it were a DC instruction. To help the assembler, we should code a **LTORG** statement in the data areas section of our program to indicate where we want our literals to be defined. Remember, we don't actually define the literal, the assembler does. Since the LTORG statement generates *DC-type* storage areas, we're simply telling the assembler where we want these areas to be defined within our program. Generally, the LTORG statement is placed just before the END statement. As long as the LTORG statement is placed after all statements containing literals, it may be defined wherever desired. The LTORG statement has no operands and it should not be commented. The coding example 4.10 contains our complete label program again, in assembly language, using literals and the LTORG statement.

As you can clearly see, all references to the field BLANKS have been changed to the literal. The LTORG statement has been coded just before the END statement, although it could have been coded anywhere within our data area.

Some companies do not wish to use literals, so you best check before using them. Literals are simply a replacement for defining a DC field and giving that field a name. There's really nothing difficult about them, but just remember to code the equals sign before you begin the literal definition and don't forget the LTORG statement. The program listing contained in Fig. 4.62 fully illustrates the assembler's reaction to literal usage and the generation of literals within your program area.

ASSEMBLY TIME AND DATE VALUES

Typical business programs place time and date values in the program so that they can keep track of when a program was developed or on what day a report was printed. The simplest method for obtaining the time and date is to use some special built-in facilities available from the standard assembler. These facilities are *not* available through the ASSIST package. The instructions are very easy to use and require only two instructions. In

```
MVC     STUFF(5),=CL5'ABCDE'
MVC     STUFF(5),=C'ABCDE'
```

Figure 4.61 Moving a literal value to an area using MVC.

```
//job card
//     EXEC     ASMFCG
//ASM.SYSIN   DD      *
LABEL      CSECT
           STM      14,12,12(13)         SAVE THE REGISTERS
           LR       12,15                MAKE R12 THE BASE
           USING    LABEL,12             FINISH THE JOB
           LA       11,REGSAVE           POINT TO OUR SAVE AREA
           ST       13,4(11)             SAVE CURRENT R13
           ST       11,8(13)             INFORM THE O.S.
           LR       13,11                ESTABLISH NEW SAVE AREA
           OPEN     (LABIN,INPUT)        OPEN INPUT FILE
           OPEN     (LABOUT,OUTPUT)      OPEN OUTPUT FILE
           GET      LABIN,PERSON         READ IN THE RECORD
           MVC      LABLINE(25),NAME     MOVE NAME TO LABEL LINE
           PUT      LABOUT,LABCC         PRINT THE NAME
           MVC      LABLINE(30),=CL30' ' CLEAR LABEL LINE
           MVC      LABLINE(25),STREET   MOVE STREET INTO LABEL
           PUT      LABOUT,LABCC         PRINT THE STREET LINE
           MVC      LABLINE(30),=CL30' ' CLEAR LABEL LINE
           MVC      LABLINE(15),CITY     MOVE CITY INTO LABEL
           PUT      LABOUT,LABCC         PRINT THE CITY LINE
           MVC      LABLINE(30),=CL30' ' CLEAR LABEL LINE
           MVC      LABLINE(2),STATE     MOVE STATE INTO LINE
           MVI      LABLINE+2,C','       MOVE COMMA AFTER STATE
           MVC      LABLINE+4(5),ZIP     MOVE ZIP AFTER STATE
           PUT      LABOUT,LABCC         PRINT STATE/ZIP LINE
           CLOSE    (LABIN)
           CLOSE    (LABOUT)
           L        13,4(13)             RESTORE R13 TO ORIGINAL
           LM       14,12,12(13)         RESTORE THE REGS
           SR       15,15                EVERYTHING WENT OK
           BCR      B'1111',14           RETURN TO THE SYSTEM
*
PERSON     DS       0CL80                DEFINE PERSON STRUCTURE
NAME       DS       CL25
STREET     DS       CL25
CITY       DS       CL15
STATE      DS       CL2
ZIP        DS       CL5
           DS       CL8
*
LABCC      DC       C' '                 SINGLE SPACING
LABLINE    DC       CL30' '              DEFINE AND INITIALIZE
REGSAVE    DS       18F
LABIN      DCB      DSORG=PS,DDNAME=LABIN,MACRF=GM
LABOUT     DCB      DSORG=PS,DDNAME=LABOUT,MACRF=PM,                  X
                    RECFM=FA,LRECL=31,BLKSIZE=31
           LTORG
           END      LABEL
//GO.SYSUDUMP       DD   SYSOUT=$
//GO.LABOUT         DD   SYSOUT=$,OUTLIM=1000
//GO.LABIN          DD   *
CHUCK KACMAR         100 OAK STREET   AUSTIN    TX    78731
//
```

Example 4.10 Mailing label program using literals.

```
  LOC  OBJECT CODE    ADDR1 ADDR2  STMT   SOURCE STATEMENT                                          ASM H V 02 10.43 08/26/85

000000                                1 LABEL    CSECT                                                               00070
000000 90EC D00C            0000C     2          STM   14,12,12(13)        SAVE REGISTERS BEFORE WE RUN              00080
000004 18CF                           3          LR    12,15               SET UP OUR BASE REGISTER                  00090
                            00000     4          USING LABEL,12            R12 WILL BE OUR BASE REG                  00100
000006 41B0 C0C8            000C8     5          LA    11,REGSAVE          POINT TO REG SAVE AREA                    00110
00000A 50DB 0004            00004     6          ST    13,4(11)            REMEMBER WHERE O.S. SAVEAREA IS           00120
00000E 50BD 0008            00008     7          ST    11,8(13)            TELL O.S. ABOUT OUR SAVEAREA              00130
000012 18DB                           8          LR    13,11               OUR SAVEAREA IS THE CURRENT ONE           00140
                                      9          OPEN  (LABIN,INPUT)       OPEN OUR INPUT FILE                       00150
000014                               10+         CNOP  0,4                           ALIGN LIST TO FULLWORD 01-OPEN
000014 4510 C01C            0001C    11+         BAL   1,*+8                         LOAD REG1 W/LIST ADDR. 01-OPEN
000018 80                            12+         DC    AL1(128)                      OPTION BYTE            01-OPEN
000019 000180                        13+         DC    AL3(LABIN)                    DCB ADDRESS            01-OPEN
00001C 0A13                          14+         SVC   19                            ISSUE OPEN SVC         01-OPEN
                                     15          OPEN  (LABOUT,OUTPUT)     OPEN OUR OUTPUT PRINT FILE                00160
00001E 0700                          16+         CNOP  0,4                           ALIGN LIST TO FULLWORD 01-OPEN
000020 4510 C028            00028    17+         BAL   1,*+8                         LOAD REG1 W/LIST ADDR. 01-OPEN
000024 8F                            18+         DC    AL1(143)                      OPTION BYTE            01-OPEN
000025 0001E0                        19+         DC    AL3(LABOUT)                   DCB ADDRESS            01-OPEN
000028 0A13                          20+         SVC   19                            ISSUE OPEN SVC         01-OPEN
                                     21          GET   LABIN,PERSON        READ THE RECORD                           00170
00002A 4110 C180            00180    22+         LA    1,LABIN                       LOAD PARAMETER REG 1   02-IHBIN
00002E 4100 C110            00110    23+         LA    0,PERSON                      LOAD PARAMETER REG 0   02-IHBIN
000032 58F0 1030            00030    24+         L     15,48(0,1)           LOAD GET ROUTINE ADDR                   01-GET
000036 05EF                          25+         BALR  14,15                LINK TO GET ROUTINE                     01-GET
000038 D218 C160 C110 00160 00110    26          MVC   LABLINE(25),NAME    MOVE NAME TO LABEL LINE                   00180
                                     27          PUT   LABOUT,LABLINE      PRINT THE NAME                            00190
00003E 4110 C1E0            001E0    28+         LA    1,LABOUT                      LOAD PARAMETER REG 1   02-IHBIN
000042 4100 C160            00160    29+         LA    0,LABLINE                     LOAD PARAMETER REG 0   02-IHBIN
000046 58F0 1030            00030    30+         L     15,48(0,1)           LOAD PUT ROUTINE ADDR                   01-PUT
00004A 05EF                          31+         BALR  14,15                LINK TO PUT ROUTINE                     01-PUT
00004C D21D C160 C240 00160 00240    32          MVC   LABLINE(30),=CL30' ' CLEAR LABEL LINE                         00200
000052 D218 C160 C129 00160 00129    33          MVC   LABLINE(25),STREET  MOVE      NTO LABEL                       00210
                                     34          PUT   LABOUT,LABLINE      PR        T LINE                          00220
000058 4110 C1E0            001E0    35+         LA    1,LABOUT                       RAMETER REG 1         02-IHBIN
00005C 4100 C160            00160    36+         LA    0,LABLINE                      AMETER REG 0          02-IHBIN
000060 58F0 1030            00030    37+         L     15,48(0,1)                     DDR                   01-PUT
000064 05EF                          38+         BALR  14,15                          E                     01-PUT
000066 D21D C160 C240 00160 00240    39          MVC   LABLINE(30),=CL30' '                                          00230
00006C D20E C160 C142 00160 00142    40          MVC   LABLINE(15),CITY               L LINE                         00240
                                     41          PUT   LABOUT,LABLINE                 E                              00250
000072 4110 C1E0            001E0    42+         LA    1,LABOUT                       AMETER REG 1          02-IHBIN
000076 4100 C160            00160    43+         LA    0,LABLINE                      ARAMETER REG 0        02-IHBIN
00007A 58F0 1030            00030    44+         L     15,48(0,1)           LO        NE ADDR               01-PUT
00007E 05EF                          45+         BALR  14,15                LINK      ROUTINE               01-PUT
000080 D21D C160 C240 00160 00240    46          MVC   LABLINE(30),=CL30' ' CLEAR LABEL LINE AGAIN                   00260
000086 D201 C160 C151 00160 00151    47          MVC   LABLINE(2),STATE    MOVE STATE INTO LINE                      00270
00008C 926B C162      00162          48          MVI   LABLINE+2,C','      MOVE COMMA AFTER STATE                    00280
000090 D204 C164 C153 00164 00153    49          MVC   LABLINE+4(5),ZIP    MOVE ZIP AFTER STATE                      00290
                                     50          PUT   LABOUT,LABLINE      PRINT STATE/ZIP LINE                      00300
000096 4110 C1E0            001E0    51+         LA    1,LABOUT                      LOAD PARAMETER REG 1   02-IHBIN
00009A 4100 C160            00160    52+         LA    0,LABLINE                     LOAD PARAMETER REG 0   02-IHBIN
00009E 58F0 1030            00030    53+         L     15,48(0,1)           LOAD PUT ROUTINE ADDR                   01-PUT
0000A2 05EF                          54+         BALR  14,15                LINK TO PUT ROUTINE                     01-PUT
                                     55          CLOSE (LABIN)                                                       00310
```

LITERALS are coded directly on the instruction.

Figure 4.62 Complete assembly language program to print mailing labels.

```
  LOC  OBJECT CODE    ADDR1 ADDR2  STMT   SOURCE STATEMENT                                  ASM H V 02 10.43 08/26/85

0000A4                              56+          CNOP  0,4                             ALIGN LIST TO FULLWORD 01-CLOSE
0000A4 4510 C0AC             000AC  57+          BAL   1,*+8                           LOAD REG1 W/LIST ADDR  01-CLOSE
0000A8 80                           58+          DC    AL1(128)                        OPTION BYTE            01-CLOSE
0000A9 000180                       59+          DC    AL3(LABIN)                      DCB ADDRESS            01-CLOSE
0000AC 0A14                         60+          SVC   20                              ISSUE CLOSE SVC        01-CLOSE
                                    61           CLOSE LABOUT                                                    00320
0000AE 0700                         62+          CNOP  0,4                             ALIGN LIST TO FULLWORD 01-CLOSE
0000B0 4510 C0B8             000B8  63+          BAL   1,*+8                           LOAD REG1 W/LIST ADDR  01-CLOSE
0000B4 80                           64+          DC    AL1(128)                        OPTION BYTE            01-CLOSE
0000B5 0001E0                       65+          DC    AL3(LABOUT)                     DCB ADDRESS            01-CLOSE
0000B8 0A14                         66+          SVC   20                              ISSUE CLOSE SVC        01-CLOSE
0000BA 58DD 0004             00004  67           L     13,4(13)              RESTORE R13 TO ITS ORIGINAL VALU    00330
0000BE 98EC D00C             0000C  68           LM    14,12,12(13)          RESTORE THE REGISTERS               00340
0000C2 1BFF                         69           SR    15,15                 TELL SYSTEM ALL WENT OK             00350
0000C4 07FE                         70           BCR   B'1111',14            RETURN CONTROL TO THE SYSTEM        00360
0000C8                              71 REGSAVE   DS    18F                   REGISTER SAVE AREA                  00370
000110                              72 PERSON    DS    0CL80                                                     00380
000110                              73 NAME      DS    CL25                                                      00390
000129                              74 STREET    DS    CL25                                                      00400
000142                              75 CITY      DS    CL15                                                      00410
000151                              76 STATE     DS    CL2                                                       00420
000153                              77 ZIP       DS    CL5                                                       00430
000158                              78           DS    CL8                                                       00440
                                    79 *                                                                         00450
000160 4040404040404040             80 LABLINE   DC    CL30                                                      00460
                                    81 *                                                                         00470
                                    82 LABIN     DCB   DSORG=PS,DDNAME=LABIN,MACRF=GM                            00480

                                    84+*                          DATA CONTROL BLOCK
                                    85+*
00017E 0000
000180                              86+LABIN     DC    0F'0'                 ORIGIN ON WORD BOUNDARY             01-DCB

                                    88+*                          DIRECT ACCESS DEVICE INTERFACE

000180 0000000000000000             90+          DC    BL16'0'               FDAD,DVTBL                          01-DCB
000190 00000000                     91+          DC    A(0)                  KEYLE,DEVT,TRBAL                    01-DCB

                                    93+*                          COMMON ACCESS METHOD INTERFACE

000194 00                           95+          DC    AL1(0)                BUFNO                               01-DCB
000195 000001                       96+          DC    AL3(1)                BUFCB                               01-DCB
000198 0000                         97+          DC    AL2(0)           BUFL                                     01-DCB
00019A 4000                         98+          DC    BL2'0100000000000000'          DSORG                      01-DCB
00019C 00000001                     99+          DC    A(1)                  ICQE/IOBAD                          01-DCB

                                   101+*                          FOUNDATION EXTENSION

0001A0 00                          103+          DC    BL1'00000000'              BFTEK,BFLN,HIARCHY             01-DCB
0001A1 000001                      104+          DC    AL3(1)                EODAD                               01-DCB
0001A4 00                          105+          DC    BL1'00000000'         RECFM                               01-DCB
0001A5 000000                      106+          DC    AL3(0)                EXLST                               01-DCB

                                   108+*                          FOUNDATION BLOCK
```

You can easily see the LABIN DCB statement and part of its' expansion by the assembler.

Figure 4.62 (cont.)

```
  LOC  OBJECT CODE     ADDR1 ADDR2  STMT    SOURCE STATEMENT                                     ASM H V 02 10.43 08/26/85

0001A8 D3C1C2C9D5404040             110+          DC    CL8'LABIN'                      DDNAME                        01-DCB
0001B0 02                           111+          DC    BL1'00000010'                   OFLGS                         01-DCB
0001B1 00                           112+          DC    BL1'00000000'                               IFLG              01-DCB
0001B2 5000                         113+          DC    BL2'0101000000000000'           MACR                          01-DCB

                                    115+*                            BSAM-BPAM-QSAM INTERFACE

0001B4 00                           117+          DC    BL1'00000000'                                           RER1  01-DCB
0001B5 000001                       118+          DC    AL3(1)                          CHECK, GERR, PERR             01-DCB
0001B8 00000001                     119+          DC    A(1)                            SYNAD                         01-DCB
0001BC 0000                         120+          DC    H'0'                            CIND1, CIND2                  01-DCB
0001BE 0000                         121+          DC    AL2(0)                          BLKSIZE                       01-DCB
0001C0 00000000                     122+          DC    F'0'                            WCPO, WCPL, OFFSR, OFFSW      01-DCB
0001C4 00000001                     123+          DC    A(1)                            IOBA                          01-DCB
0001C8 00                           124+          DC    AL1(0)                          NCP                           01-DCB
0001C9 000001                       125+          DC    AL3(1)                          EOBR, EOBAD                   01-DCB

                                    127+*                            QSAM INTERFACE

0001CC 00000001                     129+          DC    A(1)                            RECAD                         01-DCB
0001D0 0000                         130+          DC    H'0'                            QSWS                          01-DCB
0001D2 0000                         131+          DC    AL2(0)           LRECL                                        01-DCB
0001D4 00                           132+          DC    BL1'00000000'                   EROPT                         01-DCB
0001D5 000001                       133+          DC    AL3(1)                          CNTRL                         01-DCB
0001D8 00000000                     134+          DC    F'0'                            PRECL                         01-DCB
0001DC 00000001                     135+          DC    A(1)                            EOB                           01-DCB
                                    136 LABOUT    DCB   DSORG=PS,DDNAME=LABOUT,MACRF=PM,                            X   00490
                                                        RECFM=F,LRECL=30,BLKSIZE=30                                     00500

                                    138+*                            DATA CONTROL BLOCK
                                    139+*
0001E0                              140+LABOUT    DC    OF'0'                           ORIGIN ON WORD BOUNDARY       01-DCB

                                    142+*                            DIRECT ACCESS DEVICE INTERFACE

0001E0 0000000000000000             144+          DC    BL16'0'                         FDAD,DVTBL                    01-DCB
0001F0 00000000                     145+          DC    A(0)                            KEYLE,DEVT,TRBAL              01-DCB

                                    147+*                            COMMON ACCESS METHOD INTERFACE

0001F4 00                           149+          DC    AL1(0)                          BUFNO                         01-DCB
0001F5 000001                       150+          DC    AL3(1)                          BUFCB                         01-DCB
0001F8 0000                         151+          DC    AL2(0)                     BUFL                               01-DCB
0001FA 4000                         152+          DC    BL2'0100000000000000'                         DSORG           01-DCB
0001FC 00000001                     153+          DC    A(1)                            ICQE/IOBAD                    01-DCB

                                    155+*                            FOUNDATION EXTENSION

000200 00                           157+          DC    BL1'00000000'                           BFTEK,BFLN,HIARCHY    01-DCB
000201 000001                       158+          DC    AL3(1)                          EODAD                         01-DCB
000204 80                           159+          DC    BL1'10000000'                   RECFM                         01-DCB
000205 000000                       160+          DC    AL3(0)                          EXLST                         01-DCB
```

Here's the remainder of the LABIN DCB expansion.

Figure 4.62 (cont.)

```
LOC    OBJECT CODE        ADDR1 ADDR2  STMT   SOURCE STATEMENT                                  ASM H V 02 10.43 08/26/85

                                       162+*                    FOUNDATION BLOCK

000208 D3C1C2D6E4E34040                164+         DC    CL8'LABOUT'             DDNAME                        01-DCB
000210 02                              165+         DC    BL1'00000010'           OFLGS                         01-DCB
000211 00                              166+         DC    BL1'00000000'                         IFLG            01-DCB
000212 0050                            167+         DC    BL2'0000000001010000'   MACR                          01-DCB

                                       169+*                 BSAM-BPAM-QSAM INTERFACE

000214 00                              171+         DC    BL1'00000000'                                    RER1 01-DCB
000215 000001                          172+         DC    AL3(1)                  CHECK, GERR, PERR             01-DCB
000218 00000001                        173+         DC    A(1)                    SYNAD                         01-DCB
00021C 0000                            174+         DC    H'0'                    CIND1, CIND2                  01-DCB
00021E 001E                            175+         DC    AL2(30)                 BLKSIZE                       01-DCB
000220 00000000                        176+         DC    F'0'                    WCPO, WCPL, OFFSR, OFFSW      01-DCB
000224 00000001                        177+         DC    A(1)                    IOBA                          01-DCB
000228 00                              178+         DC    AL1(0)                  NCP                           01-DCB
000229 000001                          179+         DC    AL3(1)                  EOBR, EOBAD                   01-DCB

                                       181+*                    QSAM INTERFACE

00022C 00000001                        183+         DC    A(1)                     RECAD                        01-DCB
000230 0000                            184+         DC    H'0'                    QSWS                          01-DCB
000232 001E                            185+         DC    AL2(30)        LRECL                                  01-DCB
000234 00                              186+         DC    BL1'00000000'           EROPT                         01-DCB
000235 000001                          187+         DC    AL3(1)                  CNTRL                         01-DCB
000238 00000000                        188+         DC    F'0'                    PRECL                         01-DCB
00023C 00000001                        189+         DC    A(1)                    EOB                           01-DCB
000240                                 190          LTORG                                                        00510
000240 4040404040404040                191                =CL30' '
000000                                 192          END   LABEL                                                  00520
```

The LTORG statement instructs the assembler to generate the literals in our program here.

Figure 4.62 (cont.)

fact, let's modify our program to place the time and date on the first line of the label. When we print the person's name, we'll skip a blank line (using carriage controls) so that our label will now appear as shown in Fig. 4.63. As you can see, we're going to place the date on the left side of the first line and the time on the right side. The date is in the form month/day/year and the time is in the military form of hours:minutes.

To obtain the current date and time *of assembly*, we use the **&SYSDATE** and the **&SYSTIME** variables, respectively. Both are coded within a DC instruction as shown in Fig. 4.64.

```
12/25/99                 12:00

CHUCK KACMAR
100 OAK STREET
AUSTIN
TX, 78731

123456789012345678901234567890
```

Figure 4.63 Mailing label with date and time.

```
         DC       CL8'&SYSDATE'
         DC       CL5'&SYSTIME'
```

Figure 4.64 Coding the &SYSDATE and &SYSTIME variables.

When our program is processed by the assembler, the current time and date are substituted for these elements and these statements will appear as shown in Fig. 4.65 (if our program is run at noon on December 25, in the year 1999).

Since these fields only occupy 13 bytes of our 30-byte label line, we'll have to place a filler field between them so that the date appears on the left and the time on the right. The snapshot program listing in Figure 4.66 illustrates the use of these facilities.

Before looking at the printout in this figure, let me reemphasize that the time and date values are dependent on the time and date of *assembly*. If a program containing these elements is assembled and stored in object or load module form in a system library, the same time and date will print *each time that the program is run,* regardless of the day of execution. In other words, these values will *not* change dynamically based on the day on which the program is run. In a later chapter, we'll study a technique for obtaining the current time and date during execution, which allows our program to print the actual date and time that the program is run, not that on which it was assembled.

```
         DC       CL8'12/25/99'
         DC       CL5'12:00'
```

Figure 4.65 Resulting &SYSDATE and &SYSTIME values after assembly.

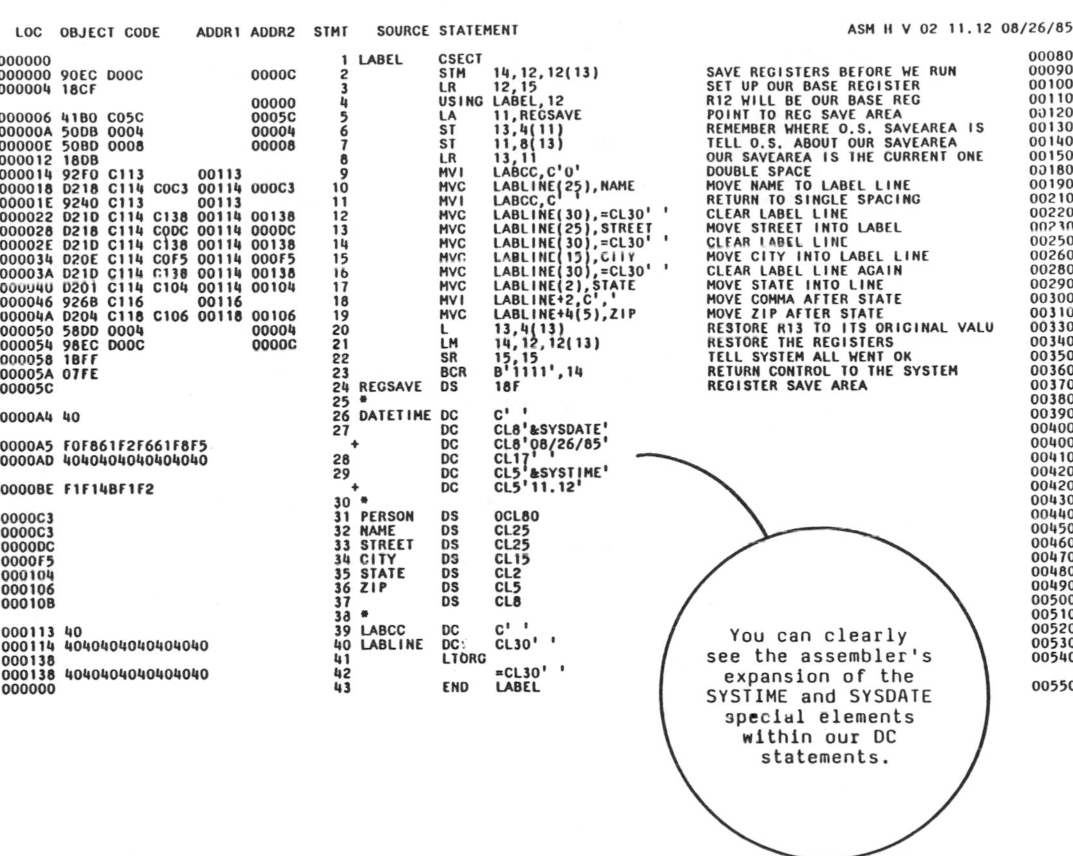

```
                                                                                                   PAGE    2

  LOC  OBJECT CODE     ADDR1 ADDR2  STMT   SOURCE STATEMENT                                 ASM H V 02 11.12 08/26/85

000000                                 1 LABEL    CSECT                                                         00080
000000 90EC D00C             0000C     2          STM   14,12,12(13)      SAVE REGISTERS BEFORE WE RUN           00090
000004 18CF                            3          LR    12,15             SET UP OUR BASE REGISTER               00100
                             00000     4          USING LABEL,12          R12 WILL BE OUR BASE REG               00110
000006 41B0 C05C             0005C     5          LA    11,REGSAVE        POINT TO REG SAVE AREA                 00120
00000A 50DB 0004             00004     6          ST    13,4(11)          REMEMBER WHERE O.S. SAVEAREA IS        00130
00000E 50BD 0008             00008     7          ST    11,8(13)          TELL O.S. ABOUT OUR SAVEAREA           00140
000012 18DB                            8          LR    13,11             OUR SAVEAREA IS THE CURRENT ONE        00150
000014 92F0 C113       00113           9          MVI   LABCC,C'0'        DOUBLE SPACE                           00180
000018 D218 C114 C0C3 00114 000C3     10          MVC   LABLINE(25),NAME  MOVE NAME TO LABEL LINE                00190
00001E 9240 C113       00113          11          MVI   LABCC,C' '        RETURN TO SINGLE SPACING               00210
000022 D21D C114 C138 00114 00138     12          MVC   LABLINE(30),=CL30' '  CLEAR LABEL LINE                   00220
000028 D218 C114 C0DC 00114 000DC     13          MVC   LABLINE(25),STREET    MOVE STREET INTO LABEL             00230
00002E D21D C114 C138 00114 00138     14          MVC   LABLINE(30),=CL30' '  CLEAR LABEL LINE                   00250
000034 D20E C114 C0F5 00114 000F5     15          MVC   LABLINE(15),CITY  MOVE CITY INTO LABEL LINE              00260
00003A D21D C114 C138 00114 00138     16          MVC   LABLINE(30),=CL30' '  CLEAR LABEL LINE AGAIN             00280
000040 D201 C114 C104 00114 00104     17          MVC   LABLINE(2),STATE  MOVE STATE INTO LINE                   00290
000046 926B C116       00116          18          MVI   LABLINE+2,C','    MOVE COMMA AFTER STATE                 00300
00004A D204 C118 C106 00118 00106     19          MVC   LABLINE+4(5),ZIP  MOVE ZIP AFTER STATE                   00310
000050 58DD 0004             00004    20          L     13,4(13)          RESTORE R13 TO ITS ORIGINAL VALU       00330
000054 98EC D00C             0000C    21          LM    14,12,12(13)      RESTORE THE REGISTERS                  00340
000058 1BFF                           22          SR    15,15             TELL SYSTEM ALL WENT OK                00350
00005A 07FE                           23          BCR   B'1111',14        RETURN CONTROL TO THE SYSTEM           00360
00005C                                24 REGSAVE  DS    18F               REGISTER SAVE AREA                     00370
                                      25 *                                                                       00380
0000A4 40                             26 DATETIME DC    C' '                                                     00390
                                      27          DC    CL8'&SYSDATE'                                            00400
0000A5 F0F861F2F661F8F5                +          DC    CL8'08/26/85'                                            00400
0000AD 4040404040404040               28          DC    CL17' '                                                  00410
                                      29          DC    CL5'&SYSTIME'                                            00420
0000BE F1F14BF1F2                      +          DC    CL5'11.12'                                               00420
                                      30 *                                                                       00430
0000C3                                31 PERSON   DS    0CL80                                                    00440
0000C3                                32 NAME     DS    CL25                                                     00450
0000DC                                33 STREET   DS    CL25                                                     00460
0000F5                                34 CITY     DS    CL15                                                     00470
000104                                35 STATE    DS    CL2                                                      00480
000106                                36 ZIP      DS    CL5                                                      00490
00010B                                37          DS    CL8                                                      00500
                                      38 *                                                                       00510
000113 40                             39 LABCC    DC    C' '                                                     00520
000114 4040404040404040               40 LABLINE  DC    CL30' '                                                  00530
000138                                41          LTORG                                                          00540
000138 4040404040404040               42                =CL30' '
000000                                43          END   LABEL                                                    00550
```


Figure 4.66 &SYSDATE and &SYSTIME assembly expansion.

STUDY QUESTIONS

1. Software programs that control the processing and execution of instructions within the computer are called __________ __________ programs.
2. The __________ __________ manages application execution within a computer system.
3. A program may be loaded into memory and executed if and only if it has been processed by either the __________ or the __________ __________.
4. The process of loading a program for execution is called __________.
5. An eight-byte area in the computer found at memory address 0 that is crucial to the execution of programs is called the __________ __________ __________.
6. The __________ __________ can be used by a program to control program flow during execution time.

7. If a program abends, the location of the abending point may be found by subtracting the ____________ from the ____________ ____________ ____________.
8. A program continues to execute until it ____________, ____________, or ____________.
9. An operator may start up a computer system by pressing the ____________ button on the computer to cause the system to begin ____________.
10. Channels may inform the computer that I/O is ready to be processed through ____________.
11. Any byte of data in the computer may be processed by ____________ data instructions.
12. Information may or may not be human understandable; it all depends on the ____________ of the data in the field.
13. The MVC instruction allows a programmer to move as many as ____________ bytes of data from one location in the computer to another.
14. The second operand of the MVI instruction is more commonly called the ____________ operand.
15. SS instructions are ____________ bytes long and RR instructions are only ____________ bytes long.
16. In general, the ____________ the instruction the ____________ that it processes.
17. One of the most common types of files processed by application programs is the ____________ file.
18. A file must be connected to an application program by using a combination of ____________, ____________, ____________, and ____________.
19. ____________ ____________ characters may be used to control line spacing when output is printed on a printer.
20. DC instructions may be replaced with ____________ when their values do not change during the course of program processing.
21. Using MVI or MVC, write the code to:
    (a) Change the carriage control character for the field called PRNTLINE from single spacing to double spacing.
    (b) Move the string "WYSIWYG" into the 25-byte area labeled XYZ.
    (c) Interchange the values of the 20-byte character fields A and B.
    (d) Initialize the variable FOUNDIT to N, meaning, "not found".
22. What will be in the 10-byte area labeled LINE after the following code is executed?

```
         MVC      LINE(10),=C'1234567890'
         MVI      LINE,C'A'
         MVC      LINE+1(9),LINE
```

23. Apply your answer and analysis of problem 22 to write the necessary code which will set the area labeled PRNTLINE to blanks. You cannot use a literal or a define constant (DC) storage area to perform this task.
24. Assume the following definitions:

```
ABC      DC       C'ALL COWS EAT GRASS'
XYZ      DS       CL10
```

(a) What will be in ABC after the following instruction is executed?

```
MVC     ABC(18),XYZ
```

(b) What will be in XYZ after this instruction is executed?

```
MVC     XYZ(10),ABC+3
```

(c) What will be in XYZ after these instructions are executed?

```
MVC     XYZ(10),=CL10'   '
MVC     XYZ(3),ABC
MVC     XYZ+3(2),ABC+5
MVC     XYZ+5(5),=C'ANCE'
```

(d) What will be in ABC after the following instructions are executed?

```
MVC     ABC+5(3),=C'ICE'
MVI     ABC+4,X'D4'
MVC     ABC+13(2),=C'CHOCOLATE'
MVC     ABC+15(3),=C'EEZEE DOES IT'
```

25. Which of the following literals are equivalent?

```
(a)   =CL25'X'
(b)   =25C'X'
(c)   =5C'XXXXX'
(d)   =25B'11100111'
(e)   =CL5'XXXXX'
```

26. Write a DCB macro instruction to allow us to direct output to the printer and to allow us to print 133 byte lines. Assume that the first byte of each line will contain the carriage control character.

27. Assume that register 12 is the base register. Two variables, LASTNAME and EMPLOYEE are defined in the program and are located at offsets 0001AC and 0002BE respectively in the program. If both fields are 25 bytes in length, write an instruction which uses explicit addressing to move the entire contents of EMPLOYEE to LASTNAME.

28. A 10-byte field contains the digits of a person's phone number. Define a data structure which can be used to separate the digits into groups so that the phone number can be printed as "(xxx)-xxx-xxxx".

29. Referring to problem 28, write the necessary instructions to extract the segments from the 10-byte phone number to derive the printable representation.

30. Two fields, X and Y, are defined in a program which uses register 3 as the base register. X is located at displacement E4 and Y is located at displacement 3F. Both fields are 5-byte fields. Write the machine code resulting from the instruction below.

```
MVC     X+2(2),Y+1
```

PROGRAMMING PROBLEMS

1. One data card contains eight words in each 10 column group. Write a program to read in the data card and print each word on a separate line of the printout.
2. Design a logo or crest to identify your family heritage. Write a program that will input the lines of the crest and echo (print an image) them to the printer. Hint: you'll have as many pairs of read/write statements as there are lines in your crest.
3. An employee's information is contained on a data card. The data card contains the employee's name (columns 1-25), street address (columns 26-50), city (51-65), state (66-67), and zip code (columns 68-72). Assuming that the employee earns $500 for the week, print a check for this employee. Make the check appear as realistic as possible by making up a company name, address, and company payment officer.
4. Five data cards contain information on automobiles for Mr. Smith, a used car dealer. Each data card contains the vehicle manufacturer (columns 1-20), model (columns 21-35), year (36-39), general condition (columns 40-60), and selling price of the car (61-65). All selling prices are greater than $1. Write a program to print a report of the vehicles that Mr. Smith has in stock. To do this, you'll have to print a centered title containing the name of Mr. Smith's firm and column headings for each of the data elements on the data card. Following this data, you should print the auto information. Assume that the report is to be centered on the output page. Note: you'll have a lot of redundant code in this program. In a later chapter, we'll learn how to reduce this redundancy by using looping techniques.
5. Write a program which will process an undetermined number of data cards by structuring your program using an infinite loop. Each data card contains a compressed social security number in the first 9 columns of the data card and a compressed 10 digit phone number in the next 10 columns. Separate the segments of both the social security number and the phone number into their more common representations and print them with 10 blank columns between the resulting fields. Use data structuring techniques throughout this project. Hint: by placing a label on your input instruction and using the instruction "B <label>" at the bottom of your loop, you'll construct an infinite loop. Your program will abnormally terminate when you exhaust your input data card supply. This will also give you an opportunity to review an abnormal termination printout caused by your program.

Processing Binary Data, Input and Output of Binary Fields, the Full IBM Linkage Conventions

5

In developing our knowledge base up to this point, we've used techniques and instructions that may or may not have been completely clear to you. This chapter is transitional in that it will tie a few loose ends, in particular, the entry and exit coding requirements for our programs. We'll look into detail as to why we do this processing and at all of the instructions involved in this code. Further, this chapter will completely cover binary data proccssing, particularly during input and output operations.

REGISTER-TO-REGISTER INSTRUCTIONS

Some of the fastest instructions in the computer system that process binary information are the register-to-register instructions. These instructions allow us to add, subtract, multiply, divide, and copy data between registers. The information processed by these instructions must be in binary format and it usually consists only of numbers with digits to the left of the decimal point (integers).

Binary information is stored in base-2 format with each position of the base-2 number equivalent to a power of 2. For example, the decimal number 17 would be written as illustrated in Fig. 5.1.

```
        Binary Number   10001

   Decimal Equivalent   2^4 + 2^0 = 17
```

Figure 5.1 Representing the decimal integer 17 in binary.

Further we always discuss and write binary numbers in either byte, halfword, or fullword format. Binary numbers are not usually stored in doubleword or other storage denominations and so we don't think of them in these formats. The decimal number 17 is written as shown in Fig. 5.2, depending on format.

Format	Representation
byte	00010001
halfword	0000000000010001
fullword	00000000000000000000000000010001

Figure 5.2 Binary representations of decimal value 17.

Negative numbers are represented in **two's complement** notation. Since the left most bit of the number indicates the sign, with bit value 0 meaning positive and bit value 1 meaning negative, negative numbers have a leftmost bit value of 1. Refer to Chapter 2 for a complete discussion of the two's complement format.

Binary data may be processed using RR instructions. They allow processing only within registers and do not allow operations between data in a register and data in memory.

The most used set of RR instructions are those in Fig. 5.3.

Mnemonic	Function
LR	Copies the contents of one register into another.
AR	Adds the contents of one register to another.
SR	Subtracts the contents of one register from another.
MR	Multiplies the contents of one register by the contents of another.*
DR	Divides the contents of a register by the contents of another.*

*Special register combinations are needed.

Figure 5.3 The most common RR instructions.

As noted, two of the instructions have an additional requirement which we'll discuss later.

The **LR (load register)** instruction copies the contents of one register into another. We've used this instruction before to copy the contents of register 15 into some other register, which we then used as the base register for our program. There's not much else you can say about this instruction since all registers are the same size and this is just a copying operation. For example, to copy the contents of register 3 into register 5, you would code the instruction as given in Fig. 5.4. Notice that this operation works from right to left. The contents of register 3 are copied *into* the contents of register 5. The contents of register 3 are not changed by this operation; hence, you'll have two copies of the same data in the registers.

```
LR    5,3
```

Figure 5.4 Copy the contents of one register into another.

The **AR (add register)** instruction adds two registers. With each register containing a binary fullword number, the instruction adds the two numbers and places the result in the first register operand. For example, suppose that register 5 contains the value 10 and register 6 contains the value 25. If we now assume that the register equates have been issued, we can add registers 5 and 6 as shown in Fig. 5.5.

```
AR      R5,R6
```

Figure 5.5 Adding the contents of register 6 to that of register 5.

The result, 35, is in register 5 since the AR instruction also works from right to left.

The **SR (subtract register)** instruction subtracts the contents of one register from another. To subtract the value 10 from 25 using registers 5 and 6, we code the instruction contained in Fig. 5.6. Note that we reverse the operands since we want to subtract 10 from 25. Register 6 contains the value 25 and register 5 contains the value 10. The subtract register instruction subtracts the contents of the second register *from* the contents of the first register, placing the result into the first register. In Fig. 5.6, register 6 will be changed to a value of 15, but register 5 will not change.

```
SR      R6,R5
```

Figure 5.6 Subtracting register contents from another.

To multiply or divide numbers, we must understand **register pairing.** Whenever we multiply or divide using registers, the first operand in the instruction must identify a pair of registers. The first register in the pair must be an even register and the second register in the pair must be an odd register. **Even/odd register pairs** are used in RR and RX instructions when performing multiply and divide operations. You'll also see even/odd pairs used in looping instructions in the next chapter.

Registers 4 and 5 constitute an even/odd pair, but registers 5 and 6 do not. Registers 4 and 7 *do not* constitute an even/odd pair because they are not consecutive numbers.

When coding the **MR (multiply register)** or **DR (divide register)** instructions, the first operand is specified by coding the even register of the even/odd pair. Although only one register number has been coded, *both* registers are actually referenced.

```
MR      E,r

DR      E,r
```

Figure 5.7 Source formats of the multiply and divide RR instructions.

The second operand in the instructions, logically described by Fig. 5.7, may refer to any other register since the second operand is not paired. Also, the second operand may be coded as either an even register or odd register number. If you do not code the first operand as an even register, your program will abend. The abend code in this case will be a **specification exception** abend.

When using the multiply register instruction, the first operand's associated odd register must contain the value to be multiplied. To multiply the value 10 times 20, we must place the value 10 (or 20) into register 5 and the value 20 (or 10) into some other register, let's say register 7. Multiplying registers 4/5 by register 7 gives a result of 200 in register 4/5. Figure 5.8 illustrates the processing using base 10 notation.

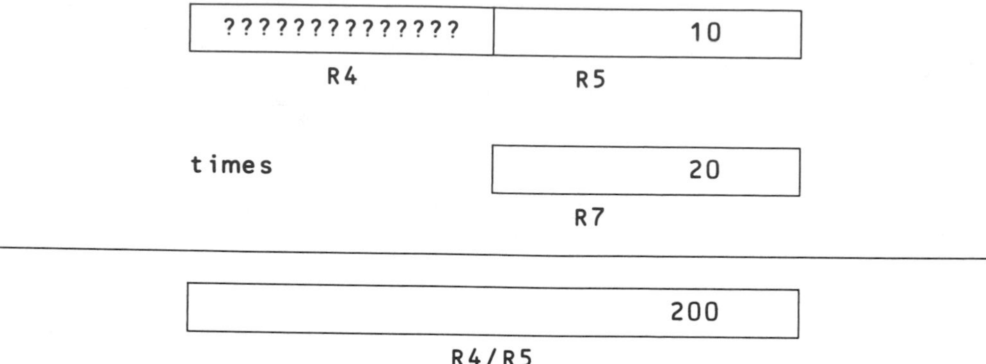

Figure 5.8 Multiplying the contents of registers.

Referring to Fig. 5.8, you can see the result of the multiplication. The odd register of the even/odd pair (in this case, register 5) contains one of the numbers to be multiplied. This number is multiplied by the contents of another register, register 7. The result is a *64-bit* number that spans *both* registers 4 and 5. Since the number 200 easily fits into register 5, register 4 contains the value 0 after the operation takes place. Registers 4 and 5 are treated as one binary doubleword field *after* the operation.

If one operand is positive and the other negative, a negative result will occur. If the result is greater than −2,147,483,648 then the even register will contain a value of −1 after the operation. If the resulting value is less than −2,147,483,648, the even register will contain the overflow from the odd register of the pair. As long as the numbers being multiplied yield a positive value less than 2,147,483,647 (X'7FFFFFFF'), the even register contains a value of zero. If the multiplication results in a number greater than 2,147,483,647, then register 4 contains the leading digits of the number. In general, most operations do not cause the even register to contain a value other than 0 or −1.

The **DR (divide register)** instruction divides two numbers. Again, an even/odd register pair is coded in the first operand and some other register is coded in the second operand. The DR instruction is slightly different in that the even/odd pair is a 64-bit number *before* the division takes place and becomes two 32-bit numbers *after* the division. The 32-bit numbers after the division are the remainder (even register) and quotient (odd register).

Before the divide register instruction is issued, the even register *must* contain a value of 0 or negative 1, depending on the sign of the number in the odd register. If the odd register contains a value greater than or equal to zero, then the even register *must* contain a value of 0. If the odd register contains a value less than zero or a negative number, then the even register *must* contain a value of negative 1. In the next chapter, we'll see a short section of code that uses comparison and branch instructions to test and set the value of the even register, depending on the value of the odd register. The process for assigning a value to the even register that is dependent on the sign of the number in the odd register is called **setting the sign of the even register.** It is a very important process if you want your divide operations to complete normally.

After the division takes place, the even/odd pair is split in half. The even register holds the **remainder** and the odd register holds the **quotient.** Obviously, if the even/odd pair is evenly divisible by the second operand, the remainder is zero.

The examples in Fig. 5.9 illustrate the result of the various divisions using the DR instruction. Rather than giving specific register numbers, the examples identify each register generically.

	Before Division	After Division	
even	0	0	remainder
odd	6	2	quotient
divisor	3	3	

	Before Division	After Division	
even	-1	0	remainder
odd	-6	-2	quotient
divisor	3	3	

	Before Division	After Division	
even	0	0	remainder
odd	6	-2	quotient
divisor	-3	-3	

	Before Division	After Division	
even	0	1	remainder
odd	9	2	quotient
divisor	4	4	

	Before Division	After Division	
even	-1	-1	remainder
odd	-9	-2	quotient
divisor	4	4	

	Before Division	After Division	
even	-1	-1	remainder
odd	-9	2	quotient
divisor	-4	-4	

	Before Division	After Division	
even	0	1	remainder
odd	9	-2	quotient
divisor	-4	-4	

Figure 5.9 Examples of division operations illustrating quotient and remainder values.

Where negative numbers are involved, the remainder always has the sign of the first operand. If the first operand is positive before the division occurs, the remainder is positive; if the first operand is negative, the remainder is negative unless, of course, the remainder is zero.

Since the even/odd pair is really a 64-bit number and can therefore hold a number larger than what would normally fit into a register, one must be careful when performing divisions. The quotient register is only 32-bits long. If the division yields a quotient that does not fit into the 32-bit register, an abend occurs. Further, an attempt to divide by zero causes a **decimal divide exception abend (OCB).**

Although register operations are generally associated only with integer processing, it is possible to simulate floating point or decimal operations quite easily. For example, dividing 11 by 4 will yield a quotient of 2 and a remainder of 3. However, if we first multiply 11 by 100 and then divide by 4, we'll obtain a quotient of 275 and a remainder of 0. In this case, the quotient logically represents 2.75 instead of 275. In fact, more significant digits can be obtained by first multiplying by a larger power of ten. That is, if four significant digits are desired, multiply the first operand by 10^4 before dividing.

Later in the chapter when we discuss data conversion, you should reflect back on this discussion and think about how you can obtain a printable 2.75 from an integer value of 275. Quite simply, by converting the integer 275 to printable form, and then using the MVC and MVI instructions to extract the ''integer'' and ''fractional'' components respectively, you can merge the halves together by adding a decimal point to construct a noninteger result. This technique is quite valuable when noninteger data must be processed. We discuss it here with respect to binary processing and again in Chapter 7 when we discuss packed-decimal processing. This technique can be used in place of floating point operations where appropriate significance can be attained through integer operations.

REGISTER-TO-STORAGE INSTRUCTIONS

The RR instructions allow processing data between registers, but not all data to be processed is inside a register when our program executes. Often, we'll have to obtain a value from memory, place it into a register, perform an operation on it, and place the result back into storage for later use. In order to obtain, process, and (re)place values into memory, we must use the register-to-storage instructions or the **RX instructions.**

RX instructions are four-byte instructions. Each instruction uses a single register or even/odd register pair in the first operand and a D(X,B) address in the second operand. Labeled storage areas may be used in the second operand since they are converted into D(0,B) addresses by the assembler. Figure 5.10 describes the logical format of an RX instruction.

```
mnemonic  R,D(X,B)
```

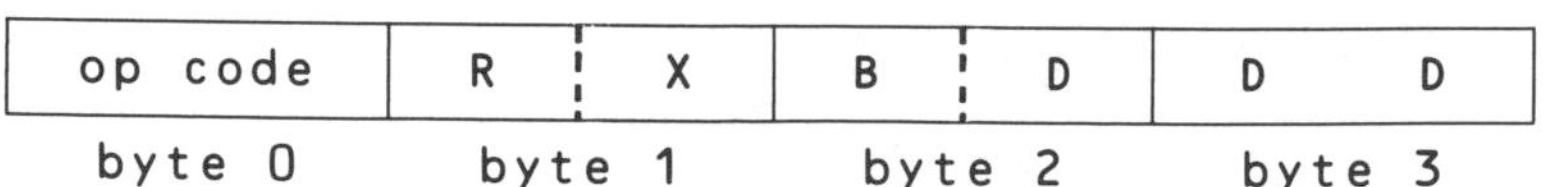

Figure 5.10 Format of an RX instruction.

A similar complement of instructions to the RR instructions exists within the RX instruction set. In fact, the operations performed are exactly like those of the RR instructions except that the data area referenced by the second operand is in memory rather than in a register. There is one difference, however, between the instructions that deal with copying data from memory into a register and copying data from a register into memory. Two instructions are required to replace the LR (load register) instruction—the L (load) and ST (store) instructions. Figure 5.11 describes the general set of commonly used RX instructions.

RX Instruction	Function
A (add)	Adds a value from memory to the contents of a register.
S (subtract)	Subtracts a value in memory from a value in a register.
M (multiply)	Multiply an even/odd pair by a value in memory.
D (divide)	Divide an even/odd pair by a value in memory.
L (load)	Copy a value from memory and place it into a register.
ST (store)	Copy a value from a register and place it into a memory area.

Figure 5.11 General set of RX instructions.

Since the RX instruction references a memory area in its second operand, we must now be concerned with boundary and alignment. All second operands coded on the RX instructions must be aligned on a halfword, fullword, or doubleword boundary for optimal processing.

There are several other RX instructions available, which we'll discuss as needed. One of immediate importance is the **LA (load address)** instruction, which is not listed in Fig. 5.11 because it is not generally associated with arithmetic processing. The load address instruction places the *address* of a data area into a register. For example, if you want to place the address of the data area STUFF into register 3, code the instruction as shown in Fig. 5.12.

```
         LA        R3,STUFF
```

Figure 5.12 Using the load address instruction.

In Fig. 5.12, the assembler converts the label reference into a D(0,B) address, which is determined by summing the displacement of STUFF with the contents of the base register used to reference STUFF.

The load address instruction may also initialize registers by placing only a displacement into a register. The instruction shown in Fig. 5.13 places the value 8 into register 4. In this example, the value 8 is being treated as the displacement of an explicit D(X,B) address. The index and base registers have not been specified and so their values are zero, 8(0,0). Displacements as high as 4095 may be used on the LA instruction in this fashion. Figure 5.14 contains several other examples of the LA instruction.

```
LA      R4,8
```

Figure 5.13 Initializing a register using the load address instruction.

LA Instruction		Value in Register
LA	R,0	zero
LA	R,5	5
LA	R,STUFF+3	address of fourth byte of STUFF

Figure 5.14 Examples of using the load address instruction.

Some programmers use the LA instruction to set a register to zero. As you've seen before, the SR instruction allows us to subtract a register from itself, thus placing a value of zero in the register. Although both instructions set the register to zero, the SR instruction, which is an RR instruction, is faster than the RX instruction LA. As a rule of thumb, use SR to set a register to zero, although it's really a matter of preference.

Let's write a simple program to add, subtract, multiply, and divide two numbers. We'll place each result in a separate fullword of storage within our program. The coding example 5.1 contains the program to perform our processing.

As you can clearly see, all storage areas referenced by the RX instructions are aligned on fullword boundaries since they are defined as fullword storage areas. Further, you see some of the elements that we've developed over the past few chapters, such as the entry and exit code, the LTORG statement, register equate use, and line comments. You can also see the setting of the sign of the even register of the even/odd pair, especially when negative 25 was divided by 5. We must always remember to set the sign for division whether we're using the RR instruction DR or the RX instruction D. We do not have to set the sign of the even register to perform multiplication since only the value in the odd register of the even/odd pair is used. In fact, you can use the even register of the even/odd pair as the second operand as shown in Fig. 5.15.

```
L       R2,VALUE2
L       R3,VALUE1
MR      R2,R2
```

Figure 5.15 Using the even register during multiplication.

The value in register 2 *after* the multiplication will be zero or negative 1 as we have discussed. Before the multiplication, however, it may be used just as any other register. Hence, if you're running short of registers, use the even register to multiply.

There is a problem with coding example 5.1 however, in that it does not allow us

```
COMPUTE  CSECT
         STM    R14,R12,12(R13)     SAVE THE REGISTERS
         LR     R12,R15             ESTABLISH BASE REG
         USING  COMPUTE,R12         TELL THE ASSEMBLER
         LA     R11,SAVEAREA        POINT TO OUR SAVE AREA
         ST     R11,8(R13)          TELL THE O.S. OR CALLER
         ST     R13,4(R11)          SAVE CURRENT R13
         LR     R13,R11             POINT TO NEW SAVEAREA
*
         L      R3,VALUE1           GET FIRST VALUE
         L      R5,VALUE2           GET SECOND NUMBER
         AR     R3,R5               ADD THEM
         ST     R3,ADDEM            SAVE VALUE IN MEMORY
*
         L      R3,VALUE1           GET FIRST NUMBER AGAIN
         S      R3,VALUE2           COMPUTE DIFFERENCE
         ST     R3,DIFFER           SAVE DIFFERENCE
*
         SR     R2,R2               SET SIGN IN R2 TO 0
         L      R3,VALUE1           GET ORIGINAL NUMBER
         M      R2,VALUE2           E/O PAIR TIMES VALUE2
         ST     R3,PRODUCT          SAVE PRODUCT VALUE
*
         L      R2,MINUS1           PLACE -1 IN R2
         L      R3,NEGVALUE         GET NEW NEGATIVE VALUE
         L      R6,VALUE2           GET SECOND OPERAND
         DR     R2,R6               DIVIDE THE NUMBERS
         ST     R2,REMAIN           SAVE REMAINDER
         ST     R3,QUOTIENT         SAVE QUOTIENT
*
         L      R13,4(R13)          RESTORE ORIGINAL R13
         LM     R14,R12,12(R13)     RESTORE ALL REGS
         SR     R15,R15             INDICATE ALL OK
         BCR    B'1111',R14         RETURN TO O.S.
*
VALUE1   DC     F'25'               ORIGINAL VALUE
VALUE2   DC     F'5'                SECOND VALUE
SUM      DS     F
DIFFER   DS     F
PRODUCT  DS     F
MINUS1   DC     F'-1'               NEGATIVE 1
NEGVALUE DC     F'-25'
REMAIN   DS     F
QUOTIENT DS     F
SAVEAREA DS     18F
         LTORG
         END    COMPUTE
```

Example 5.1 Coding example of a general arithmetic processing program.

to print any results. We can compute anything that we want, but we can't see the results. We'll resolve this problem shortly by learning how to convert binary numbers into a printable format. Before doing so, let's complete our study of the entry and exit code so that we fully understand these instructions.

THE IBM LINKAGE CONVENTIONS

The program code that initiates and exits our program was presented in Chapter 3 in a "here it is—use it" manner. Although some instructions were explained, it was not complete for a full understanding. The following explanation will correct that deficiency.

The IBM **linkage conventions**, as they are called, are rules to follow when implementing programs in an IBM environment. As we stated earlier, it is the option of the programmer as to whether or not to code the conventions. Some examples were given in which the linkage conventions were not used, such as the case when using ASSIST or when the program was not performing I/O or calling a subroutine of some sort. Since ASSIST manages our environment by preserving and restoring the registers, there is no need to adhere to the linkage conventions when coding programs under ASSIST. Also, if our program does not request services from the operating system or call any other subprogram, then the linkage conventions are not necessary.

Clearly, there are many cases where we do not have to adhere to the linkage conventions. These cases allow shortcuts in coding, but, in general, we will follow the linkage conventions in full. It is good practice to code with the conventions so that later program modifications will not fail because the linkage conventions have been omitted or shortened to save a little time.

When our program begins execution, it is actually called by either the loader or the operating system. We can think of our program as being a subroutine to either of these elements. Since both the operating system and the loader are programs, they use the general-purpose registers for processing. When our program begins execution, we inherit whatever values are in the registers. We can use the information in the registers if it is meaningful but, in general, the registers have nothing of value. The registers do contain valuable information for the operating system or the loader, however. If we destroy or change the values in the registers and return control to the operating system, we could impact processing and may in fact cause an error. For this reason, the linkage conventions require us to save all of the registers into a special register save area before we use them and to restore the registers to their original state before we exit our program. What we do with the registers between those times is our business.

If our program calls a subroutine, then it is the responsibility of the subroutine to preserve the registers *for us*. If we view the execution of programs as a chain, with the operating system as its first link, we can say that somewhere in the chain is our link. If we use the linkage conventions as defined by IBM, then we preserve the chain and allow it to continue. If we do not use the linkage conventions, then we may weaken the chain—our program or subroutine would be the weak link.

One of the first instructions issued by our program when we obtained control was to save the contents of the registers. By issuing the instruction given in Figure 5.16, we are saving registers 14 through 12 into a storage area addressed by register 13.

```
STM      R14,R12,12(R13)
```

Figure 5.16 Preserving the register contents.

The STM (store multiple) instruction works like a clock with each position on the clock being a register number. Starting at the register specified in the first operand and continuing clockwise until the second operand is reached, all registers are stored into the area addressed by register 13 (see Fig. 5.17).

As you can see from the clock in Fig. 5.17, register 13 has not been stored. From Fig. 5.16, the STM instruction does not store the registers at the address addressed by register 13, rather, it stores the registers at a displacement 12 bytes from the address contained in register 13. Figure 5.18 describes the general format of the register save area, which you know is 18 fullwords long.

The second and third fullwords of the save area hold current and future values of register 13. Therefore, all registers are stored, but they are not stored in sequential order. Register 13 is a special register that must always address a register save area. Further, it must always address an 18-fullword-register save area in the program that is

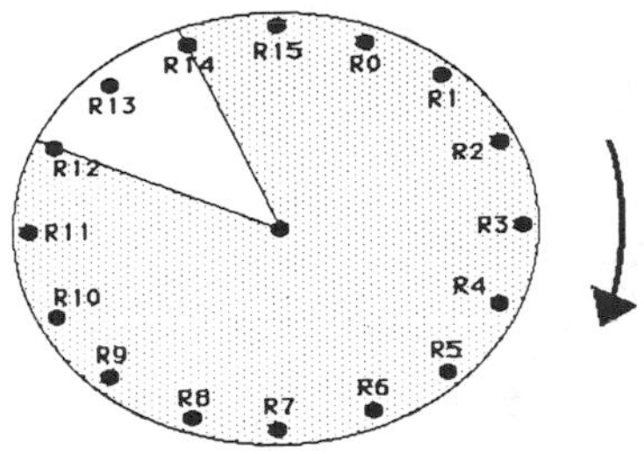


```
STM   R14,R12,12(R13)
```

Figure 5.17 Logical register storing using STM. The STM instruction stores all registers from register 14 through register 12 (in a clockwise direction) into the area addressed by register 13 with a displacement of 12 bytes.

WORD 1	RESERVED
WORD 2	PREVIOUS SAVE AREA ADDRESS
WORD 3	NEXT PROGRAM'S SAVEAREA ADDR.
WORD 4	REGISTER 14
WORD 5	REGISTER 15
WORD 6	REGISTER 0
WORD 7	REGISTER 1
WORD 8	REGISTER 2
WORD 9	REGISTER 3
WORD 10	REGISTER 4
WORD 11	REGISTER 5
WORD 12	REGISTER 6
WORD 13	REGISTER 7
WORD 14	REGISTER 8
WORD 15	REGISTER 9
WORD 16	REGISTER 10
WORD 17	REGISTER 11
WORD 18	REGISTER 12

Figure 5.18 The 18-fullword register save area.

currently executing. When the operating system is executing, register 13 addresses a save area within the operating system; when our program is executing, register 13 addresses a save area within our program. Whenever a program begins execution, a new register save area must be established and it becomes the *active* save area. When a program ends execution, a register save area is deactivated and a previous register save area becomes effective. The establishment and disestablishment of register save areas is directly related to the number of links in the program execution chain. The more programs on the chain, the more save areas there are that have been established; the fewer programs on the chain, the fewer established save areas. Figure 5.19 illustrates this relationship.

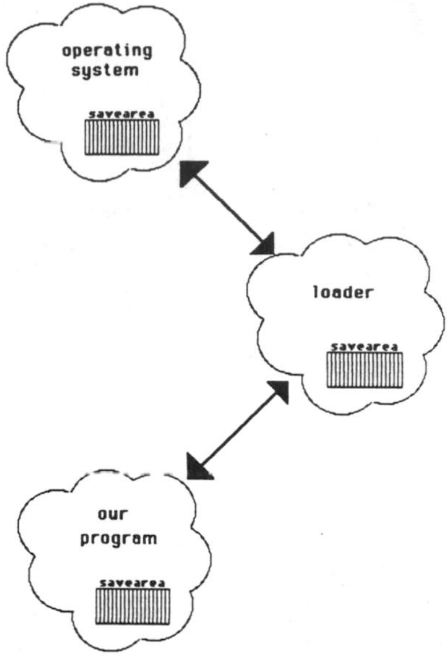

All programs on the program chain have their own register save areas.

Figure 5.19 Hierarchical program-to-program relationship.

Each program on our program chain is chained together through the register contents. When a new program obtains control, register 15 contains the **entry point address** of that program. Register 14 contains an address that allows the new program to return control to the invoking program. Register 15 connects (links) the two programs and register 14 separates the programs. See Fig. 5.20.

The connection of programs via register 15 and the separation of programs via register 14 parallels the use of register 13 and the establishment of register save areas.

The third fullword of the register save area holds the address of the *next* or *subordinate* program's register save area. The second fullword of a register save area holds the *previous* program's register save area address. The register save areas are linked

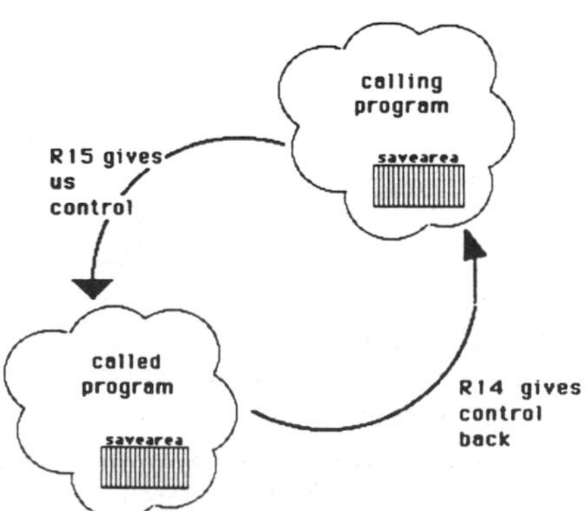

Figure 5.20 R14 and R15 usage during linkage.

through the second and third fullwords of the save areas. This is why this entire process is called the **register *link*age convention.**

In Fig. 5.21, several program links are illustrated. The operating system has invoked the loader, the loader has invoked a program called STUDMSTR (student master), and STUDMSTR has invoked our program called CLASSLST (class list).

Register save areas are found in all components in this program chain. For every two adjacent components, each knows the address of the other's register save area. The operating system knows the address of the loader's save area and the loader knows the address of the operating system's save area. The same holds true for the relationships loader-STUDMSTR and STUDMSTR-CLASSLST.

The responsibility for chaining the register save areas is given to the *subordinate* or *called program.* When the loader is called, the loader tells the operating system where the loader's save area is located. This is done by executing the entry linkage code that you've already seen. STUDMSTR tells the loader where its save area is located and STUDMSTR stores the loader's save area address. Our program, CLASSLST, stores the address of STUDMSTR's save area *into our save area* and CLASSLST places the address of its save area into the 18-fullword save area *of STUDMSTR.* The responsibility for register save area chaining is assigned to the program being called, not to the calling program.

The instructions to perform the chaining are given in Fig. 5.22. Incidentally, you've coded them before; I hope that now you understand them.

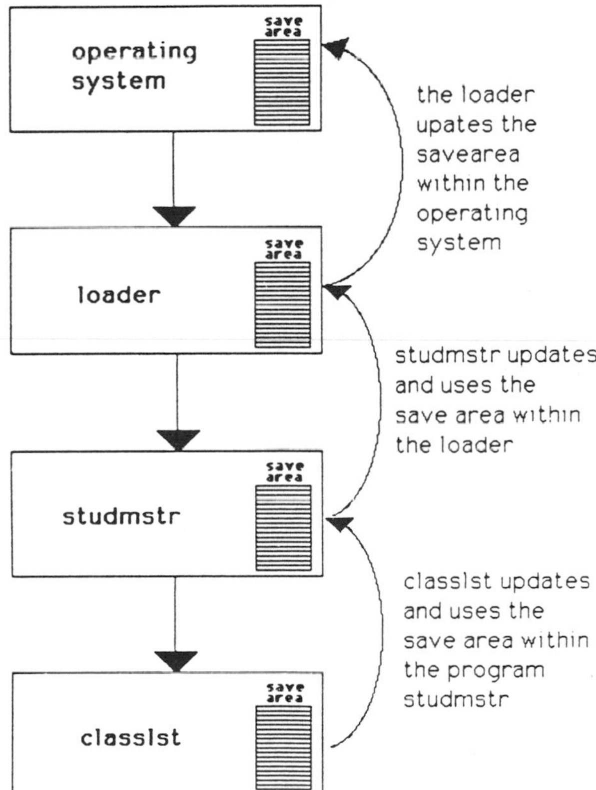

Figure 5.21 Save area maintenance responsibility.

```
LA      Rx,SAVEAREA
ST      Rx,8(R13)
ST      R13,4(Rx)
LR      R13,Rx
```

Figure 5.22 Instructions to chain register save areas.

The first instruction places the address of the 18-fullword storage area into Rx (one of registers 2 through 12). This storage area can have any name as long as it is a valid label name. We've used the name SAVEAREA.

The second and third instructions may be coded in any order, but as shown in Figure 5.22, the second instruction places the save area address in our program into the third fullword of the save area in the *previous program* (the program that called our program). The program that called us now knows the location of our save area. Half of the link is completed. Informing the calling program of our save area is referred to as **forward chaining**.

The third instruction stores the current value of register 13 into the second fullword of *our* register save area. Hence, we will know where the save area is located in the previous program. Saving and remembering the address of the calling program's save area is called **backward chaining**.

Finally, register 13 is assigned the address of our save area, which establishes register 13 and our save area as the current or most active register save area. Figure 5.23 illustrates the impact of chaining on the register save areas between two executing programs.

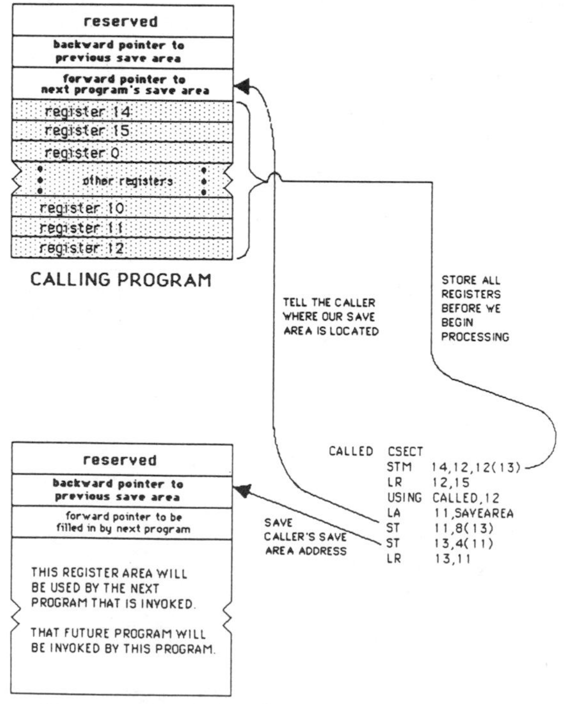

Figure 5.23 Instructions and impact of the linkage conventions.

We now perform whatever processing we want within our program. As long as all programs adhere to these conventions, we don't have to worry about the contents of our registers being altered. If our base register value was altered by a program that we called because that program did not adhere to the linkage conventions, all references to data areas by our program from that point on would result in incorrect data or could result in a program abend.

When our program is finished processing, we *unchain* ourselves from both the program chain and the register save area chain. We do this by issuing the instructions given in Fig. 5.24.

```
L       R13,4(R13)
LM      R14,R12,12(R13)
SR      R15,R15
BCR     B'1111',R14
```

Figure 5.24 Exit linkage convention instructions.

Here, the old value of register 13 is obtained from within our register save area. If you recall, we saved the previous program's register 13 value into the second fullword of our save area, which is located at a displacement four bytes from the beginning of our save area (addressed by the current value of register 13). By simply loading register 13 with this value, we've returned R13 to its original value (the value when our program first began execution).

The second instruction, **LM (load multiple)**, returns all registers to their original values. The load multiple instruction loads registers in a clockwise method based on the register numbers specified in the first and second operands. As you can see, the address from which the registers are reloaded is our familiar 12-byte displacement from the address in register 13.

We clear register 15 to set our condition code or return code using the SR (subtract register) instruction. A condition code of zero informs the program that called us that everything is alright.

Finally, the BCR (branch on condition register) instruction returns control to the calling program by branching to the address that is contained in register 14. This address is where execution *within the calling* will now continue. We'll talk more about this instruction in the next chapter. These instructions unchain our program from the program execution chain and return control to the program that called us.

Let's suppose that our program did not work properly or did not complete all of its processing. If this were the case, we would not want to return a value of zero in register 15. In fact, we may want to set register 15 to one of several values, depending on the circumstances encountered during the execution of our program.

To return a value of 4 in register 15, we can use the LA (load address) instruction discussed earlier in the chapter. Figure 5.25 contains a complete example of this technique.

```
L       R13,4(R13)
LM      R14,R12,12(R13)
LA      R15,4
BCR     B'1111',R14
```

Figure 5.25 Returning a nonzero value in register 15.

On the other hand, if our program sets register 15 to one of many different values, it would seem that we would need many exit points from our program, depending on the processing conditions that we encounter. However, this is not true.

To adhere to the guidelines of structured programming, our programs should have one entry point and one exit point. If this code was found more than once in our program, then we would be violating structured programming guidelines. It is not necessary for this code to appear more than once. By altering our standard exit code slightly, we can use one exit point in our program, regardless of the number of values that may be returned via register 15. Figure 5.26 illustrates the proper coding.

```
L       R13,4(R13)
L       R14,12(R13)
LM      R0,R12,20(R13)
BCR     B'1111',R14
```

Figure 5.26 Restoring all but register 15 before returning control.

Register 14 is reloaded through the L (load) instruction and registers 0 through 12 are reloaded through the LM (load multiple) instruction. Previously, the LM instruction reloaded all registers between register 14 and register 12 *including register 15.* However, since register 15 may be set at an earlier point within the program code, we may not want to reload it, thus risking the possibility of changing our return code value during the exit code. By reloading all registers *except* register 15, we ensure that the proper return code is placed into register 15 before returning to the calling program.

We must remember to set register 15. If we do not return a proper value to register 15 (a value from 0 through 4095), our program may communicate to the calling program that we did not succeed in processing when in reality we may have processed and completed normally. Somewhere within the program, we must assign some value to register 15 either through the LA (load address) instruction, through the L (load) instruction, or by setting register 15 to zero by using the SR (subtract register) instruction. Figure 5.27 illustrates several methods for placing a value into register 15.

	Instruction	Explanation
LA	R15,4	Set R15 to a value of 4.
SR	R15,R15	Set R15 to zero.
L	R15,RTNCODE	Place the value in the field called return code into register 15.

Figure 5.27 Methods to place a return code value into register 15.

One important term to remember in this entire process is **addressability**. It is, of course, the ability to reference information, and it is particularly important when labels reference storage areas. Addressability is important within the linkage conventions because remember that no data area within our program may be referenced *after* we have reloaded the registers with their original contents. Once the registers are reloaded, the base register that we established is no longer in effect, which means that we cannot use it to reference labeled fields. This means that we *cannot* assign a value to register 15 using the L (load) instruction as shown in Fig. 5.28.

```
This section of code will not work.
----------------------------------------
        L       R13,4(R13)
        LM      R14,R12,12(R13)
        L       R15,ZERO                ← illogical
        BCR     B'1111',R14
```

Figure 5.28 Incorrect method of placing a return code value in register 15.

The *third* instruction in Fig. 5.28, L (load), either causes bad data to be placed into register 15 or causes our program to abend. We cannot reference a field in our program after the LM instruction has been issued since the LM instruction destroys our base register(s), causing us to lose the ability to address information.

INPUT AND OUTPUT OF BINARY INFORMATION

As we've learned, data may be stored and processed within the computer in many different formats. Data may also be stored and processed in these formats outside of the computer unless human readable information is desired. When information must be understandable by humans, data must be converted from its internal processing format to one that is human readable. For example, binary and packed-decimal information may not be printed directly to a line printer since it is not in a format that humans can understand. Let's take, for example, the number +123. This number may be represented by the two-byte packed-decimal number X'123C' or by the two-byte binary number X'007B'. If either of these fields are printed to a line printer, the output would be something to the effect of C'. . ' and C'.#', respectively. Whenever the printer cannot properly represent a byte of data, a period, blank, or some strange character is printed in its place. Here I've used periods to represent nonprintable information. As you can see, both bytes of the packed-decimal field are nonprintable and only one byte of the binary representation is nonprintable since X'7B' does represent the character #. These examples clearly illustrate that the number +123 is not human readable when printed in internal format.

In order for us to communicate with computers in an understandable format, we must write programs that perform conversion operations. The program must accept information in human readable form, convert it into information that can be processed within the computer, and convert the output from processing into a format that we can again understand.

Character data is the only information that does not have to be converted for processing within the computer. All numeric information must be converted into either packed decimal, floating point, or binary format. Since this chapter is devoted to binary data processing, let's study the method for converting and processing binary data.

When we input numeric data to the computer that is in human readable form, that information is said to be in **character format**. In order to convert our numeric-character data to internal binary format, we must issue the machine instructions PACK (convert character to packed-decimal) and CVB (convert packed-decimal format to binary) so that it can be processed. A byproduct of our conversion process is information in packed-decimal format. If we knew how to process information using packed-decimal instructions, we wouldn't have to continue the conversion to binary. However, since we are discussing binary processing, we'll issue the CVB instruction to convert from packed-decimal format to binary format so that our data can be processed in true binary format.

The **PACK instruction** is an SS instruction (six bytes) and requires two operands. Both operands must be addressable fields by the program. Both operands may be up to 16 bytes long, but, generally, the first operand is a *doubleword* and the second operand is the field to be converted. For example, suppose that two numbers come into the computer through a GET instruction (XREAD in ASSIST). Assume that the format of our input data is shown in Fig. 5.29.

```
INPUT     DS      0CL80
VALUE1    DS      CL5
VALUE2    DS      CL5
          DS      CL70
```

Figure 5.29 Example of a numeric input data structure.

VALUE1 and VALUE2 are numbers in character format that have been typed on the data card in a right justified format. VALUE1 is found in the first five positions of the input record and VALUE2 is found in the next five positions. If our data cannot be described through a data structure, the inputting and processing of data in any format becomes very difficult. Only if the ASSIST package were used could we process information that is input in a **free formatted** manner based on what we have already studied. In a later section, we'll discuss the ASSIST instructions and the formatting of input and output data in and outside of ASSIST. For now, assume a structured data input format so that we can easily convert these numbers to packed-decimal format by using the PACK instructions shown in Figure 5.30.

```
         PACK     NUM1(8),VALUE1(5)
         PACK     NUM2(8),VALUE2(5)
           .        .
           .        .
           .        .
NUM1     DS       D
NUM2     DS       D
```

Figure 5.30 Step 1: converting input character fields to packed-decimal format.

NUM1 and NUM2 are defined in our program as doublewords. Although they do not have to be defined as doublewords, it is good practice to do so since the next instructions *require* that our packed-decimal information be stored in a doubleword and be aligned on a doubleword boundary.

The PACK instructions convert our five-byte character data into eight-byte packed-decimal values. If we assume that VALUE1 is C'00020' and VALUE2 is C'00008', the PACK instructions convert these values into doubleword values of X'000000000000020F' and X'000000000000008F', respectively.

Once our values have been converted from character to packed decimal, we can continue the conversion process by using the **CVB (convert to binary)** instruction shown in Fig. 5.31. The instruction converts our packed-decimal numbers into binary fullwords, placing the converted binary values into their separate *registers.* What better place to put binary numbers but in registers. We can then use the RR or RX instructions discussed earlier to add, subtract, multiply, or divide our values.

```
CVB     R3,NUM1
CVB     R4,NUM2
```

Figure 5.31 Step 2: converting packed-decimal fields to binary.

After the CVBs, our input values will be in register(s) and in binary format. To convert this information into a printable format, reverse the conversion process going from binary format to character format. This may be done by using the CVD (convert to packed decimal) and the UNPK (unpack—convert from packed decimal to character format) instructions. Actually, we'll use one more instruction so that our data is human readable. The UNPK instruction converts *most* of the packed-decimal information into character format, but it does not convert the rightmost byte of the unpacked number properly. As a result, we issue the OI (or immediate) instruction to fully convert our number to human readable format.

Let's assume that our results are held in registers. To convert from the binary representation within the registers to packed-decimal format, we issue the **CVD (convert to decimal)** instruction. Assuming that our result is in register 6, we issue the instruction given in Fig. 5.32. The binary number in register 6 is converted into packed-decimal and placed into the *doubleword* area called RESULT. RESULT *must be defined as a doubleword* or must be defined as an eight-byte area, aligned on a doubleword boundary. The best method for defining RESULT is to define it as a doubleword.

```
CVD     R6,RESULT
```

Figure 5.32 Converting binary values to packed-decimal for conversion to a proper output format.

Our value is now in packed-decimal format and since our value is stored in an eight-byte area, there are a total of 15 possible digits within the area called RESULT. For example, if we add our values 20 and 8 and then convert them into the area called RESULT, RESULT would appear as shown in Fig. 5.33.

```
X '0 0 0 0 0 0 0 0 0 0 0 0 0 2 8 C'
```

Figure 5.33 Internal value of an eight-byte packed-decimal field.

As you can see, thirteen leading zeros appear before our value 28. These zeros plus the two digits that make up the number 28 account for 15 digits within the field called RESULT. Therefore, to convert this field into character format, we must allow for 15 digits or 15 bytes of storage.

```
OUTPUTVL   DS     CL15
```

Figure 5.34 Output conversion area to character format.

This field called OUTPUTVL, shown in Fig. 5.34, holds our result in character format. To convert the value in RESULT from packed-decimal to character format, we issue the SS instruction **UNPK (unpack)** as shown in Fig. 5.35.

```
UNPK     OUTPUTVL(15),RESULT(8)
```

Figure 5.35 Converting the packed-decimal result into character format.

After the UNPK instruction is issued, OUTPUTVL contains the hexadecimal value X'F0F0F0F0F0F0F0F0F0F0F0F0F2C8'. Look at this value carefully. All digits, except for the rightmost digit, contain a zone of **F**. The rightmost byte in RESULT has simply been switched around so that the sign is now in the left half of the rightmost byte and the digit portion is in the right half of the rightmost byte. The format of OUTPUTVL is called a **zoned-decimal format** since all digits except the rightmost digit have a proper zone of F and the rightmost byte contains the *sign* of the number and the rightmost digit of the number. If OUTPUTVL is printed, the output has the value shown in Fig. 5.36.

```
0000000000002H
```

Figure 5.36 Printed value of zoned decimal 28.

The H occurs because of the rightmost byte. This byte, whose hexadecimal value is X'C8', is the representation for the *letter* H. OUTPUTVL is not yet in a human readable format.

To complete the conversion from binary to character format, we must use the **OI (or immediate) instruction,** which fixes the rightmost byte of the field by converting it from X'C8' to X'F8'. Hence, the rightmost byte is converted from the character H to the character 8, thus allowing the rightmost digit in our number to print properly. Figure 5.37 shows us how this is accomplished.

```
OI       OUTPUTVL+14,X'F0'
```

Figure 5.37 Fixing the rightmost byte of a converted field.

In the instruction given in Fig. 5.37, OUTPUTVL is referenced with a displacement of 14. OUTPUTVL+14 addresses the fifteenth byte of OUTPUTVL, which is the rightmost byte of the field. To that byte, we change all bits in the left half of the byte to ones and leave all bits in the right half alone. The left half value of C is changed to F and the right half value of 8 is left alone. Thus, X'C8' becomes X'F8', which is now a printable value 8.

The label-plus-displacement technique used above to reference the last byte of OUTPUTVL is one of many methods in which the last byte of OUTPUTVL can be referenced. Although the instruction works, it may not be the most maintainable technique possible. In other words, if the length of the field called OUTPUTVL changes, the OI instruction also has to be changed in order for it to work. Using other methods, some of which are shown in Fig. 5.38, we can write code that is more maintainable but yet performs the same task. For example, the instructions in Fig. 5.38 reformat the last byte of OUTPUTVL, but they address the rightmost byte in a different manner. Incidentally, implicit lengths for both OUTPUTVL and RESULT are supplied by the assembler in this code.

```
          UNPK    OUTPUTVL,RESULT
          OI      LASTDIGT,X'F0'
          .       .
          .       .
          .       .
OUTPUTVL  DS      0CL15
          DS      CL14
LASTDIGT  DS      C
```

Figure 5.38 Alternate method to fix the last digit in a converted field.

All 15 digits of OUTPUTVL reside within the structure called OUTPUTVL, which consists of an unnamed 14-byte area and a 1-byte area called LASTDIGT. Clearly, the length of OUTPUTVL is taken from its definition. Further, if the definition changes, the instructions automatically change, thus making the code much more maintainable than that of the previous example.

Figure 5.39 contains yet another example. Using the EQU instruction to produce a **relocatable symbol**, this code accomplishes the same task. Again, implicit lengths are used on the UNPK instruction.

```
          UNPK    OUTPUTVL,RESULT
          OI      LASTDIGT,X'F0'
          .       .
          .       .
          .       .
OUTPUTVL  DS      CL15
LASTDIGT  EQU     OUTPUTVL+14
```

Figure 5.39 Alternate method of fixing the rightmost digit.

In Fig. 5.39, the symbol LASTDIGT is equated to OUTPUTVL+14. In reality, a label-plus-displacement format is being used on the OI instruction. Through the use of the relocatable symbol LASTDIGT, the OI instruction avoids the explicit label-plus-displacement technique and places the definition of LASTDIGT closer to the definition of OUTPUTVL. By doing so, a programmer is less likely to change one and not the other. Also, since no explicit displacements or lengths are coded on any instructions, only the two definition fields need be changed to impact the length or displacements throughout the remainder of the program.

To summarize our original discussion, the conversion process from character to binary and back again takes place as follows:

Converting from Character to Binary

1. Issue the PACK instruction to convert the input-character data to a packed-decimal format. The field to hold the converted value should be defined as a doubleword.
2. Issue the CVB instruction to convert the packed-decimal value to binary. The binary value is placed into a register and is ready for processing.
3. Process the value in the register as desired using either RR or RX instructions.

Converting from Binary to Character

1. Issue the CVD instruction to convert the binary result, stored in a register, to a packed-decimal format. The field to hold the converted packed-decimal number must be defined as a doubleword.
2. Issue the UNPK instruction to convert the packed-decimal 8-byte field into a 15-byte-character format number. All digits within the packed-decimal field are converted into a character format except for the rightmost byte, which must be manually converted in the next step.
3. Convert the rightmost byte of the 15-byte character field by using the OI instruction to change the zone portion of the field from its current sign value to a zone of F. This completes the conversion process and results in a number that is printable and in human readable form.

For the time being, let's assume that all numbers that we process are positive numbers. It's not as easy to convert negative numbers from input and output format to packed-decimal or binary. We'll discuss the processing of negative numbers in Chapter 7 where we discuss packed-decimal processing in more detail.

You should have realized that OUTPUTVL is a character field and that it can be further processed using the MVC instruction. Since there is no reason to print all 13 leading zero digits for our result, we can reduce the amount of data printed for OUTPUTVL by moving only the digits that will appear in the result to our output area. For example, if we think that our result will be less than or equal to a five-digit number, then we can move only the last five digits of OUTPUTVL to a print area and send that to the printer. We could also unpack a shorter field. For example, only the rightmost five digits of the number could be unpacked instead of the entire 15-digit field. This further helps the readability of our printouts and enhances the overall appearance of our output.

HALFWORD PROCESSING INSTRUCTIONS

The RR and RX instructions discussed so far allow the processing of binary data stored in a fullword format. Another set of RX instructions allow processing of data stored in a halfword format. These RX instructions are commonly called **halfword instructions**.

Binary data may be stored within bytes, halfwords, fullwords, and doublewords. In fact, you've seen instructions to process binary data at the byte level (MVI, MVC, and OI), fullword level (RR and RX instructions), and doubleword level (CVB and CVD). The halfword instructions allow storing, loading, adding, subtracting, and multiplying data stored in halfword binary fields. Note that you cannot divide using halfword instructions.

Since the halfword instructions are RX instructions, they have the RX format. The second operand, a D(X,B) address, now refers to a halfword area instead of a fullword area. This allows us to save some storage within our program by using halfword fields instead of fullword fields for arithmetic processing. On the other hand, halfwords only hold values up to 32,767, which may impact their use, depending on the size of data to be processed.

Although a full complement of instructions are available to process in halfword format, they generally aren't used as often as they could be. Even though they are less restrictive in terms of alignment, their limitation on value size seems to undermine their usefullness.

The most advantageous halfword instruction is the multiply halfword (MH) instruction. If you recall, the fullword version required an even/odd register pair to multiply values. The MH instruction does not require an even/odd pair, which allows us to use any register in the first operand. This reduces the number of registers required for a multiply and also reduces the attachment of one register to another. We can use registers more freely as long as the resulting value is within the bounds of the register.

The halfword instructions operate on positive and negative values stored in halfwords within memory. For the operations LH, AH, SH, and MH, the second operand is expanded to a full 32-bit binary number before the operation occurs. This is done by propagating the sign bit of the halfword number throughout the high order 16 bits of the register. Thus, the resulting operations occur using fullword binary values. Figure 5.40 summarizes the halfword instructions.

Instruction Mnemonic	Function
LH (load halfword)	Copy a halfword value from memory into a register.
STH (store halfword)	Copy the rightmost two bytes of a register into memory.
AH (add halfword)	Add a halfword value in memory to the contents of a register.
SH (subtract halfword)	Subtract the halfword value of a data area in memory from the contents of a register.
MH (multiply halfword)	Multiply the contents of a register by the value stored in a halfword in memory.

Figure 5.40 The most commonly used halfword instructions.

You'll notice that the mnemonics for the halfword instructions are almost identical to the standard RX instructions to process fullwords of data. The only difference is the extra letter H on the end of the mnemonic to specify *halfword* instruction. The small section of code in the coding example 5.2 illustrates poor use of the halfword instructions.

Your attention is immediately focused on the instructions that reference the data areas through label-plus-displacement addressing. Since the halfword instructions process and work with only halfword data, we must make sure that we reference the data properly. After the input values are converted into packed decimal and then into binary format, they are stored respectively into the fields called BINVAL1 and BINVAL2 through the STM instruction that references the generic name BINVALUE. Each of these operands are stored in binary fullword format, which means that the numbers are *right* justified within these fields. The decimal number 25 would be stored as X'00000019' within one of these fullwords. If we referenced BINVAL1 without the displacement qualifier, we'd be referring to the *first two bytes* of the field, which in this case would be X'0000'. Only the rightmost two bytes of our fields contain values; in order to reference our data properly, we must refer to the rightmost two bytes of both the BINVAL1 and BINVAL2 fields by using a displacement of 2 whenever they are referenced.

The use of displacements to qualify references is yet another reason why halfword instructions are not as commonly used as RX instructions. Input data must be converted to binary using fullword formats, but may then be referenced using halfword formats.

```
         GET     DATAIN,VALUES           READ THE INPUT RECORD
         PACK    NUM1(8),VALUE1(3)       CONVERT FIRST NUMBER TO PACKED
         PACK    NUM2(8),VALUE2(3)       CONVERT SECOND NUMBER TO PACKED
         CVB     R3,NUM1                 CONVERT FIRST NUMBER TO BINARY
         CVB     R4,NUM2                 CONVERT NUMBER 2 TO BINARY
         STM     R3,R4,BINVALUE          SAVE VALUES IN FULLWORD BINARY
         AH      R3,BINVAL2+2            ADD THE VALUES
         STH     R3,SUM                  SAVE SUM IN MEMORY
         LH      R3,BINVAL1+2            RESTORE FIRST OPERAND VALUE
         SH      R3,BINVAL2+2            SUBTRACT
         STH     R3,DIFFER               SAVE THE DIFFERENCE
         L       R3,BINVAL1              RESTORE FIRST OPERAND, FULLWORD
         MH      R3,BINVAL2+2            MULTIPLY THE VALUES
         STH     R3,PRODUCT              SAVE THE PRODUCT

         .       .
         .       .
         .       .

VALUES   DS      0CLnn                   INPUT RECORD AREA
VALUE1   DS      CL3                     FIRST VALUE
VALUE2   DS      CL3                     SECOND VALUE
         DS      CLnn                    UNKNOWN FILLER LENGTH
NUM1     DS      D
NUM2     DS      D
BINVALUE DS      0F                      GENERIC NAME FOR VALUES
BINVAL1  DS      F
BINVAL2  DS      F
SUM      DS      H
DIFFER   DS      H
PRODUCT  DS      H
```

Example 5.2 Poor technique when using halfword instructions for processing.

```
         GET     DATAIN,VALUES           READ THE INPUT RECORD
         PACK    NUM1(8),VALUE1(3)       CONVERT FIRST NUMBER TO PACKED
         PACK    NUM2(8),VALUE2(3)       CONVERT SECOND NUMBER TO PACKED
         CVB     R3,NUM1                 CONVERT FIRST NUMBER TO BINARY
         CVB     R4,NUM2                 CONVERT NUMBER 2 TO BINARY
         STH     R3,BINVAL1              SAVE VALUES IN FULLWORD BINARY
         STH     R4,BINVAL2
         AH      R3,BINVAL2              ADD THE VALUES
         STH     R3,SUM                  SAVE SUM IN MEMORY
         LH      R3,BINVAL1              RESTORE FIRST OPERAND VALUE
         SH      R3,BINVAL2              SUBTRACT
         STH     R3,DIFFER               SAVE THE DIFFERENCE
         L       R3,BINVAL1              RESTORE FIRST OPERAND, FULLWORD
         MH      R3,BINVAL2              MULTIPLY THE VALUES
         STH     R3,PRODUCT              SAVE THE PRODUCT

         .       .
         .       .
         .       .

VALUES   DS      0CLnn                   INPUT RECORD AREA
VALUE1   DS      CL3                     FIRST VALUE
VALUE2   DS      CL3                     SECOND VALUE
         DS      CLn                     UNKNOWN FILLER LENGTH
NUM1     DS      D
NUM2     DS      D
BINVAL1  DS      H
BINVAL2  DS      H
SUM      DS      H
DIFFER   DS      H
PRODUCT  DS      H
```

Example 5.3 Coding example to illustrate the proper use of halfword instructions.

This inconsistency, and, quite simply, the bother of converting to and from halfword, fullword, packed, and character formats makes halfword instruction use somewhat cumbersome. On the other hand, practice makes perfect. The more you use and become familiar with these instructions, the more you'll find yourself using and appreciating their capabilities. Again, this is not an appropriate way to use the halfword instructions. As an example, let's redo the previous program example using halfword instructions as they should be used. As you can see in the coding example 5.3, the halfword instructions are no more difficult to use and understand than any other set of instructions as long as they are used properly.

The problem in the code given in example 5.2 was not in our use of the halfword instructions, but in the manner in which we stored our binary values. By replacing the STM instruction with two STH instructions, we place the two values to be processed into memory in halfword format. Anytime that we now need to reference the fields, we may do so without the additional label-plus-displacement qualifications that we used before. Clearly, this code is as readable as any that we've used so far. Halfword instructions are powerful and can be very useful and understandable if used properly. These two examples clearly illustrate the difference between muddy and clear programming techniques.

FULLWORD AND HALFWORD LITERALS

Our discussion of character data included a brief discussion of character data literals. Literals may be used wherever an equivalent storage definition (DC instruction) may be used. Literal values do not change and so we cannot use a literal where we may want a value to change. Further, we should always use the LTORG statement to inform the assembler where and when to generate the literals for our program. Typically, the LTORG statement comes just before the END statement or just after the program code to exit from our program (just before our data areas).

Fullword and halfword literals may be used within the fullword or halfword RX instructions when appropriate. To code a fullword literal, you must use the equals sign and then define a fullword field with a value. For example, to add 3 to the contents of register 6, we code the instruction as illustrated in Fig. 5.41. We could use the halfword instruction AH and its equivalent literal to perform the same operation as shown in Fig. 5.42.

```
         A       R6,=F'3'
```

Figure 5.41 Using fullword literals.

```
         AH      R6,=H'3'
```

Figure 5.42 Example of coding and using halfword literals.

Since the value of 3 easily fits into a halfword of storage and since a halfword occupies less storage than a fullword, it might be better to use the second instruction (Fig. 5.42) over the first (Fig. 5.41), although one could argue either way.

To subtract 5 from the contents of register 9, we could use the subtract instruction to subtract 5, or use the add instruction to add negative 5. Several techniques are given in Fig. 5.43.

```
S         R9,=F'5'
SH        R9,=H'5'
A         R9,=F'-5'
AH        R9,=H'-5'
```

Figure 5.43 Decreasing the contents of a register by a value of 5.

The MVC instruction can process any type of data as well as character information. Therefore, suppose that we have fields STUFF and STUHH that are defined as a fullword and halfword, respectively. To set each of these fields to the value 0, we could code the instructions given in Fig. 5.44.

```
MVC       STUFF(4),=F'0'
MVC       STUHH(2),=H'0'
```

Figure 5.44 Setting a fullword and a halfword field to zero.

Clearly, the literals define appropriate fields by which the MVC instructions can set their respective fields to zero. On the other hand, are two separate literal definitions necessary? Isn't the halfword value of zero the same as the fullword value of zero? Let's redo the code in Fig. 5.44 by using just the literal F'0' for both operations as shown in Fig. 5.45.

```
MVC       STUFF(4),=F'0'
MVC       STUHH(2),=F'0'
```

Figure 5.45 Modified version of the code contained in Fig. 5.44.

The first two bytes of the fullword value zero are exactly the same as the literal **H'0'**. The length qualifier indicates that only two bytes are to be moved and so only one literal needs to be coded on each of these two instructions. I bring up this aspect of programming because it is a technique used by programmers to save storage. Two bytes of storage are saved, but the program readability may be hindered. Someone who reads this program may be confused and may not understand this distinction between fullword and halfword literals. It is not immediately clear that a halfword of storage is being moved in the second MVC instruction, unless you look carefully at the length operand or the definition of STUHH. Although you'll have to decide whether or not you approve of this programming practice and whether or not you take these shortcuts, let me suggest that this code may not be as readable as it could be. The two bytes of storage saved may not be worth the potential readability problem that someone may encounter.

REPORT FORMATTING AND CARRIAGE CONTROLS

One of the most common business printouts is the report. Reports may detail payroll information, stock trends, employee benefit allowances or many other informational items that vary in content. However, the overall format of a report is generally the same. At this point, we can discuss the formatting of reports since we have most of the tools to produce a very simple report. Now that we understand how to perform I/O operations, how to set up input and output structures, define elements, utilize carriage control values, and process some of the different types of data, we can begin to think more seriously of full-fledged processing activities.

The format of a report may vary from company to company, but the basic report contains the following information:

- a title such as a company name
- a subtitle that describes or identifies the report
- the date of the report
- a page number if the report has multiple pages
- an identifier used by a programmer or a user when information or the layout of the report is discussed

The content of the report will, of course, vary with the information to be processed.

The manner in which a report is produced is relatively the same from company to company and from language to language. A program defines the layout of the report and the information to be printed. Through assignment statements and I/O statements, the report is constructed and printed. The first position of each line sent to the printer is the carriage control, which defines the line spacing. The width of the line ranges from a few characters to several hundred, depending on the paper width and the size of the printed letters. Generally, print lines contain 132 characters plus one for carriage control—133 characters in all. At 10 characters per inch (pica type), that yields a line length of just over 13 inches. Printing 86-character lines (85 information characters and 1 carriage control character) provides reports formatted for $8^{1}/_{2}$-inch wide paper.

Vertically, reports are usually 60 to 66 lines per page, depending on the amount of information. Let's look at a typical report shown in Fig. 5.46.

This simple report can be produced with what we learned to this point. By processing two values and by performing the common arithmetic operations on those numbers, we can produce this report. The program contained in the coding example 5.4 processes and produces this report.

Note that this program does not work in ASSIST since we are obtaining the date from the system using SYSDATE.

Most of this program should be clear except for the ORG instruction found just after the definition of the line called TITLE. As you can see, TITLE is defined as a 133-byte line and it is initialized with a report identifier and our title value. Rather than counting 125 positions into the field called TITLE, I've simply used the ORG instruction to inform the assembler to go back into the area called TITLE, at offset 125, and define the field whose value is &SYSDATE. The ORG instruction, after the definition of the &SYSDATE value, returns the assembler to standard processing. The ORG instruction saves counting and can be used to place information within an already defined field. You must remember to return to standard processing by coding the ORG instruction, with no operands, after you have completed your definition.

The ORG instruction alters the location counter on the left side of our printouts. The location counter value is altered so that the current location referenced matches the operand that we code on the ORG instruction. Defining a data field after the ORG specification places the data area into our program at the location specified on the

```
REPORT                     A R I T H M E T I C   P R O C E S S I N G   R E P O R T                              09/05/85
 NAME:  MATH                                  BASIC   MATH   OPERATIONS

----- OPERATION -----     ----- FIRST VALUE -----    ----- SECOND VALUE -----    ---------------- RESULT ---------------
      ADD                         00020                      00008              0000000000000028
      SUBTRACT                    00020                      00008              0000000000000012
      MULTIPLY                    00020                      00008              0000000000000160
      DIVIDE                      00020                      00008              0000000000000002     REMAINDER  0000004
```

Figure 5.46 Sample output from assembler program.

```
PROCESS  CSECT
         STM   R14,R12,12(R13)        SAVE INVOKING REGISTERS
         LR    R12,R15                R12 WILL BE OUR BASE
         USING PROCESS,R12
         LA    R10,SAVEAREA           POINT TO OUR SAVEAREA
         ST    R13,4(R10)             REMEMBER CURRENT R13
         ST    R10,8(R13)             INFORM ABOUT OUR R13
         LR    R13,R10                ESTABLISH NEW R13
*
         OPEN  (DATAIN,INPUT)         OPEN INPUT DATA FILE
         OPEN  (PRNT,OUTPUT)          OPEN PRINT FILE
*
         GET   DATAIN,INPUTREC        GET INPUT RECORD DATA
         PACK  VALUE1(8),NUM1(5)      CONVERT FIRST NUMBER
         PACK  VALUE2(8),NUM2(5)      CONVERT SECOND VALUE
         CVB   R3,VALUE1              CONVERT TO BINARY
         CVB   R4,VALUE2              CONVERT TO BINARY
         STM   R3,R4,VALUES           SAVE THE VALUES
         AR    R3,R4                  COMPUTE THE SUM
         CVD   R3,SUMP                CONVERT TO PACKED
         UNPK  SUM(15),SUMP(8)        CONVERT TO CHARACTER
         OI    SUM+14,X'F0'           FIX RIGHT DIGIT
*
         LM    R3,R4,VALUES           RESTORE VALUES
         SR    R3,R4                  COMPUTE DIFFERENCE
         CVD   R3,DIFFERP             CONVERT TO PACKED
         UNPK  DIFFER(15),DIFFERP(8) CONVERT TO CHARACTER
         OI    DIFFER+14,X'F0'        FIX RIGHTMOST DIGIT
*
         LH    R3,VALUES+2            RESTORE FIRST VALUE
         MH    R3,VALUES+6            TIMES SECOND VALUE
         CVD   R3,PRODUCTP            TO PACKED DECIMAL
         UNPK  PRODUCT(15),PRODUCTP(8)  TO CHARACTER
         OI    PRODUCT+14,X'F0'       FIX RIGHT DIGIT
*
         LM    R3,R4,VALUES           RESTORE THE VALUES
         SR    R2,R2                  SET SIGN FOR DIVIDE
         DR    R2,R4                  PERFORM DIVIDE
         CVD   R2,REMAINP             CONVERT REMAINDER
         UNPK  REMAIN(15),REMAINP(8)   TO CHARACTER FORMAT
         OI    REMAIN+14,X'F0'        FIX RIGHT DIGIT
         CVD   R3,QUOTENTP            QUOTIENT TO PACKED
         UNPK  QUOTIENT(15),QUOTENTP(8) TO CHARACTER FORMAT
         OI    QUOTIENT+14,X'F0'      FIX DIGIT
*
         PUT   PRNT,TITLE             PRINT TITLE LINE
         PUT   PRNT,SUBTITLE          PRINT THE SUBTITLE
         PUT   PRNT,SKIP2             SKIP A FEW LINES
         PUT   PRNT,HEADINGS          PRINT COLUMN HEADINGS
         PUT   PRNT,UNDERLIN          UNDERLINE COLUMNS
*
         MVC   OP1(5),NUM1            MOVE TO PRINT LINE
         MVC   OP2(5),NUM2            MOVE TO PRINT LINE
         MVC   COMMAND(15),=CL15'ADD'
         MVC   RESULT(15),SUM         MOVE RESULT INTO LINE
         PUT   PRNT,PLINE             PRINT THE LINE
*
         MVC   COMMAND(15),=CL15'SUBTRACT'
         MVC   RESULT(15),DIFFER      MOVE RESULT INTO LINE
         PUT   PRNT,PLINE             PRINT THE LINE
*
         MVC   COMMAND(15),=CL15'MULTIPLY'
         MVC   RESULT(15),PRODUCT     MOVE RESULT INTO LINE
         PUT   PRNT,PLINE             PRINT THE LINE
*
         MVC   COMMAND(15),=CL15'DIVIDE'
         MVC   RESULT(15),QUOTIENT  MOVE RESULT INTO LINE
         MVC   RESULT+20(9),=C'REMAINDER'
         MVC   RESULT+31(15),REMAIN
         PUT   PRNT,PLINE             PRINT THE LINE
```

Example 5.4 Coding example for the program to produce the report shown in Fig. 5.46.

```
*
          CLOSE   (DATAIN,,PRNT)          CLOSE ALL FILES
          L       R13,4(R13)              RESTORE R13
          LM      R14,R12,12(R13)         RESTORE ALL REGS
          SR      R15,R15                 SET RETURN CODE = 0
          BCR     B'1111',R14             RETURN CONTROL
*
          LTORG
*
TITLE     DC      CL133'1NAME: MATH                                X
                              A R I T H M E T I C   P R O C X
                  E S S I N G   R E P O R T'
          ORG     TITLE+125
          DC      CL8'&SYSDATE'
          ORG
*
SUBTITLE  DC      CL133'                                          X
                                                BASIC   MATX
                  H   OPERATIONS'
*
SKIP2     DC      CL133'-'
*
HEADINGS  DC      CL133'          ----- OPERATION -----       X
                  ----- FIRST VALUE -----       ----- SECOND VAX
                  LUE -----          --------------- RESULT -X
                  -------------'
UNDERLIN  DC      CL133'+         ______________________       X
                  ___________________________     _____________X
                  ___________       '    ______________________X
                  _________________
*
PLINE     DS      0CL133
CC        DC      C' '
          DC      CL16' '
COMMAND   DC      CL15' '
          DC      CL14' '
OP1       DC      CL5' '
          DC      CL26' '
OP2       DC      CL5' '
          DC      CL17' '
RESULT    DC      CL34' '
*
SAVEAREA  DS      18F
INPUTREC  DS      0CLnnn
NUM1      DS      CL5
NUM2      DS      CL5
          DS      CLnnn
*
VALUE1    DS      D
VALUE2    DS      D
VALUES    DS      2F
*
SUM       DS      CL15
DIFFER    DS      CL15
PRODUCT   DS      CL15
QUOTIENT  DS      CL15
REMAIN    DS      CL15
SUMP      DS      D
DIFFERP   DS      D
PRODUCTP  DS      D
QUOTENTP  DS      D
REMAINP   DS      D
DATAIN    DCB     DSORG=PS,DDNAME=INPUT,MACRF=GM
PRNT      DCB     DSORG=PS,DDNAME=PRINT,MACRF=PM,                X
                  RECFM=FBA,LRECL=133,BLKSIZE=1330
          END     PROCESS
```

Example 5.4 (cont.)

ORG. The location counter is returned to its normal displacement by coding the ORG with no operands. Many consecutive fields may be defined between the bounds of the ORG instruction.

Incidentally, the construction and layout of a report can be greatly simplified through the use of a **printer spacing chart.** This coding form allows you to draw an image of your report and assists in converting your image into the assembly language coding format. In particular, the fields called HEADINGS and UNDERLIN are very difficult to understand and make the report difficult to modify. Rather than defining these lines as shown in Ex. 5.4, I would redefine them in a format similar to the print line called PLINE. Both formats have been used to illustrate programming techniques that yield code that is easy and not so easy to modify.

When this program is processed by the assembler, a very large listing is obtained since we've used many macro instructions throughout. We can reduce the size of our printout by telling the assembler *not* to show the full expansion of all macros. Suppressing macro expansion is easily coded by using the instruction given in Fig. 5.47 at the beginning of your program.

```
PRINT   NOGEN
```

Figure 5.47 Suppressing macro expansion.

This instruction causes the program listing shown in Fig. 5.48. Look closely at the use of line comments, TITLE statement, line spacing, and block commenting. Line comments and full block comments highlight sections of code within the program.

ASSIST ARITHMETIC CONVERSION INSTRUCTIONS—XDECI AND XDECO

Since SYSDATE is used in the program shown in Fig. 5.48, ASSIST cannot format and print this report. Removing SYSDATE allows us to do so, however. At this time we'll discuss some capabilities of ASSIST that are not found in standard assembly language. They are very powerful and are some of the most useful features within the ASSIST package.

The **XDECI (decimal input)** instruction converts character input data to binary and the **XDECO (decimal output)** instruction converts binary data to character for printing.

XDECO is the easiest to use, so let's look at it first. A number in a register may be converted into character printable format using the XDECO instruction. It converts a number in a register into a *12-byte* character value. Earlier we dealt with 15-digit numbers, but if you recall, registers can only hold numbers up to 10 digits long. Hence, a 12-byte area is sufficient to hold our results.

XDECO converts both positive and negative values into character format. The number +23 is converted to ƀƀƀƀƀƀƀƀƀƀ23 and the number −23 is converted to ƀƀƀƀƀƀƀƀƀ−23. We avoided negative numbers earlier since they are difficult to format without the XDECO command. We will discuss negative numbers in Chapter 7.

XDECO has two operands, the first being a register and the second a D(X,B) address. The value in the register is converted and placed into the area specified by the address, but the value in the register is not changed. If register 3's value is to be converted and placed into the area called TOTAL, which is 12 bytes long, we'd issue the instruction given in Fig. 5.49.

```
  LOC  OBJECT CODE    ADDR1 ADDR2  STMT   SOURCE STATEMENT                                          ASM H V 02 10.34 09/05/85

                              00000     2 R0         EQU   0
                              00001     3 R1         EQU   1
                              00002     4 R2         EQU   2
                              00003     5 R3         EQU   3
                              00004     6 R4         EQU   4
                              00005     7 R5         EQU   5
                              00006     8 R6         EQU   6
                              00007     9 R7         EQU   7
                              00008    10 R8         EQU   8
                              00009    11 R9         EQU   9
                              0000A    12 R10        EQU   10
                              0000B    13 R11        EQU   11
                              0000C    14 R12        EQU   12
                              0000D    15 R13        EQU   13
                              0000E    16 R14        EQU   14
                              0000F    17 R15        EQU   15
                                       18            PRINT NOGEN
                                       19 ***********************************************************************
                                       20 *    THIS PROGRAM WILL COMPUTE THE SUM, DIFFERENCE, PRODUCT, AND       *
                                       21 *    QUOTIENT OF TWO INPUT VALUES.  RESULTS WILL BE PRINTED IN A       *
                                       22 *    NICE REPORT FORMAT.  THE REMAINDER OF THE DIVISION WILL ALSO      *
                                       23 *    BE PRINTED.                                                       *
                                       24 ***********************************************************************
000000                                 25 PROCESS    CSECT
000000 90EC D00C              0000C    26            STM   R14,R12,12(13)        SAVE CALLER'S REGISTERS
000004 18CF                            27            LR    R12,R15               R12 WILL BE OUR BASE REG
                              00000    28            USING PROCESS,R12           TELL THE ASSEMBLER ABOUT R12
000006 41A0 C4F4              004F4    29            LA    R10,SAVEAREA          POINT TO REGISTER SAVE AREA
00000A 50AD 0008              00008    30            ST    R10,8(R13)            TELL CALLER ABOUT OUR SAVEAREA
00000E 50DA 0004              00004    31            ST    R13,4(R10)            REMEMBER CALLER'S SAVEAREA ADDR.
000012 18DA                            32            LR    R13,R10               ESTABLISH NEW SAVE AREA
                                       33 ***********************************************************************
                                       34 *  OPEN THE INPUT AND OUTPUT FILES AND PREPARE TO PROCESS.             *
                                       35 ***********************************************************************
                                       36            OPEN  (DATAIN,INPUT)        OPEN OUR INPUT FILE
                                       42            OPEN  (PRNT,OUTPUT)         OPEN OUR REPORT FILE
                                       48 ***********************************************************************
                                       49 *  OBTAIN THE INPUT VALUES FROM OUR FILE AND CONVERT THEM INTO         *
                                       50 *  BINARY FORMAT FOR PROCESSING.                                       *
                                       51 ***********************************************************************
                                       52            GET   DATAIN,INPUTREC       GET OUR RECORD
000038 F274 C590 C53C 00590 0053C      57            PACK  VALUE1(8),NUM1(5)     CONVERT FIRST NUMBER
00003E F274 C598 C541 00598 00541      58            PACK  VALUE2(8),NUM2(5)     CONVERT SECOND NUMBER
000044 4F30 C590              00590    59            CVB   R3,VALUE1             FINISH THE CONVERSION TO BINARY
000048 4F40 C598              00598    60            CVB   R4,VALUE2             ..SAME FOR SECOND NUMBER
00004C 9034 C5A0              005A0    61            STM   R3,R4,VALUES          SAVE VALUES FOR LATER USAGE
```



```
  LOC  OBJECT CODE    ADDR1 ADDR2  STMT   SOURCE STATEMENT                                          ASM H V 02 10.34 09/05/85

                                       63 ***********************************************************************
                                       64 *        COMPUTE THE SUM AND CONVERT IT FOR OUTPUT PRINTING.         *
                                       65 ***********************************************************************
000050 1A34                            66            AR    R3,R4                 COMPUTE THE SUM
000052 4E30 C5F8              005F8    67            CVD   R3,SUMP               CONVERT TO PACKED
000056 F3E7 C5A8 C5F8 005A8 005F8      68            UNPK  SUM(15),SUMP(8)       CONVERT TO CHARACTER FORMAT
00005C 96F0 C5B6        005B6          69            OI    SUM+14,X'F0'          FIX RIGHT MOST DIGIT
                                       70 ***********************************************************************
                                       71 *        COMPUTE THE DIFFERENCE BETWEEN THE NUMBERS AND PREPARE      *
                                       72 *        TO BE PRINTED.                                              *
                                       73 ***********************************************************************
000060 9834 C5A0              005A0    74            LM    R3,R4,VALUES          RESTORE BINARY VALUES IN REGS.
000064 1B34                            75            SR    R3,R4                 COMPUTE DIFFERENCE
000066 4E30 C600              00600    76            CVD   R3,DIFFERP            CONVERT TO PACKED DECIMAL
00006A F3E7 C5B7 C600 005B7 00600      77            UNPK  DIFFER(15),DIFFERP(8) CONVERT TO CHARACTER
000070 96F0 C5C5        005C5          78            OI    DIFFER+14,X'F0'       FIX REIGHTMOST DIGIT
                                       79 ***********************************************************************
                                       80 *        COMPUTE THE PRODUCT BY USING THE HALFWORD MULTIPLY          *
                                       81 *        INSTRUCTION.  PREPARE FOR PRINTING AFTER MULTIPLYING.       *
                                       82 ***********************************************************************
000074 4830 C5A2              005A2    83            LH    R3,VALUES+2           RESTORE FIRST VALUE
000078 4C30 C5A6              005A6    84            MH    R3,VALUES+6           TIMES SECOND VALUE
00007C 4E30 C608              00608    85            CVD   R3,PRODUCTP           CONVERT TO PACKED DECIMAL
000080 F3E7 C5C6 C608 005C6 00608      86            UNPK  PRODUCT(15),PRODUCTP(8) NOW TO CHARACTER
000086 96F0 C5D4        005D4          87            OI    PRODUCT+14,X'F0'      FIX RIGHTMOST DIGIT
                                       88 ***********************************************************************
                                       89 *      DIVIDE THE TWO NUMBERS AND PREPARE BOTH THE QUOTIENT AND      *
                                       90 *      REMAINDER FOR PRINTING ON OUR REPORT.                         *
                                       91 ***********************************************************************
00008A 9834 C5A0              005A0    92            LM    R3,R4,VALUES          RESTORE THE VALUES
00008E 1B22                            93            SR    R2,R2                 SET THE SIGN FOR DIVIDE
000090 1D24                            94            DR    R2,R4                 PERFORM THE DIVISION
000092 4E20 C618              00618    95            CVD   R2,REMAINP            CONVERT REMAINDER TO PACKED
000096 F3E7 C5E4 C618 005E4 00618      96            UNPK  REMAIN(15),REMAINP(8) NOW TO CHARACTER
00009C 96F0 C5F2        005F2          97            OI    REMAIN+14,X'F0'       FIX RIGHTMOST REMAINDER DIGIT
0000A0 4E30 C610              00610    98            CVD   R3,QUOTENTP           QUOTIENT TO PACKED
0000A4 F3E7 C5D5 C610 005D5 00610      99            UNPK  QUOTIENT(15),QUOTENTP(8) CONVERT TO CHARACTER
0000AA 96F0 C5E3        005E3         100            OI    QUOTIENT+14,X'F0'     FIX RIGHTMOST QUOTIENT DIGIT
```

Figure 5.48 The complete program to produce the report shown in Fig. 5.46.

```
  LOC  OBJECT CODE    ADDR1 ADDR2  STMT   SOURCE STATEMENT                                              ASM H V 02 10.34 09/05/85

                                    102 **********************************************************************   00950
                                    103 *     PRINT THE TITLE LINES ON THE OUTPUT PAGE AND SET UP THE REPORT  *   00960
                                    104 *     FOR OUR OUTPUT INFORMATION.                                     *   00970
                                    105 **********************************************************************   00980
                                    106          PUT   PRNT,TITLE               PRINT TITLE LINE                 00990
                                    111          PUT   PRNT,SUBTITLE            PRINT THE SUBTITLE               01000
                                    116          PUT   PRNT,SKIP2               SKIP A FEW LINES                 01010
                                    121          PUT   PRNT,HEADINGS            PRINT COLUMN HEADINGS            01020
                                    126          PUT   PRNT,UNDERLIN            UNDERLINE COLUMN HEADINGS        01030
                                    131 **********************************************************************   01040
                                    132 *     MOVE THE INPUT VALUES INTO THE OUTPUT LINE AND PRINT THE        *   01050
                                    133 *     INFORMATION FOR THE ADD OPERATION.                              *   01060
                                    134 **********************************************************************   01070
0000F4 D204 C497 C53C 00497 0053C   135          MVC   OP1(5),NUM1              MOVE FIRST NUMBER TO PRINT LINE  01080
0000FA D204 C4B4 C541 004B4 00541   136          MVC   OP2(5),NUM2              MOVE SECOND NUMBER SIMILARLY     01090
000100 D20E C475 C190 00475 00190   137          MVC   COMMAND(15),=CL15'ADD'   FIRST COMMAND IS TO ADD          01100
000106 D20E C4C7 C5A8 004C7 005A8   138          MVC   RESULT(15),SUM           MOVE SUM INTO PRINT LINE         01110
                                    139          PUT   PRNT,PLINE               PRINT SUM VALUE                  01120
                                    144 **********************************************************************   01130
                                    145 *     PRINT THE RESULTS OF THE SUBTRACT.                              *   01140
                                    146 **********************************************************************   01150
00011A D20E C475 C19F 00475 0019F   147          MVC   COMMAND(15),=CL15'SUBTRACT'  COMMAND IS NOW SUBTRACT      01160
000120 D20E C4C7 C5B7 004C7 005B7   148          MVC   RESULT(15),DIFFER        MOVE DIFFERENCE TO PRINT LINE    01170
                                    149          PUT   PRNT,PLINE               PRINT SUM VALUE                  01180
                                    154 **********************************************************************   01190
                                    155 *     PRINT THE RESULTS OF THE MULTIPLICATION.                        *   01200
                                    156 **********************************************************************   01210
000134 D20E C475 C1AE 00475 001AE   157          MVC   COMMAND(15),=CL15'MULTIPLY'  MOVE IN MULTIPLY COMMAND     01220
00013A D20E C4C7 C5C6 004C7 005C6   158          MVC   RESULT(15),PRODUCT       MOVE PRODUCT INTO PRINT LINE     01230
                                    159          PUT   PRNT,PLINE               PRINT SUM VALUE                  01240
                                    164 **********************************************************************   01250
                                    165 *     PRINT THE QUOTIENT AND REMAINDER FROM THE DIVISION.             *   01260
                                    166 **********************************************************************   01270
00014E D20E C475 C1BD 00475 001BD   167          MVC   COMMAND(15),=CL15'DIVIDE'    MOVE IN DIVIDE COMMAND       01280
000154 D20E C4C7 C5D5 004C7 005D5   168          MVC   RESULT(15),QUOTIENT      MOVE QUOTIENT INTO PRINT LINE    01290
00015A D208 C4DB C1CC 004DB 001CC   169          MVC   RESULT+20(9),=C'REMAINDER'   MOVE IN HEADER FOR REMAIN.   01300
000160 D206 C4E6 C5EC 004E6 005EC   170          MVC   RESULT+31(7),REMAIN+8        NOW MOVE IN REMAINDER        01310
                                    171          PUT   PRNT,PLINE               PRINT QUOTIENT/REMAINDER VALUES  01320
                                    176 **********************************************************************   01330
                                    177 *      WE'RE ALL DONE.  CLOSE THE FILES, RESTORE THE REGISTERS,       *   01340
                                    178 *      SET OUR RETURN CODE AND THEN EXIT.                             *   01350
                                    179 **********************************************************************   01360
                                    180          CLOSE (DATAIN,,PRNT)           CLOSE ALL FILES                  01370
000182 58DD 0004            00004   188          L     R13,4(R13)               RESTORE ORIGINAL R13 VALUE       01380
000186 98EC D00C            0000C   189          LM    R14,R12,12(R13)          RESTORE ALL REGS                 01390
00018A 1BFF                         190          SR    R15,R15                  SET RETURN CODE TO ZERO          01400
00018C 07FE                         191          BCR   B'1111',R14              RETURN CONTROL TO CALLER         01410
                                    192 *                                                                         01420
000190                              193          LTORG                                                            01430
000190 C1C4C44040404040             194                =CL15'ADD'
00019F E2E4C2E3D9C1C3E3             195                =CL15'SUBTRACT'
0001AE D4E4D3E3C9D7D3E8             196                =CL15'MULTIPLY'
0001BD C4C9E5C9C4C54040             197                =CL15'DIVIDE'
0001CC D9C5D4C1C9D5C4C5             198                =C'REMAINDER'
```

Figure 5.48 (cont.)

```
LOC    OBJECT CODE       ADDR1 ADDR2  STMT   SOURCE STATEMENT                                      ASM H V 02 10.34 09/05/85
                                       200 ******************************************************************
                                       201 *                     DATA AND STORAGE AREA DEFINITIONS                  *
                                       202 ******************************************************************
0001D5 F1D9C5D7D6D9E340                203 TITLE    DC    CL133'1REPORT                                       A R I TX
0001DD 4040404040404040                               H M E T I C    P R O C E S S I N G    R E P O R T'
00025A                   00252         204          ORG   TITLE+125
                                       205          DC    CL8'&SYSDATE'
00025A                   0025A         206          ORG
00025A 40400D5C1D4C57A40               207 SUBTITLE DC    CL133'  NAME:  MATH                                          X
000262 40D4C1E3C8404040                                       BASIC   MATH   OPERATIONS'
0002DF 6040404040404040                208 SKIP2    DC    CL133'-'
000364 4060606060604006                209 HEADINGS DC    CL133' ----- OPERATION -----                  ----- FIRST VALUE -X
00036C D7C5D9C1E3C9D6D5                                ----       ----- SECOND VALUE -----          --------------- RX
000374 4060606060604040                               ESULT ---------------'
0003E9 4E6D6D6D6D6D6D6D                210 UNDERLIN DC    CL133'+________________________          ________________________X
0003F1 6D6D6D6D6D6D6D6D                               ____   _____________________            ______________________X
0003F9 6D6D6D6D6D6D4040                               ______________________________'
                                       211 *
00046E                                 212 PLINE    DS    OCL133
00046E 40                              213 CC       DC    C' '
00046F 404040404040                    214          DC    CL6' '
000475 4040404040404040                215 COMMAND  DC    CL15' '
000484 4040404040404040                216          DC    CL19' '
000497 4040404040                      217 OP1      DC    CL5' '
00049C 4040404040404040                218          DC    CL24' '
0004B4 4040404040                      219 OP2      DC    CL5' '
0004B9 4040404040404040                220          DC    CL14' '
0004C7 4040404040404040                221 RESULT   DC    CL44' '
                                       222 *
0004F4                                 223 SAVEAREA DS    18F                           REGISTER SAVE AREA
00053C                                 224 INPUTREC DS    OCL80                         ****
00053C                                 225 NUM1     DS    CL5                              **** INPUT RECORD DESCRIPTION
000541                                 226 NUM2     DS    CL5                              *
000546                                 227          DS    CL70                          ****
000590                                 228 VALUE1   DS    D
000598                                 229 VALUE2   DS    D
0005A0                                 230 VALUES   DS    2F                            HOLDING AREA FOR INPUT VALUES
0005A8                                 231 SUM      DS    CL15                          ****
0005B7                                 232 DIFFER   DS    CL15                             *
0005C6                                 233 PRODUCT  DS    CL15                             **** OUTPUT RESULT AREAS
0005D5                                 234 QUOTIENT DS    CL15                             *
0005E4                                 235 REMAIN   DS    CL15                          ****
0005F8                                 236 SUMP     DS    D                             ****
000600                                 237 DIFFERP  DS    D                                *
000608                                 238 PRODUCTP DS    D                                **** CONVERSION AREAS
000610                                 239 QUOTENTP DS    D                                *
000618                                 240 REMAINP  DS    D                             ****
                                       241 DATAIN   DCB   DSORG=PS,DDNAME=INPUT,MACRF=GM
                                       295 PRNT     DCB   DSORG=PS,DDNAME=PRINT,MACRF=PM,RECFM=FA,LRECL=133,       X
                                                          BLKSIZE=1330
000000                                 349          END   PROCESS
```

Figure 5.48 (cont.)

```
XDECO  R3,TOTAL
```

Figure 5.49 Converting a binary value to character format using XDECO.

The value in TOTAL is ready to be printed and its rightmost byte does not have to be fixed by the OI instruction. *XDECO formats the number completely*—no other processing is required. Again, if our numbers are of a certain size, the MVC instruction can extract only the number of digits expected from the converted data area. For example, if TOTAL has a value less than 1000, its last three digits can be extracted and placed into the field called OUTPUTVL as shown in Fig. 5.50. A displacement of nine bytes into the 12-byte TOTAL area allows us to reference the last three bytes of TOTAL.

```
MVC     OUTPUTVL(3),TOTAL+9
```

Figure 5.50 Extracting only a portion of a converted result using MVC.

XDECI, which is used for input conversion under ASSIST, is a very powerful but dangerous instruction. XDECI handles both negative and positive numbers as long as they are separated by either a blank column or a comma on the input record. For example, previously we used a data structure to define two values that were to come into our program from an 80-byte line image. These values were five bytes long, right justified, and completely filled fields. Figure 5.51 shows this earlier definition.

```
INPUTVAL  DS    0CL80
VALUE1    DS    CL5
VALUE2    DS    CL5
          DS    CL70
```

Figure 5.51 Defining two adjacent input numeric fields using a structure.

Assume that VALUE1 is equal to C'00020' and VALUE2 is C'00008'. When discussing the processing of these fields, we used the PACK and CVB instructions to convert them from character to binary format. Although XDECI does convert fields in the same manner, it *cannot* process VALUE1 and VALUE2 since they are adjacent and are not separated by a blank or a comma. If XDECI were used, ASSIST would think that there was only one field on this input record whose value was C'0002000008' or 2,000,008.

In general, we do not use a data structure for describing input data when using XDECI since XDECI has the added ability to scan for input data. XDECI scans our input record area, finds the input value, converts it to binary, and places it into our desired register. The section of code in Fig. 5.52 obtains an 80-byte input record and extracts the first numeric field from that record, placing that value into register 4.

```
XREAD    INPUTREC,80
XDECI    R4,INPUTREC
```

Figure 5.52 Obtaining and converting an input numeric value in ASSIST.

After the XDECI instruction is issued, register *1* is set to an address within the field called INPUTREC. The location addressed by register 1 is illustrated in Fig. 5.53.

If our 80-byte input record contains another value, we can issue the instruction

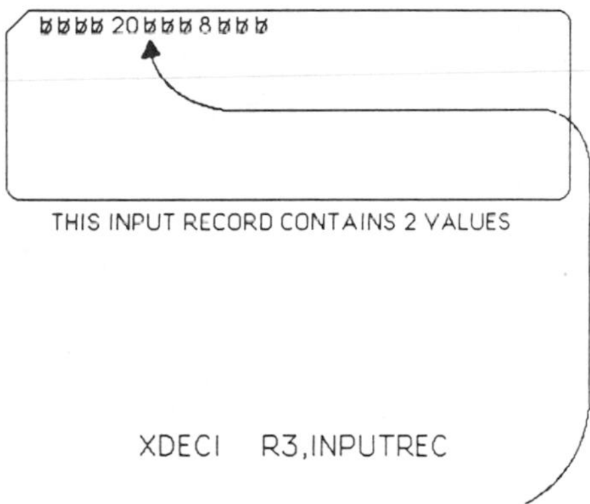

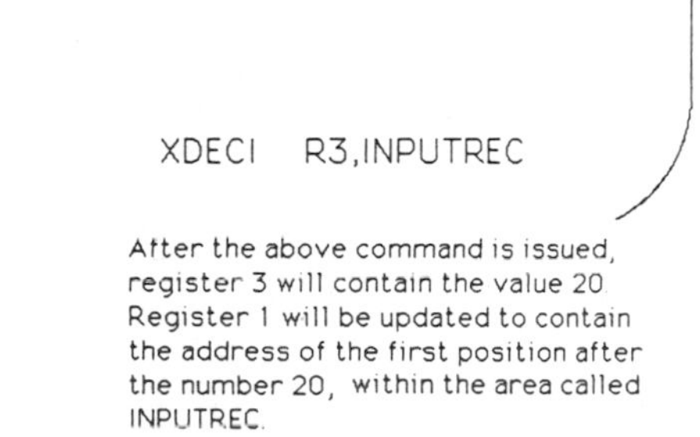

Figure 5.53 The address in register 1 after issuing XDECI.

given in Fig. 5.54 to cause ASSIST to scan our input record, starting at the location addressed by register 1.

```
XDECI    R6,0(R1)
```

Figure 5.54 Extracting subsequent values from a single data card using XDECI.

The next value found is converted and placed into register 6 as specified in this instruction. If our input record contained only one value, the XDECI instruction would continue to scan whatever information was located in memory after our record definition. Eventually, some number in memory would be found and converted or our program would abend with a protection exception when XDECI attempted to scan past the boundaries of our program memory. If you use XDECI, be sure that all input records contain exactly the proper number of values to be extracted. XDECI expects to find a value and continues scanning until it finds something, valid or invalid. This is a negative feature of XDECI.

If we omit the system date from our report, the program to compute the sum, difference, product, and quotient/remainder of two input values may be written in ASSIST as shown in the coding example 5.5.

```
PROCESS  CSECT
         STM    R14,R12,12(R13)       SAVE INVOKING REGISTERS
         LR     R12,R15               R12 WILL BE OUR BASE
         USING  PROCESS,R12
         LA     R10,SAVEAREA          POINT TO OUR SAVEAREA
         ST     R13,4(R10)            REMEMBER CURRENT R13
         ST     R10,8(R13)            INFORM ABOUT OUR R13
         LR     R13,R10               ESTABLISH NEW R13
*
         XREAD  INPUTREC,80           GET INPUT RECORD DATA
         XDECI  R3,INPUTREC           CONVERT TO BINARY
         XDECI  R4,0(R1)              CONVERT TO BINARY
         XDECO  R3,NUM1               SAVE FIRST INPUT NUM
         XDECO  R4,NUM2               SAVE SECOND INPUT NUM
*
         STM    R3,R4,VALUES          SAVE THE VALUES
         AR     R3,R4                 COMPUTE THE SUM
         XDECO  R3,SUM                CONVERT TO PRINTABLE
*
         LM     R3,R4,VALUES          RESTORE VALUES
         SR     R3,R4                 COMPUTE DIFFERENCE
         XDECO  R3,DIFFER             CONVERT TO CHARACTER
*
         LH     R3,VALUES+2           RESTORE FIRST VALUE
         MH     R3,VALUES+6           TIMES SECOND VALUE
         XDECO  R3,PRODUCT            TO CHARACTER
*
         LM     R3,R4,VALUES          RESTORE THE VALUES
         SR     R2,R2                 SET SIGN FOR DIVIDE
         DR     R2,R4                 PERFORM DIVIDE
         XDECO  R2,REMAIN             CONVERT REMAINDER
         XDECO  R3,QUOTIENT           QUOTIENT TO CHARACTER
*
         XPRNT  TITLE,133             PRINT TITLE LINE
         XPRNT  SUBTITLE,133          PRINT THE SUBTITLE
         XPRNT  SKIP2,133             SKIP A FEW LINES
         XPRNT  HEADINGS,133          PRINT COLUMN HEADINGS
         XPRNT  UNDERLIN,133          UNDERLINE COLUMNS
```

Example 5.5 Coding example for the ASSIST program to compute arithmetic values.

```
*
         MVC    OP1(5),NUM1+7          MOVE TO PRINT LINE
         MVC    OP2(5),NUM2+7          MOVE TO PRINT LINE
         MVC    COMMAND(15),=CL15'ADD'
         MVC    RESULT(12),SUM         MOVE RESULT INTO LINE
         XPRNT  PLINE,133              PRINT THE LINE
*
         MVC    COMMAND(15),=CL15'SUBTRACT'
         MVC    RESULT(12),DIFFER      MOVE RESULT INTO LINE
         XPRNT  PLINE,133              PRINT THE LINE
*
         MVC    COMMAND(15),=CL15'MULTIPLY'
         MVC    RESULT(12),PRODUCT     MOVE RESULT INTO LINE
         XPRNT  PLINE,133              PRINT THE LINE
*
         MVC    COMMAND(15),=CL15'DIVIDE'
         MVC    RESULT(12),QUOTIENT    MOVE RESULT INTO LINE
         MVC    RESULT+15(9),=C'REMAINDER'
         MVC    RESULT+26(12),REMAIN
         XPRNT  PLINE,133              PRINT THE LINE
*
         L      R13,4(R13)             RESTORE R13
         LM     R14,R12,12(R13)        RESTORE ALL REGS
         SR     R15,R15                SET RETURN CODE = 0
         BCR    B'1111',R14            RETURN CONTROL
*
         LTORG
*
TITLE    DC     CL133'1NAME: MATH                                     X
                           A R I T H M E T I C   P R O C X
               E S S I N G   R E P O R T'
*
SUBTITLE DC     CL133'                                                X
                                             BASIC   MATX
               H   OPERATIONS'
*
SKIP2    DC     CL133'-'
*
HEADINGS DC     CL133'          ----- OPERATION -----                X
               ----- FIRST VALUE -----      ----- SECOND VAX
               LUE -----          --------------- RESULT -X
               -------------'
UNDERLIN DC     CL133'+          _____________________               X
               _________________________    ________________X
               __________              ,   _____________________X
               _______________
*
PLINE    DS     0CL133
CC       DC     C' '
         DC     CL16' '
COMMAND  DC     CL15' '
         DC     CL14' '
OP1      DC     CL5' '
         DC     CL26' '
OP2      DC     CL5' '
         DC     CL17' '
RESULT   DC     CL34' '

*
SAVEAREA DS     18F
INPUTREC DS     CL80
*
NUM1     DS     CL12
NUM2     DS     CL12
*
VALUES   DS     2F
*
SUM      DS     CL12
DIFFER   DS     CL12
PRODUCT  DS     CL12
QUOTIENT DS     CL12
REMAIN   DS     CL12
         END    PROCESS
```

Example 5.5 (cont.)

You can see the power behind the ASSIST instructions. XDECI scans the INPUTREC field and extracts the first value, placing it into register 3. XDECI is called a second time, using the address in register 1, to obtain the second value from the input record area. All conversions using the PACK, CVB, CVD, UNPK, and OI instructions are eliminated with the use of XDECI and XDECO. ASSIST provides very powerful features to the student assembly language programmer.

Did it occur to you that ASSIST was using one of the special registers? Register 1 is a special register that our program should not use. However, ASSIST is using this register to support the execution of our program rather than our program using it for processing. The use of register 1 by XDECI must be noted because if you are planning to use it and if you use the XDECI instruction, you'll have a problem. As before, registers 2 through 12 are the only registers that our program should use for processing and registers 13, 14, 15, 0, and 1 are to be used only by the supporting software (operating system, access method, ASSIST).

This chapter has moved us even closer to performing complete assembly language data processing. After the next few chapters, we should be able to implement almost any type of problem in assembly language or under ASSIST. Processing character data and binary data and producing readable reports constitute a significant portion of any programmer's processing. More importantly, our complete understanding of the linkage conventions allows us to move in the direction of more modular systems to solve our problems. We will continue to build on our foundations as we discuss techniques for improving the performance and readability of our programs.

STUDY QUESTIONS

1. The _______ instruction may be used to copy the contents of a register into storage.
2. The literal _______ defines a fullword of storage and initializes that fullword to the value −1.
3. The process for coupling register save areas together is more commonly called _______.
4. The special register used by ASSIST to convert input character data into binary format is _______.
5. The _______ instruction alters the program location counter to allow storage area definitions within an already defined storage area.
6. R15 contains the _______ _______ _______ of our program when our program gets control and informs the calling program of our success or failure through a value called the _______ _______.
7. The _______ assembly language instruction informs the assembler which register will be our base register.
8. Macro expansion may be suppressed by coding the _______ _______ statement earlier in the program.
9. Register _______ contains the return address into the invoking program, where control is given following the execution of our program.
10. The first fullword of the 18-fullword-register save area is _______ or _______ _______.

11. Program A calls program B. The program responsible for establishing and linking the two programs through the linkage conventions is program _______.
12. Halfword instructions may reference memory areas because the second operand is a _______ address, which may also be coded as a _______.
13. After a binary value is converted to packed decimal and then unpacked, the resulting data is represented in _______ _______ format.
14. To fix the zone portion of the rightmost byte of an unpacked field, the _______ instruction changes the zone from its current _______ value to a zone of _______.
15. The RECFM DCB operand indicates that the first position of each line is to be treated as the carriage control if the RECFM value contains the letter _______, which stands for _______ carriage control.
16. When a division operation is to be performed, the even register within the even/odd pair must have the same sign as _____________.
17. The even register of an even/odd pair may not be used during _______, but may be used when performing _______.
18. Typical report output lines are _______ or _______ bytes in length, with the first character of each line being used for the carriage control.
19. If not used properly, halfword instructions may hinder program readability since _______ may have to be used to properly address data fields.
20. ASSIST supports many of the assembly language features that we've discussed except for _______.
21. Write a section of code which will obtain an input record containing three integers. Compute the average of the numbers and store the result into the field labeled AVERAGE.
22. Code the instructions which will center the company title on an 8.5-inch line of output. The company name is ACME COMPUTER CORPORATION.
23. Write instructions to do the following.
    (a) Reactivate macro expansion during assembly.
    (b) Convert the halfword value in R5 to printable format, placing the result in the 15-byte area labeled RUNSUM.
    (c) Set the return code value to 16.
    (d) Multiply the contents of R5 by 3.1416, truncating all fractional components following the operation.
    (e) Establish R15 as the base register in an ASSIST program.
24. Register 5 contains a positive number that represents the amount of cents from a purchase. Convert the value in R5 to printable format placing a decimal point between the dollars and cents portions of the number. Your result should be in the 10-byte field called CASH.

25. Find the error(s) in the following code segment.

```
MAINPGM  CSECT
         STM    R12,R14,12(R13)     SAVE THE REGISTERS
         LA     R11,R15             COPY THE E.P.A.
         USING  MAINPGM,R11         ESTABLISH R11 AS THE BASE REG.
         LA     R11,SAVEAREA        ADDRESS OUR REGISTER SAVE AREA
         ST     R13,8(R11)          SAVE CURRENT R13 ADDRESS
         ST     R11,4(R13)          CHAIN BACKWARD
         LR     R13,R11             ESTABLISH A NEW SAVE AREA
```

PROGRAMMING PROBLEMS

1. Input three values. Compute the sum, product, and average of the numbers. Print each of the numbers and your results. Use output labels to identify each of the output values.
2. Input the length, width, and height of a room (in feet). Compute the number of square yards required to carpet the room, and compute the number of cubic feet of air to be cooled by air conditioning to keep the room at a comfortable temperature.
3. If carpeting costs $9 per square yard and air conditioning $2 per cubic foot, how much does it cost to carpet and air condition the room as processed in Programming Problem 2? Write a program to perform the processing based on this modification.
4. Input the number of miles driven and the number of gallons of gasoline required to go that distance. To the nearest mile, compute the average number of miles per gallon obtained by the vehicle used for the trip.
5. Modify Programming Problem 4 from Chapter 4. Compute the average selling price for each of the five vehicles on the car lot and compute the total retail value of Mr. Smith's inventory. Include these items on your report.
6. Input a number called N. Compute the sum of all integers between 1 and including the number. For example, if the input number is 5, then you'll compute the sum of 1 + 2 + 3 + 4 + 5 and print this result. Hint: use the formula (N*(N+1))/2 to get your result.
7. Input two values. The first value is the interest rate and the second is the amount invested. Ten percent interest is expressed as the value 10 and $100.50 is expressed as 10050 cents. Compute the value of the investment in one year if simple interest is used. Output your results.
8. Input the weight of a package in ounces. Compute the cost of mailing the package if the cost is 10¢ per ounce. Output your results in dollars and cents. Hint: see problem 24.
9. A fence is to be constructed around a lot. Given the dimensions of the lot in terms of feet, compute the; number of boards needed, number of fence posts needed, number of support beams required, and number of pounds of nails required. Assume that the fence is built in 8-foot sections with each section requiring 25 boards, 1 post, 3 beams, and 1 pound of nails.
10. Redo any of the above problems but construct the program using an infinite loop implementation similar to problem 5 in Chapter 4. Again, this logic will result in abnormal termination of your program but your results will be printed before termination occurs.

Controlling Program Flow: Looping, Comparisons, and Branching

6

As we know, the three basic logical constructs that are needed to develop an application program are sequence, decision, and iteration. In the previous chapters, we discussed sequential file processing and sequential instruction execution. We noted that instructions and data are processed one after the other until our program ends normally, abends, or is terminated by the system for some reason. Sequential instruction processing is important, but it does not give us enough tools to develop more sophisticated applications. In this chapter, we will round out our study of the logical constructs by learning how to use branching, decisions, and looping within our application programs to control processing.

OVERVIEW OF PROGRAM CONTROL

The focal point for program control within any application program is within the PSW (program status word). Specifically, bits 34 and 35 are dedicated to the **condition code** field, which can have a value of 0, 1, 2, or 3 (00, 01, 10, or 11, respectively). As we process, some instructions may change the value of the condition code to one of its possible values and other machine instructions may not change the condition code value. Figure 6.1 illustrates some of these instructions. After the instruction name, there is a lower case letter **c, p,** or both **(c,p).** The letter **c** indicates that the instruction *changes* the value of the condition code in the PSW. Instructions with the letter **p** can only be used by the operating system. Instructions labeled **(c,p)** can only be used by the operating system even though they also change the value of the condition code. Since we are limited to using nonprivileged instructions (instructions without the **p** designation), we will focus our attention on the instructions that change the condition code value.

The condition code is set depending on the outcome of the instruction. For example, an AR (add register) instruction sets the condition code to 0 (B'00') if the result is equal to zero, to 1 (B'01') if the result is less than zero, to 2 (B'10') if the result is greater than zero, and to 3 (B'11') if an overflow occurs. For each instruction that sets the condition code, we can refer to the IBM manual to obtain a list of all instruction types and how they affect the condition code value. In Fig. 6.2, the add instructions A, AR, and AH, set the condition code as stated above. Each of the four columns represents a possible condition code setting.

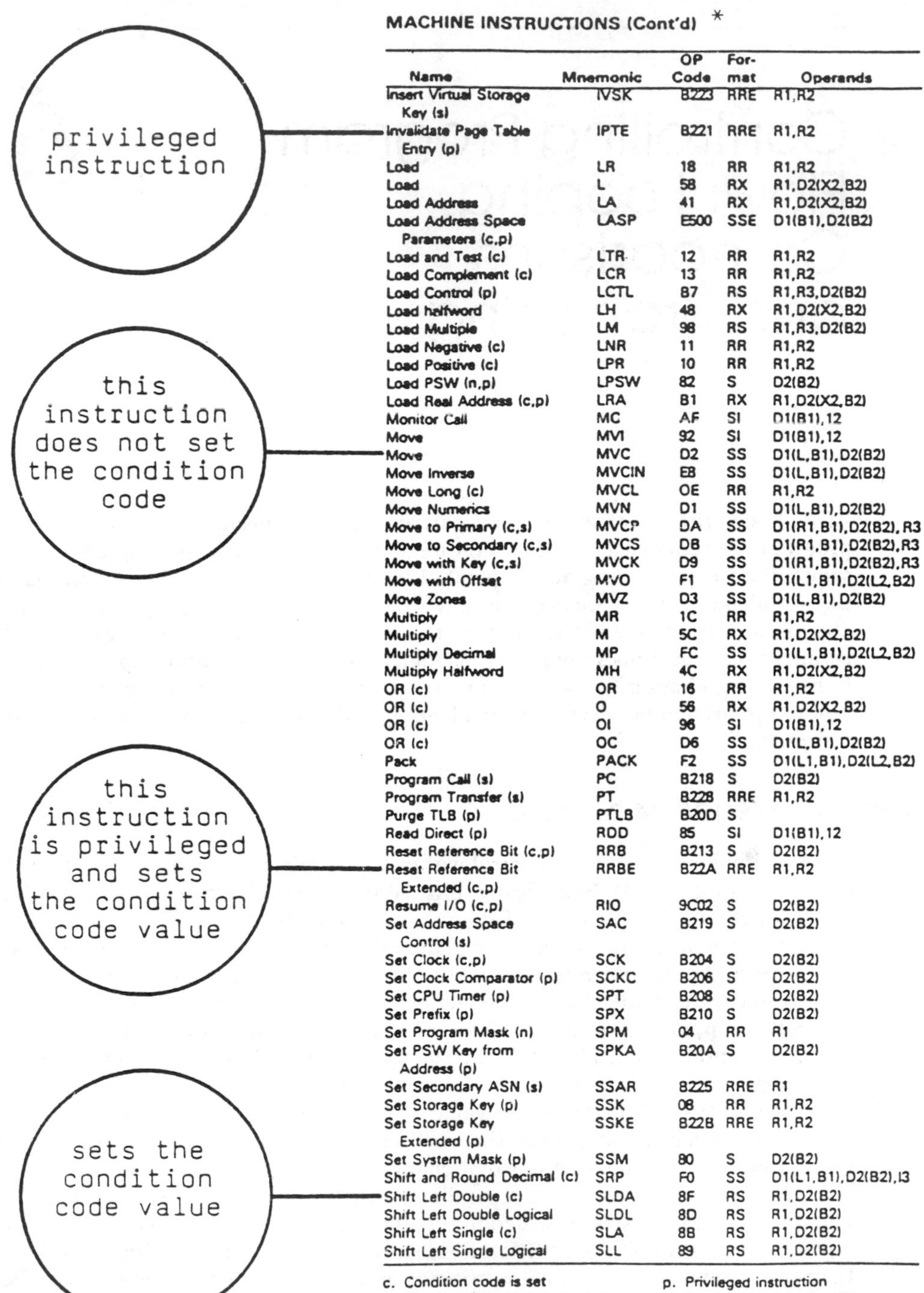

MACHINE INSTRUCTIONS (Cont'd) *

Name	Mnemonic	OP Code	Format	Operands
Insert Virtual Storage Key (s)	IVSK	B223	RRE	R1,R2
Invalidate Page Table Entry (p)	IPTE	B221	RRE	R1,R2
Load	LR	18	RR	R1,R2
Load	L	58	RX	R1,D2(X2,B2)
Load Address	LA	41	RX	R1,D2(X2,B2)
Load Address Space Parameters (c,p)	LASP	E500	SSE	D1(B1),D2(B2)
Load and Test (c)	LTR	12	RR	R1,R2
Load Complement (c)	LCR	13	RR	R1,R2
Load Control (p)	LCTL	B7	RS	R1,R3,D2(B2)
Load halfword	LH	48	RX	R1,D2(X2,B2)
Load Multiple	LM	98	RS	R1,R3,D2(B2)
Load Negative (c)	LNR	11	RR	R1,R2
Load Positive (c)	LPR	10	RR	R1,R2
Load PSW (n,p)	LPSW	82	S	D2(B2)
Load Real Address (c,p)	LRA	B1	RX	R1,D2(X2,B2)
Monitor Call	MC	AF	SI	D1(B1),I2
Move	MVI	92	SI	D1(B1),I2
Move	MVC	D2	SS	D1(L,B1),D2(B2)
Move Inverse	MVCIN	E8	SS	D1(L,B1),D2(B2)
Move Long (c)	MVCL	OE	RR	R1,R2
Move Numerics	MVN	D1	SS	D1(L,B1),D2(B2)
Move to Primary (c,s)	MVCP	DA	SS	D1(R1,B1),D2(B2),R3
Move to Secondary (c,s)	MVCS	DB	SS	D1(R1,B1),D2(B2),R3
Move with Key (c,s)	MVCK	D9	SS	D1(R1,B1),D2(B2),R3
Move with Offset	MVO	F1	SS	D1(L1,B1),D2(L2,B2)
Move Zones	MVZ	D3	SS	D1(L,B1),D2(B2)
Multiply	MR	1C	RR	R1,R2
Multiply	M	5C	RX	R1,D2(X2,B2)
Multiply Decimal	MP	FC	SS	D1(L1,B1),D2(L2,B2)
Multiply Halfword	MH	4C	RX	R1,D2(X2,B2)
OR (c)	OR	16	RR	R1,R2
OR (c)	O	56	RX	R1,D2(X2,B2)
OR (c)	OI	96	SI	D1(B1),I2
OR (c)	OC	D6	SS	D1(L,B1),D2(B2)
Pack	PACK	F2	SS	D1(L1,B1),D2(L2,B2)
Program Call (s)	PC	B218	S	D2(B2)
Program Transfer (s)	PT	B228	RRE	R1,R2
Purge TLB (p)	PTLB	B20D	S	
Read Direct (p)	RDD	85	SI	D1(B1),I2
Reset Reference Bit (c,p)	RRB	B213	S	D2(B2)
Reset Reference Bit Extended (c,p)	RRBE	B22A	RRE	R1,R2
Resume I/O (c,p)	RIO	9C02	S	D2(B2)
Set Address Space Control (s)	SAC	B219	S	D2(B2)
Set Clock (c,p)	SCK	B204	S	D2(B2)
Set Clock Comparator (p)	SCKC	B206	S	D2(B2)
Set CPU Timer (p)	SPT	B208	S	D2(B2)
Set Prefix (p)	SPX	B210	S	D2(B2)
Set Program Mask (n)	SPM	04	RR	R1
Set PSW Key from Address (p)	SPKA	B20A	S	D2(B2)
Set Secondary ASN (s)	SSAR	B225	RRE	R1
Set Storage Key (p)	SSK	08	RR	R1,R2
Set Storage Key Extended (p)	SSKE	B22B	RRE	R1,R2
Set System Mask (p)	SSM	80	S	D2(B2)
Shift and Round Decimal (c)	SRP	F0	SS	D1(L1,B1),D2(B2),I3
Shift Left Double (c)	SLDA	8F	RS	R1,D2(B2)
Shift Left Double Logical	SLDL	8D	RS	R1,D2(B2)
Shift Left Single (c)	SLA	8B	RS	R1,D2(B2)
Shift Left Single Logical	SLL	89	RS	R1,D2(B2)

c. Condition code is set
n. New condition code is loaded
p. Privileged instruction
s. Semiprivileged instruction
x. Extended-precision floating-point

Figure 6.1 IBM 370 instruction reference. Reprinted by permission from *IBM System/370 Reference Summary* (GX20-1850). Copyright 1981 by the International Business Machines Corporation.

CONDITION CODES *

Condition Code Setting	0	1	2	3
Mask Bit Value	8	4	2	1
General Instructions				
Add, Add Halfword	zero	<zero	>zero	overflow
Add Logical	zero, no carry	not zero, no carry	zero, carry	not zero, carry
AND	zero	not zero	—	—
Compare, Compare Halfword	equal	1st op low	1st op high	—
Compare and Swap Double	equal	not equal	—	—
Compare Logical	equal	1st op low	1st op high	—
Exclusive OR	zero	not zero	—	—
Insert Characters under Mask	all zero	1st bit one	1st bit zero	—
Load and Test	zero	<zero	>zero	—
Load Complement	zero	<zero	>zero	overflow
Load Negative	zero	<zero	—	—
Load Positive	zero	—	>zero	overflow
Move Long	count equal	count low	count high	overlap
OR	zero	not zero	—	—
Shift Left Double/ Single	zero	<zero	>zero	overflow
Shift Right Double/ Single	zero	<zero	>zero	—
Store Clock	set	not set	error	not oper
Subtract, Subtract Halfword	zero	<zero	>zero	overflow
Subtract Logical	—	not zero, no carry	zero, carry	not zero, carry
Test and Set	zero	one	—	—
Test under Mask	zero	mixed	—	ones
Translate and Test	zero	incomplete	complete	—
Decimal Instructions				
Add Decimal	zero	<zero	>zero	overflow
Compare Decimal	equal	1st op low	1st op high	—
Edit, Edit and Mark	zero	<zero	>zero	—
Shift and Round Decimal	zero	<zero	>zero	overflow
Subtract Decimal	zero	<zero	>zero	overflow
Zero and Add	zero	<zero	>zero	overflow
Floating-Point Instructions				
Add Normalized	zero	<zero	>zero	—
Add Unnormalized	zero	<zero	>zero	—
Compare	equal	1st op low	1st op high	—
Load and Test	zero	<zero	>zero	—
Load Complement	zero	<zero	>zero	—
Load Negative	zero	<zero	—	—
Load Positive	zero	—	>zero	—
Subtract Normalized	zero	<zero	>zero	—
Subtract Unnormalized	zero	<zero	>zero	—

Figure 6.2 Condition code settings table. Reprinted by permission from *IBM System/370 Reference Summary* (GX20-1850). Copyright 1981 by the International Business Machines Corporation.

TESTING THE CONDITION CODE VALUE

Instructions set the condition code to one of four possible values based on the outcome of the instruction. For the add instruction, our program uses the condition code to determine if a resulting sum was equal to zero, less than zero, greater than zero, or if overflow occurred. Also, our program takes action based on this value by using the BC or BCR instructions to alter the processing flow within our code.

The **BC (branch on condition)** and **BCR (branch on condition register)** instructions are the condition code testing instructions. The BC instruction is an RX instruction and the BCR is an RR instruction. Regardless of type, both compare the current condition code value to what is expected, and transfer control to another section of code in your program depending on the comparison. As much as I shouldn't say this, the BC and BCR instructions are "GO TO" instructions.

After issuing an add instruction, let's suppose that you want to perform some special processing depending on the outcome. If the result is zero, then you want to use the code at the location labeled ZERO to act on the result. The location GTZERO acts on the value if the result is greater than zero, and the code at location LTZERO acts on a less-than-zero result. These decisions, and the actions to be taken as a result of the add, are handled through the BC or BCR instructions.

Since it is an RX instruction, BC has two operands. The first operand is called the **mask** field and the second specifies a D(X,B) location within your program to which control is to be transferred. See Fig. 6.3.

```
BC      mask,D(X,B)
```

Figure 6.3 General format of the branch-on-condition instruction.

The mask is compared to the condition code. If the mask setting matches the condition code value in the PSW, then the system starts processing at location D(X,B). If the mask does not match the condition code, then the next instruction is executed, which comes immediately after the BC instruction within your program.

The mask is a four-bit value to which any or all of the bits may be set to zero or one. The mask bits are "on" or "off" as related to a particular condition code column setting. If the mask bit value is set to 1, then the condition code value for that mask position is tested. A mask setting of B'1000' (decimal 8) tests for a condition code value of zero (column 1 in the condition code chart of Fig. 6.2), B'0100' (decimal 4) tests for a setting of 1, B'0010' (decimal 2) tests for a setting of 2, and B'0001' (decimal 1) tests for a setting of 3. Again, each mask *position* is related directly to a *column* found in the IBM manual. Let's look at the condition code settings in Fig. 6.4.

At the top of chart, you see the relationship between condition code settings and mask bit values. Each column relates to one condition code setting. Although we can test condition code settings using single-bit mask settings, we can also combine mask bit settings to test multiple conditions. For example, B'0111' (decimal 7) takes action only if the condition code is *not* zero. Therefore, after issuing the add instruction, we would code the BC instructions shown in Fig. 6.5 to branch to appropriate places within our program depending on the outcome of the add.

The code in Fig. 6.5 clearly defines the action to be taken when the condition code is zero, one, or two. Since a condition code setting of three is not specifically tested, should it occur, the section of code labeled OVERFLOW is executed. Here we **fall** condition code values and mask settings

CONDITION CODES *				
Condition Code Setting	0	1	2	3
Mask Bit Value	8	4	2	1
General Instructions				
Add, Add Halfword	zero	<zero	>zero	overflow
Add Logical	zero, no carry	not zero, no carry	zero, carry	not zero, carry
AND	zero	not zero	—	—
Compare, Compare Halfword	equal	1st op low	1st op high	—
Compare and Swap Double	equal	not equal	—	—
Compare Logical	equal	1st op low	1st op high	—
Exclusive OR	zero	not zero	—	—
Insert Characters under Mask	all zero	1st bit one	1st bit zero	—
Load and Test	zero	<zero	>zero	—
Load Complement	zero	<zero	>zero	overflow
Load Negative	zero	<zero	—	—
Load Positive	zero	—	>zero	overflow
Move Long	count equal	count low	count high	overlap
OR	zero	not zero	—	—
Shift Left Double/ Single	zero	<zero	>zero	overflow
Shift Right Double/ Single	zero	<zero	>zero	—
Store Clock	set	not set	error	not oper
Subtract, Subtract Halfword	zero	<zero	>zero	overflow
Subtract Logical	—	not zero, no carry	zero, carry	not zero, carry
Test and Set	zero	one	—	—
Test under Mask	zero	mixed	—	ones
Translate and Test	zero	incomplete	complete	—
Decimal Instructions				
Add Decimal	zero	<zero	>zero	overflow
Compare Decimal	equal	1st op low	1st op high	—
Edit, Edit and Mark	zero	<zero	>zero	—
Shift and Round Decimal	zero	<zero	>zero	overflow
Subtract Decimal	zero	<zero	>zero	overflow
Zero and Add	zero	<zero	>zero	overflow
Floating-Point Instructions				
Add Normalized	zero	<zero	>zero	—
Add Unnormalized	zero	<zero	>zero	—
Compare	equal	1st op low	1st op high	—
Load and Test	zero	<zero	>zero	—
Load Complement	zero	<zero	>zero	—
Load Negative	zero	<zero	—	—
Load Positive	zero	—	>zero	—
Subtract Normalized	zero	<zero	>zero	—
Subtract Unnormalized	zero	<zero	>zero	—

Figure 6.4 Another look at the condition code settings table. Reprinted by permission from *IBM System/370 Reference Summary* (GX20-1850). Copyright 1981 by the International Business Machines Corporation.

```
            (Add instruction)
            BC         B'1000',ZERO
            BC         B'0100',LTZERO
            BC         B'0010',GTZERO
OVERFLOW    .          .
            .          .
            .          .
ZERO        .          .
            .          .
            .          .
LTZERO      .          .
            .          .
            .          .
GTZERO      .          .
            .          .
            .          .
```

Figure 6.5 Branching logic after an arithmetic operation.

through or **fall into** these instructions since we do not test for a specific match on any of the conditions.

The code in Fig. 6.5 is not logically sound. As coded, a problem may occur because it appears that ZERO falls into LTZERO, LTZERO falls into GTZERO, and GTZERO falls into whatever code comes after it. In order to process only the code related to the action to be taken, we must branch out of the functional code by using the **unconditional branch instruction**—a GOTO instruction.

A mask value of all ones (B'1111') (decimal 15) causes a branch to occur regardless of the condition code value. The condition code can only have one of four values, and, according to the mask B'1111', we are branching on *any* of those four values. A branch is taken to wherever specified if a mask of B'1111' is coded. Rewriting our code to eliminate the fall-through logic problem, we arrive at the implementation shown in Fig. 6.6.

Each routine directly supporting the add processing advances to the location called CONTINUE when its processing is completed. This eliminates the problem of LTZERO falling into the GTZERO code, possibly causing problems or incorrect results. Of course, each label in column 1 is attached to some assembly language instruction.

```
            Add instruction
            BC         B'1000',ZERO
            BC         B'0100',LTZERO
            BC         B'0010',GTZERO
OVERFLOW    .          .
            .          .
            .          .
            BC         B'1111',CONTINUE
ZERO        .          .
            .          .
            .          .
            BC         B'1111',CONTINUE
LTZERO      .          .
            .          .
            .          .
            BC         B'1111',CONTINUE
GTZERO      .          .
            .          .
            .          .
CONTINUE    .          .
            .          .
            .          .
```

Figure 6.6 Branching logic with functional exiting.

At this time, it's appropriate to discuss a more effective and maintainable method for placing labels within our programs. Although statement labels may be placed directly on any assembly language or machine instruction, it's better to use the EQU or DS instructions as shown in Fig. 6.7.

Either technique allows adding or deleting code from within each component without altering the location of the label or risking the possibility of mistyping or forgetting the label altogether. Although both techniques and the method of placing labels directly on machine instructions result in the same statement reference, the second technique shown in Fig. 6.7 (using the DS 0H instructions) is most common. Since all machine instructions are aligned on a halfword boundary by the assembler, the DS 0H does not waste any memory, but labels the instructions appropriately.

```
         Add instruction
         BC        B'1000',ZERO
         BC        B'0100',LTZERO
         BC        B'0010',GTZERO
OVERFLOW EQU       *
         .         .
         .         .
         BC        B'1111',CONTINUE
ZERO     EQU       *
         .         .
         .         .
         BC        B'1111',CONTINUE
LTZERO   EQU       *
         .         .
         .         .
         BC        B'1111',CONTINUE
GTZERO   EQU       *
         .         .
         .         .
CONTINUE EQU       *
         .         .
         .         .
```

```
         Add instruction
         BC        B'1000',ZERO
         BC        B'0100',LTZERO
         BC        B'0010',GTZERO
OVERFLOW DS        0H
         .         .
         .         .
         BC        B'1111',CONTINUE
ZERO     DS        0H
         .         .
         .         .
         BC        B'1111',CONTINUE
LTZERO   DS        0H
         .         .
         .         .
         BC        B'1111',CONTINUE
GTZERO   DS        0H
         .         .
         .         .
CONTINUE DS        0H
         .         .
         .         .
```

Figure 6.7 Techniques for labeling sections of code using DS and EQU instructions.

The EQU instruction equates the label with the operand * (asterisk or star). The * or asterisk is a special operand that effectively means, "the current address." Since the EQU instruction is an assembly language instruction and thus generates no machine code, the "current address" is the "next instruction." Hence, the label OVERFLOW, in the instruction "OVERFLOW EQU *", is effectively placed on the instruction that immediately follows the EQU.

Returning to our main discussion, the BC instruction forces a branch to some other point in the program or controls the flow of processing in a program by testing certain condition code settings. It is the most common instruction for testing the condition code setting as compared to the BCR instruction.

If you recall, we've used the BCR instruction before, as shown in Fig. 6.8. Do you remember where it was used?

```
BCR     B'1111',R14
```

Figure 6.8 Branching to the address contained in a register.

In this instruction, we are unconditionally branching to the *address* that is contained in register 14. The basic difference between the BCR and BC instructions is in the second operand. The BC instruction defines a D(X,B) location where control is to be given and the BCR instruction specifies a register number. The register specified in the BCR instruction is assumed to contain a valid address where control is to be transferred if the condition code testing yields a true result. If the register does not contain a valid address, some type of abend will undoubtedly occur. Implementing the add processing logic using the BCR instruction is shown in Fig. 6.9.

As you can see, we *load up* a group of registers with addresses where control is to be transferred depending on the testing of the condition code by the BCR instruction. If the condition code matches our mask value, a branch is taken to the address in the register

```
               LA       R3,ZERO
               LA       R4,LTZERO
               LA       R5,GTZERO
               Add instruction
               BCR      B'1000',R3
               BCR      B'0100',R4
               BCR      B'0010',R5
OVERFLOW       DS       0H
               .        .
               .        .
               BC       B'1111',CONTINUE
ZERO           DS       0H
               .        .
               .        .
               BC       B'1111',CONTINUE
LTZERO         DS       0H
               .        .
               .        .
               BC       B'1111',CONTINUE
GTZERO         DS       0H
               .        .
               .        .
CONTINUE       DS       0H
               .        .
               .        .
```

Figure 6.9 Branching implementation using BCR instructions.

```
          LM        R3,R5,=A(ZERO,LTZERO,GTZERO)
          Add instruction
          BCR       B'1000',R3
          BCR       B'0100',R4
          BCR       B'0010',R5
OVERFLOW  DS        0H
          .         .
          .         .
          BC        B'1111',CONTINUE
ZERO      DS        0H
          .         .
          .         .
          BC        B'1111',CONTINUE
LTZERO    DS        0H
          .         .
          .         .
          BC        B'1111',CONTINUE
GTZERO    DS        0H
          .         .
          .         .
CONTINUE  DS        0H
          .         .
          .         .
```

Figure 6.10 Loading registers with addresses when using BCR.

specified. Hence, if the result of the add is greater than zero, then we branch to the address in register 5, which happens to be the location of the first instruction labeled GTZERO.

The code in Fig. 6.9 is not as clear as the previous code. Not only do you have to remember to set each register appropriately, but you must remember which register contains each address so that you can branch to the proper place. In fact, this programming technique, and the readability associated with the BCR instruction, causes it to be one of the least used instructions in the IBM instruction set. We can't do without it, however, since it is the easiest method for returning control after program processing.

Figure 6.10 illustrates yet another method for implementing the same section of code. It performs exactly as the code in Fig. 6.9, but one LM (load multiple) instruction is used instead of three LA (load address) instructions. Registers 3 through 5 are loaded with the addresses of ZERO, LTZERO, and GTZERO, respectively, by using an address literal to specify each address.

You could also use the data areas section of your program to define three fullwords of storage holding each of the address constants for ZERO, LTZERO, and GTZERO. With the load multiple instruction, you could place the addresses into their respective registers so that the BCR instructions transfer control to the proper place within your program depending on the result (and condition code testing) of the addition.

As I stated earlier, the programming techniques shown are a matter of preference. However, you may run out of registers if you select any of the BCR options instead of the BC condition code testing process.

If you select the BCR instruction, be very careful about coding it correctly. Remember that the second operand is a register and it must contain a valid address that can be referenced by your program. Carefully review the instruction in Fig. 6.11 at this time. Do you see anything wrong with it?

```
BC      B'1111',R14
```

Figure 6.11 Incorrectly coding the BCR instruction to exit a program.

The assembler does not generate an error from the above instruction, but your program will not work properly during execution. We coded a BC instruction in Fig. 6.11 instead of the BCR instruction. The second operand references register 14, but as far as the assembler is concerned, we are unconditionally branching to location 14 (displacement 14) in the computer. Location 14 resides within the operating system, which means that any attempt to branch into that area results in some type of abend. The miscoding of mnemonic BC in place of BCR is a very common coding error. With BC or BCR, double-check your first operand to see that you've coded the proper mask for the condition that you want to test and double-check your second operand to ensure a proper D(X,B) address (or label) or a proper register.

COMPARING FIELDS AND TESTING VALUES (IF-THEN CONSTRUCTS)

The earlier examples of using the BC and BCR instructions to test condition code settings are *not* typical of their use. Although the condition code may be tested anytime during program execution or immediately after an instruction that sets the condition code, the most common time to code the BC or BCR instruction is after issuing a compare instruction.

A compare occurs in each of the following instructions: the CR instruction compares two register values, the C instruction compares a register value to an aligned fullword binary value in storage, CH provides halfword binary comparisons, CLC compares two character values in storage, CLI compares a byte in storage to an immediate value, and CP compares two packed-decimal fields. These are the major instructions used to determine how one field relates to another. They also set the condition code so that control may be transferred to the proper section of code depending on how the two values relate to each other. Hence, a comparison instruction, followed by one or more branch instructions, enables the programmer to construct IF-THEN and IF-THEN-ELSE constructs. By selectively executing sections of code, the programmer can effectively implement THEN and ELSE **clauses,** that is, one or more instructions associated with a resulting decision. This logic parallels that found in higher-level languages.

We must also distinguish between the two types of comparisons that can be made. The instructions C, CR, and CH compare **arithmetically** while CLI and CLC compare **logically.** As a general rule, arithmetic comparisons are performed against numeric signed data and logical comparisons are performed against character or non-numeric data. For example, the bit string B'0001' would constitute a positive number because the leftmost bit is zero. The string B'1110' would be a negative number because the leftmost bit is one. Arithmetically, B'0001' would be greater than B'1110'. Logically, B'0001' would be less than B'1110' because the first bit of B'0001' is a zero bit which is less than the one bit found in the first position of B'1110'.

In a limited sense, logical comparisons can be used for numeric field processing. If your numeric values are non-negative, the slower C and CR instructions can be replaced with CL and CLR, respectively, to provide value comparison. Condition code settings and the outcome of a comparison will be identical to that of C and CR for non-negative values.

In the case of the add processing logic that we've been using throughout this chapter, let's modify it slightly to use the compare instruction (C) to illustrate the IF-THEN construct. Figure 6.12 illustrates the logic.

After the add instruction is issued, we compare the value in the result register with the fullword literal value of zero. The branch instructions are now related to the compare instruction, but we can clearly see that we are comparing the result to a value of zero.

```
          Add instruction
          C         Rx,=F'0'
          BC        B'1000',ZERO
          BC        B'0100',LTZERO
          BC        B'0010',GTZERO
OVERFLOW  DS        0H
          .         .
          .         .
          BC        B'1111',CONTINUE
ZERO      DS        0H
          .         .
          .         .
          BC        B'1111',CONTINUE
LTZERO    DS        0H
          .         .
          .         .
          BC        B'1111',CONTINUE
GTZERO    DS        0H
          .         .
          .         .
CONTINUE  DS        0H
          .         .
          .         .
```

Figure 6.12 Using the RX compare instruction.

Don't think that this is a "better" technique than what you've seen before. In fact, it isn't. There is no reason to compare the resulting value after addition since the add instruction sets the condition code appropriately. The compare instruction is not necessary *for this example.* Each section of code such as OVERFLOW, ZERO, LTZERO, and GTZERO forms a **clause** or **do-group** within this logical construct. The branch instructions pass control to the appropriate clause depending on the outcome of the comparison. Since this example allows three possible outcomes, we more commonly call such an implementation a **case construct.** Logic allowing only one or two outcomes is more closely associated with IF-THEN and IF-THEN-ELSE logic respectively.

Let's suppose that we didn't want to see how the result relates to zero, but how it

```
          Add instruction
          C         Rx,=F'100'
          BC        B'1000',EQUAL
          BC        B'0100',LT100
          BC        B'0010',GT100
OVERFLOW  DS        0H
          .         .
          .         .
          BC        B'1111',CONTINUE
EQUAL     DS        0H
          .         .
          .         .
          BC        B'1111',CONTINUE
LT100     DS        0H
          .         .
          .         .
          BC        B'1111',CONTINUE
GT100     DS        0H
          .         .
          .         .
CONTINUE  DS        0H
          .         .
          .         .
```

Figure 6.13 Comparing to a non-zero value.

compares to 100. Since the add instruction does not base its condition code settings on any value other than zero, we now *must* use a compare instruction to see how the result relates to 100. Figure 6.13 illustrates this logic. Incidentally, if the resulting value after addition is less than 32,768 we could use the **CH (compare halfword)** instruction in this example. The mnemonic would change to CH and the second operand would specify a halfword literal instead of a fullword literal.

As you can see, we've changed the labels to relate to the new conditions being

CONDITION CODES *

Condition Code Setting	0	1	2	3
Mask Bit Value	8	4	2	1
General Instructions				
Add, Add Halfword	zero	<zero	>zero	overflow
Add Logical	zero, no carry	not zero, no carry	zero, carry	not zero, carry
AND	zero	not zero	—	—
Compare, Compare Halfword	equal	1st op low	1st op high	—
Compare and Swap Double	equal	not equal	—	—
Compare Logical	equal	1st op low	1st op high	—
Exclusive OR	zero	not zero	—	—
Insert Characters under Mask	all zero	1st bit one	1st bit zero	—
Load and Test	zero	<zero	>zero	—
Load Complement	zero	<zero	>zero	overflow
Load Negative	zero	<zero	—	—
Load Positive	zero	—	>zero	overflow
Move Long	count equal	count low	count high	overlap
OR	zero	not zero	—	—
Shift Left Double/ Single	zero	<zero	>zero	overflow
Shift Right Double/ Single	zero	<zero	>zero	—
Store Clock	set	not set	error	not oper
Subtract, Subtract Halfword	zero	<zero	>zero	overflow
Subtract Logical	—	not zero, no carry	zero, carry	not zero, carry
Test and Set	zero	one	—	—
Test under Mask	zero	mixed	—	ones
Translate and Test	zero	incomplete	complete	—
Decimal Instructions				
Add Decimal	zero	<zero	>zero	overflow
Compare Decimal	equal	1st op low	1st op high	—
Edit, Edit and Mark	zero	<zero	>zero	—
Shift and Round Decimal	zero	<zero	>zero	overflow
Subtract Decimal	zero	<zero	>zero	overflow
Zero and Add	zero	<zero	>zero	overflow
Floating-Point Instructions				
Add Normalized	zero	<zero	>zero	—
Add Unnormalized	zero	<zero	>zero	—
Compare	equal	1st op low	1st op high	—
Load and Test	zero	<zero	>zero	—
Load Complement	zero	<zero	>zero	—
Load Negative	zero	<zero	—	—
Load Positive	zero	—	>zero	—
Subtract Normalized	zero	<zero	>zero	—
Subtract Unnormalized	zero	<zero	>zero	—

Figure 6.14 Condition code settings for the compare instruction. Reprinted by permission from *IBM System/370 Reference Summary* (GX20-1850). Copyright 1981 by the International Business Machines Corporation.

tested: equal to 100, less than 100, or greater than 100. Referring to the condition code settings table shown in Fig. 6.14, we see the values for the C (compare), CR (compare register), and CH (compare halfword) instructions.

A mask of B'1000' tests for values that are equal, B'0100' tests for the first operand having a value less than the second operand, and B'0010' tests for the first operand having a value greater than the second. Since the first operand is the result register and the second operand is the literal value of 100, the condition code settings compare each possible condition to 100. The compare instruction has no condition code setting of three and so there is no reason to test using a mask of B'0001'.

We can alter the problem slightly to branch to the location labeled GE100 if the value is greater than or equal to 100 by coding the instructions as shown in Fig. 6.15.

The mask in our branch on condition instruction B'1010' is testing for two possibilities: equal to 100 or greater than 100. If the result in register Rx is less than 100, then we will fall into the code labeled LT100. Again, this illustrates how mask bit settings can be combined to test for multiple conditions within the same branch instruction.

```
          Add instruction
          C        Rx,=F'100'
          BC       B'1010',GE100
LT100     DS       0H
          .        .
          .        .
          BC       B'1111',CONTINUE
GE100     DS       0H
          .        .
          .        .
CONTINUE  DS       0H
          .        .
          .        .
```

Figure 6.15 Branching after a comparison.

The **CLC (compare logical character)** and **CLI (compare logical immediate)** instructions compare two data areas. They may compare any two types of data, such as binary, packed decimal, and character, but in general, they compare only character data. In fact, if either compares two numeric areas (as discussed earlier), you may obtain incorrect results.

The CLC instruction is coded with two operands, both of which are D(B) addresses. A length qualifier specifies the number of bytes that are to be compared. A maximum of 256 bytes may be compared using a CLC.

The CLI instruction uses a format very similar to MVI—the first operand specifies a D(B) address and the second defines an immediate byte. CLI may only compare a single byte in memory against an immediate byte value. Even though CLC also supports single byte comparisons, a programmer should utilize the faster CLI if a situation warrants a comparison against a known data value.

Suppose that two fields, A and B, are defined as five byte character fields. Figs. 6.16 and 6.17 illustrate various applications of the CLI and CLC instructions.

The length operand should be coded on the CLC instruction to indicate the number of storage bytes to be compared. After the CLC or CLI instructions are issued, the condition code may be tested using the BC or BCR instruction against the mask settings listed in Fig. 6.18.

```
CLI   A,C'M'              IS FIRST BYTE OF A EQUAL TO 'M'?
CLI   B+2,X'00'           IS THE THIRD BYTE OF B X'00'?
CLI   A+4,B'11110000'     IS LAST BYTE OF A = C'0'?
```

Figure 6.16 Comparing data using CLI.

```
CLC   A(5),B              IS FIELD A EQUAL TO B?
CLC   A,B                 USE AN IMPLICIT LENGTH TO DETERMINE
                           IF A AND B ARE EQUAL
CLC   A+2(2),B            ARE BYTES 3 & 4 FROM A EQUAL
                           TO THE FIRST TWO BYTES OF B?
```

Figure 6.17 Comparing character fields using CLC.

Mask Setting	Relationship
B'1000'	operand 1 = operand 2
B'0100'	operand 1 < operand 2
B'0010'	operand 1 > operand 2

Figure 6.18 Mask settings for the CLC and CLI instructions.

Character literals may also be used on the CLC instruction. In Fig. 6.19, field A is compared to the value ASMƀƀ.

```
CLC      A(5),=CL5'ASM'
```

Figure 6.19 Comparing a field to a literal character string using CLC.

Finally, registers may be compared by using another comparison instruction, **CR (compare register)**. For example, the contents of register 3 may be compared to register 7 by using the CR instruction illustrated in Fig. 6.20.

```
CR      R3,R7
```

Figure 6.20 Comparing the contents of two registers.

The contents of register 3 is compared to that of register 7 and the condition code is set as before—B'1000' (if they are equal), B'0100' (contents of R3 are less than that of R7), B'0010' (contents of R3 are greater than that of R7). Again, there is no condition code setting for B'0001'.

EXTENDED MNEMONIC INSTRUCTIONS

To construct the mask field for the BC and BCR instructions, refer to the condition code settings table in the IBM manual until you become familiar with the settings. However, there's an easier and more meaningful method for testing condition code settings using

BC and BCR instructions. It involves another set of instructions called the **extended mnemonic instructions.** These are not completely different instructions, but simply nicknames for the BC and BCR instructions.

The common mask settings for the BC and BCR instructions have been incorporated into the extended mnemonic instructions. Instead of coding the mnemonic BC or BCR and a mask, code a single mnemonic which defines *both.* For example, to compare two storage areas and take action if they're equal, we normally code the instructions shown in Fig. 6.21.

```
CLC     A(5),B
BC      B'1000',EQUAL
```

Figure 6.21 Character comparison followed by conditional testing.

As you can see, we code the proper mask for testing equality between the two storage areas. Using extended mnemonics, we replace the BC instruction and its mask as shown in Fig. 6.22.

```
CLC     A(5),B
BE      EQUAL
```

Figure 6.22 Character comparison followed by use of an extended mnemonic instruction.

The mnemonic **BE (branch on equal)** replaces *both* the mnemonic BC and the mask B'1000'. *The BE instruction is an alternate form of the BC instruction,* and when processed by the assembler, is converted into the standard BC instruction machine code with a mask of B'1000'. The mnemonic BE is a little more meaningful since we can refer to it as the **branch on equal instruction.**

If we are using BCR to control program flow instead of the BC instruction, we could use the **BER (branch on equal register) instruction** to transfer control in a similar manner. Assuming that register 5 contains our branch point, code the instructions as shown in Fig. 6.23.

```
CLC     A(5),B
BER     R5
```

Figure 6.23 Character compare followed by an extended mnemonic RR branch instruction.

A set of extended mnemonic instructions exists for testing most typical program masks. In general, branch on condition instructions are used after comparisons, arithmetic instructions, or after issuing the special **test under mask** instruction that we'll discuss in a later chapter. Figure 6.24 lists all of the RX extended mnemonic instructions, their equivalent mask bit values (if you are using BC), and their meanings. By appending the letter R to each mnemonic, you have the complete set of RR extended mnemonic instructions. That is, each instruction listed in Fig. 6.24 may be used in an RX format (second operand is a D(X,B) address) or an RR format (second operand specifies a register).

Extended Mnemonic	Mask	Meaning
B	B'1111'	unconditional branch
After a comparison:		
BH	B'0010'	branch on first operand > second
BL	B'0100'	branch on first operand < second
BE	B'1000'	branch if first operand = second
BNH	B'1101'	branch if first operand is not higher than the second; in other words, less than or equal to
BNL	B'1011'	branch if first operand is not lower than the second; in other words, greater than or equal to
BNE	B'0111'	branch if first operand is not equal to the second operand
After an arithmetic operation:		
BO	B'0001'	branch if overflow has occurred
BP	B'0010'	branch if result is positive
BM	B'0100'	branch if result is negative (minus)
BNP	B'1101'	branch if not positive; in other words, less than or equal to 0
BNM	B'1011'	branch if not minus (negative); in other words, greater than or equal to zero
BNZ	B'0111'	branch if result is not equal to 0
BZ	B'1000'	branch if result is equal to 0

Figure 6.24 The extended mnemonic RX instructions.

The various branch mnemonics are grouped into their respective categories, but this does not mean that you have to use them as intended. You can use any instruction at any time if it meets your needs. To help the readability and to be consistent with the coding practices, you should use the extended mnemonics whenever possible and as they are intended.

Returning to our example, we control branching in our program through extended mnemonics as shown in Fig. 6.25.

The extended mnemonics eliminate the mask bit coding used with either the BC or BCR instructions. Further, they add meaning to the branch instructions such as *branch on equal, branch on positive,* or *branch on minus (negative)* as we've been discussing and as illustrated in Fig. 6.25.

DEFINING YOUR OWN MNEMONICS (OPSYN)

As you review extended mnemonics, you may find that you do not agree with the wording associated with a particular mnemonic. Additionally, you may find that a mnemonic

```
              Add instruction
              BZ          ZERO
              BP          GTZERO
              BM          LTZERO
OVERFLOW      DS          0H
              .           .
              .           .
              BC          B'1111',CONTINUE
ZERO          DS          0H
              .           .
              .           .
              BC          B'1111',CONTINUE
GTZERO        DS          0H
              .           .
              .           .
              BC          B'1111',CONTINUE
LTZERO        DS          0H
              .           .
              .           .
CONTINUE      DS          0H
              .           .
              .           .
```

Figure 6.25 Using extended mnemonics.

does not exist for a situation peculiar to your program's processing. For example, the extended mnemonic BNL (branch on first operand not low) would be more appropriately called "branch on first operand greater than or equal to the second operand." However, there is no mnemonic called BGE (branch greater than or equal to).

With a special assembly language instruction, however, you can define your own mnemonics. Be careful. I am *not* saying that you can define your own instructions, rather, I am saying that you can define your own mnemonics. The IBM instruction set is not changeable; you must work within its boundaries. With this command, you can give a nickname or alternate name for an *existing* instruction in assembly language. This capability is not available in ASSIST.

The instruction that performs this request is called **OPSYN.** This instruction defines a new mnemonic to act as an existing mnemonic. Be sure to understand that you're simply *modeling* a new mnemonic after an existing one. Mnemonic BGE is going to act the same as the current mnemonic BNL. To define and equate BGE with BNL, code the instruction given in Fig. 6.26.

```
BGE      OPSYN   BNL
```

Figure 6.26 Defining the BGE mnemonic using OPSYN.

We can now use the BGE mnemonic wherever we would normally use the BNL mnemonic. In fact, we can also continue to use BNL if desired, thus allowing the use of two different mnemonics for the same operation. Although this seems impressive, stop and consider what you're doing. By defining new or redefining mnemonics, you are introducing a level of confusion for those who have to read and maintain your programs. Since BGE is not a standard instruction, a programmer may be confused by this instruction if they did not know that it has been defined using OPSYN. Again, we're discussing a tradeoff between coding and readability/maintenance. You have to decide the path to select when coding your programs.

Some other examples of OPSYN use are given in Fig. 6.27.

```
LOAD        OPSYN   L
SUBTRACT    OPSYN   S
COMPARE     OPSYN   C
STOREREG    OPSYN   ST
LOADREGS    OPSYN   LM
SAVEREGS    OPSYN   STM
FIXDIGIT    OPSYN   OI
ADDRESS     OPSYN   LA
```

Figure 6.27 Examples of OPSYN use.

Clearly, many confusing instructions can be clarified with the OPSYN instruction. Again, the original mnemonic and the new mnemonic are *both* available to your program. However, be careful when using OPSYN because you can destroy an existing mnemonic. In the example given in Fig. 6.28, a new mnemonic ZAP is defined as equivalent to mnemonic MVC (move character). However, *there is a machine instruction already called ZAP,* and so issuing the OPSYN instruction destroys the real ZAP instruction that may be needed in your program.

```
Be careful about using this example.

         ZAP      OPSYN   MVC
```

Figure 6.28 Potentially dangerous use of the OPSYN instruction.

LOOP CONSTRUCTS: A GENERAL OVERVIEW

One of the three basic logical constructs in structured programming is the loop construct, which allows an algorithm to perform a series of operations many times. The number of times that processing is to be done depends on several conditions. For example, I may want to perform a series of statements 10 times. Although I could make 10 copies of the series in my program and execute them sequentially, it is more logical to establish a looping environment that contains the statements that are to be performed 10 times.

The statements within the loop are said to be within the **range** or **body** of the loop. The number of statements or type of statements in the range is of no concern; in fact, loops can contain loops or any other logical constructs that we desire (sequence or decision). If a loop contains another loop, we say that loops are **nested,** that is, one is within the range of the other. How we organize loops depends on the processing to be done within our algorithms. In order to understand how loops are used, we must first understand the different looping situations that may be encountered.

For our purposes, we will study three types of loop constructs, although some may argue that there are fewer or more than three. The constructs are **while** looping, **until** looping, and **count** looping. A possible fourth category is the **end-of-file** loop construct, but this construct can be made with the **while** loop format.

The loop construct selected depends on the looping situation you are trying to implement. If you are to perform an operation *n* times, then select the **count** loop construct. If you are to perform a series of statements *zero or more times,* as long as a condition is *true,* then select the **while** construct. Finally, if you are to perform a series of statements *at least once* and to continue performing those statements as long as a condition has *not* been reached, then select the **until** loop construct.

The while, until, and count loop constructs are found in many other high-level languages. Also, instructions with these logical names exist in those languages to easily implement these constructs. In assembly language, the instructions to perform loop processing do not have related mnemonics. However, there is a set of macros that allows establishment of these constructs. In either case, we'll need to learn how these constructs are established using the typical machine language instructions available.

COUNTER LOOPS

The first loop construct that we'll discuss is the **counting** loop, which is used whenever the exact number of times that a series of operations will be performed is known. To set up this construct, we need a storage area to hold a counter value (also called **control variable**), the increment value, and the limit value used to determine when we should exit the loop. Figure 6.29 contains the logical format of the counting loop construct.

```
Repeat the following steps 10 times

  a) . . .
  b) . . .
  c) . . .
  d) . . .

endloop
```

Figure 6.29 Logical structure of the counting loop construct.

There are several ways to implement this construct in assembly language. If we count by ones, then by starting at 1 and ending at 10, we have gone through the loop 10 times. If we start at 5 and count by fives, then we stop at 50. In this case, our increment is 5, our limit is 50, and our loop begins counting from 5. No matter how we begin, increment, or limit our loop, we must do so in a manner that causes our loop to execute steps *a through d* 10 times. The most natural place to maintain a loop control variable is within a register. Hence, let's implement this loop structure using a register as shown in Fig. 6.30.

Register 3 is used as the loop control variable. It is initially set to 1 using the LA

```
                   LA      R3,1         SET CURRENT COUNT TO 1
LOOP               DS      0H           STARTING POINT OF THE LOOP
                   C       R3,=F'10'    REACHED THE LIMIT YET?
                   BH      ALLDONE      IF > 10 THEN LIMIT REACHED

                   a)
                   b)
                   c)
                   d)

                   A       R3,=F'1'     INCREMENT COUNT BY 1
                   B       LOOP         RETURN TO TOP OF LOOP
ALLDONE            DS      0H           END OF THE LOOP
```

Figure 6.30 Implementation of the counting loop.

(load address) instruction and is incremented by 1 each time through the loop using the A (add) instruction. Just inside the body of the loop, we check to see if we have reached our limit, and, if so, we exit from the loop. If our limit has not been reached, we continue executing steps *a through d* until we eventually reach it.

This loop can be implemented in many ways as we said earlier. Most often we'll see the LA (load address) instruction initialize the loop control variable *and* increment it each time through the loop. Figure 6.31 illustrates this implementation.

Loops may also be controlled in a reverse manner. In other words, rather than counting from 1 *up to* 10, we can count from 10 *down to* 1 as shown in Fig. 6.32. At times, the manner in which we count is very helpful to the processing within the loop since the control variable's value may be used within the body of the loop. Further, we can alter the value of either the control or limit value, but this is not typically done within a loop construct.

We've used a register to control the processing within loops. Although we could have used some other data type to control the number of times that we performed our loop, it is more efficient to use registers and binary data instructions. If you recall, binary data processing is one of the fastest forms on the IBM machines. Whenever possible, it should be used for numeric operations such as this. Additionally, we could have used the halfword instructions to implement our counter loop examples. As long as the starting, increment, and limit values are less than or equal to 32,767, halfword instructions may be used.

As you can see from our examples so far, the limit value that controls the number of times through the loop is tested *before* any statements within the loop are executed. If we test the limit value at the end of the loop, the logical structure of our loop processing is

```
                 LA     R3,1          SET CURRENT COUNT TO 1
LOOP             DS     0H            STARTING POINT OF THE LOOP
                 C      R3,=F'10'     REACHED THE LIMIT YET?
                 BH     ALLDONE       IF > 10 THEN LIMIT REACHED

                 a)
                 b)
                 c)
                 d)

                 LA     R3,1(R3)      INCREMENT COUNT BY 1
                 B      LOOP          RETURN TO TOP OF LOOP
ALLDONE          DS     0H            END OF THE LOOP
```

Figure 6.31 Alternate implementation of the counting loop.

```
                 LA     R3,10         SET CURRENT COUNT TO 10
LOOP             DS     0H            STARTING POINT OF THE LOOP
                 C      R3,=F'0'      REACHED ZERO YET?
                 BE     ALLDONE       IF YES, THEN EXIT THE LOOP

                 a)
                 b)
                 c)
                 d)

                 S      R3,=F'1'      DECREMENT COUNT BY 1
                 B      LOOP          RETURN TO TOP OF LOOP
ALLDONE          DS     0H            END OF THE LOOP
```

Figure 6.32 Counting backwards to control loop flow.

altered. The limit test at the end of the loop executes the statements in the range of the loop at least once. If this is not to occur, two decisions to control entry into the loop and exit from the loop have to be used. This is not the type of loop construction that we will be following in this text. Further, the limit value may have been set earlier in our program by some other processing. In fact, it may come from an input data record that tells our program the number of data records to be processed. Not knowing in advance the number of times that our loop should be executed may cause a problem depending on where our limit decision was made. In other words, if our limit value specifies that we are not to loop at all, then a loop constructed with a limit decision at the beginning will abide by this specification whereas a limit decision at the end of the loop will not. We'll execute the statements within the range of the loop once. During the development of your algorithm, you have to decide where to place your limit decision as well as how to count (forward or backward) and construct the loop according to your needs.

The **BCT (branch on count)** and **BCTR (branch on count register)** instructions also support the looping construct. Both BCT and BCTR count backwards by ones and both are normally coded at the bottom of the loop construct. The first operand specifies a register, which is used to determine the number of times that the statements in the body of the loop are to be executed. The second operand of the BCT instruction specifies a D(X,B) address whereas the second operand of the BCTR instruction specifies a register (which is assumed to contain an address).

When the BCT or BCTR instructions are executed, the register contents specified in the first operand are *decreased* by *one.* If the resulting value in the register is not equal to zero, a branch occurs to the address specified in the second operand. Only when the contents of the first operand register are zero will branching not occur, thus terminating the looping operation. Figure 6.33 illustrates the construction of a branch-on-count loop construct in which the statements in the body of the loop are to be executed 10 times.

```
         LA     R3,10       SET LIMIT VALUE TO 10
LOOP     DS     0H
         .
         .
         .
         BCT    R3,LOOP     REPEAT 9 TIMES
```

Figure 6.33 Looping using the BCT instruction.

Implementing the same loop using the BCTR instruction requires us to load the address of our loop return point into a register as well as initialize the limit control register. Figure 6.34 contains this implementation.

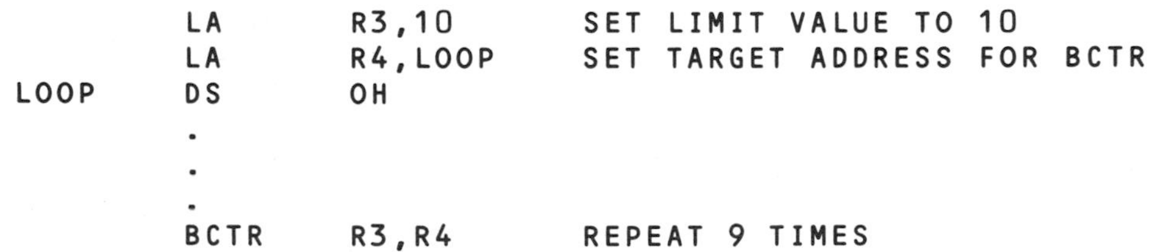

```
         LA     R3,10       SET LIMIT VALUE TO 10
         LA     R4,LOOP     SET TARGET ADDRESS FOR BCTR
LOOP     DS     0H
         .
         .
         .
         BCTR   R3,R4       REPEAT 9 TIMES
```

Figure 6.34 Looping using the BCTR instruction.

Again, the BCT and BCTR instructions decrement the first operand register by one. They cannot be used to advance through a loop by two's, three's, five's, and so on. However, the next instructions that we'll study *will* support such processing.

The IBM 370 computer series has two more instructions that allow easy loop construction. They are generally used to make the limit decision at the end of the loop unless the programmer uses reverse logic to place these instructions at the beginning of the loop construct. The instructions are **BXLE (branch on index low or equal)** and **BXH (branch on index high).**

The BXLE and BXH instructions generally require three registers for implementation. The register requirements, compared to the examples we looked at earlier, may cause you to select the earlier looping forms rather than these instructions. BXLE and BXH are RS instructions, which means that they are four bytes long. Both instructions have three operands.

```
<mnemonic>    R,Re/o,D(B)
```

Figure 6.35 General format of the RS instructions BXLE and BXH.

As Fig. 6.35 describes, the first operand is a register, the second defines an even/odd register pair, and the third specifies an address in your program. The last operand may use either an explicit D(B) address form or an implicit address form if you code a label.

The key to these instructions is understanding the role of the even/odd register pair (second operand). The even register is the *increment value* (which can be a value other than one) and the odd register specifies the *limit value* (which can also specify any value). The first register is the control variable that is incremented each time through the loop.

The BXLE instruction continues looping as long as the first register's value is *less than or equal* to the value in the odd register of the even/odd pair. The BXH instruction continues looping as long as the first register's value is *greater than* (higher than) the value in the odd register of the even/odd pair. Generally, BXLE is used for counting in a forward direction and BXH is used when counting in a backward direction.

Let's carefully review the code given in Fig. 6.36. At the bottom of the loop and each time through the loop, register 3 is incremented by the value in register 4, which in this case is 1. After incrementing, register 3's value is compared to register 5. As long as its value is less than or equal to that of register 5, a branch occurs to the location specified in the third operand of the BXLE instruction—LOOP. When register 3's value is greater than that of register 5, the loop exits. Since the control, increment, and limit values are arbitrary, BXLE and BXH can both be used to support looping by increments other than

```
         LA    R3,1         SET CURRENT COUNT TO 1
         LA    R4,1         SET INCREMENT VALUE
         LA    R5,10        SET LIMIT VALUE
LOOP     DS    0H           STARTING POINT OF LOOP

         a)
         b)
         c)
         d)

         BXLE  R3,R4,LOOP   REPEAT UNTIL LIMIT REACHED
```

Figure 6.36 Counting loop implementation using BXLE.

one. This is quite different from the BCT and BCTR instructions in which the control variable could only change by one each time through the loop.

Both instructions improve the readability of the code within the loop by eliminating the compare/branch and the increment for the loop counter. However, the programmer must remember to initialize each register before using the instructions and must remember that a register pair comprises the second operand.

There is a technique for reducing the number of registers required for either BXLE or BXH. The second operand does not have to be an even/odd pair. If an odd register is specified, it is used as *both* the increment value and the limit value. The same loop from Fig. 6.36 can be constructed using only two registers by altering the starting value for the loop counter. This implementation is shown in Fig. 6.37.

Register 5 is used as both the increment register and the limit register. With the loop counter starting at −8 and incrementing by positive 1 each time through, it assumes the values −8, −7, −6, −5, −4, −3, −2, −1, 0, and 1 before the loop is terminated. Since 10 different values are assumed by the control register until we exit from the loop, the loop is performed 10 times just as required. Would you have been able to determine this by looking at the code below? Again, shortcuts in coding and techniques to save registers may not help the overall understanding or readability of your programs. In fact, assembly language is difficult enough without further complicating it with these techniques.

The BXH instruction is generally used to count backwards. The same problem implemented with the BXH instruction appears as coded in Fig. 6.38.

Did you notice that the limit value was set to 0? You might think that we'll loop 11 times instead of 10, but try it. Since the BXH instruction loops as long as register 3 is greater than the limit value, setting register 5 to an initial value of 1 allows us only to loop nine times. We must set our limit value to one less than what we think so that we loop the proper number of times. Will you remember to do this when you construct your BXH loops?

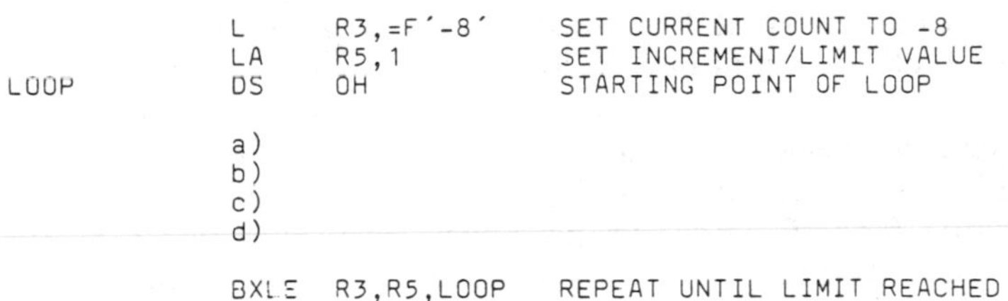

```
         L     R3,=F'-8'    SET CURRENT COUNT TO -8
         LA    R5,1         SET INCREMENT/LIMIT VALUE
LOOP     DS    0H           STARTING POINT OF LOOP

         a)
         b)
         c)
         d)

         BXLE  R3,R5,LOOP   REPEAT UNTIL LIMIT REACHED
```

Figure 6.37 Using BXLE without the even/odd pair.

```
         LA    R3,10        SET CURRENT COUNT TO 10
         L     R4,=F'-1     SET INCREMENT VALUE
         LA    R5,0         SET LIMIT VALUE
LOOP     DS    0H           STARTING POINT OF LOOP

         a)
         b)
         c)
         d)

         BXH   R3,R4,LOOP   REPEAT UNTIL LIMIT REACHED
```

Figure 6.38 Counting loop implementation using BXH.

Counter loops are very common in applications development, are easy to understand, and may be implemented in a variety of ways. Due to the large number of implementing techniques, counter loops can be difficult constructs to code in assembly language. The two remaining loop constructs are very easy to implement with our standard assembly language instructions.

WHILE AND UNTIL LOOP CONSTRUCTS

The **while** and **until** loop constructs allow program looping depending on a condition to be met or tested. The **while** construct continues looping as long as the condition is true and the **until** construct loops at least once and continues looping as long as the condition is *not* true. Logical representations of these loops are shown in Fig. 6.39.

```
        WHILE Construct                                   UNTIL Construct
   ______________________                            ______________________
Repeat as long as (expression) is true           Repeat
    a)                                                a)
    b)                                                b)
    c)                                                c)
endloop                                           as long as (expression) is false
```

Figure 6.39 The WHILE and UNTIL logical constructs.

If we use a flowchart to illustrate the processing within the two loop constructs, you can clearly see the differences. Figure 6.40 illustrates the relationship between these constructs.

The flowcharts clearly illustrate that the primary differences between these two constructs is where the decision to continue looping is made and how the loop is exited. In the case of the WHILE loop construct, the loop continues as long as the condition *is true.* The UNTIL loop continues as long as the condition *is not true.*

For example, suppose that we want to control looping based on the relationship between two elements, A and B. Further, assume that both A and B have the same value, that is, they are equal. Since they are equal, the expression $(A = B)$ is **true,** that is, it is true that A and B have the same value. The expression $(A \neq B)$ is **false** since in fact A does equal B. In this case, it is not true that A and B are not equal.

The construction of expressions to control looping for the WHILE and UNTIL constructs is done by expressing relationships between data elements, such as A and B. The WHILE construct continues to process statements contained in the body of the loop as long as the expression is evaluated to a true condition. The UNTIL construct continues processing as long as the expression evaluates to a false condition. Again, this logical structure parallels that found in higher-level languages. Your implementation may actually reverse the normal logical structures of either of these constructs. However, the presentation here attempts to provide an understanding and relationship to other languages that you may encounter.

Referring to Fig. 6.40, the statements within the range of the loop are executed *after* the condition is tested with the WHILE construct and *before* the condition is tested with the UNTIL construct. If the statements in the range *may not* be executed, then the programmer should select the WHILE construct since the UNTIL construct always allows the statements in the range of the loop to be executed at least once.

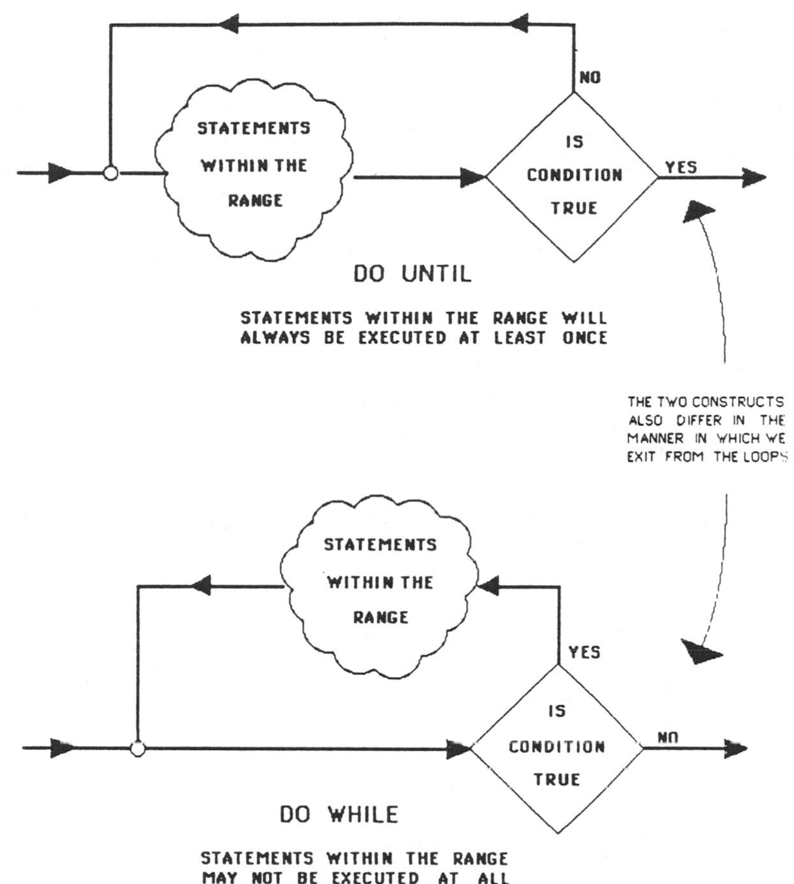

Figure 6.40 A graphic representation of the UNTIL and WHILE logical constructs.

The primary use of these two constructs is to process information when you don't know how many times you need to go through the loop. Contrary to the counter loop construct reviewed earlier, the UNTIL and WHILE constructs may not involve counting at all, rather, they are most often associated with **end-of-file** and **trailer record** processing.

END-OF-FILE AND TRAILER RECORD PROCESSING

End-of-file processing reads and processes data from a file when you do not know the number of records in that file. **Trailer record** logic processes data in a file until a certain value or values are reached within the input data stream. When these values are reached, the program terminates processing or goes on to some other activity as a result of reaching this point in the file.

If there are an undetermined number of records in a file to be processed, then the end-of-file loop construct processes all the records, attempting to read one more record after the program has processed the last record. The system then informs the program that the end of the data file has been reached. The program can then act accordingly since it now knows that all records have been processed.

Implementing the end-of-file loop construct is very simple since much of the work is automatically performed by the I/O instructions. In assembly language (not ASSIST), the DCB instruction provides assistance in recognizing the end of file and the XREAD instruction in ASSIST provides much the same capability. The code in Fig. 6.41 illustrates this implementation technique.

As you can see, the DCB instruction contains the operand **EODAD (end of data).** This operand specifies the label on the instruction where control is to be transferred when the end of file is reached. Although any label can be used, the name *EOF* is quite suitable to denote the place to resume processing when the end of file is reached.

As you look at the loop structure, you may question the use of two GET instructions. One appears just before the loop and the other just at the bottom of the loop. Although another structure could be used, our philosophy is to develop assembly language programs in a manner similar to any other language. Hence, this implementation for end-of-file processing is most similar to that used in other languages.

If the end of file is reached on the first record, then statements a, b, c, and d are not executed since these steps are probably related to processing data obtained from a record. If the end of file is encountered on the second GET statement, then processing is immediately transferred to EOF, not allowing the program to accidentally process the last record twice.

The next implementation, shown in Fig. 6.42 also works and is a more common form of coding end-of-file logic within an assembly language program. Although this logic is not typical of completely structured programs, it works here because of the forced branch caused by the EODAD operand in the DCB. In fact, the only reason that this implementation does work is because the *access method* forces a transfer of control to the label EOF. As you'll soon see in the ASSIST implementation, problems can arise when using this implementation technique.

When the end of file is encountered on the GET instruction, control is transferred to the routine labeled EOF and steps a, b, c, and d are not performed.

What loop construct is used here? Is the WHILE construct being used or the UNTIL construct? By thinking carefully, you can see that the WHILE construct is being used. Remember, if the end of file is reached on the *first* GET statement, then steps a, b, c, and d are *not* performed. If we implement our logic using the UNTIL construct, steps a, b, c, and d would be executed at least once. This is not acceptable if the end of file is

```
                GET     DCBIN,RECIN
LOOPTOP         DS      0H

                a)
                b)
                c)
                d)

                GET     DCBIN,RECIN
                B       LOOPTOP
EOF             DS      0H

   .             .       .
   .             .       .

DCBIN           DCB     DSORG=PS,DDNAME=....,EODAD=EOF
```

Figure 6.41 End-of-file implementation in standard assembly language.

```
Warning:  This implementation is not typical
          of the end of file processing
          techniques used in fully structured
          programs.



LOOPTOP   DS     0H
          GET    DCBIN,RECIN

          a)
          b)
          c)
          d)

          B      LOOPTOP
EOF       DS     0H

   .      .      .
   .      .      .

DCBIN     DCB    DSORG=PS,DDNAME=...,EODAD=EOF
```

Figure 6.42 Alternate end-of-file implementation in standard assembly language.

encountered on the first record that we attempt to process. Incidentally, if we reach the end of file on the first record, it means that we have no data in our file to process.

Since ASSIST does not use DCB's, another technique must test for the end of file, namely, the condition code. When an ASSIST program issues an XREAD instruction, the condition code indicates whether or not the end of file has been reached. A mask of B'1000' tests for a successful read and a mask of B'0100' tests for the end of file. Given this, we can now implement an end-of-file loop construct in ASSIST as shown in Fig. 6.43.

There really isn't much difference between the loop construct in assembler and this loop construct. The input instructions are in the same position as before and the label EOF is still the target of processing when the end of file is reached. The important difference is the function of the DCB as compared to testing the condition code. In assembler, the programmer must specify (in the DCB instruction using the EODAD operand) where control is to be given when the end of file is reached whereas the branch instruction specifies the end-of-file target address in ASSIST.

We can implement our logic in yet another manner as illustrated in Fig. 6.44. However, let me warn you about this implementation.

This loop implementation works, but, as I stated before, it is not similar in tech-

```
          XREAD  RECIN,80
LOOPTOP   BC     B'0100',EOF

          a)
          b)
          c)
          d)

          XREAD  RECIN,80
          B      LOOPTOP
EOF       DS     0H
```

Figure 6.43 End-of-file implementation in ASSIST.

```
warning:  be careful when implementing programs
          as shown below.  Make sure that you
          code the BC instruction properly



LOOPTOP   DS     0H
          XREAD  RECIN,80
          BC     B'0100',EOF

          a)
          b)
          c)
          d)

          B      LOOPTOP
EOF       DS     0H
```

Figure 6.44 Alternate end-of-file implementation in ASSIST.

nique to the end-of-file implementation in other languages. What is coded here is an infinite loop with a decision structure to exit from within the loop. The loop itself does not end naturally, rather, control is forced out of the loop to the label called EOF through *our* coding of a branch instruction. Neither ASSIST nor the access method is forcing a branch as was the case in assembler. Here, *we* must control the flow of execution in our program and miscoding or incorrect coding of the BC instruction could be disastrous. Some programmers would argue that this is not a correct implementation of the end-of-file loop structure for these reasons. Logically, Fig. 6.45 contains what this loop structure is to do.

```
     Repeat forever

          Input a record
          If end of file has been reached, then
               go to the statement labeled EOF

          a)
          b)
          c)
          d)

     endloop

EOF: continue processing. . . .
```

Figure 6.45 Logical representation of the code contained in Fig. 6.44.

The loop itself does not determine the flow of control within the program, rather, the decision as to whether or not the end of file has been reached is embedded within the loop and controls the program's flow. If you are concerned about consistency and carry-over from one language to another, select the input-loop-process-input-endloop structure rather than the technique shown in Figs. 6.44 and 6.45. However, keep in mind that the single-input end-of-file processing form presented above is a very common method for implementing the end-of-file processing logic in assembly language. If properly coded, it *will* work and it *will* exit your logic from within the loop construct when the end of file is reached.

Suppose that we use the UNTIL structure to implement our end-of-file loop construct. Using ASSIST, our implementation appears as given in Fig. 6.46.

In this example, the decision as to whether the end of file has been reached is made at the bottom of the loop. Steps a, b, c, and d are always executed at least once. Furthermore, the condition being tested is the reverse of that before. In other words, "if the end of file has not been reached, then return to the top of the loop, otherwise fall through into the end-of-file routine." In fact, the label EOF is not needed since there aren't any instructions that refer to it.

This implementation also works unless we reach the end of file on the *first* XREAD. If this is the case, we process steps a, b, c, and d even though we do not read a valid record from our input file. Can you imagine what results our program produces in this case? Since a, b, c, and d are probably dependent on the data obtained during the XREAD, it's anyone's guess as to what happens. Most likely, the program would abend.

Trailer record processing, a very important structure, continues looping as long as a certain input value has not been reached. Although its frequency of use is quite small, the technique nonetheless should be considered since there are applications in which it is a valid data processing feature.

If we assume that there are at least two records in our file and that our trailer value is not on the first record, we can implement the trailer record processing technique using the UNTIL loop construct shown in Fig. 6.47.

After the second input instruction, we look for the record that contains our trailer value. As long as it is not found, processing continues within the loop called LOOPTOP.

```
         XREAD   RECIN,80
LOOPTOP  DS      0H

         a)
         b)
         c)
         d)

         XREAD   RECIN,80
         BC      B'1011',LOOPTOP
EOF      DS      0H
```

Figure 6.46 UNTIL loop construction for end-of-file processing in ASSIST.

```
         XREAD   RECIN,80
LOOPTOP  DS      0H

         a)
         b)
         c)
         d)

         XREAD   RECIN,80
         CLC     field,=C'value'
         BNE     LOOPTOP
GOTIT    continue processing ...
```

Figure 6.47 UNTIL loop implementation for trailer record processing in ASSIST.

When the trailer value is reached, we exit the loop by falling into the program logic labeled GOTIT.

Although Fig. 6.47 shows trailer record processing with UNTIL logic, this is not necessarily the technique in which to implement trailer record processing. We could use WHILE logic by placing our decision at the top of the loop to look for our trailer record. The code in Fig. 6.48 illustrates this processing.

```
         XREAD   RECIN,80
LOOPTOP  CLC     field,=C'value'
         BE      GOTIT

         a)
         b)
         c)
         d)

         XREAD   RECIN,80
         B       LOOPTOP
GOTIT    continue processing ...
```

Figure 6.48 Trailer record processing with WHILE logic in ASSIST.

COMPOUND CONDITIONS

Occasionally, loop and decision processing requires several tests against data before processing a decision clause or exiting a loop. For example, a decision or loop may process as long as A is equal to B *and* C is greater than D. If either A is not equal to B or C is not greater than D, then we exit the construct as shown in Fig. 6.49. Such situations, called **compound conditions,** are very important for many computer applications.

```
IF A = B and C > D THEN
.
.
.
endif
---------------------------
Repeat while A = B and C > D

.
.
.
endloop
```

Figure 6.49 Compound logical conditions.

Let's consider how to implement the loop shown in Fig. 6.49. Obviously, decision logic tests the values of A and C against B and D, respectively. As long as *both* conditions are true, we continue processing within the loop. If either condition is false, then we exit from the loop.

Let's get a general overview by implementing each decision separately in its own loop structure as shown in Fig. 6.50. We combine the two decision structures to form the compound loop condition as shown in Fig. 6.51.

```
LOOPTOP     DS      OH
            Cx      A,B           COMPARE A TO B
            BNE     LOOPEXIT      IF NOT EQUAL THEN EXIT

            .       .
            .       .             body of the loop
            .       .

            B       LOOPTOP       RETURN TO TOP OF LOOP
LOOPEXIT    DS      OH            EXIT POINT FROM LOOP
```

```
LOOPTOP     DS      OH
            Cx      C,D           COMPARE C AND D
            BNH     LOOPEXIT      IF C IS NOT MORE; EXIT

            .       .
            .       .             body of the loop
            .       .

            B       LOOPTOP       RETURN TO TOP OF LOOP
LOOPEXIT    DS      OH            EXIT POINT FROM LOOP
```

Figure 6.50 Separate implementations of compound decisions.

```
LOOPTOP     DS      OH
            Cx      A,B           COMPARE A TO B
            BNE     LOOPEXIT      IF NOT EQUAL THEN EXIT
            Cx      C,D           COMPARE C AND D
            BNH     LOOPEXIT      IF C NOT MORE THEN EXIT
            .       .
            .       .             body of the loop
            .       .

            B       LOOPTOP       RETURN TO TOP OF LOOP
LOOPEXIT    DS      OH            EXIT POINT FROM LOOP
```

Figure 6.51 Implementing the compound conditions from Figures 6.49 and 6.50.

Two conditional decisions are made at the top of the loop. As long as A is equal to B and C is greater than D, then we remain in the loop and continue processing. If A is not equal to B or C is not greater than D, then we exit from the loop and resume processing at the location LOOPEXIT.

Compound conditions involve complex relationships. For example, elements may have to be compared to several other elements before we can determine if a loop is continued or exited. Typically, compound loops involve **AND** and **OR** decisions between two or more pairs of elements. Such relationships are commonly called **boolean relationships** since they compare the outcomes of two conditions. In Fig. 6.51, you see an **and** loop condition, that is, the loop continues as long as *both* A is equal to B *and* C is greater than D. Some loops may be dependent on one or the other decision, but not both. For example, our loop may state that we continue processing as long as A is equal to B *or* as long as C is greater than D. Hence, if A is equal to B, we continue within the loop. If C is greater

```
LOOPTOP    DS    0H
           Cx    A,B          COMPARE A TO B
           BE    CONTINUE     CONTINUE LOOP IF EQUAL
           Cx    C,D          COMPARE C AND D
           BNH   LOOPEXIT     IF C NOT MORE THEN EXIT
CONTINUE   DS    0H           INTERMEDIATE TARGET
           .     .
           .     .            body of the loop
           .     .

           B     LOOPTOP      RETURN TO TOP OF LOOP
LOOPEXIT   DS    0H           EXIT POINT FROM LOOP
```

Figure 6.52 Logical OR compound conditions.

than D, we continue within the loop. Implementing this compound condition is shown in Fig. 6.52.

If A equals B, we don't have to compare C and D since the loop is to continue anyway. If A and B are not equal, then we must compare C and D: if C is *not* greater than D, then we exit the loop; otherwise, we fall into the loop and continue processing.

MAILING LABEL PRINT PROGRAM EXAMPLE

We end this chapter with a program to print mailing labels from input data records. Each mailing label has six lines, with each label separated by two blank lines. Each label allows 30 characters per line and carriage control is *not* to be used during output. Carefully look at the following items within the program:

1. End-of-file processing is used.
2. Each input record contains many pieces of data.
3. Based on the input data, a salutation is added to each name before the person's name is printed on the label.
4. All labels occupy six lines on output, and carriage control is not used.
5. The ORG instruction assigns two different names to the same storage area within the program.

The program example is implemented in both ASSIST (see Example 6.1) and standard assembly language (see Example 6.2) for your reference. Important items are labeled. Finally, the main purpose of this program example is to illustrate the use of end-of-file processing logic.

```
*** ASSIST 4.0/A-12/21/77  370/145.OS/VS2  INS=SDFP/X=BGHO, CHECK/TRC/=1130, OPTS=CMPRX  PENN STATE UNIV ***
$JOB                                                                      |  00140
                                                                                                      PAGE    1
  LOC  OBJECT CODE    ADDR1 ADDR2  STMT   SOURCE STATEMENT
                                      1 ************************************************************  |  00150
                                      2 *  THIS PROGRAM WILL INPUT MAILING LABEL INFORMATION CONSISTING OF   *  |  00160
                                      3 *  A PERSON'S NAME, MARITAL STATUS, SEX CODE, STREET ADDRESS, CITY,  *  |  00170
                                      4 *  STATE, AND ZIP.  FROM THIS INFORMATION THE PROGRAM WILL BUILD     *  |  00180
                                      5 *  A SERIES OF MAILING LABEL LINES AND OUTPUT THEM SO THAT THEY MAY  *  |  00190
                                      6 *  BE PRINTED ON LABELS TO BE USED IN MAILING.                       *  |  00200
                                      7 ************************************************************  |  00210
000000                                8 R0        EQU   0                                            |  00220
000001                                9 R1        EQU   1                                            |  00230
000002                               10 R2        EQU   2                                            |  00240
000003                               11 R3        EQU   3                                            |  00250
000004                               12 R4        EQU   4                                            |  00260
000005                               13 R5        EQU   5                                            |  00270
000006                               14 R6        EQU   6                                            |  00280
000007                               15 R7        EQU   7                                            |  00290
000008                               16 R8        EQU   8                                            |  00300
000009                               17 R9        EQU   9                                            |  00310
00000A                               18 R10       EQU   10                                           |  00320
00000B                               19 R11       EQU   11                                           |  00330
00000C                               20 R12       EQU   12                                           |  00340
00000D                               21 R13       EQU   13                                           |  00350
00000E                               22 R14       EQU   14                                           |  00360
00000F                               23 R15       EQU   15                                           |  00370

000004                               25 ENDFILE   EQU   B'0100'             REPLACE MASK WITH MEANING TO   |  00390
                                     26 *                                   ...INDICATE END OF FILE        |  00400

000000                               28 LABELS    CSECT                                                    |  00420
000000 90EC D00C          0000C      29           STM   R14,R12,12(R13)     SAVE INVOKER'S REGISTERS       |  00430
000004 18CF                          30           LR    R12,R15             R12 WILL BE OUR BASE REG       |  00440
000000                               31           USING LABELS,R12          TELL THE ASSEMBLER             |  00450
000006 47F0 C05C          0005C      32           B     SKIPOVER            SKIP AROUND SAVE AREA          |  00460
00000A D3C1C2C5D3E24040              33           DC    CL8'LABELS'         NAME OF THE MODULE             |  00470
000014 FFFFFFFFFFFFFFFF              34 SAVEAREA  DC    18F'-1'             18 FULLWORD SAVE AREA          |  00480
00005C                               35 SKIPOVER  DS    0H                                                 |  00490
00005C 41B0 C014          00014      36           LA    R11,SAVEAREA        POINT TO OUR SAVE AREA         |  00500
000060 50BD 0008          00008      37           ST    R11,8(R13)          TELL CALLER ABOUT OUR AREA     |  00510
000064 50DB 0004          00004      38           ST    R13,4(R11)          REMEMBER WHERE CALLER'S IS AT  |  00520
000068 18DB                          39           LR    R13,R11             ESTABLISH NEW R13 SAVEAREA     |  00530
```


Example 6.1 Mailing label program and output in ASSIST.

```
                                                                                                              PAGE    2
  LOC  OBJECT CODE     ADDR1 ADDR2  STMT   SOURCE STATEMENT

                                      41 ***********************************************************************  | 00550
                                      42 * READ THE FIRST RECORD IN THE FILE AND BEGIN PROCESSING ALL PEOPLE. *  | 00560
                                      43 ***********************************************************************  | 00570
00006A E000 C148 0050 00148           44          XREAD PERSON,80              GET A PERSON'S RECORD              | 00580
000070 4740 C13C            0013C     45 MAINLOOP BC    ENDFILE,EOF            MAIN LOOP FOR THE PROGRAM          | 00590
                                      46 ***********************************************************************  | 00600
                                      47 * IF THE PERSON IS A MALE THEN THE SALUTATION IS 'MR.'.               *  | 00610
                                      48 ***********************************************************************  | 00620
000074 95D4 C15C      0015C           49          CLI   SEXCODE,C'M'           IF MALE THEN SALUTATION='MR.'      | 00630
000078 4770 C08C            0008C     50          BNE   FEMALE                 ELSE IT'S A FEMALE                 | 00640
00007C D21D C199 C220 00199 00220     51          MVC   PNAME(30),=CL30'MR.'   SUPPLY SALUTATION AND CLEAR LINE   | 00650
000082 D213 C19D C148 0019D 00148     52          MVC   PNAME+4(20),NAME       MOVE NAME INTO LABEL OUTPUT LINE   | 00660
000088 47F0 C0B0            000B0     53          B     MOVEREST               MOVE REST OF NAME                  | 00670

00008C                                55 FEMALE   DS    0H                                                        | 00690
                                      56 ***********************************************************************  | 00700
                                      57 * IF FEMALE THEN WE MUST DETERMINE IF SHE IS MARRIED OR NOT SO THAT   *  | 00710
                                      58 * WE WILL SUPPLY THE CORRECT SALUTATION (MRS. IF MARRIED,             *  | 00720
                                      59 * MS. IF NOT MARRIED).                                                *  | 00730
                                      60 ***********************************************************************  | 00740
00008C 95E2 C15D      0015D           61          CLI   MARITAL,C'S'           SINGLE OR MARRIED FEMALE?          | 00750
000090 4770 C0A4            000A4     62          BNE   MARRIED                IF NOT SINGLE THEN MUST BE MARRY   | 00760
000094 D21D C199 C23E 00199 0023E     63          MVC   PNAME(30),=CL30'MS.'   SUPPLY FEMALE SINGLE SALUTATION    | 00770
00009A D213 C19D C148 0019D 00148     64          MVC   PNAME+4(20),NAME       MOVE IN THE PERSON'S NAME          | 00780
0000A0 47F0 C0B0            000B0     65          B     MOVEREST                                                  | 00790

0000A4                                67 MARRIED  DS    0H                                                        | 00810
0000A4 D21D C199 C25C 00199 0025C     68          MVC   PNAME(30),=CL30'MRS.'  MARRIED FEMALE SALUTATION          | 00820
0000AA D213 C19E C148 0019E 00148     69          MVC   PNAME+5(20),NAME       FINISH MOVING IN THE NAME          | 00830
```

here is our branch instruction with the equated symbol ENDFILE in place of the standard mask value for end of file. This may help the readability of this code to indicate that loop is being controled by end of file logic.

```
LOC    OBJECT CODE      ADDR1 ADDR2  STMT   SOURCE STATEMENT

0000B0                                71 MOVEREST DS    0H                                                       00850
                                      72 ********************************************************************** 00860
                                      73 * MOVE THE STREET INFORMATION INTO THE LABEL LINE TO BE PRINTED.     * 00870
                                      74 ********************************************************************** 00880
0000B0 D21D C1B8 C1F6 001B8 001F6     75          MVC   PSTREET(30),BLINE        CLEAR STREET OUTPUT LINE        00890
0000B6 D213 C1B8 C15E 001B8 0015E     76          MVC   PSTREET(20),STREET       MOVE STREET INTO OUTPUT LINE    00900
0000BC D21D C1D7 C1F6 001D7 001F6     77          MVC   PCITY(30),BLINE          CLEAR CITY, STATE,ZIP LINE      00910

                                      79 ********************************************************************** 00930
                                      80 * TO MAKE THE LABEL LOOK NICE WE MUST MOVE THE CITY NAME ONE LETTER  * 00940
                                      81 * AT A TIME INTO THE TARGET LABEL SO THAT WE CAN APPEND A COMMA, THE * 00950
                                      82 * STATE, AND THEN THE ZIP TO THE END OF THE CITY NAME.               * 00960
                                      83 ********************************************************************** 00970
0000C2 4130 C172              00172   84          LA    R3,CITY                  POINT TO START OF CITY LINE     00980
0000C6                                85 CITYLOOP DS    0H                                                       00990
0000C6 D501 3000 C27A 00000 0027A     86          CLC   0(2,R3),=C'  '           FIND DOUBLE BLANK TO END CITY   01000
0000CC 4780 C0E0              000E0   87          BE    CITYEND                  IF FOUND END THEN EXIT          01010
0000D0 5930 C218              00218   88          C     R3,=A(CITY+19)           END OF CITY YET?                01020
0000D4 4720 C0E0              000E0   89          BH    CITYEND                  IF YES THEN EXIT                01030
0000D8 4130 3001              00001   90          LA    R3,1(,R3)                POINT TO NEXT POSITION          01040
0000DC 47F0 C0C6              000C6   91          B     CITYLOOP                 CONTINUE UNTIL CITY END IS FOUND 01050

                                      93 ********************************************************************** 01070
                                      94 * ONCE WE FIND THE END OF THE CITY NAME WE CAN COMPUTE ITS LENGTH    * 01080
                                      95 * AND THEN USE A COUNTER LOOP TO MOVE EACH CHARACTER OF THE CITY     * 01090
                                      96 * NAME TO THE OUTPUT LABEL AREA.                                     * 01100
                                      97 *                                                                    * 01110
                                      98 * NOTE THAT THE FIELDS CANNOT BE REFERENCED BY SYMBOLIC NAMES WHEN   * 01120
                                      99 * THIS TYPE OF PROCESSING IS BEING USED.                             * 01130
                                     100 ********************************************************************** 01140
0000E0                               101 CITYEND  DS    0H                       MOVE CITY INTO LABEL LINE       01150
0000E0 5B30 C21C              0021C  102          S     R3,=A(CITY)              COMPUTE LENGTH OF CITY NAME     01160
0000E4 4140 C171              00171  103          LA    R4,CITY-1                POINT TO START OF CITY          01170
0000E8 4150 C1D6              001D6  104          LA    R5,PCITY-1               POINT TO TARGET LABEL LINE      01180
0000EC                               105 CITYLP2  DS    0H                       MOVE CITY NAME ONE AT A TIME    01190
0000EC 4144 0001              00001  106          LA    R4,1(R4)                 POINT TO NEXT CITY CHARACTER    01200
0000F0 4155 0001              00001  107          LA    R5,1(R5)                 POINT TO NEXT TARGET ADDRESS    01210
0000F4 D200 5000 4000 00000 00000    108          MVC   0(1,R5),0(R4)            MOVE ONE CHARACTER FROM CITY    01220
0000FA 4630 C0EC              000EC  109          BCT   R3,CITYLP2               CONTINUE LENGTH OF CITY TIMES   01230
```

the code in lines 79-109 is quite complex. Review it very carefully in order to understand.

```
                                                                                                 PAGE    4
  LOC  OBJECT CODE    ADDR1 ADDR2  STMT   SOURCE STATEMENT

                                    111 **********************************************************************   |  01250
                                    112 * AFTER THE CITY NAME HAS BEEN MOVED INTO THE LABEL WE CAN NOW MOVE   *   |  01260
                                    113 * IN THE COMMA, STATE, AND ZIP CODE AT PROPER OFFSETS FROM THE LAST   *   |  01270
                                    114 * CHARACTER OF THE CITY NAME.                                          *   |  01280
                                    115 **********************************************************************   |  01290
0000FE 926B 5001       00001        116          MVI   1(R5),C','                MOVE COMMA AFTER CITY NAME      |  01300
000102 D201 5003 C186 00003 00186   117          MVC   3(2,R5),STATE             MOVE IN STATE CODE              |  01310
000108 D204 5006 C188 00006 00188   118          MVC   6(5,R5),ZIPCODE           MOVE IN ZIP CODE                |  01320

                                    120 **********************************************************************   |  01340
                                    121 * PRINT THE ENTIRE MAILING LABEL AT THIS TIME.                         *   |  01350
                                    122 *                                                                      *   |  01360
                                    123 * SINCE ASSIST ALWAYS REQUIRES CARRIAGE CONTROL WE MUST ALLOW FOR      *   |  01370
                                    124 * A CARRIAGE CONTROL.  HOWEVER, ALL OF OUR CONTROL CHARACTERS ARE      *   |  01380
                                    125 * BLANKS AND SO NO CARRIAGE CONTROL IS REALLY BEING USED.              *   |  01390
                                    126 **********************************************************************   |  01400
00010E E020 C198 001F 00198         127          XPRNT PNAME-1,31                PRINT PERSON'S NAME LINE        |  01410
000114 E020 C1B7 001F 001B7         128          XPRNT PSTREET-1,31              PRINT STREET LINE               |  01420
00011A E020 C1D6 001F 001D6         129          XPRNT PCITY-1,31                PRINT CITY,STATE,ZIP LINE       |  01430
000120 E020 C1F5 001F 001F5         130          XPRNT BLINE-1,31                SKIP A BLANK LINE               |  01440
000126 E020 C1F5 001F 001F5         131          XPRNT BLINE-1,31                SKIP A BLANK LINE               |  01450
00012C E020 C1F5 001F 001F5         132          XPRNT BLINE-1,31                SKIP A BLANK LINE               |  01460

                                    134 **********************************************************************   |  01480
                                    135 * GET THE NEXT INPUT RECORD SO THAT WE MAY CONTINUE LABEL PROCESSING.*   |  01490
                                    136 **********************************************************************   |  01500
000132 E000 C148 0050 00148         137          XREAD PERSON,80                 GET THE NEXT PERSON'S RECORD    |  01510
000138 47F0 C070             00070  138          B     MAINLOOP                  CONTINUE TO PROCESS ALL RECORDS |  01520

                                    140 **********************************************************************   |  01540
                                    141 * AFTER ALL RECORDS HAVE BEEN PROCESSED WE'RE DONE.  RETURN CONTROL    *   |  01550
                                    142 * TO THE OPERATING SYSTEM AFTER SETTING THE RETURN CODE.               *   |  01560
                                    143 **********************************************************************   |  01570
00013C                              144 EOF      DS    0H                        TARGET POINT WHEN END OF FILE   |  01580
00013C 58DD 0004             00004  145          L     R13,4(R13)                RESTORE SAVE AREA POINTER       |  01590
000140 98EC D00C             0000C  146          LM    R14,R12,12(R13)           RESTORE ALL OTHER REGISTERS     |  01600
000144 1BFF                         147          SR    R15,R15                   CLEAR REGISTER 15 BEFORE WE EXIT|  01610
000146 07FE                         148          BR    R14                       RETURN CONTROL TO THE O.S.      |  01620
```

At the bottom of the main loop in the program we read the next record and continue.

When end of file is reached we arrive here so that we can end the execution of our program

```
LOC   OBJECT CODE      ADDR1 ADDR2  STMT   SOURCE STATEMENT

                                    150 ***********************************************************************  | 01640
                                    151 *     D A T A     A R E A S    &    W O R K    E L E M E N T S       *  | 01650
                                    152 ***********************************************************************  | 01660

                                    154 ***********************************************************************  | 01680
                                    155 * THE AREA CALLED PERSON IS SIMPLY A GLOBAL NAME FOR A SET OF FIELDS.*  | 01690
                                    156 * THE ORG ALLOWS THE FIELDS CALLED NAME THROUGH ZIPCODE TO RENAME    *  | 01700
                                    157 * THE AREA CALLED PERSON INTO MEANINGFUL FIELDS THAT CAN BE USED.    *  | 01710
                                    158 ***********************************************************************  | 01720
000148                              159 PERSON   DS    CL80                 INPUT RECORD HOLDING AREA           | 01730
000148                              160          ORG   PERSON               RENAME THE AREA CALLED PERSON       | 01740
000148                              161 NAME     DS    CL20                 PERSON'S NAME IN FIRST 30 COLS      | 01750
00015C                              162 SEXCODE  DS    C                    M-MALE, F-FEMALE                    | 01760
00015D                              163 MARITAL  DS    C                    MARITAL STATUS S-SINGLE,M-MARRY     | 01770
00015E                              164 STREET   DS    CL20                 STREET ADDRESS                      | 01780
000172                              165 CITY     DS    CL20                 NAME OF THE CITY                    | 01790
000186                              166 STATE    DS    CL2                  STATE CODE                          | 01800
000188                              167 ZIPCODE  DS    CL5                  ZIP CODE                            | 01810
000198                              168          ORG                                                          | 01820

                                    170 ***********************************************************************  | 01840
                                    171 * THE FOLLOWING AREAS ARE USED TO BUILD THE VARIOUS LINES OF THE     *  | 01850
                                    172 * LABEL AND TO PROVIDE PROPER SPACING BETWEEN EACH LABEL SINCE       *  | 01860
                                    173 * CARRIAGE CONTROL CHARACTERS CANNOT BE USED.                        *  | 01870
                                    174 ***********************************************************************  | 01880
000198 40                           175          DC    C' '                                                   | 01890
000199                              176 PNAME    DS    CL30                 OUTPUT NAME LINE                    | 01900
0001B7 40                           177          DC    C' '                                                   | 01910
0001B8                              178 PSTREET  DS    CL30                 OUTPUT STREET LINE                  | 01920
0001D6 40                           179          DC    C' '                                                   | 01930
0001D7                              180 PCITY    DS    CL30                 OUTPUT CITY,STATE,ZIP LINE          | 01940

0001F5 40                           182          DC    C' '                                                   | 01960
0001F6 4040404040404040             183 BLINE    DC    CL30' '              BLANK LINE FOR LABEL SPACING        | 01970

                                    185          LTORG                                                        | 01990
000218 00000185                     186                =A(CITY+19)
00021C 00000172                     187                =A(CITY)
000220 D4D94B4040404040             188                =CL30'MR.'
00023E D4E24B4040404040             189                =CL30'MS.'
00025C D4D9E24B40404040             190                =CL30'MRS.'
00027A 4040                         191                =C'  '
                                    192          END   LABELS                                                 | 02000
*** NO   STATEMENTS FLAGGED -  NO   WARNINGS,  NO   ERRORS

*** DYNAMIC CORE AREA USED:  LOW:    15100 HIGH:     1200 LEAVING:  503892 FREE BYTES. AVERAGE:       84 BYTES/STMT ***

*** ASSEMBLY TIME =     0.027 SECS,      7148 STATEMENTS/SEC ***

*** PROGRAM EXECUTION BEGINNING - ANY OUTPUT BEFORE EXECUTION TIME MESSAGE IS PRODUCED BY USER PROGRAM ***


MR. JOHN DOE
101 W. MARKET
SOMEWHERE, TX 78777


MR. BILL SMYTHE
#3 PLEASANT LANE
NOWHERE, IL 61616


MS. MARY JONES
100 E. MAPLE #2
SOMEWHERE, TX 78777


MRS. BETTY BOOP
#3 CONCORD AVENUE
NOWHERE, IL 61616


MR. JIMMY BOOP
#3 CONCORD AVENUE
NOWHERE, IL 61616


MR. NNNNNNNNNNNNNNNNNNNN
SSSSSSSSSSSSSSSSSSSS
CCCCCCCCCCCCCCCCCCCC, XX 55555


*** EXECUTION TIME =     0.010 SECS.       764 INSTRUCTIONS EXECUTED -    76400 INSTRUCTIONS/SEC ***

*** AM004 - NORMAL USER TERMINATION BY RETURN ***
```

ORG allows the same area of storage to be named by different labels as shown here.

Output from the program. Note the city, state and zip output line.

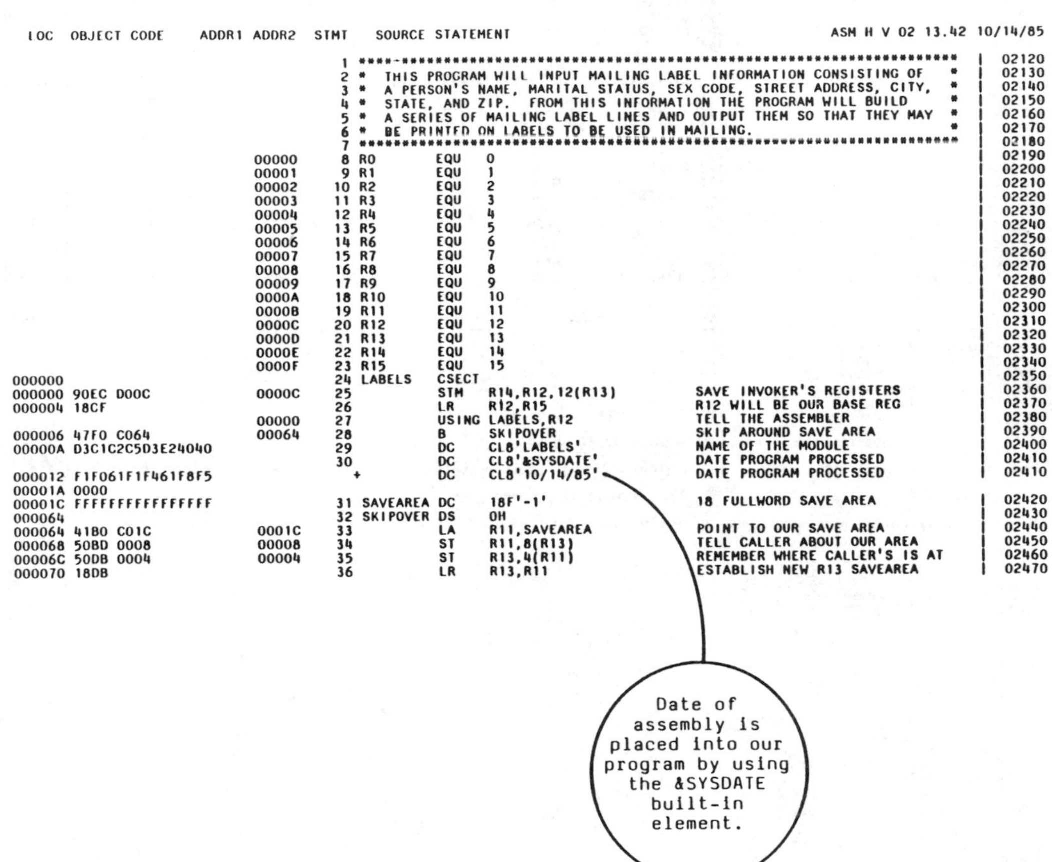

```
                                                                                                          PAGE    2

LOC  OBJECT CODE     ADDR1 ADDR2  STMT   SOURCE STATEMENT                                    ASM H V 02 13.42 10/14/85

                                     1 ****-**********************************************************   | 02120
                                     2 *  THIS PROGRAM WILL INPUT MAILING LABEL INFORMATION CONSISTING OF  *  | 02130
                                     3 *  A PERSON'S NAME, MARITAL STATUS, SEX CODE, STREET ADDRESS, CITY, *  | 02140
                                     4 *  STATE, AND ZIP.  FROM THIS INFORMATION THE PROGRAM WILL BUILD    *  | 02150
                                     5 *  A SERIES OF MAILING LABEL LINES AND OUTPUT THEM SO THAT THEY MAY *  | 02160
                                     6 *  BE PRINTED ON LABELS TO BE USED IN MAILING.                     *  | 02170
                                     7 ****************************************************************   | 02180
                           00000     8 R0        EQU   0                                                    | 02190
                           00001     9 R1        EQU   1                                                    | 02200
                           00002    10 R2        EQU   2                                                    | 02210
                           00003    11 R3        EQU   3                                                    | 02220
                           00004    12 R4        EQU   4                                                    | 02230
                           00005    13 R5        EQU   5                                                    | 02240
                           00006    14 R6        EQU   6                                                    | 02250
                           00007    15 R7        EQU   7                                                    | 02260
                           00008    16 R8        EQU   8                                                    | 02270
                           00009    17 R9        EQU   9                                                    | 02280
                           0000A    18 R10       EQU   10                                                   | 02290
                           0000B    19 R11       EQU   11                                                   | 02300
                           0000C    20 R12       EQU   12                                                   | 02310
                           0000D    21 R13       EQU   13                                                   | 02320
                           0000E    22 R14       EQU   14                                                   | 02330
                           0000F    23 R15       EQU   15                                                   | 02340
000000                              24 LABELS    CSECT                                                      | 02350
000000 90EC D00C           0000C    25           STM   R14,R12,12(R13)      SAVE INVOKER'S REGISTERS        | 02360
000004 18CF                         26           LR    R12,R15              R12 WILL BE OUR BASE REG        | 02370
                           00000    27           USING LABELS,R12           TELL THE ASSEMBLER              | 02380
000006 47F0 C064           00064    28           B     SKIPOVER             SKIP AROUND SAVE AREA           | 02390
00000A D3C1C2C5D3E24040             29           DC    CL8'LABELS'          NAME OF THE MODULE              | 02400
                                    30           DC    CL8'&SYSDATE'        DATE PROGRAM PROCESSED          | 02410
000012 F1F061F1F461F8F5              +           DC    CL8'10/14/85'        DATE PROGRAM PROCESSED          | 02410
00001A 0000
00001C FFFFFFFFFFFFFFFF             31 SAVEAREA  DC    18F'-1'              18 FULLWORD SAVE AREA           | 02420
000064                              32 SKIPOVER  DS    0H                                                   | 02430
000064 41B0 C01C           0001C    33           LA    R11,SAVEAREA         POINT TO OUR SAVE AREA          | 02440
000068 50BD 0008           00008    34           ST    R11,8(R13)           TELL CALLER ABOUT OUR AREA      | 02450
00006C 50DB 0004           00004    35           ST    R13,4(R11)           REMEMBER WHERE CALLER'S IS AT   | 02460
000070 18DB                         36           LR    R13,R11              ESTABLISH NEW R13 SAVEAREA      | 02470
```


Example 6.2 Mailing label program and output in standard assembly language.

```
  LOC  OBJECT CODE    ADDR1 ADDR2  STMT   SOURCE STATEMENT                                       ASM H V 02 13.42 10/14/85

                                     38 ************************************************************************  |  02490
                                     39 * OPEN THE FILES AND BEGIN PROCESSING THE LABEL DATA FROM THE INPUT  *  |  02500
                                     40 * FILE.                                                               *  |  02510
                                     41 ************************************************************************  |  02520
                                     42          OPEN  (LABELIN,INPUT,LABELOUT,OUTPUT)                            |  02530
000072 0700                          43+         CNOP  0,4                                ALIGN LIST TO FULLWORD 01-OPEN
000074 4510 C080            00080    44+         BAL   1,*+12                             LOAD REG1 W/LIST ADDR. 01-OPEN
000078 00                            45+         DC    AL1(0)                             OPTION BYTE            01-OPEN
000079 000274                        46+         DC    AL3(LABELIN)                       DCB ADDRESS            01-OPEN
00007C 8F                            47+         DC    AL1(143)                           OPTION BYTE            01-OPEN
00007D 0002D4                        48+         DC    AL3(LABELOUT)                      DCB ADDRESS            01-OPEN
000080 0A13                          49+         SVC   19                                 ISSUE OPEN SVC         01-OPEN
                                     50          GET   LABELIN,PERSON             GET A PERSON'S RECORD          |  02540
000082 4110 C274            00274    51+         LA    1,LABELIN                          LOAD PARAMETER REG 1   02-IHBIN
000086 4100 C1AA            001AA    52+         LA    0,PERSON                           LOAD PARAMETER REG 0   02-IHBIN
00008A 58F0 1030            00030    53+         L     15,48(0,1)                  LOAD GET ROUTINE ADDR         01-GET
00008E 05EF                          54+         BALR  14,15                       LINK TO GET ROUTINE           01-GET
000090                               55 MAINLOOP DS    0H                         MAIN LOOP FOR THE PROGRAM      |  02550
                                     56 ************************************************************************  |  02560
                                     57 * IF THE PERSON IS A MALE THEN THE SALUTATION IS 'MR.'.              *  |  02570
                                     58 ************************************************************************  |  02580
000090 95D4 C1BE      001BE          59          CLI   SEXCODE,C'M'               IF MALE THEN SALUTATION='MR.'  |  02590
000094 4770 C0A8            000A8    60          BNE   FEMALE                     ELSE IT'S A FEMALE             |  02600
000098 D21D C1FA C340 001FA 00340    61          MVC   PNAME(30),=CL30'MR.'       SUPPLY SALUTATION AND CLEAR LINE | 02610
00009E D213 C1FE C1AA 001FE 001AA    62          MVC   PNAME+4(20),NAME           MOVE NAME INTO LABEL OUTPUT LINE | 02620
0000A4 47F0 C0CC            000CC    63          B     MOVEREST                   MOVE REST OF NAME              |  02630

0000A8                               65 FEMALE   DS    0H                                                        |  02650
                                     66 ************************************************************************  |  02660
                                     67 * IF FEMALE THEN WE MUST DETERMINE IF SHE IS MARRIED OR NOT SO THAT  *  |  02670
                                     68 * WE WILL SUPPLY THE CORRECT SALUTATION (MRS. IF MARRIED,            *  |  02680
                                     69 * MS. IF NOT MARRIED).                                               *  |  02690
                                     70 ************************************************************************  |  02700
0000A8 95E2 C1BF      001BF          71          CLI   MARITAL,C'S'               SINGLE OR MARRIED FEMALE?      |  02710
0000AC 4770 C0C0            000C0    72          BNE   MARRIED                    IF NOT SINGLE THEN MUST BE MARRY | 02720
0000B0 D21D C1FA C35E 001FA 0035E    73          MVC   PNAME(30),=CL30'MS.'       SUPPLY FEMALE SINGLE SALUTATION | 02730
0000B6 D213 C1FE C1AA 001FE 001AA    74          MVC   PNAME+4(20),NAME           MOVE IN THE PERSON'S NAME      |  02740
0000BC 47F0 C0CC            000CC    75          B     MOVEREST                                                  |  02750

0000C0                               77 MARRIED  DS    0H                                                        |  02770
0000C0 D21D C1FA C37C 001FA 0037C    78          MVC   PNAME(30),=CL30'MRS.'      MARRIED FEMALE SALUTATION      |  02780
0000C6 D213 C1FF C1AA 001FF 001AA    79          MVC   PNAME+5(20),NAME           FINISH MOVING IN THE NAME      |  02790
```

Files must be opened before they can be processed in assembler. Note the expansion of OPEN.

```
LOC    OBJECT CODE       ADDR1 ADDR2  STMT   SOURCE STATEMENT                                           ASM H V 02 13.42 10/14/85
0000CC                                  81 MOVEREST DS    0H                                                            02810
                                        82 ***********************************************************************      02820
                                        83 * MOVE THE STREET INFORMATION INTO THE LABEL LINE TO BE PRINTED.      *      02830
                                        84 ***********************************************************************      02840
0000CC D21D C218 C254 00218 00254       85          MVC   PSTREET(30),BLINE        CLEAR STREET OUTPUT LINE             02850
0000D2 D213 C218 C1C0 00218 001C0       86          MVC   PSTREET(20),STREET       MOVE STREET INTO OUTPUT LINE         02860
0000D8 D21D C236 C254 00236 00254       87          MVC   PCITY(30),BLINE          CLEAR CITY, STATE,ZIP LINE           02870

                                        89 ***********************************************************************      02890
                                        90 * TO MAKE THE LABEL LOOK NICE WE MUST MOVE THE CITY NAME ONE LETTER   *      02900
                                        91 * AT A TIME INTO THE TARGET LABEL SO THAT WE CAN APPEND A COMMA, THE  *      02910
                                        92 * STATE, AND THEN THE ZIP TO THE END OF THE CITY NAME.                *      02920
                                        93 ***********************************************************************      02930
0000DE 4130 C1D4               001D4    94          LA    R3,CITY                  POINT TO START OF CITY LINE          02940
0000E2                                  95 CITYLOOP DS    0H                                                            02950
0000E2 D501 3000 C39A 00000 0039A       96          CLC   0(2,R3),=C'  '           FIND DOUBLE BLANK TO END CITY        02960
0000E8 4780 C0FC               000FC    97          BE    CITYEND                  IF FOUND END THEN EXIT               02970
0000EC 5930 C338               00338    98          C     R3,=A(CITY+19)           END OF CITY YET?                     02980
0000F0 4720 C0FC               000FC    99          BH    CITYEND                  IF YES THEN EXIT                     02990
0000F4 4130 3001               00001   100          LA    R3,1(,R3)                POINT TO NEXT POSITION               03000
0000F8 47F0 C0E2               000E2   101          B     CITYLOOP                 CONTINUE UNTIL CITY END IS FOUND     03010

                                       103 ***********************************************************************      03030
                                       104 * ONCE WE FIND THE END OF THE CITY NAME WE CAN COMPUTE ITS LENGTH      *      03040
                                       105 * AND THEN USE A COUNTER LOOP TO MOVE EACH CHARACTER OF THE CITY      *      03050
                                       106 * NAME TO THE OUTPUT LABEL AREA.                                      *      03060
                                       107 *                                                                     *      03070
                                       108 * NOTE THAT THE FIELDS CANNOT BE REFERENCED BY SYMBOLIC NAMES WHEN    *      03080
                                       109 * THIS TYPE OF PROCESSING IS BEING USED.                              *      03090
                                       110 ***********************************************************************      03100
0000FC                                 111 CITYEND  DS    0H                       MOVE CITY INTO LABEL LINE            03110
0000FC 5B30 C33C               0033C   112          S     R3,=A(CITY)              COMPUTE LENGTH OF CITY NAME          03120
000100 4140 C1D3               001D3   113          LA    R4,CITY-1                POINT TO START OF CITY               03130
000104 4150 C235               00235   114          LA    R5,PCITY-1               POINT TO TARGET LABEL LINE           03140
000108                                 115 CITYLP2  DS    0H                       MOVE CITY NAME ONE AT A TIME         03150
000108 4144 0001               00001   116          LA    R4,1(R4)                 POINT TO NEXT CITY CHARACTER         03160
00010C 4155 0001               00001   117          LA    R5,1(R5)                 POINT TO NEXT TARGET ADDRESS         03170
000110 D200 5000 4000 00000 00000      118          MVC   0(1,R5),0(R4)            MOVE ONE CHARACTER FROM CITY         03180
000116 4630 C108               00108   119          BCT   R3,CITYLP2               CONTINUE LENGTH OF CITY TIMES        03190
```



```
LOC    OBJECT CODE       ADDR1 ADDR2  STMT   SOURCE STATEMENT                                           ASM H V 02 13.42 10/14/85
                                       121 ***********************************************************************      03210
                                       122 * AFTER THE CITY NAME HAS BEEN MOVED INTO THE LABEL WE CAN NOW MOVE   *      03220
                                       123 * IN THE COMMA, STATE, AND ZIP CODE AT PROPER OFFSETS FROM THE LAST   *      03230
                                       124 * CHARACTER OF THE CITY NAME.                                         *      03240
                                       125 ***********************************************************************      03250
00011A 926B 5001         00001         126          MVI   1(R5),C','               MOVE COMMA AFTER CITY NAME           03260
00011E D201 5003 C1E8 00003 001E8      127          MVC   3(2,R5),STATE            MOVE IN STATE CODE                   03270
000124 D204 5006 C1EA 00006 001EA      128          MVC   6(5,R5),ZIPCODE          MOVE IN ZIP CODE                     03280

                                       130 ***********************************************************************      03300
                                       131 * PRINT THE ENTIRE MAILING LABEL AT THIS TIME.                        *      03310
                                       132 ***********************************************************************      03320
                                       133          PUT   LABELOUT,PNAME           PRINT PERSON'S NAME LINE             03330
00012A 4110 C2D4               002D4   134+         LA    1,LABELOUT                          LOAD PARAMETER REG 1  02-IHBIN
00012E 4100 C1FA               001FA   135+         LA    0,PNAME                             LOAD PARAMETER REG 0  02-IHBIN
000132 58F0 1030               00030   136+         L     15,48(0,1)                LOAD PUT ROUTINE ADDR               01-PUT
000136 05EF                            137+         BALR  14,15                     LINK TO PUT ROUTINE                 01-PUT
                                       138          PUT   LABELOUT,PSTREET         PRINT STREET LINE                    03340
000138 4110 C2D4               002D4   139+         LA    1,LABELOUT                          LOAD PARAMETER REG 1  02-IHBIN
00013C 4100 C218               00218   140+         LA    0,PSTREET                           LOAD PARAMETER REG 0  02-IHBIN
000140 58F0 1030               00030   141+         L     15,48(0,1)                LOAD PUT ROUTINE ADDR               01-PUT
000144 05EF                            142+         BALR  14,15                     LINK TO PUT ROUTINE                 01-PUT
                                       143          PUT   LABELOUT,PCITY           PRINT CITY,STATE,ZIP LINE            03350
000146 4110 C2D4               002D4   144+         LA    1,LABELOUT                          LOAD PARAMETER REG 1  02-IHBIN
00014A 4100 C236               00236   145+         LA    0,PCITY                             LOAD PARAMETER REG 0  02-IHBIN
00014E 58F0 1030               00030   146+         L     15,48(0,1)                LOAD PUT ROUTINE ADDR               01-PUT
000152 05EF                            147+         BALR  14,15                     LINK TO PUT ROUTINE                 01-PUT
                                       148          PUT   LABELOUT,BLINE           SKIP A BLANK LINE                    03360
000154 4110 C2D4               002D4   149+         LA    1,LABELOUT                          LOAD PARAMETER REG 1  02-IHBIN
000158 4100 C254               00254   150+         LA    0,BLINE                             LOAD PARAMETER REG 0  02-IHBIN
00015C 58F0 1030               00030   151+         L     15,48(0,1)                LOAD PUT ROUTINE ADDR               01-PUT
000160 05EF                            152+         BALR  14,15                     LINK TO PUT ROUTINE                 01-PUT
                                       153          PUT   LABELOUT,BLINE           SKIP A BLANK LINE                    03370
000162 4110 C2D4               002D4   154+         LA    1,LABELOUT                          LOAD PARAMETER REG 1  02-IHBIN
000166 4100 C254               00254   155+         LA    0,BLINE                             LOAD PARAMETER REG 0  02-IHBIN
00016A 58F0 1030               00030   156+         L     15,48(0,1)                LOAD PUT ROUTINE ADDR               01-PUT
00016E 05EF                            157+         BALR  14,15                     LINK TO PUT ROUTINE                 01-PUT
                                       158          PUT   LABELOUT,BLINE           SKIP A BLANK LINE                    03380
000170 4110 C2D4               002D4   159+         LA    1,LABELOUT                          LOAD PARAMETER REG 1  02-IHBIN
000174 4100 C254               00254   160+         LA    0,BLINE                             LOAD PARAMETER REG 0  02-IHBIN
000178 58F0 1030               00030   161+         L     15,48(0,1)                LOAD PUT ROUTINE ADDR               01-PUT
00017C 05EF                            162+         BALR  14,15                     LINK TO PUT ROUTINE                 01-PUT
```

```
                                                                                                       PAGE    6

  LOC  OBJECT CODE    ADDR1 ADDR2  STMT   SOURCE STATEMENT                                 ASM H V 02 13.42 10/14/85

                                   164 *********************************************************************  |  03400
                                   165 * GET THE NEXT INPUT RECORD SO THAT WE MAY CONTINUE LABEL PROCESSING.*  |  03410
                                   166 *********************************************************************  |  03420
                                   167          GET   LABELIN,PERSON          GET THE NEXT PERSON'S RECORD    |  03430
00017E 4110 C274            00274  168+         LA    1,LABELIN                         LOAD PARAMETER REG 1  02-IHBIN
000182 4100 C1AA            001AA  169+         LA    0,PERSON                          LOAD PARAMETER REG 0  02-IHBIN
000186 58F0 1030            00030  170+         L     15,48(0,1)               LOAD GET ROUTINE ADDR          01-GET
00018A 05EF                        171+         BALR  14,15                    LINK TO GET ROUTINE            01-GET
00018C 47F0 C090            00090  172          B     MAINLOOP                CONTINUE TO PROCESS ALL RECORDS |  03440

                                   174 *********************************************************************  |  03460
                                   175 * AFTER ALL RECORDS HAVE BEEN PROCESSED WE'RE DONE.  CLOSE ALL FILES *  |  03470
                                   176 * AND RETURN CONTROL TO THE OPERATING SYSTEM.                         *  |  03480
                                   177 *********************************************************************  |  03490
000190                             178 EOF      DS    0H                      TARGET POINT WHEN END OF FILE   |  03500
                                   179          CLOSE (LABELIN,,LABELOUT)     CLOSE ALL FILES                 |  03510
000190                             180+         CNOP  0,4                               ALIGN LIST TO FULLWORD 01-CLOSE
000190 4510 C19C            0019C  181+         BAL   1,*+12                            LOAD REG1 W/LIST ADDR  01-CLOSE
000194 00                          182+         DC    AL1(0)                            OPTION BYTE            01-CLOSE
000195 000274                      183+         DC    AL3(LABELIN)                      DCB ADDRESS            01-CLOSE
000198 80                          184+         DC    AL1(128)                          OPTION BYTE            01-CLOSE
000199 0002D4                      185+         DC    AL3(LABELOUT)                     DCB ADDRESS            01-CLOSE
00019C 0A14                        186+         SVC   20                                ISSUE CLOSE SVC        01-CLOSE
00019E 58DD 0004            00004  187          L     R13,4(R13)              RESTORE SAVE AREA POINTER       |  03520
0001A2 98EC D00C            0000C  188          LM    R14,R12,12(R13)         RESTORE ALL OTHER REGISTERS     |  03530
0001A6 1BFF                        189          SR    R15,R15                 CLEAR REGISTER 15 BEFORE WE EXIT |  03540
0001A8 07FE                        190          BR    R14                     RETURN CONTROL TO THE O.S.      |  03550
```

When end of file is reached we must CLOSE all files before returning control back to the operating system. Again, note the expansion of the I/O macros used in this program.

```
  LOC  OBJECT CODE    ADDR1 ADDR2  STMT   SOURCE STATEMENT                                          ASM H V 02 13.42 10/14/85

                                    192 ************************************************************************ | 03570
                                    193 *     D A T A     A R E A S     &     W O R K     E L E M E N T S      * | 03580
                                    194 ************************************************************************ | 03590

                                    196 ************************************************************************ | 03610
                                    197 * THE AREA CALLED PERSON IS SIMPLY A GLOBAL NAME FOR A SET OF FIELDS.  * | 03620
                                    198 * THE ORG ALLOWS THE FIELDS CALLED NAME THROUGH ZIPCODE TO RENAME       * | 03630
                                    199 * THE AREA CALLED PERSON INTO MEANINGFUL FIELDS THAT CAN BE USED.       * | 03640
                                    200 ************************************************************************ | 03650
0001AA                              201 PERSON   DS    CL80                  INPUT RECORD HOLDING AREA            | 03660
0001FA                       001AA  202          ORG   PERSON                RENAME THE AREA CALLED PERSON        | 03670
0001AA                              203 NAME     DS    CL20                  PERSON'S NAME IN FIRST 30 COLS       | 03680
0001BE                              204 SEXCODE  DS    C                     M-MALE, F-FEMALE                     | 03690
0001BF                              205 MARITAL  DS    C                     MARITAL STATUS S-SINGLE,M-MARRY      | 03700
0001C0                              206 STREET   DS    CL20                  STREET ADDRESS                       | 03710
0001D4                              207 CITY     DS    CL20                  NAME OF THE CITY                     | 03720
0001E8                              208 STATE    DS    CL2                   STATE CODE                           | 03730
0001EA                              209 ZIPCODE  DS    CL5                   ZIP CODE                             | 03740
0001EF                       001FA  210          ORG                                                            | 03750

                                    212 ************************************************************************ | 03770
                                    213 * THE FOLLOWING AREAS ARE USED TO BUILD THE VARIOUS LINES OF THE       * | 03780
                                    214 * LABEL AND TO PROVIDE PROPER SPACING BETWEEN EACH LABEL SINCE         * | 03790
                                    215 * CARRIAGE CONTROL CHARACTERS CANNOT BE USED.                          * | 03800
                                    216 ************************************************************************ | 03810
0001FA                              217 PNAME    DS    CL30                  OUTPUT NAME LINE                     | 03820
000218                              218 PSTREET  DS    CL30                  OUTPUT STREET LINE                   | 03830
000236                              219 PCITY    DS    CL30                  OUTPUT CITY,STATE,ZIP LINE           | 03840
000254 4040404040404040             220 BLINE    DC    CL30' '               BLANK LINE FOR LABEL SPACING         | 03850

                                    222          PRINT NOGEN                                                    | 03870
                                    223 ************************************************************************ | 03880
                                    224 * LABELIN IS THE NAME OF THE INPUT FILE AND USES EODAD TO TRANSFER     * | 03890
                                    225 * CONTROL TO THE LABEL EOF WHEN END OF FILE IS REACHED.                * | 03900
                                    226 *                                                                      * | 03910
                                    227 * LABELOUT IS THE NAME OF THE OUTPUT FILE WHICH DIRECTS THE BUILT      * | 03920
                                    228 * LABEL LINES TO THE PROPER OUTPUT ELEMENT TO PRINT MAILING LABELS.    * | 03930
                                    229 ************************************************************************ | 03940
                                    230 LABELIN  DCB   DSORG=PS,DDNAME=LABELIN,MACRF=GM,EODAD=EOF                 | 03950
                                    284 LABELOUT DCB   DSORG=PS,DDNAME=LABELOUT,MACRF=PM,RECFM=F,LRECL=30,      X| 03960
                                                       BLKSIZE=30                                               | 03970
000338                              338          LTORG                                                          | 03980
000338 000001E7                     339                =A(CITY+19)
00033C 000001D4                     340                =A(CITY)
000340 D4D94B4040404040             341                =CL30'MR.'
00035E D4E24B4040404040             342                =CL30'MS.'
00037C D4D9E24B40404040             343                =CL30'MRS.'
00039A 4040                         344                =C'  '
000000                              345          END   LABELS                                           | 03990
```

The DCB macros are not expanded due to the fact that a PRINT NOGEN preceded the DCB commands. NOGEN means "do not generate or expand".

```
SYMBOL     LEN    VALUE  DEFN  REFERENCES                                              ASM H V 02 13.42 10/14/85

BLINE     00030   000254 0220  0085 0087 0150 0155 0160
CITY      00020   0001D4 0207  0094 0113 0339 0340
CITYEND   00002   0000FC 0111  0097 0099
CITYLOOP  00002   0000E2 0095  0101
CITYLP2   00002   000108 0115  0119
EOF       00002   000190 0178  0252
FEMALE    00002   0000A8 0065  0060
LABELIN   00004   000274 0234  0046 0051 0168 0183
LABELOUT  00004   0002D4 0288  0048 0134 0139 0144 0149 0154 0159 0185
LABELS    00001 00000000 0024  0027 0345
MAINLOOP  00002   000090 0055  0172
MARITAL   00001   0001BF 0205  0071
MARRIED   00002   0000C0 0077  0072
MOVEREST  00002   0000CC 0081  0063 0075
NAME      00020   0001AA 0203  0062 0074 0079
PCITY     00030   000236 0219  0087 0114 0145
PERSON    00080   0001AA 0201  0052 0169 0202
PNAME     00030   0001FA 0217  0061 0062 0073 0074 0078 0079 0135
PSTREET   00030   000218 0218  0085 0086 0140
R11       00001 0000000B 0019  0033 0034 0035 0036
R12       00001 0000000C 0020  0025 0026 0027 0188
R13       00001 0000000D 0021  0025 0034 0035 0036 0187 0187 0188
R14       00001 0000000E 0022  0025 0188 0190
R15       00001 0000000F 0023  0026 0189 0189
R3        00001 00000003 0011  0094 0096 0098 0100 0100 0112 0119
R4        00001 00000004 0012  0113 0116 0116 0118
R5        00001 00000005 0013  0114 0117 0117 0118 0126 0127 0128
SAVEAREA  00004   00001C 0031  0033
SEXCODE   00001   0001BE 0204  0059
SKIPOVER  00002   000064 0032  0028
STATE     00002   0001E8 0208  0127
STREET    00020   0001C0 0206  0086
ZIPCODE   00005   0001EA 0209  0128
=A(CITY+19)
          00004   000338 0339  0098
=A(CITY)  00004   00033C 0340  0112
=C' '     00002   00039A 0344  0096
=CL30'MR.'
          00030   000340 0341  0061
=CL30'MRS.'
          00030   00037C 0343  0078
=CL30'MS.'
          00030   00035E 0342  0073
```

The cross reference page lists all elements and in what lines each element was used. As you can see, the fields called PERSON and NAME are defined in the program at offset X'0001AA' as a result of the ORG command. The ORG command allows you to name a storage area in many different ways. Here, the storage area at X'0001AA' is named by either NAME or by the element PERSON.

```
MR. JOHN DOE
101 W. MARKET
SOMEWHERE, TX 78777


MR. BILL SMYTHE
#3 PLEASANT LANE
NOWHERE, IL 61616


MS. MARY JONES
100 E. MAPLE #2
SOMEWHERE, TX 78777


MRS. BETTY BOOP
#3 CONCORD AVENUE
NOWHERE, IL 61616


MR. JIMMY BOOP
#3 CONCORD AVENUE
NOWHERE, IL 61616


MR. NNNNNNNNNNNNNNNNNNNN
SSSSSSSSSSSSSSSSSSSS
CCCCCCCCCCCCCCCCCCCC, XX 55555
```

STUDY QUESTIONS

1. The condition code is found in the PSW and is used to control the processing flow within a program. It has four possible values and they are _______, _______, _______, and _______.
2. A four-bit mask may be coded on the _______ or the _______ instructions to test the value of the condition code.
3. _______ _______ instructions are used in place of the BC or BCR mnemonic and the mask value to help overall program readability.
4. The instruction to give more than one name to the same area of storage is the _______ instruction.
5. The logical construct that executes a loop within the range at least once is the _______ logical structure.
6. Although end-of-file processing is typically implemented with two input commands, it is generally implemented with only one command in assembler language since the _______ operand on the DCB *forces* a branch to logic generally located outside of the loop construct.
7. In ASSIST, the end of file is tested using the condition code and an appropriate branch instruction. The instruction to branch to the location BYEBYE when the end of file is reached is _______________________.
8. Two register values are subtracted. If the result is negative, then we want to transfer control to the location labeled SCHARGE to assess a service charge on the person's account. Write the instructions to implement this logic.
9. If register 2 is the loop control register, register 6 is the increment register, and register 7 is the limit register, the BXLE instruction to continue looping to the label called AGAIN is _______________.
10. The instruction that allows us to place a label on a storage area without actually defining any storage for the area is _______________________. This instruction also allows us to label instructions within our program to allow later insertion or deletion of code very easily.
11. Write instructions to perform the following operations.
    (a) Branch to the location TOOBIG if overflow occurs after a subtraction operation.
    (b) Determine if the value in the halfword field PSN is equal to 10 and set the condition code appropriately.
    (c) Transfer control to the location labeled KEEPGOIN if the value of the field SSN (social security number) does not begin with the digits 123.
    (d) Transfer control to the location KEEPGOIN if the contents of register 3 are positive or negative but not zero.
    (e) Add the three fullword values NUM1, NUM2, and NUM3 and set the condition code based on the value of the result; zero, less than zero, greater than zero, overflow.
12. The following counting loop structure is found in many higher-level languages. Implement the same structure in assembly language.

```
FOR I := 1 TO 50 BY 5 DO
   {body of the loop}
ENDFOR
```

13. Implement the following WHILE loop structure in assembly language. Assume that any variables are 20 byte character fields.

```
WHILE (LASTNAME ≠ 'JONES' AND LASTNAME ≠ 'SMITH') DO
   {body of the loop}
ENDWHILE
```

14. Implement the following loop construct in assembly language. Assume that any variables are 20 byte character fields.

```
REPEAT
   {body of the loop}
UNTIL (LASTNAME > 'ZACHRY')
```

15. Implement the following construct in assembly language. Assume that all accumulation variables are to be processed using registers.

```
IF SEX = 'F' THEN
   FEMALES := FEMALES + 1
ELSE
   MALES := MALES + 1
ENDIF
```

PROGRAMMING ASSIGNMENTS

1. Write a program to read data cards until the end of file and echo them to the printer. In other words, don't process any data on each data card, just send it to the printer so that you can see what it contains. This is a modification of the logo or crest program of an earlier chapter.
2. Write a program that computes the sum of all integers between 1 and 100 and output this value.
3. Modify the mailing label program so that a letter is sent to each person informing them of a new product on the market. Use the same data format that you saw in the programming examples within the chapter, but output a letter instead of mailing labels. Attempt to make the letter personalized by imbedding the person's name within the letter at appropriate points.
4. An unknown number of data cards contains two values typed in each of the first five columns. The first value is the number of miles driven and the second is the number of gallons of gasoline used to go that distance. For each pair of numbers, use integer arithmetic to compute the approximate average miles per gallon for each pair of values. Output each pair of numbers and the result.
5. Each data card contains a single number in the first five columns. For 50 data cards, compute the average of all of the numbers. Output each number and the final average.
6. Write a program to read cards until the end of file is reached. Each data card contains a single number. Using the formula (N*(N+1)/2), compute the sum of all integers between 1 and the number. Print each number and output your results.
7. Modify Program Problem 6 to eliminate the formula by using a counting loop to sum the numbers between 1 and the input value.
8. Several room measurements have been entered on data cards. Each room measurement consists of the room's length, width, and height (in feet). For each room, compute the total square

yards of carpeting needed to carpet the room and the number of cubic feet of air conditioning required to maintain the room at an adequate temperature. Total the values for all rooms and provide a summary report at the end of all processing.

9. An unknown number of data cards contains integer numbers. Read in each data card and determine which numbers are the largest and smallest in the set of input values. Print out all of the numbers followed by the largest and smallest values that you find.
10. Mr. Smith's auto sales has increased the size of his inventory. In fact, Mr. Smith has so many cars that he doesn't know the exact count on the lot. Refer to the problems in the earlier chapters and write a program to report on Mr. Smith's current inventory using end-of-file logic. Compute and report on the same data that you did in Programming Assignment 5 in Chapter 5.
11. Input a five-digit number. The first two digits represent a year and the last three digits represent the day of the year. For example, February 10, 1999 is represented by the input value 99041 since February 10 is the forty-first day of 1999. For each input value, convert the value into the two most common date formats. In other words, you're going to write a program to convert from Julian date format to Gregorian date format and what we'll call "computer date format." With an input value of 99041, your program would print out this number and the two converted dates as follows:

    99041   02/10/99   February 10, 1999

12. Process input records until end of file. Each input record contains an integer number. Extract the integer and proceed to approximate the square root of the integer using the algorithm below.

    assume that X represents the input integer value.

    first approximation: F = X * 0.5

    next approximation: NA = 0.5 * (F + (X / F))

    Subsequent approximations utilize the second equation to compute a new NA value based on the previous NA value. In other words, the second equation will be embedded in a loop. Each time through the loop, the old NA value will be used for F in order to compute a new NA value. When the difference between the last approximation and current approximation is zero, you've found the square root of the number.
13. Process input records until end of file. For each input value, compute the factorial of the number. Print the original number and its factorial value.
14. Process input records until end of file. Each input record consists of an unknown number of numbers on the record. The first number of each data record specifies the number of numbers that follow it. For example, the numbers 3, 10, 20, and 50 would be found on a data record. The first number, 3, indicates that three numbers follow it.

    For each data record, compute the average of the numbers on the record, excluding the first number. Referring to our example, we'd average the numbers 10, 20, and 50. Print all input values, including the first number on the data record, followed by the average.

    Compute the average of all averages when end of file is reached and print this value as the last element of your printout.
15. Read the first data record in a data file. Extract the integer number from this data record. This number indicates the number of data records that are to be processed. In other words, the first data record value will set the limit value for a counting loop structure.

    For each subsequent data record, extract an integer number from the record. Determine if the number is even or odd. Print the data record number, the number from the data record, and "even" or "odd" depending on what your program determined.

7

Processing with Packed-Decimal Data

In terms of data processing, packed-decimal data ranks as one of the most used. Payroll information, inventory reports, and many other day-to-day applications rely on packed-decimal data as the basis for their processing. Why is packed-decimal data so widely used and so important? The answer lies in that it is common to most standard languages, it is typically faster as compared to floating-point operations, and finally, it is easy to understand since the instructions used for its processing are logically related to the operation being performed.

REVIEW OF PACKED-DECIMAL FORMAT

In Chapter 2, we discussed the internal format and some general processing of packed-decimal data. We learned that packed-decimal information is stored within the computer in a somewhat *compressed* manner. Two packed-decimal digits are stored in one byte of storage except for the rightmost byte, which is used to hold the sign of the number. Logically, a packed-decimal field has a representation as described in Fig. 7.1.

```
dd dd dd . . . dd ds
```

Figure 7.1 Format of a packed-decimal field.

The format illustrates that each pair of digits (dd) occupies one byte and the rightmost byte (ds—digit and sign) holds the rightmost digit and sign of the number.

Generally, packed-decimal fields are 1 to 15 digits long, although fields as large as 31 digits may be processed. The numbers are stored without any relationship to a decimal point. If a decimal point is to exist, special instructions must be used. In other words, the numbers 1,234 and 12.34 are stored in *exactly* the same format within a packed-decimal field. The instructions to process the data are the same except those to print the number. During printing, the number is converted to character format (output format), and a decimal point or a comma is inserted between digits so that the number is printed as desired. Decimal points are maintained by the programming instructions and appear only after processing has occurred and the results have been printed. Recall a similar discussion in chapter 5 where we discussed binary data processing.

DEFINING AND INITIALIZING PACKED-DECIMAL FIELDS

A packed-decimal field may be defined in a number of ways, but it is typically defined using the **P** type. For example, a packed-decimal field three *bytes* long is defined as shown in Fig. 7.2.

```
ABC      DS      PL3
```

Figure 7.2 Defining a three-byte packed-decimal field.

This field holds five digits (three times two minus one). For numbers with 10 digit positions, we define a field six bytes long. Actually, a six-byte field allows 11 digit positions rather than 10. Remember, the rightmost byte of a packed-decimal field only holds one digit position, so that the total number of digits is always an odd number, regardless of the number of bytes.

Packed-decimal fields are also defined in many other ways, too. A **DS CL1** statement defines a one-byte field holding one packed-decimal digit. In this example, we must recall that instructions may be used to process any type of data. Further, the definition of a field does not necessarily have to match the use of the field, although we tend to coordinate them to enhance program understanding and readability. Defining a packed-decimal field as CL1 works, but it is more acceptable to define it as PL1, which means a packed-decimal field of one byte.

Earlier in the text, we discussed the input and output of information so that it could be processed in binary format. We saw that character data was converted into packed decimal and then into binary so it could be processed in binary. For output, the binary data is converted to packed-decimal format and then to character format so that it could be printed in an understandable form. We also remarked that the instructions **CVD (convert to decimal)** and **CVB (convert to binary)** require a field definition aligned on a doubleword boundary and is eight bytes long (doubleword). At that time, we defined the field as shown in Fig. 7.3.

```
This is not the method to use when
 defining packed-decimal fields.

        CONVERT   DS     D
```

Figure 7.3 Defining a packed-decimal field in a non-standard manner.

The field labeled CONVERT is defined as a *binary* field rather than a packed-decimal field (logically, of course). Again, what matters is not how we define the field, but what information the field contains and what instructions process the data. The only constraint is that the field has to be aligned on a doubleword boundary.

We can define CONVERT in another way to give more meaning to our program. This is done by using the P type and a null-boundary alignment instruction as shown in Fig. 7.4.

```
          DS     0D
CONVERT   DS     PL8
```

Figure 7.4 Standard method for defining and aligning an 8-byte packed-decimal field.

The first field in Fig. 7.4 defines no storage since it only forces the field to align on a doubleword boundary. CONVERT is defined as an eight-byte packed-decimal field and so the end result is an eight-byte, doubleword aligned field. The result is the same as using DS D, but it is clear that CONVERT is being used to hold packed-decimal data (P data type) rather than binary information (D data type).

Packed-decimal fields are initialized in a manner similar to the other data storage types. After the P directive and the length designator, the initial value of the field is within quotes. For example, to initialize the field called TOTAL to zero, code the instruction shown in Fig. 7.5.

```
TOTAL    DC     PL5'0'
```

Figure 7.5 Defining and initializing a field.

Here, the DC (define constant) assembly language instruction allows us to give a default or initial value to a field. The field called TOTAL is five bytes long and is set to zero. Suppose that we define TOTAL as a doubleword and initialize it using the code given in Fig. 7.6.

```
This example will not work correctly.

TOTAL    DC     D'0'
```

Figure 7.6 Incorrect packed-decimal definition and initialization.

Yes, TOTAL is initialized to zero, but TOTAL is defined as a *binary field.* Since TOTAL is *not* defined as a packed-decimal field, it cannot be processed using packed-decimal instructions. If we attempt to process any field containing nonpacked-decimal data with packed-decimal instructions, our program abends with a **data exception** abend code (0C7). If we look carefully at the hexadecimal representation of TOTAL as defined above, X'0000000000000000', we see that it does not have a valid sign in the rightmost half byte of the field. This causes the definition to be invalid. All packed-decimal fields must have a valid sign in the rightmost half byte and contain only digits 0 through 9 in all positions to the left of the sign position.

Defining and initializing packed-decimal fields is quite easy, but aligning them on proper boundaries to convert data from input to internal format may cause difficulty. Another accepted technique for aligning fields is to use the **CNOP (conditional, no operation) assembly language instruction.** By itself it is not an executable instruction, but it generates instructions that cause alignment.

The CNOP instruction has two operands. The first operand is usually coded with a value of 0 and the second operand with a value of 4 or 8. These values *do not* refer to registers. For example, to align a storage area on a doubleword boundary, the programmer could code the instructions given in Fig. 7.7.

```
         CNOP  0,8
CONVERT  DS    PL8
```

Figure 7.7 Aligning and defining a field using CNOP.

In this example, the second operand indicates that the storage area that follows is to be aligned on an eight-byte boundary address (a doubleword boundary). If we code a 4 in the second operand, then CONVERT aligns on a fullword boundary. A value of 2 aligns CONVERT on a halfword boundary.

The CNOP instruction generates a null branch-on-condition register instruction (BCR). The machine code and mnemonic for the null BCR instruction is shown in Fig. 7.8.

Machine Code	Instruction Mnemonic
0700	BCR 0,0

Figure 7.8 Code generation using the CNOP instruction.

As you can see from the mnemonic, no program mask is specified in the instruction since a value of zero is coded. Register 0, specified as a target of a branch, yields a null branch, that is, a branch is never taken since register 0 cannot be used in addressing. Hence, this instruction does nothing but occupy storage. But this is exactly the goal of CNOP. It causes enough bytes to be filled with X'0700' so that the field that follows the CNOP is aligned on the designated boundary.

Here's an example. Assume that CONVERT is defined at location X'001013'. By placing a CNOP 0,8 instruction just before CONVERT, bytes X'001013' through X'001017' are filled with X'0007000700', thus causing CONVERT to align with the next address X'001018', which is a doubleword boundary. If the address of CONVERT is X'001012', then the CNOP 0,8 fills locations X'001012' through X'001017' with X'070007000700' to again force CONVERT on a doubleword boundary.

CNOP allows the programmer to align storage areas on designated boundaries to reduce the chances of program failure. If an instruction requires alignment, but the data area referenced by the instruction is not aligned, then the program abends with an **0C6 (specification exception)** abend code.

When the first operand of CNOP is not zero, the storage area that follows is aligned on a boundary *within* the overall alignment specified in the second operand. Figure 7.9 describes the various CNOP settings and the impact of those definitions on the allocation and filling of intermediate storage.

The second operand indicates overall alignment—fullword (4) or doubleword (8). The first operand then specifies which even-numbered byte within the fullword or doubleword is to be used for alignment.

Regardless of alignment technique, we must remember to align packed-decimal fields in certain cases. The null storage definition instruction (DS 0D) or the CNOP instruction may be used as a matter of preference. One last factor to consider is the contents of the null bytes in memory. CNOP ensures that the bytes are filled with either X'00' or X'07' and the null storage definition instruction simply causes alignment without storage fill. This difference may assist you in determining the source of a program abend or the source of erroneous data. Knowing what is in each memory location compared to not knowing this information may make the difference between finding and resolving a program problem and not resolving the problem by yourself.

CNOP Setting	Result
0,4	Fullword alignment (address ends in 0, 4, 8, or C).
2,4	Halfword alignment within a fullword (address ends in 2, 6, A or E).
0,8	Doubleword alignment (address ends in 0 or 8).
2,8	Halfword alignment within a doubleword (address ends in 2 or A).
4,8	Fullword alignment within a doubleword (address ends in 4 or C).
6,8	Halfword alignment within a doubleword (address ends in 6 or E).

Figure 7.9 Results of using the CNOP instruction.

INPUT AND OUTPUT OF PACKED-DECIMAL FIELDS

Packed-decimal information may be stored on disk, tape, or some other external storage medium. On the other hand, packed-decimal information may not be sent to the printer, input from data cards, or input from terminal devices since these units only allow character data to be represented. With this in mind, we'll review the conversion of character data input to packed-decimal format and packed-decimal data to character data output format for printing since we'll undoubtedly be using card image input and printed output for most processing tasks.

Suppose that a number is typed in columns one to five of a data card and that the number is right justified within the field. To convert this number to packed-decimal format, we use the instruction in Fig. 7.10 and the field called CONVERT defined earlier.

```
PACK   CONVERT(8),field(5)
```

Figure 7.10 Converting a character field value to packed-decimal.

The character data that is five bytes long is converted into packed-decimal format and is stored in the field called CONVERT. If the input field is C'bbb25', then the value in CONVERT is X'000000000000025F' since the PACK instruction reverses the zone and digit portions of the rightmost byte and removes the zones from all bytes to the left of the rightmost byte.

Suppose that **field** contains the value C'bbb@$', which is equivalent to X'4040407C5B'. The PACK instruction does not concern itself with valid and invalid source data. Hence, packing this field places X'0000000000000**CB**5' in CONVERT. As you can see, two of the digit portions are not digits and the sign is also not valid. If our program now attempts to use packed-decimal instructions to reference CONVERT, it abends with a **data exception** (0C7) abend.

Now suppose that the value 25 is *not* right justified in the first five columns of our input data. Packing C'bb25b' (X'4040F2F540'), for example, places X'000000000000250**4**' into CONVERT. The rightmost half byte of CONVERT is not a valid sign (since it's not A through F). Again, the program abends when CONVERT is referenced with a packed-decimal instruction.

Consider a number containing a decimal point. Packing C'12.34' (X'F-1F24BF3F4') gives a value of X'000000000012**B**34F' to CONVERT. Here, a problem lies with the decimal point since its digit portion **B** is treated as a digit by the PACK instruction. The resulting number in CONVERT is *not* valid and causes a program to abend when referenced. To eliminate this problem, ignore the decimal point as shown in Fig. 7.11.

```
         MVC    PART1(2),field
         MVC    PART2(2),field+3
         PACK   CONVERT(8),PARTS(4)
         .      .
         .      .
         .      .
PARTS    DS     0CL4
PART1    DS     CL2
PART2    DS     CL2
```

Figure 7.11 Managing the decimal point on an input field.

By removing the decimal point, we can now pack the number as if it were an integer. The resulting value in CONVERT is X'000000000001234F', which must be processed to retain the *logical* decimal point desired by the user and the input data. We'll see how to do this later.

After processing, we must convert our packed-decimal result(s) into character (printable) format. As discussed in Chapter 5, the UNPK (unpack) and OI (or immediate) instructions are used for this purpose. The UNPK instruction reverses the sign and digit portions of the rightmost byte in the packed-decimal field and supplies zone portions to all remaining digit positions. If properly done, X'0012345C' is converted into X'F0F0F1F2F3F4C5' after unpacking. When printed, the output of this field is C'001234E'. The last byte is printed as the letter E, not the digit 5, since X'C5' is the representation for E, not 5. To fix this problem, the OI instruction changes the zone on the rightmost byte from C to F so that the byte becomes X'F5' instead of X'C5'. The rightmost byte of our printable character field is at offset 6 within this field (since our field is seven bytes long). Hence, the instruction given in Fig. 7.12 fixes the rightmost byte and allows the field to be printed properly.

```
OI      field+6,X'F0'
```

Figure 7.12 Fixing the rightmost byte after conversion using OI.

Now suppose that our field is to be converted to 123.45. To edit this field and to supply a decimal point, we must build a new field that contains digits to the left of the decimal, the decimal point, and digits to the right as illustrated in Fig. 7.13.

```
         UNPK    ALMOST(7),field
         OI      ALMOST+6,X'F0'
         MVC     LEFT(5),ALMOST
         MVC     RIGHT(2),ALMOST+5
         pnum is the field in proper form
         .       .
         .       .
         .       .
field    DS      PL4
ALMOST   DS      CL7
PNUM     DS      0CL8
LEFT     DS      CL5
         DC      C'.'
RIGHT    DS      CL2
```

Figure 7.13 Converting a decimal field (with a decimal point) for output.

After converting the number into printable format, we must move the digits to the left and right of the decimal place into their respective locations within PNUM. Sandwiched between the two halves is the decimal point. If we now move PNUM to an output line, we can print C'00123.45' as desired.

Let's take this one step further. Suppose that we want to add commas between groups of three digits and that leading zeros are not to be printed. As we continue to complicate the output formatting procedure, we soon find that the formatting can be tedious as well as complex. There's a much easier method. Special formatting instructions in assembly language allow us to easily convert packed-decimal numbers into ones that have leading zeros suppressed, commas between digits, decimal points, floating characters, negative signs, and so on. In fact, this method is so powerful that you'll immediately abandon the UNPK/OI technique in its favor.

Editing or Formatting Numeric Output

The two instructions that provide an easy method of formatting packed-decimal data for output are **ED (edit)** and **EDMK (edit and mark).** Both instructions have two operands and both are SS instructions. Figure 7.14 describes their general format.

```
ED      D1(L,B1),D2(B2)

EDMK    D1(L,B1),D2(B2)
```

Figure 7.14 Format of the ED and EDMK instructions.

Since both operands contain a D(B) address form, we often find them used with labeled storage areas. Further, both instructions contain a **length** operand that refers to the length of the *first* operand.

The first operand designates a character field and the second designates the packed-decimal field to be converted for output. The second operand can be as long as 31 digits, but its length directly impacts on the length of the first operand (in bytes).

Before issuing either instruction, the first operand must contain the **edit pattern.** From the common meaning of the word *pattern,* you understand how these instructions work. The edit pattern *guides* the editing of the packed-decimal field. Information in the edit pattern is used during editing so that leading zeros can be suppressed, commas and decimal points placed within the field, and dollar or negative signs floated before the first digit. In fact, the edit pattern is the key to the successful use of these instructions. If you build the edit pattern incorrectly, you do not get the results desired. If you build it correctly, it works very well. Don't be fooled since at first it *is* difficult to understand and to build an edit pattern. However, the number of instructions, fields required, and time involved to accomplish the same activity using UNPK/OI/MVC/MVI makes it worthwhile to learn how to use ED and EDMK.

To use the ED and EDMK instructions, here's what you must do:

1. Create an edit pattern and place it into the field referenced by the first operand.
2. Issue the ED or EDMK instruction to convert the packed-decimal field into the desired output format.
3. Move (if necessary) the converted character field into the output line for printing.

The edit pattern is a character field consisting of special *hexadecimal* field values. Depending on these values, the packed-decimal field is edited and converted into a representation as selected by the programmer. The resulting character valued number *replaces* the original edit pattern. Hence, if many numbers are to be converted using the same edit pattern, you'll have to recreate the edit pattern since it is destroyed during *each* editing operation.

The edit pattern consists of several field types. The name of each field type, its hexadecimal value, and its meaning are given in Fig. 7.15.

Field Type	Hex Value	Meaning
fill character	selected by user	First character in the edit pattern used to replace or fill any nondigit areas.
digit selector	X'20'	Edits a digit from the packed field.
digit selector and significance starter	X'21'	Edits a digit from the packed-decimal field and forces the significance indicator to turn "on."
message character	selected by user	Special characters to allow the user to place commas, decimal points, or other characters into the resulting number.

Figure 7.15 Components of the edit pattern.

Some terminology must be understood when using ED or EDMK. The packed-decimal field X'0000234C' has three significant digits, 2, 3, and 4. Four nonsignificant digits, all zeros, appear before the first significant digit. The field X'0001034D' has four significant digits, 1, 0, 3, and 4. The fourth zero is significant since it appears between two other nonzero digits. The first three zeros on the front of the number are not significant. Considering these two numbers, we want X'0000234C' to be converted into C'ƀƀƀƀ 234' and X'0001034D' to be converted into C'ƀƀ−1034'. Constructing a proper edit pattern and using the proper sequence of instructions allow this to occur.

The first character in the edit pattern is the **fill character.** It is used as the *replacement* character within the edited result. If all positions before the first significant digit are to be filled with blanks or spaces, then the fill character is a blank (X'40',C'ƀ'). If you want to fill with a dollar sign, asterisk, or dash before the first significant digit, then use a fill character of a dollar sign, asterisk, or dash, respectively. As you can see, the fill character is used in place of leading zeros. Wherever a leading zero would appear, the fill character appears after editing.

Following the fill character, define X'20' characters for as many digits as you expect to be in the result minus two. If you expect seven digits in your result, then you should have 5 X'20' characters. An expected result of five digits causes you to use three digit selector bytes. In planning the number of digit selector bytes to be placed into your edit pattern, remember that, usually, the total number of digit selector bytes (X'20') is an even number and the total number of digits converted for printing is an odd number. Although the total length of your edit pattern may be even or odd, the number of X'20' edit character positions is usually an even number.

The next selector byte is X'21', which is the *digit selector and significance starter* byte. This field in the edit pattern selects and edits a digit position (just as does X'20'), *and* turns on the significance indicator. The primary purpose of the X'21' byte is to allow a value of zero to be produced properly during editing.

Finally, end your edit pattern with a X'20' character. Thus, a basic pattern to edit a packed-decimal field containing N digits (N being an odd number) will consist of: a fill character, N−2 X'20' characters, X'21', and X'20'. The total length of the edit pattern will be N+1 bytes.

Suppose that a three-byte packed-decimal field is to be edited. Within this field there are five digits (three times two minus one). An edit pattern of at least six characters is needed—the fill character, three X'20' bytes, one X'21' byte, and 1−X'20' byte. A fill character and five X'20' bytes could be used, but we wouldn't get the same result. Let's see what happens and how the editing process works.

To begin, the system sets the significance indicator to "off." The **significance indicator** is a special field that determines whether or not a significant digit has been reached within the number. The significance indicator is "off" until a significant digit is found *or* until a X'21' is encountered. Either will turn the significance indicator "on."

In terms of editing, the fill character is used as the editing character as long as the significance indicator is "off." When the indicator is "on," a digit is edited and becomes a printable digit.

Suppose that our three-byte packed-decimal field contains the value +123 (X'00123C'). We want to convert it into a printable format using the ED instruction. The instruction in Fig. 7.16 provides the editing of this field, but let's see how the ED instruction works.

```
         ED     RESULT(6),FIELD

RESULT   DC     X'402020202120'
FIELD    DC     PL3'123'
```

Figure 7.16 Example of an editing operation using ED.

FIELD is defined and initialized as a packed-decimal field with a value of +123. RESULT is a six-byte field that is initialized with a proper edit pattern. The ED instruction edits FIELD and *changes the value of RESULT* to the edited number. It is important to remember that the edit pattern is destroyed during editing. If your program contains a loop and you must edit several numbers within the loop, you have to restore the edit pattern to its original value by using an MVC instruction as shown in Fig. 7.17.

```
MVC    RESULT(6),=X'402020202120'
```

Figure 7.17 A method of restoring an edit pattern using MVC.

When the editing of FIELD begins, the significance indicator is set to "off." The first byte in RESULT is noted as the fill character and processing continues to the next byte. The next byte is X'20', which indicates that a digit is to be selected. Within FIELD, the first digit selected is the first zero in the field X'**0**0123C'. Since the significance indicator is "off," this zero is not significant and so the fill character *replaces* the X'20' in RESULT. RESULT is now X'40**40**20202120'. Notice how the edit pattern is being changed.

The next byte in RESULT is a X'20', another digit selector. The digit X'0**0**123C' is selected from FIELD to be edited. Since the significance indicator is still "off" and this digit is a zero, the fill character replaces X'20' within RESULT so that RESULT is now X'4040**40**202120'.

The next byte in RESULT is X'20', a digit selector. The next digit in FIELD to be selected is X'00**1**23C'. The digit 1 is selected and edited, but since it is a significant digit, the digit is converted into X'F1' and is placed into the edit pattern, replacing the X'20'. Thus, RESULT now becomes X'404040**F1**2120'. Since a significant digit is encountered, the significance indicator is set "on."

Now that the significance indicator is "on," editing occurs on *every* digit selected from this point on whether or not it has a value of zero. In fact, X'21' has no impact on the significance indicator since the significance indicator has already been turned "on."

Continuing with our example, the next field in the edit pattern is X'21', which selects the digit X'001**2**3C' from FIELD. Since the SI (significance indicator) is "on" and since 2 is a significant digit, the digit is converted into X'F2' (by adding a zone of F) and placed into the edit pattern over top of X'21'. The edit pattern now becomes X'404040F1**F2**20'.

The next byte in the edit pattern is X'20', a digit selector. The digit X'0012**3**C' is selected from FIELD to be edited. Since the SI is "on" and since the digit 3 is significant, the digit is converted into X'F3' and replaces the X'20' in the edit pattern field. RESULT is now X'404040F1F2**F3**'. Since the edit pattern has been exhausted, the editing process ends. The value in RESULT is C'ƀƀƀ123'. The number has been properly edited, leading zeros have been suppressed, and the number is ready for printing.

Incidentally, if RESULT were defined within our print line storage area, we could immediately write our output to the printer (if FIELD was the only field to be edited). If the edit pattern is defined within the print line, you do not have to move the edited number into the print line storage area in order to send it to the printer.

Now suppose that FIELD has a value of zero, X'00000C'. Using the same edit pattern, X'402020202120', we'll edit this value.

The SI is set to "off." The fill character is noted and editing begins. X'20' selects a digit X'**0**0000C'. Since the SI is "off," the X'20' is replaced with the fill character. The edit pattern field becomes X'40**40**20202120'.

X'20' selects the digit X'00000C'. The SI is still "off" and so the fill character replaces X'20' within the edit pattern to give X'404040202120'.

The next byte in the edit pattern is X'20', which selects the digit X'00000C' from the field to be edited. Since the SI is "off," the fill character replaces X'20' in the edit pattern to give X'404040402120'.

X'21' selects the digit X'00000C' from the field, but since SI is still "off," the fill character replaces X'21' within the edit pattern to give X'404040404020'. After this digit is edited, the SI is turned to "on" since a X'21' was encountered during editing.

The next edit pattern byte is X'20', which says to select a digit. X'00000C' is selected for editing. Since the SI is now "on," the digit is converted into X'F0' and replaces X'20' within the edit pattern to give X'4040404040F0'. Therefore, our result is C'ƀƀƀƀƀ0', which prints as a value of zero.

In this example, the significance indicator was turned "on" by the X'21' byte. Having the SI "on" causes the digit zero to be edited into X'F0' and placed into the edit pattern instead of being replaced with the fill character. Had we used an original pattern of X'402020202020', we would have obtained a result of C'ƀƀƀƀƀƀ'. Since this field appears blank when printed, it is probably more appropriate to at least print a single zero digit if the result is zero. This is the reason why the X'21' character is used, namely, to force a digit of zero in the conversion when the field to be edited is zero.

Now let's turn to numbers with digits to the left and right of the decimal point. As we said earlier, the contents of a packed-decimal field have no indication of a decimal point. The only method for maintaining the decimal point is to edit the field in a manner that inserts a decimal point into the proper field position. Hence, the primary method builds an edit pattern to do the job. Also, remember that a value of zero is to be printed instead of all blanks as before. At this time we want to print a value of zero as 0.00 rather than 0.

Suppose that the field to be edited is four bytes long. A four-byte packed-decimal field contains seven digits. Let's suppose that of these seven digits, five are to the left of the decimal and two are to the right. We must, therefore, build our edit pattern to allow for this situation. If we write each digit position as shown in Fig. 7.18, we can easily see how the edit pattern is to be constructed.

Figure 7.18 An edit pattern for a seven-digit packed-decimal number.

Each of the seven digit positions is defined within the edit pattern. The first field in the edit pattern is still the fill character, which we provided. For all but one digit position, we use the X'20' to select and edit the digit. Just prior to the location where we want a value of zero to be printed, we place the X'21' character, which turns "on" the significance indicator. Incidentally, placing the X'21' is very important in this application because it provides both the digit zero before the decimal point and the decimal point. For example, we want 25 cents to be printed as '0.25', not as '25' or '.25'.

The basic method to construct an edit pattern is to draw a series of lines for each digit position to be edited. Just *before* the position where a zero is to be generated, place the X'21' character. Insert decimal points or commas into the edit pattern between the digit positions where desired or appropriate. Add a fill character to the front of the edit pattern and it's complete. Count the number of bytes in the edit pattern and write your instruction to edit the packed-decimal field.

Let's use different edit patterns on the same packed-decimal field. Suppose that we have an eight-byte packed-decimal field, but only the last five bytes (nine digits) are to be edited. If the field is called TOTAL, then the edit instruction appears as given in Fig. 7.19.

```
ED     pattern(length),TOTAL+3
```

Figure 7.19 Editing the last five bytes of an eight-byte field.

Figure 7.20 shows the results of the edited 5-byte field, depending on different edit patterns.

TOTAL+3 = X'000347092C'

Original Edit Pattern	Result (in characters)
40202020202020202120	ƀƀƀƀ347092
402020202020202120	ƀƀƀƀ34709
5B202020202020202120	$$$$347092
4020202020202120 4B2020	ƀƀƀƀ3470.92
5B20202020202120 4B2020	$$$$3470.92
5B206B2020206B202120 4B2020	$$$$$3,470.92
5C205B2020202120 4B202020	**$**347.092
402020206B2020206B202120	ƀƀƀƀƀ347,092
40202120	ƀƀƀ0

Figure 7.20 Sample edit patterns and their results.

The last pattern yields rather odd results. Did you notice that the number is truncated (chopped off) if there aren't enough digit selector bytes to select all the digits?

Did you notice the results when a fill character other than a blank is used? Finally, direct your attention to the decimal point patterns. Did you notice that the position of the decimal point within the pattern does not have to have any relationship to the packed-decimal field? These examples illustrate what can happen during editing, depending on the edit pattern field. Again, the contents of the packed-decimal field are almost forgotten since it is the edit pattern that controls the format of the number after editing.

During editing, the fields within the edit pattern are changed by the edit process. In fact, they are changed in one of three ways: first, the edit pattern byte could be replaced with the fill character; second, the edit pattern byte could be replaced with an edited digit from the packed-decimal field; or third, the edit pattern byte could be left alone as is the case with the decimal point or commas that appeared after the SI was turned "on."

The edit pattern may also be constructed so that several fields may be edited simultaneously. With X'22', the **field separator** edit character, the application program may edit two or more adjacent source packed fields using one edit pattern. For example, suppose that the two packed-decimal fields given in Fig. 7.21 are to be edited.

```
TOTA     DS     PL2
TOTB     DS     PL3
```

Figure 7.21 Editing adjacent fields.

TOTA contains three digits and TOTB contains five. We can edit them simultaneously using one edit pattern if and only if they are adjacent to each other in memory as shown in Fig. 7.21. If some other field is defined between TOTA and TOTB, then we cannot use this technique.

To build an edit pattern for this situation, we must account for all digits within *both* fields. Using one fill character and using X'22' to indicate where field separation occurs, our edit pattern logically appears as shown in Fig. 7.22.

```
fill character—TOTA pattern—X'22'—TOTB pattern
```

Figure 7.22 Logical pattern for dual field editing.

Using this logical representation, we now construct the digit selection patterns for TOTA and TOTB as X'202120' and X'2020202120', respectively. Combining the individual patterns into our logical representation, we have the edit pattern given in Fig. 7.23.

```
40 202120 22 2020202120
```

Figure 7.23 Resulting edit pattern for the data fields of Fig. 7.21.

(I've separated the components of the pattern for purposes of illustration.) If our edit pattern is stored in the field called NUMOUT, then we use the edit instruction in Fig. 7.24 to edit both fields simultaneously.

```
ED      NUMOUT(10),TOTA
```

Figure 7.24 Instruction to perform dual field editing.

Remember that the fields to be edited *must* be adjacent to each other and that only one fill character may be used for the entire edit pattern. If your application requires a fill character of a blank for one field and a fill character of $ for another, then you cannot use this technique. Finally, more than two fields may be edited by simply using several field separators within a single edit pattern.

Negative Signs and Floating Characters

Suppose that we want to edit a packed-decimal field that is either positive or negative. In all previous examples, we edited only positive fields and have not worried about the negative sign. However, negative numbers may result in our processing and we should be able to handle them properly. Further, suppose that we're processing monetary fields and we want a dollar sign to appear immediately before the first digit. In both of these cases, the ED instruction is not sufficient for our needs. However, the EDMK instruction, and our knowledge of edit pattern construction, will provide the necessary tools to process negative and monetary field values.

Negative numbers require the insertion of a negative sign before the first significant digit. The negative number 25 should be printed as −25 and the negative number 3 should be printed as −3. Suppose that we are editing a negative number and use an edit pattern of X'60202120' (note that the fill character, hex 60, is a negative sign or minus). The negative number 25 is edited as C'−−25' and the negative number 3 is edited as C'−−−3'. This isn't a standard form for representing a negative number and so we must adopt a technique that places the negative sign only before the first significant digit. In fact, using *this* edit pattern to edit the *positive* number 25 also gives a result of C'−−25'. Would you realize that this value was *positive*? Clearly, using a fill character of a minus does not properly distinguish between positive and negative values.

In order to format negative numbers for printing, we use our standard, edit pattern building techniques and a new instruction to edit negative numbers. This is done using the instruction called **EDMK (edit and mark)**.

Edit and mark may be used for negative numbers *or* positive numbers. The primary difference between ED and EDMK is that EDMK modifies register 1 so as to provide a location (within the resulting edit pattern) where the negative sign or some other floating character can be placed.

We must be careful when using EDMK since register 1 is *not* always modified. Register 1 is modified automatically when the significance indicator is turned "on" as a result of selecting and editing a significant digit. Register 1 is *not* modified if the SI was turned "on" as a result of encountering a X'21' edit pattern character. This ambiguity can cause problems if you don't plan for this before using EDMK. What we do is to adopt a technique by which register 1 is set properly by our program (before the EDMK instruction is issued) or by the EDMK instruction. In either case, R1 addresses a valid location, *within the edit pattern,* where we can then insert a negative sign (if the number is negative) or another floating character (such as a dollar sign).

Suppose that TOTAL is a three-byte packed-decimal field (five digits). TOTAL may be positive or negative. The edit pattern that we use to edit TOTAL is X'402020202120', which is identical to that used in the past. Actually, the edit pattern used with EDMK is exactly the same as that used with ED. The only difference between ED and EDMK is the modification made to register 1 as you'll soon see.

Suppose that our edit pattern is called PATTERN and is located in memory at location X'000500'. Figure 7.25 lists each byte in the edit pattern and its associated memory location.

Location	Edit pattern byte
000500	40
000501	20
000502	20
000503	20
000504	21
000505	20

Figure 7.25 Memory values prior to editing.

If TOTAL has a value of X'00123C' (positive 123) or X'00123D' (negative 123), then register 1 addresses location X'00503' *after* the EDMK instruction is completed (see Fig. 7.26.).

```
EDMK      PATTERN(6),TOTAL
```

Figure 7.26 Using the EDMK instruction.

If we now use an MVI instruction to move a negative sign into the memory location addressed by register 1, our edited result becomes C'ƀƀƀ−23'. But we chopped off the first digit. Register 1 contains the address of the digit 1, X'000503'. If register 1 contains the address X'000502', we move the negative sign into the edit pattern just *before* the first digit. This gives a result of C'ƀƀ−123'. This is what we need to do. Whenever we use EDMK, we must *back up* register 1 by one byte before inserting a negative sign or a dollar sign. R1 always addresses the first significant digit and so by backing up register 1, we address the byte just before the first significant digit. *Backing up* a register is easily done by subtracting 1 from it. Therefore, the code to insert a negative sign or a dollar sign before the first significant digit is given in its entirety in Fig. 7.27.

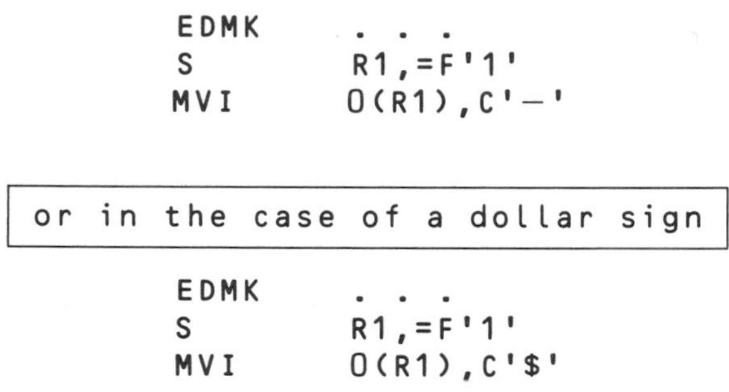

```
EDMK      . . .
S         R1,=F'1'
MVI       0(R1),C'-'

or in the case of a dollar sign

EDMK      . . .
S         R1,=F'1'
MVI       0(R1),C'$'
```

Figure 7.27 Editing followed by character insertion.

Subtracting 1 from our address of X'000503' gives an address of X'000502' in register 1. This happens to be the address of the field just before the first significant digit. Using MVI to move in either a negative sign or a dollar sign *floats* the appropriate character before the first digit.

Suppose that TOTAL has a value of zero. Using the same edit pattern, TOTAL is edited and the result is C'ƀƀƀƀƀ0' in the field called PATTERN. In this case, however, register 1 *is not* changed since the digit zero is not significant and the SI was turned "on" due to the X'21' edit character, not by encountering a significant digit. If we follow the EDMK instruction with a subtract and a move-immediate instruction, the program probably abends since register 1 may not contain a valid address (since it has not been set by a significant digit found during editing). To avoid such a problem, we can initiate some defensive programming. Since EDMK may or may not set register 1, we can eliminate any potential problem by setting register 1 *before* we issue the EDMK instruction. If EDMK changes the value in register 1, use the updated value. If no change is made to R1 by EDMK, then use *our* value to properly place the negative or dollar sign. In fact, the only time that EDMK does not change R1 is when the SI is turned "on" due to the X'21' edit character. Whenever a significant digit causes the SI to be turned "on," register 1 is set.

Before issuing the EDMK instruction, address register 1 to the byte in the edit pattern just after the X'21' character. This is where the SI is forced "on" and where the first significant digit in our number will be forced to occur. Since PATTERN is six bytes long, the address of the byte following the X'21' is at location PATTERN+5. This is the address to place in register 1. Combining all the elements of this discussion, we arrive at the code in Fig. 7.28 to properly insert a negative sign before the first significant digit. This code works if the number is large enough to turn "on" the SI by itself or if the SI is turned "on" as a result of EDMK encountering the X'21' pattern byte.

```
Warning: this code is not complete and may not
  fully handle negative numbers as desired.

           LA      R1,PATTERN+5
           EDMK    PATTERN(6),TOTAL
           S       R1,=F'1'
           MVI     0(R1),C'-'
```

Figure 7.28 Placing a negative sign into an edited result.

We have a slight problem here, however. What if TOTAL is positive? The code of Fig. 7.28 inserts a negative sign before the first digit *regardless* of the sign of the number. Further, a value of zero is edited as C'ƀƀƀƀ−0', which is illogical. This code alone is not sufficient. We need a method to test the value of TOTAL to see if it is equal to or greater than zero; and, if so, not to insert a negative sign before the number.

In order to determine whether or not a negative sign should be inserted before a number, we can use the condition code. Both the ED and EDMK instructions set the condition code based on the value in the *packed-decimal field* that is being edited. If that value is zero, then the condition code is set to B'1000'. A negative packed-decimal field sets the condition code to B'0100' and a positive packed-decimal field sets the condition code to B'0010'. Knowing this, we can now change our code to insert a negative sign before the number only if the number is negative as illustrated in Fig. 7.29.

```
         LA      R1,PATTERN+5
         EDMK    PATTERN(6),TOTAL
         BNM     NOTLT0
         S       R1,=F'1'
         MVI     0(R1),C'-'
NOTLT0   DS      0H
```

Figure 7.29 Complete method for editing a negative packed field.

In the code of Fig. 7.29, the packed-decimal field labeled TOTAL is to be edited. Register 1 initially addresses the last digit position in PATTERN should the value of TOTAL be only a single digit. After EDMK is issued, the condition code is tested for B'1011' (zero or greater than zero). If the value in TOTAL is not less than zero, then a branch is taken to the location called NOTLT0. If it is less than zero, then we fall into the code that adjusts register 1 appropriately and moves a negative sign into the edit pattern field just before the first significant digit.

This almost concludes our discussion on packed-decimal field editing. However, let's introduce a few more techniques related to their editing using the ED and EDMK instructions.

The first technique deals with subtracting 1 from register 1. If you recall, we did this to back up the address in register 1 to a point just before the first significant digit.

Although the subtract instruction does work very well to back up R1's value, this is not the typical method for subtracting 1 from the contents of a register. Another instruction is used, but you may not find it as meaningful or as understandable as the subtract.

The instruction is BCTR (branch on count register). In the discussion on looping in Chapter 6, we used BCTR to subtract 1 from a register and to branch to a location specified in BCTR's second operand. The BCTR instruction has two operands and both are registers as shown in Fig. 7.30.

```
BCTR    Ra,Rb
```

Figure 7.30 General format of the BCTR instruction.

As we said in Chapter 6, BCTR is not a commonly used instruction for branching purposes since the second operand identifies a register—and registers are not often used as branch targets. The RX counterpart of BCTR is BCT, which is used much more although it performs the same function as BCTR.

In any case, we can use BCTR to subtract 1 from a register. If the second operand in the BCTR instruction is zero, then the second operand is simply ignored by the system and no branch is taken. In the code given in Fig. 7.31, there are three instructions. The instructions before and after the BCTR are executed normally. Since no branch is taken with the BCTR, the instructions are an example of sequential instruction execution logic, that is, one instruction is executed after the other.

```
mnemonic     . . .
BCTR         R5,0
mnemonic     . . .
```

Figure 7.31 Sequential execution logic with BCTR.

A value of 1 is subtracted from register 5 and execution continues. You might ask, "Why do I need to know this rather than using the standard subtract instruction?" The answer is *performance.* BCTR is a much faster instruction than the subtract (S). If your logic simply calls for a register to be decreased by 1, then use the BCTR rather than the subtract. Finally, remember that the register's value can only be decreased by one. You cannot use BCTR to decrease a register's value by 10, or 8, or 20, or whatever. It has very limited use in this instance and can only be used to subtract a value of one from the register.

Integrating the BCTR into our editing code, we arrive at the next example for editing a packed-decimal field and supplying a valid sign before the number. Figure 7.32 shows this implementation.

```
         LA    R1,PATTERN+5
         EDMK  PATTERN(6),TOTAL
         BNM   NOTLTO
         BCTR  R1,0
         MVI   0(R1),C'-'
NOTLTO   DS    0H
```

Figure 7.32 Replacing S with BCTR during editing.

Our final example places either a positive sign before the number (if the number is greater than zero) or a negative sign (if the number is less than zero). Occasionally, you may want the number signed whether it's positive or negative. Figure 7.33 shows how this is done.

```
         LA    R1,PATTERN+5
         EDMK  PATTERN(6),TOTAL
         BZ    CONTINUE
         BP    POSITIVE
         BCTR  R1,0
         MVI   0(R1),C'-'
         B     CONTINUE
POSITIVE DS    0H
         BCTR  R1,0
         MVI   0(R1),C'+'
CONTINUE DS    0H
```

Figure 7.33 Forcing a sign into an edited result.

Incidentally, if you refer to the reference card, notice that the BCTR instruction does not set the condition code. Using this information, we can rewrite the code of Fig. 7.33 to centralize the BCTR instruction and eliminate duplicate coding by locating the BCTR just after the EDMK instruction. Figure 7.34 gives this implementation.

```
         LA    R1,PATTERN+5
         EDMK  PATTERN(6),TOTAL
         BCTR  R1,0
         BZ    CONTINUE
         BP    POSITIVE
         MVI   0(R1),C'-'
         B     CONTINUE
POSITIVE DS    0H
         MVI   0(R1),C'+'
CONTINUE DS    0H
```

Figure 7.34 Centralizing the BCTR instruction.

The last item to be discussed is using the field separator and the EDMK instruction. If two or more fields are edited simultaneously using a large edit pattern and field separators, you must be careful about testing the condition code. The condition code setting is based upon the *last* packed-decimal field edited. In other words, if you are editing three packed-decimal fields, the condition code is set based on the value in the *last* packed-decimal field. You cannot use register 1 or the condition code to place a negative or floating dollar sign into the first two fields that were edited. You can only move those signs into the last field.

To move a negative or dollar sign into the first two fields, you have to write a short section of code that will examine each byte in the resulting edit patterns for the first two fields one at a time. When the first significant character is found, you *BCTR the address* (as you did before) and insert your special character. The end result is what you wanted, but with a little more work. In fact, it's much more work than issuing three separate EDMK instructions and eliminating the use of the field separator edit pattern byte. The code in Fig. 7.35 illustrates the search and insert technique.

Note that in the code register 2 looks through the edit pattern to find the first significant digit. Again, R1 cannot be used since we're assuming that multiple fields were edited simultaneously. We're trying to go into the edit pattern for each individual field and add appropriate signs to each edited result. Incidentally, we only want to use this code if the packed-decimal number is less than zero.

In order to determine if the field is positive or negative, use the packed-decimal compare instruction (CP) that is discussed in a later section. Clearly, this is considerable work and quite confusing. I'd suggest using individual ED or EDMK instructions for each packed-decimal field rather than editing several packed fields simultaneously using field separator characters.

EDMK forces R1 to change if a significant digit is found during editing. However, you must be careful when using this instruction if you are programming under the ASSIST package. If you recall, ASSIST uses register 1 with the XDECI instruction to assist in locating data within an input area. If XDECI and EDMK are used in the same program, problems may result between their coordination. Therefore, it may be necessary to temporarily store the XDECI register 1 value into a fullword before issuing the EDMK instruction. The stored value may be reloaded before subsequent XDECI instructions are used.

```
         edit instruction has been issued earlier

         LA    R2,PATTERN+1       POINT TO SECOND BYTE OF AREA
LOOP     DS    0H                 START OF THE LOOP
         CLC   0(1,R2),PATTERN    NEXT BYTE = FILL CHARACTER?
         BNE   SIGNIF             IF NOT, IT'S A DIGIT
         LA    R2,1(,R2)          IF SO, MOVE TO NEXT BYTE
         B     LOOP               CONTINUE SEARCHING
SIGNIF   DS    0H                 A DIGIT HAS BEEN FOUND
         BCTR  R2,0               BACK UP ONE BYTE
         MVI   0(R2),C'-'         INSERT A MINUS SIGN
NOTMINUS DS    0H
```

Figure 7.35 Scanning fields to locate point of negative sign insertion.

PACKED-DECIMAL INSTRUCTIONS

The set of instructions that process packed-decimal data consists of the full complement of arithmetic and comparison instructions. Additionally, two other instructions exist to assist the programmer in managing **logical** decimal points within the packed-decimal data being processed and to copy packed-decimal fields from one location in memory to another. You'll most likely find that the packed-decimal instructions are easy to use and be disappointed that we didn't talk about them sooner. However, if you think about what we did to get to this point, such as converting input and output, editing packed-decimal fields, placing signs into the numbers, and so on, you begin to see why we waited until this point to discuss packed-decimal processing.

The basic packed-decimal instructions allow you to add, subtract, multiply, and divide packed-decimal numbers. These instructions are very simple and work similarly to their binary data counterparts. The only instructions within this set that may cause some difficulty are multiply and divide. They have some peculiar rules, but if used correctly, they are no more difficult than any instructions that we've used before.

The packed-decimal instructions are often referred to as the "packed" instructions. On the other hand, the IBM manuals refer to them as the "decimal" instructions. This ambiguity can lead to some confusion. Since the last letter of the mnemonic for each instruction is the letter P, it seems more appropriate to refer to them as the "packed" instructions. We'll label them as the "decimal/packed" instructions, thus treating the two references as being synonomous.

Two packed-decimal fields called NUM1 and NUM2 are defined in Fig. 7.36. Both are eight-byte fields, although fields as large as 16 bytes may be used during processing. Eight-byte fields allow up to 15 digits and 16-byte fields allow 31.

```
NUM1     DC     PL8'376'
NUM2     DC     PL8'22'
```

Figure 7.36 Fields to be used in later examples.

NUM1 and NUM2 are compared by using the **CP (compare decimal/compare packed)** instruction, which is an SS instruction with two operands as shown in Fig. 7.37. The lengths of both operands must be specified within the instruction. On the other hand, the assembler can also supply lengths to the instruction implicitly, depending on the definition of the field. Explicit and implicit lengths were discussed in Chapter 4 where we discussed the move instruction. Here, the lengths indicate the number of *bytes* that a field occupies and not the number of *digits* within the field. Also, notice that both operands are D(B) addresses, which means that explicit addresses may be specified or an implicit address (such as a label) may be used within the instruction.

```
CP     D1(L1,B1),D2(L2,B2)
```

Figure 7.37 General form of the CP instruction.

The CP instruction sets the condition code as defined in Fig. 7.38.

Condition Code	Meaning
0	The operands are equal.
1	The first operand has a value less than the second operand.
2	The first operand has a value that is greater than the second operand.

Figure 7.38 Condition code settings from the CP instruction.

Extended mnemonics may also be used in place of the BC/BCR instruction and mask bit setting to test the condition code values. BE determines if the two operands are equal, BL branches to a location if the first operand is less than the second, and BH tests if the first operand is greater than the second.

Figure 7.39 shows some examples of the CP instruction and how it is used.

As you can see, referencing a packed-decimal field may be done in many ways, but it must be done carefully to ensure a valid packed-decimal field. Abends are frequent since programmers tend to forget to initialize fields before using them, use the wrong instruction when processing them, specify field lengths incorrectly, or end with a result in a packed-decimal field that is too large to be adequately processed.

Another common mistake made by beginning programmers is to use the incorrect instruction when processing packed-decimal data. Suppose, for example, that the CLC (compare logical character) instruction compares two packed fields instead of the CP instruction. If you recall, CLC was used to compare character data. If we now try to use this instruction to compare two packed fields, Fig. 7.40 illustrates what may happen.

```
CP      NUM1(8),NUM2(8)        compare the two eight byte
                               fields and set the condition
                               code appropriately

CP      NUM1,NUM2              compare the two eight byte
                               fields as above but in this
                               case the implicit lengths
                               of the fields are supplied
                               to the instruction by the
                               assembler

CP      NUM1,NUM2+3            THIS WILL NOT WORK!!  It
                               appears that we are trying
                               to compare the full value
                               of NUM1 to the last five
                               bytes of NUM2.  Although both
                               are packed decimal fields we
                               have not specified the length
                               of any of the fields.  Whenever
                               we reference a field through
                               an offset we must always
                               remember to explicitly code the
                               length operand.  This compare
                               would have worked if we had
                               coded:
                                   CP   NUM1(8),NUM2+3(5) or
                                   CP   NUM1,NUM2+3(5)
                               NUM1's length need not be
                               specified since we want to
                               look at the full value of
                               NUM1.

CP      NUM1(5),=P'0'          THIS WILL NOT WORK!!  The first
                               five bytes of NUM1 do not make
                               up a valid packed decimal value
                               since there's no sign in the
                               first five bytes.  The sign of
                               NUM1 is located in byte 8 which
                               causes this instruction to abend
                               with an 0C7 (data exception).

CP      NUM1(8),=P'123'        compare the value of NUM1 to
                               the value +123 and set the
                               condition code appropriately.
                               The length does not have to be
                               specified on the second operand
                               since the second operand is a
                               literal and literals have
                               implicit lengths.
```

Figure 7.39 Using the compare packed instruction.

```
                CLC       NUMA(3),NUMB

NUMA            DC        PL3'123'
NUMB            DC        PL3'-123'
```

Figure 7.40 Incorrect use of the CLC instruction to compare packed fields.

NUMA and NUMB are valid packed-decimal fields. If we look at their values in hexadecimal, X'00123C' and X'00123D', respectively, we see that they only differ by their signs, that is, NUMA is positive and NUMB is negative. The CLC instruction evaluates fields on a bit-by-bit basis. Hence, when it compares these two fields, they differ in the bit location shown in Fig. 7.41.

```
NUMA  =  X'00123C'  =  B'0000 0000 0001 0010 0011 1100'
NUMB  =  X'00123D'  =  B'0000 0000 0001 0010 0011 1101'
```

Figure 7.41 Bit representation of two packed fields.

Looking at the italicized bit values, we see that NUMB's bit value is one and the same bit position in NUMA is zero. When using the CLC instruction to compare these fields, the condition code is set to indicate that **NUMB is greater than NUMA.** But wait, NUMB is a *negative number.* As far as the computer is concerned, the CLC instruction has worked flawlessly since it has properly compared the fields. The problem is that the wrong instruction was used to compare packed-decimal data. This example further stresses the importance of using the proper instruction with the appropriate data type being processed. It is especially important with packed decimals that you define their fields properly and that you use the correct instructions when processing them.

ADDING AND SUBTRACTING PACKED-DECIMAL FIELDS

Packed decimal fields may be added or subtracted using **AP (add decimal/add packed)** and **SP (subtract decimal/subtract packed)** instructions. These instructions also have two operands and two D(B) addresses. Using our NUM1 and NUM2 values again, we can add and subtract the two values as illustrated in Fig. 7.42.

The AP and SP instructions set the condition code based on the value of the result in the *first operand* location. If the first operand is zero, then the condition code is tested using a mask of B'1000'; if less than zero, the mask will be B'0100'; if greater than zero, the mask will be B'0010'; and if an overflow occurs, the mask will be B'0001'.

HANDLING DECIMAL OVERFLOW CONDITIONS

The **overflow** situation occurs when the result is too large to fit into the first operand's storage area. For example, if we have two packed-decimal fields, both defined as one-byte long, and we add them as shown in Fig. 7.43, the result does not fit into the first field's storage area.

instruction		result
AP	NUM1(8),NUM2(8)	Add the two packed decimal fields. Explicit lengths have been specified.
SP	NUM1(8),NUM2(8)	Subtract the two values.
AP	NUM1(8),=P'5'	Add 5 to the value of NUM1.
SP	NUM2(8),=PL8'1'	Subtract 1 from the value of NUM2. I coded the literal a little differently just to show you a different form.
AP	NUM1+3(5),NUM2+3(5)	**Poor technique.** NUM1 and NUM2 are added together but only the last 5 bytes of both fields are added. If any of the left three bytes of either field contained digits those digits would <u>not</u> be used in the addition.

Figure 7.42 AP and SP coding examples.

```
Warning, this code will cause an overflow condition.

                 AP      VAL1,VAL2
                 .       .
                 .       .
                 .       .
        VAL1     DC      PL1'6'
        VAL2     DC      PL1'7'
```

Figure 7.43 Overflow during packed-decimal processing.

The result, a value of 13, is too large to fit into a one-byte packed-decimal field. Overflow occurs and, most likely, the program abends with a **0CA (decimal overflow)** abend. As a programmer, make sure that your fields are defined large enough to hold your results to avoid overflow. In fact, digits *are lost* when overflow occurs. For example, adding 6 and 7 gives a value of 3 since VAL1 is too small.

Although the computer typically abends the program when a decimal overflow exception occurs, we can tell the system to ignore this condition and to continue executing as if nothing had happened. This is not a good technique since we will lose digits and our results will be incorrect. However, there are situations where this is a desired form of processing (modular arithmetic), so let's see how we tell the system to ignore such conditions.

Within the PSW, a series of bits called **program masks** are set to allow interrupts to occur. One such bit in the program mask field causes our program to abend if the decimal overflow condition occurs. If we simply turn this bit "off," then we can continue processing even if a decimal overflow occurs. This program mask bit is located in the PSW at bit position 37. To turn this bit "off," we use the **SPM (set program mask)** instruction.

The SPM instruction changes the condition code *and* the program mask bits in the

PSW. Although we can change the condition code and several other program mask bits, we're only concerned with one bit at this point. The condition code is located in bit positions 34 and 35 and the program mask bits are located in bits 36 through 39. Hence, SPM changes six bits in the PSW.

Each program mask bit controls some other type of interrupt, but we're concerned only with the decimal overflow bit. To change the bit values, we must place a value into a register that matches the bit configuration required and then issue the SPM instruction to change the PSW program mask bits.

The SPM instruction has one operand, a register. In the *leftmost* byte of the register, we must place the bit settings required. In particular, we want bits 0 and 1 in the register to be zero since they have no meaning and do not alter the PSW, bits 2 and 3 to be zero (condition code bits), bit 4 to be 1 (to allow a fixed-point overflow interrupt to occur), *bit 5 to be zero (to turn off the decimal overflow interrupt),* and bits 6 and 7 to be 1 (to allow for exponent and significance interrupts when using floating-point data). Clearly, the only bits that we are really concerned with arc bits 4 through 7. Their values must be B'1011' with the zero bit specifying that the decimal overflow should be turned "off."

To establish these values in the register properly, load a value into a register that matches the bit settings that we require. After loading this value, issue the SPM instruction to turn off the decimal overflow condition. The instructions in Fig. 7.44 perform the desired processing.

```
         L      Rx,BITS
         SPM    Rx
         .      .
         .      .
         .      .
         DS     0F
BITS     DC     B'00001011'
         DC     XL3'00'
```

Figure 7.44 Modifying the PSW program mask bits to prevent overflow abends.

BITS is an aligned fullword value. The first byte is defined using the **B (bit)** data type definition, which defines individual bit values. The last three bytes are set to zero although their values are of no concern since they are not used in the SPM instruction.

Loading the resulting fullword into *any* usable register and issuing the SPM instruction sets the program mask as desired. Although you might think that we're finished, remember that *you* are now responsible for any overflow conditions. You should design your code to test for a condition code of B'0001' (overflow) after all the packed-decimal instructions to determine if overflow has occurred. Should it occur, you can print a message and terminate your program execution (if you desire) in a *normal* manner rather than with an abend.

MULTIPLYING, DIVIDING AND ZAPPING PACKED-DECIMAL DATA

Packed-decimal data may be multiplied or divided using **MP (multiply decimal/multiply packed)** or **DP (divide decimal/divide packed)** instructions. These instructions also have two operands, two lengths, and are used similarly as CP, AP, and SP. Although they are very similar to the other packed-decimal instructions, they have a few more quirks that can cause problems.

The multiply instruction allows you to multiply two packed-decimal fields. The second operand *cannot* be longer than eight bytes and *cannot* be as large as the first operand. The first operand can be as large as 31 digits (16 bytes). Additionally, the number of leading zeros in the first operand must be equal to the size of the second operand or else a data exception abend (0C7) occurs. For example, suppose that we want to multiply NUMA by NUMB as defined in Fig. 7.45.

```
NUMA     DC     PL5'3UU'
NUMB     DC     PL5'25'
```

Figure 7.45 Field definitions for later examples.

In hexadecimal, the values of these fields are X'000000300C' and X'000000025C', respectively. NUMA has three bytes of X'00' before the first significant digit in the field. Since there are only three bytes of leading zeros in NUMA, then the *largest* field that we can use to multiply NUMA is a three-byte field. Hence, we *cannot* multiply NUMA by NUMB directly since NUMB is too large.

On the other hand, we see that NUMB is not a full field. In fact, only the last two bytes contain digits. If we multiply NUMA by only the last two bytes of NUMB, then we have a valid multiply since two bytes is less than or equal to three, thus satisfying the length limitation. We can now issue the multiply instruction as given in Fig. 7.46.

```
MP     NUMA(5),NUMB+3(2)
```

Figure 7.46 Multiplying two packed-decimal fields.

We *must* code the length element on the second operand since we are using offset referencing. The first operand, NUMA, does not have to be specified with the length operand unless desired.

The length rule prevents overflow and allows referencing a valid packed-decimal field. Further, the MP instruction does not set the condition code to allow testing for the result value or to see if overflow occurred. Since the instruction allows sufficient room in the resulting field to hold the result, overflow should not occur.

Figure 7.47 defines pairs of fields that are to be multiplied. It also indicates whether these are legal multiplications or whether they will fail due to insufficient room or incorrect definition within the instruction. Carefully review these examples to familiarize yourself with the legal and illegal multiply situations. For each A/B pair in the figure, field A is the first operand and field B is the second operand.

Dividing packed-decimal numbers can also lead to problems before and after the division. Before the division, the packed-decimal fields must be valid. If they are invalid, then a data exception abend occurs. Again, the second operand must be less than or equal to eight bytes (15 digits) and must be less than the length of the first operand.

Following the division, the first operand consists of *two* fields instead of one. Part of the first operand is the quotient and the other is the remainder. In other words, dividing an eight-byte packed-decimal field by a four-byte packed-decimal field results in two 4-byte fields, a quotient and a remainder. Figure 7.48 illustrates this occurrence.

Fields to be Multiplied			Validity
A	DC	PL16'256'	Not legal unless a portion of field B was referenced.
B	DC	PL16'100'	
A	DC	PL2'25'	Not legal at all. Field A does not have any full bytes of leading zeros to accommodate field B.
B	DC	PL1'3'	
A	DC	PL3'25'	Legal multiply.
B	DC	PL1'3'	
A	DC	PL8'1024'	Legal. There are enough bytes of leading zeros within field A to equal the length of B.
B	DC	PL5'40936'	

Figure 7.47 Valid and invalid multiplications.

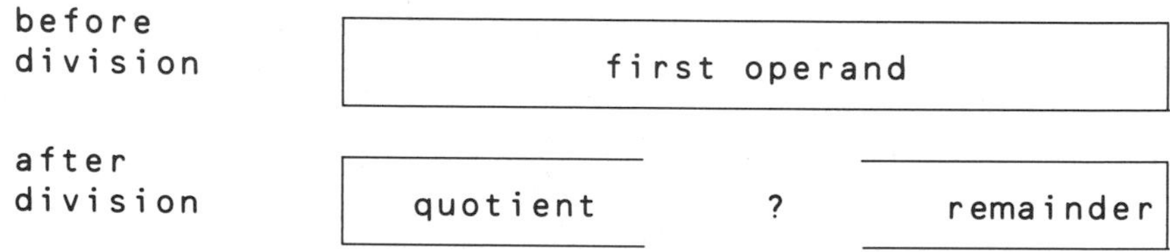

The first operand field is split in two after the division, but not necessarily into identical or equal-sized parts

Figure 7.48 Values before and after division.

The quotient occupies the left portion of the first operand field after the division and the remainder occupies the right. The number of bytes occupied by the quotient field is equal to the original length of the first field minus the original length of the second field (L1 − L2). The remainder occupies the remaining bytes of the entire first operand field.

It is important for you understand that the first operand is transformed into *two* packed decimal fields. If you attempt to reference the first operand field as a whole after the division, an abend occurs (0C7 data exception) since the first operand contains a sign somewhere in the middle of it.

Suppose that NUM1 and NUM2, which are defined as shown in Fig. 7.49, are to be divided. The values before and after the division are shown to illustrate the generation of the two quotient/remainder fields following the division.

The quotient field becomes five bytes long after the division since its length is determined by the difference in lengths of the original fields (8 and 3). The remainder occupies the rest of the original first operand's storage area.

The length of both operands has not changed, it's just that the first operand is now subdivided into two fields. In this example, 37 divided by 6 yields a quotient of 6 with a remainder of 1. The first operand's full value is now X'000000006C00001C', which is clearly not a valid packed-decimal field. To use the field, we must move the quotient or

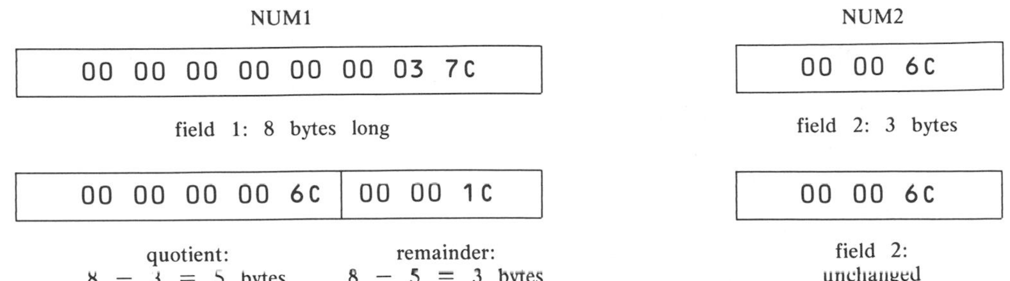

Figure 7.49 Field values before and after division (an example).

remainder to another field(s) in our program and convert this original field into a valid packed-decimal field. This is done with the **ZAP (zero and add packed)** instruction.

The ZAP instruction is somewhat like the MVC instruction except that it works on packed-decimal data. ZAP *copies* the contents of a field from one location in memory to another, thus replacing the target field's original value. Hence, if we copy the contents of the first five bytes of our result field above, the quotient is isolated. If we do the same for the remainder, it's also isolated. The code in Fig. 7.50 performs the tasks described.

```
         DP      NUM1(8),NUM2(3)
         ZAP     QUOT(8),NUM1(5)
         ZAP     REMAIN(8),NUM1+5(3)
         .       .
         .       .
         .       .
NUM1     DC      PL8'37'
NUM2     DC      PL3'6'
QUOT     DS      PL8
REMAIN   DS      PL8
```

Figure 7.50 Isolating the quotient and the remainder.

The DP instruction is issued, which forms the quotient and remainder. The first five bytes of NUM1 are zapped (copied) into the eight-byte area called QUOT, and the last three bytes of NUM1 (NUM1+5) are copied into the location called REMAIN. Although QUOT and REMAIN are defined as eight-byte fields, they need not be. They could be defined from 1 to 16 bytes as long as they are sufficiently large to hold their respective quotient and remainder values. Additionally, overflow can occur if the target field is too small.

Once the quotient and remainder are isolated, we can now reuse the NUM1 field by resetting it back to its original value using the instruction given in Fig. 7.51.

```
         ZAP     NUM1(8),=P'37'
```

Figure 7.51 Initializing or restoring the value of a packed field using ZAP.

In this case, the ZAP instruction is used as an initialization instruction. The field called NUM1 is initialized to the value 37 and whatever was in NUM1 is destroyed.

Now suppose that we don't care about the remainder and just want to keep the quotient value. Further, suppose that we don't want to define another field called QUOT to hold the quotient, but instead want NUM1 to hold the resulting quotient value. By zapping the first five bytes of NUM1 *into itself*, we change the value of NUM1 so that it only contains the quotient value. Figure 7.52 illustrates this technique.

```
DP       NUM1(8),NUM2(3)
ZAP      NUM1(8),NUM1(5)
```

Figure 7.52 Eliminating the remainder by zapping a field into itself.

This code is rather difficult, so consider it carefully. Before the division, NUM1 was an eight-byte field. After the division, NUM1 consisted of a five-byte and three-byte field. The address of the quotient portion (five bytes long) was at location NUM1 and the address of the remainder portion (three bytes long) was at location NUM1+5. The ZAP instruction simply copies data from one location in memory to another. Hence, the value in the first five bytes of NUM1 is expanded to a length of eight bytes and is placed into location NUM1. The end result is an eight-byte packed-decimal field that contains only the quotient of the division. Figure 7.53 illustrates this process graphically.

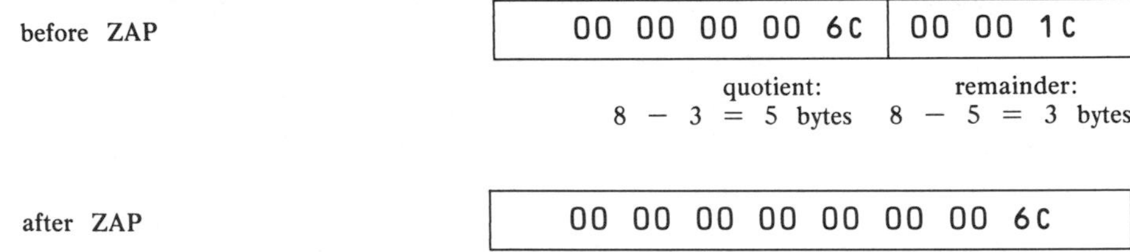

Figure 7.53 A graphical view of the zapping process.

The length of the quotient field after the division is equal to the difference in lengths of the two fields being divided. Another way to remember the lengths is that the length of the remainder field is *equal to* the length of the second operand. If the second operand is five bytes long, then the length of the remainder field is five bytes.

Now that you understand how the DP instruction works and how the original operand is divided in two pieces, we can now turn our attention to positive and negative division operations.

To divide numbers that are positive and negative, the resulting quotient and remainder assume different signs, which depend on the signs of the original dividend (first operand) and divisor (second operand). The sign of the remainder is always the same as the original dividend. Figure 7.54 illustrates various results when dividing positive and negative values.

Dividend Sign	Divisor Sign	Quotient Sign	Remainder Sign
+	+	+	+
−	+	−	−
+	−	−	+
−	−	+	−

Figure 7.54 Quotient and remainder signs following division.

To illustrate this aspect of the DP instruction, let's divide the value 37 (positive and negative) by the value 6 to see what is the remainder and how the signs are impacted by the results of the division. Figure 7.55 contains our results.

Dividend	Divisor	Quotient	Remainder
37	6	6	1
-37	6	-6	-1
37	-6	-6	1
-37	-6	6	-1

Figure 7.55 Component results following division (an example).

DIGITS TO THE LEFT AND RIGHT OF THE DECIMAL

When processing values in which digits are to be retained to the left and right of the decimal, it is important to understand the results of division, the quotient and remainder. Although the quotient can be thought of as the value to the left of the decimal, the remainder *cannot* be thought of as being the digit(s) to the right. In the example of Fig. 7.55 using the numbers 37 and 6, we see that when 37 is divided by 6, we get 6 with a remainder of 1. Actually, 37 divided by 6 is a repeating decimal value of $6.16666\underline{6}$ and is not 6.1. Depending on the number of digit positions to be retained, we use another technique for dividing to obtain digits to the left and right of the decimal.

One of the easiest techniques for performing division that results in more significant digits is to expand the dividend (first operand). Instead of dividing 37 by 6, we divide 370 by 6 to get 61 remainder 4. Dividing 3700 by 6, we get 616 remainder 4. If we continue to expand the first operand by a power of ten before the division, we obtain more and more digits in the resulting quotient.

Looking at the quotient more closely, remember that it has no imbedded or physical decimal point. Hence, a quotient of 61 can mean 61., 6.1, .61, .061, and so on. The manner in which we *edit* the number determines how the result is represented. Basically, if we want to retain **N** digits to the right of the decimal, then we must multiply the original first operand value (dividend) by 10 to the **N**th power. This results in a number that has the appropriate number of significant digits. Multiplying by 10 to the **N + 1** power provides an additional digit position on which we can perform some sort of rounding (if desired) to achieve more satisfactory results.

The first operand can be multiplied by a power of 10 by using the MP instruction or by using the **SRP (shift and round decimal/packed)** instruction. The SRP instruction can multiply or divide numbers by a power of ten *and* add an appropriate rounding factor to the rightmost digit in the number. For example, 37 divided by 6 yields $6.1666\underline{6}$. For most purposes, this result is represented as 6.17. Using the SRP instruction, we can first raise the dividend by a power of 10. We then issue the divide, and then adjust the rightmost digit by a round factor to achieve the 6.17 result. Figure 7.56 illustrates how it is done.

```
SRP     DIVIDEND(8),3,0              MULTIPLY BY 1000
DP      DIVIDEND(8),SIX(1)           DIVIDE BY 6
ZAP     DIVIDEND(8),DIVIDEND(7)      EXPAND QUOTIENT
SRP     DIVIDEND(8),64-1,5           SHIFT AND ROUND
```

Figure 7.56 Handling digits to the right of the decimal.

The first SRP instruction multiplies the dividend 37 by 10^3 (1000) to give 37000. As you can see, the second operand of the SRP instruction indicates the power of 10 by which the dividend should be multiplied, in this case, 3. The dividend 37000 is then divided by the single-byte element, called SIX, to give a seven-byte quotient and a one-byte remainder field. The next ZAP instruction reformats the quotient field so that it now fills the entire original field called DIVIDEND. Performing the ZAP at this point loses the remainder. Finally, the last SRP instruction divides the DIVIDEND by 10 to the first power, but before doing so, a value of 5 is added to the last digit lost from this number, causing a rounding operation to occur. The quotient value 6166 is therefore converted into 6171 and then into 617 when the SRP instruction completes. Our result, if edited properly using an edit pattern of 402021204B2020, comes out to 6.17 as we wanted.

While the SRP instruction looks as if it is multiplying or dividing by a power of 10, in reality it is simply *shifting* the digits from one position within the packed-decimal field to another and filling in vacant positions with zeros. For example, the packed-decimal field X'00123C' can be shifted to the left to give X'01230C' or to the right to give X'00012C' as illustrated in the instructions contained in Fig. 7.57.

```
SRP      HEX123(3),1,0         SHIFT TO THE LEFT
SRP      HEX123(3),64-1,0      SHIFT TO THE RIGHT
```

Figure 7.57 Examples of using the SRP instruction.

The shifting process is controlled by the second operand of the SRP instruction. A value between 0 and 31 shifts the first operand to the *left* 0 to 31 positions, respectively, and a value between 64 and 32 causes a shift to the *right* 0 to 31 places, respectively. Although the second operand is converted into a binary number by the assembler, it is easier to represent the number of positions shifted by a familiar decimal number. A left shift is specified by coding a value of 1, 2, 3, . . . , 31, and a right shift is represented by coding 64−1, 64−2, 64−3, . . . , 64−31 to indicate shifting 1, 2, 3, . . . , 31 digit positions, respectively. Figure 7.58 shows several examples of shifting fields and specifying the second operand of the SRP instruction.

SRP Second Operand	Result of the Shifting
3	Shift to left three positions (multiply by 1000).
B'0010'	Shift to left two positions (multiply by 100).
64-5	Shift to right five positions (divide by 100000).
0	Don't shift.
64-4	Shift to right four positions (divide by 10000).

Figure 7.58 Specifying the second operand of SRP.

When shifting to the right, digits are lost. The *leftmost digit lost* is rounded, if rounding has been indicated in the third operand (a nonzero value). For example, suppose that we have the value X'000123456C'. If this value is shifted to the right three positions, we end up with X'000000123C'. The last digit shifted is the digit 4. Rounding, if specified, applies to *this* digit and not to 5 or 6. A rounding value of 5 does not change the next highest digit position (currently a value of 3), but a rounding factor of 8 causes a carry into the next highest digit position, thus changing the digit 3 to 4. In general, a rounding factor of 5 is used and is specified as the third operand on the SRP instruction when shifting to the right. The third operand of SRP is ignored when shifting left and for that reason is normally coded as a value of zero.

As we've been discussing, the SRP instruction is used primarily to manage numbers with digits to the left and right of the decimal. On the other hand, it can serve as a quick method to multiply or divide numbers by a power of 10. Although processing numbers with digits to the left and right of the decimal may seem difficult, you should now understand how to expand (SRP to left), divide (DP), reformat (ZAP), round if desired (SRP to right), and edit for output (ED, EDMK) to produce the desired results.

Now suppose that we want to divide 100 by 2.5. Since decimal numbers are simply represented as integers within the packed-decimal fields, we really have 100 divided by 25. Clearly, we've changed the meaning of the digits 2 and 5 by losing the logical decimal position. To compensate for this, we must multiply 100 by 10 since we moved the decimal point of the value 2.5 to the right (multiplied by 10). Now we can divide 1000 by 25 to get 40, which is the same as dividing 100 by 2.5.

Clearly, managing information with digits to the left and right of the decimal requires that you know the data. You have to know the full field length and how many digits within that field are to the right of the decimal. Compensation will often have to be made to obtain proper precision or to increase the number of significant digits in the result.

DECIMAL DATA PROGRAMMING EXAMPLE

We end this chapter with a programming example. This program should be familiar since it is identical to the add, subtract, multiply, and divide program that we did in Chapter 5 when we discussed binary data processing. We simply replace the binary instructions with decimal instructions to process the same data. Although you may be inclined to skim over the code, I strongly urge you to review it carefully. The program handles positive and negative numbers on both input and output. It contains code that searches the incoming values for a negative sign and converts the numbers into proper packed-decimal form as related to the sign of the number. Editing is used to output the results and to place negative signs before the first significant digit. This program is truly a classic example of handling input and output of character data and processing data in packed-decimal format. To further enhance the understanding of this program, I've implemented the program in ASSIST and have again labeled the various aspects of the program. See Example 7.1.

Finally, let me strongly encourage you to complete the study questions and programming problems at the end of the chapter. They are very important for your understanding of packed-decimal data since this is one of the most used data types in industry. Packed decimals also prove to be very important in the next chapter where we discuss debugging techniques. As I've said over and over, incorrect processing or invalid packed-decimal data is one of the most common sources of program failures.

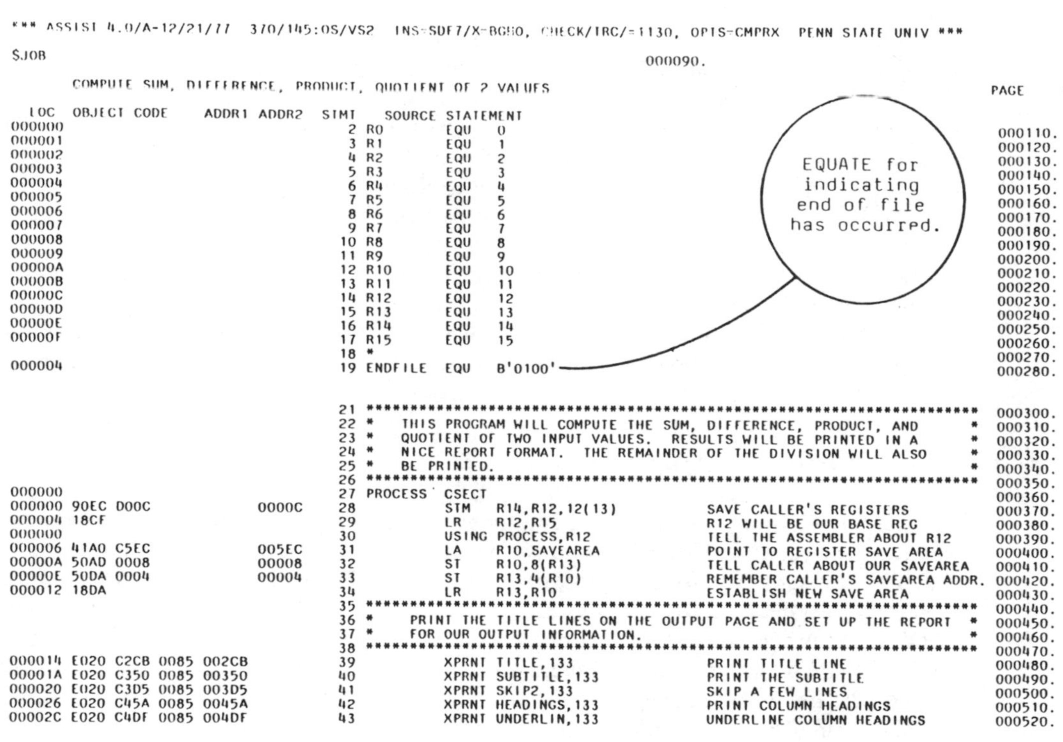

```
*** ASSIST 4.0/A-12/21/77  370/145:OS/VS2  INS=SDF7/X=BGHO, CHECK/TRC/=1130, OPTS=CMPRX  PENN STATE UNIV ***
$JOB                                                                               000090.
      COMPUTE SUM, DIFFERENCE, PRODUCT, QUOTIENT OF 2 VALUES                                                          PAGE    1
  LOC  OBJECT CODE     ADDR1 ADDR2  STMT   SOURCE STATEMENT
000000                                 2 R0       EQU   0                                                              000110.
000001                                 3 R1       EQU   1                                                              000120.
000002                                 4 R2       EQU   2                                                              000130.
000003                                 5 R3       EQU   3                                                              000140.
000004                                 6 R4       EQU   4                                                              000150.
000005                                 7 R5       EQU   5                                                              000160.
000006                                 8 R6       EQU   6                                                              000170.
000007                                 9 R7       EQU   7                                                              000180.
000008                                10 R8       EQU   8                                                              000190.
000009                                11 R9       EQU   9                                                              000200.
00000A                                12 R10      EQU   10                                                             000210.
00000B                                13 R11      EQU   11                                                             000220.
00000C                                14 R12      EQU   12                                                             000230.
00000D                                15 R13      EQU   13                                                             000240.
00000E                                16 R14      EQU   14                                                             000250.
00000F                                17 R15      EQU   15                                                             000260.
                                      18 *                                                                             000270.
000004                                19 ENDFILE  EQU   B'0100'                                                        000280.

                                      21 ************************************************************************     000300.
                                      22 *   THIS PROGRAM WILL COMPUTE THE SUM, DIFFERENCE, PRODUCT, AND         *     000310.
                                      23 *   QUOTIENT OF TWO INPUT VALUES.  RESULTS WILL BE PRINTED IN A         *     000320.
                                      24 *   NICE REPORT FORMAT.  THE REMAINDER OF THE DIVISION WILL ALSO        *     000330.
                                      25 *   BE PRINTED.                                                         *     000340.
                                      26 ************************************************************************     000350.
000000                                27 PROCESS  CSECT                                                               000360.
000000 90EC D00C             0000C    28          STM   R14,R12,12(13)          SAVE CALLER'S REGISTERS               000370.
000004 18CF                           29          LR    R12,R15                 R12 WILL BE OUR BASE REG              000380.
000000                                30          USING PROCESS,R12             TELL THE ASSEMBLER ABOUT R12          000390.
000006 41A0 C5EC             005EC    31          LA    R10,SAVEAREA            POINT TO REGISTER SAVE AREA           000400.
00000A 50AD 0008             00008    32          ST    R10,8(R13)              TELL CALLER ABOUT OUR SAVEAREA        000410.
00000E 50DA 0004             00004    33          ST    R13,4(R10)              REMEMBER CALLER'S SAVEAREA ADDR.      000420.
000012 18DA                           34          LR    R13,R10                 ESTABLISH NEW SAVE AREA               000430.
                                      35 ************************************************************************     000440.
                                      36 *    PRINT THE TITLE LINES ON THE OUTPUT PAGE AND SET UP THE REPORT    *     000450.
                                      37 *    FOR OUR OUTPUT INFORMATION.                                       *     000460.
                                      38 ************************************************************************     000470.
000014 E020 C2CB 0085 002CB           39          XPRNT TITLE,133               PRINT TITLE LINE                      000480.
00001A E020 C350 0085 00350           40          XPRNT SUBTITLE,133            PRINT THE SUBTITLE                    000490.
000020 E020 C3D5 0085 003D5           41          XPRNT SKIP2,133               SKIP A FEW LINES                      000500.
000026 E020 C45A 0085 0045A           42          XPRNT HEADINGS,133            PRINT COLUMN HEADINGS                 000510.
00002C E020 C4DF 0085 004DF           43          XPRNT UNDERLIN,133            UNDERLINE COLUMN HEADINGS             000520.
```


Example 7.1 Sum, difference, product, and quotient/remainder program.

```
  LOC  OBJECT CODE    ADDR1 ADDR2  STMT   SOURCE STATEMENT

                                     45 ********************************************************************  000540.
                                     46 *   OBTAIN THE INPUT VALUES FROM OUR FILE AND CONVERT THEM INTO      *  000550.
                                     47 *   BINARY FORMAT FOR PROCESSING.                                    *  000560.
                                     48 ********************************************************************  000570.
000032                               49 CONTINUE DS    OH                                                       000580.
000032 E000 C634 0050 00634          50          XREAD  INPUTREC,80            GET OUR RECORD                   000590.
000038 4740 C1D6            001D6    51          BC     ENDFILE,EOF            WHEN END OF FILE, ALL DONE       000600.
00003C 9240 C564      00564          52          MVI    PLINE,C' '             CLEAR FIRST BYTE OF PLINE        000610.
000040 D283 C565 C564 00565 00564    53          MVC    PLINE+1(132),PLINE     CLEAR REST OF PRINT LINE         000620.
000046 F274 C688 C634 00688 00634    54          PACK   VALUE1(8),NUM1(5)      CONVERT FIRST NUMBER             000630.
00004C F274 C690 C639 00690 00639    55          PACK   VALUE2(8),NUM2(5)      CONVERT SECOND NUMBER            000640.

                                     57 ********************************************************************  000660.
                                     58 *   IF VALUE1 OR VALUE2 ARE TO BE NEGATIVE, THEN CONVERT THE PACKED  *  000670.
                                     59 *   VALUES INTO NEGATIVE NUMBERS.                                    *  000680.
                                     60 ********************************************************************  000690.
000052 4130 C634            00634    61          LA     R3,NUM1                POINT TO FIRST INPUT NUMBER      000700.
000056                               62 LOOP1    DS     OH                     FIND NEGATIVE SIGN               000710.
000056 5930 C1E8            001E8    63          C      R3,=A(NUM1+4)          HAVE WE LOOKED AT ENTIRE NUM1    000720.
00005A 4720 C080            00080    64          BH     NUM1POS                IF SO, THEN NUM1 IS POSITIVE     000730.
00005E 9560 3000      00000          65          CLI    0(R3),C'-'             NEGATIVE SIGN?                   000740.
000062 4780 C06E            0006E    66          BE     MINUS1                 IF YES, THEN NEGATIVE FIRST NUM  000750.
000066 4130 3001            00001    67          LA     R3,1(,R3)              ADVANCE TO NEXT ADDRESS          000760.
00006A 47F0 C056            00056    68          B      LOOP1                  CONTINUE LOOKING                 000770.
00006E F870 C698 C1F0 00698 001F0    69 MINUS1   ZAP    WORK(8),=P'0'          SET WORK EQUAL TO ZERO           000780.
000074 FB77 C698 C688 00698 00688    70          SP     WORK(8),VALUE1(8)      SUBTRACT VALUE1 FROM 0           000790.
00007A F877 C688 C698 00688 00698    71          ZAP    VALUE1(8),WORK         VALUE1 IS NOW NEGATIVE           000800.
000080                               72 NUM1POS  DS     OH                                                      000810.

000080 4130 C639            00639    74          LA     R3,NUM2                POINT TO FIRST INPUT NUMBER      000830.
000084                               75 LOOP2    DS     OH                     FIND NEGATIVE SIGN               000840.
000084 5930 C1EC            001EC    76          C      R3,=A(NUM2+4)          HAVE WE LOOKED AT ENTIRE NUM1    000850.
000088 4720 C0AE            000AE    77          BH     NUM2POS                IF SO, THEN NUM1 IS POSITIVE     000860.
00008C 9560 3000      00000          78          CLI    0(R3),C'-'             NEGATIVE SIGN?                   000870.
000090 4780 C09C            0009C    79          BE     MINUS2                 IF YES, THEN NEGATIVE FIRST NUM  000880.
000094 4130 3001            00001    80          LA     R3,1(,R3)              ADVANCE TO NEXT ADDRESS          000890.
000098 47F0 C084            00084    81          B      LOOP2                  CONTINUE LOOKING                 000900.
00009C F870 C698 C1F0 00698 001F0    82 MINUS2   ZAP    WORK(8),=P'0'          SET WORK EQUAL TO ZERO           000910.
0000A2 FB77 C698 C690 00698 00690    83          SP     WORK(8),VALUE2(8)      SUBTRACT VALUE1 FROM 0           000920.
0000A8 F877 C690 C698 00690 00698    84          ZAP    VALUE2(8),WORK         VALUE1 IS NOW NEGATIVE           000930.
0000AE                               85 NUM2POS  DS     OH                                                      000940.
```

Convert input numbers to positive and negative packed values as appropriate.

We've changed program structure to match our second form of e-o-f logic.

```
    COMPUTE SUM, DIFFERENCE, PRODUCT, QUOTIENT OF 2 VALUES                                                    PAGE    3

  LOC  OBJECT CODE    ADDR1 ADDR2  STMT   SOURCE STATEMENT

                                     87 ************************************************************************  000960.
                                     88 *       COMPUTE THE SUM AND CONVERT IT FOR OUTPUT PRINTING.            *  000970.
                                     89 ************************************************************************  000980.
0000AE F877 C6F0 C688 006F0 00688    90          ZAP   SUMP(8),VALUE1(8)        COMPUTE THE SUM                   000990.
0000B4 FA73 C6F0 C694 006F0 00694    91          AP    SUMP(8),VALUE2+4(4)      ...JUST A DIFFERENT FORMAT        001000.
0000BA D20F C6A0 C236 006A0 00236    92          MVC   SUM(16),PATTERN          MOVE IN EDIT PATTERN              001010.
0000C0 4110 C6AF              006AF  93          LA    R1,SUM+15                POINT TO LAST DIGIT POSITION      001020.
0000C4 DF0F C6A0 C6F0 006A0 006F0    94          EDMK  SUM(16),SUMP             EDIT THE SUM VALUE                001030.
0000CA 47B0 C0D4              000D4  95          BNM   SUMPOS                   IF NOT < 0, DON'T MOVE IN SIGN    001040.
0000CE 0610                          96          BCTR  R1,0                     BACK UP ONE POSITION              001050.
0000D0 9260 1000        00000        97          MVI   0(R1),C'-'               MOVE IN NEGATIVE SIGN             001060.
0000D4                               98 SUMPOS   DS    0H                       SKIP NEGATIVE MOVE IF POSITIVE    001070.
                                     99 ************************************************************************  001080.
                                    100 *       COMPUTE THE DIFFERENCE BETWEEN THE NUMBERS AND PREPARE         *  001090.
                                    101 *       TO BE PRINTED.                                                 *  001100.
                                    102 ************************************************************************  001110.
0000D4 F877 C6F8 C688 006F8 00688   103          ZAP   DIFFERP(8),VALUE1(8)     RESTORE BINARY VALUES IN REGS.    001120.
0000DA FB77 C6F8 C690 006F8 00690   104          SP    DIFFERP(8),VALUE2(8)     COMPUTE DIFFERENCE                001130.
0000E0 D20F C6B0 C236 006B0 00236   105          MVC   DIFFER(16),PATTERN       MOVE IN THE EDIT PATTERN          001140.
0000E6 4110 C6BF              006BF 106          LA    R1,DIFFER+15             POINT TO LAST DIGIT POSITION      001150.
0000EA DF0F C6B0 C6F8 006B0 006F8   107          EDMK  DIFFER(16),DIFFERP       CONVERT TO DISPLAY                001160.
0000F0 47B0 C0FA              000FA 108          BNM   DIFFPOS                  IF NOT < 0, DON'T MOVE IN SIGN    001170.
0000F4 0610                         109          BCTR  R1,0                     BACK UP ONE POSITION              001180.
0000F6 9260 1000        00000       110          MVI   0(R1),C'-'               MOVE IN NEGATIVE SIGN             001190.
0000FA                              111 DIFFPOS  DS    0H                       SKIP NEGATIVE MOVE IF POSITIVE    001200.
```

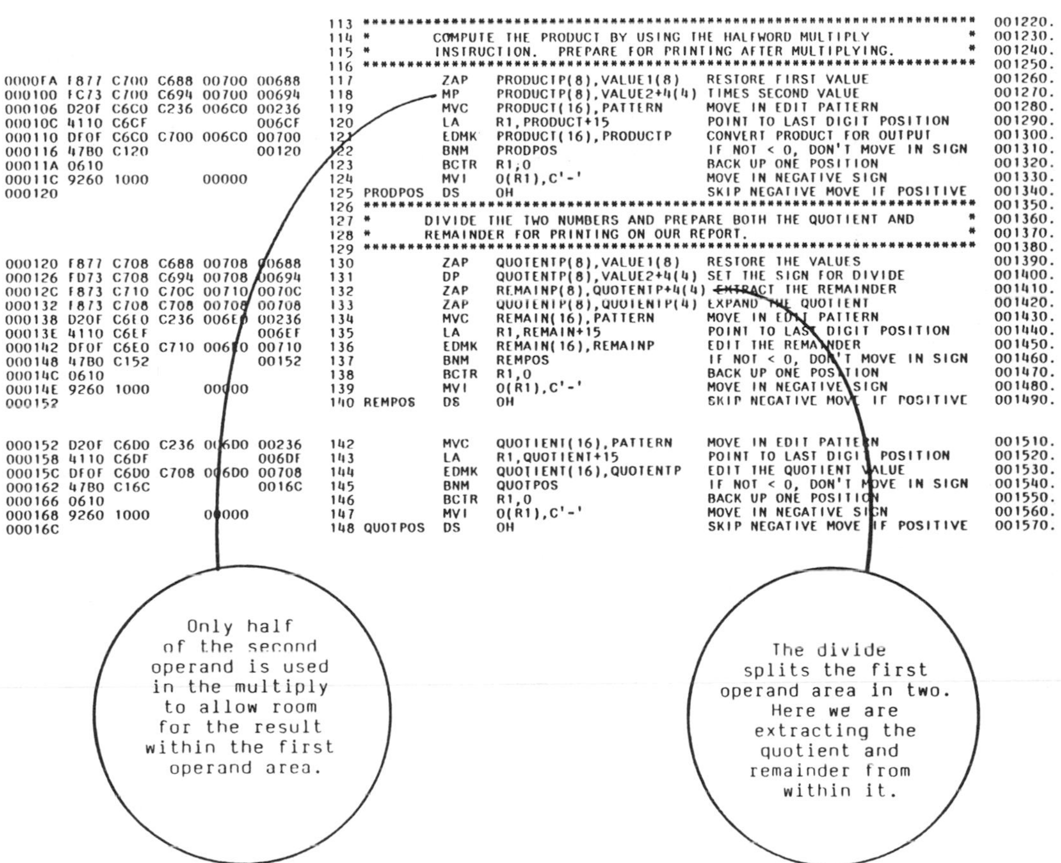

```
     COMPUTE SUM, DIFFERENCE, PRODUCT, QUOTIENT OF 2 VALUES                                                    PAGE    4

  LOC  OBJECT CODE     ADDR1 ADDR2  STMT   SOURCE STATEMENT

                                     113 ******************************************************************* 001220.
                                     114 *        COMPUTE THE PRODUCT BY USING THE HALFWORD MULTIPLY         * 001230.
                                     115 *        INSTRUCTION.  PREPARE FOR PRINTING AFTER MULTIPLYING.      * 001240.
                                     116 ******************************************************************* 001250.
0000FA F877 C700 C688 00700 00688    117          ZAP   PRODUCTP(8),VALUE1(8)   RESTORE FIRST VALUE        001260.
000100 FC73 C700 C694 00700 00694    118          MP    PRODUCTP(8),VALUE2+4(4) TIMES SECOND VALUE         001270.
000106 D20F C6C0 C236 006C0 00236    119          MVC   PRODUCT(16),PATTERN     MOVE IN EDIT PATTERN       001280.
00010C 4110 C6CF             006CF    120          LA    R1,PRODUCT+15           POINT TO LAST DIGIT POSITION 001290.
000110 DF0F C6C0 C700 006C0 00700    121          EDMK  PRODUCT(16),PRODUCTP    CONVERT PRODUCT FOR OUTPUT 001300.
000116 47B0 C120             00120    122          BNM   PRODPOS                 IF NOT < 0, DON'T MOVE IN SIGN 001310.
00011A 0610                          123          BCTR  R1;0                    BACK UP ONE POSITION       001320.
00011C 9260 1000       00000         124          MVI   0(R1),C'-'              MOVE IN NEGATIVE SIGN      001330.
000120                               125 PRODPOS  DS    0H                      SKIP NEGATIVE MOVE IF POSITIVE 001340.
                                     126 ******************************************************************* 001350.
                                     127 *      DIVIDE THE TWO NUMBERS AND PREPARE BOTH THE QUOTIENT AND     * 001360.
                                     128 *      REMAINDER FOR PRINTING ON OUR REPORT.                        * 001370.
                                     129 ******************************************************************* 001380.
000120 F877 C708 C688 00708 00688    130          ZAP   QUOTENTP(8),VALUE1(8)   RESTORE THE VALUES         001390.
000126 FD73 C708 C694 00708 00694    131          DP    QUOTENTP(8),VALUE2+4(4) SET THE SIGN FOR DIVIDE    001400.
00012C F873 C710 C70C 00710 0070C    132          ZAP   REMAINP(8),QUOTENTP+4(4) EXTRACT THE REMAINDER     001410.
000132 F873 C708 C708 00708 00708    133          ZAP   QUOTENTP(8),QUOTENTP(4) EXPAND THE QUOTIENT        001420.
000138 D20F C6E0 C236 006E0 00236    134          MVC   REMAIN(16),PATTERN      MOVE IN EDIT PATTERN       001430.
00013E 4110 C6EF             006EF    135          LA    R1,REMAIN+15            POINT TO LAST DIGIT POSITION 001440.
000142 DF0F C6E0 C710 006E0 00710    136          EDMK  REMAIN(16),REMAINP      EDIT THE REMAINDER         001450.
000148 47B0 C152             00152    137          BNM   REMPOS                  IF NOT < 0, DON'T MOVE IN SIGN 001460.
00014C 0610                          138          BCTR  R1,0                    BACK UP ONE POSITION       001470.
00014E 9260 1000       00000         139          MVI   0(R1),C'-'              MOVE IN NEGATIVE SIGN      001480.
000152                               140 REMPOS   DS    0H                      SKIP NEGATIVE MOVE IF POSITIVE 001490.

000152 D20F C6D0 C236 006D0 00236    142          MVC   QUOTIENT(16),PATTERN    MOVE IN EDIT PATTERN       001510.
000158 4110 C6DF             006DF    143          LA    R1,QUOTIENT+15          POINT TO LAST DIGIT POSITION 001520.
00015C DF0F C6D0 C708 006D0 00708    144          EDMK  QUOTIENT(16),QUOTENTP   EDIT THE QUOTIENT VALUE    001530.
000162 47B0 C16C             0016C    145          BNM   QUOTPOS                 IF NOT < 0, DON'T MOVE IN SIGN 001540.
000166 0610                          146          BCTR  R1,0                    BACK UP ONE POSITION       001550.
000168 9260 1000       00000         147          MVI   0(R1),C'-'              MOVE IN NEGATIVE SIGN      001560.
00016C                               148 QUOTPOS  DS    0H                      SKIP NEGATIVE MOVE IF POSITIVE 001570.
```

```
     COMPUTE SUM, DIFFERENCE, PRODUCT, QUOTIENT OF 2 VALUES                                        PAGE    5
  LOC  OBJECT CODE     ADDR1 ADDR2  STMT   SOURCE STATEMENT

                                     150 ********************************************************************** 001590.
                                     151 *    MOVE THE INPUT VALUES INTO THE OUTPUT LINE AND PRINT THE        * 001600.
                                     152 *     INFORMATION FOR THE ADD OPERATION.                             * 001610.
                                     153 ********************************************************************** 001620.
00016C D204 C58D C634 0058D 00634    154           MVC   OP1(5),NUM1            MOVE FIRST NUMBER TO PRINT LINE 001630.
000172 D204 C5AA C639 005AA 00639    155           MVC   OP2(5),NUM2            MOVE SECOND NUMBER SIMILARLY    001640.
000178 D20E C56B C1F1 0056B 001F1    156           MVC   COMMAND(15),=CL15'ADD' FIRST COMMAND IS TO ADD         001650.
00017E D20E C5B7 C6A1 005B7 006A1    157           MVC   RESULT(15),SUM+1       MOVE SUM INTO PRINT LINE        001660.
000184 E020 C564 0085 00564          158           XPRNT PLINE,133              PRINT SUM VALUE                 001670.
                                     159 ********************************************************************** 001680.
                                     160 *    PRINT THE RESULTS OF THE SUBTRACT.                              * 001690.
                                     161 ********************************************************************** 001700.
00018A D20E C56B C200 0056B 00200    162           MVC   COMMAND(15),=CL15'SUBTRACT'  COMMAND IS NOW SUBTRACT   001710.
000190 D20E C5B7 C6B1 005B7 006B1    163           MVC   RESULT(15),DIFFER+1    MOVE DIFFERENCE TO PRINT LINE   001720.
000196 E020 C564 0085 00564          164           XPRNT PLINE,133              PRINT SUM VALUE                 001730.
                                     165 ********************************************************************** 001740.
                                     166 *    PRINT THE RESULTS OF THE MULTIPLICATION.                        * 001750.
                                     167 ********************************************************************** 001760.
00019C D20E C56B C20F 0056B 0020F    168           MVC   COMMAND(15),=CL15'MULTIPLY'  MOVE IN MULTIPLY COMMAND  001770.
0001A2 D20E C5B7 C6C1 005B7 006C1    169           MVC   RESULT(15),PRODUCT+1   MOVE PRODUCT INTO PRINT LINE    001780.
0001A8 E020 C564 0085 00564          170           XPRNT PLINE,133              PRINT SUM VALUE                 001790.
                                     171 ********************************************************************** 001800.
                                     172 *    PRINT THE QUOTIENT AND REMAINDER FROM THE DIVISION.             * 001810.
                                     173 ********************************************************************** 001820.
0001AE D20E C56B C21E 0056B 0021E    174           MVC   COMMAND(15),=CL15'DIVIDE'    MOVE IN DIVIDE COMMAND    001830.
0001B4 D20E C5B7 C6D1 005B7 006D1    175           MVC   RESULT(15),QUOTIENT+1  MOVE QUOTIENT INTO PRINT LINE   001840.
0001BA D208 C5CB C22D 005CB 0022D    176           MVC   RESULT+20(9),=C'REMAINDER'  MOVE IN HEADER FOR REMAIN. 001850.
0001C0 D206 C5D6 C6E9 005D6 006E9    177           MVC   RESULT+31(7),REMAIN+9       NOW MOVE IN REMAINDER      001860.
0001C6 E020 C564 0085 00564          178           XPRNT PLINE,133          PRINT QUOTIENT/REMAINDER VALUES     001870.
0001CC E020 C3D5 0085 003D5          179           XPRNT SKIP2,133                                              001880.
0001D2 47F0 C032             00032   180           B     CONTINUE               CONTINUE UNTIL END OF FILE      001890.
```

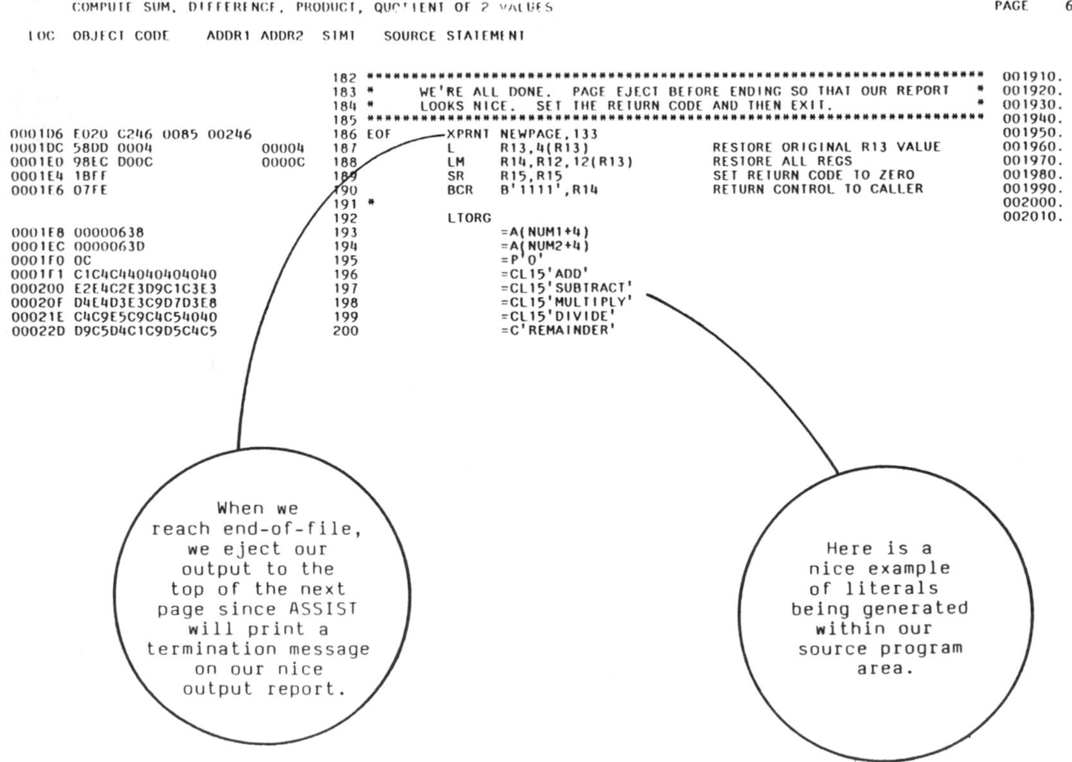

```
     COMPUTE SUM, DIFFERENCE, PRODUCT, QUOTIENT OF 2 VALUES                                        PAGE    6
  LOC  OBJECT CODE     ADDR1 ADDR2  STMT   SOURCE STATEMENT

                                     182 ********************************************************************** 001910.
                                     183 *     WE'RE ALL DONE.  PAGE EJECT BEFORE ENDING SO THAT OUR REPORT   * 001920.
                                     184 *     LOOKS NICE.  SET THE RETURN CODE AND THEN EXIT.                * 001930.
                                     185 ********************************************************************** 001940.
0001D6 E020 C246 0085 00246          186 EOF       XPRNT NEWPAGE,133                                        001950.
0001DC 58DD 0004             00004   187           L     R13,4(R13)             RESTORE ORIGINAL R13 VALUE      001960.
0001E0 98EC D00C             0000C   188           LM    R14,R12,12(R13)        RESTORE ALL REGS                001970.
0001E4 1BFF                          189           SR    R15,R15                SET RETURN CODE TO ZERO         001980.
0001E6 07FE                          190           BCR   B'1111',R14            RETURN CONTROL TO CALLER        001990.
                                     191 *                                                                      002000.
                                     192           LTORG                                                        002010.
0001E8 00000638                      193                 =A(NUM1+4)
0001EC 0000063D                      194                 =A(NUM2+4)
0001F0 0C                            195                 =P'0'
0001F1 C1C4C44040404040              196                 =CL15'ADD'
000200 E2E4C2E3D9C1C3E3              197                 =CL15'SUBTRACT'
00020F D4E4D3E3C9D7D3E8              198                 =CL15'MULTIPLY'
00021E C4C9E5C9C4C54040              199                 =CL15'DIVIDE'
00022D D9C5D4C1C9D5C4C5              200                 =C'REMAINDER'
```

```
COMPUTE SUM, DIFFERENCE, PRODUCT, QUOTIENT OF 2 VALUES                                                PAGE    7

LOC    OBJECT CODE      ADDR1 ADDR2  STMT   SOURCE STATEMENT

                                     202 ********************************************************************* 002030.
                                     203 *                    DATA AND STORAGE AREA DEFINITIONS             *  002040.
                                     204 ********************************************************************* 002050.
000236 4020202020202020              205 PATTERN  DC    X'40202020202020202020202020202120'                    002060.
000246 F140404040404040              206 NEWPAGE  DC    CL133'1'                                               002070.
                                     207 *                                                                     002080.
0002CB F1D9C5D7D6D9E340              208 TITLE    DC    CL133'1REPORT                                 A R I TX002090.
                                                          H M E T I C    P R O C E S S I N G    R E P O R T'    002100.
000350 4040D5C1D4C57A40              209 SUBTITLE DC    CL133'  NAME:  MATH                                    X002110.
                                                               BASIC   MATH   OPERATIONS'                       002120.
0003D5 6040404040404040              210 SKIP2    DC    CL133'-'                                               002130.
00045A 40606060606040D6              211 HEADINGS DC    CL133' ----- OPERATION -----        ----- FIRST VALUE -X002140.
                                                      ----      ----- SECOND VALUE -----      --------------- RX002150.
                                                      ESULT ---------------'                                   002160.
0004DF 4E6D6D6D6D6D6D6D              212 UNDERLIN DC    CL133'+_______________________        ________________X002170.
                                                      _____    ______________________      __________________X002180.
                                                      ____________________________                            002190.
                                     213 *                                                                     002200.
000564                               214 PLINE    DS    0CL133                                                 002210.
000564 40                            215 CC       DC    C' '                                                   002220.
000565 404040404040                  216          DC    CL6' '                                                 002230.
00056B 4040404040404040              217 COMMAND  DC    CL15' '                                                002240.
00057A 4040404040404040              218          DC    CL19' '                                                002250.
00058D 4040404040                    219 OP1      DC    CL5' '                                                 002260.
000592 4040404040404040              220          DC    CL24' '                                                002270.
0005AA 4040404040                    221 OP2      DC    CL5' '                                                 002280.
0005AF 4040404040404040              222          DC    CL8' '                                                 002290.
0005B7 4040404040404040              223 RESULT   DC    CL50' '                                                002300.
                                     224 *                                                                     002310.
0005EC                               225 SAVEAREA DS    18F                REGISTER SAVE AREA                  002320.

000634                               227 INPUTREC DS    0CL80              ****                                002340.
000634                               228 NUM1     DS    CL5                    **** INPUT RECORD DESCRIPTION   002350.
000639                               229 NUM2     DS    CL5                    *                               002360.
00063E                               230          DS    CL70               ****                                002370.
```

This edit pattern is used for editing all of our results during processing.

```
COMPUTE SUM, DIFFERENCE, PRODUCT, QUOTIENT OF 2 VALUES                                                PAGE    8

LOC    OBJECT CODE      ADDR1 ADDR2  STMT   SOURCE STATEMENT

000688                               232          DS    0D                                                     002390.
000688                               233 VALUE1   DS    PL8                                                    002400.
000690                               234 VALUE2   DS    PL8                                                    002410.
000698                               235 WORK     DS    PL8                                                    002420.
0006A0 4040404040404040              236 SUM      DC    CL16' '              ****                              002430.
0006B0 4040404040404040              237 DIFFER   DC    CL16' '                 *                              002440.
0006C0 4040404040404040              238 PRODUCT  DC    CL16' '                 **** OUTPUT RESULT AREAS       002450.
0006D0 4040404040404040              239 QUOTIENT DC    CL16' '                 *                              002460.
0006E0 4040404040404040              240 REMAIN   DC    CL16' '              ****                              002470.
0006F0 000000000000000C              241 SUMP     DC    PL8'0'               ****                              002480.
0006F8 000000000000000C              242 DIFFERP  DC    PL8'0'                  *                              002490.
000700 000000000000000C              243 PRODUCTP DC    PL8'0'                  **** CONVERSION AREAS          002500.
000708 000000000000000C              244 QUOTENTP DC    PL8'0'                  *                              002510.
000710 000000000000000C              245 REMAINP  DC    PL8'0'               ****                              002520.
                                     246          END   PROCESS                                                002530.

***  NO   STATEMENTS FLAGGED -  NO   WARNINGS,  NO   ERRORS

*** DYNAMIC CORE AREA USED:  LOW:   20184 HIGH:    1660 LEAVING:  498348 FREE BYTES. AVERAGE:      88 BYTES/STMT ***

*** ASSEMBLY TIME =    0.038 SECS,     6500 STATEMENTS/SEC ***

*** PROGRAM EXECUTION BEGINNING - ANY OUTPUT BEFORE EXECUTION TIME MESSAGE IS PRODUCED BY USER PROGRAM ***
```

```
REPORT                          A R I T H M E T I C   P R O C E S S I N G   R E P O R T
 NAME:  MATH                                     BASIC   MATH   OPERATIONS


----- OPERATION -----      ----- FIRST VALUE -----   ----- SECOND VALUE -----   --------------- RESULT ---------------
      ADD                         00020                     00008                  28
      SUBTRACT                    00020                     00008                  12
      MULTIPLY                    00020                     00008                 160
      DIVIDE                      00020                     00008                   2     REMAINDER         4


      ADD                            -6                         4                  -2
      SUBTRACT                       -6                         4                 -10
      MULTIPLY                       -6                         4                 -24
      DIVIDE                         -6                         4                  -1     REMAINDER        -2


      ADD                            25                        -3                  22
      SUBTRACT                       25                        -3                  28
      MULTIPLY                       25                        -3                 -75
      DIVIDE                         25                        -3                  -8     REMAINDER         1


      ADD                           -66                        -7                 -73
      SUBTRACT                      -66                        -7                 -59
      MULTIPLY                      -66                        -7                 462
      DIVIDE                        -66                        -7                   9     REMAINDER        -3


      ADD                           370                        -9                 361
      SUBTRACT                      370                        -9                 379
      MULTIPLY                      370                        -9               -3330
      DIVIDE                        370                        -9                 -41     REMAINDER         1
```

You can clearly see our input values. Some appear differently (leading zeros) since these fields came directly from the character input.

Carefully review the results paying particular attention to the signs of the various results.

```
*** EXECUTION TIME =    0.008 SECS.        601 INSTRUCTIONS EXECUTED -      75125 INSTRUCTIONS/SEC ***
*** AM004 - NORMAL USER TERMINATION BY RETURN ***
```

These messages would have appeared on our output report if we had not performed a page eject before returning control to the operating system.

STUDY QUESTIONS

1. Write the number +376 as a four-byte packed-decimal number.
2. NUMA contains the value X'00246801357C'. Write an edit pattern that converts NUMA into its character equivalent of 2,468,013.57.
3. Write the instruction to convert NUMA into its character equivalent using the edit pattern developed in Study Question 2.
4. What is the most number of digits that can be processed using packed-decimal data?
5. NUMA is a six-byte field and NUMB is a four-byte field. If NUMA is divided by NUMB, what does the format of NUMA look like after the division?
6. VAL1 has a value of X'000003451C' and VAL2 has a value of X'023C'. If VAL1 is divided by VAL2, what is the result in VAL1?
7. VALA has a value of 24.5 and VALB has a value of 2.4. Write the necessary code to divide VALA by VALB and leave a result with three digits to the right of the decimal point. Assume that VALA is eight bytes long and VALB is four bytes long.
8. Write the necessary code to set the condition code to B'11' in the PSW.
9. If ABC is X'003456834D', what will be in ABC after
   SRP ABC,64−5,7
10. Write the instruction to decrease the value in register 6 by one.
11. What will be in the five-byte area called ABC if the following instruction is issued?
    PACK ABC(5),=C'004.5'
12. What will be in the five-byte area called ABC if the following instruction is issued?
    PACK ABC(5),=C'−2345679'
13. Use the EQU instruction to equate the symbol ALLDONE with the symbol B'0111'.

14. Initialize the three-byte packed-decimal area labeled XYZ to the value 14.
15. What will be in the five-byte area called ABC if the following instruction is issued?
    UNPK ABC(5),=X'002413579D'
16. The CLC instruction can compare any type of field, including packed-decimal fields (although it may not work as desired). Can the CP instruction compare any type of character data areas?
17. Suppose that an input value was typed in columns 10 through 16 as C'ƀƀ23ƀƀƀ'. If this value were packed, would the resulting number be a valid or an invalid packed-decimal field?
18. What abend code is most commonly associated with packed-decimal processing?
19. How is the third operand of the SRP instruction used?
20. What is the first field in the edit pattern called?

PROGRAMMING ASSIGNMENTS

1. Write a program to balance a checkbook. Input records containing a code of D (deposit) or W (withdrawal) in column 1 of a data card and an amount in columns 2 through 10. The first card in the data deck has the opening balance in columns 1 through 10. Apply deposits and withdrawals to the account and print out a balance statement for each transaction processed.
2. Data cards contain two values. The first value is the number of miles driven and the second value is the number of gallons of gasoline required to go that distance. For each pair of numbers, compute the miles per gallon for that fillup. For all pairs of numbers in the data deck, compute an overall average miles per gallon. Assume that the miles are in the format xxx.x (columns 1 to 5) and the gallons are in the format xx.xx (columns 6 to 10).
3. A large auto parts distributor collects data on each branch in the region. For each branch, a data card is typed that identifies the branch (columns 1 to 40), the total yearly sales to date (columns 41 to 50), and the number of current sales (columns 51 to 53). Following this "header" card, each sale is listed. A sales record consists of the item name (columns 1 to 30), the number of these items sold (columns 31 to 33), and the unit price of the item (columns 34 to 40 in the format xxxxx.xx). Process each branch by printing the opening sales amount and the branch name, itemizing each item sold and adjusting the total yearly sales within that branch, and by summarizing the average cost per unit item within that branch. Produce a master summary report for all branches that gives the distributor an overall view of all sales, items sold, and year-to-date values. Construct your reports in a very readable fashion oriented toward a real business environment.
4. Modify the carpet/air conditioning problems that we've done in the previous chapters by allowing the room measurements to be expressed with digits to the left and right of the decimal point.
5. Write a program to compute the future value of an investment if simple interest is used. Input to your program should consist of the amount of the investment, the number of years to be invested, and the annual interest rate. Using simple interest and annual compounding, compute the value of the investment over the time period specified.
6. A loan is secured from a bank using simple interest compounding. If a certain principle is borrowed at x% for N years, how many payments will be required to pay off the loan? Input to your program should consist of the principle borrowed, annual interest rate, length of the loan, and maximum monthly payment. Print a report showing the original principle and each month's balance, assuming a fixed monthly payment. Also print the current year, the month of the payment, and the resulting principle.

7. Data contains a student's name and five exam scores. For each student, compute the student's average exam score for the semester. Print all student data in a report format that lists each student, their exam scores, and their average scores. For each student, assign the student a semester letter grade based on the scale 90, 80, 70, and 60.
8. A furniture company maintains an inventory of all items in their warehouse. Each item's data is recorded on a single data card and consists of the item description, number in stock, wholesale price, and retail price. Write a program that computes the total wholesale and retail value of the inventory for the furniture company.
9. Write a program to generate a list of all prime numbers between 1 and 100.
10. Write a program that totals the items in a shopping cart. In other words, assume that each data card contains a description of the item and its price. For each item in the grocery cart, print the item description and price on a receipt while accumulating the item's price into the total. After totaling all the items, compute the tax on the total. Print the tax and the final bill.
11. Process input records until end of file. Each input record contains a letter in column 1 of the input record and an integer number, right justified in the next five columns of each input record. If the letter in column 1 is the letter C, convert the integer number from celsius to fahrenheit by applying the formula F = ((9/5) * C) + 32. If the letter is F, convert the fahrenheit number to celsius by applying the formula C = (5/9) * (F − 32). Print the original number and its converted value in a column report fashion.
12. A package delivery firm charges based on the weight of each package. Items weighing less than 1 pound are charged at the rate of 10 cents per ounce. Items between one and five pounds are charged a flat $2, plus 10 cents per ounce. Items over 5 pounds are charged $3 for each five pound denomination or fraction of a denomination plus 10 cents per ounce for the first 5 pounds and 15 cents per ounce for any weight over five pounds. Given the weight of the package in ounces, compute the cost for mailing the item. Print your results using dollars and cents representation. Float a dollar sign before the first significant digit of your result.
13. A brass musical instrument manufacturing company rewards employees based on the quality of the instruments manufactured. If the clearance between the instrument valves and their casings fall within the allowable ranges, employees receive payment bonuses. Clearance measurements for each instrument are collected and fed into the computer each evening to determine the day's bonus allowance. Measurements are very small and generally fall between .0005 and .0010 inches. A daily average tolerance greater than .0009 is considered unacceptable. Given six digit input fields with all digits to the right of the decimal, determine the average tolerance for the day. If the average tolerance exceeds the allowable limit, indicate that no bonus pay will be received for the day. If tolerance is acceptable, indicate that bonus will be received.
14. Referring back to programming problem 12 in Chapter 6, approximate the square root of an input number to 4 places to the right of the decimal.
15. Input an integer number and convert it to hexadecimal representation. For example, the input number 123 would be converted to 7B after processing. Process an undetermined number of input values and for each one, print the input number and its converted value.

8

Program Debugging

Following program development and implementation, we begin to test our computer solutions. If our program runs the first time, then we generally assume that it contains no "bugs." On the other hand, a program should be tested thoroughly to ensure that it works against *all* possible data values. The first successful execution of a program should not be regarded as total completion of an assignment.

While testing our computer solutions, we may soon find that our program contains an error. The error, commonly called a **bug,** must be fixed to obtain full credit on an assignment or to produce the correct results. What then is **debugging** and what does it involve in assembly language?

To most of us, debugging is removing errors from a program. Further, debugging is a negative experience. Every error frustrates us and causes us to question our competency as a programmer. On the other hand, debugging can be positive if viewed differently. In other words, it *should* be viewed as a process of "discovery." Every bug found should be a rewarding experience since you have uncovered a slight flaw or oversight in a component of your computer solution. Looking at debugging in this manner, we should treat it as an important phase during the development of a computer solution. In fact, we should plan for the debugging of our programs.

Planning for debugging is an important aspect of program development. Constructing data to test our program and determining what results our program should produce is done during analysis and design. Debugging is not an afterthought, but an ongoing and normal part of the problem solving process.

Let's look at program development and debugging realistically for a minute. In general, you feel that you do not have enough time to develop a computer solution to a problem. As a result, you take shortcuts. Typically, you skimp during analysis, design, and all other phases of preparation so that you may enter your program on the computer as quickly as possible. Once entered, you begin testing and debugging your program. This is the time when you think about how your program should act and what it should produce. As you work toward a final solution, you are under pressure to attend your other classes, use only the computer time or budget allocated, and yet produce a perfect product. On one hand, you're encouraged (or forced) to follow a structured program implementation procedure, and, on the other, you're discouraged from using the computer as a discovery tool. Debugging requires computer time and an adequate budget. For proper debugging to be practiced, appropriate resources and encouragement should be given.

Do you continue to test your program after you've obtained the correct results? Of course not. What if your first run was successful? Are you done with the assignment? Yes. Will your program handle all processing situations based on the data that you're to process? Maybe. The idea is *thoroughness.* A programmer should fully test as many aspects of the program as possible to ensure that it contains no flaws. If you're working under a time constraint, then you're obviously not going to be as thorough. Since reality takes precedence over theory, what I hope to provide in this chapter is direction. Assembly language is one of the most difficult languages in which to debug and without a direction or strategy for debugging, you'll most likely fail at an attempt. For this reason, I will propose several debugging facilities which can be integrated into your program *during program development.* Hopefully, this will aid in successful program completion by providing you with information about the execution of your program. By doing so, we hope to minimize the debugging process as much as possible.

Many languages provide debugging aids such as tracing facilities, number of instructions executed, and program failure reports. In other words, they provide the programmer with sufficient information to debug his program. This is not the case in assembly language, where all debugging aids must be built into the program *by the programmer.* Assembly language does not provide any automatic debugging facilities because of performance. Debugging aids, tracing services, and other facilities add to the processing overhead of a program. Assembly language's goal is fast processing and these aids tend to hinder the performance of a program. On the other hand, *a program cannot run efficiently if it can't run at all.*

In order to perform debugging, we must understand the various errors that can occur during program development. There are two general types, **syntax errors** and **execution errors.** Each type occurs as a result of a particular situation. We need to understand when each type of error can occur and how to resolve the problem(s) that caused the error.

SYNTAX ERRORS

A **syntax error** occurs in the program *before* execution. A syntax error occurs because the programmer has not typed a statement correctly. For example, the AP (add decimal) instruction discussed in Chapter 7 requires two operands. If a programmer wants to add three fields, N1, N2, and N3, he might attempt to code the instruction given in Fig. 8.1. This causes a syntax error because the AP instruction is not designed for three operands.

```
This instruction causes a syntax error.

          AP      N1(8),N2(8),N3(8)
```

Figure 8.1 Example of a syntax error.

Since syntax errors occur *before* execution, this means that the assembler, interpreter, compiler, or preprocessor has detected a coding error in a statement and indicates that error via an error message. The manner in which syntax errors are pointed out differs between versions of the assembler and ASSIST. The sample sections of printouts in Figs. 8.2 through 8.5 illustrate the different message formats that are obtained from ASSIST and the various assembler versions. In Fig. 8.2, ASSIST indicates the error and its reason directly under the statement that has been coded incorrectly. The latest assembler versions also indicate errors in a similar manner as shown in Fig. 8.3. Older assem-

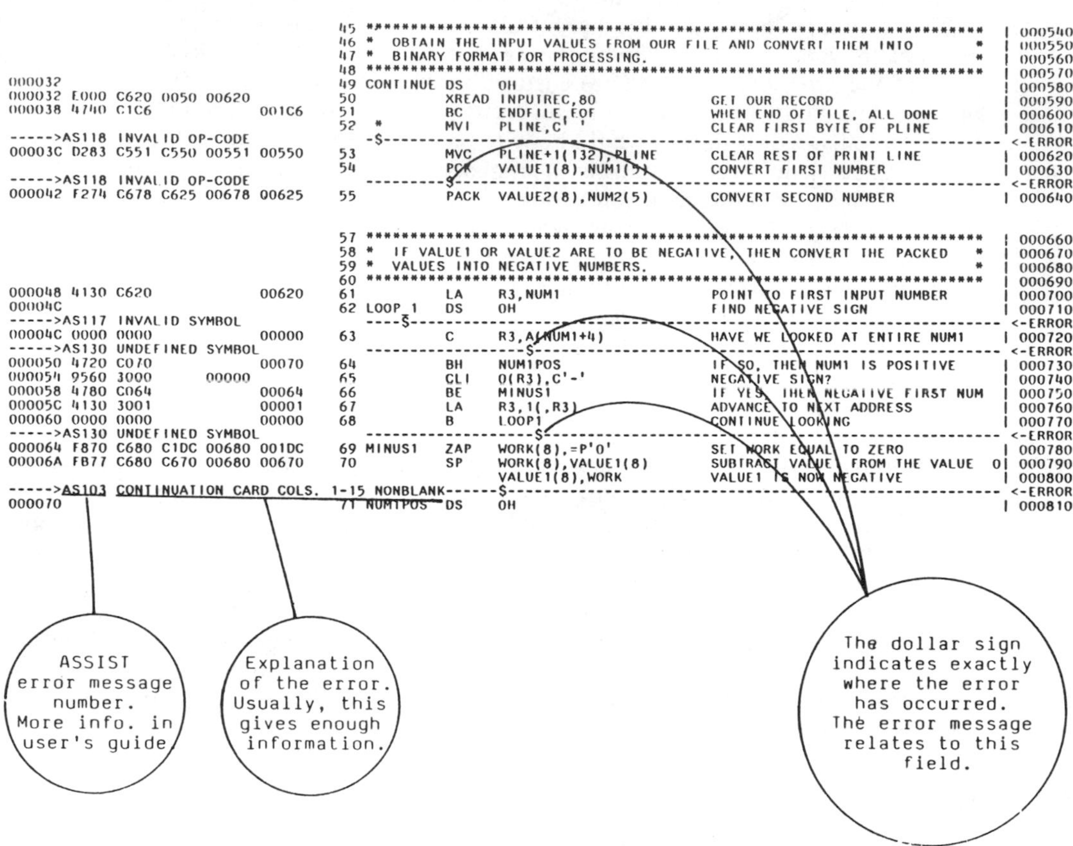

```
   COMPUTE SUM, DIFFERENCE  PRODUCT, QUOTIENT OF 2 VALUES                                                         PAGE    2

LOC   OBJECT CODE     ADDR1 ADDR2  STMT   SOURCE STATEMENT

                                   45 ***************************************************************   | 000540
                                   46 *  OBTAIN THE INPUT VALUES FROM OUR FILE AND CONVERT THEM INTO   *   | 000550
                                   47 *  BINARY FORMAT FOR PROCESSING.                                *   | 000560
                                   48 ***************************************************************   | 000570
000032                             49 CONTINUE DS    0H                                                  | 000580
000032 E000 C620 0050 00620        50          XREAD INPUTREC,80          GET OUR RECORD                | 000590
000038 4740 C1C6             001C6 51          BC    ENDFILE,EOF          WHEN END OF FILE, ALL DONE    | 000600
                                   52  *       MVI   PLINE,C' '           CLEAR FIRST BYTE OF PLINE     | 000610
----->AS118 INVALID OP-CODE        -$---------------------------------------------------------------- <-ERROR
00003C D283 C551 C550 00551 00550  53          MVC   PLINE+1(132),PLINE   CLEAR REST OF PRINT LINE      | 000620
                                   54          PCK   VALUE1(8),NUM1(5)    CONVERT FIRST NUMBER          | 000630
----->AS118 INVALID OP-CODE        ---------$-------------------------------------------------------- <-ERROR
000042 F274 C678 C625 00678 00625  55          PACK  VALUE2(8),NUM2(5)    CONVERT SECOND NUMBER         | 000640

                                   57 ***************************************************************   | 000660
                                   58 *  IF VALUE1 OR VALUE2 ARE TO BE NEGATIVE, THEN CONVERT THE PACKED *   | 000670
                                   59 *  VALUES INTO NEGATIVE NUMBERS.                                *   | 000680
                                   60 ***************************************************************   | 000690
000048 4130 C620             00620 61          LA    R3,NUM1              POINT TO FIRST INPUT NUMBER   | 000700
00004C                             62 LOOP_1   DS    0H                   FIND NEGATIVE SIGN            | 000710
----->AS117 INVALID SYMBOL         ----$------------------------------------------------------------- <-ERROR
00004C 0000 0000             00000 63          C     R3,A(NUM1+4)         HAVE WE LOOKED AT ENTIRE NUM1 | 000720
----->AS130 UNDEFINED SYMBOL       -----------------$------------------------------------------------ <-ERROR
000050 4720 C070             00070 64          BH    NUM1POS              IF SO, THEN NUM1 IS POSITIVE  | 000730
000054 9560 3000       00000       65          CLI   0(R3),C'-'           NEGATIVE SIGN?                | 000740
000058 4780 C064             00064 66          BE    MINUS1               IF YES, THEN NEGATIVE FIRST NUM | 000750
00005C 4130 3001             00001 67          LA    R3,1(,R3)            ADVANCE TO NEXT ADDRESS       | 000760
000060 0000 0000             00000 68          B     LOOP1                CONTINUE LOOKING              | 000770
----->AS130 UNDEFINED SYMBOL       -----------------$------------------------------------------------ <-ERROR
000064 F870 C680 C1DC 00680 001DC  69 MINUS1   ZAP   WORK(8),=P'0'        SET WORK EQUAL TO ZERO        | 000780
00006A FB77 C680 C670 00680 00670  70          SP    WORK(8),VALUE1(8)    SUBTRACT VALUE1 FROM THE VALUE 0| 000790
                                                     VALUE1(8),WORK       VALUE1 IS NOW NEGATIVE        | 000800
----->AS103 CONTINUATION CARD COLS. 1-15 NONBLANK------$--------------------------------------------- <-ERROR
000070                             71 NUM1POS  DS    0H                                                  | 000810
```


Figure 8.2 Error message location in an ASSIST program listing.

blers "flag" the statement as having an error and describe the error at a later point in the listing under the heading ASSEMBLER DIAGNOSTICS AND STATISTICS as shown in Figs. 8.4 and 8.5. Although both processors indicate which statement is in error and for what reason, it's easier to identify statements in error in ASSIST and in the latest assembler versions since the messages appear directly under the statements. Programmers do not have to go back and forth within the listing to refer to the error messages and then to the source statement to correlate the error with the source code.

There are hundreds of syntax errors possible during program development. It's not worthwhile to memorize all the error messages, but it is worthwhile to understand why the errors occur and how to fix the source program statements. The basic technique for resolving syntax errors is to read the message(s) carefully, review the source statement, and use your reference summary card or a manual (such as *IBM 370 Principles of Operation*) to obtain the correct coding format of the statement. If further assistance is needed, look up the error message in an error manual or ask for help. IBM (developers of the

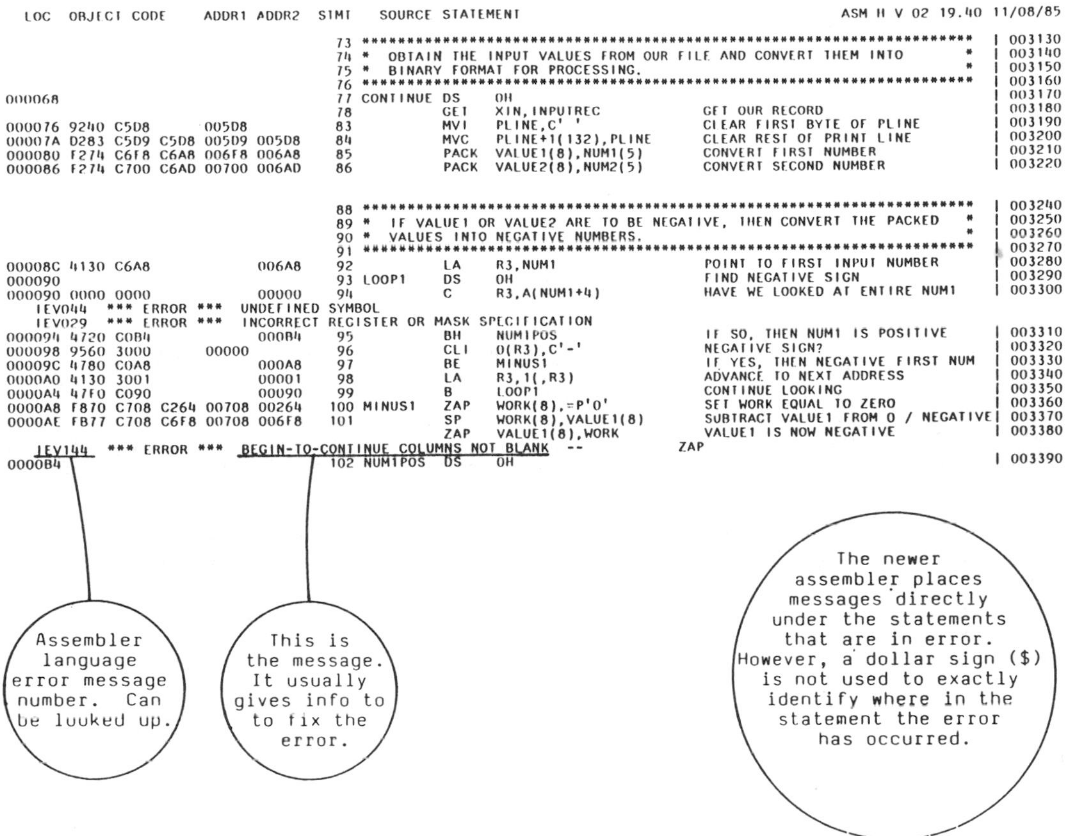

```
COMPUTE SUM, DIFFERENCE, PRODUCT, QUOTIENT OF 2 VALUES                                                     PAGE    4

  LOC  OBJECT CODE    ADDR1 ADDR2  STMT   SOURCE STATEMENT                                   ASM H V 02 19.40 11/08/85

                                    73 ********************************************************************  | 003130
                                    74 *  OBTAIN THE INPUT VALUES FROM OUR FILE AND CONVERT THEM INTO      *  | 003140
                                    75 *  BINARY FORMAT FOR PROCESSING.                                     *  | 003150
                                    76 ********************************************************************  | 003160
000068                              77 CONTINUE DS    0H                                                      | 003170
                                    78          GET   XIN,INPUTREC           GET OUR RECORD                   | 003180
000076 9240 C5D8        005D8       83          MVI   PLINE,C' '             CLEAR FIRST BYTE OF PLINE        | 003190
00007A D283 C5D9 C5D8 005D9 005D8   84          MVC   PLINE+1(132),PLINE     CLEAR REST OF PRINT LINE         | 003200
000080 F274 C6F8 C6A8 006F8 006A8   85          PACK  VALUE1(8),NUM1(5)      CONVERT FIRST NUMBER             | 003210
000086 F274 C700 C6AD 00700 006AD   86          PACK  VALUE2(8),NUM2(5)      CONVERT SECOND NUMBER            | 003220

                                    88 ********************************************************************  | 003240
                                    89 *  IF VALUE1 OR VALUE2 ARE TO BE NEGATIVE, THEN CONVERT THE PACKED   *  | 003250
                                    90 *  VALUES INTO NEGATIVE NUMBERS.                                     *  | 003260
                                    91 ********************************************************************  | 003270
00008C 4130 C6A8              006A8 92          LA    R3,NUM1                POINT TO FIRST INPUT NUMBER      | 003280
000090                              93 LOOP1    DS    0H                     FIND NEGATIVE SIGN               | 003290
000090 0000 0000              00000 94          C     R3,A(NUM1+4)           HAVE WE LOOKED AT ENTIRE NUM1    | 003300
   IEV044   *** ERROR ***  UNDEFINED SYMBOL
   IEV029   *** ERROR ***  INCORRECT REGISTER OR MASK SPECIFICATION
000094 4720 C0B4              000B4 95          BH    NUM1POS                IF SO, THEN NUM1 IS POSITIVE     | 003310
000098 9560 3000        00000       96          CLI   0(R3),C'-'             NEGATIVE SIGN?                   | 003320
00009C 4780 C0A8              000A8 97          BE    MINUS1                 IF YES, THEN NEGATIVE FIRST NUM  | 003330
0000A0 4130 3001              00001 98          LA    R3,1(,R3)              ADVANCE TO NEXT ADDRESS          | 003340
0000A4 47F0 C090              00090 99          B     LOOP1                  CONTINUE LOOKING                 | 003350
0000A8 F870 C708 C264 00708 00264  100 MINUS1   ZAP   WORK(8),=P'0'          SET WORK EQUAL TO ZERO           | 003360
0000AE FB77 C708 C6F8 00708 006F8  101          SP    WORK(8),VALUE1(8)      SUBTRACT VALUE1 FROM 0 / NEGATIVE| 003370
                                                ZAP   VALUE1(8),WORK         VALUE1 IS NOW NEGATIVE           | 003380
   IEV144   *** ERROR ***  BEGIN-TO-CONTINUE COLUMNS NOT BLANK  --         ZAP
0000B4                             102 NUM1POS  DS    0H                                                      | 003390
```


Figure 8.3 Error messages in the latest versions of the assembler.

assembler) and Penn State University (developers of ASSIST) provide manuals that contain all of the error messages and general explanations about each. From these manuals, you should be able to determine why the error occurred and successfully fix the problem.

Some companies and schools have on-line systems to assist debugging. When an error occurs, the user enters an on-line command (such as ABND) to request information about a particular error message. Using the error message number or the error message phrase, the facility describes why the error occurred and gives several suggestions to correct the problem. Obviously, this system is very useful since it may be accessed from any terminal and is always available when needed.

When coding assembly language programs, programmers generally make the same type of errors. In particular, let's identify several of the common errors so that you are aware of their sources when coding your assembly language programs. Figure 8.6 lists these errors.

```
 COMPUTE SUM, DIFFERENCE, PRODUCT, QUOTIENT OF 2 VALUES                                                  PAGE    5

  LOC  OBJECT CODE     ADDR1 ADDR2  STMT   SOURCE STATEMENT                                      ASM 0201 19.39 11/08/85

                                      92 ************************************************************************ | 000650
                                      93 *   IF VALUE1 OR VALUE2 ARE TO BE NEGATIVE, THEN CONVERT THE PACKED       * | 000660
                                      94 *   VALUES INTO NEGATIVE NUMBERS.                                         * | 000670
                                      95 ************************************************************************ | 000680
000094 4130 C6BC        006BC         96          LA    R3,NUM1              POINT TO FIRST INPUT NUMBER       | 000690
000098                                97 LOOP1    DS    0H                   FIND NEGATIVE SIGN                | 000700
000098 5930 C270        00270         98          C     R3,=A(NUM1+4)        HAVE WE LOOKED AT ENTIRE NUM1     | 000710
00009C 4720 C0C2        000C2         99          BH    NUM1POS              IF SO, THEN NUM1 IS POSITIVE      | 000720
0000A0 9560 3000        00000        100          CLI   0(R3),C'-'           NEGATIVE SIGN?                    | 000730
0000A4 4780 C0B0        000B0        101          BE    MINUS1               IF YES, THEN NEGATIVE FIRST NUM   | 000740
0000A8 4130 3001        00001        102          LA    R3,1(,R3)            ADVANCE TO NEXT ADDRESS           | 000750
0000AC 47F0 C098        00098        103          B     LOOP1                CONTINUE LOOKING                  | 000760
0000B0 F870 C720 C278 00720 00278    104 MINUS1   ZAP   WORK(8),=P'0'        SET WORK EQUAL TO ZERO            | 000770
0000B6 FB77 C720 C710 00720 00710    105          SP    WORK(8),VALUE1(8)    SUBTRACT VALUE1 FROM 0 / NEGATIV  | 000780
0000BC F877 C710 C720 00710 00720    106          ZAP   VALUE1(8),WORK       VALUE1 IS NOW NEGATIVE            | 000790
0000C2                               107 NUM1POS  DS    0H                                                     | 000800

0000C2 4130 C6C1        006C1        109          LA    R3,NUM2              POINT TO FIRST INPUT NUMBER       | 000820
0000C6                               110 LOOP_2   DS    0H                   FIND NEGATIVE SIGN                | 000830
          *** ERROR ***
0000C6 5930 C274        00274        111          C     R3,=A(NUM2+4)        HAVE WE LOOKED AT ENTIRE NUM1     | 000840
0000CA 4720 C0F0        000F0        112          BH    NUM2POS              IF SO, THEN NUM1 IS POSITIVE      | 000850
0000CE 9560 3000        00000        113          CLI   0(R3),C'-'           NEGATIVE SIGN?                    | 000860
0000D2 4780 C0DE        000DE        114          BE    MINUS2               IF YES, THEN NEGATIVE FIRST NUM   | 000870
0000D6 4130 3001        00001        115          LA    R3,1(,R3)            ADVANCE TO NEXT ADDRESS           | 000880
0000DA 0000 0000        00000        116          B     LOOP2                CONTINUE LOOKING                  | 000890
          *** ERROR ***
0000DE 0000 0000 0000 00720 00000    117 MINUS2   ZAP   WORK(8),P'0'         SET WORK EQUAL TO ZERO            | 000900
          *** ERROR ***
0000E4 FB77 C720 C718 00720 00718    118          SP    WORK(8),VALUE2(8)    SUBTRACT VALUE1 FROM 0            | 000910
0000EA F877 C718 C720 00718 00720    119          ZAP   VALUE2(8),WORK       VALUE1 IS NOW NEGATIVE            | 000920
0000F0                               120 NUM2POS  DS    0H                                                     | 000930
```

The older assemblers simply indicate that an error has occurred. You must look on the next page to see what the error actually is in each of your source statements.

Figure 8.4 Older assemblers only indicate that the statement is in error. Full descriptions are found later in the listing.

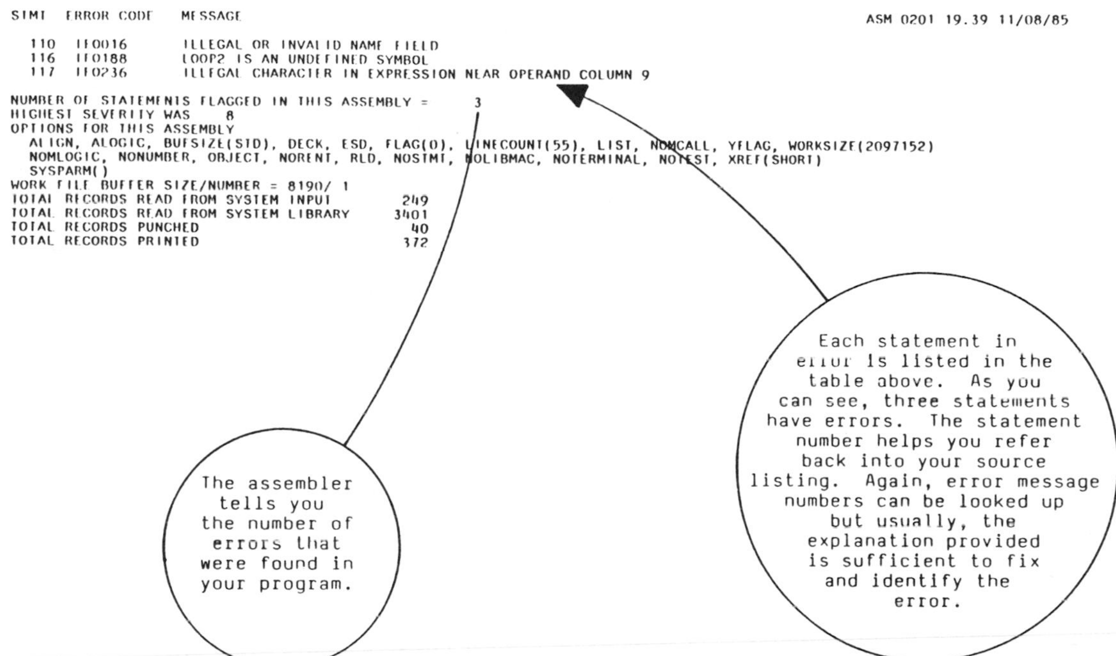

```
                                   ASSEMBLER DIAGNOSTICS AND STATISTICS                          PAGE   15

STMT  ERROR CODE   MESSAGE                                                               ASM 0201 19.39 11/08/85

  110  IEO016       ILLEGAL OR INVALID NAME FIELD
  116  IEO188       LOOP2 IS AN UNDEFINED SYMBOL
  117  IEO236       ILLEGAL CHARACTER IN EXPRESSION NEAR OPERAND COLUMN 9

NUMBER OF STATEMENTS FLAGGED IN THIS ASSEMBLY =      3
HIGHEST SEVERITY WAS     8
OPTIONS FOR THIS ASSEMBLY
  ALIGN, ALOGIC, BUFSIZE(STD), DECK, ESD, FLAG(0), LINECOUNT(55), LIST, NOMCALL, YFLAG, WORKSIZE(2097152)
  NOMLOGIC, NONUMBER, OBJECT, NORENT, RLD, NOSTMT, NOLIBMAC, NOTERMINAL, NOTEST, XREF(SHORT)
  SYSPARM()
WORK FILE BUFFER SIZE/NUMBER = 8190/ 1
TOTAL RECORDS READ FROM SYSTEM INPUT          249
TOTAL RECORDS READ FROM SYSTEM LIBRARY       3401
TOTAL RECORDS PUNCHED                          40
TOTAL RECORDS PRINTED                         372
```


Figure 8.5 Older assemblers describe all errors on the diagnostics page.

The register equates always seem to be omitted, thus causing syntax errors throughout the program whenever a register is referenced with the R prefix.

The programmer defines a storage area as DS instead of DC, and attempts to give a default or initial value to the field. Initial values may only be given to constant fields (DC).

Coding statements in the wrong columns cause many problems. Labels must begin in column 1, mnemonics are usually coded in column 10, and operands in column 16. The statement must end before column 71 unless the statement is to be continued. When continuing an assembler statement, place a non-blank character in column 72 and begin on the next line in column 16. If you start before or after column 16, you'll either generate a syntax error or not accomplish your task.

Labels may only be eight characters long. Although this rule has changed for the latest assembler versions, it still applies for ASSIST programs. In general, follow the eight-character rule since this is the industry standard.

Literals also present some problems. Programmers forget to code the LTORG statement, which may cause literals not to be generated or to be generated in the wrong CSECT. Further, programmers forget the equals sign before the literal when coding it on a statement. In fact, programmers also err in using literals when immediate data is to be coded and vice versa. As a general rule, if the mnemonic ends with the letter I, then a literal may not be coded.

Figure 8.6 Common causes of syntax errors.

EXECUTION ERRORS

Debugging an execution error is one of the most difficult tasks until you become proficient at debugging, which, as with most tasks, takes practice. Debugging your own programs and working through an execution problem is the best way to become familiar with debugging assembly language programs.

Execution errors are further classified based on their cause. **Invalid data** or **logical errors** are the two most common reasons for program failure at execution. Invalid data generally causes a data exception (0C7) abend during program execution. Invalid data can occur because you did not properly type input data into a field, your program did not validate or check a field before using it, you did not define the field correctly, you did not convert the data to proper internal format, or you used a wrong instruction to process a particular data type.

As we saw in Chapter 7, packed-decimal data must be in the proper format to be processed. Often, 0C7 abends occur because an input data field was not typed correctly and is converted into an invalid packed field or because the programmer used a wrong instruction to process a packed field. For example, suppose an input data card containing two numbers is to be processed. Instead of making sure that all positions within the input numbers are valid, the programmer blindly issues the PACK instruction and continues to process the data using arithmetic instructions. The program abends.

We might ask whether the problem is in the program or in the data. In fact, the problem could be caused by both. If the programmer is told that the data is valid, then the program may not be at fault since it works on that assumption. Clearly, a misunderstanding has occurred between the programmer and the person who entered the data. In any case, the problem must be resolved and the program rerun.

Logical errors are the most difficult to fix since they occur as a result of an error within the solution (program). Your code does not perform the processing that you wanted, and, for some reason, the processing performed results in an error.

Logical errors can occur for so many different reasons that it is difficult to give general guidelines as to possible causes. However, logical errors do occur in assembler due to many reasons, such as incorrect use of assembly language instructions. For example, the L (load) and LA (load address) instructions are often confused and are coded where the other should have been. Although such confusion may be regarded as syntax errors, the assembler or ASSIST may not find them when evaluating the coding of these statements, even if they are not being used properly. Hence, the errors do not occur before execution and so they become categorized as execution or logic errors.

If your program fails during execution, look for some of the symptoms outlined in Fig. 8.7.

DIAGNOSING ERRORS: ABEND CODES

Almost each logical or execution error abnormally terminates your program. You must be able to diagnose and fix your program based on the information given to you by the system. The standard system response to an abnormal program activity is to abend the program and to give a reason for the abend as an error message. The error message form varies, depending on whether or not the programmer has implemented the program in ASSIST or in assembly language. However, both ASSIST and the operating system issue abend messages with the same code numbers. Hence, if you become familiar with the abend codes in ASSIST, they also apply to assembly language.

It's important to realize that when your assembly language program fails during execution, it is *not* the assembler that is issuing the error message(s). The assembler only converts the program from source to object form. During execution, the assembler has already completed processing your program. Hence, assembly language program failures are diagnosed and reported by the *operating system,* not the assembler. As a result, you cannot look up the abend code messages in an ASSIST or assembly language manual, but you must refer to the IBM publications *System Codes* or *Messages and Codes.*

Although there are two categories of abend codes, we will discuss one in this chapter. The two categories are **user** and **system** abends. System abend codes are our main concern since they are issued by the system when our program has done something wrong. User abend codes are issued *by our program* when it detects something incorrect. For example, we may want to forcefully abend our program if we find that there isn't any data to be processed. Although we could have ended normally by printing a message on our output pages, we have the option of issuing an abend message to attract attention. A program that abends generally attracts more attention than one that ends without abending.

System abend codes are issued by the system to assist the programmer in finding the problem within the program. Generally, they appear as *Sxxx* at the top of the com-

Infinite loop. The program is to perform a series of operations N times or until the end of file is reached, but for some reason, it continues to process beyond the point of termination.

Incorrect return of control to the operating system. This logical error would seem to be another example of a misplaced syntax error. Basically, the program attempts to return control to the operating system but because you used the wrong instruction or did not reload your registers correctly, it does not return as desired.

File processing problems. Before issuing any GET or PUT instructions, remember to open your files for either input or output processing. Also remember to close your files before returning control to the operating system. Failure to perform these activities at the appropriate times usually results in abends.

Incorrect output. This is the most common method of determ ining a logical error in your program. Although the program doesn't abend, it does not produce the desired results. The only way to determine what is wrong is to play computer and attempt to process data yourself by mimicking the results that will be produced by your code. This is a time consuming process, but usually results in success. In fact, the act of playing computer is commonly called desk checking. Incidentally, it can also be done on programs before execution. Desk checking in this manner can discover many syntax errors as well as logical errors. Errors discovered before execution are much easier and take less time to fix than those found during execution.

Incorrect addressing. This is a major problem in assembly language programming and less of a concern in higher level languages. Whenever you reference a storage area, an address is used. If you have not properly referenced the field or computed its address, the program attempts to address an unauthorized location. An abend results and you must find the invalid storage reference.

Figure 8.7 Common failures at execution time.

puter listing. The letter S means **system** and xxx is a three-digit number that identifies what you did wrong. Figure 8.8 lists the most common system abend codes and general reasons why the program terminates with each abend.

These are the most common abend codes, which should be a permanent part of your vocabulary so that you can reduce the time analyzing the program abend. The program listings in Figs. 8.9 through 8.11 show you where the abend codes may be found and how to recognize an abend when your program has failed.

Abend Code	Reason for Program Termination
0C1	operation exception (a) Program attempts to execute an instruction for which there is no valid op code. This occurs when the program's logic carries the program into a data area definition where instruction execution is attempted. (b) You did not open your files before issuing a GET or PUT.
0C4	protection exception (a) You are trying to access a storage area outside the bounds of the program. In other words, your address is not correct or you've destroyed the base register.
0C6	specification exception (a) The storage area that you are trying to reference is not aligned on the proper boundary.
0C7	data exception (a) The data that you are trying to process is invalid. (b) You have not allowed sufficient bytes in the first operand for a packed-decimal operation.
0CA	decimal overflow (a) As discussed in Chapter 7, you are processing packed data and the results of your computation are too large to fit into the target field.
0CB	decimal divide exception (a) You've attempted to divide by zero.
322	time-out condition (a) Your program could not do all of its processing in the time allowed. Most likely you have an infinite loop.

Figure 8.8 Common abend codes at execution time.

```
ASSIST COMPLETION DUMP
PSW AT ABEND FFC50007 D00000B4        COMPLETION CODE    SYSTEM = 0C7 DATA
** TRACE OF INSTRUCTIONS JUST BEFORE TERMINATION: PSW BITS SHOWN ARE THOSE BEFORE CORRESPONDING INSTRUCTION DECODED ***
  IM LOCATION     INSTRUCTION :  IM = PSW BITS 32-39(ILC,CC,MASK) BEFORE INSTRUCTION EXECUTED AT PROGRAM LOCATION SHOWN
  10  000094      4130 3001
  90  000098      47F0 C084
  90  000084      5930 C1EC
  90  000088      4720 C0AE
  90  00008C      9560 3000
  80  000090      4780 C09C
  80  00009C      F870 C698 C1F0
  C0  0000A2      FB77 C698 C690
  D0  0000A8      F877 C690 C698
  D0  0000AE      F877 C6F0 C688  <-- LAST INSTRUCTION DONE - PROBABLE CAUSE OF TERMINATION

** TRACE OF LAST 10 BRANCH INSTRUCTIONS EXECUTED: PSW BITS SHOWN ARE THOSE BEFORE CORRESPONDING INSTRUCTION DECODED ***
  IM LOCATION     INSTRUCTION :  IM = PSW BITS 32-39(ILC,CC,MASK) BEFORE INSTRUCTION EXECUTED AT PROGRAM LOCATION SHOWN
  10  00006A      47F0 C056
  90  00006A      47F0 C056
  A0  00006A      47F0 C056
  A0  00006A      47F0 C056
  90  00006A      47F0 C056
  A0  00005A      4720 C080
  90  000098      47F0 C084
  90  000098      47F0 C084
  90  000098      47F0 C084
  80  000090      4780 C09C
REGS 0-7      F4F4F4F4  000006DE  F4F4F4F4  0000063C  F4F4F4F4  F4F4F4F4  F4F4F4F4  F4F4F4F4
REGS 8-15     F4F4F4F4  F4F4F4F4  000005EC  F4F4F4F4  00000000  000005EC  FFFE7960  00C00000

FLTR 0-6      F4F4F4F4F4F4F4F4    F4F4F4F4F4F4F4F4    F4F4F4F4F4F4F4F4    F4F4F4F4F4F4F4F4
```

If your ASSIST printout contains an ASSIST COMPLETION DUMP, you knew that your ASSIST program has abended during execution.

Figure 8.9 ASSIST traces the last ten branch and executed instructions.

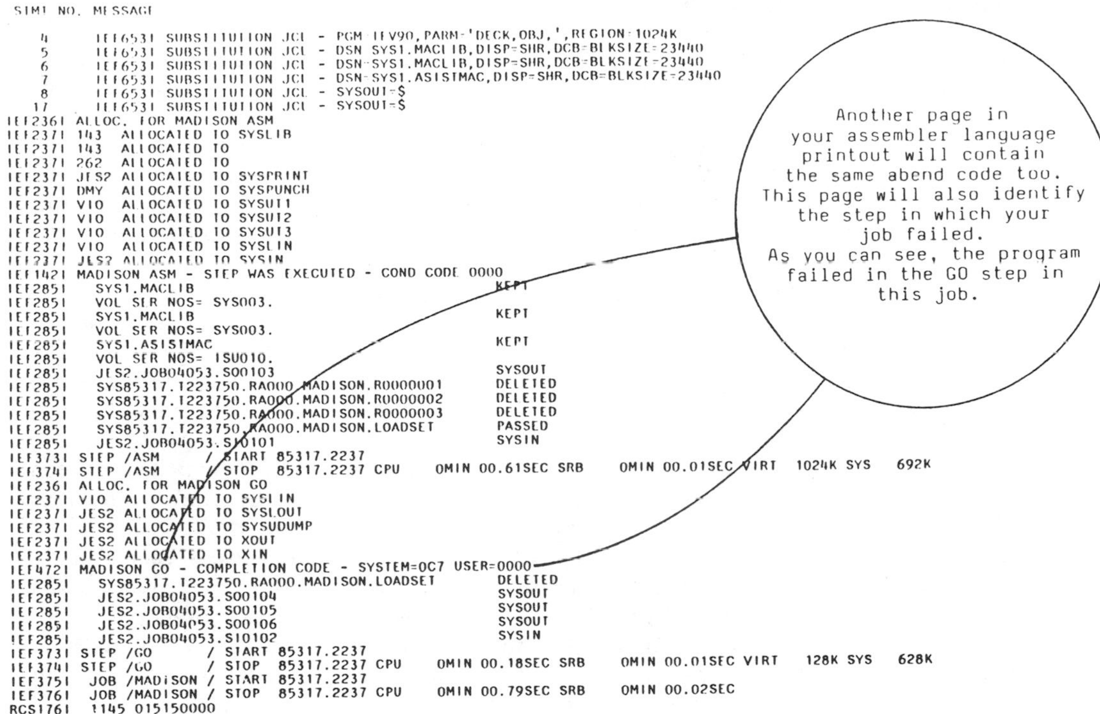

```
STMT NO. MESSAGE

    4     IEF653I SUBSTITUTION JCL - PGM=IEV90,PARM='DECK,OBJ,',REGION=1024K
    5     IEF653I SUBSTITUTION JCL - DSN=SYS1.MACLIB,DISP=SHR,DCB=BLKSIZE=23440
    6     IEF653I SUBSTITUTION JCL - DSN=SYS1.MACLIB,DISP=SHR,DCB=BLKSIZE=23440
    7     IEF653I SUBSTITUTION JCL - DSN=SYS1.ASISTMAC,DISP=SHR,DCB=BLKSIZE=23440
    8     IEF653I SUBSTITUTION JCL - SYSOUT=$
   17     IEF653I SUBSTITUTION JCL - SYSOUT=$
IEF236I ALLOC. FOR MADISON ASM
IEF237I 143  ALLOCATED TO SYSLIB
IEF237I 143  ALLOCATED TO
IEF237I 262  ALLOCATED TO
IEF237I JES2 ALLOCATED TO SYSPRINT
IEF237I DMY  ALLOCATED TO SYSPUNCH
IEF237I VIO  ALLOCATED TO SYSUT1
IEF237I VIO  ALLOCATED TO SYSUT2
IEF237I VIO  ALLOCATED TO SYSUT3
IEF237I VIO  ALLOCATED TO SYSLIN
IEF237I JES2 ALLOCATED TO SYSIN
IEF142I MADISON ASM - STEP WAS EXECUTED - COND CODE 0000
IEF285I   SYS1.MACLIB                                     KEPT
IEF285I   VOL SER NOS= SYS003.
IEF285I   SYS1.MACLIB                                     KEPT
IEF285I   VOL SER NOS= SYS003.
IEF285I   SYS1.ASISTMAC                                   KEPT
IEF285I   VOL SER NOS= ISU010.
IEF285I   JES2.JOB04053.S00103                            SYSOUT
IEF285I   SYS85317.T223750.RA000.MADISON.R0000001         DELETED
IEF285I   SYS85317.T223750.RA000.MADISON.R0000002         DELETED
IEF285I   SYS85317.T223750.RA000.MADISON.R0000003         DELETED
IEF285I   SYS85317.T223750.RA000.MADISON.LOADSET          PASSED
IEF285I   JES2.JOB04053.S10101                            SYSIN
IEF373I STEP /ASM      / START 85317.2237
IEF374I STEP /ASM      / STOP  85317.2237 CPU    0MIN 00.61SEC SRB    0MIN 00.01SEC VIRT  1024K SYS   692K
IEF236I ALLOC. FOR MADISON GO
IEF237I VIO  ALLOCATED TO SYSLIN
IEF237I JES2 ALLOCATED TO SYSLOUT
IEF237I JES2 ALLOCATED TO SYSUDUMP
IEF237I JES2 ALLOCATED TO XOUT
IEF237I JES2 ALLOCATED TO XIN
IEF472I MADISON GO - COMPLETION CODE - SYSTEM=0C7 USER=0000
IEF285I   SYS85317.T223750.RA000.MADISON.LOADSET          DELETED
IEF285I   JES2.JOB04053.S00104                            SYSOUT
IEF285I   JES2.JOB04053.S00105                            SYSOUT
IEF285I   JES2.JOB04053.S00106                            SYSOUT
IEF285I   JES2.JOB04053.S10102                            SYSIN
IEF373I STEP /GO       / START 85317.2237
IEF374I STEP /GO       / STOP  85317.2237 CPU    0MIN 00.18SEC SRB    0MIN 00.01SEC VIRT   128K SYS   628K
IEF375I  JOB /MADISON / START 85317.2237
IEF376I  JOB /MADISON / STOP  85317.2237 CPU    0MIN 00.79SEC SRB    0MIN 00.02SEC
RCS176I  1145 015150000
```


Figure 8.10 Abends are indicated on the allocation and messages page.

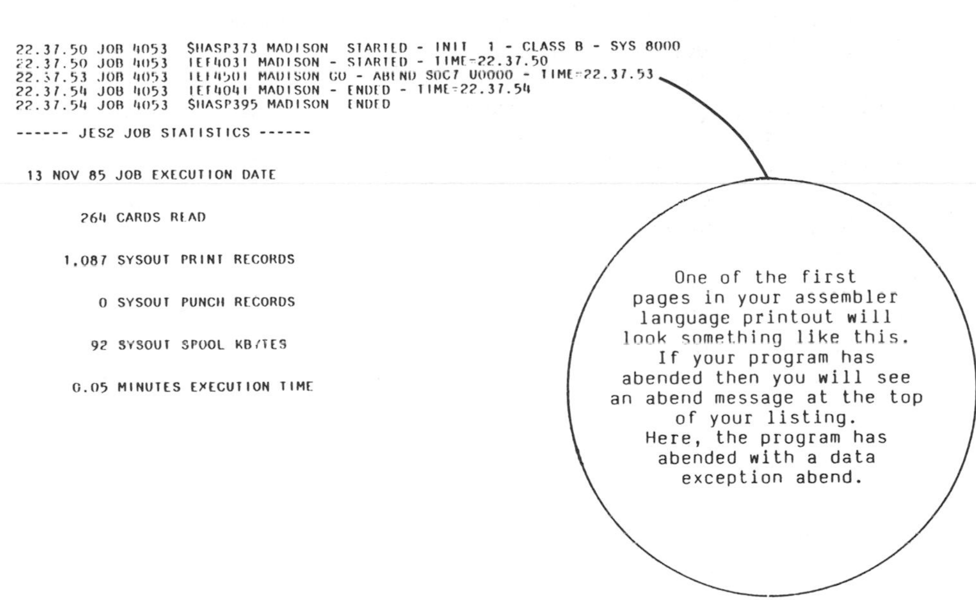

```
                    J E S 2   J O B   L O G   --   S Y S T E M   8 0 0 0   --   N O D E   A S 8 0 0 0

22.37.50 JOB 4053  $HASP373 MADISON  STARTED - INIT  1 - CLASS B - SYS 8000
22.37.50 JOB 4053  IEF403I MADISON - STARTED - TIME=22.37.50
22.37.53 JOB 4053  IEF450I MADISON GO - ABEND S0C7 U0000 - TIME=22.37.53
22.37.54 JOB 4053  IEF404I MADISON - ENDED - TIME=22.37.54
22.37.54 JOB 4053  $HASP395 MADISON  ENDED

------ JES2 JOB STATISTICS ------

 13 NOV 85 JOB EXECUTION DATE

       264 CARDS READ

     1,087 SYSOUT PRINT RECORDS

         0 SYSOUT PUNCH RECORDS

        92 SYSOUT SPOOL KBYTES

      0.05 MINUTES EXECUTION TIME
```


Figure 8.11 The job log page also indicates if an abend has occurred.

DEFENSIVE PROGRAMMING: DEBUGGING TOOLS

The first step in program debugging is to understand what the problem might be. If you have no idea as to why your program abended, you'll soon discover that you won't be able to debug your program without difficulty. The first step in this process is understanding the abend code and recognizing why a program has failed. Since we've already discussed the various abend codes, let's assume that you've already done this step.

Although it's true that debugging assembly language programs generally requires you to read a **dump,** let's first learn how to build debugging aids into our program so that we can debug most of our programs without referring to a dump.

The primary debugging tools in ASSIST and assembly language are the I/O instructions. Throughout your program, you can print out various messages and values of storage elements to monitor the execution and changing of data within the program. The more you print, the better understanding you'll have about program execution. Of course, these instructions clutter your code and your output, but the advantages far outweigh this disadvantage.

ASSIST has two instructions that can be used. The first, XPRNT, which we've seen before, prints various messages or lines as we process through the program. In previous chapters, we used XPRNT to only print our reports. In fact, we adopted a standard printed line length of 86 or 133 bytes long, which included the carriage control character in column 1. We *cannot* ignore that XPRNT requires a carriage control, but we can ignore the line standards when using this instruction for debugging purposes. For example, if we are processing input cards and we suspect that one input card has an incorrect value, we can print an image of the card to the printer each time through the processing loop. This technique of **echoing** is one of the basic techniques for checking input data validity. Figure 8.12 illustrates this coding technique.

Note that we had to allow for a carriage control character before the card image data to be printed. If we do not allow for this carriage control position, XPRNT uses the first character of our input as a carriage control. Hence, the first character is **truncated** and would not print. Clearly, if some data is not printed, this may impact the success or failure of our debugging.

The next example in Fig. 8.13 performs the same processing, but the XPRNT instruction is coded differently. Let's look at this example and discuss its use.

The XPRNT instruction again prints 81 characters. The first character is used as a carriage control and the next 80 are printed. This XPRNT instruction is slightly different, however, since it refers to an unnamed field that appears before INPUT. Fortunately, we remembered to define a one-byte field just before the field labeled INPUT. Either technique works, provided of course, that you remember to define the carriage control field. Clearly, a specific reference to the field CARDIMG more likely causes you to remember to define the extra one-byte field rather than the implicit reference to the field as shown in the second example.

XPRNT can also be used to print literal values as shown in Fig. 8.14.

```
MAINLOOP    DS       0H
            XREAD    INPUT,80
            BC       B'0100',EOF
            XPRNT    CARDIMG,81
            .        .
            .        .
            .        .
            B        MAINLOOP


CARDIMG     DC       C' '
INPUT       DS       0CL80
```

Figure 8.12 Echoing input data images to the printer can help program debugging.

```
MAINLOOP    DS       0H
            XREAD    INPUT,80
            BC       B'0100',EOF
            XPRNT    INPUT-1,81
            .        .
            .        .
            .        .
            B        MAINLOOP


            DC       C' '
INPUT       DS       0CL80
```

Figure 8.13 Modification to the code presented in Figure 8.12.

```
XPRNT  =CL50' I AM READING AN INPUT RECORD',50
```

Figure 8.14 Printing literal values using XPRNT to aid in debugging.

Here, XPRNT prints the 50-byte literal shown. As you can see, the first byte of the literal is a blank, thus allowing for a carriage control. By placing statements such as this throughout your program, you can easily follow its execution simply by following the sequence of your printed messages. An infinite loop is very easy to find with this technique since it results in hundreds or thousands of identical messages printed.

XPRNT can be used to print messages, input data, or storage areas *as long as the data is in character format.* As we have discussed, packed-decimal, binary, floating-point, and bit data cannot be printed in a human readable format unless they are first converted into character representation by your program. Therefore, let's suppose that a field SUBTOTAL is not coming out correctly on our report. To monitor the changing values of SUBTOTAL, print out its value at various stages during processing. Assuming that SUBTOTAL is a five-byte packed-decimal field, we can do this as shown in Fig. 8.15.

```
MVC      STPATERN(10),=X'40202020202020202120'
ED       STPATERN(10),SUBTOTAL
XPRNT    STPATERN,10
```

Figure 8.15 Converting and printing a single field value in ASSIST.

To print the value of SUBTOTAL, we convert it to character format using the ED instruction (or the UNPK/OI instructions). With the first character of the edit pattern (the fill character) as a carriage control, the converted value is printed using the XPRNT instruction. Although this does print the value of SUBTOTAL, it always prints SUBTOTAL as a *positive* number or zero. Appropriate code has to be added to convert SUBTOTAL to a negative value.

In a similar manner, binary elements can be printed through a conversion process as discussed in the past chapters. The binary number is converted to packed decimal and then unpacked or edited as shown in Fig. 8.15. On the other hand, ASSIST has a useful instruction to display the *hexadecimal* representation or internal representation of any field, whether character, packed, binary, bit, or whatever. This instruction, called **XDUMP,** is one of the most powerful debugging facilities available in ASSIST.

The XDUMP instruction prints the value of a storage area in hexadecimal and character format. In other words, XDUMP prints the value of a storage area in a **dump format.** This is our first exposure to an actual dump output and we'll have to learn how to read dump formatted output to understand how to use the XDUMP instruction effectively.

The XDUMP instruction allows dumping any storage area within our program or dumping the contents of the registers. If you code the mnemonic XDUMP with no operands and *no comments,* ASSIST gives you a dump of the registers. If you code XDUMP with a storage area and a length, ASSIST dumps the storage area and gives you its value in hexadecimal and in character formats. Figure 8.16 describes the two general formats of the XDUMP instruction.

```
Dump the register contents (do not comment!).

          XDUMP

Dump the contents of a storage area.

          XDUMP   area,length
```

Figure 8.16 General format of the XDUMP ASSIST instruction.

For example, the storage area SUBTOTAL is defined as a five-byte packed-decimal field. Using the XPRNT and conversion instructions shown earlier, we note that we did not print positive and negative values of SUBTOTAL. XDUMP prints the field in hexadecimal, thus allowing *us* to determine if SUBTOTAL is positive or negative. The instruction is shown in Fig. 8.17.

```
          XDUMP   SUBTOTAL,5
```

Figure 8.17 Dumping five bytes from the area SUBTOTAL using XDUMP.

The output from an ASSIST program given in Fig. 8.18 illustrates the format of XDUMP output. In Fig. 8.18, the registers and a field labeled SUBTOTAL are dumped so that we may review their values.

But where is the value for SUBTOTAL? From the first five bytes of the XDUMP output, SUBTOTAL is not a valid packed-decimal field. Although our initial analysis is

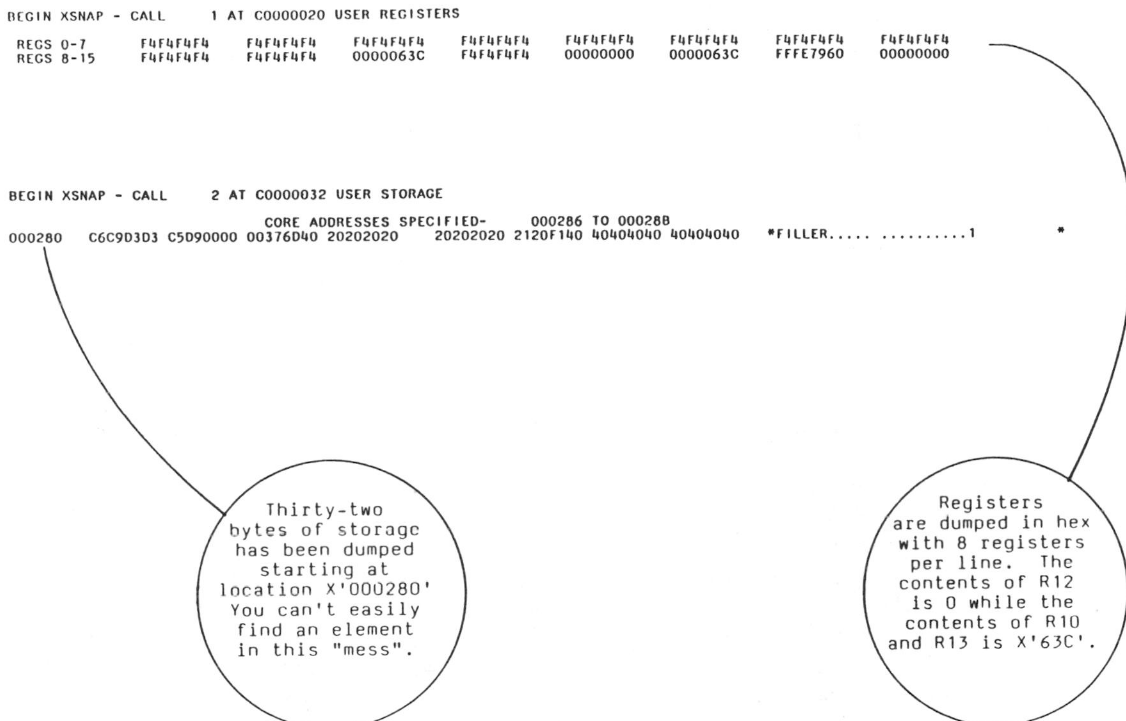

Figure 8.18 Sample output from an XDUMP instruction.

correct, you must first understand that the XDUMP instruction does not dump memory locations as you might think. To understand how XDUMP works, let's discuss the format of the dumped output and return to SUBTOTAL later.

As you can see in Fig. 8.19, the basic format of dumped output consists of three major components. The **address displacement** or **address offset** field is the first field in the dump and whose address is a multiple of 32. In other words, the XDUMP instruction does not dump out just the area that you requested. Instead, it starts at a memory location evenly divisible by 32 and dumps past your storage area to the next highest memory location evenly divisible by 32. If your storage area is not on an address evenly divisible by 32, then you must look for your data area within the storage that was dumped. This is not convenient and can be very misleading. It is very important to remember this since it can lead to problems if you look at the wrong area in the output dump.

Address Displacement	Hexadecimal Translation	Character Translation
XXXXXX	XX XX XX XX XX XX XX XX	XXXXXXXXXXXXXXXX

Figure 8.19 Format of dumped output.

All addresses are given as six digit addresses. If the first area dumped is X'000280', then the next line will begin at address X'0002A0' and so on since each line represents 32 bytes of data.

The rightmost section in the dump is a character representation of the bytes that were dumped. Packed-decimal, binary, bit, and most nonprintable bytes are represented within this area by a period. Any legitimate characters are printed in their normal manner. In other words, byte X'C3' is printed as the letter C and the byte X'3C' is printed as a period (since there isn't a human representable character in the EBCDIC character set for the byte code 3C).

Between the address/displacement section and the character representation section is the hexadecimal representation of the data area that you dumped. Each byte in memory is represented by two characters within this portion of the printout. Further, this section is divided into groups of eight characters to represent four bytes of memory for each group. From my representation, there are eight sets of four-byte fields. Hence, 32 bytes of data are displayed on each line of the dump printout. Within this area, a total of 64 characters are printed to represent the 32 bytes of storage that were dumped.

As you read across each line of this dump, remember that each byte displayed is at a different memory location in the computer. If the first byte on the line is at location X'000280', then the first byte of the second group of storage is at location X'000284'. Group 3 is at location X'000288' and group 4 is at location X'00028C'. The middle of the page has groups found at locations X'000290', X'000294', X'000298', and X'00029C'.

We can now find the value of SUBTOTAL by referring to our original XDUMP output. As you can see in Fig. 8.20, the message **"CORE ADDRESSES SPECIFIED-,"** just before the dumped output, tells us that SUBTOTAL is to begin at location X'000286' and continues until location X'00028B'. Using this information, we can now find the value of SUBTOTAL as shown in Fig. 8.21.

```
BEGIN XSNAP - CALL      1 AT C0000020 USER REGISTERS

 REGS 0-7     F4F4F4F4   F4F4F4F4   F4F4F4F4   F4F4F4F4   F4F4F4F4   F4F4F4F4   F4F4F4F4   F4F4F4F4
 REGS 8-15    F4F4F4F4   F4F4F4F4   0000063C   F4F4F4F4   00000000   0000063C   FFFE7960   00000000
```

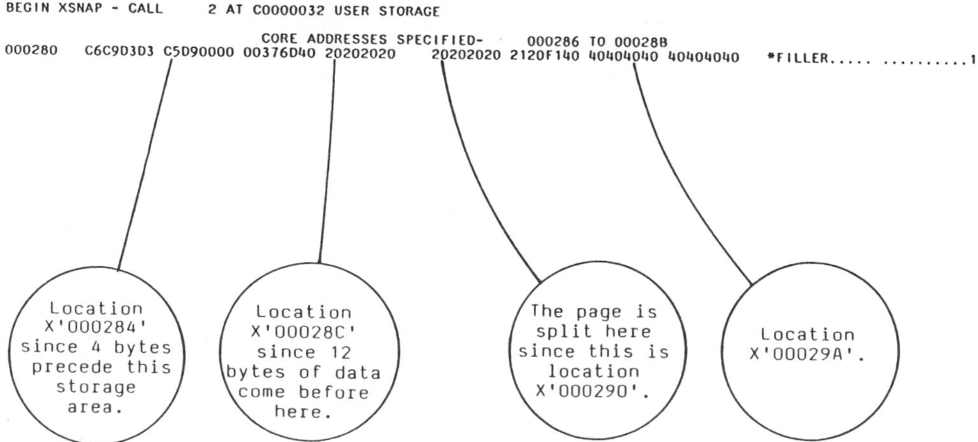

```
BEGIN XSNAP - CALL      2 AT C0000032 USER STORAGE

                               CORE ADDRESSES SPECIFIED-     000286 TO 00028B
000280    C6C9D3D3 C5D90000 00376D40 20202020     20202020 2120F140 40404040 40404040    *FILLER..... ..........1          *
```


Figure 8.20 The dumped output is grouped into four-byte segments with 32 bytes printed on each line.

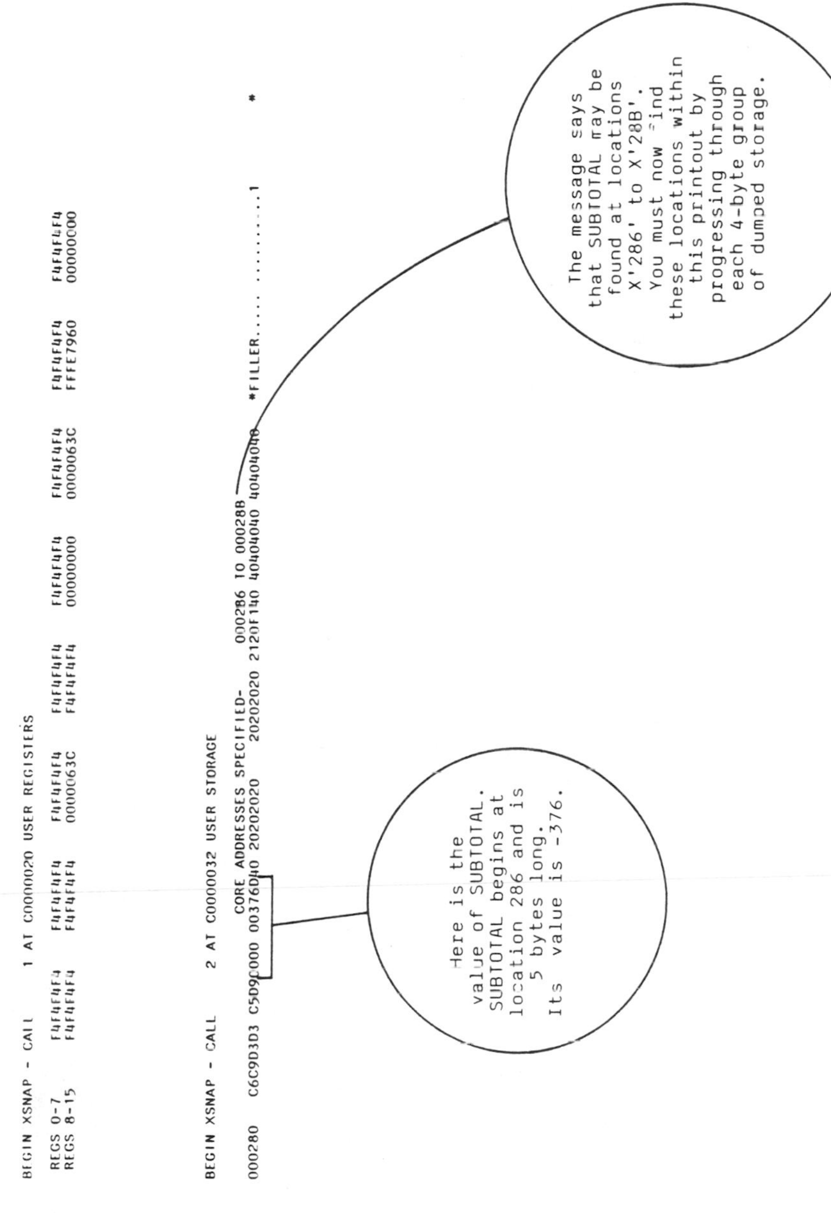

Figure 8.21 Locating elements in an ASSIST XDUMP can be difficult.

Finding elements in dumped output can be rather difficult. Again, the more experience that you have finding values, the easier it becomes. As long as you remember that each group of four bytes increases the address/displacement value by four, you should have no trouble finding your desired storage areas.

The XPRNT and XDUMP instructions are the primary tools for program debugging in ASSIST. By placing these instructions throughout your program, you provide messages and intermediate values during its execution. It's very important not to skimp on this aspect of program debugging or development. The more time spent on defensive techniques, the less time spent in front of a terminal or looking at a printout trying to figure out what happened.

Debugging programs in assembly language is slightly more difficult since the instructions to perform I/O and to dump storage areas are more complex. Also, the number of lines of output generated using this technique can run into the hundreds or thousands, especially if the program goes into an infinite loop. Therefore, before we discuss how to print messages and obtain dumped output in assembler, let's first discuss limiting this output.

For every output file in our program, we can use another defensive debugging feature that the operating system allows. This technique limits the number of lines printed for *each* file if we choose to do so. The operand is called **OUTLIM** and it is coded on our JCL statements. If you recall, we discussed this JCL parameter in Chapter 4. Since it is an important feature, let's review it.

```
//GO.FILE1   DD   SYSOUT=$,OUTLIM=1000
//GO.SNAP    DD   SYSOUT=$,OUTLIM=5000
```

Figure 8.22 Restricting printed output with OUTLIM.

In the JCL statements coded in Fig. 8.22, we are limiting the output lines for FILE1 to no more than 1000 lines and for SNAP to no more than 5000 lines. We must be able to predict or anticipate the amount of output our program will produce. If we underestimate the number of lines, the program abnormally terminates even though it is working correctly. Overestimating is almost as bad since a loop can cause many output lines to be printed. Therefore, we must have a good understanding of how much data will be processed so that the OUTLIM parameter can abnormally terminate the program *if we try to exceed that limit.* When the program attempts to write record 1001 to file FILE1 *or* record 5001 to file SNAP, the operating system terminates the program with an abend code of S722. Although we could write our program without the OUTLIM parameter, this is not recommended during initial testing and development in assembly language.

ASSIST has similar page and line limit features that are usually set by your systems programming staff when ASSIST was installed. Hence, we aren't concerned about coding the OUTLIM parameter under ASSIST. In assembly language, however, we should code the OUTLIM parameter on every output file for our program during testing.

A second method to control our program is to limit the time that it can execute in the computer. Typically, programs require only a few seconds to assemble and process the data that we've defined. Therefore, a time limit of 15 to 30 seconds for assembly language programs is excessive. We can reduce this time to a few seconds by coding the **TIME** parameter on our job card. For example to limit the time for a job to three seconds, we use the TIME parameter on our job card as shown in Fig. 8.23.

```
//jobname  JOB  . . . ,TIME=(0,3), . . . .
```

Figure 8.23 Limiting the job execution time.

This parameter also works when developing programs in ASSIST. Hence, infinite program loops do not waste computer time needlessly. Rather, infinite loops are terminated in three seconds by abending our program with an S322 abend code (time out).

These are two of the basic tools to control runaway loops in your program. As we've discussed, the XDUMP and XPRNT instructions are used in ASSIST to provide debugging assistance. Let's now look at similar instructions in standard assembly language to provide additional debugging assistance during program testing.

First, data areas are only printed if you use the PUT instruction. You must code a DCB to direct the data to be printed to the printer. Also, the PUT instruction (as we've discussed so far) only prints *fixed-length* storage areas. For example, you must print 100-byte or 50-byte messages and you cannot mix varying line lengths within one output file. This is definitely a disadvantage as compared to ASSIST since the XPRNT instruction prints any amount of data.

For example, if you want to print a field called STPATERN that is 10 bytes long with the PUT instruction, you must also print 90 bytes of data before or after this field to account for a full-line length of 100. Although we'll find a method to handle varying line lengths in a later chapter, let's limit ourselves to printing lines of the same length.

The line length limitation can be worked around by using the MVC instruction. The example in Fig. 8.24 edits the field SUBTOTAL and prints its value as desired.

```
         MVC    STPATERN(10),=X'40202020202020202120'
         ED     STPATERN(10),SUBTOTAL
         MVC    DBUGLINE(100),=CL100' '
         MVC    DBUGLINE(10),STPATERN
         PUT    DBUGDCB,DBUGLINE
```

Figure 8.24 Printing an element's value in assembly language.

DBUGLINE is a 100-character area. STPATERN and SUBTOTAL are defined as we've been discussing throughout the chapter. As you can see, the field is converted from packed-decimal format. DBUGLINE is cleared and the edited field is moved into the debugging output line for printing. The PUT instruction sends the line to the printer. This technique also works for messages simply by moving a message into DBUGLINE and printing this area.

We did not have to allow for a carriage control in this example since the programmer controls the carriage control use through the DCB. The **RECFM** parameter in the DCB may be coded so that a carriage control is not used. If you recall, a RECFM value containing the character A requires use of ANSI carriage control characters whereas a RECFM value without the letter A allows us to build and send lines to the printer without a carriage control. The full DCB for DBUGDCB is shown in Fig. 8.25.

```
DBUGDCB  DCB  DSORG=PS,DDNAME=DBUG,MACRF=PM,RECFM=F,        X
              LRECL=100,BLKSIZE=100
```

Figure 8.25 A DCB instruction that may be used to support debugging.

If we know that the maximum message or output values to be sent to the printer is 50 bytes, then we can change the LRECL and BLKSIZE parameters to 50 instead of 100.

As with ASSIST, packed-decimal, binary, bit, and floating-point numbers cannot be sent to the printer in human readable format. They must be converted into character representation before they may be written.

The ASSIST XDUMP instruction has a counterpart in assembly language called **SNAP.** This *macro* dumps the contents of the registers, dumps the current PSW, and dumps storage areas in your program. Although it is coded much differently than XDUMP, it nonetheless performs the same functions.

SNAP requires a DCB that must be opened and closed. Further, a JCL statement must be coded to direct the output from SNAP to the printer. The general structure for a program using the SNAP instruction appears as coded in Fig. 8.26.

```
               .          .
               .          .
               .          .
               OPEN       (SNAPDCB,OUTPUT)
               .          .
               .          .
               SNAP       DCB=SNAPDCB,other operands
               .          .
               .          .
               CLOSE      (SNAPDCB)
               .          .
               .          .
      SNAPDCB  DCB        DSORG=PS,RECFM=VBA,MACRF=(W),          X
                          LRECL=125,BLKSIZE=882,DDNAME=SNAP
               .          .
               .          .


      //GO.SNAP    DD   SYSOUT=$,OUTLIM=nnnn
```

Figure 8.26 Format of an assembly language program using SNAP.

Operand	Meaning
ID=	Allows assignment of an ID number to each set of SNAP output. This easily identifies where in your program the SNAP instruction was issued.
PDATA=PSW PDATA=REGS PDATA=ALL	Allows dumping the program status word, the registers, or all storage associated with the job. Do not use the ALL operand since a large amount of unnecessary information is dumped.
STORAGE=(a,b)	Dumps all storage between the areas a and b. As with ASSIST, the storage areas have to be found in the dump since SNAP dumps storage on fullword boundaries.

Figure 8.27 Common operands on the SNAP instruction.

```
SNAP    DCB=SNAPDCB,STORAGE=(SUBTOTAL,SUBTOTAL+5)
```

Figure 8.28 Snapping the first five bytes of SUBTOTAL.

The SNAP instruction requires the operand DCB to identify the associated DCB for which I/O is to be performed. Other operands on the SNAP statement are described in Fig. 8.27. For example, to dump the five-byte storage area called SUBTOTAL, the SNAP instruction coded in Fig. 8.28 would be used.

As you can see, the STORAGE operand requires two arguments. The first argument indicates where the dumping is to start and the second identifies where the storage dumping is to end. Although the ID operand is not coded in this example, I strongly suggest that you code it when you use the SNAP instruction. Further, by placing SNAP instructions coded with ID numbers throughout your code, you can use the SNAP instruction both as a dumping facility and as a logical trace facility. Figures 8.29 through 8.31 illustrate output produced by the SNAP instruction and what operands were coded.

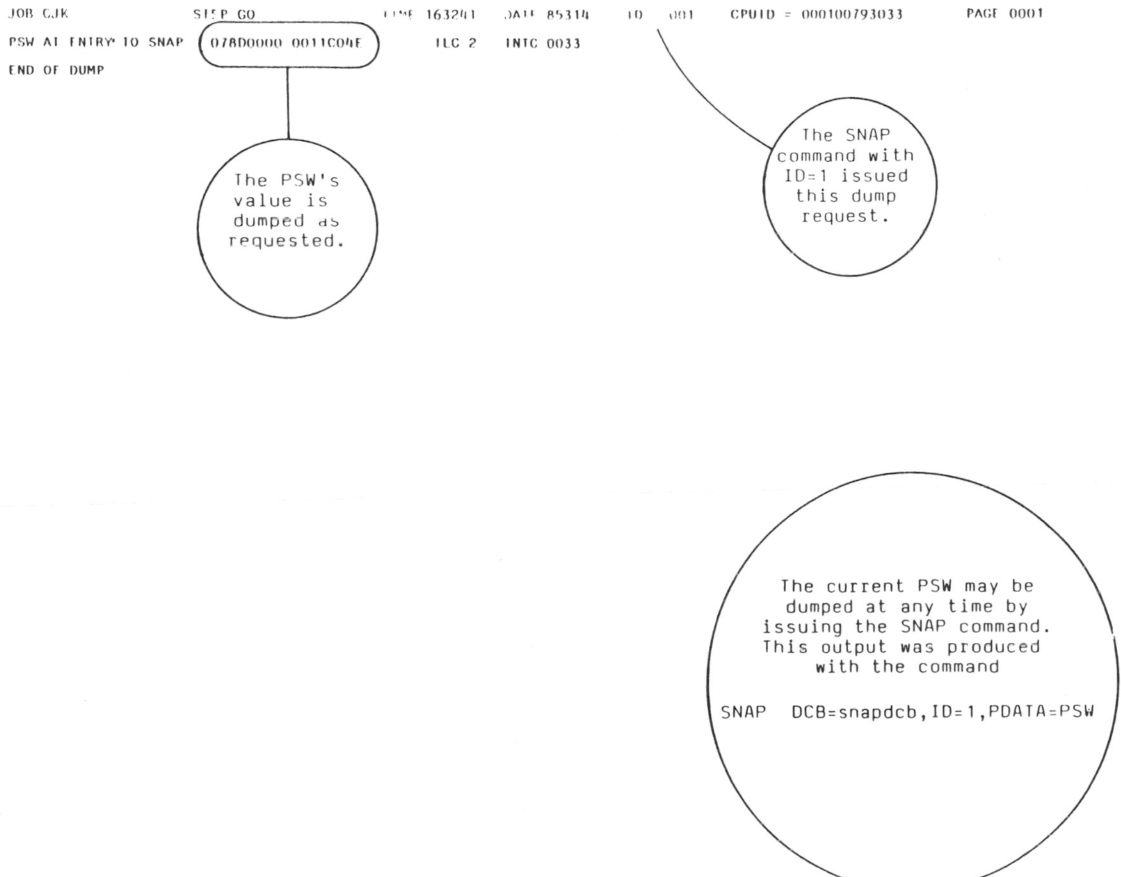

Figure 8.29 The current PSW may be snapped to the debugging file.

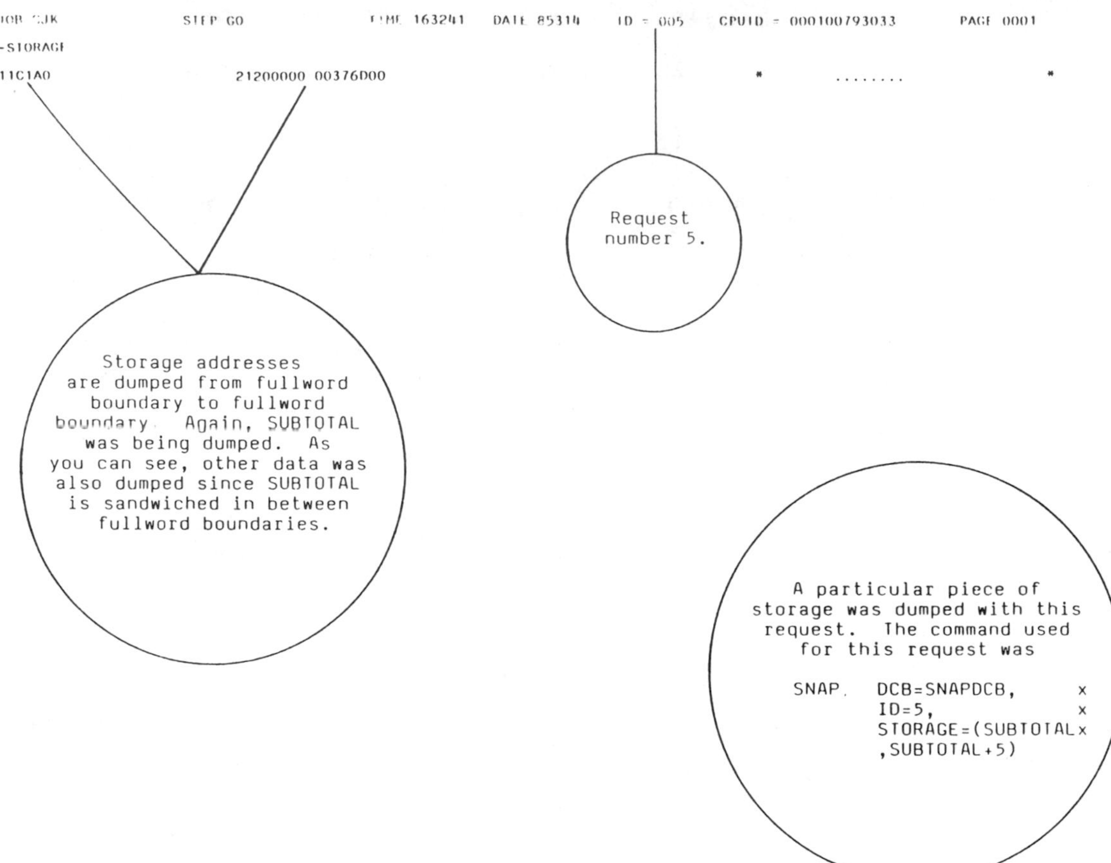

Figure 8.30 Only the storage specified is dumped using the assembly language SNAP instruction.

THE DEBUGGING PROCESS USING DUMPS

When *any* program abnormally terminates, whether it is written in assembly language, COBOL, PL/I or FORTRAN, the system can provide an abend dump to help in debugging. ASSIST provides such a dump automatically, but it must be requested in other languages by the proper coding of a JCL statement as shown in Fig. 8.32.

The **SYSUDUMP** ddname is the key element in the debugging process. Without this ddname, dumps are not produced when assembly language programs abnormally terminate. Clearly, this JCL statement is placed in the same vicinity as the other GO. statements discussed earlier. Although the order to the GO. statements usually doesn't matter, you may want to order them in the order in which you want your output, SNAP dump, or abend dump output to be printed. Finally, do *not* code the OUTLIM parameter on this DD statement. If you limit the amount of dumped output, you may truncate some important areas that you'll need to debug your program.

Dump reading, a skill that comes with practice, can be condensed into a few steps for most dump situations. Although the more complex dumps may require substantial

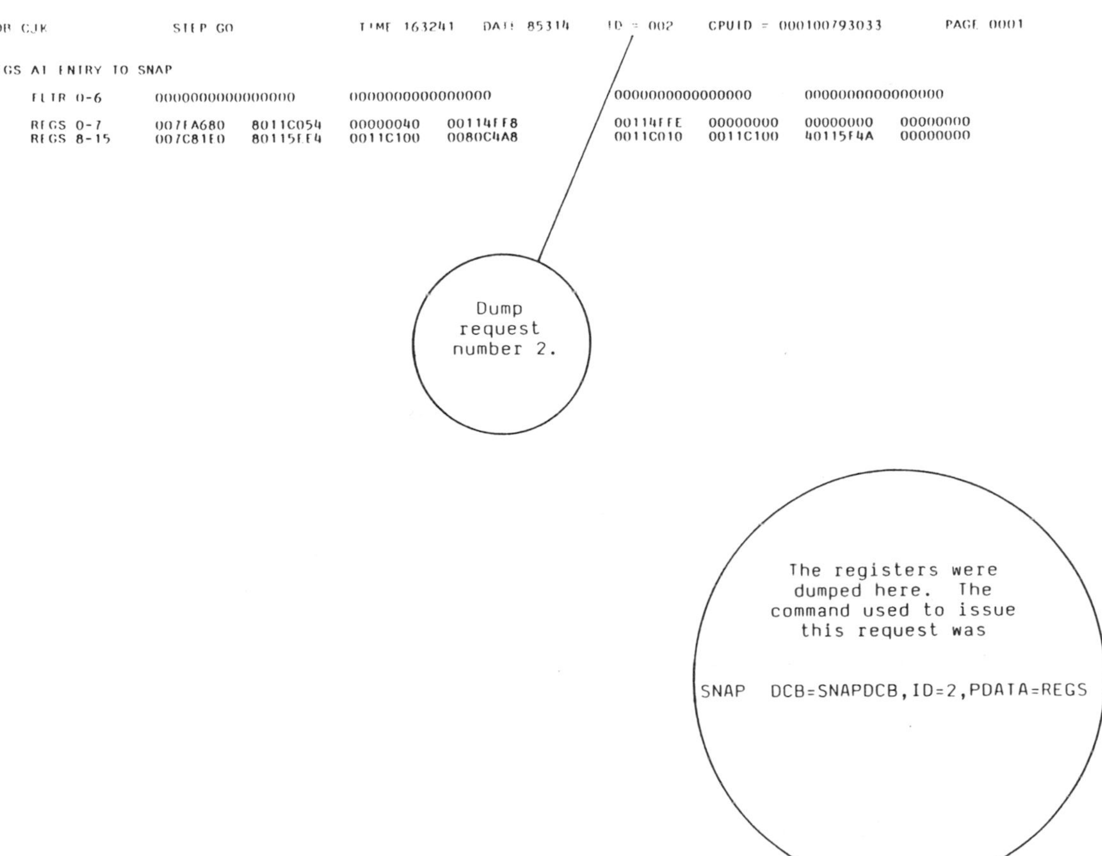

Figure 8.31 Dump ID's help identify dump output.

```
//GO.SYSUDUMP   DD   SYSOUT=$
```

Figure 8.32 A JCL statement to request storage dumps.

more analysis, the technique that follows is simple and will get you through most program abends.

The first thing to do when looking at a dump is to review the reason behind the failure. Clearly, this involves looking at the abend code and trying to get an overview of why the program failed.

Next, locate the **program status word (PSW)** in the dump. It contains the address of the *next instruction to be executed.* The PSW does *not* contain the address of the current instruction or the instruction that may have caused the problem. It's very important to remember this.

Find the **instruction length code** (also located in the PSW or printed separately within the dump) so that you can determine the length of the last instruction. The *last* instruction executed is the one that caused the abend. Therefore, the combination of the next instruction address and the instruction length code points us to the instruction that caused the failure. In other words, the address of the failing instruction is found by subtracting the instruction length code value from the next instruction address value as shown in Fig. 8.33.

```
  address of the next instruction to be executed
- instruction length code value
------------------------------------------------
  address of the instruction that failed
```

Figure 8.33 Locating the point of program failure.

Let's look at a PSW and determine which components are valuable during debugging. A PSW is an eight-byte area, which when printed in a program dump, appears as two pieces, each four bytes long as shown in Fig. 8.34.

FFC50007   D011C038

Figure 8.34 Sample PSW value at abnormal program termination.

Let's split the PSW to identify the valuable parts as shown in Fig. 8.35. All boldface pieces are important to debugging. Working from left to right, let's start with the value X'0007'.

FFC5 **0007**   **D0 11C038**

Figure 8.35 Isolating the important parts of the PSW.

The right half of the left four bytes of the PSW contains the field called the **interrupt code.** This value is X'0007', which means that our program abended with an 0C7 abend code (data exception). If our program had abended with a protection exception, this value would be X'0004'. The value in this portion of the PSW may be cross-referenced with your reference summary card by looking under the section entitled *Program Interruption Codes.*

The next byte in the PSW is found in the right half. This byte has many fields, but, in particular, the first two *bits* of this byte give the value of the instruction length code. The byte value X'D0' can be converted into the bit representation **11**010000, which means that the instruction length code for this example is **11.** This value indicates that the instruction that we were executing was three halfwords long, that is, six bytes. Instruction length code values of 01 and 10 indicate one halfword (two bytes) and two halfwords (four bytes), respectively. If you recall, most SS instructions are six bytes long; therefore, we can initially assume that our program failed on a packed-decimal or MVC instruction.

The rightmost three bytes of the right half of the PSW give the **next instruction address** value. In this example, the address is at location X'11C038'. Now that we have both the next instruction address and the length of the failing instruction, we can compute the address of the point of abend as follows:

```
  11C038 next instruction address
-      6 instruction length code value
--------------------------------------
  11C032 address of the failing instruction
```

If we look into the dump at this location, we can find the instruction that caused our program to abend. However, before we do this, there's one more computation to do. Our source program is most likely less than 4096 bytes long, which makes the largest address in our program less than X'001000'. As you can see, the address of the failing instruction is *much* larger than this. Clearly, something must be wrong.

We have computed the failing address location properly. However, to relate this address to our source program, we must perform another computation. We must subtract the **entry point address** of our program from the address that we just derived to find the offset of the instruction within our source code listing. In ASSIST, the entry point address is usually X'000000', but in assembler, it must be located in the dump.

```
   address of the failing instruction
 —entry point address of our program
 ------------------------------------
   offset into our source program of the
      failing instruction
```

In Fig. 8.37 we'll see how to determine the entry point address for our program. For now, let's assume that it is X'11C010'.

With respect to the example above,

```
  11C032
 -11C010
 -------
      22
```

If we look at the source code listing at offset 22, we'll find the instruction that failed.

ASSIST also has several other features for debugging that assembly language does not. ASSIST maintains a list of the last 10 branch instructions executed by your program and it maintains a trace of the last 10 instructions executed. Traces are very helpful in debugging since they help determine how you got into the predicament. Again, tracing is not automatically provided in assembler unless you use the SNAP instruction to dump the PSW at various intervals during the execution of your program.

Let's now look at the ASSIST dump of Fig. 8.36 and identify the various components within the dump.

Now let's turn our attention to an assembler dump as shown in Fig. 8.37 and locate each of the components that are needed in the debugging process. Actually, the dump in Fig. 8.37 is not an "assembler" dump at all, rather, it is a dump produced by the operating system. Since this dump was produced by an assembly language program, we'll just refer to it from now on as an "assembler" dump. In fact, the dump shown in Fig. 8.37 would be obtained if a COBOL, PL/I, FORTRAN, or assembly language program failed on an IBM system.

The operating system dump is much longer than the ASSIST dump. On the other hand, most of the information in the dump is not needed for typical program abends. Therefore, you'll skip over most of the material and learn to look quickly for what you need. In fact, the worksheet of Fig. 8.38 may prove helpful in debugging assembly language or ASSIST programs.

```
ASSIST COMPLETION DUMP
PSW AT ABEND FFC50004 900000CE        COMPLETION CODE    SYSTEM = 0C4 PROTECTION
** TRACE OF INSTRUCTIONS JUST BEFORE TERMINATION: PSW BITS SHOWN ARE THOSE BEFORE CORRESPONDING INSTRUCTION DECODED ***
  IM LOCATION     INSTRUCTION :   IM = PSW BITS 32-39(ILC,CC,MASK) BEFORE INSTRUCTION EXECUTED AT PROGRAM LOCATION SHOWN
  20  000098      47F0 C084
  A0  000084      5930 C1CC
  A0  000088      4720 C0AE
  A0  0000AE      1B11
  40  0000B0      F877 C6D0 C668
  D0  0000B6      FA73 C6D0 C674
  D0  0000BC      D20F C680 C216
  D0  0000C2      DF0F C680 C6D0
  D0  0000C8      0610
  50  0000CA      9260 1000       <-- LAST INSTRUCTION DONE - PROBABLE CAUSE OF TERMINATION

** TRACE OF LAST 10 BRANCH INSTRUCTIONS EXECUTED: PSW BITS SHOWN ARE THOSE BEFORE CORRESPONDING INSTRUCTION DECODED ***
  IM LOCATION     INSTRUCTION :   IM = PSW BITS 32-39(ILC,CC,MASK) BEFORE INSTRUCTION EXECUTED AT PROGRAM LOCATION SHOWN
  10  00006A      47F0 C056
  90  00006A      47F0 C056
  90  00006A      47F0 C056
  80  000062      4780 C06E
  90  000098      47F0 C084
  90  000098      47F0 C084
  90  000098      47F0 C084
  90  000098      47F0 C084
  A0  000098      47F0 C084
  A0  000088      4720 C0AE
REGS 0-7     F4F4F4F4   FFFFFFFF   F4F4F4F4   0000061E   F4F4F4F4   F4F4F4F4   F4F4F4F4   F4F4F4F4
REGS 8-15    F4F4F4F4   F4F4F4F4   000005CC   F4F4F4F4   00000000   000005CC   FFFE7960   00000000
FLTR 0-6     F4F4F4F4F4F4F4F4      F4F4F4F4F4F4F4F4      F4F4F4F4F4F4F4F4      F4F4F4F4F4F4 4F4
```

PSW and abend code message indicating the abend.

This is a trace of the last 10 instructions that were executed. Look this over carefully to help find errors.

Here is instruction where the program failed.

The last 10 branch instructions are traced. This is a good area to look for infinite loops.

The REGS are dumped for your reference.

Figure 8.36 A complete ASSIST program dump.

```
USER STORAGE

                              CORE ADDRESSES SPECIFIED-    000000 TO 000840
000000   90ECD00C 18CF41A0 C5CC50AD 000850DA   000418DA E020C2AB 0085E020 C3300085   *........E...............B.... C...*
000020   E020C3B5 0085E020 C43A0085 E020C4BF   0085E000 C6140050 4740C1B0 9240C544   *..C.....D.....D.....F.... A.. F.*
000040   D283C545 C544F274 C668C614 F274C670   C6194130 C6145930 C1C84720 C0809560   *K.F.E.2.F.F.2.F.F...F...AH......*
000060   30004780 C06E4130 300147F0 C056F870   C678C1D0 FB77C678 C668F877 C668C678   *...........0..8.F.A...F.F.8.F.F.*
000080   4130C619 5930C1CC 4720C0AE 95603000   4780C09C 41303001 47F0C084 F870C678   *..F...A....................0..8.F.*
0000A0   C1D0FB77 C678C670 F877C670 C6781B11   F877C6D0 C668FA73 C6D0C674 D20FC680   *A...F.F.8.F.F...8.F.F...F.F.K.F.*
0000C0   C216DF0F C680C6D0 06109260 1000F877   C6D8C668 FB77C6D8 C670D20F C690C216   *B...F.F........8.FQF...FQF.K.F.B.*
0000E0   DF0FC690 C6D80610 92601000 F877C6E0   C668FC73 C6E0C674 D20FC6A0 C216DF0F   *..F.FQ......8.F.F...F.F.K.F.3...*
000100   C6A0C6E0 06109260 1000F877 C6E8C668   FD73C6E8 C674F373 C6F0C6EC F873C6E8   *F.F.......8.FYF...FYF.8.FOF.8.FY*
000120   C6E8D20F C6C0C216 DF0FC6C0 C6F00610   92601000 D20FC6B0 C216DF0F C6B0C6E8   *FYK.F.B...F.FO......K.F.B...F.FY*
000140   06109260 1000D204 C56DC614 D204C58A   C619D20E C54BC1D1 D20EC597 C681E020   *.......K.E.F.K.E.F.K.E.AJK.E.F...*
000160   C5440085 D20EC54B C1E0D20E C597C691   E020C544 0085D20E C54BC1EF D20EC597   *E...K.E.A.K.E.F...E...K.E.A.K.E.*
000180   C6A1E020 C5440085 D20EC54B C1FED20E   C597C6B1 D208C5AB C20DD206 C5B6C6C9   *F...E...K.E.A.K.E.F.K.E.B.K.E.FI*
0001A0   E020C544 0085E020 C3B50085 47F0C032   E020C226 008558DD 000498EC D00C1BFF   *..E.....C....0....B.............*
0001C0   07FEF5F5 F5F5F5F5 00000618 0000061D   0CC1C4C4 40404C40 40404040 40404040   *..555555.........ADD            *
0001E0   E2E4C2E3 D9C1C3E3 40404040 404040D4   E4D3E3C9 D7D3E840 40404040 4040C4C9   *SUBTRACT        MULTIPLY      DI*
000200   E5C9C4C5 40404040 40404040 40D9C5D4   C1C9D5C4 C5D94020 20202020 20202020   *VIDE          REMAINDER .........*
000220   20202020 2120F140 40404040 40404040   40404040 40404040 40404040 40404040   *......1                         *
000240   40404040 40404040 40404040 40404040   40404040 40404040 40404040 40404040   *                                *
  LINES    000260-000280     SAME AS ABOVE
0002A0   40404040 40404040 404040F1 D9C5D7D6   D9E34040 40404040 40404040 40404040   *             1REPORT            *
0002C0   40404040 40404040 40404040 40404040   40404040 4040C140 D940C940 E340C840   *                      A R I T H *
0002E0   D440C540 E340C940 C3404040 D740D940   D640C340 C540E240 E240C940 D540C740   *M E T I C   P R O C E S S I N G *
000300   4040D940 C540D740 D640D940 E3404040   40404040 40404040 40404040 40404040   *  R E P O R T                   *
000320   40404040 40404040 40404040 40404040   4040D5C1 D4C57A40 40D4C1E3 C8404040   *                    NAME.  MATH  *
000340   40404040 40404040 40404040 40404040   40404040 40404040 40404040 40404040   *                                *
000360   40404040 40404040 C2C1E2C9 C3404040   D4C1E3C8 404040D6 D7C5D9C1 E3C9D6D5   *        BASIC   MATH   OPERATION*
000380   E2404040 40404040 40404040 40404040   40404040 4040404D 40404040 40404040   *S                               *
0003A0   40404040 40404040 40404040 40404040   40404040 40604040 40404040 40404040   *                                *
0003C0   40404040 40404040 40404040 40404040   40404040 40404040 40404040 40404040   *                                *
  LINES    0003E0-000400     SAME AS ABOVE
000420   40404040 40404040 40404040 40404040   40404040 40404040 40404060 60606060   *                           .....*
000440   40D6D7C5 D9C1E3C9 D6D54060 60606060   40404040 40404040 40606060 606040C6   * OPERATION .....          ..... F*
000460   C9D9E2E3 40E5C1D3 E4C54060 60606060   40404040 40406060 60606040 E2C5C3D6   *IRST VALUE .....        ..... SECO*
000480   D5C440E5 C1D3E4C5 40606060 60604040   40404060 60606060 60606060 60606060   *ND VALUE .....      ...............*
0004A0   606040D9 C5E2E4D3 E3406060 60606060   60606060 60606060 60404040 4040404E   *.. RESULT ...............        .*
0004C0   6D6D6D5D 6D6D6D6D 6D6D6D6D 6D6D6D6D   6D6D6D6D 6D404040 40404040 40406D6D   *.....................        ..*
0004E0   6D6D6D6D 6D6D6D6D 6D6D6D6D 6D6D6D6D   6D6D6D6D 6D404040 4040406D 6D6D6D6D   *.....................      .....*
000500   6D6D6D6D 6D6D6D6D 6D6D6D6D 6D6D6D6D   6D6D6D40 40404040 6D6D6D6D 6D6D6D6D   *...................      ........*
000520   6D6D6D6D 6D6D6D6D 6D6D6D6D 6D6D6D6D   6D6D6D6D 6D6D6D6D 6D6D6D6D 6D6D4040   *..............................  *
000540   40404040 40404040 40404040 40404040   40404040 40404040 40404040 40404040   *                                *
  LINES    000560-0005A0     SAME AS ABOVE
0005C0   40404040 40404040 40F5F5F5 F5F5F5F5   000006F8 F5F5F5F5 F5F5F5F5 F5F5F5F5   *          5555555...8555555555555*
0005E0   F5F5F5F5 F5F5F5F5 F5F5F5F5 F5F5F5F5   F5F5F5F5 F5F5F5F5 F5F5F5F5 F5F5F5F5   *55555555555555555555555555555555*
000600   F5F5F5F5 F5F5F5F5 F5F5F5F5 F5F5F5F5   F5F5F5F5 40404060 F6404040 40F44040   *5555555555555555555   .6    4   *
000620   40404040 40404040 40404040 40404040   40404040 40404040 40404040 40404040   *                                *
000640   40404040 40404040 40404040 40404040   40404040 40404040 40404040 F0F1F0F2   *                            0102*
000660   F4F04B40 F5F5F5F5 00000000 0000006D   00000000 0000004F 00000000 0000006D   *40. 5555........................*
000680   40404040 40404040 40404040 404040F2   40404040 40404040 40404040 4060F1F2   *               2             .12*
0006A0   40404040 40404040 40406060 60F1F6F0   40404040 40404040 40404040 404040F2   *            ...160             2*
0006C0   40404040 40404040 40404040 404040F4   00000000 0000002D 00000000 0000012C   *               4................*
0006E0   00000000 0000160C 00000000 0000002C   00000000 0000004C F5F5F5F5 000000C0   *............................5555....*
000700   000005CC FFFE7960 00000000 F4F4F4F4   F4F4F4F4 F4F4F4F4 F4F4F4F4 F4F4F4F4   *............44444444444444444444*
000720   F4F4F4F4 F4F4F4F4 F4F4F4F4 F4F4F4F4   F4F4F4F4 F4F4F4F4 F4F4F4F4 F4F4F4F4   *44444444444444444444444444444444*
000740   F5F5F5F5 F5F5F5F5 F5F5F5F5 F5F5F5F5   F5F5F5F5 F5F5F5F5 F5F5F5F5 F5F5F5F5   *55555555555555555555555555555555*
  LINES    000760-000800     SAME AS ABOVE
```

This is a dump of your complete program and all data areas within your program. You'll have to learn how to read this in order to debug your programs.

Figure 8.36 (continued)

```
JOB MADISON          STEP GO              TIME 062530   DATE 85310    ID = 000    CPUID = 000100793033         PAGE 0001

COMPLETION CODE      SYSTEM = 322

PSW AT ENTRY TO ABEND  078D0000 0011C266          ILC 2    INTC 0014

ASCB 00FD8EA0
        +0     ASCB    C1E2C3C2   FWDP    00000000   BWDP   00FD9528   CMSF   00000000   SVRB   0080D248   SYNC   00001E49
        +18    IOSP    00000000   INEW    007D4470   CPUS   00000001   IDSQ   000D0015   IODP   00000100   RESV   00000000
        +30    LDA     0080F548   RSM     00FD8C60   CSCB   00FD9060   TSB    00000000   EJST   00000001   KJST   1B592009
        +48    EWST    99FE85CE   XWST    9A145000   JSTL   00000001   ECB    8080D7E0   UBET   00000000   ILCH   00000000
        +60    DUMP    0080CD90   FW1     FFFF0100   TMCH   00000000   ASXB   0080F300   FW2    00C20000   SRBS   00000000
        +78    VSC     0002000E   RCTP    0080DA68   LOCK   00000000   LSQH   00000000   QECB   00000000   MECB   40000000
        +90    OUCB    00FD8DB8   OUXB    00FCBB38   FMCT   00270000   XMPQ   00000000   IQEA   00000000   RIMC   00000000
        +A8    MCC     00000000   JBNI    00F80008   JBNS   00FD9070   SRQ    00000000   VGTT   00000000   PCTT   00000000
        +C0    SMCT    00000007   SWTL    0000035A   SRBT   00000000   ATME   0077F000   LSMQ   00000000   LSPL   00000000
        +D8    TCBS    00000001   TCBL    00000000   WPRB   0080EA08   SRDP   00FFFF00   LOCI   00000000   CMLH   00000000
        +F0    CMLC    00000000   SSOM    00000000   ASTE   00FC90D0   LTOV   0080A000   ATOV   0080CC50   ETC    00000000
        +108   LXR     00000000   STKH    0080EA18   GQEL   00000000   LQEL   00201110   GSYN   00000000   XTCB   007D4470
        +120   FW3     00000000   GXL     00000000   EATT   00000000   EAT1   A9411006   INTS   99FE85CA   INT1   EA76C000
        +138   FW4     00000000   RCMS    00000000   IOSC   00000008   PKXC   008001F4   NSQA   00000000   ASM    00FD8C90
        +150   RESV    00000000   TCME    00000000

*** ADDRESS SPACE SWITCH EVENT MASK OFF (ASTESSEM = 0) ***

TCB  7D4470
        +0     RBP     0080D158   PIE     00000000   DEB  007D8608   TIO 007DB000   CMP    88322000   TRN  C0000000
        +18    MSS     007FAE00   PK-FLG  80850000   FLG  0000FFFF   LLS 007FA530   JLB    00000000   JPQ  C07C3D98
        +70    FSA     00114FB0   TCB     00000000   TME  00000000   JST 007D4470   NTC    00000000   OTC  007FAEA8
        +88    LTC     00000000   IQE     00000000   ECB  007C3FB4   TSF 20000000   D-PQE  0080F548   AQE  007C3038
        +A0    STAB    0080C7D0   TCT     807FA288   USER 00000000   SDF 00000000   MDID   00000000   JSCB 0080C25C
        +B8    RESV    00022D78   IOBRC   00000000   XCPD 00000000   EXT 00000000   BITS   00000000   DAR  00000000
        +D0    EXT2    007D45A8   AECB    00000000   XSB  0080D228   BCK 007FAEA8   RTMWA  007FA5A8   NSSP 00000000
        +E8    TMSAV   00000000   ABCR    00000000   XSCT 80000040   FOE 00000000   SWA    007FADC0   STAW 00000000
        +100   BID     E3C3C240   RTM1    00000000   ESTA 00000000   UKY 007FABD0   SQAF   0005FFFF   BYT1 88840000
        +118   RPT     00000000   DBTB    00000000   SWAS 00809F50   SCB 00000000
        EXT2   GTF     00000000   SVAB    00000000   EVNT 00000000   RTM 00000000   TQE    00000000   CAUF 00000000
               PERCP   80000000   PERCT   00000000

ACTIVE RBS

PRB  7C3DE8   XSB     007C3E50   RESV 00000000   RTPSW1 078D0000   0011C266   RTPSW2 00020014   007C6000
              FLG1    00000000   WC-L-IC 00020014
              RESV    00000000   APSW    00000000   SZ-STAB 00110082      FL-CDE 0080C4A8   PSW 078D0000   0011C266
              Q/TTR   00000000   WT-LNK  007D4470
              RG 0-7    0080C010   00114FF8   00000040   007FD474   007FD450   007FAEA8   007DAFF8   FD000000
              RG 8-15   007C3F90   807FA288   00000000   0080EFB8   50D7BAD2   00114FB0   40D7BE6C   007C3FC0

XSB AT 007C3E50
        +0     XSB    E7E2C240   LINK   00000000   KM    8080   SASID   000D       AX   0000   PASID   000D   XLSRB   00000000
        +14    XLAS   00000000   TKN    0000       ASD   0000   SEL     00000000

SVRB 80D040   XSB   0080D110   RESV 00000000   RTPSW1 00000000   00000000   RTPSW2 00000000   00000000
```

Abend code. 322 means out of time.

The PSW and instruction length code are separated. You must remember this when computing the point of abend.

Figure 8.37 A complete assembly language program dump.

```
JOB MADISCN          STEP GO              TIME 062530   DAT: 85310    ID = 000                                 PAGE 0002

            FLG1  20000000   WC-L-IC 00020033
            RESV  00000000   APSW     00000000   SZ-STAB 001ED022     FL-CDE 00000000   PSW 070C1000    00CE7D60
            Q/TTR 00000000   WT-LNK   007C3DE8
            RG 0-7     000001B0   007D9E50   00000040   0011C6BC   00114FFE   00000000   00000000   00000000
            RG 8-15    007C3F90   80115EE4   0011C66C   0080EFB8   0011C010   0011C66C   4011C256   00000094
            EXTSA      000001B0   007D9E50   00022F58   007D4470   0080D040   00FD8EA0   0004F828   00FDC800
                       007FA5A8   FF0004D4   40001001   88322000
            SCB        00000000   00000000   1580D040   0380D040   2400DB00   XPTR     0080D100
            FEPARM     00000000   80E1D844   00000000   00000884   0004F828   00000000
            SCBX       00000000   00000000

XSB AT 0080D110
       +0    XSB    E7E2C240    LINK    00000000    KM    0080    SASID    000D    AX    0000    PASID    000D    XLSRB    00000000
       +14   XLAS   00000000    TKN     0000        ASD   0000    SEL      00000000

SVRB 80D158  XSB  0080D228    RESV 00000000    RTPSW1 00000000      00000000    RTPSW2 00000000      00000000
            FLG1  02000000   WC-L-IC 0002000C
            RESV  00000000   APSW     00000000   SZ-STAB 001ED022     FL-CDE 00000000   PSW 070C1000    00C9210A
            Q/TTR 00000000   WT-LNK   0080D040
            RG 0-7     000001A0   007FA6A8   007DB028   007D9EC0   007FA6A8   00CE8019   50CE701A   007FA5A8
            RG 8-15    007D9E68   00000000   00CE83B0   007FA6A8   007C3F28   007FA71C   00FD376C   00000000
            EXTSA      00000000   007C3110   00000440   0080D1BC   20FD0000   00000000   00000000   00000000
                       00000000   00000000   00000000   00000000
            SCB        00000000   00000000   16FC24C0   0380D158   6400DB00   XPTR     0080D218
            FEPARM     00000000   80E1D844   80E1D864   00000884   0004F828   00000000
            SCBX       00000000   00000000

XSB AT 0080D228
       +0    XSB    E7E2C240    LINK    00000000    KM    0080    SASID    000D    AX    0000    PASID    000D    XLSRB    00000000
       +14   XLAS   00000000    TKN     0000        ASD   0000    SEL      00000000


LOAD LIST

       NE 007D4000    RSP-CDE 00FB3730    CNT 00010001          NE 00000000    RSP-CDE 007C3D98    CNT 00010000


CDE

    80C4A8       NCDE 00000000    RBP 007C3DE8 NM ISULOADR    EPA 00115E78    XL/MJ 0080C000    USE 0001C0FB    ATTR 0B22000
    FB3730       NCDE 00FB3910    RBP 00000000 NM IGG019DK    EPA 00AFF850    XL/MJ 00FB3750    USE 00020000    ATTR B122000
    7C3D98       NCDE 0080C4A8    RBP 00000000 NM **GO        EPA 0011C010    XL/MJ 007C3DB8    USE 00010000    ATTR 01A0000

XL                                                LN          ADR          LN          ADR          LN          ADR

    80C000    SZ 00000010    NO 00000001      80000188    00115E78
    FB3750    SZ 00000010    NO 00000001      800007B0    00AFF850
    7C3DB8    SZ 00000010    NO 00000001      80000858    0011C000

TIOT   7DB000         JOB  MADISON     STEP     GO
         OFFSET       LN-STA       DDNAME       TTR-STC      STB-UCB
         + 0018       14010100     SYSIN        7E788000     807E64E0
         + 002C       14010102     SYSLOUT      7E758000     80000000
         + 0040       14010102     SYSUDUMP     7E740000     80000000
         + 0054       14010102     XOUT         7E728000     80000000
```

Entry point address of your program. Very important in assembler debugging.

Figure 8.37 (continued)

```
JOB MADISON          STEP GO              TIME 062530   DATE 85310    ID = 000                                  PAGE 0003

        + 0068    14010102    XIN         7E6F4000    80000000


VSM
  SPQE   007FAE00 NSPQE 007FAC50  DQE 00000000  FL/RS 0000  SPID  252  KEY  0

  SPQE   007FAC50 NSPQE 007FAC20  DQE 007C39B0  FL/RS 0000  SPID  251  KEY  8
DQE 7C39B0 FQE 7FAD90  NDQE 000000  BLK 00115000  LN 00001000  FQE 7FAD90  FQE 80000000  LN 00000E78  AREA 00115E78
  SPQE   007FAC20 NSPQE 00000000  DQE 007FABC0  FL/RS C000  SPID  000  KEY  8
  SPQE   007FABC0 NSPQE 00000000  DQE 007FAAD0  FL/RS 6000  SPID  000  KEY  8
DQE 7FAAD0 FQE 7FAE60  NDQE 7FAA80  BLK 00114000  LN 00001000  FQE 7FAE60  FQE 807FACB0  LN 00000108  AREA 00114DE8
                                                               FQE 7FACB0  FQE 80000000  LN 00000AB8  AREA 00114AB8
DQE 7FAA80 FQE 7FAC10  NDQE 000000  BLK 0011C000  LN 00001000  FQE 7FAC10  FQE 80000000  LN 00000148  AREA 0011C9A0

D-PQE  80F548      FIRST 0080F418

PQE   80F418    FFB 007FAAA0   LFB 007FAE70   NPQ 00000000   PPQ 00000000
                TCB 007FAEA8   RSI 006FC000   RAD 00114000   FLG 00000000
FBQE 7FAAA0     NFB 007FADF0   PFB 0080F418   SZ  00006000   AREA 00116000
FBQE 7FADF0     NFB 007C39D0   PFB 007FAAA0   SZ  00694000   AREA 0011D000
FBQE 7C39D0     NFB 007FAE70   PFB 007FADF0   SZ  00011000   AREA 007B2000
FBQE 7FAE70     NFB 0080F418   PFB 007C39D0   SZ  0000E000   AREA 007C4000

SSAT    022D78
        SSAT   E2E2C1E3   LNK    00000000   CT   00000000   HIDX   00000000
        00000000    00000000    00FB5260    40E3D8C5    00022D98    00FE4000    00000310    FFFFFFFF
        FFFFFFFF    40E3D8C5    00FE4000    00FC3010    00000301    99FF7181    28000000    40E3D8C5

                                       ***TCB SUMMARY***
                                          -----------
TCB AT 80DA68    CMP 00000000    PKF-FLG 00000080   DSP 0400FFFF    SDY 00000000    RTM 00000000    FBYT 00000000
TCB AT 80CD90    CMP 00000000    PKF-FLG 00000080   DSP 0400FFFF    SDY 00000000    RTM 00000000    FBYT 00040000
TCB AT 80CAF8    CMP 00000000    PKF-FLG 00000080   DSP 0400FFFF    SDY 00000000    RTM 00000000    FBYT 00040000
TCB AT 7FAEA8    CMP 00000000    PKF-FLG 80000000   DSP 0400FFFF    SDY 00000000    RTM 00000000    FBYT 00040000
TCB AT 7D4470    CMP 88322000    PKF-FLG 80850000   DSP 0000FFFF    SDY 00000000    RTM 007[illegible]A5A8    FBYT 88840000

                                        ***** LOCAL QUEUE CONTROL BLOCK PRINT *****
                                        -------------------------------------------

     MAJOR NAME-SYSIEA01

          MINOR NAME-IEA
               STATUS-EXCLUSIVE/OWN        SCOPE-STEP        ASID-000D     TCB-007D4470     SVRB-0080D158

                                        ***** GLOBAL QUEUE CONTROL BLOCK PRINT *****
                                        --------------------------------------------
NO GLOBAL RESOURCES EXIST


-DEB--------------------------------------AT LOCATION   007D8608
-----

-8      EXTNSION 007D8680 LENGTH   10       AMTYPE   81       TBLOF    0002
+0      TCBADR   007D4470 NEXTDEB  00000000 IRBADR   087D6DA0 PATB     0F000900
```

Figure 8.37 (continued)

```
JOB MADISON          STEP CO              TIME 062530   DATE 85310    ID = 000                        PAGE 0004

+10     USRPG    00000000 RRQ      007D9E68 DCBADR   81114E68 APPADR   00EE33E8
+20     000011D8 E2E2C9C2 00240000 D1C5E2F2
+30     00000000 00000000 00000000 00000000
+40     00000000 00000000 E2E2D6C2 00140010
+50     007D862C 00000000 007D8664 001C0000
+60     00000000 007D87B4 007D8608 007D6DA0
+70     00000000 00000000


*** FOR THIS DEB THERE IS NO DCB, THE CONTROL BLOCK POINTED TO BY THE DEB IS AN ACB ***


-RTM2WA-----------------------------------AT LOCATION  007FA5A8
 ------

+0      D9E3D4F2 007FA5A8 FF0004D4 00022F58 007D4470 0080D040 00FD8EA0 80322000
+20     00000000 00000000 00000000 00000000 007D4470 0080D040 00FD3680

-EED TYPE1 REGS AND PSW
+3C     007D4470 88322000 00000000 0080C324 00FD8EA0 007C3F10 007FA288 00000322
+5C     007D4470 00000000 00022FA8 007D4470 4008B082 007FA028 5008B264 00042460
+7C     00000000 00000000 00000000 00000000
-----

+8C     00000000 00000000 00000000

-EED TYPE3 MACHINE CHECK
+98     00000000 00000000 00000000 00000000 00000000 00000000 00000000
-----

+B4     08040001 000D0000 00000000 00000000 00000000 00000001 00000000 00000000
+D4     00000000 00000000 00000000 00000000 00000000 00000000 00000000 00000000
+F4     00000000 00000000 007FA6A8

-SNPPARMS
+100    006C0000 0F40EE00 007D9E68 007D4470 007FA98C
-----

+114    00000000 00000000 00000000 00000000 00000000 00000000 00000000 00000000
+134    E2E8E2E4 C4E4D4D7 00000000 007D4470 007FA6FC 007FA700 007FA704 007FA708
+154    00000000 00000000 00000000 00000000 00000000 00000000 00000000 00000000

-SUBFUNCTION REGISTER SAVE AREA
+174    00000000 00000000 00000000 50CE99DC 00CE6FF8 D9E3F104 007FA5A8 007D4470
+194    00CEA139 007D4470 0080D040 40CE913A 00000000 007FA5A8 00CE9A0C 00000000
+1B4    007FA910 007FA6A8
-----

+1BC    00480000 00FE0000 00000000 00000000 00080000 000C0000 00000000 E0100000
+1DC    00000000 00CE83B0 00CE9A0C 00000000 00CE3F20 000C0800

-RECURSION REGISTERS
+1F4    000001A0 007D8E60 007DB028 007D9EC0 00000000 00CE8019 50CE701A 007FA5A8
```

Figure 8.37 (continued)

```
JOB MADISON          STEP GO              TIME 062530   DATE 85310    ID = 000                          PAGE 0005

+214     007D9E68 00000000 00CE83B0 007D9EC0 007C3F28 007FA71C 007D4470 00000000

-SAVE AREA FOR VTRI2
+234     00000000 00000000 00000000 40CE3BCA 00CE9118 D9E3F104 00000000 00FDC800
+254     00CE401F 007D4470 0080D040 40CE3020 0080D0A0 007FA5A8 00000000 00000000
+274     007FA910 00000000

-SAVE AREA FOR TAS2/TAS3
+27C     00000000 00000000 00000000 00000000 00000000 00000000 00000000 00000000
+29C     00000000 00000000 00000000 00000000 00000000 00000000 00000000 00000000
+2BC     00000000 00000000
-----

+2C4     007FA870

-RMPL
+2C8     8400000D 00FD8EA0 007D4470 00000000 007FA888 00000000

-WORK AREA FOR RESOURCE MANAGER
+2E0     FF030100 007FA894 007FA89C E2E8E2C9 C5C1F0F1 C9C5C100 00047880 00000D08
+300     00000000 00000000 00000000 00000000 00000000 00000000 00000000 00000000

-SAVE AREA FOR RESOURCE MANAGER
+320     007FA910 007FA71C 00809F58 50CE735A 00D80BA0 007D9ED8 007D9EC4 007DB028
+340     007DB028 007D4470 00CE8019 50CE701A 007FA5A8 007D9E68 007D9E68 007FA5A8
+360     007D9EC4 007C3F28

+368     000F0000 000D0003 87850000 00000000 00000000 00000000 00000000 00000000
+388     00000000 00000000 00000000 00000000 00000000 00000000 00000000 00000000
+3A8     00000000 00000000 00000000 00000000 00000000 00000000 00000000 00000000
+3C8     00000000 8080000D 0000000D 00000000 00000000 00000000 00000000

                                DUMP STORAGE RANGES
                                -------------------

+0       00000000 00000000 00000000 00000000 00000000 00000000 00000000 00000000
+20      00000000 00000000 00000000 00000000 00000000 00000000 00000000 00000000
+40      00000000 00000000 00000000 00000000 00000000 00000000 00000000 00000000
+60      00000000 00000000 00000000 00000000 00000000 00000000 00000000 00000000
+80      00000000 00000000 00000000 00000000 00000000 00000000 00000000 00000000
+A0      00000000 00000000 00000000 00000000 00000000 00000000 00000000 00000000
+C0      00000000 00000000 00000000 00000000 00000000 00000000 00000000 00000000
+E0      00000000 00000000 00000000 00000000

                                RTM2WA SUMMARY
                                --------------

+1C      COMPLETION CODE           80322000
+8C      ABENDING PROGRAM NAME       N/A
+94      ABENDING PROGRAM ADDR     00000000

+3C      REGS AT TIME OF ERROR     007D4470 88322000 00000000 0080C324 00FD8EA0 007C3F10 007FA288 00000322   (0-7)
+5C                                007D4470 00000000 00022FA8 007D4470 4008B082 007FA028 5008B264 00042460   (8-F)
+7C      EC PSW AT TIME OF ERROR   00000000 00000000 00000000 00000000
+DC      SDWACOMP                  00000000
```

Figure 8.37 (continued)

```
JOB MADISON          STEP GO              TIME 062530    DATE 85310     ID   000                             PAGE 0006

+E8     RETURN CODE FROM RECOVERY ROUTINE-00,CONTINUE WITH TERMINATION-IMPLIES PERCOLATION
+E0     RETRY ADDR RETURNED FROM RECOVERY EXIT  00000000
+E4     RB ADDR FOR RETRY                       00000000

+C      CVT  ADDR                  00022F58
+38     RTCT ADDR                  00FD3680
+C8     SCB  ADDR                  00000001
+D4     SDWA ADDR                  00000000
+14     SVRB ADDR                  0080D040
+16C    PREV RTM2WA FOR THE TASK   00000000
+170    PREV RTM2WA FOR RECURSION  00000000

+B8     ASID OF ERROR IF CROSS MEMORY ABTERM       000D
+36C    ERROR ASID                 000D

+37C    CURRENT TRACE ENTRY FOR SAVED TRACE TABLE  00000000
+380    FIRST TRACE ENTRY FOR SAVED TRACE TABLE    00000000
+384    LAST TRACE ENTRY FOR SAVED TRACE TABLE     00000000

                              RTM2WA BIT FLAG SUMMARY
                              -----------------------

+2C8    TASK TERMINATION
        ABNORMAL TERMINATION
        TERMINATING TASK IS JOBSTEP
+B4     ENTRY TO RTM2 VIA ABTERM
+B5     ENABLED RB IN CONTROL AT ERROR
+B7     ERROR ID INFORMATION AVAILABLE

                              ESA BIT FLAG SUMMARY (RTM1 RELATED INFORMATION) FROM SVRB AT 0080D040
                              ----------------------------------------------------------

+88     RTM2 ENTERED VIA ABTERM
+8A     RTM1 ENTERED FOR  CROSS MEMORY ABNORMAL TERMINATION
+8B     SYSTEM STATE: TASK MODE



-STAE CONTROL BLOCK------------------------AT LOCATION 00E0C7D0
 ------------------

+0      NEXTSCB 00000000 USEREXIT 00C8B150 PARMLIST 167C3264 TCB/RB 0380D158 SCBDATA 4000DB0C SCBXPTR 0080C7E8

+0      SCBX    XKMSK  0080   XRSV   000D0000000D   XTOKN  0000000F   XRSV2  00000000

                              SCB BIT FLAG SUMMARY
                              --------------------

+8      ALLOW ASYNCHRONOUS INTERRUPTS
        BYPASS I/O INTERVENTION
        ESTAE INDICATOR ON
+C      USER IN KEY 0-7
        USER IN SUPERVISOR STATE
```

Figure 8.37 (continued)

```
JOB MADISON           STEP GO              TIME 062530    DATE 85310    ID = 000                    PAGE 0007


-STAE CONTROL BLOCK-------------------------AT LOCATION 0080C7F8
 ------------------

+0      NEXTSCB 0080C7D0 USEREXIT 0011E48E PARMLIST 167D48F0 TCB/RB 0380D158 SCBDATA 0000DB00 SCBXPTR 0080C810

+0      SCBX    XKMSK  0080    XRSV    000D0000000D    XTOKN  0000000C    XRSV2  00000000

                              SCB BIT FLAG SUMMARY
                              --------------------

+8      ALLOW ASYNCHRONOUS INTERRUPTS
        BYPASS I/O INTERVENTION
        ESTAE INDICATOR ON
+C      USER IN KEY 0-7
        USER IN SUPERVISOR STATE


SAVE AREA TRACE

ISULOADR WAS ENTERED VIA LINK

**GO     WAS ENTERED VIA CALL

UNKNOWN  WAS ENTERED VIA CALL         AT EP 05..05..05.........................K.................................

INTERRUPT AT 11C266

PROCEEDING BACK VIA REG 13

UNKNOWN  WAS ENTERED VIA CALL         AT EP 05..05..05.........................K.................................

**GO     WAS ENTERED VIA CALL

VSAM TCBVAT  7D458C 000004

7D4580                              00000000                                   *            ....              *

NO VSAM VGTT CHAIN PRESENT FOR THIS ASCB

NO VSAM VSI CHAIN PRESENT

END OF VSAM DATA


REGS AT ENTRY TO ABEND
```

Figure 8.37 (continued)

```
JOB MADISON         STEP GO            TIME 062530   DATE 85310    ID = 000                    PAGE 0008

    FLTR 0-6     0000000000000000    0000000000000000         0000000000000000    0000000000000000

    REGS 0-7     000001B0  007D9E50  00000040  0011C6BC       00114FFE  00000000  00000000  00000000
    REGS 8-15    007C3F90  80115EE4  0011C66C  0080EFB8       0011C010  0011C66C  4011C256  00000004

ACTIVE LOAD MODULES

JPA MODULE        ISULOADR
115E60                                                                 90ECD00C 18AF50D0   *                          ........*
115E80   A08041C0 A07C50CD 000818DC 18315843   00004144 00001B55 48540000 1B774100   *................................*
115EA0   A02E47F0 A036C8C5 E6D3D6C1 C4401B11   0A0818F0 4590A0E4 181305EF 42F0A0D4   *...0..HEWLOAD .....0...U:.....0.M*
115EC0   9504A0D4 4720A06C D207A0DC 10004500   A062C8C5 E6D3D6C1 C4400A09 4590A0EE   *...M....K.........HEWLOAD ......*
115EE0   4590A0C4 58D0A08D 58ED000C 980CD014   07FE0358 00FB5CA8 00114FB0 0011C66C   *...D.........................F.*
115F00   40115F4A 0011C010 0011C010 00114FF8   00000040 00114FF8 00114FFE 00000000   * ................8...  ...8........*
115F20   00000000 00000000 007C3F90 80115EE4   00115E78 0080EFB8 00115EF4 4100A0DC   *..................U.............4....*
115F40   1B110A08 18F01813 05EF07F9 0000D200   40024001 5C5CC7D6 40404040 9200A14A   *.....0.....9..K. . ...GO     ....*
115F60   12774780 A11A4177 00021B57 125547B0   A1001B55 47F0A116 D201A0DA A1804A70   *.....................0..K........*
115F80   A0DA4070 A0DA4450 A0D64155 00014054   00001874 18651255 4780A146 95617002   *.. .......0.... ..................*
115FA0   4770A13E 1B744074 00001277 4780A148   92FFA14A 07F94177 00014660 A1241B74   *...... ....................9..........*
115FC0   07F90040 40404040 40404040 40404040   40404040 40404040 40404040 40404040   *.9.                              *
115FE0   40404040 40404040 40404040 40404040   40404040 40F6D3E2 4001D5A0 00000000   *                       6LS .N.....*

JPA MODULE        **GO
11C000   5C5CC7D6 40404040 00000000 00000000   90ECD00C 18CF41A0 C65C50AD 000850DA   *..GO      ..................F.......*
11C020   000418DA 4510C020 0011C798 8F11C7F8   0A134110 C7E84100 C33B58F0 103005EF   *...........G...G8....GY..C..0.....*
11C040   4110C7E8 4100C3C0 58F01030 05EF4110   C7E84100 C44558F0 103005EF 4110C7E8   *..GY..C..0.......GY..D..0.......GY*
11C060   4100C4CA 58F01030 05EF4110 C7E84100   C54F58F0 103005EF 4110C788 4100C6A4   *..D..0......GY..E..0.......G...F.*
11C080   58F01030 05EF9240 C5D4D283 C5D5C5D4   F274C6F8 C6A4F274 C700C6A9 4130C6A4   *.0.....  EMK.ENEM2.F8F.2.G.F...F.*
11C0A0   5930C258 4720C0BA 95603000 4780C0A8   41303001 47F0C090 F870C708 C260FB77   *..B....................0..8.G.B...*
11C0C0   C708C6F8 F877C6F8 C7084130 C6A95930   C25C4720 C0E89560 30004780 C0D64130   *G.F88.F8G...F...B....Y.......0..*
11C0E0   300147F0 C0BEF870 C708C260 FB77C708   C700F877 C700C708 F877C760 C6F8FA73   *...0..8.G.B...G.G.8.G.G.8.G.F8..*
11C100   C760C704 D20FC710 C2A64110 C71FDF0F   C710C760 47B0C10E C6109260 1000F877   *G.G.K.G.B...G...G.G...A........8.*
11C120   C768C6F8 FB77C768 C700D20F C720C2A6   4110C72F DF0FC720 C76847B0 C1340610   *G.F8..G.G.K.G.B...G...G.G...A...*
11C140   92601000 F877C770 C6F8FC73 C770C704   D20FC730 C2A      C73FDF0F C730C770   *....8.G.F8..G.G.K.G.B...G...G.G.*
11C160   47B0C15A 06109260 1000F877 C778C6F8   FD73C778              0C77C F873C778   *..A.......8.G.F8..G.G.8.G.G.8.G.*
11C180   C778D20F C750C2A6 4110C75F DF0FC750   C78047B                 000 D20FC740   *G.K.G.B...G...G.G...A.......K.G *
11C1A0   C2A64110 C74FDF0F C740C778 47B0C1A6   06109                     4 D204C61A   *B...G...G G...A.......K.E.F.K.F.*
11C1C0   C6A9D20E C5DBC261 D20EC627 C7114110   C7E8                        D20EC5DB   *F.K.E.B.K.F.G...GY..EM.0....K.E.*
11C1E0   C270D20E C627C721 4110C7E8 4100C5D4   58F0                        D20EC627   *B.K.F.G...GY..EM.0....K.E.B.K.F.*
11C200   C7314110 C7E84100 C5D458F0 103005EF   D20E                        D208C63B   *G...GY..EM.0....K.E.B.K.F.G.K.F.*
11C220   C29DD206 C646C759 4110C7E8 4100C5D4   58F0                        C44558F0   *B.K.F.G...GY..EM.0......GY..D..0*
11C240   103005EF 47F0C068 4110C7E8 4100C2B6   58F0                        0011C798   *.....0....GY..B..0.........B...G.*
11C260   8011C7F8 0A1407FE 0011C6B8 0011C6BD   0CC1                      0 40404040   *..G8.......F...F..ADD             *
11C280   E2E4C2E3 D9C1C3E3 40404040 404040D4   E4D3E                     0 4040C4C9   *SUBTRACT          MULTIPLY       DI*
11C2A0   E5C9C4C5 40404040 40404040 40D9C5D4   C1C9D5                  020 20202020   *VIDE          REMAINDER .........*
11C2C0   20202020 2120F140 40404040 40404040   40404040               4040 40404040   *......1                          *
11C2E0   40404040 40404040 40404040 40404040   40404040 40          404040 40404040   *                                 *
      LINES 11C300-11C320 SAME AS ABOVE
11C340   40404040 40404040 404040F1 D9C5D7D6   D9E34040 40404040 40404040 40404040   *               1REPORT           *
11C360   40404040 40404040 40404040 40404040   40404040 4040C140 D940C940 E340C840   *                        A R I T H *
11C380   D440C540 E340C940 C3404040 D740D940   D640C340 C540E240 E240C940 D540C740   *M E T I C   P R O C E S S I N G *
11C3A0   4040D940 C540D740 D640D940 E3404040   40404040 40404040 40404040 40404040   *  R E P O R T                    *
11C3C0   40404040 40404040 40404040 40404040   4040D5C1 D4C57A40 40D4C1E3 C8404040   *                   NAME.   MATH   *
11C3E0   40404040 40404040 40404040 40404040   40404040 40404040 40404040 40404040   *                                 *
11C400   40404040 40404040 C2C1E2C9 C3404040   D4C1E3C8 404040D6 D7C5D9C1 E3C9D6D5   *          BASIC   MATH   OPERATION*
```

Dump of the register contents.

Dump of your program's storage areas.

Figure 8.37 (continued)

```
JOB MADISON          STEP GO               TIME 062530   DATE 85310    ID = 000                                PAGE 0009

11C420   E2404040 40404040 40404040 40404040    40404040 40404040 40404040 40404040   *S                              *
11C440   40404040 40404040 40404040 40404040    40404040 40604040 40404040 40404040   *                               *
11C460   40404040 40404040 40404040 40404040    40404040 40404040 40404040 40404040   *                               *
     LINES 11C480-11C4A0 SAME AS ABOVE
11C4C0   40404040 40404040 40404040 40404040    40404040 40404040 40404060 60606060   *                          .....*
11C4E0   40D6D7C5 D9C1E3C9 D6D54060 60606060    40404040 40404040 40606060 606040C6   * OPERATION .....       ..... F*
11C500   C9D9E2E3 40E5C1D3 E4C54060 60606060    40404040 40406060 60606040 E2C5C3D6   *IRST VALUE .....     ..... SECO*
11C520   D5C440E5 C1D3E4C5 40606060 60604040    40404060 60606060 60606060 60606060   *ND VALUE .....    ..............*
11C540   606040D9 C5E2E4D3 E3406060 60606060    60606060 60606060 60404040 4040404E   *.. RESULT ...............      .*
11C560   6D6D6D6D 6D6D6D6D 6D6D6D6D 6D6D6D6D    6D6D6D6D 6D404040 40404040 40406D6D   *..................            ..*
11C580   6D6D6D6D 6D6D6D6D 6D6D6D6D 6D6D6D6D    6D6D6D6D 6D404040 4040406D 6D6D6D6D   *..................          .....*
11C5A0   6D6D6D6D 6D6D6D6D 6D6D6D6D 6D6D6D6D    6D6D6D40 40404040 6D6D6D6D 6D6D6D6D   *................     ........*
11C5C0   6D6D6D6D 6D6D6D6D 6D6D6D6D 6D6D6D6D    6D6D6D6D 6D6D6D6D 6D6D6D6D 6D6D4040   *..............................  *
11C5E0   40404040 40404040 404040C4 C9E5C9C4    C5404040 40404040 40404040 40404040   *           DIVIDE              *
11C600   40404040 40404040 40404040 404040F3    F7F04040 40404040 40404040 40404040   *               370             *
11C620   40404040 40404040 40404040 4060F940    40404040 40404040 40404040 40404040   *              .9               *
11C640   40404060 F4F14040 404040D9 C5D4C1C9    D5C4C5D9 40404040 40404040 F1404040   *   .41     REMAINDER        1   *
11C660   40404040 40404040 40000000 00000000    00115EF4 00000000 4011C256 92E5D9D2   *          ..........4.... .B..VRK*
11C680   0011C2C6 0011C2C6 00000040 0011C6BC    00114FFE 00000000 00000000 00000000   *..BF..BF... ..F.................*
11C6A0   007C3F90 80115EE4 0011C66C 0080EFB8    0011C010 4040F3F7 F0404040 60F94040   *.......U..F.........  370   .9  *
11C6C0   40404040 40404040 40404040 40404040    40404040 40404040 40404040 40404040   *                               *
11C6E0   40404040 40404040 40404040 40404040    40404040 40404040 40404040 F0F1F5F5   *                           0155*
11C700   F1F04B40 00000000 00000000 0000370F    00000000 0000009D 00000000 0000009D   *10. ... ........................*
11C720   40404040 40404040 40404040 40F3F6F1    40404040 40404040 40404040 40F3F7F9   *             361            379*
11C740   40404040 40404040 40404060 F3F3F3F0    40404040 40404040 40404040 4060F4F1   *            .3330           .41*
11C760   40404040 40404040 40404040 404040F1    00000000 0000361C 00000000 0000379C   *               1................*
11C780   00000000 0003330D 00000000 0000041D    00000000 0000001C 00000000 00000000   *....... ........................*
11C7A0   00000000 00000000 00000000 00114B48    00004000 00000001 0411C248 00000000   *....... ................B.....*
11C7C0   E7C9D540 40404040 02005000 00000001    00000001 00080000 00000000 00000001   *XIN     ........................*
11C7E0   00114BA0 00114B50 00000000 00000001    00000000 00000001 00000000 00000000   *....... ........................*
11C800   00000000 00000000 00000000 00114AB8    00004000 00000001 04000001 84000000   *....... ........................*
11C820   E7D6E4E3 40404040 02000050 00000001    00000001 00080085 00000000 00000001   *XOUT    ........................*
11C840   00114B45 00114B45 00000085 00000001    00000000 00000001                     *.......................        *

SP 000

114AA0                                                            00114AC0 00010085   *                        ........*
114AC0   00000000 00000000 00000000 00000000    00000000 00000000 00000000 00000000   *................................*
     LINES 114AE0-114B20 SAME AS ABOVE
114B40   00000000 00000000 00114B50 00050050    00114BA0 00000000 00000000 00000000   *................................*
114B60   00000000 00000000 00000000 00000000    00000000 00000000 00114E68 8F114D00   *................................*
114B80   D1C5E2F2 4BD1D6C2 F0F0F0F7 F74BE2C9    F0F1F0F2 40404040 40404040 40404040   *JES2.JOB00077.SI0102           *
114BA0   00114BF0 40404040 40404040 40404040    40404040 28000000 5C5C5C5C 00000000   *...0                ............*
114BC0   00000200 80000000 00000000 00000000    55013600 000000C1 00020000 00000000   *.........................A.......*
114BE0   00004000 90000050 00500000 5C5C5C5C    00114C40 00004040 40404040 40404040   *.. ................ ..          *
114C00   40404040 40404040 40404040 40404040    40404040 00000000 00000000 00000000   *                    ............*
114C20   00000000 00000000 00000000 00000100    D1C5E2F2 4BD1D6C2 F0F0F0F7 F74BE2D6   *................JES2.JOB00077.SO*
114C40   00114C90 40404040 40404040 40404040    40404040 40404040 40404040 40404040   *....                            *
114C60   40404040 20000000 5C5C5C5C 00000000    00000200 00000000 00000000 00000000   *     ...........................*
114C80   55013600 00000081 00020000 00000000    00000000 84000085 00850000 5C5C5C5C   *..... ..........................*
114CA0   00000000 00004040 40404040 40404040    40404040 40404040 40404040 40404040   *.....                           *
114CC0   40404040 00000000 00000000 00000000    00000000 00000000 00000000 00000100   *     .. ........................*

SP 000

114DE0                     7F000000 00200000    007D9E68 0011C9A0 00000000 007D0000   *        ..............'.........*
```

Figure 8.37 (continued)

```
JOB MADISON          STEP GO             TIME 062530   DATE 85310    ID = 000                                PAGE 0010

114E00   5C5C5C5C 007FA028 00004040 40C92194   00AFF88A 00000020 00114DE8 00114E00   *..........  I....8.......Y....*
114E20   0011C9A0 0011C9A4 00110000 00000038   007C3110 0000000A 00114DE8 00022FA8   *..I...I..................Y....*
114E40   00000038 50C92024 00114E48 40000000   00000000 00114E4C 00000000 00000000   *.....I........................*
114E60   00000000 007D9E68 A000004C 00000000   00EE33E8 52000000 00000000 00000000   *..................Y...........*
114E80   2A540008 00000000 00000000 00000000   00400041 007D8608 92000000 00114D94   *..............................*
114EA0   00000000 0660007D 00000000 00000000   00000000 C9C7C7F0 F1F9C1C8 00000000   *...................IGG019AH....*
114EC0   00114EC0 00000000 50AFFD7C 00000000   00000001 00114F08 00114F08 00000078   *..............................*
114EE0   00114E48 0011CF80 00114E68 00114DE8   007D9E68 00000079 0011C9A0 40AFF8C8   *...............Y.........I. .8H*
114F00   0011CF84 00000000 0000014C 00000000   40000000 00000200 00000000 0011CF84   *..............................*
114F20   00114EE8 00000000 0011CF85 00000000   20000000 00000000 00000078 00000658   *..............................*
114F40   000000C0 00010E13 07000010 00000000   00114F64 00114E48 00000000 00114DE8   *.............................Y*
114F60   000000C0 00000000 00000000 00000000   00000000 00000000 00000000 0000007D   *..............................*
114F80   000000C0 00000000 00000000 00000000   00000000 00114E68 08000000 00000000   *..............................*
114FA0   04000000 00000000 00000000 00000000   00000000 00000000 00115EF4 00022FA8   *...........................4....*
114FC0   00115E78 0080C010 00114FF8 00000040   007FD474 007FD450 007FAEA8 007DAFF8   *...........8... ..M...M.........8*
114FE0   FD000000 007C3F90 807FA288 00000000   0080EFB8 50D7BAD2 80114FFE 00000000   *.....................P.K........*

11C9A0   055D4040 007D0000 40F1F1F4 C6F8F040   4040F0F0 F0F0F0F0 F0F040F0 F0F0F0F0   *..  .... 114F80    00000000 00000*
11C9C0   F0F0F040 F0F0F0F0 F0F0F0F0 40F0F0F0   F0F0F0F0 F0404040 40F0F0F0 F0F0F0F0   *000 00000000 00000000      0000000*
11C9E0   F040F0F0 F1F1F4C5 F6F840F0 F8F0F0F0   F0F0F040 F0F0F0F0 F0F0F0F0 4040405C   *0 00114E68 08000000 00000000    .*
11CA00   4B4B4B4B 4B4B4B4B 4B4B4B4B 4B4B4B4B   4B4B4B4B 4B4B4B4B 4B4B4B4B 4B4B4B4B   *................................*
11CA20   5C007D00 0040F1F1 F4C6C1F0 404040F0   F4F0F0F0 F0F0F040 F0F0F0F0 F0F0F0F0   *..... 114FA0    04000000 00000000*
11CA40   40F0F0F0 F0F0F0F0 F040F0F0 F0F0F0F0   F0F04040 4040F0F0 F0F0F0F0 F0F040F0   * 00000000 00000000     00000000 0*
11CA60   F0F0F0F0 F0F0F040 F0F0F1F1 F5C5C6F4   40F0F0F0 F2F2C6C1 F8404040 5C4B4B4B   *0000000 00115EF4 00022FA8    ....*
11CA80   4B4B4B4B 4B4B4B4B 4B4B4B4B 4B4B4B4B   4B4B4B4B 4B4B4B4B F44B4B4B 4B5C007D   *.........................4.......*
11CAA0   000040F1 F1F4C6C3 F0404040 F0F0F1F1   F5C5F7F8 40F0F0F8 F0C3F0F1 F040F0F0   *.. 114FC0    00115E78 0080C010 00*
11CAC0   F1F1F4C6 C6F840F0 F0F0F0F0 F0F4F040   404040F0 F0F7C6C4 F4F7F440 F0F0F7C6   *114FF8 00000040      007FD474 007F*
11CAE0   C4F4F5F0 40F0F0F7 C6C1C5C1 F840F0F0   F7C4C1C6 C6F34040 405C4B4B 4B4B4B4B   *D450 007FAEA8 007DAFF8     .......*
11CB00   4B4B4B4B 4BF84B4B 4B404B4B D44B4B4B   D44B4B4B 4B434B4B 4BF85C00 7D000040   *.....8... ..M...M.........8.....  *
11CB20   F1F1F4C5 C5F04040 40C6C4F0 F0F0F0F0   F040F0F0 F7C3F3C6 F9F040F8 F0F7C6C1   *114FE0    FD000000 007C3F90 807FA*
11CB40   F4C6F040 C6F0C6F0 C6F0C6F0 40404040   C6F0F4F0 C6F0C6F0 40C6F7C3 F3C6F3C3   *4F0 F0F0F0F0      F040F0F0 F7C3F3C*
11CB60   F640C6F9 C6F0F4F0 C6F840C6 F0C6F7C3   F6C3F140 40405CF1 F1F4C6C5 F0404040   *6 F9F040F8 F0F7C5C1    .114FE0    *
11CB80   C6C4F0F0 F0F0F0F0 40F0F0F7 C3F3C6F9   F040F8F0 F7C6C15C 007D0000 40F1F1C3   *FD000000 007C3F90 807FA..... 11C*
11CBA0   C2F4F040 4040C6F4 C3F6C6F0 F4F040C3   F6C6F0C3 F6C6F040 C3F6C6F0 C3F6C6F0   *B40    F4C6F040 C6F0C6F0 C6F0C6F0*
11CBC0   40F4F0F4 F0F4F0F4 F0404040 40C3F6C6   F0C6F4C6 F040C3F6 C6F0C3F6 C6F040F4   * 40404040      C6F0F4F0 C6F0C6F0 4*
11CBE0   F0C3F6C6 F7C3F340 C6F3C3F6 C6F3C3F3   4040405C F4C6F040 C6F0C6F0 C6F0C6F0   *0C6F7C3 F3C6F3C3    .4F0 F0F0F0F0*
11CC00   40404040 C6F0F4F0 C6F0C6F0 40C6F7C3   F3C6F3C3 5C007D00 0040F1F1 C3C2F6F0   *      F040F0F0 F7C3F3C.....  11CB60*
11CC20   404040C6 F6F4F0C3 F6C6F940 C3F6C6F0   C6F4C6F0 40C3F6C6 F8F4F0C3 F640C6F0   *     F640C6F9 C6F0F4F0 C6F840C6 F0*
11CC40   C3F6C6F7 C3F34040 4040C6F6 C3F3C6F1   F4F040F4 F0F4F0F5 C3C6F140 C6F1C6F4   *C6F7C3      F6C3F140 40405CF1 F1F4*
11CC60   C3F6C3F5 40C6F0F4 F0F4F0F4 F0404040   5CF640C6 F9C6F0F4 F0C6F840 C6F0C6F7   *C6C5 F0404040    .6 F9F040F8 F0F7*
11CC80   C3F6C3F1 4040404B F1F1F4C6 C5F04040   405C007D 000040F1 F1C3C2F8 F0404040   *C6C1    .114FE0    .....  11CB80    *
11CCA0   C3F6C3F4 C6F0C6F0 40C6F0C6 F0C6F0C6   F040F4F0 C6F0C6F0 C6F740C3 F3C6F3C3   *C6C4F0F0 F0F0F0F0 40F0F0F7 C3F3C*
11CCC0   F6C6F940 404040C6 F0F4F0C6 F8C6F040   C6F7C3F6 C3F1F5C3 40F0F0F7 C4F0F0F0   *6F9     F040F8F0 F7C6C15C 007D000*
11CCE0   F040F4F0 C6F1C6F1 C3F34040 405CC5C4   F0F0F0F0 F0F040F0 F0F7C3F3 C6F9F040   *0 40F1F1C3    .FD000000 007C3F90 *
11CD00   F8F0F7C6 C14B4B4B 4B4B40F1 F1C35C00   7D000040 F1F1C3C2 C1F04040 40C3F2C6   *807FA..... 11C..... 11CBA0    C2F*
11CD20   F4C6F0F4 F040F4F0 F4F0C3F6 C6F440C3   F3C6F6C3 F6C6F040 C6F4C6F0 F4F0C3F3   *4F040 4040C6F4 C3F6C6F0 F4F040C3*
11CD40   40404040 C6F6C3F6 C6F0C3F3 40C6F6C3   F6C6F0F4 F040C3F3 C6F6C3F6 C6F040C3   *     F6C6F0C3 F6C6F040 C3F6C6F0 C*
11CD60   F6C6F0F4 F0C3F340 40405C40 404040C6   F6C3F6C6 F0C3F340 C6F6C3F6 C6F0F4F0   *6F040C3    .      F6C6F0C3 F6C6F040*
11CD80   40C3F3C6 F6C3F6C6 F040C35C 007D0000   40F1F1C3 C4F6F040 4040C6F6 C3F6C6F0   * C3F6C6F0 C.....  11CD60     F6C6F0*
11CDA0   C6F440C6 F0C3F3C6 F3F4F040 F4F0F4F0   F5C3F4F0 40F4F0F4 F0F4F0C3 F6404040   *F4 F0C3F340 40405C40 404040C6     *
11CDC0   40C6F6C3 F3C6F6C3 F640C6F0 C3F3C6F3   F4F040C3 F6C6F6C3 F3C6F640 C3F6C6F0   * F6C3F6C6 F0C3F340 C6F6C3F6 C6F0*
11CDE0   C6F4C6F0 4040405C F6C6F0F4 F0C3F340   40404B40 404040C6 F6C3F6C6 F0C3F340   *F4F0    .6F040C3    .      F6C6F0C3 *
11CE00   C6F6C3F6 C6F0F4F0 5C007D00 0040F1F1   C3C4F8F0 404040F4 F0C3F3C6 F3C3F640   *F6C6F040.....  11CD80     40C3F3C6 *
11CE20   C6F6C3F3 C6F6C3F6 40C6F0F4 F0C3F3F5   C340F0F0 F7C4F0F0 F0F04040 4040F4F0   *F6C3F6C6 F040C35C 007D0000      40*
11CE40   C6F1C6F1 C3F340C3 F4C6F6C6 F0F4F040   F4F0F4F0 C3F6C6F6 40C3F3C6 F6C3F6C6   *F1F1C3 C4F6F040 4040C6F6 C3F6C6F*
11CE60   F0404040 5C40C3F3 C6F6C3F6 C6F040C3   4B4B4B4B 4B4CF1F1 C3C4F6F0 404040C6   *0    . C3F6C6F0 C.....  11CDE0     F*
```

Figure 8.37 (continued)

```
JOB MADISON         STEP GO              TIME 062530   DATE 85310     ID = 000                          PAGE 0011

11CE80    F6C3F6C6 F05C007D 000040F1 F1C3C4C1    F0404040 C3F6C6F4 F4F0C3F6 40C6F0C3   *6C6F0.....  11CDA0   C6F440C6 F0C*
11CEA0    F3C6F3C3 F640C6F3 C6F4C6F0 F4F040C6    F4C6F0C6 F4C6F040 404040C6 F5C3F3C6   *3F3C6 F3F4F040 F4F0F4F0     F5C3F*
11CEC0    F4C6F040 F4F0C6F4 C6F0C6F4 40C6F0C6    F4C6F0C3 F340C6F5 F4F0F4F0 F4F04040   *4F0 40F4F0F4 F0F4F0C3 F6404040  *
11CEE0    405CC6F4 40C6F0C3 F3C6F3F4 F040F4F0    F4F0F5C3 F4F040F4 F0F4F0F4 F0C3F640   * .F4 F0C3F340 40405C40 404040C6 *
11CF00    40405C00 7D000040 F1F1C3C4 C3F04040    40F4F0C3 F6C6F6C3 F340C6F3 C3F6C6F6   *  ..... 11CDC0   40C6F6C3 F3C6F6*
11CF20    C3F340C6 F6F4F0C3 F6C6F040 C3F3C6F3    C3F6C6F3 40404040 C6F4C6F0 F4F0C3F3   *C3 F640C6F0 C3F3C6F3     F4F040C3*
11CF40    40F4F0F4 F0F4F0F4 F040C3F6 C6F4C3F6    C6F040C6 F4C6F0C3 F3C6F340 40405CC3   * 40404040 C6F4C6F0 F4F0C3F3    .C*
11CF60    F340C6F6 F4F0C3F6 C6F040C3 F3C6F3C3    F6C6F340 404040C6 F4C6F0F4 F0C3F35C   *3 F640C6F0 C3F3C6F3     F4F040C3.*
11CF80    007D0000 40F1F1C3 C6F4F040 4040F4F0    C6F4C6F0 C6F440C6 F0C6F4C6 F0C6F440   *.... 11CF40   40F4F0F4 F0F4F0F4 *
11CFA0    C6F0F4F0 C3F3C6F6 40C3F6C6 F4C3F3C6    F6404040 40C3F6C6 F0F4F0C3 F640C6F4   *F040C3F6 C6F4C3F6     C6F040C6 F4*
11CFC0    C3F6C6F0 C3F340C6 F3C3F6C6 F3F4F040    F4F0F4F0 F5C3C3F3 4040405C 40F4F0F4   *C6F0C3 F3C6F340 40405CC3    . 404*
11CFE0    F0F4F0F4 F040C3F6 C6F4C3F6 C6F040C6    F4C6F0C3 F3C6F340 40404BC3 5C000000   *04040 C6F4C6F0 F4F0C3F3    .C....*


 JOB MADISON        STEP GO              TIME 062530   DATE 85310     ID = 000                          PAGE 0012
                 DUMP INDEX
                 ----------

 DATA AREAS                        PAGE NUMBER
 ----------                        -----------

 ENQ/DEQ CONTROL BLOCKS................  0003
 DATA MANAGEMENT CONTROL BLOCKS........  0003
 RTM CONTROL BLOCKS....................  0004
 PCLINK STACKS / SAVE AREAS............  0007
 INSTALLATION/SUBSYSTEM AREAS..........  0007
 REGISTERS.............................  0007
 MODULES...............................  0008
 USER SUBPOOLS.........................  0009

 END OF DUMP
```

Since the assembler dumps are so large, the assembler usually provides an index or table of contents for the dump.

Figure 8.37 (continued)

DEBUGGING WORKSHEET

Abend code____________ PSW________________________ ________________________

Next instruction address ____________________________________

Instruction length code ____________________________________

Entry point address ____________________________________

Next instruction address ________________________

minus instruction length code

failing instruction address ________________________

failing instruction address ________________________

minus entry point address

source code instruction offset ________________________

Source code instruction ____________________________________

Figure 8.38 A debugging worksheet.

At this point, we've identified the reason behind the failure and the instruction in our program that caused the abend. To determine why the program failed, we must now look at the values of each operand used in the source code instruction.

To locate operand values in a dump, we must convert from the source code format or dump format into the more familiar D(B) or D(X,B) address forms. For example, let's suppose that our base register is R12 and that the data area SUBTOTAL is located at offset X'1A4' from the beginning of our program. Another field TOTAL is located at offset X'1B8'. The instruction causing the failure is given in Fig. 8.39.

```
AP      TOTAL(8),SUBTOTAL(5)
```

Figure 8.39 Sample failing instruction.

If we convert this instruction into machine code format, we arrive at the code given in Fig. 8.40.

```
FA74 C1B8 C1A4
```

Figure 8.40 The machine code representation for the instruction of Fig. 8.39.

The op code (first byte) is FA, which means add decimal/packed. The next byte consists of the two length operands 7 and 4. Even though we coded length values of 8 and 5 in our instruction, the assembler (or ASSIST) converts our length values used in the SS instructions to one less than coded. Hence, the length of the area TOTAL is 8 bytes (7 + 1) and the length of SUBTOTAL is 5 (4 + 1). SS instructions always store lengths as one less than their actual value. *You must remember this when debugging or converting SS instructions.*

The first operand, TOTAL, is located in memory at displacement X'1B8' from the beginning of our program (X'1B8' off from R12). SUBTOTAL is at displacement X'1A4' off from register 12. We can find both data areas in a dump if we only know the value of register 12. If you refer to the dump printouts shown earlier, you can find the values in the registers. Assuming that register 12 contains our entry point address (since it's our base register), the value in register 12 is X'0001C010'. Therefore, the addresses of TOTAL and SUBTOTAL may be found by the performing the additions listed in Fig. 8.41.

```
     base register value
   + displacement value
   ----------------------------
     memory location of the operand

TOTAL's location              SUBTOTAL's location

   1C010                          1C010
 +   1B8                        +   1A4
 -------                        -------
   1C1C8                          1C1B4
```

Figure 8.41 Locating data values in a dump.

If we now refer to the dump at these memory locations (see Fig. 8.37), we can find the values of TOTAL and SUBTOTAL. Instead of analyzing the contents of these fields at this time, let's instead save this procedure for the next section. At this time, let's concentrate on the debugging worksheet, first presented in Fig. 8.38. If you refer back to this figure, you'll notice that the worksheet did not provide for the computation of field addresses nor for a place to record the value of fields from within the dump. Let's update our worksheet, as shown in Fig. 8.42, so that we have a place to compute the location of each operand and record its value.

As you can see, the lower section of the worksheet now includes a section which will enable us to locate each operand and determine its value at the time of program failure. Since most operands are either registers or addresses, the location and resulting value of each operand can be determined. In the case of register operands, the value of a register can be immediately located in the dump and recorded on the worksheet. For addressed operands, the base, index, and displacement values are computed to determine the location of the operand within memory. From this address, the value of the operand can be extracted from the dump and recorded on the worksheet. With all operands and their values now available, the programmer can proceed to analyze the operand contents and determine the cause of the program failure.

It's important to remember that some operands may be addresses and have a base register, an index register, and a displacement value. You must locate the values of the base and index registers in the dump, and obtain the displacement value from your source code instruction or from the machine code instruction within the dump.

Before we begin looking at some debugging examples, note that ASSIST does one more thing that does not occur in assembly language—it tells you which instruction caused the abend. As a result, there's no reason to go through many of the computations to find *which* instruction caused the abend. However, you still must determine where in memory your values are to be found and locate them to determine *why* your program failed.

The worksheet that we've developed can help significantly in diagnosing a program failure. Through proper analysis, information extracted from a program dump will identify and help correct a program problem. Let's review the steps in the debugging process

```
                      DEBUGGING WORKSHEET

Abend code__________      PSW_______________    _________________

Next instruction address ________________________________________

Instruction length code _________________________________________

Entry point address _____________________________________________


               Next instruction address     _____________________
      minus    instruction length code
      ___________________________________________________________
               failing instruction address  _____________________


               failing instruction address  _____________________
      minus    entry point address
      ___________________________________________________________
               source code instruction offset ___________________


Source code instruction _________________________________________

First operand D(B)/D(X,B) _______________________________________

Length of first operand (bytes) _________________________________


Second operand D(B)/D(X,B) ______________________________________

Length of second operand (bytes) ________________________________

   first operand                                  second operand
    ___________ '--- base register value ---`   ____________
    ___________ '-- index register value ---`   ____________
    ___________ '------- displacement ------`   ____________
 +_____________                              +_______________

  _____________ '----- memory location -----` _______________

 ____________________       value        ____________________

Why did the program abend?  (comments)
```

Figure 8.42 Completed debugging worksheet.

and then use this knowledge to debug some actual program failures in the next section. Remember, the number of steps below that you may have to perform will vary from failure to failure. You may be able to diagnose the problem after step 1. On the other hand, you may not be able to diagnose the problem even after performing all 14 steps below. Your understanding and the nature of the problem will determine how quickly the problem can be resolved and how soon you can resume normal processing.

1. Determine why the program failed by locating the abend code for the failure. Understand the abend code and anticipate why the program abended.
2. Locate the PSW in the dump and extract the next instruction address and instruction length code.
3. Compute the address of the failing instruction by subtracting the instruction length code from the next instruction address.

4. Determine the entry point address for the program by looking on the loader messages page or in the CDE (contents directory entry) in the dump. If you're running your programs in ASSIST, look at the first storage address of the dump.
5. Compute the displacement of the failing source instruction in the program by subtracting the entry point address from the failing instruction address.
6. Locate the failing source instruction in the program and speculate as to why it caused the failure.
7. Convert the instruction to machine code and isolate the various operands.
8. Obtain base and index register values from the dump and if necessary, compute addresses for each operand in the failing instruction.
9. Locate data values in the dump using the addresses derived from step 8.
10. Analyze the values of the operands and determine why the program failed.
11. Trace back through the program instructions (if necessary) to determine why the operand values became illegal.
12. Correct the problem in the program.
13. Add additional debugging facilities to the program to aid in future failures.
14. Rerun the program.

PROGRAM DEBUGGING EXAMPLES

The first program debugging example is in ASSIST. Let's look at Example 8.1, which is a complete program and dump from this particular program failure.

```
*** ASSIST 4.0/A-12/21/77  370/145:OS/VS2  INS=SDFT/X=B[illegible]O, CHECK/TRC/=1130, OPTS=CMPRX  PENN STATE UNIV ***
$JOB                                                                                    005270.
        COMPUTE SUM, DIFFERENCE, PRODUCT, QUOTIENT OF 2 VALUES                                                    PAGE    1
  LOC  OBJECT CODE     ADDR1 ADDR2  STMT   SOURCE STATEMENT
000000                                 2 R0       EQU   0                                                      005290.
000001                                 3 R1       EQU   1                                                      005300.
000002                                 4 R2       EQU   2                                                      005310.
000003                                 5 R3       EQU   3                                                      005320.
000004                                 6 R4       EQU   4                                                      005330.
000005                                 7 R5       EQU   5                                                      005340.
000006                                 8 R6       EQU   6                                                      005350.
000007                                 9 R7       EQU   7                                                      005360.
000008                                10 R8       EQU   8                                                      005370.
000009                                11 R9       EQU   9                                                      005380.
00000A                                12 R10      EQU   10                                                     005390.
00000B                                13 R11      EQU   11                                                     005400.
00000C                                14 R12      EQU   12                                                     005410.
00000D                                15 R13      EQU   13                                                     005420.
00000E                                16 R14      EQU   14                                                     005430.
00000F                                17 R15      EQU   15                                                     005440.
                                      18 *                                                                     005450.
000004                                19 ENDFILE  EQU   B'0100'                                                005460.

                                      21 ********************************************************************** 005480.
                                      22 *   THIS PROGRAM WILL COMPUTE THE SUM, DIFFERENCE, PRODUCT, AND      * 005490.
                                      23 *   QUOTIENT OF TWO INPUT VALUES.  RESULTS WILL BE PRINTED IN A      * 005500.
                                      24 *   NICE REPORT FORMAT.  THE REMAINDER OF THE DIVISION WILL ALSO     * 005510.
                                      25 *   BE PRINTED.                                                      * 005520.
                                      26 ********************************************************************** 005530.
000000                                27 PROCESS  CSECT                                                        005540.
000000 90EC D00C             0000C    28          STM   R14,R12,12(13)        SAVE CALLER'S REGISTERS          005550.
000004 18CF                           29          LR    R12,R15               R12 WILL BE OUR BASE REG         005560.
000000                                30          USING PROCESS,R12           TELL THE ASSEMBLER ABOUT R12     005570.
000006 41A0 C5F4             005F4    31          LA    R10,SAVEAREA          POINT TO REGISTER SAVE AREA      005580.
00000A 50AD 0008             00008    32          ST    R10,8(R13)            TELL CALLER ABOUT OUR SAVEAREA   005590.
00000E 50DA 0004             00004    33          ST    R13,4(R10)            REMEMBER CALLER'S SAVEAREA ADDR. 005600.
000012 18DA                           34          LR    R13,R10               ESTABLISH NEW SAVE AREA          005610.
                                      35 ********************************************************************** 005620.
                                      36 *    PRINT THE TITLE LINES ON THE OUTPUT PAGE AND SET UP THE REPORT  * 005630.
                                      37 *    FOR OUR OUTPUT INFORMATION.                                     * 005640.
                                      38 ********************************************************************** 005650.
000014 E020 C2D3 0085 002D3           39          XPRNT TITLE,133             PRINT TITLE LINE                 005660.
00001A E020 C358 0085 00358           40          XPRNT SUBTITLE,133          PRINT THE SUBTITLE               005670.
000020 E020 C3DD 0085 003DD           41          XPRNT SKIP2,133             SKIP A FEW LINES                 005680.
000026 E020 C462 0085 00462           42          XPRNT HEADINGS,133          PRINT COLUMN HEADINGS            005690.
00002C E020 C4E7 0085 004E7           43          XPRNT UNDERLIN,133          UNDERLINE COLUMN HEADINGS        005700.
```

Example 8.1 An ASSIST program and its abend dump.

```
  LOC  OBJECT CODE    ADDR1 ADDR2  STMT   SOURCE STATEMENT

                                    45 *********************************************************************** 005720.
                                    46 *  OBTAIN THE INPUT VALUES FROM OUR FILE AND CONVERT THEM INTO        * 005730.
                                    47 *  BINARY FORMAT FOR PROCESSING.                                      * 005740.
                                    48 *********************************************************************** 005750.
000032                              49 CONTINUE DS    0H                                                        005760.
000032 E000 C63C 0050 0063C         50          XREAD INPUTREC,80               GET OUR RECORD                  005770.
000038 4740 C1D6            001D6   51          BC    ENDFILE,EOF               WHEN END OF FILE, ALL DONE      005780.
00003C 9240 C56C      0056C         52          MVI   PLINE,C' '                CLEAR FIRST BYTE OF PLINE       005790.
000040 D283 C56D C56C 0056D 0056C   53          MVC   PLINE+1(132),PLINE        CLEAR REST OF PRINT LINE        005800.
000046 F274 C690 C63C 00690 0063C   54          PACK  VALUE1(8),NUM1(5)         CONVERT FIRST NUMBER            005810.
00004C F274 C698 C641 00698 00641   55          PACK  VALUE2(8),NUM2(5)         CONVERT SECOND NUMBER           005820.

                                    57 *********************************************************************** 005840.
                                    58 *  IF VALUE1 OR VALUE2 ARE TO BE NEGATIVE, THEN CONVERT THE PACKED    * 005850.
                                    59 *  VALUES INTO NEGATIVE NUMBERS.                                      * 005860.
                                    60 *********************************************************************** 005870.
000052 4130 C63C            0063C   61          LA    R3,NUM1                   POINT TO FIRST INPUT NUMBER     005880.
000056                              62 LOOP1    DS    0H                        FIND NEGATIVE SIGN              005890.
000056 5930 C1F0            001F0   63          C     R3,=A(NUM1+4)             HAVE WE LOOKED AT ENTIRE NUM1   005900.
00005A 4720 C080            00080   64          BH    NUM1POS                   IF SO, THEN NUM1 IS POSITIVE    005910.
00005E 9560 3000      00000         65          CLI   0(R3),C'-'                NEGATIVE SIGN?                  005920.
000062 4780 C06E            0006E   66          BE    MINUS1                    IF YES, THEN NEGATIVE FIRST NUM 005930.
000066 4130 3001            00001   67          LA    R3,1(,R3)                 ADVANCE TO NEXT ADDRESS         005940.
00006A 47F0 C056            00056   68          B     LOOP1                     CONTINUE LOOKING                005950.
00006E F870 C6A0 C1F8 006A0 001F8   69 MINUS1   ZAP   WORK(8),=P'0'             SET WORK EQUAL TO ZERO          005960.
000074 FB77 C6A0 C690 006A0 00690   70          SP    WORK(8),VALUE1(8)         SUBTRACT VALUE1 FROM 0          005970.
00007A F877 C690 C6A0 00690 006A0   71          ZAP   VALUE1(8),WORK            VALUE1 IS NOW NEGATIVE          005980.
000080                              72 NUM1POS  DS    0H                                                        005990.

000080 4130 C641            00641   74          LA    R3,NUM2                   POINT TO FIRST INPUT NUMBER     006010.
000084                              75 LOOP2    DS    0H                        FIND NEGATIVE SIGN              006020.
000084 5930 C1F4            001F4   76          C     R3,=A(NUM2+4)             HAVE WE LOOKED AT ENTIRE NUM1   006030.
000088 4720 C0AE            000AE   77          BH    NUM2POS                   IF SO, THEN NUM1 IS POSITIVE    006040.
00008C 9560 3000      00000         78          CLI   0(R3),C'-'                NEGATIVE SIGN?                  006050.
000090 4780 C09C            0009C   79          BE    MINUS2                    IF YES, THEN NEGATIVE FIRST NUM 006060.
000094 4130 3001            00001   80          LA    R3,1(,R3)                 ADVANCE TO NEXT ADDRESS         006070.
000098 47F0 C084            00084   81          B     LOOP2                     CONTINUE LOOKING                006080.
00009C F870 C6A0 C1F8 006A0 001F8   82 MINUS2   ZAP   WORK(8),=P'0'             SET WORK EQUAL TO ZERO          006090.
0000A2 FB77 C6A0 C698 006A0 00698   83          SP    WORK(8),VALUE2(8)         SUBTRACT VALUE1 FROM 0          006100.
0000A8 F877 C698 C6A0 00698 006A0   84          ZAP   VALUE2(8),WORK            VALUE1 IS NOW NEGATIVE          006110.
0000AE                              85 NUM2POS  DS    0H                                                        006120.
```



```
  LOC  OBJECT CODE    ADDR1 ADDR2  STMT   SOURCE STATEMENT

                                    87 *********************************************************************** 006140.
                                    88 *        COMPUTE THE SUM AND CONVERT IT FOR OUTPUT PRINTING.          * 006150.
                                    89 *********************************************************************** 006160.
0000AE F877 C6F8 C690 006F8 00690   90          ZAP   SUMP(8),VALUE1(8)         COMPUTE THE SUM                 006170.
0000B4 FA73 C6F8 C69C 006F8 0069C   91          AP    SUMP(8),VALUE2+4(4)       ...JUST A DIFFERENT FORMAT      006180.
0000BA D20F C6A8 C23E 006A8 0023E   92          MVC   SUM(16),PATTERN           MOVE IN EDIT PATTERN            006190.
0000C0 4110 C6B7            006B7   93          LA    R1,SUM+15                 POINT TO LAST DIGIT POSITION    006200.
0000C4 DF0F C6A8 C6F8 006A8 006F8   94          EDMK  SUM(16),SUMP              EDIT THE SUM VALUE              006210.
0000CA 47B0 C0D4            000D4   95          BNM   SUMPOS                    IF NOT < 0, DON'T MOVE IN SIGN  006220.
0000CE 0610                         96          BCTR  R1,0                      BACK UP ONE POSITION            006230.
0000D0 9260 1000      00000         97          MVI   0(R1),C'-'                MOVE IN NEGATIVE SIGN           006240.
0000D4                              98 SUMPOS   DS    0H                        SKIP NEGATIVE MOVE IF POSITIVE  006250.
                                    99 *********************************************************************** 006260.
                                   100 *        COMPUTE THE DIFFERENCE BETWEEN THE NUMBERS AND PREPARE       * 006270.
                                   101 *        TO BE PRINTED.                                               * 006280.
                                   102 *********************************************************************** 006290.
0000D4 F877 C700 C690 00700 00690  103          ZAP   DIFFERP(8),VALUE1(8)      RESTORE BINARY VALUES IN REGS.  006300.
0000DA FB77 C700 C698 00700 00698  104          SP    DIFFERP(8),VALUE2(8)      COMPUTE DIFFERENCE              006310.
0000E0 D20F C6B8 C23E 006B8 0023E  105          MVC   DIFFER(16),PATTERN        MOVE IN THE EDIT PATTERN        006320.
0000E6 4110 C6C7            006C7  106          LA    R1,DIFFER+15              POINT TO LAST DIGIT POSITION    006330.
0000EA DF0F C6B8 C700 006B8 00700  107          EDMK  DIFFER(16),DIFFERP        CONVERT TO DISPLAY              006340.
0000F0 47B0 C0FA            000FA  108          BNM   DIFFPOS                   IF NOT < 0, DON'T MOVE IN SIGN  006350.
0000F4 0610                        109          BCTR  R1,0                      BACK UP ONE POSITION            006360.
0000F6 9260 1000      00000        110          MVI   0(R1),C'-'                MOVE IN NEGATIVE SIGN           006370.
0000FA                             111 DIFFPOS  DS    0H                        SKIP NEGATIVE MOVE IF POSITIVE  006380.
```

```
           COMPUTE SUM, DIFFERENCE, PRODUCT, QUOTIENT OF 2 VALUES                                                                PAGE    4

  LOC  OBJECT CODE     ADDR1 ADDR2  STMT   SOURCE STATEMENT

                                     113 ***********************************************************************  006400.
                                     114 *       COMPUTE THE PRODUCT BY USING THE HALFWORD MULTIPLY            *  006410.
                                     115 *       INSTRUCTION.  PREPARE FOR PRINTING AFTER MULTIPLYING.         *  006420.
                                     116 ***********************************************************************  006430.
0000FA F877 C708 C690 00708 00690    117          ZAP   PRODUCTP(8),VALUE1(8)   RESTORE FIRST VALUE               006440.
000100 FC73 C708 C69C 00708 0069C    118          MP    PRODUCTP(8),VALUE2+4(4) TIMES SECOND VALUE                006450.
000106 D20F C6C8 C23E 006C8 0023E    119          MVC   PRODUCT(16),PATTERN     MOVE IN EDIT PATTERN              006460.
00010C 4110 C6D7             006D7   120          LA    R1,PRODUCT+15           POINT TO LAST DIGIT POSITION      006470.
000110 DF0F C6C8 C708 006C8 00708    121          EDMK  PRODUCT(16),PRODUCTP    CONVERT PRODUCT FOR OUTPUT        006480.
000116 47B0 C120             00120   122          BNM   PRODPOS                 IF NOT < 0, DON'T MOVE IN SIGN    006490.
00011A 0610                          123          BCTR  R1,0                    BACK UP ONE POSITION              006500.
00011C 9260 1000       00000         124          MVI   0(R1),C'-'              MOVE IN NEGATIVE SIGN             006510.
000120                               125 PRODPOS  DS    0H                      SKIP NEGATIVE MOVE IF POSITIVE    006520.
                                     126 ***********************************************************************  006530.
                                     127 *      DIVIDE THE TWO NUMBERS AND PREPARE BOTH THE QUOTIENT AND       *  006540.
                                     128 *      REMAINDER FOR PRINTING ON OUR REPORT.                          *  006550.
                                     129 ***********************************************************************  006560.
000120 F877 C710 C690 00710 00690    130          ZAP   QUOTENTP(8),VALUE1(8)   RESTORE THE VALUES                006570.
000126 FD73 C710 C69C 00710 0069C    131          DP    QUOTENTP(8),VALUE2+4(4) SET THE SIGN FOR DIVIDE           006580.
00012C F873 C718 C714 00718 00714    132          ZAP   REMAINP(8),QUOTENTP+4(4) EXTRACT THE REMAINDER            006590.
000132 F873 C710 C710 00710 00710    133          ZAP   QUOTENTP(8),QUOTENTP(4) EXPAND THE QUOTIENT               006600.
000138 D20F C6E8 C23E 006E8 0023E    134          MVC   REMAIN(16),PATTERN      MOVE IN EDIT PATTERN              006610.
00013E 4110 C6F7             006F7   135          LA    R1,REMAIN+15            POINT TO LAST DIGIT POSITION      006620.
000142 DF0F C6E8 C718 006E8 00718    136          EDMK  REMAIN(16),REMAINP      EDIT THE REMAINDER                006630.
000148 47B0 C152             00152   137          BNM   REMPOS                  IF NOT < 0, DON'T MOVE IN SIGN    006640.
00014C 0610                          138          BCTR  R1,0                    BACK UP ONE POSITION              006650.
00014E 9260 1000       00000         139          MVI   0(R1),C'-'              MOVE IN NEGATIVE SIGN             006660.
000152                               140 REMPOS   DS    0H                      SKIP NEGATIVE MOVE IF POSITIVE    006670.

000152 D20F C6D8 C23E 006D8 0023E    142          MVC   QUOTIENT(16),PATTERN    MOVE IN EDIT PATTERN              006690.
000158 4110 C6E7             006E7   143          LA    R1,QUOTIENT+15          POINT TO LAST DIGIT POSITION      006700.
00015C DF0F C6D8 C710 006D8 00710    144          EDMK  QUOTIENT(16),QUOTENTP   EDIT THE QUOTIENT VALUE           006710.
000162 47B0 C16C             0016C   145          BNM   QUOTPOS                 IF NOT < 0, DON'T MOVE IN SIGN    006720.
000166 0610                          146          BCTR  R1,0                    BACK UP ONE POSITION              006730.
000168 9260 1000       00000         147          MVI   0(R1),C'-'              MOVE IN NEGATIVE SIGN             006740.
00016C                               148 QUOTPOS  DS    0H                      SKIP NEGATIVE MOVE IF POSITIVE    006750.
```

```
           COMPUTE SUM, DIFFERENCE, PRODUCT, QUOTIENT OF 2 VALUE                                                                 PAGE    5

  LOC  OBJECT CODE     ADDR1 ADDR2  STMT   SOURCE STATEMENT

                                     150 ***********************************************************************  006770.
                                     151 *    MOVE THE INPUT VALUES INTO THE OUTPUT LINE AND PRINT THE         *  006780.
                                     152 *    INFORMATION FOR THE ADD OPERATION.                               *  006790.
                                     153 ***********************************************************************  006800.
00016C D204 C595 C63C 00595 0063C    154          MVC   OP1(5),NUM1             MOVE FIRST NUMBER TO PRINT LINE   006810.
000172 D204 C5B2 C641 005B2 00641    155          MVC   OP2(5),NUM2             MOVE SECOND NUMBER SIMILARLY      006820.
000178 D20E C573 C1F9 00573 001F9    156          MVC   COMMAND(15),=CL15'ADD'  FIRST COMMAND IS TO ADD           006830.
00017E D20E C5BF C6A9 005BF 006A9    157          MVC   RESULT(15),SUM+1        MOVE SUM INTO PRINT LINE          006840.
000184 E020 C56C 0085 0056C          158          XPRNT PLINE,133               PRINT SUM VALUE                   006850.
                                     159 ***********************************************************************  006860.
                                     160 *    PRINT THE RESULTS OF THE SUBTRACT.                               *  006870.
                                     161 ***********************************************************************  006880.
00018A D20E C573 C208 00573 00208    162          MVC   COMMAND(15),=CL15'SUBTRACT'  COMMAND IS NOW SUBTRACT      006890.
000190 D20E C5BF C6B9 005BF 006B9    163          MVC   RESULT(15),DIFFER+1     MOVE DIFFERENCE TO PRINT LINE     006900.
000196 E020 C56C 0085 0056C          164          XPRNT PLINE,133               PRINT SUM VALUE                   006910.
                                     165 ***********************************************************************  006920.
                                     166 *    PRINT THE RESULTS OF THE MULTIPLICATION.                         *  006930.
                                     167 ***********************************************************************  006940.
00019C D20E C573 C217 00573 00217    168          MVC   COMMAND(15),=CL15'MULTIPLY'  MOVE IN MULTIPLY COMMAND     006950.
0001A2 D20E C5BF C6C9 005BF 006C9    169          MVC   RESULT(15),PRODUCT+1    MOVE PRODUCT INTO PRINT LINE      006960.
0001A8 E020 C56C 0085 0056C          170          XPRNT PLINE,133               PRINT SUM VALUE                   006970.
                                     171 ***********************************************************************  006980.
                                     172 *    PRINT THE QUOTIENT AND REMAINDER FROM THE DIVISION.              *  006990.
                                     173 ***********************************************************************  007000.
0001AE D20E C573 C226 00573 00226    174          MVC   COMMAND(15),=CL15'DIVIDE'    MOVE IN DIVIDE COMMAND       007010.
0001B4 D20E C5BF C6D9 005BF 006D9    175          MVC   RESULT(15),QUOTIENT+1   MOVE QUOTIENT INTO PRINT LINE     007020.
0001BA D208 C5D3 C235 005D3 00235    176          MVC   RESULT+20(9),=C'REMAINDER'   MOVE IN HEADER FOR REMAIN.   007030.
0001C0 D206 C5DE C6F1 005DE 006F1    177          MVC   RESULT+31(7),REMAIN+9        NOW MOVE IN REMAINDER        007040.
0001C6 E020 C56C 0085 0056C          178          XPRNT PLINE,133               PRINT QUOTIENT/REMAINDER VALUES   007050.
0001CC E020 C3DD 0085 003DD          179          XPRNT SKIP2,133                                                 007060.
0001D2 47F0 C032             00032   180          B     CONTINUE                CONTINUE UNTIL END OF FILE        007070.
```

```
      COMPUTE SUM, DIFFERENCE, PRODUCT  QUOTIENT OF 2 VALUES                                                    PAGE    6

  LOC   OBJECT CODE     ADDR1 ADDR2  STMT    SOURCE STATEMENT

                                      182 ********************************************************************** 007090.
                                      183 *     WE'RE ALL DONE.  PAGE EJECT BEFORE ENDING SO THAT OUR REPORT   *  007100.
                                      184 *     LOOKS NICE.  SET THE RETURN CODE AND THEN EXIT.                *  007110.
                                      185 ********************************************************************** 007120.
0001D6 E020 C24E 0085 0024E           186 EOF      XPRNT NEWPAGE,133                                              007130.
0001DC 58DD 0004            00004     187          L     R13,4(R13)             RESTORE ORIGINAL R13 VALUE         007140.
0001E0 98EC D00C            0000C     188          LM    R14,R12,12(R13)        RESTORE ALL REGS                   007150.
0001E4 1BFF                           189          SR    R15,R15                SET RETURN CODE TO ZERO            007160.
0001E6 47F0 000E            0000E     190          BC    B'1111',R14            RETURN CONTROL TO CALLER           007170.
                                      191 *                                                                       007180.
                                      192          LTORG                                                          007190.
0001F0 00000640                       193                =A(NUM1+4)
J001F4 00000645                       194                =A(NUM2+4)
0001F8 0C                             195                =P'0'
0001F9 C1C4C44040404040               196                =CL15'ADD'
000208 E2E4C2F3D9C1C3E3               197                =CL15'SUBTRACT'
000217 D4E4D3E3C9D7D3E8               198                =CL15'MULTIPLY'
000226 C4C9E5C9C4C54040               199                =CL15'DIVIDE'
000235 D9C5D4C1C9D5C4C5               200                =C'REMAINDER'
```

```
      COMPUTE SUM, DIFFERENCE, PRODUCT, QUOTIENT OF 2 VALUES                                                    PAGE    7

  LOC   OBJECT CODE     ADDR1 ADDR2  STMT    SOURCE STATEMENT

                                      202 ********************************************************************** 007210.
                                      203 *                         DATA AND STORAGE AREA DEFINITIONS          *  007220.
                                      204 ********************************************************************** 007230.
00023E 4020202020202020               205 PATTERN  DC    X'40202020202020202020202020202120'                      007240.
00024E F140404040404040               206 NEWPAGE  DC    CL133'1'                                                 007250.
                                      207 *                                                                       007260.
0002D3 F1D9C5D7D6D9E340               208 TITLE    DC    CL133'1REPORT                                  A R I TX007270.
                                                          H M E T I C   P R O C E S S I N G   R E P O R T'        007280.
000358 4040D5C1D4C57A40               209 SUBTITLE DC    CL133'  NAME:  MATH                                     X007290.
                                                                BASIC   MATH   OPERATIONS'                        007300.
0003DD 6040404040404040               210 SKIP2    DC    CL133'-'                                                 007310.
000462 4060606060606040D6             211 HEADINGS DC    CL133' ----- OPERATION -----       ----- FIRST VALUE -X007320.
                                                         ----      ----- SECOND VALUE -----    --------------- RX007330.
                                                         ESULT ---------------'                                   007340.
0004E7 4E6D6D6D6D6D6D6D               212 UNDERLIN DC    CL133'+______________________     ____________________X007350.
                                                                                           ____________________X007360.
                                                         ____   _____________'___________  ____________________ 007370.
                                                         ______________________                                   007380.
                                      213 *                                                                       007390.
00056C                                214 PLINE    DS    0CL133                                                   007400.
00056C 40                             215 CC       DC    C' '                                                     007410.
00056D 404040404040                   216          DC    CL6' '                                                   007420.
000573 4040404040404040               217 COMMAND  DC    CL15' '                                                  007430.
000582 4040404040404040               218          DC    CL19' '                                                  007440.
000595 4040404040                     219 OP1      DC    CL5' '                                                   007450.
00059A 4040404040404040               220          DC    CL24' '                                                  007460.
0005B2 4040404040                     221 OP2      DC    CL5' '                                                   007470.
0005B7 4040404040404040               222          DC    CL8' '                                                   007480.
0005BF 4040404040404040               223 RESULT   DC    CL50' '                                                  007490.
                                      224 *                                                                       007500.
0005F4                                225 SAVEAREA DS    18F                    REGISTER SAVE AREA

00063C                                227 INPUTREC DS    0CL80                  ****                              007520.
00063C                                228 NUM1     DS    CL5                       **** INPUT RECORD DESCRIPTION  007530.
000641                                229 NUM2     DS    CL5                       *                              007540.
000646                                230          DS    CL70                   ****                              007550.
```

```
      COMPUTE SUM, DIFFERENCE, PRODUCT, QUOTIENT OF 2 VALUES                                                    PAGE    8

  LOC   OBJECT CODE     ADDR1 ADDR2  STMT    SOURCE STATEMENT

000690                                232          DS    0D                                                       007570.
000690                                233 VALUE1   DS    PL8                                                      007580.
000698                                234 VALUE2   DS    PL8                                                      007590.
0006A0                                235 WORK     DS    PL8                                                      007600.
0006A8 4040404040404040               236 SUM      DC    CL16' '                ****                              007610.
0006B8 4040404040404040               237 DIFFER   DC    CL16' '                   *                              007620.
0006C8 4040404040404040               238 PRODUCT  DC    CL16' '                   **** OUTPUT RESULT AREAS       007630.
0006D8 4040404040404040               239 QUOTIENT DC    CL16' '                   *                              007640.
0006E8 4040404040404040               240 REMAIN   DC    CL16' '                ****                              007650.
0006F8 000000000000000C               241 SUMP     DC    PL8'0'                 ****                              007660.
000700 000000000000000C               242 DIFFERP  DC    PL8'0'                    *                              007670.
000708 000000000000000C               243 PRODUCTP DC    PL8'0'                    **** CONVERSION AREAS          007680.
000710 000000000000000C               244 QOUTENTP DC    PL8'0'                    *                              007690.
000718 000000000000000C               245 REMAINP  DC    PL8'0'                 ****                              007700.
                                      246          END   PROCESS                                                  007710.

***  NO   STATEMENTS FLAGGED -  NO   WARNINGS,  NO   ERRORS

*** DYNAMIC CORE AREA USED:  LOW:    20184 HIGH:     1660 LEAVING:  498348 FREE BYTES. AVERAGE:       88 BYTES/STMT ***

*** ASSEMBLY TIME =    0.037 SECS,     6675 STATEMENTS/SEC ***

*** PROGRAM EXECUTION BEGINNING - ANY OUTPUT BEFORE EXECUTION TIME MESSAGE IS PRODUCED BY USER PROGRAM ***
```

```
REPORT                          A R I T H M E T I C   P R O C E S S I N G   R E P O R T
 NAME:  MATH                                BASIC   MATH   OPERATIONS

----- OPERATION -----        ----- FIRST VALUE -----     ----- SECOND VALUE -----     -------------- RESULT --------------
      ADD                           00020                        00008                      28
      SUBTRACT                      00020                        00008                      12
      MULTIPLY                      00020                        00008                     160
      DIVIDE                        00020                        00008                       2     REMAINDER        4


      ADD                              -6                            4                      -2
      SUBTRACT                         -6                            4                     -10
      MULTIPLY                         -6                            4                     -24
      DIVIDE                           -6                            4                      -1     REMAINDER       -2


      ADD                              25                           -3                      22
      SUBTRACT                         25                           -3                      28
      MULTIPLY                         25                           -3                     -75
      DIVIDE                           25                           -3                      -8     REMAINDER        1


      ADD                             -66                           -7                     -73
      SUBTRACT                        -66                           -7                     -59
      MULTIPLY                        -66                           -7                     462
      DIVIDE                          -66                           -7                       9     REMAINDER       -3


      ADD                             370                           -9                     361
      SUBTRACT                        370                           -9                     379
      MULTIPLY                        370                           -9                   -3330
      DIVIDE                          370                           -9                     -41     REMAINDER        1


ASSIST COMPLETION DUMP

PSW AT ABEND FFC50004 80000012        COMPLETION CODE   SYSTEM = 0C4 PROTECTION

** TRACE OF INSTRUCTIONS JUST BEFORE TERMINATION: PSW BITS SHOWN ARE THOSE BEFORE CORRESPONDING INSTRUCTION DECODED ***
  IM LOCATION     INSTRUCTION :  IM = PSW BITS 32-39(ILC,CC,MASK) BEFORE INSTRUCTION EXECUTED AT PROGRAM LOCATION SHOWN
  10  0001CC      E020 C3DD 0085
  D0  0001D2      47F0 C032
  90  000032      E000 C63C 0050
  D0  000038      4740 C1D6
  90  0001D6      E020 C24E 0085
  D0  0001DC      58DD 0004
  90  0001E0      98EC D00C
  90  0001E4      1BFF
  40  0001E6      47F0 000E
  80  00000E      50DA 0004        <-- LAST INSTRUCTION DONE - PROBABLE CAUSE OF TERMINATION


** TRACE OF LAST 10 BRANCH INSTRUCTIONS EXECUTED: PSW BITS SHOWN ARE THOSE BEFORE CORRESPONDING INSTRUCTION DECODED ***
  IM LOCATION     INSTRUCTION :  IM = PSW BITS 32-39(ILC,CC,MASK) BEFORE INSTRUCTION EXECUTED AT PROGRAM LOCATION SHOWN
  10  000098      47F0 C084
  90  000098      47F0 C084
  90  000098      47F0 C084
  80  000090      4780 C09C
  A0  0000CA      47B0 C0D4
  A0  0000F0      47B0 C0FA
  A0  000148      47B0 C152
  90  0001D2      47F0 C032
  90  000038      4740 C1D6
  80  0001E6      47F0 000E
REGS 0-7      F4F4F4F4   F4F4F4F4   F4F4F4F4   F4F4F4F4   F4F4F4F4   F4F4F4F4   F4F4F4F4   F4F4F4F4
REGS 8-15     F4F4F4F4   F4F4F4F4   F4F4F4F4   F4F4F4F4   F4F4F4F4   00000720   FFFE7960   00000000

FLTR 0-6      F4F4F4F4F4F4F4F4       F4F4F4F4F4F4F4F4       F4F4F4F4F4F4F4F4       F4F4F4F4F4F4F4F4
```

```
USER STORAGE

                         CORE ADDRESSES SPECIFIED-     000000 TO 000868
000000   90ECD00C 18CF41A0 C5F450AD 000850DA   000418DA E020C2D3 0085E020 C3580085   *........E4............BI....C...*
000020   E020C3DD 0085E020 C4620085 E020C4E7   0085E000 C63C0050 4740C1D6 9240C56C   *..C.....D.....DX....F.... AO. F.*
000040   D283C56D C56CF274 C690C63C F274C698   C6414130 C63C5930 C1F04720 C0809560   *K.F.F.2.F.F.2.F.F...F...AO......*
000060   30004780 C06E4130 300147F0 C056F870   C6A0C1F8 FB77C6A0 C690F877 C690C6A0   *...........0..8.F.A8..F.F.8.F.F.*
000080   4130C641 5930C1F4 4720C0AE 95603000   4780C09C 41303001 47F0C084 F870C6A0   *..F...A4................0..8.F.*
0000A0   C1F8FB77 C6A0C698 F877C698 C6A0F877   C6F8C690 FA73C6F8 C69CD20F C6A8C23E   *A8..F.F.8.F.F.8.F8F...F8F.K.F.B.*
0000C0   4110C6B7 DF0FC6A8 C6F847B0 C0D40610   92601000 F877C700 C690FB77 C700C698   *..F...F.F8...M......8.G.F...G.F.*
0000E0   D20FC6B8 C23E4110 C6C7DF0F C6B8C700   47B0C0FA 06109260 1000F877 C708C690   *K.F.B...FG..F.G..........8.G.F.*
000100   FC73C708 C69CD20F C6C8C23E 4110C6D7   DF0FC6C8 C70847B0 C1200610 92601000   *..G.F.K.FHB..;FP..FHG...A.......*
000120   F877C710 C690FD73 C710C69C F873C718   C714F873 C710C710 D20FC6E8 C23E4110   *8.G.F...G.F.8.G.G.8.G.G.K.FYB...*
000140   C6F7DF0F C6E8C718 47B0C152 06109260   1000D20F C6D8C23E 4110C6E7 DF0FC6D8   *F7..FYG...A.......K.FQB...FX..FQ*
000160   C71047B0 C16C0610 92601000 D204C595   C63CD204 C5B2C641 D20EC573 C1F9D20E   *G...A.......K.E.F.K.E.F.K.E.A9K.*
000180   C5BFC6A9 E020C56C 0085D20E C573C208   D20EC5BF C6B9E020 C56C0085 D20EC573   *E.F...E...K.E.B.K.E.F...E...K.E.*
0001A0   C217D20E C5BFC6C9 E020C56C 0085D20E   C573C226 D20EC5BF C6D9D208 C5D3C235   *B.K.E.FI..E...K.E.B.K.E.FRK.ELB.*
0001C0   D206C5DE C6F1E020 C56C0085 E020C3DD   008547F0 C032E020 C24E0085 58DD0004   *K.E.F1..F.....C....0....B.......*
0001E0   98ECD00C 1BFF47F0 000EF5F5 F5F5F5F5   00000640 00000645 0CC1C4C4 40404040   *.......0..555555... .....ADD    *
000200   40404040 40404040 E2E4C2E3 D9C1C3F3   40404040 404040D4 E4D3E3C9 D7D3E840   *         SUBTRACT       MULTIPLY *
000220   40404040 4040C4C9 E5C9C4C5 40404040   40404040 40D9C5D4 C1C9D5C4 C5D94020   *      DIVIDE          REMAINDER .*
000240   20202020 20202020 20202020 2120F140   40404040 40404040 40404040 40404040   *..............1                 *
000260   40404040 40404040 40404040 40404040   40404040 40404040 40404040 40404040   *                                *
  LINES    000280-0002A0      SAME AS ABOVE
0002C0   40404040 40404040 40404040 40404040   404040F1 D9C5D7D6 D9E34040 40404040   *                   1REPORT      *
0002E0   40404040 40404040 40404040 40404040   40404040 40404040 40404040 4040C140   *                              A *
000300   D940C940 E340C840 D440C540 E340C940   C3404040 D740D940 D640C340 C540E240   *R I T H M E T I C   P R O C E S *
000320   E240C940 D540C740 4040D940 C540D740   D640D940 E3404040 40404040 40404040   *S I N G   R E P O R T           *
000340   40404040 40404040 40404040 40404040   40404040 40404040 4040D5C1 D4C57A40   *                           NAME *
000360   40D4C1E3 C8404040 40404040 40404040   40404040 40404040 40404040 40404040   * MATH                           *
000380   40404040 40404040 40404040 40404040   C2C1E2C9 C3404040 D4C1E3C8 404040D6   *                BASIC   MATH   O*
0003A0   D7C5D9C1 E3C9D6D5 E2404040 40404040   40404040 40404040 40404040 40404040   *PERATIONS                       *
0003C0   40404040 40404040 40404040 40404040   40404040 40404040 40404040 40604040   *                                *
0003E0   40404040 40404040 40404040 40404040   40404040 40404040 40404040 40404040   *                                *
  LINES    000400-000440      SAME AS ABOVE
000460   40404060 60606060 40D6D7C5 D9C1E3C9   D6D54060 60606060 40404040 40404040   *   ..... OPERATION .....        *
000480   40606060 606040C6 C9D9E2E3 40E5C1D3   E4C54060 60606060 40404040 40406060   * ..... FIRST VALUE .....      ..*
0004A0   60606040 E2C5C3D6 D5C440E5 C1D3E4C5   40606060 60604040 40404060 60606060   *... SECOND VALUE .....     .....*
0004C0   60606060 60606060 606040D9 C5E2E4D3   E3406060 60606060 60606060 60606060   *.......... RESULT ..............*
0004E0   60404040 4040404E 6D6D6D6D 6D6D6D6D   6D6D6D6D 6D6D6D6D 6D6D6D6D 6D404040   *.       ....................    *
000500   40404040 40406D6D 6D6D6D6D 6D6D6D6D   6D6D6D6D 6D6D6D6D 6D6D6D6D 6D404040   *      ....................      *
000520   4040406D 6D6D6D6D 6D6D6D6D 6D6D6D6D   6D6D6D6D 6D6D6D6D 6D6D6D40 40404040   *   ....................         *
000540   6D6D6D6D 6D6D6D6D 6D6D6D6D 6D6D6D6D   6D6D6D6D 6D6D6D6D 6D6D6D6D 6D6D6D6D   *................................*
000560   6D6D6D6D 6D6D4040 40404040 40404040   404040C4 C9E5C9C4 C5404040 40404040   *......            DIVIDE        *
000580   40404040 40404040 40404040 40404040   40404040 404040F3 F7F04040 40404040   *                    370         *
0005A0   40404040 40404040 40404040 40404040   40404040 4060F940 40404040 40404040   *                    .9          *
0005C0   40404040 40404040 40404060 F4F14040   404040D9 C5D4C1C9 D5C4C5D9 40404040   *           .41   REMAINDER      *
0005E0   40404040 F1404040 40404040 40404040   40F5F5F5 F5F5F5F5 00000720 F5F5F5F5   *    1           5555555....5555*
000600   F5F5F5F5 F5F5F5F5 F5F5F5F5 F5F5F5F5   F5F5F5F5 F5F5F5F5 F5F5F5F5 F5F5F5F5   *55555555555555555555555555555555*
000620   F5F5F5F5 F5F5F5F5 F5F5F5F5 F5F5F5F5   F5F5F5F5 F5F5F5F5 F5F5F5F5 4040F3F7   *555555555555555555555555555555 37*
000640   F0404040 60F94040 40404040 40404040   40404040 40404040 40404040 40404040   *0   .9                          *
000660   40404040 40404040 40404040 40404040   40404040 40404040 40404040 40404040   *                                *
000680   40404040 F0F0F7F7 F7F04B40 F5F5F5F5   00000000 0000370F 00000000 0000009D   *    007770. 5555................*
0006A0   00000000 0000009D 40404040 40404040   40404040 40F3F6F1 40404040 40404040   *........          361           *
0006C0   40404040 40F3F7F9 40404040 40404040   40404060 F3F3F3F0 40404040 40404040   *     379         .3330          *
0006E0   40404040 4060F4F1 40404040 40404040   40404040 404040F1 00000000 0000361C   *     .41             1.........*
000700   00000000 0000379C 00000000 0003330D   00000000 0000041D 00000000 0000001C   *................................*
000720   F5F5F5F5 00000000 000005F4 FFFE7960   00000000 F4F4F4F4 F4F4F4F4 F4F4F4F4   *5555.......4........444444444444*
000740   F4F4F4F4 F4F4F4F4 F4F4F4F4 F4F4F4F4   F4F4F4F4 F4F4F4F4 F4F4F4F4 F4F4F4F4   *44444444444444444444444444444444*
000760   F4F4F4F4 F4F4F4F4 F5F5F5F5 F5F5F5F5   F5F5F5F5 F5F5F5F5 F5F5F5F5 F5F5F5F5   *44444444555555555555555555555555*
```

After extracting all information from the program dump, our worksheet may be filled out as shown in Fig. 8.43.

Although you may think that we've found the problem, we haven't. Yes, we did realize that the second operand was invalid, but we must now find out why. Where did the second operand's value come from and how did it get that way?

This is a rather difficult dump, but it is a common problem in assembly language. To answer this question, we must look at the source program itself. At offset 00000E, we find the ST instruction just as expected. Further, the second operand is an explicit address, 4(R10) (a displacement off from an *index* register). Hence, we must determine where R10's value came from and how it became invalid.

If we look at our complete program listing, we see that our program did process some data. Why then did we abend in our linkage section on *entry* to our program? You should begin to recognize a potential problem. First, the program produced output. This means that we correctly entered our program and processed before abending. According to the dump, we abended in the linkage convention code that *begins* our program. Hence, we must have branched back into this code from some other point in our program.

If we turn our attention to the tracing facilities of ASSIST, we see that the last instructions executed were at locations 1CC, 1D2, 32, 38, 1D6, 1DC, 1E0, 1E4, 1E6, and

```
                        DEBUGGING WORKSHEET

Abend code  0C4        PSW  FFC50004         80000012

Next instruction address      000012

Instruction length code             4

Entry point address          000000  (since we're in ASSIST)

             Next instruction address              000012
   minus     instruction length code               000004
             failing instruction address           00000E

             failing instruction address           00000E
   minus     entry point address                   000000
             source code instruction offset        00000E

Source code instruction                    ST   R13,4(R10)

First operand D(B)/D(X,B)                  register 13

Length of first operand (bytes)            4

Second operand D(B)/D(X,B)                 4(R10)

Length of second operand (bytes)           4

   first operand                                  second operand
   ___________  '--- base register value ---`      000000
   ___________  '-- index register value ---`      F4F4F4
   ___________  '------- displacement ------`          4
 +_____________                                 +__________

  _____________ '----- memory location -----`      F4F4F8

     00000720               value      value is outside program

Why did the program abend?  (comments)

The address into which we are storing the value of R13
is outside of our program area.  How could this happen?
```

Figure 8.43 Completed debugging worksheet for the dump in Example 8.1.

then the abend point of E. Hence, our program came from the instruction at location 1E6 before it abended. Figure 8.44 highlights this for us.

Looking back at the instruction at location 1E6 (as shown in Fig. 8.45), we see that it is our exit instruction. But it's not coded correctly. Instead of coding

```
BCR      B'1111',R14
```

we coded

```
BC       B'1111',R14
```

This caused our program to branch to location 14 in the computer and not to the address *contained* within register 14. Hence, when we branched back to location 14 (E), we began executing our program all over again from the middle of our linkage conven-

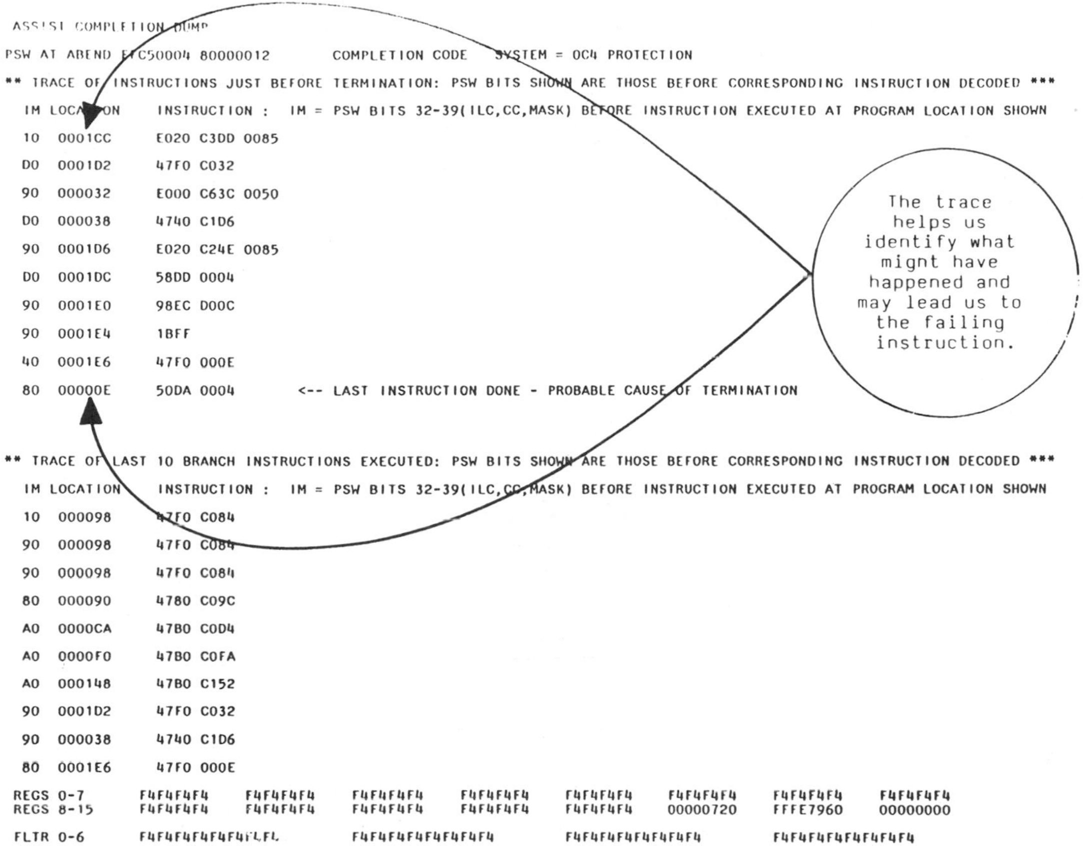

```
ASSIST COMPLETION DUMP
PSW AT ABEND FFC50004 80000012        COMPLETION CODE   SYSTEM = 0C4 PROTECTION
** TRACE OF INSTRUCTIONS JUST BEFORE TERMINATION: PSW BITS SHOWN ARE THOSE BEFORE CORRESPONDING INSTRUCTION DECODED ***
  IM LOCATION     INSTRUCTION :  IM = PSW BITS 32-39(ILC,CC,MASK) BEFORE INSTRUCTION EXECUTED AT PROGRAM LOCATION SHOWN
  10  0001CC      E020 C3DD 0085
  D0  0001D2      47F0 C032
  90  000032      E000 C63C 0050
  D0  000038      4740 C1D6
  90  0001D6      E020 C24E 0085
  D0  0001DC      58DD 0004
  90  0001E0      98EC D00C
  90  0001E4      1BFF
  40  0001E6      47F0 000E
  80  00000E      50DA 0004       <-- LAST INSTRUCTION DONE - PROBABLE CAUSE OF TERMINATION

** TRACE OF LAST 10 BRANCH INSTRUCTIONS EXECUTED: PSW BITS SHOWN ARE THOSE BEFORE CORRESPONDING INSTRUCTION DECODED ***
  IM LOCATION     INSTRUCTION :  IM = PSW BITS 32-39(ILC,CC,MASK) BEFORE INSTRUCTION EXECUTED AT PROGRAM LOCATION SHOWN
  10  000098      47F0 C084
  90  000098      47F0 C084
  90  000098      47F0 C084
  80  000090      4780 C09C
  A0  0000CA      47B0 C0D4
  A0  0000F0      47B0 C0FA
  A0  000148      47B0 C152
  90  0001D2      47F0 C032
  90  000038      4740 C1D6
  80  0001E6      47F0 000E
REGS 0-7     F4F4F4F4   F4F4F4F4   F4F4F4F4   F4F4F4F4   F4F4F4F4   F4F4F4F4   F4F4F4F4   F4F4F4F4
REGS 8-15    F4F4F4F4   F4F4F4F4   F4F4F4F4   F4F4F4F4   F4F4F4F4   00000720   FFFE7960   00000000

FLTR 0-6     F4F4F4F4F4F4F4F4      F4F4F4F4F4F4F4F4      F4F4F4F4F4F4F4F4      F4F4F4F4F4F4F4F4
```


Figure 8.44 ASSIST traces the last 10 instructions executed.

tions. Therefore, we'll fix the branch instruction to BCR and rerun our program to see if it will now work correctly.

Incidentally, the value of R10 was X'F4F4F4F4'. You should remember this value when programming in ASSIST since ASSIST sets most registers to this value when your program *begins* execution. You can then determine which registers have been altered by your processing by simply looking at their values. If a register's value is not X'F4F4F4F4', then you know that you used or changed its value. If it's still X'F4F4F4F4', then it *probably* has not been used. Further, ASSIST initializes all storage to X'F5'. You can use this indicator to determine if you've correctly modified or processed a storage area when looking at a dump.

This example clearly illustrates that finding the point of abend does not necessarily point you directly to the problem. Additionally, it clearly illustrates the power of tracing facilities. Without the instruction trace, we would have had more difficulty in finding the problem within this program.

Most of the time, the process of finding the point of failure and identifying why the program fails is relatively straightforward. The process of analyzing why a particular data element or register became bad requires yet another level of experience. Again, through practice, you will be able to debug your programs remarkably fast. Don't be

```
COMPUTE SUM, DIFFERENCE, PRODUCT, QUOTIENT OF 2 VALUES                                          PAGE    6

  LOC  OBJECT CODE     ADDR1 ADDR2  STMT   SOURCE STATEMENT
```

```
                                     182 ********************************************************************** 007090.
                                     183 *      WE'RE ALL DONE.  PAGE EJECT BEFORE ENDING SO THAT OUR REPORT   * 007100.
                                     184 *      LOOKS NICE.  SET THE RETURN CODE AND THEN EXIT.                * 007110.
                                     185 ********************************************************************** 007120.
0001D6 E020 C24E 0085 0024E          186 EOF      XPRNT NEWPAGE,133                                            007130.
0001DC 58DD 0004           00004     187          L     R13,4(R13)         RESTORE ORIGINAL R13 VALUE          007140.
0001E0 98EC D00C           0000C     188          LM    R14,R12,12(R13)    RESTORE ALL REGS                    007150.
0001E4 1BFF                          189          SR    R15,R15            SET RETURN CODE TO ZERO             007160.
0001E6 47F0 000E           0000E     190          BC    B'1111',R14        RETURN CONTROL TO CALLER            007170.
                                     191 *                                                                     007180.
                                     192          LTORG                                                        007190.
0001F0 00000640                      193                =A(NUM1+4)
0001F4 00000645                      194                =A(NUM2+4)
0001F8 0C                            195                =P'0'
0001F9 C1C4C4404040404040            196                =CL15'ADD'
000208 E2E4C2E3D9C1C3E3              197                =CL15'SUBTRACT'
000217 D4E4D3E3C9D7D3E8              198                =CL15'MULTIPLY'
000226 C4C9E5C9C4C54040              199                =CL15'DIVIDE'
000235 D9C5D4C1C9D5C4C5              200                =C'REMAINDER'
```


Figure 8.45 Finding the source instruction that failed.

afraid to read a dump. Use the suggested worksheet as an aid. Work backwards through your program to determine why a field became bad.

The debugging technique that we just discussed works for both ASSIST and assembly language program debugging if you've built tracing or debugging features into your program since they are not provided automatically. As you've seen, the primary difference between debugging in the two processors is the amount of excess information that the operating system gives you and the tracing facilities provided by ASSIST.

Before we look at the next debugging example in assembler, let's discuss another debugging hint. If your program fails with a S322 (time-out, infinite loop) or a S0C4 (protection exception), look carefully at the PSW. If the PSW has a location that is outside the bounds of your program or if it appears that you're going back through your program again and again, look for an improper return to the operating system. One of the most common mistakes attempts to return control by issuing the instruction given in Fig. 8.46.

```
This does not work.
___________________

BC    B'1111',R14
```

Figure 8.46 Incorrect method of returning control to the operating system.

Although it appears correct, the mnemonic is not. As you've seen, you are attempting to return control to location 14 in the computer and not to the location *in* register 14. The mnemonic should have been coded BCR instead of BC. In general, any PSW address less than X'001000' (in *assembler*) is regarded as invalid and you should immediately look at register 14's value to help determine where the problem might be.

On the other hand, ASSIST begins your program at address 000000. A location less than X'001000' is normal in ASSIST and this general rule does not apply. For this reason, the START instruction is a useful feature when using ASSIST. With it, you can begin an ASSIST program at a higher address. Therefore, if the program branches to a location less than this address, you'll know immediately that it's branching outside its bounds.

The START instruction replaces the CSECT instruction as we discussed in Chapter 3. Any location higher than X'001000' should be sufficient to recognize such a wild branch. If we code the instruction shown in Fig. 8.47, our program begins at location 1000.

```
PROCESS  START  X'001000'
```

Figure 8.47 Altering the starting location of a program using START.

This starting address allows easy reference to offsets or displacements within our code since the last three digits of the ending address are zero. It also allows us to immediately recognize wild branches if our program attempts to return to process at location 14 in the computer.

Additionally, register 14 helps in other abends, especially in assembler (not ASSIST). Register 14 is one of the primary registers that communicates with the operating system file access routines. It is also used as a **return address** into your program when an operating system module is called to perform a function. A GET or PUT instruction that fails can be easily found by looking at the contents of register 14. In other words, if the next instruction address in the PSW does not point to an address within your program, look at the contents of R14. It should address an instruction within your program and, in fact, it should address the instruction immediately following the failing instruction. If R14 doesn't point to an address within your program, good luck!

The next program, as shown in Example 8.2, has also failed, but this time an 0C7 (data exception) abend code is given. Looking at *selected* pages from the dump, we can fill in our worksheet as shown in Fig. 8.48.

At this point, we return to the assembly language source program to find the instruction at location E8. As you can see, I've removed many of the unnecessary pages within a typical operating system dump and within the source listing. Looking just at selected pages, we find our instruction as shown in Fig. 8.49 and can complete our worksheet as shown in Fig. 8.50.

This program failed because the second operand was not valid. The ZAP instruction requires the second operand (not the first) to be a valid packed-decimal field. Since it wasn't, a data exception (bad data) abend occurred. Although we've found the problem, we're not done. Why was the value of VALUE1 invalid? If we step back through our program, we see that VALUE1 came from an input record that was obtained through a GET instruction (statement number 78). Figure 8.51 highlights this for us.

Since VALUE1 obtained its value from the PACK instruction in line 85, we have now identified the potential problem as being the value of NUM1. Let's now find NUM1 in memory.

```
JOB MADISON          STEP GO              TIME 223753   DATE 85317    ID = 000    CPUID = 000100793033          PAGE 0001

COMPLETION CODE      SYSTEM = 0C7

PSW AT ENTRY TO ABEND  078D2000 0011C0FE          ILC 6    INIC 0007

ASCB 00FE4948
      +0    ASCB  C1E2C3C2   IWDP  00F830C0   BWDP  00F8B018   CMSF  00000000   SVRB  0080D248   SYNC  0046300C
      +18   IOSP  00000000   TNEW  007B2038   CPUS  00000001   IDSQ  000C0011   IODP  00000105   RESV  00000000
      +30   LDA   0080F548   RSM   00FE4538   CSCB  00FD2320   TSB   00000000   EJST  00000000   XJST  0DD2E000
      +48   EWST  9A082C35   XWST  19D87000   JSTL  00000001   ECB   8080D7E0   UBET  9A082B0C   TLCH  00000000
      +60   DUMP  0080CD90   FW1   FFFF0000   TMCH  00000000   ASXB  0080F300   FW2   D9600000   SRBS  00000000
      +78   VSC   0002002E   RCTP  0080DA68   LOCK  00000000   LSQH  00000000   QECB  00000000   MECB  40000000
      +90   OUCB  00FE4690   OUXB  00FD1DB8   FMCT  005C0000   XMPQ  00000000   IQEA  00000000   RTMC  00000000
      +A8   MCC   00000000   JBNI  00F852C0   JBNS  00FD2330   SRQ   00000000   VGTT  00000000   PCTT  00000000
      +C0   SMCT  00000007   SWTL  0000035A   SRBT  00000000   ATME  00668000   LSMQ  00000000   LSPL  00000000
      +D8   TCBS  00000001   TCBL  00000000   WPRB  0080EA08   SRDP  05FFFF00   LOCI  00000000   CMLH  00000000
      +F0   CMLC  00000000   SSOM  00000000   ASTE  00FC90C0   LTOV  0080A000   ATOV  0080CC50   ETC   00000000
      +108  LXR   00000000   STKH  0080EA18   GQEL  00000000   LQEL  002D22F0   GSYN  00000000   XTCB  007B2038
      +120  FW3   00000000   GXL   00000000   EATT  00000000   EAT1  B1D2B007   INTS  9A082C32   INT1  62713000
      +138  FW4   00000000   RCMS  00000000   IOSC  00000006   PKXC  000001F4   NSQA  00000000   ASM   00FE4568
      +150  RESV  00000000   TCME  00000000

*** ADDRESS SPACE SWITCH EVENT MASK OFF (ASTESSEM = 0) ***

TCB  7B2038
      +0    RBP   0080D158   PIE    00000000   DEB  007CE608   TIO 00795000   CMP   900C7000   TRN  00000000
      +18   MSS   007B74B0   PK-FLG 80010000   FLG  0000FFFF   LLS 007AF000   JLB   00000000   JPQ  00793000
      +70   FSA   00114FB0   TCB    00000000   TME  00000000   JST 007B2038   NIC   00000000   OTC  007FAEA8
      +88   LTC   00000000   IQE    00000000   ECB  0078CB94   TSF 20000000   D-PQE 0080F548   AQE  007C0900
      +A0   STAB  0080C7D0   TCT    807DD0A0   USER 00000000  SDF 00000000   MDID  00000000   JSCB 007D8C74
      +B8   RESV  00022D78   IOBRC  00000000   XCPD 00000000  EXT 00000000   BITS  00000000   DAR  00000000
      +D0   EXT2  007B2170   AECB   00000000   XSB  0080D228   BCK 007FAEA8   RTMWA 0078A2A8   NSSP 00000000
      +E8   TMSAV 00000000   ABCR   00000000   XSCT 80000040  FOE 00000000   SWA   007FAB00   STAW 00000000
      +100  BID   E3C3C240   RTM1   00000000   ESTA 00000000  UKY 007D5CF0   SQAF  0005FFFF   BYT1 08040000
      +118  RPT   00000000   DBTB   00000000   SWAS 00809F50  SCB 00000000
      EXT2  GTF   00000000   SVAB   00000000   EVNT 00000000  RTM 00000000   TQE   00000000   CAUF 00000000
            PERCP 80000000   PERCT  00000000


ACTIVE RBS

PRB  78E318   XSB   0078E380   RESV 00000000   RTPSW1 078D2000   0011C0FE   RTPSW2 00060007   0034C000
              FLG1  00000000   WC-L-IC 00060007
              RESV  00000000   APSW    00000000   SZ-STAB 00110082       FL-CDE 0079D4D8   PSW 078D2000   0011C0FE
              Q/TTR 00000000   WT-LNK  007B2038
              RG 0-7   0080C010   00114FF8   00000040   007FD474   007FD450   007FAEA8   00794FF8   FD000000
              RG 8-15  0078CB70   807DD0A0   00000000   0080C4A8   50D7BAD2   00114FB0   40D7BE6C   0078CBA0

XSB AT 0078E380
      +0    XSB   E7E2C240   LINK   00000000   KM   0080   SASID  000C   AX   0000   PASID  000C   XLSRB  00000000
      +14   XLAS  00000000   TKN    0000       ASD  0000   SEL    00000000

SVRB 80D040   XSB   0080D110   RESV 00000000   RTPSW1 00000000   00000000   RTPSW2 00000000   00000000
```

Example 8.2 Selected pages from an assembler program dump.

```
JOB MADISON          STEP GO            TIME 223753   DATE 85317    ID = 000                    PAGE 0002

            FLG1   20000000   WC-L-IC 00020033
            RESV   00000000   APSW     00000000   SZ-STAB 001ED022     FL-CDE 00000000   PSW 070C1000     00CE7D60
            Q/TTR  00000000   WT-LNK   0078E318
            RG 0-7    0011C6C4   0011C6C4   00000040   0011C6CE   00114FFE   00000000   00000000   00000000
            RG 8-15   0078CB70   80115EE4   0011C67C   0080C4A8   0011C010   0011C67C   4011C086   12E5D9C6
            EXTSA     0011C6C4   0011C6C4   00022F58   007B2038   0080D040   00FE4948   0004F828   00FD4874
                      0078A2A8   FF0004D4   40000101   900C7000
            SCB       00000000   00000000   1580D040   0380D040   2400DB00   XPTR     0080D100
            FEPARM    00000000   80E1D844   00000000   00000884   0004F828   00000000
            SCBX      00000000   00000000

XSB AT 0080D110
      +0    XSB    E7E2C240   LINK   00000000   KM   0000   SASID   000C   AX   0000   PASID   000C   XLSRB   00000000
      +14   XLAS   00000000   TKN    0000       ASD  0000   SEL     00000000

SVRB 80D158   XSB   0080D228   RESV 00000000   RTPSW1 00000000    00000000   RTPSW2 00000000    00000000
            FLG1   02000000   WC-L-IC 0002000C
            RESV   00000000   APSW     00000000   SZ-STAB 001ED022     FL-CDE 00000000   PSW 070C1000     00C9210A
            Q/TTR  00000000   WT-LNK   0080D040
            RG 0-7    000001A0   0078A3A8   00795028   0078DEC0   0078A3A8   00CE8019   50CE701A   0078A2A8
            RG 8-15   0078DE68   00000000   00CE83B0   0078A3A8   007AB2B0   0078A41C   00FE01D4   00000000
            EXTSA     00000000   00.8BBC0   00000440   0080D1BC   20FD0000   000000C0   00000000   00000000
                      00000000   00000000   00000000   00000000
            SCB       00000000   00000000   16FE62C8   0380D158   6400DB00   XPTR     0080D218
            FEPARM    00000000   80E1D844   80E1D864   00000884   0004F828   00000000
            SCBX      00000000   00000000

XSB AT 0080D228
      +0    XSB    E7E2C240   LINK   00000000   KM   0000   SASID   000C   AX   0000   PASID   000C   XLSRB   00000000
      +14   XLAS   00000000   TKN    0000       ASD  0000   SEL     00000000

LOAD LIST

      NE 007D5F68   RSP-CDE 00FB1940   CNT 00010001          NE 007D5F98   RSP-CDE 00FB1B50   CNT 00010001
      NE 007FA000   RSP-CDE 00FDD490   CNT 00020002          NE 00000000   RSP-CDE 00793000   CNT 00010000

CDE

    79D4D8      NCDE 00000000   RBP 0078E318 NM ISUILOADR   EPA 00115E78   XL/MJ 0080C000   USE 000100FB   ATTR 0B22000
    FB1940      NCDE 00FDD490   RBP 00000000 NM IGG019DK    EPA 00AFF850   XL/MJ 00FB1960   USE 00020000   ATTR B922000
    FB1B50      NCDE 00FB1940   RBP 00000000 NM IGG019AQ    EPA 00ADEDC0   XL/MJ 00FB1B70   USE 00020000   ATTR B922000
    FDD490      NCDE 00FDD3A0   RBP 00000000 NM IGG019DJ    EPA 00E5D968   XL/MJ 00FDD4B0   USE 001A0000   ATTR B922000
    793000      NCDE 0079D4D8   RBP 00000000 NM **GO        EPA 0011C010   XL/MJ 00793020   USE 00010000   ATTR 01A0000

XL                                             LN         ADR        LN         ADR        LN         ADR

    80C000   SZ 00000010   NO 00000001        80000188   00115E78
    FB1960   SZ 00000010   NO 00000001        800007B0   00AFF850
    FB1B70   SZ 00000010   NO 00000001        80000240   00ADEDC0
    FDD4B0   SZ 00000010   NO 00000001        80000698   00E5D968
    793020   SZ 00000010   NO 00000001        80000868   0011C000

TIOT   795000       JOB   MADISON    STEP   GO
```

```
JOB MADISON          STEP GO              TIME 223753   DATE 85317    ID = 000                        PAGE 0008

+8      ALLOW ASYNCHRONOUS INTERRUPTS
        BYPASS I/O INTERVENTION
        ESTAE INDICATOR ON
+C      USER IN KEY 0 7
        USER IN SUPERVISOR STATE


SAVE AREA TRACE

ISULOADR WAS ENTERED VIA LINK

**GO     WAS ENTERED VIA CALL

IGG019DJ WAS ENTERED VIA CALL        AT EP 05..05..01..05..05..05.........................K......................

INTERRUPT AT 11C0FE

PROCEEDING BACK VIA REG 13

IGG019DJ WAS ENTERED VIA CALL        AT EP 05..05..01..05..05..05.........................K......................

**GO     WAS ENTERED VIA CALL

VSAM TCBVAT  7B2154 000004

7B2140                                             00000000                  *                  ....      *

NO VSAM VGTT CHAIN PRESENT FOR THIS ASCB

NO VSAM VSI CHAIN PRESENT

END OF VSAM DATA


REGS AT ENTRY TO ABEND

     FLTR 0-6      0000000000000000     0000000000000000             0000000000000000     0000000000000000

     REGS 0-7      0011C6C4   0011C6C4  00000040   0011C6CE          00114FFE   00000000  00000000   00000000
     REGS 8-15     0078CB70   80115EE4  0011C67C   0080C4A8          0011C010   0011C67C  4011C086   12E5D9C6

ACTIVE LOAD MODULES

JPA MODULE          ISULOADR
115E60                                                               90ECD00C 18AF50D0    *                        ........*
115E80    A08041C0 A07C50CD 000818DC 18315843     00004144 00001B55 48540000 1B774100    *................................*
115EA0    A02E47F0 A036C8C5 E6D3D6C1 C4401B11     0A0818F0 4590A0E4 181305EF 42F0A0D4    *...0..HEWLOAD .....0...U.....0.M*
115EC0    9504A0D4 4720A06C D207A0DC 10004500     A062C8C5 E6D3D6C1 C4400A09 4590A0EE    *...M....K.........HEWLOAD ......*
```

```
JOB MADISON          STEP GO                TIME 223753   DATE 65317    ID = 000                             PAGE 0009

115EE0   4590A0C4 58D0A080 58ED000C 980CD014    07FE0358 00FB5CA8 00114FB0 0011C67C   *...D..........................F.*
115F00   40115F4A 0011C010 0011C010 00114FF8    00000040 00114FF8 00114FFE 00000000   * ..............8... ...8........*
115F20   00000000 00000000 0078CB70 80115EE4    00115E78 0080C4A8 00115EF4 4100A0DC   *...............U......D....4....*
115F40   1B110A08 18F01813 05EF07F9 0000D200    40024001 5C5CC7D6 40404040 9200A14A   *.....0.....9..K. . ...GO    ....*
115F60   12774780 A11A4177 00021B57 125547B0    A1001B55 47F0A116 D201A0DA A1804A70   *.......................0..K.......*
115F80   A0DA4070 A0DA4450 A0D64155 00014054    00001874 18651255 4780A146 95617002   *.. ......0... ...................*
115FA0   4770A13E 1B744074 00001277 4780A148    92FFA14A 07F94177 00014660 A1241B74   *...... ...............9..........*
115FC0   07F90040 40404040 40404040 40404040    40404040 40404040 40404040 40404040   *.9.                             *
115FE0   40404040 40404040 40404040 40404040    40404040 40F6D3E2 4001D5A0 00000000   *                        6LS .N.....*

JPA MODULE          **GO
11C000   5C5CC7D6 40404040 00000000 00000000    90ECD00C 18CF41A0 C66C50AD 000850DA   *..GO    ...............F.......*
11C020   000418DA 4510C020 0011C7A8 8F11C808    0A134110 C7F84100 C34B58F0 103005EF   *..........G...H.....G8..C..0....*
11C040   4110C7F8 4100C3D0 58F01030 05EF4110    C7F84100 C45558F0 103005EF 4110C7F8   *..G8..C..0......G8..D..0......G8*
11C060   4100C4DA 58F01030 05EF4110 C7F84100    C55F58F0 103005EF 4110C798 4100C6B4   *..D..0......G8..E..0......G...F.*
11C080   58F01030 05EF9240 C5E4D283 C5E5C5E4    F274C708 C6B4F274 C710C6B9 4130C6B4   *.0..... EUK.EVEU2.G.F.2.G.F...F.*
11C0A0   5930C268 4720C0BA 95603000 4780C0A8    41303001 47F0C090 F870C718 C270FB77   *..B..................0..8.G.B...*
11C0C0   C718C708 F877C708 C7184130 C6B95930    C26C4720 C0E89560 30004780 C0D64130   *G.G.8.G.G...F...B....Y.......0..*
11C0E0   300147F0 C0BEF870 C718C270 FB77C718    C710F877 C710C718 F877C770 C708A73    *...0..8.G.B...G.G.8.G.G.8.G.G...*
11C100   C770C714 D20FC720 C2B64110 C72FDFDF    C720C770 47B0C10E 06109260 1000F877   *G.G.K.G.B...G...G.G...A.......8.*
11C120   C778C708 FB77C778 C710D20F C730C2B6    4110C73F DF0FC730 C77847B0 C1340610   *G.G...G.G.K.G.B...G...G.G...A...*
11C140   92601000 F877C780 C708FC73 C780C714    D20FC740 C2B64110 C74FDF0F C740C780   *....8.G.G...G.G.K.G B...G...G G.*
11C160   47B0C15A 06109260 1000F877 C788C708    FD73C788 C714F873 C790C78C F873C788   *..A.......8.G.G...G.G.8.G.G.8.G.*
11C180   C788D20F C760C2B6 4110C76F DF0FC760    C79047B0 C18C0610 92601000 D20FC750   *G.K.G.B...G...G.G...A.......K.G.*
11C1A0   C2B64110 C75FDF0F C750C788 47B0C1A6    06109260 1000D204 C60DC6B4 D204C62A   *B...G...G.G...A.......K.F.F.K.F.*
11C1C0   C6B9D20E C5EBC271 D20EC637 C7214110    C7F84100 C5E458F0 103005EF D20EC5EB   *F.K.E.B.K.F.G...G8..EU.0....K.E.*
11C1E0   C280D20E C637C731 4110C7F8 4100C5E4    58F01030 05EFD20E C5EBC28F D20EC637   *B.K.F.G...G8..EU.0....K.E.B.K.F.*
11C200   C7414110 C7F84100 C5E458F0 103005EF    D20EC5EB C29ED20E C637C751 D208C64B   *G...G8  EU.0....K.E.B.K.F.G.K.F.*
11C220   C2ADD206 C656C769 4110C7F8 4100C5E4    58F01030 05EF4110 C7F84100 C45558F0   *B.K.F.G...G8..EU.0......G8..D..0*
11C240   103005EF 47F0C068 4110C7F8 4100C2C6    58F01030 05EF0700 4510C254 0011C7A8   *.....0....G8..BF.0........B...G.*
11C260   8011C808 0A1458DD 000498EC D00C1BFF    07FE0000 00000000 0011C6C8 0011C6CD   *..H.......................FH..F.*
11C280   0CC1C4C4 40404040 40404040 40404040    E2E4C2E3 D9C1C3E3 40404040 404040D4   *.ADD                SUBTRACT   M*
11C2A0   E4D3E3C9 D7D3E840 40404040 4040C4C9    E5C9C4C5 40404040 40404040 40D9C5D4   *ULTIPLY         DIVIDE       REM*
11C2C0   C1C9D5C4 C5D94020 20202020 20202020    20202020 2120F140 40404040 40404040   *AINDER ...............1         *
11C2E0   40404040 40404040 40404040 40404040    40404040 40404040 40404040 40404040   *                                *
     LINES 11C300-11C320 SAME AS ABOVE
11C340   40404040 40404040 40404040 40404040    40404040 40404040 404040F1 D9C5D7D6   *                           1REPO*
11C360   D9E34040 40404040 40404040 40404040    40404040 40404040 40404040 40404040   *RT                              *
11C380   40404040 4040C140 D940C940 E340C840    D440C540 E340C940 C3404040 D740D940   *      A R I T H M E T I C   P R *
11C3A0   D640C340 C540E240 E240C940 D540C740    4040D940 C540D740 D640D940 E3404040   *O C E S S I N G   R E P O R T   *
11C3C0   40404040 40404040 40404040 40404040    40404040 40404040 40404040 40404040   *                                *
11C3E0   4040D5C1 D4C57A40 40D4C1E3 C8404040    40404040 40404040 40404040 40404040   *  NAME.  MATH                   *
11C400   40404040 40404040 40404040 40404040    40404040 40404040 C2C1E2C9 C3404040   *                         BASIC  *
11C420   D4C1E3C8 404040D6 D7C5D9C1 E3C9D6D5    E2404040 40404040 40404040 40404040   *MATH   OPERATIONS               *
11C440   40404040 40404040 40404040 40404040    40404040 40404040 40404040 40404040   *                                *
11C460   40404040 40604040 40404040 40404040    40404040 40404040 40404040 40404040   *                                *
11C480   40404040 40404040 40404040 40404040    40404040 40404040 40404040 40404040   *                                *
     LINES 11C4A0-11C4C0 SAME AS ABOVE
11C4E0   40404040 40404040 40404060 60606060    40D6D7C5 D9C1E3C9 D6D54060 60606060   *               ..... OPERATION .....*
11C500   40404040 40404040 40606060 606040C6    C9D9E2E3 40E5C1D3 E4C54060 60606060   *             ..... FIRST VALUE .....*
11C520   40404040 40406060 60606040 E2C5C3D6    D5C440E5 C1D3E4C5 40606060 60604040   *          ..... SECOND VALUE .....  *
11C540   40404060 60606060 60606060 60606060    606040D9 C5E2E4D3 E3406060 60606060   *     ............... RESULT ......*
11C560   60606060 60606060 60404040 4040404E    6D6D6D6D 6D6D6D6D 6D6D6D6D 6D6D6D6D   *.........      .................*
11C580   6D6D6D6D 6D404040 40404040 40406D6D    6D6D6D6D 6D6D6D6D 6D6D6D6D 6D6D6D6D   *.....      ......................*
11C5A0   6D6D6D6D 6D404040 4040406D 6D6D6D6D    6D6D6D6D 6D6D6D6D 6D6D6D6D 6D6D6D6D   *.....   .........................*
11C5C0   6D6D6D40 40404040 6D6D6D6D 6D6D6D6D    6D6D6D6D 6D6D6D6D 6D6D6D6D 6D6D6D6D   *...     ..........................*
```

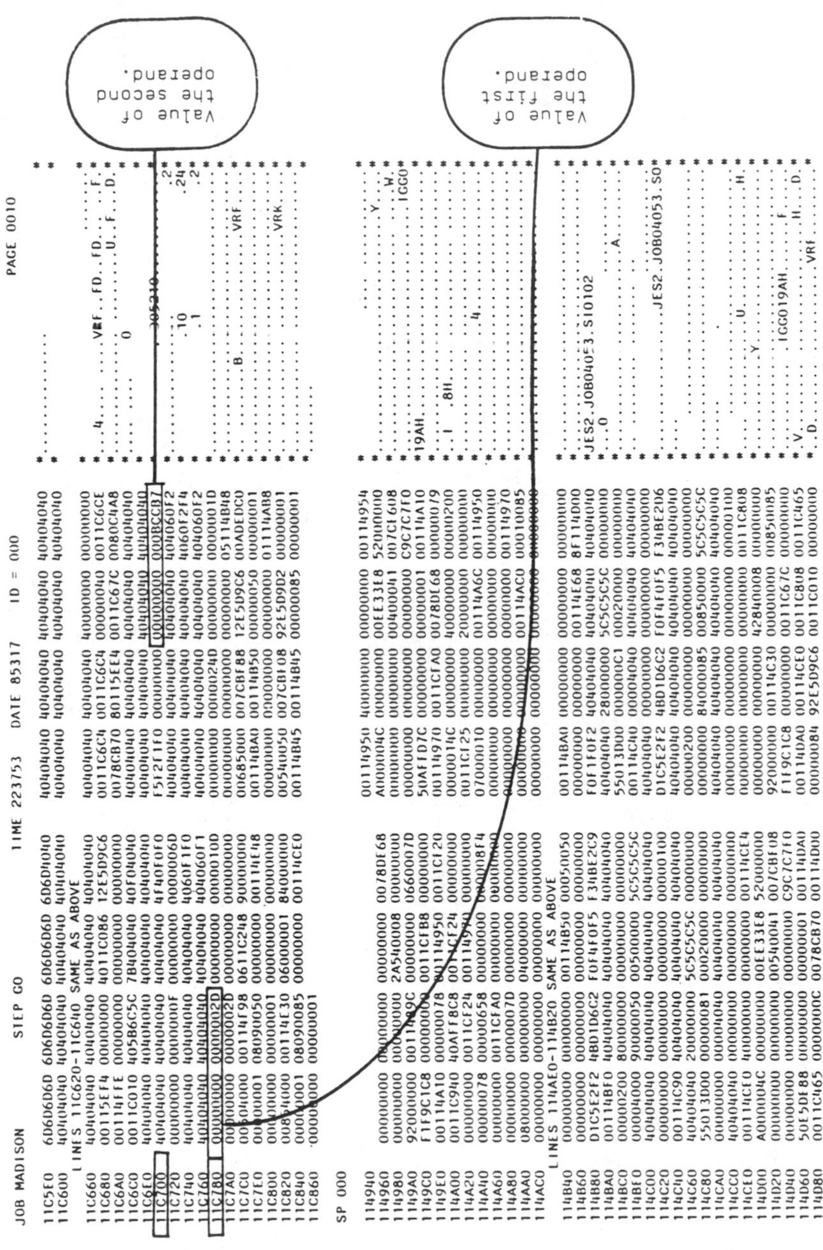
Value of the second operand.
Value of the first operand.

```
                         DEBUGGING WORKSHEET

Abend code____0C7_____   PSW___078D2000______   ____0011C0FE________

Next instruction address ___________11C0FE___________________________

Instruction length code ______________6______________________________

Entry point address _____________11C010______________________________


            Next instruction address    ______________11C0FE_________
   minus    instruction length code     _________________6___________
   ---------failing instruction address ______________11C0F8_________


            failing instruction address ______________11C0F8_________
   minus    entry point address         ______________11C010_________
   ---------source code instruction offset _____________E8___________

Source code instruction _____________________________________________

First operand D(B)/D(X,B) ___________________________________________

Length of first operand (bytes) _____________________________________

Second operand D(B)/D(X,B) __________________________________________

Length of second operand (bytes) ____________________________________

   first operand                                     second operand
   ___________ '--- base register value ---` ___________
   ___________ '-- index register value ---` ___________
   ___________ '------- displacement ------` ___________
 +_____________                            +_____________

 _____________'----- memory location -----`_____________

 ______________________      value      ______________________

Why did the program abend? (comments)
```

Figure 8.48 Partially completed debugging worksheet for Example 8.2.

NUM1's reference in the PACK instruction on line 85 indicates that it is at location 6B4 off from register 12. Adding register 12's value and X'0006B4', we obtain memory location X'01C6C4'. Referring to our dump, we find that the five-byte field called NUM1 has the value X'405B6C5C7B' or a character value of C'b$%*#'. Clearly, this is not a valid number.

If we refer to the output of our program (see Fig. 8.52), we see that two sets of numbers have already been processed and their results printed on the printer. This leads us to assume that the third input data card is invalid.

We must now return to our input data cards and correct card three's first value so that it is a valid numeric field.

We could go on, but at this point I'm going to leave the rest of the program debugging up to you. Hopefully, you've gained some insight into the various problems that can occur during program development as you've seen a few debugging techniques. Regardless of the technique or strategy used, the more assistance that you can provide yourself through messages and dumps of intermediate storage, the faster and more accurately you'll find and resolve the problem(s) in your failing program.

```
     COMPUTE SUM, DIFFERENCE, PRODUCT, QUOTIENT OF ? VALUES                                                    PAGE    5

   LOC  OBJECT CODE    ADDR1 ADDR2  STMT   SOURCE STATEMENT                                        ASM H V 02 22.37 11/13/85

                                     118 **********************************************************************  | 003540
                                     119 *        COMPUTE THE SUM AND CONVERT IT FOR OUTPUT PRINTING.            *  | 003550
                                     120 **********************************************************************  | 003560
0000E8 F877 C770 C708 00770 00708    121          ZAP   SUMP(8),VALUE1(8)       COMPUTE THE SUM                  | 003570
0000EE FA73 C770 C714 00770 00714    122          AP    SUMP(8),VALUE2+4(4)     ...JUST A DIFFERENT FORMAT       | 003580
0000F4 D20F C720 C2B6 00720 002B6    123          MVC   SUM(16),PATTERN         MOVE IN EDIT PATTERN             | 003590
0000FA 4110 C72F            0072F    124          LA    R1,SUM+15               POINT TO LAST DIGIT POSITION     | 003600
0000FE DF0F C720 C770 00720 00770    125          EDMK  SUM(16),SUMP            EDIT THE SUM VALUE               | 003610
000104 47B0 C10E            0010E    126          BNM   SUMPOS                  IF NOT < 0, DON'T MOVE IN SIGN   | 003620
000108 0610                          127          BCTR  R1,0                    BACK UP ONE POSITION             | 003630
00010A 9260 1000      00000          128          MVI   0(R1),C'-'              MOVE IN NEGATIVE SIGN            | 003640
00010E                               129 SUMPOS   DS    0H                      SKIP NEGATIVE MOVE IF POSITIVE   | 003650
                                     130 **********************************************************************  | 003660
                                     131 *        COMPUTE THE DIFFERENCE BETWEEN THE NUMBERS AND PREPARE         *  | 003670
                                     132 *        TO BE PRINTED.                                                 *  | 003680
                                     133 **********************************************************************  | 003690
00010E F877 C778 C708 00778 00708    134          ZAP   DIFFERP(8),VALUE1(8)    RESTORE BINARY VALUES IN REGS.   | 003700
000114 FB77 C778 C710 00778 00710    135          SP    DIFFERP(8),VALUE2(8)    COMPUTE DIFFERENCE               | 003710
00011A D20F C730 C2B6 00730 002B6    136          MVC   DIFFER(16),PATTERN      MOVE IN THE EDIT PATTERN         | 003720
000120 4110 C73F            0073F    137          LA    R1,DIFFER+15            POINT TO LAST DIGIT POSITION     | 003730
000124 DF0F C730 C778 00730 00778    138          EDMK  DIFFER(16),DIFFERP      CONVERT TO DISPLAY               | 003740
00012A 47B0 C134            00134    139          BNM   DIFFPOS                 IF NOT < 0, DON'T MOVE IN SIGN   | 003750
00012E 0610                          140          BCTR  R1,0                    BACK UP ONE POSITION             | 003760
000130 9260 1000      00000          141          MVI   0(R1),C'-'              MOVE IN NEGATIVE SIGN            | 003770
000134                               142 DIFFPOS  DS    0H                      SKIP NEGATIVE MOVE IF POSITIVE   | 003780
```

The instruction causing the abend is at offset E8 in the program. As you can see, the instruction is a ZAP.

Figure 8.49 Locating the failing instruction in the source program.

```
                         DEBUGGING WORKSHEET

Abend code____0C7_____   PSW___078D2000______   ____0011C0FE______

Next instruction address  ___________11C0FE____________________

Instruction length code  ________________6_____________________

Entry point address  ________________11C010____________________

                  Next instruction address  ____________11C0FE___
         minus    instruction length code                     6
                  failing instruction address  _________11C0F8___

                  failing instruction address  _________11C0F8___
         minus    entry point address                    11C010
                  source code instruction offset  _________E8____

Source code instruction  ______ZAP   SUMP(8),VALUE1(8)__________

First operand D(B)/D(X,B)  ___________770(8,12)_________________

Length of first operand (bytes)  _______8_______________________

Second operand D(B)/D(X,B)  __________708(8,12)_________________

Length of second operand (bytes)  ______8_______________________

   first operand                                 second operand
  ___11C010___  '--- base register value ---`   ___11C010___
  ____________  '-- index register value ---`   ____________
  _____770____  '------- displacement ------`   _____708____
 +_____________                                +_____________

  ___11C780____'----- memory location -----`____11C718______

 ___NOT RELEVANT______       value        ____00000000000BCCB7_

Why did the program abend?  (comments)

  The first operand is not relevant since a ZAP instruction
  is being executed.  However, the second operand is not a
  valid packed decimal field...hence, the abend!
```

Figure 8.50 Completed debugging worksheet for Example 8.2.

```
COMPUTE SUM, DIFFERENCE, PRODUCT, QUOTIENT OF 2 VALUES                                                       PAGE    4

  LOC  OBJECT CODE     ADDR1 ADDR2  STMT   SOURCE STATEMENT                                       ASM H V 02 22.37 11/13/85

                                      73 ********************************************************************** | 003130
                                      74 *  OBTAIN THE INPUT VALUES FROM OUR FILE AND CONVERT THEM INTO         * | 003140
                                      75 *  BINARY FORMAT FOR PROCESSING.                                      * | 003150
                                      76 ********************************************************************** | 003160
000068                                77 CONTINUE DS    0H                                                       | 003170
                                      78          GET   XIN,INPUTREC             GET OUR RECORD                  | 003180
000076 9240 C5E4       005E4          83          MVI   PLINE,C' '               CLEAR FIRST BYTE OF PLINE       | 003190
00007A D283 C5E5 C5E4 005E5 005E4     84          MVC   PLINE+1(132),PLINE       CLEAR REST OF PRINT LINE        | 003200
000080 F274 C708 C6B4 00708 006B4     85          PACK  VALUE1(8),NUM1(5)        CONVERT FIRST NUMBER            | 003210
000086 F274 C710 C6B9 00710 006B9     86          PACK  VALUE2(8),NUM2(5)        CONVERT SECOND NUMBER           | 003220

                                      88 ********************************************************************** | 003240
                                      89 *  IF VALUE1 OR VALUE2 ARE TO BE NEGATIVE, THEN CONVERT THE PACKED    * | 003250
                                      90 *  VALUES INTO NEGATIVE NUMBERS.                                      * | 003260
                                      91 ********************************************************************** | 003270
00008C 4130 C6B4             006B4    92          LA    R3,NUM1                  POINT TO FIRST INPUT NUMBER     | 003280
000090                                93 LOOP1    DS    0H                       FIND NEGATIVE SIGN              | 003290
000090 5930 C268             00268    94          C     R3,=A(NUM1+4)            HAVE WE LOOKED AT ENTIRE NUM1   | 003300
000094 4720 C0BA             000BA    95          BH    NUM1POS                  IF SO, THEN NUM1 IS POSITIVE    | 003310
000098 9560 3000       00000          96          CLI   0(R3),C'-'               NEGATIVE SIGN?                  | 003320
00009C 4780 C0A8             000A8    97          BE    MINUS1                   IF YES, THEN NEGATIVE FIRST NUM | 003330
0000A0 4130 3001             00001    98          LA    R3,1(,R3)                ADVANCE TO NEXT ADDRESS         | 003340
0000A4 47F0 C090             00090    99          B     LOOP1                    CONTINUE LOOKING                | 003350
0000A8 F870 C718 C270 00718 00270    100 MINUS1   ZAP   WORK(8),=P'0'            SET WORK EQUAL TO ZERO          | 003360
0000AE FB77 C718 C708 00718 00708    101          SP    WORK(8),VALUE1(8)        SUBTRACT VALUE1 FROM 0          | 003370
0000B4 F877 C708 C718 00708 00718    102          ZAP   VALUE1(8),WORK           VALUE1 IS NOW NEGATIVE          | 003380
0000BA                               103 NUM1POS  DS    0H                                                       | 003390

0000BA 4130 C6B9             006B9   105          LA    R3,NUM2                  POINT TO FIRST INPUT NUMBER     | 003410
0000BE                               106 LOOP2    DS    0H                       FIND NEGATIVE SIGN              | 003420
0000BE 5930 C26C             0026C   107          C     R3,=A(NUM2+4)            HAVE WE LOOKED AT ENTIRE NUM1   | 003430
0000C2 4720 C0E8             000E8   108          BH    NUM2POS                  IF SO, THEN NUM1 IS POSITIVE    | 003440
0000C6 9560 3000       00000         109          CLI   0(R3),C'-'               NEGATIVE SIGN?                  | 003450
0000CA 4780 C0D6             000D6   110          BE    MINUS2                   IF YES, THEN NEGATIVE FIRST NUM | 003460
0000CE 4130 3001             00001   111          LA    R3,1(,R3)                ADVANCE TO NEXT ADDRESS         | 003470
0000D2 47F0 C0BE             000BE   112          B     LOOP2                    CONTINUE LOOKING                | 003480
0000D6 F870 C718 C270 00718 00270    113 MINUS2   ZAP   WORK(8),=P'0'            SET WORK EQUAL TO ZERO          | 003490
0000DC FB77 C718 C710 00718 00710    114          SP    WORK(8),VALUE2(8)        SUBTRACT VALUE1 FROM 0          | 003500
0000E2 F877 C710 C718 00710 00718    115          ZAP   VALUE2(8),WORK           VALUE1 IS NOW NEGATIVE          | 003510
0000E8                               116 NUM2POS  DS    0H                                                       | 003520
```

Tracing backwards we see that VALUE1 came from NUM1 which came from our input data card.

Figure 8.51 Tracing back to find the bug.

REPORT
NAME: MATH

A R I T H M E T I C   P R O C E S S I N G   R E P O R T
BASIC MATH OPERATIONS

----- OPERATION -----	----- FIRST VALUE -----	----- SECOND VALUE -----	--------------- RESULT ---------------		
ADD	00020	00008	28		
SUBTRACT	00020	00008	12		
MULTIPLY	00020	00008	160		
DIVIDE	00020	00008	2	REMAINDER	4
ADD	-6	4	-2		
SUBTRACT	-6	4	-10		
MULTIPLY	-6	4	-24		
DIVIDE	-6	4	-1	REMAINDER	-2

Figure 8.52 Program output can help to locate errors.

STUDY QUESTIONS

1. Give an example of an instruction that causes an OC1 abend when executed.
2. What abend code is obtained if your program tries to store data into location X'000000' within the operating system?
3. What abend code is obtained in the following example?

```
MVC  PACKED1(4),=PL4'25'
MP   PACKED1(4),=H'5'
```

4. What register should be looked at if the PSW points to an address outside of your program?
5. Field NUM1 is located at displacement 1B0 off from register 10 and NUM2 is located at displacement 1B9 off from register 10. If NUM1 is five bytes long and NUM2 is two bytes long, write the *machine code* from the following instruction:

```
AP  NUM1(5),NUM2(2)
```

6. An infinite loop is recognized immediately because an abend code of _____ is obtained.
7. Give an example of an instruction that uses an index register.
8. If I want to initialize a register to the value 5, but instead code the instruction shown below, what happens?

```
L  R2,5
```

9. What are the primary fields found in a dump needed to determine the address of the failing instruction?
10. Register 6 is used as a loop counter and we suspect that it is not incrementing properly. How might we dump register 6 so that we can monitor its value as we process within our loop?
11. The following PSW was printed when our program failed. What is the address of the instruction that caused the abend?

```
078D0004  8008CFB2
```

12. With respect to Study Question 11, what might have caused the program to abend?
13. A programmer forgets to code the instructions to properly exit from a program and instead "falls into" the DS and DC storage areas. What abend code may result from this situation?
14. What is the title of the section in the dump where we find the entry point address of our program if the dump is produced by the operating system?
15. A fullword of storage called LOOPCTR is used as a binary counter in a program to accumulate input values. We assume that its value is not correct. How do we print this value in order to monitor it?
16. What instruction is used in assembly language to print messages to yourself as your program executes?

17. To support the SNAP instruction, a DCB had to be coded. Does the name of this DCB have to be SNAPDCB for the instruction to work correctly?
18. What JCL statement is used in assembly language to allow the operating system to generate a dump for your program?
19. How can you limit the number of output lines printed in assembly language programming?
20. How can you reduce the computer time used by a program in the event that it goes into an infinite loop?

```
The following program applies to questions 21 - 30.

          COMPUTE    CSECT
                     USING    *,R15
                     PACK     VALUE(8),N(5)
                     ZAP      LIMIT(8),VALUE(8)
                     DP       LIMIT(8),=PL4'2'
                     ZAP      LIMIT(8),LIMIT(4)
          LOOP       DS       0H
                     CP       I(8),LIMIT(8)
                     BH       YES
                     ZAP      WORK(8),VALUE(8)
                     DP       WORK(8),I+4(4)
                     ZAP      WORK(8),WORK(4)
                     MP       WORK(8),I+4(4)
                     CP       WORK(8),VALUE(8)
                     BE       NO
                     AP       I(8),=P'1'
                     B        LOOP
          YES        XPRNT    YESLINE,10
                     B        OUT
          NO         XPRNT    NOLINE,10
          OUT        BR       R14
          YESLINE    DC       CL10' YES'
          NOLINE     DC       CL10' NO'
          LIMIT      DS       D
          VALUE      DS       D
          N          DS       CL5'00025'
          WORK       DS       D
          I          DC       D'2'
                     LTORG
                     END      COMPUTE
```

21. Play computer and derive the statement displacements (offsets) and object code for each instruction in the program. Hint: the XPRNT instruction is a 6 byte instruction. The first two bytes are E020 and the last two bytes are the length (in hexadecimal) of the area to be printed. The middle two bytes contain the D(B) address of the first operand.
22. What is the purpose of the program? In other words, what does the program attempt to do?
23. Since the program will undoubtedly abend, what abend code do you expect to receive from this program?
24. At what instruction will the program fail? Why?
25. What will the LTORG statement generate?

26. The asterisk in the USING statement is similar to the * on the EQU instruction. What does this operand mean?
27. Does this program adhere to normal linkage conventions? How can you tell.
28. The program uses extended mnemonics as you can see. What source code instruction could be used to replace the BH instruction in line 9 of the program?
29. The program currently utilizes decimal instructions to process. Could this program be rewritten to utilize only binary instructions to perform the processing?
30. When the program attempts to return control to the program by executing the "BR R14" instruction, what will be in register 3 at this point during processing?

9

Internal and External Subroutines

Throughout we've emphasized the importance of a top-down structured development process. Placement of input statements, construction of loops, and adherence to the three basic logical constructs have been of primary concern. We're now going to extend this development process to a larger scale by **modularizing** or **functionalizing** our computer solutions. This should allow us to develop programs that are

(a) easier to change or modify if need be
(b) easier to debug
(c) easier to understand
(d) smaller in size

In fact, these components are important for all programs. Therefore, we're not going to do anything new, rather, we're simply going to *package* our program solutions differently.

WHAT IS A MODULE OR A FUNCTION?

When we use the terms **module** or **function,** we do so in many different ways when talking about computer solutions. Basically, a function is a task or unit of work that must be done. Adding, subtracting, multiplying, or dividing two numbers may all be thought of as functions. Converting internal data to a format to be printed can also be regarded as a function. Hence, a program may have many different functions, all related to solving a particular problem.

When we develop computer algorithms and eventually programs, we want to watch for programs that have too many functions. In other words, programs that perform many activities or have many different functions tend to be more difficult to understand, maintain, and debug. As illustrated in Fig. 9.1, we want to develop programs that isolate functions so that the inputs and outputs of each can be verified as we progress through our development process.

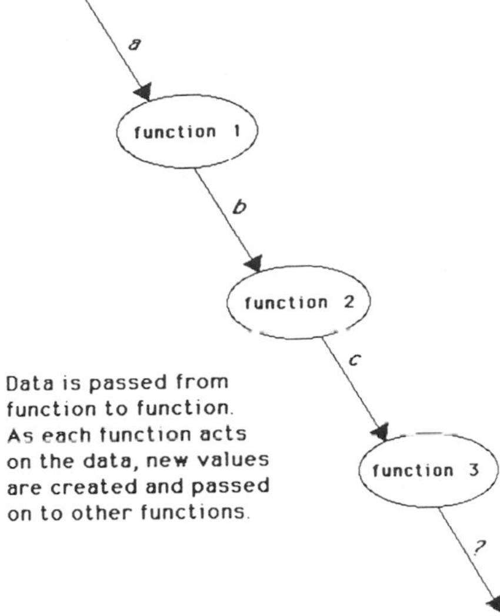

Figure 9.1 A logical view of module-to-module communications.

From the figure, each function is uniquely identified on the flow diagram. Function 1 processes *a* and produces *b*. After each function, we can use the XPRNT, XDUMP, PUT or SNAP instruction to verify that function 1 actually did what it was supposed to do. If our output is incorrect, we can only speculate as to which function is in error. By analyzing the inputs and outputs of *each* function during program development, we can more accurately identify a problem area within our computer solution if we're getting incorrect results from our program.

The process of constructing an algorithm gradually uncovers each function within a computer solution. As the algorithm progresses, we should step back and look at it as a whole. In particular, we should look at the functions within the algorithm to see if any are duplicated within the algorithm or if any are similar to functions developed in other programs. If we find such situations, we can **package** these functions into **modules.** That is, we implement these functions as separate programs. By doing so, we only code them *once* and use them over and over again. Clearly, this results in a savings in coding time since the coding of repetitive functions is eliminated. In fact, we'll save coding time in this project and in all other projects that use these functions within their solution.

For example, the program that computed the sum, difference, product, and quotient/remainder of two input numbers required a section of code to convert the results into character representation so that the results could be printed. At each phase of processing, instructions were coded which performed this conversion and placed a negative sign (if applicable) before the first significant digit. This process was obviously an example of duplicate coding since each set of instructions was identical except for the input and output fields being processed. This program is an obvious choice for **modularization**.

Although you may agree with this discussion, you may be doubting its value. The program that we cited worked. Why not leave it alone? At this point, I'd agree since the program has already been written. However, suppose that we were just beginning to develop a program or were about to modify a program by adding exponentiation, square root, and cube root processing. If we had a module to convert the resulting values from internal form to external form, we wouldn't have to write that component. We could devote our efforts to making sure that we correctly computed the appropriate new values, knowing full well that our conversion routine worked properly.

This is perhaps the greatest advantage of modularization. Namely, it gives you the opportunity to concentrate your efforts on the functions. It also allows you to look at each function individually and not worry about that function's impact on any other within the solution. This results in programs that contain fewer errors and solutions that are easier to debug and expand.

When we modularize, we must be careful since there's a tendency to construct modules with multiple functions, thus defeating the idea of modularization. We want to adopt the strategy that the fewer functions performed by a module, the better it will be. Hence, modules that perform one function are optimal whereas modules that perform several functions are not as desirable.

PACKAGING LOGICAL FUNCTIONS INTO MODULES

As we said before, a module is a program. It may be a complete program or it may be a partial program. In general, we commonly refer to modules as **subroutines, subprograms,** or **procedures.** Further, the module may be located *outside* the bounds of the CSECT in which it is used (external) or it may be located *within* the CSECT (internal). Where we locate the module determines whether it is internal or external to the primary program.

The manner in which we package modules is very critical to long-term problem development. If we know that a particular function is to be used in later projects, then *external* implementation is the best choice. On the other hand, an *internal* subroutine is used if we know that this function is unique to this problem or if all other uses of this function require a slight modification to adapt it to the new situation.

Regardless of the implementation technique, the basic format of a module is shown in Fig. 9.2.

```
Save all registers to be used.
. . .
Perform the desired processing.
. . .
Restore registers as they were.
Return to the calling module.
```

Figure 9.2 General format of a subroutine.

This is familiar. In fact, it is the basic format of any assembly language program. When the program gets control, it preserves the processing environment by saving all the registers. The module (program) then does its job, and, when completed, restores all the registers to their original states. The module then returns control to the calling module and its task is completed.

The only thing missing in this representation is the input and output of data. Although modules can read and print data just as any other programs can, they generally obtain their data from those modules that called them and pass their results back to them.

Figure 9.3 shows a computer solution consisting of several different functions. Let's assume that each has been implemented as a separate module.

Module TOP is the highest level module in the system. It obtains control from the operating system and is the last module to execute. Thus, TOP gives control back to the operating system.

The **system** or **collection of modules** operates by invoking I, L1, L2, L3, and O. L1 and L2 must both call X1 to do their jobs. L3 has no module subordinate to it.

The data processed by this system must come from somewhere. At least one module must input data and at least one module must output data. Although all modules could perform both input and output, this is not generally the case for a system designed in this manner. Typically, one module obtains data and another outputs data. Let's assume that module I inputs all data for the system and module O outputs all data.

We can now ask from where do L1, L2, L3, and X1 obtain the values that they must process? Clearly, the elements processed by these modules must come *from I through TOP*. Hence, TOP calls I to obtain data and distributes it, as needed, to L1, L2, and L3. L1 and L2 then distribute the data needed by X1 so that X1 can perform its processing. Following processing within each module, the results are passed back through the module hierarchy to TOP and then over to O for printing.

Clearly, TOP is the controlling module for this system. TOP, which is called the **driver,** determines the order of processing and determines which data elements are to be distributed to the subordinate modules. In fact, L1 may only need four of the original 10 input values to perform its task(s). Although all 10 input values could be passed to L1, thus allowing it to choose which values it needs to process, we generally limit a module's access to data by giving it only what it needs. In other words, TOP can be designed to control the values given to subordinate modules. Such control can *only* occur when the modules are implemented as *external* subroutines, not *internal* subroutines. This is yet another very important distinction for the use of internal and external subroutines.

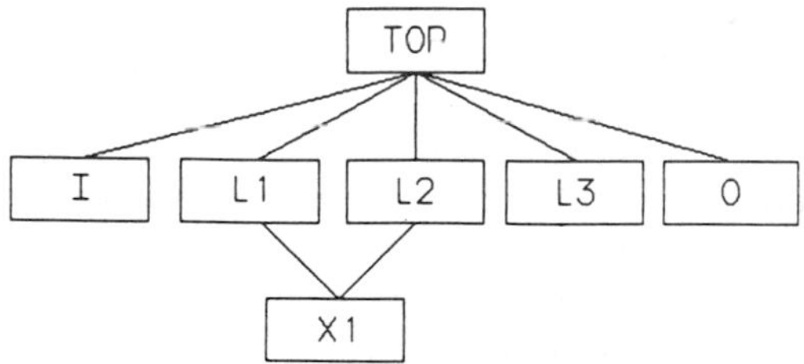

Figure 9.3 Module hierarchy for a proposed system.

Limiting the **scope** of data for a module helps in debugging and module verification. If L1 has access to all data, it is possible for L1 to inadvertently change a value that it does not need. Hence, when L3 obtains this altered value and fails, you believe that the problem resides in L3 and do not suspect L1. In fact, you probably wouldn't dump out or verify all 10 values after L1 is done processing, rather, you're more likely to dump only the four elements that you believe L1 modified, further averting your suspicion of L1 when L3 fails.

The act of limiting a data element's access by modules within a system is commonly referred to as **limiting the scope of a data element.** If a module has access to all data, whether it needs it or not, we say that the *data* has **global scope.** (Note that it is the data that is global and not the module.) When a data element is not known by all modules but is known only by the module in which it is used, then that data element has **local scope.** As we've just seen, local scope is preferred since it isolates problems through data restriction.

Although data may be global or local with respect to subroutine access, both internal and external subroutines share a common data attribute—**static data.** When a subroutine is called, local data areas within the subroutine may be modified during the course of processing. When the subroutine returns and is called again, the values of the data areas inherit their values from the last execution of the subroutine. For example, suppose that a field has been assigned an initial value of F'0' through the DC instruction. During the course of processing, the value is changed to F'25' to support the processing of the subroutine. The next time that the subroutine is called, the data field inherits its last value 25 and not the original value of 0. If it's necessary for the value of 0 to be present when the subroutine is called, the programmer must use other techniques to initialize this field.

Hence, it is necessary for the developer of the subroutine to use execution-time initialization procedures instead of assembly-time procedures. In other words, the DC instruction may be used to initialize data but this will only be effective on the first call to the subroutine. On all other calls, the value of the data will be as it was when the subroutine was previously called. Thus, the programmer must utilize MVC, ZAP, or some other instruction to initialize all data areas before the subroutine begins processing. On the other hand, the static data characteristic may be a wanted feature in some applications. Therefore, depending on the needs of the application and subroutine, the programmer should construct the subroutine to use or not use the static data attribute to the benefit of program development.

The manner in which we implement subroutines (internal or external) directly impacts the scope of data elements. If we implement them as an external routine, then we are automatically restricting our routine to localized data or to data passed to the module from another module. If all modules in our example are implemented as internal subroutines, then they have access to data within themselves (local data) as well as access to *all* data in *any* of the other modules (global data). Clearly, we are generalizing here. Logically, these general guidelines and restrictions apply to the construction of subroutines. However, the ability to address memory in assembly language does not prevent one module from accessing data from another, even if they are internal or external. Although we may have an external routine, its data can be addressed by another subroutine, but usually unintentionally. Further, it can access data in other routines even if it shouldn't.

Why then would we ever implement a subroutine as an internal module? Quite simply, it's easier and it requires less coding. Although the basic structure of the module is the same for internal and external subroutines, we generally find that internal routines do not strictly adhere to the full module structure. Typically, an internal subroutine has the structure shown in Fig. 9.4 and an external routine has the structure previously illustrated.

```
Process as desired.
. . .
Return to the calling module.
```

Figure 9.4 General format of an internal subroutine.

As you can see, the primary difference between the two structures is the preservation of the processing environment. Internal routines generally do not save and restore the registers but external routines generally do. Further, data accessed by the internal routine is openly available but data needed by the external routine must be passed and received by that routine.

The next sections discuss the processing and coding format for internal and external subroutines. As you read these sections, you'll begin to understand the usefulness of modular programming. However, remember that data element labels used in any internal or external subroutine must be unique. Although your design separates functions through module definition, the assembler makes no such distinction when it comes to data area names or statement labels. For all modules within a multimodule system, every label or data area name must be unique. Failure to abide by this rule will cause you great frustration when you obtain your first printout that indicates many duplicate labels within your system. Incidentally, this also applies to the register equates. Only one set of register equates need be coded for the entire assembly of modules.

INTERNAL SUBROUTINES

The situation that we related earlier concerning the converting of internal values to character representation is a good candidate for an internal routine. The amount of processing required by this subroutine is small, it has few data elements to work with, and it performs one function. Although we can implement this subroutine as an external module, let's concentrate on internal routines at this time.

The module consists of the logic as described in Fig. 9.5.

```
(a) build an edit pattern field
(b) edit the packed number
(c) if negative then
       place sign before first digit
(d) exit the module
```

Figure 9.5 Logic for a data conversion module.

This logic may look straightforward, but there are a few unanswered questions. How does this routine know *which* value to edit? In other words, how will this routine know whether to edit the field called SUMP, DIFFERP, QUOTENTP, REMAINP, or PRODUCTP? How will this routine know whether it was called by the ADD function, SUBTRACT function, or from some other function? Finally, where is the result to be placed? Will each of the calling functions know which field contains the result?

This routine needs at least two fields for processing, an input field and an output field. Before this routine is called, the arithmetic processing function places the number to be converted into a generic packed-decimal field, *also* known by this module, and then calls this module. After processing, the arithmetic module accesses another field known by both functions to obtain the character representation of the converted value.

How does this routine know whether it was called from the ADD function, SUBTRACT function, or some other function? Clearly, we must find a method for calling and returning control to the proper module. The code in Fig. 9.6 illustrates how this may be accomplished.

```
ADD       ZAP    SUMP(8),VALUE1(8)
          AP     SUMP(8),VALUE2(8)
          ZAP    GENERIC(8),SUMP(8)
          BAL    R14,CONVERT
          MVC    SUM(16),PATTERN

          .      .
          .      .

CONVERT   DS     0H
          MVC    PATTERN(16),CONVPATT
          LA     R1,PATTERN+15
          EDMK   PATTERN(16),GENERIC
          BNM    NOTLTO
          BCTR   R1,0
          MVI    0(R1),C'-'
NOTLTO    DS     0H
          BR     R14
CONVPATT  DC     X'40202020202020202020202020202120'
GENERIC   DS     PL8
PATTERN   DS     CL16
```

Figure 9.6 Implementation of the data conversion module.

After the ADD function computes the sum of the two input values, it places the resulting packed-decimal sum into the field called GENERIC. The **BAL (branch and link)** instruction transfers control to the internal subroutine called CONVERT, but *before* doing so, the address of the next instruction within ADD is placed into register 14. In other words, the address of the MVC instruction within ADD (just after the BAL instruction) is placed into register 14, which acts as our **link register.**

CONVERT is given control and converts the value of GENERIC into character representation with a proper sign (if the number is negative). The resulting character representation is placed into the field called PATTERN. Both fields, GENERIC and PATTERN, must be known by both modules.

After the conversion is completed, CONVERT branches back to the address contained in register 14, which returns control to the MVC instruction and so the ADD function continues. ADD now moves the converted value into the print line and processing proceeds to the next function.

CONVERT is called as many times as needed by each functional module in the mainline code. Each time that it is called, the function uses the BAL instruction to establish a return address in register 14 and then to transfer control to the module. Although register 14 was used in this example, any valid register can be used. Especially with internal subroutines, the register used between the routines is a matter of preference. On the other hand, register 14 is the industry standard link register. If two people wrote these routines, the one who wrote CONVERT would most likely have used R14 as the return register since it is the industry standard. As a matter of note, don't use your base register as the linking register. I'm sure you understand why.

As you look at the code within CONVERT, you see that register 1 is altered. If the ADD function has used register 1 for something else, it is destroyed by the CONVERT routine. With a slight modification, CONVERT can be designed so that it does not alter any register when it is invoked. Figure 9.7 contains this implementation.

If we look at CONVERT now, we see that it does not alter any registers used by the routine that called it. Hence, this example of CONVERT is along the lines of our external routines that preserve the processing environment. Further, if CONVERT uses several registers, we might see something like the code given in Fig. 9.8.

In this case, registers 1 through 5 are used within CONVERT. These registers are saved before processing is started and are reloaded before control is returned. As we remarked before, you do not have to develop your routines in this manner. However, this form is similar to that of developing external routines. If internal and external routines are developed in a similar manner, you'll have better consistency and be less prone to errors.

The BAL instruction, shown in Fig. 9.9, places the address of the routine to be branched to into the rightmost three bytes of the register specified. The leftmost byte of the register contains the instruction length code, condition code, and program mask fields from the PSW. In other words, the register contains the *entire* right half of the

```
CONVERT  DS    0H
         ST    R1,R1SAVE
         MVC   PATTERN(16),CONVPATT
         LA    R1,PATTERN+15
         EDMK  PATTERN(16),GENERIC
         BNM   NOTLTO
         BCTR  R1,0
         MVI   0(R1),C'-'
NOTLTO   DS    0H
         L     R1,R1SAVE
         BR    R14
CONVPATT DC    X'40202020202020202020202020202120'
GENERIC  DS    PL8
PATTERN  DS    CL16
R1SAVE   DS    F
```

Figure 9.7 Preserving the register contents (a modification to the code contained in Fig. 9.6).

```
CONVERT  DS    0H
         STM   R1,R5,REGSAVE

         processing

         LM    R1,R5,REGSAVE
         BR    R14
CONVPATT DC    X'40202020202020202020202020202120'
GENERIC  DS    PL8
PATTERN  DS    CL16
REGSAVE  DS    5F
```

Figure 9.8 Preserving the contents of several registers.

```
BAL      Rx,routinename
```

Figure 9.9 General form of the BAL instruction.

PSW. This information may be used when returning control, but also, it can be used to restore the condition code to its original state after the subroutine is called. This can be done using the SPM instruction.

Since the ADD routine may cause an overflow, it might be desirable to alter the program mask field to turn "off" the overflow mask bit. Hence, if an overflow condition occurs, the ADD function does not cause an abend. However, if the program mask is modified by ADD, then it remains modified for the remainder of the program unless it is restored to its original state. Hence, ADD can be designed to set the program mask *for its processing*, perform the addition as desired, and then restore the program mask to its original state so as to not impact processing in any other module. Figure 9.10 contains this implementation.

When this function is called, the registers used by this routine are saved. Next, the decimal overflow bit in the PSW is turned "off" so that an overflow abend does not result. The two fields are then added and CONVERT is called to convert the resulting packed field into character format. Notice that an internal subroutine is calling another internal subroutine. When CONVERT finishes, ADD restores the registers and returns the PSW mask to its original state by issuing the SPM instruction using R14. Since R14 is the link register, its leftmost byte contains the condition code and program mask, set by the function that called ADD. Finally, ADD returns control to the mainline logic and processing continues.

If you recall, our original ADD routine built our output lines and printed results. I've taken out that code in Fig. 9.10 so that we could concentrate on the processing within ADD and especially the processing to preserve and alter the program mask.

The SPM instruction also preserves the condition code value. Hence, an internal subroutine may be called between a comparison and a branch as long as the subroutine preserves and restores the condition code value. The example in Fig. 9.11 illustrates this concept by calling a subroutine between a character compare instruction and the associated branch instruction for the compare.

Internal subroutines may also be called by the **BALR (branch and link register)** instruction instead of the BAL instruction. The only difference between the two is the second operand. The BAL instruction requires that the second operand be a D(X,B) address and the BALR instruction requires the second operand to be a register. Further, the register specified in the second operand of the BALR instruction must contain a valid

```
ADD      DS    0H
         ST    R3,ADDR3
         ST    R14,ADDR14
         L     R3,BITS
         SPM   R3
         ZAP   ADDWORK(8),VALUE1
         AP    ADDWORK(8),VALUE2
         ZAP   SUMP(8),ADDWORK(8)
         BAL   R14,CONVERT
         L     R3,ADDR3
         L     R14,ADDR14
         SPM   R14
         BR    R14
ADDWORK  DS    PL8
ADDR3    DS    F
ADDR14   DS    F
BITS     DC    B'00001011',AL3(0)
```

Figure 9.10 Preserving the program mask by the function.

```
Warning: this code requires special consideration.

         CLC      fielda,fieldb
         BAL      Rx,subroutine
         Bxx      TARGET
```

Figure 9.11 Gambling with the condition code.

address so that proper calling of the routine can occur. Figure 9.12 contains our ADD functional code using the BALR instruction instead of the BAL instruction.

There really isn't that much difference between the two implementations except for the LA (load address) just before the BALR instruction. Again, CONVERT returns control to the ADD function using R14 as the return register.

Another instruction can be used in place of BALR if the leftmost byte of the link register is *not* to be used for resetting the program mask or the condition code. Also, this instruction may be used on 31-bit address systems (extended architecture) whereas the BAL and BALR instructions only support 24-bit addresses. The instructions that we're discussing are the **BAS (branch and save)** and the **BASR (branch and save register)** instructions.

The BAS and BASR instructions are used for module linkage exactly as are the BAL and BALR instructions. However, the leftmost byte of the link register does not contain the program mask and condition code since the link register contains a 31-bit address. From the subroutine's viewpoint, control is returned in exactly the same manner as if the BAL or BALR instructions were used. These instructions may not be used in ASSIST.

```
ADD      ZAP      SUMP(8),VALUE1(8)
         AP       SUMP(8),VALUE2(8)
         ZAP      GENERIC(8),SUMP(8)
         LA       R15,CONVERT
         BALR     R14,R15
         MVC      SUM(16),PATTERN
```

Figure 9.12 Using the BALR instruction in place of BAL.

INTERNAL SUBROUTINE PACKAGING AND DATA ACCESS

In our previous discussion, we noted that internal subroutines have access to all data since they typically operate on a global data scale. The reason behind this generalization centers around the manner and location in which internal subroutines are coded. If we look at the skeleton program in Fig. 9.13 that contains internal subroutines, we'd generally find the subroutines in an area where they could not be executed by default.

As you can see, the subroutines are located just before the data areas. Further, they are located where they cannot be executed unless they are explicitly called from the mainline code or from some other subroutine. Further, we see a single CSECT housing the mainline logic, one or more subroutines, and all data areas for *all* modules in the system (mainline and subroutines). Needless to say, the coding within this CSECT can be quite extensive. For that reason, it's a good idea to begin each module at the top of a new page within your source listing (using EJECT or TITLE) and to supply each module with a

```
MAINPGM     CSECT
            ...main program linkage

            ...main program processing

            ...main program linkage out and
               return of control to o.s.


SUBa        DS      0H
            ...subroutine a


SUBb        DS      0H
            ...subroutine b

            ...data areas for all modules

            END     MAINPGM
```

Figure 9.13 Format of a program utilizing internal subroutines.

meaningful comment block to describe the function, inputs and outputs, and processing performed by that subroutine.

Data shared between internal subroutines or mainline code is controlled only through responsible programming. Internal subroutines can access data easily since *any data* within the bounds of the control section is available to the routine. Formal parameter passing is not usually followed since the developer is also usually the developer of the mainline program. With the broad flexibility for internal subroutine implementation, it's no wonder there are so many methods for invoking and passing data to such routines. Although this can be a concern in a development environment, most uses of internal routines see few if any data access problems during implementation.

Another concern at this point is the size of your program. A single-base register may only be used to reference up to 4096 bytes of program area. Programs larger than this require multiple-base registers. Although additional base registers are easy to establish, they clearly impact on the number of available registers that you may use to perform processing. The fewer registers that you have available, the more difficult it is to process data. Hence, we want to design programs that require few base registers, which may not be possible with internal subroutines but is with external routines. If you have to define more than one base register, let's see how it's done.

DEFINING MULTIPLE-BASE REGISTERS

A program usually needs as many base registers as there are 4096-byte segments within the program. In other words, a program 10,000 bytes long needs three base registers, but a program 8,000 bytes long needs only 2. A program that is 5,000 bytes may only need one base register as long as the last field in the program begins before byte 4096.

To define additional base registers, you must modify your USING statement and code additional instructions to initialize your alternate base registers. For example, the USING statement to define registers 10, 11, and 12 as base registers is coded as shown in Fig. 9.14.

```
USING   MAINPGM,10,11,12
```

Figure 9.14 Specifying three base registers on the USING statement.

You must be careful, however, because the order of the registers in the USING statement is important. Since register 10 is the first register coded, it is considered as the **primary** base register. If R12 was our primary base register, then we code the USING statement shown in Fig. 9.15 to specify primary and secondary base registers.

```
USING   MAINPGM,12,10,11
```

Figure 9.15 Specifying three base registers with R12 as the primary base register.

The primary base register probably contains the entry point address since we loaded the contents of R15 into the primary base register to begin processing. If R10 is our first *secondary* base register, then it must contain the value of 4096 added to register 12. R11 must contain the value 4096 added to R10. This is done as shown in Fig. 9.16.

```
MAINPGM     CSECT
            STM       R14,R12,12(R13)
            LR        R12,R15
            USING     MAINPGM,R12,R10,R11
            LA        R10,4095(R12)
            LA        R10,1(R10)
            LA        R11,4095(R10)
            LA        R11,1(R11)
```

Figure 9.16 Establishing base registers upon entering a program.

Since the largest displacement is 4095, two load address instructions are required to add 4096 to a register's value. R10 obtains its value from R12 and R11 obtains its value from R10. Hence, the addresses in R12, R10, and R11, respectively, are

R12—the entry point address

R10—the entry point address + 4096

R11—the entry point address + 4096 + 4096

R12 references all fields within the first 4096 bytes of the program. R10 references all fields from byte 4096 to byte 8191. R11 references all fields from byte 8192 to the end of the program.

PASSING DATA TO SUBROUTINES BY FOLLOWING THE LINKAGE CONVENTIONS

Again, the data areas processed by internal subroutines are contained within the same CSECT as the data areas used and processed by the mainline code. Hence, transferring data between one module and another becomes trivial since all instructions within a CSECT can easily address any data areas also contained within that CSECT. On the other hand, IBM has developed guidelines by which information is passed between one module and another. These rules are an extension of the *linkage conventions,* and they are the guidelines by which modules are developed and communicate in business environments.

Clearly, the easiest method for passing and addressing data using internal subroutines is to utilize the label(s) on the area(s) to be processed. In most cases, the person writing the internal subroutine is also the one writing the mainline code and so coordination between field names and usage is immediate. On the other hand, if several people are developing modules for a system, it is usually more difficult to coordinate data usage and access. Hence, the linkage conventions provide guidelines in which data may be communicated across module boundaries. In fact, software developed in different languages is able to communicate by adhering to the linkage guidelines. Although you can adhere to these guidelines when developing internal subroutines, it's not usually done.

As we discussed in Chapters 3 and 5, the linkage conventions cover the use of the registers, establishing register save areas, preserving the processing environment, and establishing a base register to gain addressability to data areas. Although we've discussed every item, we have not gone into enough detail for register use, especially by multimodule systems.

Registers 2 through 12 are for general use by any program. Registers 13, 14, 15, 0, and 1 are reserved for special use. In particular, register 14 contains the return address to a calling module, register 15 contains the entry point address or address of a module that is being called, and register 13 contains the address of the current register save area.

Registers 0 and 1 are now valuable to our processing since they are used to pass data to and from modules. Information passed between modules is commonly called **parameter data** or, simply, **parameters.** Specifically, register 0 passes an individual value and register 1 passes many values (in the form of an address list). For example, suppose that we have a binary number four bytes long and we want to compute the square of this number. We can place the value into register 0, call our squaring subroutine, and obtain the resulting square through register 0 as shown in Fig. 9.17.

```
L      R0,ORIGINAL
BAL    R14,SQUARE
CVD    R0,NTIMESN
```

Figure 9.17 Using register 0 to pass a single parameter.

The original number is placed into register 0 and is passed to the SQUARE subroutine. The square of the number is computed and its value is returned in register 0. As long as we only have one binary value and as long as we have a number that is small enough to fit into a single register, register 0 can be used to pass this parameter.

Now let's consider the ADD and CONVERT routines discussed before. Can we pass our result to CONVERT through register 0? The answer is no. If you recall, the data that we were processing was in packed-decimal format. Further, our numbers were eight bytes long—much larger than the four-byte register. Hence, register 0 cannot pass the number to be converted to CONVERT.

Suppose that we also want our result in a specific place rather than in a generic field as before. Again, another parameter must be introduced. However, since register 0 only holds one value at a time, it clearly cannot be used as our parameter register. To solve this problem, we use register 1 to pass our parameters between the calling and called modules. Although register 1 is a register, it is *not* used to hold *values*. Instead, it holds an

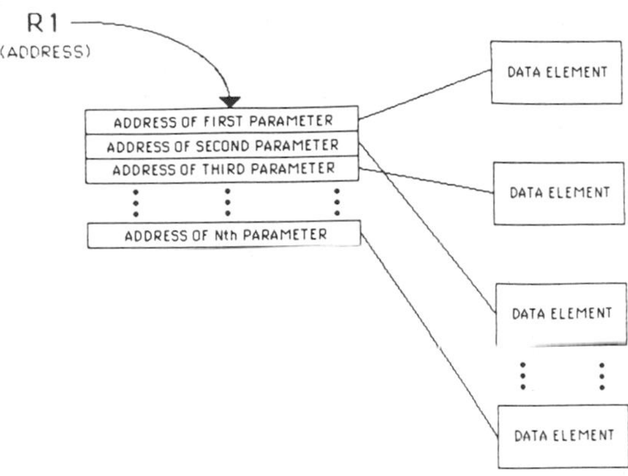

Figure 9.18 Format for the register 1 parameter list. R1 contains the address of a parameter list when a module is called. Through that list, the called program accesses the data elements via explicit addressing techniques.

address that points to a list of addresses (one for each parameter) by which we can then reference or address our data.

As Fig. 9.18 illustrates, register 1 addresses a **parameter list** or **list of parameters,** which contains addresses that address each data element. The longer the list, the more elements that can be addressed by the *called* module. In our example of the ADD and CONVERT routines, two elements must be passed from ADD to CONVERT. These elements are the number to be converted and the area into which the character representation is to be placed. CONVERT must obtain the addresses properly and use the input parameter value to produce the output parameter value. This is done as shown in Fig. 9.19.

The addresses of the packed-decimal field (SUMP) and the area into which the character representation is to be placed (SUM) are passed via register 1 to the subroutine. CONVERT first saves the registers that it will use and then obtains the addresses of the two data areas. Once acquired, the target character area is formatted with an edit pattern and the number is edited. Following processing, the registers are reloaded and control is returned to the ADD module.

You probably noticed that explicit addressing was used to access the parameter data values once their addresses were obtained from the parameter list. Explicit addressing is a natural element when constructing external subroutines and an addressing technique with which you must become familiar. In Chapter 13 we'll discuss a method by which DSECTs can be used to supply field names in situations like this. You could also use the EXTRN assembly language instruction to define fields as external so that they

```
 ADD       ZAP      SUMP(8),VALUE1(8)        INITIALIZE FIRST VALUE
           AP       SUMP(8),VALUE2(8)        COMPUTE THE SUM
           LA       R1,PARMLIST              ADDRESS THE PARM LIST
           LA       R15,CONVERT              OBTAIN SUBROUTINE ADDRESS
           BALR     R14,R15                  CALL THE SUBROUTINE

           .        .

 PARMLIST  DS       0F
           DC       A(SUMP)                  FIRST PARAMETER
           DC       A(SUM)                   SECOND PARAMETER

           .        .

CONVERT    DS       0H
           STM      R1,R3,REGSAVE            PRESERVE CALLER'S REGS
           L        R2,0(R1)                 ADDRESS THE FIRST PARM
           L        R3,4(R1)                 ADDRESS THE SECOND PARM
           MVC      0(16,R3),CONVPATT        REFRESH EDIT PATTERN
           LA       R1,15(R3)                ADDRESS LAST BYTE
           EDMK     0(16,R3),0(R2)           EDIT THE 8-BYTE NUMBER
           BNM      NOTLTO                   IF NOT NEGATIVE, DONE
           BCTR     R1,0                     SET TO INSERT MINUS SIGN
           MVI      0(R1),C'-'               INSERT MINUS IF NEGATIVE
NOTLTO     DS       0H
           LM       R1,R3,REGSAVE            RESTORE CALLER'S REGS
           BR       R14                      RETURN CONTROL TO CALLER
CONVPATT   DC       X'40202020202020202020202020202120'
REGSAVE    DS       3F                       SUBROUTINE SAVE AREA
```

Figure 9.19 Passing parameters via register 1—a coding example.

may be referenced in other CSECTs. However, this is not the standard approach for addressing data in external subroutines. Thus, we'll continue our discussion using explicit addressing methods and assume that after practice, you will have no difficulty in accessing your parameter values.

Each address in the parameter list is a fullword. The order in which the addresses are stored in the list must be known by both the calling module (in this case, ADD) and the called module (CONVERT). If CONVERT has the order of the parameters reversed, it's obvious that incorrect results or an abend occurs.

Register 1 is the parameter address register, which in this case, points to two parameter addresses. In larger systems, it may address several hundred parameter addresses. For our example however, two is sufficient.

Parameter lists may become quite lengthy as you can well imagine. In fact, the linkage conventions also specify that parameter lists should be ended. In other words, the last address in the parameter list is supposed to contain a leftmost bit value of 1. However, look carefully at our examples (Figures 9.18 and 9.19) and notice that we have not followed this guideline.

This guideline is generally ignored in day to day program development. In most cases, the developers of the calling and called programs agree on the number of parameters to be passed between the routines. Thus, it is not necessary to indicate the end of the parameter list since the routines know what to expect. However, software purchased from computer software manufacturers usually requires the end-of-list indicator to be present. Such software also allows a variable number of parameters instead of the fixed number of parameters that we'll normally use. In this case, it is necessary for the end of the parameter list to be noted. Thus, when calling a subroutine of this type, the routine scans for the end-of-list indicator to determine how many parameters it must process. If the end-of-list indicator is not found in a reasonable period of time, the software aborts processing, computes incorrectly, or communicates a return code through register 15 as to what went wrong. Your program can then inspect the R15 value and communicate its value to you so that you know why the software did not work as intended.

Since our approach in this textbook is to utilize software that we'll develop, we will not have to worry about the end of list designator. If we had to or wanted to, the last element in the parameter list labeled PARMLIST, Figure 9.19, would be changed to the instruction "DC X'80',AL3(SUM)".

This is the basic format of module-to-module linkage. Register 0 is rarely used and register 1 is the primary register for passing parameters between modules. R14 is the link register containing the return point into the calling program and register 15 is the "link to" register to give control to the called module.

Figure 9.20 implements our solution once more using the different instructions that we've been discussing. This shows another common method for calling subroutines.

This solution is a little different in that literals replace the explicitly defined parameter list. Further, the individual load instructions to obtain the addresses from within the parameter list are replaced by a single-load multiple instruction. Although the code is workable, it may not be as easy to understand as the first solution where the parameters were referenced using labels (see Figure 9.6 or 9.7).

We should also note that using literals to formulate a parameter list is a common technique, but one that does not allow easy insertion of the end of list indicator. As you can see by referring to the third line of Figure 9.20, the address constant literal is very clear and it's easy to determine what elements are being passed to the subroutine. Adding the end of list indicator may confuse the reader and lead them to believe that more than two parameters are to be passed to the subroutine.

```
ADD       ZAP   SUMP(8),VALUE1(8)         INITIALIZE FIRST VALUE
          AP    SUMP(8),VALUE2(8)         COMPUTE THE SUM
          LA    R1,=A(SUMP,SUM)           ADDRESS & BUILD PARM LIST
          L     R15,=A(CONVERT)           OBTAIN SUBROUTINE ADDRESS
          BALR  R14,R15                   CALL THE SUBROUTINE

          .     .
          .     .

CONVERT   DS    0H
          STM   R1,R3,REGSAVE             PRESERVE CALLER'S REGS
          LM    R2,R3,0(R1)               ADDRESS BOTH PARAMETERS
          MVC   0(16,R3),CONVPATT         REFRESH EDIT PATTERN
          LA    R1,15(R3)                 ADDRESS LAST BYTE
          EDMK  0(16,R3),0(R2)            EDIT THE 8-BYTE NUMBER
          BNM   NOTLTO                    IF NOT NEGATIVE, DONE
          BCTR  R1,0                      SET TO INSERT MINUS SIGN
          MVI   0(R1),C'-'                INSERT MINUS IF NEGATIVE
NOTLTO    DS    0H
          LM    R1,R3,REGSAVE             RESTORE CALLER'S REGS
          BR    R14                       RETURN CONTROL TO CALLER
CONVPATT  DC    X'40202020202020202020202020202120'
REGSAVE   DS    3F                        SUBROUTINE SAVE AREA
```

Figure 9.20 Establishing a parameter list using address constants.

ESTABLISHING BASE REGISTERS USING BALR

Our base register has always been established with the LR instruction. Although this is a workable and accepted technique, another common method is used for subroutines. The reason for this alternate method is that R15 may not always contain the entry point or first instruction address of your subroutine. That is, some applications do not adhere to the linkage conventions and thus they invoke modules in a different manner, causing R15 to be invalid. Clearly, if your routine relies on a valid entry point address in R15, an invalid address surely causes an abend.

A safer technique for establishing a base register uses the BALR instruction. Although this instruction typically transfers control to subroutines, it is also used to establish a base register. It places the address of the next instruction into the first operand (a register) and transfers control to the address contained in the second register. However, if the second operand is coded with a value of zero, no branch occurs. Processing continues with the next instruction.

If you recall, the BCTR instruction works in a similar manner. A second operand of zero on the BCTR instruction gives us a quick method for subtracting one from the value in a register. As in this case, a zero value in the second operand of the BALR instruction places the address of the next instruction into the register but then falls into the next instruction.

If we use the BALR instruction in this manner, we must alter the USING statement slightly. If you recall, the reference point on the USING statement (first operand) must match the address in our primary base register. When the entry point address was contained in our base register and when the label on the USING statement addressed our CSECT statement, the two reference points agreed, thus allowing our program to process properly. When we use the BALR instruction to establish our base register, the address in our base register is the address of the instruction that *follows* the BALR instruction. In other words, the address in R12 is the address of the LA instruction with respect to the code shown in Fig. 9.21.

```
MAINPGM  CSECT
         STM    R14,R12,12(R13)
         BALR   R12,0
         using statement goes here
         LA     R10,SAVEAREA
```

Figure 9.21 Using BALR to establish a base register.

We must now adjust our USING statement so that it also addresses the LA instruction. The easiest way to do this is to use the code given in Fig. 9.22.

```
MAINPGM  CSECT
         STM    R14,R12,12(R13)
         BALR   R12,0
         USING  *,R12
         LA     R10,SAVEAREA
```

Figure 9.22 The USING statement when using BALR to establish a base register.

The * parameter in the USING statement informs the assembler that the current instruction serves as the reference point for computing displacements within the program. However, since the USING instruction does not generate object code, the * parameter actually addresses the load address instruction. Since the base register and the USING statement both address the same instruction, we have established our base register correctly.

If desired, you may label the LA instruction and use the code given in Fig. 9.23 to establish your base register. Again, both reference points are identical; we've just identified them in a slightly different manner.

```
MAINPGM  CSECT
         STM     R14,R12,12(R13)
         BALR    R12,0
         USING   BASEREF,R12
BASEREF  LA      R10,SAVEAREA
```

Figure 9.23 Using BALR with a labeled USING statement.

This technique works, but you must be careful. The displacements for all storage area references do not match the location counter values produced by the assembler. The location counter begins at offset 0 and begins with the first instruction of the program. From the code in Fig. 9.23, displacements for all storage areas are computed from the LA instruction and not from the CSECT instruction. Hence, there is a difference of six between the two values since the STM instruction is four bytes long and the BALR instruction is two bytes long.

EXTERNAL SUBROUTINES

With our development so far, the transition from internal to external subroutines is relatively simple. Data is passed between the calling and called subroutine using registers 0 and 1 as compared to the standard manner in which data is accessed in an internal subroutine (label reference). However, we've seen how to pass data using R1 as the parameter register. Therefore, there is little difference in passing data to an external routine based on what you've seen so far.

An external subroutine is a separate program that should adhere to the IBM linkage conventions by establishing a base register and a new register save area. Since we know how to set up a base register and a register save area, let's look at the basic format of an external subroutine using Fig. 9.24. It should be familiar since it has the same format as our mainline program.

The external subroutine establishes a base register and a register save area when called. In this case, R12 is selected as the base register and uses our more familiar method of establishing a base register. The calling function is not concerned whether or not it uses R12 as a base register since the registers are saved and reloaded when this external subroutine obtains and relinquishes control.

As stated earlier, this routine is a complete program containing all data areas needed for processing and all literals used within this routine. That is why the LTORG statement is coded at the bottom of this module.

The primary difference between this module and a mainline module is its data source. As you can see, the parameters are addressed at the beginning of the module so that the routine can process the data within the body of the module. As is the case with internal subroutines, data may also be sent back to the calling module if expected. Of

```
SUBX      CSECT
          STM     R14,R12,12(R13)
          LR      R12,R15
          USING   SUBX,R12
          LA      R10,SUBXSAVE
          ST      R10,8(R13)
          ST      R13,SUBXSAVE+4
          LR      R13,R10

          address parm values
          .       .
          process as required
          .       .
          indicate success or failure
            via R15
          .       .
          .       .

          L       R13,4(R13)
          L       R14,12(R13)
          LM      R0,R12,20(R13)
          BR      R14

          .       .
SUBXSAVE  DS      18F
          .       .
          other data areas
          LTORG
```

Figure 9.24 Format of an external subroutine.

course, the complete parameter list consisting of input and output parameters must be known by both the calling and the called routines.

The registers are saved and reloaded to preserve the processing environment of the calling module. Data is passed between the modules through register 0 (single value) or register 1 (one or more values in the form of an address list). Let's suppose that SUBX requires three input parameters and produces one output value. The code needed to invoke SUBX is shown in Fig. 9.25.

The code introduces several new techniques used to call external subroutines. First, the literal **=V(SUBX),** called a **V-constant** or **V-type address constant,** allows our calling routine to obtain the address of an external subroutine (another CSECT). If SUBX were an internal subroutine and did not begin with a CSECT statement, we would use the more familiar **A-type address constant.**

Another new instruction is the **LTR (load and test register)** instruction, which copies the contents of the second register into the first register and causes the condition code to be set depending on the value in the first register. Although the two registers may be different, this example illustrates that the contents of R15 are copied into R15 and the condition code is set. Actually, R15 did not change, but we did set the condition code. *As*

```
LA   R1,PARMLIST          ADDRESS THE PARAMETER LIST
L    R15,=V(SUBX)         OBTAIN ADDRESS OF SUBX
BALR R14,R15              CALL THE SUBROUTINE
LTR  R15,R15              DID SUBX WORK OK?
BNZ  PROBLEM              IF NOT, WE HAVE A PROBLEM
```

Figure 9.25 Code to invoke an external subroutine called SUBX.

used above, this instruction may more appropriately be called the "condition code setting instruction."

The LTR instruction determines whether a module completed its task correctly or not. Since R15 is the first register specified, a value of 0 in R15 sets the condition code to a value of B'1000'. If the contents of R15 are less than zero, then the condition code is set to B'0100', and a value greater than zero in R15 sets the condition code to B'0010'. Basically, the LTR determines if R15 has a value equal to or greater than zero. If your subroutine sets R15 to several different values before returning, depending on the outcome of the processing within the module, use the more familiar C (compare) or CL (compare logical) instructions to determine *what* value is in R15 when a module returns control.

The value returned in R15 is commonly called the **return code,** appropriately named since the value is placed into the register before a module returns to the higher level module. When a mainline program returns control to the operating system, the value in R15 is used as a return code to the operating system. This value is then printed by the operating system on the allocation and messages section of the printout under the **condition code** category.

The capability to indicate module success or failure is very useful to determine the success or failure of your program. Figure 9.26 illustrates two examples of return code values. One value indicates a "successful" return from a program and the other indicates a potential problem.

Invoking the subroutine and passing parameters is similar to our previous examples where register 1 pointed to our parameter list and registers 14 and 15 were used as linking registers. There is one important factor to note here, however. For internal subroutines, we noted that the link register did not have to be register 14 and that register 15 did not have to be used at all. The BAL or BAS instructions could provide linkage without using a register in the second operand. This is *not* the case here. Linkage conventions specify that register 14 *will be* the link register and that register 15 *should* be the target of the BALR instruction. As we discussed earlier, some programs may not follow the linkage conventions fully. In general, R14 is mostly adhered to, but R15 may not be used as the target of the linking process.

Again, the BASR instruction is used in place of BALR if 31-bit addressing is used on your system or if your external subroutine does not preserve the condition code and program mask bits in the PSW. BASR is not supported in ASSIST.

As compared to the placement of internal subroutines within our mainline program, it is again very important to code your external subroutines in their correct places. If you imbed an external subroutine in the middle of your mainline CSECT, you can have problems and lose addressability to various elements within your program. The example in Fig. 9.27 illustrates the typical area in which to place external subroutines. As you can see, it is generally located just before the END statement of the mainline code.

The subroutines are contained within the bounds of the END statement, but they are *completely* outside of the mainline code. They are separate CSECT's and *they must have their own LTORG statements.* Each module must now have its own LTORG statement since each is a separate CSECT. If only one LTORG statement is coded just before the END statement, then *all* literals for *all* routines are generated at that point. Hence, all literals used in the routines called MAINLINE and SUBX belong to SUBY. Further, references to the literals used in MAINLINE and SUBX result in errors since the literals are not contained within their CSECT. Figure 9.28 shows the incorrect format for using literals in a program containing external subroutines.

The label on the END statement is very important when external subroutines are coded. It indicates which CSECT is to be given control *first*. If the label on the END

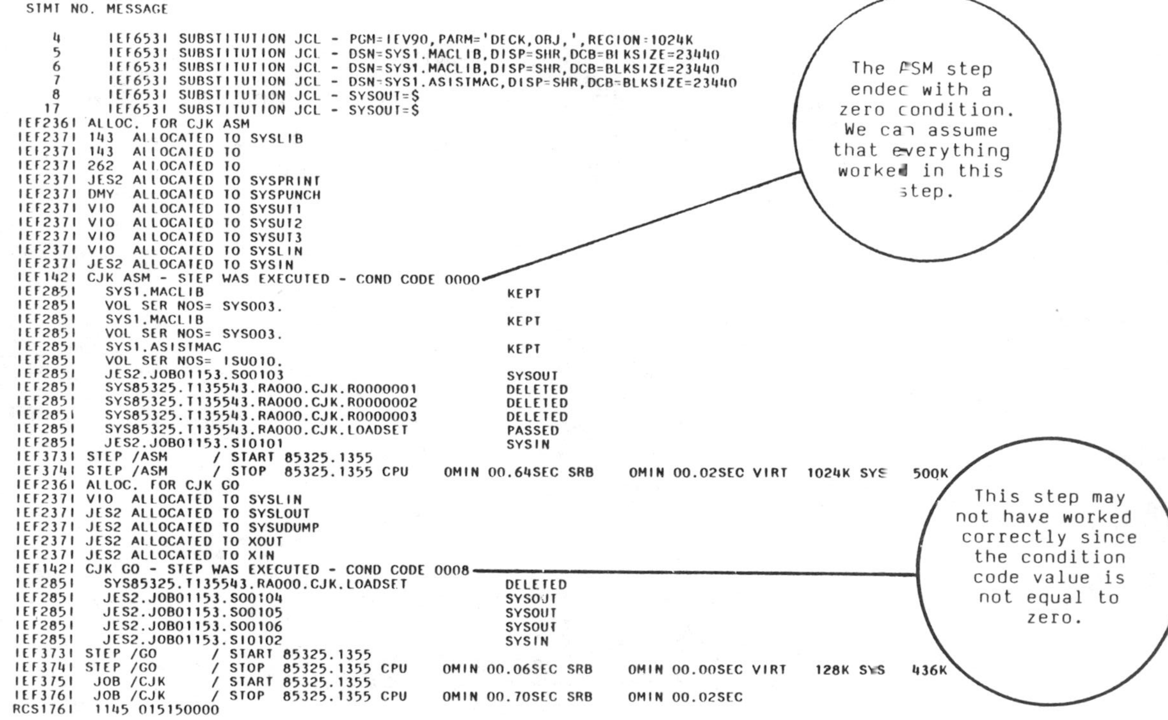

```
STMT NO. MESSAGE

   4      IEF653I SUBSTITUTION JCL - PGM=IEV90,PARM='DECK,OBJ,',REGION=1024K
   5      IEF653I SUBSTITUTION JCL - DSN=SYS1.MACLIB,DISP=SHR,DCB=BLKSIZE=23440
   6      IEF653I SUBSTITUTION JCL - DSN=SYS1.MACLIB,DISP=SHR,DCB=BLKSIZE=23440
   7      IEF653I SUBSTITUTION JCL - DSN=SYS1.ASISTMAC,DISP=SHR,DCB=BLKSIZE=23440
   8      IEF653I SUBSTITUTION JCL - SYSOUT=$
  17      IEF653I SUBSTITUTION JCL - SYSOUT=$
IEF236I ALLOC. FOR CJK ASM
IEF237I 143  ALLOCATED TO SYSLIB
IEF237I 143  ALLOCATED TO
IEF237I 262  ALLOCATED TO
IEF237I JES2 ALLOCATED TO SYSPRINT
IEF237I DMY  ALLOCATED TO SYSPUNCH
IEF237I VIO  ALLOCATED TO SYSUT1
IEF237I VIO  ALLOCATED TO SYSUT2
IEF237I VIO  ALLOCATED TO SYSUT3
IEF237I VIO  ALLOCATED TO SYSLIN
IEF237I JES2 ALLOCATED TO SYSIN
IEF142I CJK ASM - STEP WAS EXECUTED - COND CODE 0000
IEF285I   SYS1.MACLIB                                     KEPT
IEF285I   VOL SER NOS= SYS003.
IEF285I   SYS1.MACLIB                                     KEPT
IEF285I   VOL SER NOS= SYS003.
IEF285I   SYS1.ASISTMAC                                   KEPT
IEF285I   VOL SER NOS= ISU010.
IEF285I   JES2.JOB01153.S00103                            SYSOUT
IEF285I   SYS85325.T135543.RA000.CJK.R0000001             DELETED
IEF285I   SYS85325.T135543.RA000.CJK.R0000002             DELETED
IEF285I   SYS85325.T135543.RA000.CJK.R0000003             DELETED
IEF285I   SYS85325.T135543.RA000.CJK.LOADSET              PASSED
IEF285I   JES2.JOB01153.SI0101                            SYSIN
IEF373I STEP /ASM     / START 85325.1355
IEF374I STEP /ASM     / STOP  85325.1355 CPU    0MIN 00.64SEC SRB    0MIN 00.02SEC VIRT  1024K SYS   500K
IEF236I ALLOC. FOR CJK GO
IEF237I VIO  ALLOCATED TO SYSLIN
IEF237I JES2 ALLOCATED TO SYSLOUT
IEF237I JES2 ALLOCATED TO SYSUDUMP
IEF237I JES2 ALLOCATED TO XOUT
IEF237I JES2 ALLOCATED TO XIN
IEF142I CJK GO - STEP WAS EXECUTED - COND CODE 0008
IEF285I   SYS85325.T135543.RA000.CJK.LOADSET              DELETED
IEF285I   JES2.JOB01153.S00104                            SYSOUT
IEF285I   JES2.JOB01153.S00105                            SYSOUT
IEF285I   JES2.JOB01153.S00106                            SYSOUT
IEF285I   JES2.JOB01153.SI0102                            SYSIN
IEF373I STEP /GO      / START 85325.1355
IEF374I STEP /GO      / STOP  85325.1355 CPU    0MIN 00.06SEC SRB    0MIN 00.00SEC VIRT   128K SYS   436K
IEF375I  JOB /CJK     / START 85325.1355
IEF376I  JOB /CJK     / STOP  85325.1355 CPU    0MIN 00.70SEC SRB    0MIN 00.02SEC
RCS176I  1145 015150000
```


Figure 9.26 Condition codes indicate program success or failure.

```
MAINLINE    CSECT
            .       .
            .       .
            LTORG

SUBX        CSECT
            .       .
            .       .
            LTORG


SUBY        CSECT
            .       .
            .       .
            LTORG

            END     MAINLINE
```

Figure 9.27 Format of a program utilizing external subroutines.

this code will not work properly !

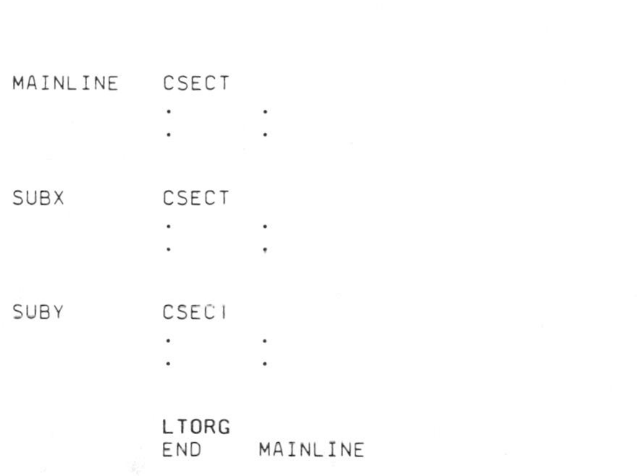

```
MAINLINE    CSECT
            .       .
            .       .


SUBX        CSECT
            .       .
            .       .


SUBY        CSECT
            .       .
            .       .


            LTORG
            END     MAINLINE
```

Figure 9.28 Incorrect coding of the LTORG with external subroutines.

statement specifies SUBY instead of MAINLINE, execution *begins* at the routine called SUBY instead of MAINLINE. Clearly, this is a problem if MAINLINE is the highest level module in the system and SUBY is subordinate to MAINLINE.

Since the END statement does allow you to specify which routine is to be given control, it is clear that the order of the routines does not matter. SUBX could be coded first followed by MAINLINE and then by SUBY. Again, the END statement identifies which module is to be given control when execution begins.

INTERNAL AND EXTERNAL SUBROUTINES IN THE SAME PROGRAM

A large-scale system may contain internal as well as external subroutines. It is very important to understand the relationship between them so that you can determine which type of subroutine best suits the problem to be solved. Since a module's address is nor-

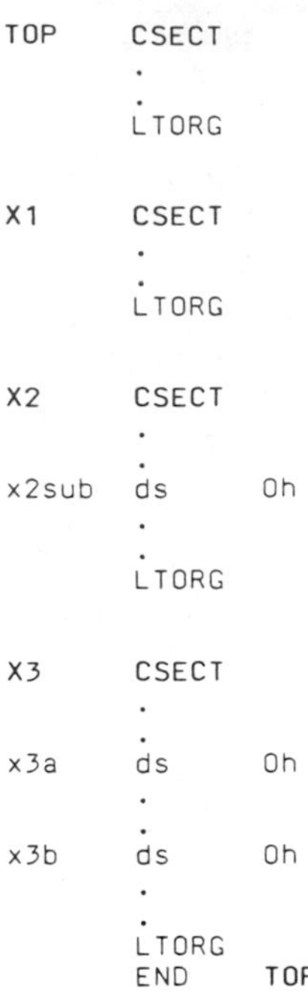

```
TOP     CSECT
        .
        .
        LTORG

X1      CSECT
        .
        .
        LTORG

X2      CSECT
        .
        .
x2sub   ds      0h
        .
        .
        LTORG

X3      CSECT
        .
        .
x3a     ds      0h
        .
        .
x3b     ds      0h
        .
        .
        LTORG
        END     TOP
```

Figure 9.29 Module calling hierarchy.

mally obtained through an A-type or V-type address constant, a module hierarchy develops when subroutines are used.

An internal subroutine is housed within the bounds of an external subroutine or within the bounds of a mainline program. An internal subroutine can call an external subroutine. It can also call another internal subroutine housed within the same control section. On the other hand, an external subroutine can call another external subroutine or it can call any internal subroutines housed inside the external subroutine.

Figure 9.29 illustrates this relationship. As you can see, TOP, X1, X2, and X3 are all external subroutines. Within X2 is the internal routine X2SUB and within X3 are two internal subroutines X3A and X3B.

The allowable calls are given in Fig. 9.30.

```
TOP     can call   X1    X2      X3
X1      can call         X2      X3
X2      can call   X1    x2sub   X3
x2sub   can call   X1            X3
X3      can call   X1    X2      x3a    x3b
x3a     can call   X1    X2             x3b
x3b     can call   X1    X2      x3a
```

Figure 9.30 Allowable calls for the code of Fig. 9.29.

Actually, a module may call itself or may call a module who called it. For example, X1 is called by TOP, and, as shown, X1 cannot call TOP. In fact, this is not true. Although other calls are allowable, we have not shown them here. Such routines are called

recursive routines, and although they have a very important role in certain types of data processing situations, we'll omit them from our discussion for now.

EXECUTE JCL STATEMENT PARAMETERS

In standard assembly language (not ASSIST), data can be directed into a program from the EXECUTE (EXEC) JCL statement. This capability allows up to 100 characters of information to be input to a program when it begins execution. Although you may not think that there is need for such a facility, it is in fact very valuable. For example, a program that prints a report may select only certain records from a file based on a beginning and ending date within the records. To supply the program with these dates, we must either change the code in the program to reflect the new dates each time that it is run or allow the program to input a data control record containing the desired date ranges. Both of these alternatives have their advantages and disadvantages.

In the case of changing the program, the obvious disadvantage is that we could make a mistake and cause an error during assembly. This is a rather trivial reason, but there's a more substantial reason. In Chapter 13 we'll learn how to place executable routines into a library for general use by all programmers or systems within a company. If the routine to print a report is used by several people simultaneously, then we do not want one person's processing to be impacted by another's. Clearly, changing the code in the program *does* impact someone else's processing when they use the program.

For values entered via a control record, the program must OPEN, GET, and CLOSE the file to be processed. These services require intervention by the operating system, thus increasing the overhead of our program and decreasing performance.

Both disadvantages are solved by using the EXEC statement parameter, provided that no more than 100 characters of data are needed by the program.

When a program begins execution, register 1 contains the address of the EXEC statement parameter data. If a program consists of several CSECT's (as shown earlier), the *first* CSECT to obtain control from the operating system has access to the parameter data through register 1. Hence, starting and ending dates to our program are supplied as shown in Fig. 9.31.

```
//    EXEC    ASMCG,PARM.GO='/mmddyymmddyy'
```

Figure 9.31 Passing parameters into a program via the EXEC JCL statement.

You must remember that we are using the assembler and loader to run our program. The slash after the first quote *is required.* Each of the six character dates are then coded for a total of 12 bytes of data to our program. If our program was in executable form and did not need to be processed by the assembler or loader, our EXEC statement parameter could be coded as illustrated in Fig. 9.32. The slash is omitted because we are not calling our program through the loader.

```
//    EXEC    PGM=OURPGM,PARM='mmddyymmddyy'
```

Figure 9.32 EXEC parameter format when not using the assemble/go procedure.

When our program obtains control, register 1 points to a fullword address. This address further points to a data area that contains our parameter (parm) information. Figure 9.33 illustrates the complete chaining process to obtain the EXEC statement data.

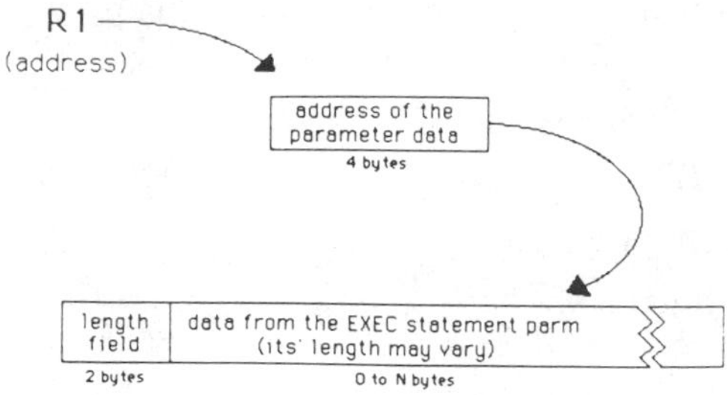

Figure 9.33 Accessing the EXEC statement parameter data. The first field of the parameter data is a binary halfword holding a value equal to the amount of data entered on the EXEC statement. The actual parameter data follows this halfword field.

The first field within the parameter data area is a two-byte *binary* field. This value indicates the number of data bytes entered into the PARM field on the EXEC statement. This value may be greater than or equal to zero, but no more than 100 bytes of data may be supplied to the program through the parm field.

A program that is to use the parm data should first check the value in the length area to determine if sufficient data was entered in the EXEC statement field. Also, the program may have to edit the data to ensure that it is in the correct format and that the correct data has in fact been entered. If the data is invalid or if insufficient data has been entered, the program may abort processing, correct the data and continue (if possible), substitute default values for any parm fields that were incorrectly entered, or possibly print out messages to the person trying to run the program. All of these measures attempt to identify problems in the parm data so that they may be corrected and the program rerun. However, if we think of the reasons for using the parm field, message printing or I/O operations were to be avoided. Hence, printing messages explaining problems in the parm field defeats the purpose of using the parm field as a substitute for input processing.

Let's write a section of code to accept our starting and ending dates from the EXEC statement parameter. Since we expect exactly 12 bytes of data to be entered, we elect to abort our program if 12 bytes have not been entered. Although we probably should check the data further to ensure that all characters are digits and that each date is a valid date, I'll leave this processing to you. Figure 9.34 contains this implementation.

The code addresses the parm data and proceeds to check it for correct length. With register 3 holding the length value, it is compared to the value of 12. If the value in R3 is 12, then a branch is taken to the label called PARMOK, but if the data is not 12 bytes long, then the branch is not taken, causing our program to "fall into" the instruction DC X'0000'. Since this is not a valid machine instruction (there is no operation code of 00), our program aborts with an OC1, operation exception (invalid instruction), abend code.

This is one of the first checks against the parm data. As stated earlier, further checks may be issued against the data if desired.

```
MAINPGM  CSECT
         STM    R14,R12,12(R13)      SAVE THE REGS
         LR     R12,R15              R12 IS OUR BASE
         USING  MAINPGM,R12
         LA     R10,SAVEM            ADDRESS SAVE AREA
         ST     R10,8(R13)           CHAIN FORWARD
         ST     R13,SAVEM+4          CHAIN BACKWARD
         LR     R13,R10              ESTABLISH NEW AREA
         L      R2,0(R1)             ADDRESS PARM DATA
         LH     R3,0(R2)             GET LENGTH OF DATA
         C      R3,=F'12'            12 BYTES ENTERED?
         BE     PARMOK               IF SO, CONTINUE
         DC     X'0000'              ABEND THE PROGRAM
PARMOK   DS     0H
         MVC    DATES(12),2(R2)      MOVE IN GOOD DATES

         .      .
         .      .
         .      .

DATES    DS     0CL12
DATE1MM  DS     CL2
DATE1DD  DS     CL2
DATE1YY  DS     CL2
DATE2MM  DS     CL2
DATE2DD  DS     CL2
DATE2YY  DS     CL2
```

Figure 9.34 EXEC parameter access program example.

I/O OPERATIONS ACROSS MODULE BOUNDARIES

Programs consisting of several modules often perform I/O operations in more than one module. Although such processing presents no problems in ASSIST, it can be disastrous in assembler. When implementing multimodule systems in assembly language, you must be very careful about issuing I/O operations against the same file in different modules.

This problem is most prevalent with external subroutines. Although there may be a concern about *design* when several internal routines access the same file, there are no real problems if I/O is done in this manner. The major problem with I/O operations is addressing the DCB.

As you know, all files must be opened and closed in assembly language. Further, a DCB is required when processing a file. Hence, the OPEN, CLOSE, GET, and PUT instructions must address or reference the DCB to do their jobs. If the DCB is housed in an external module, then it is not available as a label and must therefore become a parameter to the external routine. Internal subroutines do not require a DCB to be passed as a parameter since it can address all elements defined within its scope and within the CSECT in which it is housed (containing the DCB).

A DCB *address* may be passed as a parameter just as any other data element. Let's assume that the third parameter in our parameter list is a DCB address. To perform I/O against this DCB, we must use explicit addressing in the GET or PUT instruction shown in Fig. 9.35.

```
L     R4,8(R1)      GET ADDRESS OF THE DCB
.     .
.     .
.     .
i/o   0(R4),LINEX   READ OR PRINT THE DATA AS NEEDED
```

Figure 9.35 Addressing and using a DCB through explicit addressing.

The third parameter is at offset 8 in the parameter list since parameters 1 and 2 are at offsets 0 and 4, respectively. We obtain the DCB address from the parameter list and begin processing within our module. When needed, our module issues either a GET or PUT instruction against the data that we are to process in the I/O operation.

There are many obvious problems when processing in this manner. First, this module must assume that the DCB has been opened by some other module. If it hasn't, the module abends. Second, the module assumes that the DCB is of the correct format for I/O processing. In other words, the module assumes that the DCB is properly defined with the correct LRECL, RECFM, and so on to allow the module to properly access the data in the file. Finally, the module assumes that the DCB is closed before the system ends. Again, an abend usually results if this is not the case.

I/O may be performed across module boundaries, but it is generally centralized within a single module. In other words, one module prints all data to the file called PRNT. This module opens, prints, and closes the file *when asked to do so* by another module in the system. Using the logic in Fig. 9.36 as an example, the mainline module could contain that logic for a design.

```
(a) Invoke I/O modules to open their respective files.
(b) Obtain first record to be processed by invoking
     the input module.
(c) Repeat until the end of file is reached:
     process the record by calling appropriate
      modules to process the data
     send output results to the print module
     obtain next record by calling the appropriate
      input module
(d) Invoke I/O modules to close their respective files.
```

Figure 9.36 Logic for a system containing a centralized I/O driver.

Now let's look at one of the I/O modules, particularly the module performing printing operations using standard 133-character lines with the ANSI carriage control.

This module requires two parameters. The first is the address of a field that indicates whether the module should open, close, or print to the file. The second parameter is the address of the line to be printed. Note that the second parameter has no value when the module is being called to open or close the file. Hence, the logic for the module appears as shown in Fig. 9.37.

As you can see, the module checks the operation code each time it is called. If an invalid code is specified, then the module returns a nonzero value in R15. Of course, the *calling* module should check the value of R15 after each call to determine if the operation completed successfully or not.

```
If operation = "open" then
   OPEN the file
else
   if operation = "close" then
      CLOSE the file
   else
      if operation = "print" then
         print the data to the file
      else
         set a bad return code in R15
```

Figure 9.37 Logic for a centralized I/O module.

The code to call the module is shown in Fig. 9.38. The code for the print module is given in Fig. 9.39 on page 366.

This module is completely self-contained. As long as it is called to open the file before printing requests occur, it works as intended. As you can see, the DCB is housed within this module. Hence, explicit addressing is not required to address the DCB, but it is required to address the line to be printed. This is slightly different than our earlier discussion in which the DCB, not the data itself, was a parameter value.

```
         LA    R1,PLIST            POINT TO PARAMETER LIST
         L     R15,PRINTIT         GET PRINTIT MODULE ADDRESS
         BALR  R14,R15             PRINT THE OUTPUT LINE
         LTR   R15,R15             WAS OPERATION OK?
         BZ    CONTINUE            IF SO, CONTINUE NORMALLY
         ...we have a problem.
         ...what do we do at this point?


PRINTIT  DC    V(PRNTMOD)          ADDRESS OF PRINT MODULE
PLIST    DC    A(PCODE)            PRINT CODE VALUE
         DC    A(PLINE)            PRINT LINE ADDRESS

PCODE    DC    C'P'                PRINT THIS LINE PLEASE
PLINE    DS    CL133               PRINT LINE AREA
```

Figure 9.38 The code to call a centralized I/O module.

TESTING DCB's WHEN USED AS PARAMETERS

Now that you've seen both forms of I/O processing with respect to modular implementation, let's discuss the more difficult technique of using the DCB as a parameter. As we said earlier, a DCB address may be passed as a parameter to a subordinate module so that I/O may be performed in more than one module. The called module usually assumes that the DCB is properly opened, but we can build checks into this module if that is not true. Our module can be designed to see if the DCB is opened. If it isn't, the module could abort, return a nonzero return code, or attempt to open the DCB. Since you know how to abend a program, pass back a nonzero return code, and open a DCB, we can concentrate on determining *if* the DCB is open or not.

To determine if a DCB is open, we only have to check one bit within the DCB itself.

```
PRNTMOD  CSECT
         STM   R14,R12,12(R13)  SAVE THE REGS
         BALR  R12,0            ESTABLISH A BASE REG
         USING *,R12
         LA    R10,PSAVE        POINT TO OUR SAVE AREA
         ST    R13,PSAVE+4      CHAIN BACKWARD
         ST    R10,8(R13)       CHAIN FORWARD
         LR    R13,R10          ESTABLISH NEW R13
*
         LM    R2,R3,0(R1)      GET PARM VALUES
*
         CLI   0(R2),C'O'       OPEN THE FILE?
         BE    POPEN            IF SO, GO OPEN IT
         CLI   0(R2),C'P'       PRINT A LINE?
         BE    PPRINT           IF SO, GO PRINT IT
         CLI   0(R2),C'C'       CLOSE THE FILE?
         BE    PCLOSE           IF SO, GO CLOSE IT
*
PBAD     DS    0H               INVALID PRINT CODE VALUE
         LA    R15,8            SET BAD RETURN CODE
         B     PEXIT            GET OUT
*
POPEN    DS    0H
         OPEN  (PRNT,OUTPUT)
         B     PEXIT
PPRINT   DS    0H
         PUT   PRNT,0(R3)       PRINT THE PARAMETER LINE
         B     PEXIT
PCLOSE   DS    0H
         CLOSE (PRNT)
*
PEXIT    DS    0H
         L     R13,PSAVE+4      RESTORE R13'S VALUE
         L     R14,12(R13)      RESTORE R14
         LM    R0,R12,20(R13)   RESTORE ALL BUT R15
         BR    R14              RETURN CONTROL TO CALLER
*
PSAVE    DS    18F              REGISTER SAVE AREA
PRNT     DCB   DSORG=PS,DDNAME=PRNT,MACRF=PM,RECFM=FBA,    X
               LRECL=133,BLKSIZE=2261
         LTORG
```

Figure 9.39 The complete code for an I/O subroutine.

This bit, located at offset 48 (base 10) into the DCB, is one if the DCB is open, or zero if it is not. To test the value of an individual bit within a byte, we use the **TM (test under mask)** instruction.

The test under mask instruction tests the value of bits in storage as associated with a bit pattern coded in the second operand. For example, we can test the first bit of a byte in memory by coding a bit mask of B'10000000'. If the matching bit in the byte being tested is one, then the condition code is set to B'0001'. We then use the extended mnemonic **BO (branch if ones)** to act on this bit value. If the bit in memory is zero, then the condition code is set to B'1000', allowing us to use the extended mnemonic **BZ (branch if zeros)** to control processing.

Several bit values may be tested by using a mask with more than one bit indicated for testing. A mask of B'10101010' tests every other bit in a byte. If *all* bits to be tested have a value of one, then the condition code is set to B'0001'. If *all* bits tested have a value of zero, then the condition code is set to B'1000'. If *some* bits are ones and some are zeros, then the condition code is set to B'0100', allowing use of the extended mnemonic **BM (branch if mixed)** to control program flow.

With respect to our discussion on DCB's, we must test the fourth bit, at offset 48, of the DCB. If this bit is one, then the DCB is open; otherwise, the DCB is not open. We code the test under mask instruction as shown in Fig. 9.40 to make this evaluation.

```
TM     dcbaddress+48,B'00010000'
BO     OPENED
```

Figure 9.40 Testing the DCB for open/close status.

The fourth bit, and only the fourth bit, has to be tested. If our program branches to the location OPENED, then we know that the DCB is open and is ready for use. If it is not open, then we can take appropriate action as described earlier.

Since the DCB address is undoubtedly a parameter, we will most likely use explicit addressing to reference it. If we assume that register 3 contains our DCB address, then the TM instruction is coded as shown in Fig. 9.41.

```
TM     48(R3),B'00010000'
BO     OPENED
```

Figure 9.41 Testing the DCB for open/close status using explicit addressing.

We can also use reverse logic to control our branch instruction after testing the storage bit against our mask value. The extended mnemonic **BNO (branch if not ones)** may control program flow if the bit tested is not one. We can use the instruction illustrated in Fig. 9.42.

```
TM      48(R3),B'00010000'
BNO     NOTOPEN
```

Figure 9.42 Reverse logic with TM.

If the bit in the DCB is not one, then the DCB is not open. We can appropriately set the return code or issue an open for the DCB with the OPEN instruction shown in Fig. 9.43.

```
OPEN     ((R3),INPUT)
```

Figure 9.43 Opening a closed DCB using explicit addressing.

If the DCB is to be opened for output, then we issue the instruction given in Fig. 9.44.

```
OPEN     ((R3),OUTPUT)
```

Figure 9.44 Opening a DCB for output using explicit addressing.

Register 3 must be enclosed in parentheses as shown in the instruction. *Do not* attempt to code the instruction given in Fig. 9.45.

This example does not work.

```
OPEN     (0(R3),OUTPUT)
```

Figure 9.45 Incorrect addressing when attempting to open a DCB.

The difference between the two forms is the added displacement in the example of Fig. 9.45. This is *not* the correct format for issuing the OPEN when explicit addressing to the DCB is used. The register must contain the true or actual address of the DCB to use this form of the OPEN instruction.

Be careful when coding the TM instruction. The second operand is not a literal, rather, it is **immediate data**. If you code a TM instruction as shown in Fig. 9.46, you obtain a syntax error.

This example causes a syntax error.

```
TM     48(R3),=B'00010000'
```

Figure 9.46 Incorrectly coding the second operand of a TM instruction.

ASSEMBLY LANGUAGE AND COBOL COMMUNICATIONS

This chapter concludes by investigating the techniques for passing data between COBOL and assembly language programs (not ASSIST). In fact, we'll find out how to pass data from an assembly language program to a COBOL program *and* from a COBOL program to an assembly language program. Although we might also have discussed how to pass parameters between assembly language and PL/I, FORTRAN, PASCAL, and many other languages, COBOL was selected since it is the most popular business oriented language. Also, most languages adhere to the linkage conventions to pass data between modules. Thus, our discussion for passing data between COBOL and assembly language routines would apply equally to a discussion on passing data between FORTRAN and assembly language and so on. As long as you adhere to the linkage conventions, modules can be written in almost any language and data can be passed between those modules for processing.

Parameters are passed between COBOL and assembly language programs just as we have been discussing. Register 1 points to a list of addresses which in turn address the data element values. Registers 14 and 15 are linkage registers and register 13 is again the save area register. Register 0 is not used to communicate between these languages. As we stated earlier, register 0 is rarely used for passing parameters since register 1 is the industry standard parameter register.

Consider the add, subtract, multiply, and divide program that we implemented earlier in assembly language. Without considering the need or design of this application, suppose that the arithmetic functions are implemented as separate modules. In other words, the actual add, subtract, multiply, and divide functions are implemented in COBOL and the mainline logic is implemented in assembly language. Conversely, the mainline logic may be implemented in COBOL and the arithmetic functions in assembly language. You'll see both implementations of this system.

Passing data from an assembly language program to a COBOL program is no different than passing data between two assembly language programs. For example, to pass

```
         BAL    R1,ADDEM        POINT TO PARM LIST AND SKIP AROUND
         DC     A(COMMAND)      COMMAND INDICATOR (ADD)
         DC     A(VALUE1)       ADDRESS OF THE FIRST ELEMENT
         DC     A(VALUE2)       ADDRESS OF THE SECOND ELEMENT
         DC     A(SUM)          AREA FOR THE RESULT VALUE
ADDEM    DS     0H
         L      R15,=V(COBSUB)     ADDRESS COBOL SUBROUTINE
         BALR   R14,R15            CALL THE COBOL ROUTINE

         .      .
         .      .

COMMAND  DC     C'A'            ADD THE TWO NUMBERS
VALUE1   DS     PL8             FIRST OPERAND VALUE
VALUE2   DS     PL8             SECOND OPERAND VALUE
SUM      DS     PL8             DATA AREA FOR THE SUM
```

Figure 9.47 Passing data from an assembly language program to a COBOL program.

two values (to be added) from our assembly language program to a COBOL program, we simply code the instructions shown in Fig. 9.47.

The code in Fig. 9.47 uses yet another technique for invoking a subroutine. The parameter list immediately follows the BAL instruction. Referring to Fig. 9.47 you can see that four parameters are passed and they are COMMAND, VALUE1, VALUE2, and SUM. The BAL instruction causes register 1 to be updated to the address of the area *following* the BAL. Thus, register 1 is changed so that it addresses the constant area containing the address of COMMAND. This effectively causes R1 to address the first element in the parameter list, just as it should.

After register 1 is updated, the BAL instruction transfers control to the location labeled ADDEM. By transferring control around the parameter list, an abend is avoided and addressability to the parameter list is established appropriately. This technique is used often because it's clear how many parameters are to be passed to the routine and what those parameters are. In a previous example (see Fig. 9.19) the parameter list was located in the data areas section of the program. To understand what elements were passed to a routine, the programmer might have to locate the parameter list later in the listing and then refer back to the calling code to coordinate the two components. Here, both the calling instructions and the parameter list definition are located in one area. This facilitates understanding and aids in overall program readability and maintenance.

The code passes four parameters to the COBOL routine. The COBOL routine uses the first parameter to determine what operation is to be performed and then uses the remaining three to perform the operation. Parameters passed to a COBOL subroutine are contained within the **LINKAGE SECTION** of the COBOL program. Since four parameters are passed, then four elements must be defined within the COBOL program's linkage section as shown in Fig. 9.48.

```
LINKAGE SECTION.

01 COMMAND-CODE       PIC X.
01 FIRST-VALUE        PIC S9(15) COMP-3.
01 SECOND-VALUE       PIC S9(15) COMP-3.
01 SUM-OF-VALUES      PIC S9(15) COMP-3.
```

Figure 9.48 LINKAGE SECTION to accept the assembler program values.

The parameters are accepted by the COBOL program only if its **PROCEDURE DIVISION** statement identifies those parameters. Figure 9.49 illustrates the proper coding of the COBOL PROCEDURE DIVISION instruction.

```
PROCEDURE DIVISION USING COMMAND-CODE, FIRST-VALUE,
          SECOND-VALUE, SUM-OF-VALUES.
```

Figure 9.49 The COBOL PROCEDURE DIVISION statement to accept parameters.

Once the linkage section is coded properly and the procedure division statement identifies the values, the COBOL program can simply work with the data as if it were contained and processed solely within the COBOL program. When the COBOL program issues the **GOBACK** (return) statement, any changed parameters are returned to the assembly language module.

A COBOL program may call an assembly language program using the COBOL **CALL** statement and specify the parameters that are to be passed to the assembly language program. Figure 9.50 gives the code to perform this calling sequence.

The COBOL program is calling the assembly language program called "asmmod" and is passing four values to it. Hence, the parameter list addressed by register 1 consists of four addresses, one for each of the parameters. As you can see, the process of passing parameters between COBOL and assembly language is identical to passing data between assembly language modules. As a result, the assembler module that processes these elements may be coded just as if these parameters were being passed from any assembler module.

Before we look at the program source code listings that exhibit the COBOL/assembly language communications process, let's first discuss how we combine the two language programs using JCL.

If the COBOL program is a subroutine to the assembler module, it must be compiled first. After compilation, the COBOL subroutine is processed by the **linkage editor** and is placed into a temporary load module library that is accessed later by the loader. JCL is the primary element to perform this processing and so it's very important to understand the function and coding of these JCL statements. Figure 9.51 contains the JCL to perform the first phase of this activity, establishing the temporary library that will hold the COBOL subroutine. You should also note that the JCL statements in the examples that follow may require slight modifications to work on your system. The allocation of file

```
WORKING-STORAGE SECTION.

01  COMMAND-CODE           PIC X.
01  FIRST-VALUE            PIC S9(15) COMP-3.
01  SECOND-VALUE           PIC S9(15) COMP-3.
01  SUM-OF-VALUES          PIC S9(15) COMP-3.

  .   .   .

PROCEDURE DIVISION.

  .   .   .

    CALL 'asmmod' USING COMMAND-CODE, FIRST-VALUE,
                  SECOND-VALUE, SUM-OF-VALUES.
```

Figure 9.50 COBOL code to call an assembler module.

```
//***********************************************************
//*    CREATE THE LOAD MODULE LIBRARY TO HOLD THE *
//*    COBOL SUB PROGRAM(S).                      *
//***********************************************************
//CREATE    EXEC    PGM=IEFBR14
//DDA       DD      DSN=&&LLIB,DISP=(NEW,PASS),
//          SPACE=(TRK,(5,5,5)),UNIT=SYSDA
```

Figure 9.51 Creating the COBOL subroutine library.

space and the assignment of device types are of particular concern. If the examples do not work as contained in this text, check with your systems programming staff to resolve any difficulties.

The program IEFBR14 is executed. This program allows the operating system to recognize and process your JCL statements, thus allowing your temporary load module library to be created.

Each COBOL subroutine is now compiled and placed into the load module library using the JCL shown in Fig. 9.52. Note that your system may consist of many such routines written in COBOL. This JCL must be coded for *each* COBOL subroutine that is to be called by your assembly language program.

```
//              EXEC   COBUCL
//COB.SYSIN    DD     *

    (place your cobol source code here)

//LKED.SYSLMOD       DD   DSN=&&LLIB(modname),DISP=(OLD,PASS)
```

Figure 9.52 JCL to place a COBOL subroutine into its library.

From Fig. 9.52, the last JCL statement must contain the name of your COBOL program. This name should match the name on the PROGRAM-ID statement within the IDENTIFICATION DIVISION of your COBOL program.

To assemble your assembly language program, attach your COBOL subroutines, and execute the entire package, now code the JCL given in Fig. 9.53.

```
//RUNIT        EXEC  ASMCG
//ASM.SYSIN    DD    *

  (place your assembly language source program here)

//GO.SYSLIB    DD     DSN=&&LLIB,DISP=(OLD,PASS)
//             DD     DSN=SYS1.COBLIB,DISP=SHR
  any other jcl statements needed to run your system
```

Figure 9.53 Assembling and executing the assembler/COBOL system.

The JCL in Fig. 9.53 calls the assembler to convert your assembly language program into machine code. The loader then forms an execution package from your assembler module and the COBOL modules referenced in your assembly language program.

Once the package is formed, it is executed. JCL statements required by this system must be coded where indicated in the example.

Now let's reverse the module heirarchy. A COBOL mainline program calls upon one or more assembly language programs as subroutines. In this case, we must first assemble each of the assembly language modules and place them into the load module library. Then we must compile the COBOL program, invoke the loader to bring in all modules of the system to form an execution package, and then execute the system.

The JCL to assemble and link edit each assembly language module is coded as shown in Fig. 9.54.

```
//              EXEC  ASMCL
//ASM.SYSIN     DD    *


  (place your assembly language
   subroutine source code here)


//LKED.SYSLMOD        DD DSN=&&LLIB(modname),DISP=(OLD,PASS)
```

Figure 9.54 The JCL to assemble and link edit an assembly language subroutine.

The last JCL statement again requires the name of the module being formed. In this case, the name on the CSECT statement of your assembly language program is placed into this area.

After all the assembly language routines have been assembled and link edited, you may now compile the mainline COBOL program and execute the resulting system by using the JCL statements shown in Fig. 9.55.

```
//              EXEC  COBUCG
//COB.SYSIN     DD    *


    (place your COBOL source program here)


//GO.SYSLIB     DD    DSN=&&LLIB,DISP=(OLD,PASS)
//              DD    DSN=SYS1.COBLIB,DISP=SHR
  any other JCL statements needed to run your system
```

Figure 9.55 Compiling the COBOL mainline program and then executing the COBOL/assembler system.

The program listings that appear in Example 9.1 illustrate the COBOL and assembler communications structure. The first listing uses an assembly language main program and a COBOL subroutine to perform the arithmetic processing used in earlier chapters. Significant components of these programs have been labeled as in previous program listings.

Example 9.2 uses a mainline COBOL program and an assembly language subroutine to compute and process in the same manner as in previous chapters using this problem example.

The COBOL and assembly language programs that you've seen are quite simple and do not involve much processing. Further, it is quite unusual for a mainline program

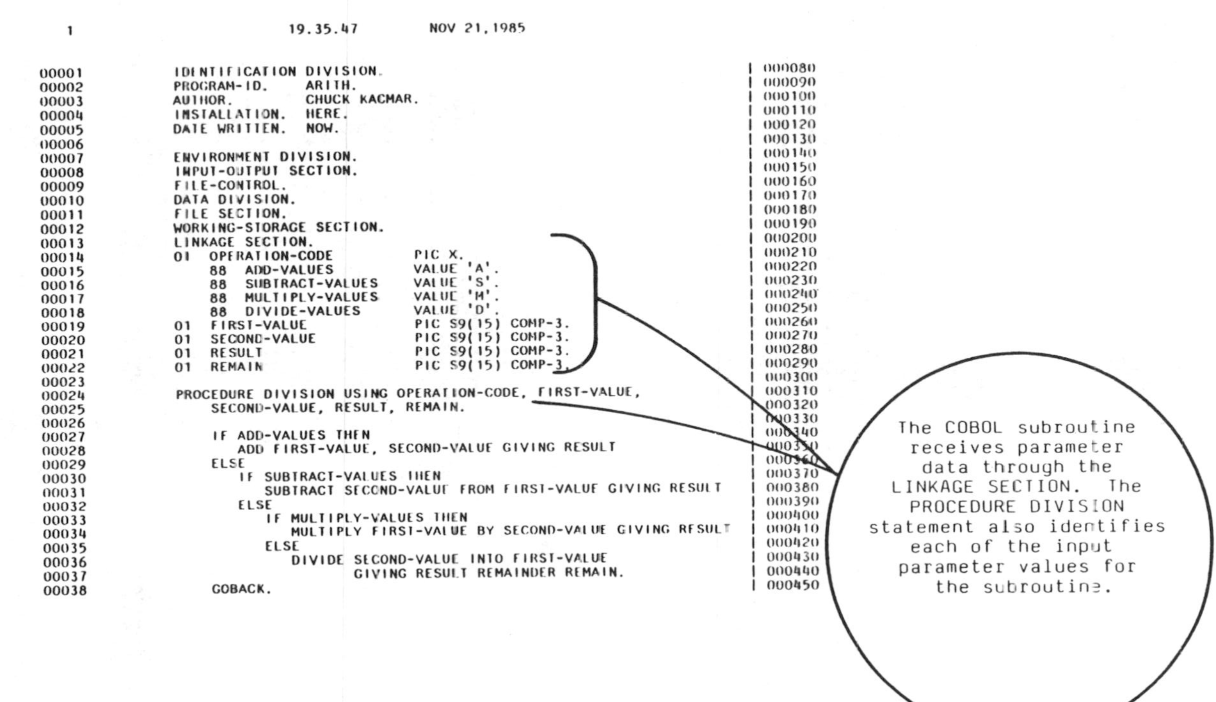

```
PP 5740-CB1 RELEASE 2.3 + PTF 8 - UP13477          IBM OS/VS COBOL  JULY 24, 1978          19.35.47  DATE NOV 21,1985

   1                    19.35.47        NOV 21,1985

               IDENTIFICATION DIVISION.
               PROGRAM-ID.     ARITH.
               AUTHOR.         CHUCK KACMAR.
               INSTALLATION.   HERE.
               DATE WRITTEN.   NOW.

               ENVIRONMENT DIVISION.
               INPUT-OUTPUT SECTION.
               FILE-CONTROL.
               DATA DIVISION.
               FILE SECTION.
               WORKING-STORAGE SECTION.
               LINKAGE SECTION.
               01  OPERATION-CODE          PIC X.
                   88  ADD-VALUES          VALUE 'A'.
                   88  SUBTRACT-VALUES     VALUE 'S'.
                   88  MULTIPLY-VALUES     VALUE 'M'.
                   88  DIVIDE-VALUES       VALUE 'D'.
               01  FIRST-VALUE             PIC S9(15) COMP-3.
               01  SECOND-VALUE            PIC S9(15) COMP-3.
               01  RESULT                  PIC S9(15) COMP-3.
               01  REMAIN                  PIC S9(15) COMP-3.

               PROCEDURE DIVISION USING OPERATION-CODE, FIRST-VALUE,
                   SECOND-VALUE, RESULT, REMAIN.

                   IF ADD-VALUES THEN
                      ADD FIRST-VALUE, SECOND-VALUE GIVING RESULT
                   ELSE
                      IF SUBTRACT-VALUES THEN
                         SUBTRACT SECOND-VALUE FROM FIRST-VALUE GIVING RESULT
                      ELSE
                         IF MULTIPLY-VALUES THEN
                            MULTIPLY FIRST-VALUE BY SECOND-VALUE GIVING RESULT
                         ELSE
                            DIVIDE SECOND-VALUE INTO FIRST-VALUE
                                   GIVING RESULT REMAINDER REMAIN.
                   GOBACK.
```


Example 9.1 COBOL subroutine and assembly language mainline.

```
COMPUTE SUM, DIFFERENCE, PRODUCT, QUOTIENT OF 2 VALUES                                   PAGE    3

  LOC  OBJECT CODE      ADDR1 ADDR2  STMT   SOURCE STATEMENT                        ASM H V 02 19.35 11/21/85

                              00000     3 R0       EQU   0                                                 000530
                              00001     4 R1       EQU   1                                                 000540
                              00002     5 R2       EQU   2                                                 000550
                              00003     6 R3       EQU   3                                                 000560
                              00004     7 R4       EQU   4                                                 000570
                              00005     8 R5       EQU   5                                                 000580
                              00006     9 R6       EQU   6                                                 000590
                              00007    10 R7       EQU   7                                                 000600
                              00008    11 R8       EQU   8                                                 000610
                              00009    12 R9       EQU   9                                                 000620
                              0000A    13 R10      EQU   10                                                000630
                              0000B    14 R11      EQU   11                                                000640
                              0000C    15 R12      EQU   12                                                000650
                              0000D    16 R13      EQU   13                                                000660
                              0000E    17 R14      EQU   14                                                000670
                              0000F    18 R15      EQU   15                                                000680
                                       19 *                                                                000690

                                       21 *******************************************************************  000710
                                       22 *   THIS PROGRAM WILL COMPUTE THE SUM, DIFFERENCE, PRODUCT, AND      *  000720
                                       23 *   QUOTIENT OF TWO INPUT VALUES.  RESULTS WILL BE PRINTED IN A      *  000730
                                       24 *   NICE REPORT FORMAT.  THE REMAINDER OF THE DIVISION WILL ALSO     *  000740
                                       25 *   BE PRINTED.                                                      *  000750
                                       26 *******************************************************************  000760
000000                                 27 PROCESS  CSECT                                                       000770
000000 90EC D00C              0000C    28          STM   R14,R12,12(13)     SAVE CALLER'S REGISTERS            000780
000004 18CF                            29          LR    R12,R15            R12 WILL BE OUR BASE REG           000790
                              00000    30          USING PROCESS,R12        TELL THE ASSEMBLER ABOUT R12       000800
000006 41A0 C6CC              006CC    31          LA    R10,SAVEAREA       POINT TO REGISTER SAVE AREA        000810
00000A 50AD 0008              00008    32          ST    R10,8(R13)         TELL CALLER ABOUT OUR SAVEAREA     000820
00000E 50DA 0004              00004    33          ST    R13,4(R10)         REMEMBER CALLER'S SAVEAREA ADDR.   000830
000012 18DA                            34          LR    R13,R10            ESTABLISH NEW SAVE AREA            000840
                                       35 *******************************************************************  000850
                                       36 *    PRINT THE TITLE LINES ON THE OUTPUT PAGE AND SET UP THE REPORT  *  000860
                                       37 *    FOR OUR OUTPUT INFORMATION.                                     *  000870
                                       38 *******************************************************************  000880
                                       39          OPEN  (XIN,INPUT)                                           000890
00001E 4130 C858              00858    45          LA    R3,XOUT                                               000900
                                       46          OPEN  ((R3),OUTPUT)                                         000910
                                       53          PUT   XOUT,TITLE         PRINT TITLE LINE                   000920
                                       58          PUT   XOUT,SUBTITLE      PRINT THE SUBTITLE                 000930
                                       63          PUT   XOUT,SKIP2         SKIP A FEW LINES                   000940
                                       68          PUT   XOUT,HEADINGS      PRINT COLUMN HEADINGS              000950
                                       73          PUT   XOUT,UNDERLIN      UNDERLINE COLUMN HEADINGS          000960
```

This is the assembler mainline program which calls the COBOL subroutine.

```
COMPUTE SUM, DIFFERENCE, PRODUCT, QUOTIENT OF 2 VALUES                                   PAGE    4

  LOC  OBJECT CODE      ADDR1 ADDR2  STMT   SOURCE STATEMENT                        ASM H V 02 19.35 11/21/85

                                       79 *******************************************************************  000980
                                       80 *  OBTAIN THE INPUT VALUES FROM OUR FILE AND CONVERT THEM INTO       *  000990
                                       81 *  BINARY FORMAT FOR PROCESSING.                                     *  001000
                                       82 *******************************************************************  001010
00007C                                 83 CONTINUE DS    0H                                                    001020
                                       84          GET   XIN,INPUTREC       GET OUR RECORD                     001030
00008A 9240 C647        00647          89          MVI   PLINE,C' '         CLEAR FIRST BYTE OF PLINE          001040
00008E D283 C648 C647 00648 00647      90          MVC   PLINE+1(132),PLINE CLEAR REST OF PRINT LINE           001050
000094 F274 C768 C714 00768 00714      91          PACK  VALUE1(8),NUM1(5)  CONVERT FIRST NUMBER               001060
00009A F274 C770 C719 00770 00719      92          PACK  VALUE2(8),NUM2(5)  CONVERT SECOND NUMBER              001070

                                       94 *******************************************************************  001090
                                       95 *  IF VALUE1 OR VALUE2 ARE TO BE NEGATIVE, THEN CONVERT THE PACKED   *  001100
                                       96 *  VALUES INTO NEGATIVE NUMBERS.                                     *  001110
                                       97 *******************************************************************  001120
0000A0 4130 C714              00714    98          LA    R3,NUM1            POINT TO FIRST INPUT NUMBER        001130
0000A4                                 99 LOOP1    DS    0H                 FIND NEGATIVE SIGN                 001140
0000A4 5930 C2B0              002B0   100          C     R3,=A(NUM1+4)      HAVE WE LOOKED AT ENTIRE NUM1      001150
0000A8 4720 C0CE              000CE   101          BH    NUM1POS            IF SO, THEN NUM1 IS POSITIVE       001160
0000AC 9560 3000        00000         102          CLI   0(R3),C'-'         NEGATIVE SIGN?                     001170
0000B0 4780 C0BC              000BC   103          BE    MINUS1             IF YES, THEN NEGATIVE FIRST NUM    001180
0000B4 4130 3001              00001   104          LA    R3,1(,R3)          ADVANCE TO NEXT ADDRESS            001190
0000B8 47F0 C0A4              000A4   105          B     LOOP1              CONTINUE LOOKING                   001200
0000BC F870 C778 C2BC 00778 002BC     106 MINUS1   ZAP   WORK(8),=P'0'      SET WORK EQUAL TO ZERO             001210
0000C2 FB77 C778 C768 00778 00768     107          SP    WORK(8),VALUE1(8)  SUBTRACT VALUE1 FROM 0             001220
0000C8 F877 C768 C778 00768 00778     108          ZAP   VALUE1(8),WORK     VALUE1 IS NOW NEGATIVE             001230
0000CE                                109 NUM1POS  DS    0H                                                    001240

0000CE 4130 C719              00719   111          LA    R3,NUM2            POINT TO FIRST INPUT NUMBER        001260
0000D2                                112 LOOP2    DS    0H                 FIND NEGATIVE SIGN                 001270
0000D2 5930 C2B4              002B4   113          C     R3,=A(NUM2+4)      HAVE WE LOOKED AT ENTIRE NUM1      001280
0000D6 4720 C0FC              000FC   114          BH    NUM2POS            IF SO, THEN NUM1 IS POSITIVE       001290
0000DA 9560 3000        00000         115          CLI   0(R3),C'-'         NEGATIVE SIGN?                     001300
0000DE 4780 C0EA              000EA   116          BE    MINUS2             IF YES, THEN NEGATIVE FIRST NUM    001310
0000E2 4130 3001              00001   117          LA    R3,1(,R3)          ADVANCE TO NEXT ADDRESS            001320
0000E6 47F0 C0D2              000D2   118          B     LOOP2              CONTINUE LOOKING                   001330
0000EA F870 C778 C2BC 00778 002BC     119 MINUS2   ZAP   WORK(8),=P'0'      SET WORK EQUAL TO ZERO             001340
0000F0 FB77 C778 C770 00778 00770     120          SP    WORK(8),VALUE2(8)  SUBTRACT VALUE1 FROM 0             001350
0000F6 F877 C770 C778 00770 00778     121          ZAP   VALUE2(8),WORK     VALUE1 IS NOW NEGATIVE             001360
0000FC                                122 NUM2POS  DS    0H                                                    001370
```

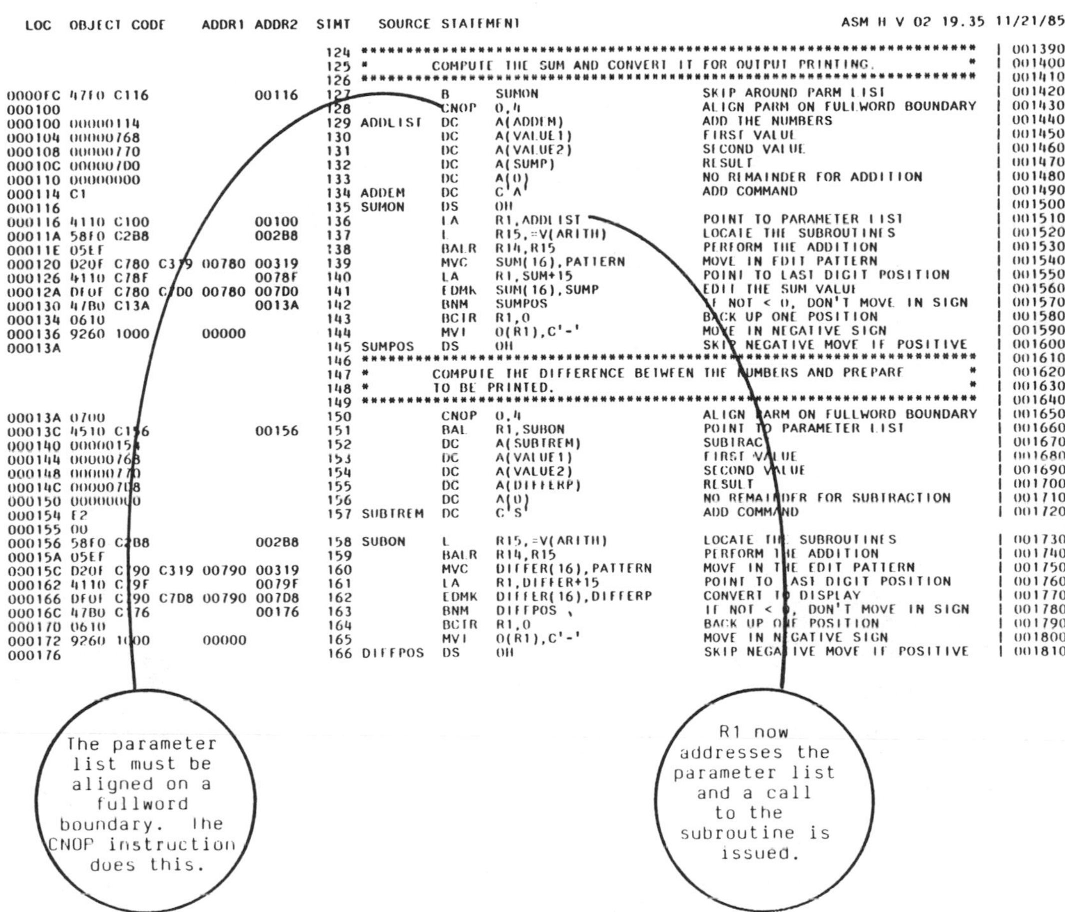

```
         COMPUTE SUM, DIFFERENCE, PRODUCT, QUOTIENT OF 2 VALUES                                                        PAGE    5

  LOC  OBJECT CODE      ADDR1 ADDR2  STMT   SOURCE STATEMENT                                        ASM H V 02 19.35 11/21/85

                                      124 ****************************************************************** | 001390
                                      125 *       COMPUTE THE SUM AND CONVERT IT FOR OUTPUT PRINTING.      * | 001400
                                      126 ****************************************************************** | 001410
0000FC 47F0 C116              00116   127               B     SUMON            SKIP AROUND PARM LIST          | 001420
000100                                128               CNOP  0,4              ALIGN PARM ON FULLWORD BOUNDARY | 001430
000100 00000114                       129 ADDLIST       DC    A(ADDEM)         ADD THE NUMBERS                | 001440
000104 00000768                       130               DC    A(VALUE1)        FIRST VALUE                    | 001450
000108 00000770                       131               DC    A(VALUE2)        SECOND VALUE                   | 001460
00010C 000007D0                       132               DC    A(SUMP)          RESULT                         | 001470
000110 00000000                       133               DC    A(0)             NO REMAINDER FOR ADDITION      | 001480
000114 C1                             134 ADDEM         DC    C'A'             ADD COMMAND                    | 001490
000116                                135 SUMON         DS    0H                                              | 001500
000116 4110 C100              00100   136               LA    R1,ADDLIST       POINT TO PARAMETER LIST        | 001510
00011A 58F0 C2B8              002B8   137               L     R15,=V(ARITH)    LOCATE THE SUBROUTINES         | 001520
00011E 05EF                           138               BALR  R14,R15          PERFORM THE ADDITION           | 001530
000120 D20F C780 C319 00780 00319     139               MVC   SUM(16),PATTERN  MOVE IN EDIT PATTERN           | 001540
000126 4110 C78F              0078F   140               LA    R1,SUM+15        POINT TO LAST DIGIT POSITION   | 001550
00012A DF0F C780 C7D0 00780 007D0     141               EDMK  SUM(16),SUMP     EDIT THE SUM VALUE             | 001560
000130 47B0 C13A              0013A   142               BNM   SUMPOS           IF NOT < 0, DON'T MOVE IN SIGN | 001570
000134 0610                           143               BCTR  R1,0             BACK UP ONE POSITION           | 001580
000136 9260 1000        00000         144               MVI   0(R1),C'-'       MOVE IN NEGATIVE SIGN          | 001590
00013A                                145 SUMPOS        DS    0H               SKIP NEGATIVE MOVE IF POSITIVE | 001600
                                      146 ****************************************************************** | 001610
                                      147 *       COMPUTE THE DIFFERENCE BETWEEN THE NUMBERS AND PREPARE   * | 001620
                                      148 *       TO BE PRINTED.                                           * | 001630
                                      149 ****************************************************************** | 001640
00013A 0700                           150               CNOP  0,4              ALIGN PARM ON FULLWORD BOUNDARY | 001650
00013C 4510 C156              00156   151               BAL   R1,SUBON         POINT TO PARAMETER LIST        | 001660
000140 00000154                       152               DC    A(SUBTREM)       SUBTRACT                       | 001670
000144 00000768                       153               DC    A(VALUE1)        FIRST VALUE                    | 001680
000148 00000770                       154               DC    A(VALUE2)        SECOND VALUE                   | 001690
00014C 000007D8                       155               DC    A(DIFFERP)       RESULT                         | 001700
000150 00000000                       156               DC    A(0)             NO REMAINDER FOR SUBTRACTION   | 001710
000154 E2                             157 SUBTREM       DC    C'S'             ADD COMMAND                    | 001720
000155 00
000156 58F0 C2B8              002B8   158 SUBON         L     R15,=V(ARITH)    LOCATE THE SUBROUTINES         | 001730
00015A 05EF                           159               BALR  R14,R15          PERFORM THE ADDITION           | 001740
00015C D20F C790 C319 00790 00319     160               MVC   DIFFER(16),PATTERN  MOVE IN THE EDIT PATTERN    | 001750
000162 4110 C79F              0079F   161               LA    R1,DIFFER+15     POINT TO LAST DIGIT POSITION   | 001760
000166 DF0F C790 C7D8 00790 007D8     162               EDMK  DIFFER(16),DIFFERP  CONVERT TO DISPLAY          | 001770
00016C 47B0 C176              00176   163               BNM   DIFFPOS          IF NOT < 0, DON'T MOVE IN SIGN | 001780
000170 0610                           164               BCTR  R1,0             BACK UP ONE POSITION           | 001790
000172 9260 1000        00000         165               MVI   0(R1),C'-'       MOVE IN NEGATIVE SIGN          | 001800
000176                                166 DIFFPOS       DS    0H               SKIP NEGATIVE MOVE IF POSITIVE | 001810
```

```
LOC    OBJECT CODE      ADDR1 ADDR2  STMT   SOURCE STATEMENT                                                 ASM H V 02 19.35 11/21/85

                                      168 ************************************************************************ | 001830
                                      169 *       COMPUTE THE PRODUCT BY USING THE HALFWORD MULTIPLY              * | 001840
                                      170 *       INSTRUCTION.  PREPARE FOR PRINTING AFTER MULTIPLYING.           * | 001850
                                      171 ************************************************************************ | 001860
00                              00304 172              LA    R1,MULTPARM            POINT TO PARAMETER LIST          | 001870
0                               002B8 173              L     R15,=V(ARITH)          LOCATE THE SUBROUTINES           | 001880
                                      174              BALR  R14,R15                PERFORM THE ADDITION             | 001890
                            A0  00319 175              MVC   PRODUCT(16),PATTERN    MOVE IN EDIT PATTERN             | 001900
                                007AF 176              LA    R1,PRODUCT+15          POINT TO LAST DIGIT POSITION     | 001910
                            A0  007E0 177              EDMK  PRODUCT(16),PRODUCTP   CONVERT PRODUCT FOR OUTPUT       | 001920
                                0019A 178              BNM   PRODPOS                IF NOT < 0, DON'T MOVE IN SIGN   | 001930
0                                     179              BCTR  R1,0                   BACK UP ONE POSITION             | 001940
00                          000       180              MVI   0(R1),C'-'             MOVE IN NEGATIVE SIGN            | 001950
000                                   181 PRODPOS      DS    0H                     SKIP NEGATIVE MOVE IF POSITIVE   | 001960
                                      182 ************************************************************************ | 001970
                                      183 *      DIVIDE THE TWO NUMBERS AND PREPARE BOTH THE QUOTIENT AND         * | 001980
                                      184 *      REMAINDER FOR PRINTING ON OUR REPORT.                            * | 001990
                                      185 ************************************************************************ | 002000
00019A 0700                           186              CNOP  0,4                    ALIGN PARM ON FULLWORD BOUNDARY  | 002010
00019C 4510 C1B6                001B6 187              BAL   R1,DIVON               POINT TO PARAMETER LIST          | 002020
0001A0 000001B4                       188              DC    A(DIVID)               DIVIDE THE NUMBERS               | 002030
0001A4 00000768                       189              DC    A(VALUE1)              FIRST VALUE                      | 002040
0001A8 00000770                       190              DC    A(VALUE2)              SECOND VALUE                     | 002050
0001AC 000007E8                       191              DC    A(QUOTENTP)            RESULT                           | 002060
0001B0 000007F0                       192              DC    A(REMAINP)             REMAINDER IS NEEDED HERE         | 002070
0001B4 C4                             193 DIVID        DC    C'D'                   ADD COMMAND                      | 002080
0001B5 00
0001B6 58F0 C2B8                002B8 194 DIVON        L     R15,=V(ARITH)          LOCATE THE SUBROUTINES           | 002090
0001BA 05EF                           195              BALR  R14,R15                PERFORM THE ADDITION             | 002100
0001BC D20F C7C0 C319 007C0 00319     196              MVC   REMAIN(16),PATTERN     MOVE IN EDIT PATTERN             | 002110
0001C2 4110 C7CF                007CF 197              LA    R1,REMAIN+15           POINT TO LAST DIGIT POSITION     | 002120
0001C6 DF0F C7C0 C7F0 007C0 007F0     198              EDMK  REMAIN(16),REMAINP     EDIT THE REMAINDER               | 002130
0001CC 47B0 C1D6                001D6 199              BNM   REMPOS                 IF NOT < 0, DON'T MOVE IN SIGN   | 002140
0001D0 0610                           200              BCTR  R1,0                   BACK UP ONE POSITION             | 002150
0001D2 9260 1000          00000       201              MVI   0(R1),C'-'             MOVE IN NEGATIVE SIGN            | 002160
0001D6                                202 REMPOS       DS    0H                     SKIP NEGATIVE MOVE IF POSITIVE   | 002170

0001D6 D20F C7B0 C319 007B0 00319     204              MVC   QUOTIENT(16),PATTERN   MOVE IN EDIT PATTERN             | 002190
0001DC 4110 C7BF                007BF 205              LA    R1,QUOTIENT+15         POINT TO LAST DIGIT POSITION     | 002200
0001E0 DF0F C7B0 C7E8 007B0 007E8     206              EDMK  QUOTIENT(16),QUOTENTP  EDIT THE QUOTIENT VALUE          | 002210
0001E6 47B0 C1F0                001F0 207              BNM   QUOTPOS                IF NOT < 0, DON'T MOVE IN SIGN   | 002220
0001EA 0610                           208              BCTR  R1,0                   BACK UP ONE POSITION             | 002230
0001EC 9260 1000          00000       209              MVI   0(R1),C'-'             MOVE IN NEGATIVE SIGN            | 002240
0001F0                                210 QUOTPOS      DS    0H                     SKIP NEGATIVE MOVE IF POSITIVE   | 002250
```

When the parms are located in the data section of the program the code to perform the linking is simple.

The BAL instruction and the parms are aligned. R1 is pointed to the parms by the BAL and processing continues at DIVON.


```
LOC    OBJECT CODE      ADDR1 ADDR2  STMT   SOURCE STATEMENT                                                 ASM H V 02 19.35 11/21/85

                                      212 ************************************************************************ | 002270
                                      213 *    MOVE THE INPUT VALUES INTO THE OUTPUT LINE AND PRINT THE           * | 002280
                                      214 *    INFORMATION FOR THE ADD OPERATION.                                 * | 002290
                                      215 ************************************************************************ | 002300
0001F0 D204 C670 C714 00670 00714     216              MVC   OP1(5),NUM1              MOVE FIRST NUMBER TO PRINT LINE | 002310
0001F6 D204 C68D C719 0068D 00719     217              MVC   OP2(5),NUM2              MOVE SECOND NUMBER SIMILARLY    | 002320
0001FC D20E C64E C2BD 0064E 002BD     218              MVC   COMMAND(15),=CL15'ADD'   FIRST COMMAND IS TO ADD         | 002330
000202 D20E C69A C781 0069A 00781     219              MVC   RESULT(15),SUM+1         MOVE SUM INTO PRINT LINE        | 002340
                                      220              PUT   XOUT,PLINE               PRINT SUM VALUE                 | 002350
                                      225 ************************************************************************ | 002360
                                      226 *    PRINT THE RESULTS OF THE SUBTRACT.                                 * | 002370
                                      227 ************************************************************************ | 002380
000216 D20E C64E C2CC 0064E 002CC     228              MVC   COMMAND(15),=CL15'SUBTRACT'  COMMAND IS NOW SUBTRACT     | 002390
00021C D20E C69A C791 0069A 00791     229              MVC   RESULT(15),DIFFER+1      MOVE DIFFERENCE TO PRINT LINE   | 002400
                                      230              PUT   XOUT,PLINE               PRINT SUM VALUE                 | 002410
                                      235 ************************************************************************ | 002420
                                      236 *    PRINT THE RESULTS OF THE MULTIPLICATION.                           * | 002430
                                      237 ************************************************************************ | 002440
000230 D20E C64E C2DB 0064E 002DB     238              MVC   COMMAND(15),=CL15'MULTIPLY'  MOVE IN MULTIPLY COMMAND    | 002450
000236 D20E C69A C7A1 0069A 007A1     239              MVC   RESULT(15),PRODUCT+1     MOVE PRODUCT INTO PRINT LINE    | 002460
                                      240              PUT   XOUT,PLINE               PRINT SUM VALUE                 | 002470
                                      245 ************************************************************************ | 002480
                                      246 *    PRINT THE QUOTIENT AND REMAINDER FROM THE DIVISION.                * | 002490
                                      247 ************************************************************************ | 002500
00024A D20E C64E C2EA 0064E 002EA     248              MVC   COMMAND(15),=CL15'DIVIDE'    MOVE IN DIVIDE COMMAND      | 002510
000250 D20E C69A C7B1 0069A 007B1     249              MVC   RESULT(15),QUOTIENT+1    MOVE QUOTIENT INTO PRINT LINE   | 002520
000256 D208 C6AE C2F9 006AE 002F9     250              MVC   RESULT+20(9),=C'REMAINDER'   MOVE IN HEADER FOR REMAIN.  | 002530
00025C D206 C6B9 C7C9 006B9 007C9     251              MVC   RESULT+31(7),REMAIN+9    NOW MOVE IN REMAINDER           | 002540
                                      252              PUT   XOUT,PLINE               PRINT QUOTIENT/REMAINDER VALUES | 002550
                                      257              PUT   XOUT,SKIP2                                               | 002560
00027E 47F0 C07C                0007C 262              B     CONTINUE                 CONTINUE UNTIL END OF FILE      | 002570
```

```
        COMPUTE SUM, DIFFERENCE, PRODUCT, QUOTIENT OF 2 VALUES                                                PAGE    8

  LOC  OBJECT CODE      ADDR1 ADDR2  STMT   SOURCE STATEMENT                                    ASM H V 02 19.35 11/21/85
                                     264 ***********************************************************************  | 002590
                                     265 *      WE'RE ALL DONE.  PAGE EJECT BEFORE ENDING SO THAT OUR REPORT    *  | 002600
                                     266 *      LOOKS NICE.  SET THE RETURN CODE AND THEN EXIT.                 *  | 002610
                                     267 ***********************************************************************  | 002620
                                     268 EOI        PUT   XOUT,NEWPAGE                                             | 002630
                                     273            CLOSE (XIN,,XOUT)                                              | 002640
00029E 58DD 0004              00004  281            L     R13,4(R13)              RESTORE ORIGINAL R13 VALUE       | 002650
0002A2 98EC D00C              0000C  282            LM    R14,R12,12(R13)         RESTORE ALL REGS                 | 002660
0002A6 1BFF                          283            SR    R15,R15                 SET RETURN CODE TO ZERO          | 002670
0002A8 07FE                          284            BCR   B'1111',R14             RETURN CONTROL TO CALLER         | 002680
                                     285 *                                                                         | 002690
0002B0                               286            LTORG                                                          | 002700
0002B0 00000718                      287                  =A(NUM1+4)
0002B4 0000071D                      288                  =A(NUM2+4)
0002B8 00000000                      289                  =V(ARITH)
0002BC 0C                            290                  =P'0'
0002BD C1C4C44040404040              291                  =CL15'ADD'
0002CC E2E4C2E3D9C1C3E3              292                  =CL15'SUBTRACT'
0002DB D4E4D3E3C9D7D3E8              293                  =CL15'MULTIPLY'
0002EA C4C9E5C9C4C54040              294                  =CL15'DIVIDE'
0002F9 D9C5D4C1C9D5C4C5              295                  =C'REMAINDER'
```

```
        COMPUTE SUM, DIFFERENCE, PRODUCT, QUOTIENT OF 2 VALUES                                                PAGE    9

  LOC  OBJECT CODE      ADDR1 ADDR2  STMT   SOURCE STATEMENT                                    ASM H V 02 19.35 11/21/85
                                     297 ***********************************************************************  | 002720
                                     298 *                  DATA AND STORAGE AREA DEFINITIONS                   *  | 002730
                                     299 ***********************************************************************  | 002740
000302 0700                          300            CNOP  0,4                     ALIGN PARM ON FULLWORD BOUNDARY  | 002750
000304 00000318                      301 MULTPARM   DC    A(TIMES)                MULTIPLY                         | 002760
000308 00000768                      302            DC    A(VALUE1)               FIRST VALUE                      | 002770
00030C 00000770                      303            DC    A(VALUE2)               SECOND VALUE                     | 002780
000310 000007E0                      304            DC    A(PRODUCTP)             RESULT                           | 002790
000314 00000000                      305            DC    A(0)                    NO REMAINDER FOR MULTIPLICATION  | 002800
000318 D4                            306 TIMES      DC    C'M'                    ADD COMMAND                      | 002810

000319 4020202020202020              308 PATTERN    DC    X'402020202020202020202020202120'                        | 002830
000329 F140404040404040              309 NEWPAGE    DC    CL133'1'                                                 | 002840
                                     310 *                                                                         | 002850
0003AE F1D9C5D7D6D9E340              311 TITLE      DC    CL133'1REPORT                                      A R I TX| 002860
0003B6 4040404040404040                                    H M E T I C   P R O C E S S I N G   R E P O R T'         | 002870
000433 4040D5C1D4C57A40              312 SUBTITLE DC      CL133'  NAME:  MATH                                          X| 002880
00043B 40D4C1E3C8404040                                       BASIC    MATH    OPERATIONS'                          | 002890
0004B8 6040404040404040              313 SKIP2      DC    CL133'-'                                                 | 002900
00053D 4060606060606040D6            314 HEADINGS DC      CL133' ----- OPERATION -----              ----- FIRST VALUE -X| 002910
000545 D7C5D9C1E3C9D6D5                                   ----       ----- SECOND VALUE -----        --------------- RX| 002920
00054D 4060606060606040                                   ESULT ---------------'                                   | 002930
0005C2 4E6D6D6D6D6D6D6D              315 UNDERLIN DC      CL133'+_______________________              ___________________X| 002940
0005CA 6D6D6D6D6D6D6D6D                                                                              _________________X| 002950
0005D2 6D6D6D6D6D6D4040                                   ----     ______________________          ___________________ | 002960
                                     316 *                                                                         | 002970
000647                               317 PLINE      DS    0CL133                                                   | 002980
000647 40                            318 CC         DC    C' '                                                     | 002990
000648 404040404040                  319            DC    CL6' '                                                   | 003000
00064E 4040404040404040              320 COMMAND    DC    CL15' '                                                  | 003010
00065D 4040404040404040              321            DC    CL19' '                                                  | 003020
000670 4040404040                    322 OP1        DC    CL5' '                                                   | 003030
000675 4040404040404040              323            DC    CL24' '                                                  | 003040
00068D 4040404040                    324 OP2        DC    CL5' '                                                   | 003050
000692 4040404040404040              325            DC    CL8' '                                                   | 003060
00069A 4040404040404040              326 RESULT     DC    CL50' '                                                  | 003070
                                     327 *                                                                         | 003080
0006CC                               328 SAVEAREA DS      18F                     REGISTER SAVE AREA               | 003090

000714                               330 INPUTREC DS      0CL80                   ****                             | 003110
000714                               331 NUM1       DS    CL5                         **** INPUT RECORD DESCRIPTION | 003120
000719                               332 NUM2       DS    CL5                         *                            | 003130
00071E                               333            DS    CL70                    ****                             | 003140
```

The parameter list for the multiplication is aligned and can be located in the data area section of the program.

```
COMPUTE SUM, DIFFERENCE, PRODUCT, QUOTIENT OF 2 VALUES                                          PAGE   10

  LOC  OBJECT CODE      ADDR1 ADDR2  STMT   SOURCE STATEMENT                                  ASM H V 02 19.35 11/21/85
000768                               335            DS    0D                                            | 003160
000768                               336 VALUE1     DS    PL8                                           | 003170
000770                               337 VALUE2     DS    PL8                                           | 003180
000778                               338 WORK       DS    PL8                                           | 003190
000780 40404040404040404040          339 SUM        DC    CL16' '          ****                         | 003200
000790 40404040404040404040          340 DIFFER     DC    CL16' '          *                            | 003210
0007A0 40404040404040404040          341 PRODUCT    DC    CL16' '          **** OUTPUT RESULT AREAS     | 003220
0007B0 40404040404040404040          342 QUOTIENT   DC    CL16' '          *                            | 003230
0007C0 40404040404040404040          343 REMAIN     DC    CL16' '          ****                         | 003240
0007D0 000000000000000C              344 SUMP       DC    PL8'0'           ****                         | 003250
0007D8 000000000000000C              345 DIFFERP    DC    PL8'0'           *                            | 003260
0007E0 000000000000000C              346 PRODUCTP   DC    PL8'0'           **** CONVERSION AREAS        | 003270
0007E8 000000000000000C              347 QUOTIENTP  DC    PL8'0'           *                            | 003280
0007F0 000000000000000C              348 REMAINP    DC    PL8'0'           ****                         | 003290
                                     349 XIN        DCB   DSORG=PS,DDNAME=XIN,MACRF=GM,EODAD=EOF        | 003300
                                     403 XOUT       DCB   DSORG=PS,DDNAME=XOUT,MACRF=PM,LRECL=133,BLKSIZE=133,    X| 003310
                                                          RECFM=FA                                      | 003320
000000                               457            END   PROCESS                                       | 003330
```

```
REPORT                         A R I T H M E T I C   P R O C E S S I N G   R E P O R T
 NAME:  MATH                                 BASIC   MATH   OPERATIONS


----- OPERATION -----      ----- FIRST VALUE -----     ----- SECOND VALUE -----    --------------- RESULT ---------------
     ADD                          00020                       00008                      28
     SUBTRACT                     00020                       00008                      12
     MULTIPLY                     00020                       00008                     160
     DIVIDE                       00020                       00008                       2     REMAINDER         4


     ADD                             -6                           4                      -2
     SUBTRACT                        -6                           4                     -10
     MULTIPLY                        -6                           4                     -24
     DIVIDE                          -6                           4                      -1     REMAINDER        -2


     ADD                             25                           5                      30
     SUBTRACT                        25                           5                      20
     MULTIPLY                        25                           5                     125
     DIVIDE                          25                           5                       5     REMAINDER         0


     ADD                            -66                          -7                     -73
     SUBTRACT                       -66                          -7                     -59
     MULTIPLY                       -66                          -7                     462
     DIVIDE                         -66                          -7                       9     REMAINDER        -3


     ADD                            370                          -9                     361
     SUBTRACT                       370                          -9                     379
     MULTIPLY                       370                          -9                   -3330
     DIVIDE                         370                          -9                     -41     REMAINDER         1
```

This assembler subroutine is called by a COBOL program. Parms for this routine are passed as usual through register 1. This routine will perform the same arithmetic functions.

```
                                                                                              PAGE    2

 LOC  OBJECT CODE    ADDR1 ADDR2  STMT   SOURCE STATEMENT                                 ASM H V 02 20.08 11/21/85

                           00000     1 R0       EQU   0                                           | 000080
                           00001     2 R1       EQU   1                                           | 000090
                           00002     3 R2       EQU   2                                           | 000100
                           00003     4 R3       EQU   3                                           | 000110
                           00004     5 R4       EQU   4                                           | 000120
                           00005     6 R5       EQU   5                                           | 000130
                           00006     7 R6       EQU   6                                           | 000140
                           00007     8 R7       EQU   7                                           | 000150
                           00008     9 R8       EQU   8                                           | 000160
                           00009    10 R9       EQU   9                                           | 000170
                           0000A    11 R10      EQU   10                                          | 000180
                           0000B    12 R11      EQU   11                                          | 000190
                           0000C    13 R12      EQU   12                                          | 000200
                           0000D    14 R13      EQU   13                                          | 000210
                           0000E    15 R14      EQU   14                                          | 000220
                           0000F    16 R15      EQU   15                                          | 000230
                                    17 *                                                          | 000240

000000                              19 PROCESS  CSECT                                             | 000260
000000 90EC D00C           0000C    20          STM   R14,R12,12(13)   SAVE CALLER'S REGISTERS    | 000270
000004 18CF                         21          LR    R12,R15          R12 WILL BE OUR BASE REG   | 000280
                           00000    22          USING PROCESS,R12      TELL THE ASSEMBLER ABOUT R12 | 000290
000006 41A0 C098           00098    23          LA    R10,SAVEAREA     POINT TO REGISTER SAVE AREA | 000300
00000A 50AD 0008           00008    24          ST    R10,8(R13)       TELL CALLER ABOUT OUR SAVEAREA | 000310
00000E 50DA 0004           00004    25          ST    R13,4(R10)       REMEMBER CALLER'S SAVEAREA ADDR. | 000320
000012 18DA                         26          LR    R13,R10          ESTABLISH NEW SAVE AREA    | 000330
000014 9826 1000           00000    27          LM    R2,R6,0(R1)      PICK UP PARM VALUES        | 000340
                                    28 *                                                          | 000350
000018 1BFF                         29          SR    R15,R15          RC=0..ASSUME IT WILL WORK  | 000360
00001A 95C1 2000     00000          30          CLI   0(R2),C'A'       ADD?                       | 000370
00001E 4780 C042           00042    31          BE    ADD                                         | 000380
000022 95E2 2000     00000          32          CLI   0(R2),C'S'       SUBTRACT?                  | 000390
000026 4780 C052           00052    33          BE    SUBTRACT                                    | 000400
00002A 95D4 2000     00000          34          CLI   0(R2),C'M'       MULTIPLY?                  | 000410
00002E 4780 C062           00062    35          BE    TIMES                                       | 000420
000032 95C4 2000     00000          36          CLI   0(R2),C'D'       DIVIDE?                    | 000430
000036 4780 C072           00072    37          BE    DIVIDE                                      | 000440
00003A 41F0 0008           00008    38          LA    R15,8            SET RETURN CODE TO BAD     | 000450
00003E 47F0 C08A           0008A    39          B     EXIT             IF NONE OF THE ABOVE THEN RETURN | 000460
                                    40 *                                                          | 000470
000042                              41 ADD      DS    0H                                          | 000480
000042 F877 5000 3000 00000 00000   42          ZAP   0(8,R5),0(8,R3)  OBTAIN FIRST VALUE         | 000490
000048 FA77 5000 4000 00000 00000   43          AP    0(8,R5),0(8,R4)  ADD SECOND VALUE TO IT     | 000500
00004E 47F0 C08A           0008A    44          B     EXIT             ALL DONE TO RETURN         | 000510
                                    45 *                                                          | 000520
000052                              46 SUBTRACT DS    0H                                          | 000530
000052 F877 5000 3000 00000 00000   47          ZAP   0(8,R5),0(8,R3)  OBTAIN FIRST VALUE         | 000540
000058 FB77 5000 4000 00000 00000   48          SP    0(8,R5),0(8,R4)  SUBTRACT SECOND VALUE FROM IT | 000550
00005E 47F0 C08A           0008A    49          B     EXIT             ALL DONE TO RETURN         | 000560
                                    50 *                                                          | 000570
000062                              51 TIMES    DS    0H                                          | 000580
000062 F877 5000 3000 00000 00000   52          ZAP   0(8,R5),0(8,R3)  OBTAIN FIRST VALUE         | 000590
000068 FC73 5000 4004 00000 00004   53          MP    0(8,R5),4(4,R4)  TIME RIGHT MOST HAVE OF VALUE 2 | 000600
00006E 47F0 C08A           0008A    54          B     EXIT             ALL DONE TO RETURN         | 000610
```

```
                                                                                              PAGE    3

 LOC  OBJECT CODE    ADDR1 ADDR2  STMT   SOURCE STATEMENT                                 ASM H V 02 20.08 11/21/85

                                    55 *                                                          | 000620
000072                              56 DIVIDE   DS    0H                                          | 000630
000072 F877 5000 3000 00000 00000   57          ZAP   0(8,R5),0(8,R3)  OBTAIN FIRST VALUE         | 000640
000078 FD73 5000 4004 00000 00004   58          DP    0(8,R5),4(4,R4)  ADD SECOND VALUE TO IT     | 000650
00007E F873 6000 5004 00000 00004   59          ZAP   0(8,R6),4(4,R5)  EXPAND REMAINDER TO FULL FORM | 000660
000084 F873 5000 5000 00000 00000   60          ZAP   0(8,R5),0(4,R5)  EXPAND QUOTIENT TO FULL FORM | 000670
                                    61 *                                                          | 000680
00008A                              62 EXIT     DS    0H                                          | 000690
00008A 58D0 C09C           0009C    63          L     R13,SAVEAREA+4   RESTORE ORIGINAL R13 VALUE | 000700
00008E 58FD 000C           0000C    64          L     R14,12(R13)      RESTORE ONLY R14           | 000710
000092 980C D014           00014    65          LM    R0,R12,20(R13)   RESTORE ALL BUT R15        | 000720
000096 07FE                         66          BR    R14              RETURN CONTROL             | 000730
                                    67 *                                                          | 000740
000098                              68 SAVEAREA DS    18F                                         | 000750
0000E0                              69          LTORG                                             | 000760
000000                              70          END   PROCESS                                     | 000770
```

Example 9.2 Assembly language subroutine and COBOL mainline.

```
PP 5740-CB1 RELEASE 2.3 + PTF 8 - UP13477           IBM OS/VS COBOL  JULY 24, 1978          20.08.12  DATE NOV 21,1985

   1                    20.08.12       NOV 21,1985

           IDENTIFICATION DIVISION.
           PROGRAM-ID.    ARITH.
           AUTHOR.        CHUCK KACMAR.
           INSTALLATION.  HERE.
           DATE WRITTEN.  NOW.

           ENVIRONMENT DIVISION.
           INPUT-OUTPUT SECTION.
           FILE-CONTROL.
               SELECT CARD-FILE ASSIGN TO UT-S-CARDS.

           DATA DIVISION.
           FILE SECTION.
           FD  CARD-FILE
               LABEL RECORDS ARE OMITTED.
           01  INPUT-DATA-CARD.
               05  VALUE1              PIC 99999.
               05  VALUE2              PIC 99999.
               05  FILLER              PIC X(70).

           WORKING-STORAGE SECTION.
           01  END-OF-FILE-INDICATOR   PIC X  VALUE 'N'.
               88  END-OF-FILE         VALUE 'Y'.

           01  OPERATION-CODE          PIC X.
               88  ADD-VALUES          VALUE 'A'.
               88  SUBTRACT-VALUES     VALUE 'S'.
               88  MULTIPLY-VALUES     VALUE 'M'.
               88  DIVIDE-VALUES       VALUE 'D'.
           01  FIRST-VALUE             PIC S9(15) COMP-3.
           01  SECOND-VALUE            PIC S9(15) COMP-3.
           01  RESULT                  PIC S9(15) COMP-3.
           01  REMAIN                  PIC S9(15) COMP-3.

           PROCEDURE DIVISION.
               OPEN INPUT CARD-FILE.
               READ CARD-FILE
                   AT END MOVE 'Y' TO END-OF-FILE-INDICATOR.

               PERFORM PROCESS-ALL-RECORDS UNTIL END-OF-FILE.
               CLOSE CARD-FILE.
               STOP RUN.

           PROCESS-ALL-RECORDS.
               DISPLAY 'THE INPUT VALUES ARE:  ', VALUE1, ',    ', VALUE2.

               MOVE VALUE1 TO FIRST-VALUE.
               MOVE VALUE2 TO SECOND-VALUE.

               MOVE 'A'     TO OPERATION-CODE.
               CALL 'PROCESS' USING OPERATION-CODE, FIRST-VALUE,
                    SECOND-VALUE, RESULT, REMAIN.
               DISPLAY 'SUM -------------- ', RESULT.
```

This COBOL mainline program will invoke the assembler subroutine by using a CALL statement. The rame of the CSECT to be called is enclosed in in single quotes and all parameters to be passed tc the subroutine are identified on the CALL statement.

```
          MOVE 'S'     TO OPERATION-CODE.
          CALL 'PROCESS' USING OPERATION-CODE, FIRST-VALUE,
               SECOND-VALUE, RESULT, REMAIN.
          DISPLAY 'DIFFERENCE ------- ', RESULT.

          MOVE 'M'     TO OPERATION-CODE.
          CALL 'PROCESS' USING OPERATION-CODE, FIRST-VALUE,
               SECOND-VALUE, RESULT, REMAIN.
          DISPLAY 'PRODUCT ---------- ', RESULT.

          MOVE 'D'     TO OPERATION-CODE.
          CALL 'PROCESS' USING OPERATION-CODE, FIRST-VALUE,
               SECOND-VALUE, RESULT, REMAIN.
          DISPLAY 'QUOTIENT --------- ', RESULT,
                  ', REMAINDER ------ ', REMAIN.
          DISPLAY ' '.
          DISPLAY ' '.
          DISPLAY ' '.
          DISPLAY ' '.

          READ CARD-FILE
               AT END MOVE 'Y' TO END-OF-FILE-INDICATOR.
```

The output from the COBOL mainline program will be slightly different than before. The COBOL DISPLAY statement is similar to the assembler XPRNT statement to dump out information in a "quick and dirty" manner.

```
THE INPUT VALUES ARE:  00020,    00008
SUM -------------- 000000000000028
DIFFERENCE ------- 000000000000012
PRODUCT ---------- 000000000000160
QUOTIENT --------- 000000000000002, REMAINDER ------ 000000000000004


THE INPUT VALUES ARE:  00005,    00030
SUM -------------- 000000000000035
DIFFERENCE ------- 00000000000002N
PRODUCT ---------- 000000000000150
QUOTIENT --------- 000000000000000, REMAINDER ------ 000000000000005


THE INPUT VALUES ARE:  00008,    00004
SUM -------------- 000000000000012
DIFFERENCE ------- 000000000000004
PRODUCT ---------- 000000000000032
QUOTIENT --------- 000000000000002, REMAINDER ------ 000000000000000


THE INPUT VALUES ARE:  00028,    00007
SUM -------------- 000000000000035
DIFFERENCE ------- 000000000000021
PRODUCT ---------- 000000000000196
QUOTIENT --------- 000000000000004, REMAINDER ------ 000000000000000


THE INPUT VALUES ARE:  00044,    00013
SUM -------------- 000000000000057
DIFFERENCE ------- 000000000000031
PRODUCT ---------- 000000000000572
QUOTIENT --------- 000000000000003, REMAINDER ------ 000000000000005
```

This is the COBOL program's output. As you can see, the packed decimal field that is printed has not been fully edited for printing. Hence, the last digit of the number is not printed properly in this case since the difference between 5 and 30 yields a negative number as a result.

to be written in assembly language and subroutines in COBOL. Although there are cases where COBOL can perform some facilities that are more difficult to perform in assembler, most COBOL-to-assembler communications involve a COBOL mainline program and assembly language subroutines.

STUDY QUESTIONS

1. Although register ____________ may be used to pass individual values from module to module, this is not a typical method of passing parameters.
2. Which assembler instruction is used to transfer control to an external subroutine?
3. If a subroutine wants to indicate to the calling program that it did not complete its processing normally, then it should ____________.
4. What two instructions determine if a module worked or didn't work once control returns to the calling module?
5. A module called STRING is to be called. Give examples of invoking STRING
   (a) internally using R3 as the return register
   (b) externally using standard linkage conventions
   (c) internally using R3 as the return register in an extended architecture environment
6. A subroutine is invoked. If the subroutine is *not* to alter either the condition code or the program mask, how might the program go about preserving these values?
7. When a parameter is to be passed into a program from the EXEC JCL statement, what is the first field in the resulting data area?
8. Five elements are to be passed to the external module called STRING. The elements are A, B, C, D, and E. Give two examples of the code needed to pass these parameters and invoke the STRING module.
9. What is the scope of data within a program that contains a mainline code and two internal subroutines?
10. When coding external subroutines, where must the LTORG statement be coded?
11. Identify any errors in the following code segment.

```
MAINPGM    CSECT
           USING    MAINPGM,10
           STM      14,12,12(13)
           LR       10,15
           LA       12,SAVEAREA
           ST       12,8(13)
           ST       13,4(12)
           LR       13,12
```

12. Fields A, B, and C are to be passed to the external subroutine labeled AVERAGE. Identify any errors in the following code segment.

```
location        program source instruction
 counter

 0000A2                   BAL      1,CALLSUB
 0000A8                   DC       A(A)
 0000AC                   DC       A(B)
 0000B0                   DC       A(C)
 0000B4         CALLSUB   L        15,=V(AVERAGE)
 0000B8                   BALR     14,15
```

13. In what cases below could register 0 be used to pass parameters to each of the subroutines?
    a. A single 4-byte packed-decimal field is to be squared.
    b. A print line is to be sent to the printer and the address of the print line is to be passed to a subroutine.
    c. The subroutine to be called does not require any input parameters but only returns the current year as a binary halfword value.
    d. A number is passed to a routine to determine if it's even or odd. The routine returns a "yes" or "no" indicator to the invoking program.
    e. The calling routine passes the subroutine N and the subroutine returns the value (N*(N−1))/2.
14. Suppose that your program is being executed using an assemble-and-go procedure. Write the JCL statement that will pass your lastname to the first module in the program.
15. A system consists of several internal subroutines, all housed within a single CSECT. Accidentally, the programmer forgets to code the label on the END statement. What do you expect will happen?
16. Write the code to enter an ASSIST program and establish registers 15 and 12 as the primary and secondary registers respectively. Do not adhere to the linkage conventions.
17. A program is currently 4000 bytes long. However, the programmer must enlarge one of the data definition fields in the program which will cause the program to expand to over 4100 bytes. In what cases will the programmer need to define another base register?
18. In what cases is it necessary for the leftmost bit of the last parameter to be "on" when communicating between modules?
19. Does the following section of code adhere to the linkage conventions? Explain your answer.

```
     LA      R1,N             ADDRESS THE PARAMETER VALUE
     L       R15,=V(SUB)      ADDRESS THE EXTERNAL SUBROUTINE
     BALR    R14,R15          CALL THE SUBROUTINE TO COMPUTE N SQUARED
     .
     .
N    DC      F'25'            THE VALUE TO BE SQUARED
```

20. In most of the examples presented in this chapter, the CSECT statement began both the mainline program and all external subroutines. In what cases can the START instruction be used in place of CSECT?

PROGRAMMING PROBLEMS

1. Twenty consecutive four-byte packed-decimal storage areas are to be added and the result placed in the field called SUM. Write an internal subroutine to perform this function if the name of the first consecutive field is called VALUE1. The return register is R2.
2. An external subroutine is to be written in ASSIST. This subroutine is called PRINTIT and it is passed a single parameter, the address of the first element in a set of 20 consecutive 4-byte packed-decimal storage areas. PRINTIT converts each of these numbers to proper format and prints their values to the printer.
3. Write an internal subroutine called FORMAT that converts an eight-byte packed-decimal number to printable format. The address of this number is in register 3 when the routine is called and the address of the 16-byte convert area is in register 4. The return register is register 2.
4. Write a complete system consisting of two modules. The mainline module inputs data cards with each card containing a date in Julian format. For each input value, the Julian date is passed to a subroutine. The subroutine converts the Julian date into mm/dd/yy format as well as into Gregorian date format. Both converted values are returned to the mainline program. The mainline program prints the input value and the converted dates on the line printer.
5. Write a program consisting of two modules, a mainline program and a subroutine (internal or external). The mainline program inputs integer numbers from a data card. For each input number, the subroutine is called and it computes the sum of all integers between 1 and the number. The computed value is returned to the mainline program and the results printed.
6. Modify Programming Problem 5 so that the product of all integers between 1 and the number is computed.
7. Develop a subroutine that computes the future value of an investment if simple interest compounding is used. In other words, the subroutine is given the amount of the investment, the annual interest rate, and the length of the investment (in years). Using simple interest computation, the subroutine computes the value of the investment over its life and returns the future value to the calling routine.
8. Write a program that computes the semester grade for students in a programming class. The mainline program inputs the student's name and 10 scores for the semester. These scores are passed to a subroutine that averages the scores and returns the semester average and the semester grade for the student. The mainline program then calls upon another module to print the results of the processing in a report format.
9. Write a program consisting of four modules. The mainline program calls an input module to read a single number from an unknown number of input data cards. For each number, the mainline program then calls upon a subroutine to transform the input number into its roman numeral representation. The mainline program then passes this transformed value and the original input number to an output module to be printed to the printer.
10. Write a system consisting of two modules. The main program inputs single numbers from data cards. For each number, a subroutine derives a list of all prime numbers between 1 and the number. The mainline program then outputs the original input value and the list of associated prime numbers as determined by the subroutine.
11. Write a system consisting of several modules. The mainline module inputs data cards consisting of words typed. Each data card contains an unknown number of words. For each card, a subroutine extracts the words. For each word, another subroutine counts the number of occur-

rences of each letter. After all the words and data cards have been processed, the system outputs the total number of data cards, the total number of words processed, and the number of occurrences of each letter in all the words.

12. Develop a mainline program which will invoke an external subroutine. Pass to the subroutine a single integer value and obtain from the subroutine the square root approximation of the number. The result should be accurate to 4 decimal places.

13. Write a mainline program with an internal subroutine. The mainline program reads input lines of text and passes each input line to the subroutine. The subroutine reformats the text so that the left and right margins are justified. The subroutine does this by inserting additional spaces between words. The insertion of blanks should be done intelligently so that the line appears balanced.

14. Develop an external subroutine that will perform the same function as XDECI in ASSIST. The routine will scan an input data area to locate a number, convert the number to binary, and update register 1 to address the first byte after the input number. Input to the subroutine is the input area address and the register number into which the input value should be placed. The routine should also set the condition code depending on the value of the number (zero, less than zero, greater than zero, invalid field or number not found).

15. An external subroutine is passed a non-fixed number of input values. All values are binary fullword integers. From this data the routine will print a horizontal bar chart. The routine should edit all data and ensure that all values are less than 100. If any illegal values are discovered, the routine should set a "failing" return code in R15 and exit, not printing the chart. For example, given the values 10, 20, 30, and 15, the routine will print the following bar chart.

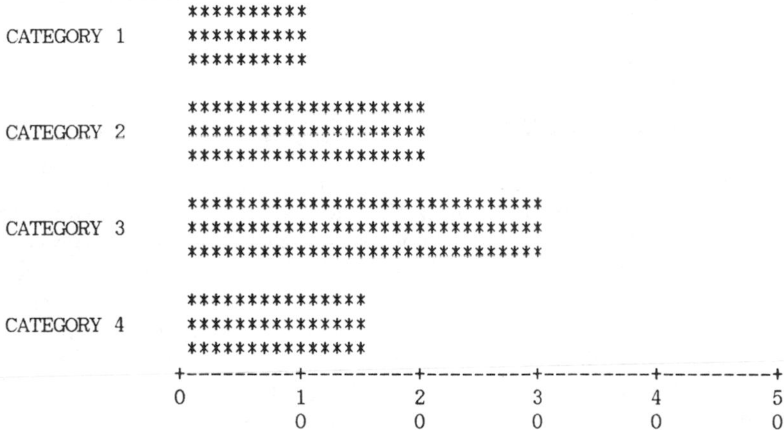

10

Macros and Conditional Assembly

Macros are not new to our discussion since we've discussed and used them many times before. In particular, we've discussed their use in assembly language and ASSIST to perform I/O operations and to help debug our programs. XREAD, XPRNT, XDECI, XDECO, OPEN, CLOSE, GET, PUT, DCB, and SNAP are macros that we've been using to this point. We will now look at macros to determine how they can further help us construct our programming solutions.

OVERVIEW OF MACRO PROCESSING

A **macro** is a special facility of the assembler that can generate instructions into our source programs *prior to assembly.* In other words, the assembler operates as a **macro processor,** which at our request, adds statements into our programs or controls which source statements are to be placed into our programs during their conversion from source to object formats. Figure 10.1 illustrates the expansion of a macro into program source code. The statements placed into our program by the assembler come from the **body** of the macro. Once placed into our program, the resulting instructions are processed as if we had typed them ourselves. Thus, during the **pre-assembly** phase of processing, the assembler locates a macro definition and **expands** the macro into our program.

Referring to Figure 10.1, we see that the CALLSUB macro definition is used to generate instructions within the user program. The programmer invokes the macro by coding the macro name in much the same manner as the programmer would code any instruction mnemonic. Following the macro call, instructions from the macro are imbedded in the program (they begin with a plus sign) and can now be used to support the processing within the program. Clearly, using the CALLSUB macro reduces the amount of coding on the part of the programmer. Instead of coding three instructions to call a subroutine (LA, L, BALR), the programmer now only has to code one instruction, that being a macro call.

A macro is constructed to promote standardization and to minimize duplicate coding in our programs. For example, the code to call a subroutine or to edit a packed-decimal field is very repetitive if several such routines are to be performed. With a macro, we write the code once and invoke the macro to generate the proper instructions to pro-

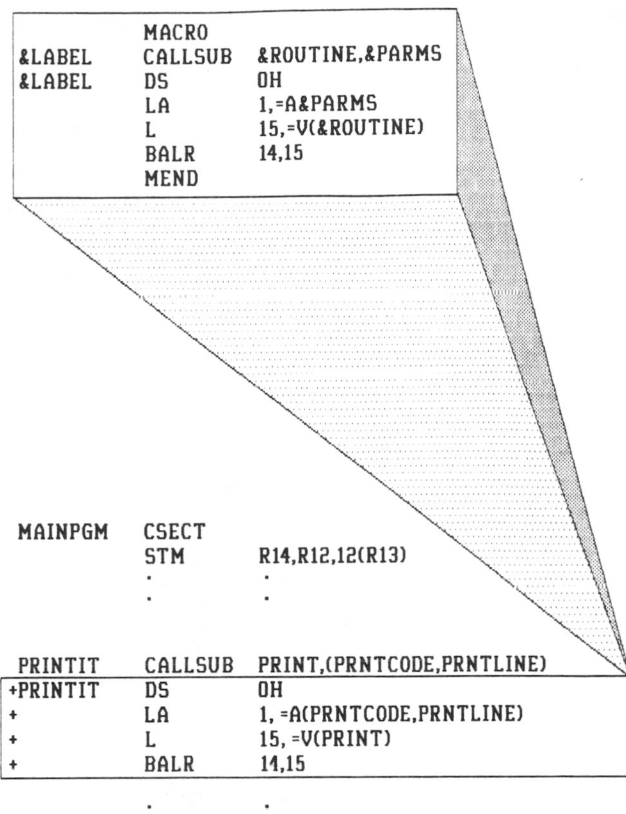

Figure 10.1 Macro expansion within an assembly language program. Macros are expanded to produce executable machine instructions within the body of the user program.

vide the calling or editing support. Although our program may have duplicate sections of code, we only had to write it once.

A macro is *not* a subroutine. Although it may seem that it is "called" in the same manner that a subroutine is called, it is not. A macro, when invoked, generates the necessary instructions to have something done. If the statements within the macro generate into code that edits a packed-decimal field, then the field is edited at *execution* time. If the macro code generates source statements to invoke an internal or external subroutine, then those subroutines are invoked at execution time.

Code generated by the macro must be assembled before it can be executed. The macro does not result in code execution, rather, it simply generates statements which are *later* assembled and executed. From the code of Fig. 10.2 you see the OPEN macro instruction. Immediately after this instruction there are several statements that begin with a plus sign (+). These statements are generated by the macro, that is, they are produced by the OPEN macro. At execution time, these five statements open the file called XIN as an input file. Once generated by the macro processor, these source code statements are now processed by the assembler.

These instructions could have been explicitly coded to open file XIN for input. However, it is much easier to code one macro call than to code the several statements to open XIN. Considering this for each I/O macro mentioned earlier, you see that a substantial amount of coding is saved. However, it's very important that you understand that

```
                                                                                         PAGE    3

  LOC  OBJECT CODE     ADDR1 ADDR2  STMT    SOURCE STATEMENT                          ASM H V 02 18.10 11/26/85

                                       4            OPEN   (XIN,INPUT)                                 I 000100
000000                                 5+           CNOP   0,4              ALIGN LIST TO FULLWORD 01-OPEN
000000 4510 F008           00008       6+           BAL    1,*+8            LOAD REG1 W/LIST ADDR. 01-OPEN
000004 80                              7+           DC     AL1(128)         OPTION BYTE            01-OPEN
000005 00000C                          8+           DC     AL3(XIN)         DCB ADDRESS            01-OPEN
000008 0A13                            9+           SVC    19               ISSUE OPEN SVC         01-OPEN
```

Figure 10.2 Generating code with the OPEN macro instruction.

the code generated by a macro is not generated over and over. In other words, consider the OPEN macro in Figure 10.2. In this figure, the generated code will open the file XIN for INPUT. The code cannot be regenerated during execution to open another file for input or output. Similarly, a macro contained in a loop will not generate code each time the code in the loop is processed. The code is generated once, at pre-assembly, and remains in the program throughout the life of the program during execution. Again, the greatest advantage of a macro is the reduction of coding requirements on the part of the programmer. As an example, let's look at the associated DCB for the XIN file. Although I coded the DCB instruction shown in Fig. 10.3, the macro generates several more lines of code as shown in Fig. 10.4.

```
XIN      DCB      DSORG=PS,MACRF=GM,DDNAME=XIN,EODAD=EOF
```

Figure 10.3 Input DCB macro instruction.

Clearly, it's much easier to code one statement and allow the macro to do the work than it is to code all the source statements needed to define a data control block. However, the macro had to be written in the first place. Hence, this is what we want to learn to do—to write macros to reduce our coding efforts by invoking them to generate repetitive or frequently used sections of code.

As you have seen, some macro expansions can occupy considerable space within a program listing. However, their expansion can be suppressed by using the instruction given in Fig. 10.5

This assembly language instruction informs the assembler not to print the macro expansion in your source listing. Don't be misled, however. The macro *is* expanded. You just don't see it in your listing.

The PRINT NOGEN instruction may be used at the beginning of your program to suppress all macro expansions or throughout the body of your program to suppress *some* macro expansions. When desired, inform the assembler to again begin printing macro expansions by using the instruction given in Fig. 10.6.

For example, to suppress only the generation of the DCB macro instruction, we code the instructions shown in Fig. 10.7.

Suppressing macro expansions works against you if your program fails *within* the code generated by the macro. If the abend point of your program identifies a location that is suppressed by the PRINT instructions, you'll have a difficult time determining what code was being processed at the time of failure. In general, few macro expansions should be suppressed, especially those that generate executable machine instructions. The DCB is a macro that does *not* generate executable instructions and so it's a good candidate for macro suppression.

```
LOC  OBJECT CODE     ADDR1 ADDR2  STMT   SOURCE STATEMENT                                  ASM H V 02 18.10 11/26/85
                                  13 XIN       DCB    DSORG=PS,MACRF=GM,DDNAME=XIN,EODAD=EOF                  | 000140

                                  15+*                         DATA CONTROL BLOCK
                                  16+*
00000A 0000
00000C                            17+XIN       DC     0F'0'                    ORIGIN ON WORD BOUNDARY       01-DCB

                                  19+*                         DIRECT ACCESS DEVICE INTERFACE

00000C 0000000000000000           21+          DC     BL16'0'                  FDAD,DVTBL                    01-DCB
00001C 00000000                   22+          DC     A(0)                     KEYLE,DEVT,TRBAL              01-DCB

                                  24+*                         COMMON ACCESS METHOD INTERFACE

000020 00                         26+          DC     AL1(0)                   BUFNO                         01-DCB
000021 000001                     27+          DC     AL3(1)                   BUFCB                         01-DCB
000024 0000                       28+          DC     AL2(0)              BUFL                               01-DCB
000026 4000                       29+          DC     BL2'0100000000000000'            DSORG                 01-DCB
000028 00000001                   30+          DC     A(1)                     ICQE/IOBAD                    01-DCB

                                  32+*                         FOUNDATION EXTENSION

00002C 00                         34+          DC     BL1'00000000'                 BFTEK,BFLN,HIARCHY       01-DCB
00002D 00000A                     35+          DC     AL3(EOF)                 EODAD                         01-DCB
000030 00                         36+          DC     BL1'00000000'            RECFM                         01-DCB
000031 000000                     37+          DC     AL3(0)                   EXLST                         01-DCB

                                  39+*                         FOUNDATION BLOCK

000034 E7C9D54040404040           41+          DC     CL8'XIN'                 DDNAME                        01-DCB
00003C 02                         42+          DC     BL1'00000010'            OFLGS                         01-DCB
00003D 00                         43+          DC     BL1'00000000'                       IFLG               01-DCB
00003E 5000                       44+          DC     BL2'0101000000000000'    MACR                          01-DCB

                                  46+*                         BSAM-BPAM-QSAM INTERFACE

000040 00                         48+          DC     BL1'00000000'                                     RER1 01-DCB
000041 000001                     49+          DC     AL3(1)                   CHECK, GERR, PERR             01-DCB
000044 00000001                   50+          DC     A(1)                     SYNAD                         01-DCB
000048 0000                       51+          DC     H'0'                     CIND1, CIND2                  01-DCB
00004A 0000                       52+          DC     AL2(0)                   BLKSIZE                       01-DCB
00004C 00000000                   53+          DC     F'0'                     WCPO, WCPL, OFFSR, OFFSW      01-DCB
000050 00000001                   54+          DC     A(1)                     IOBA                          01-DCB
000054 00                         55+          DC     AL1(0)                   NCP                           01-DCB
000055 000001                     56+          DC     AL3(1)                   EOBR, EOBAD                   01-DCB

                                  58+*                         QSAM INTERFACE

000058 00000001                   60+          DC     A(1)                     RECAD                         01-DCB
00005C 0000                       61+          DC     H'0'                     QSWS                          01-DCB
00005E 0000                       62+          DC     AL2(0)              LRECL                              01-DCB
000060 00                         63+          DC     BL1'00000000'            EROPT                         01-DCB
000061 000001                     64+          DC     AL3(1)                   CNTRL                         01-DCB
000064 00000000                   65+          DC     F'0'                     PRECL                         01-DCB
000068 00000001                   66+          DC     A(1)                     EOB                           01-DCB
```

Figure 10.4 DCB macro expansion.

```
         PRINT  NOGEN
```

Figure 10.5 Reducing the expansion of macro code using PRINT.

```
         PRINT  GEN
```

Figure 10.6 Using PRINT to produce a full macro expansion.

```
         PRINT  NOGEN
XIN      DCB    DSORG=PS,DDNAME=XIN, . . . .
         PRINT  GEN
```

Figure 10.7 Suppressing only the DCB macro expansion.

BASIC STRUCTURE AND CODING OF A MACRO

A macro consists of four components:

macro header
macro prototype statement
body of the macro
macro trailer

Macro statements are coded as any other assembly language statement with labels beginning in column 1, mnemonics in column 10, operands in column 16, comments beginning around column 40, and continuations indicated with a nonblank character in column 72. Line comments may be coded on the macro prototype statement or on statements within the body of the macro, but they are not coded on the header or trailer statements.

A macro may invoke other macros as well. In other words, macros can be constructed so that one macro invokes another to assist in generating code. Most macros that we write are self-contained and do not invoke others. However, many macros developed by IBM, for example, invoke subordinate macros to complete the processing by the macro. Regardless of how many macros are required to produce the necessary code, they are all constructed in the same format.

The **macro header** is the first statement in the macro definition. This statement is very easy to code since all you have to code is the word **MACRO** starting in column 10.

The **macro trailer** or **macro end** statement is as easy to code since it too has just one element, **MEND,** coded in column 10. Figure 10.8 illustrates the proper coding of both the macro header and trailer instructions.

```
MACRO
. . .
. . .
. . .
MEND
```

Figure 10.8 Instructions for the macro header and trailer.

These statements define the **bounds of the macro.** All statements between these two statements are part of a single **macro definition.** In fact, *each* macro must begin and end with these statements in much the same manner that a program begins and ends with a CSECT and an END statement, respectively.

Line comments and labels should not be used on these statements. Although the MEND statement allows for a label in column 1, it is not commonly used.

The **macro prototype statement** follows *immediately* after the macro header. This statement identifies the name of the macro and all parameters used within its body to generate source code. The prototype statement can (and usually does) contain a label in column 1, a one- to eight-character **macro name** in column 10, operands beginning in column 16, and a line comment if desired. Also, the prototype statement is continued if the number of operands for the macro do not fit on a single line. Macro continuation is identical to standard source statement continuation with column 72 indicating continuation and column 16 continuing the operands on the next statement(s). Figure 10.9 describes the general format of a macro language statement.

```
1           10          16          40          72

<label>     mnemonic    operands    comments    continuation
```

Figure 10.9 Format of a macro statement.

Statements within the body of the macro consist of macro statements, machine instructions, and assembly language instructions. Macro statements are special instructions within the body of the macro to control macro processing and the expansion of the source code. Since the macro often produces source code that can then be assembled, it is quite obvious that machine instructions or assembly language instructions are allowed within the body of the macro. As we discuss the macro further, we'll learn more about the various macro statements that support macro expansion.

USING MACROS IN YOUR PROGRAM

The macros that we've been using thus far have not been written by us and they have not been contained within our programs. Clearly, the I/O macros that we've been using in ASSIST or in assembly language were written by others, but now we will investigate how macros can be used in our programs and how to create macros that may be used by others.

As you've seen, all macros begin with the MACRO statement and end with the MEND statement. The macro is completely contained within the bounds of these two statements. If we want to use a macro in our program, then the macro must be in one of two places:

(a) at the very beginning of our source statements
(b) in a macro library

Macros written by you are placed just after the $JOB ASSIST control statement or after the ASM.SYSIN JCL statement. Further, these macros are *only* available to *your* program. They cannot be used by any other program unless they are copied and placed at the beginning of the other program.

Suppose that we have written two macros called ADD and SUBTRACT. To define and use these macros in an ASSIST program, we use the format as shown in Fig. 10.10.

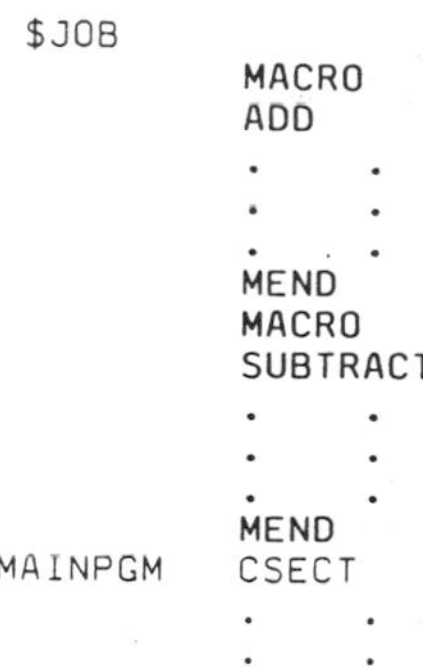

Figure 10.10 Format for placing macros in an ASSIST job stream.

The macros *must* come before any machine instructions used by our program. We can use the TITLE, EJECT, SPACE, EQU, or comment instructions before, between, or after each macro definition, but we may not code any machine instructions in these locations. The macros follow each other in any order and each must have its own MACRO and MEND statements.

A macro is invoked simply by coding its name. XPRNT, GET, PUT, and DCB are all invoked by coding their respective names. If you attempt to invoke an undefined macro, an error occurs as shown in Fig. 10.11.

```
                                                                                    PAGE    3

LOC  OBJECT CODE    ADDR1 ADDR2  STMT   SOURCE STATEMENT                 ASM H V 02 18.10 11/26/85
                                    4          OPIN  (XIN,INPUT)                         | 000100
 IEV057  *** ERROR ***  UNDEFINED OP-CODE  --  OPIN
```

Figure 10.11 The OPEN macro is not coded correctly, so the assembler flags the statement as an error.

Since the macro is undefined, the assembler is not aware of the macro. When the assembler encounters any illegal mnemonic, an error results.

Macros are coded just after the ASM.SYSIN JCL statement within an assembly language program as shown in Fig. 10.12.

```
//         EXEC    ASMCG
//ASM.SYSIN   DD   *
           MACRO
           ADD
           . . .
           . . .
           MEND
           MACRO
           SUBTRACT
           . . .
           . . .
           MEND
MAINPGM    CSECT
           . . .
           . . .
```

Figure 10.12 Format for placing macros in a standard assembly language job stream.

Although macros can be written on a program-to-program basis, their real power is that they may be shared among many programmers and across many software systems. This occurs when they are placed into a **macro library.**

A **macro library** is a disk dataset where many macros are stored. Whenever a stored macro is to be used, the programmer simply codes the name of the macro. For example, you code XPRNT or GET whenever you want to use these macros. The appropriate macro is pulled from the macro library and processed by the assembler. All of the I/O macros are of this type, that is, they have been previously written and placed into a macro library for general use. Whenever a programmer wants to use these macros, he simply codes the macro name. The assembler locates the macro in the library and processes it accordingly.

Macros written and contained within your program area have priority over those contained in a macro library. For example, suppose that a macro called CLEAR is contained in both the macro library and just before your source program. When your code invokes CLEAR, the assembler uses that macro contained within your program area. The CLEAR macro in the macro library is not processed since the system assumes that the call to the CLEAR macro is for the one written by you.

It's very easy to place a macro into a macro library. In fact, the special IBM utility called **IEBUPDTE** is used for this purpose, but this is not its only function.

To place a macro into a macro library, you must know the name of the macro library. In most installations, the main macro library for ASSIST is **SYS1.ASISTMAC** or **ASSIST.MACLIB** and the main macro library for assembly language programs is **SYS1.MACLIB**. If a macro is to be used by both ASSIST and assembly language programs, it *may* (but not necessarily) have to be placed into both libraries. Check with your systems programming staff to determine which libraries are to contain your macros.

The macro called SUBTRACT may be placed into SYS1.MACLIB by coding the JCL shown in Fig. 10.13.

```
//      EXEC  PGM=IEBUPDTE,PARM=NEW
//SYSPRINT   DD   SYSOUT=$
//SYSUT2     DD   DSN=SYS1.MACLIB,DISP=SHR
//SYSIN      DD   *
./    ADD   NAME=SUBTRACT,LIST=ALL
          MACRO
          SUBTRACT
          . . .
          . . .
          MEND
./    ENDUP
```

Figure 10.13 Storing a macro in a macro library using IEBUPDTE.

If you want to place a copy of this macro into the ASSIST macro library, simply change the DSN operand on the SYSUT2 JCL statement so that it specifies the ASSIST macro library. This is done as shown in Fig. 10.14.

```
//SYSUT2   DD   DSN=SYS1.ASISTMAC,DISP=SHR
```

Figure 10.14 Directing IEBUPDTE output to an ASSIST macro library.

As you can see, it's very simple to place a macro into a library for general use. However, since macros may contain errors or bugs just as any other program, it may be necessary to replace a defective macro with an updated version. The example of Fig. 10.13 can also be used, just as it is, to replace a macro that has been revised.

If you are not allowed to use these libraries, then you may have to create your own library to share your macros with others. The JCL in Fig. 10.15 creates a macro library called MY.MACRO.LIBRARY. This library has similar characteristics to the standard system macro library and holds about 300 fifty-statement macros. Since macros are usually short, this library size will support your processing for quite some time.

```
//       EXEC    PGM=IEFBR14
//DDA    DD      DSN=MY.MACRO.LIBRARY,DISP=(NEW,CATLG),
//       UNIT=SYSDA,SPACE=(CYL,(2,,36)),DCB=SYS1.MACLIB
```

Figure 10.15 JCL to create a macro library.

You can change the name of the dataset coded on the DDA JCL statement in Fig. 10.15 based on your own needs by changing the DSN parameter from MY.MACRO.LIBRARY to one more applicable. A much larger macro library is created by increasing the value of the SPACE parameter. For example, SPACE=(CYL,(5,,108)) creates a very large library capable of holding upwards of 700 fifty-statement macros.

The DCB parameter in this example may look strange, but it is a very common method to define the characteristics of your macro library. This format informs the system to define this library with the same characteristics as SYS1.MACLIB. This prevents any incompatibility problems if I later attempt to access macros from both libraries within the same program.

Once your macro library is created, you must now code the appropriate JCL to cause ASSIST and the assembler to look to your libraries for your macros. In other words, the assembler and ASSIST do not automatically search all libraries for your macros. You must inform them that a macro library exists so that it can be used. For the library that I created, I would code the JCL given in Figs. 10.16 and 10.17 for access by ASSIST and the assembler, respectively.

```
//  EXEC        ASSIST
//SYSLIB        DD   DSN=MY.MACRO.LIBRARY,DISP=SHR
//              DD   DSN=SYS1.ASISTMAC,DISP=SHR
//              DD   DSN=SYS1.MACLIB,DISP=SHR
//SYSIN         DD   *
$JOB
*SYSLIB    macro1,macro2,macro3

       .    .    .
       .    .    .
```

Figure 10.16 Accessing a macro library in ASSIST.

```
//          EXEC  ASMCG
//ASM.SYSLIB  DD   DSN=MY.MACRO.LIBRARY,DISP=SHR
//            DD   DSN=SYS1.MACLIB,DISP=SHR
//ASM.SYSIN   DD   *

       .    .    .
       .    .    .
```

Figure 10.17 Accessing a macro library by the assembler.

In the ASSIST example of Fig. 10.16, the *SYSLIB statement is required when using any macro other than XREAD, XPRNT, and so on. As you can see, the *SYSLIB statement is coded beginning in column 1 and *after* the $JOB statement. Hence, the *SYSLIB statement is not a JCL statement—it is an ASSIST control statement. For each macro to be used from a library, its name *must* be coded on a SYSLIB statement. Of course, the standard ASSIST macros such as XPRNT, XDUMP and so on do not have to be referenced in this manner.

The *SYSLIB control statement is not required when using library macros in standard assembly language. In fact, no other control statements similar to *SYSLIB are required since the assembler will automatically search the specified macro libraries to find your macros. Since macro usage in standard assembly language requires no additional considerations, we devote the remaining discussion in this section to handling ASSIST macro libraries and the *SYSLIB control statement.

The *SYSLIB statement must come immediately after the $JOB statement. The *SYSLIB statement can identify several macros or just one. The examples in Fig. 10.18 illustrate how the macros called CALL and FORMAT are referenced from the macro libraries.

```
*SYSLIB     CALL,FORMAT
```

or

```
*SYSLIB     CALL
*SYSLIB     FORMAT
```

Figure 10.18 Causing ASSIST to recognize library macros by coding the *SYSLIB statement.

Also, the order in which you code the macro names or where the macro names appear on the *SYSLIB statement does not matter as long as one blank follows the control word *SYSLIB. If your program uses both library macros and program macros, then the *SYSLIB statement(s) must come before any of these macros. Again, the *SYSLIB statement is not required in standard assembly language.

The boldface JCL statements in Figs. 10.16 and 10.17 define each of the macro libraries to be used within your program. Also, these libraries are **concatenated** to form a very large collection of macros. By coding this JCL in this and other programs, macros may be shared by many programming groups. Although each programming group can define and use its own macro library, you begin to realize that macro libraries of this type quickly proliferate and become difficult to track and manage. This is the reason why there are typically just one or two macro libraries to support all programmers and all systems within a company.

THE MACRO PROTOTYPE STATEMENT

The macro prototype statement is very important to the macro definition. It identifies the name of the macro, which must be unique within your program, and it also identifies the information elements or **symbolic parameters** that supply information to the body of the macro. For example, the DCB macro instruction has many different parameters. From a sample DCB statement, we can identify each of the macro variables by their names as shown in Fig. 10.19.

XIN   DCB   *DSORG*=PS, *DDNAME*=XIN, *MACRF*=GM, *EODAD*=EOF

Figure 10.19 Keyword parameter DCB macro variables (in italics).

DSORG, DDNAME, MACRF, and EODAD are some of the symbolic parameters used by the DCB macro. These parameters can have any name, but when the macro was written, these names were selected.

Clearly, the macro name in this case is **DCB,** which you should already know means **data control block.** Again, this name was selected when the macro was originally developed.

The symbolic parameters in the DCB macro are called **keyword parameters** because the name of the parameter must be coded followed by the value assigned to that parameter. To read records from a file, code MACRF=GM, and to write records to a file, code MACRF=PM. The keyword parameter **MACRF** is assigned the value GM or PM depending on the type of processing to be performed.

Keyword parameters are used heavily in macros that have many operands, as is the case with the DCB macro. The order in which you code the keyword parameters does not matter since the keyword itself identifies which parameter is to be assigned a particular value. For example, the DCB instructions in Fig. 10.20 yield the same results.

```
XIN      DCB    DSORG=PS,DDNAME=XIN,MACRF=GM,EODAD=EOF

XIN      DCB    EODAD=EOF,MACRF=GM,DSORG=PS,DDNAME=XIN
```

Figure 10.20 The order of keyword macro parameters does not matter (a coding example).

Data is also supplied to a macro by **positional parameters,** where each parameter is not identified by a keyword or variable name, but by the *order* (position) in which it must be coded when the macro is invoked. All of the X-macro instructions in ASSIST (XDUMP, XPRNT, XREAD, XDECI, XDECO, and so on) are excellent examples of macros using positional parameters. Let's look at the XREAD instruction, for example.

The XREAD instruction requires two parameters. The first identifies the area into which the data is to be read, and the second identifies the amount of data to be read. The XREAD instruction shown in Fig. 10.21 causes the first 50 bytes of the next data card to be read and placed into the area called FIFTY.

```
XREAD   FIFTY,50
```

Figure 10.21 XREAD uses positional macro parameters.

What happens if we reverse the two parameters? Most likely, an error occurs since the second operand would now be FIFTY and would probably not be a valid length.

As you can see, it is important that positional parameters are coded in *exactly* the order that they are expected. Can you imagine how much more difficult it would be to code the DCB parameter if all of its parameters were positional? Although the amount of coding would be substantially reduced (since we wouldn't have to code the keyword parameter names), a slight mistake in order between any two parameters would most likely mean disaster.

Positional parameters are generally used when the number of parameters supplied to the macro is small or when ordering does not pose too much of a problem. Keyword parameters are used when many parameters are to be supplied to the macro or when ordering is not desired when a macro is invoked.

Each parameter used within the macro must be defined on the prototype statement in either positional or keyword parameter form. A symbolic parameter must begin with an ampersand (&), and must be followed by one to seven characters, the first of which must be a letter of the alphabet and the remaining characters can either be letters or digits. Figure 10.22 contains several examples of valid and invalid macro parameter names.

```
Macro Parameters           Validity

    &A                     valid
    &1                     invalid (illegal first character)
    &TOTAL                 valid
    &TOTAL1                valid
    &TOTALTIMES            invalid (too long)
    SUM                    invalid (doesn't begin with &)
```

Figure 10.22 Valid and invalid symbolic parameter names.

Suppose that a macro called CLEAR is to be constructed to clear a print line, that is, move spaces to each position of a print line. The macro requires at least one parameter, the name of the storage area to be cleared. Will we be clearing 133-byte or 86-byte print lines? Will we be clearing lines of mailing labels, which are 30 characters? Since we aren't sure of the length of the print area to be cleared, we need another parameter to give the length of the area.

Let's call our two parameters FIELD and LENGTH. The prototype statement for the CLEAR macro using positional parameters is coded as shown in Fig. 10.23. The prototype statement for the macro using keyword parameters is shown in Fig. 10.24.

```
CLEAR   &FIELD,&LENGTH
```

Figure 10.23 Example of a prototype statement using positional parameters.

```
CLEAR   &FIELD=,&LENGTH=
```

Figure 10.24 Example of a prototype statement using keyword parameters.

From the programmer's point of view, it's easier to use the macro with positional parameters. However, let's develop the macro using both formats to illustrate the difference in using each.

With positional symbolic parameters, a 133-byte print line called PLINE is cleared by coding the macro call in Fig. 10.25. The same area is cleared using the instruction shown in Fig. 10.26 if keyword symbolic parameters are used.

```
CLEAR   PLINE,133
```

Figure 10.25 Invoking the macro with positional parameters.

```
CLEAR   FIELD=PLINE,LENGTH=133
```

Figure 10.26 Invoking the macro with keyword parameters.

Again, more coding is required with keyword parameters than with positional parameters. Regardless of how the values are supplied to the macro, the values are the same. Hence, within the body of the macro, FIELD and LENGTH are processed in exactly the same manner.

It may be worthwhile to code the prototype statement with comments to identify the use of each symbolic parameter as shown in Fig. 10.27. Comments may not be too valuable for small macros with few parameters, but for larger macros, this technique is strongly encouraged.

```
positional symbolic parameter format with comments

         CLEAR    &FIELD,         AREA TO BE CLEARED              X
                  &LENGTH         LENGTH OF AREA TO CLEAR

cols:    10       16              40                              72



keyword symbolic parameter format with comments

         CLEAR    &FIELD=,        AREA TO BE CLEARED              X
                  &LENGTH=        LENGTH OF AREA TO CLEAR
```

Figure 10.27 Coding a prototype statement with comments.

Another difference between keyword and positional parameters is that keyword parameters may be assigned a default value on the prototype statement, *positional parameters may not.* This means that the programmer may not have to code all the parameters whenever the macro is invoked. For example, the CLEAR macro could assume that 133-byte print lines are to be cleared most often. Hence, a default value of 133 is assigned to the symbolic parameter LENGTH, thus, not requiring the programmer to code the parameter when the macro is called. Only when the print lines are *not* 133 bytes does the LENGTH parameter have to be coded. To accomplish this task, we code the prototype statement differently to accommodate our 133 LENGTH default as shown in Fig. 10.28.

```
Keyword parameters with default values and comments.

   CLEAR   &FIELD=,       AREA TO BE CLEARED        X
           &LENGTH=133    LENGTH OF AREA TO CLEAR
```

Figure 10.28 Supplying a default value to a keyword parameter.

As long as the print area to be cleared matches the default length value, the programmer calls this macro by simply coding the macro call given in Fig. 10.29.

```
         CLEAR   FIELD=PLINE
```

Figure 10.29 Invoking a macro and accepting macro default values.

Keyword and positional parameters may be utilized in the same macro definition if desired. Although all of our examples have utilized only keyword or only positional parameters in the construction of a macro, this need not be the case. You can develop a macro which can utilize keyword parameters in order to supply default values to fields, and utilize positional parameters for most of the other parameters needed by the macro.

When invoking such a macro, the user must code the positional parameters in the order expected. However, the user can also code keyword parameters intermixed among the positional parameters or centralized in one area of the macro call to supply values to these parameters used by the macro. You'll have to determine if your processing needs require positional, keyword, or mixed parameter definitions and implement your macro accordingly.

THE MACRO BODY AND A COMPLETE MACRO EXAMPLE

What is to happen within the body of the CLEAR macro that we've been developing? Quite simply, blanks or spaces are moved to the area identified by &FIELD. Hence, the *machine instruction* necessary to cause this move is shown in Fig. 10.30.

```
MVC    field(length),=CL133' '
```

Figure 10.30 Instruction to initialize a character field.

The literal presents a problem since a 30-byte field does not need a 133-byte literal of blanks and so we are wasting program storage. Using another technique discussed in an earlier chapter, we can clear an area by moving a single blank to the first position of the field and then propagate that byte to every other byte within the field as shown in Fig. 10.31.

```
MVI   field,C' '                 CLEAR FIRST BYTE
MVC   field+1(length-1),field    CLEAR REMAINING BYTES
```

Figure 10.31 Another method for initializing a character field.

This solution does not require a literal and works with any area up to 257 bytes long. For now, let's assume that all areas to be cleared will be less than 257 bytes.

Since our symbolic parameters identify the field to be processed and the length of data to be moved, we can now code the statements shown in Fig. 10.32 within the body of our macro. Note that these statements are coded in the same manner whether keyword or positional parameters are used.

```
MVI   &FIELD,C' '                  CLEAR FIRST BYTE
MVC   &FIELD+1(&LENGTH-1),&FIELD   CLEAR REMAINING BYTES
```

Figure 10.32 The body of the CLEAR macro.

When the macro, which is defined with positional parameters by the code in Fig. 10.33, is called, the assembler generates the associated machine instructions also shown in this figure. The machine instructions are then assembled into the executable program to clear the area called PLINE during program execution.

```
         CLEAR   PLINE,86
+        MVI     PLINE,C' '
+        MVC     PLINE+1(86-1),PLINE
```

Figure 10.33 Macro call and generated instructions.

The same macro defined with keyword parameters is called and produces the code shown in Fig. 10.34. Again, note that the same machine instructions are generated with the keyword parameters.

```
        CLEAR   FIELD=PLINE,LENGTH=86
+       MVI     PLINE,C' '
+       MVC     PLINE+1(86-1),PLINE
```

Figure 10.34 Calling the CLEAR macro with keyword parameters.

This macro can also be modified to clear any area with a value other than a blank. Although the default value can be a blank, there may be times when we want to clear an area by using X'00' or X'FF'. Using a symbolic parameter name of &BYTE, we code the modified macro as shown in Fig. 10.35.

```
MACRO
CLEAR    &FIELD=,                          AREA TO BE CLEARED        X
         &LENGTH=133,                      LENGTH OF AREA            X
         &BYTE=40                          DEFAULT FIELD VALUE
MVI      &FIELD,X'&BYTE'                   CLEAR FIRST BYTE
MVC      &FIELD+1(&LENGTH-1),&FIELD
MEND
```

Figure 10.35 Complete macro to initialize data areas with any programmer-supplied value.

The hexadecimal value X'40' is the character—blank. Therefore, the default parameters clear a 133-byte area to blanks. A four-byte area is cleared to binary zeros by calling the macro shown in Fig. 10.36. This macro call generates the machine code shown in Fig. 10.37.

```
CLEAR   FIELD=TOTAL,BYTE=00,LENGTH=4
```

Figure 10.36 Initializing a four-byte field to X'00' using the macro from Fig. 10.35.

```
+    MVI   TOTAL,X'00'
+    MVC   TOTAL+1(4-1),TOTAL
```

Figure 10.37 Generated code from the macro call in Fig. 10.36.

The MVI sets the first byte of the field called TOTAL to X'00'. The second instruction propagates the value in the first byte of TOTAL, now X'00', to each of the other three bytes in TOTAL. Hence, TOTAL becomes four bytes of X'00'.

Since most machine instructions allow labels to be placed in column 1, it's only appropriate for our macro to also allow this capability. The label coded then becomes yet another parameter to our macro and should be placed on the first machine instruction statement generated by our macro. Let's call the symbolic parameter associated with the label &LABEL. Our modified CLEAR macro is coded as shown in Fig. 10.38. Note that a slightly different prototype statement is used.

When the macro is invoked using a label of LOOP, the code shown in Fig. 10.39 is generated.

```
                MACRO
&LABEL          CLEAR     &FIELD=,&LENGTH=133,&BYTE=40
&LABEL          MVI       &FIELD,X'&BYTE'
                MVC       &FIELD+1(&LENGTH-1),&FIELD
                MEND
```

Figure 10.38 The CLEAR macro that accepts a user label.

```
 LOOP      CLEAR   FIELD=TOTAL,BYTE=00,LENGTH=4
+LOOP      MVI     TOTAL,X'00'
+          MVC     TOTAL+1(4-1),TOTAL
```

Figure 10.39 Code generated by the CLEAR macro (with a label).

In Chapter 6, we remarked that EQU and DS instructions also hold and define labels. The CLEAR macro, rewritten once more to adhere to this guideline, is shown in Figure 10.40.

```
                MACRO
&LABEL          CLEAR     &FIELD=,&LENGTH=133,&BYTE=40
&LABEL          DS        0H
                MVI       &FIELD,X'&BYTE'
                MVC       &FIELD+1(&LENGTH-1),&FIELD
                MEND
```

Figure 10.40 The CLEAR macro that supports label definition.

THE LENGTH ATTRIBUTE

To assist in field processing, ASSIST and the assembler use special attribute elements to reference fields. These elements, called **data attributes,** are used within macros or within **open code** (standard machine instructions not contained within macros). One attribute, called the **length attribute** and also called the **L' attribute** (pronounced ell-quote), supplies values to your instructions related to the lengths of fields defined within your program. For example, consider a four-byte binary field called TOTAL. The length attribute gives a value of 4 when used with a reference to this field. In other words, the load address instruction in Fig. 10.41 places a value of 4 into register 7 after it is executed.

```
         LA      R7,L'TOTAL
         . . .
         . . .
TOTAL    DS      F
```

Figure 10.41 Using the L' attribute.

The manner in which a field is defined directly impacts the value of the length attribute. Specifically, repetition (duplication) factors *do not* impact the value of the length attribute. If TOTAL is defined as four 1-byte fields, the length attribute gives a value of 1 for TOTAL instead of 4 as shown earlier.

The length attribute is very helpful in the CLEAR macro that we discussed earlier. If we assume that fields are not defined with repetition factors, the length attribute can determine the length of the print line to be cleared. By integrating this capability into the CLEAR macro, we eliminate the &LENGTH symbolic parameter used before, and so our macro can now be implemented as shown in Fig. 10.42.

```
           MACRO
&LABEL     CLEAR    &FIELD=,&BYTE=40
&LABEL     DS       0H
           MVI      &FIELD,X'&BYTE'
           MVC      &FIELD+1(L'&FIELD-1),&FIELD
           MEND
```

Figure 10.42 CLEAR macro with L' integration.

The length attribute may also be used within our standard assembly language statements, outside the bounds of our macro. In fact, the length attribute *should* be used since it helps greatly in maintaining our code. If all lengths are coded with the length attribute instead of *hard coded* within our machine instructions, a change in length to the associated data area automatically updates all length attribute values when the program is reassembled. For example, suppose that two 5-byte packed-decimal fields called NUM1 and NUM2 are to be added using the instruction given in Fig. 10.43.

```
AP      NUM1(5),NUM2(5)
```

Figure 10.43 Explicitly coded length operands.

The length operands are explicitly coded within this instruction. If we have to increase the size of either field, we have to change this instruction *and all other* instructions that reference either of these fields where the lengths have been explicitly coded. If this instruction is coded with the L' operand, any reassembly automatically updates the associated field lengths. Clearly, when changes of this type are made, they decrease or eliminate problems. Our instruction is, therefore, coded as shown in Fig. 10.44.

```
AP      NUM1(L'NUM1),NUM2(L'NUM2)
```

Figure 10.44 Using L' in standard machine instructions.

If either NUM1 or NUM2 are redefined, the length attribute automatically updates the add instruction to reflect the new length(s) of the field(s).

THE MACRO LANGUAGE

As we've discussed, any machine instruction (such as MVI or MVC) and assembly language instruction (such as TITLE, EJECT, or SPACE) may be coded within the body of the macro. There are other instructions that may be coded within a macro. These instructions, which are new to our discussion, are called **macro instructions.**

Macro instructions or macro statements are special instructions that perform macro processing. Further, they use **macro variables** to process data within the macro.

These variables are not the same as the data areas that we have been using since they are not created with the DS or DC instructions. Macro variables are elements within the macro that process character data, numeric data, or bit information to generate machine instructions.

Macro variables may be **local** or **global** to the macro. Local macro variables are used only within a single macro and are defined with either the **LCLC, LCLA,** or **LCLB** macro instructions. The LCLC (local macro character variable) instruction, LCLA (local macro arithmetic variable), and LCLB (local macro boolean variable) are coded at the beginning of the macro to **declare** each local macro variable. For example, the code in Fig. 10.45 defines &C as a local character variable, &A as a local arithmetic variable, and &B as a local boolean variable.

```
          MACRO
prototype statement
          LCLA      &A
          LCLB      &B
          LCLC      &C
```

Figure 10.45 Declaring local macro variables.

Depending on which data type declares the variable, it is also given a default value. Arithmetic variables are assigned an initial value of 0, character variables are assigned an initial value of the null string (no data), and boolean variables are assigned an initial value of 0.

Global macro variables are defined with the **GBLA, GBLB,** and **GBLC** macro instructions. These variables are also initialized in the same manner as locally declared variables.

A local variable may only be used within the macro in which it is declared. A global variable may be used across several macros as long as it is declared in each macro. For example, suppose that several macros produce the register equates. It would not be wise for each macro to blindly generate the register equates when it is called since duplicate equates result in syntax errors. By using a single global variable declared in each macro, each macro knows whether or not the register equates have been generated. If they have, the macro does not generate them again; if they haven't, the macro generates the equates and then changes the value of the global variable to indicate that the equates have been produced.

Global variables are usually declared before local variables and immediately following the prototype statement. Further, all macro variables must be unique. You cannot define two macro variables with the same name and you cannot define a macro variable with the same name as one of the symbolic parameters on your prototype statement. Incidentally, symbolic parameters are not declared using the LCLx or GBLx statements. Symbolic parameters are implicitly defined as character variables by their presence on the prototype statement.

Macro variables may be used on any machine instruction or on a macro instruction. The various macro instructions with their functions are summarized in Fig. 10.46.

These instructions make up the macro instruction set. The general format of each instruction is given in Fig. 10.47.

macro instruction	function it performs
AIF	decision statement identical to the IF-THEN logical construct
ANOP	null statement similar to the DS 0H or EQU * instruction to identify a target of a branch instruction
AGO	unconditional branch instruction similar to the GOTO
ACTR	process control element to limit the number of AIF or AGO instructions that can be executed within the macro. It is most often used as a debugging aid to trap infinite loops within macros.

SET macro instructions (assignment statements)	
SETA	assign a value to an arithmetic macro variable
SETB	assign a value to a boolean macro variable
SETC	assign a value to a character macro variable

Figure 10.46 Summary of the macro instructions.

```
.label      ANOP
.label      AGO      .target
.label      ACTR     nnnn
.label      AIF      (expression).target
variable    SETx     variable
```

Figure 10.47 Format for each macro instruction.

Labels on macro statements begin with a period and may be followed by one to seven characters. The first character (following the period) must be a letter of the alphabet and the remaining characters can be letters or digits. Each macro label must be unique within the body of the macro.

As you can see, every macro instruction can contain a macro label. Remember, these are *macro labels,* not labels on machine code instructions. For example, you cannot use the BC instruction to branch to a *macro* label.

Most of the macro statements are quite simple. The only statement of any concern is the AIF statement since it is the primary statement to control processing within the body of the macro. The AIF statement requires an expression, enclosed in parentheses, as part of the statement. This expression uses **logical operators** to compare values to determine if they are equal to (EQ), not equal to (NE), less than or equal to (LE), greater than or equal to (GE), less than (LT), or greater than (GT). The boolean operators AND, OR, and NOT are also used within the AIF expression to form **compound expressions** or **compound conditions.** We'll see some examples of AIF statement coding later.

Let's construct a simple macro to illustrate the use of macro instructions. Without concern for meaning, let's write a simple macro to generate 10 fullwords of storage with each fullword initialized to the binary value zero. The *logic* to perform this processing is as follows:

```
do i = 10 to 1 by -1
   generate a fullword
enddo
```

Since variable i will assume more than one arithmetic value, we'll use an arithmetic macro variable called &I to represent the variable above. With statement numbers serving as reference, Fig. 10.48 contains the macro to generate our fullwords.

```
 1                   MACRO
 2                   FULLWRDS
 3                   LCLA      &I
 4         &I        SETA      10
 5         .LOOP     ANOP
 6                   AIF       (&I EQ 0).DONE
 7                   DC        F'0'
 8         &I        SETA      &I-1
 9                   AGO       .LOOP
10         .DONE     ANOP
11                   MEND
```

Figure 10.48 Macro to generate and initialize 10 fullwords of storage.

The arithmetic variable called &I is declared and is given an initial value of 0. Statement 4 changes the default value from 0 to 10. The ANOP in statement 5 is the target of the AGO in statement 9. In other words, statements 5 through 9 form the loop within our macro. Statement 6 determines if the value of &I is equal to 0. If it is, a branch is taken to the macro label called .DONE, which is in line 10. If &I is not equal to zero, then we fall into the DC instruction and generate a fullword of storage. A value of 1 is then subtracted from &I and the loop continues by branching from statement 9 back to statement 5.

As you can see, most of the statements are quite simple. The only statement that is complex is the AIF statement. In this example, the AIF compares &I to the value of 0. Although only two arithmetic elements are compared, the AIF instruction can also compare boolean or character macro variables as well. If &A and &X represent arithmetic variables, &B represents a boolean variable, and &C represents a character variable, the statements in Fig. 10.49 illustrate the basic form for coding the AIF macro statement.

```
AIF     (&A EQ 5).TARGET

AIF     (&A EQ 5 AND &B).TARGET

AIF     (&A GT &X OR '&C' EQ 'ABC').TARGET

AIF     (NOT &B).TARGET

AIF     ((&A EQ 5) AND NOT ('&C' LT 'ABC')).TARGET

AIF     (&B OR NOT (&A EQ 5)).TARGET

AIF     (&A NE &X).TARGET
```

Figure 10.49 Examples of coding the AIF instruction.

Clearly, macro variables can be compared to constant terms or to other macro variables. Whenever a *character* macro variable is coded or referenced in an AIF statement, enclose the variable in single quotes as illustrated in Fig. 10.49. Although most of the AIF instructions are straightforward, the boolean expressions may be difficult to understand. Remember that the AIF expression is evaluated and yields either a "true" or a "false" result. If the expression evaluated is true, a branch is taken to the target label. If it is false, processing continues with the instruction that follows. For example, suppose that &B, our boolean variable, is 0. Zero means "false" and 1 means "true." The examples in Fig. 10.50 indicate the value of the expression when &B is used.

```
&B      SETB    0
        AIF     (&B).target          false, no branch
        AIF     (NOT &B).target      not 0 is 1, 1 is true,
                                     the branch is taken

&B      SETB    1
        AIF     (&B).target          B is 1, true, the
                                     branch is taken
```

Figure 10.50 Evaluating boolean macro variables.

Now let's write a macro to generate the register equates. The logic for this macro is as follows:

```
do i = 0 to 15
   Ri     EQU   i
enddo
```

The logic for this macro is similar to our previous macro. Hence, we implement the macro called EQUATES in much the same way as shown in Fig. 10.51.

```
         MACRO
         EQUATES
         LCLA     &REG
.LOOP    AIF      (&REG GT 15).OUT
R&REG    EQU      &REG
&REG     SETA     &REG+1
         AGO      .LOOP
.OUT     ANOP
         MEND
```

Figure 10.51 Macro to generate the register equates.

For each value of the arithmetic macro variable ® between 0 and 15, the value is concatenated to the letter R to form R0, R1, R2, and so on. These symbols are then equated to the respective values of 0, 1, 2, and so on, thus generating the register equates. This macro is called by coding the instruction shown in Fig. 10.52.

```
EQUATES
```

Figure 10.52 Instruction to invoke the register equates macro.

It may be wise to introduce a global variable at this point in our discussion. As we remarked earlier, several different macros may be constructed to generate the register equates. If more than one macro attempts to generate the equates, syntax errors result. To prevent this, we can use a global variable, *declared in all macros that generate the equates,* to indicate whether or not the equates have been generated. Since there are only two possible values in this situation, generated or not generated, a boolean variable is an excellent choice for this application. We use a value of 0 to indicate that the equates *have not* been generated and a value of 1 to indicate that they have been generated. Figure 10.53 contains our revised implementation.

```
         MACRO
         EQUATES
         GBLB      &REGS
         LCLA      &REG
         AIF       (&REGS EQ 1).OUT
&REGS    SETB      1
.LOOP    AIF       (&REG GT 15).OUT
R&REG    EQU       &REG
&REG     SETA      &REG+1
         AGO       .LOOP
.OUT     ANOP
         MEND
```

Figure 10.53 EQUATES macro with the global check variable ®S.

The macro variable ®S is used as the global variable. Don't confuse the two variables ®S and ®. ®S is the global variable to indicate whether or not the equates have been generated and ® is the local variable within the macro that generates the equates if they have not been generated already.

If the value of ®S is already 1 when this macro is processed, the register equates have been generated and so an immediate exit is taken from the macro. If the value of ®S is 0, then it is immediately set to 1, the register equates are generated, and the macro is ended.

Remember that when an expression is evaluated within the AIF instruction, the result of the expression is either "true" or "false." If the expression is "true," a branch is taken to the target label identified on the AIF instruction. A false result causes macro processing to continue with the next instruction. A boolean value of 1 is considered "true" and a value of 0 is considered "false." Since ®S is a boolean variable and can constitute an expression itself, we can modify our previous example as shown in Fig. 10.54.

```
         MACRO
         EQUATES
         GBLB      &REGS
         LCLA      &REG
         AIF       (&REGS).OUT
&REGS    SETB      1
.LOOP    AIF       (&REG GT 15).OUT
R&REG    EQU       &REG
&REG     SETA      &REG+1
         AGO       .LOOP
.OUT     ANOP
         MEND
```

Figure 10.54 Revised EQUATES macro utilizing boolean expressions.

Now that you've seen an example of using arithmetic and boolean macro variables, let's turn our attention to character variable processing. Character variables process character strings up to 255 characters long. They may also extract one string from another or form larger strings by concatenating two or more variables or strings.

Suppose that a macro is to construct an edit pattern for a packed-decimal field. Given the name of the packed-decimal field, its length (in bytes), and the name of the field to hold the edited value, we construct the necessary *machine instructions* to generate a standard edit pattern, edit the field, and place a negative sign before the first digit if the number is negative. Here's what this macro must do.

```
digits = (field length * 2) - 1
pattern = X'40'
do i = 1 to digits - 2
   pattern = pattern + X'20'
enddo
pattern = pattern + X'2120'
move edit pattern into edit field
edit and mark the number
move in negative sign if required
```

The macro generates an edit pattern of the correct type to allow all values, including zero, to print properly on output. Although this macro does not handle numbers with digits to the right of the decimal point, it could be modified to do so.

Clearly, character processing must form the edit pattern since the edit characters are represented as character data. Further, the edit pattern generated by this macro is of a different length, depending on the size of the field to be edited. Clearly, this macro would have been useful in Chapter 7 when we processed packed-decimal fields. Figure 10.55 contains the macro called EDIT.

```
                MACRO
&LABEL          EDIT      &FIELD,&LENGTH,&TARGET
                LCLC      &PATTERN
                LCLA      &DIGITS
                LCLA      &P1LEN
&DIGITS         SETA      &LENGTH
&DIGITS         SETA      &DIGITS*2
&DIGITS         SETA      &DIGITS-1
&P1LEN          SETA      &DIGITS-2
.*
&PATTERN        SETC      '40'
.LOOP           AIF       (&P1LEN EQ 0).PART2
&PATTERN        SETC      '&PATTERN.20'
&P1LEN          SETA      &P1LEN-1
                AGO       .LOOP
.PART2          ANOP
&PATTERN        SETC      '&PATTERN.2120'
&LABEL          MVC       &TARGET.(L'&TARGET),=X'&PATTERN'
                LA        1,&TARGET+L'&TARGET-1
                EDMK      &TARGET.(L'&TARGET),&FIELD
                BNM       NOTLTO
                BCTR      1,0
                MVI       0(1),C'-'
NOTLTO          DS        0H
                MEND
```

Figure 10.55 Macro to construct an edit pattern and edit a packed-decimal field.

There are many parts of this macro to investigate closely. Lines 11 to 15 of the macro form the first part of the edit pattern, that is, they form all of the edit characters before the significance starter (X'21'). Line 17 adds the last two characters to the edit pattern to complete the pattern definition. Line 18 generates a machine instruction. The edit pattern is moved into the target field and the length attribute is used in the moving process to specify the length of the target field for the MVC instruction. Register 1 addresses the rightmost byte in the target area, again through the use of the length attribute. Incidentally, register 1 is not coded with the R prefix since this macro does not check if the register equates are generated. If they are not and if we use the R prefix, a syntax error results in the program. In general, it's *not* good practice to use the R suffix on register references within machine instructions contained in a library macro.

The standard code to edit the field and place a negative sign before the first digit is then generated by the macro (lines 20–24). Only when the MEND statement is encountered is the macro terminated. If this macro is called more than once, we have a problem since the label called NOTLT0 is generated *each time* that the macro is called. Obviously, this causes assembly errors since a statement label may only be used once within a program. To solve this problem, we use a special facility provided by the assembler to generate unique labels on machine code instructions. The facility, called **&SYSNDX,** provides a unique four-digit number wherever it is coded.

If we concatenate &SYSNDX onto another one- to four-character label, such as NLT0, then each time this macro is invoked a new label is generated. NLT0**0001** is generated on the first call, NLT0**0002** on the second call, and so on. We only have to code NLT0&SYSNDX in place of the current label NOTLT0 within our program to prove this facility. &SYSNDX can be used in many macros to provide unique labels on all machine instructions. Whenever there is a possibility for a macro to be called more than once and for the macro to generate duplicate labels, &SYSNDX should be used. Figure 10.56 contains our modified implementation.

```
1                      MACRO
2   &LABEL             EDIT      &FIELD,&LENGTH,&TARGET
3                      LCLC      &PATTERN
4                      LCLA      &DIGITS
5                      LCLA      &P1LEN
6   &DIGITS            SETA      &LENGTH
7   &DIGITS            SETA      &DIGITS*2
8   &DIGITS            SETA      &DIGITS-1
9   &P1LEN             SETA      &DIGITS-2
10  .*
11  &PATTERN           SETC      '40'
12  .LOOP              AIF       (&P1LEN EQ 0).PART2
13  &PATTERN           SETC      '&PATTERN.20'
14  &P1LEN             SETA      &P1LEN-1
15                     AGO       .LOOP
16  .PART2             ANOP
17  &PATTERN           SETC      '&PATTERN.2120'
18  &LABEL             MVC       &TARGET.(L'&TARGET),=X'&PATTERN'
19                     LA        1,&TARGET+L'&TARGET-1
20                     EDMK      &TARGET.(L'&TARGET),&FIELD
21                     BNM       NLT0&SYSNDX
22                     BCTR      1,0
23                     MVI       0(1),C'-'
24  NLT0&SYSNDX        DS        0H
25                     MEND
```

Figure 10.56 EDIT macro using &SYSNDX.

Line 10 within the macro is a macro comment. Macro comments do not appear within the generated program when the macro is processed by the assembler. Standard comments can be coded in a macro, but they are generated when processed by the assembler. If you want to generate comments each time the macro is called, then use the standard comment beginning with a * in column 1. If you want comments to be found only within the macro and not generated outside, then code a macro comment with a .* in columns 1 and 2 of your statement line.

Speaking of comments, macros should be commented as if they were programs or modules. Just after the declaration of your global and local variables, a comment block should be coded to define the function of the macro. This comment block is information to someone who may have to modify your macro at a later time. Also, comments placed throughout the body of the macro help readability and understanding of the macro code. They are especially valuable when the processing performed by the macro is rather complex or when the macro is quite large.

The programmer calls the macro by coding the instruction given in Fig. 10.57. The expansion of the EDIT macro is shown in Fig. 10.58.

```
SUMEDIT   EDIT   SUMP,8,SUM
```

Figure 10.57 Calling the EDIT macro.

```
                                                                                                      PAGE    3

  LOC  OBJECT CODE     ADDR1 ADDR2  STMT   SOURCE STATEMENT                                 ASM H V 02 10.47 12/02/85

                                     29 SUMEDIT  EDIT  SUMP,8,SUM                                            | 000350
000000 D20F F0B0 F0C0 000B0 000C0    30+SUMEDIT  MVC   SUM(L'SUM),=X'40202020202020202020202020202120'    01-00016
000006 4110 F0BF            000BF    31+             LA    1,SUM+L'SUM-1                                       01-00017
00000A DF0F F0B0 F0A8 000B0 000A8    32+             EDMK  SUM(L'SUM),SUMP                                     01-00018
000010 47B0 F01A            0001A    33+             BNM   NLT00001                                            01-00019
000014 0610                          34+             BCTR  1,0                                                 01-00020
000016 9260 1000      00000          35+             MVI   0(1),C'-'                                           01-00021
00001A                               36+NLT00001     DS    0H                                                  01-00022
```

Figure 10.58 Code generated by the EDIT macro.

The **ACTR** instruction is not a frequently used macro instruction. Its primary purpose is to limit the number of AIF and AGO statements that are processed during macro expansion. This limitation prevents infinite loops when macro or conditional assembly processing occurs. For example, the macro shown in Fig. 10.59 generates many fullwords of storage.

```
DO NOT USE THIS MACRO, IT IS DESIGNED TO FAIL!

          MACRO
          BOMB
.LOOP     ANOP
          DS         F
          AGO        .LOOP
          MEND
```

Figure 10.59 Macro to generate many fullwords.

The macro generates fullwords of storage until the ACTR limit is reached. At that point, the assembler terminates the expansion of this macro. Although this macro is intended to fail, the macros you write are not designed to act in this manner. However, they may contain a bug causing them to loop longer than desired.

Occasionally, a very large or complex macro may exceed the ACTR value. The typical ACTR value is 4096, but if your macro loops 8,000 times, you obviously have to increase the ACTR value. This is done by coding the ACTR instruction as shown in Fig. 10.60.

```
ACTR    10000
```

Figure 10.60 Increasing the ACTR limit.

The ACTR limit is set to 10,000 in this example. This allows our 8,000-loop macro to operate normally and yet prevents any infinite loops within any other macro. You can also use ACTR during testing of a macro. In this case, the ACTR limit is set upon entering your macro and reset when your macro finishes. If your macro doesn't operate as you intended, you've provided a method for controlling the code generation by the macro.

CHARACTER VARIABLES, CONCATENATION, AND STRING PROCESSING

The capabilities of macro variables and statements to perform string processing are quite amazing. Characters or portions of strings are extracted or concatenated to form new strings that can be used to generate code or to process within the body of the macro. To gain a better understanding of string processing features, let's look closely at character variables.

Suppose that a character macro variable has a value of 'ASSIST'. The sample SETC instructions in Fig. 10.61 illustrate some of the other character processing facilities within the macro language.

macro statement			result
&C	SETC	'&C&C'	'ASSISTASSIST'
&C	SETC	'&C+1'	'ASSIST+1' (no addition will be performed!)
&C	SETC	'&CABC'	error, illegal concatenation
&C	SETC	'&C.ISFUN'	'ASSISTISFUN'
&C	SETC	'&C..ISFUN'	'ASSIST.ISFUN'
&C	SETC	'&C'.'ISFUN'	'ASSISTISFUN'
&C	SETC	'&C'(3,2)	'SI'

Figure 10.61 Character string manipulation using macro variables.

The period is the macro symbol for **concatenation,** which is the joining of strings to form a larger string. Whenever a macro variable is to be concatenated, the concatenation symbol may or may not be required. The list in Fig. 10.62 specifies when the concatenation symbol is required during string processing. Assume that &C is a macro character variable and that its value is 'ASSIST'.

```
          concatenation symbols are required when...

a)  a standard alphanumeric character follows
    a macro variable

                 '&C.ABC'          = 'ASSISTABC'

b)  a macro variable comes immediately before a
    left parenthesis

                 '&C.(4)'          = 'ASSIST(4)'

c)  a period is to be generated within the
    resulting character string

                 '&C..ABC'         =  'ASSIST.ABC'


       concatenation symbols are not required when...

a)  a macro variable follows a character string

                 'ABC&C'           = 'ABCASSIST'

b)  a special character follows the macro variable

                 'ABC&C-1'         = 'ABCASSIST-1'

c)  one macro variable follows another

                 '&C&C'            = 'ASSISTASSIST'
```

Figure 10.62 Rules for string concatenation.

One example shown earlier in Fig. 10.61 is of particular interest and is shown again in Fig. 10.63. This example illustrates how **substring notation** is used when processing macro character variables. Using the form (3,2), the macro processor takes characters 3 and 4 from the string and assigns them to &C. In other words, starting at location 3 within the string, extract two characters and assign them to &C.

```
&C      SETC   '&C'(3,2)      =>   'SI'
```

Figure 10.63 Example of substring notation.

What will the example in Fig. 10.64 produce if we still assume that &C originally contains ASSIST? The resulting string is 'HAVING FUN YET?'. The string 'HAVING ' is concatenated with three characters, starting in position 9 of the string 'ASSISTISFUN', and concatenated with the string ' YET?'. As you can see, some rather sophisticated string processing in the macro language can be performed. However, remember that strings must be between 0 and 255 characters long.

```
&C       SETC   'HAVING '.'&C.ISFUN'(9,3).' YET?'
```

Figure 10.64 What is produced by this SETC instruction?

SUBLISTS WITHIN MACRO PARAMETERS

Another useful application of macros is to call subroutines. Given the name of the subroutine and the various parameters to be passed, the macro constructs a parameter list and invokes the subroutine appropriately. On the other hand, the macro must be flexible to handle a varying number of parameters, that is, each subroutine called may not require the same number of parameters. Hence, the macro must build a parameter list that varies in length depending on the number of parameters to be passed to and from the subroutine.

To support this processing, we use the **sublist** facility provided by the assembler. A sublist is a list of parameters enclosed in parentheses and separated by commas. For example, (A,B,C,D) is a sublist with four **entries.** Using this facility, we can determine the number of entries in the sublist and obtain the value of each entry by using the **number attribute,** the **SYSLIST** symbolic parameter, or **sublist symbolic parameters.**

Suppose that sublist (A,B,C,D) defines the parameters to be passed to a subroutine. A macro called CALLSUB is constructed to perform the subroutine call, provided that it allows two arguments—the name of the module to be called and the parameters to be passed between the modules. Figure 10.65 shows the call to this macro.

```
CALLSUB  READRTN,(A,B,C,D)
```

Figure 10.65 Invoking the subroutine call macro.

Within the assembler, a special system symbolic parameter called **SYSLIST** is available. You do not have to define this parameter on your prototype statement, you can simply use it within your macro as needed. In this example, there are two SYSLIST argument values. SYSLIST(1) has a value of **READRTN** and SYSLIST(2) has a value of **(A,B,C,D)**. (The number in parentheses just after SYSLIST is the symbolic parameter **subscript.**) Without defining any other parameters on our macro prototype statement, we can write the complete macro using only the SYSLIST system parameter as shown in Fig. 10.66.

```
         MACRO
&LABEL   CALLSUB
&LABEL   DS       0H
         LA       1,=A&SYSLIST(2)
         L        15,=V(&SYSLIST(1))
         BALR     14,15
         MEND
```

Figure 10.66 Macro to invoke subroutines with SYSLIST support.

The instruction containing the load address instruction concatenates our sublist onto the "=A" to form the address reference "=A(A,B,C,D)". The first SYSLIST value is concatenated between "=V(" and ")" to form "=V(READRTN)" when this statement is fully converted by the assembler. We did not define any parameters on the prototype statement since the SYSLIST variable accesses any data entered by the programmer. However, this technique can only be used if *positional parameters* have been coded to invoke the macro.

Again, a statement label can be coded by the programmer on the macro call statement. Although we allowed for this in previous examples by using the symbolic parameter &LABEL, we can also eliminate this parameter by using the SYSLIST element. Access to the label is made by referencing SYSLIST(0). Incorporating this into our macro definition, we supply the statement label onto a machine instruction as shown in Fig. 10.67.

```
                MACRO
                CALLSUB
&SYSLIST(0)     DS          0H
                LA          1,=A&SYSLIST(2)
                L           15,=V(&SYSLIST(1))
                BALR        14,15
                MEND
```

Figure 10.67 Referencing all user parameters with SYSLIST.

Although the DS 0H instruction may look rather odd since it doesn't appear in our standard coding format, it works. If desired, we can also reference the individual values *within* the sublist operand. SYSLIST(2,1) gives a value of A, SYSLIST(2,2) a value of B, and SYSLIST(2,4) a value of D. We can extract values from within the sublist by using this alternate form of the SYSLIST directive.

If our macro is designed to use keyword parameters, we cannot use SYSLIST. However, elements within a sublist can still be extracted using a similar reference with our keyword parameter. Figure 10.68 shows a typical macro prototype statement containing keyword parameters.

```
&LABEL   CALLSUB   &ROUTINE=,&PARMS=
```

Figure 10.68 Prototype statement with keyword parameters.

Assume that the PARMS keyword parameter will hold our sublist value. If this macro is invoked by coding the instruction shown in Fig. 10.69, then &PARMS(1) has a value of A and &PARMS(4) has a value of D.

```
CALLSUB   ROUTINE=READRTN,PARMS=(A,B,C,D)
```

Figure 10.69 Assigning a sublist value to a keyword parameter.

Again, values within a sublist are extracted using a subscript reference as illustrated.

The number of entries in the sublist is determined by the **number attribute**. Considering the example in Fig. 10.69 and the parameter called &PARMS, a sublist of (A,B,C) yields a **N'&PARMS** value of 3 and a sublist of (A,B,C,D,,E) yields a **N'&PARMS** value of 6. If a value is assigned to a symbolic parameter without using sublist notation, then the number attribute has a value of 1 as shown in Fig. 10.70.

```
CALLSUB   ROUTINE=READRTN,PARMS=A

N'&PARMS would be equal to 1 in this case
```

Figure 10.70 Value of N' when sublists are not coded.

The number attribute is a very important value to control processing within the macro. Depending on the value obtained from the number attribute, a loop within the macro can be constructed to process each sublist element in some manner. For example, let's reconstruct our CALLSUB macro to incorporate the use of sublist values within our subroutine call logic as shown in Fig. 10.71.

```
              MACRO
&LABEL        CALLSUB  &ROUTINE=,&PARMS=
              LCLA     &PCOUNT
              LCLA     &I
.*
.*    THIS MACRO WILL GENERATE THE NECESSARY CODE
.*    TO PASS PARAMETERS TO A SUBROUTINE THROUGH R1
.*
&PCOUNT       SETA     N'&PARMS
&I            SETA     1
&LABEL        DS       OH
              CNOP     0,4                         ALIGN PARMS
              BAL      1,PSKP&SYSNDX               SKIP OVER PARMS
.LOOP         AIF      (&I GT &PCOUNT).OVER        CONTINUE?
              AIF      ('&PARMS(&I)' EQ '').AO
              DC       A(&PARMS(&I))               GENERATE PARM
              AGO      .ROUND
.AO           ANOP
              DC       A(0)                        NO PARM HERE
.ROUND        ANOP
&I            SETA     &I+1                        INCREMENT
              AGO      .LOOP
.OVER         ANOP
PSKP&SYSNDX DS           OH                        BAL TARGET
              L        15,=V(&ROUTINE)
              BALR     14,15
              MEND
```

Figure 10.71 CALLSUB macro with sublist inclusion.

The instructions generated by this macro for an associated macro call statement are illustrated in Fig. 10.72.

```
 CALLX1       CALLSUB   ROUTINE=X1,PARMS=(VALUE1,,VALUE3)
+CALLX1       DS        OH
+             CNOP      0,4
+             BAL       1,PSKP0001
+             DC        A(VALUE1)
+             DC        A(0)
+             DC        A(VALUE3)
+PSKP0001     DS        OH
+             L         15,=V(X1)
+             BALR      14,15
```

Figure 10.72 Macro call and code generation with the CALLSUB macro.

THE TYPE AND COUNT DATA ATTRIBUTES

Two other data attributes are used during macro processing. They determine what type of data can be stored in a field and how many characters of information are assigned to a symbolic parameter. These data attributes are called the **type attribute** and the **count attribute,** respectively.

The type attribute determines the type of field that you are processing. Suppose that we have a field called FLD defined within our program. We already know that FLD can be defined as a binary, packed, hexadecimal, character, bit, or as an address field. Once the field is defined, it's difficult for an *instruction* to determine what type of data the field can hold. For example, consider the CLEAR macro that we developed earlier. Initially, this macro only moved blanks into a character area. We later changed the macro so that it could move any hexadecimal value into a field. However, it was up to the programmer to know what type of field was to be initialized in order to provide the macro with the correct hexadecimal value. With the type attribute, the *macro* could determine how a field is defined and could use the proper data type and the proper instructions to initialize the field. The responsibility for field initialization is now left to the macro. If the macro is coded correctly, fields are initialized with little effort on the part of the programmer. If the macro is not correct, it's quite obvious that a field can be initialized with a wrong value.

Using character macro variables, the type attribute assigns a *single* character into the character variable depending on how a field is defined. If we assume that &TYPE is defined as a local character macro variable, the SET statement given in Fig. 10.73 determines the type of data in the symbolic parameter called FIELD.

```
&TYPE    SETC  T'&FIELD
```

Figure 10.73 Using the type attribute.

The value assigned to &TYPE depends on the definition of &FIELD. Possible resulting values for &TYPE are listed in Fig. 10.74.

Type Attribute Values	Definition of the Field
A	address
C	character
F	fullword
H	halfword
P	packed-decimal
V	V-type address
X	hexadecimal field

Figure 10.74 Values returned by the T' (type) attribute.

These values are then tested within your macro code using the AIF instruction to determine what instructions are to be used for certain types of processing. The CLEAR macro can be modified so that it can clear any of our typical data fields—character, binary, or packed-decimal. Using the type attribute, we determine the type of data in the field and use the appropriate instruction(s) to clear the value of the field. Figure 10.75 contains our new version of the CLEAR macro.

What if the field to be cleared is not one of the types supported by the macro? As coded, the macro does nothing. However, the macro should probably issue an error message so that the programmer knows that the CLEAR macro cannot properly initialize the field specified. Using the **MNOTE** facility, we can issue error messages from within the

```
         MACRO
&LABEL   CLEAR  &FIELD
         LCLC   &TYPE
         LCLA   &LEN
&LEN     SETA   L'&FIELD
&TYPE    SETC   T'&FIELD
         AIF    ('&LABEL' EQ '').NOLABL
&LABEL   DS     0H
.NOLABL  ANOP
         AIF    ('&TYPE' NE 'C').NEXT1
         MVI    &FIELD,X'40'
         MVC    &FIELD+1(&LEN-1),&FIELD
         AGO    .EXIT
.NEXT1   AIF    ('&TYPE' NE 'P').NEXT2
         ZAP    &FIELD.(&LEN),=P'0'
         AGO    .EXIT
.NEXT2   AIF    ('&TYPE' NE 'F' AND '&TYPE' NE 'H').BOMB
         MVC    &FIELD.(&LEN),=XL&LEN'00'
         AGO    .EXIT
.BOMB    ANOP
.EXIT    ANOP
         MEND
```

Figure 10.75 CLEAR macro with "typing" capability.

macro expansion to notify the programmer of a problem. The MNOTE instruction has two operands as illustrated in Fig. 10.76.

```
MNOTE   number,'message'
```

Figure 10.76 The MNOTE macro instruction.

The first operand is a number between 0 and 255. The higher the number, the more severe the error in the statement coded by the programmer. A severity level of 4 generally means that processing is alright, but the programmer should review the code produced by the macro to make sure that it is correct. A severity level of 8 or 12 means that some-

```
         MACRO
&LABEL   CLEAR  &FIELD
         LCLC   &TYPE
         LCLA   &LEN
&LEN     SETA   L'&FIELD
&TYPE    SETC   T'&FIELD
         AIF    ('&LABEL' EQ '').NOLABL
&LABEL   DS     0H
.NOLABL  ANOP
         AIF    ('&TYPE' NE 'C').NEXT1
         MVI    &FIELD,X'40'
         MVC    &FIELD+1(&LEN-1),&FIELD
         AGO    .EXIT
.NEXT1   AIF    ('&TYPE' NE 'P').NEXT2
         ZAP    &FIELD.(&LEN),=P'0'
         AGO    .EXIT
.NEXT2   AIF    ('&TYPE' NE 'F' AND '&TYPE' NE 'H').BOMB
         MVC    &FIELD.(&LEN),=XL&LEN'00'
         AGO    .EXIT
.BOMB    ANOP
         MNOTE  8,'INVALID FIELD TYPE FOR THIS MACRO'
         MNOTE  'FIELD HAS NOT BEEN INITIALIZED'
.EXIT    ANOP
         MEND
```

Figure 10.77 CLEAR macro with MNOTE integration.

thing is wrong with the information supplied to the macro and that the macro cannot generate the code properly. In general, a severity level of 8 or higher will not allow the program to finish assembly or execute since something is definitely wrong. The first operand may also be omitted to cause the message to be generated but to not indicate an error within the user's program; in other words, it becomes a comment.

We now modify the CLEAR macro to issue an error message when an invalid type is encountered as shown in Fig. 10.77.

The first MNOTE generates a severity level of 8, meaning that something is definitely wrong. At this point in the macro, instructions have not been generated to clear the programmer's field, so it is quite reasonable to issue a severe message since the macro cannot generate valid instructions. The second MNOTE is simply a comment since it is not coded with a level value. Figures 10.78 and 10.79 illustrate a printout in which the programmer has used this macro in a manner which generated an error.

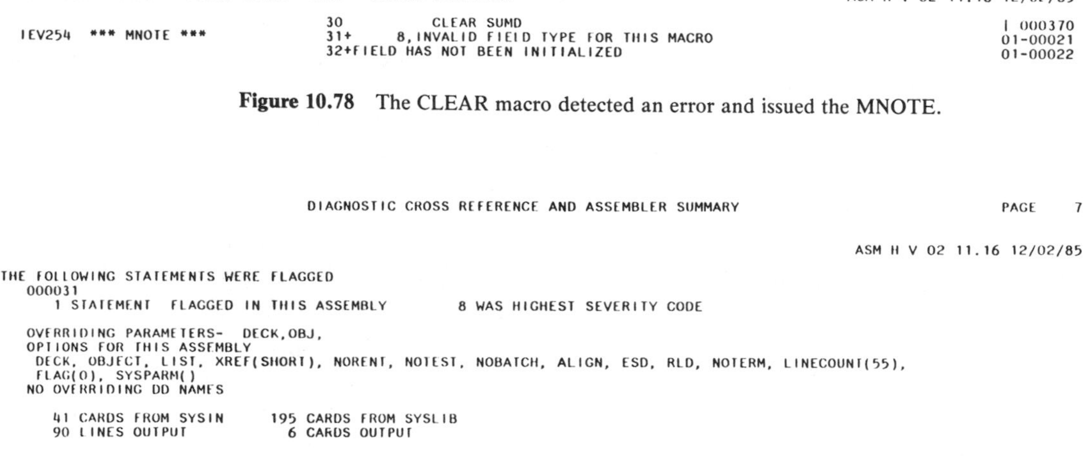

```
                                                                                     PAGE    3

LOC  OBJECT CODE    ADDR1 ADDR2  STMT   SOURCE STATEMENT                 ASM H V 02 11.16 12/02/85

                                 30          CLEAR SUMD                                   000370
 IEV254  *** MNOTE ***           31+     8,INVALID FIELD TYPE FOR THIS MACRO            01-00021
                                 32+FIELD HAS NOT BEEN INITIALIZED                      01-00022
```

Figure 10.78 The CLEAR macro detected an error and issued the MNOTE.

```
                    DIAGNOSTIC CROSS REFERENCE AND ASSEMBLER SUMMARY                 PAGE    7

                                                                 ASM H V 02 11.16 12/02/85

THE FOLLOWING STATEMENTS WERE FLAGGED
   000031
     1 STATEMENT  FLAGGED IN THIS ASSEMBLY        8 WAS HIGHEST SEVERITY CODE

   OVERRIDING PARAMETERS-  DECK,OBJ,
   OPTIONS FOR THIS ASSEMBLY
    DECK, OBJECT, LIST, XREF(SHORT), NORENT, NOTEST, NOBATCH, ALIGN, ESD, RLD, NOTERM, LINECOUNT(55),
    FLAG(0), SYSPARM()
   NO OVERRIDING DD NAMES

      41 CARDS FROM SYSIN       195 CARDS FROM SYSLIB
      90 LINES OUTPUT             6 CARDS OUTPUT
```

Figure 10.79 MNOTE's are also flagged on the diagnostics page by the assembler.

Reviewing the CLEAR macro, we see several places where it simply branches to the last statement so that it terminates. This is unnecessary since the macro language provides a statement called **MEXIT** to allow the macro to end without processing through the MEND statement.

Whenever the macro is to be terminated, the MEXIT instruction can be coded. If we adhere to structured programming rules, this statement would not be used since a component should only have one entry and one exit point. Placing MEXIT statements throughout our macro allows several exit points. Disregarding this argument, we can modify the CLEAR macro again to exit at each of the termination points as shown in Fig. 10.80.

The count attribute **(K')** can be used to determine *how much* data has been assigned to a macro parameter. To understand the use of the count attribute, let's return to an earlier discussion in the chapter. Consider the CLEAR macro illustrated in Figures 10.35, 10.38, and 10.40. In each of these implementations, a parameter labeled &BYTE

```
         MACRO
&LABEL   CLEAR  &FIELD
         LCLC   &TYPE
         LCLA   &LEN
&LEN     SETA   L'&FIELD
&TYPE    SETC   T'&FIELD
&LABEL   DS     0H
         AIF    ('&TYPE' NE 'C').NEXT1
         MVI    &FIELD,X'40'
         MVC    &FIELD+1(&LEN-1),&FIELD
         MEXIT
.NEXT1   AIF    ('&TYPE' NE 'P').NEXT2
         ZAP    &FIELD.(&LEN),=P'0'
         MEXIT
.NEXT2   AIF    ('&TYPE' NE 'F' AND '&TYPE' NE 'H').BOMB
         MVC    &FIELD.(&LEN),=XL&LEN'00'
         MEXIT
.BOMB    ANOP
         MNOTE  8,'INVALID FIELD TYPE FOR THIS MACRO'
         MNOTE  'FIELD HAS NOT BEEN INITIALIZED'
         MEND
```

Figure 10.80 CLEAR macro using the MEXIT statement.

allowed the user to supply a hexadecimal value to this parameter which was then used as the initialization value for the field to be cleared. Since all bytes contain two hexadecimal digits, what if the user coded only a single character for this parameter when invoking the macro? What if the user coded a non-hexadecimal digit when invoking the macro? Clearly, we could leave the responsibility for correct coding up to the user but it would be more appropriate to build checks within the macro to validate the user input. The count attribute helps us provide this ability.

The count attribute supplies a numeric value equal to the number of characters assigned to a macro parameter. Hence, **K'&BYTE** can be assigned to a local arithmetic variable and then evaluated to determine if it has a value equal to two. Obviously, if it isn't two, MNOTEs should be issued to inform the user that the macro has been invoked incorrectly. If it is two, we can build a loop into the macro and use substring processing to extract each character of &BYTE and determine if it's a valid hexadecimal digit. If the macro variable &I assumes values of 1 and 2 within the loop, '&BYTE'(&I,1) would return each character of &BYTE which we can then evaluate to determine validity.

The length, number, type, and count attributes are among the most used of the data attributes available in macro programming. Several other attributes are also available but we will not discuss them here. Please refer to the IBM manuals for more on attribute processing and how it can be used in macro construction.

CONDITIONAL ASSEMBLY

We conclude the chapter by discussing a feature provided by the assembler called **conditional assembly**. Conditional assembly allows the programmer to construct programs consisting of different formats depending on the values of macro variables. The assembly of machine instructions is conditional, that is, it is based on whether or not machine instructions are to be generated.

Conditional assembly applies to open code and not to macro processing. This means that macro instructions are used within a standard assembly language program to allow instructions to be assembled or not assembled to form the final execution package. Conditional assembly is used quite frequently by companies that market software products. By setting the value of a macro variable, certain functions within a software package are generated into a system or eliminated from a system. For example, consider a software package that offers seven major processing capabilities, but your needs are for four of those functions. Rather than generating a full system housing three unused functions, conditional assembly is built into the package so as to not generate any code associated with any particular function. By eliminating unnecessary coding, the system generally requires less memory for execution (since the resulting system is smaller) and it probably runs faster (since there's less code to be executed).

At the beginning of each module in such a system you'd probably find seven local or global macro variables. Although they can be defined as arithmetic, boolean, or character, they are most likely defined as boolean variables. Let's suppose that these variables are as defined in Fig. 10.81.

```
LCLB   &FUNC1
LCLB   &FUNC2
LCLB   &FUNC3
LCLB   &FUNC4
LCLB   &FUNC5
LCLB   &FUNC6
LCLB   &FUNC7
```

Figure 10.81 Defining conditional assembly variables.

If you want functions 1, 2, 5, and 7 to be part of your system, then you use SET statements to indicate which functions are to be generated and which are not. Figure 10.82 shows how this is done.

```
&FUNC1    SETB   1
&FUNC2    SETB   1
&FUNC3    SETB   0
&FUNC4    SETB   0
&FUNC5    SETB   1
&FUNC6    SETB   0
&FUNC7    SETB   1
```

Figure 10.82 Selecting the functions to be generated through macro variable value assignment.

We didn't have to assign a value to each variable, but it's usually a more explicit method of indicating which functions are to be generated. Within the code of the system, we can now use the macro instructions AIF, ANOP, and AGO to control the generation of the code within this system.

To use these instructions within open code, we simply code the statements as we normally would within the body of a macro. For example, the related code for each function is "surrounded" by statements as shown in Fig. 10.83.

This module is then generated with only the code needed for the functions desired within your system. The code for each function is generated based on the value of the macro variable. Note that each section of code for each function is surrounded by the AIF/ANOP combination. This may require a significant amount of coding to provide conditional assembly capabilities for all components of a system.

```
MODULEX      CSECT
             .     .
             .     .

             AIF    (NOT &FUNC1).NOT1
             code for function 1
.NOT1        ANOP
             AIF    (NOT &FUNC2).NOT2
             code for function 2
.NOT2        ANOP
             .     .
             .     .

             AIF    (NOT &FUNC1).MORE1
             more code for function 1
.MORE1       ANOP

             .     .
             .     .

             END    MODULEX
```

Figure 10.83 Code to provide conditional assembly support.

After assembly, only the functions that are needed are integrated into the system. Hence, the system contains functions 1, 2, 5, and 7 and does not contain functions 3, 4, and 6.

Incidentally, the other functions can be added later by simply changing the values of the macro variables and reassembling the entire system. As each module is reassembled, the specified functions are incorporated into the system.

STUDY QUESTIONS

1. The first statement in the macro definition is called the ______________________.
2. What macro statements can also be used in open code?
3. The full-line macro comment begins with what characters?
4. What are the rules for defining a macro variable or a symbolic parameter?
5. If a macro is used in many programs throughout a company, how can it be made available to the other programmers?
6. What character is used for concatenating macro variables or values?
7. Portions of strings may be extracted from others by using ____________ processing on the character data.
8. Infinite loops may be controlled by using the ____________ statement within the macro language.
9. The ____________ data attribute provides a single character that indicates the type of data that may be used within a certain data field.
10. Can macros invoke other macros in the same manner that modules can call other modules?
11. When macro statements suppress or generate machine instructions in open code, we say that the program is being ____________ assembled.

12. Structured programming guidelines may be violated if the ____________ macro instruction is used throughout the macro.
13. If a macro variable has two values, then it should probably be declared as a ____________ variable.
14. The longest character string that can be processed by a macro variable is ____________ bytes.
15. If more than one macro needs to know about a certain condition, then a macro variable can be declared ____________ so that the value of the variable can be known by other macros.
16. What code is generated by the following macro?

```
         MACRO
         WHATIS
         LCLA    &I
&I       SETA    193
.LOOP    AIF     (&I GT 198).BYEBYE
         DC      AL1(&I)
&I       SETA    &I+1
         AGO     .LOOP
.BYEBYE  ANOP
         MEND
```

17. Write a macro which will use the SPM instruction to set the condition code to a value specified. Make sure that the macro doesn't alter any registers in the process. The macro accepts one parameter having a value of 0, 1, 2, or 3.
18. Write macro instructions to do the following:
    (a) Branch to the macro label .ALLOK.
    (b) Determine if the local arithmetic variables &A and &B are equal. If they are, set the value of the local arithmetic variable &C to one more than its current value. Otherwise, set it to one less.
    (c) Define a macro which will accept three keyword parameters, all packed-decimal fields, and compute the average of the fields. Don't write the complete macro; write only its definition.
    (d) Issue a message to the programmer indicating that the macro parameter &FIELDL is too large and cause execution to be suspended.
    (e) Exit from the macro prematurely.
19. Find the errors in the following macro instructions. Assume that &A is an arithmetic variable, &B is boolean, and &C is character.

```
(a) &A    SETA   &A*3+4-6*25

(b)       AIF    (&B)&C  SETA  'YES'

(c) &C    SETC   '&A'

(d) &B    SETB   ('&C' EQ 'ASSIST')

(e)       AIF    ('&C' EQ 'ASSIST' AND &A EQ 1).CONTINUE
```

20. Write a macro called TRACE which can be used to help debug programs. Given an input string, the macro prints an input string of characters during debugging. The macro uses a global boolean parameter DBUG to determine if tracing should be done for this execution of a program.

PROGRAMMING ASSIGNMENTS

1. Develop a macro that exits from a program using standard linkage conventions and allows the programmer to place a nonzero return code in R15 before control is returned. Use keyword parameters and call the return code parameter RC. Give RC a default value of 0.
2. Develop a macro to enter a program and generate the necessary code to establish a base register and a register save area. This macro invokes the EQUATES macro so that the register equates can be generated by the program. One positional parameter, the base register number, is the input to the macro.
3. Write a macro to generate each of the 256 different character representations in the EBCDIC character set.
4. Write a macro that converts an input character field from a data card into packed-decimal format with the proper sign on the number. The macro is given the name of the character field on the data card and the name of the packed-decimal field into which the value is to be placed. The macro determines the lengths of both fields if needed during instruction generation. (Incidentally, this macro is similar to XDECI.)
5. Write a macro that converts a packed-decimal field of any length into a printable output field. Input to the macro consists of the name of the packed field to be converted, the target area into which the converted value is to be placed, and the number of digits to the right of the decimal point. The macro should *not* assume that all digits within the packed-decimal field will be placed into the output area.
6. Write a macro that accepts an integer as a parameter. When invoked, the macro determines the sum of all integers between 1 and the number. The resulting value is stored in a fullword of storage, also passed as a parameter to the macro. Follow the development of this macro by writing a program that prints the value of each of these fullwords.
7. Develop two macros XREAD and XPRNT that can be used in standard assembly language to perform input and output operations. These macros in turn invoke the OPEN, CLOSE, GET, PUT, and DCB macros to generate the appropriate instructions to allow I/O to occur in assembly language.
8. Write a macro called DDUMP that can be used in standard assembly language to provide dumped output of storage areas or register contents. This macro replaces or invokes the OPEN, SNAP, CLOSE, and DCB macro instructions normally required to perform dumping operations outside of ASSIST.
9. Develop a macro called INDEX. This macro accepts two parameters to support its processing. Both arguments are character data fields. The macro determines if the value of the second argument is contained within the field specified in the first. The macro then sets the condition code to zero if the second argument is not within the first argument field or sets the condition code to 1 if it is.
10. Develop a macro called SUBSTRNG. This macro processes a character field by allowing all or a portion of that field to be moved to another location in memory. Input to the macro consists of the name of the source field, the position within the source field where data is to be extracted, the number of characters of data to be obtained from the field, and the target field address. When invoked, the character string specified is copied from the source field and placed into the target field.
11. Develop a macro which can be invoked in a program to perform modulo arithmetic on a value in a register. The parameters to the macro are the register as the first operand, the base number as the second operand, and the string MOD or DIV in the third operand. The macro will generate the necessary code which will leave the integer remainder in the register if the MOD operand is specified or the integer quotient value in the register of the DIV operand is specified. The macro should preserve the registers during this operation.
12. Develop a macro called NEWPAGE which can be used to cause the output to be advanced to a new page during printing. The macro should suppress printing of any instructions generated

by the macro. Assume that the macro is to be developed for use in ASSIST. Hence, no parameters are necessary for the macro call.

13. Develop a macro called PRNTLINE which will generate the necessary DC instructions to construct a print line to be used during report generation. Input to the macro consists of two primary elements, the length of the line to be generated and the fields to be imbedded within the line. The second operand is further subdivided and requires the use of sublist processing to extract each operand value and its position within the print line. For example, suppose that the phrase "PHONE" is to appear in columns 20 to 24 of a report line and "NAME" is to appear in columns 50 to 53 of the same line. The macro would be invoked as shown below to place these elements within an 86 byte print line.

```
PRNTLINE   86,(PHONE,20,NAME,50)
```

An unlimited number of elements should be able to be entered in the second operand. This will allow the programmer to easily format print lines and to design reports using printer spacing charts.

14. Construct two macros called FOR and ENDFOR which will construct a counting loop within an assembly language program. Three parameters are input to the FOR macro: the starting value, the limit value, and the increment value (which may be a negative number). No parameters are needed for the ENDFOR macro. Edit all input parameters for validity. Hint: share a global variable between the two macros which will communicate the return point label between the two macros. As a FOR macro is encountered, generate a return point label and concatenate it onto the global character variable. When the ENDFOR macro is encountered, "peel off" the return point labels in reverse order to generate the code to branch back to the return point. This technique will allow nested loops to be supported. Incidentally, you can extend this problem by developing DOWHILE-ENDWHILE, IFTHEN-ENDIF, and DOUNTIL-ENDUNTIL macros to support all of the structured logical constructs.

15. Develop a macro called DECIMALP which will edit a packed-decimal field and supply a decimal point within the number. Input parameters are the name of the field to be edited, the target area into which the printable number is to be placed, and the number of digits within the field that are to be to the right of the decimal. You might want to allow the user to enter an additional parameter, a floating point character which is to be inserted just before the first significant digit.

11 Extended Instructions and Advanced Techniques

The many instructions and techniques learned so far have allowed implementation of most typical applications. Although the amount of work to perform some functions varied depending on the instructions available, we nonetheless were able to implement our applications. This chapter is devoted to a set of techniques and instructions that go beyond the typical instruction set. It includes instructions that are not as commonly used as the ones that we've studied. With each technique and set of instructions presented, I'll give some suggestions as to where and how they might be used.

USING R13 AS A BASE REGISTER

When we began our study of assembly language, one of our first tasks was to establish a base register for our program. Typically, one base register was sufficient for most programs, but occasionally more than one register had to be established if we needed addressability beyond 4096 bytes. As more and more registers were assigned to various tasks, fewer registers were available for general processing. The first section of this chapter describes a method in which R13 is used as both the base register for your program and as the required register save area pointer.

Establishing a base register requires two elements—a register and a USING statement. As long as the two elements agree as to the reference point in the program, almost any register can be used as a base register. Our previous discussions eliminated registers 0, 1, 13, 14, and 15 as candidates since they're used by the operating system and for subroutine linkage. Actually, R13 should not have been excluded. As long as R13 addresses a save area and as long as the USING statement uses the same reference point as the base register, there's no reason why R13 can't serve as both.

The register save area is 18 fullwords long, or 72 bytes. Consider the section of code given in Fig. 11.1.

The first instruction, STM (store multiple), saves the contents of the registers in the calling program's save area. The next instruction, BAL (branch and link), places the address of the *next instruction* into register 14 and branches to a location 80 bytes from the address contained in R15. The *next instruction* is the 18-fullword save area since the USING statement is not a machine instruction and therefore does not generate any object code. As a result, R14 will address the register save area.

```
MAINPGM  CSECT
         STM    R14,R12,12(R13)     SAVE THE REGS
         BAL    R14,80(R15)         SKIP OVER SAVE AREA
         USING  *,R13               R13 WILL BE OUR BASE
         DS     18F                 REGISTER SAVE AREA
```

Figure 11.1 Using R13 as a base register and as a save area pointer.

In this example, we're assuming that R15 contains the entry point address of our program since this is a linkage convention standard. The STM (store multiple) instruction is 4 bytes long, the BAL instruction is 4 bytes long, and the 18-fullword save area is 72 bytes long, and so the sum of these instructions and save area length is 80 bytes. Therefore, the branch takes us to the instruction that *follows* the 18-fullword save area. Although we haven't coded any instructions after the save area, we can do so as shown in Fig. 11.2.

```
MAINPGM  CSECT
         STM    R14,R12,12(R13)     SAVE THE REGS
         BAL    R14,80(R15)         SKIP OVER SAVE AREA
         USING  *,R13               R13 WILL BE OUR BASE
         DS     18F                 REGISTER SAVE AREA
         ST     R13,4(R14)          CHAIN BACKWARD
         ST     R14,8(R13)          CHAIN FORWARD
         LR     R13,R14             ESTABLISH R13
```

Figure 11.2 Entry code with R13 as the base register.

The branch-and-link instruction takes us to the first store instruction (in boldface) in the code given in Fig. 11.2. At this point, R13 is saved into the second fullword of this program's 18-fullword save area. The next instruction, another ST (store) instruction, informs the calling program of the save area and the load register instruction copies the contents of R14 into R13. Since R14 addressed the 18-fullword save area, R13 now addresses this area. Thus, R13 addresses the save area as desired. If we now look at the USING instruction, we see that it too addresses the 18-fullword save area since the *, current instruction reference, has been used in the first operand. Since both the USING and R13 address the same location, R13 can be used for both the register save area pointer and as the base register for our program.

This technique saves one more register in our normal set of available registers (2 through 12) and allows that register to be used for some other type of processing.

BYTE-PROCESSING RS INSTRUCTIONS—ICM, STCM, AND CLM

When we used the SPM instruction to change or restore the condition code and program mask bits in the PSW, we preceded this instruction with one that obtained the mask values. Also, the mask values had to be located in the leftmost byte of the register that was going to be used on the SPM instruction. To accomplish this, we defined a one-byte field, aligned on a fullword boundary that contained our mask values, and followed this field by a three-byte field of anything (since its value didn't matter when using the SPM instruction). Let's review this code as shown in Fig. 11.3.

The only reason for adding the AL3 field after the bit definition is to account for four bytes of storage. Since the load instruction brings four bytes of data from memory into a register, we want to ensure that we are obtaining and processing the correct

```
         L       R3,BITS
         SPM     R3
         .       .
         .       .
BITS     DS      0F
         DC      B'00001011'
         DC      AL3(0)
```

Figure 11.3 Instructions to set the mask in the PSW.

amount of data and not impacting the processing for any other field in our program. With a new RS instruction called **ICM (insert characters under mask)**, this technique can be greatly modified and simplified.

The ICM instruction does not require alignment and places any number of bytes into a register as desired. One, two, three, or four bytes of memory can be placed into a register depending on how the ICM instruction is coded.

The ICM instruction consists of three operands: a register into which the data is to be placed, a bit mask (four *bits* long), and a D(B) storage area address (a label is acceptable also). The mask (second operand) determines which bytes in the register are to be modified with data from the storage area. The first bit in the mask is associated with the leftmost byte in the register and the rightmost mask bit is associated with the rightmost byte in the register. If any mask bit is 1, then the corresponding byte in the register is modified with a byte from the memory area (third operand).

```
ICM     R3,B'0111',AREA
```

Figure 11.4 Example of the ICM instruction.

This instruction shown in Fig. 11.4 modifies three bytes in R3. In fact, only the rightmost three bytes of R3 are modified. The leftmost byte in R3, byte 0, is not changed. To modify R3, the instruction obtains three *consecutive* bytes of data from the location called AREA. The three bytes are placed into bytes 1, 2 and 3 of R3, respectively. Byte 0 is not loaded with data. Again, alignment is not a factor since the ICM instruction is not concerned with storage alignment.

A single byte in a register can be modified by coding only one 1-bit in the 4-bit mask operand. In the example given in Fig. 11.5, only the leftmost byte of register 3 is modified. Its value comes from the area called BITS, which, coincidentally, contains valid data to modify and set the mask fields in the PSW.

```
ICM     R3,B'1000',BITS
```

Figure 11.5 Using ICM to alter only the leftmost byte in R3.

If we follow this instruction with the SPM instruction, we can easily set the program mask. Incidentally, the third operand of the ICM instruction given in Figure 11.6 could have been coded as a literal. Instead of referencing the storage area BITS, =B'00001011' could have been coded for a literal value. Don't forget the equals sign.

The ICM instruction may also load a register with four bytes of data in a manner similar to the standard L (load) instruction. However, the load instruction usually requires alignment and the ICM instruction does not. Figure 11.6 shows this implementation.

```
ICM    R7,B'1111',FULLWORD
```

Figure 11.6 Using ICM to load a register with a fullword value.

A byte from memory is inserted into the rightmost byte of a register by coding the ICM instruction given in Fig. 11.7.

```
ICM    Rx,B'0001',AREA
```

Figure 11.7 Altering the rightmost byte of a register with ICM.

This task can also be accomplished through the more common **IC (insert character)** instruction, which is an RX instruction that copies one byte from memory and places it into the rightmost byte of the register. The IC instruction is given in Fig. 11.8. Although the two instructions have similar mnemonics, they are quite different. IC only inserts 1 byte and *only* into the rightmost byte of a register. ICM inserts one to four bytes and into any or all of the bytes in the register. The second operand of the IC instruction may also be coded as a literal.

```
IC     Rx,AREA
```

Figure 11.8 The general format of the IC instruction.

Data from a register may be copied into storage in a manner opposite to that of the IC and ICM instructions. Using **STC (store character)** and **STCM (store characters under mask),** one byte and one to four bytes, respectively, can be copied from the register into storage.

The store character instruction copies the rightmost byte from a register into storage. For example, to replace the first byte at location XYZ with the value in the rightmost byte of register 6, code the instruction shown in Fig. 11.9.

```
STC    R6,XYZ
```

Figure 11.9 Copying the rightmost byte from R6 to XYZ using STC.

The STCM instruction stores one to four bytes from a register into memory. To copy bytes 0 and 2 from the register into the *first two consecutive* bytes of an area called XYZ, code the instruction given in Fig. 11.10.

```
STCM   R6,B'1010',XYZ
```

Figure 11.10 Copying two bytes from R6 to XYZ using STCM.

The STCM instruction is used to save the current program mask contained in the leftmost byte of R14 when a module is called. If you recall, a module is normally called via the BALR instruction. BALR places the address of the next instruction into the rightmost three bytes of the link register and the program mask data from the PSW in the leftmost byte of the register. The data in the leftmost byte of the register may be saved by coding the instruction shown in Fig. 11.11.

```
STCM    R14,B'1000',LINKDATA
```

Figure 11.11 Saving PSW linking information after a BALR.

To restore the condition code and program mask to their original status, use the ICM and SPM instructions as shown earlier.

Another instruction of this type is the **CLM (compare logical characters under mask).** Using a format identical to that of ICM and STCM, the CLM instruction allows the programmer to perform *logical comparisons* between selected bytes in registers and contiguous bytes in storage. A mask value of B'0011' would compare the right half of the first operand register with the two contiguous bytes of storage specified by the third operand. A mask value of B'0001' would provide a comparison between the rightmost byte in the register and the byte located at the location specified by the third operand.

The CLM instruction is used most frequently to compare byte values after performing the TRT instruction (which we'll describe in a later section in this chapter) and in supporting byte-oriented arithmetic operations. For example, we normally process binary data using halfword and fullword fields. However, using the ICM, STCM, and CLM instructions, we now have the ability to process binary data that occupies only one byte. Although data of this type is normally limited to positive values and to values less than 256, nonetheless, if our processing calls for such needs we can utilize these instructions to process data in this format.

This processing capability is further enhanced when one realizes that fifty to seventy-five percent of the storage space needed for a field can now be saved. In other words, instead of using a halfword or fullword to hold a field value that ranges between 1 and 100, we can now reduce the storage requirements of the field by at least half. Using the IC or ICM instructions to obtain the value, standard RR or RX arithmetic instructions to operate on the data, STC or STCM to update, and CLM to analyze the contents of a field, we have full processing capabilities with reduced storage requirements. For small files, the instruction overhead associated with such processing may not be worth the trouble, but for large files, the benefits may be significant. You'll have to decide how these instructions can be used in your environment and use them appropriately.

THE EXECUTE INSTRUCTION

One of the former uses for the STC and IC instructions was to modify instructions *during execution* to give different results. This technique has almost vanished since this practice does not follow structured programming practice. Programs that modify themselves during execution result in inconsistent processing each time they are run.

Consider the MVC instruction, which is an SS instruction with the object code format as illustrated in Fig. 11.12.

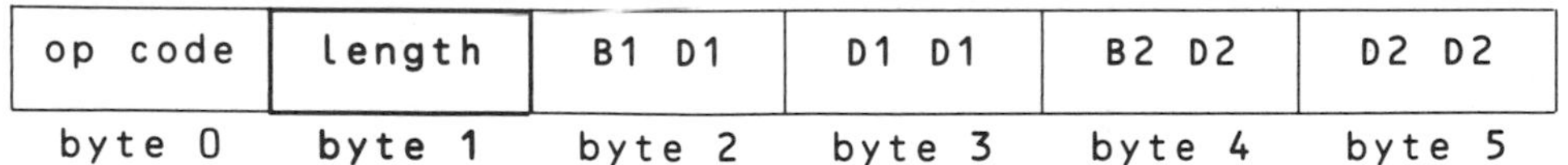

Figure 11.12 Object code format of the MVC instruction.

The second byte of the MVC instruction contains the number of bytes to be moved. If this field is modified during execution, then a different number of bytes are moved than what was originally coded on the instruction, unless, of course, the modified length is the same as the coded length. For example, suppose that the input data is separated by commas and is not coded in specific columns on the input data records. Data typed in a "free floating" format is difficult to process and requires changeable instructions.

Suppose that processing has established register 6 such that it contains the address of the data field on the data record and register 7 contains the actual length of the field. We move the input field to the area called OPERANDX by using the instructions coded in Fig. 11.13.

```
         BCTR   R7,0                     DECREASE LENGTH BY 1
         STC    R7,MVC+1                 MODIFY THE MVC
MVC      MVC    OPERANDX(0),0(R6)        MOVE THE DATA
```

Figure 11.13 Modifying an MVC instruction during execution.

The first instruction, BCTR, subtracts one from the value in R7. We must do this because all SS instructions represent field lengths as one less than their coded value. If we want to move 10 bytes of data, then the value in the second byte of the MVC instruction *must be* X'09'.

The STC instruction modifies the second byte (offset 1) of the MVC instruction. After the STC instruction is executed, the modified MVC instruction is executed to move the appropriate amount of data to OPERANDX. Although the MVC instruction (as coded) indicates that zero bytes of data are to be moved, you must remember that this value is modified during execution (by the STC instruction) to move the correct amount of data.

If you look at this code, however, you can't tell how many bytes are moved from the location in R6 to OPERANDX. Further, the next time this code is executed, it will probably modify itself again to move a different number of bytes. Clearly, it is difficult to determine what this code will do each time that it is executed unless we print the value in register 7 just before we process these instructions.

Although we're not going to help readability, we can use a different instruction to modify the MVC during execution. This instruction, which is called the **EX (execute)** instruction, basically performs the same function as the STC instruction.

The execute instruction can *temporarily* modify another instruction. Using the example shown in Fig. 11.13, we'll use the RX-format EX (execute) instruction to accomplish the same task as shown in Fig. 11.14.

The system copies the MVC instruction into a special system work area, changes the length of the copied MVC instruction based on the value in the rightmost byte of R7, and then executes the copied-modified MVC. After execution, the branch instruction following the EX causes processing to continue at the location called MVCSKIP. Notice that we don't fall into the MVC instruction as before. In fact, you want to *make sure* that you don't fall into the instruction. For that reason, you'll typically find executed instructions at the bottom of a program within the data areas section. Hence, the MVC is lo-

```
         BCTR   R7,0                     CORRECT LENGTH OF DATA
         EX     R7,MVC                   EXECUTE THE MVC INSTRUCTION
         B      MVCSKIP                  SKIP OVER THE MVC
MVC      MVC    OPERANDX(0),0(R6)        EXECUTED INSTRUCTION
MVCSKIP  DS     0H
```

Figure 11.14 Using the execute instruction.

cated in that area and you only see the executed code in the main logic section of the program. Figure 11.15 illustrates this coding technique.

```
         BCTR  R7,0                      CORRECT LENGTH OF DATA
         EX    R7,MVC                    EXECUTE THE MVC INSTRUCTION

          .     .
          .     .
          .     .


**** data areas section of the program ****

MVC      MVC   OPERANDX(0),0(R6)        EXECUTED INSTRUCTION
```

Figure 11.15 Executed instructions may be located in the data areas section of your program.

With this code, it may be difficult to determine what has happened and what instruction is executed by the execute instruction unless you refer to the data areas section of your program. However, to find the instruction that is executed, you may have to go through several pages of listing to find the instruction labeled MVC. This may be distracting, causing you to lose your train of thought, and possibly lead to an error. For that reason, the executed instruction can be incorporated into the program "in line" as shown in Fig. 11.14. Yet another format for incorporating the executed instructions into the mainline code is shown in Fig. 11.16.

```
         BCTR  R7,0                      CORRECT LENGTH OF DATA
         EX    R7,MVC                    EXECUTE THE MVC INSTRUCTION
         B     *+10                      SKIP OVER THE MVC
MVC      MVC   OPERANDX(0),0(R6)         EXECUTED INSTRUCTION
```

Figure 11.16 Locating executed instructions close to the EX instruction.

From Fig. 11.16, the unconditional branch instruction transfers control to a location 10 bytes beyond the *current* instruction. Since the current instruction is the branch instruction that is four bytes long and the next instruction (the MVC) is 6 bytes long, the **B *+10** transfers control to the instruction that follows the MVC. This has the same effect as the previous code in which MVCSKIP was used as the branch and target label. Since this method is usually difficult to understand and can be disastrous if coded incorrectly, I'd suggest using either of the earlier versions.

The execute instruction does not permanently alter the MVC instruction as the STC instruction did. However, the MVC instruction does change in a different manner. The execute instruction does not *replace* the second byte of the MVC with the rightmost byte in the register, but the rightmost byte in the register specified and the second byte of the instruction to be executed are **OR'd.** To understand the OR process, let's look at Fig. 11.17.

OR	0	1
0	0	1
1	1	1

Figure 11.17 The OR logic table.

The table shows what happens when bits of different values are OR'd, and can be summarized as described in Figure 11.18.

```
0 OR 0 = 0
0 OR 1 = 1
1 OR 0 = 1
1 OR 1 = 1
```

Figure 11.18 An alternate format for the OR logic table.

Any time that a 1 bit is OR'd with either a 0 bit or a 1 bit, the result is a 1 bit. Only when both bits are zeros is the result zero. As you can see, ORing is a bit operation. With respect to the execute instruction, each bit in the rightmost byte of the register is OR'd respectively against each bit in the second byte of the executed instruction to produce its results. Reviewing our MVC instruction, we see that the original MVC has a coded length of 0. This means that the length value in the MVC instruction is B'00000000'—all zeros. If the rightmost byte of R7 contains the value 5, B'00000101', then the result of ORing the rightmost byte of R7 with the second byte of the MVC yields a length of 5 in the MVC. This means that six bytes of data are moved since the length field in the SS instruction is one less than the actual number of bytes to be moved.

You might be asking, "Why does this matter?" It's very important that you understand how the execute instruction works and that it uses an ORing process rather than a replacement process to execute instructions. Let's use the example in Fig. 11.19 to illustrate. Suppose that R6 now addresses a numeric field that is to be converted from character format on an input data record into packed-decimal format. The instruction used for this conversion is the PACK instruction, but it requires two lengths.

```
PACK   NUMBER(L1),0(L2,R6)
```

Figure 11.19 Using the PACK instruction.

We know the length of NUMBER since it is defined in our program, but we don't know the length of the incoming field, and so we must again code a length of 0. Figure 11.20 contains the instruction for our program.

```
PACK   NUMBER(8),0(0,R6)
```

Figure 11.20 Specifying SS instruction lengths when using EX.

The second byte of the PACK instruction contains the lengths of *both* operands. The value of this byte is X'70' since the first operand's length is 8, and the second's length is 0.

If R7 contains the length (in bytes) of the number on the input data record, the EX instruction can be used to convert the input data value into packed format properly. The instructions given in Fig. 11.21 perform this task.

If we can assume that the value in R7 is originally 4, then we OR the value of 3 with the second byte of the PACK instruction. Figure 11.22 shows the result.

```
          BCTR   R7,0                  SET LENGTH FOR EXECUTE
          EX     R7,PACKIT             PACK THE NUMBER
          B      PACKSKIP              SKIP OVER PACK INSTRUCTION
PACKIT    PACK   NUMBER(8),0(0,R6)
PACKSKIP  DS     0H
          LA     R7,1(R7)              RETURN R7 TO ORIGINAL VALUE
```

Figure 11.21 Packing an incoming value with the execute instruction.

```
   right most byte of R7          00000011
OR second byte of PACKIT          01110000
------------------------------------------
   new value for PACKIT byte      01110011
```

Figure 11.22 Result of ORing X'03' and X'70'.

The resulting byte packs a four-byte field into an eight-byte field, which is exactly what we wanted. After the instruction is executed, we restore R7 back to its original length in case it is needed somewhere else in our program.

TRANSLATING DATA AREAS

Earlier in the text, we discussed the various ways in which data can be input to a computer. Card punches/readers and on-line terminals were identified as some of the primary devices to supply data. Any of these devices can be attached to a computer, but the software may not be able to process or recognize data from the device because it may be in the wrong format. For example, let's take something as simple as upper and lower case letters. To some software programs, lower case letters are not valid information that may be processed by the program. Hence, the lower case data must be converted to upper case to be processed. Output going back to the terminal from the computer program will be in upper case since the program probably only operates in upper case in both directions.

A lower case letter **a** has the hexadecimal value X'81' and an upper case **A** has the hexadecimal value X'C1'. If we evaluate each bit between each lower and upper case letter, we see that the only difference is a single bit value as shown in Fig. 11.23.

```
lower case a    1000    0001
upper case A    1100    0001

lower case s    1010    0010
upper case S    1110    0010
```

Figure 11.23 Bit differences between upper and lower case letters.

The second bit, bit 1, of each character is the only bit that's different between upper and lower case letters. To convert from lower case to upper case (or vice versa), we simply change the value of this bit. To accomplish this easily, we can use the **TR (translate)** instruction.

The translate instruction is an SS instruction, but the second operand does not have a length. With the format of the TR instruction as shown in Fig. 11.24, only one length is specified, which means that its value can be as large as 256.

```
TR      D1(L,B1),D2(B2)
```

Figure 11.24 General format of the translate instruction.

This means that up to 256 bytes of data may be translated at a time. The second operand is a "table" that is 256 bytes in length. Although there are techniques for reducing the size of this table, it is generally 256 bytes in length. To understand the TR instruction, you must first understand the construction of the table.

Each eight-bit configuration in the EBCDIC character set has an equivalent decimal value. The bit configuration B'00000010' has a base-10 or decimal value of 2 and the bit configuration B'00001010' has a decimal value of 10. The lower case **a** has a bit configuration of B'10000001' or a decimal value of 129. If we place an *upper* case **A** at offset 129 into our table, the translate instruction converts all lower case **a**'s within the first operand to upper case **A**'s. If we code the table similarly for each lower case letter, all lower case letters translate to upper case.

To translate a field, the translate instruction uses each byte of the first operand as a *displacement* into the table specified in the second operand. If the translate instruction selects a lower case **a** from the first operand, it then uses the value of the lower case **a** as a displacement into the table. Since the value of the lower case **a** is 129, the translate instruction *replaces* the lower case **a** in the first operand with the *value* located at displacement 129 in the second operand, which we've defined as an upper case **A**. Again, the construction of the table defined in the second operand is the key to successful translation.

The table specified in the second operand is easily constructed using a macro to generate each EBCDIC character. The macro shown in Fig. 11.25 generates each EBCDIC character.

Line 6 generates each byte within the table. After the table macro is initiated, a complete 256-byte table is generated, a portion of which is shown in Fig. 11.26.

This table is *not* ready to be used for translation however since we haven't changed any character values. The EBCDIC macro has only performed a preliminary table definition which can be used to support the translate instruction. Thus, we must follow the

```
 1                  MACRO
 2      &LABEL      EBCDIC
 3                  LCLA      &I
 4      &LABEL      DS        0H
 5      .LOOP       AIF       (&I GT 255).DONE
 6                  DC        AL1(&I)
 7      &I          SETA      &I+1
 8                  AGO       .LOOP
 9      .DONE       ANOP
10                  MEND
```

Figure 11.25 Macro to generate the EBCDIC character set.

```
LOWER          EBCDIC
+LOWER         DS         0H
+              DC         AL1(0)
+              DC         AL1(1)
+              DC         AL1(2)

       .         .        .
       .         .        .

+              DC         AL1(254)
+              DC         AL1(255)
```

Figure 11.26 Code generated by the EBCDIC macro.

```
ORG         LOWER+C'a'
DC          C'ABCDEFGHI'
ORG         LOWER+C'j'
DC          C'JKLMNOPQR'
ORG         LOWER+C's'
DC          C'STUVWXYZ'
ORG
```

Figure 11.27 Altering table values after EBCDIC macro expansion.

expansion of this macro by the ORG instruction to alter the location counter to refer back into the table. This will enable us to modify the appropriate bytes, changing each lower case letter to upper case. Figure 11.27 shows how this is done.

Since the letters of the alphabet are not represented as a contiguous set of bytes, three sets of redefinitions are required to change the lower case letters to upper case. At offset C'**j**', for example, the lower case letters **j** through **r** are changed to upper case letters **J** through **R**. Don't forget the final ORG to return the location counter back to its original offset within your program.

Once our table is constructed, we issue the TR instruction. Assuming our input device is a terminal, let's call our input data area a "terminal input/output area." We'll use the label TIOA for the name of the area. Assuming that TIOA is 100 bytes long, we translate the area by issuing the instruction given in Fig. 11.28.

```
TR      TIOA(100),LOWER
```

Figure 11.28 Translating input data to upper case.

Another application of the translate instruction is to fix the rightmost digit of a numeric field after it has been unpacked. If you recall, the rightmost byte of a zoned-decimal number commonly has a value of C0, C1, C2, C3, . . . , C9 or D0 through D9 after it is unpacked. Although the OI instruction can clean up this byte, the translate instruction is also used for this purpose. Incidentally, OI is much faster and so is recommended over the TR instruction.

To perform this translation, we again need a translation table for each byte value. Let's use our EBCDIC macro again and use ORG to change the rightmost zoned byte values to the digits 0 through 9. Figure 11.29 illustrates this implementation.

We now convert the rightmost digit of an unpacked number by issuing the sequence of instructions shown in Fig. 11.30. Incidentally, these instructions also form the basis for a much more sophisticated dumping routine. By using the UNPK instruction to unpack any storage area and by using the TR instruction (with an appropriate table) to convert each unpacked byte into a printable format, you can write a routine to perform the same function as XDUMP.

```
LSTDIGIT    EBCDIC
            ORG         LSTDIGIT+X'C0'
            DC          C'0123456789'
            ORG         LSTDIGIT+X'D0'
            DC          C'0123456789'
            ORG
```

Figure 11.29 Translate table to reformat the rightmost byte of a zoned-decimal field.

```
UNPK    AREA(15),VALUE(8)
TR      AREA+14(1),LSTDIGIT
```

Figure 11.30 Instructions to unpack and reformat the rightmost byte of a zoned-decimal field using TR.

SEARCHING FOR CHARACTERS WITHIN FIELDS

The **TRT (translate and test)** machine instruction scans fields to look for certain characters. Suppose, for example, that you are going to rearrange a person's name from the format "last, first" into "first last". The character that separates the first and last names in the "last, first" form is the comma. Hence, our code searches for the comma's location to find where the last name ends and where the first name begins.

The searching can be accomplished by using the CLC or CLI instructions as well. However, the TRT instruction is faster, requires less coding, and can search for more than one character in the same operation. The TRT instruction uses a 256-byte table as the second operand, but this table has a different format and use than the tables used with the TR instruction. Further, the TRT instruction does *not* change or alter the first operand as does the TR instruction.

The TRT instruction evaluates each character in the first operand with respect to the values in the table contained in the second operand. Each byte in the first operand again acts as a displacement into the table in the second operand. If the value in the table, based on the displacement for each first operand character, is X'00', the TRT instruction continues scanning. If the value is not X'00', then register 1 is set to the address *in the first operand* of the current byte, and the nonzero byte from within the table is inserted into the rightmost byte of register *2.* The rightmost byte of register 2 can then be analyzed using CLM to determine which character was found in the field being scanned since it caused the TRT instruction to terminate.

Suppose that our table used for the second operand is defined as shown in Fig. 11.31. As defined, the TRT instruction will not "find a match" on any character in the first operand with this table. For each byte selected from the first operand, the corresponding byte in the table has a value of X'00'.

```
SCAN      DC    256X'00'
```

Figure 11.31 Table for TRT processing.

If our table was defined as shown in Fig. 11.32, then the only byte in the table that is not equal to X'00' is the byte at offset C',', or offset 107.

```
COMMA     DC    256X'00'
          ORG   COMMA+C','
          DC    C','
          ORG
```

Figure 11.32 Translate table to search for a comma.

Suppose that we used this table to issue the TRT instruction given in Fig. 11.33 against the field called NAMEIN, which is located in memory at location X'2000'.

```
          TRT   NAMEIN(20),COMMA
          .     .
          .     .
          .     .
NAMEIN    DS    CL20
```

Figure 11.33 Searching for the comma within a field.

Suppose that the value in NAMEIN is "SMITH,   JOHN   ". The TRT instruction finds a value of X'00' for each of the characters S, M, I, T, and H. When the TRT instruction encounters the character C',' within NAMEIN, it also encounters a value not equal to X'00' within the table called COMMA at this offset (offset 107, the decimal value of a comma). At this point, the TRT instruction places the value of C',' *(from the table)* into the rightmost byte of *register 2* and places the address of the comma, *within NAMEIN,* into register 1. The address of the comma within NAMEIN is at location 2005 as shown in Fig. 11.34.

Letters within NAMEIN	Their Address
S	2000
M	2001
I	2002
T	2003
H	2004
,	2005
b̸	2006
J	2007

and so on

Figure 11.34 Internal contents of the name field.

The address in register 1 will be 2005.

Suppose that a blank can also separate the first and last names. In this case, we have a table in which two elements in the table are not zero as shown in Fig. 11.35.

From Fig. 11.35, the TRT instruction stops scanning if *either* a blank or a comma is found. Since John Smith's name contains both, the comma is found first since it appears within the name field before the blank. Also, since the rightmost byte of R2 contains the character that caused the scanning to stop, we can check R2 (using CLM) to see if it contains a blank or a comma. From this, we can determine *which* character was found during scanning.

Let's finish the task of reordering the input name from last-first into first-last. Note that the execute instruction is used within this code (see Fig. 11.36) to extract the proper number of characters in either the first or last names.

This code is rather complex, so you have to spend some time reviewing it. Let's run through the code to understand how it works. Figure 11.37 describes the code in Fig. 11.36 in detail.

For your information, we can use another table to find the end of the first name. Since the first name contains only letters of the alphabet, the end of the first name can also be indicated by finding a character that is *not* a letter. The TRT table in Fig. 11.38 stops the scanning process whenever a nonletter is found.

The table is initialized to hexadecimal FF, which means that *any* character *stops*

```
FINDFRST     DC      256X'00'
             ORG     FINDFRST+C' '
             DC      C' '
             ORG     FINDFRST+C','
             DC      C','
             ORG
```

Figure 11.35 Translate table to search for a blank or a comma.

```
         MVI    FRSTLAST,C' '             CLEAR TARGET FIELD
         MVC    FRSTLAST+1(19),FRSTLAST   ...FINISH THE JOB
         TRT    NAMEIN(20),COMMA          FIND THE COMMA
         LR     R3,R1                     NOTE WHERE LAST NAME
*                                            ENDS
         LA     R4,2(R1)                  POINT TO FIRST NAME
         TRT    0(20,R4),COMMA            FIND END OF FIRST NAME
         SR     R1,R4                     COMPUTE LENGTH OF FIRST
*                                            NAME
         BCTR   R1,0                      SET UP FOR EXECUTE
         EX     R1,FRSTMOVE               MOVE IN FIRST NAME
         B      *+10                      SKIP OVER MVC
FRSTMOVE MVC    FRSTLAST(0),0(R4)         EXECUTED
         LA     R1,FRSTLAST+2(R1)         FIND LOCATION WHERE LAST
*                                           NAME GOES WITHIN THE
*                                           RESULT FIELD
         S      R3,=A(NAMEIN)             COMPUTE LENGTH OF THE
*                                           LAST NAME
         BCTR   R3,0                      SET UP FOR EXECUTE
         EX     R3,LASTMOVE               MOVE IN LAST NAME
         B      *+10
LASTMOVE MVC    0(0,R1),NAMEIN            EXECUTED
```

Figure 11.36 Code to rearrange a name from "last, first" to "first last".

```
MVI        Clear first byte of the rearranged field.
MVC        Finish clearing the rearranged field.
TRT        Find the location of the comma within the
              input name field.
LR         Save the location of the comma since it
              will help us extract the first name
              and compute the length of the last
              name field.
LA         Point R4 to the start of the first name
              field.
TRT        Using R4 as the starting point, scan the
              first name to find the end of it.  The
              end will be denoted by a blank.
SR         After the TRT, R1 will point to the end
              of the first name.  The length of the
              first name may now be computed by
              subtracting the ending address from
              the starting address.
BCTR       Subtract 1 from the length of the first
              name.
EX         Move the first name, and only the first
              name, into the target field.  Since R4
              points to the start of the first name
              then R4 is the source on the MVC.
B          Skip around the executed MVC instruction.
LA         Point R1 into the target name field after
              the first name.  A displacment of 2 is
              coded to allow for a blank between the
              names and because R1 was BCTR'd
              earlier.
S          Compute the length of the last name.  R3
              points to the end of the first name
              and so by subtracting the starting
              address we obtain the length.
BCTR       Subtract 1 from the last name length to
              get ready for the execute.
EX         Move the last name into the target area
              after the first name and after the
              blank that separates the two names.
B          Skip around the executed MVC instruction.
```

Figure 11.37 Explanation of the code in Fig. 11.36.

```
NOTLETTR  DC    256X'FF'
          ORG   NOTLETTR+C'A'
          DC    9X'00'
          ORG   NOTLETTR+C'J'
          DC    9X'00'
          ORG   NOTLETTR+C'S'
          DC    8X'00'
          ORG
```

Figure 11.38 TRT table that "stops" on something that is not a letter.

the TRT instruction. Using the ORG instruction, we go back into the table and replace each letter offset with X'00'. Hence, any time that TRT encounters a letter when scanning, it continues scanning. Only when something other than a letter is found does TRT stop and set registers 1 and 2. X'FF' is used as the "stopping character" in this case since it's very unlikely that we'll check the value of R2 to determine exactly which character terminated our scanning. Since only 26 of the 256 characters do not stop the scan, there are a large number of comparisons to make to determine which character terminated the scan.

With the TRT instruction, R1 and R2 are modified. Clearly, if you are using TRT, make sure that nothing of value is in R1 or R2 before issuing the instruction.

TRT is also used to scan text for words. This paragraph, for example, can be scanned for occurrences of the word "the." However, be careful when using TRT for this purpose. TRT operates on a letter-by-letter basis, not on a word-by-word basis. The first letter of **TRT** causes the instruction to stop scanning as well as the first letter of the word "**The**". When scanning for words, use TRT in combination with CLC to determine if you've found a searched word. The section of code in Fig. 11.39 reads input data cards until the end of file and counts the number of "the's" on each input card.

Each TRT scan table uses a character value equal to the character to search for to

```
         SR     R10,R10           COUNTER FOR NUMBER OF T'S
MLOOP    XREAD  CARDIN,80         INPUT A DATA CARD
         BNZ    EOF               IF END OF FILE THEN QUIT
         LA     R3,CARDIN         POINT TO INPUT CARD AREA
         LA     R4,80             R4 = LENGTH OF CARD AREA
SLOOP    DS     0H
         EX     R4,SCAN           LOOK FOR A 'T'
         B      *+10              SKIP OVER TRT INSTRUCTION
SCAN     TRT    0(0,R3),FINDT     LOOK FOR A LETTER T
         BZ     NOTHES            IF CC=0, NO MORE THE'S ON THIS
*                                 INPUT DATA CARD
         CLC    0(3,R1),=C'THE'   IS IT A "THE"?
         BNE    NOPE              IF NOT, DON'T COUNT IT
         LA     R10,1(R10)        IF SO,  COUNT IT!
NOPE     DS     0H
         LA     R3,1(R1)          POINT TO NEXT BYTE TO BEGIN
*                                 SCANNING ON THIS CARD
         LA     R4,CARDIN+79      POINT TO LAST BYTE OF CARD
         SR     R4,R1             COMPUTE LENGTH OF CARD LEFT
*                                 TO BE SEARCHED
         B      SLOOP             SCAN FOR MORE OCCURRANCES
NOTHES   B      MLOOP             PROCESS ALL INPUT RECORDS
         .      .
         .      .
FINDT    DC     256X'00'          SKIP ALL BYTES EXCEPT T
         ORG    FINDT+C'T'        STOP ON A T
         DC     C'T'
         ORG
```

Figure 11.39 Code to count the number of "the" words on an input set of data cards.

stop the scanning process. It is *not* necessary for you to use this value in your scan tables. Some programmers use X'FF' to stop the scanning process since the value in register 2 is not generally tested after the TRT instruction. Often, R2 is needlessly modified and causes you to reserve this register unnecessarily as a result of using TRT. Finally, notice that the condition code may be tested after the TRT instruction to determine if the scanning process "found" any characters. A zero condition code means that the characters were *not* found. The condition code is B'0100' if the TRT instruction "finds" a character before the end of the first argument. Finally, the condition code is B'0010' if TRT "finds" a character in the last byte of the first operand.

SINGLE-DIMENSIONAL ARRAY PROCESSING

A list of elements having identical properties is called an **array.** For example, a list of names with each name able to store up to 20 characters and a list of numbers with each number able to hold any integer value between −999 and +999 are called arrays. Arrays appear under many other names such as **vectors** or **lists.** Regardless of the name, we're discussing lists of elements with similar properties. The instruction in Fig. 11.40 defines an array of five elements, with each element able to hold one halfword of data.

```
ARRAY    DS    5H
```

Figure 11.40 An array of five halfword elements.

The repetition factor is the first clue to the definition of an array in assembly language. Although the same array may be defined as shown in Fig. 11.41, it is more likely to be defined as illustrated in Fig. 11.40.

```
ARRAY       DS    H
            DS    H
            DS    H
            DS    H
            DS    H
ARRAYEND    EQU   *
```

Figure 11.41 Alternate definition of a five halfword array.

Arrays are processed in assembly language in several manners: first, an index register references appropriate elements within the array; second, a D(B) address is constructed to reference each array element; and third, array elements are accessed by their displacement within the array. For example, the label ARRAY+4 references the *third* element in the array of Fig. 11.41. The displacement, 4, indicates that four bytes of storage come *before* this reference. Since each element of the array is two bytes long, an offset of four bytes places us at the third element in the array.

It is more common to reference an array element using an explicit address reference or an index register than with using a specific label-plus-displacement reference. If register 4 contains the address of the first element within the array, then increasing the value of R4 by two each time through a loop moves from the first element address to the last element. The code in Fig. 11.42 illustrates this processing.

From figure 11.42, addressability to the array is first obtained so that each element

```
         LA      R4,ARRAY            ADDRESS THE FIRST ELEMENT
LOOP     DS      0H
         MVC     0(2,R4),=H'0'       CLEAR THIS ARRAY POSITION
         LA      R4,2(R4)            MOVE TO NEXT ARRAY POSITION
         C       R4,=A(ARRAYEND)     END OF THE ARRAY YET?
         BL      LOOP                IF NOT, CONTINUE CLEARING
```

Figure 11.42 Code to initialize an array using looping.

in the array can be set to zero. The MVC initializes the array element addressed by R4 to binary zeros. R4 is then incremented to address the next array element and processing continues until R4 is beyond the bounds of the array. Since each element in the array is two bytes long, R4 is incremented by two each time through the loop to allow R4 to reference the next element within the array.

Since an MVC instruction initializes each array element, an index register *cannot* be used. The MVC instruction only allows D(B) addresses in each operand. Let's perform the same processing but with the STH (store halfword) instruction to initialize each array element. Figure 11.43 contains this implementation.

```
         SR      R6,R6               SET R6 TO ZERO
         SR      R7,R7               SET INDEX REGISTER TO ZERO
LOOP     DS      0H
         STH     R6,ARRAY(R7)        CLEAR THE ARRAY POSITION
         LA      R7,2(R7)            MOVE TO NEXT ARRAY POSITION
         C       R7,=F'8'            END OF THE ARRAY YET?
         BNH     LOOP                IF NOT, INITIALIZE NEXT ELEMENT
```

Figure 11.43 Modification to the code of Fig. 11.42.

Since STH allows the second operand to be a D(X,B) address, we can introduce an index register to move through each array element. The index register R7 is initially set to zero before the loop begins. Each pass through the loop increments this register by two, the length of each array element. Register 4 is not needed to address the array since the array may be referenced through the format *ARRAY(R7)*. In this format, the label ARRAY is still a D(B) address. However, R7 is acting as the index register. Hence, ARRAY(R7) is a D(X,B) address. Each time that STH executes, the system computes the effective address by adding the value in R7 to the D(B) address identified by ARRAY. The halfword value in R6 is then stored into this memory location, thus initializing the desired array element to zero.

The loop is controlled by comparing the index register value to the last offset that can be used when referencing the array. In other words, the first element position in the array is at offset 0, the second at offset 2, and the last at offset 8. When the index register's value is larger than 8, then we terminate the loop or risk the possibility of destroying other areas in our program. Our program can also fail with an 0C4 (protection exception) if the index register references a storage area outside the bounds of our program.

Although the last form for referencing array elements is clearer than the earlier form, it cannot be used on all instructions. Again, not all instructions permit the use of D(X,B) addresses. Therefore, we may have to convert this format into a D(B) format as illustrated by the code in Fig. 11.44.

Before using the MVC instruction to move the data into the array position desired, register 4 is assigned the value of the array position's *address*. This address is then used to reference the array position as a D(B) address.

```
         SR      R6,R6                 SET R6 TO ZERO
         SR      R7,R7                 SET INDEX REGISTER TO ZERO
LOOP     DS      0H
         LA      R4,ARRAY(R7)          ADDRESS THE ARRAY POSITION
         MVC     0(2,R4),=H'0'         CLEAR THE ARRAY POSITION
         LA      R7,2(R7)              MOVE TO NEXT ARRAY POSITION
         C       R7,=F'8'              END OF THE ARRAY YET?
         BNH     LOOP                  IF NOT, INITIALIZE NEXT ELEMENT
```

Figure 11.44 Another version of Figure 11.42.

When an index register is combined with the array label name, the index register is used as a **subscript** into the array. As R7 assumes the values of 0, 2, 4, 6, and 8, ARRAY(R7) moves from element 1 through element 5 of the array. Logically, the index register references the array as if we were using the notation $ARRAY_1$, $ARRAY_2$, $ARRAY_3$, $ARRAY_4$, and $ARRAY_5$.

In a higher-level language such as COBOL, PL/I, or FORTRAN, we reference each position of the array as shown in Fig. 11.45.

```
ARRAY(1), ARRAY(2), ARRAY(3), ARRAY(4), ARRAY(5)
```

Figure 11.45 Referencing array elements in higher-level languages.

As you can see, using an index register in combination with the array label is very similar to processing arrays in other languages. In fact, through the EQU instruction, we can further enhance our assembly language code to parallel the processing found in a higher-level language. Figure 11.46 contains this implementation.

The reference on the STH instruction to ARRAY(I) is identical to the format used in higher-level languages. Logically, the code in Fig. 11.46 is similar to the loop structure in Fig. 11.47. However, a slight adjustment in representation is made since the value of the index register actually begins at 0, increments by 2, and ends when it exceeds 8.

```
I        EQU     7                     R7 WILL BE USED AS "I"
         SR      R6,R6                 SET R6 TO ZERO
         SR      I,I                   SET I TO ZERO
LOOP     DS      0H
         STH     R6,ARRAY(I)           CLEAR ARRAY POSITION
         LA      I,2(I)                MOVE TO NEXT ARRAY POSITION
         C       I,=F'8'               END OF THE ARRAY YET?
         BNH     LOOP                  IF NOT, INITIALIZE NEXT ELEMENT
```

Figure 11.46 Using EQU when processing arrays.

```
DO I = 1 TO 5
  ARRAY(I) = 0
ENDDO
```

Figure 11.47 Array initialization logic in a higher-level language.

MULTIDIMENSIONAL ARRAYS

Arrays of unlimited dimensions can be constructed in assembly language since it has no dimensional limit as do some of the higher-level languages. All array references and processing are handled with the same set of machine instructions that we've been using throughout the text. These instructions can reference an array of 50 dimensions if required. For our purposes, arrays of one, two, and three dimensions will be discussed.

An array of 2 or 3 dimensions is only slightly more difficult to process than a single-dimensional array. Using several registers or storage areas to hold each subscript reference, an address of an array element can be computed and used to reference the array position. Consider an array of two dimensions that is defined as shown in Fig. 11.48.

```
ARRAY2    DS     15H
```

Figure 11.48 Defining an array of 15 elements.

Although this definition can indicate that a single-dimensional array is defined, it can also define an array that *logically* represents five rows by three columns (two dimensions) or three rows by five columns. Suppose the array is five rows by three columns. This array allows 15 element positions, each holding a halfword value. The first dimension of the array is the number of rows and the second dimension of the array is the number of columns. To process the array, we'll want to reference logical positions (1,1), which is row 1, column 1, and (1,2), (1,3), (2,1), (2,2), (2,3), . . . , (5,1), (5,2), and (5,3), which is row 5, column 3. Again, there are several options to reference each array element, but not as many as before.

Each array element is referenced by the array name and its offset into the array. The first element may be referenced by ARRAY2 or ARRAY2+0 and the fifth element may be referenced by ARRAY2+8. However, the fifth element is logically associated with row 2, column 2 as shown in Fig. 11.49.

```
Fifth element in a 5-by-3 array.
---------------------------------
      (1,1)     (1,2)     (1,3)
      (2,1)     (2,2)     (2,3)
      (3,1)     (3,2)     (3,3)
      (4,1)     (4,2)     (4,3)
      (5,1)     (5,2)     (5,3)
```

Figure 11.49 Representation of a 15-element array.

Displacement array referencing does not clearly identify the row/column relationship with respect to the array. Therefore, it is not generally used with arrays having more than one dimension.

Another form of array referencing uses an index register to move through the array in conjunction with an explicit register reference or with a label. With D(X,B) or label (index) formats, each element of the single-dimensional array can be referenced based on the current value of the index register. This form, too, falls short when processing arrays of more than one dimension since the D(B) or D(X,B) address forms only permit one or two registers to be used. Hence, we cannot easily use this format when referencing multidimensional arrays.

Finally, we arrive at the referencing form that can be used to process multidimensional arrays, a form that uses either registers or storage areas to maintain dimensional referencing. Further, it requires a series of computations before the actual address of the element within the array is determined as related to the various array subscript elements. To illustrate this technique, let's implement the logic given in Fig. 11.50 to initialize our multidimensional array to zero. Implementing this logic in assembly language, we arrive at the solution given in Fig. 11.51.

```
do i = 1 to 5
   do j = 1 to 3
      array2(i,j) = 0
   enddo
enddo
```

Figure 11.50 Array initialization logic to be implemented in assembly language.

```
I        EQU   6
J        EQU   7

         SR    I,I                 CLEAR FIRST SUBSCRIPT
         SR    J,J                 CLEAR SECOND SUBSCRIPT
LOOP     DS    0H
         L     R2,=A(ARRAY2)       ADDRESS THE TABLE
         AR    R2,I                ADD FIRST SUBSCRIPT OFFSET
         AR    R2,J                ADD SECOND SUBSCRIPT
         MVC   0(2,R2),=H'0'       CLEAR THIS ELEMENT
         LA    J,2(J)              BUMP TO NEXT COLUMN
         C     J,=F'4'             LAST COLUMN IN THIS ROW?
         BNH   LOOP                IF NOT, FINISH THIS ROW
         SR    J,J                 START AT BEGINNING OF ROW
         LA    I,6(I)              BUMP TO NEXT ROW
         C     I,=F'24'            LAST ROW IN ARRAY?
         BNH   LOOP                IF NOT, PROCESS NEXT ROW
```

Figure 11.51 Implementing the logic of Fig. 11.50.

Each element (column) occupies two bytes of storage and each row occupies six bytes of storage (two bytes for each of the three elements). Hence, **J** increments by two to move from element to element (column to column) and **I** increments by six to move from row to row. The address of the element referenced is computed by adding the location of the array to the row and column offsets. The registers denoted by **I** and **J** are used as displacements to address the elements within the array.

Clearly, more registers could be added to increase the number of dimensions within this array. However, we soon find that as we increase the number of registers used as subscripts, the number of registers available for normal processing becomes smaller. Therefore, rather than using registers to maintain each subscript offset, we accomplish the same thing using storage areas. The code in Fig. 11.52 illustrates this technique.

With this technique, the number of dimensions in the array is impacted only by the number of storage area offsets added to R2 to reference the array. For example, a third dimension can be added to our array to allow 10 levels of the five-by-three rows and columns. A total of 150 positions are needed for the complete array at this point. The code in Fig. 11.53 processes all positions as we've been doing, with the boldface code indicating the third dimensional processing.

Figure 11.53 allows us to discuss another *peculiar* aspect of array processing, namely, the offsets that increment and reference each array position. In this code, each subscript element is incremented by either 2, 6, or 30 to progress from column to column, row to row, or level to level within the array. The values that increment each subscript element are dependent on the length of each array position, the number of elements in each row, and the number of rows/columns per level. Clearly, any change to the array

```
LOOP     DS     0H
         L      R2,=A(ARRAY2)     ADDRESS THE TABLE
         A      R2,I              ADD FIRST SUBSCRIPT OFFSET
         A      R2,J              ADD SECOND SUBSCRIPT
         MVC    0(2,R2),=H'0'     CLEAR THIS ELEMENT
         L      R3,J              OBTAIN ROW OFFSET
         LA     R3,2(R3)          BUMP TO NEXT COLUMN
         ST     R3,J              UPDATE OFFSET VALUE
         C      R3,=F'4'           LAST COLUMN IN THIS ROW?
         BNH    LOOP              IF NOT, FINISH THIS ROW
         MVC    J(4),=F'0'        START AT BEGINNING OF ROW
         L      R3,I              OBTAIN ROW VALUE
         LA     R3,6(R3)          BUMP TO NEXT ROW
         ST     R3,I              UPDATE VALUE IN STORAGE
         C      R3,=F'24'         LAST ROW IN ARRAY?
         BNH    LOOP              IF NOT, PROCESS NEXT ROW

I        DC     F'0'              ROW OFFSET REFERENCE
J        DC     F'0'              COLUMN OFFSET REFERENCE
```

Figure 11.52 Maintaining array subscripts using storage areas.

```
LOOP     DS     0H
         L      R2,=A(ARRAY2)     ADDRESS THE TABLE
         A      R2,DIM1           ADD FIRST DIMENSION
         A      R2,I              ADD ROW OFFSET
         A      R2,J              ADD COLUMN OFFSET
         MVC    0(2,R2),=H'0'     CLEAR THIS ELEMENT
         L      R3,J              OBTAIN ROW OFFSET
         LA     R3,2(R3)          BUMP TO NEXT COLUMN
         ST     R3,J              UPDATE OFFSET VALUE
         C      R3,=F'4'           LAST COLUMN IN THIS ROW?
         BNH    LOOP              IF NOT, FINISH THIS ROW
         MVC    J(4),=F'0'        START AT BEGINNING OF ROW
         L      R3,I              OBTAIN ROW VALUE
         LA     R3,6(R3)          BUMP TO NEXT ROW
         ST     R3,I              UPDATE VALUE IN STORAGE
         C      R3,=F'24'         LAST ROW IN ARRAY?
         BNH    LOOP              IF NOT, PROCESS NEXT ROW
         MVC    I(4),=F'0'        RESET ROW REFERENCE FOR
*                                   THE NEXT LEVEL
         L      R3,DIM1           GET CURRENT LEVEL VALUE
         LA     R3,(5*3)*2(R3)    BUMP TO NEXT LEVEL
         ST     R3,DIM1           SAVE LEVEL OFFSET VALUE
         C      R3,=F'270'        ALL LEVELS PROCESSED?
         BNH    LOOP              IF NOT THEN CONTINUE

DIM1     DC     F'0'              LEVEL OFFSET REFERENCE
I        DC     F'0'              ROW OFFSET REFERENCE
J        DC     F'0'              COLUMN OFFSET REFERENCE
```

Figure 11.53 Three-dimensional array processing.

length, such as adding another column or row within a level or increasing the size of each element, dramatically impacts the operation of our code. To build programs that are easily maintained, try to use **relocatable symbols** to supply these values to our code.

A relocatable symbol is an element whose value is dependent on that of another element or elements. Further, it dynamically changes its value each time the program is reassembled if there has been a change to any one of the elements on which it is based. Consider the example in Fig. 11.54 that uses the element ARRAYLEN. This symbol is defined as the difference between the two address references * and **ARRAY**.

```
ARRAY       DS     15H
ARRAYLEN    EQU    *-ARRAY
```

Figure 11.54 Defining relocatable symbols to create maintainable array processing code.

In this example, the * attribute again refers to the current value of the location counter. If the location counter value for ARRAY is X'0000A0', then the location counter value for ARRAYLEN is X'0000A0'+X'1E' or X'0000BE'. ARRAYLEN is the difference between X'0000BE' and X'0000A0', or X'1E'. Therefore, the value of ARRAYLEN is equal to the number of bytes in the array. As long as ARRAYLEN immediately follows the definition of ARRAY as shown, its value always equals 30. If, on the other hand, the definition of ARRAY is changed to add more elements or to increase the size of each element, ARRAYLEN changes appropriately when the program is reassembled.

ARRAYLEN is called a relocatable symbol since its value is dependent on the value of the location counter and the location of ARRAY within the program. If code is added to or removed from the program prior to the definition of these elements, the location counter values for both elements change or are "relocated." ARRAYLEN changes appropriately since it is a symbol based on the current value of the location counter.

Suppose that the array being processed holds 150 elements and is defined as shown in Fig. 11.55.

```
ARRAY2     DS      150H
```

Figure 11.55 Array to hold 150 elements.

Relocatable symbols add more meaning and increase the maintainability of our code. In particular, relocatable symbols can be used to provide the length of each element, the size of each row, the size of each level, and the number of levels, which are all very valuable to our program. They are defined as illustrated in Fig. 11.56.

```
ROWS         EQU    5                      NUMBER OF ROWS
COLUMNS      EQU    3                      NUMBER OF COLUMNS
LEVELS       EQU    10                     NUMBER OF LEVELS
TSIZE        EQU    LEVEL*ROWS*COLUMNS     TOTAL ELEMENTS IN TABLE
LSIZE        EQU    ROWS*LEVELS            # ELEMENTS ACROSS A ROW
ARRAY2       DS     150H                   TABLE DEFINITION
ARRAYEND     EQU    *-ARRAY2               BYTES IN ENTIRE ARRAY
ELEMENTL     EQU    (*-ARRAY2)/TSIZE       SIZE OF EACH ELEMENT
COLUMNL      EQU    (*-ARRAY2)/TSIZE       BYTES IN EACH COLUMN
ROWL         EQU    (*-ARRAY2)/LSIZE       BYTES IN EACH ROW
LEVELL       EQU    (*-ARRAY2)/LEVELS      BYTES PER LEVEL
```

Figure 11.56 Relocatable symbol definitions to provide more maintainable coding.

Based on the instructions in Fig. 11.56, the values assigned to each of the relocatable symbols are as follows:

ELEMENTL	2
COLUMNL	2
ROWL	6
LEVELL	30

Hence, we can use these symbols within our code to help readability and to assist in creating maintainable code. By simply changing the value of ROWS, COLUMNS, LEVELS, or our array definition, we can redefine the array to make it larger or smaller and automatically cause *all* other variables to be reassigned during assembly. These changes are immediately reflected within the code to support processing with the new array size. Figure 11.57 contains this implementation.

Array processing can be accomplished yet another way if you do not like any of the methods proposed so far. In all previous methods, we used offsets or displacements to advance through the array elements. Although this technique works, it may cause confusion in some cases due to the size of the array and the number of elements in the various levels. In most languages, array subscripts begin with a value of 1 and increase by 1 until they reach their maximum value. In other words, a subscript referring to the rows within each level normally starts at 1 and continues until it reaches 5. In our examples so far, the subscript value began at 0 and ended when it exceeded 24 or became 30, since each iteration through the loop increased this value by 6. Clearly, it may be more meaningful to go from 1 through 5 by ones, instead of 0 through 24 by sixes.

To use this incrementing technique in array processing, we use the multiply or multiply-halfword instructions to convert these increments into offsets. The offset still has to be the ultimate value that we need to arrive at. Whether we increment our subscripts by displacements or increment by 1 and multiply by the appropriate displacement value, we obtain the same result. However, our subscripts can proceed in a more logical manner and in a manner typical of that found in higher-level languages. The code in Fig. 11.58 uses this technique to process arrays. Incidentally, the multiply-halfword instruction is valuable in this case since it allows only one register to be used for the multiply operation. The standard multiply instruction, however, requires yet another register for this code.

Although many techniques can process arrays, some array processing can be accomplished in a much easier manner. For example, the array(s) that we've processed could be defined with the DC statement, thus freeing us from writing all of the code that

```
LOOP     DS    0H
         L     R2,=A(ARRAY2)      ADDRESS THE TABLE
         A     R2,DIM1            ADD FIRST DIMENSION
         A     R2,I               ADD ROW OFFSET
         A     R2,J               ADD COLUMN OFFSET
         MVC   0(2,R2),=H'0'      CLEAR THIS ELEMENT
         L     R3,J               OBTAIN ROW OFFSET
         LA    R3,COLUMNL(R3)     BUMP TO NEXT COLUMN
         ST    R3,J               UPDATE OFFSET VALUE
         C     R3,=F'6'           LAST COLUMN IN THIS ROW?
         BL    LOOP               IF NOT, FINISH THIS ROW
         MVC   J(4),=F'0'         START AT BEGINNING OF ROW
         L     R3,I               OBTAIN ROW VALUE
         LA    R3,ROWL(R3)        BUMP TO NEXT ROW
         ST    R3,I               UPDATE VALUE IN STORAGE
         C     R3,=F'30'          LAST ROW IN ARRAY?
         BL    LOOP               IF NOT, PROCESS NEXT ROW
         MVC   I(4),=F'0'         RESET ROW REFERENCE FOR
*                                   THE NEXT LEVEL
         L     R3,DIM1            GET CURRENT LEVEL VALUE
         LA    R3,LEVELL(R3)      BUMP TO NEXT LEVEL
         ST    R3,DIM1            SAVE LEVEL OFFSET VALUE
         C     R3,=F'300'         ALL LEVELS PROCESSED?
         BL    LOOP               IF NOT THEN CONTINUE
DIM1     DC    F'0'               LEVEL OFFSET REFERENCE
I        DC    F'0'               ROW OFFSET REFERENCE
J        DC    F'0'               COLUMN OFFSET REFERENCE
```

Figure 11.57 Three-dimensional array processing using relocatable symbols.

```
LOOP     DS    0H
         L     R2,=A(ARRAY2)     ADDRESS THE TABLE
         L     R3,DIM1           OBTAIN LEVEL NUMBER
         MH    R3,=H'30'         TIMES BYTES PER LEVEL
         AR    R2,R3             ADD LEVEL OFFSET TO ADDRESS
         L     R3,I              OBTAIN ROW SUBSCRIPT VALUE
         MH    R3,=H'6'          TIMES LENGTH OF EACH ROW
         AR    R2,R3             ADD ROW OFFSET
         L     R3,J              ADD COLUMN OFFSET
         MH    R3,=H'2'          TIMES COLUMN ELEMENT LENGTH
         AR    R2,R3             ADD COLUMN OFFSET
         MVC   0(2,R2),=H'0'     CLEAR THIS ELEMENT
         L     R3,J              OBTAIN ROW OFFSET
         LA    R3,1(R3)          BUMP TO NEXT COLUMN
         ST    R3,J              UPDATE OFFSET VALUE
         C     R3,=F'3'          LAST COLUMN IN THIS ROW?
         BL    LOOP              IF NOT, FINISH THIS ROW
         MVC   J(4),=F'0'        START AT BEGINNING OF ROW
         L     R3,I              OBTAIN ROW VALUE
         LA    R3,1(R3)          BUMP TO NEXT ROW
         ST    R3,I              UPDATE VALUE IN STORAGE
         C     R3,=F'5'          LAST ROW IN ARRAY?
         BL    LOOP              IF NOT, PROCESS NEXT ROW
         MVC   I(4),=F'0'        RESET ROW REFERENCE FOR NEXT LEVEL
         L     R3,DIM1           GET CURRENT LEVEL VALUE
         LA    R3,1(R3)          BUMP TO NEXT LEVEL
         ST    R3,DIM1           SAVE LEVEL OFFSET VALUE
         C     R3,=F'10'         ALL LEVELS PROCESSED?
         BL    LOOP              IF NOT THEN CONTINUE


DIM1     DC    F'0'              LEVEL OFFSET REFERENCE
I        DC    F'0'              ROW OFFSET REFERENCE
J        DC    F'0'              COLUMN OFFSET REFERENCE
```

Figure 11.58 Processing a three-dimensional array using subscript values beginning at 0 and incrementing by 1.

we've written. Also, the arrays could be initialized through a simple MVC instruction as shown in Fig. 11.59.

```
MVC    ARRAY2(30),=30X'00'
```

Figure 11.59 Initializing a 15-element array using MVC.

TABLE PROCESSING

The terms *array* and *table* are often used synonymously. However, we're going to make a distinction between these terms in a manner similar to that made in higher-level languages. It will characterize arrays and tables so that they do not have similar meanings and are not used in identical processing situations.

Tables have the characteristic that all elements within a row are *not* of the same type and of the same size. Although rows or levels within a table may have the same characteristics, columnar data is not necessarily similar. Further, elements within each row of a table are not only different, but they are typically related in some manner. Hence, a logical relationship exists between the various elements within a row of a table. On the other hand, tables *do* have the advantage in that they are usually (not necessarily) processed in single dimensions.

Consider a student in a class whose information consists of her name, social security number, and her average score. Clearly, these three pieces of information are all related to one student. A classroom typically has more than one student and therefore the information related to this student/class data can be stored in a **table.**

Defining a table can be rather difficult since each row contains different data types. Assuming that we're going to store the student data in a single-dimensional array, each row contains a student name, social security number, and class average. In fact, the table data can be considered as a series or group of arrays. In this example, one array can hold the student names, another the social security numbers, and another the student scores. If each array were processed in **parallel** or in **tandem,** we have a logical organization similar to that of a table.

```
ROW      DS    0CL28
NAME     DS    CL20
SSNUM    DS    PL5
SCORE    DS    PL3
```

Figure 11.60 Defining a single row in a table.

One row of the table is defined as shown in Fig. 11.60. Defining several rows in this manner requires repetitive coding of each of the elements in the table. The example in Fig. 11.61 *does not work* in defining a table to hold student data of this type.

```
     This example does not work.
STUDENTS  DS    50(CL20,PL5,PL3)
```

Figure 11.61 Incorrect method for defining a 50-row table.

The definition of our student information seems quite reasonable, *but it is not allowed.* A duplication factor may not be applied to more than one element. Using another method shown in Fig. 11.62, we still have a problem with the definition of this table. We've defined three separate arrays, *not* a table. How then might we define such a table? Our options are to code 50 statements to define each row of the table or to use a macro to generate as many table elements as desired. Since a macro requires less coding, we define our table with the macro shown in Fig. 11.63.

```
This example will assemble, but is incorrect.
-----------------------------------------------
     STUDENTS  DS    50CL20,50PL5,50PL3
```

Figure 11.62 Another incorrect method for defining a 50-row table.

```
         MACRO
&LABEL   STUDENTS  &SIZE
         LCLA      &I
&I       SETA      &SIZE            CONVERT # STUDENTS IN CLASS
&LABEL   DS        0H               DEFINE START OF THE TABLE
.LOOP    AIF       (&I EQ 0).DONE   IF ALL DONE THEN EXIT MACRO
         DS        CL20             GENERATE A NAME IN THIS ROW
         DS        PL5              GENERATE A SS NUMBER
         DS        PL3              GENERATE A SCORE FIELD
&I       SETA      &I-1             ACCOUNT FOR THIS STUDENT
         AGO       .LOOP            GENERATE AS MANY AS NEEDED
.DONE    ANOP
         MEND
```

Figure 11.63 Macro to define a table of 50 rows.

With the macro call in Fig. 11.64, 50 rows will be defined to hold the student data. Each row of the table holds 28 bytes of data. Using relocatable symbols, we again define elements to process the table data in a more readable manner. Figure 11.65 contains our macro call and relocatable symbol definitions.

```
STUDTBL    STUDENTS  50
```

Figure 11.64 Invoking the STUDENTS macro (Figure 11.63) to generate 50 rows of student data.

```
STUDTBL   STUDENTS  50                GENERATE THE TABLE
STUDEND   EQU       *-STUDTBL         LENGTH OF THE TABLE
ROWBYTES  EQU       (*-STUDTBL)/50    BYTES PER ROW
TBLNAME   EQU       0                 OFFSET OF NAME INTO ROW
TBLSSN    EQU       20                OFFSET OF SSN  INTO ROW
TBLSCORE  EQU       25                OFFSET OF SCORE INTO ROW
NAMESIZE  EQU       20                SIZE OF THE NAME FIELD
SSNSIZE   EQU       5                 SIZE OF THE SSN FIELD
SCORSIZE  EQU       3                 SIZE OF THE SCORE FIELD
```

Figure 11.65 Student table relocatable symbols.

Let's write a program to read records from an input file and fill this table with data. Since only one subscript is required to reference each student in this one-dimensional array, let's begin the subscript value at 1 and increment by 1 for each student in the table. Figure 11.66 contains this implementation

The input card is read and register **I** (R10) is used as the subscript into the table. As **I** increments from 1 by 1, each student is placed into the table as data for that student is obtained. Register 3 is introduced to compute the offset into the table where the student data is to be placed. Using the value of **I,** R3 is multiplied by the number of bytes in each row of the table ($28 = 20 + 5 + 3$). Hence, R3 assume the values 0, 28, 56, 84, . . . , 1344, and 1372. Adding this displacement to the table's location in memory addresses each row of the table.

In this example, the relocatable symbols TBLNAME, TBLSSN, and TBLSCORE define displacements with respect to each *column* within the table. For example, TBLNAME has a value of zero, which means that it is located in the first 20 bytes of each row. TBLSSN has a value of 20, which places each social security number in bytes 21 to 25 of each row. Therefore, each set of data for each student is placed into its corresponding column within the table.

After all student records are input and stored into the table, the value of **I** is stored into a fullword storage area for later reference. In other words, this code does *not* assume that all 50 table rows will be filled with student data. Instead, a variable maintains a value equal to the number of student rows within the table that are filled. This value can then be used later to process only as much student data as there are students in the class.

This application can be converted into a multidimensional table application by considering each class offered within a school system. The first dimension of the table can be associated with a particular class and the second dimension contains the data for each student in a class. Expanding further, the third dimension can be associated with schools in a school district. As you can see, we quickly move from single to multidimensional tables by expanding the scope of our application.

```
I        EQU    10
         LA     I,0                 SET SUBSCRIPT TO 0 (NO STUDENTS)
         XREAD  CARDIN,80           READ IN AN INPUT RECORD
LOOP     DS     0H
         BNZ    EOF                 WHEN DONE THE TABLE IS LOADED
         LA     I,1(I)              INCREMENT SUBSCRIPT VALUE
*-------------------------------------------------------------------*
*  CONVERT THE SUBSCRIPT VALUE INTO AN OFFSET TO STORE THIS        *
*  STUDENT'S DATA INTO THE TABLE PROPERLY.                          *
*-------------------------------------------------------------------*
         LR     R3,I                OBTAIN SUBSCRIPT VALUE
         BCTR   R3,0                COMPUTE THE OFFSET
         MH     R3,=H'28'           ...TIMES BYTES PER ROW
         LA     R3,STUDTBL(R3)      POINT TO ROW IN THE TABLE
*-------------------------------------------------------------------*
*  THE INSTRUCTIONS BELOW PLACE THE STUDENT INPUT DATA INTO THE *
*  APPROPRIATE ROW WITHIN THE TABLE.                                *
*-------------------------------------------------------------------*
         MVC    TBLNAME(NAMESIZE,R3),NAMEIN        STORE THE NAME
         PACK   TBLSSN(SSNSIZE,R3),SSNIN(9)        STORE THE SSN
         PACK   TBLSCORE(SCORSIZE,R3),SCOREIN(5)   STORE THE SCORE
         XREAD  CARDIN,80                          GET NEXT STUDENT
         B      LOOP
         .      .
         .      .
         .      .
EOF      DS     0H
         ST     I,SCOUNT            SAVE I VALUE FOR LATER USE
         .      .
         .      .
         .      .
SCOUNT   DS     F
CARDIN   DS     0CL80               INPUT CARD AREA
NAMEIN   DS     CL20                INPUT NAME AREA
SSNIN    DS     CL9                 INPUT SOCIAL SECURITY NUMBER
SCOREIN  DS     CL5                 INPUT AVERAGE SCORE
         DS     CL46                REST OF INPUT CARD, UNUSED
```

Figure 11.66 Code to read input cards and fill the student table.

THE MOVE AND COMPARE LONG INSTRUCTIONS

The MVC and CLC instructions process data areas less than or equal to 256 bytes. Once beyond this length, groups of MVC or CLC instructions are used to move or compare the data fields that we're processing or we use the extended instructions **MVCL (move character long)** and **CLCL (compare logical character long).** Suppose that we are processing a very large array or lengthy storage area that must be reinitialized for processing. If the area is longer than 256 bytes, several MVC instructions are required. The code in Fig. 11.67 illustrates this aspect by clearing a 1,000-byte area with blanks.

The first two instructions clear the first 256 bytes of the area. The next two instructions clear 512 bytes, and, finally, the last instruction clears the remaining 232 bytes.

```
MVI      AREA,C' '
MVC      AREA+1(255),AREA
MVC      AREA+256(256),AREA
MVC      AREA+512(256),AREA
MVC      AREA+768(232),AREA
```

Figure 11.67 Initializing a 1000-byte area with MVC instructions.

Clearly, this process is rather cumbersome, especially if the area to be processed is larger than that cleared above. In fact, it is better to use a loop to set this area to blanks as shown in Fig. 11.68.

The area is divided into equal-length 200-byte segments that are cleared within the body of the loop. However, this code is no shorter than the code of Fig. 11.67, and, in fact, it may be more difficult to understand.

The MVCL instruction solves our problem. It processes areas up to 16,777,215 bytes, which should be more than adequate for most of our processing.

The MVCL instruction, although appearing to be the answer to our problems, has a severe drawback: it requires four registers. Not many programs can spare four registers during processing, especially for only one instruction. More likely, loops (as shown in Fig. 11.68) are used to process large areas of data instead of using the MVCL.

```
         LA    R3,AREA             ADDRESS THE AREA TO CLEAR
LOOP     DS    0H                  START THE LOOP
         MVI   0(R3),C' '          CLEAR FIRST BYTE OF 200
         MVC   1(199,R3),0(R3)     CLEAR REMAINING 199 BYTES
         LA    R3,200(R3)          MOVE TO NEXT GROUP
         C     R3,=A(AREA+1000)    ARE WE DONE YET?
         BL    LOOP                IF NOT, DO IT AGAIN
```

Figure 11.68 Initializing a large character area using a loop structure.

The four registers used by the MVCL consist of two even/odd register pairs. This pairing places yet another restriction on the selection of registers for this instruction. R2/R3 constitutes an even/odd pair, but R5/R6 does not since the first register, R5, is not an even register. Each register pair is coded in one of the two MVCL operands. Therefore, the MVCL instruction is an RR instruction with the format described in Fig. 11.69.

```
MVCL  Ra,Rb
```

Figure 11.69 General format of the MVCL instruction.

Ra and Rb relate to the first and second even/odd register pair, respectively.

Before the MVCL instruction is issued, the even/odd pairs are initialized to specific values so that the instruction can work as desired. With Ra representing the even register in the first pair and Ra+1 representing the odd register, the values in the register pairs are as described in Fig. 11.70.

```
Ra      Twenty-four-bit address of the target field and located in
         the rightmost three bytes of the register.

Ra+1    Twenty-four-bit value representing the length of the
         field defined in Ra.

Rb      Twenty-four-bit address representing the area from
         which data is to be moved.

Rb+1    The leftmost byte is the pad character
         and fills the first operand if
         the first operand is longer than the second.
        The rightmost three bytes contain the length of the
         second operand field.
```

Figure 11.70 MVCL register requirements.

Suppose that the MVCL instruction is to clear the 1,000-byte storage area as we had done before. The code in Fig. 11.71 performs this operation.

From Fig. 11.71, the first two instructions identify the area to be cleared and the length of this area. R2 is supplied with the address of the AREA and the odd register R3 is initialized to the length of the area, 1,000. The next three instructions place null values into the second operand even/odd pair by setting both registers to zero. The ICM instruction places a pad character value of a blank in the *leftmost* byte of R5. When the MVCL instruction is issued, the pad character is placed in each byte of the first operand's location, clearing the area as we desired. Incidentally, the pad character could be any value.

This is a unique application of the MVCL instruction. Since the second operand is null, the pad character is used to supply values to all positions within the first operand. Thus, this is an effective method for initializing a storage area. However, this is not the only application for using the MVCL instruction. More typically, MVCL is used to move one storage area to another.

In the code of Fig. 11.72, SOURCE and TARGET are the fields to be processed. SOURCE contains data to be moved into the area called TARGET. Again, assume that both fields are longer than 256 bytes, allowing MVCL to be used to move the data.

In Fig. 11.72, we are assuming that both the target and source areas are *shorter* than 4096 bytes since the length attribute (L'), combined with the load address (LA) instruction, was used to obtain the length of each field. If the fields are longer than 4095 bytes, then place the lengths into the registers by loading a fullword value into the register as illustrated earlier.

If the length of the first operand is shorter than the length of the second, then only the number of characters specified by the first operand length is moved. This means that not all the data in the second operand necessarily appears in the first operand location. If the first operand is longer than the second, then the pad character fills the remaining bytes within the first operand location. Clearly, it's important to select a pad character appropriate to your processing needs should pad filling occur during the MVCL instruction.

The **CLCL (compare logical long)** instruction uses the same register format as MVCL to compare two storage areas. Depending on the values in each area, the condition code may be tested as described in Fig. 11.73.

```
LA      R2,AREA             ADDRESS THE AREA TO BE CLEARED
L       R3,=F'1000'         SET LENGTH OF THE FIRST OPERAND

SR      R4,R4               SECOND OPERAND DOES NOT EXIST
SR      R5,R5               NO SECOND OPERAND LENGTH
ICM     R5,B'1000',=C' '    PAD CHARACTER IS A BLANK

MVCL    R2,R4               CLEAR THE STORAGE AREA
```

Figure 11.71 Using MVCL to initialize a 1,000-byte area.

```
LA      R4,TARGET           SET UP THE FIRST OPERAND
LA      R5,L'TARGET         OBTAIN LENGTH OF TARGET AREA
LA      R6,SOURCE           POINT TO SOURCE AREA
LA      R7,L'SOURCE         OBTAIN LENGTH OF SOURCE AREA
ICM     R7,B'1000',=X'00'   USE A BINARY ZERO PAD
MVCL    R4,R6               MOVE SOURCE TO TARGET
```

Figure 11.72 Using MVCL to move one field value into another.

```
B'1000'    The operands are equal.
B'0100'    The first operand is less than the second.
B'0010'    The first operand is greater than the second.
```

Figure 11.73 Testing the condition code when using the CLCL instruction.

The CLCL instruction compares the two fields in a logical *not* arithmetical manner. As you saw in Chapters 6 and 7, a logical comparison between two packed-decimal fields caused a negative field to have a value *greater* than a positive field. A similar situation can happen with the CLCL instruction since a logical comparison is made.

The CLCL instruction also uses the pad character to expand or lengthen *either* of the shorter fields so that both fields are the same length. Again, the selection of the pad character is significant in that it can determine the outcome of the comparison. The code in Fig. 11.74 illustrates the use of the CLCL instruction against two small fields. Although the CLCL instruction is most likely used on fields larger than 256 bytes, there's no reason why it can't be used on very small fields as shown.

Since both fields are the same length, the padding character is not a factor that influences the comparison. However, NUM2 is *greater* than NUM1 since the leftmost bit of NUM2 is 1 and the leftmost bit of NUM1 is 0. Again, the compare logical instructions are not good choices to compare data arithmetically.

```
         LA    R4,NUM1             POINT TO FIRST FIELD
         LA    R5,L'NUM1           OBTAIN LENGTH OF FIRST FIELD
         LA    R2,NUM2             ADDRESS THE SECOND FIELD
         LA    R3,L'NUM2           OBTAIN SECOND FIELD LENGTH
         ICM   R3,B'1000',HEX00    SET PAD CHARACTER
         CLCL  R4,R2               COMPARE THE FIELDS
         BE    EQUAL               BRANCH APPROPRIATELY
         BL    LESSTHAN
         B     GREATER

         .     .
         .     .
         .     .

NUM1     DC    F'100'
NUM2     DC    F'-100'
HEX00    DC    X'00'
```

Figure 11.74 Comparing fields with the CLCL instruction.

AND, OR, AND EXCLUSIVE OR PROCESSING

Earlier, we discussed the EX (execute) instruction that performed an ORing operation on the second byte of an instruction. ORing is just one of three bit-oriented operations used on IBM computer systems to process data. The operations are AND, OR, and EXCLUSIVE OR, and they are performed between registers, between a register and a storage area, between a single byte in storage and an immediate byte within the instruction, or between two storage areas.

Using RR, RX, SI, or SS instructions, the programmer issues instructions to perform the bit-processing requests. In most cases, bit data are used as flags to indicate whether or not a condition has occurred. Further, the outcome of an event is tested using the test-under-mask instruction discussed in Chapter 9. Since we already know how to use the TM instruction, we can immediately begin our study of the bit-processing techniques.

Instructions to perform ORing between data areas consist of the **OR (OR register), OI (OR immediate), O (OR),** and **OC (OR character)** instructions. The OR instructions primarily turn bits "on" within a byte of storage. If you recall our discussion earlier, any bit with a value of 1 OR'd with any other bit produces a bit with a value of 1. Figure 11.75 reviews these relationships.

```
0 OR 0 = 0
1 OR 0 = 1
0 OR 1 = 1
1 OR 1 = 1
```

Figure 11.75 Results of bit ORing.

If R3 contains the value 1 and R4 contains the value 2, then ORing R3 with R4 using the OR instruction yields a value of 3 in register 3 as shown in Fig. 11.76.

```
                   OR       R3,R4

          R3    00000000 00000000 00000000 00000001
          R4    00000000 00000000 00000000 00000010
-----------------------------------------------------
Result in R3    00000000 00000000 00000000 00000011
```

Figure 11.76 ORing two general-purpose registers.

A single byte of storage may hold eight different flags. The logic in Fig. 11.77 sets the fourth bit of the storage area to 1 as a result of using the OI instruction.

```
            OI      BYTE,B'00010000'

BYTE        DC      X'00'
```

Figure 11.77 Turning "on" the fourth bit of a byte.

The TM instruction tests the fourth bit of BYTE as illustrated in Fig. 11.78.

```
TM      BYTE,B'00010000'
BO      ITSONE
```

Figure 11.78 Using TM to test the fourth bit of a byte.

As you recall, the OI instruction was often used when performing packed-decimal conversion to fix the rightmost byte of a zoned-decimal number. Since the UNPK instruction does not provide a correctly formatted number, OI is used to provide this result.

OC may be used to OR data between two different storage areas. Since OC is an SS instruction, a length operand is coded when it is used. Figure 11.79 illustrates use of this instruction.

```
         OC    A(3),B

A        DC    C'ABC'
B        DC    C'3210'
```

Figure 11.79 ORing two character fields with OC.

Although A is smaller than B, only the first three bytes of B are used in the ORing process since the length operand for the instruction specifies a value of 3. Field A is changed as shown in Fig. 11.80. As you can see, A is changed based on the location of bits with a value of 1 within A and B.

```
A before OC    11000001   11000010   11000011   C'ABC'
B before OC    11110011   11110010   11110001   C'321'
-----------------------------------------------------
A after OC     11110011   11110010   11110011   C'323'
B is not changed
```

Figure 11.80 Result of ORing two character fields.

ANDing turns bits "off" or reverses the ORing operation. As is the case with OR, ANDing is performed between registers using the **NR (AND register)** instruction, between one byte of storage and an immediate byte of data by using the **NI (AND immediate)** instruction, between a register and a storage area using the **N (AND)** instruction, and between two storage areas using the **NC (AND character)** instruction.

ANDing yields a value of 1 only if *both* bits are 1. Figure 11.81 illustrates the ANDing operation.

```
0 AND 0 = 0
0 AND 1 = 0
1 AND 0 = 0
1 AND 1 = 1
```

Figure 11.81 Results of ANDing bit values.

Most often, ANDing turns flags "off" or adjusts addresses so that they are on fullword, doubleword, or some other boundary address. Let's look at examples of this processing.

Consider the field called BYTE whose fourth bit was turned "on" earlier with the OI instruction. If we now decide to turn "off" this bit, we can AND against the field called BYTE. However, we don't want to impact the value of any other bits in the area and so we must AND the other bits against a value of 1. Figure 11.82 shows how this is accomplished.

```
NI      BYTE,B'11101111'
```

Figure 11.82 Turning "off" the fourth bit of a byte using AND.

All bits but the fourth bit are 1 so that the remaining bits do not change their values. Since the fourth bit in our immediate data byte is 0, then the fourth bit in the area called BYTE is set to 0 (anything ANDed with 0 is 0).

ANDing may also be used to adjust addresses so that they provide proper alignment when accessing data areas. Consider, for example, the XDUMP instruction used in ASSIST to dump storage areas. This instruction dumps areas on 32-byte boundaries, which causes a slight problem in reading the XDUMP output since more output (than desired) is usually produced, and the area to be dumped is not necessarily the first field within the dumped output. If we place our data area on a 32-byte boundary to begin with, we are assured that it would be the first field within the XDUMP output even though more data may be dumped than required.

A field on a 32-byte boundary address contains zeros in the rightmost five bits of the address. An address of X'000020' (0000 0000 0000 0000 001**0 0000**) is aligned on a 32-byte boundary, but the address X'000030' is not (0000 0000 0000 0000 001**1 0000**) since not all of the rightmost five bits are zero.

To alter an address so that it is on a proper boundary, use the N or NR instructions. Examples of performing this ANDing operation are shown in Figs. 11.83 and 11.84.

```
         N        Rx,BYTE32            ALIGN ON 32-BYTE BOUNDARY

BYTE32   DS       0F
         DC       X'FFFFFF'
         DC       B'11100000'
```

Figure 11.83 ANDing addresses to force alignment.

```
         L        Ry,BYTE32            PLACE PROPER BITS INTO Ry
         NR       Rx,Ry                ALIGN ON 32-BYTE BOUNDARY
```

Figure 11.84 Alternate method to Fig. 11.83.

Again, the ANDing process is most often used to turn individual bits "off" within a byte. Although it can align addresses in the manner illustrated, this is not its common use. You'll see other examples of the ANDing process later in this chapter when other forms of the move instruction are discussed.

Exclusive ORing is another bit-processing facility that interchanges two values or alters a value to binary zeros. Again, the four primary exclusive OR instructions are **X (exclusive OR), XR (exclusive OR register), XI (exclusive OR immediate),** and **XC (exclusive OR character).** The process of exclusive ORing is illustrated in Fig. 11.85.

```
0 exclusive OR 0 = 0
0 exclusive OR 1 = 1
1 exclusive OR 0 = 1
1 exclusive OR 1 = 0
```

Figure 11.85 Exclusive ORing bit values.

As you can see, the result of exclusive ORing two bits is 1 only if both bits are of different values. Consider the bytes of storage in Fig. 11.86 and the result of exclusive ORing these areas against each other.

```
A        DC       B'01010101'
B        DC       B'01100110'

         XC       A(1),B

A = B'00110011'   ← result
```

Figure 11.86 Example of exclusive ORing.

Now suppose that A and B are exclusive OR'd several times. Figure 11.87 shows the value of each field before and after each exclusive OR instruction. Altered values are in boldface.

As you can see, A and B have swapped original values. Although this may not seem impressive, it is a very valuable technique when performing sorting operations. For example, a bubble sort interchanges elements to place them in sorted order. To perform this interchanging operation, a "work area" is generally used to hold one value temporarily, allowing the values to be interchanged. For example, to interchange the values of A and B, we normally code the logic shown in Fig. 11.88.

instruction	value of A before	value of A after	value of B before	value of B after
	01010101		01100110	
XC A(1),B				
		00110011		01100110
	00110011		01100110	
XC B(1),A				
		00110011		01010101
	00110011		01010101	
XC A(1),B				
		01100110		01010101

Figure 11.87 Performing the exclusive OR operation three times on two fields to interchange their values.

```
Move A to a field called HOLD.
Move B into A, replacing the old value of A.
Move HOLD into B, replacing the old value of B.
```

Figure 11.88 Standard logic contained in the interchange or bubble sort.

This process interchanges the values, but requires a third element, HOLD (a work area), to act as a holding area for one element value. With exclusive OR, this third element does *not* have to be introduced since the two areas may be interchanged through a series of three exclusive OR instructions.

Exclusive OR is a valuable technique to interchange the values between two registers. As we just discussed, the XC instruction can swap two storage values. In a similar manner, XR can interchange two register values. For example, registers 6 and 7 are interchanged through the instruction sequence shown in Fig. 11.89.

```
XR       R6,R7
XR       R7,R6
XR       R6,R7
```

Figure 11.89 Interchanging two register values using XR.

Exclusive OR is also commonly used to set a storage area to binary zeros. Consider a storage area that is exclusive OR'd *with itself* as shown in Fig. 11.90.

```
                 01010101
exclusive OR     01010101
                 --------
                 00000000
```

Figure 11.90 Exclusive ORing a value with itself.

Any field that is exclusive OR'd with itself is changed to binary zeros. Therefore, a register can be cleared or initialized to zero by issuing the instruction shown in Fig. 11.91.

```
XR    Rx,Rx
```

Figure 11.91 Initializing a register to zero using XR.

A fullword storage area called **I** may be set to binary zeros by issuing the instruction given in Fig. 11.92.

```
XC    I(4),I
```

Figure 11.92 Initializing a field to binary zeros using XC.

ALTERNATE MOVE INSTRUCTIONS—MVO, MVN, AND MVZ

Before the IBM 370 computer systems arrived, the shift and round packed (SRP) instruction was not available. As you can imagine, shifting packed-decimal fields was a little more difficult and the process of rounding values while shifting was even more complex. Although the process may seem difficult, several instructions to provide this facility did exist if they were used in the proper sequence and manner. First, the multiply and divide packed-decimal instructions could be used to multiply or divide by powers of 10. This provided the shifting capability, but it had the disadvantage (when dividing) of splitting fields into their quotient and remainder. To avoid this problem, a programmer could use the the **MVO (move with offset)** instruction, **MVN (move numerics)** instruction, and the **MVZ (move zones)** instruction. Since the primary purpose of these instructions is to process (by shifting) packed-decimal fields, we'll discuss their use in this respect. In particular, we'll process eight-byte packed-decimal fields, which have been common in our discussions throughout the text when considering packed-decimal fields.

The MVZ and MVN instructions are quite simple in their operation since they move the zone and numeric portions of a packed-decimal field, respectively. Suppose that an eight-byte packed-decimal field called NUM1 has a value of +12345. This field is represented in hexadecimal as shown in Fig. 11.93.

```
X'0 0 0 0 0 0 0 0 0 0 1 2 3 4 5 C'
```

Figure 11.93 Hexadecimal representation of the packed-decimal value +12345.

Fifteen digit positions and one sign position fill the eight-byte field area. In this case, the number is positive and so the sign is assumed to be C. Using italics in Fig. 11.94, let's indicate which halves of the bytes within this field are the zone and numerics (digit) portions.

```
zone portion        X'000000000012345C'
 (left half)

numerics portion    X'000000000012345C'
 (right half)
```

Figure 11.94 Analysis of the field contents of Fig. 11.93.

To illustrate the MVN and MVZ instructions, suppose that another eight-byte field called HEXFA has the value shown in Fig. 11.95.

```
X'F A F A F A F A F A F A F A F A'
```

Figure 11.95 Contents of a field to be used in later examples.

Using these two fields, let's issue the MVZ and MVN instructions to show the two move instructions moving their respective half bytes between the fields. Figures 11.96 and 11.97 illustrate the results of these moving operations.

```
              MVZ    NUM1(8),HEXFA

NUM1 becomes X'F 0 F 0 F 0 F 0 F 0 F 2 F 4 F C'
```

Figure 11.96 Using the MVZ instruction.

```
              MVN    NUM1(8),HEXFA

NUM1 becomes X'0 A 0 A 0 A 0 A 0 A 1 A 3 A 5 A'
```

Figure 11.97 Using the MVN instruction.

In Fig. 11.96, the zone portions of the HEXFA field are moved to the zone portions of the NUM1 field. Figure 11.97 illustrates the MVN instruction, which moves the digit portions of the HEXFA fields over to the digit portions of the NUM1 field. The relevance of these instructions may not be immediate until we discuss their use with respect to the MVO instruction.

The move offset instruction moves all half bytes in one field in a diagonal manner into another field. From the MVO instruction in Fig. 11.98, we see that moving field X'00123C' into X'00567D' changes the second field to X'0123CD'.

```
                 MVO    FIELD2(3),FIELD1(3)

        FIELD1   DC     X'00123C'
        FIELD2   DC     X'00567D'

  0 0 5 6 7 D      becomes     0 1 2 3 C D
```

Figure 11.98 Using the MVO instruction.

Since both fields are the same length, you can see how FIELD 1 is offset (shifted) by a *half byte* during the moving operation. Although this illustrates how the instruction works, it doesn't provide an adequate perspective of how to use it for day-to-day processing. For this reason, we'll present several examples using the MVO, MVN, and MVZ instructions that may be helpful when processing packed-decimal fields. Again, these instructions, when combined with some of the other advanced instructions that we've studied, simply replace the SRP instruction. Obviously, it's much easier to use the SRP instruction rather than using the several instructions that follow to accomplish the same function. Further, the instructions in Figs. 11.99 through 11.106 do not give examples of incorporating rounding into our decimal shifting operations; I'll leave that task to you. However, if you do not have an IBM 370 computer system, you'll have to learn how to use these instructions to shift your packed-decimal fields appropriately. In Figs. 11.99 through 11.106, assume that NUM1 contains the eight-byte packed-decimal number +12345 to be processed and that NUM2 holds the result after processing.

```
MVC    NUM2+7(1),NUM1+7       MOVE IN THE SIGN OF THE NUMBER
MVO    NUM2(8),NUM1(8)        SHIFT LEFT ONE POSITION
NI     NUM2+7,X'0F'           FIX LAST BYTE TO BE ZERO/SIGN

X'000000000012345C'     will become     X'000000000123450C'
```

Figure 11.99 Shifting one packed-decimal digit to the left (multiplying by 10).

```
MVC    NUM2+7(1),NUM1+7       MOVE IN THE SIGN OF THE NUMBER
MVO    NUM2(7),NUM1(8)        SHIFT LEFT 3 POSITIONS
NC     NUM2+6(2),=X'000F'     CHANGE LAST DIGITS TO ZERO

X'000000000012345C'     will become     X'000000012345000C'
```

Figure 11.100 Shifting three packed-decimal digits to the left (multiplying by 1,000).

```
ZAP    NUM2(8),NUM1(8)        OBTAIN THE NUMBER
MVC    NUM2(7),NUM2+1         MOVE LEFT ONE FULL BYTE
NC     NUM2+6(2),=X'F00F'     CHANGE LAST 2 DIGITS TO 0

X'000000000012345C'     will become     X'000000001234500C'
```

Figure 11.101 Shifting two packed-decimal digits to the left (multiplying by 100).

```
ZAP    NUM2(8),NUM1(8)        OBTAIN THE NUMBER
MVC    NUM2(6),NUM2+2         MOVE LEFT TWO FULL BYTES
NC     NUM2+5(3),=X'F0000F'   CHANGE LAST 4 DIGITS TO 0

X'000000000012345C'     will become     X'000000123450000C'
```

Figure 11.102 Shifting four packed-decimal digits to the left (multiplying by 10,000).

```
MVC    NUM2+7(1),NUM1+7       OBTAIN THE LAST DIGIT AND SIGN
MVO    NUM2(8),NUM1(7)        SHIFT ALL BYTES BUT LAST ONE DIGIT

X'000000000012345C'     will become     X'000000000001234C'
```

Figure 11.103 Shifting one packed-decimal digit to the right (dividing by 10).

```
         MVC    NUM2+7(1),NUM1+7       OBTAIN THE LAST DIGIT AND SIGN
         MVO    NUM2(8),NUM1(6)        MOVE ALL BUT LAST 3 DIGITS

X'000000000012345C'      will become    X'00000000000012C'
```

Figure 11.104 Shifting three packed-decimal digits to the right (dividing by 1,000).

```
         MVC    NUM2+1(7),NUM1         OBTAIN ALL BUT THE RIGHT BYTE
         NI     NUM2+7,X'F0'           ELIMINATE THE SIGN
         MVN    NUM2+7(1),NUM1+7       OBTAIN THE SIGN OF THE NUMBER

X'000000000012345C'      will become    X'00000000000123C'
```

Figure 11.105 Shifting two packed-decimal digits to the right (dividing by 100).

```
         MVC    NUM2+2(6),NUM1         OBTAIN ALL BUT RIGHTMOST 2 BYTES
         NI     NUM2+7,X'F0'           ELIMINATE THE SIGN
         MVN    NUM2+7(1),NUM1+7       OBTAIN THE SIGN OF THE NUMBER

X'000000000012345C'      will become    X'000000000000001C'
```

Figure 11.106 Shifting four packed-decimal digits to the right (dividing by 10,000).

From these examples, notice that different techniques are used to shift an even number of digits as compared to an odd number. Also notice that the sign of the number is preserved in different ways that may involve using the AND or MVN instructions to supply the sign. Work through each of these examples yourself and implement them in ASSIST. By placing XDUMP statements between each instruction, you can monitor the changes in the NUM1 field so that you can understand how the shifting takes place.

THE LOGICAL INSTRUCTIONS

In Chapter 6, we used the CLC instruction to compare two storage areas and in this chapter we studied the CLCL instruction. We noted that these instructions did not consider the arithmetic value of a data element during the compare and could yield a result indicating that a negative number has a larger value than a positive number. With this in mind, we now study another set of logical instructions to add, subtract, or compare data between two registers or between a register and a storage area. The instructions are listed in Fig. 11.107.

The two comparison instructions operate in the same manner as the CLC and CLCL instructions except that the comparison is made between two registers or between a register and a storage area. Since the manner of comparison is identical, refer to the discussion in Chapter 6 or earlier in this chapter for details.

A logical addition occurs by adding each bit within the fields *without regard to the sign of the number.* A program exception does not occur if an overflow condition results during addition. Any bits carried *beyond* the register are simply lost. Let's illustrate the process of logical addition using Fig. 11.108.

The last example in Fig. 11.108 adds two *negative* numbers, which normally yields a negative result. But the result is a positive number. Again, logical addition has no regard for sign or for overflow bits. The examples in Fig. 11.109 further illustrate this situation using 32-bit values to perform addition.

CL (compare logical)	logically compare a value in a register to a value in storage
CLR (compare logical register)	logical compare the values in two registers
AL (add logical)	logically add a value in storage to a value in a register
ALR (add logical register)	logically add two registers together
SL (subtract logical)	logically subtract a value in storage from a value in a register
SLR (subtract logical register)	logically subtract a value in one register from a value in another register

Figure 11.107 The compare, add, and subtract logical instructions.

```
    0 0 0 1
+   0 1 1 0
   ---------
    0 1 1 1     (positive)

    0 0 0 1
+   0 1 1 1
   ---------
    1 0 0 0     (negative)

    0 1 1 1
+   0 1 1 1
   ---------
    1 1 1 0     (negative)

    1 0 1 1
+   1 0 1 1
   ---------
  1 0 1 1 0     (positive, lost bit)
```

Figure 11.108 Examples of logical addition.

```
  7     00000000 00000000 00000000 00000111
  5     00000000 00000000 00000000 00000101
----   -------------------------------------
 12     00000000 00000000 00000000 00001100


 -7     11111111 11111111 11111111 11111001
 -5     11111111 11111111 11111111 11111011
----   -------------------------------------
-12    111111111 11111111 11111111 11110100   (bit lost)


 -7     11111111 11111111 11111111 11111001
  5     00000000 00000000 00000000 00000101
----   -------------------------------------
 -2    111111111 11111111 11111111 11111110   (bit lost)


  7     00000000 00000000 00000000 00000111
 -5     11111111 11111111 11111111 11111011
----   -------------------------------------
  2    100000000 00000000 00000000 00000010   (bit lost)
```

Figure 11.109 Examples of 32-bit logical addition.

As you can see, the operations proceed normally. Further, the condition code may be used to determine if a carry occurred by testing the condition code values B'0010' or B'0001' (both indicate a carry).

Logical subtraction is performed by adding the complement of the second number to the first. Therefore, if B is to be subtracted from A, then −B is added to A to give the result. The condition code is also used in subtraction to determine if a carry occurred during the "addition." To illustrate, let's assume that 5 is to be subtracted from 7. To perform this subtraction, using either the SL or SLR instructions, the complement of 5, −5, is added to 7 as shown in Fig. 11.110.

```
     7   00000000 00000000 00000000 00000111
  + -5   11111111 11111111 11111111 11111011
  ------------------------------------------
     2   00000000 00000000 00000000 00000010
```

Figure 11.110 Logical subtraction.

The logical instructions are used primarily for integer processing. They are slightly faster than their arithmetic counterparts since sign management is not performed by the instructions. The logical instructions may also be used to process 64-bit binary numbers. Although values of this size are more easily processed using the packed-decimal or floating point formats, processing values of this size can be done. Consider an operation in which the resulting value now spans two registers. Normal addition or subtraction instructions can only operate on values contained in a single register. However, the logical instructions can be used to process values spanning both registers thus supporting 64-bit processing. For example, suppose that a 64-bit addition is to be performed. By adding logically to the "right" register, the program can determine if any carry should occur into the "left" by evaluating the condition code after the addition. If the condition code is B'0010' or B'0001', the program should then add an additional value of 1 to the "left" register since a carry occurred. Thus, a 64-bit result will be obtained.

The IBM instruction set also provides a few other instructions to assist in logical or arithmetic processing on binary fullword data. The **LCR (load complement register)** instruction converts the value in one register to its complement and places the result in a register. The **LPR (load positive register)** instruction converts a value in one register to its positive value (absolute value) and places it into a register. And finally, the **LNR (load negative register)** instruction converts a value in a register to its negative value and places it into a register. Incidentally, the source register (second operand) can also be specified as the target register (first operand) since each of these instructions is an RR instruction. Since the instructions are RR instructions and their functions are straightforward, they should be easy to understand by referring to Figure 11.111.

THE SHIFT INSTRUCTIONS

Earlier in this chapter, we discussed the shifting of packed-decimal fields to the left and right, which allowed us to easily multiply or divide a number by a power of 10. A similar procedure exists for processing binary data, thus allowing us to multiply or divide by a power of 2.

The instructions that perform this processing operate on single register values or double register values (even/odd pairs). Hence, we may shift fullword or doubleword values in either a right direction (divide by a power of 2) or left direction (multiply by a power of 2). Consider the number and shifting process as illustrated in Fig. 11.112.

```
LCR     Rx,Ry          Copy the complement value of Ry into Rx.

LNR     Rx,Ry          Copy the two's complement of the value in
                       Ry into Rx.   If the value in Ry is
                       already negative, the value is copied
                       directly. The resulting value in Rx is a
                       negative number.

LPR     Rx,Ry          The absolute value of the contents of Ry
                       are copied into Rx.  The resulting value
                       in Rx is a positive number.
```

```
L       R2,=F'17'      PLACE POSITIVE 17 INTO R2
L       R3,=F'-17'     PLACE NEGATIVE 17 INTO R3

LPR     R4,R2          R4 WILL CONTAIN POSITIVE 17
LPR     R5,R3          R5 WILL CONTAIN POSITIVE 17

LNR     R6,R2          R6 WILL CONTAIN NEGATIVE 17
LNR     R7,R3          R7 WILL CONTAIN NEGATIVE 17

LCR     R8,R2          R8 WILL CONTAIN NEGATIVE 17
LCR     R9,R3          R9 WILL CONTAIN POSITIVE 17
```

Figure 11.111 LCR, LNR, and LPR instructions.

result	bit value	decimal value
	0 0 0 0 0 1 1 0	6
shifted left one bit	0 0 0 0 1 1 0 0	12
	0 0 0 0 0 1 1 0	6
shifted right one bit	0 0 0 0 0 0 1 1	3

Figure 11.112 Binary shifting operations.

In Fig. 11.112, the original number 6 is shifted one bit. When shifted to the left by one bit, the number is multiplied by 2 to the first power. Shifting the number to the right by one bit divides it by 2 to the first power. In fact, the number of bit positions shifted is the power value of 2 that is applied to the number. In other words, if the number is shifted three bit positions, then the number is multiplied or divided by 2^3, or 8.

Two types of shifting are performed on either fullword or doubleword register values (even/odd register pairs). **Arithmetic shifting** moves the number in either direction, but recognizes and maintains its sign. In particular, arithmetic shifting is most important when shifting to the right, dividing by a power of 2. As the bits move to the right within the register(s), the sign bit fills vacated bit positions. If the sign bit is 0, then each position vacated is filled with a 0 whereas a sign bit of 1 continues the 1's value into subsequent bit positions. Figures 11.113 and 11.114 illustrate this concept.

Since arithmetic shifting retains the sign bit when shifting to the right, negative numbers remain negative and positive numbers remain positive when divided by a power of 2. However, when dividing by a power of 2 in this manner, remember that this process is an integer form of division. Remainders are not maintained as illustrated in the example given in Fig. 11.115, which divides 7 by 4.

```
0  0  0  0  1  1  1  0

0  0  0  0  0  0  1  1    1  0
                          lost bits
```

shifting right 2 positions causes 2 bits to be lost on the right and two positions on the left to be filled in with 0's

Figure 11.113 Shifting right arithmetically with a positive number.

```
1  1  1  1  1  1  0  1

1  1  1  1  1  1  1  1    0  1
                          lost bits
```

again, shifting right 2 positions causes 2 bits to be lost on the right and two positions on the left to be filled. This time the left bits are filled with 1's since the sign bit was 1.

Figure 11.114 Shifting right arithmetically with a negative number.

```
                      0  0  0  0  0  1  1  1    (7)
shift right two       0  0  0  0  0  0  0  1    (1)
bit positions
```

Figure 11.115 Shifting is an integer form of division as shown by dividing 7 by 4 resulting in 1.

Seven divided by 2 to the second power (4) is 1. Clearly, a substantial loss in accuracy may occur when dividing in this fashion.

When shifting to the left arithmetically, positions on the right are filled with zeros. However, the sign of the number is not changed, that is, only the data bits are shifted. The example in Fig. 11.116 shifts a bit pattern to the left three bit positions.

Logical shifting can also be performed on single or double registers. Logical shifting moves *all* bits in the register including the sign bit, and fills all positions, whether shifting right or left, with zeros. The examples in Figs. 11.117 and 11.118 illustrate logical shifting to the left and right.

Now that you have a general understanding of the shifting process, let's study the instructions used to perform this processing. In all the formats given in Fig. 11.119, the

```
                  1  1  0  0  0  0  0  1

1  0  0           1  0  0  0  1  0  0  0
lost bits                        filled
```

shifting left arithmetically causes zeros to be added on to the right hand side of the number but the sign of the field is retained. Only the data bits are shifted when performing a shift to the left of N bits.

Figure 11.116 Shifting left three bit positions is the same as multiplying by eight.

```
              0  0  1  1  1  0  1  0

0  0          1  1  1  0  1  0  0  0
lost bits                       fill

   in this example, notice that the number was
     originally positive but after shifting,
          it became a negative number!
```

Figure 11.117 Logically shifting left by two positions.

```
0  0  1  1  1  0  1  0

0  0  0  0  1  1  1  0     1  0
fill                      lost bits

shifting right does not retain the sign of the
 number since all vacated positions are filled
 with zeros.  The resulting number will always
   be positive!  Bits shifted off are lost.
```

Figure 11.118 Logically shifting right by two positions.

```
SRL     R,n            shift right logical
                       shift the contents of the register
                       to the right N logical positions

SRA     R,n            shift right arithmetic
                       shift right arithmetic N bit
                       positions

SRDL    Re/o,n         shift right double logical
                       shift the even/odd register pair
                       to the right logically, N positions

SRDA    Re/o,n         shift right double arithmetic
                       shift the even/odd pair to the
                       right N positions arithmetically

SLL     R,n            shift left logical
                       shift left logical N positions

SLA     R,n            shift left arithmetic
                       shift left arithmetically N
                       bit positions

SLDL    Re/o,n         shift left double logical
                       shift the even/odd pair to the
                       left N positions logically

SLDA    Re/o,n         shift left double arithmetic
                       shift the even/odd pair to the
                       left N positions arithmetically
```

Figure 11.119 The shift instructions.

second operand is actually a D(B) address. However, it is generally coded to represent the number of bit positions which the first operand is to be shifted.

The primary use of the shifting instructions is to multiply or divide by a power of 2. Using these facilities, the programmer can perform some rather sophisticated processing. One use is to establish a **branch table** to control program flow during processing. For example, suppose that input data contains an employee name, address, hourly wage, hours worked, and tax rate code. After computing an employee's earnings for the week, the program now computes the taxes based on the value of the tax rate code. This is most likely done by branching to a routine based on the value of the tax code. If the input data has many tax codes, the logic to determine which tax code applies to this employee can be quite extensive. However, if the tax rate codes have consecutive values such as 0, 1, 2, 3, and 4, we can construct a branch table and use the shift instructions to transfer control to the various routines. Assuming that the field TAXCODE is a halfword binary number holding the tax code value, the logic presented in Fig. 11.120 transfers control to the appropriate routine to compute the employee's taxes.

```
         LH    R3,TAXCODE          OBTAIN THE TAX CODE VALUE
         SLL   R3,2                MULTIPLY BY 4
         L     R3,BRTAB(R3)        OBTAIN THE ADDRESS OF TAX ROUTINE
         BR    R3                  BRANCH TO THE TAX ROUTINE
BRTAB    DC    A(NOTAXES)
         DC    A(T3PERCNT)
         DC    A(T5PERCNT)
         DC    A(T7PERCNT)
         DC    A(T9PERCNT)
```

Figure 11.120 Implementing a logical branch table.

The value of the tax code, when multiplied by 4 becomes 0, 4, 8, 12, or 16. This value is then used as a displacement into a list of addresses. If the tax code value is 2, then a displacement of 8 from the beginning of the table called BRTAB obtains the address of the routine called T5PERCNT. Since this is the third address in the table, it's the correct address associated with this employee's tax code. Once the address of the routine is determined, we branch to the routine to perform the desired processing using the BR instruction.

This logic reduces the coding normally required to compare each tax code value to determine which routine should be given control. However, this form of processing can only be used if the tax code values (or other values used in this manner) are relatively consistent. Incidentally, this code could have been presented earlier without using the shifting instructions. Because of the rather advanced logic involved, it is more appropriately presented in a chapter on advanced topics.

STUDY QUESTIONS

1. What is the result of ANDing B'01101111' with B'00101010'?
2. Register 4 contains a binary integer value. Write an instruction to place the complement of R4's value into R3.
3. Two registers are to be compared arithmetically. Which instruction(s) can be used to compare them?
4. A large storage area called BUFFER is to be moved into an area called INPUTREC. Both areas are 2500 bytes long. Write the code, using MVCL, to perform this move.
5. The third byte of R8 (from the left) is to be modified with the single byte of data addressed by register 9. Perform this modifying process.

6. Register 3 contains a carriage control character in the leftmost byte of the register. Without using the STCM instruction, store this character into the first byte of the area called PRNTLINE.
7. An array called POWERS is defined to hold 31 fullword values. Each value is the corresponding value of 2 raised to the position in the table. Write a section of code to fill each of the 31 positions. Process the array using subscript notation.
8. Construct a table to be used with TRT to scan a data area, stopping at all end-of-sentence punctuation characters.
9. The following elements are defined in a program. What will the value of X be after assembly? What type of element is X called?

```
STUDENTS    DS    0CL28
NAME        DS    CL20
SSN         DS    PL5
SCORE       DS    PL3
X           EQU   SSN-NAME
```

10. Using the binary data definition element and the length modifier, define a series of bits within the byte called FLAGS that can be tested to determine if an employee belongs to the Christmas club, the retirement foundation, the credit union, the insurance program, or the bowling league.
11. Can R14 be used as a base register for your program? Explain.
12. Give four examples in which a value of zero may be placed into a register.
13. Give two examples in which control may be transferred to the routine called MINUS if the value in register 3 is negative.
14. An unknown amount of input data is to be translated from upper/lower case letters to all upper case letters. Which instructions would you most likely use to perform this conversion?
15. If an area consisting of hexadecimal digits is unpacked and its resulting value is X'FAFBFCFDFEFF', how might this area be converted into printable characters?

PROGRAMMING PROBLEMS

1. Write a subroutine that produces a hexadecimal dump of a storage area when given the length of the area and the address of the area to be dumped. Assume that both parameters are stored in fullwords within the calling program.
2. Write a subroutine that performs a bubble sort on a single-dimensional array of elements. Given the number of elements in the array, the size of each element, and the address of the array, the routine places the elements in ascending order based on the element values. This routine must use the EX instruction to compare the elements and use exclusive-OR instructions to interchange their values if a swap between two array positions is to occur.
3. Write a macro and a corresponding subroutine to perform the same function as the ASSIST XDECI macro.
4. Write a macro and a corresponding subroutine to perform the same function as the ASSIST XDECO macro.

5. Write a program to produce a student grade report for the semester. Given input data consisting of a student's name and 10 scores, compute the average score and the semester grade for each student. Print two reports for the class: the first report is an alphabetical listing by the student's name and the second report is ordered by the semester average score. Both reports are to follow acceptable report formatting standards as discussed in an earlier chapter.
6. From problems in an earlier chapter, Mr. Smith owns an automobile used car sales business. Using the application, write a program that inputs information on the autos in Mr. Smith's inventory and produces a report ordered by the make of vehicle.
7. Write a program that reads a series of numbers and places them in the order read. In other words, the program uses a technique for sorting called **insertion sorting.** This means that a single array is used. For each input value, the program scans the array and "inserts" the value into its proper position within the array. When all values are processed, print the contents of the array.
8. Using Programming Problem 7 as a reference, assume that each input value is not located in a fixed position on the input data card. In other words, each input value is coded in a "free format" within the input records. Hence, write a routine that scans the input record for the value, determines the length of the input value, and uses the EX instruction to pack the value so that it can be placed in its proper order.
9. A paragraph from a book has been typed onto data cards. However, the shift key was broken on the terminal when the data was entered and so all data is entered in lower case letters. Write a program to read the text and capitalize it appropriately. Hint: analyze the text for punctuation and capitalize each letter that begins a sentence.
10. Develop a program that inputs integer values from data cards. For each input value, convert the value into a fullword binary format. Count the number of 1 bits in each binary number and print the original number and the number of 0 and 1 bits within this number. For example, the input value 25 is represented in binary as B'00000000000000000000000000011001'. In this number there are three 1 bits and twenty-nine 0 bits. Your program determines the number of 0 and 1 bits by analyzing the contents of the resulting fullword value.
11. Write a program that plays a game of tic-tac-toe with itself. To perform this processing, the program reads a single input value of either 0 or 1. This determines which piece will move first. Using a subroutine, the program makes the next move for the player. Clearly, the subroutine makes moves for both players and must be told which piece is to move next. As each move is performed, the program is to print the 3×3 array of the game board. Finally, the program is to analyze the status of the game and determine if anyone has won or if the game is a draw.
12. Write a program that prints a graph of the function $F(x) = x^2 + 3x + 2$. The program is to compute values for both x and F(x) and then "map" each of these coordinates into a graphic array. Plot 25 values and then print the graph.
13. Develop a program that multiplies matrices of various sizes. Each matrix is typed on data cards and is preceded by a card that contains the size of the matrix. In other words, the first data card contains the size of the first matrix and is followed by each row of the matrix. The values for each row are contained on a single data card. Following the last row, another matrix is defined again beginning with the data card that defines its size. Perform matrix multiplication on each pair of matrices after first determining if the matrices can, in fact, be multiplied.
14. Write a program that prints customer mailing labels in an "X-UP" format. Let me explain. Suppose that customer data contains the person's name, address, city, state, and zip code. Given this information, the program prints one, two, or three sets of labels for each person. If one set of labels is printed, then we say that the labels are printed in a "1-up" format. If three sets of labels are printed, then the format is "3-up." The greater the "up" value, the more copies of the label that are printed across the page. Assuming that each label occupies five lines—one blank line, the name line, the address line, the city-state-zip line, and another blank line—3-up labels print three copies of each label across the page. Understand that the labels are not printed three times from top to bottom on the page, but they are printed *across* the page. Hence, the person's name will be printed one, two, or three times *on the same line,* depending on the value of the "up" parameter.

The first input record to the program indicates the "up" parameter and the order of the labels. If the labels are to be ordered by zip code and are to be printed in a 2-up format, then the first control card contains the values 2 and 5. The value 2 indicates the "up" value and the value 5 specifies the field number on which to sort. A field number of 0 indicates that the labels are to be printed in their input order. Field numbers greater than 5 result in an error as determined by the program.

If you're implementing the program in standard assembly language, use the JCL EXEC statement parameter to supply the control values to the program.

15. Develop a program which prints a horizontal bar chart to represent sales in each of the months reported within the input data. Input data consists of the month name, the number of sales, and the total dollar value of sales during that month. Use either of the last two fields to formulate the bar chart and use the execute (EX) instruction to produce the lines within the chart. The example below illustrates total unit sales for the first 5 months of the year.

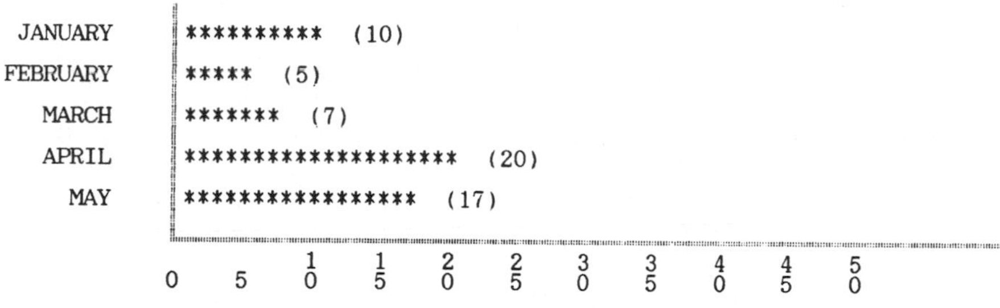

12

Floating-Point Processing

Numeric data is usually processed with binary or packed-decimal instructions. However, when extreme accuracy is required, when a result will consist of many digits to the left and right of the decimal point, or when you desire automatic decimal point handling, floating-point data and instructions should be used to process your data.

Floating-point processing provides for over 28 digits in our results, which is quite a large number and will definitely support most processing needs. In a business environment, far fewer digits are normally required for most applications. As a result, floating-point processing is normally used in scientific or experimental environments where very precise results are required.

Floating-point processing has the advantage of providing many significant digits, but it also has many glaring disadvantages. The primary disadvantage is that it's difficult to understand since the representation of a fractional number is in base-16 notation. If you were analyzing an abend dump of a program and encountered a floating-point number, you would not immediately know its value as you would with a packed-decimal number. Further, it is very difficult to convert from human readable format into floating-point format (and vice versa) to perform your processing. Since there are no instructions, such as PACK, UNPK, CVB, CVD, ED, or EDMK, to easily convert values to or from floating-point format, the conversion process is difficult and is one of the main reasons why floating-point processing is not more widely used. As you'll see later, our conversion process is simplified through the use of two macros. A macro called FLOATIN converts from character format into floating-point format and FLOATOUT does the reverse. These macros eliminate the need to study the conversion process, thus allowing us to concentrate strictly on the floating-point instructions available. Incidentally, we should note that the use of conversion macros or external subroutines, sometimes developed in higher-level languages, are commonly used to provide the necessary conversion from human readable to floating-point format. Thus, our study will parallel that commonly used in business environments.

INTERNAL REPRESENTATION AND CONVERSIONS

Floating-point values are processed using a special set of registers called the **floating-point registers.** There are four floating-point registers specified by register numbers 0, 2, 4, and 6. Although these numbers are similar to general-purpose register numbers, the machine uses the proper register (floating point or general purpose) depending on the instruction being processed. In other words, if you're using the L (load) instruction, then a general-purpose register is referenced whereas if you're using the LD (load long) instruction, the machine uses a floating-point register for your processing.

A floating-point register is 64 bits long. The leftmost bit in the register is used as the sign bit for the floating-point number. A sign bit value of 0 indicates that the number is positive and a sign bit of 1 indicates that it is negative. Although the floating-point number itself is represented in base-16 notation, negative numbers are *not* represented in two's complement notation. All floating-point numbers are stored in their positive value format with only the sign bit indicating positive or negative.

Three sizes of floating-point numbers are available with the floating-point instructions and the floating-point registers. The size of the floating-point number is directly related to the number of significant digits maintained during processing. A 32-bit (fullword) floating-point number processes 6-digit values, a 64-bit (doubleword) floating-point number processes 14-digit values, and a 128-bit (16-byte) floating-point number processes 28-digit numbers. Depending on your needs, select and use the appropriate set of instructions to provide the accuracy required.

Since all floating-point values are processed in a floating-point register, you may be confused by the 128-bit sized number since a floating-point register is only 64 bits long. To provide **extended precision,** paired floating-point registers are used. Since there are only four floating-point registers, only two register pairs may be constructed. Registers 0/2 and 4/6 constitute the two register pairs. When using extended precision, specify either register 0 or register 4 to indicate the appropriate pair for your processing.

Floating point numbers are represented in scientific notation and thus consist of an exponent (**characteristic**), fractional component (**mantissa**), and of course the sign bit. The characteristic occupies the second through eighth bits of a floating-point number, thus placing the characteristic just after the sign of the number. Figure 12.1 illustrates the general format of a floating-point number.

sign	characteristic	fractional component
0	1	8

Figure 12.1 General format of a floating-point number.

The characteristic is very similar to the exponent value in scientific notation. For example, the number +123.45 can be represented as a power of 10 in many ways. Figure 12.2 gives us examples of several different representations. Floating-point values, however, are always represented as shown in the *last* format of Fig. 12.2. In other words, all

Scientific Notation	Our Method of Thinking
12345.E-02	12345. times 10 to the -2 power
1234.5E-01	1234.5 times 10 to the -1 power
123.45E+00	123.45 times 10 to the 0 power
12.345E+01	12.345 times 10 to the 1 power
1.2345E+02	1.2345 times 10 to the 2 power
.12345E+03	.12345 times 10 to the 3 power

Figure 12.2 Different representations of +123.45.

values are represented with digits to the *right* of the decimal and the characteristic reflecting the "exponential value" of the number. Keep in mind that this example is related to base-10 notation and powers of 10. Floating-point numbers are represented in base-16 notation with the characteristic represented similarly.

The characteristic represents exponential values in **excess-64 notation.** This means that the "zero" value of the characteristic is 64 (X'40'). As numbers get larger, the value of the characteristic increases whereas smaller values cause the characteristic to approach zero (X'00'). The largest value for the seven-bit characteristic is B'x**1111111**', or 127 (base 10), and the smallest characteristic is the value zero, B'x**0000000**'.

A value of zero is represented using a sign bit of zero, a characteristic of zero, and a fractional component of zero. In other words, the value zero is represented in a format called **true zero** in which each component of the floating-point number is zero.

To further illustrate the representation of a floating-point number, let's consider the number 123 (base 10). The hexadecimal value of 123 is 7B. In the three different floating-point formats, this value is stored as shown in Fig. 12.3.

```
Short form        X'427B0000'
Long form         X'427B000000000000'
Extended form     X'427B0000000000000000000000000000'
```

Figure 12.3 Floating-point representation of the base-10 number +123.

The characteristic, X'42', specifies that both digits, 7 and B, are to the left of the decimal since the current characteristic, X'42', minus the initial characteristic, X'40', yields a value of 2. In other words, the characteristic value X'42' is equal to 66 (base 10). The difference between 66 and 64 is 2, which means that the first two hexadecimal digits of the fractional component are to the *left* of the decimal. Now let's change the value by moving the location of the decimal point (also called the **radix point**) and see how this value changes in representation. The examples shown in Fig. 12.4 are analyzed not only in terms of their characteristic, but also in terms of their sign and fractional component.

Decimal Value	Floating-point Representation
12.3	41C4CCCCCCCCCCCD
-12.3	C1C4CCCCCCCCCCCD
1.23	4113AE147AE147AE
.123	401F7CED916872B0
.0123	3F32617C1BDA511A

Figure 12.4 Decimal values and their floating-point equivalents.

The first byte of a floating-point number contains the sign and characteristic of the number. For the values 12.3 and −12.3, the sign and characteristics are X'41' and X'C1, repectively. The difference between these two bytes is in the leftmost bit, the sign bit. Negative numbers have a sign bit of 1 and positive numbers zero. The characteristic is not impacted by the sign of the floating-point number. In other words, the characteristic for 12.3 and −12.3 is B'1000001', which means that the first digit in the fractional component is to the left of the decimal. Looking closely at both numbers again, 41**C**4CCCCCCCCCCCD or C1**C**4CCCCCCCCCCCD, we see that the first digit in the fractional component is X'C', or 12. Since the characteristic is greater than 64 (X'40'), we know that this value of 12 is to the left of the decimal. Hence, the number above is between 12.0 and 13.0 or between −12.0 and −13.0 if we consider the negative representation of the number.

To further help our understanding of floating-point representation, let's learn a method to convert from base 10 to floating-point format. This method has many similarities to the conversion procedures discussed in Chapter 2. The algorithm that we'll use to convert from base 10 to floating-point is given in Fig. 12.5.

```
1. Split the number into its sign and value components.
2. Separate the values to the left and right of the
   decimal point.
3. Convert the digits to the left of the decimal into
   hexadecimal representation exactly as we did in Chapter 2.
4. Convert the digits to the right of the decimal by repeating
   the following steps depending on the significance to be
   obtained:
   (a) Multiply the remaining digits to the right
       of the decimal by 16. Perform all operations
       using base 10 arithmetic.
   (b) Extract the value to the left of the decimal
       obtained from step 4a. Convert this value to
       hexadecimal representation and concatenate all
       such digits to form the right-half of the number.
5. Concatenate the halves from steps 3 and 4.
6. Form a preliminary sign and characteristic (exponent)
   byte by concatenating a 0-bit (positive number) or
   1-bit (negative number) with an initial exponential
   value of B'100 0000'.
7. Normalize the number and adjust the exponent accordingly.
```

Figure 12.5 Algorithm to convert from base 10 to floating-point.

Let's use the algorithm to convert the number +123.45 to floating point representation. Using a tree structure to illustrate the separation and joining of components, Fig. 12.6 performs the conversion.

Referring to Fig. 12.6, you'll notice that the left and right converted halves are joined, normalized, and signed to construct the floating point number. The digits to the right of the decimal, .45, are multiplied by 16 depending on the number of significant digits that are needed. Since the characteristic occupies 1 byte and the converted value to the left of the decimal occupies 1 byte, only 2 bytes of the remaining short-form number must be derived. Since 4 hexadecimal digits are contained in two bytes, step 4 from our algorithm is performed 4 times.

Now let's convert the base 10 number −.05 to floating point. Fig. 12.7 illustrates the conversion procedure for this number. However, please note that the number is a repeating decimal and so step 4 is not repeated individually for each digit position in the fractional right half.

Referring to Fig. 12.7, you'll notice that each time .80 is multiplied by 16, the resulting value is 12.80. The value to the left of the decimal, 12, is converted to the hexadecimal digit C and becomes part of the converted number. The remaining portion to the

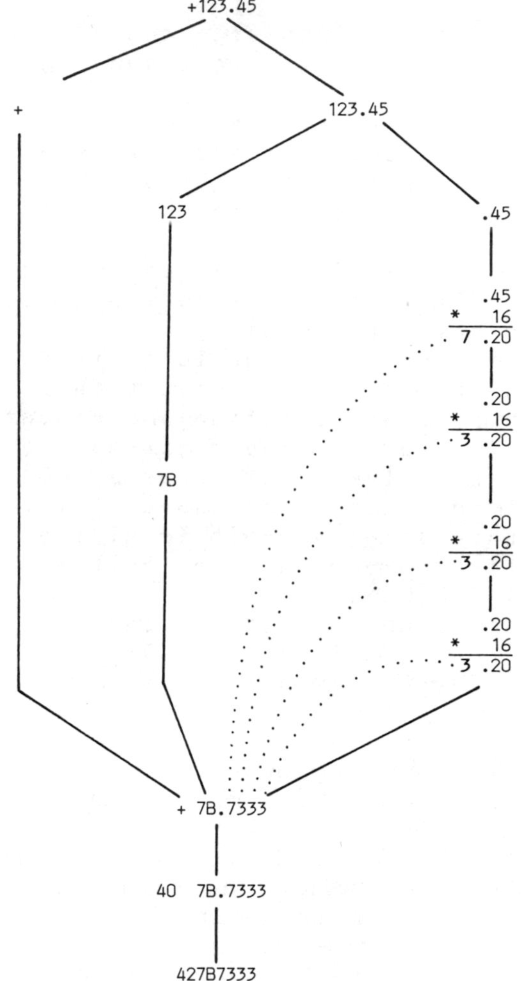

Figure 12.6 Converting +123.45 to floating-point representation.

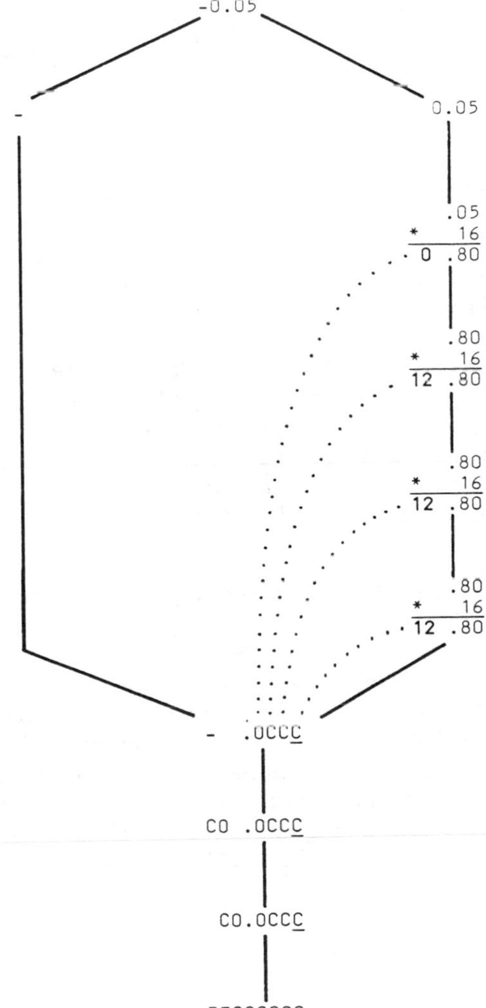

Figure 12.7 Converting −.05 to floating-point representation.

right of the decimal, .80, is used during the next iteration of step 4 described by the conversion algorithm. However, since the conversion process results in a repeating decimal, we can assume that all resulting digits will be C.

Converting from floating-point representation to base 10 is described in the algorithm given in Fig. 12.8.

```
1. Separate the sign from the number.
2. Analyze the characteristic and separate the number
   into the components to the left and right of the
   decimal point. If the characteristic is less than
   X'40', add leading zeros to the number and adjust
   the exponent respectively (by one) until the
   characteristic is equal to X'40'.
3. Convert the value to the left of the decimal using
   the procedure discussed in Chapter 2.
4. Convert the value to the right of the decimal by
   using the following algorithm.
   (a) Set I = 1.
   (b) Set SUM = 0.
   (c) For each digit to be converted:
       1. Divide the digit's base 10 value by
          16^I and add this value to SUM.
       2. Add 1 to I.
5. Concatenate the converted value from step 3 to the
   value of SUM derived from step 4.
6. Place the appropriate sign on the number.
```

Figure 12.8 Algorithm to convert from floating-point to base 10.

Using the algorithm given in Fig. 12.8, let's convert the short-form floating-point number X'41280000' to base 10 representation. Fig. 12.9 converts this value.

Clearly, a calculator can be extremely helpful in the conversion process. However, since most calculators provide less than 10 significant digits, it becomes difficult to derive the powers of 16 beyond a certain point. For that reason we must understand that for long-form or extended-precision floating-point numbers, this process may not provide total accuracy. In fact, since the FLOATIN and FLOATOUT macros utilize a process

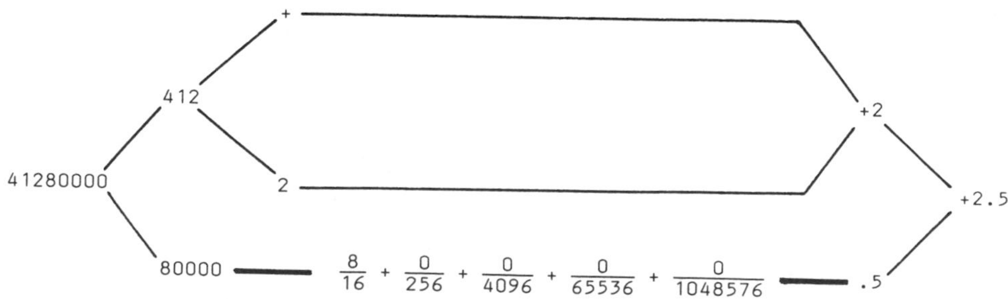

Figure 12.9 Converting a floating-point number to base 10.

similar to that presented, we can easily see why they too are limited to short or long-form floating-point values.

Our final example converts the floating point number X'3F147AE1' to base 10 representation. As you review the conversion of this value in Figure 12.10, please notice that the resulting value is not quite .005 even though +.005 is the derived value. Since short-form numbers do not have a sufficient number of digits to accurately represent certain numbers, a slight error in precision will often result. Thus, we adjust the value of .004999998 to .005 (by rounding) to compensate for this inaccuracy. If we had converted a long-form or extended-precision number, we would find our approximation converging to the value .005. Again, the more significant digits that you retain in your results, the more accurate your processing will be.

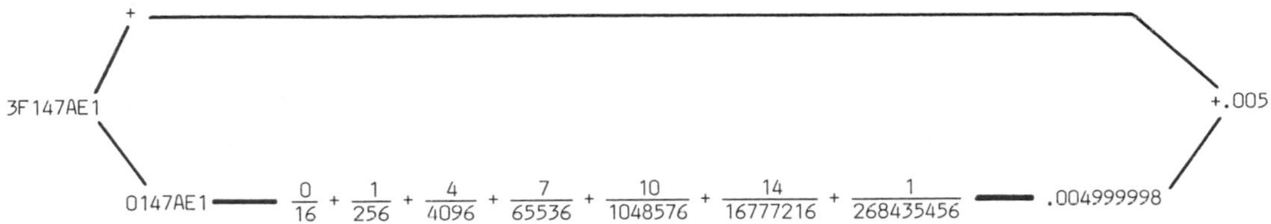

Figure 12.10 Converting a floating-point number to base 10.

DEFINING FLOATING-POINT STORAGE AREAS

To support each of the three floating-point formats, three different data types are defined with the DS or DC instructions. Short-form (32-bit) floating-point numbers are defined using the **E (floating-point short)** storage data type, 64-bit numbers are defined using the **D (floating-point long)** data type, and 128-bit floating-point storage areas are defined using the **L (extended floating-point)** data type. Extended-precision numbers are not supported in ASSIST.

As before, the DS and DC instructions define storage and align floating-point areas. The DC instruction also can initialize a floating-point storage area if needed for your processing. The examples in Fig. 12.11 illustrate coding techniques for defining and initializing floating-point fields. Note that all values specified on the DC instruction to initialize floating-point fields are specified in base-10 notation. The assembler converts these values into proper floating-point form before your program begins execution. Additionally, initialization values may be specified in scientific notation as illustrated in Fig. 12.2 earlier in the chapter. Since both formats are supported by the assembler you'll have to decide which initialization format you'll use to define and initialize your floating-point storage areas.

Another type of floating-point storage area is a literal. Literals are used on any floating-point instruction in which the second operand is a D(B) or D(X,B) address. Incidentally, almost all floating-point instructions that allow processing between a register and storage utilize a D(X,B) address in the second operand. You won't have to be concerned with which address form to use, D(X,B) or D(B), since only one form is used on the floating-point instructions that we will discuss in this chapter.

Floating-point literals are coded using the E, D, and L data types as described in Fig. 12.11. Hence, the value 12.3 is coded as =D'12.3' if used as a long-form floating-point number and the value 1.25 is coded as =E'1.25' if used as a short-form floating-point number.

Instruction	Resulting Storage
DC E'1.2345'	Four-byte (fullword) floating-point storage area initialized to the value 1.2345. Here, a short-form floating point number is defined.
DC D'12.3'	Eight-byte (doubleword) floating-point area initialized to the value 12.3. A long-form number is defined in this example.
DS L	Sixteen-byte floating-point storage area used for extended precision processing. This area is not initialized. In this example, an extended precision storage area is defined.

Figure 12.11 Defining and initializing floating-point data areas.

LOAD AND STORE INSTRUCTIONS

Now that we have storage for floating-point numbers, we can begin to process them. First, we place at least one floating-point value into a floating-point register. All processing is done through register-to-register or register-to-storage instructions.

Values are loaded into registers using the appropriate floating-point load instruction. Remember, there are three different types of floating point formats: short, long, and extended. Therefore, load the values into the registers depending on how they are to be processed and the number of digits in the fractional component that are to be maintained.

Short floating-point numbers are loaded into the left half of a floating-point register using the **LE (load short).** This is somewhat confusing since the instruction ends with the letter E, which might be mistaken for "extended." Do not make this error since your results will be severely impacted if you do.

With the LE instruction, the first operand specifies a floating-point register and the second specifies a D(X,B) address. The value from the memory location specified is copied into the *left half* of the floating-point register. Since the right half of the register is unchanged, the accuracy of your processing can be impacted by the load. Therefore, it's generally good practice to first clear the register by either subtracting it from itself or loading it with true zero before loading the value that you want to process. The instructions in Fig. 12.12 illustrate this technique by placing 45.6 into floating-point register 4.

```
SDR    R4,R4              CLEAR FLOATING-POINT REGISTER 4
LE     R4,=E'45.6'        LOAD THE SHORT VALUE
```

Figure 12.12 Loading a 32-bit value into a register.

In this example, the **SDR (subtract normalized long)** instruction clears floating-point register 4. The load instruction then places the short value 45.6 into the left half of register 4. It is now ready to be processed.

The example in Fig. 12.13 illustrates another technique, using literals, to clear register 4 and load it with our value. Note that two different load instructions are used since all 64 bits of register 4 are to be cleared using the long-form load instruction (LD) before R4 may be loaded with the short floating-point number.

```
         LD     R4,=D'0.0'          CLEAR ALL OF REGISTER 4
         LE     R4,=E'45.6'         INITIALIZE R4 TO 45.6
```

Figure 12.13 Alternate method of loading a 32-bit value into a register.

There are many other methods to clear register 4 as I'm sure you're well aware. In fact, it's probably much easier to simply use the **LD (load long)** instruction to place the value into register 4 in the first place. This implementation is given in Fig. 12.14.

```
         LD     R4,=D'45.6'         INITIALIZE R4 TO 45.6
```

Figure 12.14 Loading floating-point register 4 with the value 45.6.

Since there isn't a single instruction to load an extended-precision value into the two registers of a floating-point pair, extended-precision processing requires two load-long instructions. The left register of a pair is loaded with the leftmost 64 bits of a floating-point number and the right register is loaded with the right half of the number. The instructions in Fig. 12.15 illustrate this loading technique.

```
         LD     R0,BIGNUM          GET LEFT HALF OF BIGNUM
         LD     R2,BIGNUM+8        NOW LOAD RIGHT HALF
         .      .
         .      .
         .      .
BIGNUM   DC     L'45.6'            16-BYTE FLOATING-POINT NUMBER
```

Figure 12.15 Loading registers with an extended precision value.

Register contents may be copied from one to the other using either the **LER (load short)** or **LDR (load long)** RR instructions. Both instructions specify floating-point registers and both instructions copy the contents of the second register operand into the first. In a manner similar to the LE instruction, LER copies only the left-half of the second operand register's value into the left-half of the first register. The right-halves of both registers remain unchanged.

During processing, it will most likely be necessary to store values into memory. Floating-point values are copied from a register to storage using the **STD (store long)** and the **STE (store short)** instructions. Again, no instruction exists to store all 128 bits of a pair into memory. Therefore, two STD instructions are required.

When storing values, alignment of the target area into which you are storing must be considered. When using the STE instruction, the target storage area should be aligned on a fullword boundary. Storage areas should be aligned on a doubleword boundary when using the STD instruction. The examples in Fig. 12.16 illustrate storing of floating-point values into memory areas.

```
         STD   R4,SUBTOTAL       SAVE SUBTOTAL UNTIL LATER
         .     .                 .
         .     .                 .
         .     .                 .
         STE   R2,TAXES          SAVE TAXES PAID UNTIL LATER
         .     .                 .
         .     .                 .
         .     .                 .
SUBTOTAL DS    D                 SUBTOTAL FLOATING POINT VALUE
TAXES    DS    E                 TAXES    FLOATING POINT VALUE
```

Figure 12.16 Storing values into memory areas.

NORMALIZATION AND THE GUARD DIGIT

The primary advantages of using floating-point numbers for processing are increased accuracy and automatic decimal point handling. To further increase accuracy during processing, two techniques are used by the floating-point instructions.

Normalization expresses a floating-point number with as many significant digits as possible. To relate this to something in everyday life, consider the act of purchasing a new shirt or blouse in a store. Suppose that the blouse costs $12.25 (tax included). You hand the clerk $15 and receive back $2. Even though you have your blouse, you've also been cheated out of 75 cents. You question the clerk about the amount tendered and are informed that all digits to the right of the decimal are dropped when it comes to giving back change. The store pockets all of the excess change from a sale.

Although you might be quite upset at the store's policy, this analogy emphasizes the need for normalization. The more digits that are retained during processing, the more accurate the results. Normalization ensures that the most digits possible are used in a floating point operation and thus would minimize occurrences of the situation described above.

Concern for normalization is most apparent when converting values to and from human readable forms. During floating-point processing, instructions can be selected to automatically perform normalization. Only when unnormalizing instructions are used or when converting to or from floating-point format may *un*normalized values result. You'll see this in the discussion of the conversion macros FLOATIN and FLOATOUT later in the chapter.

To illustrate the normalization process, consider the number 12.3. In long form, it is represented as 41C4CCCCCCCCCCCD, which is a normalized value.

Now consider the number 43**00**C4CCCCCCCCCD. This is also the value 12.3, but it is not normalized since the leftmost fractional digits are zero. Also notice that the characteristic is different, reflecting the digits to the left of the decimal. To normalize this number, shift it to the left one fractional digit at a time and reduce the characteristic by 1 for each shift. The stages given in Fig. 12.17 illustrate the transformation of a number from unnormalized to normalized form.

As the fractional component is shifted to the left, vacant positions on the right must be filled. They are filled with values representative of the number, although they are not

beginning value	action	resulting value
4300C4CCCCCCCCCD	shift left	420C4CCCCCCCCCDx
420C4CCCCCCCCCDx	shift left	41C4CCCCCCCCCDxx

```
41C4CCCCCCCCCDxx   is a normalized floating point number
```

Figure 12.17 Normalizing a floating-point value.

filled in the example. As you can see, the normalized version of this number has two more digits in its representation than the unnormalized number. This may not seem important, but in a scientific environment or one requiring a high degree of precision, it is.

Again, normalization is most often a consideration during conversion to or from floating-point format. Since we are using two macros to perform conversion operations, we aren't concerned about normalization during processing since we'll use instructions that automatically normalize our results. During conversion, the macros take care of normalizing our values, allowing us to concentrate on solving the problem.

The **guard digit** is another technique used during processing to increase accuracy. Depending on the instructions, an additional fractional digit used during an operation increases the number of digits in the floating-point number. Short-form numbers then have 7 fractional digits instead of 6 and extended-form numbers have 29 fractional digits instead of 28. For example, when adding two normalized floating-point numbers an additional digit is added to the numbers to increase accuracy. Although the result must still be contained in a register, the guard digit is added to the numbers during the operation to increase accuracy. After the operation is completed and the result obtained, the guard digits(s) are dropped and the result is placed into the register appropriately. Again, the guard digit is maintained by the instructions themselves. Since the guard digit facility is provided automatically and occurs only on selected instructions, we generally don't concern ourselves with its occurrence. We simply understand that it exists and that it increases the accuracy of our floating-point computations.

ARITHMETIC FLOATING-POINT OPERATIONS

Floating-point numbers may be added, subtracted, multiplied or divided using various floating-point instructions. Each instruction operates on short-, long-, or extended-form floating-point numbers. Therefore, *you* must select the appropriate instructions depending on the accuracy required. Generally, the short- or long-form instructions most likely meet your processing needs.

Since almost all floating-point instructions are RR and RX instructions, there's no need to investigate each instruction individually. Hence, the table given in Fig. 12.18 simply lists each normalizing instruction and its format. You should be able to determine which instruction you'd use to perform your floating-point processing. Unnormalized instructions are not listed since they are usually only used in the conversion process. Therefore, refer to the IBM publication *IBM System/370 Principles of Operation (GA22-7000)* for further information on floating-point unnormalized instructions.

As briefly described in the Fig. 12.18, the halve instructions allow the programmer to divide the contents of a register by two. Specifically, the *second* operand is divided by

function	instruction	
ADD SHORT	AE	R,D(X,B)
ADD SHORT (register)	AER	R,R
ADD LONG	AD	R,D(X,B)
ADD LONG (register)	ADR	R,R
ADD EXTENDED (register)	AXR	R,R
SUBTRACT SHORT	SE	R,D(X,B)
SUBTRACT SHORT (register)	SER	R,R
SUBTRACT LONG	SD	R,D(X,B)
SUBTRACT LONG (register)	SDR	R,R
SUBTRACT EXTENDED (register)	SXR	R,R
MULTIPLY LONG	MD	R,D(X,B)
MULTIPLY LONG (register)	MDR	R,R
MULTIPLY EXTENDED (register)	MXR	R,R
DIVIDE SHORT	DE	R,D(X,B)
DIVIDE SHORT (register)	DER	R,R
DIVIDE LONG	DD	R,D(X,B)
DIVIDE LONG (register)	DDR	R,R
HALVE (divide by 2, register)	HER	R,R
HALVE (divide by 2, register)	HDR	R,R

Figure 12.18 Floating-point arithmetic and normalizing instructions.

two and is placed into the first operand register. However, if the first and second operands specify the same register number, it's quite clear that these instructions can be used to divide the contents of a register by two. As you can also see, halving can be performed on both short- and long-form floating-point numbers.

Several other instructions not given in Fig. 12.18 relate to multiplication. These instructions utilize operands that have different lengths than the resulting values and are described in Fig. 12.19.

instruction		explanation
MXD	R,D(X,B)	Multiply two long floating point numbers together to obtain an extended precision result. The resulting extended precision number is placed into the first operand.
MXDR	R,R	Same as above except that the operation involves only registers.
ME	R,D(X,B)	Multiply two short form floating point numbers to produce a long form result.
MER	R,R	Same effect as ME except that the operation involves only registers.

Figure 12.19 Multiplication instructions with automatic normalization.

Most arithmetic instructions are straightforward except for the multiply and the divide. With division, the floating-point instructions operate differently than any of the binary or packed-decimal division instructions studied so far. Remember that the binary division requires an even/odd pair and results in a quotient and a remainder. This is not the case in floating-point processing since results contain digits to the left and right of the decimal. Hence, the result of a floating-point division is a single number, not a quotient and remainder. Further, neither the division nor the result use even/odd pairs. A floating-point division occurs between a single floating-point register and another or between a floating-point register and a value in storage. However, short- or long-form divisions can be performed, thus impacting the significance of your floating-point result.

ADDITIONAL FLOATING-POINT LOAD INSTRUCTIONS

Several other load instructions process floating-point numbers. They allow us to complement floating-point numbers, obtain the absolute value of a number, or convert the number to positive or negative value format. Again, these instructions are quite similar to the RR and RX counterparts and so, little explanation is needed. Figure 12.20 lists and describes these instructions.

ROUNDING FLOATING-POINT VALUES

After performing a floating-point operation, you may want to convert the result into a shorter floating-point form. For example, suppose that two long-form numbers are multiplied to produce an extended floating-point number. This number can be converted back to a long-form number using the **rounding floating-point instructions.**

As we convert from a longer value to a shorter one, we don't want to simply throw away all of the extra significant digits in the right half of the extended precision number.

instruction	explanation
LTER R,R	load the short floating point number in the second register into the first register and set the condition code depending on the resulting value
LTDR R,R	load and test using a long floating point number
LCER R,R	load the complement value of the second operand into the register specified in the first operand
LCDR R,R	load complement for long floating point numbers
LNER R,R	load negative short
LNDR R,R	load negative long
LPER R,R	load positive short
LPDR R,R	load positive long

Figure 12.20 Load positive, negative, and complementary instructions.

Therefore, we use them to round the value in the left half to give a more accurate representation of the result.

To illustrate, when 1.25 and 1.75 are multiplied, we obtain the number 2.1875. If we only want to retain two digits to the right of the decimal, the value 2.18 is our result. However, 2.1875 is closer to 2.19 than it is to 2.18. Therefore, it's more reasonable to give a result of 2.19 than 2.18. By **rounding** the original result (2.1875), the final value becomes 2.19.

Two instructions are used to round floating-point numbers. The **LRER (load rounded long to short)** instruction rounds a long-form floating-point number into a short floating-point number. The **LRDR (load rounded extended to long)** rounds an extended-precision floating-point number into a long-form floating-point number. In both cases, we end with a shorter floating-point number than what we started with and the values are rounded to obtain our final result.

COMPARISON BETWEEN FLOATING-POINT VALUES

As with any type of data, the compare instruction can be used so that we can make decisions about the data we are processing. Again, these instructions relate to the size of the floating-point data to be compared. Since only short or long floating-point data can be compared, extended-precision floating-point data has to be compared using a dual-instruction technique.

The floating-point comparison instructions are similar to the RR and RX instructions, compare and compare register. Figure 12.21 summarizes these instructions.

CONVERSION OF FLOATING-POINT DATA FOR I/O

One of the most difficult aspects of floating point-processing is converting the numbers for input and output. There are no instructions that easily convert from character to floating-point format and vice versa. Therefore, an algorithm must be utilized to perform the necessary conversions. We discussed procedures for performing these conversions earlier in the chapter (see Fig. 12.5 and 12.8) but we did not develop the necessary code to

instruction		explanation
CE	R,D(X,B)	Compare a short floating point number in a register to a value in storage and set the condition code appropriately.
CER	R,R	Compare two short floating point numbers in registers.
CD	R,D(X,B)	Compare a long floating point number in a register with a long number in storage.
CDR	R,R	Compare two floating point registers using a long form comparison.

Figure 12.21 Floating-point compare instructions.

carry out the conversion process. This section will review each conversion algorithm and provide the implementation of those algorithms in the form of a macro. The FLOATIN macro provides conversion from character-format to floating-point and the FLOATOUT macro provides conversion from floating-point to character-format. Both macros are limited to short- or long-form floating-point numbers. However, these macros may be modified as needed to provide extended-precision support or to provide a conversion format other than that implemented within each macro. At this time, let's review the procedure for converting from character-format to floating-point representation. This procedure is reviewed in Fig. 12.22.

```
1. Separate the character data into the digits to
   the left and right of the decimal point.
2. Convert each half into packed decimal and then
   into binary format.
3. Change the representation of the binary halves
   to that of a floating-point number.
4. Normalize each half.
5. Add the two halves together.
```

Figure 12.22 Algorithm to convert from character to floating-point format.

The process is quite complex, especially step 3 where the binary numbers must be converted into floating-point format. Additionally, since standard instructions are generally used in the conversion process, numbers larger than nine digits cannot be easily handled using this method. In fact, if your processing requires extended-precision processing or processing numbers with more than nine digits to the right or left of the decimal, I'd suggest using a higher-level language to implement your solution.

Converting from floating-point form to character requires a reverse technique. The algorithm in Fig. 12.23 summarizes this conversion process.

```
1. Separate the digits to the left of the decimal from
   those to the right of the decimal. This splits the
   floating-point number into two components.
2. Convert each half to standard binary format.
3. Convert each binary number to packed decimal and
   then to character format.
4. Concatenate the halves to form a printable floating-
   point number.
```

Figure 12.23 Algorithm to convert from floating-point to character format.

To help us convert data from character to floating point, we're going to use two macros that I've developed. The FLOATIN macro converts from character to floating-point format and the FLOATOUT macro converts from floating point to character. Clearly, these macros are coded within your program code or contained in a macro library to perform the conversion when invoked. Figure 12.24 describes the general format to invoke each macro.

```
<label>   FLOATIN    area,length,register

<label>   FLOATOUT   register,area,length,rt
```

Figure 12.24 Format of the floating-point conversion macro's call instructions.

The FLOATIN macro identifies an area (first operand) containing a number in character format. The length of this area is specified in the second operand so that the macro knows how long the value might be. Using this information, the macro converts base-10 input numbers, with or without decimal points, into floating-point format. For example, a value of 12.5 is converted properly by the macro into floating-point format. However, .125E+02 is not converted properly since the macro does not "understand" scientific notation.

After the value is converted, it is loaded in *long* form into the floating-point register specified by the last operand.

A long-form floating-point number in a register is converted to character format using the FLOATOUT macro. Given the register containing the value to be converted in the first operand, the macro converts the value and places it into the area specified by the second operand. The length of the target area is coded in the third operand so that the macro knows how long a number is to be represented in the final result. The last operand for the FLOATOUT macro specifies the number of digits to the right of the decimal. By coding a consistent value for this operand, you can easily align your printed output values.

After conversion, the FLOATOUT macro places the number, right justified, into the area indicated. The appropriate number of digits to the right of the decimal is supplied with leading and trailing zeros in the number suppressed. Since the macro can only process numbers with nine digits to the right of the decimal, it's not reasonable to code a value having more than nine digits in the last operand.

Both macros can be used in ASSIST or in standard assembly language. In assembly language however, an additional operand may be coded to reduce the storage requirements of the macros. By coding the operand ASSIST=NO as a parameter to the macro, the macro expansion results in a separate CSECT definition for each conversion routine. Since imbedded CSECT's are not allowed in ASSIST, this operand *cannot* be coded when using these macros in ASSIST programming projects. Figure 12.25 illustrates the method for calling each macro and specifying the ASSIST= keyword parameter.

```
FLOATIN    NUM1IN,15,R2,ASSIST=NO
.          .
.          .
.          .
FLOATOUT   R0,TAXESOUT,10,5,ASSIST=NO
```

Figure 12.25 Calling the conversion macros and specifying that separate CSECT's are to be generated.

Coding Examples 12.1 and 12.2 contain the two conversion macros. These macros should provide support for most processing situations that you might encounter in your programming class. Clearly, they may be modified to suit your needs so that more significant digits may be represented. They may also be modified to accept and output numbers in scientific notation if required.

FLOATING-POINT PROGRAMMING EXAMPLE

We conclude this chapter with a complete floating-point program that computes the sum, difference, product, and quotient of two floating-point numbers. We've seen this sample program before when we discussed binary and packed-decimal processing. Here it is using floating-point instructions. The FLOATIN and FLOATOUT macros are used to input and output the results of processing.

As you look at the program and partial output that follows, notice that the program uses long-form floating-point instructions for processing. This provides a number with 14 fractional digits, which is the largest number that can be converted by these macros. The program is implemented in ASSIST and a listing of the complete program (see Example 12.3), the input data (see Example 12.3), and partial program output (see Example 12.4) are provided for reference. This should further help in understanding floating-point processing and floating-point instructions.

```
         MACRO
&LAB     FLOATIN &AREA,&LEN,&REG,&ASSIST=YES
.*********************************************************************
.*  THIS MACRO CONVERTS A NUMBER OF THE FORMAT  SDDDDDDDD.DDDDDDDD   *
.*  INTO A FLOATING POINT NUMBER AND PLACES THE FLOATING POINT       *
.*  VALUE INTO THE SPECIFIED FLOATING POINT REGISTER.                *
.*                                                                   *
.*  OPERANDS FOR THE MACRO CONSIST OF THE FOLLOWING:                 *
.*      --  ADDRESS OF A CHARACTER AREA THAT CONTAINS THE NUMBER     *
.*          THAT IS TO BE CONVERTED INTO FLOATING POINT FORMAT       *
.*      --  LENGTH OF THE AREA SPECIFIED IN OPERAND 1                *
.*      --  FLOATING POINT REGISTER NUMBER WHERE THE CONVERTED       *
.*          NUMBER IS TO BE PLACED                                   *
.*                                                                   *
.*********************************************************************
         GBLB  &FITIME
         LCLC  &CSECT
         AIF   ('&REG' EQ '0' OR '&REG' EQ '2').REGOK
         AIF   ('&REG' EQ '4' OR '&REG' EQ '6').REGOK
         AIF   ('&REG' EQ 'R0' OR '&REG' EQ 'R2').REGOK
         AIF   ('&REG' EQ 'R4' OR '&REG' EQ 'R6').REGOK
         MNOTE 8,'THE FLOATING POINT REGISTER SPECIFIED IS NOT VALID.
         MNOTE 0,'ONLY REGISTERS 0, 2, 4, OR 6 MAY BE CODED IN THE
         MNOTE 0,'FLOATING POINT REGISTER NUMBER FIELD.
         MEXIT
.REGOK   ANOP
&CSECT   SETC  '&SYSECT'                       GET CURRENT CSECT NAME
         AIF   ('&LAB' EQ '').NOLAB
&LAB     DS    0H
.NOLAB   ANOP
         CNOP  4,8                             ALIGN FOR PARM LIST
         BAL   1,*+20                          SKIP OVER THE PARM LIST
         DS    A                               LOCATION OF THE AREA
         DS    A                               LENGTH VALUE
         DS    D                               ANSWER
         LA    14,&AREA                        WHERE IS THE NUMBER
         ST    14,0(1)                         SAVE IN PARM LIST
         LA    14,&LEN                         GET LENGTH OF DATA AREA
         ST    14,4(1)                         SAVE IN PARM LIST
         AIF   ('&ASSIST' EQ 'YES').ADDR
         L     15,=V(FLTIN)                    ADDRESS OUR ROUTINE
         AGO   .ADDRE
.ADDR    ANOP
         L     15,=A(FLTIN)                    ADDRESS OUR ROUTINE
.ADDRE   ANOP
         BALR  14,15                           CONVERT THE NUMBER
         LD    &REG,8(1)                       PLACE VALUE INTO REGISTER
         B     FI&SYSNDX                       SKIP AROUND LITERALS
         LTORG
FI&SYSNDX DS   0H
         AIF   (&FITIME EQ 0).FIRST
         MEXIT
.FIRST   ANOP
&FITIME  SETB  1
         AIF   ('&ASSIST' EQ 'YES').ASST1
         PUSH  USING,PRINT
```

Example 12.1 The FLOATIN conversion macro.

```
FLTIN    CSECT
         STM   R14,R12,12(R13)               SAVE CALLER'S REGISTERS
         BAL   R11,80(R15)                   SKIP OVER THE SAVE AREA
         USING *,R13,R12,R11                 TELL THE ASSEMBLER
         DS    18F                           REGISTER SAVE AREA
         ST    R13,4(R11)                    SAVE CURRENT R13 VALUE
         ST    R11,8(R13)                    CHAIN BACKWARD
         LR    R13,R11                       ESTABLISH R13 AS BASE
         AIF   ('&ASSIST' EQ 'NO').ASSTX
.ASST1   ANOP
         B     FLT@ROND                      SKIP AROUND THIS ROUTINE
FLTIN    DS    0H
         STM   R0,R15,FLT@SAVE               SAVE THE REGS
         B     FLT@SKIP                      SKIP AROUND SAVE AREA
FLT@SAVE DS    16F                           REGISTER SAVE AREA
FLT@SKIP DS    0H
.ASSTX   ANOP
         ST    R1,FLT@REG1                   SAVE PARM LIST REGISTER
.*********************************************************************
.*   CONVERT THE FIRST HALF OF THE NUMBER (DIGITS TO THE LEFT OF     *
.*   THE DECIMAL) INTO PACKED FORMAT.  THEN DETERMINE IF THERE ARE   *
.*   ANY DIGITS TO THE LEFT TO BE CONVERTED.                         *
.*********************************************************************
         ZAP   FLT@PAK1,FLT@ZERO             CLEAR FIRST HALF OF NUM
         ZAP   FLT@PAK2,FLT@ZERO             CLEAR RIGHT HALF OF NUM
         XC    FLT@PKL1,FLT@PKL1             CLEAR ALL FIELDS
         XC    FLT@PKL2,FLT@PKL2             ....
         XC    FLT@HXL1,FLT@HXL1
         XC    FLT@HXL2,FLT@HXL2
         LM    R3,R4,0(R1)                   ADDRESS VALUE AND LENGTH
         LA    R4,0(R3,R4)                   FIND END OF THE NUMBER
         TRT   0(200,R3),FLT@DGIT            FIND FIRST DIGIT OR SIGN
         MVI   FLT@NEG,B'00000000'           INDICATE POSITIVE
         CLI   0(R1),C'-'                    NEGATIVE NUMBER?
         BNE   *+8                           IF NOT, SKIP MOVE
         MVI   FLT@NEG,B'10000000'           INDICATE NEGATIVE NUMBER
         CLI   0(R1),C'.'                    FIRST CHAR A DOT?
         BNE   FJT@&SYSNDX                   IF SO, NO FIRST HALF
         LR    R6,R1                         SAVE STARTING ADDRESS
         B     FAT@&SYSNDX                   SKIP FIRST HALF CONVERSION
FJT@&SYSNDX DS 0H
         CLI   0(R1),C'0'                    FIRST CHAR A DIGIT?
         BNL   *+8                           IF NOT, BUMP ONE BYTE
         LA    R1,1(R1)                      SKIP OVER SIGN INDICATOR
         LR    R3,R1                         REMEMBER STARTING LOC.
         TRT   0(200,R3),FLT@DOT             LOOK FOR DOT
         LR    R5,R1                         REMEMBER WHERE WE STOPPED
         BZ    F88@&SYSNDX                   IF NO END THEN FORCE END
         CR    R5,R4                         PAST END OF NUMBER?
         BNH   F99@&SYSNDX                   IF NOT, TAKE CURRENT LOC.
F88@&SYSNDX DS 0H
         LR    R5,R4                         ELSE TAKE ENDING LOC.
F99@&SYSNDX DS 0H
         LR    R6,R5                         REMEMBER FOR LATER
         SR    R5,R3                         COMPUTE LENGTH OF PART 1
```

```
         STH   R5,FLT@PKL1                 SAVE LENGTH OF FIRST FIELD
         LTR   R5,R5                       SEE IF EQUAL TO ZERO
         BZ    FAT@&SYSNDX                 IF ZERO, FIRST HALF DONE
         BCTR  R5,0                        SET UP FOR EXECUTE
         EX    R5,FMT@&SYSNDX              CONVERT FIRST HALF
         B     *+10                        SKIP OVER PACK INSTRUCTION
FMT@&SYSNDX PACK  FLT@PAK1(8),0(0,R3)      PACK THE VALUE
FAT@&SYSNDX DS    0H
.*********************************************************************
.*  CONVERT DIGITS TO THE RIGHT OF THE DECIMAL INTO BINARY FORMAT.   *
.*  REMEMBER HOW MANY DIGITS THERE WERE SO THAT WE CAN DIVIDE BY     *
.*  10 TO THE POWER OF DIGITS TO FORM OUR FLOATING POINT NUMBER.     *
.*********************************************************************
         ZAP   FLT@PAK2,FLT@ZERO           CLEAR SECOND HALF
         LR    R3,R6                       GET BACK ENDING LOC
         CLI   0(R3),C'.'                  LOOKING AT A DOT?
         BNE   FXT@&SYSNDX                 IF NOT, NO SECOND HALF
         LA    R3,1(R3)                    BUMP TO FIRST DIGIT
         LR    R6,R3                       SAVE FOR LATER
         CR    R3,R4                       PAST END OF NUM?
         BNL   FXT@&SYSNDX                 IF SO, WE'RE DONE  GETTING
         TRT   0(200,R3),FLT@BLNK          LOOK FOR NON-DIGIT
         LR    R5,R1                       REMEMBER WHERE WE STOPPED
         CR    R5,R4                       PAST END OF NUMBER?
         BNH   FAA@&SYSNDX                 IF NOT, TAKE CURRENT LOC.
         LR    R5,R4                       ELSE TAKE ENDING LOC.
         LA    R5,1(R5)                    ADJUST ONE BYTE
FAA@&SYSNDX DS 0H
         SR    R5,R6                       COMPUTE LENGTH OF PART 2
         STH   R5,FLT@PKL2                 SAVE LENGTH FOR DIVIDE
         LTR   R5,R5                       IS SECOND HALF LENGTH 0?
         BZ    FBT@&SYSNDX                 IF SO, SKIP CONVERSION
         BCTR  R5,0                        SET UP FOR EXECUTE
         EX    R5,FNT@&SYSNDX              CONVERT FIRST HALF
         B     *+10                        SKIP OVER PACK INSTRUCTION
FNT@&SYSNDX PACK  FLT@PAK2(8),0(0,R3)      PACK THE VALUE
FBT@&SYSNDX DS    0H
.*********************************************************************
.* BOTH PARTS OF THE NUMBER ARE IN PACKED FORMAT.  PROCEED TO        *
.* CONVERT THE NUMBER INTO BINARY FORMAT AND THEN INTO FLOATING      *
.* POINT FORM.                                                       *
.*********************************************************************
FXT@&SYSNDX DS    0H
         CVB   R3,FLT@PAK1                 CONVERT LEFT HALF TO BINARY
         ST    R3,FLT@BIN1                 SAVE IN MEMORY
.*********************************************************************
.*  DETERMINE THE NUMBER OF HEX DIGITS IN THE NUMBER SO THAT THE     *
.*  EXPONENT FOR THE NUMBER CAN BE FORMED.                           *
.*********************************************************************
         LA    R2,64                       R2 = STANDARD EXPONENT
F4T@&SYSNDX DS 0H
         LTR   R3,R3                       IS R3 ZERO YET?
         BZ    F5T@&SYSNDX                 IF SO, WE'RE DONE
         LA    R2,1(R2)                    INCREMENT EXPONENT
         SRL   R3,4                        SHIFT R3 ONE HEX DIGIT
```

```
         B      F4T@&SYSNDX                    KEEP SHIFTING
F5T@&SYSNDX DS  0H
         S      R2,FLT@64                      COMPUTE HEX DIGIT LENGTH
         STH    R2,FLT@HXL1                    SAVE UPDATED VALUE
         A      R2,FLT@64                      BACK TO EXPONENT VALUE
.*********************************************************************
.*  SHIFT THE LEFT HALF OF THE NUMBER TO THE LEFT TO NORMALIZE IT    *
.*  AND TO ADJUST IT TO MATCH THE EXPONENT VALUE.  NORMALIZING WILL  *
.*  MOVE THE LEFT MOST DIGIT TO THE FAR LEFT.                         *
.*********************************************************************
         L      R3,FLT@BIN1                    GET BACK ORIGINAL VALUE
         CLC    FLT@BIN1(4),FLT@0              VALUE OF ZERO?
         BE     FRT@&SYSNDX                    IF SO, SKIP SHIFTING
FQT@&SYSNDX DS  0H
         TM     FLT@BIN1,B'11110000'           ANY FIRST FOUR BITS ONE?
         BNZ    FRT@&SYSNDX                    ALL DONE SHIFTING SO EXIT
         SLL    R3,4                           MOVE LEFT 4 BITS
         ST     R3,FLT@BIN1                    SAVE UPDATED VALUE
         B      FQT@&SYSNDX                    REPEAT
FRT@&SYSNDX DS  0H
         SLDL   R2,24                          MOVE R2/R3 BACK TO LEFT
         STM    R2,R3,FLT@D1                   SAVE LEFT NUMBER
.*********************************************************************
.* NOW CONVERT THE RIGHT HALF.  START BY COUNTING THE NUMBER OF HEX  *
.* DIGITS IN THE NUMBER TO DERIVE THE EXPONENT VALUE FOR THE RIGHT   *
.* HALF.                                                              *
.*********************************************************************
         CVB    R3,FLT@PAK2                    CONVERT RIGHT HALF TO BIN.
         ST     R3,FLT@BIN2                    SAVE IT FOR LATER
         LA     R2,64                          R2 = STANDARD EXPONENT
F6T@&SYSNDX DS  0H
         LTR    R3,R3                          IS R3 ZERO YET?
         BZ     F7T@&SYSNDX                    IF SO, WE'RE DONE
         LA     R2,1(R2)                       INCREMENT EXPONENT
         SRL    R3,4                           SHIFT R3 ONE HEX DIGIT
         B      F6T@&SYSNDX                    KEEP SHIFTING
F7T@&SYSNDX DS  0H
         S      R2,FLT@64                      COMPUTE HEX DIGIT LENGTH
         STH    R2,FLT@HXL2                    SAVE UPDATED VALUE
         A      R2,FLT@64                      BACK TO EXPONENT VALUE
.*********************************************************************
.*  NORMALIZE THE RIGHT HALF BY SHIFTING IT TO THE LEFT UNTIL THE    *
.*  LEFT MOST POSITION IS NOT ZERO.                                   *
.*********************************************************************
         L      R3,FLT@BIN2                    GET BACK BINARY VALUE
         CLC    FLT@BIN2(4),FLT@0              VALUE OF ZERO?
         BE     FST@&SYSNDX                    IF SO, SKIP SHIFTING
FTT@&SYSNDX DS  0H
         TM     FLT@BIN2,B'11110000'           ANY FIRST FOUR BITS ONE?
         BNZ    FST@&SYSNDX                    ALL DONE SHIFTING SO EXIT
         SLL    R3,4                           MOVE LEFT 4 BITS
         ST     R3,FLT@BIN2                    SAVE UPDATED VALUE
         B      FTT@&SYSNDX                    REPEAT
FST@&SYSNDX DS  0H
         SLDL   R2,24                          MOVE R4/R5 TO LEFT
```

```
         STM   R2,R3,FLT@D2                    SAVE SECOND VALUE
.*********************************************************************
.*  BOTH VALUES ARE CONVERTED.  PROCEED TO ADD THE LEFT AND RIGHT    *
.*  HALVES TOGETHER TO FORM THE FULL FLOATING POINT VALUE.           *
.*********************************************************************
         STD   R2,FLT@REG2                     SAVE CURRENT R2 VALUE
         STD   R4,FLT@REG4                     SAVE CURRENT R4 VALUE
         LD    R2,FLT@D1                       GET FIRST HALF
         LD    R4,FLT@D2                       GET SECOND HALF
         LH    R2,FLT@PKL2                     OBTAIN LENGTH OF LAST HALF
.*********************************************************************
.*  DIVIDE THE RIGHT HALF BY 10 TO THE XTH POWER WHERE X IS THE      *
.*  NUMBER OF DIGITS IN THE RIGHT HALF.                              *
.*********************************************************************
         LTR   R2,R2                           IS IT ZERO?
         BZ    F8T@&SYSNDX                     IF SO, DON'T DIVIDE
F9T@&SYSNDX DS 0H
         DD    R4,FLT@10                       DIVIDE BY 10
         BCT   R2,F9T@&SYSNDX                  REPEAT FOR ALL POWERS
F8T@&SYSNDX DS 0H
         STD   R4,FLT@D2                       SAVE SECOND HALF
.*********************************************************************
.*  MAKE SURE THAT BOTH HALVES ARE NORMALIZED.  THEN ADD THE TWO     *
.*  HALVES.  RESTORE FLOATING POINT REGS 2 AND 4 TO THEIR ORIGINAL   *
.*  VALUES BEFORE LOADING THE SPECIFIED REGISTER WITH THE RESULT.    *
.*********************************************************************
         AD    R2,FLT@D0                       NORMALIZE
         AD    R4,FLT@D0                       NORMALIZE
         ADR   R2,R4                           ADD THE TWO HALVES
         STD   R2,FLT@RSLT                     SAVE RESULT IN MEMORY
         LD    R2,FLT@REG2                     RESTORE REGS TO ORIGINAL
         LD    R4,FLT@REG4                     RESTORE REGS TO ORIGINAL
         OC    FLT@RSLT(1),FLT@NEG             SIGN THE NUMBER
         L     R1,FLT@REG1                     GET PARM LIST ADDRESS
         MVC   8(8,R1),FLT@RSLT                MOVE VALUE INTO PARM LIST
         AIF   ('&ASSIST' EQ 'NO').ASSTM
         LM    R0,R15,FLT@SAVE                 RESTORE THE REGS
         BR    R14                             RETURN TO THE CALLER
         AGO   .ASSTR
.ASSTM   ANOP
         L     R13,4(R13)                      RESTORE THE SAVEAREA PTR.
         LM    R14,R12,12(R13)                 RESTORE ALL REGS
         BR    R14                             RETURN TO CALLER
.ASSTR   ANOP
FLT@REG1 DS    F
FLT@PAK1 DS    D                               VALUE LEFT OF DECIMAL
FLT@PAK2 DS    D                               VALUE RIGHT OF DECIMAL
FLT@PKL1 DS    H                               DIGITS IN FLT@PAK1
FLT@PKL2 DS    H                               DIGITS IN FLT@PAK2
FLT@HXL1 DS    H                               HEX DIGITS IN NUMBER HALFS
FLT@HXL2 DS    H                               HEX DIGITS IN NUMBER HALFS
FLT@BIN1 DS    F                               BINARY CONVERSION AREA
FLT@BIN2 DS    F                               BINARY CONVERSION AREA
FLT@D1   DS    D                               DOUBLEWORD WORK AREA
FLT@D2   DS    D                               DOUBLEWORD WORK AREA
```

```
FLT@RSLT DS    D                                  THE RESULT
FLT@REG2 DS    D                                  HOLD AREA FOR FLOAT REG2
FLT@REG4 DS    D                                  HOLD AREA FOR FLOAT REG4
FLT@ZERO DC    P'0'                               CONSTANT OF ZERO
FLT@D0   DC    D'0'                               FLOATING POINT ZERO VALUE
FLT@64   DC    F'64'                              STANDARD EXPONENT
FLT@0    DC    F'0'                               CONSTANT ZERO
FLT@10   DC    D'10.0'                            VALUE OF 10
FLT@NEG  DC    X'00'                              FLAG TO INDICATE NEGATIVE
FLT@DOT  DC    256X'FF'                           STOP ON A NON-DIGIT
         ORG   FLT@DOT+C'0'
         DC    10X'00'
         ORG
FLT@BLNK DC    256X'00'                           STOP ON A SPACE
         ORG   FLT@BLNK+C' '
         DC    X'FF'
         ORG
FLT@DGIT DC    256X'00'                           STOP ON ANYTHING THAT IS
         ORG   FLT@DGIT+C'0'                      ...A VALID DIGIT OR SIGN
         DC    C'0123456789'
         ORG   FLT@DGIT+C'+'
         DC    C'+'
         ORG   FLT@DGIT+C'-'
         DC    C'-'
         ORG   FLT@DGIT+C'.'
         DC    C'.'
         ORG
FLT@LEN  EQU   *-FLT@PAK1
         LTORG
         AIF   ('&ASSIST' EQ 'NO').ASSTE
FLT@ROND DS    0H
         AGO   .OUT
.ASSTE   ANOP
         POP   USING,PRINT
&CSECT   CSECT
.OUT     ANOP
         MEND
```

Example 12.1 (cont.)

```
         MACRO
&LAB     FLOATOUT &REG,&AREA,&LEN,&RIGHT,&ASSIST=YES
.*********************************************************************
.* THIS MACRO CONVERTS FLOATING POINT VALUES CONTAINED IN A REGISTER *
.* INTO A PRINTABLE NUMBER IN THE FORMAT   SDDDDDDDD.DDDDDDDD        *
.* WHERE S IS THE SIGN OF THE NUMBER.                                *
.*                                                                   *
.* THIS USER INVOKES THE MACRO BY CODING THE FOLLOWING PARAMETERS:   *
.*      -- FLOATING POINT REGISTER CONTAINING THE NUMBER TO CONVERT  *
.*      -- ADDRESS IN THE USER'S PROGRAM WHERE THE RESULTING NUMBER  *
.*         IS TO BE PLACED.                                          *
.*      -- LENGTH OF THE AREA IDENTIFIED IN OPERAND 2                *
.*      -- NUMBER OF DIGITS TO THE RIGHT OF THE DECIMAL THAT THE     *
.*         USER WANTS IN THE RESULT.  THIS ALLOWS THE USER TO        *
.*         JUSTIFY NUMBERS AND OBTAIN CONSISTENT CONVERTED RESULTS   *
.*********************************************************************
         GBLB  &FOTIME
         LCLC  &CSECT
         LCLA  &MAX
&CSECT   SETC  '&SYSECT'                      GET CURRENT CSECT NAME
&MAX     SETA  &LEN
         AIF   (&MAX GE 15).LENOK
         MNOTE 8,'THE AREA THAT WILL CONTAIN THE CONVERTED FLOATING  '
         MNOTE 0,'POINT NUMBER MUST BE AT LEAST 15 BYTES LONG.  THE  '
         MNOTE 0,'LENGTH OF YOUR AREA IS LESS THAN THIS.  FLOATING   '
         MNOTE 0,'POINT CONVERSION SUSPENDED DUE TO ERRORS.          '
         MEXIT
.LENOK   ANOP
         AIF   ('&REG' EQ '0' OR '&REG' EQ '2').REGOK
         AIF   ('&REG' EQ '4' OR '&REG' EQ '6').REGOK
         AIF   ('&REG' EQ 'R0' OR '&REG' EQ 'R2').REGOK
         AIF   ('&REG' EQ 'R4' OR '&REG' EQ 'R6').REGOK
         MNOTE 8,'THE FLOATING POINT REGISTER SPECIFIED IS NOT VALID.'
         MNOTE 0,'ONLY REGISTERS 0, 2, 4, OR 6 MAY BE CODED IN THE   '
         MNOTE 0,'FLOATING POINT REGISTER NUMBER FIELD.              '
         MEXIT
.REGOK   ANOP
         AIF   ('&LAB' EQ '').NOLAB
&LAB     DS    0H
.NOLAB   ANOP
         CNOP  4,8                            ALIGN FOR PARM LIST
         BAL   1,*+24                         SKIP OVER THE PARM LIST
         DS    A                              LOCATION OF THE AREA
         DS    A                              LENGTH VALUE
         DS    D                              VALUE IN THE REGISTER
         DS    F                              DIGITS TO RIGHT OF DECIMAL
         LA    14,&AREA                       WHERE IS THE NUMBER
         ST    14,0(1)                        SAVE IN PARM LIST
         LA    14,&LEN                        GET LENGTH OF DATA AREA
         ST    14,4(1)                        SAVE IN PARM LIST
         LA    14,&RIGHT                      DIGITS TO THE RIGHT
         ST    14,16(1)                       SAVE IN PARM LIST
         STD   &REG,8(1)                      SAVE FLOATING POINT VALUE
         AIF   ('&ASSIST' EQ 'YES').ADDR
         L     15,=V(FLTOUT)                  ADDRESS OUR ROUTINE
```

Example 12.2 The FLOATOUT conversion macro.

```
         AGO    .ADDRE
.ADDR    ANOP
         L      15,=A(FLTOUT)                 ADDRESS OUR ROUTINE
.ADDRE   ANOP
         BALR   14,15                         CONVERT THE NUMBER
         B      FO&SYSNDX                     SKIP AROUND LITERALS
         LTORG
FO&SYSNDX DS    0H
         AIF    (&FOTIME EQ 0).FIRST
         MEXIT
.FIRST   ANOP
&FOTIME  SETB   1
         AIF    ('&ASSIST' EQ 'YES').FOTASST
         PUSH   USING,PRINT
FLTOUT   CSECT
         STM    R14,R12,12(R13)               SAVE CALLER'S REGISTERS
         BAL    R11,80(R15)                   SKIP OVER THE SAVE AREA
         USING  *,R13,R12,R11                 TELL THE ASSEMBLER
         DS     18F                           REGISTER SAVE AREA
         ST     R13,4(R11)                    SAVE CURRENT R13 VALUE
         ST     R11,8(R13)                    CHAIN BACKWARD
         LR     R13,R11                       ESTABLISH R13 AS BASE
         AGO    .NOTASST
.FOTASST ANOP
         B      FOT@ROND                      SKIP AROUND THIS ROUTINE
FLTOUT   DS     0H
         STM    R0,R15,FOT@SAVE               SAVE CALLER'S REGS
         B      FOT@SKIP                      SKIP AROUND SAVE AREA
FOT@SAVE DS     16F                           REGISTER SAVE AREA
FOT@SKIP DS     0H
.NOTASST ANOP
         ST     R1,FOT@REG1                   SAVE PARM LIST REGISTER
*
         LM     R2,R3,0(R1)                   GET LOCATION AND LENGTH
         MVI    0(R2),C' '                    CLEAR TARGET AREA
         BCTR   R3,0                          SET FOR EXECUTE
         EX     R3,FOT@CLR                    CLEAR REST OF THE AREA
         B      *+10                          SKIP OVER EXECUTE
FOT@CLR  MVC    1(0,R2),0(R2)                 CLEAR REST OF AREA
.*
.*********************************************************************
.*  DON'T ALTER THE CURRENT CONTENTS OF THE FLOATING POINT REGS      *
.*  THAT WE'LL BE USING TO SUPPORT THIS MODULE.  OBTAIN THE VALUE    *
.*  TO BE CONVERTED FROM THE PARAMETER LIST.                         *
.*********************************************************************
         STD    R0,FOT@F0                     SAVE FLOATING PT. REG0
         STD    R2,FOT@F2                     SAVE FLOATING PT. REG2
         LD     R0,8(R1)                      GET FLOATING PT. NUMBER
         STD    R0,FOT@NUM                    SAVE IN OUR PROGRAM AREA
         XC     FOT@R000(4),FOT@R000          NO DIGITS AFTER DECIMAL
         MVI    FOT@NEG,C'+'                  INDICATE POSITIVE
         ZAP    FOT@LEFT,=P'0'                SUPPLY DEFAULT VALUES
         ZAP    FOT@RGHT,=P'0'                ...TO LEFT AND RIGHT HALVES
         CD     R0,=D'0.0'                    IS THE VALUE ZERO?
         BE     FOT@NOR                       IF SO, CONVERSION IS DONE
```

```
.*
.************************************************************************
.*  DETERMINE IF THE NUMBER IS POSITIVE OR NEGATIVE AND SET A FLAG   *
.*  TO INDICATE ITS SIGN.                                            *
.************************************************************************
         TM    FOT@NUM,B'10000000'          NEGATIVE NUMBER?
         BNO   *+8                          IF NOT, DON'T SET FIELD
         MVI   FOT@NEG,C'-'                 ELSE CHANGE TO NEGATIVE
         NI    FOT@NUM,B'01111111'          CHANGE NUMBER TO POSITIVE
.*
.************************************************************************
.*  SET DEFAULT VALUES FOR BOTH THE LEFT AND RIGHT HALVES OF THE      *
.*  NUMBER.  SEE IF THERE ARE ANY DIGITS TO THE LEFT OF THE DECIMAL  *
.*  AND IF SO, SEE HOW MANY THERE MAY BE BY LOOKING AT THE EXPONENT. *
.************************************************************************
         LD    R0,FOT@NUM                   GET POSITIVE NUMBER BACK
         CD    R0,FOT@BIG                   IS NUMBER TO BIG FOR US?
         BH    FOT@TOOB                     IF SO, EXIT
         SR    R2,R2                        CLEAR R2 FOR WORKING
         IC    R2,FOT@NUM                   GET EXPONENT VALUE
         S     R2,=F'64'                    COMPUTE DIFFERENCE
         ST    R2,FOT@POWR                  SAVE POWER VALUE
.*
.************************************************************************
.*  IF THE NUMBER IS LESS THAN 1 THEN THERE'S NO REASON TO LOOK FOR  *
.*  DIGITS TO THE LEFT OF THE DECIMAL.  PROCEDE TO CONVERT THE       *
.*  RIGHT HALF INTO REASONABLE FORMAT.                               *
.************************************************************************
         CD    R0,FOT@ONE                   IS NUMBER LESS THAN ONE?
         BNL   FOT@GT1                      YES, SKIP LEFT HALF
         LCR   R2,R2                        TAKE POWER COMPLEMENT
         ST    R2,FOT@POWR                  SAVE FOR LATER
         B     FOT@LT1
.*
.************************************************************************
.* IF THERE ARE DIGITS TO THE LEFT OF THE DECIMAL THEN CONVERT THEM  *
.* INTO PACKED DECIMAL FORM.  THIS IS DONE BY NORMALIZING AND THEN   *
.* SHIFTING BY THE VALUE OF THE EXPONENT.                            *
.************************************************************************
FOT@GT1  DS    0H                           ...DIGITS LEFT OF DECIMAL
         SR    R4,R4                        SHIFT REGISTER
         ICM   R5,B'1111',FOT@NUM+1         GET ALL LEADING DIGITS
FOT@LP1  DS    0H
         SLDL  R4,4                         EXTRACT LEADING VALUE
         BCT   R2,FOT@LP1                   REPEAT FOR ALL LEADING DGTS
         CVD   R4,FOT@LEFT                  SAVE LEFT HALF VALUE
FOT@LL1  DS    0H
         STCM  R4,B'1111',FOT@WORK+1        NORMALIZE THIS VALUE
         TM    FOT@WORK+1,B'11110000'       LEFT DIGIT NON-ZERO?
         BNZ   FOT@LL2                      IF SO, WE'RE DONE
         SLL   R4,4                         SHIFT R4 LEFT
         B     FOT@LL1                      REPEAT FOR ALL DIGITS
FOT@LL2  DS    0H
.************************************************************************
.* SAVE THE NUMBER OF PLACES SHIFTED SO THAT WE CAN DETERMINE THE    *
```

```
.* NUMBER OF DIGITS IN THE LEFT HALF.  CONTINUE TO SUBTRACT THE      *
.* LEFT HALF FROM THE TOTAL NUMBER TO ISOLATE THE RIGHT HALF ONLY.    *
.*********************************************************************
         XC    FOT@WORK+5(3),FOT@WORK+5      CLEAR RIGHT HALF
         L     R4,FOT@POWR                   OBTAIN POWER VALUE
         A     R4,=F'64'                     CONSTRUCT FULL EXPONENT
         STC   R4,FOT@WORK                   ...FINISH CONSTRUCTION
         LD    R2,FOT@WORK                   GET LEFT HALF VALUE
         SDR   R0,R2                         RESULT IS ONLY RIGHT HALF
         CD    R0,=D'0.0'                    IS RIGHT HALF ZERO?
         BE    FOT@NOR                       IF SO, CONTINUE CONVERSION
.*
FOT@LT1  DS    0H
.*********************************************************************
.* NOW CONVERT THE RIGHT HALF INTO PACKED FORMAT.  THIS IS DONE BY   *
.* FIRST RAISING THE EXPONENT VALUE TO X'40' AND THEN BY MULTIPLYING *
.* BY 10 TO THE SEVENTH POWER.                                       *
.*********************************************************************
.* THIS DIFFERENCE BETWEEN THE RIGHT HALF EXPONENT VALUE AND X'40'   *
.* WILL TELL US THE NUMBER OF LEADING ZEROS ON THE FRONT OF THE      *
.* RIGHT HALF OF THE NUMBER.                                         *
.*********************************************************************
         STD   R0,FOT@WORK                   SAVE TO EXTRACT EXPONENT
         XC    FOT@R000(4),FOT@R000          CLEAR LEADING DIGIT COUNT
FOT@LP3  DS    0H
         STD   R0,FOT@WORK                   SAVE VALUE IN MEMORY
         SR    R2,R2                         CLEAR R2
         IC    R2,FOT@WORK                   CHECK THE EXPONENT
         S     R2,=F'64'                     WHAT IS THE DIFFERENCE
         LTR   R2,R2                         IS RESULT +, -, 0 ?
         BZ    FOT@STOR                      IF ZERO WE'RE DONE
         BP    FOT@DIVD                      POSITIVE THEN DIVIDE
         L     R2,FOT@R000                   GET LEADING DIGIT COUNTER
         LA    R2,1(R2)                      REFLECT MULTIPLY
         ST    R2,FOT@R000                   TURN VALUE TO MEMORY
         MD    R0,=D'10.0'                   TIMES 10
         B     FOT@LP3                       REPEAT TILL DONE
FOT@DIVD DS    0H
         L     R2,FOT@R000                   GET LEADING DIGIT COUNTER
         BCTR  R2,0                          REFLECT DIVIDE
         ST    R2,FOT@R000                   TURN VALUE TO MEMORY
         DD    R0,=D'10.0'                   DIVIDE BY 10
         B     FOT@LP3                       REPEAT IF NECESSARY
FOT@STOR DS    0H
         STD   R0,FOT@WORK                   SAVE BACK IN MEMORY
FOT@LX   DS    0H
         SR    R2,R2                         CLEAR R2 VALUE
         SR    R3,R3                         GET READY TO MULTIPLY
         ICM   R3,B'0111',FOT@WORK+1         GET RIGHT HALF
         M     R2,=F'10000000'               TIMES 10,000,000
         SLDA  R2,8                          FINISH THE CONVERSION
         CVD   R2,FOT@RGHT                   SAVE RIGHT HALF IN MEMORY
.*
.*********************************************************************
.* IF RIGHT MOST DIGIT IN RIGHT HALF IS A NINE THEN ROUND THE NUMBER *
```

```
.* BY ADDING A VALUE OF 1.  THIS WILL COMPENSATE FOR ANY CONVERSION  *
.* ERRORS OR IN THE REPRESENTATION OF THE FLOATING POINT NUMBER.     *
.*********************************************************************
FOT@NOR  DS    0H
         CP    FOT@RGHT+7(1),=P'9'         LAST DIGIT A NINE?
         BNE   *+10                        IF NOT, DON'T ADD ONE
         AP    FOT@RGHT,=P'1'              ROUND UP IF APPROPRIATE
         CLC   FOT@RGHT(4),=F'0'           FIRST HALF, RIGHT HALF 0?
         BE    *+10                        IF SO, DON'T ROUND
         AP    FOT@LEFT,=P'1'              ROUND UP LEFT HALF
.*********************************************************************
.*  NOW PROCEDE TO CONVERT THE HALVES INTO PRINTABLE FORMAT.         *
.*********************************************************************
         MVC   FOT@CHRL(16),=X'40202020202020202020202020202120'
         MVC   FOT@CHRR(16),=X'40212020202020202020202020202020'
         LA    R1,FOT@CHRL+15              POINT TO LAST DIGIT
         EDMK  FOT@CHRL(16),FOT@LEFT       EDIT LEFT HALF
         LR    R2,R1                       SAVE FIRST DIGIT ADDR.
         CLI   FOT@NEG,C'-'                NEGATIVE NUMBER?
         BNE   FOT@NOTN                    IF NOT, DON'T MOVE/ADJUST
         BCTR  R2,0                        BACK UP ONE BYTE
         MVI   0(R2),C'-'                  SUPPLY NEGATIVE SIGN
FOT@NOTN DS    0H
         ED    FOT@CHRR(16),FOT@RGHT       EDIT RIGHT HALF
         LA    R3,FOT@CHRR+9               SAVE FIRST DIGIT ADDR.
.*********************************************************************
.* ADD LEADING ZEROS TO SECOND HALF IF NECESSARY.                    *
.*********************************************************************
         CLC   FOT@R000(4),=F'0'           ANY LEADING DIGITS?
         BE    FOT@NOLD                    IF NOT, SKIP NEXT CODE
         S     R3,FOT@R000                 MINUS LEADING DIGITS
FOT@NOLD DS    0H                          LEADING ZEROS SUPPLIED
.*********************************************************************
.* MOVE SECOND HALF INTO OUR WORK AREA.                              *
.*********************************************************************
         LA    R4,FOT@CHRL+16              ADDRESS END OF FIRST HALF
         SR    R4,R2                       COMPUTE LENGTH OF PART 1
         LA    R5,FOT@CHRR+16              LENGTH OF PART 2
         SR    R5,R3                       GET THIS LENGTH
         L     R1,FOT@REG1                 GET BACK PARM ADDRESS
         LA    R8,FOT@CHAR+19              ADDRESS END OF BUILD AREA
         L     R6,16(R1)                   GET DIGITS TO RIGHT
         MVI   FOT@CHAR,C' '               CLEAR BUILDING AREA
         MVC   FOT@CHAR+1(L'FOT@CHAR-1),FOT@CHAR  ...FINISH
         MVI   FOT@DP,C'N'                 NO DIGITS TO RIGHT OF DP
         LTR   R6,R6                       ANY DIGITS TO RIGHT?
         BZ    FOT@NORT                    IF NOT, DON'T USE ANY
         SR    R8,R6                       FIND PLACEMENT ADDRESS
         LR    R7,R6                       COPY AMOUNT INTO R7
         BCTR  R7,0                        SET TO EXECUTE
         EX    R7,FOT@FILL                 FILL IN WITH ZEROS
         B     *+10                        SKIP OVER EXECUTE
FOT@FILL MVC   0(0,R8),=10C'0'             FILL WITH ZEROS
.*********************************************************************
 *  GIVE USER THE NUMBER OF DIGITS THAT THEY WANTED.                 *
```

```
***************************************************************************
         CR    R5,R6                           WHICH IS LARGER, OURS/USER
         BNH   *+6                             TAKE OURS IF NOT GREATER
         LR    R5,R6                           TAKE THEIRS INSTEAD
         CLI   0(R3),C' '                      FIX FIRST POSITION FOR BIG
         BNE   *+8                             ...NUMBERED RESULTS
         MVI   0(R3),C'0'                      FORCE A ZERO
         BCTR  R5,0                            SET TO MOVE RIGHT HALF
         EX    R5,FOT@RTMV                     MOVE IN RIGHT HALF
         B     *+10
FOT@RTMV MVC   0(0,R8),0(R3)                   BUILD RIGHT HALF VALUE
         BCTR  R8,0                            NOW SUPPLY DECIMAL POINT
         MVI   0(R8),C'.'                      ...FINISH THE JOB
         MVI   FOT@DP,C'Y'                     THERE ARE DIGITS TO RT DP.
         LA    R5,FOT@CHAR+19                  ADDRESS END OF BUILD AREA
         SR    R5,R8                           COMPUTE LENGTH
.**************************************************************************
.* SEE HOW MANY DIGITS ARE TO THE RIGHT OF THE DECIMAL.  IF MORE          *
.* THAN 8 THEN THROW AWAY ALL BUT 8 DIGITS SINCE WE CAN'T ACCURATELY      *
.* REPRESENT VALUES WITH MORE THAN 8 DIGITS                               *
.**************************************************************************
         C     R5,=F'9'                        LARGER THAN 8 DIGITS?
         BNH   FOT@NORT                        IF NOT, ACCEPT AS IS
         LA    R5,9(R8)                        FIND LAST VALID DIGIT LOC
FOT@INVD DS    0H
         C     R5,=A(FOT@CHAR+19)              PAST END OF LAST DIGIT?
         BH    FOT@NORT                        YES, THEN WE'RE DONE FIXING
         MVI   0(R5),C'0'                      SUPPLY TRAILING ZERO
         LA    R5,1(R5)                        MOVE TO NEXT BYTE
         B     FOT@INVD                        CONTINUE LOOKING
FOT@NORT DS    0H
.**************************************************************************
.*  MOVE IN THE LEFT HALF OF THE NUMBER                                   *
.**************************************************************************
         SR    R8,R4                           LOCATE TARGET AREA FOR P1
         BCTR  R4,0                            SET UP TO MOVE.
         EX    R4,FOT@MVP1                     MOVE IN PART 1
         B     *+10
FOT@MVP1 MVC   0(0,R8),0(R2)                   MOVE IN FIRST HALF
         LA    R9,FOT@CHAR+19                  POINT TO END OF OUR AREA
         SR    R9,R8                           COMPUTE OUR LENGTH
         L     R7,4(R1)                        GET USER LENGTH FIELD
.**************************************************************************
.*  SEE IF USER'S AREA IS TOO SMALL FOR THE COMPLETE RESULT.              *
.**************************************************************************
         CR    R7,R9                           GREATER?  USERS/OURS
         BL    FOT@TOOB                        IF TOO SMALL THEN ABORT
         L     R6,0(R1)                        GET TARGET ADDRESS
         A     R6,4(R1)                        ADD THE LENGTH
         LR    R3,R6                           REMEMBER FOR LATER
         SR    R6,R9                           DETERMINE MOVE LOCATION
         BCTR  R9,0                            SET TO MOVE FINAL RESULT
         EX    R9,FOT@FINL                     MOVE DATA TO USER PGM.
         B     *+10
FOT@FINL MVC   0(0,R6),0(R8)                   MOVE FINAL RESULT TO USER
.**************************************************************************
.* IF THERE ARE DIGITS TO THE RIGHT OF THE DECIMAL THEN ELIMINATE         *
.* ALL UNSIGNIFICANT ZEROS TO THE RIGHT OF THE RIGHT MOST DIGIT.          *
.**************************************************************************
         CLI   FOT@DP,C'Y'                     REMOVE ENDING ZEROS?
         BNE   FOT@DPAL                        IF NOT THEN WE'RE DONE
         BCTR  R3,0                            POINT TO END OF USER FIELD
```

```
FOT@ZRDP DS     0H
         CLI    0(R3),C'0'                     IS IT A ZERO?
         BNE    FOT@DPAL                       IF NOT WE'RE DONE
         MVI    0(R3),C' '                     CHANGE TO A BLANK
         BCTR   R3,0                           BACK UP TO NEXT BYTE
         B      FOT@ZRDP                       KEEP LOOKING
FOT@DPAL DS     0H
         B      FOT@BYE                        FORCE AN EXIT
.*
.*********************************************************************
.*  IF THE NUMBER IS LARGER THAN 2 TO THE THIRTY-FIRST POWER MINUS 1 *
.*  THEN SET THE USER AREA TO X'FF' TO INDICATE THIS PROBLEM.        *
.*********************************************************************
FOT@TOOB DS     0H
         L      R1,FOT@REG1                    POINT TO PARM AREA
         LM     R2,R3,0(R1)                    ADDRESS AREA AND LENGTH
         MVI    0(R2),C'0'                     CLEAR TARGET AREA
         BCTR   R3,0                           SET FOR EXECUTE
         EX     R3,FOT@CLR2                    INDICATE TOO BIG
         B      *+10                           SKIP OVER EXECUTE
FOT@CLR2 MVC    1(0,R2),0(R2)                  SET ENTIRE AREA TO C'0'
.*
.*********************************************************************
.*  AFTER ALL CONVERSION IS DONE THEN LEAVE THE ROUTINE.  BEFORE     *
.*  DOING SO MAKE SURE THAT ALL REGISTERS ARE BACK TO THEIR          *
.*  ORIGINAL VALUES.                                                 *
.*********************************************************************
FOT@BYE  DS     0H                             EXIT POINT FROM PROGRAM
         LD     R0,FOT@F0                      RELOAD FLOATING PT. REG0
         LD     R2,FOT@F2                      RELOAD FLOATING PT. REG2
         AIF    ('&ASSIST' EQ 'NO').ASSTA
         LM     R0,R15,FOT@SAVE                RESTORE THE REGS
         BR     R14                            RETURN TO THE CALLER
         AGO    .ASSTB
.ASSTA   ANOP
         L      R13,4(R13)                     RESTORE THE SAVEAREA PTR.
         LM     R14,R12,12(R13)                RESTORE ALL REGS
         BR     R14                            RETURN TO CALLER
.ASSTB   ANOP
.*
FOT@REG1 DS     F                              ADDRESS OF PARM LIST
FOT@F0   DS     D                              HOLDING AREA FOR FLT R0
FOT@F2   DS     D                              HOLDING AREA FOR FLT R2
FOT@NUM  DS     D                              NUMBER TO BE CONVERTED
FOT@PACK DS     D                              AREA TO UNPACK VALUES
FOT@LEFT DS     D                              VALUE TO LEFT OF DECIMAL
FOT@RGHT DS     D                              VALUE TO RIGHT OF DECIMAL
FOT@WORK DS     D                              WORK AREA
FOT@POWR DS     F                              POWER OF 10
FOT@R000 DS     F                              LEADING ZEROS TO RIGHT
FOT@CHRL DS     CL16                           AREA TO CONVERT LEFT HALF
FOT@CHRR DS     CL16                           AREA TO CONVERT RIGHT HALF
FOT@CHAR DS     CL19                           PUT NUMBER TOGETHER HERE
FOT@BIG  DC     D'2147483648.0'                LARGEST POSSIBLE NUMBER
FOT@ONE  DC     D'1.0'                         CONSTANT VALUE OF 1
FOT@NEG  DS     X                              POSITIVE/NEGATIVE FLAG
FOT@DP   DS     X                              DECIMAL POINT PRESENT
         LTORG
         AIF    ('&ASSIST' EQ 'NO').NTASST
FOT@ROND DS     0H
         AGO    .OUT
.NTASST  ANOP
         POP    USING,PRINT
&CSECT   CSECT
.OUT     ANOP
         MEND
```

```
MYPGM    CSECT
         STM    R14,R12,12(R13)        SAVE CALLER'S REGISTERS
         BAL    R11,80(R15)            SKIP OVER THE SAVE AREA
         USING  *,R13,R12,R11          TELL THE ASSEMBLER
         DS     18F                    REGISTER SAVE AREA
         ST     R13,4(R11)             SAVE CURRENT R13 VALUE
         ST     R11,8(R13)             CHAIN BACKWARD
         LR     R13,R11                ESTABLISH R13 AS BASE
         XPRNT  NEWPAGE,1
LOOP     DS     0H
         XREAD  CARD,80
         BL     BYEBYE
         FLOATIN F1IN,10,R2
         FLOATIN F2IN,10,R4
         FLOATOUT R2,P1OUT,20,9
         FLOATOUT R4,P2OUT,20,9
         LDR    R6,R2
         ADR    R6,R4
         FLOATOUT R6,P3OUT,20,9
         XPRNT P1OUT,133
*
         FLOATOUT R2,P1OUT,20,9
         FLOATOUT R4,P2OUT,20,9
         LDR    R6,R2
         SDR    R6,R4
         FLOATOUT R6,P3OUT,20,9
         XPRNT P1OUT,133
*
         FLOATOUT R2,P1OUT,20,9
         FLOATOUT R4,P2OUT,20,9
         LDR    R6,R2
         MDR    R6,R4
         FLOATOUT R6,P3OUT,20,9
         XPRNT P1OUT,133
*
         FLOATOUT R2,P1OUT,20,9
         FLOATOUT R4,P2OUT,20,9
         LDR    R6,R2
         DDR    R6,R4
         FLOATOUT R6,P3OUT,20,9
         XPRNT P1OUT,133
         B      LOOP
BYEBYE   DS     0H
         XPRNT NEWPAGE,1
         L      R13,4(R13)             GET BACK R13 VALUE
         LM     R14,R12,12(R13)        RESTORE CALLER'S REGS
         SR     R15,R15                SET RETURN CODE = 0
         BR     R14                    BYE BYE
CARD     DS     0CL80
F1IN     DS     CL10
F2IN     DS     CL10
         DS     CL60
P1OUT    DS     CL20
         DC     CL5'
P2OUT    DS     CL20
```

Example 12.3 Program to add, subtract, multiply, and divide in floating-point.

```
         DC    CL5' '
P3OUT    DS    CL20
         DC    CL100' '
NEWPAGE  DC    C'1'
         LTORG
         EQUREGS
         END   MYPGM
$ENTRY
   50        100
   30         6
   4.75      .346
  -3.5        -4.2
  -1.0       -1.0
   0           14
   14.3        .000001
   123.45     2.0
 123.45        1.0
 123.45     123.45
 .0003       .0004
 .25         .25
 1.25        100
  42.77      3.0004
  -333      .2
  100       .001
  .00001    10000
 .003        1000
  .02         200
  .9          50
  .04        100
  .03        100
//
```

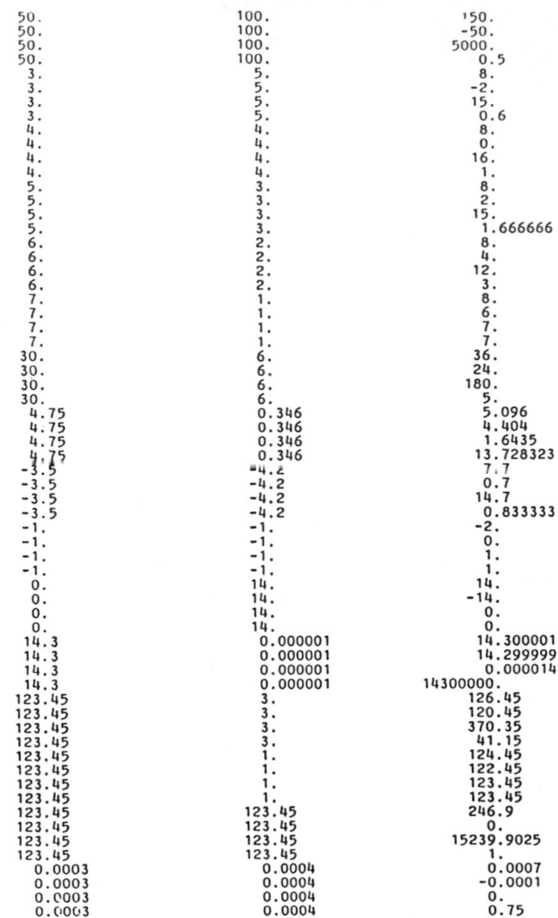

```
    50.          100.          150.
    50.          100.          -50.
    50.          100.         5000.
    50.          100.            0.5
     3.            5.            8.
     3.            5.           -2.
     3.            5.           15.
     3.            5.            0.6
     4.            4.            8.
     4.            4.            0.
     4.            4.           16.
     4.            4.            1.
     5.            3.            8.
     5.            3.            2.
     5.            3.           15.
     5.            3.            1.666666
     6.            2.            8.
     6.            2.            4.
     6.            2.           12.
     6.            2.            3.
     7.            1.            8.
     7.            1.            6.
     7.            1.            7.
     7.            1.            7.
    30.            6.           36.
    30.            6.           24.
    30.            6.          180.
    30.            6.            5.
     4.75          0.346         5.096
     4.75          0.346         4.404
     4.75          0.346         1.6435
     4.75          0.346        13.728323
    -3.5          -4.2           7.7
    -3.5          -4.2           0.7
    -3.5          -4.2          14.7
    -3.5          -4.2           0.833333
    -1.           -1.           -2.
    -1.           -1.            0.
    -1.           -1.            1.
    -1.           -1.            1.
     0.           14.           14.
     0.           14.          -14.
     0.           14.            0.
     0.           14.            0.
    14.3           0.000001     14.300001
    14.3           0.000001     14.299999
    14.3           0.000001      0.000014
    14.3           0.000001 14300000.
   123.45          3.          126.45
   123.45          3.          120.45
   123.45          3.          370.35
   123.45          3.           41.15
   123.45          1.          124.45
   123.45          1.          122.45
   123.45          1.          123.45
   123.45          1.          123.45
   123.45        123.45        246.9
   123.45        123.45          0.
   123.45        123.45      15239.9025
   123.45        123.45          1.
     0.0003        0.0004        0.0007
     0.0003        0.0004       -0.0001
     0.0003        0.0004        0.
     0.0003        0.0004        0.75
```

Example 12.4 Selected output from the program of Example 12.3.

STUDY QUESTIONS

1. What are the various storage formats for representing a floating-point number?
2. How are positive and negative floating-point numbers represented?
3. What are the three components of a floating-point number?
4. Two doubleword floating-point numbers called A and B are added. The result is placed into the area called SUM. Write the code to perform this activity.
5. How is the value zero represented in floating-point format?
6. What facilities increase the accuracy of floating-point operations?
7. How do the floating-point multiply and divide instructions differ from those of binary or packed-decimal processing?
8. What is the largest characteristic value for a floating-point number?
9. How many fractional digits are contained in each floating-point number format?

10. What instruction obtains the absolute value of a four-byte floating-point number?
11. Normalize the following floating-point values.

```
(a)   43001AF7
(b)   3F268900
(c)   C0123456
```

12. Convert the following base 10 numbers to short-form floating-point.

```
(a)   4321
(b)   .543
(c)   4321.543
```

13. Convert the floating-point numbers below to base 10 representation.

```
(a)   C1500000
(b)   3F800000
(c)   441234CC
```

14. Convert the following base 10 numbers to long-form floating-point representation.

```
(a)   .5
(b)   3.1416
(c)   123.123
```

15. Convert the following long-form floating-point numbers to base 10 representation.

```
(a)   3FCCCCCCCCCCCCCC
(b)   4413880000000000
(c)   C1255551D68C692D
```

PROGRAMMING PROBLEMS

1. Modify the FLOATIN and FLOATOUT macros to support numbers in scientific notation.
2. During automobile manufacturing, each part for an automobile is cataloged with its part number, cost, function, and weight. If the input to a program is all of the parts, write a program to compute the total weight of an automobile if each part weight is accurate to five digits to the right of the decimal.
3. Given each car part in Programming Problem 2, suppose that the weight of each part may be reduced by 7% if its weight is over 1.5 pounds. For parts weighing less than 1.5 pounds, the weight can only be reduced by 0.1%. Write a program to compute the new weight of each part and print a report listing the part number, function, old weight, and expected new weight value.
4. A computer is made up of many different circuit parts. The time for an electrical signal to be transferred or processed by a part impacts the overall speed of the computer. Assume that a

new computer is to be built and you are given each component and its average processing speed, accurate to six digits to the right of the decimal. Compute the expected speed of the computer if we assume that a signal is processed by each part in succession.

5. Each instruction on a computer takes a certain time for processing. In fact, if we know the time that each instruction requires, it would be possible to anticipate or predict the amount of processing time required by a program. Suppose that each instruction and its time requirement can be input to our program. Following this input, we then read in a complete program and proceed to compute the expected time requirement. For each program instruction, print the expected time value alongside the instruction. Keep a running total of the expected time values and print the overall program time requirement at the end. Warning: How will you predict looping requirements by the program?

6. Daily air samples are taken in a community to measure the amount of pollen and other particles in the atmosphere. The samples are analyzed and the particles are separated and weighed based on type and category. Since some particles are not captured in great quantities, the measurements must be very precise and require an accuracy of at least five digits to the left and right of the decimal. Each sample measurement is recorded and is processed by a computer program that you must develop. The program reports on each particle found, its total weight within any given sample, and the total weight of all particle measurements for the day, week, and month. The program also plots the total weight of each daily sample in a graphic format to further illustrate any increase or decrease in particle collection.

7. Obsolete or broken computer systems are placed in the basement of a local university. Without the knowledge of the administration or staff, students in the computer department go into the basement each night and scrape the gold plating off the electrical circuits within the old computers. During the next day, the students weigh the gold particles and determine how much their effort was worth. Using very precise scales in the chemistry and physics departments, students weigh the gold to an accuracy of seven decimal places. After weighing, the weights are entered into a computer program (developed by you, of course) that computes the earnings for the evening. Assuming that gold is worth $400 per ounce, make up some weight values and process them through your program.

8. The square root approximation of a number was presented in several programming problems in previous chapters. Rewrite any of your former implementations to utilize floating-point processing.

9. It is common to refer to the floating point registers using FLT2, FP2, or F2 instead of the R2 notation. Revise the EQUATES macro to generate floating point register equates or develop a completely new macro to provide this facility.

10. Process input records until end of file. Each input record contains a single integer value that represents the radius of a circle. If pi represents the number 3.1416, use this value to compute the diameter, area, and circumference of a circle using the formulas below:

```
     diameter = 2 * radius
         area = pi * (radius * radius)
circumference = 2 * pi * radius
```

13

More Advanced Topics

This chapter continues to extend our processing capabilities by investigating some very advanced assembly language processing services. Specifically, this chapter discusses the construction and use of dummy control sections, locate mode processing, program reentrancy, variable-length record processing, communicating with the operator, and tape processing techniques. Although many of these facilities are invaluable, there are limitations on these processing capabilities when using ASSIST. Specifically, although dummy control sections can be used under ASSIST, the other topics require operating system services not supported under ASSIST. Therefore, we begin with dummy control sections, giving you the option of skipping the rest of the chapter if you are limited to ASSIST.

DUMMY CONTROL SECTIONS (DSECT's)

As you know, we generally use labels to reference storage areas within our programs since they allow easier referencing as compared to explicit addressing techniques. However, we did encounter some difficulty in referencing data elements using labels. If you recall, the construction of a two-dimensional array yields a situation in which labels cannot reference each of the various elements within the array in a meaningful manner. In fact, referencing any element other than the first requires offsets or register references. The situation discussed in Chapter 11 involves student data consisting of student names, social security numbers, and a class score. What we attempted to do was to define a table to store 50 sets of student data. However, the assembler does not permit the definition of a table as shown in Fig. 13.1. Therefore, we are forced to reference the elements within the table using explicit addressing.

```
This example will not work.
STUDENTS  DS   50(CL20,CL9,PL3)
```

Figure 13.1 Incorrect definition of a 50-element table.

Through the use of DSECT's, this dilemma is easily solved. A **DSECT (dummy control section)** is a data structure that references storage areas using labels without defining storage for the DSECT itself. For example, a simple data structure to reference one student's data is constructed as shown in Fig. 13.2. However, this structure sets aside 32 bytes of storage and it only allows us to reference one student's data using labels. If we convert this data structure into a DSECT, we can use the labels within this structure to reference *any* student's data and yet we do not set aside any storage for this definition. See the code of Fig. 13.3.

```
NAME    DS   CL20
SSN     DS   CL9
SCORE   DS   PL3
```

Figure 13.2 Structure to reference student/class data.

```
STUDENT   DSECT
NAME      DS        CL20
SSN       DS        CL9
SCORE     DS        PL3
```

Figure 13.3 Student data structure implemented as a DSECT.

Again, DSECT's do not define storage, but they address other storage areas in your program. Therefore, to access the data elements in a storage area with a DSECT, we establish addressability to the storage area by coding a USING statement as shown in Fig. 13.4.

```
USING   STUDENT,R3
```

Figure 13.4 Establishing addressability to the student DSECT.

Whenever we reference any of the labeled areas called NAME, SSN, or SCORE, we're actually referring to the respective storage areas 0(R3), 20(R3), and 29(R3), all of which are addressed by register 3. In fact, a DSECT can be thought of as a template floating around the computer's memory. Whenever addressability is established to the DSECT through the USING statement, the template overlays the storage area address contained in the register. This allows us to reference the storage area using the labels in the DSECT. If the address in the DSECT register changes, the DSECT moves to a new location within the computer. Let's illustrate this concept using the program segment shown in Fig. 13.5.

The definition of the area called TABLE does not allow easy label referencing of each student's data within this table. With the DSECT however, labels *can* provide this reference. Although the DSECT does not define any storage, it does provide addressability to some other storage area, in this case, TABLE. This occurs through the DSECT definition and its associated USING statement.

The register associated with the DSECT, in this example R3, changes during processing. R3 originally addresses the first row in the table, but as each new student's record is read from the input card file, R3 moves to the next row within the table. The relocatable symbol ROWLEN provides the length of each row in the table. After all input student data is loaded into the table and the end of file is reached, R3 is returned to the beginning of the table for further processing.

```
         .       .
         .       .
         LA      R3,TABLE           ADDRESS THE TABLE STORAGE AREA
         USING   STUDENT,R3         ESTABLISH DSECT ADDRESSABILITY
FILLTBL  DS      0H                 BEGIN TABLE FILLING CODE
         XREAD   CARDIN,80          READ IN AN INPUT DATA CARD
         BL      EOF                STOP WHEN EOF IS REACHED
         MVC     NAME(20),CNAME     MOVE CARD NAME INTO THE TABLE
         MVC     SSN(9),CSSN        MOVE SSN INTO THE TABLE
         PACK    SCORE,CSCORE       STORE SCORE INTO THE TABLE
         LA      R3,ROWLEN(R3)      MOVE DSECT TO NEXT ROW
         B       FILLTBL

EOF      DS      0H
         LA      R3,TABLE           POINT TO BEGINNING OF TABLE

         .       .
         .       .

CARDIN   DS      0CL80
CNAME    DS      CL20
CSSN     DS      CL9
CSCORE   DS      CL5
REST     DS      CL46

TABLE    DS      100CL32            ALLOW FOR 100 STUDENTS

STUDENT  DSECT
NAME     DS      CL20
SSN      DS      CL9
SCORE    DS      PL3
ROWLEN   EQU     *-NAME
```

Figure 13.5 Code segment that uses DSECT processing.

Each element in each table row is referenced using the labels NAME, SSN, and SCORE. Without the DSECT, we'd have to fill the table using explicit addressing such as 0(R3), 20(R3), and 29(R3). Labels allow us to attach much more meaning to the data being processed as compared to the displacement-register forms normally used. To further illustrate the use of DSECT's, consider the same program that uses a DSECT to reference the table elements as well as a DSECT to reference the input data records as shown in Fig. 13.6.

The definition of the input area is not structured into individual field definitions. Instead, a DSECT, used as a template, subdivides the area labeled CARDIN into the fields CNAME, CSSN, CSCORE, and CREST. The DATAIN DSECT does not define or set aside a storage area, it is simply used as a template to rename the bytes within the area labeled CARDIN.

Additionally, several DSECT's may be used to address the same storage location. Considering the area labeled CARDIN, several DSECT's may be used to define this 80-byte storage area in different ways. All DSECT's may be active at the same time as well. This capability allows the input card area to consist of several different record formats. Each record format can be referenced through labels with its respective DSECT.

DSECT's are very powerful when developing programs with subroutines. In particular, they are very useful when referencing the parameters being passed from the calling to the called routine. For the subroutine to reference each element, the address of the parameter's value must be obtained through an offset from register 1 (since R1 is the link address register). Addressability to the data elements can then be accomplished by coding a USING statement for the associated DSECT. For example, assume that a complete employee record is passed to a subroutine to compute the employee's taxes for the weekly

```
         .        .
         .        .
         LA       R3,TABLE            ADDRESS THE TABLE STORAGE AREA
         USING    STUDENT,R3          ESTABLISH DSECT ADDRESSABILITY
         LA       R4,CARDIN           ADDRESS INPUT RECORD AREA
         USING    DATAIN,R4           ESTABLISH DSECT ADDRESSABILITY
FILLTBL  DS       0H                  BEGIN TABLE FILLING CODE
         XREAD    CARDIN,80           READ IN AN INPUT DATA CARD
         BL       EOF                 STOP WHEN EOF IS REACHED
         MVC      NAME(20),CNAME      MOVE CARD NAME INTO THE TABLE
         MVC      SSN(9),CSSN         MOVE SSN INTO THE TABLE
         PACK     SCORE,CSCORE        STORE SCORE INTO THE TABLE
         LA       R3,ROWLEN(R3)       MOVE DSECT TO NEXT ROW
         B        FILLTBL

EOF      DS       0H
         LA       R3,TABLE            POINT TO BEGINNING OF TABLE

         .        .
         .        .

CARDIN   DS       CL80

TABLE    DS       100CL32             ALLOW FOR 100 STUDENTS

STUDENT  DSECT
NAME     DS       CL20
SSN      DS       CL9
SCORE    DS       PL3
ROWLEN   EQU      *-NAME

DATAIN   DSECT
CNAME    DS       CL20
CSSN     DS       CL9
CSCORE   DS       CL5
CREST    DS       CL46
```

Figure 13.6 Using DSECT's for input and table processing.

payroll. Although the address of the record can be passed as a single parameter, many fields within the employee record may have to be referenced by the subroutine to compute the taxes. Since field referencing is most understandable using labels, a DSECT is an excellent choice here. Figure 13.7 shows the program segment related to this discussion.

DSECT's are very powerful, but they require the use of registers. As we know, the registers available may dwindle to the point of not allowing processing because of the many facilities and uses that require registers. For that reason, it may be necessary to use

```
         L        R2,0(R1)            GET ADDRESS OF THE DATA RECORD
         USING    EMPLOYEE,R2         ESTABLISH ADDRESSABILITY

         .        .
         compute the taxes using named fields in the DSECT
         .        .

EMPLOYEE DSECT
NAME     DS       CL30
IDNUM    DS       F
GROSSPAY DS       PL7
TAXRATE  DS       H
TAXES    DS       PL7
         .        .
         .        .
```

Figure 13.7 Using a DSECT for subroutine parameters.

a single register to address multiple DSECT's as long as only one DSECT is to be addressed at any given time. Suppose, for example, that DSECT's DS1 and DS2 are to be used in a program but not simultaneously. Addressability is established for DS1 so that its fields are addressed within the program code using labels. When it's time to address fields using DS2, addressability to DS1 is dropped and addressability to DS2 is established. This is accomplished through the **DROP** and USING instruction sequence as shown in Fig. 13.8.

Regardless of the number of DSECT's used by your program, they are all coded in the same manner. The DSECT begins with the DSECT statement and contains DS instructions. DC instructions may be coded in the DSECT, but remember that storage is not reserved and initialization *does not occur.*

DSECT's are generally defined before your CSECT statement and after your macro definitions. They may also be defined just before the END statement. The placement of DSECT definitions is a matter of preference unless you're using the next form of DSECT definition that we're about to discuss.

If a DSECT is defined before the start of your CSECT, the USING statement can be contained within the DSECT definition. This eliminates the need to code the USING statement within the program since the entire program has addressability to the DSECT. Referring to our earlier discussion of the student table, Fig. 13.9 illustrates DSECT coding when the DSECT definition *precedes* that of the program.

The DSECT is defined before the start of the program, thus allowing the USING statement to be contained within the DSECT. Therefore, throughout the program, R3 is used as the base register for this DSECT. Since addressability to the DSECT is contained within the DSECT, a USING statement does not have to be coded within the program.

COPY LIBRARIES

When using external subroutines, it is often necessary for both the calling and called modules to share fields during processing. To standardize references to these fields, one or more DSECT's can be utilized by the modules to reduce the coding required by the programmer(s). Since a DSECT can address any storage area, only the USING statement may have to change in the modules to establish addressability to the shared field values.

Sharing a DSECT among modules helps in standardization since programmers use the same labels to reference the fields and become more familiar with the names associated with the data to be processed. In fact, DSECT's or other common sections of code can be placed into a **copy library** so that they are available to anyone. Remember, a

```
LA       R7,AREA1             POINT TO FIRST STORAGE AREA
USING    DS1,R7               ESTABLISH ADDRESSABILITY TO DS1
.        .
.        .
  process data using the DS1 DSECT
.        .
.        .

DROP     R7
LA       R7,AREA2             ADDRESS THE SECOND STORAGE AREA
USING    DS2,R7               ESTABLISH THE DS2 DSECT
.        .
.        .
  now process data using the DS2 DSECT
```

Figure 13.8 Multiple DSECT support from a single register.

```
STUDENT    DSECT
           USING  *,R3
NAME       DS     CL20
SSN        DS     CL9
SCORE      DS     PL3
ROWLEN     EQU    *-NAME

MAINPGM    CSECT
           .      .
           .      .

           LA     R3,TABLE             ADDRESS THE TABLE STORAGE AREA
FILLTBL    DS     0H                   BEGIN TABLE FILLING CODE
           XREAD  CARDIN,80            READ IN AN INPUT DATA CARD
           BL     EOF                  STOP WHEN EOF IS REACHED
           MVC    NAME(20),CNAME       MOVE CARD NAME INTO THE TABLE
           MVC    SSN(9),CSSN          MOVE SSN INTO THE TABLE
           PACK   SCORE,CSCORE         STORE SCORE INTO THE TABLE
           LA     R3,ROWLEN(R3)        MOVE DSECT TO NEXT ROW
           B      FILLTBL

EOF        DS     0H
           LA     R3,TABLE             POINT TO BEGINNING OF TABLE

           .      .
           .      .

CARDIN     DS     0CL80
CNAME      DS     CL20
CSSN       DS     CL9
CSCORE     DS     CL5
REST       DS     CL46

TABLE      DS     100CL32              ALLOW FOR 100 STUDENTS
```

Figure 13.9 Defining the DSECT before the start of the program.

macro can be placed into a macro library to allow many programmers to use it. The same situation can occur with DSECT's or even sections of code. Such code can be placed into a library and copied into your program using the assembly language **COPY instruction.** Figure 13.10 illustrates this technique. For example, wherever the copy statement is coded, a DSECT called EMPLOYEE is copied into your program (the mnemonic COPY begins in column 10).

```
COPY   EMPLOYEE
```

Figure 13.10 Including a code segment or DSECT into your program using the COPY instruction.

Of course, we're assuming that such a DSECT exists in a copy library. Should you want to create a copy library, the JCL shown in Fig. 13.11 performs this function.

DSECT's or program code can be placed into a copy library using the IEBUPDTE utility as described in Chapter 10. For example, the EMPLOYEE DSECT can be added to our copy library using the JCL shown in Fig. 13.12.

Incidentally, the example in Fig. 13.12 can also be used to replace the current copy of the EMPLOYEE DSECT with an updated version if necessary.

```
//    EXEC  PGM=IEFBR14
//DDA       DD  DSN=MY.COPY.LIBRARY,DISP=(NEW,CATLG),
//          UNIT=SYSDA,SPACE=(CYL,(2,,36)),DCB=SYS1.MACLIB
```

Figure 13.11 JCL to create a copy library.

```
//       EXEC   PGM=IEBUPDTE,PARM=NEW
//SYSPRINT      DD    SYSOUT=$
//SYSUT2        DD    DSN=MY.COPY.LIBRARY,DISP=SHR
//SYSIN         DD    *
./    ADD       NAME=EMPLOYEE,LIST=ALL
EMPLOYEE        DSECT
NAME            DS         CL30
                 .          .
                 .          .
./    ENDUP
```

Figure 13.12 Adding a DSECT to a copy library.

Finally, one additional JCL modification is required to use copy libraries during our processing. Typically, we invoke the assembler to process our programs by using the JCL shown in Fig. 13.13. This JCL is now changed to reference our copy library. This is accomplished by coding the JCL as illustrated in Fig. 13.14.

```
//          EXEC   ASMFCG
//ASM.SYSIN        DD   *
```

Figure 13.13 Typical JCL to assemble and execute assembly language programs.

```
//          EXEC   ASMFCG
//ASM.SYSLIB   DD   DSN=MY.COPY.LIBRARY,DISP=SHR
//ASM.SYSIN    DD   *
```

Figure 13.14 JCL to access a copy library.

As you can see, the associated DDNAME for the assembler to access our copy library is **SYSLIB.** If you recall, this is the same DDNAME used to reference macro libraries. In fact, a copy library and a macro library have the same characteristics and can be used interchangeably. Usually, one library is used for both purposes. Finally, the name that I selected for my copy library may, of course, not meet your needs or the standards within your organization. The name may be changed to suit your processing environment.

LOCATE MODE PROCESSING

All file processing operations performed up to this point have used **move mode** processing techniques. Although you may not have understood what this meant, we will now discuss the details of move mode versus locate mode I/O. Further, you'll see that DSECT's can be very valuable when using locate mode processing.

Data external to our programs is usually stored on disk, tape, or on cards. As we process this data, each record is retrieved from the device and presented to our program. In other words, each time that we issue a GET instruction, the data is retrieved from the device and moved into an area in our program to be processed. To write records, data is taken from our program area and written to the printer or to some other external storage device.

What we don't see happening during processing are some services provided by the access method. In particular, the access method obtains the data from the device and moves it into our program area. To help perform this task, the access method uses an area of memory to hold our records, which is called a **buffer,** that is large enough to hold our largest *physical* record. In other words, data stored outside the program is stored as **physical records.** Our program, however, processes **logical records.**

The size of each buffer is equal to the size of our largest physical record. However, since our program can only process one logical record at a time, the size of the area in our program is equal to the size of the logical records to be processed. Hence, as we issue GET or PUT instructions, the access method extracts a logical record from within the physical record and moves the data from the buffer into our program area (for input processing) or from our program area to the buffer (for output processing). When a buffer becomes empty (input) or full (output), the access method fills or empties the buffer, respectively, by obtaining another physical record from the device or writing the record in the buffer to the device. In any case, our program processes each data record within the bounds of the program, thus causing the access method to move the data to or from the program during processing. This activity, called **move mode processing,** requires additional overhead on the part of the access method to support our I/O requests. Figure 13.15 further illustrates this relationship.

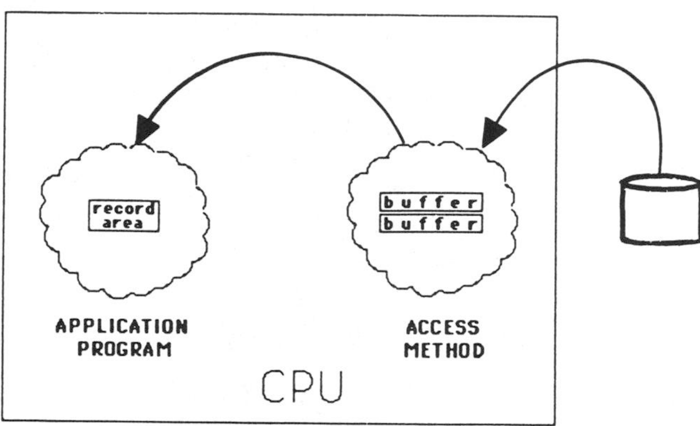

RECORDS ARE MOVED FROM THE ACCESS METHOD'S BUFFER INTO THE PROGRAM'S AREA WHERE THE RECORDS ARE PROCESSED.

Figure 13.15 I/O movement through the buffer area.

Generally, two buffers are set aside by the access method for each file to be processed. Consider, for example, a dataset with a logical record length of 100 and a physical record length of 500. In this situation, each physical record consists of five logical records. This situation is called **blocked data** or, simply, **blocking.** If the ratio of logical to physical records is 1 : 1, then each logical record requires a separate physical record for storing. Data is said to be **nonblocked** in this situation.

The size of each logical and physical record is determined by two parameters that we've been coding on our DCB instructions or on our JCL when our datasets were created, **LRECL (logical record length)** and **BLKSIZE (physical record length).** When the value of the LRECL and BLKSIZE parameters are equal, the records in our file are processed in nonblocked format. When the LRECL is an integer multiple of the BLKSIZE, the records are processed in blocked format.

If we assume that we have blocked data in the ratio of 5 : 1, then for every five I/O operations issued by our program, the access method performs only one I/O. Since I/O operations are expensive in terms of processing time, the fewer physical I/O operations required, the faster the program processes. Hence, packing more logical records into each physical record generally increases the performance of our program. Further, larger physical record sizes generally increases storage efficiency as well. That is, a storage device holds more records if the data is blocked than if the data is nonblocked.

If data is nonblocked, then a 1 : 1 relationship exists between logical and physical records. Clearly, the access method performs as many physical I/O operations as the number of I/O requests that are issued. In general, nonblocked data files are very inefficient although they are required in some processing situations. For each I/O operation, our program must wait for the access method to obtain the data and move it into our program area for processing. As a result, the access method usually suspends our processing until the data has been moved into (input) or removed from (output) our program area.

We can increase program performance by processing the data directly in the access method's buffer area. Since a buffer is nothing more than an area of memory, there's no reason why another area has to be defined within our program to process records. With **locate mode processing,** the records are processed within the access method's buffer area, saving the access method the overhead of moving the data to or from our program area. Eliminating this extra movement of data allows our program to process faster.

Before discussing locate mode processing, let's first recall how we performed move mode processing. Assuming that our program processes employee records, the program shown in Fig. 13.16 performs move mode sequential record processing.

The DCB instruction contains the MACRF parameter that indicates that move mode processing is to be used. Specifically, the MACRF value, **GM** (get move), indicates that input (G) and move mode processing (M) are to be used on this file. Also, the definition of the employee record is contained within our program area, that is, the data structure called EMPLOYEE defines a storage area within the program and it describes each logical record to be processed.

This program may be easily converted into locate mode processing. First, the EMPLOYEE logical record description is converted into a DSECT definition. Since the logi-

```
MAINPGM     CSECT
            .         .
            .         .
LOOP        GET       EMPIN,EMPLOYEE      GET AN EMPLOYEE RECORD
            .         .
               process the employee record
            .         .
            B         LOOP                GET THE NEXT RECORD

EOF         DS        0H
            .         .

EMPIN       DCB       DSORG=PS,DDNAME=EMPLOYEE,MACRF=GM,EODAD=EOF

EMPLOYEE    DS        0CL100
NAME        DS        CL30
            .         .
            .         .
```

Figure 13.16 Program format for move mode processing.

cal records are not moved into our program area, they are processed outside in the access method's buffer. Since buffers reside outside of our program area, a DSECT is needed to address this data and to allow us to use labels to reference the fields within each logical record. Explicit addressing techniques may also be used to reference the data in the buffer. However, since DSECT's provide more meaningful field referencing capabilities, let's use this technique.

Next, the MACRF parameter on the DCB is changed from GM to **GL (get locate),** which informs the access method that locate mode input processing is to access this dataset.

Finally, the GET instruction itself must be changed. Referring back to Fig. 13.16, the GET instruction references the logical record description called EMPLOYEE. Since this structure no longer exists within our program, the GET instruction cannot refer to it. Hence, the GET instruction must provide an *address* to the logical record. This occurs through register 1. By copying the address of the record into another register and by using this register to address the DSECT, we can process logical records in almost the same manner as we did before. This technique is illustrated in Fig. 13.17.

```
MAINPGM     CSECT
            .         .
            .         .
LOOP        GET       EMPIN               GET AN EMPLOYEE RECORD
            LR        R3,R1               GET ADDR OF LOGICAL RECORD
            USING     EMPLOYEE,R3         ESTABLISH ADDRESSABILITY
            .         .
               process the employee record
            .         .
            B         LOOP                GET THE NEXT RECORD

EOF         DS        0H
            .         .

EMPIN       DCB       DSORG=PS,DDNAME=EMPLOYEE,MACRF=GL,EODAD=EOF

EMPLOYEE    DSECT
NAME        DS        CL30
            .         .
            .         .
```

Figure 13.17 Locate mode program format.

The actual code to process the employee records has not changed. The program can still reference the fields within the employee records using labels since the DSECT provides addressability with the assistance of register 3. On the other hand, this slight change in coding has probably increased the I/O processing performance by almost 50%.

Locate mode processing may also be used on output. Suppose that the same program prints a report on each employee record. Integrating locate mode output in the program given in Fig. 13.17, we arrive at the solution given in Fig. 13.18.

The PUT instruction returns the address to an area where a print line may be constructed. Since the DSECT called PLINE is to be used to construct the output lines within the report, a USING statement establishes addressability to the DSECT with register 5 as the base register for this DSECT. Note that a PUT instruction begins the program even though nothing is printed on the first PUT instruction. The first PUT instruction *only* returns the address of the first area into which subsequent print lines may be constructed. After a print line is built, it may then be printed using another PUT instruction. Later, PUT instructions not only print the previous line constructed, but also supply a new buffer area address into which the next print line may be built.

As you can see from the REPORT DCB, the MACRF operand contains the value **PL (put locate).** Clearly, this means that output (P) operations are to be issued and that locate mode processing (L) is to be used. You'll also notice that the records are blocked

```
MAINPGM  CSECT
         .        .
         .        .
         PUT      REPORT              OBTAIN AREA ADDRESS
         LR       R5,R1               GET PRINT LINE ADDRESS
         USING    PLINE,R5            ESTABLISH DSECT REFERENCE
LOOP     GET      EMPIN               GET AN EMPLOYEE RECORD
         LR       R3,R1               GET ADDR OF LOGICAL RECORD
         USING    EMPLOYEE,R3         ESTABLISH ADDRESSABILITY
         .        .
           process the employee record
         .        .
           move data into the print line
         .        .
         PUT      REPORT              PRINT LINE AND GET NEW
*                                       AREA ADDRESS
         LR       R5,R1               GET NEXT OUTPUT AREA ADDR
         B        LOOP                GET THE NEXT RECORD
EOF      DS       0H
         .        .
EMPIN    DCB      DSORG=PS,DDNAME=EMPLOYEE,MACRF=GL,EODAD=EOF
REPORT   DCB      DSORG=PS,DDNAME=PRINT,MACRF=PL,RECFM=FBA,          X
                  LRECL=133,BLKSIZE=1330
EMPLOYEE DSECT
NAME     DS       CL30
         .        .
         .        .
PLINE    DSECT
CC       DS       C
         .        .
         .        .
```

Figure 13.18 Input and output using locate mode processing.

for this dataset. Ten logical records of 133 bytes each are contained in each physical record. Again, blocking improves program performance and storage efficiency when processing files sequentially.

Although you may think that locate mode output will again yield a 50% performance improvement, this is not likely the case. Each time that a line is to be printed, the program must *fully* construct the entire print line. Remember, DSECT's do not recognize constants on DC instructions. Therefore, a value must be supplied to every column in the print line during execution time. Since this processing might require many MVC or MVI instructions on the part of the programmer, it is generally accepted that locate mode processing is not used on output since the savings in processing overhead are not significant. However, locate mode processing is strongly encouraged for input processing regardless of the type of file being processed.

TAPE PROCESSING

Processing a dataset on tape is not much different than processing one on cards or disk. Sequential processing must be used and either move mode or locate mode can be used to process the records. Further, data is stored on tape in blocked or nonblocked format as described in the previous section.

The primary difference between tape, card, and disk processing is in the coding of the JCL needed to reference the datasets. However, two general formats are used when storing data on a tape volume. Therefore, your program must know which format is to be processed so that the appropriate JCL operands can be coded when trying to access the tape.

The two most common formats for storing tape data are **standard label** tape format and **nonlabeled** tape format. Processing records in either format is almost identical except for the JCL parameters that access the data. Standard label tape format stores information about the records themselves. Specifically, standard label tape format contains information on the record format (RECFM), logical record length (LRECL), and physical record length (BLKSIZE). Hence, these parameters do not have to be coded when processing an *existing* standard label tape file. On the other hand, values for these parameters *must* be specified when *creating* a standard label tape file or when processing *any* nonlabeled tape file.

Let's assume that all parameters for processing a tape file are specified on the JCL and not on the DCB within our program. By doing so, we can simplify the coding discussion by simply saying that a tape file is processed just as any other file discussed earlier. The input and output DCB's using locate mode input and move mode output are shown in Fig. 13.19 for reference. Since the GET and PUT instructions are coded exactly as in previous examples, no discussion is necessary.

```
INPUT    DCB   DSORG=PS,DDNAME=TAPEIN,MACRF=GL,EODAD=EOF

OUTPUT   DCB   DSORG=PS,DDNAME=TAPEOUT,MACRF=PM
```

Figure 13.19 Sample DCB's for tape processing.

Since JCL is of primary concern when processing tape files, let's discuss its coding. A summary of the required parameters are given in Fig. 13.20 and a summary of the optional parameters is given in Figure 13.21.

Required JCL Parameter	Explanation
VOL=SER	Tape identification number.
UNIT=TAPE	Specifies that a tape dataset is to be processed.
DISP	Specifies the dataset disposition. If processing an existing tape dataset, then the value of this parameter should be (OLD,KEEP). Creating a dataset requires coding (NEW,KEEP).
LABEL	Tape volumes may contain several tape files. This parameter identifies the file on the tape to be processed.

Figure 13.20 Required tape processing JCL parameters.

Optional JCL Parameter	Explanation
DSN	Name of the tape dataset that is to be processed. This parameter is not coded when processing nonlabeled tapes, but is required when processing standard label tapes.
DCB	Always required when processing nonlabeled tapes or when creating a standard label tape dataset.

Figure 13.21 Optional tape processing JCL parameters.

Suppose that a tape dataset is to be processed. The tape identification number is 123456. The data in this file consists of fixed-length blocked records having a logical record length of 100 and a physical record length of 500. Finally, assume that there is only one file on the tape. Again the code and logic in our program does not change when processing tape files as compared to card or disk files. Hence, we will not review the program logic to process the data on this tape but rather we only have to code the appropriate JCL to reference the tape and data properly. The JCL statements in Figs. 13.22 through 13.25 process the dataset described. Note that each example relates to the DCB instructions coded earlier (see Fig. 13.19).

```
//GO.TAPEOUT    DD  DSN=tape.dataset.name,VOL=SER=123456,
//                  DISP=(NEW,KEEP),UNIT=TAPE,LABEL=(1,SL),
//                  DCB=(RECFM=FB,LRECL=100,BLKSIZE=500)
```

Figure 13.22 Creating a standard label tape dataset.

```
//GO.TAPEIN      DD   DSN=tape.dataset.name,VOL=SER=123456,
//                    DISP=(OLD,KEEP),UNIT=TAPE,LABEL=(1,SL)
```

Figure 13.23 Accessing an existing standard label tape dataset.

```
//GO.TAPEOUT     DD   VOL=SER=123456,DISP=(NEW,KEEP),
//                    UNIT=TAPE,LABEL=(1,NL),
//                    DCB=(RECFM=FB,LRECL=100,BLKSIZE=500)
```

Figure 13.24 Creating a nonlabeled tape dataset.

```
//GO.TAPEIN      DD   VOL=SER=123456,DISP=(OLD,KEEP),
//                    UNIT=TAPE,LABEL=(1,NL),
//                    DCB=(RECFM=FB,LRECL=100,BLKSIZE=500)
```

Figure 13.25 Accessing an existing nonlabeled tape dataset.

VARIABLE-LENGTH RECORD PROCESSING

Since the beginning of the text, we've been concerned with processing records of the same length. Although this has served our needs well, fixed-length record processing does not meet all of our processing needs. Consider, for example, a bank where a person's deposit and check records must be maintained. Since the number of deposits or checks written are not the same every month, it's more appropriate to consider the data associated with this application to be of variable length. In other words, the amount of data maintained by the bank for a particular account varies depending on the activity within that account for the month.

Since the amount of data to be processed is not fixed, another technique is used to capture the data regardless of the number of checks or deposits issued. To perform such processing, programs may use **variable-length record processing** to store and process data of this type. In other words, variable-length record processing allows each record in a file to be a different length. Further, records can "grow" or "shrink" as data is added or removed from a record.

A variable-length record consists of two primary components, a **root portion** and a **variable portion**. The root portion consists of all the data that has a consistent length and is present each time the record is processed. In the case of our bank, the root portion most likely consists of the account number, account owner information, and the current balance. The variable portion of the record consists of the deposit or check data, specifically, the date of the transaction, the amount of the transaction, the name of the person to whom the check was written, and at which facility the deposit was made. If we think of each check or deposit as a **segment** of data, we can picture a variable-length record as a root portion with many segments of data attached to the root. Clearly, the number of segments varies from month to month, depending on the number of checks and deposits processed. Figure 13.26 illustrates the variable-length record.

Although the amount of information contained in a deposit segment can differ from that in a check segment, they are usually the same length. If the length of each segment is also variable, the complexity of processing becomes quite substantial. For our purposes, let's assume that segments have the same length and proceed to process records of this type.

Variable-length record files are processed using a record format of **V (variable)** or

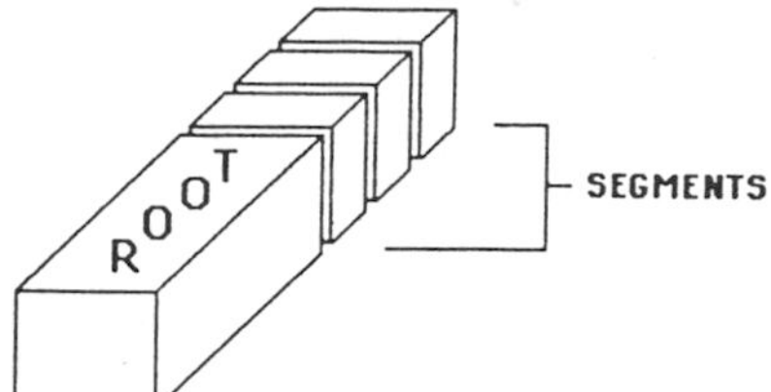

Figure 13.26 General format of the variable-length record.

VB (variable blocked). With respect to the logical and physical record sizes, *maximum* values for the logical record length (LRECL) and block size (BLKSIZE) are coded when the dataset is defined. The LRECL and BLKSIZE values must also account for two special fields that support variable-length record processing. These fields, **record descriptor word (RDW)** and **block descriptor word (BDW),** specify the length of each logical record to be processed by the program and the length of each physical record to be stored in the dataset, respectively. All other fields in the DCB are not changed with respect to variable-length record processing.

During processing, the RDW determines the length of a logical record to be processed. This field is also used by your program to tell the system the length of a record that you've just created or modified. Hence, if you add or delete a segment within a variable-length record, your code must update the RDW appropriately. Figure 13.27 describes this additional field.

As you issue GET or PUT instructions, you obtain or provide records to the access method. The access method uses both the RDW and BDW fields to form blocks of data that can be stored into a dataset. During input processing, these fields are used by the access method to extract logical records from within physical blocks. Regardless of the direction of processing, both fields are crucial to successful variable-length record processing.

Figures 13.28 and 13.29 illustrate nonblocked and blocked variable length records, respectively. As you can see, *each* logical record contains an associated RDW. Each block of data contains one BDW. Since each RDW and BDW is a four-byte field, the LRECL and BLKSIZE values must allow for these fields within the record definition. In other words, if your logical records contain 100 bytes of data, your LRECL field should be defined as 104. The BLKSIZE should be equal to 108 if only one logical record is to be

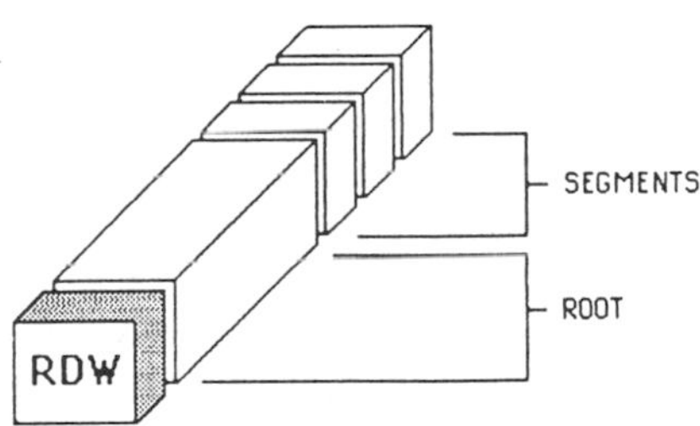

Figure 13.27 The record descriptor word.

Figure 13.28 Nonblocked variable-length record format.

Figure 13.29 Blocked variable-length record format.

stored per block. However, if several logical records are to be stored per block to increase storage efficiency and increase program performance, the value of the BLKSIZE parameter should be equal to a value as determined by the formula in Fig. 13.30. This allows room for *n* complete logical records in each block and allows room for the required block descriptor word.

```
BLKSIZE = 4 + (number of records per block * (maximum logical record length + 4))
```

Figure 13.30 Computing the BLKSIZE for variable-length processing.

As we process, we obtain and supply values to the RDW field for each record. The BDW field is managed by the access method, so we do not have to supply values to that field. Assuming that we're processing bank data consisting of a bank master file and a daily transaction file, Fig. 13.31 illustrates the components involved.

Three files are processed in this application. In fact, this processing is called a **master file update** since a master file is updated with data supplied from a transaction file. Incidentally, master file update processing does not have to involve variable-length records.

Fields in the root portion of the master file records are described using the record description given in Fig. 13.32. Note that this record description is aligned on a fullword boundary, thus placing the RDW on a fullword boundary, too.

A DSECT addresses the data in a check or deposit segment. Since two DSECT's are needed, their descriptions are in Fig. 13.33. The skeleton program presented in Fig. 13.34 processes the check data. You should note that the program is not a complete master file update. The code presented concentrates on managing the RDW during master file update processing. Check or deposit segments are *added* to each master record and the RDW is updated appropriately. This program code does not *update* root or segment data, typical of most master file update systems.

The code prior to line 5 attempts to match each incoming transaction against its associated master file record. If a match does not occur, the transaction record is rejected. Undoubtedly, a message is printed to inform the user of this problem. If a match is found, the associated master record is read using a GET macro instruction (line 4),

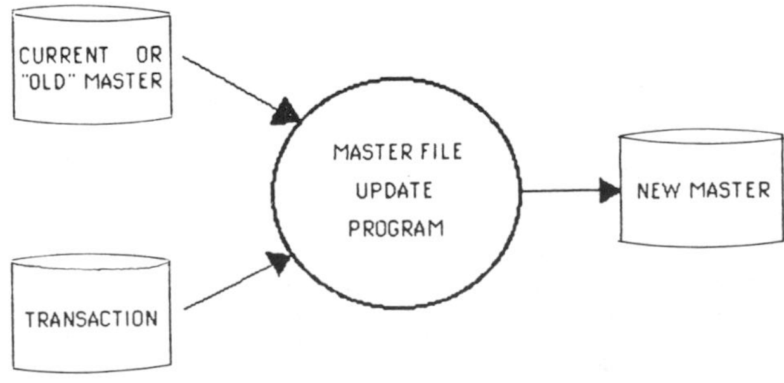

Figure 13.31 Components for a master-file update application.

```
MASTER      DS     0F                 START OF MASTER RECORD
RDW         DS     0CL4               RDW FIELD STARTS RECORD
RECLEN      DS     H                  LENGTH OF RECORD (FROM RDW)
            DS     H                  LAST HALF OF RDW IS UNUSED
ACCOUNT     DS     CL10               ACCOUNT NUMBER
OWNRNAME    DS     CL30               ACCOUNT OWNER NAME
STREET      DS     CL30               STREET ADDRESS
CITY        DS     CL20               CITY
STATE       DS     CL2                STATE CODE
ZIP         DS     CL9                FULL FORMAT ZIP CODE
BALANCE     DS     PL7                CURRENT BALANCE
SEGCOUNT    DS     H                  NUMBER OF SEGMENTS THAT FOLLOW
SEGMENTS    DS     100CL43            START OF SEGMENT DATA THAT
*                                        ALLOWS UP TO 100 SEGMENTS
```

Figure 13.32 Record description for a banking application.

```
CHECK       DSECT
CDATE       DS     CL8                DATE CHECK WAS WRITTEN
CAMOUNT     DS     PL5                AMOUNT OF CHECK
CWHOM       DS     CL30               CHECK PAYEE


DEPOSIT     DSECT
DDATE       DS     CL8                DATE OF THE DEPOSIT
DAMOUNT     DS     PL5                AMOUNT OF THE DEPOSIT
DBRANCH     DS     CL30               FACILITY WHERE DEPOSIT MADE
```

Figure 13.33 Check and deposit DSECT's to support the banking application.

```
BANK        CSECT
            .        .
            .        .

MAINLOOP    DS       0H
            GET      TRANS,TRANSREC        OBTAIN TRANSACTION RECORD
            .        .

            GET      OLDMSTR,MASTER        GET OLD MASTER RECORD

            .        .
            obtain master record that matches that
            account number for this transaction

            if there isn't a master record that has
            the same account number then reject this
            transaction and continue processing
            .        .

            LH       R3,SEGCOUNT           GET SEGMENT COUNTER
            CH       R3,=H'100'            TOO MANY SEGMENTS?
            BH       TOOMANY               IF SO, ABORT
            MH       R3,=H'43'             TIMES SEGMENT LENGTH
            A        R3,=A(SEGMENTS)       FIND WHERE NEW SEGMENT
*                                             IS TO BE PLACED
```

Figure 13.34 Skeleton banking program to process variable-length records.

```
         CLI   TCODE,C'C'         IS IT A CHECK?
         BE    CHECKS             YES, GO PROCESS
         CLI   TCODE,C'D'         IS IT A DEPOSIT?
         BE    DEPOSITS           YES, GO PROCESS
         .     .
         error in transaction data, reject transaction
         .     .

CHECKS   DS    0H
         USING CHECK,R3           ADDRESS CHECK SEGMENT
         ZAP   CAMOUNT,TAMOUNT    SAVE TRANSACTION AMOUNT
         MVC   CDATE,TDATE        MOVE TRANSACTION DATE INTO
*                                    SEGMENT AREA
         MVC   CWHOM,TPAYEE       MOVE PAYEE NAME TO CHECK
*                                  SEGMENT AREA
         SP    BALANCE,CAMOUNT    SUBTRACT AMOUNT OF CHECK
*                                  FROM ACCOUNT BALANCE
         DROP  R3                 ALL DONE WITH CHECK DSECT
         B     WRITMSTR           GO WRITE MASTER RECORD

DEPOSITS DS    0H
         USING DEPOSITS,R3        ADDRESS DEPOSIT SEGMENT
         ZAP   DAMOUNT,TAMOUNT    SAVE TRANSACTION AMOUNT
         MVC   DDATE,TDATE        MOVE TRANSACTION DATE INTO
*                                       SEGMENT AREA
         MVC   DBRANCH,TBRANCH    MOVE BRANCH LOCATION INTO
*                                       SEGMENT AREA
         AP    BALANCE,CAMOUNT    ADD AMOUNT OF DEPOSIT TO
*                                       ACCOUNT BALANCE
         DROP  R3                 ALL DONE WITH CHECK DSECT
         B     WRITMSTR           GO WRITE MASTER RECORD
WRITMSTR DS    0H
         LH    R4,RECLEN          GET OLD RECORD LENGTH
         AH    R4,=H'43'          ADD LENGTH OF NEW SEGMENT
         STH   R4,RECLEN          UPDATE RDW
         LH    R4,SEGCOUNT        GET CURRENT SEGMENT COUNT
         LA    R4,1(R4)           ADJUST FOR ADDED SEGMENT
         STH   R4,SEGCOUNT        UPDATE SEGMENT COUNTER
         PUT   NEWMSTR,MASTER     WRITE OUT UPDATED MASTER
         B     MAINLOOP           CONTINUE PROCESSING

TOOMANY  DS    0H
         .     .
         the master record is full of segments and more
         cannot be added.  Reject this transaction and
         inform the bank officers of this situation by
         printing messages
         .     .

TRANS    DCB   DSORG=PS,DDNAME=TRANS,MACRF=GM,EODAD=EOF

OLDMSTR  DCB   DSORG=PS,DDNAME=OLDMSTR,MACRF=GM

NEWMSTR  DCB   DSORG=PS,DDNAME=NEWMSTR,MACRF=PM,               X
               RECFM=VB,LRECL=4414,BLKSIZE=17660
```

Figure 13.34 (continued)

thus placing the master record data in the area called MASTER. Before master record processing can continue, the record is checked to determine if there's any room to add a check or deposit segment (lines 5 to 7). If not, the record is again rejected (line 7). If room does exist, the address of the available segment area is computed using the segment count field (SEGCOUNT) and the starting address of the segment data area (SEGMENTS) (lines 8 and 9, respectively). The segment count field (SEGCOUNT) is simply a binary number that indicates the number of check and deposit segments currently "attached" to the root portion of the master record. Once the address of the unused segment area is located, addressability to the CHECK or DEPOSIT DSECT is established through the appropriate USING statement in lines 16 or 27, depending on the transaction type processed. Note that R3 serves as the base register for both of these DSECT's.

Depending on the transaction to be processed, addressability to the CHECK or DEPOSIT DSECT is made and processing for that transaction type occurs. After the check or deposit is applied to the master record (lines 17 to 23 or 28 to 34), the updated master record is now written to the new master file (line 44) using the NEWMSTR DCB (line 49). Clearly, we're assuming that only one check or deposit transaction is applied to a master record for each processing run.

Before the master record is written to the master file, the RDW is updated to reflect the new record length (lines 38 to 40). Since the length of each check or deposit segment is 43 bytes, the first two bytes of the RDW, the logical record length field, is updated by this amount. Once the RDW reflects the true length of the updated record, the record can be written to the new master file (line 44). Since the segment count field (SEGCOUNT) must reflect the number of segments attached to the record, it too *must* be updated before the master record is written to the updated master file. Lines 41 to 43 reflect this processing. This code is very important since lines 5 to 7 depend on a correct value in the SEGCOUNT field. Also, the address computations in lines 9 and 10 assume that SEGCOUNT reflects the proper value. Clearly, any error in coordinating either SEGCOUNT or the RDW could lead to incorrect results.

Clearly, the major aspects of variable-length record processing involve addressing the segments and managing the RDW field. Once you understand and master updating and accessing these fields, you've mastered variable-length record processing.

SYSTEM SUPPORT MACROS AND SERVICES

Many support services are provided by the operating system through macros and special routines. These services allow us to abnormally terminate a program, obtain the current time and date, invoke subroutines, or send messages to the computer operator. Using these macros and routines, we can make a program more flexible and powerful in the solution of programming problems. Although we're only going to discuss a few such system services, complete details of these and other services may be found in the IBM publication *OS/VS2 Supervisor Services and Macro Instructions* (GC28-0683).

Abnormal Program Termination

A program abend or failure has been regarded throughout the text as something to be avoided. In fact, Chapter 8 was devoted to debugging and fixing programs that failed. Although we usually want programs to run without abending, it may be appropriate for our program to end abnormally in certain situations.

Suppose that our program is to process an input transaction file. We expect the first data record in the transaction file to contain processing information. Clearly, if this record is not present, our program cannot continue its processing tasks. On the other hand, is it necessary for our program to abend if this situation is discovered?

In a business production environment, programs are usually executed by operations or production control staff. Since these individuals cannot be completely familiar with the output and execution of every program, a program that ends normally (does not abend) is assumed to have completed correctly. Hence, even though a required control record is not found by the program, normal termination would be regarded as "successful" execution. Causing the program to abnormally terminate would draw attention to the program and may enable the production control staff to initiate corrective measures in order to attain successful execution.

We can abend our program very easily by coding and executing the instruction given in Fig. 13.35.

```
DC    X'0000'
```

Figure 13.35 Instruction to abend a program with a S0C1 abend code.

This storage area is an invalid *machine* instruction since the first two bytes of the area do not contain a valid instruction op code. Hence, when the computer encounters this "instruction," the system abends our program with a *system abend code* of **S0C1.** Although this does abend our program, it's not the best method. System abend codes are generally associated with coding errors or logical errors within the program. They are not usually associated with **program detected errors** as in our example.

A program can also terminate abnormally by using the **ABEND** macro instruction. This instruction allows our program to abnormally terminate itself, but it's *not* the system that abnormally terminates the program. Therefore, the program abends with a **user abend code** as compared with the system abend code, S0C1. This distinction causes the staff to focus on problems *outside* the program rather than on a problem within the program instructions.

The ABEND instruction can be called with one or two parameters. The number of parameters coded depends upon the severity of the situation causing the abend. Figure 13.36 illustrates the general format of the ABEND instruction.

```
ABEND   code,DUMP
```

Figure 13.36 Format of the ABEND macro instruction.

The first parameter in the instruction specifies a value less than or equal to 4095, which becomes the **user abend code** when this instruction is executed. The second parameter is optional and should be coded when a complete abend dump of your program's area is necessary. The DUMP operand should be coded in situations that require analysis of a problem and require someone to read a dump of your program to fix the problem. Of course, the DUMP operand requires coding the SYSUDUMP JCL DD statement discussed in Chapter 8.

In most cases, the second operand is not required. The abend code identifies the problem found by the program (which is all you want) and a dump is not usually necessary. If staff members are familiar with the abend codes or if they have a manual that describes the various abend codes issued by your program, they may be able to take corrective measures when your program uses this instruction.

With respect to our example of an invalid control card, let's assume that an abend code value of 1 indicates a missing or invalid transaction control record, which is obtained with the instruction given in Fig. 13.37.

```
ABEND    1
```

Figure 13.37 Forcing an abend with a user abend code value of 1.

When our program terminates, a message is displayed on the operator's console indicating an abnormal termination of our program. Our printout also reflects this abnormal termination and contains a message on the JOB LOG page of our output listing as shown in Fig. 13.38.

Since this abend code is displayed in two places, it usually can't be missed by staff members. Hopefully, they can then fix the problem with our program and rerun the program so that it can complete successfully.

Invoking External Subroutines

External subroutines are called using another system service macro, **CALL.** This macro instruction transfers control to a subroutine and passes parameters to the subroutine. In other words, this instruction builds a parameter list, places the address of the parameter list in register 1, places the address of our subroutine in register 15, and transfers control to our routine using the BALR 14,15 instruction. Summarizing, this instruction gener-

```
                    J E S 2   J O B   L O G  --  S Y S T E M  8 0 0 0  --  N O D E  A S 8 0 0 0

08.36.19 JOB   96  $HASP373 CJK      STARTED - INIT  2 - CLASS B - SYS 8000
08.36.19 JOB   96  IEF403I CJK - STARTED - TIME=08.36.19
08.36.25 JOB   96  IEF450I CJK GO - ABEND S000 U0001 - TIME=08.36.25
08.36.26 JOB   96  IEF404I CJK - ENDED - TIME=08.36.26
08.36.26 JOB   96  $HASP395 CJK      ENDED
------ JES2 JOB STATISTICS ------

 31 JAN 86 JOB EXECUTION DATE

        64 CARDS READ

       354 SYSOUT PRINT RECORDS

         0 SYSOUT PUNCH RECORDS

        29 SYSOUT SPOOL KBYTES

      0.10 MINUTES EXECUTION TIME
```

This program used the ABEND instruction to abort its processing. The abend code value supplied to the ABEND instruction was a value of 1.

Figure 13.38 User abend codes are displayed on the JOB LOG page.

ates the standard linkage instructions that transfer control to a subroutine.

Suppose that three parameters are to be passed to a subroutine. The parameters are P1, P2, and P3, and the subroutine is ABC. This routine is called through the CALL instruction given in Fig. 13.39.

```
CALL   ABC,(P1,P2,P3)
```

Figure 13.39 Using the CALL macro instruction.

The CALL instruction can call an external subroutine stored in a load module library as well. However, for the operating system to locate and load this subroutine into memory for execution, we must code a JCL statement that identifies the library containing our module.

Suppose that module ABC is stored in the load module library called STUDENT.LOADLIB. The JCL given in Fig. 13.40 assembles and executes our main program with the associated ABC subroutine.

We must remember to supply the additional JCL statement (in boldface) when using subroutines stored in load module libraries. If our main program *and all* of our subroutines are in line (not stored in a library), the additional JCL statement is not needed.

```
 //       EXEC    ASMFCG
 //ASM.SYSIN     DD       *

   ...   main program code

//GO.SYSLIB     DD       DSN=STUDENT.LOADLIB,DISP=SHR
// ...   other jcl needed by either routine
```

Figure 13.40 Using preassembled external subroutines.

If several subroutines, each in different load module libraries, are to be invoked, slightly different JCL is required. With a technique called **JCL concatenation,** many libraries can be searched to locate all routines needed to support the execution of our program. This is done using the JCL shown in Fig. 13.41.

Three load module libraries are concatenated. Subroutines are located and pulled from these libraries as needed by the program. In fact, modules written in higher-level languages can also be invoked from assembly language programs using this same technique if parameters are passed between the modules in the correct manner.

```
 //       EXEC    ASMFCG
 //ASM.SYSIN     DD       *

   ...   main program code

//GO.SYSLIB     DD       DSN=STUDENT.LOADLIB,DISP=SHR
//              DD       DSN=SECOND.LOADLIB,DISP=SHR
//              DD       DSN=PRODUCT.LOADLIB,DISP=SHR
// ...   other jcl needed by either routine
```

Figure 13.41 Concatenating subroutine libraries.

Obtaining the Current Date and Time

During execution, a program may ask the operating system for the current date and time using the **TIME** macro instruction. With this instruction, the system supplies the current time and date through registers 0 and 1, respectively. These values must then be converted into the format needed by your program.

In Chapter 4, we discussed the &SYSDATE and &SYSTIME variables. We noted that they can obtain the current date and time during *assembly* of your program. If your program is assembled and placed in a load module library on January 1, the value of the &SYSDATE variable when your program is run on January 30 is still January 1. In other words, &SYSDATE and &SYSTIME should *not* be used to obtain the *current* time and date when your program is executed unless your program is assembled *every* time it is run.

Using the instruction shown in Fig. 13.42, the system returns the current time in register 0 and the current date in register 1. You must be careful, however, since the values returned may not be in the format needed by your program.

```
TIME  DEC
```

Figure 13.42 Using the TIME macro instruction.

The time value returned in register 0 is in the form HHMMSSth, where *t* and *h* are tenths and hundredths of a second, respectively. If the current time is 9:18:27 A.M., the value returned in R0 is X'09182734' (assuming that the current tenth and hundredth of a second value are 3 and 4, respectively). As you can see, this value is not in binary format and it's not in packed-decimal format since it doesn't have a valid sign. Therefore, we must convert it into a format that can be used by storing it into a memory location and editing the field to form a valid packed-decimal number. Once it is converted into a packed-decimal format, we can use the EDIT instruction to convert the field into the form HH:MM:SS.

Let's assume that we don't need the tenths and hundredths of a second values. The instructions given in Fig. 13.43 convert the value in R0 into the more common time format and place the resulting value in the area called CURRTIME.

The current date is returned in register 1 in packed-decimal format. Although the current date is already in packed-decimal format, it too probably has to be converted into a usable format. Since the current date is returned in **Julian date format,** your

```
          SRL    R0,4                       GET RID OF HUNDREDTHS VALUE
          O      R0,=X'0000000F'            CHANGE TENTHS VALUE TO SIGN
          ST     R0,TIMEPD                  SAVE TIME VALUE
          ED     TIMEPATT(10),TIMEPD        EDIT THE TIME VALUE
          MVC    CURRTIME(8),TIMEPATT+2     MOVE VALUE INTO OUR FIELD

          .      .
          .      .

TIMEPD    DS     PL4                        PACKED TIME VALUE
TIMEPATT  DC     X'402021207A20207A2020'    EDIT PATTERN
CURRTIME  DS     CL8                        FINAL TIME VALUE
```

Figure 13.43 Obtaining and converting the current time.

program has to convert from Julian date to Gregorian date or mm/dd/yy format as needed by your program.

Register 1's value has the following format: 00 YY DDD S, where YY is the current year, DDD is the current day, and S is the sign value of F. Since January has 31 days, the Julian date for February 10, 1999 is X'0099041F'. In other words, February 10 is the forty-first day of the year.

Since this date format may not meet your needs, write a routine to convert this date into your desired format. I'll leave this problem as a programming assignment.

Sending Messages to the Operator

While your program is executing, it may be necessary to send messages to the computer operator. The messages can inform the operator of a situation that needs correcting or can indicate why your program is not running correctly. For example, we may want to send a message to the operator to inform him that a required control card is missing and that processing cannot continue normally. Through the following instructions, your program can supply information to the operator to resolve such a problem detected by your program.

The **WTO (write-to-operator)** macro instruction should *not* be used to send *unimportant* messages to the operator, who is usually quite busy and does not need the additional distraction of noncritical messages. However, if you need to communicate important messages to the operator, this instruction can be used.

The write-to-operator instruction displays messages up to 120 characters in length to the operator's console, your job listing, or to both locations. Since messages can be routed to two destinations, the WTO instruction identifies where your messages are to be sent. For example, the master console operator is notified that a required data control card is missing through the WTO instruction shown in Fig. 13.44.

```
WTO   'MISSING TRANSACTION CONTROL CARD',ROUTCDE=1
```

Figure 13.44 Routing a message to the console operator.

The message to be sent is enclosed in single quotes (apostrophes) and is followed by the ROUTCDE operand. A **ROUTCDE (routing code)** value of 1 indicates that this message is to be sent to the master console operator. Simultaneously, this message is also sent to your JOB LOG listing, thus allowing you to also see the messages sent by your program to the operator.

Messages may be directed to your JOB LOG (and not to the operator) by using a different ROUTCDE value. A value of 11 provides messages to you and does not disrupt the activity at the computer console. In this case, the WTO instruction may be used to supply information about the execution of your program. For example, by placing WTO instructions throughout the body of the program, you'll be able to follow its logical execution. Hopefully, the placement and usage of WTO instructions can assist in debugging. Figure 13.45 illustrates the JOB LOG page with WTO messages used in this fashion.

Another macro instruction, similar to WTO, *interacts* with the operator. However, this instruction should be used with *extreme* care since it *requires* a response from the console operator.

The **WTOR (write-to-operator-with-reply)** instruction requests information from the operator to be used by your program. For example, suppose that your program

```
                    J E S 2  J O B  L O G  --  S Y S T E M  8 0 0 0  --  N O D E  A S 8 0 0 0

08.40.30 JOB   103   $HASP373 CJK        STARTED - INIT  2 - CLASS B - SYS 8000
08.40.30 JOB   103   IEF403I CJK - STARTED - TIME=08.40.30
08.40.37 JOB   103   +JUST ABOUT TO OPEN THE FILES
08.40.37 JOB   103   +BEGINNING MAIN LOOP PROCESSING
08.40.37 JOB   103   +READING A RECORD
08.40.37 JOB   103   +PROCESSING THE RECORD
08.40.37 JOB   103   +PRINTING RESULTS
08.40.37 JOB   103   +READING A RECORD
08.40.37 JOB   103   +PROCESSING THE RECORD
08.40.37 JOB   103   +PRINTING RESULTS
08.40.37 JOB   103   +READING A RECORD
08.40.37 JOB   103   +END OF FILE HAS BEEN REACHED, ENDING PGM.
08.40.37 JOB   103   +FILES BEING CLOSED
08.40.37 JOB   103   IEF404I CJK - ENDED - TIME=08.40.37
08.40.37 JOB   103   $HASP395 CJK        ENDED

------ JES2 JOB STATISTICS ------

 31 JAN 86 JOB EXECUTION DATE

        74 CARDS READ

       497 SYSOUT PRINT RECORDS

         0 SYSOUT PUNCH RECORDS

        44 SYSOUT SPOOL KBYTES

      0.12 MINUTES EXECUTION TIME
```

These messages were printed from the program by issuing the WTO instruction. As you can see, these messages form the basis for an audit trail printout that can be used in debugging.

Figure 13.45 Using WTO as a tracing facility.

produces billing reports for a set of customers served by your company. Before processing, the program must know the starting and ending billing days so that the proper records are retrieved from the file and used in generating the billing report. Clearly, this information could be supplied to your program through a data card or through the parm operand on the EXEC statement. For illustration purposes, let's assume that eight-character starting and ending billing dates in the form mm/dd/yy are to be supplied to your program directly from the master console operator. The WTOR instruction in Fig. 13.46 illustrates the technique for requesting these dates from the console operator.

```
WTOR   'PLEASE ENTER STARTING AND ENDING BILLING DATES',     X
       DATES,16,WTORECB,ROUTCDE=(1,11)
```

Figure 13.46 Requesting data from the console operator using WTOR.

The WTOR instruction sends the message to the operator. From Fig. 13.46, the instruction also indicates that a 16-byte reply is expected and that the reply is to be placed in the field called DATES. The message is to be routed to both the operator and our program listing so that we see the message and the operator's reply. Finally, the field called WTORECB identifies the name of a fullword area in our program. This field is called an **event control block**, which helps suspend the execution of our program until the operator replies to our request. That is, the WTOR instruction sends a message to the operator, but our program can't continue executing until a response is received. Therefore, the operating system uses the field called WTORECB to notify our program when the operator has responded.

After issuing the WTOR instruction, our program *must* test the value in the WTORECB field to determine when the operator has responded. This is done using the

WAIT macro instruction as shown in Fig. 13.47. The complete set of instructions to send a message to the operator and request a reply are shown in Fig. 13.48.

```
WAIT   ECB=WTORECB
```

Figure 13.47 Waiting for the operator's response.

```
          .          .
          .          .
          .          .
          WTOR       'PLEASE ENTER STARTING AND ENDING BILX
                     LING DATES',DATES,16,WTORECB,        X
                     ROUTCDE=(1,11)
          WAIT       ECB=WTORECB
          .          .
          .          .
          .          .
WTORECB   DC         F'0'

DATES     DS         0CL16
STARTING  DS         0CL8
SMM       DS         CL2
SSLASH1   DS         C
SDD       DS         CL2
SSLASH2   DS         C
SYY       DS         CL2
ENDING    DS         0CL8
EMM       DS         CL2
ESLASH1   DS         C
EDD       DS         CL2
ESLASH2   DS         C
EYY       DS         CL2
```

Figure 13.48 Code segment to request an operator response using WTOR and WAIT instructions.

The program is suspended until the operator responds to our message. If the operator responds within 15 minutes, the data entered by the operator is returned to our program. If the operator takes longer than 15 minutes, our program is abended by the operating system with an abend code of **S522.**

After responding, the area labeled DATES contains the operator's response. The maximum number of characters that the operator may enter is 16, but if the operator enters fewer characters, only the number of characters entered is returned into our program field in a left-justified manner. Therefore, following the operator's response, our program should edit the date values to ensure validity. In the event that incorrect or invalid dates are supplied to the program, the ABEND instruction may be used to abort processing, thus notifying the operator of the error. On the other hand, the program can edit the dates and upon determining that they are invalid, request a new set of dates from the operator using the same WTOR/WAIT instruction sequence.

Reentrant Programming

The development of our assembly language programs has been oriented toward a single-user environment. In other words, we've developed programs that are executed by a single user to process a set of data. If we expand our scope, it may be desirable for many users to execute our program simultaneously. Therefore, multiple copies of our program and the associated data areas are required to support the processing needed by the many users.

We can develop programs more efficiently using **reentrant programming.** With this method, many users can execute the same program concurrently, but only *one* copy of the instructions for the program is required to support all the users. As the program executes, the program acquires unique data areas for each user, thus maintaining integrity and uniqueness across user boundaries. Figure 13.49 illustrates this concept.

The process of developing reentrant programs is quite complex. Further, the payoff in using these programs may not be worth the investment in time required to make a program reentrant. Large computer systems using virtual memory may not justify the construction of reentrant programs since sufficient memory is usually available for the execution of programs for each user request. Therefore, reentrant programming is more of a concern in smaller systems or in on-line environments where memory and programs may be shared among many concurrent users, thus placing a premium on available storage.

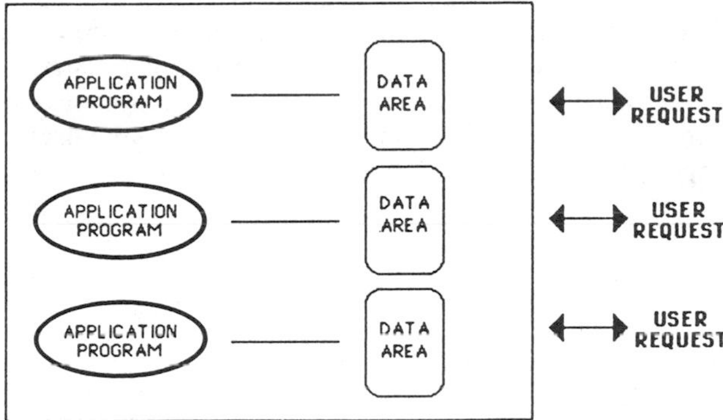

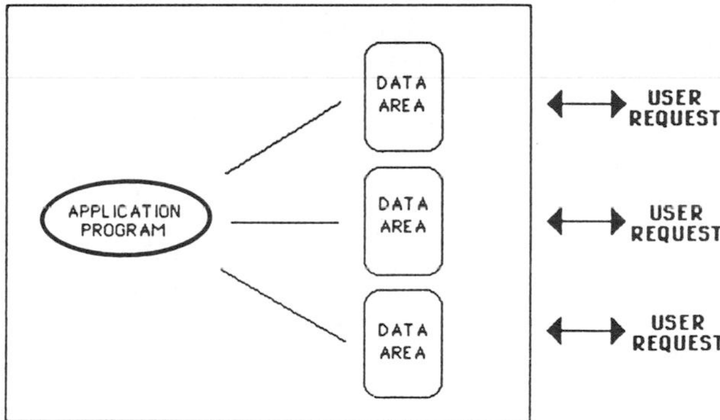

Figure 13.49 Comparing nonreentrant programs to reentrant programs.

Assembly language programs are developed in a reenterable manner by writing programs that do not contain modifiable data areas. This means that *all* data areas that will be modified by the program must be contained *outside* of the CSECT containing the instructions. This does *not* simply mean that another CSECT needs to be addressed by the program. Instead, the program acquires storage *during execution* and uses it for processing. Also, this means that the program uses instructions that do not store information into areas within the program. For example, different forms of the OPEN, CLOSE, and DCB instructions are required in the development of reentrant programs.

During processing, the data control block is modified by the access method to contain information about the I/O request. Since the DCB is contained within our CSECT, programs performing I/O as we've used throughout the text are nonreentrant programs. Further, programs containing DS storage areas whose values are supplied to the area during execution are nonreentrant. Therefore, all data areas and modified control blocks must be located *outside* the bounds of the instruction CSECT. This can be accomplished through the **GETMAIN** macro instruction.

The GETMAIN macro instruction requests storage from the operating system at execution time. Once obtained, the storage area can be used to build print lines, contain control blocks, or house any other data areas that change during the execution of the program. Since GETMAINed storage is *not* considered part of a program's instruction set, programs using it and adhering to the nonmodify rules meet the reentrancy standards. That is, the instructions for a program may be shared by more than one user and so only one copy is needed to support multiuser processing.

```
STORAGE     DSECT
REGSAVE     DS        18F

    ....other storage definitions needed by the program

STLENGTH    EQU       *-STORAGE


MAINPGM     CSECT
            STM       R14,R12,12(R13)      SAVE CALLER'S REGISTERS
            LR        R12,R15              R12 IS OUR BASE REG
            USING     MAINPGM,R12          ESTABLISH ADDRESSABILITY
            L         R0,DATALEN           GET LENGTH OF MEMORY NEEDED
            GETMAIN   R,LV=(0)             GET MEMORY FROM O.S.
            ST        R13,4(R1)            SAVE CURRENT R13 VALUE
            ST        R1,8(R13)            CHAIN BACKWARD
            LR        R13,R1               POINT TO SAVE AREA
            USING     STORAGE,R13          ADDRESS SEPARATE STORAGE
            .         .
            .         .
            .         .

            L         R0,DATALEN           PLACE STORAGE LENGTH IN R0
            LR        R1,R13               R1 = ADDRESS OF STORAGE
            L         R13,4(R13)           GET BACK OLD R13 VALUE
            FREEMAIN  R,A=(1),LV=(0)       GIVE STORAGE BACK
            LM        R14,R12,12(R13)      RESTORE THE REGISTERS
            SR        R15,R15              SET THE RETURN CODE
            BR        R14
DATALEN     DC        A(STLENGTH)          LENGTH OF MEMORY
            LTORG

    definition of constant data areas used by the program

            END       MAINPGM
```

Figure 13.50 General format of a reentrant program.

The GETMAIN instruction is usually found at the very beginning of a program. Before the major bulk of program processing begins, the program acquires storage from the operating system and uses it to hold the register save area, control blocks, and *all* other modified storage areas needed by the program. Since this storage area is not contained within the same CSECT as the instructions, addressability is achieved through DSECT references or through explicit addressing. Clearly, this can make for difficult programming as compared to our normal form of program development.

When a program completes execution, the acquired storage area is returned to the operating system *before* program termination. Storage may be returned to the operating system with the **FREEMAIN** macro instruction. Therefore, a reentrant program generally begins and ends as illustrated in Fig. 13.50.

This program uses a relocatable symbol (STLENGTH) to determine the amount of memory needed to support execution. As you can see, R0 is used in the GETMAIN instruction to inform the operating system as to the number of bytes of memory needed by the program. The programmer must know the amount of storage needed since that number must be coded on the GETMAIN instruction. The length of storage needed is indicated as shown in Fig. 13.50, or the programmer may request a specific amount of storage by coding the instruction as shown in Fig. 13.51.

```
GETMAIN  R,LV=500
```

Figure 13.51 Requesting 500 bytes of storage through the GETMAIN instruction.

After the GETMAIN instruction is executed, the address of the area that can be used by the program is returned in register 1. The program in Fig. 13.50 then proceeds to use the first 18 fullwords of this area as a register save area. Therefore, R13 addresses the register save area *and* provides addressability to the acquired storage. The use of R13 to address this area is convenient since it saves us from assigning another register to this task.

Throughout the body of the program, the fields contained within the acquired storage may be addressed through the DSECT called STORAGE (as given in Fig. 13.50). This area contains all the fields that may be modified during execution.

Finally, the program returns control to the system, but, before doing so, it frees the acquired storage. This requires that the length of the storage area be placed in R0 and the address of the storage area be placed in register 1. Since R13 was used as the base register for this area, R13 contains the address of the area to be freed. Therefore, the address in R13 is copied into R1.

The caller's save area address is then loaded into R13, which must be done before the area is freed since the acquired storage area contains the caller's save area address. If we issue the FREEMAIN instruction before obtaining this address, we cannot restore the caller's registers since the associated address is lost. The FREEMAIN instruction then frees the acquired storage area.

Incidentally, a *main* program does not have to use the FREEMAIN instruction to free the acquired storage. Storage is automatically reclaimed by the operating system when a program terminates. However, a *subroutine* should acquire and free its storage area(s). If the subroutine doesn't free storage when it completes and if the subroutine is called many times, a program can use up all of its available storage. When a program requests storage and not enough is available, the program is abended with an **S80A** abend code.

Let's write a simple reentrant subroutine that obtains the current time and converts the time in the form HH:MM:SS and returns this eight-character field to the calling program. Upon entry to this routine, R1 addresses the data area into which the current time is to be placed. The program is coded as shown in Example 13.1.

All storage areas that build and process the time value are contained within the DSECT used to address the acquired storage area. The only data areas within the program are EDITPTN and STSIZE. Neither area is modified by the program during execution. The address of the parameter from the calling program to this subroutine is passed via register 1. This address is moved to register 5 since the TIME macro instruction uses R1. Thus, R5 addresses the area in the caller's program into which the formatted time value is to be placed.

Generally, reentrant programs are developed as illustrated above. Constants are contained within the program area and modified data areas are processed in the acquired storage area. Although this is typical of reentrant programs, it is also possible to develop reentrant programs that perform I/O operations. The program in Example 13.2 reads and prints records using reentrant programming techniques.

Each storage area within the DSECT labeled STORAGE and following the area labeled MYDATA corresponds in a 1:1 ratio. In fact, if any fields are added, changed, or deleted from either area, corresponding changes *must* be made to the respective fields within the other structure.

```
 STORAGE   DSECT
 REGSAVE   DS       18F
 TIMEPD    DS       PL4                 PACKED TIME VALUE
 TPATT     DS       CL10                EDIT PATTERN
 TAMOUNT   EQU      *-REGSAVE

 TIMERTN   CSECT
           STM      R14,R12,12(R13)     SAVE CALLER'S REGISTERS
           LR       R12,R15             R12 IS OUR BASE REG
           LR       R5,R1               SAVE PARM ADDRESS
           USING    TIMERTN,R12         ESTABLISH ADDRESSABILITY
           L        R0,STSIZE           OBTAIN SIZE OF MEM. NEEDED
           GETMAIN  R,LV=(0)            GET STORAGE FROM O.S.
           ST       R13,4(R1)           SAVE CURRENT R13 VALUE
           ST       R1,8(R13)           CHAIN BACKWARD
           LR       R13,R1              POINT TO SAVE AREA
           USING    STORAGE,R13         ADDRESS SEPARATE STORAGE

           L        R5,0(R5)            GET ADDRESS OF CALLER'S
*                                         DATA AREA INTO WHICH
*                                         THE TIME VALUE IS TO BE
*                                         PLACED
           TIME     DEC
           SRL      R0,4                ELIMINATE HUNDREDTHS
           O        R0,=X'0000000F'     ADD PACKED DECIMAL SIGN
           ST       R0,TIMEPD           SAVE INTO MY DATA AREA
           MVC      TPATT(10),EDITPTN   MOVE IN EDIT PATTERN
           ED       TPATT(10),TIMEPD    EDIT THE FIELD
           MVC      0(8,R5),TPATT+2     GIVE TIME TO CALLER

           L        R0,STSIZE           PLACE STORAGE LENGTH IN R0
           LR       R1,R13              R1 = ADDRESS OF STORAGE
           L        R13,4(R13)          GET BACK OLD R13 VALUE
           FREEMAIN R,A=(1),LV=(0)      GIVE STORAGE BACK
           LM       R14,R12,12(R13)     RESTORE THE REGISTERS
           SR       R15,R15             SET THE RETURN CODE
           BR       R14
 EDITPTN   DC       X'402021207A20207A2020'
 STSIZE    DC       A(TAMOUNT)
           LTORG
```

Example 13.1 Reentrant time conversion routine.

```
STORAGE   DSECT
REGSAVE   DS      18F
STDATA    DS      0C
XIN       DCB     DSORG=PS,DDNAME=XIN,MACRF=GM,EODAD=EOF
XOUT      DCB     DSORG=PS,DDNAME=XOUT,MACRF=PM,RECFM=FA,           X
                  LRECL=133,BLKSIZE=133
PLINE     DS      0CL133
CC        DC      C' '
CARDAREA  DS      CL80
REST      DC      CL52' '
OPENWORK  OPEN    (XIN,INPUT),MF=L
CLOSWORK  CLOSE   (XOUT),MF=L

READPRNT  CSECT
          STM     R14,R12,12(R13)      SAVE CALLER'S REGISTERS
          LR      R12,R15              R12 IS OUR BASE REG
          LR      R5,R1                SAVE PARM ADDRESS
          USING   READPRNT,R12         ESTABLISH ADDRESSABILITY
          L       R0,DATALEN           GET SIZE OF STORAGE NEEDED
          GETMAIN R,LV=(0)             ASK O.S. FOR MEMORY
          ST      R13,4(R1)            SAVE CURRENT R13 VALUE
          ST      R1,8(R13)            CHAIN BACKWARD
          LR      R13,R1               POINT TO SAVE AREA
          USING   STORAGE,R13          ADDRESS SEPARATE STORAGE

          LA      R2,STDATA            ADDRESS DSECT AREA
          L       R3,DATALEN           OBTAIN LENGTH OF DATA
          LR      R5,R3                PLACE SAME VALUE IN R5
          LA      R4,MYDATA            ADDRESS CONSTANT AREA
          MVCL    R2,R4                FORMAT DSECT STORAGE AREA

          OPEN    (XIN,INPUT),MF=(E,OPENWORK)    OPEN THE DCB
          OPEN    (XOUT,OUTPUT),MF=(E,OPENWORK) OPEN THE DCB

 LOOP     DS      0H
          GET     XIN,CARDAREA         INPUT A RECORD
          PUT     XOUT,PLINE           PRINT AN IMAGE
          B       LOOP

 EOF      DS      0H
          CLOSE   (XIN),MF=(E,CLOSWORK)    CLOSE THE INPUT FILE
          CLOSE   (XOUT),MF=(E,CLOSWORK)   CLOSE OUTPUT FILE

          L       R0,DATALEN           PLACE STORAGE LENGTH IN R0
          LR      R1,R13               R1 = ADDRESS OF STORAGE
          L       R13,4(R13)           GET BACK OLD R13 VALUE
          FREEMAIN R,A=(1),LV=(0)      GIVE STORAGE BACK
          LM      R14,R12,12(R13)      RESTORE THE REGISTERS
          SR      R15,R15              SET THE RETURN CODE
          BR      R14

EDITPTN   DC      X'402021207A20207A2020'
MYDATA    DS      0C
          DCB     DSORG=PS,DDNAME=XIN,MACRF=GM,EODAD=EOF
          DCB     DSORG=PS,DDNAME=XOUT,MACRF=PM,RECFM=FA,           X
                  LRECL=133,BLKSIZE=133
          DS      0CL133
          DC      C' '
          DS      CL80
          DC      CL52' '
          OPEN    (*,INPUT),MF=L
          CLOSE   (*),MF=L
MYDATAE   EQU     *
DATALEN   DC      A(MYDATAE-MYDATA)
          LTORG
          END     READPRNT
```

Example 13.2 Reentrant program to read and print records.

The fields between MYDATA and MYDATAE are moved into their corresponding locations within the DSECT. Note that the fields are named within the DSECT, but have *not* been named within the program area. This further emphasizes that processing occurs in the acquired area of storage and not within the program's CSECT area.

Next, special forms of the OPEN instruction open the two files for processing. These forms are called **execute forms** and are used when reentrant programming is being used. The area called OPENWORK is used by the instructions to build the appropriate parameter list for the operating system. Referring to OPENWORK in the DSECT, you see that this label is attached to an OPEN instruction. However, this instruction is slightly different in that it contains the operand **MF=L.** This operand generates a **list form** of the OPEN instruction that is used in combination with the execute form to provide reentrant execution of the desired function.

Processing within the body of the program occurs normally through GET and PUT instructions. Note that the GET and PUT instructions do not have to be modified to reference the fields or DCB's in the DSECT. The code generated by the GET and PUT macros automatically supports reentrant programming. Hence, whether or not a reentrant program is used, the same form of the GET and PUT I/O macros can be used.

When the end of file is reached, **execute forms** of the CLOSE instruction disconnect the files from our program. These instructions are in turn associated with the **list form** of the CLOSE instruction contained in the DSECT. This area is called CLOSWORK. Again, the two forms of the CLOSE instruction allow the operating system to provide file closure properly. Finally, our program frees the acquired storage area and returns control to the operating system.

When developing programs, it may be difficult to determine if a program is truly reentrant. To help answer this question we call upon the assembler to check our program for reentrancy. In fact, since reentrant programs are undoubtedly link edited, let's look at the complete JCL to assemble and link edit a reentrant program as shown in Fig. 13.52.

The RENT parameter is supplied to both the assembler and the linkage editor. If the assembler determines that the program is not reentrant, then warning messages are issued and the assembler identifies the instructions in the program that do *not* pass reentrancy. If the program is reentrant and no other errors are found, the program is link edited and placed into a load module library by the linkage editor. The RENT parameter during link editing is used to "mark" the module as reentrant. Therefore, when the operating system loads this program for execution, it recognizes that the program is reentrant and only loads one copy of the program regardless of the number of users executing it.

```
//        EXEC         ASMFCL,PARM.ASM='OBJECT,RENT',
//                     PARM.LKED='XREF,LET,CALL,RENT'
//ASM.SYSIN            DD  *

      .... program to be assembled

//LKED.SYSLMOD  DD  DSN=MY.LOADLIB(modulename),DISP=SHR
```

Figure 13.52 The JCL to assemble, link edit a program, and test the progran. for reentrancy.

STUDY QUESTIONS

1. How can addressability be established to a DSECT?
2. When processing in locate mode, what register supplies your program the address of the record read from a file?
3. What are the MACRF values when performing locate mode input or output processing?
4. The length of a variable-length record to be written to a file must be placed into the _______ before the I/O instruction is issued for that record.
5. The length of a variable-length physical record is found in the _______ field within that physical block.
6. When creating a variable-length dataset, the value of the BLKSIZE parameter must be _______ as compared to the value of the LRECL parameter.
7. What are the two most common types of tape formats?
8. Which tape format does not require coding of the DCB operands each time that a dataset on the tape is referenced?
9. How many datasets can be stored on a single tape volume?
10. When processing a tape dataset, how do the instructions within an assembly language program differ as compared to processing disk datasets?
11. A subroutine called GREGDATE is called to obtain the current date from the system and return the Gregorian date form to your program. How would you call this routine using the CALL macro if the name of the area that is to hold the Gregorian date is called PRNTDATE?
12. What JCL statement obtains a dump of a program in the event of failure during execution?
13. If the WTO instruction is used, what routing code value is used most often by your program?
14. What are the two primary macro instructions used to provide program reentrancy?
15. What types of programs are most suited for reentrant coding format?

PROGRAMMING PROBLEMS

1. Write a subroutine that obtains the current time and date and converts the Julian date into the form MM/DD/YY. The address of an area in the caller's program into which the converted date is to be placed is supplied to the subroutine via register 1.
2. Rewrite the subroutine of Programming Problem 1 into a reentrant module.
3. Write a reentrant subroutine that computes the future value of an investment. If you recall, this was a problem in Chapter 9. If you still have the code, convert it to a reentrant module. See Programming Problem 7 in Chapter 9.
4. Using any of your previous program implementations, integrate the WTO instruction into your code to provide tracing facilities during execution. *Do not* route your trace messages to the console operator.
5. Refer to any of the student class/grade programming projects from earlier chapters. In these projects, we processed student data consisting of the student's name and semester scores. From this input data, we computed the student's average score and semester grade. Rewrite any of these implementations to use DSECT's and/or locate mode processing.

6. In several previous chapters you were asked to write a square root approximation program. Rewrite this code into an external subroutine and develop a macro called SQRT to invoke the routine. At your option, choose the parameters to the subroutine and determine whether the subroutine will be reentrant.
7. The MVCL and CLCL instructions require four registers for implementation. Develop two external subroutines called MVCLSUB and CLCLSUB to perform the same functions as MVCL and CLCL but do not alter *any* registers during processing. CLCLSUB should set the condition code appropriately and MVCLSUB should move and pad the fields as required. At your option, implement the subroutines using reentrant coding procedures.
8. Develop a subroutine which will provide field editing capabilities. Given the address, length, and type of editing to be performed, the routine will determine if the field contains only numeric data, only letters of the alphabet, or alphanumeric data (any valid character) within the field contents. The subroutine should set the condition code depending on the field contents; B'00'—if the field is valid, B'01'—if the field is not valid.
9. Develop a subroutine which will determine if a number is even or odd. Given the number, the subroutine will set the condition code so that the extended mnemonic instruction BO can be used if the number is odd and BE can be used to control flow if the number is even. Implement the routine as a reentrant program.
10. Develop a subroutine which can be used by assembly or higher-level language programs. The subroutine is called BYTES and has two parameters. The first parameter is a byte of storage and the second is an 8-byte storage area. Given the first parameter, the subroutine will set the values in the 8-byte area to character values of 0 or 1 depending on the respective bit values in the first parameter byte. This will enable higher-level language programs to perform "bit" analysis even though such facilities may not be directly supported. Extend this project by allowing the routine to accept another parameter. This parameter will indicate whether the 8-byte area is to be determined from the single byte area or if the 8-byte area will be used to set the bit values within the single byte data area. This will allow bits within the byte to be analyzed or updated through the capabilities of this subroutine.

14

Random File Processing

The need to access information directly requires us to study random file processing. In this and the following chapter, we'll be looking at most of the methods for accessing records in a random manner on an IBM system. Specifically, we'll study the **BDAM (basic direct access method)** and **ISAM (index sequential access method)** in this chapter, and leave the **VSAM (virtual storage access method)** for the next chapter.

GENERAL OVERVIEW

Random file processing allows us to process any record in a file without first having to process some other record. Suppose that a file contains 100 records and that record 75 is to be processed. Using a **sequential** or **queued** file structure as we have in all previous chapters, we have to read through the first 74 records to get to record 75 before we can begin processing. With a random file structure, we go directly to record 75, which not only eliminates the program code to skip over the first 74 records, but also saves many I/O operations since only one record has to be read instead of 75. Additionally, our program can access the record more quickly since less processing is done and fewer I/O operations are required.

Not all application files should be implemented using a random structure, however. From this discussion, you might have the impression that random files should be used for all applications. This is not true. Random processing is used when *selected* records in the file are to be accessed. Generally, less than half of the records in a random file are processed during any given program execution. If your application calls for most records in a file to be processed, select sequential file processing to support your application.

Random files are stored on direct access storage devices while sequential files may be placed virtually anywhere. In general, only disk devices support random file processing whereas cards, disk, tape, drum, or paper tape support sequential file processing. The cost of storing data on the various storage devices and their availability also impact on the selection of your file structure.

Random files require us to specify a **key field** to identify each record in the file. If it is not possible to specify a field that uniquely identifies each record, random file processing cannot be used. A single field or a group of fields in the record form the **record key.** The *value* of the record key in one record cannot be the same as that in another record.

Hence, if your application does not allow you to form a record key, and, in fact, a unique key value for each record, random files cannot be used for your processing.

Although the tradeoffs in performance, storage requirements, record structure, and program processing can be argued, there are applications that require random file processing. To understand random file processing, we must be familiar with each type of file structure available. These file structures and their corresponding access methods are listed in Fig. 14.1.

File Structure	Access Method
sequential	QSAM: queued sequential access method
sequential	BSAM: basic sequential access method
relative	BDAM: basic direct access method
direct	BDAM: basic direct access method
indexed	ISAM: indexed sequential access method

Figure 14.1 Traditional file structures and associated IBM access method routines.

As you can see, each file structure is associated with a specific access method. In general, selecting a file structure also determines the access method to be used. However, the VSAM access method, not listed above, supports three file structures: sequential, relative, and indexed. The power of this access method requires a careful discussion, which is given in the next chapter.

The three most common file structures used on IBM systems are the sequential, relative, and indexed structures. Therefore, we're omitting direct file processing from our discussion. For information on direct file processing, refer to the IBM publication *OS/VS Data Management Services Guide* (GC26-3783 or GC26-4058).

RELATIVE FILE PROCESSING

Each record in a relative file is identified by its *position* within the file. The first record is at location 0 and the one-hundredth record is at location 99. Therefore, when processing a relative file in a random manner, identify the record to be processed using a numeric value. This value is the "record identifier" discussed earlier and is more commonly called the **relative record number (RRN).**

The relative record number is a three-byte binary number. As a relative file is processed, you must supply this value to the BDAM access method and BDAM retrieves or stores records into the file. The relative record number uniquely identifies each record in the file, that is, no two records can have the same relative record number value. When defining the structure of your records, you must be able to derive a value from the data in the record for the relative record number. For example, information related to students in a university can be identified through the student's social security number. In theory, no two students have the same social security number. Therefore, each student is uniquely identified.

The relative record number does not have to be part of the data record itself. Fields in the record can construct the relative record number, but it does not have to be stored with the other data in the record. This saves a few bytes of space for each record which can amount to a significant amount of storage in a large file.

Records in a relative file are fixed length. If you recall, sequential files allow us to store and process variable-length records. This is not possible when storing and processing records in a relative dataset.

Defining a Relative Record Dataset

A relative record dataset can be defined using standard IBM JCL coding techniques. To define a dataset, we execute the utility called **IEFBR14,** which causes the operating system to process our JCL. Note that IEFBR14 is not defining the dataset, but it is the operating system that is responding to our request. IEFBR14 is simply an "agent" that causes the operating system to respond and act on the JCL.

Assuming that our records are 81 bytes long and that the name of the relative file is RELATIVE.FILE, the JCL given in Fig. 14.2 can create our dataset.

The dataset is cataloged, thus allowing its easy reference later using only the DSN and DISP JCL parameters. Each record is of fixed length (RECFM=F) and the logical and physical record sizes are the same, 81 bytes. Records in a relative dataset cannot be blocked, which is why the values of the LRECL and BLKSIZE parameters are the same.

The dataset is a direct access file (DSORG=DA) to be placed on the disk device called DISK01. The operand OPTCD=R specifies that records are to be processed using a relative record number.

The SPACE parameter is slightly different than what we coded before. In this example, we're asking for space to hold one hundred 81-byte records. Coding the SPACE parameter in this fashion is called **block allocation.** We could have used the more familiar forms of the SPACE parameter such as SPACE=(TRK,(p,s)) or SPACE =(CYL,(p,s)), where *p* and *s* are the primary and secondary space allocation amounts. However, these forms require use of a table or formula to determine how much space is to be allocated to hold the records that we plan to store. Using the block allocation method, we can easily determine and specify the number of records that are to be stored in the dataset.

A secondary allocation can be coded when defining a relative record dataset, but it's not usually done. Generally, the primary space allocation allows for the current file needs and allows for growth of the dataset. Secondary extents or secondary allocations fragment the dataset, thus increasing processing time. Contiguous space allocation allows for a more controlled and consistent processing environment.

Once space for the dataset has been defined, we may now **format** the dataset using the **BSAM (basic sequential access method).** This process requires us to write empty records or **dummy records** into the dataset, thus filling the entire dataset with these records. When we add, delete, or update records, we simply *change* the contents of the records in the dataset at the relative position that we are processing. Formatting the dataset not only simplifies our add, delete, and update processing later, but it also eliminates any unusual processing problems that can occur when processing a nonformatted relative dataset.

If we continue to assume that our records are 81 bytes long, the program in Example 14.1 formats a relative record dataset that can hold 100 records.

```
//     EXEC  PGM=IEFBR14
//DDA   DD   DSN=RELATIVE.FILE,DISP=(NEW,CATLG),
//           DCB=(RECFM=F,LRECL=81,BLKSIZE=81,
//           DSORG=DA,OPTCD=R),UNIT=SYSDA,VOL=SER=DISK01,
//           SPACE=(81,(100))
```

Figure 14.2 JCL to create a relative record dataset.

```
//       EXEC    ASMFCG
//ASM.SYSIN    DD   *
FORMAT      CSECT
            STM    R14,R12,12(R13)    SAVE THE CALLER'S REGS
            LR     R12,R15            USE R12 AS OUR BASE REGISTER
            USING  FORMAT,R12         TELL THE ASSEMBLER
            LA     R11,SAVEAREA       POINT TO OUR SAVEAREA
            ST     R13,SAVEAREA+4     SAVE CURRENT R13 VALUE
            ST     R11,8(R13)         TELL CALLER ABOUT OUR SAVEAREA
            LR     R13,R11            ESTABLISH NEW R13 VALUE

            OPEN   (RRDS,OUTPUT)      OPEN OUR RELATIVE RECORD D.S.
            LA     R3,100             INDICATE NUMBER OF RECORDS
LOOP        DS     0H
            WRITE  ADECB,SF,RRDS,DUMMYREC
            CHECK  ADECB
            BCT    R3,LOOP

            CLOSE  (RRDS)             CLOSE THE FILE
            L      R13,4(R13)
            LM     R14,R12,12(R13)
            SR     R15,R15
            BR     R14                RETURN CONTROL TO O.S.

DBUG        DS     0H
            LR     R2,R0                        ADDRESS CONTROL DATA
            MVC    DBUGWORK(2),1(R2)            OBTAIN STATUS BITS
            UNPK   DBUGCHAR(5),DBUGWORK(3)      CONVERT TO DISPLAY
            TR     DBUGCHAR(4),DBUGTBL-240      FINISH THE CONVERSION
            MVC    DBUGWTO+8+33(4),DBUGCHAR     MOVE INTO WTO MESSAGE
DBUGWTO     WTO    'SYNAD ENTERED, EXPECTION VALUE =          ',     X
                   ROUTCDE=11
            ABEND  1234
DBUGWORK    DS     CL3
DBUGCHAR    DS     CL5
DBUGTBL     DC     C'0123456789ABCDEF'
SAVEAREA    DS     18F

RRDS        DCB    DSORG=PS,DDNAME=RRDS,MACRF=WL,SYNAD=DBUG
DUMMYREC    DC     X'FF',80X'00'
            LTORG
            END    FORMAT

//GO.SYSUDUMP     DD SYSOUT=$
//GO.RRDS         DD DSN=RELATIVE.FILE,DISP=SHR
```

Example 14.1 Program to format a relative dataset.

The **WRITE** instruction writes records into a relative record dataset. This instruction specifies an event control block (ECB), the type of output operation to be performed, the name of the DCB, and the record contents to be written. In Example 14.1, the event control block is named ADECB. The operand SF specifies that records are to be processed sequentially and in a forward direction.

The dummy record area DUMMYREC is 81 bytes long and contains a value of X'FF' in the first byte and a value of X'00' in all remaining bytes. We'll discuss why the record is formatted in this manner shortly.

The DCB called RRDS indicates that the dataset is a PS (physical sequential) dataset. Although this contradicts the DSORG=DA operand that we coded when the dataset was defined, it *is* the proper value that should be coded when *formatting* a relative record dataset.

The MACRF parameter specifies that output operations (W—write) are to be performed and that the BSAM access method is to be used in the formatting process (L).

The **SYNAD (synchronous error routine exit)** operand is new to our discussion.

This operand identifies a label that is to be given control if any I/O operations fail. Since there's only one output instruction in the program, the area called DBUG obtains control if the WRITE instruction fails.

The SYNAD routine can determine why an I/O request failed. The routine can analyze various bits in the event control block to determine what went wrong. Further, the routine can take corrective action and retry an I/O operation if appropriate. In our example, we simply convert the **exception code bits** in the event control block into a readable format and then use the WTO instruction to display a hexadecimal representation of the bits to the job log. This technique is easier than opening, closing, and writing to a message file, especially since we don't expect our program to fail.

The **event control block** and the **CHECK macro instruction** suspend execution of the program until the I/O operation is complete. This action is very similar to the WAIT instruction processing required after issuing the WTOR instruction as discussed in the last chapter. After completion, the second and third bytes of the event control block contain information about the status of our I/O operation. If it is *not* successful, control goes to our SYNAD routine. As long as we continue to write records into the file successfully, our SYNAD routine is *not* called.

If an I/O operation fails, the event control block contains information that helps us determine why the operation failed. The two-byte area in the event control block that contains I/O status information is called the **exception code** area. Figure 14.3 describes the bits and their meanings within the exception code bytes. If a bit in this area is "on" or has a value of 1, an error occurred during processing.

If the DBUG routine is given control, the code extracts the exception code bits from the event control block and converts them into human readable format. The routine then moves this information *into* the WTO instruction and displays the exception code values to our program job log. (Note that the WTO instruction message is modified during processing.)

Following the execution of the ABEND instruction, we can evaluate the exception code bits and determine why our program failed by reviewing the messages on the job log page. We can then fix any problem in our program and rerun it to finish formatting the dataset. More detailed information on the exception code bits are found in IBM's *OS/VS Data Management Macro Instructions* (GC26-3793 or GC26-4057).

Dumping the Contents of a Relative Dataset

To verify the contents and processing against your relative dataset, it may be necessary to obtain a dump of the contents of your file. One method is to write a program to read the dataset sequentially, form a hexadecimal print of each record image, and print the converted images. However, there's an easier method.

The VSAM utility called **IDCAMS** can dump the contents of almost any dataset, including our relative dataset. With just a few JCL statements and control cards, IDCAMS produces character, hexadecimal, or dump formatted output of each record in our file. With respect to our relative dataset, the JCL and IDCAMS commands given in Fig. 14.4 accomplish the task.

This example uses the most common IDCAMS operands to dump a file. The INFILE parameter identifies a DDNAME contained on an associated DD statement that references the file. The DD statement with the DDNAME RELFILE does indeed address the dataset to be dumped.

The operand DUMP specifies that a formatted dump is to be produced. The output from this job step looks very similar to that of a program abend dump. If you don't like

Bit Number	Meaning
0	The record that you tried to access was not found in the dataset.
1	The length of the record that you're trying to add to the dataset is not the same length as all other records in the dataset.
2	The dataset is full; no more records can be added.
3	Invalid request. See bits 9 to 15 for more information.
4	I/O error on the disk drive.
5	End of file or end of data.
6	Severe error.
7	You're trying to update a record in your dataset by issuing a WRITE instruction, but you did not first issue a READ instruction on the record.
8	Not used.
9	Dataset is opened as input, but you're trying to write to it.
10	Not used in our manner of processing.
11	The key of the record that you tried to access is outside the bounds of the dataset.
12	Not applicable for our purposes.
13	Not applicable for our purposes.
14	Invalid DCB.
15	Not applicable for our purposes.

Figure 14.3 Exception code bit meanings within the ECB.

```
//     EXEC    PGM=IDCAMS,REGION=1024K
//SYSPRINT    DD  SYSOUT=$
//RELFILE     DD  DSN=RELATIVE.DATASET,DISP=SHR
//SYSIN       DD  *
  PRINT INFILE(RELFILE) DUMP COUNT(10) SKIP(2)
```

Figure 14.4 Dumping a relative file using IDCAMS.

reading dumped output, specify the operands HEX or CHAR instead. HEX prints an image of your records in hexadecimal and CHAR prints them in character format. Obviously, DUMP or CHAR are used most often.

The COUNT operand indicates the number of records to be dumped. If you omit this operand, then IDCAMS prints an image of all records in the dataset.

The SKIP operand specifies the number of records to be skipped *before* printing begins. Hence, if you only want records 10 through 20 printed, you can specify COUNT and SKIP to perform this service. You cannot use SKIP to skip every other record, however. In other words, it is not possible to print records 1, 3, 5, 7, 9, . . . , and so on using a value of two in the SKIP operand.

Updating a Relative Dataset

A relative dataset can be updated using BDAM direct access processing. Records may be added or deleted from the dataset but only in a logical manner. In other words, we're going to set aside the first byte of every record to indicate whether or not the record contains valid information. If you look back to our formatted program example, you'll notice that the first byte of every record contains the value X'FF', which means that the record contains no data—it is **logically empty** or **logically deleted.** When we add a record to the dataset, we simply read the block, move our data into the block, and change the value from X'FF' to X'00' before we rewrite the record to the dataset. If a record has a value of X'00' in the first byte, we must assume that it contains valid information that can be processed by our programs. When processing sequentially, we skip records with X'FF' in the first byte because they do not contain application data.

It's not necessary to define your relative datasets to use the logical delete byte. This field is optional and is based on the needs of your application. Therefore, if your processing or application does not require this field, simply omit it from your record definition.

The *complete* program in Example 14.2 illustrates random relative record processing. The program inputs data from a transaction file that contains a transaction identification in the first byte of the record. The value of the transaction code is A, C, or D to add a record, change a record, or delete a record, respectively. Therefore, the program shown is again an example of a master file update application. Records are processed based on requirements contained in the transaction records.

The program begins with normal linkage conventions. After opening the files, the program processes each transaction by sending an image of the transaction to the audit trail report. The relative record number contained on each transaction record is then converted into the binary relative record number that accesses records in the master file. Once converted, the program attempts to read the corresponding block (record) from the file so that it can be processed.

If the READ instruction is successful, processing continues by evaluating the transaction code contained in the first byte of the transaction record. Depending on that value, a routine is called to add, change, or delete the associated master record. However, an unsuccessful READ causes the SYNAD routine, DBUG, to be called to determine why the READ request failed.

Inside each functional module, the record is processed. If a record is to be added to the file, the logical delete byte is checked to make sure that the block does not already contain a record. If it does, the program rejects the transaction since there must have been an error. If the record is empty, then the data from the transaction is moved into the master record and the new master record is written to the master file.

```
//      EXEC    ASMFCG
//ASM.SYSIN    DD   *
RRDSUPDT    CSECT
            STM     R14,R12,12(R13)   SAVE CALLER'S REGISTERS
            LR      R12,R15           USE R12 FOR A BASE REG
            USING   RRDSUPDT,R12      TELL THE ASSEMBLER
            LA      R11,SAVEM         ADDRESS OUR SAVE AREA
            ST      R13,4(R11)        SAVE CALLER'S SAVEAREA ADDR.
            ST      R11,8(R13)        TELL CALLER ABOUT OURS
            LR      R13,R11           OBTAIN NEW SAVE AREA
*
            OPEN    (RRDS,UPDAT)      OPEN OUR RELATIVE RECORD D.S.
            OPEN    (TRANS,INPUT)     OPEN OUR TRANSACTION FILE
            OPEN    (AUDIT,OUTPUT)    OPEN PRINT AUDIT TRAIL
*
LOOP        DS      0H
            GET     TRANS,TREC        INPUT A TRANSACTION
            PUT     AUDIT,SKIP3       SEPARATE EACH TRANSACTION
            PUT     AUDIT,DASHES      . WITH SPACES AND DASHED LINE
            MVC     AUDITKEY,TKEY     SAVE RECORD KEY VALUE
            MVC     AUDITMSG,TREC     MOVE TRANS REC TO AUDIT LINE
            PUT     AUDIT,AUDITLIN    PRINT AUDIT LINE
            XC      MASTER,MASTER     CLEAR THE RECORD AREA
            PACK    WORK,TKEY         CONVERT INPUT RELATIVE RECORD
            CVB     R2,WORK           ...NUMBER TO BINARY AND SAVE
            LA      R2,1(R2)          COMPENSATE FOR RR# OF ZERO
            ST      R2,RRNHOLD        STORE RRN IN MEMORY
*---------------------------------------------------------------*
*   SINCE THE RECORD MUST BE READ IN ALL CASES, GO AHEAD AND    *
*   OBTAIN THE RECORD FROM THE DATASET HAVING THE RELATIVE      *
*   RECORD NUMBER AS SPECIFIED ON THE TRANSACTION RECORD.       *
*---------------------------------------------------------------*
            READ    RDECB,DI,RRDS,MASTER,'S',0,RRN
            CHECK   RDECB
*---------------------------------------------------------------*
*  DETERMINE WHAT IS TO BE DONE WITH THIS TRANSACTION AND       *
*  BRANCH TO THE APPROPRIATE ROUTINE TO CARRY OUT THE REQUEST.  *
*---------------------------------------------------------------*
            CLI     TCODE,C'A'        ADD A RECORD?
            BE      ADD               IF SO, GO ADD A RECORD
            CLI     TCODE,C'C'        CHANGE?
            BE      CHANGE            IF SO, GO TO CHANGE ROUTINE
            CLI     TCODE,C'D'        DELETE A RECORD?
            BE      DELETE            IF SO, GO DELETE IT
            B       LOOP              SKIP TRANSACTION IF NOT VALID
*---------------------------------------------------------------*
*             ADD A NEW RECORD INTO THE MASTER FILE.            *
*---------------------------------------------------------------*
ADD         DS      0H
            CLI     MASTER,X'FF'      IS THIS RECORD EMPTY?
            BE      ADDOK             IF SO, CONTINUE NORMALLY
            PUT     AUDIT,CANTADD     IF NOT, CANT ADD RECORD
            B       LOOP              PROCESS NEXT TRANSACTION
ADDOK       DS      0H
            MVI     MASTER,X'00'      TURN OFF DELETE INDICATOR
            MVC     MDATA,TDATA       MOVE DATA INTO MASTER RECORD
            B       REWRITE           ALL DONE, GO REWRITE RECORD
*---------------------------------------------------------------*
*           CHANGE THE DATA IN A MASTER RECORD.                 *
*---------------------------------------------------------------*
CHANGE      DS      0H
            CLI     MASTER,X'00'      DOES RECORD CONTAIN DATA?
            BE      CHANGOK           IF SO, CONTINUE
            PUT     AUDIT,NOMSTR      IF NOT, PRINT PROBLEM MESSAGE
            B       LOOP              PROCESS NEXT TRANSACTION
CHANGOK     DS      0H
            MVC     MDATA,TDATA       UPDATE MASTER RECORD
            B       REWRITE
```

Example 14.2 Master file update program that uses random relative record access.

```
*-------------------------------------------------------------*
*          DELETE A RECORD IN THE MASTER FILE.                 *
*-------------------------------------------------------------*
DELETE    DS    0H
          CLI   MASTER,X'00'       CAN RECORD BE DELETED?
          BE    DELOK              IF SO, CONTINUE
          PUT   AUDIT,CANTDEL      IF NOT, WE CANT DELETE IT
          B     LOOP               PROCESS NEXT TRANSACTION
DELOK     DS    0H
          XC    MASTER,MASTER      CLEAR DATA FROM MASTER RECORD
          MVI   MASTER,X'FF'       INDICATE IT IS DELETED
          B     REWRITE            NOW REWRITE THE RECORD
*-------------------------------------------------------------*
*   AFTER ALL PROCESSING ON THE RECORD IS COMPLETED, REWRITE   *
*   THE RECORD INTO THE MASTER FILE.                           *
*-------------------------------------------------------------*
REWRITE   DS    0H
          WRITE WDECB,DI,RRDS,MASTER,'S',0,RRN
          CHECK WDECB
          PUT   AUDIT,WRITTEN       RECORD WRITTEN OK MESSAGE
          B     LOOP
*-------------------------------------------------------------*
*  AFTER ALL TRANSACTIONS HAVE BEEN PROCESSED, CLOSE THE FILES *
*  AND RETURN CONTROL TO THE OPERATING SYSTEM.                 *
*-------------------------------------------------------------*
EOF       DS    0H
          CLOSE (AUDIT,,TRANS,,RRDS)  CLOSE ALL FILES
          L     R13,4(R13)         GET BACK ORIGINAL R13
          LM    R14,R12,12(R13)    RESTORE CALLER'S REGS
          SR    R15,R15            SET RETURN CODE
          BR    R14                RETURN CONTROL TO O.S.
*-------------------------------------------------------------*
*  THE SYNAD ROUTINE BELOW TRAPS ALL UNUSUAL CONDITIONS THAT   *
*  MAY OCCUR WHILE PROCESSING THE DATASET RANDOMLY.  MESSAGES  *
*  ARE DISPLAYED FOR PROBLEMS THAT ARE ANTICIPATED.  IF AN     *
*  UNANTICIPATED ERROR OCCURS, THE PROGRAM DISPLAYS THE BITS   *
*  IN THE EXCEPTION BYTES AND CONTINUES PROCESSING OTHER       *
*  TRANSACTIONS.                                               *
*-------------------------------------------------------------*
DBUG      DS    0H
          LR    R1,R0                         POINT TO ECB ADDRESS
          TM    1(R1),B'10000000'             RECORD NOT FOUND?
          BNO   DBUG1                         IF NOT, SKIP PRINT
          PUT   AUDIT,DBUGMSG1                PRINT MESSAGE
          B     LOOP                          PROCESS NEXT RECORD
DBUG1     DS    0H
          TM    1(R1),B'01000000'             LENGTH ERROR?
          BNO   DBUG2                         IF NOT, SKIP PRINT
          PUT   AUDIT,DBUGMSG2                PRINT MESSAGE
          B     LOOP                          PROCESS NEXT RECORD
DBUG2     DS    0H
          TM    1(R1),B'00100000'             NO SPACE?
          BNO   DBUG3                         IF NOT, SKIP PRINT
          PUT   AUDIT,DBUGMSG3                PRINT MESSAGE
          B     LOOP                          PROCESS NEXT RECORD
DBUG3     DS    0H
          TM    2(R1),B'00000100'             OUTSIDE DATASET?
          BNO   BIGBUG                        IF NOT, FORCE ABEND
          PUT   AUDIT,DBUGMSG4                IF SO, PRINT MESSAGE
          B     LOOP
*-------------------------------------------------------------*
*  THE CODE BELOW IS STILL PART OF THE SYNAD ROUTINE.  IF AN   *
*  UNANTICIPATED ERROR OCCURS THEN ABORT PROGRAM PROCESSING.   *
*-------------------------------------------------------------*
BIGBUG    DS    0H
          LR    R2,R0                         ADDRESS CONTROL DATA
          MVC   DBUGWORK(2),1(R2)             OBTAIN STATUS BITS
          UNPK  DBUGCHAR(5),DBUGWORK(3)       CONVERT TO DISPLAY
          TR    DBUGCHAR(4),DBUGTBL-240       FINISH THE CONVERSION
          MVC   DBUGBITS(4),DBUGCHAR          MOVE INTO PRINT LINE
          PUT   AUDIT,DBUGLINE                PRINT INFORMATION
          B     LOOP                          CONTINUE PROCESSING
```

```
DBUGWORK     DS      CL3
DBUGCHAR     DS      CL5
DBUGTBL      DC      C'0123456789ABCDEF'
DBUGLINE     DS      0CL133
             DC      C' '                      CARRIAGE CONTROL
DBUGBITS     DS      CL4                       CONVERTED EXCEPTION CODE
             DC      CL128' - UNUSUAL ERROR OCCURRED DURING PROCESSIX
                     NG.  EXCEPTION BITS DISPLAYED.'
DBUGMSG1     DC      CL133' RECORD HAVING THIS TRANSACTION KEY IS NOX
                     T IN THE DATASET'
DBUGMSG2     DC      CL133' LENGTH OF RECORD BEING WRITTEN DOES NOT X
                     MATCH DATASET CHARACTERISTICS'
DBUGMSG3     DC      CL133' NO MORE SPACE IN THE DATASET'
DBUGMSG4     DC      CL133' KEY SPECIFIED IS OUTSIDE THE BOUNDS OF TX
                     HE DATASET'
*-------------------------------------------------------------------*
*          DATA AND STORAGE AREAS NEEDED BY THE PROGRAM.            *
*-------------------------------------------------------------------*
SAVEM        DS      18F
WORK         DS      D
RRNHOLD      DS      0F
             DS      X                        THIS MUST FOLLOW RRNHOLD
RRN          DS      AL3                      THIS MUST FOLLOW RRNHOLD+1
*
RRDS         DCB     DSORG=DA,DDNAME=RRDS,MACRF=(RIC,WIC),              X
                     SYNAD=DBUG,OPTCD=R
AUDIT        DCB     DSORG=PS,DDNAME=AUDIT,MACRF=PM
TRANS        DCB     DSORG=PS,DDNAME=SYSIN,MACRF=GM,EODAD=EOF
*
TREC         DS      0CL80                    TRANSACTION RECORD AREA
TCODE        DS      C                        TRANSACTION CODE: A,C,D
TKEY         DS      CL5                      RELATIVE RECORD NUMBER
TDATA        DS      CL50                     DATA FOR MASTER RECORD
             DS      CL24                     UNUSED AREA IN TRANSACTION
*
MASTER       DS      0CL81                    MASTER RECORD AREA
MDELBYTE     DS      X                        LOGICAL DELETE BYTE
MDATA        DS      CL50                     MASTER RECORD DATA AREA
             DS      CL30                     UNUSED MASTER RECORD AREA
*
AUDITLIN     DS      0CL133                   AUDIT TRAIL OUTPUT LINE
             DC      C' '                     CARRIAGE CONTROL
AUDITKEY     DS      CL5                      KEY OF THE TRANSACTION
             DC      CL5' '                   SPACING AREA
AUDITMSG     DS      CL80                     AUDIT MESSAGE AREA
             DC      CL42' '                  FILLER AREA
*-------------------------------------------------------------------*
*   THE FOLLOWING MESSAGES ARE PRINTED OUT DURING PROCESSING        *
*   TO HELP DETERMINE HOW VARIOUS TRANSACTIONS WERE PROCESSED.      *
*-------------------------------------------------------------------*
CANTADD      DC      CL133' CAN''T ADD MASTER RECORD SINCE CURRENT RX
                     ECORD IS ALREADY OCCUPIED.'
NOMSTR       DC      CL133' MASTER RECORD CANNOT BE CHANGED SINCE CUX
                     RRENT MASTER RECORD IS EMPTY.'
CANTDEL      DC      CL133' CAN''T DELETE MASTER RECORD SINCE THE CUX
                     RRENT MASTER RECORD IS EMPTY.'
WRITTEN      DC      CL133' RECORD WRITTEN SUCCESSFULLY TO THE MASTEX
                     R FILE'
DASHES       DC      C' ',132C'-'
SKIP3        DC      CL133'-'
             LTORG
             END     RRDSUPDT
//GO.SYSUDUMP   DD SYSOUT=$
//GO.RRDS       DD DSN=RELATIVE.FILE,DISP=SHR
//GO.AUDIT      DD SYSOUT=$,DCB=(RECFM=FA,LRECL=133,BLKSIZE=133)
//GO.SYSIN      DD *
   'transaction file is placed here
```

Example 14.2 (cont.)

The logical delete byte is tested in each functional module and appropriate action is taken if it is not the value expected. If processing continues normally, then the master record is written back to the master file, replacing the old image of the record. Again, the SYNAD routine called DBUG may be called if the WRITE instruction fails.

When all transactions are processed, the program terminates processing by closing the files and returning to the operating system. Random master file update processing is completed once all transactions have been applied.

From the SYNAD routine, you see that bytes 2 and 3 of the event control block are being tested. When the SYNAD routine is invoked, register 0 contains the address of the event control block. After copying this address into register 2, the routine analyzes why the I/O request failed. Using the test-under-mask instruction, the routine analyzes the exception code bits to determine what may have happened.

Clearly, this routine does not check all possible conditions. If an unexpected condition occurs, control is transferred to the location called BIGBUG. Here, the exception code bytes are converted into printable format (hexadecimal dump format) and displayed to the audit report. Note that they are *not* written to the job log using the WTO instruction as in the previous program example. Since the audit trail report contains an activity log of each transaction and its processing sequence, the exception code values are sent to this report instead of to the job log. The programmer can review the output from the program to further analyze why the transaction could not be applied to the master file.

The READ and WRITE instructions are the primary instructions that process a relative record dataset. As shown, the READ and WRITE instructions contain seven operands, which are explained in Fig. 14.5.

Any address area can be specified through a label or a register number. For example, if register 4 contains the address of the DCB for our file, then code **(R4)** in place of

```
READ
          ecbname,DI,dcbname,record,'S',0,rrn
WRITE


ecbname  --  label to be assigned to an event control
             block generated by this instruction.  The
             name of your ECB may be any standard statement
             label as long as it is not duplicated in the
             program.

DI       --  indicates that direct access processing will
             occur against this dataset.

dcbname  --  label of the DCB for the relative record
             dataset.

record   --  location of the area where the records are
             to be processed.

'S'      --  the length of each record will be the same
             as the current standard within the dataset.

0        --  zero -- this field is used when processing
             a direct dataset.  Since we're processing a
             relative dataset we code a value of 0 here.

rrn      --  relative record number.  This must be a
             three byte binary field.
```

Figure 14.5 The READ and WRITE BDAM instructions.

the DCB label. In fact, this allows use of reentrant programming techniques if desired.

Let's look at the DCB instruction for the relative file. Specifically, the MACRF parameter contains values quite different than any we've used so far. These values, RIC and WIC, mean that read and write operations are to be performed, relative record number access is to be used, and that the CHECK macro instruction is to be used to suspend program execution until the I/O operations complete. It's very important that these values be coded as shown. The omission of a single letter within this parameter will almost certainly guarantee failure when processing your relative files. In fact, the complexity of the READ, WRITE, and DCB instructions clearly make relative file processing much more difficult than sequential file processing.

Sequentially Processing Records in a Relative File

After randomly processing your relative file, it may be necessary to develop a program to process it sequentially as in the case of printing a report. Surprisingly, standard *sequential* processing methods can be used to process a relative record file sequentially. This means that standard QSAM macro instructions (GET) can be used in place of the READ instructions if we're processing the file sequentially. Further, standard QSAM DCB's can be used when accessing such datasets. Since we're more familiar with the QSAM method of processing than with BSAM or BDAM, it's easier and faster to implement an application that performs sequential processing.

Your application program, however, should check the first byte of each record processed. If you use the logical delete indicator, the program should not process and display information contained in "deleted" records. Clearly, your reports will be inaccurate if you blindly process all records in a relative file in which logical delete processing has been used.

If you process records sequentially, but also want the ability to update records, design your application similar to the update program shown earlier. Your program can access the records "sequentially" by randomly reading record 0, followed by records 1, 2, 3, 4, 5, . . . , and so on. As each record is read, it can be updated and written back to the dataset as your program advances through the file.

INDEXED FILE PROCESSING USING ISAM

The **indexed sequential access method (ISAM)** offers yet another method of processing data. Records may be accessed randomly or sequentially in a manner similar to that of the relative record dataset. However, records in an ISAM dataset are not accessed through a relative record number. Instead, the key field in an ISAM record can consist of any field or group of fields in the record. In fact, the key field in an ISAM record can be up to 255 bytes long. However, each record key value must be unique, that is, no two records in an ISAM dataset may have the same key value.

ISAM supports fixed- or variable-length record storage. Records stored in an ISAM dataset can be blocked, quite contrary to the nonblocked requirement when processing relative record datasets. Based on these characteristics, you should see the increased capabilities available when using ISAM for your processing. Better storage utilization, increased flexibility in record definition and key selection, and the ability to process records sequentially or randomly combine to support almost any processing need. For these reasons, ISAM is one of the most used random access methods. However, it is gradually being phased out in favor of VSAM due to the ever-increasing capabilities of this newer access method.

Structure of an ISAM Dataset

There are three primary components of an ISAM dataset: the index area, the prime data area, and the overflow area. The prime data area stores our application records. Again, these records may be accessed sequentially or randomly, depending on our processing needs.

The **index area** supports random processing. Through its hierarchical organization, we can access records randomly. In other words, ISAM uses the index component much like the guide words in a dictionary. For example, to look up the word "file" in the dictionary, you open to a particular page. Since it's very unlikely to open to the very page on which this word is defined, you now page backward or forward to locate the word. It's not necessary to advance page by page, however, since each page contains a pair of words that help lead you to the desired word. Therefore, you can advance by groups of pages until you get closer and closer to the page containing the word "file."

The process of looking up a word in the dictionary is very similar to the method used by ISAM to find a record in a dataset. Using three levels of index, ISAM locates a record by evaluating **entries** in the index records. The entries, consisting of record key values, allow ISAM to get closer and closer to your record. Eventually, ISAM locates the record or determines that it is not in the dataset.

The highest level of index in an ISAM dataset is called the **master index.** This level of index is optional and its existence is based on the overall size of your ISAM file. Large files achieve better performance if a master index is established.

The next level of index is the **cylinder index,** which is usually the highest level when a master index is not present. Again, cylinder indexes are only present when your ISAM dataset occupies considerable space on a disk device. The generation of a cylinder index is automatically done by ISAM and does not have to be requested as with the master index.

The lowest and most common index level is the **track index,** which is found in all ISAM files. The track index is the last index level searched when accessing a record in an ISAM dataset. As Fig. 14.6 illustrates, the track index is the component closest to that of the application data records.

The track index is also very important when using the overflow component in an ISAM dataset. As records are added to an ISAM dataset, they are placed in keyed order on the disk device. Further, records are stored in areas called **tracks.** The size of a track depends on the type of disk used. For example, a 3330-model disk drive contains 13,030 bytes on each track, a 3350 contains 19,069 bytes per track, and a 3380 contains 47,467 bytes per track. Therefore, if we're storing 100-byte records on a 3330, the maximum number of records to fit on a track is 130. Actually, fewer records than this can fit on a track due to hardware and software requirements.

If the last record on a track contains the key value 'SMITH' and the first record contains the key value 'OLSON', then clearly the record whose key is 'QWERTY' must be placed on this track to maintain key ordering. If the track is full, however, then one of the records must be "bumped" off of the track. ISAM bumps the *last* record off the track and places it into the **overflow area.** This allows the record whose key is 'QWERTY' to be placed in its proper order on the track. The track index is updated to reflect the "bumping" action, thus maintaining the order of the records. Hence, the record whose key is 'SMITH' is now contained in the overflow area.

As more records are added to the various tracks in the dataset, it is possible that the overflow area eventually becomes full due to this "bumping" activity. Clearly, it's important to have an overflow area, but it's also very important to keep the overflow area as

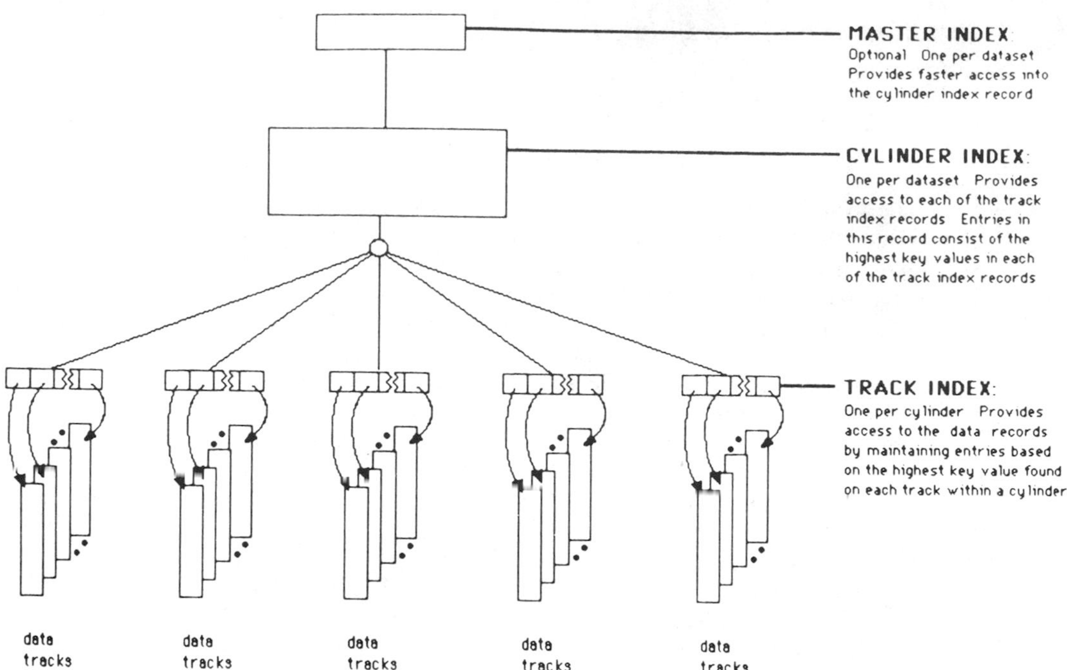

Figure 14.6 Structure of an ISAM dataset.

empty as possible. As the overflow area becomes full, it takes more time for ISAM to add and bump records from the various tracks in the dataset. Bumping may not occur on each record addition, but it can occur more often than planned. Therefore, it is very important that an ISAM dataset be reorganized periodically to reduce the number of records in the overflow area.

Records can be added to an ISAM dataset or updated once they've been added. Records can also be deleted if the first byte of each record has been set aside as the delete indicator. Again, X'FF' is used in the **logical delete byte** to indicate that a record is deleted. It is the responsibility of the program to place and maintain the logical delete byte. However, ISAM acts differently than BDAM with respect to this byte. If you recall, records are retrieved from a BDAM dataset even if they contain the "deleted" indicator. As a result, your program has to continually check the value of the delete byte before processing a record to determine if the record can be processed.

When processing records in an ISAM dataset, a record is not returned to the program if it is deleted. ISAM evaluates the first byte of the record to determine if it is deleted. If so, the program is told that the record cannot be found. The program does not have to check the delete byte since deleted records are not presented to the program for processing.

Creating an ISAM Dataset

An ISAM dataset is again created using standard IBM JCL language. Again, IEFBR14 will allow the operating system to recognize and process our JCL. Therefore, an ISAM dataset is created by allocating space for the dataset and describing its characteristics as we did before.

Records in an ISAM dataset contain record keys that require several more operands within the DCB parameter on our JCL statements. Specifically, we have to specify the length of the record key **(KEYLEN, key length)** and where the key is located within the record **(RKP, relative key position).** If the first field in the record is the record key, then the relative key position (RKP) is specified as zero. If the key occupies bytes 5 to 10, then the relative key position is specified as 4 and the key length is specified as 6.

ISAM also allows creating and processing variable-length records. If an ISAM dataset is defined to support such a record structure, then the record descriptor word is allowed for on the front of each logical record. This moves the relative key position four bytes farther into the record. Hence, if the first field in the record serves as the record key, then the relative key position is specified as 4 instead of 0. The key length value does not change when processing fixed- or variable-length records.

Once you've decided where your record key is to be located, you can proceed to allocate space for the dataset. Since an ISAM dataset consists of three components, we allocate space for an index, prime, and overflow area. The amount of space for each depends on the size and activity in our dataset. Since this varies from application to application, let's just assume that all components are defined as one cylinder in size. Incidentally, space for ISAM datasets must be allocated in cylinders. Track and block allocation are not permitted. Figure 14.7 contains our ISAM file definition.

Space for this dataset is allocated on DISK01. Each record is 81 bytes long and the records are not blocked. The first byte of each record is used as the delete indicator (OPTCD=L), thus placing the key at relative key position 1 rather than at relative key position 0. The key is four bytes long.

Each component of this dataset occupies one cylinder. More space should probably be allocated to the prime area since that's where most of our records are stored. Finally, it's important to note the order of allocation. Just after the dataset name, in parentheses, is the name of the component being allocated. The three components of an ISAM dataset must be allocated in the order shown in our example. The index must be allocated first, followed by the prime data area, and finally the overflow area. If the components are not allocated in this order, you will have difficulty processing your ISAM dataset.

Processing an ISAM Dataset Sequentially

An ISAM dataset is processed sequentially using the **QISAM (queued index sequential access method).** The term *queued* is most synonomous with the phrases "one after another" or "one at a time." In other words, records processed using the QISAM access method are processed in keyed order, that is, they are not processed randomly. With this

```
//        EXEC   PGM=IEFBR14
//DDA       DD   DSN=ISAM.MASTER.FILE(INDEX),DISP=(,CATLG),
//               UNIT=3350,VOL=SER=DISK01,SPACE=(CYL,(1)),
//               DCB=(RECFM=F,LRECL=81,BLKSIZE=81,DSORG=IS,
//               RKP=1,KEYLEN=4,OPTCD=L)
//          DD   DSN=ISAM.MASTER.FILE(PRIME),DISP=(,CATLG),
//               UNIT=3350,VOL=SER=DISK01,SPACE=(CYL,(1)),
//               DCB=(RECFM=F,LRECL=81,BLKSIZE=81,DSORG=IS,
//               RKP=1,KEYLEN=4,OPTCD=L)
//          DD   DSN=ISAM.MASTER.FILE(OVFLOW),DISP=(,CATLG),
//               UNIT=3350,VOL=SER=DISK01,SPACE=(CYL,(1)),
//               DCB=(RECFM=F,LRECL=81,BLKSIZE=81,DSORG=IS,
//               RKP=1,KEYLEN=4,OPTCD=L)
```

Figure 14.7 JCL to create an ISAM dataset.

access method, we can load records into an empty ISAM dataset, read through the records in the file from beginning to end, and add records on to the *end* of the dataset. Although it's not necessary to format an ISAM dataset as we did with the BDAM file, it may be appropriate to place some records into the file before we begin our random processing. Therefore, the QISAM access method can load records into an empty ISAM dataset as illustrated in Example 14.3.

This program assumes that the input transaction records are in the correct format for loading directly into the ISAM file. The first four bytes of each record are used as the key. The first byte of the master record is set aside for the delete indicator. As you can see by referring to this code, the first byte of each record added to the file is X'00', which indicates that these records are not deleted.

An ISAM file can be processed sequentially using a similar program to access each record in the file based on its key order. Assuming that we're processing the same file loaded in Example 14.3, the program in Example 14.4 prints an image of each record to the printer.

You should notice that this program is almost identical to that of a standard sequential (QSAM) program from previous chapters. Except for the DSORG=IS operand on the DCB statement, the programs are identical. The QISAM access method allows easy sequential processing of an ISAM file using standard GET and PUT instructions. Its processing techniques parallel that of standard QSAM, thus making sequential ISAM processing rather trivial.

```
//       EXEC     ASMFCG
//ASM.SYSIN    DD     *
ISAMLOAD    CSECT
            STM      R14,R12,12(R13)       SAVE CALLER'S REGISTERS
            BAL      R11,80(R15)           SKIP OVER SAVE AREA
            USING    *,R13                 USE R13 AS A BASE REG
            DS       18F                   REGISTER SAVE AREA
            ST       R13,4(R11)            SAVE CALLER'S SAVEAREA ADDR.
            ST       R11,8(R13)            TELL CALLER ABOUT OURS
            LR       R13,R11               ADDRESS OUR SAVE AREA

            OPEN     (IMAGEIN,INPUT,ISAM,OUTPUT)
MAINLOOP    DS       0H
            GET      IMAGEIN,MASTER+1      GET A MASTER RECORD
            PUT      ISAM,MASTER           WRITE OUT THE RECORD
            B        MAINLOOP

EOF         DS       0H
            CLOSE    (IMAGEIN,,ISAM)       CLOSE ALL FILES
            L        R13,4(R13)            RESTORE SAVE AREA POINTER
            LM       R14,R12,12(R13)       RESTORE CALLER'S REGS.
            SR       R15,R15               SET RETURN CODE TO ZERO
            BR       R14                   RETURN TO O.S.

MASTER      DC       X'00'                 DELETE BYTE -- NOT DELETED
            DS       CL80                  MASTER RECORD AREA

IMAGEIN     DCB      DSORG=PS,DDNAME=SYSIN,MACRF=GM,EODAD=EOF
ISAM        DCB      DSORG=IS,DDNAME=ISAM,MACRF=PM
            LTORG
            END      ISAMLOAD
//GO.ISAM   DD       DSN=ISAM.MASTER.FILE,DISP=OLD
//GO.SYSIN  DD       *
     'place master file records here'
```

Example 14.3 Program to load records sequentially into an ISAM dataset.

```
//       EXEC    ASMFCG
//ASM.SYSIN    DD    *
ISAMPRNT    CSECT
            STM      R14,R12,12(R13)      SAVE CALLER'S REGISTERS
            BAL      R11,80(R15)          SKIP OVER SAVE AREA
            USING    *,R13                USE R13 AS A BASE REG
            DS       18F                  REGISTER SAVE AREA
            ST       R13,4(R11)           SAVE CALLER'S SAVEAREA ADDR.
            ST       R11,8(R13)           TELL CALLER ABOUT OURS
            LR       R13,R11              ADDRESS OUR SAVE AREA

            OPEN     (IMAGE,OUTPUT,ISAM,INPUT)
MAINLOOP    DS       0H
            GET      ISAM,MASTER          GET A MASTER RECORD
            PUT      IMAGE,MASTER         WRITE RECORD TO PRINTER
            B        MAINLOOP

EOF         DS       0H
            CLOSE    (IMAGE,,ISAM)        CLOSE ALL FILES
            L        R13,4(R13)           RESTORE SAVE AREA POINTER
            LM       R14,R12,12(R13)      RESTORE CALLER'S REGS.
            SR       R15,R15              SET RETURN CODE TO ZERO
            BR       R14                  RETURN TO O.S.

MASTER      DS       CL81                 MASTER RECORD AREA

IMAGE       DCB      DSORG=PS,DDNAME=IMAGE,MACRF=PM,RECFM=F,           X
                     LRECL=81,BLKSIZE=81
ISAM        DCB      DSORG=IS,DDNAME=ISAM,MACRF=GM,EODAD=EOF

            LTORG
            END      ISAMPRNT
//GO.ISAM   DD       DSN=ISAM.MASTER.FILE,DISP=OLD
//GO.IMAGE  DD       SYSOUT=$
```

Example 14.4 Program to copy ISAM record images to the printer.

Obtaining a Dump of an ISAM Dataset

An ISAM dataset can be dumped to the printer using a utility called **IEBISAM.** This utility can copy, reorganize, print, and dump the contents of an ISAM dataset. In this text, we're only going to produce a hexadecimal dump of an ISAM file. Therefore, refer to the IBM publication *Utilities* (GC28-6586) for more information on using IEBISAM or any other IBM utility (except IDCAMS).

An ISAM file is dumped to the printer using JCL statements. A single EXEC parameter is directed to the IEBISAM utility to request a printed dump of the ISAM dataset. The example in Fig. 14.8 illustrates the method for dumping the contents of our ISAM dataset created above.

```
//      EXEC    PGM=IEBISAM,PARM='PRINTL,N',REGION=512K
//SYSPRINT      DD   SYSOUT=$
//SYSIN         DD   DUMMY
//SYSUT1        DD   DSN=ISAM.MASTER.FILE,DISP=OLD
//SYSUT2        DD   SYSOUT=$
```

Figure 14.8 Obtaining a hexadecimal dump of an ISAM file using IEBISAM.

Randomly Processing an ISAM File

One of our major goals when we began this chapter was to learn how to process files in a random manner. As we've discussed, ISAM file structures process records sequentially or randomly. With the QISAM access method, records can be processed in key order. Records are randomly added, deleted, or updated in an ISAM dataset using the BISAM **(basic indexed sequential access method).** Since an ISAM dataset does not have to be formatted before random processing may begin, the techniques for processing a random ISAM file are much different than for processing a relative file.

Records can be added to an ISAM dataset without first having to read the record. To add a record, the program constructs the record to be added and writes the record into the file. If successful, the program continues normally. If the write operation fails, the CHECK macro transfers control to a SYNAD routine to analyze the problem. Corrective measures can be taken or the transaction can be rejected by the SYNAD routine. In general, the program does not have to abort processing when an exceptional condition occurs. With the SYNAD routine, the program can handle almost any I/O failure when processing an ISAM dataset.

The program in Example 14.5 is a typical ISAM master file update application. The logic in this program is very similar to that of the relative file example shown earlier, although there are some differences. Let's look at the program and then comment on those differences.

The READ and WRITE instructions are again used when processing an ISAM dataset randomly. However, their formats are slightly different. Specifically, the delete

```
//       EXEC    ASMFCG
//ASM.SYSIN    DD    *
ISAMUPDT   CSECT
           STM     R14,R12,12(R13)   SAVE CALLER'S REGISTERS
           LR      R12,R15           USE R12 FOR A BASE REG
           USING   ISAMUPDT,R12      TELL THE ASSEMBLER
           LA      R11,SAVEM         ADDRESS OUR SAVE AREA
           ST      R13,4(R11)        SAVE CALLER'S SAVEAREA ADDR.
           ST      R11,8(R13)        TELL CALLER ABOUT OURS
           LR      R13,R11           OBTAIN NEW SAVE AREA
*
           OPEN    (ISAM,INOUT)      OPEN OUR ISAM FILE
           OPEN    (TRANS,INPUT)     OPEN OUR TRANSACTION FILE
           OPEN    (AUDIT,OUTPUT)    OPEN PRINT AUDIT TRAIL
*
LOOP       DS      0H
           GET     TRANS,TREC        INPUT A TRANSACTION
           PUT     AUDIT,SKIP3       SEPARATE EACH TRANSACTION
           PUT     AUDIT,DASHES        WITH SPACES AND DASHED LINE
           MVC     AUDITKEY,TKEY     SAVE RECORD KEY VALUE
           MVC     AUDITMSG,TREC     MOVE TRANS REC TO AUDIT LINE
           PUT     AUDIT,AUDITLIN    PRINT AUDIT LINE
           XC      MASTER,MASTER     CLEAR THE RECORD AREA
*-------------------------------------------------------------------*
*  DETERMINE WHAT IS TO BE DONE WITH THIS TRANSACTION AND           *
*  BRANCH TO THE APPROPRIATE ROUTINE TO CARRY OUT THE REQUEST.      *
*-------------------------------------------------------------------*
           CLI     TCODE,C'A'        ADD A RECORD?
           BE      ADD               IF SO, GO ADD A RECORD
           CLI     TCODE,C'C'        CHANGE?
           BE      CHANGE            IF SO, GO TO CHANGE ROUTINE
           CLI     TCODE,C'D'        DELETE A RECORD?
           BE      DELETE            IF SO, GO DELETE IT
           B       LOOP              SKIP TRANSACTION IF NOT VALID
```

Example 14.5 A random access master file update program using ISAM.

```
*------------------------------------------------------------------*
*            ADD A NEW RECORD INTO THE MASTER FILE.                *
*------------------------------------------------------------------*
ADD          DS      0H
             MVC     MKEY,TKEY          MOVE IN TRANSACTION KEY
             MVC     MDATA,TDATA        SUPPLY DATA TO RECORD
             MVI     MDELBYTE,X'00'     RECORD IS NOT DELETED
             WRITE   ADECB,KN,ISAM,MASTER-16,'S',MKEY
             CHECK   ADECB,DSORG=IS
             PUT     AUDIT,ADDED        DISPLAY AUDIT MESSAGE
             B       LOOP
*------------------------------------------------------------------*
*            CHANGE THE DATA IN A MASTER RECORD.                   *
*------------------------------------------------------------------*
CHANGE       DS      0H
             READ    CDECB,KU,ISAM,MASTER,'S',TKEY,MF=E
             CHECK   CDECB,DSORG=IS
             MVC     MDATA,TDATA        MOVE NEW DATA INTO MASTER REC
             WRITE   CDECB,K,ISAM,MASTER-16,'S',TKEY,MF=E
             CHECK   CDECB,DSORG=IS
             PUT     AUDIT,CHANGED      DISPLAY COMPLETED MESSAGE
             B       LOOP               GO PROCESS NEXT TRANSACTION
CFORMAT      READ    CDECB,KU,ISAM,MASTER,'S',TKEY,MF=L
*------------------------------------------------------------------*
*            DELETE A RECORD IN THE MASTER FILE.                   *
*------------------------------------------------------------------*
DELETE       DS      0H
             READ    DDECB,KU,ISAM,MASTER,'S',TKEY,MF=E
             CHECK   DDECB,DSORG=IS
             MVI     MASTER,X'FF'       TURN ON DELETE BYTE
             WRITE   DDECB,K,ISAM,MASTER-16,'S',TKEY,MF=E
             CHECK   DDECB,DSORG=IS
             PUT     AUDIT,DELETED      PRINT AUDIT MESSAGE
             B       LOOP               PROCESS NEXT RECORD
DFORMAT      READ    DDECB,KU,ISAM,MASTER,'S',TKEY,MF=L
*------------------------------------------------------------------*
*  AFTER ALL TRANSACTIONS HAVE BEEN PROCESSED, CLOSE THE FILES     *
*  AND RETURN CONTROL TO THE OPERATING SYSTEM.                     *
*------------------------------------------------------------------*
EOF          DS      0H
             CLOSE   (AUDIT,,TRANS,,ISAM)  CLOSE ALL FILES
             L       R13,4(R13)         GET BACK ORIGINAL R13
             LM      R14,R12,12(R13)    RESTORE CALLER'S REGS
             SR      R15,R15            SET RETURN CODE
             BR      R14                RETURN CONTROL TO O.S.
*------------------------------------------------------------------*
*  THE SYNAD ROUTINE BELOW TRAPS ALL UNUSUAL CONDITIONS THAT       *
*  MAY OCCUR WHILE PROCESSING THE DATASET RANDOMLY.  MESSAGES      *
*  ARE DISPLAYED FOR PROBLEMS THAT ARE ANTICIPATED.  IF AN         *
*  UNANTICIPATED ERROR OCCURS, THE PROGRAM DISPLAYS THE BITS       *
*  IN THE EXCEPTION BYTES AND CONTINUES PROCESSING OTHER           *
*  TRANSACTIONS.                                                   *
*------------------------------------------------------------------*
DBUG         DS      0H
             TM      24(R1),B'00000010'        OVERFLOW RECORD?
             BNO     DBUG0                     IF NOT, SKIP PRINT
             PUT     AUDIT,DBUGMSG0            PRINT MESSAGE
             BR      R14                       CONTINUE NORMALLY!
DBUG0        DS      0H
             TM      24(R1),B'10000000'        RECORD NOT FOUND?
             BNO     DBUG1                     IF NOT, SKIP PRINT
             PUT     AUDIT,DBUGMSG1            PRINT MESSAGE
             B       LOOP                      PROCESS NEXT RECORD
DBUG1        DS      0H
             TM      24(R1),B'01000000'        LENGTH ERROR?
             BNO     DBUG2                     IF NOT, SKIP PRINT
             PUT     AUDIT,DBUGMSG2            PRINT MESSAGE
             B       LOOP                      PROCESS NEXT RECORD
```

```
DBUG2    DS    0H
         TM    24(R1),B'00100000'          NO SPACE?
         BNO   DBUG3                       IF NOT, SKIP PRINT
         PUT   AUDIT,DBUGMSG3              PRINT MESSAGE
         B     LOOP                        PROCESS NEXT RECORD
DBUG3    DS    0H
         TM    24(R1),B'00000100'          OUTSIDE DATASET?
         BNO   DBUG4                       IF NOT, SKIP PRINT
         PUT   AUDIT,DBUGMSG4              IF SO, PRINT MESSAGE
         B     LOOP
DBUG4    DS    0H
         TM    24(R1),B'00000001'          DUPLICATE RECORD KEY
         BNO   BIGBUG                      IF NOT, FORCE ABEND
         PUT   AUDIT,DBUGMSG5              IF SO, PRINT MESSAGE
         B     LOOP
*-----------------------------------------------------------------*
*  THE CODE BELOW IS STILL PART OF THE SYNAD ROUTINE.  IF AN      *
*  UNANTICIPATED ERROR OCCURS THEN ABORT PROGRAM PROCESSING.      *
*-----------------------------------------------------------------*
BIGBUG   DS    0H
         MVC   DBUGWORK(2),24(R1)          OBTAIN STATUS BITS
         UNPK  DBUGCHAR(5),DBUGWORK(3)     CONVERT TO DISPLAY
         TR    DBUGCHAR(4),DBUGTBL-240     FINISH THE CONVERSION
         MVC   DBUGBITS(4),DBUGCHAR        MOVE INTO PRINT LINE
         PUT   AUDIT,DBUGLINE              PRINT INFORMATION
         B     LOOP                        CONTINUE PROCESSING
DBUGWORK DS    CL3
DBUGCHAR DS    CL5
DBUGTBL  DC    C'0123456789ABCDEF'
DBUGLINE DS    0CL133
         DC    C' '                   CARRIAGE CONTROL
DBUGBITS DS    CL4                    CONVERTED EXCEPTION CODE
         DC    CL128' - UNUSUAL ERROR OCCURRED DURING PROCESSIX
               NG.  EXCEPTION BITS DISPLAYED.'
DBUGMSG0 DC    CL133' THIS RECORD WAS FOUND IN THE OVERFLOW ARX
               EA OF THE DATASET'
DBUGMSG1 DC    CL133' RECORD HAVING THIS TRANSACTION KEY IS NOX
               T IN THE DATASET'
DBUGMSG2 DC    CL133' LENGTH OF RECORD BEING WRITTEN DOES NOT X
               MATCH DATASET CHARACTERISTICS'
DBUGMSG3 DC    CL133' NO MORE SPACE IN THE DATASET'
DBUGMSG4 DC    CL133' KEY SPECIFIED IS OUTSIDE THE BOUNDS OF TX
               HE DATASET'
DBUGMSG5 DC    CL133' RECORD ALREADY EXISTS WITH THIS KEY.  REX
               CORD CANNOT BE ADDED'
*-----------------------------------------------------------------*
*          DATA AND STORAGE AREAS NEEDED BY THE PROGRAM.          *
*-----------------------------------------------------------------*
SAVEM    DS    18F
*
ISAM     DCB   DSORG=IS,DDNAME=ISAM,MACRF=(RUC,WUAC),                  X
               SYNAD=DBUG
AUDIT    DCB   DSORG=PS,DDNAME=AUDIT,MACRF=PM
TRANS    DCB   DSORG=PS,DDNAME=SYSIN,MACRF=GM,EODAD=EOF
*
TREC     DS    0CL80                  TRANSACTION RECORD AREA
TCODE    DS    C                      TRANSACTION CODE: A,C,D
TKEY     DS    CL5                    INCOMING RECORD KEY
TDATA    DS    CL50                   DATA FOR MASTER RECORD
         DS    CL24                   UNUSED AREA IN TRANSACTION
*
         DS    0F                     MASTER RECORD WORK AREA
         DS    4F                     ...REQUIRED BY ISAM
MASTER   DS    0CL81                  MASTER RECORD AREA
MDELBYTE DS    X                      LOGICAL DELETE BYTE
MKEY     DS    CL5                    KEY OF THE MASTER RECORD
MDATA    DS    CL50                   MASTER RECORD DATA AREA
         DS    CL25                   UNUSED MASTER RECORD AREA
*
AUDITLIN DS    0CL133                 AUDIT TRAIL OUTPUT LINE
         DC    C' '                   CARRIAGE CONTROL
```

```
AUDITKEY   DS      CL5                        KEY OF THE TRANSACTION
           DC      CL5' '                     SPACING AREA
AUDITMSG   DS      CL80                       AUDIT MESSAGE AREA
           DC      CL42' '                    FILLER AREA
*------------------------------------------------------------------*
*   THE FOLLOWING MESSAGES ARE PRINTED OUT DURING PROCESSING      *
*   TO HELP DETERMINE HOW VARIOUS TRANSACTIONS WERE PROCESSED.    *
*------------------------------------------------------------------*
CANTADD    DC      CL133' CAN''T ADD MASTER RECORD SINCE CURRENT RX
                   ECORD IS ALREADY OCCUPIED.'
NOMSTR     DC      CL133' MASTER RECORD CANNOT BE CHANGED SINCE CUX
                   RRENT MASTER RECORD IS EMPTY.'
CANTDEL    DC      CL133' CAN''T DELETE MASTER RECORD SINCE THE CUX
                   RRENT MASTER RECORD IS EMPTY.'
ADDED      DC      CL133' RECORD ADDED SUCCESSFULLY TO THE MASTER X
                   FILE'
CHANGED    DC      CL133' CONTENTS OF THIS RECORD HAVE BEEN CHANGEX
                   D SUCCESSFULLY'
DELETED    DC      CL133' RECORD DELETED AS REQUESTED'
DASHES     DC      C' ',132C'-'
SKIP3      DC      CL133'-'
           LTORG
           END     ISAMUPDT
//GO.SYSUDUMP   DD SYSOUT=$
//GO.ISAM       DD DSN=ISAM.MASTER.FILE,DISP=OLD
//GO.AUDIT      DD SYSOUT=$,DCB=(RECFM=FA,LRECL=133,BLKSIZE=133)
//GO.SYSIN      DD *
   'transaction file is placed here'
```

Example 14.5 (cont.)

and update logic uses a rather peculiar form of the READ and WRITE instructions. Let's look again at the code to change the contents of an ISAM master record as contained in Fig. 14.9.

The code begins by reading the record from the master file having a key equal to that specified in the transaction record. The name of the event control block is CDECB, the operation is KU (which means read-for-update), and the DCB label for our file is ISAM. The area into which the record is to be read is called MASTER and the key field is located in the area called TKEY. The 'S' operand is coded to indicate that our record length does not change during processing. The last operand on the instruction indicates that the **execute form** of the READ macro is to be generated. If you notice, both the READ and WRITE macros reference the same event control block. Further, just after the code for this routine, there is a **list form** of the READ instruction. Although this instruction is never actually executed, it generates the event control block used by the other macro instructions.

ISAM *requires* that the READ and WRITE instructions address the same event control block. To adhere to this requirement, execute forms of the READ and WRITE are used in the code to address the list form generated later. Through the coordination of

```
CHANGE     DS      0H
           READ    CDECB,KU,ISAM,MASTER,'S',TKEY,MF=E
           CHECK   CDECB,DSORG=IS
           MVC     MDATA,TDATA        MOVE NEW DATA INTO MASTER REC
           WRITE   CDECB,K,ISAM,MASTER-16,'S',TKEY,MF=E
           CHECK   CDECB,DSORG=IS
           PUT     AUDIT,CHANGED      DISPLAY COMPLETED MESSAGE
           B       LOOP               GO PROCESS NEXT TRANSACTION
CFORMAT    READ    CDECB,KU,ISAM,MASTER,'S',TKEY,MF=L
```

Figure 14.9 Extracted code from Example 14.5 highlighting the READ and WRITE instructions.

a single event control block, ISAM provides update and delete record processing against your ISAM dataset. If you look carefully, the ADD routine does not require the execute form of the WRITE instruction. Since this WRITE instruction is not preceded by a READ instruction, no coordination between event control blocks is needed.

The WRITE instruction has also changed in yet another manner. The fourth operand does not address the master record area directly, rather, 16 bytes before the master record are referenced. ISAM requires a 16-byte area on the front of your master records when records are to be processed randomly in an ISAM dataset. Although you don't have to allow or be concerned about this area any other time, you must allow for it when processing randomly.

Finally, let's look at the SYNAD routine called DBUG. This routine again analyzes the contents of the exception code bytes contained in the event control block to determine why an I/O operation failed. The exception codes, however, are not located in the same location as when we processed a relative record dataset. Instead of register 0 containing the address of the exception codes, register *1* contains the address of the event control block. The exception code bytes are contained in bytes 25 and 26 of the event control block, which is why you see a reference to location 24(R1) when evaluating the reason for an I/O failure. Figure 14.10 describes the various exception bit meanings. As you can see, only the first byte of the exception bytes actually contains meaningful information.

Bit Number	Meaning
0	Record with key specified cannot be found in the dataset.
1	Incorrect record length. This should not occur in our program since we're processing fixed-length data.
2	Dataset is full. No more records can be added.
3	Invalid request. Usually, this means that you've attempted a WRITE instruction without a preceding READ instruction. Usually, it occurs when trying to update or delete.
4	I/O error.
5	Record requested is outside the bounds of the dataset.
6	When a record is read from the overflow area, an exception condition occurs. Usually, this condition is ignored as shown above.
7	There's already a record in the dataset with this key. Record can't be added.
8-15	Reserved for system usage.

Figure 14.10 Exception code bit meanings when processing an ISAM dataset randomly.

When the SYNAD routine obtains control, it first determines if the condition raised was due to an overflow record being read. If so, a message is printed and the SYNAD routine returns to the statement that follows the READ request. In other words, the program continues executing normally, but a notation is made on the audit report that a record was read from overflow. The programmer can monitor the number of records read from overflow, which may help the programmer determine if it's time to reorganize the ISAM dataset. On the other hand, the programmer can also use some other built-in facilities to monitor overflow conditions. More information on the monitoring and reorganizing of an ISAM dataset is found in the *Data Management Services Guide* and the *Data Management Macro Instructions* manuals.

EVENT COMPLETION USING THE WAIT MACRO INSTRUCTION

The CHECK macro instruction was used throughout the chapter to suspend the execution of our programs until an I/O operation completed. Another macro, **WAIT,** is used in a similar manner. However, there is a significant difference between the two macros as you shall see.

The WAIT macro is coded just after the I/O instruction, just like the corresponding CHECK macro. However, the program operates differently when WAIT is used. The primary difference between the two instructions is that the program does not have to contain a SYNAD routine. After an I/O operation completes, control returns to the next instruction after the WAIT. Hence, it's very typical to find code to test exception code bits immediately after the WAIT instruction and before any other processing continues. Figure 14.11 is a portion of a program that illustrates the use of the WAIT instruction when processing an ISAM dataset. Using the ISAM master file update code as an example, you see that the exception code bits are tested after each READ and WRITE instruction contained in the update logic. Depending on the value of the exception code bits, control may or may not proceed to the WRITE instruction after the READ instruction is executed.

The code becomes quite lengthy when using the WAIT instruction. I/O success or failure must be tested after each READ or WRITE instruction by evaluating the exception code bits. If no errors are found, processing continues normally. If anything other than overflow occurs, further testing analyzes the problem and a message is displayed to assist in problem analysis. Incidentally, it may be appropriate to branch to the location called BIGBUG to convert the exception code bits into display format and print them on the audit report. Clearly, this would only have to be done if the exception bits were something other than expected.

If the WAIT instruction is used in place of the CHECK macro instruction, the programmer must also change the MACRF parameters on the DCB instructions. In all examples contained in this chapter, the MACRF operand contained the letter C to indicate that the CHECK macro is being used to monitor I/O success or failure. This letter must be eliminated if WAIT is now to be used in testing I/O completion.

Finally, the testing for I/O success following the WAIT instruction can be simplified through a macro. Instead of coding the test-under-mask and branch instructions after each I/O instruction, a macro can generate the appropriate machine instructions. If a macro of this type is developed for one application, it can be used over and over in other programs by placing it in a macro library.

```
CHANGE    DS      0H
          READ    CDECB,KU,ISAM,MASTER,'S',TKEY,MF=E
          WAIT    ECB=CDECB
          TM      24(R1),X'FD'              TEST FOR ANY ERROR
          BZ      NOERR                     ...EXCEPT OVERFLOW
          TM      24(R1),B'10000000'        RECORD NOT FOUND?
          BNO     CBUG1                     IF NOT, SKIP PRINT
          PUT     AUDIT,DBUGMSG1            PRINT MESSAGE
          B       LOOP                      PROCESS NEXT RECORD
CBUG1     DS      0H
          TM      24(R1),B'01000000'        LENGTH ERROR?
          BNO     CBUG2                     IF NOT, SKIP PRINT
          PUT     AUDIT,DBUGMSG2            PRINT MESSAGE
          B       LOOP                      PROCESS NEXT RECORD
CBUG2     DS      0H
          TM      24(R1),B'00000100'        OUTSIDE DATASET?
          BNO     CBUG3                     IF NOT, SKIP PRINT
          PUT     AUDIT,DBUGMSG4            IF SO, PRINT MESSAGE
          B       LOOP
CBUG3     DS      0H
NOERR     DS      0H
          MVC     MDATA,TDATA       MOVE NEW DATA INTO MASTER REC
          WRITE   CDECB,K,ISAM,MASTER-16,'S',TKEY,MF=E
          WAIT    ECB=CDECB
          TM      24(R1),X'FD'              CHECK FOR ALL BUT
          BZ      LOOP                      ...OVERFLOW ERROR
          TM      24(R1),B'01000000'        LENGTH ERROR?
          BNO     CBUG2                     IF NOT, SKIP PRINT
          PUT     AUDIT,DBUGMSG2            PRINT MESSAGE
          B       LOOP                      PROCESS NEXT RECORD
CBUG2     DS      0H
          TM      24(R1),B'00100000'        NO SPACE?
          BNO     CBUG3                     IF NOT, SKIP PRINT
          PUT     AUDIT,DBUGMSG3            PRINT MESSAGE
          B       LOOP                      PROCESS NEXT RECORD
CBUG3     DS      0H
          TM      24(R1),B'00000100'        OUTSIDE DATASET?
          BNO     CBUG4                     IF NOT, SKIP PRINT
          PUT     AUDIT,DBUGMSG4            IF SO, PRINT MESSAGE
          B       LOOP
CBUG4     DS      0H
          TM      24(R1),B'00000001'        DUPLICATE RECORD KEY
          BNO     BIGBUG                    IF NOT, FORCE ABEND
          PUT     AUDIT,DBUGMSG5            IF SO, PRINT MESSAGE
          B       LOOP
CFORMAT   READ    CDECB,KU,ISAM,MASTER,'S',TKEY,MF=L
```

Figure 14.11 Update logic using the WAIT macro instruction.

STUDY QUESTIONS

1. What access methods can be used to process a relative dataset?
2. What type of field distinguishes each record in a relative dataset?
3. Normally, a relative dataset is _______ before it is processed in a random manner.
4. How are records deleted in a relative dataset?
5. How many records can be stored in a block within a relative dataset?
6. What operand is coded on the OPEN instruction to begin random processing of a relative dataset?
7. During random processing of a relative dataset, an exception condition occurs. How can we determine what happened on the I/O instruction that we issued?
8. To define a relative dataset, space is usually allocated in terms of _______.

9. What are the three components of an ISAM dataset?
10. Space for an ISAM dataset must be allocated in ______.
11. What characteristics can records have when processed using the indexed sequential access method?
12. If a record is added to an ISAM dataset, what can occur?
13. Why must the execute forms of the READ and WRITE instructions be used when processing an ISAM dataset?
14. What data can be used to construct a record key for records stored in an ISAM dataset?
15. What utility can manage and print the contents of an ISAM file?

PROGRAMMING PROBLEMS

1. Bank accounts are maintained using a relative record dataset. Each bank client is assigned an account number that is used when processing transactions against their account. Suppose that the master records in the account file consist of the owner's name, address, number of transactions applied to the account for the current month, and the current balance. Write a program that applies deposit and withdrawal transactions against such a master file. Print a report of the master file before the transactions are applied. Follow the report by applying each transaction to the accounts. Finally, print the contents of the account master file a second time to verify the processing performed.
2. Develop a complete system to maintain a parts inventory for a manufacturing company. Using the part catalog number as the key to each record in the file, maintain data on the parts based on their catalog number, description, wholesale price, retail price, and quantity in stock. Develop a program to create records having this format and store the records in an ISAM file.

   Next, create a series of transactions that process the parts master file. In this case, parts can be sold, thus decreasing the inventory; purchased, thus increasing the inventory; or the fields within the part records can be changed (description or prices). Apply your transactions to the master file using a master file update program. Make sure that your transaction file is extensive and attempts to update parts that do not exist, sell items that are not in stock, and order parts that are not in the inventory.

   After all transactions are applied to the inventory, use a sequential processing program to produce a report of the inventory. The program should also compute the total wholesale and retail costs of the inventory.
3. Modify Programming Problem 2 so that automatic ordering occurs when the number of parts in stock drops below two in the inventory. For this application, develop another report that is generated by the master file update program to identify parts that have to be ordered.
4. Pairs of letters are typed on data cards. The first letter on the data card is entered in column 1 and the second letter in column 2. Using the first letter as the key, the program accesses a master file record. The program then analyzes an array within the record to determine if the second letter is within it. If it is, the transaction is completed and processing continues. If the second letter is not in the array, then the second letter is added (in alphabetical order) and the master record is written back to the master file. Processing continues until all letter pair transactions are processed.

   When all processing is completed, print a report of all letter associations.
5. A magazine publisher maintains a master file of subscribers. Information in the master file consists of the name and address as well as the expiration date of the subscription. Write a program that adds, cancels, or updates subscription information. Subscribers should be able to cancel subscriptions; renew or extend subscriptions, thus changing the expiration date; or

make address or name changes. Develop your own transaction format and test data to be used against your master file. Your program should maintain subscription data as well as print reports or mailing labels on the client data.

6. Modify Programming Problem 5 so that each subscriber may subscribe to more than one magazine. Maintain information for each magazine subscription in much the same manner as you maintained the single subscription as specified in Programming Problem 5.
7. Develop an airline reservation system for a small commuter airline. Each plane in the airline is able to hold 10 passengers. Passenger reservations should be accepted, cancelled, or may be changed by the reservation system. Flight schedules should also be supported by the system with all reservations being checked against the flight schedule before a reservation may be made.
8. In Chapter 11 we discussed array and table processing techniques. Since a random file is logically processed much like an array, we can practice random file processing by implementing an array application. Develop a program which will load twenty-file records into a random file. Using a bubble sort technique and update processing logic, place the records in the file into ascending or descending order. After all records are sorted, print the contents of the file using sequential access processing.
9. A restaurant offers its customers fifteen different entrees on the menu. To assist in inventory planning and to monitor the selection of items by customers, each customer order is used to update a master file which contains information on each entree. For each customer purchase, the date and entree ordered by the customer are used to update the master file. This information is used by a master file update program to keep track of the number of orders for each entree for the day. Month-end and year-end reports are produced which allow the restaurant to determine which entrees are most popular and which ones should be discontinued or replaced on the menu.
10. Develop a real estate system for a realtor. This system should keep track of all listings and sales for the realtor for the year. As new listings are obtained by the realtor, they should be added to the master file. As houses are sold, they should be changed from "listing" status to "sold" status. Listing records may also be updated to reflect any changes in their status such as changes in price, availability date, and showing restrictions. Support programs should provide the realtor with year-to-date sales information and searching capability to assist in serving clients.

15

VSAM File Processing

Sequential files are used heavily throughout all areas of business. However, as we discussed in the last chapter, the need to access information immediately causes us to investigate random access methods to support our applications processing. In Chapter 14, we focused our discussion on IBM's BDAM and ISAM access methods. Although they are still very popular in many academic and business environments, another access method, VSAM, has arrived and is fast becoming the premier access method in IBM environments. For this reason, we cannot omit it from this text.

The **virtual storage access method (VSAM)** can process files sequentially or randomly as needed by the application program. Although you may think that such a powerful access method is extremely complex and difficult to use, I hope to surprise you by showing just how straightforward it is to process VSAM files. The internal structure of a VSAM dataset, however, *is* very complex. Although a brief overview of the VSAM dataset structure is presented, it is not our purpose to concentrate on this structure. Hence, a brief introduction of the VSAM dataset structure is presented and most of our attention is focused on processing the most common VSAM dataset types in assembly language.

OVERVIEW OF THE VSAM FILE STRUCTURES

The VSAM access method supports three file organizations: sequential, relative, and indexed. As with all file organizations and access methods, you select the structure suited to your processing needs. If your application requires random access to records that are identified by a unique nonnumeric field, the indexed file structure should be selected. If random access is needed for your data and each data record can be identified by a unique number, then the relative file structure can be used. Finally, sequential record access can be achieved by selecting the sequential file structure.

A sequential VSAM dataset is more commonly called an **entry sequenced dataset (ESDS),** a relative VSAM dataset is more commonly called a **relative record dataset (RRDS),** and the indexed dataset structure is called a **key sequenced dataset (KSDS).** No matter which file organization is selected, only one access method, VSAM, processes the dataset.

VSAM datasets are more commonly referred to as **clusters** since their internal structure is made up of several connected components. Depending on the type of VSAM dataset to be processed, they are comprised of two or three components. The highest logical component found in all VSAM datasets is the **cluster component,** which controls access into the dataset and supplies VSAM with information about the dataset, such as record length, key position, key length, record count, and so on. Subordinate to the cluster component and found in all VSAM datasets is the **data component,** which contains the application records that are to be processed by your application programs. The last component of a VSAM dataset is the **index component,** which exists only when using the indexed VSAM dataset structure. The index component allows VSAM to access records randomly using fields within the record to uniquely identify each record in the data component. Consisting of a hierarchical directory into the data component, the indexed VSAM dataset structure is one of the most powerful methods of processing data provided by any of IBM's access methods.

To illustrate the purpose of the index component, consider the index at the back of this textbook. The textbook index provides immediate page referencing to a particular topic. Without the index, you'd have to flip through the book page by page until you found the topic that you desired. Clearly, situations requiring random access to data through a key field use the indexed dataset structure. Figure 15.1 illustrates the logical relationships between each component and the dataset types.

An entry sequenced VSAM dataset is a sequential dataset. Fixed- or variable-length data stored in an ESDS is processed in the order stored. In other words, record 25 cannot be processed until records 1 through 24 are processed. Although an ESDS may be processed randomly using special processing facilities of VSAM, the management and coordination required to support this processing is more easily accomplished using another VSAM dataset type. For this reason, random processing using an ESDS is not discussed in this text. Information on this processing technique is found in the IBM publications *MVS/370 VSAM Reference* (GC26-4074) or *OS/VS2 VSAM Programmer's Guide* (GC26-3868).

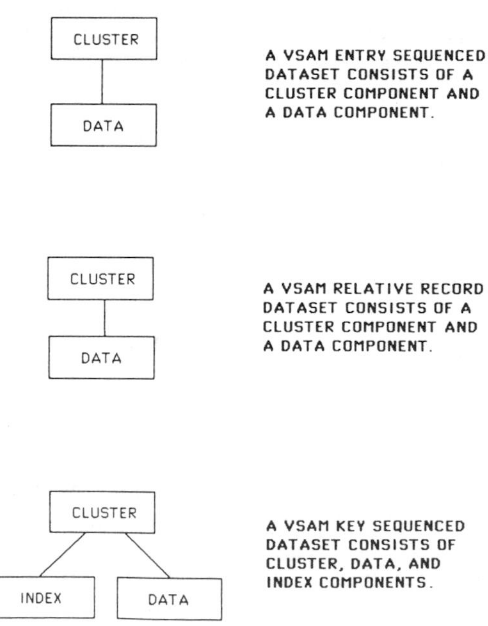

Figure 15.1 Types of VSAM datasets and their components.

A VSAM relative record dataset can be processed sequentially or randomly. Each record in the dataset must be of fixed length. Further, each record is referenced by its location in the dataset. For example, the fiftieth record in the dataset can be accessed randomly by requesting record 50 from VSAM, which obtains the record, returns it to your program, and allows you to process this record as desired.

Record position or record "slot" location is the primary method used when processing an RRDS. Typically, relative record datasets are used in conjunction with data that may be accessed through a numeric key. A social security number is an excellent example of such a key. If a social security number is 000-00-0005, your program would ask for the fifth record in the file to process this record.

Although all RRDS records are accessed by the record's position or slot within the file, relative record datasets can also be used with character key fields. With a technique called **hashing,** the character key is converted into a numeric record number by a section of code or subroutine that *you've* written. Although hashing can expand the processing capabilities of the relative record dataset, it is generally easier to simply define and process records having keys of this type using the key sequenced dataset structure.

Key sequenced datasets support fixed-length and variable-length records. Each record must have a unique key field value that distinguishes it from all others in the file. Since key fields can be up to 256 bytes long, it becomes very easy to construct records with unique identifiers.

Access to records in a KSDS occurs through the use of the **index component** of the cluster. The index of a VSAM dataset is a hierarchical series of records containing keys from selected records stored in the data component. Based on the values of these selected keys, VSAM "funnels" into the data component and locates the record having the identification that you've described. Figure 15.2 illustrates the index structure and its relationship to the data component.

The data records stored in the file are found at the lowest level in the dataset. This

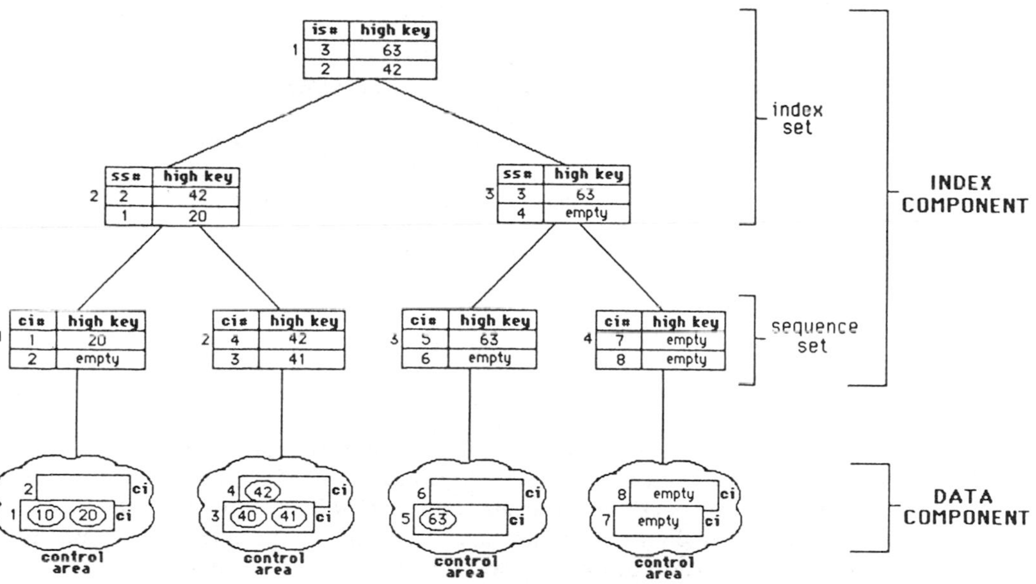

Figure 15.2 The VSAM key sequenced dataset structure.

level, the data component, consists of physical records called **control intervals.** Each control interval can hold one or more of our application data records, depending on the size of the control interval and the size of our application records. Control interval size can be specified by the programmer or it can be selected for you by VSAM when a dataset is created. To reduce the work required to properly select a control interval size, we let VSAM select an optimal control interval size for our datasets.

Control intervals are grouped into **control areas.** The number of control intervals in a control area is dependent on many factors, all beyond the realm of this text.

The highest record key in each control interval is stored in a **sequence set record.** This is an index record and it contains record key values from our application data records. When VSAM is searching for a record, it can quickly determine which control interval may contain the record we want by comparing the key of the record to be found with the key entries in the sequence set records. With sequential processing, control intervals in the data component are processed in order, thus eliminating the need to continually traverse the entire index structure.

The highest key values from a group of sequence set records are collected into progressively higher level index records. Records in the index component that contain sequence set entries comprise the **index set** of a VSAM cluster. Together, the index set and sequence set make up the entire index component for a VSAM indexed dataset.

The index structure resembles an inverted tree. The highest index record can be considered the "trunk" and each subordinate index record as a "branch." As the data component grows, so does the index component. Clearly, the index component must reflect the contents of the data component. Therefore, to process a KSDS randomly, VSAM traverses the tree structure to locate the control interval in which a record may be added, located for processing, or deleted. VSAM simultaneously maintains the index based on the processing that was performed.

This brief overview of VSAM has just scratched the surface of its internal structure. For further details on the VSAM dataset internal structure, consult the IBM publications listed in Fig. 15.3.

```
MVS/370 VSAM Reference (GC26-4074)
OS/VS2 VSAM Programmer's Guide (GC26-3868)
OS/VS2 VSAM Logic (SY26-3825)
OS/VS VSAM Options for Advanced Applications (GC26-3819)
Data Facility Extended Function:
 Access Method Services Reference (SC26-3967)
```

Figure 15.3 Suggested references on VSAM.

OVERVIEW OF IDCAMS

A VSAM dataset can be defined and placed on a system volume using a utility called **IDCAMS.** IDCAMS is the *only* utility needed to support VSAM activity. Among others, this utility creates, prints, backs up, recovers, and deletes VSAM clusters. IDCAMS is very powerful, but we will discuss only the basic commands to perform processing. For more information on IDCAMS processing, see the manual *Data Facility Extended Function: Access Method Services Reference* (SC26-3967).

IDCAMS requires very few JCL statements to support its execution. Specifically, it requires only the JCL statements given in Fig. 15.4 for most VSAM requests that we will issue.

```
//        EXEC   PGM=IDCAMS,REGION=512K
//SYSPRINT  DD   SYSOUT=$
//SYSIN     DD   *
```

Figure 15.4 Typical JCL to execute IDCAMS.

All requests for IDCAMS' services are issued through special control statements. A dataset can be created using the DEFINE command or it can be printed using the PRINT command. Figure 15.5 briefly summarizes the commands that we will be discussing.

IDCAMS Command	Activity or Command Function
DEFINE CLUSTER	Creates a VSAM dataset.
DEFINE AIX	Creates an alternate index dataset.
DEFINE PATH	Connects an alternate index dataset to its corresponding base cluster.
BLDINDEX	Prepares an alternate index dataset for processing by loading it with associated alternate index key values and base cluster keys.
PRINT	Prints the contents of a VSAM dataset.
DELETE	Deletes a VSAM cluster.
VERIFY	Updates the processing status so that a VSAM dataset can be opened and accessed.
LISTCAT	Prints a report on the status and characteristics of a cluster.
REPRO	Copies a VSAM cluster.

Figure 15.5 Summary of selected IDCAMS control commands.

Before we discuss methods to create each of the VSAM dataset types, let me point out that all VSAM datasets support password protection. By coding the appropriate operands on the IDCAMS commands, passwords may be specified at several levels to restrict access to the dataset. For example, it is possible to specify passwords to restrict access to read-only, update-only (read and write), or to allow full processing support. However, since many installations utilize dataset security packages to provide a more global protection mechanism, it is more common to see dataset protection enforced by dataset naming conventions or through account billing methods. For this reason, we will not discuss VSAM password facilities in this text. Should your facility not offer security measures as mentioned, please refer to the manuals in Fig. 15.3 for details on the READPW, UPDATEPW, CONTROLPW, and MASTERPW operands.

CREATING AN ESDS

An entry sequenced dataset can be created with the IDCAMS control statements given in Fig. 15.6. The dash at the end of each line indicates continuation of the command (a plus sign (+) can also be used). As you can see, only the last line is not continued since it is the end of the command structure.

An entry sequenced dataset consists of a cluster component and a data component. The DEFINE CLUSTER command defines only these two components. The first line identifies the name of the cluster and the last line identifies the name of the data component for the ESDS. Typically, the name of the data component is almost the same as that of the cluster except for the addition of the suffix .DATA. Although this naming convention is not a hard-and-fast rule, it is very meaningful when naming each dataset component. If you do not name each component of your VSAM dataset, a name is assigned by IDCAMS. The assigned name is not meaningful, as such, it does not relate to your clusters. For this reason, assign the name of each component within your clusters.

The second line contains the parameter **NONINDEXED**, which informs IDCAMS that an ESDS is to be created.

VOLUMES specifies which disk volume is to contain your cluster. The value supplied for this parameter varies from installation to installation. Check with your computer center staff to determine where you may place your VSAM clusters.

SHAREOPTIONS controls the number of programs that may concurrently process or update your cluster. The values specified, (2 3), usually offer the best protection against loss of data.

RECORDSIZE specifies the *average* and *maximum* lengths of your data records. If your records are of fixed length, the two numbers are usually coded with the same value. If you are using variable-length records, you have to estimate the average size of most of your records to be stored and you have to know the length of the largest record in your cluster.

The space parameter is specified in three ways. You can allocate space by **TRACKS, CYLINDERS,** or **RECORDS.** For example, if the dataset contains exactly 100 records, then allocate space by coding RECORDS(100 0). The second value is used as a **secondary space allocation** parameter. In the event that the primary space allocated is full, VSAM acquires enough disk space to hold your secondary allocation.

TRACKS and CYLINDERS are probably the most common methods of allocating space for VSAM clusters. However, without the proper background and understanding of each of the possible disk devices on which our clusters may be placed, these two allocation parameters are commonly misused. Since we have not discussed proper techniques for allocating space on devices with these parameters, let's simply use the RECORDS allocation parameter for now. However, the CYLINDERS parameter is the most efficient method of allocating VSAM space.

Let's look at a complete example for defining an ESDS. Suppose that an ESDS

```
DEFINE CLUSTER(NAME(esds-name)                    -
          NONINDEXED                              -
          VOLUMES(volume)                         -
          SHAREOPTIONS(2 3)                       -
          RECORDSIZE(avg max)                     -
          space(primary secondary))               -
   DATA(NAME(esds-name.DATA))
```

Figure 15.6 IDCAMS commands to create an ESDS.

called CARDFILE is to hold 100 records with 10 percent growth. Each record has a fixed length of 80 characters. Space for this dataset is allocated on the disk volume called DISK01. This cluster is allocated using the job step shown in Fig. 15.7.

Referring to Fig. 15.7, you should immediately notice the simplicity of the JCL required to define and execute an IDCAMS request. Although the parameters have been moved from JCL statements to IDCAMS commands, you should notice a striking similarity between the parameters. Whether a non-VSAM or a VSAM dataset is to be defined, the programmer still identifies the name, location, size, and characteristics of the

```
//        EXEC       PGM=IDCAMS,REGION=512K
//SYSPRINT      DD    SYSOUT-$
//SYSIN         DD    *
    DEFINE   CLUSTER(NAME(CARDFILE)         -
             NONINDEXED                     -
             VOLUMES(DISK01)                -
             SHAREOPTIONS(2 3)              -
             RECORDSIZE(80 80)              -
             RECORDS(100 10))               -
        DATA(NAME(CARDFILE.DATA))
```

Figure 15.7 Creating an ESDS.

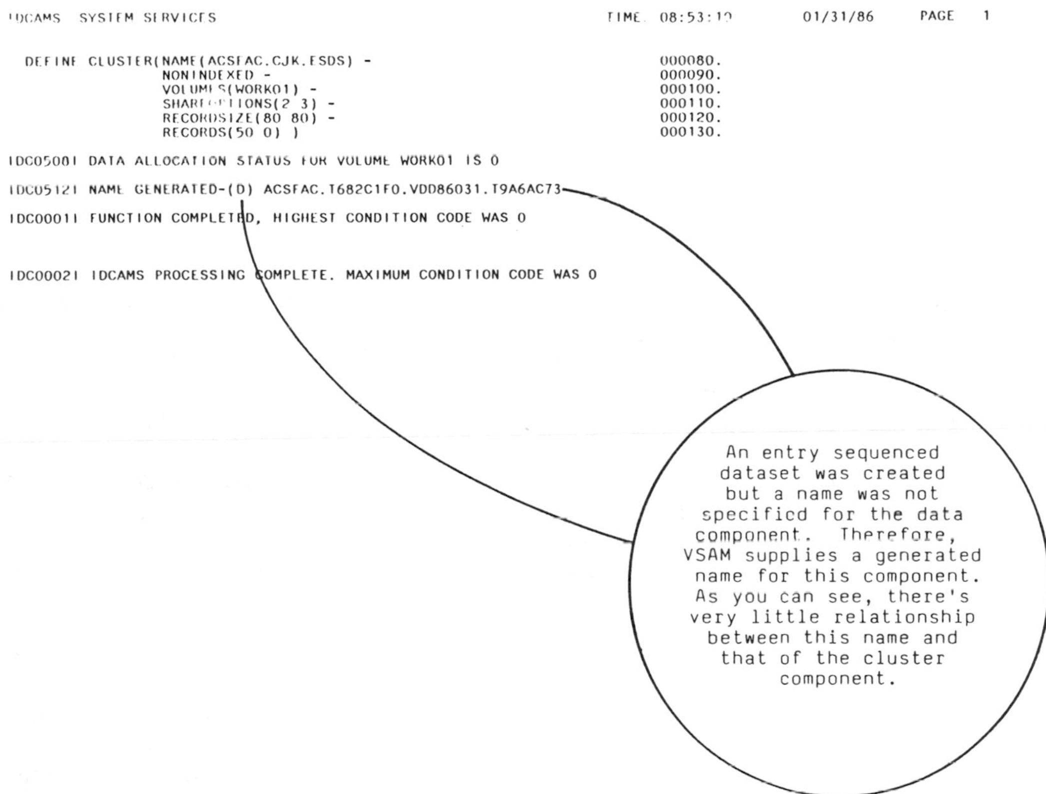

```
IDCAMS  SYSTEM SERVICES                                   TIME. 08:53:19        01/31/86        PAGE    1

  DEFINE CLUSTER(NAME(ACSFAC.CJK.ESDS) -                  000080.
                 NONINDEXED -                             000090.
                 VOLUMES(WORK01) -                        000100.
                 SHAREOPTIONS(2 3) -                      000110.
                 RECORDSIZE(80 80) -                      000120.
                 RECORDS(50 0) )                          000130.

IDC0500I DATA ALLOCATION STATUS FOR VOLUME WORK01 IS 0

IDC0512I NAME GENERATED-(D) ACSFAC.T682C1F0.VDD86031.T9A6AC73

IDC0001I FUNCTION COMPLETED, HIGHEST CONDITION CODE WAS 0


IDC0002I IDCAMS PROCESSING COMPLETE. MAXIMUM CONDITION CODE WAS 0
```


Figure 15.8 Defining an entry sequenced dataset (with sample output).

dataset. Missing however, is the DISP (disposition) JCL parameter which normally specified cataloging information when defining non-VSAM datasets. Since all VSAM datasets are cataloged, this parameter is no longer required when VSAM datasets are defined.

The sample output in Fig. 15.8 illustrates the creation of an ESDS. Note, however, that the data component was not given a meaningful name and so VSAM generated a meaningless name for this component of our cluster.

CREATING AN RRDS

A relative record dataset can be defined using a similar DEFINE CLUSTER command format. Again, an RRDS consists of only the cluster and data components. From Fig. 15.9, these components are defined and named as described earlier.

When defining an RRDS, remember that data records *cannot* be defined as variable length. Only fixed-length records can be processed using a relative record VSAM dataset. Hence, the average and maximum record lengths are equal.

The second parameter, **NUMBERED,** specifies that an RRDS is to be created. Most of the other operands are identical to those discussed when creating an ESDS and so will not be discussed.

```
DEFINE CLUSTER(NAME(rrds-name)                  -
       NUMBERED                                 -
       VOLUMES(volume)                          -
       SHAREOPTIONS(2 3)                        -
       RECORDSIZE(avg max)                      -
       space(primary secondary))                -
  DATA(NAME(rrds-name.DATA))
```

Figure 15.9 Command format to create an RRDS.

CREATING A KSDS

Since a key sequenced VSAM dataset contains an index component, we must now name all three components when defining it. Although many of the operands are familiar, some are new. Figure 15.10 illustrates the statements to define a KSDS.

The second parameter, **INDEXED,** indicates that a KSDS is to be created. As a result, all three components of a VSAM dataset are present. Therefore, the statements in Fig. 15.10 name the cluster, data, and index components for this dataset.

The KEYS operand specifies the length and position (offset) of the key field within our record. Suppose that the key of our record is five bytes long and is located in bytes 2 through 6. Since the offset of the key is specified with respect to zero, the KEYS parameter for this example is coded as KEYS(5 1), which indicates that a five-byte key is contained within the record and begins at the second byte.

The **FREESPACE** parameter allows you to plan for growth in the KSDS. Roughly speaking, this example allows for 10% growth over the life of the dataset. Larger or smaller values can be coded appropriate to your processing.

Key sequenced datasets support fixed- or variable-length records. The RECORDSIZE parameter again specifies the *average* and *maximum* record sizes to be stored in our cluster. Fixed-length records are normally specified by coding equal values in these operand fields.

Figure 15.11 shows sample output from an IDCAMS define request. The KSDS

```
DEFINE CLUSTER(NAME(ksds-name)                -
       INDEXED                                -
       VOLUMES(volume)                        -
       SHAREOPTIONS(2 3)                      -
       RECORDSIZE(avg max)                    -
       KEYS(length offset)                    -
       FREESPACE(10 10)                       -
       space(primary secondary))              -
  DATA(NAME(ksds-name.DATA))                  -
 INDEX(NAME(ksds-name.INDEX))
```

Figure 15.10 Command format to define a KSDS.

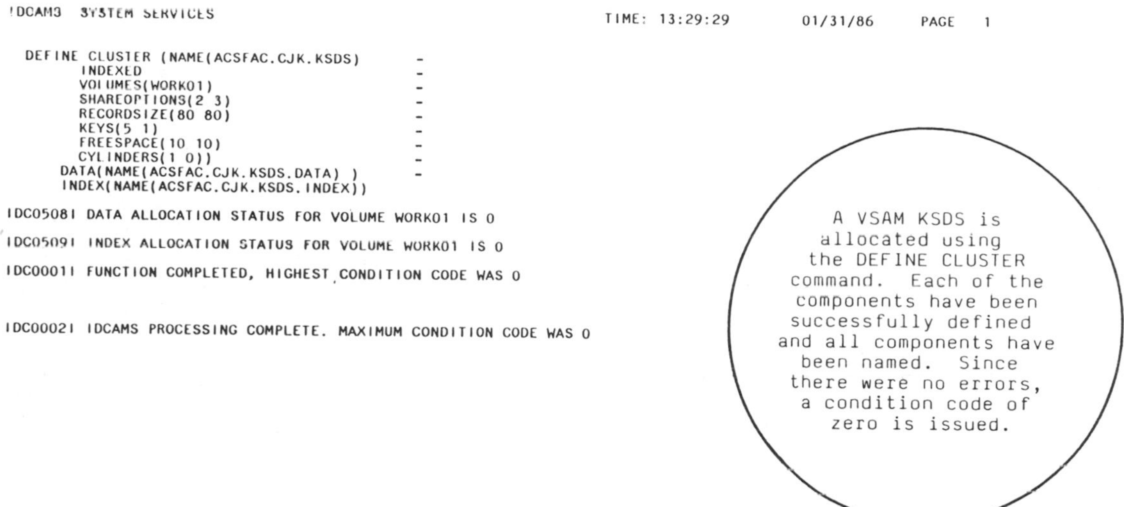

```
IDCAM3  SYSTEM SERVICES                                  TIME: 13:29:29       01/31/86     PAGE   1

  DEFINE CLUSTER (NAME(ACSFAC.CJK.KSDS)          -
         INDEXED                                 -
         VOLUMES(WORK01)                         -
         SHAREOPTIONS(2 3)                       -
         RECORDSIZE(80 80)                       -
         KEYS(5 1)                               -
         FREESPACE(10 10)                        -
         CYLINDERS(1 0))                         -
      DATA(NAME(ACSFAC.CJK.KSDS.DATA) )          -
      INDEX(NAME(ACSFAC.CJK.KSDS.INDEX))

IDC0508I DATA ALLOCATION STATUS FOR VOLUME WORK01 IS 0

IDC0509I INDEX ALLOCATION STATUS FOR VOLUME WORK01 IS 0

IDC0001I FUNCTION COMPLETED, HIGHEST CONDITION CODE WAS 0


IDC0002I IDCAMS PROCESSING COMPLETE. MAXIMUM CONDITION CODE WAS 0
```


Figure 15.11 Defining a key sequenced dataset (with sample output).

being created matches that of our discussion except that it's being placed on the disk volume WORK01 and its name is slightly different. Pay particular attention to the output messages received from IDCAMS for this request.

DEFINING AN ALTERNATE INDEX

An alternate index is a VSAM dataset that accesses primary data records through a secondary key value. Suppose that a VSAM KSDS is accessed through a **primary key** contained in bytes 2 through 6 of the record. Another field within the record can also be used to access the records in the dataset. This field, called the **secondary key,** can be defined as an alternate index, thus allowing access to records in our dataset two ways. Our primary dataset, accessed through the primary key, is commonly called the **base cluster,** and the second dataset, allowing access to records using the secondary key, is called the **alternate index.**

An alternate index is defined, loaded, and connected to a base cluster using three IDCAMS commands. First, the alternate index dataset is created with the **DEFINE AIX** command. Next, the alternate index is loaded with base cluster keys by coding the

BLDINDEX command. Finally, the alternate index is connected to the base cluster through the **DEFINE PATH** command.

Before defining and attempting to build an alternate index, make sure that you have a nonempty base cluster. An attempt to define an alternate index against an empty base cluster may result in an error.

Suppose that we already have a KSDS called CARDFILE and that we want to create an alternate index called AIX.CARDFILE. Bytes 10 to 13 of each record in CARDFILE contain the alternate index key value. The statements in Fig. 15.12 define the alternate index.

```
DEFINE AIX(NAME(AIX.CARDFILE)                         -
       RELATE(CARDFILE)                               -
       NONUNIQUEKEY                                   -
       UPGRADE                                        -
       VOLUMES(DISK01)                                -
       RECORDSIZE(avg max)                            -
       KEYS(4 9)                                      -
       FREESPACE(10 10)                               -
       SHAREOPTIONS(2 3)                              -
       space(primary secondary))                      -
    DATA(NAME(AIX.CARDFILE.DATA))                     -
   INDEX(NAME(AIX.CARDFILE.INDEX))
```

Figure 15.12 Defining an alternate index.

The alternate index is related to the base cluster called CARDFILE through the **RELATE** operand. As coded, more than one base cluster record may contain the same alternate index key value **(NONUNIQUEKEY).** If each secondary key were unique, the operand **UNIQUEKEY** could have been specified instead of NONUNIQUEKEY.

The operand **UPGRADE** is very important and coordinates the alternate index and the base cluster. Anytime a record is added, changed, or deleted within the base cluster, a corresponding update is made to the alternate index (or vice versa). This parameter should always be specified.

The **KEYS** parameter has the same format as before with the first value indicating the length of the alternate index key and the second indicating the offset within the base cluster records where this key value is located.

FREESPACE is again specified to allow for 10% growth. This matches the growth expected within the base cluster.

The **RECORDSIZE** parameter must be coded carefully. The values are determined from the length of the alternate index key and the length of the base cluster keys. In general, the average value for the RECORDSIZE parameter is computed using the formula given in Fig. 15.13.

```
average recordsize = 5 + (length of AIX key) + ((length of base cluster key) * A)

          where A is the average number of base cluster records
          expected to have this alternate index key value.
```

Figure 15.13 Computing the average AIX record length.

For example, if you think that *on the average* 10 base cluster records have the same alternate index key value, then use a value of 10 for **A.** With a base cluster key of five bytes and an alternate index key length of four bytes, the average record size for the alternate index dataset is 5 + 4 + (5 * 10), or 59.

The maximum record size is computed by using the same formula, but replacing the value of **A** with **M. M** is the maximum number of base cluster records that you expect to have the same alternate index key value. For example, if you expect no more than 25 base cluster records to have the same alternate index key value, then **M** is equal to 25. Using **M** in the equation of Fig. 15.13, we arrive at a maximum alternate index record length of 134.

Once the alternate index is defined, it can be loaded with key relationship records, which is done by issuing the **BLDINDEX** command as shown in Fig. 15.14. In this example, we're assuming that the base cluster is called CARDFILE and the alternate index is called AIX.CARDFILE.

```
BLDINDEX   IDS(CARDFILE) ODS(AIX.CARDFILE)
```

Figure 15.14 IDCAMS command to load an alternate index dataset.

The input dataset **(IDS)** specifies the base cluster name and the output dataset **(ODS)** is specified as the alternate index. Each record from the base cluster is analyzed and its alternate index key is recorded in the alternate index dataset. If many base cluster records have the same alternate index key value, they are all grouped together under a single alternate index key value.

Once the alternate index is loaded, a path can now be defined to connect the two datasets and to access base cluster records using the secondary key value. This is done through the **DEFINE PATH** command as illustrated in Fig. 15.15.

```
DEFINE   PATH(NAME(CARDFILE.PATH) -
         PATHENTRY(AIX.CARDFILE) UPDATE)
```

Figure 15.15 Defining the path to connect an AIX and associated base cluster.

This command defines a **path** which associates the base cluster with the alternate index dataset. The UPDATE option indicates that the base cluster and alternate index are to be coordinated, thus reflecting all adds, changes, or deletes. You are now ready to process your alternate index by specifying the *path name.* Do not try to process an alternate index by specifying the alternate index dataset name. On all JCL statements, the *path* is the entity that is processed when attempting to process base cluster records using an alternate index.

USING IDCAMS TO PRINT A VSAM DATASET

The IDCAMS utility can print records contained in a VSAM dataset. IDCAMS can print records in non-VSAM datasets as well. Don't expect a fancy report since IDCAMS is not a report generator. However, IDCAMS can print a dataset in three ways: character format, hexadecimal format, and dump format (combination of hex and character). Dumps of datasets can be used to determine if your application program is operating correctly or if your dataset has been created properly.

IDCAMS can also selectively print records. Using the SKIP and COUNT options, you can skip the first *n* records in the dataset and print only the number of records specified in the COUNT operand. For example, to print records 5 through 15 in the dataset called CARDFILE, we code the PRINT command as illustrated in Fig. 15.16.

```
PRINT  IDS(CARDFILE) SKIP(4) COUNT(11) DUMP
```

Figure 15.16 Printing selected records from a dataset using IDCAMS.

Since printing is to start with record 5, I skipped the first four records. Records 5 through 15 account for 11 records not 10, and so the COUNT option specifies this value. The operand DUMP indicates that records are to be printed in DUMP format (hex and character) and the options HEX or CHAR specify only hexadecimal or character formatted output printing, respectively. Finally, SKIP and COUNT are optional and can be used singly or together. The sample output in Fig. 15.17 illustrates a DUMP of three records from a VSAM dataset.

A print request can be issued using another operand, INFILE. This operand replaces the IDS operand and specifies a JCL DD name instead of the cluster name to be printed. The example in Fig. 15.18 illustrates use of the INFILE operand.

The INFILE operand requires an additional DD statement that references the dataset called CARDFILE. Figure 15.16, using the operand IDS, does *not* require this additional DD statement. Although both methods for dumping the file work, remember that there are two techniques to call IDCAMS for processing.

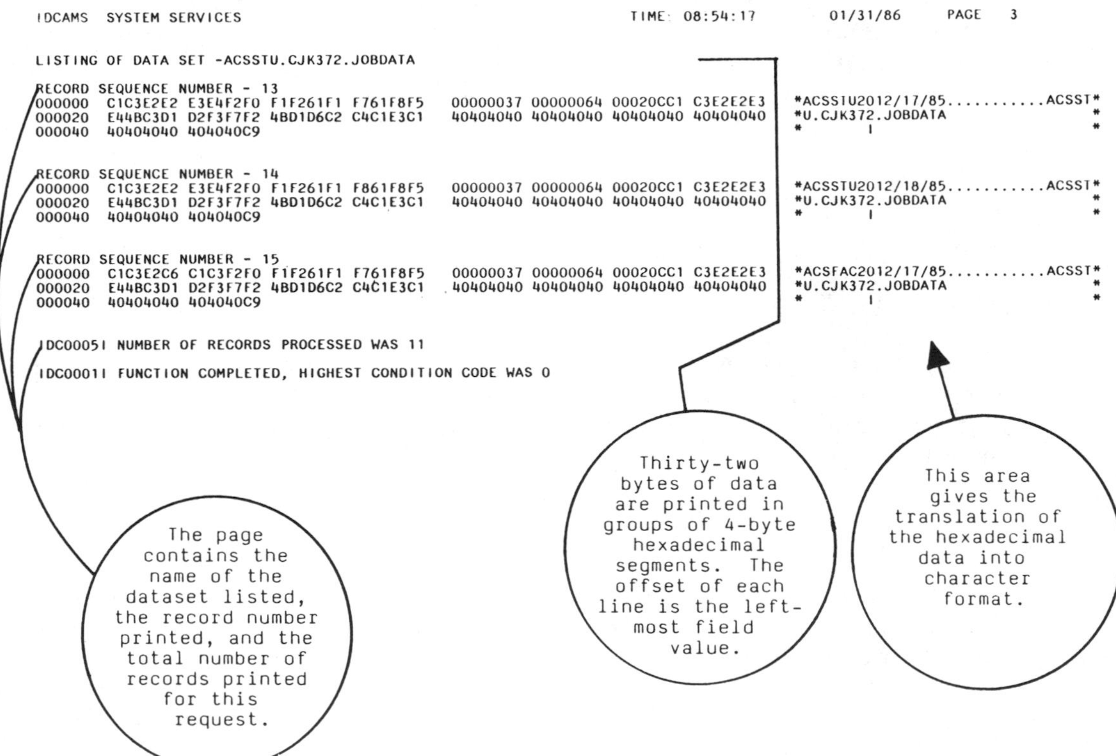

Figure 15.17 Sample output from an IDCAMS dump request.

```
//         EXEC   PGM=IDCAMS,REGION=512K
//SYSPRINT  DD    SYSOUT=$
//MYFILE    DD    DSN=CARDFILE,DISP=SHR
//SYSIN     DD    *
  PRINT  INFILE(MYFILE)  SKIP(4)  COUNT(11)  DUMP
```

Figure 15.18 Using the INFILE parameter in place of IDS on the PRINT command.

DELETING A VSAM CLUSTER

A VSAM dataset can be deleted using the IDCAMS **DELETE** command. As illustrated in Fig. 15.19, the cluster called CARDFILE is to be deleted from the system.

```
DELETE   CARDFILE
```

Figure 15.19 Deleting a VSAM cluster.

As you can see, the DELETE command is very simple. It is also very powerful since the deletion of a base cluster deletes not only the base cluster, but all associated alternate indexes as well.

VSAM DATASET VERIFICATION

VSAM maintains a series of special fields within each cluster to indicate the status of a dataset. During processing, these fields are updated to reflect the status of the dataset. If your job abends during processing, the fields are marked to prevent access to the dataset unless the integrity of the dataset is **verified. Dataset verification** is unique to VSAM datasets and is accomplished through the IDCAMS **VERIFY** command.

Let's again assume that our cluster is called CARDFILE. This dataset is verified by coding either example shown in Figs. 15.20 and 15.21.

The verify process is very important to the integrity of VSAM clusters. It is strongly suggested that all VSAM clusters be verified prior to processing. Typically, the first step of a multistep job stream contains the verification process for all datasets to be processed. This ensures that all datasets are properly verified prior to processing in a later job step. In fact, you may want to verify your VSAM clusters between job steps to ensure processing integrity.

```
//       EXEC      PGM=IDCAMS,REGION=512K
//SYSPRINT         DD   SYSOUT=$
//SYSIN            DD   *
         VERIFY    DATASET(CARDFILE)
```

Figure 15.20 Method 1 for verifying a cluster.

```
//       EXEC      PGM=IDCAMS,REGION=512K
//SYSPRINT         DD   SYSOUT=$
//MYFILE           DD   DSN=CARDFILE,DISP=SHR
//SYSIN            DD   *
         VERIFY    FILE(MYFILE)
```

Figure 15.21 Method 2 for verifying a cluster.

Verify processing does not have to be performed if your system contains some of the latest VSAM releases. They provide automatic file verification when a VSAM file is opened, thus eliminating the need to use the IDCAMS VERIFY command.

OBTAINING DATASET STATISTICS

Detailed information about a VSAM dataset can be obtained with the IDCAMS **LISTCAT** command. This command provides many statistics about your dataset that can be reviewed to ensure that your dataset or alternate index is defined properly. These statistics include the record length, key length, key position, number of records in the dataset, number of records deleted, number of records updated, and many other statistics. From this information, you can also determine the amount of space left in your dataset or determine if your dataset should be reorganized to reclaim lost space.

To obtain this information, invoke IDCAMS to process the command as shown in Fig. 15.22. Figure 15.23 contains a LISTCAT printout for a VSAM KSDS. Carefully review its contents.

```
LISTCAT  ENT(CARDFILE)  ALL
```

Figure 15.22 Coding the LISTCAT command.

COPYING APPLICATION DATA

IDCAMS can copy data from within a VSAM dataset to an external source or from an external source into your cluster using the **REPRO** command. Suppose that two datasets having the same characteristics are named DS1 and DS2. If data in DS1 is to be copied into DS2, the REPRO command as illustrated in Fig. 15.24 is used.

The input dataset (IDS) DS1 is copied to the output dataset (ODS) DS2. We now have two copies of the same data, assuming that DS2 was empty to start.

REPRO can also back up or restore a dataset by copying data from a dataset to tape or from a tape into an empty cluster. Using Fig. 15.25, let's illustrate this procedure by copying the data from the cluster called CARDFILE to the magnetic tape volume called BACKUP. Note that a slightly different form of the REPRO command is required since its operands must now refer to DDNAMES and not to cluster or dataset names.

The COUNT and SKIP operands may also be coded on the REPRO command to restrict the amount of data to be copied. Further, the operands **FROMKEY** and **TOKEY** may be coded to identify key ranges that are to be copied. These and other operands for the REPRO command offer the programmer the ability to control which data in a cluster is to be copied or backed up. Please refer to the manuals for a complete discussion of these additional copy-control facilities.

Again, we've just scratched the surface of the IDCAMS commands. Refer to the access method services manual listed earlier to assist in issuing any of the commands previously described.

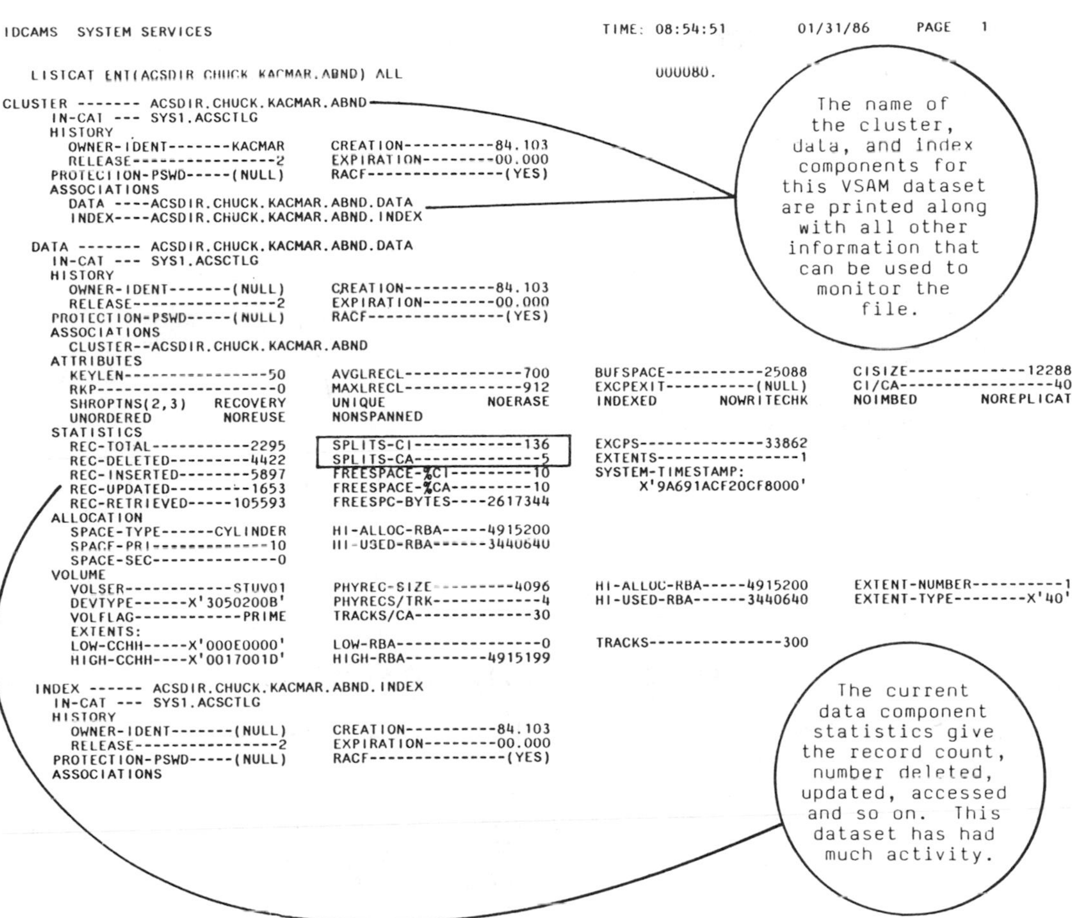

```
IDCAMS  SYSTEM SERVICES                                                   TIME: 08:54:51        01/31/86      PAGE    1

   LISTCAT ENT(ACSDIR.CHUCK.KACMAR.ABND) ALL                               000080.

CLUSTER ------- ACSDIR.CHUCK.KACMAR.ABND
     IN-CAT --- SYS1.ACSCTLG
     HISTORY
       OWNER-IDENT-------KACMAR        CREATION----------84.103
       RELEASE----------------2        EXPIRATION--------00.000
     PROTECTION-PSWD-----(NULL)        RACF---------------(YES)
     ASSOCIATIONS
       DATA ----ACSDIR.CHUCK.KACMAR.ABND.DATA
       INDEX----ACSDIR.CHUCK.KACMAR.ABND.INDEX

   DATA ------- ACSDIR.CHUCK.KACMAR.ABND.DATA
     IN-CAT --- SYS1.ACSCTLG
     HISTORY
       OWNER-IDENT-------(NULL)        CREATION----------84.103
       RELEASE----------------2        EXPIRATION--------00.000
     PROTECTION-PSWD-----(NULL)        RACF---------------(YES)
     ASSOCIATIONS
       CLUSTER--ACSDIR.CHUCK.KACMAR.ABND
     ATTRIBUTES
       KEYLEN----------------50        AVGLRECL-------------700        BUFSPACE-----------25088        CISIZE-------------12288
       RKP--------------------0        MAXLRECL-------------912        EXCPEXIT----------(NULL)        CI/CA-----------------40
       SHROPTNS(2,3)   RECOVERY        UNIQUE            NOERASE       INDEXED         NOWRITECHK      NOIMBED         NOREPLICAT
       UNORDERED        NOREUSE        NONSPANNED
     STATISTICS
       REC-TOTAL-----------2295        SPLITS-CI------------136        EXCPS--------------33862
       REC-DELETED---------4422        SPLITS-CA--------------5        EXTENTS----------------1
       REC-INSERTED--------5897        FREESPACE-%CI---------10        SYSTEM-TIMESTAMP:
       REC-UPDATED---------1653        FREESPACE-%CA---------10             X'9A691ACF20CF8000'
       REC-RETRIEVED-----105593        FREESPC-BYTES----2617344
     ALLOCATION
       SPACE-TYPE------CYLINDER        HI-ALLOC-RBA-----4915200
       SPACE-PRI-------------10        HI-USED-RBA------3440640
       SPACE-SEC--------------0
     VOLUME
       VOLSER------------STUV01        PHYREC-SIZE---------4096        HI-ALLOC-RBA-----4915200        EXTENT-NUMBER----------1
       DEVTYPE------X'3050200B'        PHYRECS/TRK------------4        HI-USED-RBA------3440640        EXTENT-TYPE--------X'40'
       VOLFLAG-----------PRIME         TRACKS/CA-------------30
       EXTENTS:
       LOW-CCHH-----X'000E0000'        LOW-RBA----------------0        TRACKS---------------300
       HIGH-CCHH----X'0017001D'        HIGH-RBA---------4915199

   INDEX ------ ACSDIR.CHUCK.KACMAR.ABND.INDEX
     IN-CAT --- SYS1.ACSCTLG
     HISTORY
       OWNER-IDENT-------(NULL)        CREATION----------84.103
       RELEASE----------------2        EXPIRATION--------00.000
     PROTECTION-PSWD-----(NULL)        RACF---------------(YES)
     ASSOCIATIONS
```


Figure 15.23 IDCAMS LISTCAT output.

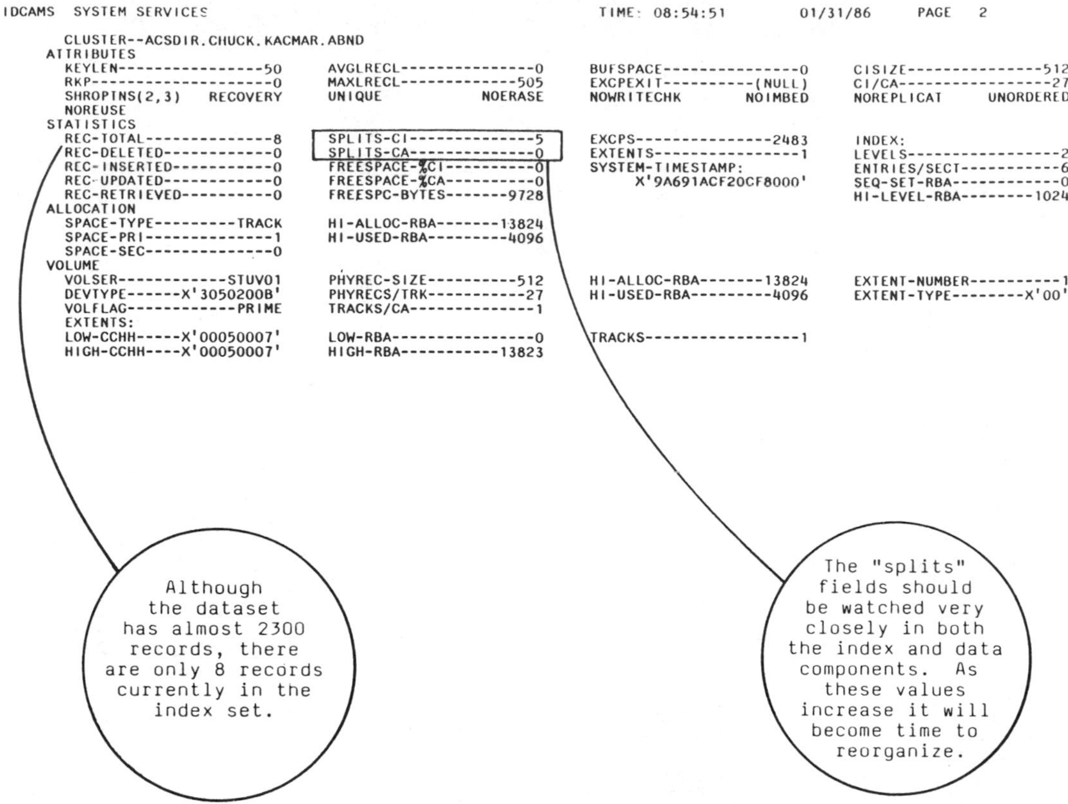


```
REPRO   IDS(DS1)   ODS(DS2)
```

Figure 15.24 Copying dataset DS1 to DS2 using the REPRO command.

```
//      EXEC       PGM=IDCAMS,REGION=512K
//SYSPRINT         DD   SYSOUT=$
//TAPEOUT          DD   UNIT=TAPE,VOL=SER=BACKUP,
//                      DISP=(NEW,KEEP),LABEL=(1,SL),
//                      DSN=BACKUP.OF.CARDFILE
//VSAMIN           DD   DSN=CARDFILE,DISP=SHR
//SYSIN            DD   *
  REPRO    INFILE(VSAMIN) OUTFILE(TAPEOUT)
```

Figure 15.25 Making a tape backup copy of a VSAM cluster.

OVERVIEW OF THE VSAM I/O MACRO INSTRUCTIONS

Many of the same I/O macro instructions that you've used before are used to process VSAM datasets. GET, PUT, OPEN, and CLOSE are among the set of instructions carried over from other dataset processing methods. However, several new instructions are needed that are unique to VSAM processing. These include RPL, SHOWCB, ACB, MODCB, and GENCB. As they are required, they will be integrated into our discussion. Further, VSAM processing will be presented from a very simple standpoint, using the fewest parameters to accomplish processing. For more information on all the various I/O instructions and their formats, consult IBM's *VSAM Programmer's Guide* (GC26-3868) or *MVS/370 VSAM Reference* (GC26-4074).

When processing non-VSAM files, a data control block (DCB) was used to access each file. For VSAM files, an **access control block (ACB)** supports our processing. Generally, only four parameters have to be coded on the ACB macro instruction (although many more parameters can be coded if desired). Also, note that these parameters are the only ones required for *any* of the VSAM dataset types. The four primary parameters on the ACB instruction are DDNAME, AM, MACRF, and EXLST.

The **DDNAME** parameter connects (as before) the ACB to our JCL DD statement. Again, the value of the DDNAME parameter is one to eight characters long, begins with a letter of the alphabet, and can contain digits after the first character.

The **AM (access method)** parameter is very simple since it is coded as AM=VSAM. Clearly, this parameter indicates that the VSAM access method is used for processing.

The **MACRF (macro facility)** parameter indicates how the file is to be processed and in which direction. Some of the most common MACRF values are listed in Fig. 15.26.

MACRF value	Meaning
SEQ	The file is to be processed sequentially.
DIR	The file is to be processed randomly.
IN	Records are to be read from the file.
OUT	Records are to be written to the file.

Figure 15.26 Common MACRF parameters.

The **EXLST (exit list)** parameter is used when processing any of the VSAM file types sequentially and when the end of file is encountered. In other words, this parameter specifies a control block which in turn specifies an EODAD address so that control may be transferred to a location in our program when the end of file is reached. Incidentally, this parameter has several other uses, but our primary use is with respect to the end-of-file processing.

Any VSAM file type can be processed sequentially for input processing using the ACB shown in Fig. 15.27. The EXLST parameter has been purposely omitted at this time since we must understand another instruction before this parameter may be used.

```
MASTER   ACB   DDNAME=MASTER,AM=VSAM,MACRF=(SEQ,IN)
```

Figure 15.27 Typical ACB for processing a VSAM cluster.

The DD statement given in Fig. 15.28 is all that is needed to complete the ACB/DD statement connection.

```
//GO.MASTER   DD   DSN=vsam-cluster-name,DISP=SHR
```

Figure 15.28 DD statement associated with the ACB given in Fig. 15.27.

As with any access method, processing begins by opening the cluster using the OPEN macro instruction. The OPEN instruction is slightly different with VSAM clusters since the parameters, INPUT, OUTPUT, or INOUT are omitted from the macro call. With respect to the ACB defined above, the ACB called MASTER can be opened by issuing the OPEN instruction as shown in Fig. 15.29.

```
OPEN   (MASTER)
```

Figure 15.29 Opening an ACB called MASTER.

After processing the VSAM dataset, your file is closed by issuing the CLOSE macro instruction. Again, this instruction is very simple since no other operands are needed. Figure 15.30 illustrates the coding of the CLOSE instruction.

```
CLOSE   (MASTER)
```

Figure 15.30 Closing a VSAM ACB.

The GET and PUT I/O macros again process the VSAM files. Their format is slightly different than that used in previous access methods, however. The GET and PUT instructions *do not* reference the ACB or our data area. Instead, they refer to another control block called the **request parameter list (RPL).** Through the RPL, I/O takes place. It is the RPL that informs VSAM *how* the dataset is to be processed. For example, if the name of our associated RPL is FILELOAD and we are going to write records into an empty VSAM cluster, the PUT instruction in Fig. 15.31 performs the desired activity.

```
PUT   RPL=FILELOAD
```

Figure 15.31 Writing a record to a VSAM cluster.

On the other hand, data can be input to our program using the GET instruction. Again, this instruction refers to an RPL, thus causing us to code the GET instruction as shown in Fig. 15.32.

```
GET   RPL=INPUTRPL
```

Figure 15.32 Reading a record from a cluster.

No matter what type of processing you are performing against your VSAM clusters, the GET and PUT instructions always reference an RPL. Since the RPL indicates how the dataset is to be processed, it is the RPL that is most important to support our VSAM dataset processing.

The **request parameter list (RPL)** is a VSAM control block that informs VSAM of the processing functions to be performed against our cluster, some of which are listed in Fig. 15.33.

Suppose that a VSAM ESDS is to be processed. The RPL in Fig. 15.34 specifies that the area called CARDIN is to hold the data records, the area is 80 bytes long, and that the dataset is to be processed in move mode and in a sequential manner.

```
1.   The name of the corresponding ACB.
2.   The area into which records are to be read or from
     which they are to be written.
3.   Whether the dataset is to be processed randomly or
     sequentially.
4.   The type of dataset that we are processing (ESDS,
     RRDS, or KSDS).
5.   The record key field for the cluster (in the case of
     RRDS or KSDS processing).
```

Figure 15.33 Functions of the request parameter list (RPL).

```
VSAMRPL   RPL   AM=VSAM,ACB=acbname,AREA=CARDIN,          X
                AREALEN=80,OPTCD=(SEQ,FWD,MVE,ADR)
```

Figure 15.34 RPL to process an ESDS.

The primary parameter of the RPL instruction is the **OPTCD (option codes)** parameter. In this RPL, the values of this parameter indicate that the cluster is to be processed sequentially (SEQ) in a forward direction (FWD) using move mode processing (MVE) and against an entry sequenced dataset (ADR). Clearly, these options are changed to allow processing RRDS or KSDS clusters. Also, the option codes vary if we are to process datasets in a backward direction, update records, or to use locate mode processing against our clusters. As we investigate each of the examples to process the different VSAM cluster types, we'll see other values for the OPTCD parameter.

PROCESSING A VSAM ESDS SEQUENTIALLY FOR OUTPUT

We begin our study of VSAM cluster processing by looking at methods to process VSAM datasets sequentially. In particular, we want to load records into an empty VSAM dataset using the PUT instruction to perform output processing requests. To do so, we define our ACB and RPL control blocks and then use the appropriate instructions to OPEN, process, and CLOSE the cluster to complete our processing. The format of a program to perform this processing is illustrated in Fig. 15.35.

The RPL and ACB options indicate that we are processing an ESDS sequentially for output in a forward direction using move mode processing. Clearly, the data area called STUFF resides in our program, and, according to the RPL, is 80 bytes long. Using this skeleton program, we could add the ability to read data from an input card file and write it to the ESDS. Since an input card file is not a VSAM cluster, standard I/O macro instructions are required to perform this processing as shown in Fig. 15.36.

The card file requires a DCB for processing and a corresponding DD statement as you can see. The main processing loop reads data cards into the area called STUFF. The PUT instruction then writes the card images into the VSAM cluster. The RPL specified on the PUT instruction is associated with the ACB called OUTACB. OUTACB is associated with the DD statement identifying our cluster. Therefore, data written using the output RPL is placed into our entry sequenced dataset.

```
//       EXEC     ASMFCG
//ASM.SYSIN       DD         *

                  OPEN       (OUTACB)
                  .          .
                  .          .

                  PUT        RPL=OUTRPL
                  .          .
                  .          .

                  CLOSE      (OUTACB)
                  .          .
                  .          .

OUTRPL            RPL        AM=VSAM,ACB=OUTACB,AREA=STUFF,           X
                             AREALEN=80,OPTCD=(SEQ,FWD,MVE,ADR)

OUTACB            ACB        AM=VSAM,DDNAME=VSAMFILE,                 X
                             MACRF=(SEQ,OUT)

//GO.VSAMFILE     DD         DSN=vsam-cluster-name,DISP=SHR
```

Figure 15.35 Program format to load a record into an ESDS.

```
//       EXEC     ASMFCG
//ASM.SYSIN       DD         *

                  OPEN       (CARDFILE,INPUT)
                  OPEN       (OUTACB)
                  .          .
                  .          .
                  GET        CARDFILE,STUFF
MAINLOOP          DS         0H
                  PUT        RPL=OUTRPL
                  GET        CARDFILE,STUFF
                  B          MAINLOOP
                  .          .
                  .          .
EOF               DS         0H
                  CLOSE      (CARDFILE)
                  CLOSE      (OUTACB)
                  .          .
                  .          .

OUTRPL            RPL        AM=VSAM,ACB=OUTACB,AREA=STUFF,           X
                             AREALEN=80,OPTCD=(SEQ,FWD,MVE,ADR)

OUTACB            ACB        AM=VSAM,DDNAME=VSAMFILE,                 X
                             MACRF=(SEQ,OUT)

CARDFILE          DCB        DSORG=PS,DDNAME=CARDIN,EODAD=EOF,        X
                             MACRF=GM

//GO.VSAMFILE     DD         DSN=vsam-cluster-name,DISP=SHR
//GO.CARDIN       DD         *
   'input card data would be placed here'
```

Figure 15.36 Loading an ESDS with input card data.

PROCESSING A VSAM RRDS SEQUENTIALLY FOR OUTPUT

Now let's turn our attention to loading an RRDS. A relative record dataset can be processed sequentially or randomly. Each record in the dataset is identified by its position within the dataset. In other words, the one-hundredth record in the dataset can be accessed directly simply by asking VSAM for record 100. Further, we do not have to process records 1 through 99 before record 100 can be accessed. Thus, a field is required to identify the record that we are processing. This field, commonly called the **relative record number,** *must* be defined as a binary fullword and must also be identified on the associated RPL.

Each record that is to be loaded into the RRDS is identified by its **relative record number.** No two records can occupy the same position or slot within an RRDS, and so we must ensure that each record's relative record number is unique. This can be done in many different ways, depending on your particular application. In the example, in Fig. 15.37, each input data card contains a number in the first five positions. This value is

```
//       EXEC      ASMFCG
//ASM.SYSIN        DD       *

                   OPEN     (CARDFILE,INPUT)
                   OPEN     (OUTACB)
                   .        .
                   .        .
                   GET      CARDFILE,STUFF
MAINLOOP           DS       0H
                   PACK     WORKAREA(8),INPUTRRN
                   CVB      R3,WORKAREA
                   ST       R3,RRN
                   PUT      RPL=OUTRPL
                   GET      CARDFILE,STUFF
                   B        MAINLOOP
                   .        .
                   .        .
EOF                DS       0H
                   CLOSE    (CARDFILE)
                   CLOSE    (OUTACB)
                   .        .
                   .        .

OUTRPL             RPL      AM=VSAM,ACB=OUTACB,AREA=STUFF,            X
                            AREALEN=80,OPTCD=(SEQ,FWD,MVE,KEY),       X
                            ARG=RRN

OUTACB             ACB      AM=VSAM,DDNAME=VSAMFILE,                  X
                            MACRF=(SEQ,OUT)

CARDFILE           DCB      DSORG=PS,DDNAME=CARDIN,EODAD=EOF,         X
                            MACRF=GM

STUFF              DS       0CL80
INPUTRRN           DS       CL5
REST               DS       CL75

WORKAREA           DS       0D
                   DS       PL8

RRN                DS       F

//GO.VSAMFILE      DD       DSN=vsam-cluster-name,DISP=SHR
//GO.CARDIN        DD       *
  'input card data would be placed here'
```

Figure 15.37 Loading an RRDS with input card data.

then used as the relative record number for the data record that is to be stored into the VSAM cluster.

The example highlights the changes in the RPL that must be made to reflect RRDS processing. As you can see, the RPL now identifies the relative record number field through the **ARG (argument)** parameter. The OPTCD parameter specifies that keyed access is used for this cluster.

Let me call your attention to the ACB. If you compare this ACB with the one used earlier when processing an ESDS, they are identical. In fact, the next example also uses the same ACB operands for processing a KSDS. This again illustrates that it is the RPL that is most important in controlling VSAM dataset processing.

PROCESSING A VSAM KSDS SEQUENTIALLY FOR OUTPUT

The key sequenced VSAM dataset is one of the most used of all VSAM dataset types. This dataset structure allows us to access records sequentially or randomly by specifying a record key. Each record key must be unique, that is, no two records may have the same key. Hence, by selecting a field within the record that guarantees uniqueness, we can use a KSDS to store the data to support our application.

Since a key must be specified when processing a KSDS, the RPL must be coded to identify the key field value. The example in Fig. 15.38 stores input data card images into

```
//        EXEC      ASMFCG
//ASM.SYSIN         DD          *

                    OPEN        (CARDFILE,INPUT)
                    OPEN        (OUTACB)
                    .           .
                    .           .
                    GET         CARDFILE,STUFF
MAINLOOP            DS          0H
                    PUT         RPL=OUTRPL
                    GET         CARDFILE,STUFF
                    B           MAINLOOP
                    .           .
                    .           .
EOF                 DS          0H
                    CLOSE       (CARDFILE)
                    CLOSE       (OUTACB)
                    .           .
                    .           .

OUTRPL              RPL         AM=VSAM,ACB=OUTACB,AREA=STUFF,          X
                                AREALEN=80,OPTCD=(SEQ,FWD,MVE,KEY),     X
                                ARG=CARDKEY

OUTACB              ACB         AM=VSAM,DDNAME=VSAMFILE,                X
                                MACRF=(SEQ,OUT)

CARDFILE            DCB         DSORG=PS,DDNAME=CARDIN,EODAD=EOF,       X
                                MACRF=GM

STUFF               DS          0CL80
CARDKEY             DS          CL20
REST                DS          CL60

//GO.VSAMFILE       DD          DSN=vsam-cluster-name,DISP=SHR
//GO.CARDIN         DD          *
   'input card data would be placed here'
```

Figure 15.38 Loading a KSDS with input card data.

the KSDS. The first 20 characters of the input data record are to be used as the key for each record in the KSDS. Although the record key value can be numeric, it need not be. Names, addresses, or any other field can be used as the key of a VSAM record as long as the key field is less than or equal to 256 bytes long and it is unique.

Again, notice that the ACB has not changed throughout the examples that we've investigated. However, the RPL has changed to indicate the type of dataset that we are processing, and if necessary, to identify the field that specifies the key of the record to be processed.

TESTING THE SUCCESS OF AN I/O OPERATION

The examples up to this point have omitted a very important aspect of VSAM processing, namely, determining if each I/O operation completed successfully. Whenever we process VSAM datasets, we should always check the value in register 15 after issuing the I/O request. Register 15 is a special register when performing VSAM processing since it communicates to our program whether or not our request was performed as desired. A value of zero in R15 indicates that the operation was successful and a nonzero value indicates a potential problem.

An I/O operation can fail for many different reasons even though register 15 can only hold one value. For this reason, we must introduce another VSAM I/O macro instruction to help us determine if our request was successful or not. The instruction is **SHOWCB (show control block)** and its function is to provide more information about our I/O requests.

For example, suppose that we issue an I/O request and after the request, register 15 contains a nonzero value. By issuing the SHOWCB instruction, VSAM provides more information about why our I/O operation failed. Specifically, the RPL control block contains a field called the **feedback code,** which, depending on its value, determines *exactly* why our request was not successful.

When opening or closing VSAM files, we must use the SHOWCB instruction to obtain the **error code** value from the ACB, which indicates specifically why a VSAM file could not be opened or closed during processing.

Either of these information fields can be accessed directly within their respective control blocks, however, it is more common to use the SHOWCB instruction to obtain these values. In other words, the SHOWCB instruction extracts the feedback code value from the RPL or the error code value from the ACB and places it into another field within our program. This field can then be interrogated to determine why our request failed.

The code generated by the SHOWCB macro instruction can extract many different values from within the RPL or the ACB and provide them to our program. However, only a very limited number of these fields are required for normal VSAM processing. In fact, there are only two fields important to us at this point: the error code field within the ACB and the feedback code field in the RPL.

The SHOWCB instruction is coded so that it is associated with a specific RPL or ACB. The SHOWCB instruction also identifies the name of the area into which the extracted fields are to be placed. For the error code or feedback code values, a four-byte area is required to hold either of these values. From Fig. 15.39, the SHOWCB instruction can extract the feedback code value from the RPL and place it into the four-byte area called FEEDBACK.

```
SHOWCB  RPL=OUTRPL,FIELDS=FDBK,AREA=FEEDBACK,LENGTH=4
```

Figure 15.39 Extracting the RPL feedback code.

The instruction indicates that the **FDBK (feedback code)** field is to be extracted from the RPL and placed into the data area called FEEDBACK whose length is four bytes. After extraction, the value of FEEDBACK can then be compared against a list of feedback codes to determine why our request failed.

Our second example in Fig. 15.40 illustrates how to extract the error code field from the ACB after opening or closing a VSAM file. In this example, the SHOWCB instruction references the appropriate *ACB* to extract the error code value.

```
SHOWCB   ACB=OURACB,AREA=ERRCODE,LENGTH=4,FIELDS=ERROR
```

Figure 15.40 Extracting the ACB error code.

For reference, Figs. 15.41 through 15.43 list the many (not all) possible error and feedback codes and give a brief explanation as to why they may have occurred. These codes should be used in comparison when the value of R15 is nonzero after issuing the associated instruction. When referring to these lists later, make sure that you reference the proper list, depending on the operation that you tried to perform. For more details on error analysis and to reference error codes not contained in the list, refer to the following IBM publications: *VSAM Programmer's Guide* (GC26-3868) or *MVS/370 VSAM Reference* (GC26-4074).

```
0      If R15 = 8, then the address given for your ACB is
        not valid.

100    You cannot open your base cluster because the as-
        sociated alternate index is empty.

104    The system and VSAM do not agree on the size of
        your dataset. Your dataset may be destroyed and
        may have to be rebuilt.

116    During the last attempt to process your dataset,
        it was not properly closed. In all likelihood,
        the last program to process the dataset abended.
        Implicit verification was not successful. Use
        IDCAMS VERIFY to reestablish the integrity of the
        dataset.

118    During the last attempt to process your dataset,
        it was not properly closed. However, implicit
        verify was successful in reestablishing dataset
        integrity.

128    You forgot to code a DD statement to reference the
        cluster that you wanted to process.

136    You did not allow enough memory to run your pro-
        gram. Increase your job's region parameter for
        this step and rerun.
```

Figure 15.41 ACB error codes after issuing an OPEN instruction.

148 The cluster that you're trying to process was not found by VSAM. Are you sure that it is a VSAM dataset?

160 The operands in your ACB or GENCB instruction are not consistent with the data in your cluster. Look carefully at your MACRF parameters.

168 You cannot process the dataset in the manner that you desire.

Figure 15.41 (continued)

4 You've already closed this dataset.

136 You did not run your job in a region of adequate size. Rerun your program and specify a larger memory region value for this job step.

Figure 15.42 ACB error codes after issuing a CLOSE instruction.

4 The end of file has been encountered.

8 You're trying to add a record into a dataset but there exists one that has this key. This may also apply to alternate index processing when UNIQUEKEY was specified and a base cluster record is being added with an identical AIX key value.

12 You're trying to add records sequentially (loading) to an RRDS or a KSDS, but the keys of the records are not in ascending order.

16 The record that you tried to access is not found in the dataset. If you're trying to access records randomly, the key of the record that you've specified is not located in the dataset.

20 Someone else is updating records in your dataset at the same time.

40 Insufficient region to run your program and process this VSAM dataset. Rerun your program in a larger region.

44 You're using move mode processing, but the area into which the input record is to be placed is too small to hold the entire record.

Figure 15.43 RPL feedback codes.

68	You're trying to process the dataset in a manner different than how it was opened. For example, you opened the dataset for input processing only, but now you're trying to write records to the file.
72	You're trying to process your dataset in the wrong manner. For example, you are trying to access RRDS records with a record key or trying to access KSDS records by specifying a relative record number.
88	You are trying to process sequentially, but the dataset was opened as random access.
92	You are trying to update a record in a dataset without first reading the record.
96	You are trying to change the key of the record. If the key of a record must be changed, then you'll have to add a record with the new key and ERASE the old record.
104	Incorrect RPL options specified.
108	The length of the record that you're trying to process is longer than the maximum record length defined for your cluster.
116	You cannot update records while loading them into an empty dataset. OPTCD=UPD is invalid during dataset loading.
148	You've exceeded the record length in your alternate index. In other words, more base cluster records have the same alternate index key than expected.
192	While trying to access a record in an RRDS, you have specified a relative record number that is not associated with an existing record.

Figure 15.43 (continued)

Once the value of the error code or feedback code has been extracted, you must now determine what action your program is going to take as a result. In the case of loading a cluster sequentially, let's assume that any nonzero R15 value terminates processing. However, before terminating, we place the code value into R15 and use R15 to set the return code as our program terminates. We can then determine why our program stopped processing by simply looking at the condition code value on the messages and codes page of our program listing (discussed in Chapters 3, 8 and 9). Figure 15.44 contains this implementation.

After each VSAM I/O request, the value of register 15 is tested for a nonzero value. If it is nonzero, control is transferred to the location called OCERROR or PROBLEM. The feedback code value is extracted from the RPL using the SHOWCB instruction and

```
//       EXEC      ASMFCG
//ASM.SYSIN        DD        *

                   OPEN      (CARDFILE,INPUT)
                   OPEN      (OUTACB)
                   LTR       R15,R15
                   BNZ       OCERROR
                   .         .
                   .         .
MAINLOOP           DS        OH
                   GET       CARDFILE,STUFF
                   PUT       RPL=OUTRPL
                   LTR       R15,R15
                   BNZ       PROBLEM
                   B         MAINLOOP
                             .
                   .         .
EOF                DS        OH
                   CLOSE     (CARDFILE)
                   CLOSE     (OUTACB)
                   LTR       R15,R15
                   BNZ       OCERROR
                   .         .
                   .         .

OCERROR            DS        OH
                   SHOWCB    RPL=OUTACB,FIELDS=ERROR,                X
                             AREA=ERRCODE,LENGTH=4
                   L         R15,ERRCODE
                   B         EXIT
ERRCODE            DS        F                  EXTRACTED ERROR VALUE

PROBLEM            DS        OH
                   SHOWCB    RPL=OUTRPL,FIELDS=FDBK,                 X
                             AREA=FEEDBACK,LENGTH=4
                   L         R15,FEEDBACK
                   B         EXIT
FEEDBACK           DS        F


EXIT               DS        OH
                   L         R13,4(R13)         RESTORE R13 VALUE
                   L         R14,12(R13)        RESTORE ALL BUT R15
                   LM        RO,R12,20(R13)     ...
                   BR        R14                RETURN CONTROL

OUTRPL             RPL       AM=VSAM,ACB=OUTACB,AREA=STUFF,          X
                             AREALEN=80,OPTCD=(SEQ,FWD,MVE,KEY),     X
                             ARG=CARDKEY

OUTACB             ACB       AM=VSAM,DDNAME-VSAMFILE,                X
                             MACRF=(SEQ,OUT)

CARDFILE           DCB       DSORG=PS,DDNAME=CARDIN,EODAD=EOF,       X
                             MACRF=GM

STUFF              DS        OCL80
CARDKEY            DS        CL20
REST               DS        CL60

//GO.VSAMFILE      DD        DSN=vsam-cluster-name,DISP=SHR
//GO.CARDIN        DD        *
   'input card data would be placed here'
```

Figure 15.44 Loading an ESDS (with provision for error and feedback code analysis).

is placed into the area called FEEDBACK, and the error code field is extracted from the ACB and is placed into the area called ERRCODE. If the error occurred during an OPEN or CLOSE, the routine OCERROR will place the value of the ERRCODE field from the ACB into R15 in order to set the program return code. An error during a GET or PUT will enable the routine PROBLEM to place the value of the FEEDBACK code field from the RPL into R15 in order to set the return code. The R15 value thus becomes the return code for the program that is printed on the messages and codes page.

The SHOWCB macro instruction generates executable instructions as you can see from the example. That is, when control is transferred to the location called PROBLEM, the SHOWCB instruction follows *in line,* thus causing generated code to be executed. This distinguishes the SHOWCB instruction from the other I/O macros that we've discussed, such as ACB and RPL. These instructions (ACB and RPL) do not generate executable code and we have to ensure that our logic does not cause us to fall into the code generated by these instructions during processing. Later, we'll investigate several other VSAM I/O macros that generate executable code.

Although the example terminated the program when a nonzero value was found in R15, this may not always be an appropriate action. In fact, some nonzero values are expected, such as the case when end of file is reached when processing records for input. Clearly, we do not want to abort processing when this situation is encountered. Therefore, it may be necessary for our program to interrogate the value in R15, the error code field in the ACB, or the feedback code field in the RPL after each I/O instruction to determine the value obtained. If an *anticipated* value is received, our program should continue processing normally. An unexpected value can still cause our program to terminate, but it may not be an automatic action as in this example.

Register 0 is also used (by VSAM) to indicate the success or failure of still other I/O request instructions. For example, suppose that the code generated by the SHOWCB instruction itself fails. If this occurs, we must not only test the value of R15, but we must also test the value of R0 to determine why the SHOWCB instruction does not work. Note that R0 is tested and not a value in the ACB or RPL. Since the SHOWCB macro instruction generates executable code, VSAM informs us of the success or failure of the SHOWCB instruction through the combination of R15 and R0. Other instructions requiring the testing of the combination R15/R0 are MODCB, GENCB, and TESTCB, which we will discuss later. Figure 15.45 lists the various R0 values and their meanings when issuing these instructions.

Another technique can determine the status of an I/O operation. This method requires the **TESTCB (test control block)** macro instruction, which generates code to set the *condition code* based on a value that we specify and the value in an associated VSAM control block field. For example, we can determine if the error code field in the ACB is equal to 8 by using the TESTCB instruction as illustrated in Fig. 15.46.

In Fig. 15.46, the code generated by the TESTCB instruction tests the ERROR field within the ACB called OURACB. If the value of this field is 8, the condition code is set appropriately to allow us to test for equality using the BE (branch if equal) instruction that follows. Clearly, many such tests against the ACB can transfer control to areas within our program to handle each possible error code value.

Fields in the RPL can be tested in a similar manner. For example, the RPL called OURRPL can be tested for a feedback code value of 4 (end of file) through the TESTCB instruction shown in Fig. 15.47.

The TESTCB macro instruction generates executable code that itself should be tested for success. After each TESTCB instruction, check the value of R15 for zero. If it is

0	Invalid request.
2	Invalid EXLST, ACB, or RPL.
3	Invalid value specified within one of the control block operands.
4	The control block being processed is not as you specified. For example, you're trying to use SHOWCB, but have requested feedback code information from an ACB.
5	The ACB that you're trying to process has not been opened.
8	Insufficient memory for your program to perform this request. Rerun your program in a larger region.
9	The work area specified is too small to hold the data or fields that you have indicated.
10	Incorrect exit list control block or the address of your EXLST control block is not valid.
12	You've attempted to use MODCB to change the information in the ACB. However, the ACB is open. Close the ACB before issuing the MODCB instruction.
14	One or more of the values specified for MACRF or OPTCD is in conflict with some other value that has been coded.
15	You were trying to extract fields from an ACB or an RPL, but the work area that you defined to hold the extracted information did not begin on a fullword boundary.

Figure 15.45 R0 values after issuing GENCB, MODCB, SHOWCB, and TESTCB.

```
TESTCB   ACB=OURACB,ERROR=8
BE       GOTA8
```

Figure 15.46 Evaluating I/O success using the TESTCB macro instruction.

```
TESTCB   RPL=OURRPL,FDBK=4
BE       EOF
```

Figure 15.47 Testing for an RPL feedback code value of 4 using TESTCB.

not zero, then R0 should be tested to determine why this instruction failed. A list of the possible R0 values and their explanations were given in Fig. 15.45.

The need to test more than one register and several different error or feedback codes can make coding cumbersome when developing VSAM applications. During development and testing, macros such as SNAP and XDUMP can be very helpful in displaying register contents in order to determine which status code values were returned by VSAM to your program. Since VSAM will not abnormally terminate an application program when an error occurs (as other access methods), it is extremely important for your code to test the values in the registers or control blocks to determine if an error occurred. A domino effect can occur if an error is left unchecked. As a last resort, you can issue the ABEND macro instruction to force program termination if an unexpected error occurs during processing.

END-OF-FILE PROCESSING

When VSAM clusters are processed for input, it is possible for your program to reach the end of file. Although the end of file may be tested using the techniques previously discussed, there's an easier method. It requires the use of the **EXLST (exit list)** *parameter* on the ACB instruction and requires a new VSAM *control block,* **EXLST.**

The EXLST macro generates a VSAM control block that specifies an address in the program where control is to be transferred when the end of file is reached. Again, this control block has many other parameters, but, for our purposes, the end-of-file parameter is of interest. Hence, the coding of this control block is very simple since only two operands need be coded as shown in Fig. 15.48.

```
EXITLIST  EXLST  AM=VSAM,EODAD=(EOF,A)
```

Figure 15.48 Coding the EXLST macro instruction to handle end of file.

You must place a label on this control block, which is shown as EXITLIST. The two parameters on the control block are **AM (access method)** and **EODAD (end of data).** As coded, EODAD indicates that control is to be transferred to the location called EOF when our program reaches the end of file. The letter **A** following the label EOF indicates that this control block is to be activated immediately. This means that the EXLST control block can be constructed so that different end-of-file locations can be in effect at various times during processing. Since our programs will most likely have only a single end-of-file location, we'll activate the control block immediately so that we don't have to worry about activating it later.

The ACB and EXLST control blocks must be associated with each other by coding the EXLST parameter on the ACB. Since the name of our exit list control block is EXITLIST, the corresponding *input* ACB is coded as shown in Fig. 15.49.

```
acbname  ACB  AM=VSAM,DDNAME=FILEIN,EXLST=EXITLIST,        X
              MACRF=(SEQ,IN)
```

Figure 15.49 Associating an ACB with an EXLST control block.

Since we are now processing our cluster for input mode, the MACRF parameter is changed to indicate input processing. The EXLST parameter associates this ACB with the exit list control block that is generated when we code the EXLST macro instruction. Since this is all that is required for input processing and for handling the end of file, we can now discuss input processing for VSAM applications.

SEQUENTIAL INPUT PROCESSING ON VSAM CLUSTERS

The ACB and EXLST control blocks discussed in the previous section can be used for *any* VSAM dataset type. Hence, the RPL is the only control block that must be changed when processing an ESDS, RRDS, or KSDS VSAM dataset. The I/O instruction that performs input processing is, of course, the GET instruction.

As is the case with the PUT instruction, the GET instruction refers to an RPL. Therefore, all VSAM datasets are processed sequentially using the common GET instruction given in Fig. 15.50.

```
GET   RPL=rplname
```

Figure 15.50 General format of the VSAM GET macro instruction.

An associated RPL then defines the type of VSAM cluster that is to be processed and identifies the record key fields that are to be used for dataset processing. In fact, the three RPL's shown in Fig. 15.51 are complete examples of RPL's that can process an ESDS, RRDS, and KSDS VSAM cluster, respectively.

Each cluster processed contains 80-byte records. As you can see, the primary differences between the RPL's are the option codes (OPTCD) values and the key field definition (ARG). For ESDS, keys are not allowed and so no ARG operand can be coded. Since both the RRDS and KSDS clusters allow keys, the OPTCD values are identical, but the key field areas are different. Again, the ARG parameter on the RRDS RPL identifies a four-byte binary area into which the relative record number of the record read is to be placed. The ARG parameter on the KSDS RPL identifies a character area that holds the record key of the record being processed. Since you should understand the relationships between I/O instruction, RPL, ACB, and EXLST at this point, I leave the construction of a program to perform sequential input processing to you.

```
ESDSIN    RPL    AM=VSAM,ACB=acbname,AREA=STUFF,AREALEN=80,     X
                 OPTCD=(SEQ,FWD,MVE,ADR)


RRDSIN    RPL    AM=VSAM,ACB=acbname,AREA=STUFF,AREALEN=80,     X
                 OPTCD=(SEQ,FWD,MVE,KEY),ARG=RRN


KSDSIN    RPL    AM=VSAM,ACB=acbname,AREA=STUFF,AREALEN=80,     X
                 OPTCD=(SEQ,FWD,MVE,KEY),ARG=RECKEY
```

Figure 15.51 RPL's used for each VSAM dataset type.

RANDOMLY PROCESSING A VSAM DATASET

The power behind the VSAM access method is in its ability to process records randomly. With GET and PUT instructions, records can be read from a VSAM cluster, updated by your program, and then rewritten into the cluster. Records can also be added or deleted from the cluster using appropriate techniques. These processing situations require slightly different control block coding techniques than before and two RPL's to process a single ACB.

All VSAM datasets can be processed randomly. However, we typically use only relative record and key sequenced datasets if we are going to process data randomly. Hence, we're going to direct our study to only these VSAM dataset types and omit random ESDS processing.

Random processing allows us to access any record in the dataset without first having to process all records before that record. For example, relative record 50 can be processed before or after any records numbered 1 through 49. The order in which records are processed is determined by the order they are supplied to our program. If the input transaction data is ordered in the same manner as the data in the cluster, we can process the records sequentially. However, if the transaction data is randomly ordered, then random processing can be used for processing.

In general, applications performing random processing add, change, or delete records from the cluster. On the other hand, application programs can be developed that perform only one or two of these functions. Regardless of the processing to be done, from the discussion that follows you should be able to analyze and construct your control blocks appropriate to the required processing.

The format of an ACB to process a KSDS randomly is identical to the format of an ACB to process an RRDS randomly. Therefore, whether we're going to process a KSDS or an RRDS, our discussion for processing both file types will be almost identical. To perform all of the functions (add, change, and delete) against our cluster, we code our ACB as shown in Fig. 15.52.

```
RANDOM   ACB   AM=VSAM,DDNAME=MASTER,MACRF=(DIR,IN,OUT)
```

Figure 15.52 ACB to randomly process a KSDS or RRDS.

The ACB identifies the DD statement that is associated with this ACB. It also indicates that direct (DIR) accessing of data in the cluster occurs and that records are read *and* written to the dataset (IN,OUT). If you are only going to add records to the cluster, you only have to code the OUT value and random retrieval only requires coding IN within the MACRF operand.

The RPL's to process the RRDS and KSDS are also similar except for identifying the record identification field as shown in Fig. 15.53. For the RRDS, a relative record

```
RRDSRPL    RPL    AM=VSAM,ACB=RANDOM,AREA=STUFF,AREALEN=80,      X
                  OPTCD=(DIR,MVE,KEY,UPD),ARG=RRN


KSDSRPL    RPL    AM=VSAM,ACB=RANDOM,AREA=STUFF,AREALEN=80,      X
                  OPTCD=(DIR,MVE,KEY,UPD),ARG=RECKEY
```

Figure 15.53 RPL's to support random processing (except record addition).

number field is specified whereas a character area is specified when performing KSDS processing.

The RPL's in Fig. 15.53 indicate that direct (random) processing is performed, move mode processing is used, records are accessed by keys, and that records will be updated within the cluster. Although you may think these RPL's are all that are needed, there's a slight problem. Specifically, these RPL's *cannot* be used to add records into the clusters. Hence, we must construct a second set of RPL's to allow records to be added to the cluster as shown in Fig. 15.54.

Using different names and omitting the UPD (update) option, these RPL's are used when records are to be added into the cluster. Hence, a single program that performs add, change, and delete requests against a VSAM cluster requires a single ACB and *two* RPL's. Also make sure that your I/O macro instructions (GET, PUT) reference the proper RPL, depending on the function being performed within your application.

The logic in Fig. 15.55 uses a transaction center to read in transactions to be applied to the records in the cluster. Depending on the first character of each input transaction record, the appropriate logic is called to add, change, or delete the record from within the cluster.

```
RRDSADD      RPL     AM=VSAM,ACB=RANDOM,AREA=STUFF,AREALEN=80,          X
                     OPTCD=(DIR,MVE,KEY),ARG=RRN


KSDSADD      RPL     AM=VSAM,ACB=RANDOM,AREA=STUFF,AREALEN=80,          X
                     OPTCD=(DIR,MVE,KEY),ARG=RECKEY
```

Figure 15.54 RPL's that allow records to be added to a cluster during random processing.

```
1.  Input a transaction record
2.  Repeat until end of file is reached

    a.  If transaction = "add a record" then
         perform add-a-record logic
        else
         if transaction = "delete a record" then
            perform delete-a-record logic
         else
            perform update-a-record logic
    b.  input the next transaction to be processed
```

Figure 15.55 Logic for random file processing.

Within each logical function records are added, updated, or deleted from the cluster. Incidentally, subroutines can also perform the processing against the cluster, thus allowing the design to be modular. However, if you implement your solution in the form of external modules, remember that the ACB must be passed as a parameter to each of the modules since a control block can only be defined in one of the routines. (We discussed the sharing of data control blocks across subroutine boundaries in Chapter 9.)

To add a record to the cluster, the record key or relative record number must be moved into the record key field identified on the RPL. The data from the transaction record is then moved into the area that is to hold the record. The program issues a PUT instruction using the RPL that does *not* specify the operand UPD (update). If you recall, this was the second set of RPL's developed.

After the PUT instruction is issued, register 15 and the feedback code should be tested. Several different conditions can occur as a result of trying to add a record. The cluster may be too full to hold the new record or a record with an identical key may already exist within the dataset. Each condition is tested using different feedback code field values. Refer to the list of feedback code values given earlier in the chapter for specific details.

When trying to update or delete a record from the cluster, first read the record from the dataset. This is done by moving the record's key or relative record number into the ARG field specified by the RPL. Clearly, this value must come from the input transaction record. With the GET instruction and the first set of RPL's that we looked at, the record is retrieved from the file and placed into the area specified on the RPL.

Your program must now move data from the transaction record into the master record to update the record. Following the changing of record data, a PUT instruction replaces the record in the cluster. If a value of 0 is returned in R15, the update was successful. If R15 is not zero, then you'll have to interrogate the feedback code field to determine why your request failed.

Deleting a record can be done with an **ERASE** macro instruction after a successful GET. The ERASE instruction refers to the same RPL as coded on the GET instruction. If successful, the record in your cluster is *physically* deleted. In other words, VSAM does not delete records by marking them with X'FF'. If you want to *logically* delete records rather than physically delete records, then *you* have to treat the delete as an update and move X'FF' into the record area and *rewrite* the record to the dataset.

It is very important that register 15 is tested after each I/O operation. Clearly, the amount of testing can be quite cumbersome and so, use of the TESTCB macro instruction becomes very important to streamlining your code.

The sample program contained in Example 15.1 performs random processing against a VSAM KSDS. Processing for an RRDS is similar except for the record identification field value. Pay particular attention to the transaction center and the logic within each of the functions (add, change, delete). Macro expansion is suppressed to help the overall readability of the program example.

GENERATING THE ACB AND RPL AT EXECUTION TIME

The ACB and RPL are the focal points of all processing against a VSAM cluster. For that reason, it is very important that these control blocks be complete and correct. Since VSAM is a relatively new access method, it is quite possible that IBM may modify the format of the ACB or RPL to allow more functions, thus extending the processing capabilities of VSAM. For this reason, another method for generating these control blocks can be used that prevents any incompatibilities between "old" and "new" releases of VSAM. This technique requires the **GENCB (generate a control block)** macro instruction.

Since an ACB must be in effect before we attempt to open our cluster, we have to generate an ACB before we issue the OPEN macro instruction. To generate an ACB at execution time, we issue the GENCB instruction and specify the same parameters on the GENCB instruction as we would normally code when generating the ACB as we did earlier. An ACB to perform sequential output processing is coded as shown in Fig. 15.56.

```
LOC  OBJECT CODE     ADDR1 ADDR2  STMT    SOURCE STATEMENT                                          ASM H V 02 12 19 02/02/86

             MACRO
    &LAB     TRACE &MSG
    .*--------------------------------------------------------------------*
    .*     THIS MACRO WILL PRINT A MESSAGE TO THE AUDIT TRAIL TO HELP      *
    .*     THE PROGRAMMER FOLLOW THE LOGICAL EXECUTION OF THE PROGRAM.     *
    .*     THIS MACRO CAN BE USED TO HELP IN PROGRAM DEBUGGING.            *
    .*--------------------------------------------------------------------*
    &LAB     MVC   AUDITMSG(50),=CL50''&MSG''
             MVC   AUDITKEY(10),TRANSKEY          REMEMBER TRANSACTION KEY
             PUT   AUDIT,AUDITLIN                 PRINT AUDIT LINE
             MEND


             MACRO
    &LAB     STATUS &AREA
    .*--------------------------------------------------------------------*
    .*     THIS MACRO WILL CONVERT BINARY FULLWORD VALUES INTO DISPLAY     *
    .*     FORMAT AND PRINT THEM ON THE AUDIT TRAIL.  THIS WILL ALLOW US   *
    .*     TO FOLLOW THE FEEDBACK AND ERROR CODE VALUES DURING PROCESSING. *
    .*--------------------------------------------------------------------*
    &LAB     L     R15,&AREA                      GET STATUS CODE VALUE
             CVD   R15,PACKED                     GET READY TO PRINT
             MVC   STATCODE(4),=X'40202120'       SET UP EDIT PATTERN
             ED    STATCODE(4),PACKED+6           EDIT STATUS CODE
             MVI   AUDITLIN+1,C' '                CLEAR AUDIT TRAIL LINE
             MVC   AUDITLIN+2(131),AUDITLIN+1     CLEAR REMAINING BYTES
             MVC   AUDITMSG(26),=C'     = STATUS CODE OBAINED'
             MVC   AUDITMSG(4),STATCODE
             PUT   AUDIT,AUDITLIN
             MEND
```

These macros are very helpful during processing since TRACE will be used to construct a printed audit trail and STATUS will be used to convert feedback and error codes into printable format.

Example 15.1 Program for the random processing of the master-file update.

```
  LOC  OBJECT CODE    ADDR1 ADDR2  STMT   SOURCE STATEMENT                                          ASM H V 02 12.19 02/02/86

                                     56 *-----------------------------------------------------------------* | 001290
                                     57 *  THIS PROGRAM WILL ADD, DELETE, AND UPDATE RECORDS IN A VSAM     * | 001300
                                     58 *  KSDS.  AN INPUT TRANSACTION FILE CONTAINS THE DATA THAT IS TO BE * | 001310
                                     59 *  USING IN PROCESSING AGAINST THE CLUSTER.                        * | 001320
                                     60 *                                                                  * | 001330
                                     61 *  A PRINTED AUDIT TRAIL IS CREATED TO ASSIST IN DEBUGGING AND IN  * | 001340
                                     62 *  FOLLOWING THE LOGIC OF THE PROGRAM.                             * | 001350
                                     63 *-----------------------------------------------------------------* | 001360
000000                               64 KSDSUPDT CSECT                                                       | 001370
000000 90EC D00C          0000C      65          STM   R14,R12,12(R13)         SAVE CALLER'S REGISTERS       | 001380
000004 18CF                          66          LR    R12,R15                 USE R12 FOR OUR BASE REG      | 001390
                          00000      67          USING KSDSUPDT,R12            TELL THE ASSEMBLER            | 001400
000006 41B0 C998          00998      68          LA    R11,SAVEM               ADDRESS OUR SAVE AREA         | 001410
00000A 50D0 C99C          0099C      69          ST    R13,SAVEM+4             SAVE CURRENT R13 VALUE        | 001420
00000E 50BD 0008          00008      70          ST    R11,8(R13)              INFORM CALLER OF OUR SAVE AREA | 001430
000012 18DB                          71          LR    R13,R11                 ESTABLISH NEW SAVE AREA       | 001440
                                     72 *-----------------------------------------------------------------* | 001450
                                     73 *  OPEN ALL FILES FOR PROCESSING.  CHECK THE STATUS OF THE VSAM    * | 001460
                                     74 *  FILE TO MAKE SURE THAT IT OPENED PROPERLY.  IF IT DID, CONTINUE. * | 001470
                                     75 *  IF IT FAILED TO OPEN, PRINT OUT THE ACB ERROR CODE THEN ABORT.  * | 001480
                                     76 *-----------------------------------------------------------------* | 001490
                                     77          OPEN  (CARDS,INPUT)           OPEN THE TRANSACTION FILE     | 001500
                                     83          OPEN  (AUDIT,OUTPUT)          OPEN AUDIT TRAIL FOR OUTPUT   | 001510
                                     89          OPEN  (VSAM)                  OPEN THE VSAM FILE            | 001520
000036 12FF                          95          LTR   R15,R15                 DID FILE OPEN OK?             | 001530
000038 4780 C0C6          000C6      96          BZ    FILEOK                  IF SO, KEEP GOING             | 001540
                                     97          TRACE 'VSAM FILE FAILED TO OPEN'                            | 001550
                                    104          SHOWCB ACB=VSAM,FIELDS=ERROR,AREA=ACBERR,LENGTH=4           | 001560
                                    122          STATUS ACBERR                                               | 001570
                                    135          ABEND 1                                                     | 001580
0000C6                              139 FILEOK   DS    0H                                                    | 001590
```

After the VSAM file is opened, R15 is tested for zero. If it is 0 then the file opened correctly. If it is not zero then we'll use the TRACE, SHOWCB, and STATUS macros to help diagnose the problem.

```
  LOC  OBJECT CODE     ADDR1 ADDR2  STMT   SOURCE STATEMENT                                              ASM H V 02 12.19 02/02/86

                                     141 *-----------------------------------------------------------------*
                                     142 *   THIS TRANSACTION CENTER WILL PASS CONTROL TO EACH PROCESSING   *
                                     143 *   ROUTINE TO ADD, DELETE, OR UPDATE RECORDS IN THE CLUSTER.      *
                                     144 *-----------------------------------------------------------------*
0000C6                               145 MAINLOOP DS    OH
                                     146          GET   CARDS,TRANS          OBTAIN A RECORD
                                     151          PUT   AUDIT,TRANSLIN       PRINT IMAGE OF TRANSACTION
0000E2 95C1 C889     00889           156          CLI   TRANS,C'A'           ADD TRANSACTION?
0000E6 4780 C0F6           000F6     157          BE    ADDIT                IF SO, GO PROCESS IT
0000EA 95C4 C889     00889           158          CLI   TRANS,C'D'           DELETE TRANSACTION?
0000EE 4780 C22C           0022C     159          BE    DELETE               IF SO, GO TO DELETE CODE
0000F2 47F0 C3C4           003C4     160          B     UPDATE               IT MUST BE UPDATE

                                     162 *-----------------------------------------------------------------*
                                     163 *   THIS SECTION OF CODE IS USED TO ADD A RECORD INTO THE CLUSTER.  *
                                     164 *   THE RECORD IS BUILT AND THEN THE PUT INSTRUCTION IS ISSUED.  R15 *
                                     165 *   AND FEEDBACK CODES ARE CHECKED TO ENSURE A SUCCESSFUL ADD.      *
                                     166 *-----------------------------------------------------------------*
                                     167 *   NOTE THAT A DIFFERENT RPL IS USED WHEN ADDING RECORDS AS COMPARED *
                                     168 *   TO DELETING AND UPDATING RECORDS.  THIS RPL DOES NOT CONTAIN THE  *
                                     169 *   OPTCD VALUE "UPD" THUS ALLOWING RECORDS TO BE ADDED TO THE FILE.  *
                                     170 *-----------------------------------------------------------------*
0000F6                               171 ADDIT    DS    OH
                                     172          TRACE 'TRYING TO ADD A NEW RECORD TO THE DATASET'
000110 D24F C838 C88A 00838 0088A    179          MVC   MASTER(80),TRANS+1          BUILD A MASTER RECORD
                                     180          PUT   RPL=ADDRPL
000128 12FF                          187          LTR   R15,R15                     ADD SUCCESSFUL?
00012A 4780 C20E           0020E     188          BZ    ADDOK                       IF SO, PROCESS NEXT RECORD
                                     189          TESTCB RPL=ADDRPL,FDBK=8          WAS FEEDBACK CODE 8?
000164 4780 C59A           0059A     207          BE    DUPREC                      IF SO, DUPLICATE RECORD
                                     208          TESTCB RPL=ADDRPL,FDBK=28         WAS FEEDBACK CODE 28?
00019C 4780 C5B8           005B8     226          BE    NOSPACE                     IF SO, DATASET IS FULL
                                     227          SHOWCB RPL=ADDRPL,FIELDS=FDBK,LENGTH=4,AREA=RPLFDBK
                                     245          STATUS RPLFDBK
                                     258          ABEND 2                           IF NONE OF ABOVE, ABORT
00020E                               262 ADDOK    DS    OH
                                     263          TRACE 'RECORD ADDED SUCCESSFULLY, CONTINUING EXECUTION'
000228 47F0 C0C6           000C6     270          B     MAINLOOP                    GET NEXT TRANSACTION
```

Two feedback code values are expected by the program. If a feedback code other than 8 or 28 occurs the program will abend after printing audit messages.

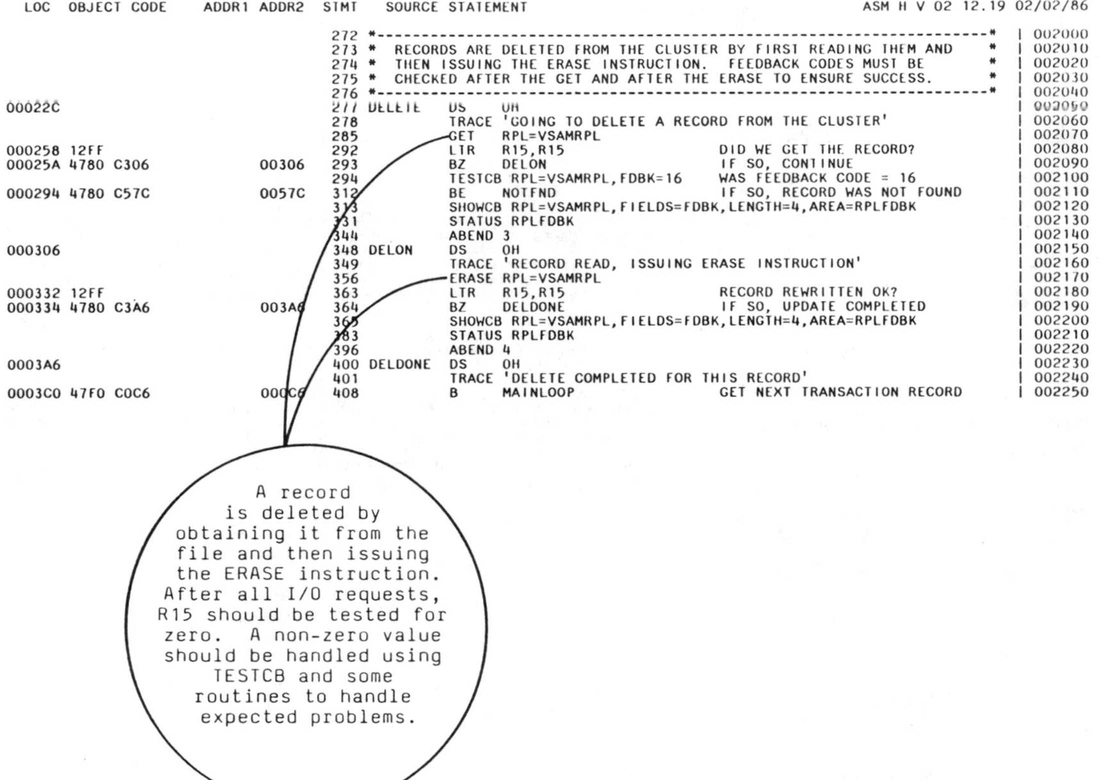

```
  LOC  OBJECT CODE    ADDR1 ADDR2  STMT   SOURCE STATEMENT                                        ASM H V 02 12.19 02/02/86

                                   272 *-----------------------------------------------------------------------*  | 002000
                                   273 *  RECORDS ARE DELETED FROM THE CLUSTER BY FIRST READING THEM AND      *  | 002010
                                   274 *  THEN ISSUING THE ERASE INSTRUCTION.  FEEDBACK CODES MUST BE         *  | 002020
                                   275 *  CHECKED AFTER THE GET AND AFTER THE ERASE TO ENSURE SUCCESS.        *  | 002030
                                   276 *-----------------------------------------------------------------------*  | 002040
00022C                             277 DELETE   DS    0H                                                          | 002050
                                   278          TRACE 'GOING TO DELETE A RECORD FROM THE CLUSTER'                 | 002060
                                   285          GET   RPL=VSAMRPL                                                 | 002070
000258 12FF                        292          LTR   R15,R15                  DID WE GET THE RECORD?             | 002080
00025A 4780 C306          00306    293          BZ    DELON                    IF SO, CONTINUE                    | 002090
                                   294          TESTCB RPL=VSAMRPL,FDBK=16     WAS FEEDBACK CODE = 16             | 002100
000294 4780 C57C          0057C    312          BE    NOTFND                   IF SO, RECORD WAS NOT FOUND        | 002110
                                   313          SHOWCB RPL=VSAMRPL,FIELDS=FDBK,LENGTH=4,AREA=RPLFDBK              | 002120
                                   331          STATUS RPLFDBK                                                    | 002130
                                   344          ABEND 3                                                           | 002140
000306                             348 DELON    DS    0H                                                          | 002150
                                   349          TRACE 'RECORD READ, ISSUING ERASE INSTRUCTION'                    | 002160
                                   356          ERASE RPL=VSAMRPL                                                 | 002170
000332 12FF                        363          LTR   R15,R15                  RECORD REWRITTEN OK?               | 002180
000334 4780 C3A6          003A6    364          BZ    DELDONE                  IF SO, UPDATE COMPLETED            | 002190
                                   365          SHOWCB RPL=VSAMRPL,FIELDS=FDBK,LENGTH=4,AREA=RPLFDBK              | 002200
                                   383          STATUS RPLFDBK                                                    | 002210
                                   396          ABEND 4                                                           | 002220
0003A6                             400 DELDONE  DS    0H                                                          | 002230
                                   401          TRACE 'DELETE COMPLETED FOR THIS RECORD'                          | 002240
0003C0 47F0 C0C6          000C6    408          B     MAINLOOP                 GET NEXT TRANSACTION RECORD        | 002250
```

```
  LOC  OBJECT CODE    ADDR1 ADDR2  STMT   SOURCE STATEMENT                                            ASM H V 02 12.19 02/02/86

                                    410 *-----------------------------------------------------------------*
                                    411 *  RECORDS ARE UPDATED BY FIRST OBTAINING THEM THROUGH A READ.  DATA *
                                    412 *  FROM THE TRANSACTION RECORD IS MOVED INTO THE MASTER RECORD AND   *
                                    413 *  THE MASTER RECORD IS REPLACED INTO THE CLUSTER.                   *
                                    414 *-----------------------------------------------------------------*
0003C4                              415 UPDATE   DS    OH                          IT MUST BE UPDATE
                                    416          TRACE 'PERFORMING AN UPDATE'
                                    423          TRACE 'ABOUT TO READ THE RECORD TO BE UPDATED'
                                    430          GET   RPL=VSAMRPL                 GET RECORD TO BE UPDATED
00040A 12FF                         437          LTR   R15,R15                     DID WE GET THE RECORD?
00040C 4780 C4B6            004B6   438          BZ    UPDON                       IF SO, CONTINUE
                                    439          TESTCB RPL=VSAMRPL,FDBK=16        WAS FEEDBACK CODE = 16
000444 4780 C57C            0057C   457          BE    NOTFND                      IF SO, RECORD WAS NOT FOUND
                                    458          SHOWCB RPL=VSAMRPL,FIELDS=FDBK,LENGTH=4,AREA=RPLFDBK
                                    476          STATUS RPLFDBK
                                    489          ABEND 5
0004B6                              493 UPDON    DS    OH
                                    494          TRACE 'RECORD READ, CONTINUING UPDATE'
0004D0 D231 C842 C894 00842 00894   501          MVC   MDATA1(50),X1               UPDATE MASTER RECORD FIELD
                                    502          PUT   RPL=VSAMRPL                 REWRITE RECORD TO MASTER FILE
0004E8 12FF                         509          LTR   R15,R15                     RECORD REWRITTEN OK?
0004EA 4780 C55E            0055E   510          BZ    UPDDONE                     IF SO, UPDATE COMPLETED
                                    511          SHOWCB RPL=VSAMRPL,FIELDS=FDBK,LENGTH=4,AREA=RPLFDBK
                                    529          STATUS RPLFDBK
                                    542          ABEND 6
00055E                              546 UPDDONE  DS    OH
                                    547          TRACE 'UPDATE COMPLETED FOR THIS RECORD'
000578 47F0 C0C6            000C6   554          B     MAINLOOP                    GET NEXT TRANSACTION RECORD
```

A record may be updated in a KSDS by first reading it, moving in the new field values, and then rewriting it to the cluster. If the record cannot be found in the cluster it cannot be updated or rewritten. It may be added although this program does not perform in this manner.

```
                                                                                                           PAGE    9

  LOC  OBJECT CODE    ADDR1 ADDR2  STMT   SOURCE STATEMENT                                      ASM H V 02 12.19 02/02/86

                                    556 *------------------------------------------------------------------*   | 002560
                                    557 *  THE FOLLOWING ROUTINES ARE USED TO TRAP EXPECTED PROBLEMS DURING  *   | 002570
                                    558 *  PROCESSING.  "RECORD NOT FOUND", "DUPLICATE RECORD KEY", AND      *   | 002580
                                    559 *  "NO SPACE LEFT IN THE DATASET" ARE THE CURRENT PROBLEMS THAT       *   | 002590
                                    560 *------------------------------------------------------------------*   | 002600
                                    561 *  MORE SUCH ROUTINES MAY BE ADDED DEPENDING ON THE NUMBER OF         *   | 002610
                                    562 *  EXCEPTIONAL CONDITIONS THAT MAY OCCURING DURING YOUR PROCESSING.  *   | 002620
                                    563 *------------------------------------------------------------------*   | 002630
                                    564 *  AFTER PRINTING THE AUDIT MESSAGE, CONTROL RETURNS TO THE MAIN      *   | 002640
                                    565 *  PROGRAM LOOP TO PROCESS THE NEXT TRANSACTION RECORD.               *   | 002650
                                    566 *------------------------------------------------------------------*   | 002660
00057C                              567 NOTFND   DS    0H                                                       | 002670
                                    568          TRACE 'RECORD WAS NOT FOUND IN THE DATASET'                    | 002680
000596 47F0 C0C6            000C6   575          B     MAINLOOP                                                 | 002690
00059A                              576 DUPREC   DS    0H                                                       | 002700
                                    577          TRACE 'RECORD ALREADY EXISTS WITH THIS KEY'                    | 002710
0005B4 47F0 C0C6            000C6   584          B     MAINLOOP                                                 | 002720
0005B8                              585 NOSPACE  DS    0H                                                       | 002730
                                    586          TRACE 'DATASET IS FULL, RECORD NOT ADDED'                      | 002740
0005D2 47F0 C0C6            000C6   593          B     MAINLOOP                                                 | 002750
```

These routines are used to handle anticipated errors during VSAM processing. Many more such routines would probably be needed in a full-scale master file update system. Further, the routines might do more than just print out a message as they do now.

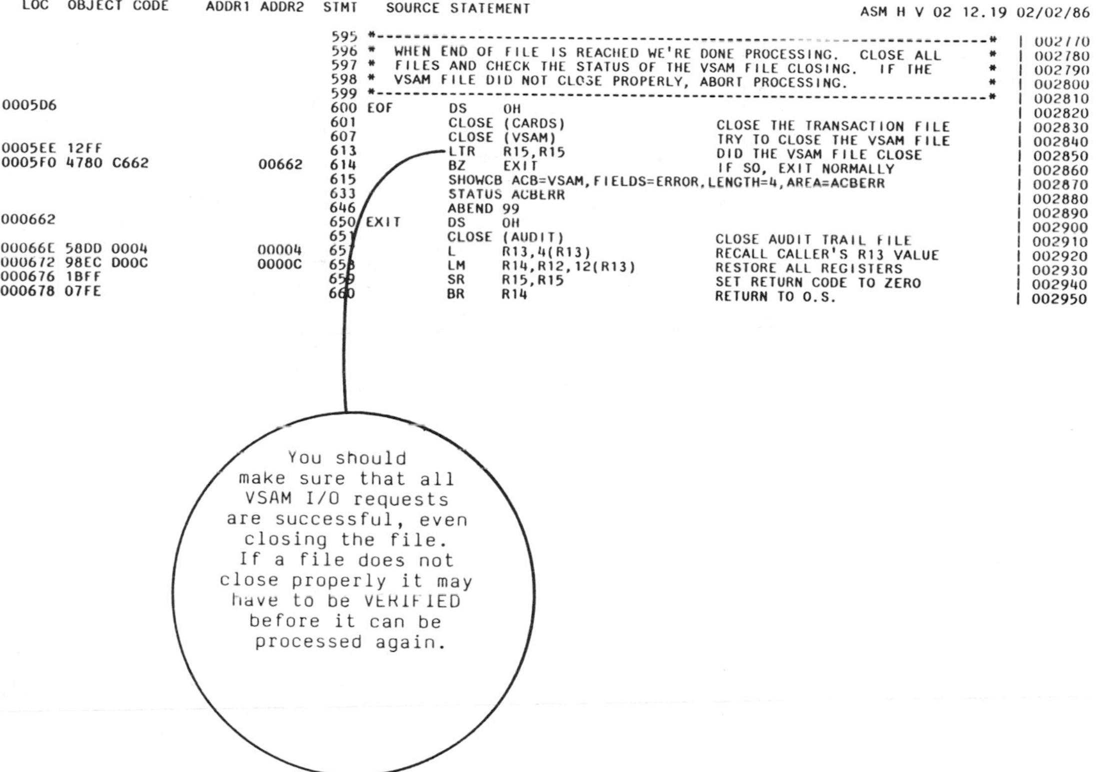

```
                                                                                                        PAGE   10

  LOC  OBJECT CODE    ADDR1 ADDR2  STMT   SOURCE STATEMENT                                  ASM H V 02 12.19 02/02/86

                                   595 *----------------------------------------------------------------*  | 002770
                                   596 *   WHEN END OF FILE IS REACHED WE'RE DONE PROCESSING.  CLOSE ALL  *  | 002780
                                   597 *   FILES AND CHECK THE STATUS OF THE VSAM FILE CLOSING.  IF THE   *  | 002790
                                   598 *   VSAM FILE DID NOT CLOSE PROPERLY, ABORT PROCESSING.            *  | 002800
                                   599 *----------------------------------------------------------------*  | 002810
0005D6                             600 EOF      DS    0H                                                 | 002820
                                   601          CLOSE (CARDS)               CLOSE THE TRANSACTION FILE     | 002830
                                   607          CLOSE (VSAM)                TRY TO CLOSE THE VSAM FILE     | 002840
0005EE 12FF                        613          LTR   R15,R15               DID THE VSAM FILE CLOSE        | 002850
0005F0 4780 C662            00662  614          BZ    EXIT                  IF SO, EXIT NORMALLY           | 002860
                                   615          SHOWCB ACB=VSAM,FIELDS=ERROR,LENGTH=4,AREA=ACBERR          | 002870
                                   633          STATUS ACBERR                                              | 002880
                                   646          ABEND 99                                                   | 002890
000662                             650 EXIT     DS    0H                                                 | 002900
                                   651          CLOSE (AUDIT)               CLOSE AUDIT TRAIL FILE         | 002910
00066E 58DD 0004            00004  657          L     R13,4(R13)            RECALL CALLER'S R13 VALUE      | 002920
000672 98EC D00C            0000C  658          LM    R14,R12,12(R13)       RESTORE ALL REGISTERS          | 002930
000676 1BFF                        659          SR    R15,R15               SET RETURN CODE TO ZERO        | 002940
000678 07FE                        660          BR    R14                   RETURN TO O.S.                 | 002950
```

```
LOC    OBJECT CODE      ADDR1 ADDR2  STMT   SOURCE STATEMENT                                                ASM H V 02 12.19 02/02/86

                                      662 *-------------------------------------------------------------------*  | 002970
                                      663 *   WORK AREAS USED BY THE PROGRAM AND MACROS TO EXTRACT THE ERROR   *  | 002980
                                      664 *   AND FEEDBACK CODE VALUES AND PREPARE THEM FOR PRINTING.          *  | 002990
                                      665 *-------------------------------------------------------------------*  | 003000
00067C                                666 ACBERR   DS    F                          FIELD TO HOLD ACB ERROR CODE      | 003010
000680                                667 RPLFDBK  DS    F                          FIELD TO HOLD RPL FEEDBACK CODE   | 003020
000688                                668 PACKED   DS    D                          WORK AREA FOR STATUS CODE CONV.   | 003030
000690                                669 STATCODE DS    CL4                        DISPLAYABLE STATUS CODE FIELD     | 003040
                                      670 *                                                                           | 003050
                                      671 *-------------------------------------------------------------------*  | 003060
                                      672 *   RPL'S, ACB'S, AND DCB'S USED BY THE PROGRAM.  NOTE THAT TWO      *  | 003070
                                      673 *   RPLS ARE NEEDED, ONE FOR ADD PROCESSING AND THE OTHER FOR        *  | 003080
                                      674 *   UPDATING AND DELETING RECORDS FROM THE CLUSTER.                  *  | 003090
                                      675 *-------------------------------------------------------------------*  | 003100
                                      676 VSAM     ACB   DDNAME=VSAM,AM=VSAM,MACRF=(DIR,IN,OUT)                      | 003110
                                      713 VSAMRPL  RPL   AM=VSAM,ACB=VSAM,AREA=MASTER,AREALEN=80,RECLEN=80,       X| 003120
                                                         OPTCD=(DIR,MVE,KEY,UPD),ARG=TRANSKEY                      | 003130
                                      747 ADDRPL   RPL   AM=VSAM,ACB=VSAM,AREA=MASTER,AREALEN=80,RECLEN=80,       X| 003140
                                                         OPTCD=(DIR,MVE,KEY),ARG=TRANSKEY                          | 003150
                                      781 CARDS    DCB   DSORG=PS,DDNAME=CARDS,MACRF=GM,EODAD=EOF                  | 003160
                                      835 AUDIT    DCB   DSORG=PS,DDNAME=AUDIT,MACRF=PM,RECFM=FA,LRECL=133,       X| 003170
                                                         BLKSIZE=133                                               | 003180
                                      889 *-------------------------------------------------------------------*  | 003190
                                      890 *  A DESCRIPTION OF THE MASTER RECORD FOLLOWS BELOW.                 *  | 003200
                                      891 *-------------------------------------------------------------------*  | 003210
000838                                892 MASTER   DS    0CL80                      MASTER RECORD DESCRIPTION         | 003220
000838                                893 MKEY     DS    CL10                       KEY OF THE MASTER RECORD          | 003230
000842                                894 MDATA1   DS    CL50                       FIRST DATA FIELD                  | 003240
000874                                895 MDATA2   DS    CL20                       SECOND DATA FIELD                 | 003250
                                      896 *                                                                           | 003260
                                      897 *-------------------------------------------------------------------*  | 003270
                                      898 * THIS AREA CONTAINS THE INPUT TRANSACTION RECORDS AND FORMS A       *  | 003280
                                      899 * PRINT LINE USED TO ECHO THE TRANSACTION RECORDS TO THE AUDIT       *  | 003290
                                      900 * TRAIL PRINTOUT.                                                    *  | 003300
                                      901 *-------------------------------------------------------------------*  | 003310
000888 60                             902 TRANSLIN DC    C'-'                       SKIP A FEW LINES BETWEEN EACH     | 003320
000889                                903 TRANS    DS    0CL80                      IMAGE OF TRANSACTION              | 003330
000889                                904          DS    C                          TRANSACTION CODE                  | 003340
00088A                                905 TRANSKEY DS    CL10                       KEY OF THE TRANSACTION RECORD     | 003350
000894                                906 X1       DS    CL50                       TRANSACTION DATA FIELD            | 003360
0008C6                                907 REST     DS    CL19                       SECOND FIELD IN TRANSACT          | 003370
0008D9 4040404040404040               908          DC    CL55' '                    END OF AUDIT TRAIL PRINT LINE     | 003380
                                      909 *                                                                           | 003390
                                      910 *-------------------------------------------------------------------*  | 003400
                                      911 *    THE FOLLOWING STORAGE AREAS ARE USED IN FORMING THE MESSAGES    *  | 003410
                                      912 *    THAT WILL BE PRINTED ON THE AUDIT TRAIL REPORT WHILE PROCESSING. * | 003420
                                      913 *-------------------------------------------------------------------*  | 003430
000910 40                             914 AUDITLIN DC    C' '                       AUDIT PRINT LINE                  | 003440
000911                                915 AUDITKEY DS    CL10                       KEY OF THE RECORD PROCESSED       | 003450
00091B 4040404040                     916          DC    CL5' '                     FILLER AREA                       | 003460
000920                                917 AUDITMSG DS    CL50                       MESSAGE TO BE PRINTED             | 003470
000952 4040404040404040               918          DC    CL70' '                    FILLER                            | 003480
```

Two RPL's and one ACB are used to process the KSDS. The RPL called ADDRPL is used when records are to be added into the KSDS. The RPL called VSAMRPL is used for update and delete requests.


```
LOC    OBJECT CODE      ADDR1 ADDR2  STMT   SOURCE STATEMENT                                                ASM H V 02 12.19 02/02/86

                                      920 *-------------------------------------------------------------------*  | 003500
                                      921 *   FINALLY, THE REGISTER SAVE AREA AND THE LITERALS FOR THE PROGRAM *  | 003510
                                      922 *   ARE GENERATED BELOW.                                             *  | 003520
                                      923 *-------------------------------------------------------------------*  | 003530
000998                                924 SAVEM    DS    18F                        REGISTER SAVE AREA FOR PROGRAM    | 003540
0009E0                                925          LTORG                                                          | 003550
0009E0 40202120                       926                =X'40202120'
0009E4 7DE5E2C1D440C6C9               927                =CL50'''VSAM FILE FAILED TO OPEN'''
000A16 40404040407E40E2               928                =C'     = STATUS CODE OBAINED'
000A30 7DE3D9E8C9D5C740               929                =CL50'''TRYING TO ADD A NEW RECORD TO THE DATASET'''
000A62 7DD9C5C3D6D9C440               930                =CL50'''RECORD ADDED SUCCESSFULLY, CONTINUING EXECUTION'
000A6A C1C4C4C5C440E2E4                                  ''
000A94 7DC7D6C9D5C740E3               931                =CL50'''GOING TO DELETE A RECORD FROM THE CLUSTER'''
000AC6 7DD9C5C3D6D9C440               932                =CL50'''RECORD READ, ISSUING ERASE INSTRUCTION'''
000AF8 7DC4C5D3C5E3C540               933                =CL50'''DELETE COMPLETED FOR THIS RECORD'''
000B2A 7DD7C5D9C6D6D9D4               934                =CL50'''PERFORMING AN UPDATE'''
000B5C 7DC1C2D6E4E340E3               935                =CL50'''ABOUT TO READ THE RECORD TO BE UPDATED'''
000B8E 7DD9C5C3D6D9C440               936                =CL50'''RECORD READ, CONTINUING UPDATE'''
000BC0 7DE4D7C4C1E3C540               937                =CL50'''UPDATE COMPLETED FOR THIS RECORD'''
000BF2 7DD9C5C3D6D9C440               938                =CL50'''RECORD WAS NOT FOUND IN THE DATASET'''
000C24 7DD9C5C3D6D9C440               939                =CL50'''RECORD ALREADY EXISTS WITH THIS KEY'''
000C56 7DC4C1E3C1E2C5E3               940                =CL50'''DATASET IS FULL, RECORD NOT ADDED'''
000000                                941          END   KSDSUPDT                                               | 003560
```

```
AEEEEEEEEEE                                                       | 003640
EEEEEEEEEE      'TRYING TO ADD A NEW RECORD TO THE DATASET'
EEEEEEEEEE      'RECORD ADDED SUCCESSFULLY, CONTINUING EXECUTION'

CBBBBBBBBBBTHIS IS A NEW VALUE                                    | 003650
BBBBBBBBBB      'PERFORMING AN UPDATE'
BBBBBBBBBB      'ABOUT TO READ THE RECORD TO BE UPDATED'
BBBBBBBBBB      'RECORD READ, CONTINUING UPDATE'
BBBBBBBBBB      'UPDATE COMPLETED FOR THIS RECORD'

CDDDDDDDDDDRECORD 4 HAS BEEN UPDATED                              | 003660
DDDDDDDDDD      'PERFORMING AN UPDATE'
DDDDDDDDDD      'ABOUT TO READ THE RECORD TO BE UPDATED'
DDDDDDDDDD      'RECORD READ, CONTINUING UPDATE'
DDDDDDDDDD      'UPDATE COMPLETED FOR THIS RECORD'

AEEEEEEEEEETHIS TRANSACTION RECORD SHOULD CAUSE A PROBLEM         | 003670
EEEEEEEEEE      'TRYING TO ADD A NEW RECORD TO THE DATASET'
EEEEEEEEEE      'RECORD ALREADY EXISTS WITH THIS KEY'

DCCCCCCCCCC                                                       | 003680
CCCCCCCCCC      'GOING TO DELETE A RECORD FROM THE CLUSTER'
CCCCCCCCCC      'RECORD READ, ISSUING ERASE INSTRUCTION'
CCCCCCCCCC      'DELETE COMPLETED FOR THIS RECORD'
```

This audit report clearly explains how each transaction is processed. As you can see, one transaction is rejected during processing. The transaction is an ADD but there's already a record in the file with a key of EEEEEEEEEE. The program uses the feedback codes to analyze processing situations such as this.

```
ACBOUT   ACB   AM=VSAM,DDNAME=CLUSTER,MACRF=(SEQ,OUT)
```

Figure 15.56 An ACB to support sequential output processing.

The equivalent ACB can be generated with the GENCB instruction as shown in Fig. 15.57.

```
GENCB   BLK=ACB,AM=VSAM,DDNAME=CLUSTER,          X
        MACRF=(SEQ,OUT)
LR      R3,R1
```

Figure 15.57 Generating the ACB of Fig. 15.56 using GENCB.

This instruction indicates that an ACB is to be constructed (BLK=ACB). The associated DDNAME is called CLUSTER and the ACB is defined for sequential output processing. After the GENCB instruction is performed, register 1 contains the address of the generated ACB. Hence, *you must* save the address of the generated ACB in a register or in a fullword storage area within your program. In this example, R3 holds the address of the generated ACB.

The GENCB instruction is also used to generate an RPL. The associated RPL to perform sequential output processing against a KSDS is generated as shown in Fig. 15.58.

```
GENCB     BLK=RPL,AM=VSAM,AREA=STUFF,                 X
          AREALEN=80,OPTCD=(SEQ,FWD,MVE,KEY),         X
          ARG=RECKEY,ACB=(3)
LR        R4,R1
```

Figure 15.58 Generating an RPL to support sequential output processing for a KSDS.

The RPL is associated with the ACB constructed in Fig. 15.57 since the GENCB instruction uses the operand ACB for the association. If you compare the GENCB operands with those on our RPL's coded earlier, there's very little difference. On the other hand, we must now use registers when referring to either the ACB or RPL during I/O processing.

Since the RPL and ACB cannot be referenced with labels unless we build a DSECT for each I/O control block, we must change the manner in which we code our VSAM I/O macro instructions to refer to these control blocks. Assuming that R3 contains the address of our ACB and R4 contains the address of our RPL, the instructions given in Fig. 15.59 perform the desired processing.

```
OPEN    ((R3))        open the ACB before beginning
                      processing

CLOSE   ((R3))        close the ACB after processing

GET     RPL=(R4)      using the RPL pointed to by R4,
                      read a record from the file

PUT     RPL=(R4)      write a record to the cluster
                      using the RPL address in R4

ERASE   RPL=(R4)      delete a record from a file
```

Figure 15.59 I/O instruction coding when using generated control blocks.

There is no difference in the outcome of processing when using the generated form of the ACB and RPL as compared to the format used earlier. However, you may find yourself running a little short of registers since they must be used to refer to these control blocks. Don't forget to check the status of your I/O operations as you have done earlier.

The SHOWCB instruction to extract the feedback code field from the RPL is now coded as shown in Fig. 15.60 since R4 addresses the RPL.

```
SHOWCB   RPL=(R4),FIELDS=FDBK,AREA=FEEDBACK,LENGTH=4
```

Figure 15.60 Extracting the feedback code from a generated RPL.

The error code field in the ACB can be tested using the TESTCB instruction shown in Fig. 15.61.

```
TESTCB     ACB=(R3),ERROR=4
BE         EOF
```

Figure 15.61 Testing for an ACB error code of 4 when using generated control blocks.

VARIABLE-LENGTH RECORD PROCESSING

Throughout our discussion, we've handled only fixed-length records in our VSAM clusters. Using entry and key sequenced datasets (RRDS datasets do not allow variable-length records), we are able to store and process records having varying lengths. To perform such processing, we use the **MODCB (modify control block)** and the SHOWCB instructions. These macro instructions generate the necessary code to obtain the length of the record to be processed (SHOWCB) or communicate to VSAM the length of a record to be stored into a cluster (MODCB).

Records in an ESDS or KSDS are stored along with their lengths. In contrast to variable-length record processing discussed in Chapters 13 and 14, the programmer does not manage records using the record or block descriptor words, RDW and BDW respectively. When obtaining records from a VSAM file, we can obtain the length of the record being processed by obtaining this value from within the RPL. In other words, the length of a record retrieved from a VSAM file through a GET instruction is made available to the program in the RPL. Using the SHOWCB instruction, we can extract the record's length from the RPL so that we may use this length in our processing. The example in Fig. 15.62 uses the SHOWCB instruction to obtain the feedback code value *and* the record length from the RPL. Once the values are extracted from the RPL and are placed into the fields called LRECL and FEEDBACK, respectively, we can use them within our program as desired.

```
         SHOWCB  RPL=rpl,FIELDS=(FDBK,RECLEN),AREA=INFO,        X
                 LENGTH=8



INFO     DS      0F
FEEDBACK DS      F
LRECL    DS      F
```

Figure 15.62 Extracting an input record's length from the RPL.

When writing records into a cluster, we must inform VSAM of the length of the record to be written. Hence, before issuing the PUT instruction to write the record into the cluster, we must first place the length of the record to be added *into the RPL.* VSAM then uses the record length value when storing the record into the cluster so that the full amount of data associated with the record is stored. To place the record length value into the RPL, use the MODCB macro instruction. In the example contained in Fig. 15.63, register 5 contains the length of the record to be written and register 4 contains the address of the RPL. The record length is placed into the RPL and then the record is written using the PUT instruction.

```
MODCB    RPL=(R4),RECLEN=(R5)
PUT      RPL=(R4)
```

Figure 15.63 Writing a variable-length record.

As long as the length of the record to be written does not exceed the maximum length record defined for the dataset, VSAM allows the request to occur. Again, your program should test the success of the I/O request by checking R15 and the feedback field after the PUT instruction is executed.

OVERVIEW OF VSAM ALTERNATE INDEXES

An **alternate index** provides a method to access data records in a VSAM cluster without knowing the *primary key* of the records. In all the previous examples concerning records with keys, each record in the file had a unique key and access to a record could only occur if our program knew the key of the record to be accessed. With an alternate index, we can access data by knowing some other value within the records. This also allows access to a particular *set* of records within the cluster (not necessarily all the records). Knowing this secondary value, we can access records in the master file as if we had known each primary record key.

VSAM is the only access method that provides alternate index processing automatically. Through various VSAM macro instructions, we can access data through either the primary key or through alternate keys (also called **secondary keys**) defined against the same set of data records.

To understand this processing, let's look at an example. Suppose that we have a VSAM KSDS containing student records identified by a nine-digit social security number. Assuming that the social security number is the primary key into the student data, we may also want to access data by the student's year in school, if an alternate index has been constructed over the data records for the year in school field. That is, if we assume that each student record contains a one-byte code of 1, 2, 3, or 4 to mean freshman, sophomore, junior, or senior, we can access all juniors in the university if an alternate index has been constructed on the class code field.

Structurally, an alternate index is a VSAM KSDS related to another VSAM dataset. The relationship between the two datasets is in the data that is accessed, in this case, the student records. Hence, one dataset is called the **base cluster,** which is accessed by the primary key (social security number), and the other is called the **alternate index cluster,** which is accessed through a secondary key (class code). Both access the *same* records but through a different record key value. In one case, we can access records only if we know the social security number of each student. In the other case, the class code field accesses many student records, all within the same academic class. In fact, other alternate keys could be defined to access the student master records in other ways as well. For example, we may want to access the records by name, city, or the zip code. Although VSAM allows us to define many fields as alternate keys, we must understand that each alternate key adds additional overhead to our processing. The more alternate keys, the more overhead. In general, fields are candidates for alternate keys if justification can be given for accessing records in that manner. An occasional access through a particular field does not justify alternate indexing.

To understand how alternate indexes are processed, we must first understand how they are developed. To begin, let's assume that we already have a VSAM dataset with data records. These records not only contain a primary key, but they also contain one or more fields that are to be used in accessing the records in another manner. Hence, we identify the fields to be used as secondary keys to the data records and construct a separate alternate index for each secondary key field.

An alternate index is constructed using IDCAMS commands. The first step in defining an alternate index is to define a new key sequenced dataset (KSDS) using the DEFINE AIX instruction as discussed earlier. Once defined, this KSDS is loaded with relationship records that allow us to access the master records. This is done through the use of the BLDINDEX command. For example, suppose that the following student records are contained in the master file.

Social Security Number	Academic Class
111-11-1111	1
222-22-2222	2
333-33-3333	1
444-44-4444	1

The four students belong to only two different academic classes. Clearly, there is not a unique one-to-one relationship between students and their class code value. As you can see, three students are within the freshman class, thus causing our alternate index key value (the class code) to be *nonunique*. Incidentally, if your secondary key is unique, processing an alternate index is easier than for the case where many base cluster records are associated with a single alternate key value.

Using IDCAMS, the alternate index is filled or loaded with records based on the cluster above. Specifically, the alternate index appears as follows:

Secondary Key Value	Base Cluster Record Associations
1	111-11-1111 333-33-3333 444-44-4444
2	222-22-2222

There are only two records in the alternate index dataset. The keys of these records are the class code values of 1 and 2. Further, these records express a relationship between the class code value and the primary keys of the base cluster. Specifically, the alternate index record, whose key is 1, indicates that there are three base cluster records having this alternate index key value. The base cluster record keys are those having social security numbers 111-11-1111, 333-33-3333, and 444-44-4444.

Suppose that a new freshman student enters the university and has a social security number of 123-45-6789. This student's record undoubtedly becomes a record in the student master file, thus causing an immediate update to the alternate index. After adding this student to the student master file, the alternate index dataset reflects this new freshman by including this student's social security number in the freshman class alternate index record. This is illustrated in the revised record structure as follows:

Secondary Key Value	Base Cluster Record Associations
1	111-11-1111 333-33-3333 444-44-4444 **123-45-6789**
2	222-22-2222

Notice that the new student's record was not added in order within the list of social security numbers. It's simply added to the end of the alternate index record. Ordering is not maintained within the alternate index records. Hence, alternate index processing cannot necessarily supply data to your program ordered by the primary key of the master records. A sort against the base cluster should be performed if ordering is required for your processing. Therefore, when processing through the "path" for this alternate index, our program processes student master records in the order 111-11-1111, 333-33-3333, 444-44-4444, and 123-45-6789.

Through the standard I/O instructions that we've been using, we can access all base cluster records that have an academic class code of 1. Note: we do not process the alternate index records, but we actually obtain and process the records in the base cluster, the student master records themselves. The alternate index is simply a "path" into the base cluster data.

The term "path" is very important to our discussion. An alternate index is a cluster that is related to another existing VSAM cluster. The relationship between the two datasets is defined through an entity called a **path**. This relationship allows a change made to the base cluster to be reflected in the alternate index. In other words, if a student moves from the freshman level to the sophomore level, the alternate index reflects this change by moving the student's social security number from record 1 in the alternate index to the record whose key is 2. The maintenance and interrelationship between the base cluster and alternate index is maintained by VSAM. In fact, we don't have to understand the internal structure of either the base cluster or the alternate index to process either of these VSAM datasets.

PROCESSING AN ALTERNATE INDEX SEQUENTIALLY

An alternate index allows you to process sequentially through base cluster records in an order based on the value of the alternate index key. For example, all junior records can be processed by simply asking VSAM for all records having an alternate index value of 3. If desired, all base cluster records can be processed by going through the complete alternate index. This provides all freshman students, then all sophomores, and so on until all students are processed. Although this processing is possible, it is not an efficient technique. If you simply want to use the alternate index as a method of ordering the base cluster records, sort your base cluster records on the secondary key field and then process in a sequential manner. This eliminates the need for an alternate index, greatly simplifies your work, and saves an enormous amount of processing time and disk space.

In any case, all records in a base cluster can be processed in alternate index order using the skeleton program contained in Fig. 15.64. Note that the only change in this program and the previous one that performed similar processing is the RPL and the JCL statements that now identify the path to be processed.

As you can see, the RPL operand OPTCD has an element highlighted in boldface. This element, **NSP (note sequential positioning),** helps VSAM remember the last record processed through the alternate index. This parameter and the fact that we are processing through the path differentiate alternate index from base cluster sequential processing.

Suppose that we want to process only junior records. This requires that we first go into the alternate index at the juniors' list and then process sequentially from that point until the end of file is reached or until we exhaust all junior records (we encounter a student that is not a junior). To perform this, we process directly and then sequentially. Since the RPL specifies direct processing, we first go into the alternate index and then use the MODCB instruction to change our processing from direct to sequential. This processing situation is illustrated in Fig. 15.65.

The program places a value of three into the alternate index key field and then reads the first record. This action causes VSAM to position itself within the alternate index and so we must now switch from random to sequential processing. For each record to be processed, we must look at the academic class value within it to make sure that we're still within the same class. If we don't and if there are senior student records in the base cluster, VSAM returns a senior's record to our program *before* the end of file is

```
//       EXEC      ASMFCG
//ASM.SYSIN      DD      *
               OPEN       (PATH)             OPEN THE PATH


               GET        RPL=VSAMPATH       OBTAIN THE FIRST RECORD
MAINLOOP       DS         0H

               print the record as desired

               GET        RPL=VSAMPATH       OBTAIN THE NEXT RECORD
               B          MAINLOOP

EOF            DS         0H
               CLOSE      (PATH)             CLOSE THE PATH, ALL DONE


PATH           ACB        DDNAME=PATH,AM=VSAM,MACRF=(KEY,SEQ,IN),       X
                          EXLST=EXITLIST
VSAMPATH       RPL        AM=VSAM,ACB=PATH,AREA=CARDIN,AREALEN=80,      X
                          ARG=CLASS,OPTCD=(KEY,SEQ,MVE,NSP)
EXITLIST       EXLST      AM=VSAM,EODAD=(EOF,A)

CARDIN         DS         0CL80              MASTER RECORD DEFINITION
SSN            DS         CL9                SOCIAL SECURITY NUMBER
CLASS          DS         C                  ACADEMIC CLASS VALUE
REST           DS         CL70               REST OF THE RECORD


//GO.PATH      DD         DSN=pathname,DISP=SHR
```

Figure 15.64 Processing sequentially through an alternate index.

reached. By looking at the academic class code field each time a record is obtained, we ensure that only junior records are processed.

This example allows us to discuss other capabilities of alternate index processing. In particular, it is possible to "skip around" within the alternate index. In other words, we could design our program to go to the freshmen students and process all of them. It can then go to the seniors and process them. This requires the execution of the MODCB instruction to change processing formats from DIR to SEQ or vice versa, depending on our needs. However, the ACB and RPL formats above support either or both processing situations.

UPDATING BASE CLUSTER RECORDS THROUGH THE ALTERNATE INDEX

Records in the base cluster can be updated by processing through the alternate index. For example, suppose that the class code for all freshmen is to be changed from "1" to "F." This requires each freshman's record to be changed so that the academic class code now contains a value of "F." By knowing the social security number of each freshman, we can write a program that reads each record given the social security number, updates the class code field, and then rewrites the record to the cluster. In a large school, the social security numbers of all freshmen is difficult and time consuming to enter. Hence, an alternate index can provide this relationship and allow the update of each freshman record as desired. Here's how this is done.

Using the path, we position ourselves into the base cluster based on the current class code of 1. Using sequential processing on the alternate index, we obtain each freshman record from the base cluster, update this record to the new academic code F, and

```
//       EXEC      ASMFCG
//ASM.SYSIN        DD       *
               OPEN      (PATH)              OPEN THE PATH

               MVI       AIXKEY,C'3'         SPECIFY JUNIORS ONLY
               GET       RPL=VSAMPATH        OBTAIN THE FIRST RECORD
               MODCB     RPL=VSAMPATH,OPTCD=(SEQ)
MAINLOOP       DS        0H
               CLC       CLASS(1),AIXKEY         VALID STUDENT?
               BNE       EOF                     IF NOT, WE'RE DONE

               print the record as desired

               GET       RPL=VSAMPATH        OBTAIN THE NEXT RECORD
               B         MAINLOOP

EOF            DS        0H
               CLOSE     (PATH)              CLOSE THE PATH, ALL DONE


PATH           ACB       DDNAME=PATH,AM=VSAM,MACRF=(KEY,DIR,IN),      X
                         EXLST=EXITLIST
VSAMPATH       RPL       AM=VSAM,ACB=PATH,AREA=CARDIN,AREALEN=80,     X
                         ARG=AIXKEY,OPTCD=(KEY,DIR,MVE,NSP)
EXITLIST       EXLST     AM=VSAM,EODAD=(EOF,A)

AIXKEY         DS        C

CARDIN         DS        0CL80               MASTER RECORD DEFINITION
SSN            DS        CL9                 SOCIAL SECURITY NUMBER
CLASS          DS        C                   ACADEMIC CLASS VALUE
REST           DS        CL70                REST OF THE RECORD


//GO.PATH      DD        DSN=pathname,DISP=SHR
```

Figure 15.65 Processing a limited set of records based on the alternate index key.

rewrite the record to the base cluster. After all freshmen records are processed, we have completed our task.

Since the path and the base cluster are to be processed, two ACB's are required. One ACB accesses the base cluster and the other references the path as illustrated earlier. Two RPL's are also required, one for the path and one for the base cluster. The skeleton program in Fig. 15.66 illustrates this processing.

Carefully review this example. The status checking to allow you to concentrate on the logic is omitted. As you can see, the alternate index is positioned into the freshman class (class code = 1). The first record is obtained and then alternate index processing is changed to sequential.

Each freshman record is read from the base cluster, updated, and replaced into the base cluster. This automatically causes a corresponding update to the alternate index dataset. The next freshman record identified through the alternate index is obtained and processing continues until the end of file is reached or until a nonfreshman record is encountered. At the end of all processing, all records that previously contained a class code of 1 now contain a class code of F. The alternate index contains a record whose key is F but does not contain a record whose key is 1. When an alternate index loses all of its associations to base cluster records, VSAM deletes the alternate index record from the AIX dataset.

Looking carefully at this code again, you'll see that it's very similar to the random processing example that was given earlier in the chapter. In fact, this code incorporates

```
//       EXEC      ASMFCG
//ASM.SYSIN        DD      *
             OPEN      (MSTR)             OPEN BASE CLUSTER
             OPEN      (PATH)             OPEN THE PATH

             MVI       AIXKEY,C'1'        SPECIFY FRESHMAN ONLY
             GET       RPL=VSAMPATH       OBTAIN THE FIRST RECORD
             MODCB     RPL=VSAMPATH,OPTCD=(SEQ)
MAINLOOP     DS        0H
             CLC       CLASS(1),AIXKEY        VALID STUDENT?
             BNE       EOF                    IF NOT, WE'RE DONE

             GET       RPL=MSTRRPL        READ RECORD FOR UPDATE
             MVI       CLASS,C'F'         CHANGE THE CLASS
             PUT       RPL=MSTRRPL        REWRITE THE RECORD
             GET       RPL=VSAMPATH       OBTAIN THE NEXT RECORD
             B         MAINLOOP

EOF          DS        0H
             CLOSE     (PATH)             CLOSE THE PATH, ALL DONE
             CLOSE     (MSTR)             CLOSE BASE CLUSTER

PATH         ACB       DDNAME=PATH,AM=VSAM,MACRF=(KEY,DIR,IN),       X
                       EXLST=EXITLIST
VSAMPATH     RPL       AM=VSAM,ACB=PATH,AREA=CARDIN,AREALEN=80,      X
                       ARG=AIXKEY,OPTCD=(KEY,DIR,MVE,NSP)

MSTR         ACB       DDNAME=MSTR,AM=VSAM,MACRF=(DIR,IN,OUT)
MSTRPATH     RPL       AM=VSAM,ACB=MSTR,AREA=CARDIN,AREALEN=80,      X
                       ARG=SSN,OPTCD=(KEY,DIR,MVE,UPD)
EXITLIST     EXLST     AM=VSAM,EODAD=(EOF,A)

AIXKEY       DS        C

CARDIN       DS        0CL80              MASTER RECORD DEFINITION
SSN          DS        CL9                SOCIAL SECURITY NUMBER
CLASS        DS        C                  ACADEMIC CLASS VALUE
REST         DS        CL70               REST OF THE RECORD


//GO.PATH    DD        DSN=pathname,DISP=SHR
//GO.MSTR    DD        DSN=baseclustername,DISP=SHR
```

Figure 15.66 Updating base cluster records via the alternate index.

the previous example, thus allowing it to be used to add, delete, or update base cluster records directly, as well as process through the alternate index. Using a transaction file containing base cluster and alternate index processing requests, this program example can become very powerful by allowing all processing situations against each dataset type.

REENTRANT VSAM CODING

To maintain program reentrancy, each I/O macro supporting VSAM processing can be coded in a reentrant format. Using the generate form of each I/O macro and control block, generated code is constructed to support reentrant programming. Specifically, the control blocks of concern are ACB and RPL. Further, the I/O macros, such as GENCB, MODCB, SHOWCB, and TESTCB, that generate or test the status of these control blocks must also be modified to support reentrancy.

To generate reentrant VSAM control blocks, each control block is generated in an external storage area using the GENCB macro instruction. Clearly, all control blocks must reside *outside* the bounds of your program. Although addressability can be obtained through DSECT labels, it is more likely that addressing the various control blocks will be done through register addresses. Hence, if we again assume that R3 addresses our ACB after it is generated and R4 addresses our RPL, we can generate an ACB using a reentrant form of the GENCB instruction as shown in Fig. 15.67.

```
GENCB    BLK=ACB,AM=VSAM,DDNAME=MASTER,MACRF=(....),        X
         MF=(G,(3))
```

Figure 15.67 Generating an ACB that may be used in a reentrant program.

If a DSECT exists to generate the ACB in a getmained area, the GENCB instruction given in Fig. 15.68 can be used. Note that the DSECT label area is called GENEDACB.

```
GENCB    BLK=ACB,AM=VSAM,DDNAME=MASTER,MACRF=(....),        X
         MF=(G,GENEDACB)
```

Figure 15.68 Generating a reentrant ACB that is referenced using a DSECT.

The format of the GENCB instruction should be familiar since it is identical to a previous example except for the MF operand. The MF operand indicates that reentrant coding is used for this control block generation and that register 3 (or a DSECT label) contains the address where the ACB is to be generated.

An RPL can be generated in a similar manner as illustrated in Fig. 15.69. Again, DSECT labeling can be used in the generation process.

```
GENCB    BLK=RPL,AM=VSAM,AREALEN=80,OPTCD=(....),        X
         ACB=(R3),MF=(G,(R4))
```

Figure 15.69 Generating a reentrant RPL.

This control block generation is slightly different than earlier examples since the address of the area into which data records are to be processed has not been specified. Therefore, we must supply this address to the control block through the MODCB instruction, which incidentally, must also be generated using an external storage address. Assuming that R5 contains an area for generation of the MODCB control block, the record area address is supplied to the generated RPL by coding the MODCB instruction contained in Fig. 15.70.

```
LA       R7,CARDAREA
MODCB    RPL=(R4),AREA=(R7),MF=(G,(R5))
```

Figure 15.70 Placing the record area address into a reentrant RPL.

Prior to executing the instruction, R7 is assigned the address of the area where the records are to be processed. R5 is assumed to contain the address of a work area for the MODCB instruction. With the RPL addressed by register 4, reentrant code is generated such that the record processing area (called CARDAREA) is placed into the externally generated RPL. Thus, reentrancy is preserved within our program.

If we are processing a keyed file, the record key address is supplied to the RPL in a similar manner. The code in Fig. 15.71 supplies both the record key address and the record area address to the associated reentrant RPL.

```
LA      R6,RECKEY                ADDRESS RECORD KEY AREA
LA      R7,MASTER                POINT TO RECORD AREA
MODCB   RPL=(R4),AREA=(R7),ARG=(R6),MF=(G,(R5))
```

Figure 15.71 Modifying the RPL to support random keyed processing.

All modifications to any control block are handled through the reentrant form of the MODCB control block. You must also remember to supply a work area for this control block (again addressed by R5). The example in Fig. 15.72 issues a SHOWCB instruction against the same RPL to extract the feedback code. Note that the feedback code target field address is supplied to the SHOWCB instruction through a register parameter.

```
LM        R5,R6,=A(WORKCB,FEEDBACK)
SHOWCB    RPL=(R4),LENGTH=4,AREA=(R6),FIELDS=FDBK,       X
          MF=(G,(R5))
```

Figure 15.72 Extracting the feedback code from the RPL when using reentrant programming techniques.

The feedback code is extracted and placed into the field called FEEDBACK. The SHOWCB argument called AREA references R6, which addresses the FEEDBACK field. The SHOWCB instruction is provided a control block work area through register 5. This area, called WORKCB, can be used by many of the instructions generating reentrant code if it is sufficiently large. The next example, shown in Fig. 15.73, uses the same area for testing the feedback code in the RPL using the TESTCB instruction.

```
LA       R5,WORKCB            POINT TO CONTROL BLOCK WORK AREA
TESTCB   RPL=(R4),FDBK=4,MF=(G,(R5))
BE       ENDFILE              IF FDBK=4, THEN END OF FILE
```

Figure 15.73 Using TESTCB in a reentrant VSAM program.

The GETMAIN instruction can also provide a work area for control block generation. Using the third parameter of the MF operand, an equate symbol is generated that contains the length of storage required to hold the desired control block. The symbol can then be used to specify the length of storage to be requested by the GETMAIN macro instruction. For example, the MODCB instruction in Fig. 15.74 alters the processing options for the RPL contained in R4. Register 5 contains the address of an area to support the MODCB instruction after storage is acquired through the GETMAIN instruction.

```
LA         R5,MODCBLEN       GET LENGTH OF MODCB AREA NEEDED
GETMAIN    R,LV=(5)          ASK FOR STORAGE
LR         R5,R1             GET LOCATION FROM O.S.
MODCB      RPL=(R4),OPTCD=(SEQ),MF=(G,(R5),MODCBLEN)
```

Figure 15.74 Obtaining VSAM control block work areas using the GETMAIN macro instruction.

The label MODCBLEN is generated as an EQU symbol by the MODCB instruction. This symbol equals the length of the storage area required by the MODCB instruction. The LA and GETMAIN instructions acquire the appropriate amount of storage for the MODCB instruction, thus allowing the MODCB instruction to execute as desired. However, this instruction uses its own control block storage area and, further, this technique is slightly less efficient due to the overhead associated with the GETMAIN instruction.

STUDY QUESTIONS

1. During random processing against a KSDS, your program receives a return code of 8 in R15 and a feedback code of 16. What may cause this situation?
2. What can happen if you try to define an alternate index using an empty base cluster dataset?
3. STUDENT.MASTER is the name of a VSAM RRDS that can be accessed by student social security numbers. How can we determine the number of records currently stored in this dataset?
4. How do nonunique alternate index keys impact processing as compared to unique alternate index keys?
5. What control blocks are most important to the definition and processing of a VSAM cluster?
6. While processing a VSAM cluster, your program fails with a data exception abend. What should you do before attempting to process this cluster again?
7. List each type of VSAM dataset and identify the various components that make up each type.
8. What instructions are used to determine if a VSAM I/O request was successful or not?
9. What registers indicate the success or failure of an I/O operation?
10. What is the name of the IBM utility used to define, delete, or perform other operations against VSAM datasets?
11. Your state government maintains data on each automobile licensed in the state. Considering the information collected by the state, what fields in this information can be used to uniquely identify your car?
12. In the latest releases of VSAM, the VERIFY instruction is not needed. Why?
13. What DDNAMEs are normally required when running the IDCAMS utility?
14. When implementing reentrant VSAM programs, what type of data structure becomes very important in addressing the various VSAM control blocks?
15. Locate mode processing may be accomplished by coding the value LOC. On what operand is this value coded?

PROGRAMMING PROBLEMS

1. Rewrite any of the programming problems from Chapter 14 using VSAM file processing techniques. In fact, return to any of the previous chapters so that you can use ESDS processing to support any sequential processing applications discussed earlier.

2. Consider student data consisting of the student's name, social security number, and 10 semester scores. Write a master-file update program that maintains the student file. Records may be added, deleted, or updated in the master file. Assume that the social security number is the key to each student's record.
3. Modify Programming Problem 2 so that an alternate index can access the student's data based on the name of the student. Assume that each student's name is unique for this problem.
4. Modify Programming Problems 2 and 3 to now support duplicate student names. Also allow the student records to be updated through the alternate index.
5. Write a single job step that creates, LISTCATs and deletes a VSAM KSDS using only IDCAMS. Run this job many times, but each time allocate the dataset in a different manner. Do not change the record size for each run. After several iterations of this process, analyze your results. In particular, notice how VSAM selects a control interval and control area size based on the allocation of the dataset. Determine which allocation yields the most efficient use of space within a control interval for the record size specified.
6. Redo Programming Problem 5 with several different record sizes to see if the results are consistent.
7. Develop a very simple program that creates and loads one record into a VSAM cluster. After the record is loaded, force the program to abend. Follow this by using LISTCAT to print the statistics on the dataset. Next, VERIFY the dataset and then LISTCAT it again. Compare the two LISTCAT printouts to determine how they are different.
8. Develop a job stream which consists of three job steps. The first job step creates a KSDS. The second uses a program to load records into the KSDS and the third performs a LISTCAT followed by a deletion of the dataset. Run the job stream several times and specify different FREESPACE parameters for each run. Evaluate the LISTCAT printouts to determine how FREESPACE allocation effects dataset loading.
9. Create a KSDS and load it with records. Define and build an alternate index for this KSDS. Write a program which will print all records in the base cluster using the alternate index. In another job step, use a sort utility to sort the records in the base cluster in the same order as defined by the alternate index. Print the records after sorting. Compare the processing times between using a sort and using an alternate index to access the records.
10. Develop a program which will help programmers choose the best control interval size for a VSAM dataset. Input to the program is the length of the records to be stored and the type of disk device on which the dataset is to be placed. For each possible control interval size, the program will print a line which gives the number of control intervals per track, number of application records per control interval, percent of the control interval space used, percent of the disk track used, and number of application records per track. Identify which control interval size is the best by choosing the control interval size which yields the most records per track. For this program, assume that every control interval has a 4-byte overhead and that every application record stored in a control interval incurs an additional 3-byte overhead.
11. Develop a two-step job stream for this problem. The first step consists of a program which enhances the printing options offered by the VSAM PRINT command. By directing a DD statement to the VSAM cluster to be printed, the program uses a single control card or EXEC statement parameter to control record printing from the dataset. Control information consists of the COUNT, SKIP, and format (CHAR, DUMP, or HEX) options normally allowed on the PRINT command. Additionally, the program accepts the operand EVERYOTHER which allows the user to specify skipping within the records to be printed. This will enable the user to print every other record, every third record, every fifth record, and so on in the dataset specified. Given this information, select the records as desired from the dataset and direct them into an ESDS. In step two of the job stream, call upon IDCAMS to print the selected records in the format specified.
12. Develop a master file update application which supports a banking environment. The root portion of each bank customer record consists of the account number, name, address, current balance, and segment count fields. Check and deposit segments may be supported through

variable-length or fixed length record processing. Each checking account owner may initiate transactions against their account for the month. Apply check and deposit transactions to each master record and update the current balance appropriately. After all transactions are applied to the master records, print a bank statement for each customer.

13. Revise problem 13 above. Create another KSDS and simulate alternate index processing by associating the bank customer's last name with their account number. Print the bank statements in order by lastname instead of by account number. Redo the problem for a third time but use standard VSAM alternate index processing to support access by the customer's last name.

14. Develop a student registration system for a university. Files containing the courses to be offered and the students that are enrolled in the university should constitute the two primary files needed by your system. Process transactions to allow students to add, change, or drop classes from their schedule. Utilize variable-length record processing for this application. Print course schedules and class lists after all transactions have been applied.

    Revise the problem by supporting alternate index processing on the student's last name. Allow students to change their registration information such as their name, address, and so on. Apply all such updates through the alternate index.

    Add another alternate index on the instructor for a course. Print a report which lists all courses taught by each instructor for the term.

15. Develop a hotel registration system. For each room in the hotel, allow the room to be reserved for a given date. Capture the client's name, address, and billing information as part of the room reservation. Allow reservations to be made, cancelled, or changed by the clients. Print a reservation report after all transactions are applied. Print billing statements for those clients requesting direct billing.

    Extend the project by allowing the client to specify room amenities that they would like to have such as a hot tub, size of bed, view, and so on. Use an alternate index over the amenity field(s) to match the customer preferences with the amenities offered.

APPENDIX A: BIBLIOGRAPHY

The following IBM publications may be consulted for additional information on the material contained within this text.

Publication	Description of Contents
IBM System/370 Principles of Operation (GA22-7000)	Explanation of all IBM 370 machine instructions as well as general descriptions of instruction processing and data types.
OS/VS Assembler Language (GC33-4010)	Overview of the assembler and an explanation of all assembly language instructions.
OS/VS JCL Reference (GC28-0692)	Description of IBM JCL coding procedures and syntax.
MVS Data Management Services Guide (GC26-4058)	Explanation of all IBM file types and file processing techniques.
MVS/370 Data Management Macro Instructions (GC26-4057)	Description of all macros needed to perform I/O operations on an IBM system: OPEN, CLOSE, DCB, GET, PUT, READ, WRITE, etc.
OS/VS Supervisor Services and Macro Instructions (GC28-0683)	Explanation of all system macros that can support the execution of your program: ABEND, CALL, SNAP, etc.
OS/VS Tape Labels (GC26-3795)	Explanation of magnetic tape processing and the various magnetic tape storage formats.
OS/VS Linkage Editor and Loader (GC26-3813) (GC26-4011)	Overview and explanation for using the linkage editor and loader.
MVS/370 VSAM Users Guide (GC26-4066)	General overview of the VSAM access method and how to use it.
MVS/370 Access Method Services Reference (GC26-4059, GC26-4074, GC26-3841, and SC26-3967)	Description of the IDCAMS utility and the commands that may be used with this utility.
Planning for Enhanced VSAM (GC26-3842)	Introduction to the VSAM access method and how it can be used in your environment.
OS/VS VSAM Programmer's Guide (GC26-3838)	Describes how to create and process a VSAM dataset.
OS/VS VSAM Options for Advanced Applications (GC26-3819)	Detailed description of the internal structure of VSAM and advanced VSAM processing.
OS/VS System Messages (GC38-1002, and GC38-1008)	List of all error messages that you may obtain while processing with explanations.
MVS/370 Utilities (GC26-4065)	Description of all of the utility programs available on an IBM system and the commands necessary to invoke them.
OS/VS Data Areas (SYB8-0606)	Explanation of all of the system control blocks used to support the execution of your program.
OS/VS Debugging Handbook (GC28-0708, GC28-0709, and GC28-0710)	Complete description of how to debug a failing program using a program dump. This is a three-volume set.

APPENDIX B: INSTRUCTION SUMMARY

mnemonic	op code	format	set CC	text page	App. C
A	5A	RX	Y	100	630
AGO		macro		404	649
AH	4A	RX	Y	169	631
AIF		macro		404	649
AL	5E	RX	Y	463	631
ALR	1E	RR	Y	463	631
ANOP		macro		404	649
AP	FA	SS	Y	254	633
AR	1A	RR	Y	149	630
B	47	RX		202	645
BAL	45	RX		344	644
BALR	05	RR		346	644
BAS	4D	RX		347	644
BASR	0D	RR		347	644
BC	47	RX		190	644
BCR	07	RR		67	644
BCT	46	RX		207	644
BCTR	06	RR		207	644
BE	47	RX		201	645
BER	07	RR		201	645
BH	47	RX		202	645
BHR	07	RR		202	645
BL	47	RX		202	645
BLR	07	RR		202	645
BM	47	RX		202	646
BMR	07	RR		202	646
BNE	47	RX		202	645
BNER	07	RR		202	645
BNH	47	RX		202	645
BNHR	07	RR		202	645
BNL	47	RX		202	645
BNLR	07	RR		202	645
BNM	47	RX		202	646
BNMR	07	RR		202	646
BNO	47	RX		467	646
BNOR	07	RR		467	646
BNP	47	RX		202	646
BNPR	07	RR		202	646
BNZ	47	RX		202	646
BNZR	07	RR		202	646
BO	47	RX		202	646
BOR	07	RR		202	646
BP	47	RX		202	646
BPR	07	RR		202	646
BR	07	RR		202	645
BXH	86	RS		208	645
BXLE	87	RS		208	645
BZ	47	RX		202	646
BZR	07	RR		202	646
C	59	RX	Y	194	640
CH	49	RX	Y	198	640
CL	55	RX	Y	463	641
CLC	D5	SS	Y	199	640
CLCL	0F	RR	Y	453	640
CLI	95	SI	Y	199	640
CLM	BD	RS	Y	429	641
CLOSE		sys macro		118	648

APPENDIX B: (continued)

mnemonic	op code	format	set CC	text page	App. C
CLR	15	RR	Y	463	641
CNOP		assembly		235	651
COPY		assembly		512	643
CP	F9	SS	Y	252	641
CR	19	RR	Y	200	641
CSECT		assembly		46	650
CVB	4F	RX		164	642
CVD	4E	RX		165	643
D	5D	RX		153	631
DC		assembly		54	643
DCB		sys macro		116	647
DP	FD	SS		256	633
DR	1D	RR		149	631
DROP		assembly		511	651
DS		assembly		58	643
DSECT		assembly		507	651
ED	DE	SS	Y	239	642
EDMK	DF	SS	Y	239	642
EJECT		assembly		86	651
END		assembly		68	651
EQU		assembly		91	643
EX	44	RX		429	637
GBLx		macro		403	649
GET		sys macro		122	648
IC	43	RX		428	638
ICM	BF	RS	Y	426	638
L	58	RX		66	629
LA	41	RX		153	629
LCLx		macro		403	649
LCR	13	RR	Y	464	630
LH	48	RX		169	629
LM	98	RS		66	630
LNR	11	RR	Y	464	630
LPR	10	RR	Y	464	630
LR	18	RR		48	629
LTORG		assembly		136	651
LTR	12	RR	Y	356	629
M	5C	RX		153	631
MACRO		macro		390	649
MEND		macro		390	649
MEXIT		macro		418	649
MH	4C	RX		169	632
MNOTE		macro		416	650
MP	FC	SS		256	633
MR	1C	RR		149	631
MVC	D2	SS		110	629
MVCL	0E	RR	Y	451	629
MVI	92	SI		101	629
MVN	D1	SS		459	633
MVO	F1	SS		459	633
MVZ	D3	SS		459	633
N	54	RX	Y	456	637
NC	D4	SS	Y	456	638
NI	94	SI	Y	456	637
NR	14	RR	Y	456	637
O	56	RX	Y	455	637
OC	D6	SS	Y	455	637

APPENDIX B: (continued)

mnemonic	op code	format	set CC	text page	App. C
OI	96	SI	Y	166, 455	637, 642
OPEN		sys macro		118	648
OPSYN		assembly		202	651
OR	16	RR	Y	455	637
ORG		assembly		434	644
PACK	F2	SS		164	642
PRINT		assembly		389	652
PUT		sys macro		122	648
READ		sys macro		551	649
S	5B	RX	Y	153	632
SETx		macro		404	650
SH	4B	RX	Y	169	632
SL	5F	RX	Y	463	632
SLA	8B	RS	Y	467	639
SLDA	8F	RS	Y	467	639
SLDL	8D	RS		467	639
SLL	89	RS		467	639
SLR	1F	RR	Y	463	632
SNAP		sys macro		294	648
SP	FB	SS	Y	254	633
SPACE		assembly		86	651
SPM	04	RR	Y	255	639
SR	1B	RR	Y	149	632
SRA	8A	RS	Y	467	639
SRDA	8E	RS	Y	467	640
SRDL	8C	RS		467	639
SRL	88	RS		467	639
SRP	F0	SS	Y	261	633
ST	50	RX		153	630
START		assembly		46, 73	650
STC	42	RX		428	639
STCM	BE	RS		428	639
STH	40	RX		169	630
STM	90	RS		49	630
TITLE		assembly		85	652
TM	91	SI	Y	366	638
TR	DC	SS		433	643
TRT	DD	SS	Y	436	652
UNPK	F3	SS		166	642
USING		assembly		47, 349	650
WRITE		sys macro		544	649
X	57	RX	Y	457	638
XC	D7	SS	Y	457	638
XDECI		ASSIST	Y	177	647
XDECO		ASSIST		177	647
XDUMP		ASSIST		288	646
XI	97	SI	Y	457	638
XPRNT		ASSIST		126	647
XR	17	RR	Y	457	638
XREAD		ASSIST	Y	126	647
ZAP	F8	SS	Y	259	632

FLOATING POINT INSTRUCTION SUMMARY

mnemonic	op code	format	set CC	text page	App. C
AD	6A	RX	Y	484	635
ADR	2A	RR	Y	484	635
AE	7A	RX	Y	484	635
AER	3A	RR	Y	484	635
AU	7E	RX	Y		635
AUR	3E	RR	Y		635
AW	6E	RX	Y		635
AWR	2E	RR	Y		635
AXR	36	RR	Y	484	635
CD	69	RX	Y	486	641
CDR	29	RR	Y	486	641
CE	79	RX	Y	486	641
CER	39	RR	Y	486	641
DD	6D	RX		484	636
DDR	2D	RR		484	636
DE	7D	RX		484	636
DER	3D	RR		484	637
HDR	24	RR		484	637
HER	34	RR		484	637
LCDR	23	RR	Y	485	634
LCER	33	RR	Y	485	634
LD	68	RX		481	633
LDR	28	RR		481	633
LE	78	RX		480	634
LER	38	RR		481	634
LNDR	21	RR	Y	485	634
LNER	31	RR	Y	485	634
LPDR	20	RR	Y	485	634
LPER	30	RR	Y	485	634
LRDR	25	RR		486	634
LRER	35	RR		486	634
LTDR	22	RR	Y	485	634
LTER	32	RR	Y	485	634
MD	6C	RX		484	636
MDR	2C	RR		484	636
ME	7C	RX		484	636
MER	3C	RR		484	636
MXD	67	RX		484	636
MXDR	27	RR		484	636
MXR	26	RR		484	636
SD	6B	RX	Y	484	635
SDR	2B	RR	Y	481	635
SE	7B	RX	Y	484	635
SER	3B	RR	Y	484	635
STD	60	RX		481	634
STE	70	RX		481	634
SU	7F	RX	Y		636
SUR	3F	RR	Y		636
SW	6F	RX	Y		636
SWR	2F	RR	Y		636
SXR	37	RR	Y	484	636

INDEX TO APPENDIX C: INSTRUCTION REFERENCE BY FUNCTION

Assignment Instructions:	App. C

- Character Data 629
- Binary Data 629
- Packed Decimal Data 632
- Floating Point Data 633
- Bit and Logical Data 637

Comparison Instructions:

- Character Data 640
- Binary Data 641
- Packed Decimal Data 641
- Floating Point Data 642

Conversion Through Assignment:

- Character to Packed Decimal 642
- Packed Decimal to Character 642
- Packed Decimal to Binary 642
- Binary to Packed Decimal 643
- Character to Character 643

Data Definition Instructions 643

Flow Control:

- Standard Instructions 644
- Extended Mnemonics 645

Input/Output Instructions:

- ASSIST 646
- Standard Assembly Language 647

Macro Instructions 649

Program Definition and Spacing 650

Scanning Text 652

Assignment Instructions

Character Data

MVI	D(B),imm	SI	**MOVE IMMEDIATE** Move the immediate byte of data from within the instruction to the area identified in the first operand.
MVC	D(L,B),D(B)	SS	**MOVE CHARACTER** Move L bytes of data from the second operand's location into the area identified by the first operand. No more than 256 bytes of data can be moved. At least one byte is moved in the event of an executed MVC instruction.
MVCL	Re/o,Re/o	RR	**MOVE CHARACTER LONG** Up to 16,777,215 bytes of data can be moved from the second operand location into the first operand. Both operands must specify even/odd register pairs. The even registers contain the address of the *from* and *to* areas and the odd registers contain the lengths of each operand. If the second operand is shorter than the first operand, then the first operand is filled with the pad character located in the leftmost byte of the odd second operand register. If the length value in the even register for the second operand is zero, the entire first operand is filled with the pad character.

Binary Data

L	R,D(X,B)	RX	**LOAD** The four-byte area identified by the second operand is copied into the general-purpose register specified. The second operand should be aligned on a fullword boundary although it is not necessary on new machines.
LA	R,D(X,B)	RX	**LOAD ADDRESS** The address of the second operand is placed into the register specified in the first operand. The address is computed by adding the contents of the index register to that of the base register and the displacement.
LH	R,D(X,B)	RX	**LOAD HALFWORD** The two-byte area specified in the second operand is placed into the rightmost two bytes of the general-purpose register specified. The leftmost bit of this value is then carried into the remaining higher bit positions of the register, thus completing the sign of the number. The second operand is aligned on a halfword boundary.
LR	R1,R2	RR	**LOAD REGISTER** The contents of the second register are copied into the first register. After the instruction, both registers contain the same value.
LTR	R1,R2	RR	**LOAD AND TEST REGISTER** The register specified in the second operand is copied into the first operand and the condition code is set depending on the resulting value. Both registers have the same value upon completion of the instruction. The condition code is set as follows: equal to zero, less than zero, greater than zero, not applicable.

Assignment Instructions

Binary Data

LCR	R1,R2	RR	**LOAD COMPLEMENT REGISTER** The complement of the second operand register is loaded into the first operand register. The condition code is set depending on the resulting value in the first operand register: equal to zero, less than zero, greater than zero, not applicable.
LNR	R1,R2	RR	**LOAD NEGATIVE REGISTER** The two's complement of the absolute value of the second operand's contents is placed into the first operand register. The condition code is set depending on the resulting value in the first register: equal to zero, less than zero, and not applicable, not applicable.
LPR	R1,R2	RR	**LOAD POSITIVE REGISTER** The absolute value of the value in the second operand register is placed into the first register. The condition code is set depending on the resulting value in the first register: equal to zero, not applicable, greater than zero, overflow.
LM	R1,R2,D(B)	RS	**LOAD MULTIPLE** Registers R1 through R2 are loaded with data from the area specified in the third operand. The third operand defines as many fullwords of storage as registers to be loaded. The third operand is aligned on a fullword boundary.
ST	R,D(X,B)	RX	**STORE** The contents of the general-purpose register specified in the first operand are placed into memory at the location identified by the second operand. The contents of the register remain unchanged. The second operand is aligned on a fullword boundary.
STH	R,D(X,B)	RX	**STORE HALFWORD** The rightmost two bytes of the general register specified are copied into memory beginning at the second operand location. The second operand is aligned on a halfword boundary.
STM	R1,R2,D(B)	RS	**STORE MULTIPLE** Registers R1 through R2 are copied into memory at the location specified by the third operand. The third operand defines as many fullwords of storage as there are register values to be stored. The third operand is aligned on a fullword boundary.
A	R,D(X,B)	RX	**ADD** The contents of the fullword area identified by the second operand are added to the contents of the general-purpose register. The second operand is aligned on a fullword boundary. The condition code is set depending on the value in the first operand: equal to zero, less than zero, greater than zero, overflow.
AR	R1,R2	RR	**ADD REGISTER** Same as the add instruction above except that the second operand is a register.

Assignment Instructions

Binary Data

AH	R,D(X,B)	RX	**ADD HALFWORD** The two-byte area identified by the second operand is added to the contents of the first operand register. The second operand is aligned on a halfword boundary. The condition code is set depending on the resulting value in the first operand: equal to zero, less than zero, greater than zero, overflow.
AL	R,D(X,B)	RX	**ADD LOGICAL** The second operand value is logically added to the contents of the first operand register. The second operand is aligned on a fullword boundary. The condition code is set depending on the resulting value in the first operand: equal to zero and no carry occurred, not equal to zero and no carry occurred, equal to zero and a carry occurred, not equal to zero and a carry occurred.
ALR	R1,R2	RR	**ADD LOGICAL REGISTER** The fullword binary value contained in the second operand register is added logically to the contents of the first register. The condition code is set depending on the value in the first register operand: equal to zero and no carry occurred, not equal to zero and no carry occurred, zero and carry occurred, not equal to zero and carry occurred.
D	Re/o,D(X,B)	RX	**DIVIDE** The contents of the even/odd register pair are divided by the value specified in the second operand. The resulting register pair consists of the remainder and quotient. Both remainder and quotient are 32-bit values in their registers. Before the operation, the even/odd register pair must consist of a 64-bit signed number. Generally, the odd register contains the value to be divided and the even register contains a value of zero or a value of negative one. These values represent the sign of the odd register. If the contents of the odd register are negative, then the even register is negative 1. A positive or zero value in the odd register requires a value of zero in the even register.
DR	Re/o,R	RR	**DIVIDE REGISTER** Same as the D instruction except that the second operand is a register and not a storage area.
M	Re/o,D(X,B)	RX	**MULTIPLY** The even/odd register pair in the first operand is multiplied by the value stored in the fullword area identified by the second operand. The resulting value is a 64-bit number spanning both even and odd registers. Before the multiplication, the odd register must contain the value of the first operand. The contents of the even register are irrelevant before the operation.
MR	Re/o,R	RR	**MULTIPLY REGISTER** Similar to the multiply instruction above except that the second operand is a register instead of a storage area.

Assignment Instructions

Binary Data

MH	R,D(X,B)	RX	**MULTIPLY HALFWORD** The contents of the first register are multiplied by the halfword value contained in memory at the second operand location. The resulting value is contained solely within the single register specified in the first operand. Even/odd pairs are not needed for this instruction.
S	R,D(X,B)	RX	**SUBTRACT** The contents of the fullword storage area identified by the second operand are subtracted from the contents of the first operand register. The resulting value is placed into the first register and the condition code is set depending on this value: equal to zero, less than zero, greater than zero, overflow.
SR	R1,R2	RR	**SUBTRACT REGISTER** Similar to subtract except that the second operand is a register. The second operand register is not altered by the instruction unless both first and second operands specify the same register.
SH	R,D(X,B)	RX	**SUBTRACT HALFWORD** The halfword value contained at the second operand location is subtracted from the contents of the first operand register. The resulting value is placed into the first operand register and the condition code is set as follows: equal to zero, less than zero, greater than zero, overflow.
SL	R,D(X,B)	RX	**SUBTRACT LOGICAL** The contents of the fullword area specified by the second operand are subtracted logically from the contents of register specified in the first operand. The condition code is set depending on the resulting value in the first operand register: not applicable, not equal to zero and no carry occurred, equal to zero and a carry occurred, not equal to zero and a carry occurred.
SLR	R,R	RR	**SUBTRACT LOGICAL REGISTER** The contents of the second operand register are complemented and added logically to the contents of the first operand register. The condition code is set depending on the outcome of the addition: not used, first operand value is not equal to zero and carry did not occur, result is equal to zero and carry occurred, result is not equal to zero and carry occurred.

Packed Decimal

ZAP	D(L,B),D(L,B)	SS	**ZERO AND ADD PACKED** The packed-decimal number contained in the second operand is assigned to the storage area identified by the first operand. Both fields have the value of the second operand after execution. The condition code is set depending on the resulting value in the first operand: equal to zero, less than zero, greater than zero, overflow.

Assignment Instructions

Packed Decimal

SRP D(L,B),D(B),imm SS **SHIFT AND ROUND PACKED**
SRP can multiply or divide a packed-decimal field by a power of 10. The field containing the packed-decimal number is contained in the first operand and the power of 10 is specified in the second operand. The last operand is added to the rightmost digit shifted off when shifting values to the right.

AP D(L,B),D(L,B) SS **ADD PACKED**
The contents of the second operand are added to the contents of the first operand. The condition code is set depending on the resulting value in the first operand: equal to zero, less than zero, greater than zero, overflow.

SP D(L,B),D(L,B) SS **SUBTRACT PACKED**
The contents of the second operand are subtracted from the contents of the first operand. The condition code is set depending on the resulting value in the first operand: equal to zero, less than zero, greater than zero, overflow.

DP D(L1,B)(L2,B) SS **DIVIDE PACKED**
The first operand is divided by the contents of the second operand. The resulting first operand field is split into the quotient and the remainder of the division. The quotient occupies the leftmost portion of the first operand field and has a length equal to L1−L2. The remainder occupies the rightmost remaining bytes in the first operand field.

MP D(L,B),D(L,B) SS **MULTIPLY PACKED**
The contents of the first operand are multiplied by the contents of the second operand with the result occupying the first operand location. The condition code is not set by this instruction.

MVN D(L,B),D(B) SS **MOVE NUMERICS**
The numerics portion (right half) of each byte in the second operand are moved to the numerics portions of the first operand bytes replacing the numeric digits in the first operand location.

MVO D(L,B),D(L,B) SS **MOVE WITH OFFSET**
Half bytes in the second operand location are moved diagonally into the bytes specified by the first operand location. If both the first and second operands specify the same field this instruction has the same effect as the SRP instruction.

MVZ D(L,B),D(B) SS **MOVE ZONES**
The zone portion (left half) of each byte in the second operand are moved to the zones portions of the first operand bytes replacing the zone digits in the first operand location.

Floating Point

LD R,D(X,B) RX **LOAD LONG**
The doubleword floating point value located at the second operand location is loaded into the floating-point register specified in the first operand.

LDR R1,R2 RR **LOAD LONG REGISTER**
The contents of floating-point register R2 are copied into floating-point register R1. Both registers now have the same contents.

Assignment Instructions

Floating Point

LE	R,D(X,B)	RX	**LOAD SHORT** The fullword (short-form) floating-point number located at operand 2 is copied into the left half of the floating-point register specified in the first operand.
LER	R1,R2	RR	**LOAD SHORT REGISTER** The left half of floating-point register R2 is copied into the left half of floating-point register R1. In other words, short-form floating-point numbers are copied in this instruction.
LNDR	R1,R2	RR	**LOAD NEGATIVE LONG REGISTER** The contents of floating-point register R2 are copied into R1 and the sign of the resulting number in R1 is set to indicate a negative number.
LNER	R1,R2	RR	**LOAD NEGATIVE SHORT REGISTER** Same as LNDR except that short-form numbers are used.
LPDR	R1,R2	RR	**LOAD POSITIVE LONG REGISTER** The contents of floating-point register R2 are copied into floating-point register R1. The sign of the result in R1 is set to indicate a positive number.
LPER	R1,R2	RR	**LOAD POSITIVE SHORT REGISTER** Same as LPDR except that short-form numbers are used.
LRDR	R,Ra/b	RR	**LOAD ROUNDED, EXTENDED TO LONG** The floating point register pair in the second operand specifies an extended precision number. This value is rounded to form a long-form number which is then copied into the first operand register.
LRER	R1,R2	RR	**LOAD ROUNDED, LONG TO SHORT** The long-form floating point number in the second operand is rounded to form a short-form number. The resulting value is loaded into the left-half of the floating point register specified in the first operand.
LTDR	R1,R2	RR	**LOAD AND TEST LONG REGISTER** The contents of floating-point register R2 are copied into R1 and the condition code is set based on the resulting value in R1: equal to zero, less than zero, greater than zero, not applicable.
LTER	R1,R2	RR	**LOAD AND TEST SHORT REGISTER** Same as LTDR except that short-form operands are used.
LCDR	R1,R2	RR	**LOAD COMPLEMENT LONG REGISTER** The long-form floating-point number in R2 is copied into R1 with the resulting number being of opposite sign to that of R2.
LCER	R1,R2	RR	**LOAD COMPLEMENT SHORT REGISTER** Same as LCDR except that short-form operands are used.
STD	R,D(X,B)	RX	**STORE LONG** The contents of the floating-point register specified are stored in the doubleword as specified by the second operand.
STE	R,D(X,B)	RX	**STORE SHORT** Same as STD except that a short-form number is stored.

Assignment Instructions

Floating Point

AD	R,D(X,B)	RX	**ADD NORMALIZED LONG** The long-form floating-point number at the second operand location is added to the contents of the floating-point register specified. The condition code is set depending on the resulting value in the floating point register: equal to zero, less than zero, greater than zero, not applicable.
ADR	R1,R2	RR	**ADD NORMALIZED LONG REGISTER** Same as AD except that a register contains the second operand value.
AE	R,D(X,B)	RX	**ADD NORMALIZED SHORT** Same as AD except that short-form numbers are used in both operands.
AER	R1,R2	RR	**ADD NORMALIZED SHORT REGISTER** Same as AD except that short-form numbers are used and the second operand is a register.
AW	R,D(X,B)	RX	**ADD UNNORMALIZED LONG** The long-form operands specified are added in an unnormalized manner with the result replacing the first operand value. The condition code is set depending on the resulting value in the first operand register: equal to zero, less than zero, greater than zero, not applicable.
AWR	R1,R2	RR	**ADD UNNORMALIZED LONG REGISTER** Same as AW except that the second operand is a register.
AU	R,D(X,B)	RX	**ADD UNNORMALIZED SHORT** The short-form operands are added in an unnormalized manner with the result replacing the first operand value. The condition code is set depending on the resulting value in the first operand: equal to zero, less than zero, greater than zero, not applicable.
AUR	R1,R2	RR	**ADD UNNORMALIZED SHORT REGISTER** Same as AU except that short-form addition is performed.
AXR	Re/o,Re/o	RR	**ADD NORMALIZED EXTENDED REGISTER** The two floating-point even/odd pairs are added in a normalized manner. The condition code is set depending on the value in the first even/odd pair: equal to zero, less than zero, greater than zero, not applicable.
SD	R,D(X,B)	RX	**SUBTRACT NORMALIZED LONG** The long-form second operand value is subtracted from the contents of the floating-point register specified. The condition code is set depending on the resulting value in the first operand: equal to zero, less than zero, greater than zero, not applicable.
SDR	R1,R2	RR	**SUBTRACT NORMALIZED LONG REGISTER** Same as SD except that the second operand is a register.
SE	R,D(X,B)	RX	**SUBTRACT NORMALIZED SHORT** The short-form value in the second operand is subtracted from the short-form number in the first operand. The resulting value in the first operand sets the condition code: equal to zero, less than zero, greater than zero, not used.
SER	R1,R2	RR	**SUBTRACT NORMALIZED SHORT REGISTER** Same as SE except that the second operand is a register.

Assignment Instructions

Floating Point

SW	R,D(X,B)	RX	**SUBTRACT UNNORMALIZED LONG** The long-form value in the second operand is subtracted from the long-form number in the first operand in an unnormalized manner. The condition code is set depending on the resulting value in the first operand: equal to zero, less than zero, greater than zero, not used.
SWR	R1,R2	RR	**SUBTRACT UNNORMALIZED LONG REGISTER** Same as SWR except that the second operand is a register.
SU	R,D(X,B)	RX	**SUBTRACT UNNORMALIZED SHORT** Same as SW except that short-form numbers are used.
SUR	R1,R2	RR	**SUBTRACT UNNORMALIZED SHORT REGISTER** Same as SWR except that short-form numbers are used.
SXR	Re/o,Re/o	RR	**SUBTRACT NORMALIZED EXTENDED REGISTER** The extended-form even/odd register value in the second operand is subtracted from the extended-precision number in the first operand. The condition code is set depending on the resulting value in the first operand: equal to zero, less than zero, greater than zero, not used.
MD	R,D(X,B)	RX	**MULTIPLY LONG** The long-form number in the first operand is multiplied by the long-form number in the second operand with the result replacing the first operand value. The condition code is not set.
MDR	R1,R2	RR	**MULTIPLY LONG REGISTER** Same as MD except that the second operand is a register value.
ME	R,D(X,B)	RX	**MULTIPLY SHORT** Same as MD except that short form numbers are multiplied.
MER	R1,R2	RR	**MULTIPLY SHORT REGISTER** Same as MDR except that short form numbers are multiplied.
MXR	Re/o,Re/o	RR	**MULTIPLY EXTENDED REGISTER** The extended-precision number in the first even/odd pair is multiplied by the extended-precision number in the second operand with the result replacing the first operand. The condition code is not set.
MXD	Re/o,D(X,B)	RX	**MULTIPLY LONG TO EXTENDED** The long-form numbers are multiplied with the resulting value being an extended-precision number occupying the first operand location. The condition code is not set.
MXDR	Re/o,R	RR	**MULTIPLY LONG TO EXTENDED REGISTER** Same as MXD except that the second operand is in a register.
DD	R,D(X,B)	RX	**DIVIDE NORMALIZED LONG** The contents of the first operand are divided (in long form) by the contents of the second operand with the result replacing the first operand value. The condition code is not set.
DDR	R1,R2	RR	**DIVIDE NORMALIZED LONG REGISTER** Same as DD except that the second operand is a register.
DE	R,D(X,B)	RX	**DIVIDE NORMALIZED SHORT** Same as DD except that short-form numbers are used.

Assignment Instructions

Floating Point

DER	R1,R2	RR	**DIVIDE NORMALIZED SHORT REGISTER** Same as DDR except that short-form numbers are divided.
HER	R1,R2	RR	**HALVE SHORT REGISTER** The contents of the *second* operand are divided by two with the normalized result replacing the first operand value. The condition code is not changed.
HDR	R1,R2	RR	**HALVE LONG REGISTER** Same as HER except that long-form numbers are halved.

Bit and Logical Operations

EX	R,D(X,B)	RX	**EXECUTE** The second operand specifies a machine instruction. The rightmost byte of the register specified in the first operand is OR'd against the second byte of the machine instruction in the second operand. The machine instruction is then executed.
OI	D(B),imm	SI	**OR IMMEDIATE** The byte located at the first operand location is OR'd against the immediate data byte contained within the instruction and specified in the second operand. The resulting OR'd byte replaces the byte at D(B). The condition code is set depending on the resulting first operand value: equal to zero, not equal zero, not used, not used.
O	R,D(X,B)	RX	**OR** The second operand is OR'd against the contents of the general-purpose register specified with the result replacing the contents of the register. The condition code is set depending on the resulting value in the general purpose register: equal to zero, not equal to zero, not used, not used.
OR	R1,R2	RR	**OR REGISTER** Same as O except that the second operand is a register.
OC	D(L,B),D(B)	SS	**OR CHARACTER** L-bytes from the first and second operand locations are OR'd and replace the L-bytes in the first operand location. The condition code is set depending on the resulting bit values after ORing: all bits are equal to zero, all bits are not equal to zero, not used, not used.
NI	D(B),imm	SI	**AND IMMEDIATE** The byte located at the first operand location is AND'd against the immediate data byte contained within the instruction and specified in the second operand. The resulting AND'd byte replaces the byte at D(B). The condition code is set depending on the resulting first operand value: equal to zero, not equal to zero, not used, not used.
N	R,D(X,B)	RX	**AND** The second operand is AND'd against the contents of the general-purpose register specified with the result replacing the contents of the register. The condition code is set depending on the resulting value in the general-purpose register: equal to zero, not equal to zero, not used, not used.
NR	R1,R2	RR	**AND REGISTER** Same as N except that the second operand is a register.

Assignment Instructions

Bit and Logical Operations

NC D(L,B),D(B) SS **AND CHARACTER**
L-bytes from the first and second operands are ANDed and replace the contents of the first operand location. The condition code is set depending on the resulting value in the first operand location: all bits are equal to zero, all bits are not equal to zero, not used, not used.

XI D(B),imm SI **EXCLUSIVE OR IMMEDIATE**
The byte located at the first operand location is exclusive OR'd against the immediate data byte contained within the instruction and specified in the second operand. The resulting exclusive OR'd byte replaces the byte at D(B). The condition code is set depending on the resulting first operand value: equal to zero, not equal to zero, not used, not used.

X R,D(X,B) RX **EXCLUSIVE OR**
The second operand is exclusive OR'd against the contents of the general-purpose register specified with the result replacing the contents of the register. The condition code is set depending on the resulting value in the general purpose register: equal to zero, not equal to zero, not used, not used.

XR R1,R2 RR **EXCLUSIVE OR REGISTER**
Same as X except that the second operand is a register.

XC D(L,B),D(B) SS **EXCLUSIVE OR CHARACTER**
L-bytes from the first and second operands are exclusive-or'd and replace the bytes in the first operand location. The condition code is set depending on the resulting bit values from the bytes processed: all bits are zero, all bits are not zero, not used, not used.

TM D(B),imm SI **TEST UNDER MASK**
The bit configuration in the immediate data byte (second operand) is used to test the value of selected bits in the first operand. All one bits in the second operand test corresponding bits in the first operand location. The condition code is determined based on the value of the bits in the first operand as related to those to be tested determined by the second operand: all bits tested were zero, some bits were one and some were zero, not used, all bits tested were ones.

IC R,D(X,B) RX **INSERT CHARACTER**
The byte of data located at the second operand location is copied into the rightmost byte of the general-purpose register specified.

ICM R,B'xxxx',D(B) RS **INSERT CHARACTERS UNDER MASK**
For each bit turned on in the second operand, data bytes from the third operand location are used to replace the respective bytes in the general-purpose register. The condition code is set depending on the resulting characters inserted into the register: all inserted bits were zero, first bit of the first inserted byte is one, first bit of the first inserted byte was a zero but all other bits were not zero, not used.

Assignment Instructions

Bit and Logical Operations

STC	R,D(X,B)	RX	**STORE CHARACTER** The rightmost byte of the general-purpose register is copied into the memory location specified by the second operand. The general-purpose register is not changed.
STCM	R,B'xxxx',D(B)	RS	**STORE CHARACTERS UNDER MASK** For each bit turned on in the second operand, corresponding bytes from the general-purpose register are stored into memory at the location specified in the last operand. The condition code is not changed nor is the contents of the GPR.
SPM	R	RR	**SET PROGRAM MASK** Bits 2 to 7 of the register specified replace bits 34 to 39 of the PSW. This allows the program to change the current condition code and program mask settings within the PSW to effect program execution.
SLL	R,i	RS	**SHIFT LEFT LOGICAL** The general-purpose register specified is shifted to the left *i* positions. This instruction has the effect of multiplying the contents of the register by 2 to the *i*th power. Vacated bit positions are filled with a 0-bit value.
SLDL	Re/o,i	RS	**SHIFT LEFT DOUBLE LOGICAL** The even/odd register pair is treated as a single 64-bit value and is shifted to the left *i* positions. This instruction is similar to SLL except that the first operand is an even/odd pair.
SLA	R,i	RS	**SHIFT LEFT ARITHMETIC** Same as SLL except that the condition code is set depending on the value in the register after shifting and the value of the sign bit in the register: equal to zero, less than zero, greater than zero, unlike sign bit was shifted out of the register (overflow).
SLDA	Re/o,i	RS	**SHIFT LEFT DOUBLE ARITHMETIC** Same as SLA except that an even/odd pair is used as the first operand.
SRL	R,i	RS	**SHIFT RIGHT LOGICAL** The GPR specified is shifted to the right *i* bit positions. This instruction has the effect of dividing the contents of the GPR by the 2 to the *i*th power. Bits shifted out of the register are lost. High-order bit positions vacated by the shift are filled with zeros.
SRDL	Re/o,i	RS	**SHIFT RIGHT DOUBLE LOGICAL** Same as SRL except that the first operand is an even/odd pair.
SRA	R,i	RS	**SHIFT RIGHT ARITHMETIC** The GPR specified is shifted to the right arithmetically. This means that all high-order vacated positions are filled with the current sign bit of the register. Although the instruction has the effect of dividing the register contents by 2 to the *i*th power, the sign of the number does not change. The condition code is set depending on the resulting value in the GPR: equal to zero, less than zero, greater than zero, not used.

Assignment Instructions

Bit and Logical Operations

SRDA	Re/o,i	RS	**SHIFT RIGHT DOUBLE ARITHMETIC** Same as SRA except that the first operand is an even/odd pair. After shifting the first operand is treated as a number of 64 bit positions with the leftmost bit position being the sign of the number.

Comparison Instructions

Character Data

CLI	D(B),imm	SI	**COMPARE LOGICAL IMMEDIATE** The byte of data identified by the first operand is compared with the byte of immediate data specified by the second operand. Both bytes are compared bit by bit, left to right until an unmatched bit position is found or the fields are exhausted. The condition code is set depending on the outcome of the comparison: operands are equal, first operand is less than the second operand, first operand is greater than the second operand, not used.
CLC	D(L,B),D(B)	SS	**COMPARE LOGICAL CHARACTER** The first L bytes of the two storage areas are compared logically. The method of comparison is identical to that of the CLI instruction. The condition code is also set like the CLI instruction. Up to 256 bytes of data may be compared in this manner.
CLCL	Re/o,Re/o	RR	**COMPARE LOGICAL CHARACTER LONG** The even/odd register pairs identify storage areas that are to be compared logically (exactly like CLI). The even registers contain the addresses of the first and second operands and the odd registers contain the lengths of each operand area. The leftmost byte of the second operand odd register also contains a pad character. This character is used to extend the shorter operand if the operands are not the same length. The condition code is set similar to that of CLI. Up to 16,777,215 bytes of data can be compared with this instruction.

Binary Data

C	R,D(X,B)	RX	**COMPARE** The binary number in the GPR is compared with the fullword binary value at the location specified. The values are compared arithmetically and not logically. The condition code is set depending on the value of the operands as follows: operands are equal, first operand is less than the second, first operand is greater than the second operand, not used.
CH	R,D(X,B)	RX	**COMPARE HALFWORD** The right half (halfword) value in the GPR is compared against the halfword value at the memory location specified. This instruction is similar to C except that halfword comparisons are performed. The condition code is also set in a similar manner.

Comparison Instructions

Binary Data

CLR	R1,R2	RR	**COMPARE LOGICAL REGISTER** The two general purpose registers specified are compared logically and the condition code is set depending on the result of the comparison: register values are equal, first register's value is less than second, first register's value is greater than the second, not used.
CL	R,D(X,B)	RX	**COMPARE LOGICAL** Similar to CLR except that the second operand now specifies a storage address instead of a register.
CLM	R,B'xxxx',D(B)	RS	**COMPARE LOGICAL UNDER MASK** Depending on the bit values specified in the second operand, selected bytes from the register contents and the storage area specified are compared logically. The condition code is set depending on the result of the comparison: all bits tested are equal, register bytes are less than the bytes in storage, register bytes are greater than the bytes in storage, not applicable.
CR	R1,R2	RR	**COMPARE REGISTER** The binary fullword values in the general-purpose registers specified are compared arithmetically. The condition code is set depending on the values in the registers: values are equal, first register value is less than the second register value, first register is greater than the second, not used.

Packed Decimal

CP	D(L,B),D(L,B)	SS	**COMPARE PACKED** The two packed-decimal values specified by the first and second operands are compared arithmetically. The condition code is set depending on the outcome of the comparison: equal, first operand is less than the second, first operand is greater than the second, not used. If the operands are not the same length, the shorter field is logically extended with high-order zeros (X'00') so that the operands will have the same length.

Floating Point

CD	R,D(X,B)	RX	**COMPARE LONG** The floating-point value in the register is compared arithmetically with the doubleword value identified by the second operand. The condition code is set depending on the differences in their values: equal, register value is less than the value in memory, register value is greater than the value in memory, not used.
CDR	R1,R2	RR	**COMPARE LONG REGISTER** The two long-form floating-point register values are compared in a manner similar to the CD instruction.
CE	R,D(X,B)	RX	**COMPARE SHORT** Similar to CD except that short-form values are compared.
CER	R1,R2	RR	**COMPARE SHORT REGISTER** Similar to CDR except that short-form values are compared.

Conversion Through Assignment

Character to Packed Decimal

PACK D(L,B),D(L,B) SS

PACK
The character data in the second operand is converted to packed-decimal format and replaces the first operand value. The conversion occurs by reversing the zone and digit portions of the rightmost byte of the field and by removing all zone portions in the bytes to the left of the rightmost byte. High-order positions are filled with zeros if the second operand does not completely fill the first operand location.

Packed Decimal to Character

ED D1(L,B1),D2(B2) SS

EDIT
The packed-decimal field specified by the second operand is converted to character representation based on the edit pattern specified in the first operand. Refer to the text for further details. The condition code is set depending on the value of the second operand: equal to zero, less than zero, greater than zero, not used.

EDMK D1(L,B1),D2(B2) SS

EDIT AND MARK
Similar to ED. After the instruction is completed, register 1 is set to address the first significant digit in the converted first operand field. This enables the programmer to provide floating characters for converted numeric values.

UNPK D(L,B),D(L,B) SS

UNPACK
The packed-decimal field identified by the second operand is converted to character format and replaces the first operand value. The conversion is done by reversing the digit and sign portions of the rightmost byte of the packed-decimal field. For all other packed-decimal digits in the second operand, a zone of X'F' is added to the digit and the resulting byte is placed into the first operand location.

OI D(B),imm SI

OR IMMEDIATE
This instruction is described earlier. In conversion, it is used following the unpack instruction to change the zone on the rightmost byte in the converted character field to a zone of F. Since the rightmost byte only consists of the reversed zone and digit portions, it is possible for the byte to contain a zone that does not allow the digit portion to be properly represented. The OI instruction is used to OR the rightmost byte of the unpacked field to construct a printable character digit.

Packed Decimal to Binary

CVB R,D(X,B) RX

CONVERT TO BINARY
The eight-byte packed-decimal number specified in the second operand is converted to binary and is placed into the GPR specified. The largest value that can be converted and placed into a register is 2,147,483,647. The smallest number that can be placed into the register is −2,147,483,648. If an attempt is made to convert a value larger or smaller than those listed, a program exception occurs.

Conversion Through Assignment

Binary to Packed Decimal

CVD	R,D(X,B)	RX	**CONVERT TO DECIMAL** The binary fullword value in the register is converted to packed-decimal format and is stored in the doubleword area identified by the second operand. The second operand is always large enough to hold the binary value. The sign of the packed-decimal number reflects the sign of the binary register value. The register is not altered.

Character to Character

TR	D(L,B),D(B)	SS	**TRANSLATE** The bytes in the first operand are used as displacements into a 256-byte table identified by the second operand. Each byte in the first operand is then replaced by its corresponding byte in the second operand. The condition code is not changed.

Data Definition

DS	definition		**DEFINE STORAGE** This assembler instruction allows you to define and label an area of storage to be used by your program during processing. The area defined is not set to an initial value. The definition operand allows you to define the following types of storage areas: A (fullword address), B (binary digit bytes), C (character), D (doubleword), E (short-form (fullword) floating-point number), F (binary fullword), H (halfword), L (16-byte, extended-precision floating-point area), P (packed-decimal area), and X (hexadecimal bytes). An additional operand called the *length qualifier* can be appended to the definition to alter the standard field length default. A repetition factor may be supplied before the field definition to cause multiple fields to be defined of this type.
DC	definition		**DEFINE CONSTANT** Similar to DS, but this assembler instruction also allows you to initialize a storage area during definition.
COPY	member name		**COPY** The assembler instruction allows you to retrieve source program instructions from an external partitioned data set (library). The source code is brought into your program at the location of the COPY statement and is treated as normal instructions originally within the definition of your program.
EQU	relocatable expression		**EQUATE** The assembler instruction equate constructs relocatable symbols throughout your program code. These values can then be used within machine instructions to further enhance program readability.

Data Definition

ORG address

SET LOCATION COUNTER

This assembler instruction alters the current location counter so that you may address an earlier defined storage area in your program. This instruction is most often used with the construction of record data structures and translation tables to support multinamed fields or to place translated data characters within a 256-byte translate table.

Flow Control

Standard Instructions

BAL R,D(X,B) RX

BRANCH AND LINK

Places the address of the next instruction into the GPR specified and transfers control to the instruction identified by the second operand. The code located at the second oper and can return to the subsequent instruction by using the BR instruction to be described later. The condition code and program mask bits from the PSW are copied into the leftmost byte of the register specified. These values may be used later to restore the PSW to its original state using the SPM instruction.

BALR R1,R2 RR

BRANCH AND LINK REGISTER

Similar to BAL except that the target instruction address in the second operand is contained in a register. An R2 value of zero causes R1 to be updated to the next instruction address, but a branch is not taken. The instruction "falls into" the next sequential executable instruction.

BAS R,D(X,B) RX

BRANCH AND SAVE

Similar to the BAL except that the leftmost byte of the first operand register specified is not loaded with PSW field values.

BASR R1,R2 RR

BRANCH AND SAVE REGISTER

Similar to BAS except that the second operand is a register.

BC B'xxxx',D(X,B) RX

BRANCH ON CONDITION

The bits in the first operand are used as a mask in a comparison against the current condition code value. The condition code values of 0, 1, 2, and 3 correspond with each bit in the mask (left to right). If a mask bit value is one and the current condition code matches that bit setting, a branch is taken to the location identified by the second operand.

BCR B'xxxx',R RR

BRANCH ON CONDITION REGISTER

Similar to BC except that the target address is in a register.

BCT R,D(X,B) RX

BRANCH ON COUNT

The GPR is reduced by one and is compared to a value of zero. If the register is not zero, then a branch is taken to the location specified in the second operand.

BCTR R1,R2 RR

BRANCH ON COUNT REGISTER

Similar to BCT except that the target address must now be contained in the GPR specified in the second operand. If the second operand is specified as zero, R1 is reduced by one but no branch is taken, even if it is nonzero.

Flow Control

Standard Instructions

BXH	R1,Re/o,D(B)	RS	**BRANCH ON INDEX HIGH** The contents of the even register in the second operand are added to R1. R1 is then compared to the odd register: if R1 is greater than the contents of the odd register, then a branch is taken to the location specified in the last operand. If R1 is not greater, then the instruction that follows is executed. If an odd register is specified in the second operand, then this register is used as the increment value for R1 and as the comparison value. If an even register is specified, an even/odd pair is used by the instruction.
BXLE	R1,Re/o,D(B)	RS	**BRANCH ON INDEX LOW OR EQUAL** Similar to BXH in operation. A branch is taken to the last operand address if the contents of R1 are less than or equal to the contents of the odd register value.

Extended Mnemonics (alternate forms of the BC, BCR instructions)

B BR	D(X,B) R	RX RR	**UNCONDITIONAL BRANCH** **UNCONDITIONAL BRANCH REGISTER** Branch to the location identified by the second operand. Similar to BC with a mask value of B'1111'.
BH BHR	D(X,B) R	RX RR	**BRANCH ON HIGH** **BRANCH ON HIGH REGISTER** If the current condition code is B'0010', a branch is taken. This is normally used after a comparison. Its mnemonic implies that a branch is to be taken if the first operand is greater than the second operand.
BL BLR	D(X,B) R	RX RR	**BRANCH ON LOW** **BRANCH ON LOW REGISTER** A branch is taken if the condition code is B'0100'. Commonly used after a comparison if the first operand is found to be less than the second.
BE BER	D(X,B) R	RX RR	**BRANCH IF EQUAL** **BRANCH IF EQUAL REGISTER** A branch is taken if the condition code is B'1000'. This instruction is used after a comparison in which the two operands have the same value.
BNH BNHR	D(X,B) R	RX RR	**BRANCH ON NOT HIGH** **BRANCH ON NOT HIGH REGISTER** B'1101'. Branch if the first operand was not greater than the second operand.
BNL BNLR	D(X,B) R	RX RR	**BRANCH ON NOT LOW** **BRANCH ON NOT LOW REGISTER** B'1011'. Branch if the first operand was not less than the second operand.
BNE BNER	D(X,B) R	RX RR	**BRANCH IF NOT EQUAL** **BRANCH IF NOT EQUAL REGISTER** B'0111'. Branch if the first and second operand do not have the same value.

Flow Control

Extended Mnemonics (alternate forms of the BC, BCR instructions)

BO	D(X,B)	RX	**BRANCH IF OVERFLOW OCCURRED, BRANCH ON ONES (TM)**
BOR	R	RR	**BRANCH IF OVERFLOW OCCURRED REGISTER, BRANCH ON ONES REGISTER (TM)** B'0001'. This instruction is generally used after an arithmetic instruction and is used to force a branch if an overflow condition occurred. Also used after a test-under-mask instruction to branch if all bits tested were ones.
BP	D(X,B)	RX	**BRANCH IF PLUS (POSITIVE)**
BPR	R	RR	**BRANCH IF PLUS REGISTER** B'0010'. If the result of an arithmetic operation results in a positive value, then a branch will be taken.
BM	D(X,B)	RX	**BRANCH IF MINUS (NEGATIVE), BRANCH IF MIXED (TM)**
BMR	R	RR	**BRANCH IF MINUS REGISTER, BRANCH IF MIXED REGISTER (TM)** B'0100'. If the result of an operation is negative, a branch is taken. Also used with the test-under-mask instruction to branch if some of the bits tested were ones and others were zero.
BNP	D(X,B)	RX	**BRANCH IF NOT PLUS (POSITIVE)**
BNPR	R	RR	**BRANCH IF NOT PLUS REGISTER** B'1101'. If the result is not a positive number, then branch to the location specified in the second operand.
BNM	D(X,B)	RX	**BRANCH IF NOT MINUS (NEGATIVE)**
BNMR	R	RR	**BRANCH IF NOT MINUS REGISTER** B'1011'. If the result is not a negative number, then branch to the location specified.
BNZ	D(X,B)	RX	**BRANCH IF NOT ZERO**
BNZR	R	RR	**BRANCH IF NOT ZERO REGISTER** B'0111'. If the resulting value is not zero, then branch.
BZ	D(X,B)	RX	**BRANCH IF ZERO, BRANCH IF ZEROS (TM)**
BZR	R	RR	**BRANCH IF ZERO REGISTER, BRANCH IF ZEROS REGISTER (TM)** B'1000'. If the resulting value is zero, then branch. Also used with the test-under-mask instruction to branch if all bits tested were zero.
BNO	D(X,B)	RX	**BRANCH IF NOT ONES, BRANCH IF NOT OVERFLOW**
BNOR	R	RR	**BRANCH IF NOT ONES REGISTER** B'1110'. Used with the test-under-mask instruction to branch if all bits tested were not ones. Used after an arithmetic instruction to branch if overflow did not occur.

Input/Output Instructions

ASSIST

XDUMP		**DUMP REGISTER CONTENTS**
XDUMP	loc,len	**DUMP A STORAGE AREA** The ASSIST XDUMP instruction can produce a hexadecimal dump of the general-purpose registers or program storage. Using the first form without operands or comments, the general-purpose registers are dumped. The second form dumps "len" bytes of storage beginning at "loc."

Input/Output Instructions

ASSIST

XDECI R,D(B)

CONVERT NUMBER FROM CHARACTER TO BINARY
The second operand identifies a character area that contains a numeric value. This instruction converts the character value into binary and places the value into the register specified. After execution, register 1 contains the address of the byte of memory that follows the converted number. Subsequent XDECI calls can use a second operand value of 0(R1) to obtain later numbers from the data area.

XDECO R,D(B)

CONVERT NUMBER FROM BINARY TO CHARACTER
The binary register value is converted to character format and is placed into the 12-byte area specified by the second operand. Make sure that the second operand is 12 bytes long. The number is right justified and contains a leading sign of minus if the number is negative. All leading zeros are suppressed. This instruction only works with integer data.

XPRNT D(B),len

PRINT A STORAGE AREA
The location specified is sent to the printer. The first byte of this area is used as a carriage control thus impacting line spacing. "len" must be greater than or equal to 1 and less than or equal to 133. See Appendix D for carriage control characters.

XREAD D(B),len

READ AN INPUT CARD
A card from the input data stream is read and "len" bytes from the data card are moved into the location specified. Each XREAD causes a new card to be read. Hence, if several pieces of data are to be extracted from a single card, use a single XREAD and use MVC instructions to extract your data.

Standard Assembly Language

DCB

DEFINE A DATA CONTROL BLOCK
A data control block is the focal point for I/O in standard assembler. Through this instruction you define the type of file to be processed and the characteristics of the dataset. The following operands are usually coded on this instruction:

OUTPUT:	DSORG	—Type of file to be processed PS—sequential DA—BDAM (relative file) IS—ISAM (index file)
	MACRF	—Type of I/O instructions to be used PM—PUT, move mode PL—PUT, locate mode WIC—WRITE, move mode, CHECK macro
	DDNAME	—Associated DD statement label
	LRECL	—Length of each logical record
	BLKSIZE	—Length of each physical block (groups of logical records)

Standard Assembly Language

			RECFM	—Format of each record F—fixed-length format V—variable-length format B—logical records are blocked A—ANSI carriage control to be used (Appendix D)
		INPUT:	DSORG	—Type of file to be processed PS—sequential DA—BDAM (relative file) IS—ISAM (index file)
			MACRF	—Type of I/O instructions to be used GM—GET, move mode GL—GET, locate mode RIC—READ, move mode, CHECK macro
			DDNAME	—Associated DD statement label
			EODAD	—Location in program where control is to be given when the end of file is reached

GET dcb,area

READ AN INPUT RECORD

An input record is read from the file identified by the DCB specified. The data is placed into the area identified by the second operand. If the area address is omitted and locate mode processing is being used, R1 returns the record address to the program.

PUT dcb,area

WRITE AN OUTPUT RECORD

The area specified in the second operand is written to the file identified by the DCB address specified in the first operand. The area should consist of a complete logical record. If the second operand is omitted and locate mode I/O is used, R1 returns the address of an area into which *you* must move the record. Another PUT is issued to actually write the record.

OPEN (dcb,direction)

PREPARE A FILE FOR PROCESSING

The DCB specified is prepared by the operating system for processing. The value of the direction depends on the file being processed. Normally, values are INPUT (bring data into the program), OUTPUT (send data out from the program), and UPDAT (update a random access file), which may be specified in the "direction" field.

CLOSE (dcb)

TERMINATE THE PROCESSING OF A FILE

When your program completes processing of a file, the program should issue the CLOSE instruction to disconnect the file from the program. The DCB name is coded as you see in the instruction. No other operands are needed.

SNAP

DUMP AN AREA OF STORAGE

This instruction can produce hexadecimal dumps of registers or storage areas. This instruction performs the same function as the ASSIST instruction XDUMP. A DCB is required as well as many operands. Refer to the discussion in the text for details on using this instruction.

Standard Assembly Language		
READ		**OBTAIN A RECORD FROM A RANDOM FILE** Similar to the GET instruction except it is used on random files. See the discussion in the text for details since there are many operands.
WRITE		**WRITE A RECORD TO A RANDOM FILE** Similar to the PUT instruction except that WRITE is used for random file processing. See the text for further details.

Macro Instructions		
AGO	label	**UNCONDITIONAL BRANCH** Transfer control to the macro label identified by the operand.
AIF	(arg1 op arg2).lab	**DECISION OR COMPARISON STATEMENT** Compare the value of argument 1 to that of argument 2 as defined in the operator element. If the comparison results in a "true" decision, then transfer control to the macro statement label identified in the last element. If "not true," then fall into the next macro instruction.
ANOP		**DUMMY INSTRUCTION** This instruction is used as the target of a branch. It does not perform any processing, it is simply used as a place holder for a macro label.
GBLA GBLB GBLC	&var &var &var	**DEFINE A GLOBAL ARITHMETIC MACRO VARIABLE** **DEFINE A GLOBAL BIT MACRO VARIABLE** **DEFINE A GLOBAL CHARACTER MACRO VARIABLE** A macro variable is defined depending on the type of data to be processed by the variable. The variable can be used across macro boundaries if each macro defines the variable as global.
LCLA LCLB LCLC	&var &var &var	**DEFINE A LOCAL ARITHMETIC MACRO VARIABLE** **DEFINE A LOCAL BIT MACRO VARIABLE** **DEFINE A LOCAL CHARACTER MACRO VARIABLE** Similar to GBLx except that a local variable is being defined. This variable cannot be used across macro boundaries.
MACRO		**BEGIN A MACRO DEFINITION** This is the first statement in a macro definition. It is called the macro header statement. Each macro must begin with this instruction. It has no operands.
MEND		**END A MACRO DEFINITION** This is the last physical statement of a macro. It informs the assembler that this is where the macro ends. Each macro must end with this instruction.
MEXIT		**EXIT THE MACRO** This instruction terminates macro processing before the MEND statement is encountered. It may be used to forcefully leave a macro if the processing for the macro has completed or if a problem has occurred where the macro cannot continue. This instruction is not needed if the MEND statement is processed to leave the macro.

Macro Instructions

MNOTE #,'lit'

DISPLAY AN INFORMATORY MESSAGE

During macro processing, the macro can issue messages depending on the outcome of processing within the macro. The first element of the MNOTE instruction is a number less than or equal to 4095. A value of zero in this area indicates that the message issued by the instruction is of a minor nature, that is, no error has occurred. Larger values usually convey a meaning of "error" to the programmer. The literal explains what problem or situation was encountered by the macro.

var SETA expression

ASSIGN A VALUE TO AN ARITHMETIC MACRO VARIABLE

var SETB expression

ASSIGN A VALUE TO A BIT MACRO VARIABLE

var SETC expression

ASSIGN A VALUE TO A CHARACTER MACRO VARIABLE

A macro variable of the appropriate type is coded in column 1 of the instruction containing this mnemonic. An expression is coded in column 16 of the instruction. The expression is evaluated and the result is assigned to the macro variable.

Program Definition and Spacing

CSECT

BEGIN AN ASSEMBLER CONTROL SECTION (PROGRAM)

This instruction begins an assembly language program. The name of the program is coded in column 1 of the instruction containing this mnemonic.

START offset

BEGIN AN ASSEMBLY LANGUAGE PROGRAM

Similar to CSECT. The offset operand sets the value of the location counter before code translation begins. This allows the programmer to adjust the location counter related to loaded memory locations for the executing program. Only one START statement can be coded per assembly. The first module of a multimodule system can utilize the START statement. All other modules must use the CSECT statement.

USING loc,R

DEFINE A BASE REGISTER TO THE ASSEMBLER

To convert all label references to base-displacement address forms, the assembler uses the information specified on the USING statement. This instruction tells the assembler that register R is the base register and that displacements are to be computed from the location identified by the first operand. Multiple-base registers can be specified by coding additional R values, separated by commas, after the one shown. An asterisk in the first operand indicates that the instruction that follows is to serve as the reference point for displacement computation.

Program Definition and Spacing

END label	**END AN ASSEMBLY LANGUAGE PROGRAM** This is the last statement of an assembly language program. Only one END statement can be coded per assembly. The label value is optional but is usually coded. The value of the operand (label) informs the operating system which module is to be executed first. In a single-module system, there is no doubt as to which one should be executed first, but in a multimodule system the END statement determines which one executes first.
new OPSYN old	**EQUATE OPERATION CODE** The instruction mnemonic specified by the operand "new" is equated to the existing mnemonic specified by the operand "old". Two instruction mnemonics now result in the same machine instruction.
CNOP m,n	**CONDITIONAL NO OPERATION** Depending on the values of m and n, the instruction has the effect of aligning storage areas on halfword, fullword, or doubleword boundaries. Refer to the discussion in the text for full details.
DROP x	**DROP BASE ADDRESS REGISTER** Informs the assembler that address computations related to the register specified are to be discontinued.
DSECT	**DEFINE A DUMMY CONTROL SECTION** The DSECT statement defines a data structure that can reference another area of memory. The DSECT itself occupies no storage since it may only be used to reference another storage area. Addressability to a DSECT is established with the USING statement. See the text for further details.
LTORG	**LITERAL GENERATION** Literals used throughout your program are generated in their full form after this instruction. In some assemblers, this instruction is not needed. Usually, this instruction is coded just before the END statement to provide proper addressability to the literal values.
SPACE n	**SKIP 1 TO 3 BLANK LINES BETWEEN SOURCE INSTRUCTIONS** The value of *n* can be coded as 1, 2, or 3. This causes the assembler to place the respective number of blank lines between source instructions in your assembly language program. This instruction cannot control spacing of output produced by your program. It can only control the listing of your instructions to enhance the readability of your program.
EJECT	**SKIP SOURCE CODE TO THE TOP OF THE NEXT PAGE** The instruction following the EJECT is placed at the top of the next page of the source listing. Again, this instruction cannot control the output produced by the program. It can only control the printing of the source code to enhance program readability.

Program Definition and Spacing

TITLE '. . . . .'

PRINT MESSAGE IN "TITLE AREA" AND EJECT TO TOP OF NEXT PAGE

The source printout from an assembly can be identified by using the TITLE instruction to place a character string into the source program title area. This instruction also causes the instruction that follows to be printed on the top of the next page. In other words, TITLE defines a printable message and causes a page eject within the source listing of your program. See the text for an example.

PRINT x

PRINT OPTIONAL DATA

This assembly language instruction allows the programmer to suppress macro expansion or printing of instructions within the program listing. An operand value of **NOGEN** suppresses macro expansion. **GEN** prints all macro expansions. **OFF** suppresses all printing. **ON** allows printing to occur.

Scanning Text

TRT D(L,B),D(B) SS

TRANSLATE AND TEST

Each byte in the first operand is used as a displacement into a 256-byte table defined by the second operand. For each byte in the first operand, the corresponding byte in operand 2 is evaluated. If the operand 2 byte is X'00', the next byte in operand 1 is evaluated. If the operand 2 byte is nonzero, then register 1 contains the address of the byte in operand 1 and the rightmost byte of register 2 contains the nonzero byte value from operand 2. The effect of this instruction is the ability to search an area (operand 1) for a particular character or characters. The text has several examples of this instruction.

The first byte of an area sent to the printer can be used as carriage control. XPRNT automatically uses the first byte for this function in ASSIST. The RECFM parameter of the DCB macro specifies whether or not the first byte will be used in this manner.

The following characters can control output spacing produced by the program. These characters cannot control source program spacing within the source listing.

Control Character	Use
1	Skip to the top of the next page of the output listing.
ƀ	Normal spacing, skip to the next line, and begin printing. Single space.
0	Leave one blank line and print on the second. Double space.
−	Leave two blank lines and print on the third. Triple spacing.
+	Do not skip. Print over the top of the current line. This may be used to highlight information on your output reports.

Abend Code	Reason for the Abend
0C1	**OPERATION EXCEPTION.** (1) The area containing the instruction did not have a valid operation code. (2) In an attempt to call a subroutine, the address of the routine to be called was not obtained correctly.
0C4	**PROTECTION EXCEPTION.** The area of memory that you're trying to access is outside of the bounds of your program. Look for a destroyed base register or for an explicit address form used incorrectly.
0C7	**DATA EXCEPTION.** The packed-decimal data that you're trying to process is not in a valid packed-decimal format. Although this abend can happen in other cases, it occurs most often when processing packed-decimal data.
0CB	**DECIMAL DIVIDE.** You tried to divide by a value of zero.
222	**OPERATOR CANCEL.** The master console operator canceled your job. Contact the console operator to determine why your program was canceled.
322	**TIME OUT.** (1) You have an infinite loop in your program. (2) You did not allow enough time for your program to execute completely.
722	**OUTLIM EXCEEDED.** The value that you coded on the OUTLIM parameter of your JCL DD statement is too small. This can also mean that your program is producing too much output or your program is in an infinite loop.
001	**DCB CONFLICT.** The LRECL and BLKSIZE parameters that you've specified on your JCL or in your program do not agree with the file that you are processing. Change your DCB values so that they are correct. If you're processing a file for input, don't code LRECL, BLKSIZE, or RECFM.
x13	**DATASET NOT FOUND.** The dataset that you are trying to process cannot be located on any of the system devices. Your dataset has been deleted or you've spelled the name incorrectly.
913	**SECURITY VIOLATION.** The dataset that you are trying to access is secured either through a password or through system protection. You are not authorized to access the dataset. Contact the owner of the dataset to get permission to access it.
30A	**INVALID FREEMAIN.** The FREEMAIN macro instruction that your program has issued is not of the correct format or does not contain the proper values. Whenever you attempt to free a storage area, make sure that the proper address and length of the area that you are freeing are in the proper registers.
706	**INVALID MODULE.** Your program is trying to execute a subroutine that is stored in a subroutine library, but the subroutine contains an error. In fact, the subroutine has been marked so that no one can use it because the error is so severe. Contact the person who wrote the module to determine what's wrong with it and to have a corrected copy of the routine placed into the library.
806	**SUBROUTINE NOT FOUND.** You are trying to invoke a subroutine written by someone else, but either the subroutine is not in the library that you thought or you've spelled the name of the subroutine incorrectly.
x37	**OUT OF SPACE.** (1) the non-VSAM disk dataset that you are trying to process is full. Either you didn't allocate enough space for the file in the first place or you've written more records than you thought. (2) The volume on which your dataset resides is completely full. Move your dataset to a volume that has more space.

ANSWERS TO CHAPTER 1 STUDY QUESTIONS

1. compiler, assembler
2. assembly language
3. COBOL, PL/I, FORTRAN, PASCAL, C, ADA, BASIC, MODULA-2
4. documentation
5. design, implementation and testing
6. memory, channels, CPU
7. EBCDIC, ASCII
8. peripherals
9. bit, byte, kilobyte, megabyte, gigabyte
10. loader, linkage editor
11. 80
12. operating system
13. 5120
14. utility or service program
15. load module
16. compile, go
17. eight
18. channel
19. analysis
20. machine language

ANSWERS TO CHAPTER 2 STUDY QUESTIONS

1. hexadecimal
2. 32 bits, two halfwords, four bytes
3. address memory, arithmetic operations, binary data
4. eight bits
5. (a) 1501
   (b) 0010 1111 1110 1101 1010
   (c) 196,314
   (d) 3AE3
   (e) 0001 1110 1011
6. (a) 1111 1101 1011 0101
   (b) 15266D
   (c) 1111 1111 1111 1111 1111 1111 1110 0111
   (d) 03274D
7. (a) 26A0
   (b) 884
   (c) 198
8. (a) 1101 0000
   (b) 0100 0010
   (c) 0000 1000

9. (a) 00005FC4
   (b) 00001234
   (c) 0007ACE2
   (d) invalid, displacement can't be negative
   (e) invalid, displacement can't be greater than 4095
10. (a) three bytes C0 00 00
    (b) eight bytes F1 F2 F5 F8 F2 F9 F1 C2
    (c) nine bytes 4E F1 F2 F5 F8 F2 F9 F1 F2
    (d) five bytes 01 25 82 91 2C
11. Each word is four bytes so 2,500 words yields 10,000 bytes of storage.
12. (a) D(X,B)
    (b) Either format. Since only a displacement has been coded, you can't tell which format has been qualified.
    (c) D(X,B)
    (d) Either format. D(B) or a D(,B) format.
    (e) Either format. Same as d.
13. Binary halfword, binary fullword, packed decimal, and floating point data types.
14. Negative numbers are represented in the binary data type using two's complement notation. Packed decimal data represents negative numbers using either the hexadecimal digits B or D in the sign portion of the number. We'll omit a discussion of floating point at this time.
15. Extended architecture supports 31 bit addressing. If your operating system, assembler or compiler, and hardware is equipped to handle 31 bit addressing, it may be used by your program.

ANSWERS TO CHAPTER 3 STUDY QUESTIONS

1. 14
2. linkage conventions
3. USING
4. 2, 12
5. 4096
6. base register, displacement
7. field, record, file
8. record, major structures, minor structures
9. DC
10. PL3 or larger
11. alignment
12. BCR B'1111',14
13. comments, SPACE, EJECT, TITLE
14. syntax or assembly errors, execution or run-time
15. 72

16. entry point address
17. assembly language, machine
18. repetition factor or duplication factor
19. left, right, blanks, right, left, zeros
20. doubleword (actually, this address would be aligned on a halfword and fullword boundary also)
21. (a) 3 times 4 = 12
    (b) 2 plus 4 = 6
    (c) 25
    (d) 4 times 8 = 32
22. (a) legal
    (b) illegal, can't use underscore
    (c) legal
    (d) illegal, can't use the period
    (e) legal
    (f) legal
23.

```
(a)              USING   QUESTION,3
(b)              LR      8,4
(c)  PROJECT1    CSECT
                 or
     PROJECT1    START   0
(d)              END     PROJECT1
(e)  LASTNAME    DS      CL20
(f)              LR      7,15
```

24. (a) illegal. The mnemonic should be A instead of AR. AR can only be used to add two registers. Since TOTAL appears to be a storage area, the A instruction must be used.
    (b) illegal. The CSECT statement cannot specify a starting value for the location counter. Omit the X'100' from the instruction to make it legal or replace the mnemonic CSECT with START.
    (c) illegal. The DS instruction is coded but the programmer has attempted to initialize the field. Incidentally, the assembler will not flag this statement as an error and the field will not be initialized.
    (d) If R25 is a legal symbol then the instruction would be legal. Most likely the instruction is not legal.
    (e) illegal. The mnemonic should be BCR instead of BC. Incidentally, this is a legal statement and will not generate an error. However, it may cause your program to fail during execution.
    (f) legal.

```
25. NOTHING   CSECT
              STM     14,12,12(13)
              LR      12,15
              USING   NOTHING,12
              LA      11,SAVEAREA
              ST      13,4(11)
              ST      11,8(13)
              LR      13,11
    *
              L       13,4(13)
              LM      14,12,12(13)
              SR      15,15
              BCR     B'1111',14
    SAVEAREA  DS      18F
              END     NOTHING
26. NOTHING   CSECT
              USING   NOTHING,15
              BCR     B'1111',14
              END     NOTHING
```

ANSWERS TO CHAPTER 4 STUDY QUESTIONS

1. micro code
2. operating system
3. loader, linkage editor
4. fetching
5. program status word (PSW)
6. condition code
7. ILC, next instruction address
8. ends normally, abends, times out
9. IPL, booting
10. interrupts
11. character
12. contents or format
13. 256
14. immediate data
15. 6, 2
16. shorter-faster, longer-slower
17. sequential
18. JCL, OPEN/CLOSE, DCB, I/O instructions
19. carriage control
20. literals

21. (a)
```
         MVI   PRNTLINE,C'-'
```
(b)
```
         MVC   XYZ(25),=CL25'WYSIWYG'
            or
         MVC   XYZ(7),=C'WYSIWYG'
```
(c)
```
         MVC   TEMP(20),A
         MVC   A(20),B
         MVC   B(20),TEMP
          .  .  .
TEMP     DS    CL20
```
(d)
```
         MVI   FOUNDIT,C'N'
```
22. The MVC moves the digits into LINE. The MVI moves the letter A into the first byte of LINE. The last MVC copies the first byte into the second to give AA, the second into the third to give AAA, the third into the fourth to give AAAA, and so on. The resulting value of LINE is AAAAAAAAAA.

23.
```
MVI PRNTLINE,C' '
MVC PRNTLINE+1(132),PRNTLINE
```
24. (a) Since XYZ is not initialized, the resulting value of ABC cannot be determined.
   (b) 'ƀCOWSƀEATƀ'
   (c) 'ALLOWANCEƀ'
   (d) 'ALLƀMICEƀEATƀCHEEZ'

25. A through D are equivalent.

26.
```
PRINTOUT  DCB   DSORG=PS,DDNAME=SYSOUT,MACRF=PM,    X
                RECFM=FA,LRECL=133,BLKSIZE=133
```
27. MVC X'1AC'(25,12),X'2BE'(12)

28.
```
PHONE     DS   0CL14
          DC   C'('
AREACODE  DS   CL3
          DC   C')-'
PREFIX    DS   CL3
          DC   C'-'
SUFFIX    DS   CL4
```
29. Assume that the compressed phone number is in the field SQZPHONE.
```
MVC AREACODE(3),SQZPHONE EXTRACT THE AREA CODE
MVC PREFIX(3),SQZPHONE+3 EXTRACT THE PHONE PREFIX
MVC SUFFIX(4),SQZPHONE+6 EXTRACT REMAINING PHONE DIGITS
```
30. The opcode for the MVC instruction is D2. Since X is located at E4, X+2 will be at location E6. Y, being at location 3F, forces Y+1 to be located at 40. Lengths are encoded in an SS instruction as one less than the coded value. Separating the fields for purposes of illustration, the resulting machine code will be:
```
D2 01 30E6 3040
```

ANSWERS TO CHAPTER 5 STUDY QUESTIONS

1. ST (store)
2. =F'−1'
3. chaining

4. register 1
5. ORG
6. entry point address, return code
7. USING
8. PRINT NOGEN
9. 14
10. reserved or not used
11. B
12. D(X,B), label
13. zoned decimal
14. OI, sign, F
15. A, ANSI
16. the odd register
17. division, multiplications
18. 86, 133
19. label-plus-displacement addressing
20. SYSDATE and SYSTIME
21. ASSIST Implementation

```
XREAD   CARDIN,80           OBTAIN AN INPUT RECORD
XDECI   R2,CARDIN           EXTRACT THE FIRST NUMBER
XDECI   R3,0(R1)            EXTRACT THE SECOND NUMBER
XDECI   R4,0(R1)            EXTRACT THE THIRD NUMBER
AR      R3,R2               ADD THE FIRST TWO NUMBERS
AR      R3,R4               ADD ON THE THIRD NUMBER
SR      R2,R2               CLEAR EVEN REGISTER FOR DIVIDE
D       R2,=F'3'            COMPUTE THE AVERAGE
ST      R3,AVERAGE          STORE QUOTIENT VALUE
```

Assembly Implementation

```
GET     INPUTDCB,CARDIN     OBTAIN AN INPUT RECORD
PACK    NUM1(8),VALUE1(5)   CONVERT FIRST NUMBER TO PACKED
PACK    NUM2(8),VALUE2(5)   CONVERT SECOND NUMBER TO PACKED
PACK    NUM3(8),VALUE3(5)   CONVERT THIRD NUMBER TO PACKED
CVB     R2,NUM1             CONVERT PACKED NUMBERS TO BINARY
CVB     R3,NUM2             ...
CVB     R4,NUM3             ...
AR      R3,R2               ADD THE FIRST TWO NUMBERS
AR      R3,R4               ADD ON THE THIRD NUMBER
SR      R2,R2               CLEAR EVEN REGISTER FOR DIVIDE
D       R2,=F'3'            COMPUTE THE AVERAGE
ST      R3,AVERAGE          STORE QUOTIENT VALUE
```

22.

```
TITLE   DS  0CL86           THIS LINE WILL BE 86 CHARACTERS
        DC  C'1'            CARRIAGE CONTROL - BEGIN ON A NEW PAGE
        DC  CL30' '         CENTER THE TITLE BY MOVING TO THE RIGHT
        DC  C'ACME COMPUTER CORPORATION'    THE TITLE
        DC  CL30' '
```

23. (a)
```
       PRINT GEN
```
(b)
```
       MVI   RUNSUM,C' '             CLEAR THE FIRST BYTE
       MVC   RUNSUM+1(14),RUNSUM     CLEAR REMAINING BYTES
       XDECO R5,RUNSUM+3             PLACE VALUE IN RIGHTMOST 12 BYTES
```

```
       CVD   R5,WORK                 CONVERT TO PACKED DECIMAL
       UNPK  RUNSUM(15),WORK(8)      CONVERT TO ZONED DECIMAL
       OI    RUNSUM+14,X'F0'         FIX RIGHTMOST DIGIT
```
(c)
```
       LA    R15,16                  SET RETURN CODE TO 16
```
(d)
```
       M     R4,=F'31416'            MULTIPLY BY PI*10,000
       D     R4,=F'10000'            DIVIDE BY 10,000 TO GET QUOTIENT
```
(e)
```
   PGM CSECT
       USING PGM,R15                 ESTABLISH R15 AS OUR BASE REG.
```
24.
```
     CVD  R5,PACKED                  CONVERT TO PACKED DECIMAL
     UNPK ZONED(15),PACKED(8)        CONVERT FROM PACKED TO ZONED
     OI   ZONED+14,X'F0'             FIX RIGHT DIGIT
     MVC  CASH+8(2),ZONED+13         MOVE CENTS TO CASH
     MVI  CASH+7,C'.'                TUCK IN THE DECIMAL POINT
     MVC  CASH(7),ZONED+6            MOVE DOLLAR AMOUNT TO CASH
```
25. (1) The first two operands on the STM should be reversed so that R14 through R12 are stored instead of R12 through R14.
(2) The second instruction should be LR instead of LA.
(3) The instructions to chain the register save areas need to be changed so that R11 is not used. R11 can't be used since it is defined as the base register for the program. The instruction "LA R11,SAVEAREA" would immediately destroy our base register, which would not be acceptable.
(4) The displacements used to chain the forward and backward save areas are reversed. Our save area address should be stored into the caller's save area list at offset eight. The caller's save area address should be stored into our save area at offset four. The correct implementation is shown below.

```
MAINPGM CSECT
        STM   R14,R12,12(R13) SAVE THE REGISTERS
        LR    R11,R15         COPY THE E.P.A.
        USING MAINPGM,R11     ESTABLISH R11 AS THE BASE REG.
        LA    R10,SAVEAREA    ADDRESS OUR REGISTER SAVE AREA
        ST    R13,4(R10)      SAVE CURRENT R13 ADDRESS
        ST    R10,8(R13)      CHAIN BACKWARD
        LR    R13,R10         ESTABLISH A NEW SAVE AREA
```

ANSWERS TO CHAPTER 6 STUDY QUESTIONS

1. 00, 01, 10, 11
2. BC, BCR
3. extended mnemonic
4. ORG
5. UNTIL

6. EODAD
7. BC B'0100',BYEBYE
8. BC B'0100',SCHARGE
   BM SCHARGE
9. BXLE 2,6,AGAIN
10. DS 0x
    EQU *
11. (a)

```
         BC    B'0001',TOOBIG
```

(b)

```
         CLC   PSN(2),=H'10'
```

(c)

```
         CLC   SSN(3),=C'123'        CHECK FIRST THREE DIGITS
         BNE   KEEPGOIN              IF NOT 123, KEEP GOING
```

(d)

```
         C     R3,=F'0'              COMPARE TO ZERO
         BNZ   KEEPGOIN              IF NOT ZERO, KEEP GOING
```

(e)

```
         L     R2,NUM1               OBTAIN THE FIRST NUMBER
         A     R2,NUM2               ADD THE SECOND NUMBER
         A     R2,NUM3               ADD THE THIRD NUMBER
```

12.

```
         LA    R3,1                  SET CONTROL VARIABLE TO 1
LOOP     DS    0H                    TOP OF THE LOOP
         C     R3,=F'50'             HAVE WE REACHED THE LIMIT
         BH    EXIT                  IF SO, EXIT THE LOOP
         [body of the loop]
         A     R3,=F'5'              INCREMENT R3 BY 5
         B     LOOP                  RETURN TO THE TOP OF THE LOOP
EXIT     DS    0H
```

13.

```
LOOP     DS    0H                    TOP OF THE LOOP
         CLC   LASTNAME(20),=CL20'JONES' IS THE NAME SMITH
         BE    EXIT                  IF SO, EXIT THE LOOP
         CLC   LASTNAME(20),=CL20'SMITH' IS THE NAME JONES
         BE    EXIT                  IF SO, EXIT THE LOOP
         [body of the loop]
         B     LOOP                  RETURN TO THE TOP OF THE LOOP
EXIT     DS    0H
```

14.

```
LOOP     DS    0H                    TOP OF THE LOOP STRUCTURE
         [body of the loop]
         CLC   LASTNAME(20),=CL20'ZACHRY'  HAVE WE PASSED ZACHRY YET?
         BNH   LOOP                        IF NOT, KEEP LOOPING
```

15. Assume that the number of females will be counted using R3 and the number of males will be counted using R4. The second implementation uses equates to make the problem look much like an implementation in a higher-level language.

    We should also note that the CLI instructions in the solutions below may be replaced with the CLC instruction. Using a literal, we can determine if the value of the field labeled SEX contains a value of F as follows:

```
                    CLC    SEX(1),=C'F'

         CLI   SEX,C'F'             IS THIS PERSON FEMALE?
         BE    SEXF                 IF SO, INCREMENT FEMALE COUNTER
         A     R4,=F'1'             ADD ONE TO R4, INCREMENT MALE COUNTER
         B     ENDIF                RETURN TO NORMAL PROCESSING
SEXF     DS    0H
         A     R3,=F'1'             INCREMENT FEMALE COUNTER.
ENDIF    DS    0H
```

```
FEMALES  EQU   3                    EQUATE THE SYMBOL "FEMALE" WITH "3"
MALES    EQU   4                    EQUATE THE SYMBOL "MALE" WITH "4"
         CLI   SEX,C'F'             IS THIS PERSON FEMALE?
         BE    SEXF                 IF SO, GO INCREMENT FEMALE COUNTER
         AH    MALES,=H'1'          IF NOT, INCREMENT MALE COUNTER BY 1
         B     ENDIF                RETURN TO NORMAL PROCESSING
SEXF     DS    0H
         AH    FEMALES,=H'1'        INCREMENT FEMALE COUNTER BY 1
ENDIF    DS    0H
```

ANSWERS TO CHAPTER 7 STUDY QUESTIONS

1. 0000376C or 0000376F
2. 40 20 20 20 6B 20 20 20 6B 20 21 20 4B 20 20
3. ED PATTERN(15),NUMA or
   EDMK PATTERN(15),NUMA
4. 31
5. two-byte quotient, 4-byte remainder
6. X'00150C001C'
7.
```
         SRP   VALA,4,0
         DP    VALA,VALB
         ZAP   VALA(8),VALA(4)
         SRP   VALA(8),64-1,5
```
8.
```
         L     R3,BITS
         SPM   R3
         .     .
         .     .
         .     .
BITS     DS    0F
         DC    B'00111111'
         DC    XL3'00'
```
9. X'00 00 00 03 5D'
10. BCTR R6,0
11. X'00 00 00 4B 5F'
12. X'00 23 45 67 9F' (a positive number !)

13. ALLDONE EQU B'0111'
14. ZAP XYZ(3),=P'14'
15. F1F3F5F7D9 (higher digits are lost because the target field is too small)
16. Usually not. CP is valid only for packed-decimal data. However, if it is known that the character fields contain data in packed format, CP can be used.
17. invalid. The sign would not be A, B, C, D, E, or F.
18. 0C7, data exception
19. When shifting left, it's not used. When shifting right, it's used as a rounding factor for the leftmost digit lost due to shifting.
20. the fill character

ANSWERS TO CHAPTER 8 STUDY QUESTIONS

1. DC X'0000'
2. 0C4 protection exception
3. 0C7 data exception. The second operand is not a packed-decimal field since it's a binary halfword.
4. R14
5. FA41 A1B0 A1B9
6. 322
7. L R3,0(R6,R7)
8. Specification exception (0C6) since you are trying to *load* the data at location 5 in the computer, and the load instruction requires halfword alignment.
9. Entry point address, next instruction address from the PSW, and the instruction length code (also from the PSW).
10. XDUMP
    SNAP DCB=SNAPDCB,PDATA=REGS
11.
next instruction address	08CFB2
− instruction length code	4
failing instruction address	08CFAE
12. Protection exception since the interrupt code is 0004.
13. Unpredictable, it depends on the contents of the data area.
14. contents directory entry (CDE)
15. XDUMP LOOPCTR,4
    SNAP DCB=SNAPDCB,STORAGE=(LOOPCTR,LOOPCTR+4)
16. PUT
17. No. A DCB may be named whatever you want as long as it's a unique name within your program.
18. //GO.SYSUDUMP DD SYSOUT=$
19. Use the OUTLIM parameter.
20. Code the TIME parameter on your JOB card.

21.

```
offset    object code              source program statement

000000                             COMPUTE  CSECT
000000                                      USING    *,R15
000000    F274 F080 F088                    PACK     VALUE(8),N(5)
000006    F877 F078 F080                    ZAP      LIMIT(8),VALUE(8)
00000C    FD73 F078 F0A0                    DP       LIMIT(8),=PL4'2'
000012    F873 F078 F078                    ZAP      LIMIT(8),LIMIT(4)
000018                             LOOP     DS       0H
000018    F977 F098 F078                    CP       I(8),LIMIT(8)
00001E    4720 F04E                         BH       YES
000022    F877 F090 F080                    ZAP      WORK(8),VALUE(8)
000028    FD73 F090 F09C                    DP       WORK(8),I+4(4)
00002E    F873 F090 F090                    ZAP      WORK(8),WORK(4)
000034    FC73 F090 F09C                    MP       WORK(8),I+4(4)
00003A    F977 F090 F080                    CP       WORK(8),VALUE(8)
000040    4780 F058                         BE       NO
000044    FA70 F098 F0A4                    AP       I(8),=P'1'
00004A    47F0 F018                         B        LOOP
00004E    E020 F060 000A           YES      XPRNT    YESLINE,10
000054    47F0 F05E                         B        OUT
000058    E020 F06A 000A           NO       XPRNT    NOLINE,10
00005E    07FE                     OUT      BR       R14
000060    40E8 C5E2 4040 4040      YESLINE  DC       CL10' YES'
00006A    40D5 D640 4040 4040      NOLINE   DC       CL10' NO'
000078                             LIMIT    DS       D
000080                             VALUE    DS       D
000088                             N        DS       CL5'00025'
000090                             WORK     DS       D
000098    0000 0000 0000 0002      I        DC       D'2'
                                            LTORG
0000A0    0000 002C                                  =PL4'2'
0000A4    1C                                         =P'1'
                                            END      COMPUTE
```

22. The program attempts to determine if a number is prime. In this particular example, the program will determine if 25 is prime. If so, the message "YES" is printed, otherwise "NO" is printed.
23. Data exception, 0C7.
24. The program fails at the first instruction because the field N is not defined properly. It should have been defined using DC instead of DS. Even though an initial value was specified, the mnemonic did not cause the field to be initialized properly.
25. Two packed-decimal literals, =PL4'2' and =P'1'.
26. The current instruction address. However, since the USING does not generate object code, the * actually references the PACK instruction that follows.
27. No. R15 is being used as the base register and no save area has been established by the program. Also, the register equates have not been coded but they are used within the program.
28. BC B'0010',YES
29. Yes. Since all operations involve integer arithmetic the conversion to binary would be no problem.
30. Since R3 has not been altered by the program, and since the program will obviously be executed in ASSIST, R3 will contain the ASSIST initialization value X'F4F4F4F4'.

ANSWERS TO CHAPTER 9 STUDY QUESTIONS

1. zero
2. BALR (branch and link register)
3. place a nonzero value into R15 just before returning control to the calling module
4. LTR (load and test register) LTR R15,R15
   C (compare) C R15,=F'0'

5. (a) BAL R3,STRING
   (b) L R15,=V(STRING)
   BALR R14,R15
   (c) BAS R3,STRING

```
(a) BAL     R3,STRING
(b) L       R15,=V(STRING)
    BALR    R14,R15
(c) BAS     R3,STRING
```

6. Use the SPM instruction to restore the condition code and program mask to their original values. The link register contains these values in the leftmost byte. Hence, if the link register is Rx, simply issue the instruction:

```
SPM     Rx
```

7. It is a halfword binary field that gives the number of bytes of parm data that was coded on the EXEC statement.
8.

```
         BAL     R1,CALLSTR
         DC      A(A)
         DC      A(B)
         DC      A(C)
         DC      A(D)
         DC      A(E)
CALLSTR  L       R15,=V(STRING)
         BALR    R14,R15
```

```
         LA      R1,=A(A,B,C,D,E)
         L       R15,=V(STRING)
         BALR    R14,R15
```

9. global
10. Place a LTORG statement at the end of ***every*** CSECT.
11. The code is correct as written. The USING statement may appear anywhere before the first label reference in the program.
12. An alignment error occurs on the first address definition for field A. Since the BAL instruction is not aligned on a fullword boundary, the BAL causes R1 to address the memory location 0000A6. However, the parameter address for field A does not begin until location A8. Thus, R1 does not address the parameter list properly. To fix the problem, the programmer should code a CNOP 0,4 instruction just before the BAL.
13. (a) R0 can be used as long as the data field is loaded and stored before the subroutine attempts to process the data. This is not a normal use of R0 to pass a single value but it is legal.
    (b) Legal. Even though the element being passed is an address, it is a single value that will fit into a register.
    (c) Legal. A halfword value can easily be returned in a fullword register.
    (d) Legal. R0 can pass the value to the subroutine and either R0 or R15 can return the "yes" or "no" indicator.
    (e) Legal. As long as the value doesn't exceed the register's limit this is a legal passing of parameters.
14. `//   EXEC   ASMFCG,PARM.GO='/SMITH'`
15. Nothing, the program will run correctly. If the label is omitted on the END statement the assembler assumes that the first CSECT in the program is to be given control. Since the program only consists of one CSECT and several internal subroutines (that do not begin with CSECT), the mainline program will be given control

properly. Some assemblers may generate a warning message on the diagnostics page but your program should still be allowed to execute.

16.
```
ASISTPGM   CSECT
           USING   ASISTPGM,15,12
           LA      12,2048(15)
           LA      12,2048(12)
```

17. If the programmer is only expanding one field, no additional base registers will be needed. By locating the largest data area in the program just before the END statement *(after the LTORG),* the program should be able to address the field properly and not require an additional base register.
18. When communicating with vendor-developed software modules that support a non-fixed number of input parameters. Such software continues to process input until the end of list indicator is found within the parameter list.
19. No. Register 1 is supposed to reference an address but if you refer to the code, R1 addresses the value directly. This is not legal. To fix the code, change the first LA instruction to "LA R1,=A(N)".
20. The START statement can only be used on the first control section within a program. All other components must begin with the CSECT statement. In general, only utilize the CSECT statement when developing multi-module systems.

ANSWERS TO CHAPTER 10 STUDY QUESTIONS

1. macro header statement
2. GBLx, LCLx, SETx, AGO, AIF, ANOP, ACTR
3. .*
4. It must begin with an ampersand (&). The next character must be a letter of the alphabet. The next one to six characters must either be letters or digits.
5. Each programmer can make a copy of the macro that is to be shared or the macro can be placed into a macro library so that it is available to all programmers.
6. the period
7. substring
8. ACTR
9. type attribute, T'
10. yes
11. conditionally
12. MEXIT
13. boolean
14. 255
15. globally
16. The WHATIS macro generates the first 6 characters of the alphabet.

```
DC   AL1(193)        C'A'
DC   AL1(194)        C'B'
DC   AL1(195)        C'C'
DC   AL1(196)        C'D'
DC   AL1(197)        C'E'
DC   AL1(198)        C'F'
```

17.
```
         MACRO
&LAB     SETCC   &VALUE
         LCLA    &I                       DECLARE A LOCAL PARAMETER
&I       SETA    &VALUE                   CONVERT PARM TO USABLE VALUE
&LAB     DS      0H                       GENERATE A LABEL IF NECESSARY
         ST      1,SCC&SYSNDX             DON'T DESTROY R1
         AIF     (&I EQ 0).ZERO           CHECK THE DESIRED CC VALUE
         AIF     (&I EQ 1).ONE            ...
         AIF     (&I EQ 2).TWO            ...
         AIF     (&I EQ 3).TREE           ...
         MNOTE   8,'ILLEGAL CONDITION CODE VALUE SPECIFIED'
         MEXIT
.ZERO    ANOP
         MVI     BITS&SYSNDX,B'00001111'  SET CC TO ZERO
         AGO     .SPM
.ONE     ANOP
         MVI     BITS&SYSNDX,B'00011111'  SET CC TO ONE
         AGO     .SPM
.TWO     ANOP
         MVI     BITS&SYSNDX,B'00101111'  SET CC TO TWO
         AGO     .SPM
.TREE    ANOP
         MVI     BITS&SYSNDX,B'00111111'  SET CC TO THREE
.SPM     ANOP
         L       1,BITS&SYSNDX            LOAD NEW CC VALUE
         SPM     1                        SET THE CONDITION CODE
         L       1,SCC&SYSNDX             RELOAD R1
         B       SKP&SYSNDX               SKIP AROUND WORK AREAS
SCC&SYSNDX  DS   F                        HOLD AREA FOR R1
BITS&SYSNDX DC   F'0'                     WORK AREA FOR THE CC
SKP&SYSNDX  DS   0H                       TARGET OF BRANCH
         MEND
```

18. (a)
```
         AGO    .ALLOK
```
(b)
```
         AIF    (&A EQ &B).EQUAL
&C       SETA   &C-1
         AGO    .GOON
.EQUAL   ANOP
&C       SETA   &C+1
.GOON    ANOP
```
(c) `&LAB  AVERAGE    &F1=,&F2=,&F3=`
(d) `MNOTE 16,'INPUT FIELD LENGTH IS TOO LARGE'`
(e) `MEXIT`

19. (a) No errors.
(b) The SETA statement cannot be issued as part of the AIF instruction. Only a macro label can appear after the last right parenthesis for the conditional expression.
(c) No errors.
(d) No errors.
(e) No errors.

20.
```
         MACRO
         TRACE   &STRING
         GBLB    &DBUG                IS DEBUGGING ON OR OFF
         LCLA    &LEN                 LENGTH OF THE STRING
         AIF     (&DBUG).OK           IF DBUG, PRINT STRING
         MEXIT                        OTHERWISE EXIT THE MACRO
.OK      ANOP
&LEN     SETA    K'&STRING            GET LENGTH OF THE MESSAGE
         XPRNT   =C&STRING,&LEN-2     PRINT ALL BUT THE QUOTES
         MEND
```

ANSWERS TO CHAPTER 11 STUDY QUESTIONS

1. B'00101010'
2. LCR R3,R4
3. CR (logical instructions may not be used here)
4.
```
         LA      R2,INPUTREC
         LA      R4,BUFFER
         L       R3,=F'2500'
         LR      R5,R3
         MVCL    R2,R4
```
5.
```
         ICM     R8,B'0010',0(R9)
```
6.
```
         SRL     R3,24
         STC     R3,PRNTLINE
```
7.
```
         SR      R5,R5
         LA      R6,1
         ST      R6,POWERS       SAVE FIRST VALUE
         LA      R7,4
LOOP     C       R5,=F'30'
         BH      DONE
         SLL     R6,1
         ST      R6,POWERS(R7)
         LA      R5,1(R5)
         LA      R7,4(R7)
         B       LOOP
DONE     .....
```
8.
```
PUNCT    DC      256X'00'
         ORG     PUNCT+C'.'
         DC      C'.'
         ORG     PUNCT+C'!'
         DC      C'!'
         ORG     PUNCT+C'?'
         DC      C'?'
         ORG
```
9. The value is 20; it is a relocatable symbol.

10.

```
FLAGS    DS     X
         ORG    FLAGS
XMAS     DS     BL1
RETIRE   DS     BL1
CREDIT   DS     BL1
INSURE   DS     BL1
BOWL     DS     BL1
         ORG
```

11. R14 is not generally used as a base register since R14 is used in calling subroutines. R14 is also used to call system routines to perform I/O operations. If your program does not do any I/O, does not call any subroutines, and does not request any services of the operating system, then R14 *can* be used as a base register.

12.

```
         LA     Rx,0
         SR     Rx,Rx
         XR     Rx,Rx
         L      Rx,-F'0'
```

13.

```
         LTR    R3,R3
         BM     MINUS

         SR     R2,R2
         SLDL   R2,1
         C      R2,=F'0'
         BNE    MINUS
```

14. Use the EXECUTE instruction to execute the TRANSLATE instruction to convert the fields appropriately.
15. Translate the area using the following translate table:

```
DUMPED   EBCDIC
         ORG    DUMPED+X'FA'
         DC     C'ABCDEF'
         ORG
```

ANSWERS TO CHAPTER 12 STUDY QUESTIONS

1. Short, long, and extended precision. Short format is a four-byte number (fullword). Long format is an eight-byte value (doubleword). Extended precision is a 16-byte value.
2. The characteristic and fractional component are both stored in positive format. Only the leftmost bit of a floating-point number represents the sign. Negative numbers are not stored in two's complement notation.
3. Sign, characteristic, fractional component.
4.

```
LD     R4,A
AD     R4,B
STD    R4,SUM
```

5. All bits in the floating-point number are zero. In other words, floating-point zero is the same as binary zero. X'0000 . . . 00'
6. Normalization, the guard digit, rounding.

7. The multiply instructions allow you to obtain a result larger than either of the original operands to be multiplied. Division instructions do not result in a quotient and remainder. Only one value results from a division operation. This value represents the number with digits to the left and right of the decimal.
8. 127
9. short form: 6 fractional digits
   long form: 14 fractional digits
   extended form: 28 fractional digits
10. LPER (load positive short register)
11. (a) 411AF700
    (b) It's already normalized.
    (c) It's already normalized.
12. (a) 4410E100
    (b) 408B020C
    (c) 4410E18B
13. (a) −5
    (b) .03125
    (c) approximately 4660.3
14. (a) 4080000000000000
    (b) 413243FE5C91D14C
    (c) 427B1F7CED916871
15. (a) .05
    (b) 5000
    (c) approximately 2.33333

ANSWERS TO CHAPTER 13 STUDY QUESTIONS

1. Place the address of a storage area into a register and use the USING statement to establish that register as a base register for the DSECT.
2. register 1
3. GL (get locate), PL (put locate)
4. RDW (record descriptor word)
5. BDW (block descriptor word)
6. Four or more. In other words, the value of the BLKSIZE parameter must be at least four more than the LRECL.
7. nonlabeled or standard labeled
8. standard labeled
9. This depends on the size of each file and the size of the tape. The smaller the files, the more that will fit on a tape. However, the maximum file number is 99,999 and so that becomes the most that may be stored.
10. Within the program, there are no differences. The only differences occur in how the JCL is coded.
11. CALL GREGDATE,(PRNTDATE)
12. //GO.SYSUDUMP DD SYSOUT=$
13. eleven, route messages to the program's job log
14. GETMAIN and FREEMAIN

15. Subroutines and modules that do not perform I/O are most suitable for reentrant design. Also, programs that have few data areas or are used to process data supplied by other programs are good candidates for reentrancy.

ANSWERS TO CHAPTER 14 STUDY QUESTIONS

1. BSAM, sequential processing; and BDAM, random processing
2. The relative record number is a three-byte binary number used to reference the records.
3. formatted
4. Records are logically deleted by placing the value X'FF' in the first byte of the record.
5. None. Records cannot be blocked.
6. UPDAT
7. Test the exception code bits to determine what happened.
8. blocks
9. index, prime, overflow
10. cylinders
11. fixed or variable length, blocked or nonblocked
12. Records added may cause other records to be bumped from a track into the overflow area of the dataset.
13. The READ and WRITE instructions must address the same event control block. This is accomplished through the use of the list and execute forms of these macros.
14. Key fields can be up to 255 bytes long and can contain any type of data as long as the value of each record's key is unique.
15. IEBISAM

ANSWERS TO CHAPTER 15 STUDY QUESTIONS

1. The record that you tried to access was not found in the dataset.
2. An error occurs and you are not able to create your alternate index.
3. Issue the LISTCAT command using IDCAMS.
4. You won't need a loop to process each record associated with that alternate index key.
5. RPL and ACB
6. You should VERIFY the dataset before attempting to process it again.
7. entry sequenced dataset — cluster, data
relative record dataset — cluster, data
key sequenced dataset — cluster, data, index
alternate index — cluster, data, index
8. LTR — load and test register
SHOWCB — extract error or feedback code values
TESTCB — set condition code based on value comparisons
9. R15 is the primary register to be tested. R0 should be tested after issuing MODCB, TESTCB, GENCB, or the SHOWCB instructions.

10. IDCAMS
11. Your vehicle's identification number and license plate number.
12. Later releases of VSAM perform an automatic verify when the dataset is opened.
13. SYSPRINT and SYSIN
14. DSECT
15. OPTCD

Index

*operand (used in addressing), 431
*SYSLIB ASSIST control statement, 394
&SYSDATE, 136, 529
&SYSNDX, 409
&SYSTIME, 136, 529
0C1 abend, 283
0C4 abend, 106
0C6 abend, 149, 236
0C7 abend, 235
0CA abend, 255
0CB abend, 152
322 abend, 283
722 abend, 124
1-dimensional arrays, 440
2-dimensional arrays, 442

A

A data type, 55
A (add) instruction, 100
abend:
  data exception, 235
  decimal divide, 152
  decimal overflow, 255
  operation exception, 283
  protection exception, 106
  322 abend (out of time), 283
  722 abend (OUTLIM exceeded), 124
  specification exception, 149, 236
abend codes, 281, 283
ABEND macro instruction, 526
abend messages (locating them in your printout), 76
absolute addressing, 21
absolute value, 464
ACB (VSAM access control block), 582
ACB error code values (VSAM), 590
access method, 115, 514
accuracy of numerical results, 261
ACTR (loop control) macro instruction, 404
AD (add long) instruction, 484
adding binary numbers, 29
adding hexadecimal numbers, 28
addition of integers using logical instructions, 463
address, 19
address literals, 356
addressability, 348
addresses (defining and using), 58
addressing, 19
  alignment, 63
  base-displacement, 21
  base-index-displacement, 21
  explicit, 44
  implicit, 44
  relative, 46
addressing data areas in a reentrant program, 535
addressing protection, 106
addressing subroutine parameters, 350
ADR (add long register) instruction, 484
advantages of assembly languages, 1
AE (add short) instruction, 484
AER (add short register) instruction, 484
AGO (GOTO) macro instruction, 404
AH (add halfword) instruction, 169
AIF (if-then) macro instruction, 404
AL (add logical) instruction, 463
algorithms, 2
aligning packed decimal fields, 234
alignment, 55, 63
allocation and messages output listing, 75, 78

alphabetic character representation, 34
ALR (add logical register) instruction, 463
alternate index (VSAM), 575
alternate keys (VSAM), 575
analysis phase of software development, 3
analyzing textual storage areas, 436
AND constructs in decision making, 217
ANDing operations, 456
ANOP (no operation) macro instruction, 404
ANSI carriage control, 132
AP (add decimal) instruction, 254
apostrophe, 86
application development tools, 1
application programs, 7
applications (master file update), 522
AR (add register) instruction, 149
arguments (passed to subroutines), 342
arithmetic comparisons, 196
arithmetic logical operations, 463
arithmetic shifting instructions, 465
array processing, 440
arrays of structures, 448
ASCII character set, 14
ASMFCG JCL procedure, 123
assemble-and-go procedure, 11
assemble-link-and-go procedure, 11
assembler, 1
  (advantages to using), 59
assembly, 11
assembly (conditional), 419
assembly language, 1
assembly language and COBOL communications, 368
assembly language dump reading, 302
assembly of macros, 386
ASSIST, 2
  dump reading, 300
  I/O instructions, 126
  macro libraries, 394
  numeric conversion instructions, 177
asterisk (used in addressing), 431
attributes:
  count, K', 415
  length, L', 401
  number, N', 414
  type, T', 415
AXR (add extended register) instruction, 484

B

B data type, 55
B (branch, GOTO) instruction, 202
backup of VSAM datasets, 580
BAL (branch and link) instruction, 344
BALR (branch and link register) instruction, 346, 354
BAS (branch and save) instruction, 347
base cluster (VSAM), 567, 575
base register, 21, 46, 348, 354
  how to select, 48
  range of, 47, 348
  using R13, 425
base-16 addition and subtraction, 28
  number system, 24
base-2 addition, 29
  number system, 26
base-displacement address, 21
base-index-displacement address, 21
basic control mode, 108
BASR (branch and save register) instruction, 347
BC (branch on condition) instruction, 190
BCR (branch on condition register) instruction, 67, 190
BCT (branch on count) instruction, 207
BCTR (branch on count register) instruction, 207
  usage during editing, 249
  used with the execute instruction, 431
BDAM file processing, 542
BDW (block descriptor word), 521
BE (branch if equal) instruction, 201
beginning a macro, 390
beginning a program, 45
BER (branch if equal register) instruction, 201
BH (branch if high) instruction, 202
BHR (branch if high register) instruction, 202
binary addition, 29
binary data shifting instructions, 464
binary number system, 26
BISAM (random ISAM processing access method), 558
bit, 13, 17
bit processing, 456
  using registers, 467
bit data (defining), 55
BL (branch if low) instruction, 202
BLKSIZE, 120
  for variable-length records, 522
block allocation when defining data sets, 543
blocking, 120, 514
BLR (branch if low register) instruction, 202
BM (branch if minus) instruction, 202
BMR (branch if minus register) instruction, 202
BNE (branch if not equal) instruction, 202
BNER (branch if not equal register) instruction, 202
BNH (branch if not high) instruction, 202
BNHR (branch if not high register) instruction, 202

BNL (branch if not low) instruction, 202
BNLR (branch if not low register) instruction, 202
BNM (branch if not minus) instruction, 202
BNMR (branch if not minus register) instruction, 202
BNP (branch if not positive) instruction, 202
BNPR (branch if not positive register) instruction, 202
BNZ (branch if not zero) instruction, 202
BNZR (branch if not zero register) instruction, 202
BO (branch on overflow) instruction, 202
boolean variables (macro processing), 406
BOR (branch on overflow register) instruction, 202
boundary, 63
boundary alignment, 55
BP (branch if positive) instruction, 202
BPR (branch if positive register) instruction, 202
BR (branch register, GOTO) instruction, 202
branching, 190
BSAM file processing, 542
buffer, 514
bug, 274
BUILDALTERNATEINDEX (BLDINDEX) (VSAM IDCAMS command), 571, 577
building a macro library, 393
building a translate and test table, 436
building a translate table, 434
BXH (branch on index high) instruction, 208
BXLE (branch on index low or equal) instruction, 208
byte, 13, 17
byte alignment, 64
byte manipulation instructions, 426
BZ (branch if zero) instruction, 202
BZR (branch if zero register) instruction, 202

C

C data type, 55
C (compare) instruction, 196
CALL instruction in COBOL, 370
CALL macro for external subroutines, 387
  CALL macro supplied with operating system, 527
calling an internal subroutine, 343
capacity of computer memory, 14
card files (processing), 119
card punch, 4
card reader, 4
carriage control characters, 132
case construct, 197
case sensitive data, 434
CD (compare long) instruction, 486
CDR (compare long register) instruction, 486
CE (compare short) instruction, 486
central processing unit, 6
CER (compare short register) instruction, 486
CH (compare halfword) instruction, 198
chaining of save areas, 160
channel, 6
channel mask, 106
character, 13
character data:
  defining character fields, 54
  floating characters, 245
  literals, 133
  macro processing, 411
  padding and justification, 56
  processing, 109
character representation table, 34
character set, 14
character to packed decimal conversions, 164
characteristic of a floating point number, 473
CHECK macro instruction (random file processing), 545
CL (compare logical) instruction, 463
clause (after THEN or ELSE logic), 197
CLC (compare logical character) instruction, 199
CLCL (compare logical character long) instruction, 453
CLI (compare logical immediate) instruction, 199
CLM (compare logical characters under mask) instruction, 429
CLOSE instruction:
  for ISAM dataset processing, 556, 558
  for QSAM dataset processing, 118, 121
  for VSAM dataset processing, 584
CLR (compare logical register) instruction, 463
cluster component of a VSAM dataset, 568
clusters (VSAM datasets), 567
CMWP, 108
CNOP (conditional no operation) instruction, 235
COBOL and assembly language communications, 368
code generation (during macro expansion), 386
coding, 3
  continuing instructions, 45
  ending a program, 68
  external subroutines, 355
  format for instructions, 43
  internal subroutines, 347
  macro statements, 391
comment, 45, 89

communication between modules, 342
comparing data fields, 196
compilation, 11
compile-and-go procedure, 11
compile-link-and-go procedure, 11
compiler, 1
complement (two's), 30
complementary load instruction, 464
components of a computer system, 4
components of a macro definition, 390
compound conditions (used in macro processing), 404
compound constructs (used in decision-making), 216
computer system components, 4
concatenated libraries, 371
concatenated source code libraries, 513
concatenating macro libraries, 394
concatenation (character data macro processing), 411
COND CODE (condition code), 75
condition code, 75, 78, 107, 187, 357
condition code table, 189
conditional assembly, 419
continuation of instructions, 45
control areas (VSAM datasets), 570
control block generation during execution (VSAM), 600
control characters, 13
control characters for output spacing, 132
control interval (VSAM datasets), 570
control language, 15
control section, 46
  dummy control section—DSECT, 507
conventions for entry and exit, 155
converting between base-10 and base-16, 24
converting between base-2 and base-10, 26
converting between base-2 and base-16, 27
converting between hexadecimal and character, 36
converting character data from one format to another, 433
converting from base 10 to floating point, 475, 487
converting from binary to packed decimal, 165
converting from binary to character in ASSIST, 177
converting from character to binary in ASSIST, 177
converting from character to packed decimal, 164
converting from floating point to base 10, 478, 487
converting from packed decimal to binary, 164
converting from packed decimal to character, 166
converting labels to machine instructions, 52
converting negative base-10 numbers to binary, 31
converting negative base-10 numbers to hexadecimal, 31
converting numbers (human-readable to machine-readable), 37
converting numeric fields for printing, 239
converting programs for execution, 8
coordinating the base register and USING, 48
COPY instruction, 512
copy library, 511
copying VSAM datasets, 580
count attribute (K' attribute), 415
counter loops, 205
CP (compare decimal) instruction, 252
CPU (central processing unit), 6
CR (compare register) instruction, 200
creating a source code library, 512
creating a subroutine library, 371
cross reference listing, 81
CSECT (begin a program or module) instruction, 46
current date, 529
current instruction being executed, 108
current time, 529
CVB (convert to binary) instruction, 164, 234
CVD (convert to decimal) instruction, 165, 234
cylinder index (ISAM datasets), 553

D

D data type, 55, 479
D (divide) instruction, 153
D(B) address, 21
data, 13
  addressing, 19
  areas (defining an array), 440
  defining data fields, 54
  immediate data operands, 101
  representing in a computer, 13
data component of a VSAM dataset, 568
data control block, 116
data exception abend, 235
data flow between modules or functions, 338
data scope, 342
data structures, 60
data types, 33
data variables, 60
dataset statistics (VSAM), 580
dataset structure:
  BDAM, 542
  ISAM, 553
  QSAM, 113

VSAM, 568
dataset verification (VSAM), 579
datasets stored on tape, 518
date (during assembly), 136
date (obtaining the current date from the system), 529
DC (define constant) instruction, 54
DCB (testing for OPEN/CLOSE status), 365
DCB instruction, 116, 212
DCB macro expansion, 125, 389
DD (divide long) instruction, 484
DDNAME JCL parameter, 116
DDR (divide long register) instruction, 484
DE (divide short) instruction, 484
debugging, 274
using dumps, 285
debugging worksheet, 313
decimal data, 37, 233
decimal divide abend, 152
decimal overflow abend, 255
decimal point, 261
decimal point handling, 238
decimal to hexadecimal conversions, 24
decimal to hexadecimal conversion table, 25
decision making, 196
defensive programming, 285
DEFINE AIX (VSAM IDCAMS command), 571, 576
DEFINE CLUSTER (VSAM IDCAMS command), 571, 572, 574, 575
DEFINE PATH (VSAM IDCAMS command), 571, 577
defined storage areas (DSECT), 507
defining a base register, 46
defining fields, 54
alignment, 63
defining floating point storage areas, 479
defining a macro, 390
defining macro variables, 403
defining several identical fields, 55
defining storage areas for a reentrant program, 535
DELETE (VSAM IDCAMS command), 571, 579
delete byte (for random file processing), 547
deleting a VSAM dataset, 579
denominations (of memory), 15, 18
DER (divide short register) instruction, 484
design phase of the software development process, 3
developing programs, 2
devices (input and output), 4
diagnosing errors, 281
diagnostic output listing, 82
digit portion of a field, 38
digit representation table, 37
digit selector, 240
disadvantages of assembly languages, 1
disk devices, 5
displacement, 21, 47
displacement values for label references, 52
dividing by powers of 10, 261
dividing by powers of 2, 467
documentation phase of software development, 3
do-group, 197
Do-until loop construct, 210
Do-while loop construct, 210
double quote, 86
doubleword, 18
alignment, 64
used in character/packed/binary conversions, 164
DP (divide decimal) instruction, 256
DR (divide register) instruction, 149
DS (define storage) instruction, 58
DS instruction (for label positioning), 193
DSECT (define a dummy control section), 507
used with locate mode processing, 515
DSORG (parameter on the DCB instruction), 119
dummy control sections (DSECT), 507
dummy records, 543
dump reading:
in ASSIST, 284
in standard assembly language, 302
dumping an ISAM dataset using IEBISAM, 557
dumps (how to request), 124
dumps of VSAM datasets, 578
duplication factor, 55
dynamic instruction building, 429

E

E data type, 479
EBCDIC character set, 14
ECB (used with WTOR), 531
echoing input record images to the printer, 286
ED (edit) instruction, 239
edit pattern, 239
edit patterns built by a macro, 408
EDMK (edit and mark) instruction, 239
effective address, 21
efficiency (when defining storage areas), 64
EJECT instruction, 86
END instruction, 68
ending a macro definition, 390
ending a program, 68

end-of-file loop construct, 211
end-of-file processing (VSAM), 596
entry point address, 48, 158
  used in debugging, 297
EODAD, 212
EPA (entry point address), 48
EQU (equate) instruction, 91
  used for label positioning, 193
EQUATES macro for register symbol definition, 406
error:
  run-time or execution time, 44
  syntax, 44, 275
  (*see also*—abend)
error codes (VSAM), 589
error messages, 82
  during macro processing, 392
  generated by MNOTE macro instruction, 416
error processing for relative files, 546
ESDS:
  how to create a VSAM ESDS, 572
  processing sequentially, 585
evaluation phase of the software development process, 4
even register (signing for division), 150
even/odd register pair, 149, 451
event control block, 530, 545
  used with WTOR, 531
  ISAM, 562
EX (execute) instruction, 429
exception code bit values (relative file processing), 545
exception code bits when processing ISAM datasets, 562
excess-64 notation, 474
exchanging character values, 433
exclusive-OR processing, 457
EXEC JCL instruction, 123
EXEC parameters, 361
execute-form of a macro, 538, 561
executing programs, 10, 103
  controlling program flow, 187
  errors at execution time, 44, 280
  fetching programs to be executed, 10
  by interpretation, 11
  simulated, 2
exiting a macro during processing, 418
exiting a program, 65
expansion of macros, 387
  suppressing macro expansion, 389
explicit address, 44, 101
exponentiation:
  by powers of 2, 465
  by powers of 10, 261
  using MVO, MVN, and MVZ, 459
exponents (floating point processing), 474
expressions (used in macro statement processing), 404
extended addressing, 19
extended architecture, 19, 58, 347
extended control mode, 108
extended-mnemonic instructions, 200
extended-precision floating point numbers, 473
external datasets (tape files), 518
external mask, 106
external subroutines, 355
external symbol dictionary, 81

F

F data type, 55
failing instruction address, 297
FDBK (feedback codes in VSAM), 589
fetching programs for execution, 10, 104
field, 60
field separator, 244
file, 60
file processing:
  keyed files, 552
  nonlabeled tape files, 518
  processing tape datasets, 518
  random, 541
  standard label tape files, 518
  (*see also* QSAM, BDAM, ISAM, VSAM)
file types, 114
fill character, 240
finding data fields within storage areas, 436
flags, 14, 17
FLOATIN macro to convert floating point numbers, 487
floating characters, 245
floating point:
  literals, 479
  numbers, 472
  numbers (rounding), 485
  registers, 20, 472
  storage areas, 479
FLOATOUT macro to convert floating point numbers, 487
format of dumped output, 289
format of instructions:
  RR instructions, 98
  RX instructions, 99
  RS instructions, 101
  SI instructions, 101
  SS instructions, 102
format of a macro statement, 391
fractional numbers, 261
FREEMAIN macro instruction, 535

fullword, 18
  alignment, 64
  literals, 171
functions, 338
future programming languages, 1

G

GBLA (global arithmetic macro variable) instruction, 403
GBLB (global bit macro variable) instruction, 403
GBLC (global character macro variable) instruction, 403
GEN (operand of the PRINT instruction), 389
GENCB (VSAM macro instruction), 600
general-purpose register, 20
generating code during macro expansion, 386
generating control blocks during execution (VSAM), 600
generic data structures, 60
GET:
  I/O macro instruction, 122
  VSAM macro instruction, 582
GETMAIN macro instruction, 534
gigabyte, 15
global data scope, 342
global macro variables, 403
GOBACK COBOL instruction, 370
GOTO instruction (unconditional branch—BC, BCR, B, BR), 192
GOTO macro instruction (AGO), 404
GPR (general purpose register), 20
guard digit (floating point processing), 483

H

H data type, 55
halfword, 18
  alignment, 64
  instructions, 168
  literals, 171
hardware, 4
hashing, 569
HDR (halve long register) instruction, 484
header of a macro, 390
HER (halve short register) instruction, 484
hexadecimal addition and subtraction, 28
  number system, 24
hexadecimal characters used as signs, 37
hexadecimal output (dump output), 289
hexadecimal to decimal conversion table, 25
hexadecimal to decimal conversions, 24
hierarchical program organization, 340
hierarchical structure of a VSAM dataset, 568
high-level languages, 1
high-level program communication, 368
high-order byte, 20
Hollerith card, 4
human-readable format, 36

I

I/O operations across module boundaries, 363
I/O processing (increasing performance), 513
I/O success or failure (VSAM), 589
IC (insert character) instruction, 428
ICM (insert characters under mask) instruction, 426
IDCAMS:
  used to dump a nonVSAM dataset, 545
  VSAM processing, 570
IEBISAM (ISAM dataset utility), 557
IEBUPDTE:
  managing a source code library, 513
  used to manage macro libraries, 393
IEFBR14, 371
  creating an ISAM dataset, 554
  defining a BDAM dataset, 542
  defining a macro library, 393
if-then macro instruction (AIF), 404
if-then-else constructs, 196
ILC (instruction length code), 107
  used in debugging, 297
immediate data, 101, 110
implicit address, 44, 101
implied length, 112
index area of an ISAM dataset, 553
index component of a VSAM dataset, 568
index register, 21
  used to process arrays, 442
index set (VSAM), 570
information (format of), 13
information storage, 6
initial program load (IPL), 105
initializing fields, 54
input instruction in ASSIST, 126
input instructions in standard assembly language, 113
input/output devices, 4
input processing:
  using locate-mode, 515
  using move-mode, 113
input-process-output software design, 6
inserting floating characters, 245
instruction abend, 297
  continuation, 45
  defining your own, 202

instruction abend (*cont.*)
execution, 104
extended mnemonics, 200
length of, 97
instruction formats:
RR instruction, 98
RS instruction, 101
RX instruction, 99
SI instruction, 101
SS instruction, 102
instruction length code, 107
instruction reference table, 188
instructions for macro processing, 404
integer, 18
integer data (minimum/maximum value), 39
integers (in packed-decimal format), 37
integrity of a VSAM dataset, 579
interchanging field values using exclusive-OR, 458
internal subroutines, 343
interpretation, 11, 104
interpreter, 2
interrupt code, 107
IPL (initial program load—starting the computer), 105
IPO (input-process-output program processing flow), 6
ISAM (indexed sequential access method), 552
ISAM datasets (random processing), 558
iteration (*see* loop constructs),

J

JCL, 15
output listing, 77
parameters, 361
to process files, 118
to process tape datasets, 519
for standard assembly language, 123
JCL page of an output listing, 75
job, 15
job control language, 15
Julian date, 529
jump instruction, 190
justification, 27, 40, 56

K

K' (count) attribute, 415
key field, 541
keyed datasets (VSAM KSDS), 567
keyed file processing, 552
KEYLEN (key length for ISAM records), 555
keyword macro parameters, 396
kilobyte, 15
KSDS (creating a VSAM KSDS), 575
KSDS (processing sequentially), 588

L

L data type, 479
L (load) instruction, 66, 153
L' (length) attribute, 401
LA (load address) instruction, 153
label:
converting into machine instructions, 52
on the END instruction, 68
implicit address, 44
positioning within a program, 193
rules for coding, 43
language generations, 1
language translator, 1
languages (control languages, JCL), 15
languages (limitations of), 17
LCDR (load complement long register) instruction, 485
LCER (load complement short register) instruction, 485
LCLA (local arithmetic macro variable) instruction, 403
LCLB (local bit macro variable) instruction, 403
LCLC (local character macro variable) instruction, 403
LCR (load complement register) instruction, 464
LD (load long) instruction, 481
LDR (load long register) instruction, 481
LE (load short) instruction, 480
leading zeros, 56 (*see also* padding)
leaving a macro during processing, 418
left shifting, 261, 467
length attribute, 401
length of instructions, 97
length qualifier, 56
LER (load short register) instruction, 481
LH (load halfword) instruction, 169
library:
copy library, 511
macro library, 392
subroutine library, 371
life cycle of software development, 2
limitations (of programming languages), 17
line comment, 45
link editing, 11
executing programs, 10
link register, 344

linkage conventions, 155
linkage editor, 8, 10, 370
LINKAGE SECTION in COBOL programs, 369
linked list (of subroutine parameters), 350
list (non-linked) processing (array processing), 440
LISTCAT (VSAM IDCAMS command), 571, 580
list-form of an I/O macro, 538, 561
listing:
  reading an output listing, 71
  suppressing macro expansion, 389
literal generation, 136
literals:
  character data, 133
  floating point, 479
  fullword, 171
  halfword, 171
LM (load multiple) instruction, 66, 161
LNDR (load negative long register) instruction, 485
LNER (load negative short register) instruction, 485
LNR (load negative register) instruction, 464
load module, 370
load-and-go processing, 11
loader, 8, 10
loading programs for execution, 104
local data scope, 342
local macro variables, 403
locate-mode processing, 513
locating data fields within storage areas (searching), 436
location counter:
  altering using the ORG instruction, 434
  on an output listing, 71
  referencing using the * operand, 431
logical:
  addressing, 21
  arithmetic instructions, 462
  comparisons, 196
  conditions (macro processing), 405
  data structures, 60
  decimal point, 251
  deletion of records, 547, 554
  file name, 117
  record length, 120
  records, 514, 522
  shifting, 466
long-form floating point numbers, 473
loop constructs, 204
looping (during macro processing), 405
lower case data, 434
LPDR (load positive long register) instruction, 485
LPER (load positive short register) instruction, 485
LPR (load positive register) instruction, 464
LR (load register) instruction, 48, 99, 148
LRDR (load rounded extended to long register) instruction, 486
LRECL DCB operand, 120
LRER (load rounded long to short register) instruction, 486
LTDR (load and test long register) instruction, 485
LTER (load and test short register) instruction, 485
LTORG instruction, 136, 355
LTR (load and test register) instruction, 356

M

M (multiply) instruction, 153
machine code, 9
machine instructions, 97
machine language, 44
machine-readable format, 36
MACRF, 120
  used with locate mode processing, 515
macro, 386
  input and output macros, 113
  instructions, 404
  library, 392
  parameters, 395
  parameters (positional), 413
  processing (conditional assembly), 419
  processor, 386
  structure, 390
  trailer, 390
  using macros from an ASSIST library, 394
  using them in your program, 391
macro expansion, 115, 387
  suppressing, 389
macro header, 390
MACRO instruction, 390
major structure, 60
mantissa of a floating point number, 473
mask, 190, 426
master file update, 522
master index (ISAM datasets), 553
MD (multiply long) instruction, 484
MDR (multiply long register) instruction, 484
ME (multiply short to long) instruction, 484
megabyte, 15
memory:
  addressing, 19, 21
  capacity of, 14
  size of, 15

MEND instruction, 390
MER (multiply short to long register) instruction, 484
message character (during numeric field editing), 240
messages:
directed to the operator, WTO, 530
generated by MNOTE macro instruction, 416
on an output listing, 75
program diagnostics, 82
syntax errors, 276
MEXIT macro instruction, 418
MH (multiply halfword) instruction, 169
micro code, 104
minor structure, 60
mnemonic, 44
defining your own, 202
extended mnemonic instruction, 200
MNOTE macro instruction, 416
MODCB (modify control block VSAM macro instruction), 611
model statement (of a macro), 390
modifying instructions during execution, 429
module, 338
coordinating I/O operations, 363
move-mode processing, 513
MP (multiply decimal) instruction, 256
MR (multiply register) instruction, 149
multidimensional array processing, 442
multi-user environments, 532
multiplying by powers of 10, 261
multiplying by powers of 2, 467
MVC instruction, 110
MVCL (move long) instruction, 451
MVI (move immediate) instruction, 101, 110
MVN (move numerics) instruction, 459
MVO (move with offset) instruction, 459
MVZ (move zones) instruction, 459
MXD (multiply long to extended) instruction, 484
MXDR (multiply long to extended register) instruction, 484
MXR (multiply extended register) instruction, 484

N

N (AND) instruction, 456
N' (number) attribute, 414
naming a macro, 390
NC (AND-character) instruction, 456
negative integer load instruction, 464
negative numbers:
binary and hexadecimal, 30
converting for printing, 245
nested constructs, 204
next instruction address, 106
used in debugging, 297
NI (AND-immediate) instruction, 456
NOGEN (operand of the PRINT instruction), 389
nonblocked records, 515
nonfixed record lengths, 520
noninitialized fields, 58
nonlabeled tape files, 518
nonprivileged instructions, 187
normalized floating point numbers, 482
NOT macro operator, 406
NR (AND-register) instruction, 456
null JCL statement, 125
number attribute, 414
number systems:
base 2 (binary), 26
base 10 (decimal), 23
base 16 (hexadecimal), 24
numeric data:
converting for printing, 239
padding and justification, 27, 40, 56

O

O (OR) instruction, 455
object code, 9
locating on an output listing, 71
object module, 9
object program, 9
OC (OR-character) instruction, 455
offset, 19
offset addressing, 47
OI (OR immediate) instruction, 166, 455
one's complement, 31
on-line terminal, 4
op code, 99
OPEN instruction:
for QSAM dataset processing, 118, 121
for VSAM dataset processing, 584
opening files for processing, 118
operands of an instruction, 44
operating system, 7
communicating with—JCL, 15
operation code, 99
operation exception, 283
operator messages (WTO, WTOR), 530
OPSYN (defining your own mnemonics), 202
OR (exclusive-OR) processing, 457
OR (OR-register) instruction, 455
OR constructs in decision making, 217

ORG (alter location counter) instruction, 434, 436
ORing data values, 431
ORing operations, 455
ORing procedures, 166
OUTLIM JCL parameter, 124, 292
output:
from link editor and loader, 10
instructions in ASSIST, 126
instructions in assembly language, 113
reading an output listing, 71
suppressing macro expansion, 389
output processing using locate mode, 517
output spacing, 132 (*see* carriage control characters)
overflow abend, 31, 254
overflow area of an ISAM dataset, 553
overlay structures (DSECT), 507

P

P data type, 55
PACK instruction, 164, 237
packaging software, 338
packed-decimal data format, 37, 39, 164, 233
packed-decimal processing, 459
padding, 27, 40, 56
paired registers, 149, 451
parallel arrays, 449
parameter list, 350
parameter passing using the linkage conventions, 349
parameters:
between COBOL and assembly language programs, 368
defining labels using DSECT definitions, 507
for internal subroutines, 344
for macro processing, 395
PARM parameter on the EXEC JCL statement, 361
passwords (for VSAM datasets), 571
pattern for editing, 239, 408
performance:
as related to data type, 32
as related to instruction type, 98
performance (execution speed), 2
performance of I/O processing, 513
peripheral devices, 5
physical deletion of records, 547
physical record length, 120
physical records, 514
variable-length processing, 522
positional macro parameters, 396, 413
positive integer load instruction, 464
powers (exponents of floating point numbers), 474
powers of 2 processing, 465
powers of 10 processing, 261
precision of floating point numbers, 482
precision of numerical data, 472
preprocessor, 1
preserving registers:
during subroutine calls, 345
upon entry to a program, 49
primary key (VSAM), 575
prime data area of an ISAM dataset, 553
PRINT (VSAM IDCAMS command), 571, 577
PRINT assembly language instruction, 389
PRINT GEN, 389
PRINT NOGEN, 389
printing a dataset using IDCAMS, 578
printing data (*see* output)
printing numeric field values, 239
privileged instructions, 187
problem solving, 2
PROCEDURE DIVISION in COBOL programs, 370
procedures, 11, 338
processing bit data, 456
processing errors for relative files, 546
program code libraries, 511
program execution, 103
by interpretation, 11
program mask, 255, 426
program status word, 105
program transformations, 8
programming:
beginning a program, 45
future of, 1
programs, 7
executing after link editing, 10
fetching for execution, 10
protection (passwords for VSAM datasets), 571
protection exception, 106
protection key, 106
prototype statement (macro definition), 390
pseudo-code, 3, 205
PSW (program status word), 105
used in debugging, 297
PTF (program temporary fix), 104
punched card, 4
PUT instruction, 122
PUT VSAM macro instruction, 582

Q

QISAM (sequential ISAM processing access method), 555

QSAM (queued sequential access method), 115
qualifier (length), 56
queued files, 541
quote, 86
quotient, 151, 258

R

R0 (register 0):
  contents after using a VSAM I/O macro, 595
  used to pass subroutine parameters, 349
R1 (register 1):
  used to address EXEC JCL parameter, 361
  used to pass subroutine parameters, 349
R13 (register 13):
  when used as a base register, 425
  when used as a register save area pointer, 48
  (*see also*—register save area)
R14 (register 14) used to return control, 66
R15 (register 15):
  when used as a base register, 48, 53
  when used to pass a return code, 66
radix point (floating point processing), 474
random access storage device, 5
random file processing, 541, 598
  BDAM datasets, 542
  ISAM datasets, 558
  VSAM datasets, 567
range of a base register, 47, 348
RDW (record descriptor word), 521
READ macro instruction (random file processing), 551
readability (improving), 85
reading data (*see* input instructions)
RECFM (parameter of the DCB instruction), 120
record, 60
record keys (random files), 541
record processing (random updating), 547
records (variable-length VSAM processing), 611
redefined storage areas (DSECT), 507
reentrant programming, 532
reference point register, 46
referencing data areas (addressing), 19
register, 19
  defining a base register, 46, 48
  floating point registers, 472
  having multiple base registers, 348
  pairing, 149, 451
  preserving values before using, 49
  used for bit processing, 467
  used for explicit addressing, 44
  using R13 as a base register, 425
register equates, 93
register equates macro, 406
register linkage conventions, 155
register save area, 49, 156
register to indexed-storage instruction, 99
register to register instruction, 98
register to storage instruction, 101
relative addressing, 46
relative file processing, 542
  sequential access, 552
relative record dataset (VSAM RRDS), 567
relocatable symbol, 167
  used in array processing, 445
remainder, 151, 258
RENT assembler parameter, 538
RENT linkage editor parameter, 538
repetition factor, 55
representing characters, 34
representing data in a computer, 13
representing digit characters, 37
representing hexadecimal numbers, 26
representing hierarchical data, 60
representing negative numbers, 30
representing numbers in hexadecimal, 24
REPRO (VSAM IDCAMS command), 571, 580
return code, 67, 161
  testing after a subroutine call, 356
returning control, 67, 158
reviewing program development, 4
right shifting, 261, 467
RKP (relative key position of an ISAM record), 555
root portion of a variable-length record, 520
rounding, 261
  floating point numbers, 485
ROUTCDE, 530
routing codes for operator messages, 530
RPL (VSAM request parameter list), 584
  feedback codes, 589, 591
RR instruction, 98, 147
RRDS creating a VSAM RRDS, 574
  processing sequentially, 587
RRN (relative record number) (random file processing), 542, 567
RS instruction, 101
RSA, 49 (*see also* register save area)
run-time error, 44
RX instruction, 99, 152

S

S (subtract) instruction, 153
save area chaining, 160
saving register values, 49
scalar variables, 60

scientific notation, 19, 473
scientific processing (floating point), 472
scope of data, 342
SD (subtract long) instruction, 484
SDLC (systems development life cycle), 2
SDR (subtract long register) instruction, 481, 484
SE (subtract short) instruction, 484
searching fields for data values, 436
secondary key processing (VSAM), 612
secondary keys (VSAM), 575
segments of a variable-length record, 520
selecting a base register, 48
sequence field (on an instruction), 45
sequence set (VSAM), 570
sequential file processing:
  BDAM, 542
  ISAM, 555
  QSAM, 115
  VSAM, 567, 585, 597
sequential files, 541
SER (subtract short register) instruction, 484
SETA (arithmetic assignment) macro instruction, 404
SETB (bit assignment) macro instruction, 404
SETC (character assignment) macro instruction, 404
SH (subtract halfword) instruction, 169
shared programs, 532
sharing code segments, 511
shift instructions for binary data, 464
shifting packed decimal fields, 459
short-form floating point numbers, 473
SHOWCB (VSAM I/O macro), 589
SI instruction, 101
sign:
  of a binary integer, 18
  packed and zoned-decimal numbers, 37
  quotient and remainder, 151
significance indicator, 240
significance starter, 240
significant digits, 152, 238, 261
signing registers for division, 150
simulated execution, 2
single-dimensional array processing, 440
size of computer memory, 15
SL (subtract logical) instruction, 463
SLA (shift left arithmetic) instruction, 467
SLDA (shift left double arithmetic) instruction, 467
SLDL (shift left double logical) instruction, 467
SLL (shift left logical) instruction, 467
SLR (subtract logical register) instruction, 463
smallest addressable unit, 14
SNAP instruction (for debugging outside of ASSIST), 294
software, 4
solving problems, 2
sorting (interchanging fields using exclusive-OR), 458
source code, 9
source code libraries, 511
source listing (controlling spacing), 86
source program, 9
source statement (on an output listing), 73
SP (subtract decimal) instruction, 254
SPACE instruction, 86
specification exception, 149, 236
SPM (set program mask) instruction, 255, 426
SR (subtract register) instruction, 149
SRA (shift right arithmetic) instruction, 467
SRDA (shift right double arithmetic) instruction, 467
SRDL (shift right double logical) instruction, 467
SRL (shift right logical) instruction, 467
SRP (shift and round decimal) instruction, 261
SS instruction, 102
ST (store) instruction, 153
standard label files, 518
standard linkage conventions, 155
START instruction, 46, 73
starting a program, 45
statement format (coding rules), 43
statement number (on an output listing), 71
statement sequence field, 45
statements (macro instruction format), 391
static data, 342
statistics for VSAM datasets, 580
STC (store character) instruction, 428, 430
STCM (store characters under mask) instruction, 428
STD (store long) instruction, 481
STE (store short) instruction, 481
STH (store halfword) instruction, 169
STM (store multiple) instruction, 49, 53
stopping program execution, 65
storage management, 534
storage to immediate instruction, 101
storage to storage instruction, 102
storing data, 6
string processing (within a macro), 411
structure chart, 339
structure of a macro, 390
structure of an ISAM dataset, 553
structure of a VSAM dataset, 568
structured arrays, 448
structured data areas, 60
structured program, 3, 212
structures (DSECT), 507
sublists, 413
subroutine, 338

subroutine (*cont.*)
accessing parameters using DSECTs, 507
calling an internal subroutine, 344
CALL macro instruction, 527
indicating success or failure, 356
linkage conventions, 349
passing data using the linkage conventions, 349
subroutine libraries, 371
subscripted macro variables, 413
subscripts (for array processing), 442
substituting data at the byte level, 433
substring (during macro processing), 411
subtracting hexadecimal numbers, 28
subtracting integers using logical instructions, 463
support programs (utilities), 7
suppressing macro expansion, 389
swapping field values using exclusive-OR, 458
SXR (subtract extended register) instruction, 484
symbolic macro parameters, 395
symbolic parameters (sublists), 413
symbols on EQU instruction, 93
SYNAD routines, 544
syntax error, 44, 275
during macro processing, 392
SYSDATE, 136, 529
SYSLIB ASSIST control statement, 394
SYSLIB JCL instruction, 513
SYSLIST, 413
SYSNDX, 409
SYSOUT, 124
system abend codes, 281
system variables, 136
systems development life cycle (SDLC), 2
SYSTIME, 136, 529
SYSUDUMP, 124, 296

T

T' (type) attribute, 415
table processing, 448
tandem arrays, 449
tape devices, 5
tape processing, 518
task, 15
terminal, 4
terminating program execution, 65
TESTCB (VSAM I/O macro), 594
testing phase of software development, 3
testing the condition code, 190
time (during assembly), 136
TIME JCL parameter, 292
TIME macro instruction, 529
time of day, 529
time-out abend, 283
TITLE instruction, 85
TM (test under mask) instruction, 366
TR (translate) instruction, 433
track index (ISAM datasets), 553
trailer loop construct, 211
trailer record processing, 211
trailing blanks, 56 (*see also* padding)
transformations, 8
trends (in programming languages), 1
TRT (translate and test) instruction, 436
true zero (floating point representation), 474
two's complement, 30, 148
type, 33, 55
type attribute, 415
type of instructions, 98
types of files, 114

U

unconditional branch (B, BR, BC, BCR), 192, 404
unit of work, 15
unnormalized floating point number, 482
UNPK (unpack) instruction, 166
until loop construct, 210
updating a relative dataset, 547, 598
upper case data, 434
user abend codes, 281
user abends, 526
USING instruction (define a base register), 47, 349, 354, 426
when defining DSECTs, 507
utility programs, 7

V

V data type, 356
variable-length records, 520
VSAM, 611
variable:
defining storage areas, 54
scalar variables, 60
structured variables, 60
used in macro processing, 402
(*see also* label)
vector processing, 440

VERIFY (VSAM IDCAMS command), 571, 579
verifying a VSAM dataset, 579
V-format records, 520
VSAM (virtual storage access method), 567
  alternate index, 612
  dataset structure, 568
  random processing, 598
  sequential processing, 597
V-type address constants, 356

W

WAIT macro instruction, 532, 563
while loop construct, 210
word, 18
WRITE macro instruction (random file processing), 544
WTO (write to operator) instruction, 530
WTOR (write to operator with reply) instruction, 530

X

X data type, 55
X (exclusive-OR) instruction, 457
XA (extended architecture), 19, 58, 347
XC (exclusive-OR character) instruction, 457
XDECI instruction, 177
XDECO instruction, 177
XDUMP instruction, 288
XI (exclusive-OR immediate) instruction, 457
XPRNT instruction, 126
  used in debugging, 286
XR (exclusive-OR register) instruction, 457
XREAD instruction, 126

Z

ZAP (zero and add decimal) instruction, 259
zone portion of a field, 38
zoned-decimal format, 37, 166
zoned digit, 38, 238